Contemporary Authors®

ISSN 0010-7468

Contemporary

Authors®

A Bio-Bibliographical Guide to
Current Writers in Fiction, General Nonfiction,
Poetry, Journalism, Drama, Motion Pictures,
Television, and Other Fields

volume 215

GALE®

THOMSON

™

GALE

Detroit • New York • San Diego • San Francisco • Cleveland • New Haven, Conn. • Waterville, Maine • London • Munich

THOMSON

GALE

Contemporary Authors, Vol. 215

Project Editor
Scot Peacock

Editorial
Katy Balcer, Shavon Burden, Sara Constantakis, Anna Marie Dahn, Alana Joli Foster, Natalie Fulkerson, Arlene M. Johnson, Michelle Kazensky, Julie Keppen, Joshua Kondek, Thomas McMahon, Jenai A. Mynatt, Judith L. Pyko, Mary Ruby, Lemma Shomali, Susan Strickland, Maikue Vang, Tracey Watson, Thomas Wiloch, Emiene Shija Wright

Research
Michelle Campbell, Tracie A. Richardson, Robert Whaley

Permissions
Lori Hines

Imaging and Multimedia
Dean Dauphinais, Robert Duncan, Leitha Etheridge-Sims, Mary K. Grimes, Lezlie Light, Dan Newell, David G. Oblender, Christine O'Bryan, Kelly A. Quin, Luke Rademacher

Composition and Electronic Capture
Carolyn A. Roney

Manufacturing
Stacy L. Melson

LIBRARY OF CONGRESS CATALOG CARD NUMBER 62-52046

ISBN 0-7876-6639-4
ISSN 0010-7468

Printed in the United States of America
10 9 8 7 6 5 4 3 2 1

Contents

Indexing note: All *Contemporary Authors* entries are indexed in the *Contemporary Authors* cumulative index, which is published separately and distributed twice a year.

As always, the most recent Contemporary Authors cumulative index continues to be the user's guide to the location of an individual author's listing.

Preface

Contemporary Authors (CA) provides information on approximately 115,000 writers in a wide range of media, including:

- Current writers of fiction, nonfiction, poetry, and drama whose works have been issued by commercial publishers, risk publishers, or university presses (authors whose books have been published only by known vanity or author-subsidized firms are ordinarily not included)

- Prominent print and broadcast journalists, editors, photojournalists, syndicated cartoonists, graphic novelists, screenwriters, television scriptwriters, and other media people

- Notable international authors

- Literary greats of the early twentieth century whose works are popular in today's high school and college curriculums and continue to elicit critical attention

A *CA* listing entails no charge or obligation. Authors are included on the basis of the above criteria and their interest to *CA* users. Sources of potential listees include trade periodicals, publishers' catalogs, librarians, and other users of the series.

How to Get the Most out of *CA*: Use the Index

The key to locating an author's most recent entry is the *CA* cumulative index, which is published separately and distributed twice a year. It provides access to *all* entries in *CA* and *Contemporary Authors New Revision Series (CANR)*. Always consult the latest index to find an author's most recent entry.

For the convenience of users, the *CA* cumulative index also includes references to all entries in these Gale literary series: *Authors and Artists for Young Adults, Authors in the News, Bestsellers, Black Literature Criticism, Black Literature Criticism Supplement, Black Writers, Children's Literature Review, Concise Dictionary of American Literary Biography, Concise Dictionary of British Literary Biography, Contemporary Authors Autobiography Series, Contemporary Authors Bibliographical Series, Contemporary Dramatists, Contemporary Literary Criticism, Contemporary Novelists, Contemporary Poets, Contemporary Popular Writers, Contemporary Southern Writers, Contemporary Women Poets, Dictionary of Literary Biography, Dictionary of Literary Biography Documentary Series, Dictionary of Literary Biography Yearbook, DISCovering Authors, DISCovering Authors: British, DISCovering Authors: Canadian, DISCovering Authors: Modules* (including modules for Dramatists, Most-Studied Authors, Multicultural Authors, Novelists, Poets, and Popular/Genre Authors), *DISCovering Authors 3.0, Drama Criticism, Drama for Students, Feminist Writers, Hispanic Literature Criticism, Hispanic Writers, Junior DISCovering Authors, Major Authors and Illustrators for Children and Young Adults, Major 20th-Century Writers, Native North American Literature, Novels for Students, Poetry Criticism, Poetry for Students, Short Stories for Students, Short Story Criticism, Something about the Author, Something about the Author Autobiography Series, St. James Guide to Children's Writers, St. James Guide to Crime & Mystery Writers, St. James Guide to Fantasy Writers, St. James Guide to Horror, Ghost & Gothic Writers, St. James Guide to Science Fiction Writers, St. James Guide to Young Adult Writers, Twentieth-Century Literary Criticism, 20th Century Romance and Historical Writers, World Literature Criticism,* and *Yesterday's Authors of Books for Children.*

A Sample Index Entry:

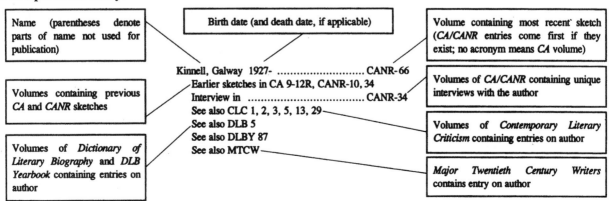

vii

How Are Entries Compiled?

The editors make every effort to secure new information directly from the authors; listees' responses to our questionnaires and query letters provide most of the information featured in *CA*. For deceased writers, or those who fail to reply to requests for data, we consult other reliable biographical sources, such as those indexed in Gale's *Biography and Genealogy Master Index*, and bibliographical sources, including *National Union Catalog, LC MARC*, and *British National Bibliography*. Further details come from published interviews, feature stories, and book reviews, as well as information supplied by the authors' publishers and agents.

An asterisk (*) at the end of a sketch indicates that the listing has been compiled from secondary sources believed to be reliable but has not been personally verified for this edition by the author sketched.

What Kinds of Information Does An Entry Provide?

Sketches in *CA* contain the following biographical and bibliographical information:

- **Entry heading:** the most complete form of author's name, plus any pseudonyms or name variations used for writing

- **Personal information:** author's date and place of birth, family data, ethnicity, educational background, political and religious affiliations, and hobbies and leisure interests

- **Addresses:** author's home, office, or agent's addresses, plus e-mail and fax numbers, as available

- **Career summary:** name of employer, position, and dates held for each career post; resume of other vocational achievements; military service

- **Membership information:** professional, civic, and other association memberships and any official posts held

- **Awards and honors:** military and civic citations, major prizes and nominations, fellowships, grants, and honorary degrees

- **Writings:** a comprehensive, chronological list of titles, publishers, dates of original publication and revised editions, and production information for plays, television scripts, and screenplays

- **Adaptations:** a list of films, plays, and other media which have been adapted from the author's work

- **Work in progress:** current or planned projects, with dates of completion and/or publication, and expected publisher, when known

- **Sidelights:** a biographical portrait of the author's development; information about the critical reception of the author's works; revealing comments, often by the author, on personal interests, aspirations, motivations, and thoughts on writing

- **Interview:** a one-on-one discussion with authors conducted especially for *CA*, offering insight into authors' thoughts about their craft

- **Autobiographical essay:** an original essay written by noted authors for *CA*, a forum in which writers may present themselves, on their own terms, to their audience

- **Photographs:** portraits and personal photographs of notable authors

- **Biographical and critical sources:** a list of books and periodicals in which additional information on an author's life and/or writings appears

- **Obituary Notices** in *CA* provide date and place of birth as well as death information about authors whose full-length sketches appeared in the series before their deaths. The entries also summarize the authors' careers and writings and list other sources of biographical and death information.

Related Titles in the *CA* Series

Contemporary Authors Autobiography Series complements *CA* original and revised volumes with specially commissioned autobiographical essays by important current authors, illustrated with personal photographs they provide. Common topics include their motivations for writing, the people and experiences that shaped their careers, the rewards they derive from their work, and their impressions of the current literary scene.

Contemporary Authors Bibliographical Series surveys writings by and about important American authors since World War II. Each volume concentrates on a specific genre and features approximately ten writers; entries list works written by and about the author and contain a bibliographical essay discussing the merits and deficiencies of major critical and scholarly studies in detail.

Available in Electronic Formats

GaleNet. *CA* is available on a subscription basis through GaleNet, an online information resource that features an easy-to-use end-user interface, powerful search capabilities, and ease of access through the World-Wide Web. For more information, call 1-800-877-GALE.

Licensing. *CA* is available for licensing. The complete database is provided in a fielded format and is deliverable on such media as disk, CD-ROM, or tape. For more information, contact Gale's Business Development Group at 1-800-877-GALE, or visit us on our website at www.galegroup.com/bizdev.

Suggestions Are Welcome

The editors welcome comments and suggestions from users on any aspect of the *CA* series. If readers would like to recommend authors for inclusion in future volumes of the series, they are cordially invited to write the Editors at *Contemporary Authors*, Gale Group, 27500 Drake Rd., Farmington Hills, MI 48331-3535; or call at 1-248-699-4253; or fax at 1-248-699-8054.

Contemporary Authors Product Advisory Board

The editors of *Contemporary Authors* are dedicated to maintaining a high standard of excellence by publishing comprehensive, accurate, and highly readable entries on a wide array of writers. In addition to the quality of the content, the editors take pride in the graphic design of the series, which is intended to be orderly yet inviting, allowing readers to utilize the pages of *CA* easily and with efficiency. Despite the longevity of the *CA* print series, and the success of its format, we are mindful that the vitality of a literary reference product is dependent on its ability to serve its users over time. As literature, and attitudes about literature, constantly evolve, so do the reference needs of students, teachers, scholars, journalists, researchers, and book club members. To be certain that we continue to keep pace with the expectations of our customers, the editors of *CA* listen carefully to their comments regarding the value, utility, and quality of the series. Librarians, who have firsthand knowledge of the needs of library users, are a valuable resource for us. The *Contemporary Authors* Product Advisory Board, made up of school, public, and academic librarians, is a forum to promote focused feedback about *CA* on a regular basis. The seven-member advisory board includes the following individuals, whom the editors wish to thank for sharing their expertise:

- **Anne M. Christensen,** Librarian II, Phoenix Public Library, Phoenix, Arizona.

- **Barbara C. Chumard,** Reference/Adult Services Librarian, Middletown Thrall Library, Middletown, New York.

- **Eva M. Davis,** Youth Department Manager, Ann Arbor District Library, Ann Arbor, Michigan.

- **Adam Janowski, Jr.,** Library Media Specialist, Naples High School Library Media Center, Naples, Florida.

- **Robert Reginald,** Head of Technical Services and Collection Development, California State University, San Bernadino, California.

- **Katharine E. Rubin,** Head of Information and Reference Division, New Orleans Public Library, New Orleans, Louisiana.

- **Barbara A. Wencl,** Media Specialist, Como Park High School, St. Paul, Minnesota.

International Advisory Board

Well-represented among the 115,000 author entries published in *Contemporary Authors* are sketches on notable writers from many non-English-speaking countries. The primary criteria for inclusion of such authors has traditionally been the publication of at least one title in English, either as an original work or as a translation. However, the editors of *Contemporary Authors* came to observe that many important international writers were being overlooked due to a strict adherence to our inclusion criteria. In addition, writers who were publishing in languages other than English were not being covered in the traditional sources we used for identifying new listees. Intent on increasing our coverage of international authors, including those who write only in their native language and have not been translated into English, the editors enlisted the aid of a board of advisors, each of whom is an expert on the literature of a particular country or region. Among the countries we focused attention on are Mexico, Puerto Rico, Germany, Luxembourg, Belgium, the Netherlands, Norway, Sweden, Denmark, Finland, Taiwan, Singapore, Spain, Italy, South Africa, Israel, and Japan, as well as England, Scotland, Wales, Ireland, Australia, and New Zealand. The sixteen-member advisory board includes the following individuals, whom the editors wish to thank for sharing their expertise:

- **Lowell A. Bangerter,** Professor of German, University of Wyoming, Laramie, Wyoming.

- **Nancy E. Berg,** Associate Professor of Hebrew and Comparative Literature, Washington University, St. Louis, Missouri.

- **Frances Devlin-Glass,** Associate Professor, School of Literary and Communication Studies, Deakin University, Burwood, Victoria, Australia.

- **David William Foster,** Regent's Professor of Spanish, Interdisciplinary Humanities, and Women's Studies, Arizona State University, Tempe, Arizona.

- **Hosea Hirata,** Director of the Japanese Program, Associate Professor of Japanese, Tufts University, Medford, Massachusetts.

- **Jack Kolbert,** Professor Emeritus of French Literature, Susquehanna University, Selinsgrove, Pennsylvania.

- **Mark Libin,** Professor, University of Manitoba, Winnipeg, Manitoba, Canada.

- **C. S. Lim,** Professor, University of Malaya, Kuala Lumpur, Malaysia.

- **Eloy E. Merino,** Assistant Professor of Spanish, Northern Illinois University, DeKalb, Illinois.

- **Linda M. Rodríguez Guglielmoni,** Associate Professor, University of Puerto Rico—Mayagüez, Puerto Rico.

- **Sven Hakon Rossel,** Professor and Chair of Scandinavian Studies, University of Vienna, Vienna, Austria.

- **Steven R. Serafin,** Director, Writing Center, Hunter College of the City University of New York, New York City.

- **David Smyth,** Lecturer in Thai, School of Oriental and African Studies, University of London, England.

- **Ismail S. Talib,** Senior Lecturer, Department of English Language and Literature, National University of Singapore, Singapore.

- **Dionisio Viscarri,** Assistant Professor, Ohio State University, Columbus, Ohio.

- **Mark Williams,** Associate Professor, English Department, University of Canterbury, Christchurch, New Zealand.

CA Numbering System and Volume Update Chart

Occasionally questions arise about the *CA* numbering system and which volumes, if any, can be discarded. Despite numbers like "29-32R," "97-100" and "214," the entire *CA* print series consists of only 264 physical volumes with the publication of *CA* Volume 215. The following charts note changes in the numbering system and cover design, and indicate which volumes are essential for the most complete, up-to-date coverage.

CA First Revision

- 1-4R through 41-44R (11 books)
  Cover: Brown with black and gold trim.
  There will be no further First Revision volumes because revised entries are now being handled exclusively through the more efficient *New Revision Series* mentioned below.

CA Original Volumes

- 45-48 through 97-100 (14 books)
  Cover: Brown with black and gold trim.
  101 through 215 (115 books)
  Cover: Blue and black with orange bands.
  The same as previous *CA* original volumes but with a new, simplified numbering system and new cover design.

CA Permanent Series

- *CAP*-1 and *CAP*-2 (2 books)
  Cover: Brown with red and gold trim.
  There will be no further Permanent Series volumes because revised entries are now being handled exclusively through the more efficient *New Revision Series* mentioned below.

CA New Revision Series

- CANR-1 through CANR-122 (122 books)
  Cover: Blue and black with green bands.
  Includes only sketches requiring significant changes; **sketches are taken from any previously published CA, CAP, or CANR volume.**

If You Have:	You May Discard:
CA First Revision Volumes 1-4R through 41-44R and *CA* Permanent Series Volumes 1 and 2	*CA* Original Volumes 1, 2, 3, 4 Volumes 5-6 through 41-44
CA Original Volumes 45-48 through 97-100 and 101 through 215	**NONE:** These volumes will not be superseded by corresponding revised volumes. Individual entries from these and all other volumes appearing in the left column of this chart may be revised and included in the various volumes of the *New Revision Series*.
CA New Revision Series Volumes *CANR*-1 through *CANR*-122	**NONE:** The *New Revision Series* does not replace any single volume of *CA*. Instead, volumes of *CANR* include entries from many previous *CA* series volumes. All *New Revision Series* volumes must be retained for full coverage.

A Sampling of Authors and Media People Featured in This Volume

F. Isabel Campoy

Campoy is the prolific author of bilingual materials for children of Hispanic heritage. Plays, poems, educational materials, picture books, biographies, and easy-readers have issued from Campoy's imagination, most of these works coauthored by Alma Flor Ada. In addition to stand-alone books, the collaborators have produced a number of book series, and several of their works have been included in the "Coleccion Puertas al Sol" series designed to introduce young readers to Hispanic culture.

Stephen Engelberg

Engelberg is a Pulitzer Prize-winning journalist who has covered critical news stories for the *New York Times* over several decades. In both his role as a reporter and later as an editor, he has been involved in most major national stories that have affected the United States and the world. In 2001, before the destruction of the World Trade Center buildings and the delivery of deadly anthrax spores to several prominent locations in the United States, Engelberg, together with two of his colleagues, wrote a book about the threat of biological warfare titled *Germs: Biological Weapons and America's Secret War.*

Terence M. Green

A Canadian science-fiction writer, Green has been praised throughout his career for his quiet, restrained style. His novels include *Children of the Rainbow,* a tale that centers on a character named Fletcher Christian IV (a descendant of the hero of the classic book *Mutiny on the Bounty*) and *Shadow of Ashland,* a time-travel story in which a man searches for his long-lost uncle. An autobiographical essay by Green is featured in this volume of *CA.*

Margaret Harkness

Harkness—or John Law, as she called herself in print—is best known for her socially radical fiction of the late nineteenth century. Her empathetic portrayal of impoverished women's lives stands her apart from such like-minded writers as George Gissing, George Bernard Shaw, and Rudyard Kipling. Harkness's fiction in such works as *A City Girl: A Realistic Story* chronicles the radical movement from a female perspective, and reveals how socialism was constructed in her day.

Kenneth Powell

Powell is an architecture critic and journalist. His many books on English architecture include studies of England's most prominent architects, Norman Foster and Richard Rogers. His works range from in-depth analyses of major structures in London, considered by many to be the architectural capital of the world, to new uses for old structures, to international urban design precepts, to the impact of modern practitioners on the house of the twenty-first century. In 2003 Powell published the volume *New Architecture in Britain.*

Malay Roy Choudhury

Poet Roy Choudhury writes both in Bangla—one of the many native languages of South Asia—and English. One of the founders of the Hungryalist literary movement, Roy Choudhury has been sought out by such notable writers as Mexican Nobel Prize winner Octavio Paz, American poet Allen Ginsberg, and Nicaraguan poet and priest Ernesto Cardenal. In addition to being a poet, Roy Choudhury is also a novelist, essayist, dramatist, short-story writer, translator, and critic. An autobiographical essay by Roy Choudhury is included in this volume of *CA.*

Alexander McCall Smith

A professor of medical law at Edinburgh University, Smith has published many works on medical ethics and criminal law, such as a study on the impact of medical advances on parental rights. He is also the author of a series of detective stories set in Zimbabwe. The first installment, *The No. 1 Ladies' Detective Agency,* became a best-selling novel in the United States after it was popularized by word of mouth. In addition, Smith has written numerous books of fiction for children. In 2003 he released the detective novel *The Kalahari Typing School for Men.*

Margaret Wild

Wild is a prolific author of children's books whose themes sometimes address serious issues: death and dying, grief, divorce, aging, and fears of being lost, overwhelmed, and bullied. Her realistic portrayals of these difficult subjects have been widely praised by critics and reviewers. Far from being morbid, Wild's other books are jubilant celebrations of grandmothers, babies, and childhood. Even her somber books, such as *Old Pig,* hold the message that children can understand and cope with a sad or scary situation.

Acknowledgments

Grateful acknowledgment is made to those publishers, photographers, and artists whose work appear with these authors' essays. Following is a list of the copyright holders who have granted us permission to reproduce material in this volume of *CA*. Every effort has been made to trace copyright, but if omissions have been made, please let us know.

Photographs/Art

Leslie Epstein: All photographs reproduced by permission of the author, except as noted: opening photo © Miriam Berkley. Reproduced by permission of Miriam Berkley.

Terence M. Green: All photographs reproduced by permission of the author.

Malay Roy Choudhury: All photographs reproduced by permission of the author.

A

Indicates that a listing has been compiled from secondary sources believed to be reliable, but has not been personally verified for this edition by the author sketched.

ACOMB, Frances (Dorothy) 1907-1984

PERSONAL: Born October 15, 1907, in Donora, PA; died 1984. *Education:* Wellesley College, A.B. 1928; Smith College, A.M., 1932; University of Chicago, Ph.D., 1943.

CAREER: High school teacher, 1929-36; University of Chicago, Chicago, IL, research assistant, 1936-43; New York State Teachers College, Albany, instructor, after 1943; Duke University, Durham, NC, assistant professor then professor, 1945-75, professor emerita of history, beginning 1975. *Wartime service:* War Department historian during World War II.

WRITINGS:

Anti-English Opinion in France (thesis), University of Chicago Library (Chicago, IL), 1943.
Anglophobia in France, 1763-1789: An Essay in the History of Constitutionalism and Nationalism, Duke University Press (Durham, NC), 1950.
Statistical Control in the Army Air Forces, History Division, U.S. Air Force (Colorado Springs, CO), 1952.
Mallet du Pan, 1749-1800: A Career in Political Journalism, Duke University Press (Durham, NC), 1973.

SIDELIGHTS: Frances Acomb was an American historian whose study *Anglophobia in France, 1763-1789: An Essay in the History of Constitutionalism and Nationalism* examines political relations between Great Britain and France during the twenty-five years before the French Revolution. In the book Acomb discusses how French writers of the period alternately admired and disliked the English, depending on political allegiances and current events. In general, French conservatives who supported the divine-right monarchy criticized English institutions, while liberals were pro-English. A reviewer for *United States Quarterly Book List* commented, "In her study, Miss Acomb has combined careful scholarship with a persistent attempt to look behind accepted interpretations, and has consequently produced a carefully documented but not pedantic study." An *American Historical Review* critic called the book a "scholarly little volume. . . . Though a bit dull in style . . . the book reveals wide research, command of nearly all pertinent material, and should make unnecessary another study of the same subject."

Subsequent publications by Acomb include *Statistical Control in the Army Air Forces,* and *Mallet du Pan, 1749-1800: A Career in Political Journalism.*

BIOGRAPHICAL AND CRITICAL SOURCES:

BOOKS

Scanlon, Jennifer, and Shaaron Cosner, *American Women Historians, 1700s-1990s: A Biographical Dictionary,* Greenwood Press (Westport, CT), 1996.

PERIODICALS

American Historical Review, October, 1950, p. 190.
United States Quarterly Booklist, September, 1950,
  p. 327.*

* * *

ADAMS, Benjamin 1966-

PERSONAL: Born 1966.

ADDRESSES: Agent—c/o Ballantine Books, 201 East
50th St., New York, NY 10022.

CAREER: Author of short fiction.

AWARDS, HONORS: Honorable mention, *The Year's
Best Fantasy and Horror,* for "Second Movement" and
"The Frieze of Life."

WRITINGS:

(Editor, with John Pelan) *The Children of Cthulhu:
Chilling New Tales Inspired by H. P. Lovecraft,*
Ballantine Books (New York, NY), 2002.

Also published numerous short stories in anthologies,
including *100 Vicious Little Vampire Stories, 100
Wicked Little Witch Stories, Midnight Journeys, Blood
Muse, Horrors! 365 Scary Stories,* and *Miskatonic
University.*

SIDELIGHTS: Benjamin Adams's short fiction has appeared in numerous horror and fantasy anthologies.
His most recent work is *The Children of Cthulhu:
Chilling New Tales Inspired by H. P. Lovecraft,* an
anthology he edited with John Pelan.

The anthology of short stories from twenty-one
contributors includes Adams and Pelan's collaboration,
"That's the Story of My Life." The book is a tribute to
H. P. Lovecraft, whom many readers consider the
master of horror/fantasy fiction. The title itself honors
Lovecraft, who popularized the Cthulhu Mythos in his

writings before his death in 1937. Cthulhu (kuh-
THOO-loo) is a godlike entity, one of the many Great
Old Ones, who sleeps beneath the ocean, but rises up
from time to time "when the stars are right," to bring
death and destruction to the human world.

Regina Schroeder described *The Children of Cthulhu*
in her *Booklist* review, "Like Lovecraft's own tales,
they exist to titillate, horrify, and confront readers
with intense descriptions of things that can't—
shouldn't—be described." A *Kirkus Reviews* critic
acknowledged a few outstanding selections in the
anthology and noted that as a whole the collection
exudes the "spirit" of Lovecraft, "the 20th-century's
weirdest and most influential horror writer."

BIOGRAPHICAL AND CRITICAL SOURCES:

PERIODICALS

Booklist, December 15, 2001, Regina Schroeder,
  review of *The Children of Cthulhu: Chilling New
  Tales Inspired by H. P. Lovecraft,* p. 709.
Kirkus Reviews, October 15, 2001, review of *The
  Children of Cthulhu,* p. 1461.
Library Journal, January, 2002, Jackie Cassada, review
  of *The Children of Cthulhu,* p. 159.

ONLINE

Eternal Night, http://www.eternalnight.co.uk/ (May
  24, 2002).
SFF Net, http://www.sff.net/ (April 16, 2002).
SFSite, http://www.sfsite.com/ (May 20, 2002).*

* * *

ADAMS, Bertha Leith 1837(?)-1912

PERSONAL: Born c. 1837, in Mottram, Longdale,
Cheshire, England; died September 5, 1912; daughter
of Frederick Grundy (a solicitor); married Andrew
Leith Adams (an army surgeon and educator), 1859
(died 1882); married Robert Stuart de Courcy Laffan
(an educator), 1883; children: (first marriage) Francis,
Harry Beardoe Adams.

CAREER: Poet, essayist, novelist, and short story writer. Edited *Kensington Magazine*, 1879-80.

WRITINGS:

Nancy's Work: A Church Story, Mowbray (London and Oxford, England), 1876.

Winstowe: A Novel, three volumes, Hurst & Blackett (London, England), 1877, published in one volume, Harper (New York, NY), 1877.

Georgie's Wooer: A Novelette, Harper (New York, NY), 1878.

Madelon Lemoine, three volumes, Hurst & Blackett (London, England), 1879, published in one volume as *Madelon Lemoine: A Novel,* Lippincott (Philadelphia, PA), 1879.

Aunt Hepsy's Foundling: A Novel, Munro (New York, NY), 1880, published in three volumes, Chapman & Hall (London, England), 1881.

Cosmo Gordon: A Novel, three volumes, Chapman & Hall (London, England), 1882.

Geoffrey Stirling: A Novel, three volumes, Chapman & Hall (London, England), 1883, published in one volume, Lippincott (Philadelphia, PA), 1887.

My Brother Sol Etc., three volumes, Tinsley (London, England), 1883.

Louis Draycott: The Story of His Life: A Novel, two volumes, Chapman & Hall (London, England), 1890.

Bonnie Kate: A Story from a Woman's Point of View, three volumes, Kegan Paul, Trench, Trübner (London, England), 1892.

(Assisted by "Stroke" and "Bow") *The Cruise of the "Tomahawk": The Story of a Summer's Holiday in Prose and Rhyme,* Eden, Remington (London, England), 1892.

A Garrison Romance, Eden, Remington (London, England), 1892.

The Peyton Romance, three volumes, Kegan Paul, Trench, Trübner (London, England), 1892.

Colour Sergeant No. 1 Company, two volumes, Jarrold (London, England), 1894.

The Old Pastures: A Story of the Woods and Fields, Kegan Paul, Trench, Trübner (London, England), 1895.

Accessory after the Fact, Digby, Long (London, England), 1899.

The Prince's Feathers: A Story of Leafy Warwickshire in the Olden Times: A Novel, Digby, Long (London, England), 1899.

The Vicar of Dale End: A Study, Digby, Long (London, England), 1906.

The Story of the Brotherhood of Hero Dogs, Madgwick, Houlston (London, England), 1910.

SHORT STORIES

My Land of Beulah, and Other Stories (comprises "My Land of Beulah," "Georgie's Wooer," and "Mabel Meredith's Love Story"), three volumes, Tinsley (London, England), 1880, published in one volume as *My Land of Beulah,* Lippincott (Philadelphia, PA), 1891.

Expiated, and Other Stories, Groombridge (London, England), 1881.

Lady Deane, and Other Stories, 3 volumes, Chapman & Hall (London, England), 1882.

Cruel Calumny, and Other Stories, Digby, Long (London, England), 1901.

What Hector Had to Say, and Other Stories, Digby, Long (London, England), 1902.

The Dream of Her Life, and Other Stories, Digby, Long (London, England), 1902.

POEMS

A Song of Jubilee, and Other Poems, Kegan Paul, Trench (London, England), 1887.

Poems, Foulis (London, England), 1907.

OTHER

(Editor) David Grant, *Metrical Tales, and Other Poems,* W. C. Leng (Sheffield, England), 1880.

Dreams Made Verity: Stories, Essays, and Memories, Elkin Mathews (London, England), 1910.

A Book of Short Plays and a Memory, Stanley Paul (London, England), 1912.

SIDELIGHTS: English poet, essayist, novelist, and short-story writer Bertha Leith Adams wrote and published prolifically during her thirty-six-year writing career. Although relatively unknown to modern readers, Adams was a familiar voice within the literary circles of Victorian and Edwardian Britain. Adams's writings, particularly her poems, display patriotic themes mixed with religious sentiments; she often described England as God's chosen country to lead the world. Commenting on Adams's work, critic Amanda Jo Pettit noted in the *Dictionary of Literary Biography* that "Her poems are by no means innovative in style, but they suggest great feeling and reveal a sensitivity to her surroundings and an active interest in the issues and people of her day."

Adams published nearly thirty books during her career, many of which were multivolume novels. Her first published story, "Keane Malcombe's Pupil," appeared in 1876 in Charles Dickens' *All the Year Round,* a publication in which a number of Adams's novels were first published, many of them anonymously. A year later she published her first novel, a three-volume tale titled *Winstowe*. Adams took her name from her first marriage in 1859 to Andrew Leith Adams, an army surgeon with the First Battalion Cheshire, a member of the Royal Society, and the author of several natural histories, including *Field and Forest Rambles, with Notes and Observations on the Natural History of Eastern Canada* (1873). Andrew Leith Leith Adams retired from the army in 1873 and accepted an appointment as a professor of zoology at the College of Science in Dublin. Through her husband's associations, Adams was able to meet many of England's most important intellectuals, including Dickens and the famous biologist Thomas Henry Huxley. Adams once told Helen C. Black in *Notable Women Authors of the Day,* that she "used to delight in meeting all the talent of this and many another country" at the Royal Society gatherings; there she gained what she called her "liberal education," which would later influence her writing.

Adams traveled extensively with her first husband and his battalion, going first to Ireland, then to Malta, where the couple's first son was born in 1862, and New Brunswick, Canada, before finally returning to England in 1871. Many of Adams's writings are based on her experiences during these travels. After publishing *Winstowe* in 1877, Adams wrote another three-volume novel, *Madelon Lemoine,* which a critic in *Pall Mall* found to have "lifelike" characters. That same year, 1879, Adams became the editor of *Kensington Magazine,* a position she held for about a year. In 1880 Adams published her third novel, *Aunt Hepsy's Foundling,* which a contributor for the *Saturday Review* called "an almost perfect novel of its kind." The book was successful, and it did not take long for it to go into a second edition.

Adams published just two more books before her first husband died. His untimely death from tuberculosis

would not be the last tragedy Adams would have to endure. In 1892 her second son, Harry, died. His death was followed a year later by that of Adams's first son, Francis, who committed suicide after suffering a hemorrhage brought on by tuberculosis and throat cancer. Ironically, it was during this time of personal loss that Adams wrote two of her most successful novels, *A Garrison Romance* and *Colour Sergeant No. 1 Company.*

In 1883 Adams married the Reverend Robert Stuart de Courcy Laffan, who would become the headmaster of the King Edward VI Grammar School and a well-known chaplain. After her marriage to Laffan, Adams published her first volume of poetry, *A Song of Jubilee, and Other Poems.* The book was issued the same year Great Britain celebrated its fiftieth year with Queen Victoria on the throne, and the book's title is a reference to that event. "Bringing greetings to our Lady— England's Queen for fifty years," Adams wrote in the title poem. "Fifty years of strong endeavor, fifty years of purpose high / Wrought out slowly to fulfillment, years whose record cannot die." While *A Song of Jubilee* also contains a number of love poems, the title poem's nationalistic tone is emblematic of much of Adams's work.

When she was not writing, Adams was active at the King Edward VI Grammar School. In addition to organizing school concerts, in which she would provide piano accompaniment, Adams designed costumes for school plays and once even composed the accompanying music to a play. These activities led her to begin a lecture series in 1889; in her talks she touted the importance of a good education. Her work at the school also influenced her 1889 novel *Louis Draycott: The Story of His Life,* which a critic for the *Athenaeum* felt contains a "tender spell and purity of purpose." Adams continued to be productive through the 1890s and into the early 1900s, publishing several more novels and collections of short stories, as well as the one-act play *Their Experiment,* which was produced.

Adams published a major volume of poetry in 1907; her *Poems* includes many previously published works as well as thirty-five new poems. As in *A Song of Jubilee,* the verses in *Poems* are filled with patriotic fervor, as in the poem "The Nation's Prayer," about England's participation in the ongoing Boer War. Adams divided the book into four sections. In the final section, "In Memoriam," she includes a number of poems in which she paid homage to several of her dead contemporaries, including statesmen and military officers whom she refers to as "knights," "beacons," and "gallant sons."

After *Poems,* Adams published only three more books: *Dreams Made Verity: Stories, Essays, and Memories* and *The Story of the Brotherhood of Hero Dogs,* both in 1910, and *A Book of Short Plays and a Memory* in 1912. She died after a long illness, on September 5, 1912.

BIOGRAPHICAL AND CRITICAL SOURCES:

BOOKS

Black, Helen C., *Notable Women Authors of the Day,* Bryce (Glasgow, Scotland), 1893, pp. 286-298.
Dictionary of Literary Biography, Volume 240: *Late-Nineteenth-and Early-Twentieth-Century British Women Poets,* Gale (Detroit, MI), 2001, pp. 3-8.*

*   *   *

ADELKHAH, Fariba 1959-

PERSONAL: Born April 25, 1959, in Teheran, Iran; immigrated to France, 1977. *Education:* University of Teheran, baccalaureat in literature, 1976; University of Humanist Science, Strasbourg, France, diploma of French studies, 1979, B.A., 1983; École des Hautes Etudes en Sciences Sociales, M.A., 1984, Ph.D. (social anthropology), 1990.

ADDRESSES: Office—National Foundation of Political Science, 56 Rue Jacob, 75006 Paris, France. *E-mail*—adelkhah@ceri-sciences-po.org.

CAREER: National Foundation of Political Science, Paris, France, researcher, 1993—.

WRITINGS:

La révolution sous le voile: femmes Islamiques d'Iran, Karthala (Paris, France), 1991.
Un péril Islamiste? Editions Complexe (Brussels, Belgium), 1994.

Etre moderne en Iran, Karthala (Paris, France), 1998, translation by Jonathan Derrick published as *Being Modern in Iran,* Columbia University Press (New York, NY), 2000.
(With François Georgeon) *Ramadan et politique,* CNRS Editions (Paris, France), 2002.

SIDELIGHTS: A longtime resident of France, Fariba Adelkhah was born in Iran and retains a strong interest in the ways Iranians, especially women, have reacted to the sweeping changes ushered in by the overthrow of the Shah. An active participant in the Iranian Revolution, Adelkhah has traveled back numerous times, bringing her sociological training to bear in studying and explaining the ways Iranians have adjusted to living in an Islamic state.

In *La révolution sous le voile: femmes Islamiques d'Iran* Fariba presents the results of numerous interviews with Iranian women conducted in the mid-1980s. Many of these women, supporters of the Iranian revolution, see Islam as an essentially egalitarian religion, though in need of new interpretation. Indeed, Adelkhah finds that the whole "women question" has been opened as never before, and the women in these pages have found a new voice as a result of their revolutionary activities and, for some, their participation in the Iran-Iraq War. The diverse voices presented in the book reflect the many ways in which people reshape official doctrines and ideologies in their actual lives. In addition to the interviews, "the book's strength is that it draws on a wide range of sources that include Iranian and Western academic literature, popular Iranian media (especially women's journals), graffiti and Islamic apologetics," explained *MAN* contributor Azam Torab Kheradpir. It "deserves to be made widely available to English-speaking readers through a competent translation, as a badly needed corrective to the prevalent view of women as mere victims of Iran's revolution," concluded *Middle East Journal* contributor Nesta Ramazani.

In 1997 the Iranians themselves dramatically exposed the social and political tensions brewing below their society's monolithic surface when they elected Mohammad Khatami as president, firmly rejecting the Islamic regime's approved candidate. For Adalkhah it was another indicator of the complexities in Iranian politics and society, and she sets out to convey some of those complexities in *Being Modern in Iran,* "a particularly sophisticated and innovative study of contemporary Iranian life," according to *Middle East Quarterly* contributor Daniel Pipes. Using case studies and an encyclopedic knowledge of Iranian politics, Adalkhah shows how officials are capable of working within supposedly medieval stricture s to administer a modern state. At the same time, she illustrates ways in which the Islamic Republic's social policies have actually created space in which private citizens can redefine and reinterpret Islamic doctrines to accommodate an increasingly urban, educated, and bureaucratic society. "This social perspective on the nature of change, moving away from an institutional and state-centered focus, is indeed refreshing, if occasionally bewildering," wrote *Times Literary Supplement* reviewer Ali Ansari. *Being Modern in Iran* "ought to be required reading for anyone wanting to understand the political and social changes in Iran during the past two decades," Eric Hoogland suggested in the *Journal of Palestine Studies.*

BIOGRAPHICAL AND CRITICAL SOURCES:

PERIODICALS

Journal of Palestine Studies, summer, 2000, Eric Hoogland, review of *Being Modern in Iran,* p. 118.
MAN, December, 1992, Azam Torab Kheradpir, review of *La révolution sous le voile: femmes Islamiques d'Iran,* p. 893.
Middle East Journal, spring, 1993, Nesta Ramazani, review of *La révolution sous le voile: femmes Islamiques d'Iran,* pp. 336-37.
Middle East Quarterly, June, 2000, Daniel Pipes, review of *Being Modern in Iran,* p. 118.
Times Literary Supplement, May 24, 2002, Ali Ansari, "There Is No Religion without Justice," p. 26.*

*   *   *

ALBANESE, Antonio 1964-

PERSONAL: Born October 10, 1964, in Olginate, Lecco, Italy. *Education:* Civica Scuola d'Arte Drammatica, Milan, Italy, graduated, 1991.

ADDRESSES: Agent—Luisa Pistoia Management, Piazza Martiri di Belfiore, 4-00195 Roma, Italy.

CAREER: Actor, director, and screenwriter. Actor in films, including *Un'anima divisa in due* (also known as *A Soul Split in Two* and *A Split Soul*), 1993; (as Antonio) *Vesna va veloce,* 1996; (as Antonio) *Uomo d'acqua dolce,* 1996; *Dead Train,* 1997; (as Felice) *Tu ridi* (also known as *You Laugh* and *You're Laughing*), RaiTrade, 1998; (as voice of Big Rat) *La Gabbianella e il gatto* (also known as *Zorba and Lucky*), Trimark Video, 1998; (as Alex/Ivo/Pacifico) *La fame e la sete* (also known as *Hunger and Thirst*), Cecchi Gori Group, 1999; (as Antonio) *La lingua del santo* (also known as *Holy Tongue*), Medusa Distribuzione, 2000; and (as Antonio) *Il nostro matrimonio è in crisi,* 2002. Director, *Il nostro matrimonio è in crisi.*

WRITINGS:

(With Vincenso Cerami; and director and actor) *Uomo d'acqua dolce* (screenplay), 1996.
(With Vincenso Cerami; and director and actor) *La fame e la sete* (screenplay), 1999.

SIDELIGHTS: Italian comedian and actor Antonio Albanese has been in films since the early 1990s. He has appeared in numerous movies in his native country, and has also co-written and directed two films, *Uomo d'acqua dolce* and *La fame e la sete. Uomo d'acqua dolce* is the story of a man—played by Albanese—who is hit on the head by a falling package when he is out buying mushrooms for his pregnant wife, Beatrice. The blow gives him amnesia, and for the next five years he wanders, not knowing who he is or what happened to him. His wife, who doesn't know what happened to him either, assumes that he has simply abandoned her and starts seeing a musician named Gotffredo. When, five years later, he returns home with the mushrooms and with no memory of being hit on the head, he "launches a determined, comical campaign to win back the naturally reticent Beatrice," wrote *MSN Entertainment* contributor Sandra Brennan.

The second film Albanese co-authored with Vincenso Cerami, *La fame e la sete,* is about three brothers who are reunited for the first time in many years when they all return to their native Sicily for their father's funeral. Albanese plays all three brothers, who are very different in personality: Alex is a fat, spoiled photographer; Salvatore has moved to the northern part of the country and become a heartless businessman; and Pacifico, a quiet, shy high school teacher.

BIOGRAPHICAL AND CRITICAL SOURCES:

BOOKS

Contemporary Theatre, Film, and Television, Volume 34, Gale (Detroit, MI), 2001.

PERIODICALS

Variety, September 18, 2000, David Rooney, review of *Holy Tongue,* p. 35.

ONLINE

Attoriitaliani.com, http://www.attoriitaliani.com/ (February 2, 2003), "Luisa Pistoia Management: Antonio Albanese."
Italica, http://www.italica.rai.it/ (January 31, 2003), "Biography of Antonio Albanese."
MSN Entertainment, http://entertainment.msn.com/ (January 31, 2003), summaries of *Tu ridi, La lingua del santo, La fame e la sete,* and *Uomo d'acqua dolce.**

*   *   *

ANDREWS, Jay
See WYNORSKI, Jim

*   *   *

ATKINS, Robert C(oleman) 1930-2003

OBITUARY NOTICE—See index for *CA* sketch: Born October 17, 1930, in Columbus, OH; died as a result of head injuries suffered in a fall April 17, 2003, in New York, NY. Physician and author. Atkins was best known for creating the Atkins diet, which emphasizes a high protein and fat, low-carbohydrate combination of foods. A cardiologist and nutritionist, he was a graduate of the University of Michigan, where he earned an A.B. in 1951, and Cornell University, where he received his medical degree in 1955. After doing an internship at Strong Hospital in Rochester, New York, for a year, and finishing his residency in cardiol-

ogy and internal medicine at hospitals in New York City, Atkins opened a private practice in 1959. During these early years, he suffered from stress and weight gain because he was depressed that he was not getting many patients at his office. He decided to go on a diet, and based his change in food intake on the research of Dr. Alfred W. Pennington, who recommended removing starch and sugar from meals. After finding success with his new diet, subsequent work as a medical consultant for American Telephone and Telegraph in which he managed to get sixty-four patients to reach their ideal weight helped spread the word of his diet. He appeared on national television in 1965 and his diet was published in *Vogue* magazine in 1970, after which it was known for a time as the Vogue diet. When he published his findings in *Dr. Atkins' Diet Revolution,* in 1972 the book became a bestseller. However, it was also quite controversial as many of his fellow doctors, advocates of a diet low in fat and including much more fruits and vegetables than Atkins called for, declared the diet unhealthy. These doctors felt that, although the Atkins diet might cause a person to lose some weight at first, it was at the sacrifice of their overall health. Nevertheless, Atkins won over many converts and continued to publish his ideas in books such as *Dr. Atkins' Superenergy Diet: The Diet Revolution's Answer to Fatigue and Depression* (1977), *Dr. Atkins' Super Energy Cookbook* (1978), *Dr. Atkins' New Diet Cookbook* (1994), *Dr. Atkins' New Diet Revolution* (1999), and the 2003 edition of his *Dr. Atkins' Diet Revolution.* Although no formal, thoroughly complete medical studies have been done on the effectiveness of the Atkins diet, a study published in the *Journal of the American Medical Association* stated that there was not enough evidence to prove it was harmful, either. Also interested in other nutrition and health issues, in 1984 Atkins opened his Atkins Center for Complementary Medicine, where he advocated the use of various alternative medicines and treatments, including the use of vitamins in place of drugs and a treatment for AIDS and cancer that used ozone. It was for the latter that he became the subject of a complaint that led to his medical license being temporarily suspended in 1993. However, he soon had his record cleared. His ideas about the use of vitamins and natural herbs in place of drugs are published in such books as *Dr. Atkins' Nutrition Breakthrough: How to Treat Your Medical Condition without Drugs* (1981) and *Dr. Atkins' Vita-Nutrient Solution: Nature's Answers to Drugs* (1998). In 2002, Atkins suffered a heart attack that was the result of an infection, not his diet, and his death was precipitated by a fall on an icy sidewalk.

OBITUARIES AND OTHER SOURCES:

PERIODICALS

Chicago Tribune, April 18, 2003, section 1, p. 6.
Los Angeles Times, April 18, 2003, p. B11.
New York Times, April 18, 2003, p. C13.
Times (London, England), April 18, 2003.
Washington Post, April 18, 2003, p. B7.

ONLINE

Atkins Center Web site, http://atkins.com/ (July 5, 2003).

B

BANNOR, Brett 1959-

PERSONAL: Born December 16, 1959, in Chicago, IL. *Education:* Southern Illinois University, B.S., 1981.

ADDRESSES: Office—Zoo Atlanta, 800 Cherokee Ave. S.E., Atlanta, GA 30315. *E-mail*—brettbannor@aol. com.

CAREER: Zoo Atlanta, Atlanta, GA, zookeeper; also worked as a zookeeper in Miami, FL, and Orlando, FL.

WRITINGS:

Bighorn Sheep, Lucent Books (San Diego, CA), 2003.

Contributor of articles to scientific journals.

WORK IN PROGRESS: Extensive research on wild animals and the law.

SIDELIGHTS: Brett Bannor told *CA:* " People ask me why I am a zookeeper *and* a freelance writer. The answer is obvious, if you have ever tried to live on what you're paid for either of these professions alone.

"To anyone wishing to embark on a career as a writer, I advise the purchase of a computer, or at least pen and paper. Perhaps someday we will control mental telepathy, and then we will be able simply to project our thoughts into the readers' minds, thereby eliminating the need for keyboards, stationery, and, best of all, editors.

"[Good writing] is all in the preparation. The only way to write informative articles or nonfiction books is to do the research, and do it thoroughly. And for goodness sake, when you do research, go to a reliable source, preferably the first place where the relevant information was published. For instance, if you pick up the *New York Times* and read some article on the effects of a new artificial sweetener on mice bladders, remember two things. One: mice have very tiny bladders. They can't sit through a half-hour of *Friends* without having to leave the couch and visit the bathroom. And two: the study of these mouse bladders was not originally published in the *Times;* it was probably published first in the *New England Journal of Medicine* or something like that. Go to a good academic library and struggle through the original article so you are really well acquainted with rodent bladders and artificial sweeteners before you try to write about this fascinating topic yourself."

*   *   *

BARGHOUTI, Mourid 1944-

PERSONAL: Born 1944, in Deir Ghassani, Palestine; married Radwa Ashour (a novelist); one child.

ADDRESSES: Home—Cairo, Egypt. *Agent*—c/o Author Mail, American University in Cairo Press, 420 Fifth Avenue, New York, NY 10018-2729.

CAREER: Worked as a teacher in Kuwait and at the Palestine Radio, Cairo, Egypt. Member, Sakakini General Assembly.

AWARDS, HONORS: Mahfouz Najib Literature Prize, American University in Cairo, 1997, for *I Saw Ramallah.*

WRITINGS:

I Saw Ramallah, translated by Ahdaf Soueif, foreword by Edward W. Said, American University in Cairo Press (New York, NY), 2000.

SIDELIGHTS: A contributor to the *Khalil Sakakini Cultural Centre Web site* called Mourid Barghouti "one of the most famous Palestinian poets." In 1997 he won the Mahfouz Najib Literature Prize from Cairo's American University for *I Saw Ramallah.*

In 1967 Barghouti left his village of Deir Ghassanah, located just outside of Ramallah, for Cairo's American University to finish his final exams before graduation. Before he had a chance to finish the exams, Israeli troops took control of Ramallah and Deir Ghassanah. Unable to return to his home and his family, Barghouti stayed in Cairo. While there, he married, but in 1977 was forced to move out of Cairo, leaving his pregnant wife behind. He settled in Budapest, separated from his wife and son. Over the following years Barghouti was not able to settle in one location for long, living in such places as Baghdad, Beirut, Budapest, Amman, and then again in Cairo. *Arab World Books* contributor Hugh Galford commented, "Rather than a place, 'home' and 'family' have become extractions and ideals," for Barghouti at this time in his life. Finally in 1996, nearly thirty years after he left, Barghouti was able to return to the village of Deir Ghassanah and nearby Ramallah for a short visit.

In *I Saw Ramallah* Barghouti describes his thirty-year ordeal and the trip back to Ramallah and Deir Ghassanah. He illustrates in great detail what he sees when he reaches his destination and how the Palestinian people have changed. "Barghouti writes in a poetic prose whose unexpected images constantly open new vistas for the reader," praised W. L. Hanaway in a *Choice* review. *Al-Ahram Weekly* contributor Youssef Rakha called the book a "beautifully constructed and moving memoir."

BIOGRAPHICAL AND CRITICAL SOURCES:

PERIODICALS

Choice, July, 2001, W. L. Hanaway, review of *I Saw Ramallah,* p. 1954.
Middle East Journal, autumn, 2001, Aida A. Bamia, review of *I Saw Ramallah,* p. 687.
New Yorker, November 19, 2001, Dana Goodyear, review of *I Saw Ramallah,* p. 22.
Times Literary Supplement, April 19, 2002, Peter Clark, "Despair of the Heart," p. 28.

ONLINE

Al-Ahram Weekly Online, http://www.ahram.org.eg/ (August 28, 2002), Maggie Morgan, "A Certain Idea of Palestine"; Youssef Rakha, "The World in Prose."
Arab World Books Web site, http://www. arabworldbooks.com/ (August 28, 2002), Hugh Galford, review of *I Saw Ramallah.*
Cairo Times Online, http://www.cairotimes.com/ (August 28, 2002), Richard Woffenden, "Reading Is Believing."
In These Times, http://www.inthesetimes.com/ (August 28, 2002), Benjamin Kunkel, "The Homecoming."
Islam Online, http://www.islamonline.net/ (August 28, 2002), Joanne McEwan, review of *I Saw Ramallah.*
Khalil Sakakini Cultural Centre Web site, http://www. sakakini.org/ (August 28, 2002), "Palestinian Poets: Mureed Barghouti."*

*   *   *

BARRY, Kevin
    See LAFFAN, Kevin (Barry)

*   *   *

BEHNKE, Robert H. 1929-

PERSONAL: Born December 30, 1929, in Stamford, CT; married 1963. *Education:* University of Connecticut, B.A. (zoology), 1957; University of California, Berkeley, M.A. 1960, Ph.D., 1964.

ADDRESSES: Office—Department of Fishery and Wildlife Biology, Colorado State University, Fort Collins, CO 80523. *E-mail*—fwb@cnr.colostate.edu.

CAREER: American Academy of Science, exchange scholar to USSR, 1964-65; University of California, Berkeley, assistant professor, 1966; Colorado State University, professor of fisheries, 1966—. Consultant to editors of *National Geographic* for articles pertaining to fish.

MEMBER: American Fisheries Society, American Society of Ichthyology and Herpetology Research.

WRITINGS:

(With D. E. Benson) *Endangered and Threatened Fishes of the Upper River Basin,* Colorado State University, Cooperative Extension Service (Fort Collins, CO), 1980.

Native Trout of Western North America, American Fisheries Society (Bethesda, MD), 1992.

Trout and Salmon of North America, illustrated by Joseph R. Tomelleri, Free Press (New York, NY), 2002.

Also writes a column for *Trout* magazine and articles for various scientific publications.

SIDELIGHTS: Robert J. Behnke has been studying and teaching the genetics and biology of endangered, threatened, and rare fish for almost fifty years. He is a professor at Colorado State University where he teaches courses such as advanced ichthyology, conservation biology, and fishery seminars. In recent years, he has attempted to reach an audience outside of academia by writing a quarterly column for the popular fishing magazine *Trout,* by advising editors at *National Geographic* on their articles pertaining to fish, and presenting his views in several scientific publications on the evolution of specific species of fish. He has also written three reference books on fish that reviewers have cited among the most intensive studies on the subject. In his books Behnke writes authoritatively about his topic, and, as a *Publishers Weekly* reviewer observed, he "also ponders some of the more philosophical aspects of ecology and human responsibility for the environments that these fish live

in. His books are filled with scholarly information, but his interest in the field is also demonstrated by many of the interesting anecdotes that he offers about the life and fate of the trout and salmon."

In 1992 Behnke published his *Native Trout of Western North America,* the result of forty years of research and practical experience with this group of fishes. In the book, Behnke discusses the evolution, taxonomy, behaviors, and current distribution of cutthroat, rainbow, Gila, and other indigenous trout found in the West. He also offers a philosophy of conservation that he believes will sustain the habitat and health of these fish. The book is illustrated with black-and-white drawings as well as color plates of the various species of fish the book focuses on. Behnke wrote the book with the hope that it will assist fisheries managers, students of salmonid evolution, taxonomists, and people interested in fishing who would like to learn more about the trout that they catch. One of the major points Behnke makes in this study is that wild stocks of trout should be left unhampered. In other words, habitats should not be altered, fish should not be introduced into waters that are not their natural environment, and native species should not be mixed with hatchery stockfish, a practice that results in hybridization. The Alvord cutthroat trout once found in native rivers along the Oregon-Nevada border, for instance, has become extinct because they were crossbred with rainbow trout local farmers introduced into the Alvord's natural environment. Behnke would like to avoid a similar disaster in the future.

Ten years after the publication of *Native Trout of Western North America,* Behnke wrote *Trout and Salmon of North America,* which a reviewer from *Forbes* found to be not only a stimulating read but also so well illustrated that the book could well be considered a work of art. Behnke, with his extensive knowledge of the topic, and illustrator Joseph R. Tomelleri, who reportedly spent anywhere from thirty-five to fifty hours on each portrait, have collaborated to create an extensive study of the more than seventy different types of trout and salmon that exist in North America. Tomelleri's illustrations, which many reviewers have claimed are some of the most beautiful ever made of fish, "are accurate down to the last fin ray and parr mark," according to the *Forbes* reviewer; and Behnke's "colorful details and anecdotes" prove to be not only educational for any professional ichthyologists or any of the thirty-five million amateur anglers in North America, but also alluring enough to "captivate casual readers."

Behnke's *Trout and Salmon of North America* includes detailed maps that demonstrate both the native freshwater locations and the bodies of water into which the fish have been introduced throughout North America. Noting that trout and salmon are among some of the most prized game fish, *Booklist*'s Mary J. Nickum referred to Behnke's study as "an excellent field guide and reference for serious anglers and naturalists."

BIOGRAPHICAL AND CRITICAL SOURCES:

PERIODICALS

Forbes, September 16, 2002, review of *Trout and Salmon of North America,* p. 120.
Library Journal, September 1, 2002, Mary J. Nickum, review of *Trout and Salmon of North American,* p. 202.
Publishers Weekly, July 29, 2002, review of *Trout and Salmon of North America,* pp. 61-62.*

*   *   *

BELL, Eudorus N. 1866-1923

PERSONAL: Born June 27, 1866, in Lake Butler, FL; died June 15, 1923, in Springfield, MO; married Katie Kimbrough, 1909. *Education:* University of Chicago, graduated, 1903.

CAREER: Minister of Southern Baptist Convention, beginning 1903; Pentecostal minister with Church of God in Christ, Malvern, AR, beginning c. 1907; Assemblies of God, minister and chair of general assembly, 1914-15; pastor of church in Galena, KA, c. 1915-16; Assemblies of God, minister, 1916-23, general secretary, 1919, chair, 1920-23. Gospel School, Findlay, OH, teacher, beginning 1914.

WRITINGS:

Questions and Answers, [Springfield, MO], 1923.

Editor of *Word and Witness* (later *Evangel*), c. 1909, and 1918-23.*

BENDER, Daniel Henry 1866-1945

PERSONAL: Born 1866, in Grantsville, MD; died 1945, in Albany, OR.

CAREER: Schoolteacher in Grantsville, MD, beginning c. 1880s; ordained Mennonite minister, 1887, later ordained bishop; minister of Mennonite congregations, 1887-1909; Hesston Academy and Bible School (later College), Hesston, KS, principal, 1909-30, president until 1930. Mennonite Board of Colonization, former president.

WRITINGS:

Author of the book *A Brief Sketch of My Life,* privately printed. Author of *Advanced Sunday School Lesson Quarterly,* beginning 1903, and *Primary Sunday School Quarterly,* beginning 1905. Editor, *Herald of Truth,* 1904-c. 1906, and *Gospel Herald,* 1908-09.*

*   *   *

BERG, James J. 1964-

PERSONAL: Born July 1, 1964, in Superior, WI. *Education:* University of Minnesota—Twin Cities, B.A. (cum laude), 1986, M.A., 1992, Ph.D. (English language and literature), 1996.

ADDRESSES: Home—3235 Bloomington Ave., Minneapolis, MN 55407. *E-mail*—bergjj@yahoo.com.

CAREER: Educator, administrator, and author. University of Maine at Orono, assistant professor and program director, 1999-2000; Minnesota State Colleges and Universities, St. Paul, program director of Center for Teaching and Learning, 2000—. Presenter at workshops.

MEMBER: Modern Language Association of America, American Association for Higher Education.

AWARDS, HONORS: Lambda Literary Award for Gay Studies, 2000, for *The Isherwood Century.*

WRITINGS:

(Editor with Chris Freeman) *The Isherwood Century: Essays on the Life and Work of Christopher Isherwood,* University of Wisconsin Press (Madison, WI), 2000.

Editor and author of introduction, with Chris Freeman) *Conversations with Christopher Isherwood,* University Press of Mississippi (University, MS), 2001.

Contributor to books, including *Cyclopedia of Literary Places,* Salem Press (Pasadena, CA), 2002, *Christopher Isherwood Encyclopedia,* McFarland & Co. (Jefferson, NC), 2003, and *Encyclopedia of Lesbian, Gay, Bisexual, and Transgender History in America,* Charles Scribner's Sons, in press; contributor to periodicals, including *West Virginia University Philological Papers, Minnesota Review, Lesbian and Gay Studies Newsletter,* and *Lambda Book Report.* Web master and editor, www.thisherwoodcentury.org.

WORK IN PROGRESS: A Writer and His World: Christopher Isherwood's Lectures in California, for University of Minnesota Press; a research project, "The American Isherwood."

BIOGRAPHICAL AND CRITICAL SOURCES:

ONLINE

James J. Berg Web site, http://jamesberg.efoliomn2.com (August 8, 2003).

*   *   *

BERG, M. C.
See BERG, Michael C(hristian)

*   *   *

BERG, Michael C(hristian) 1955-
(M. C. Berg)

PERSONAL: Born August 16, 1955, in Curitiba, Brazil; U.S. citizen; son of W. A. and A. M. Berg; married Barbara J. Peyton, June 27, 1992; children: Joseph, Charles, Samuel. *Ethnicity:* "White." *Educa-*

tion: University of California, Los Angeles, B.A., 1978; University of California, San Diego, Ph.D., 1985. *Religion:* Roman Catholic. *Hobbies and other interests:* Judo (second-degree black belt), jazz guitar, art (painting).

ADDRESSES: Home—6707 West 87th Pl., Los Angeles, CA 90045. *Office*—Department of Mathematics, Loyola Marymount University, Los Angeles, CA 90045. *E-mail*—mberg@lmu.edu.

CAREER: Saint Mary's College, Moraga, CA, assistant professor of mathematics, 1985-87; Loyola Marymount University, Los Angeles, CA, visiting assistant professor, 1988-89, assistant professor, 1989-94, associate professor, 1994-99, professor of mathematics, 1999—, instructor in judo, 1996-97. Visiting docent at El Camino College and California State University, Long Beach, both 1988.

MEMBER: American Mathematical Society, Mathematical Association of America, U.S. Judo Association, Sigma Xi, Pi Mu Epsilon.

WRITINGS:

The Fourier-Analytic Proof of Quadratic Reciprocity, Wiley Publishing Group (New York, NY), 2000.

Contributor of articles and reviews to mathematics journals, including *Integral Transforms and Special Functions, Journal of Number Theory,* and *Far East Journal of Mathematical Sciences.* Some writings appear under the name M. C. Berg.

WORK IN PROGRESS: Research on "the open question of the analytic proof of higher reciprocity laws (for global fields)."

SIDELIGHTS: Michael C. Berg told *CA:* "I am a professional mathematician whose research focuses on Fourier analytic methods in the theory of algebraic number (and, recently, function) fields. The problem that has occupied me throughout my career to date is that of the analytic approach to general reciprocity laws, going back some eighty years to Erich Heeke.

My work has been greatly influenced by the work of André Weil, Tomio Kubata, and, most recently, Alexandre Grothendieck, Pierre Delique, and Gérard Laumon."

*   *   *

BERG, William J. 1942-

PERSONAL: Born October 26, 1942, in Dunkirk, NY; son of Francis J. (a department store manager) and Adalyn H. (a registered nurse; maiden name, Goodwin) Berg; married Laurey Kramer Martin, February 1, 1986; children: Jennifer Berg Duffy, Jessica, Stirling Martin (stepson), Hunter Martin (stepson). *Education:* Hamilton College, B.A., 1964; Princeton University, M.A., 1966, Ph.D., 1969. *Politics:* Democrat. *Hobbies and other interests:* Tennis, guitar.

ADDRESSES: Home—5201 Pepin Pl., Madison, WI 53705. *Office*—Department of French, University of Wisconsin—Madison, Madison, WI 53706. *E-mail*—wjberg@facstaff.wisc.edu.

CAREER: University of Wisconsin—Madison, assistant professor, 1967-73, associate professor, 1973-79, professor of French, 1979—, Halverson-Bascom Professor, 1995-2000, director of academic year abroad in Paris, 1973-74, chair of Department of French and Italian, 1982-85, honors fellow, 1994—. Summa Publications, member of editorial board, 1983—.

MEMBER: Modern Language Association of America, American Council on the Teaching of Foreign Languages.

AWARDS, HONORS: Vilas associate, 1991-93; Chancellor's Award for excellence in teaching, University of Wisconsin, 1995.

WRITINGS:

(With Peter Schofer and Donald Rice) *Poèmes, pièces, prose: introduction a l'analyse de textes litterarires français,* Oxford University Press (New York, NY), 1973.

(With Michel Grimaud and George Moskos) *Saint/Oedipus: Psychocritical Approaches to Flaubert's Art,* Cornell University Press (Ithaca, NY), 1982.

(With Laurey K. Martin) *Images,* Holt, Rinehart & Winston (New York, NY), 1989.

The Visual Novel: Emile Zola and the Art of His Times, Pennsylvania State University Press (University Park, PA), 1992.

(With Laurey K. Martin) *Emile Zola Revisited,* Twayne (New York, NY), 1992.

(With Laurey K. Martin) *Gustave Flaubert,* Twayne (New York, NY), 1997.

(With Magnan, Ozzello, and Laurey K. Martin-Berg) *Paroles,* with video and CD-ROM, Harcourt (New York, NY), 1999.

Member of editorial board, *Sub-Stance.*

WORK IN PROGRESS: From Image to Ideology: Modern French Literature and Painting.

SIDELIGHTS: William J. Berg told *CA:* "Educational writing involves not just the clear expression of ideas, but the discovery, creation, interpretation, integration, analysis, synthesis, application, and transmission of knowledge to the broadest possible audience. Scholarship in its highest form (which I don't claim to practice, only emulate) brings new knowledge not only to experts in a given field, but to any intelligent reader interested in that field."

BIOGRAPHICAL AND CRITICAL SOURCES:

PERIODICALS

Choice, June, 1993, R. Merker, review of *Emile Zola Revisited,* p. 1630, and J. C. McLaren, review of *The Visual Novel: Emile Zola and the Art of His Times,* p. 1631.

French Review, April, 2000, Kenneth E. Kintz, review of *Paroles,* p. 981.

French Studies, April, 1994, Joy Newton, review of *The Visual Novel,* p. 219.

Modern Language Review, October, 1994, F. W. J. Hemmings, review of *The Visual Novel,* p. 1015.

Times Literary Supplement, November 5, 1993, Paul Griffiths, review of *The Visual Novel,* p. 16.

BERGSON, Abram 1914-2003

OBITUARY NOTICE—See index for *CA* sketch: Born April 21, 1914, in Baltimore, MD; died April 23, 2003, in Cambridge, MA. Economist, consultant, and author. Bergson was a former Harvard professor and authority on the Soviet economy. He earned his bachelor's degree from Johns Hopkins University in 1933 and his doctorate from Harvard University in 1940. While working on his degree at Harvard, he was an economics instructor, and at the age of twenty-three published an important paper that measured a population's well being given economic factors. After graduating he was a faculty member at the University of Texas at Austin for two years. During World War II, Bergson worked for the federal government in Washington, D.C., including time at the Office of Strategic Services, the precursor of the Central Intelligence Agency, where he was chief of the Russian economic subdivision. He then taught at Columbia University for ten years, returning to Harvard in 1956 as a professor of economics and directing the university's Russian Research Center (now the Davis Center for Russian and Eurasian Studies) from 1964 to 1968. He left academia in 1968, but continued working as a consultant for years afterward. Along with Paul A. Samuelson, Bergson became well known in the field for creating the Bergson-Samuelson social welfare function, a formula for calculating social well-being that is still commonly used by economists. His continuing interest in the Soviet economy led to his writing frequently on the subject, comparing the communist methods of management with nations using a free market economy. Bergson was the author of several books on this and other economics subjects, including *Real National Income of Soviet Russia since 1928* (1961), *Soviet Post-War Economic Development* (1974), *Welfare, Planning, and Employment: Selected Essays in Economic Theory* (1982), and *Planning and Performance in Socialist Economies: The USSR and Eastern Europe* (1989); he also edited several economics books.

OBITUARIES AND OTHER SOURCES:

BOOKS

Writers Directory, 18th edition, St. James Press (Detroit, MI), 2003.

PERIODICALS

Los Angeles Times, May 4, 2003, p. B17.
New York Times, April 25, 2003, p. B11.
Washington Post, May 2, 2003, p. B7.

*   *   *

BERMAN, Alex 1914-2000

PERSONAL: Born February 7, 1914, in New York, NY; died June 29, 2000; son of Benjamin (in sales) and Batya (a homemaker; maiden name, Simon) Berman; married Hortense Behr, August 9, 1943. *Ethnicity:* "White." *Education:* Fordham University, B.S., 1946; University of Wisconsin, Ph.D., 1954. *Politics:* Liberal. *Religion:* Jewish. *Hobbies and other interests:* History, music, French history and language, literature.

CAREER: University of Wisconsin—Madison, assistant professor of history, 1955-57; University of Texas—Austin, associate professor of pharmacy, 1961-68; University of Cincinnati, Cincinnati, OH, professor of history and historical studies in pharmacy, 1968-75. *Military service:* U.S. Army Air Forces, 1943-46; became sergeant.

AWARDS, HONORS: Guggenheim fellowship, 1958-59; Kremers Award for history of pharmacy; grants from National Science Foundation and National Library of Medicine.

WRITINGS:

(With Michael A. Flannery) *America's Botanico-Medical Movements, Vox Populi,* Haworth Press (Hazleton, PA), 2001.

SIDELIGHTS: Alex Berman's widow, Hortense Berman, told *CA:* "Professor Berman was always interested in both science and the humanities. He was not limited by his early work in pharmacy; he explored literature, history, music, and the theater. His personal library contained many valuable books and prints from the seventeenth, eighteenth, and nineteenth centuries, which he had discovered in Paris and London.

"He was keenly concerned with promising students in his courses, and he served as a kindly mentor to them."

[Date of death provided by wife, Hortense Berman.]

*   *   *

BETTI, Laura 1934-

PERSONAL: Original name, Laura Trombetti; born May 1, 1934, in Bologna, Italy.

ADDRESSES: Agent—c/o Artmedia, 10 avenue George V, 75008 Paris, France.

CAREER: Actress, singer, director, and screenwriter. Actress in films, including *Era notte a Roma* (also known as *Escape by Night,* and *Wait for the Dawn*), 1960; (as Teresa) *It Was Night in Rome,* 1960; (as the painter) *Labbra rosse* (also known as *Red Lips*), Rotor/ Gray/Orsay, 1960; (as Laura) *La dolce vita* (also known as *La douceur de vivre*), Astor/American International, 1960; *Laviamoci il cervello* (also known as *Let's Have a Brainwash* and *RoGoPaG*), Arco, 1962; *Mondo di notte numero 3* (also known as *Ecco* and *The Shocking World*), 1963; (as Desdemona) "Che cosa sono le nuvole?" (also known as "A Night like Any Other"), *Capriccio all'italiana* (also known as *Caprice Italian Style*), Dino de Laurentiis Cinematografica, 1966; (as tourist) "Senso civico," *Le streghe* (also known as *The Witches* and *Les Sorcieres*), Dino de Laurentiis Cinematografica, 1967; *Paulina s'en va,* 1969; (as Mildred Harrington) *Hatchet for the Honeymoon* (also known as *Il Rooso segno della follia, Un'accetta per la luna di miele, Blood Brides, The Red Mark of Madness, The Red Sign of Madness,* and *An Axe for the Honeymoon*), G.G.P., 1969; *La Battaglia del deserto* (also known as *Desert Battle*), 1969; (as Emilia, the servant) *Teorema* (also known as *Theorem*), Continental Distributing, 1969; (as sister) *A Man Called Sledge* (also known as *Sledge*), Columbia, 1971; (as Franco's mother) *Nel nome del Padre* (also known as *In the Name of the Father*), Vides International, 1971; (as Mrs. Fusadi) *Antefatto* (also known as *Reazione a catena, A Bay of Blood, Twitch of the Death Nerve, Before the Fact—The Ecology of a Crime, Bloodbath Bay of Blood, Bloodbath Bay of Death, Bloodbath, Carnage, Ecologia del delitto, The Ecology of a Crime, New House on the Left,* and *Last*

House on the Left, Part II), New Realm Distributors, 1971; (as the wife from Bath) *Canterbury Tales* (also known as *I racconti di Canterbury*), United Artists, 1972; *La polizia ringrazia* (also known as *Execution Squad*), 1972; (as Zigaina) *Sbatti il mostro in prima pagina* (also known as *Slap the Monster on Page One*), Euro International, 1972; (as Miss Blandish) *Last Tango in Paris,* United Artists, 1973; *Sepolta viva,* 1973; (as Donna Aparacito) *Sonny and Jed* (also known as *J. and S.-storia criminale del far west* and *Bandera Bandits*), Loyola Cinematography/Terra K-Tel, 1974; (as Tisa Borghi) *Fatti di gente perbene* (also known as *Drama of the Rich, La grande bourgeoise,* and *The Murri Affair*), Produzioni Atlas Consorziate, 1974; (as Leonore) *La Femme aux bottes rouges* (also known as *The Woman with Red Boots, The Lady with Red Boots, La ragazza con gli stivali rossi,* and *La ragazza dagli stivali rossi*), Union General Cinematographique/Sirius, 1974; *La cugina* (also known as *The Cousin*), 1974; (voice of Signora Vaccari) *Salo o le centiventi giornate di Sodoma* (also known as *Salò, or the 120 Days of Sodom* and *Salo o le 120 giornate di Sodoma.*), United Artists/Cinecenta, 1975; (as Esther Imbriani) *Allonsanfan,* Artificial Eye, 1975; *Bertolucci secondo il cinema* (also known as *The Cinema according to Bertolucci* and *The Making of "1900"*), 1975; (as Regina) *Amelia's Daughter, 1900* (also known as *Novecento* and *Nineteen Hundred*), Paramount/United Artists/Twentieth Century-Fox, 1976; (as Felicia) *Le gang* (also known as *La gang del parigino*), Warner Bros., 1976; (as Therese) *Vizi privati, pubbliche virtu* (also known as *Private Vices and Public Virtue; Private Vices, Public Pleasures;* and *Vices and Pleasures*), Fida Cinematografica, 1976; (as Jacqueline) *La Nuit tous les chat sont gris* (also known as *At Night All Cats Are Gray*), Societe Nouvelle Prodis/Exportation Francaise Cinematographique, 1977; (as Madame Carrabo) *Un papillon sur l'epaule* (also known as *A Butterfly on the Shoulder*), Gaumont, 1978; (as Ludovica) *La luna* (also known as *Luna*), Twentieth Century-Fox, 1979; (as Madame Bondi) *Il piccolo Archimede* (also known as *The Little Archimedes*), RAI-TV Channel 2, 1979; (as Laura) *Lovers and Liars* (also known as *Viaggio con Anita, A Trip with Anita,* and *Travels with Anita*), Levitt-Pickman, 1979; (as Madame Hanska) *Loin de Manhattan,* 1980; *Le ali della colomba,* RAI-TV, 1980; *La certosa di Parma,* RAI-TV, 1981; (narrator) *Whoever Says the Truth Shall Die* (documentary), Minnesota Film Center, 1981; (as Virginia Capacelli) *La nuit de Varennes* (also known as *Il mondo nuovo* and *That Night in Varennes*), Triumph, 1983; (as Clio) *L'Art d'aimer* (also known as *The Art of Love* and *Ars*

Amandi-L'arte di amare), Parafrance, 1983; (as Leonide) *La fuite en avant,* 1983; (as Carlotta Battucelli) *Retenez-moi . . . ou je fais un malheur* (also known as *Hold Me Back or I'll Have an Accident* and *To Catch a Cop*), Gaumont, 1984; (as Brunelda) *Klassenverhältnisse* (also known as *Amerika, rapports de classe* and *Class Relations*), Artificial Eye/New Yorker, 1984; (as Lidia Corradi) *Mamma Ebe,* Clemi Cinematografica, 1985; (as social worker) Tutta colpa del paradiso (also known as Blame It on Paradise and All the Fault of Paradise), CEIAD, 1985; (as Laurie) *Corps et biens* (also known as *Lost with All Hands*), Films du Semaphore, 1986; (as Miss Von Planta) *Jenatsch* (also known as *Jenach*), Films Plain Chant/Metropolis, 1987; *Caramelle da un sconosciuto* (also known as *Sweets from a Stranger* and *Sweets of One Unknown*), Numero Uno Cinematografica, 1987; (as herself) *A Futura memoria di Pier Paolo Pasolini* (also known as *In Remembrance of Pier Paolo Pasolini;* documentary), Pegaso Inter-Communication, 1987; (as Keli) *Noyade interdite* (also known as *Widow's Walk* and *L'Estate impura*), Bac, 1987; (as Paulina, Anna's mother) *I cammelli* (also known as *The Camels*), Medusa Distribuzione, 1988; *Jane B. par Agnès V.* (also known as *Jane B. by Agnes V.*), Capital Cinema/Cene-Tamaris, 1988; (as astrologer) *Il Segno di fuoco,* Boa Cinematografica, 1989; *Le ros blu* (also known as *The Blue Rose*), Kitchen, 1989; (as Signora Bonelli) *Courage Mountain* (also known as *A Heidi Adventure* and *The Adventures of Heidi*), Emerald Films International/Trans World Entertainment, 1989; *Le champignon des carpates,* 1990; (As Catherine de Medicis) *Dames galantes* (also known as *Donne di piacere* and *Gallant Ladies*), 1990; (as Aida) *Il grande cocomero* (also known as *The Great Pumpkin*), 1993; *Mario, Maria e Mario,* 1993; (as Sister Valida) *La Ribelle* (also known as *The Rebel*), 1993; (as Beatrice) *Con gli occhi chiusi* (also known as *With Closed Eyes*), 1994; (as Dottoressa Trebbi) *Un eroe borghese* (also known as *An Ordinary Hero*), 1995; (as Giuseppa) *Marianna Ucrèa* (also known as *La Vie silencieuse de Marianna Ucria*), 1996; *I Magi randagi* (also known as *We Free Kings*), 1996; *Un air si pur . . .* (also known as *An Air So Pure*), 1997; (as judge) *The Protagonists,* Medusa Distribuzione, 1998; *Paradiso e inferno,* 1999; *E insieme vivremo tutte le stagioni,* 1999; *L'amore era una cosa meravigliosa,* 1999; (as Fernando's mother) *À ma soeur!* (also known as *Fat Girl, A mia sorella!,* and *For My Sister*), 2001; *Il Diario di Matilde Manzoni,* 2002; and (as Contessa Celi Sanguineti) *Il quaderno della spesa,* 2002.

Actress in stage productions, including *I Saltimbanchi* (revue); *Il ventaglio,* 1958; *Il crogiuolo,* Italy, 1958; *Giro a vuoto* (recital), Teatro Gerolamo, Milan, Italy, 1959; *Le donne al parlamento,* Italy, 1960; *Potentissima signora,* Italy, 1963; *Il Candelaio,* Italy, 1968; *Orgia,* Italy, 1968; *Not I,* Italy, 1970; *Orgia,* Italy, 1984.

Actress in made-for-television movies, including (as Clara) *Ritorno* (also known as *Return*), 1973; *L'Eroe,* 1974; (as Irina) *Il Gabbiano* (also known as *The Seagull*), RAI-TV Channel 1, 1977; *La Certosa di Parma,* 1977; (as Maria) *The Word* (miniseries), 1978; *Venise en hiver,* [France], 1982; *Chambre d'amie,* [France], 1985; and (as herself) *Pasolini, el poeta en la playa,* 2000. Head of Pasolini Foundation, 1980—.

AWARDS, HONORS: Golden Lion, Venice Film Festival, for *Teorema.*

WRITINGS:

(Editor) *Pasolini: cronaca giudiziaria, persecuzione, morte,* Garzanti (Milan, Italy), 1977.
Teta velata, second edition, Garzanti (Milan, Italy), 1979.
(And director) *Film* (screenplay), 2000.
(And director) *Pier Paolo Pasolini e la ragione di un sogno* (screenplay; also known as *Pier Paolo Pasolini and the Reason of a Dream*), 2001.

SIDELIGHTS: Laura Betti has been appearing on stage in her native Italy since 1958, and on screen since 1960. She is best known for her acting, but in the course of her life Betti has also done some writing. In 2001 she wrote and directed a tribute to one of her favorite film directors, Pier Paolo Pasolini. Betti acted in five films for Pasolini during her career, including *Teorema,* which won the actress a Golden Lion award at the Venice Film Festival. Pasolini was murdered in 1975, possibly by people who were threatened by his outspoken support of Marxism or because of his homosexuality. Since 1980 Betti has headed a foundation named after him which strives to keep his work and his dreams alive. The film she made in tribute to him, *Pier Paolo Pasolini e la ragione di un sogno* (*Pier Paolo Pasolini and the Reason of a Dream*), screened at several film festivals at 2001 and was generally well received. The film, which consists of archival footage of Pasolini talking about life, art, and culture interspersed with interviews with those who knew Pasolini in life, is "lively and stimulating" and illustrates "Pasolini's astute grasp of the consumerist, superficial direction in which Italian society was headed prior to his death," David Rooney wrote in a review for *Variety.*

BIOGRAPHICAL AND CRITICAL SOURCES:

BOOKS

Contemporary Theatre, Film, and Television, Volume 34, Gale (Detroit, MI), 2001.
Stewart, John, *Italian Film: A Who's Who,* McFarland & Co. (Jefferson, NC), 1994.

PERIODICALS

Guardian (London, England), December 7, 2001, review of *À ma soeur!* p. 18.
Los Angeles Times, May 12, 1984, Kevin Thomas, review of *Whoever Says the Truth Shall Die,* p. 9.
New Yorker, March 21, 1983, Pauline Kael, review of *La nuit de Varennes,* pp. 121-123.
New York Times, February 16, 1983, Janet Maslin, review of *La nuit de Varennes,* p. 20; February 27, 1987, Vincent Canby, review of *Class Relations,* p. 28.
Record (Bergen County, NJ), October 12, 2001, Laurence Chollet, review of *Fat Girl,* p. 9.
Scotsman (Edinburgh, Scotland), August 11, 2001, review of *À ma soeur!* p. 8.
Variety, December 21, 1983, review of *L'art d'aimer,* p. 14; November 28, 1984, review of *Whoever Says the Truth Shall Die,* p. 21; January 15, 1986, review of *Tutta colpa del paradiso,* p. 26; August 7, 2000, Derek Elley, review of *Film,* p. 19; October 1, 2001, David Rooney, review of *Pier Paolo Pasolini and the Reason of a Dream,* p. 40.

ONLINE

San Francisco International Film Festival Web site, http://www.sffs.org/ (February 22, 2003), review of *Pier Paolo Pasolini.*
São Paolo International Film Festival Web site, http://www.mostra.org/ (February 22, 2003), review of *Pier Paolo Pasolini and the Reason of a Dream.**

BEYTAGH, Francis (X.) 1935-

PERSONAL: Born July 11, 1935, in Savannah, GA; son of Frank X. and Martha G. Beytagh; married Diane Griffin, November 30, 1957; children: Patrick A., Kathleen B., Maureen E. *Ethnicity:* "White." *Education:* University of Notre Dame, B.A., 1956; University of Michigan, S.D., 1963. *Religion:* Roman Catholic. *Hobbies and other interests:* Travel, golf, reading, walking, swimming.

ADDRESSES: Home—49 Marsh Creek Rd., Amelia Island, FL 32034. *Office*—Florida Coastal School of Law, 7555 Beach Blvd., Jacksonville, FL 32226; fax 904-680-7777. *E-mail*—fbeytagh@fcsl.edu.

CAREER: U.S. Supreme Court, Washington, DC, senior law clerk, 1963-64; associate of a law firm in Cleveland, OH, 1964-66; Office of the Solicitor General, Washington, DC, assistant solicitor general, 1966-70; professor of law and law school administrator, beginning in 1970; Florida Coastal School of Law, Jacksonville, currently professor of law. *Military service:* U.S. Navy, 1956-60. U.S. Naval Reserve, 1960-78; became captain.

MEMBER: American Bar Association, Florida Bar Association, Jacksonville Bar Association.

AWARDS, HONORS: Fulbright fellow; fellow of American Bar Foundation.

WRITINGS:

Constitutional Law: Cases and Materials, 3rd edition, Little, Brown (Boston, MA), 1980.
Constitutionalism in Contemporary England, Round Hall/Sweet & Maxwell, 1997.

WORK IN PROGRESS: Comparative Constitutional Law: Cases and Comments, and *Warren and the Warren Court: A Retrospective.**

*   *   *

BLACKWELL, Antoinette (Louisa) Brown 1825-1921

PERSONAL: Born May 20, 1825, in Henrietta, NY; died November 5, 1921, in Elizabeth, NJ; daughter of Joseph and Abby (Morse) Brown; married Samuel Charles Blackwell (in business), January 24, 1856 (died 1901); children: six (some sources cite seven), including Florence Brown, Mabel, Edith Brown, Grace Brown, Agnes Brown, and Ethel Brown. *Education:* Oberlin College, graduated, 1847, graduate study in theology, 1847-50, M.A., 1978.

CAREER: Ordained Congregational minister, 1853; pastor of Congregational church in South Butler, NY, c. 1853-54; volunteer among the poor and in prisons, New York, NY, 1855; All Souls Unitarian Church, Elizabeth, NJ, preacher, 1908-21. Lecturer on abolition, temperance, and women's suffrage. World Temperance Convention, delegate, 1853.

AWARDS, HONORS: Oberlin College, 1908, honorary D.D.

WRITINGS:

Shadows of Our Social System, 1856.
Studies in General Science, Putnam (New York, NY), 1869.
A Market Woman, 1870.
The Island Neighbors: A Novel of American Life, Harper (New York, NY), 1871.
The Sexes throughout Nature, Putnam (New York, NY), 1875.
The Physical Basis of Immortality, Putnam (New York, NY), 1876.
The Philosophy of Individuality, Putnam (New York, NY), 1893.
Sea Drift; or, Tribute to the Ocean, J. T. White and Co. (New York, NY), 1902.
The Making of the Universe: Evolution, the Continuous Process Which Derives the Finite from the Infinite, Gorham Press (Boston, MA), 1914.
The Social Side of Mind and Action, Neale Publishing Co. (New York, NY), 1915.
Soul Mates: The Oberlin Correspondence of Lucy Stone and Antoinette Brown, 1846-1850, edited by Carol Lasser and Marlene Merrill, Oberlin College (Oberlin, OH), 1983.
Friends and Sisters: Letters between Lucy Stone and Antoinette Brown Blackwell, 1846-93, edited by Carol Lasser and Marlene Deahl Merrill, University of Illinois Press (Urbana, IL), 1987.

Contributor to periodicals, including *Woman's Journal, Oberlin Quarterly Review,* and *New York Tribune.* The Blackwell Family Papers can be found in the Schlesinger Library, Radcliffe College.

BIOGRAPHICAL AND CRITICAL SOURCES:

BOOKS

Cazden, Elizabeth, *Antoinette Brown Blackwell,* Feminist Press (Old Westbury, NY), 1983.
Encyclopedia of World Biography Supplement, Volume 21, Gale (Detroit, MI), 2001.
Lasser, Carol, and Marlene Deahl Merrill, editors, *Soul Mates: The Oberlin Correspondence of Lucy Stone and Antoinette Brown, 1846-1850,* Oberlin College (Oberlin, OH), 1983.
Lasser, Carol, and Marlene Deahl Merrill, editors, *Friends and Sisters: Letters between Lucy Stone and Antoinette Brown Blackwell, 1846-93,* University of Illinois Press (Urbana, IL), 1987.

PERIODICALS

Journal of Women's History, spring, 1998, Elizabeth Munson and Greg Dickinson, "Hearing Women Speak: Antoinette Brown Blackwell and the Dilemma of Authority," p. 108.

OBITUARIES:

PERIODICALS

Newark Evening News, November 5, 1921.*

*   *   *

BLANCHARD, Charles Albert 1848-1925

PERSONAL: Born November 8, 1848, in Galesburg, IL; died December 20, 1925, in Wheaton, IL; son of Jonathan (a minister and educator) and Mary Avery (Bent) Blanchard; married Ella Milligan, 1873. *Education:* Wheaton College, graduated, 1870.

CAREER: National Christian Association, lecturer against Freemasonry, c. 1870-72; Wheaton College, Wheaton, IL, principal of preparatory school, 1872-78, professor of English language and literature and vice president of the college, 1878-82, president, 1882-1925. Ordained Congregational minister, 1882; College Church of Christ, pastor, 1882-83; Chicago Avenue Church (also known as Moody Church), preacher, c. 1883-85. Conservative Protestant Colleges of America (later Association of Conservative Evangelical Colleges), founding member, 1924.

MEMBER: National Christian Association (president, 1903).

WRITINGS:

Educational Papers, Fleming H. Revell (New York, NY), 1883.
Modern Secret Societies, National Christian Association (Chicago, IL), 1903, 8th edition, 1938.
Light on the Last Days: Being Familiar Talks on the Book of Revelation, Bible Institute Colportage Association (Chicago, IL), 1913.
Getting Things from God, Bible Institute Colportage Association (Chicago, IL), 1915.
Visions and Voices, Christian Alliance Publishing (New York, NY), 1916.
An Old Testament Gospel: A Prophet's Message to Men of Today, Bible Institute Colportage Association (Chicago, IL), 1918.

BIOGRAPHICAL AND CRITICAL SOURCES:

BOOKS

Blanchard, F. C., *The Life of Charles Albert Blanchard,* Fleming H. Revell (New York, NY), 1932.*

*   *   *

BLEASDALE, Alan 1946-

PERSONAL: Born March 23, 1946, in Liverpool, England; son of George (a foreman) and Margaret (a shop assistant; maiden name, Grant) Bleasdale; married Julia Moses, December 28, 1970; children: Timothy, Jamie, Tamana.

ADDRESSES: Home—Liverpool, England. *Agent*—Lemon, Unna & Durbridge, 24 Pottery Lane, Holland Park, London W11 4LZ, England.

CAREER: Producer and screenwriter. Teacher, St. Columbus Secondary Modern School, Huyton, England, 1967-71, King George V School, Gilbert and Ellice Islands, 1971-74, and Halewood Grange Comprehensive School, Lancashire, 1974-75; Liverpool Playhouse, Liverpool, England, resident playwright, 1975-76, joint artistic director, 1981-84, and associate director, 1984-86; Contact Theatre, Manchester, England, resident playwright, 1976-78.

Producer of film *Soft Sand, Blue Sea,* 1997. Producer of television movies *Self Catering* (also known as *Alan Bleasdale Presents Self Catering*), 1994; *Requiem Apache* (also known as *Alan Bleasdale Presents Requiem Apache*), 1994; and *Blood on the Dole* (also known as *Alan Bleasdale Presents Blood on the Dole*), 1994. Producer of television miniseries *GBH,* 1991. Executive producer of television miniseries *Melissa,* 1997, and *Oliver Twist,* 1999.

AWARDS, HONORS: Broadcasting Press Guild award, 1982; Royal Television Society award, 1982; British Academy of Film and Television Arts award, 1982, for *Boys from the Blackstuff; Evening Standard* award for musical, 1985; ITV Achievement-of-the-Decade award, 1989; Broadcasting Press Guild Television and Radio award, 1991.

WRITINGS:

PLAYS

Fat Harold and the Last Twenty-six, produced at Liverpool Playhouse, Liverpool, England, 1975.
The Party's Over, produced at Playhouse Theatre, Liverpool, England, 1975.
(With others) *Scully* (adaptation of Bleasdale's novel of the same title), produced at Everyman Theatre, Liverpool, England, 1975.
Down the Dock Road, produced at Playhouse Theatre, Liverpool, England, 1976.
(With Kenneth Alan Taylor) *Franny Scully's Christmas Stories,* produced at Playhouse Theatre, Liverpool, England, 1976.
It's a Madhouse, produced at Contact Theatre, Manchester, England, 1976.
Should Auld Acquaintance, produced at Contact Theatre, Manchester, England, 1976.

No More Sitting on the Old School Bench (produced at Contact Theatre, Manchester, England, 1977), Woodhouse, 1979, published with David Calcutt's *Detention*, Heinemann (London, England), 1987.

Crackers, produced at The Playhouse, Leeds, England, 1978.

Pimples, produced at Contact Theatre, Manchester, England, 1978.

Love Is a Many Splendoured Thing (for children; produced in Redditch, Worcestershire, England, 1986), in *Act I,* edited by David Self and Ray Speakman, Hutchinson (London, England), 1979.

Having a Ball, produced at the Coliseum, Oldham, Lancashire, England, 1981.

Young People Today (sketch), produced with *The Big One* in London, England, 1983.

Are You Lonesome Tonight? (musical; produced at Liverpool Playhouse, 1985), Faber (London, England), 1985.

Having a Ball [and] It's a Madhouse, Faber (London, England), 1986.

On the Ledge, Faber (London, England), 1993.

TELEVISION SERIES

Scully (adapted from Bleasdale's novel of the same title; produced 1984), edited by David Self, Hutchinson (London, England), 1984.

The Monocled Mutineer (four-part series; adapted from the book by William Allison and John Farley; produced by British Broadcasting Company (BBC), 1986), Hutchinson (London, England), 1986.

TELEVISION MINISERIES

Boys from the Blackstuff (produced by British Broadcasting Company), edited by David Self, Hutchinson (London, England), 1985.

GBH, 1991.

Jake's Progress, 1995.

Melissa, 1997.

Oliver Twist, 1999.

TELEVISION MOVIES

Early to Bed, British Broadcasting Company (BBC), 1975.

Dangerous Ambition, British Broadcasting Company (BBC), 1976.

The Black Stuff, British Broadcasting Company (BBC), 1980.

The Muscle Market, British Broadcasting Company (BBC), 1981.

TELEVISION SPECIALS

Scully's New Years Eve (also known as *Play for Today: Scully's New Year's Eve*), British Broadcasting Company (BBC), 1978.

SCREENPLAYS

No Surrender, Norstar, 1986, published as *No Surrender: A Deadpan Farce,* Faber (London, England), 1986.

NOVELS

Scully, Hutchinson (London, England), 1975.

Who's Been Sleeping in My Bed? Hutchinson (London, England), 1977, revised edition published as *Scully and Mooey,* Corgi (London, England), 1984.

SIDELIGHTS: Liverpool native Alan Bleasdale has been chronicling life in England on stage and on television for many years. His dramatic social commentaries include *Boys from the Blackstuff,* a miniseries about unemployed British laborers in the early 1980s; *GBH,* a fictional miniseries about fascists taking over a British city; and *Having a Ball,* a play about three men who are about to have vasectomies. More recently, Bleasdale has also updated the work of an earlier social commentator, nineteenth century British author Charles Dickens, in his television adaptation of Dickens's novel *Oliver Twist.*

Boys from the Blackstuff began as a play Bleasdale wrote in the 1970s and later expanded into a popular British Broadcasting Company (BBC) miniseries. The central characters are five unemployed road workers who are struggling to make ends meet between their welfare money and illegal, under-the-table employment. The shout of one of these men, Yosser, "Gissa job!," became a rallying cry for workers under the administration of Tory Prime Minister Margaret

Thatcher, and the series so stuck in Liverpudlian's collective imagination that the published scripts of the show were voted Liverpool's favorite book in a 2003 poll.

Bleasdale's other major critical success, *GBH*, is a sprawling political epic that aired over the course of seven weeks and required a production crew of more than one hundred people. Yet despite the "immense scale" of the narrative, it "remains accessible at all times. It is simultaneously overawing, yet understated; outlandishly funny, and tearfully poignant; angry, defiant, but never polemical, or self-righteous—and never ever self-indulgent," Ian Jones wrote in *Off the Telly*.

Bleasdale's adaptation of *Oliver Twist* fleshes out Oliver's backstory in a way Dickens did not: the entire first segment of the four-part series is devoted to explaining how Oliver came to be an orphan, a subject Dickens deals with only briefly. This segment "tie[s] up a lot of loose ends, making the plot less confusing than the original or any of the subsequent screen versions," Sam Wollaston wrote in the *Guardian*. Besides, as Wollaston wrote, "If anyone is going to tamper with *Oliver Twist* it may as well be Bleasdale, being perhaps the nearest thing we've got to Dickens today."

BIOGRAPHICAL AND CRITICAL SOURCES:

BOOKS

Berney, K. A., editor, *Contemporary British Dramatists,* St. James Press (London, England), 1994.
Contemporary Dramatists, 6th edition, St. James Press (Detroit, MI), 1999.
Dictionary of Literary Biography, Volume 245: *British and Irish Dramatists since World War II, Third Series,* Gale (Detroit, MI), 2001.
Drabble, Margaret, editor, *The Oxford Companion to English Literature,* 6th edition, Oxford University Press (Oxford, England), 2000.
Parker, Peter, editor, *A Reader's Guide to Twentieth-Century Writers,* Oxford University Press (Oxford, England), 1996.
Stringer, Jenny, editor, *The Oxford Companion to Twentieth-Century Literature in English,* Oxford University Press (New York, NY), 1996.

PERIODICALS

Birmingham Evening Mail (Birmingham, England), March 9, 2001, Fred Norris, interview with Bleas-dale, p. 64; March 19, 2001, Alison Jones, interview with Bleasdale, p. 12; March 22, 2001, Fred Norris, review of *Having a Ball,* p. 55.
Birmingham Post (Birmingham, England), March 23, 2001, Terry Grimley, review of *Having a Ball,* p. 16.
Coventry Evening Telegraph (Coventry, England), September 11, 2001, Barbara Goulden, review of *Having a Ball,* p. 11.
Daily Post (Liverpool, England), October 1, 2001, Amanda Dale, "Bleasdale Pulls out of BBC Drama Series," p. 11; January 28, 2002, Alan Weston, "Angry Bleasdale Pulls out of Pounds 6m TV Drama," p. 14.
Daily Record (Glasgow, Scotland), October 10, 1998, "Whatever Happened to *The Boys from the Blackstuff*?," p. 22; July 6, 1999, Kathleen Morgan, review of *Oliver Twist,* p. 17.
Evening News (Edinburgh, Scotland), May 1, 2001, Thom Dibdin, review of *Having a Ball,* p. 24.
Evening Times (Glasgow, Scotland), December 3, 1999, Brian Beacom, review of *Oliver Twist,* p. 38; December 10, 1999, review of *Oliver Twist,* p. 38.
Guardian (London, England), May 10, 1997, Maggie Brown, interview with Bleasdale, p. 24; July 6, 1999, Janine Gibson, review of *Oliver Twist,* p. 7; November 22, 1999, Maggie Brown, interview with Bleasdale, p. 2, Sam Wollaston, review of *Oliver Twist,* p. 3; November 30, 1999, review of *Oliver Twist,* p. 7; October 1, 2001, "Bleasdale Anger as BBC Ditches Series," p. 16; November 19, 2001, Gareth McLean, review of *The Boys from Blackstuff,* p. 13.
Herald (Glasgow, Scotland), December 8, 1999, William Russell, review of *Oliver Twist,* p. 17; May 5, 2001, "Making a Drama out of a Crisis," p. 52.
Independent (London, England), March 12, 1997, review of *Melissa,* p. 2; July 6, 1999, Paul McCann, review of *Oliver Twist,* p. 10; December 1, 1999, James Rampton, review of *Oliver Twist,* p. 10; May 15, 2001, Alan Bleasdale, "Election 2001: How I Will Vote," p. 7; October 29, 2002, Gerard Gilbert, "TV Heroes: Alan Bleasdale," p. 23.
Independent Sunday (London, England), April 13, 1997, Jasper Rees, interview with Bleasdale, p. 14; January 3, 1999, Jasper Rees, review of *Oliver Twist,* p. 3; November 28, 1999, Nick Smurthwaite, interview with Bleasdale and Julie Walters, p. 76.
Mirror (London, England), May 10, 1997, "In Heaven with Ehle," p. 4.

News of the World (London, England), May 18, 1997, Charlie Catchpole, review of *Melissa,* p. 48; December 5, 1999, review of *Oliver Twist,* p. 76.

New Statesman, June 12, 1981, Benedict Nightingale, review of *Having a Ball,* pp. 21-22; January 18, 1985, Hugo Williams, review of *South Bank Show,* pp. 36-37; May 24, 1985, Paul Allen, review of *Are You Lonesome Tonight?* pp. 37-38; September 5, 1986, profile of Bleasdale, p. 12; March 5, 1993, Boyd Tonkin, review of *On the Ledge,* pp. 33-34.

New Statesman & Society, June 14, 1991, Jaci Stephen, review of *GBH,* p. 30; July 19, 1991, Peter Jukes, review of *GBH,* pp. 29-30.

New York Times, September 14, 1986, Vincent Canby, review of *No Surrender,* p. H17; October 7, 2000, Neil Genzlinger, review of *Oliver Twist,* p. A27.

North American Review, March-April, 1994, Robert L. King, review of *On the Ledge,* pp. 18-19.

Observer (London, England), November 28, 1999, Vanessa Thorpe, "Costume War Declared on TV," p. 9.

Off the Telly, March, 2000, Ian Jones, review of *Boys from the Blackstuff;* October, 2000, Graham Kibble, review of *The Monocled Mutineer,* Ian Jones, review of *GBH.*

People (London, England), May 18, 1997, Dave Lanning, review of *Melissa,* p. 51.

School Library Journal, May, 2001, Kathy Akey, review of *Oliver Twist,* p. 69.

Scotsman (Edinburgh, Scotland), July 6, 1999, Matt Wells, "ITV Gives Dickens Classic a Twist," p. 8; July 17, 1999, Katrina Dixon, "Living Obituary: Alan Bleasdale," p. 2; September 21, 2000, "Where Eliot Meets Nick Hornby," p. 5; September 15, 2001, "Brush up on Alan Bleasdale," p. 26.

Sight and Sound, spring, 1987, Julian Petley, review of *The Monocled Mutineer,* pp. 126-131.

Spectator, May 8, 1993, Sheridan Morley, review of *On the Ledge,* pp. 38-39; October 14, 1995, Nigella Lawson, review of *Jake's Progress,* p. 58; May 17, 1997, James Delingpole, review of *Melissa,* p. 53.

Sunday Times (London, England), September 1, 1996, Margarette Driscoll, "Class of 88," p. S9; January 17, 1999, Nicholas Hellen, review of *Oliver Twist,* p. 7; November 28, 1999, John Dugdale, review of *Oliver Twist,* p. 67; June 4, 2000, "Scousers' Reunion Has the Blairites Running Scared," p. 19.

Time, September 8, 1986, Richard Corliss, review of *No Surrender,* p. 83.

Times (London, England), October 4, 1995, Alan Franks, interview with Bleasdale, p. 35; May 20, 1997, Joe Joseph, review of *Melissa,* p. 55; July 6, 1999, Carol Midgley, review of *Oliver Twist,* p. 2; November 19, 1999, Paul Nathanson, review of *Oliver Twist,* p. 49; November 30, 1999, Paul McCann, review of *Oliver Twist,* p. 11.

Times Literary Supplement, July 5, 1991, Mick Imlah, review of *GBH,* p. 16; May 7, 1993, Peter Kemp, review of *On the Ledge,* p. 8; December 24, 1999, John Bowen, review of *Oliver Twist,* pp. 16-17.

Variety, August 21, 1985, review of *Are You Lonesome Tonight?* p. 130.

Wall Street Journal, August 14, 1986, Julie Salamon, review of *No Surrender,* pp. 14, 16.

ONLINE

Museum of Broadcast Communications Web site, http://www.museum.tv/ (May 11, 2003), "Bleasdale, Alan."*

*   *   *

BOMPAS, William C(arpenter) 1834-1906

PERSONAL: Born January 20, 1834, in London, England; died June 9, 1906, in Cariboo Crossing, Yukon Territory (now British Columbia), Canada; married.

CAREER: Church Missionary Society, England, staff member, c. 1860s; ordained priest of Church of England in Canada, c. 1865; missionary priest in Northwest Territories, Canada, 1865-74; bishop of diocese of Athabasca, Northwest Territories (now Alberta, Canada), 1874-83, diocese of MacKenzie River, Northwest Territories (now Yukon Territory, Canada), 1883-91, and diocese of Selkirk, Yukon Territory, Canada, 1891-1905.

WRITINGS:

History of the Diocese of MacKenzie River, SPCK (London, England), 1888.

Lessons and Prayers in the Tenni or Slavi Language of the Indians of MacKenzie River, in the North-West Territory of Canada, SPCK (London, England), 1889.

BIOGRAPHICAL AND CRITICAL SOURCES:

BOOKS

Cody, H. A., *An Apostle of the North,* Seeley and Co. (Toronto, Ontario, Canada), 1908.*

* * *

BOYDEN, Linda 1948-

PERSONAL: Born July 6, 1948, in Attleboro, MA; daughter of Ray and Marie (Dargis) Simmons; married John P. Boyden (an engineer), 1988; children: A. Rachel, Eámon, Maeve; (stepchildren) Luanne, John, Jr. *Ethnicity:* "Caucasian/Native American." *Education:* Framingham State College, B.S.Ed., 1970; University of Virginia, M.Ed., 1992. *Hobbies and other interests:* Volunteer work at Makawao Public Library, hiking in national parks, reading, sewing.

ADDRESSES: Home—151 Alalani St., Pukalani, HI 96768. *E-mail*—lindadw@hawaii.rr.com.

CAREER: Self-employed storyteller and writer, specializing in American Indian stories. Elementary schoolteacher, 1970-97; teacher of writing at a private middle school on the island of Maui, Hawaii; gives readings from her works. United Lumbee Nation, enrolled member; Intertribal Council of Hawaii, member of Maui chapter.

MEMBER: Society of Children's Book Writers and Illustrators, Wordcraft Circle of Native American Writers and Storytellers, Children's Literature Hawaii, Maui Live Poets Society.

AWARDS, HONORS: New Voices Award, Lee & Low Books, 2000, for *The Blue Roses.*

WRITINGS:

The Blue Roses, illustrated by Amy Córdova, Lee & Low Books (New York, NY), 2002.

Work represented in anthologies, including *Through the Eye of a Deer,* Auntlute Books, 1999; and *Woven on the Wind,* Houghton Mifflin (Boston, MA), 2001.

WORK IN PROGRESS: Several picture-book manuscripts; three middle-reader manuscripts; a picture-book biography of Sarah Winnemucca; poetry for adults and children.

SIDELIGHTS: Linda Boyden told *CA:* "For as long as I can remember, I have loved words. Before I could read, I told myself stories to fall asleep or stories for my dolls to enact. The first most important discovery of my life was learning how to read. It changed everything! I still loved to make up my own stories, but now I could enjoy what others had imagined, too.

"Sometimes in my storytelling jaunts, though, important adults misunderstood me. To be good, they pointed out, I must learn the difference between telling the truth and telling lies. As I grew older and emerged as a writer, I discovered one of the truths of fiction writing: readers *approve* of the 'lies'! This is definitely for me, I decided.

"But I also wanted to teach, and I did for over twenty years. During snow days or when I was an at-home mom with my own babies, I wrote at every opportunity. When circumstances moved my husband and me to Maui in 1997, I abandoned teaching and began to try to market my writings in earnest.

"After many, many rejections, one of my manuscripts, *The Blue Roses,* hit the jackpot by winning the Lee & Low Books first New Voices Award in 2000. A traditional Cherokee myth says that the first stories came to people in dreams. My first book is based on a dream I had after my maternal grandfather passed on. I was thirty at the time, about to have my third child, and I couldn't travel the long distance to my grandfather's funeral. I was heartbroken. One night, Grandpa came to me in a dream. He stood in a beautiful garden (gardening had been his life-long hobby). Grandpa told me he was happy and to stop my carrying-on. It sounds strange, but I awoke with a new-found sense of contentment.

"Until then, death had terrified me. Seeing how happy he was changed that. Later I thought how poorly death is explained to most children. Wouldn't gardening be a great metaphor to help kids understand, to give them comfort and hope? These thoughts led to my book.

"Kids are still as hungry for good books as I was. Leading them to their own literacy is what I enjoy doing most, next to writing. Children have stories to tell. Teaching them to express their words aloud or on paper and to enjoy the written words of others empowers them and enriches the world."

BIOGRAPHICAL AND CRITICAL SOURCES:

PERIODICALS

Kirkus Reviews, April 1, 2002, review of *The Blue Roses,* p. 486.
School Library Journal, March, 2001, "New Voice in Children's Literature Honored," p. 22; June, 2002, Kathy Piehl, review of *The Blue Roses,* p. 88.

*   *   *

BREVARD, Aleshia 1937-

PERSONAL: Original name, Alfred Crenshaw; born December 9, 1937, in Erwin, TN; son of James Upshaw (a gentleman farmer and city clerk) and Mozelle Gillentine (a nurse) Crenshaw. *Ethnicity:* "Caucasian." *Education:* Middle Tennessee State University, B.A. (speech, theater, and education), 1967; Marshall University, M.A. (communication science), 1973. *Politics:* "Democrat (on a good year), otherwise anything that isn't Republican." *Hobbies and other interests:* Theatre.

ADDRESSES: Office—521 Tuttle Ave., Watsonville, CA 95076. *Agent*—Erika Wain, Erika Wain Agency, 3228 Craig Dr., Hollywood, CA 90068. *E-mail*—ababc@aol.com.

CAREER: Actress and teacher. Actress, 1966—; East Tennessee State University, Johnson City, acting professor, 1989-94; Pajaro Valley Unified School District, Watsonville, CA, teacher, 1999-2001.

MEMBER: Screen Actors Guild, Actors Equity Association, American Federation of Television and Radio Artists, American Guild of Variety Artists.

WRITINGS:

The Woman I Was Not Born to Be: A Transsexual Journey, Temple University Press (Philadelphia, PA), 2001.

Also coauthor of plays, including *A Grinnich Christmas, Caught Dead in Chattanooga,* and *RIP and Cancel Your Credit Cards;* author of play *Everything I Know, I Learned in Heels: A One-Woman Show,*

WORK IN PROGRESS: Bilbo's Bend, a fictional examination of a young gay man's life as he struggles to find his place on the gender scale.

SIDELIGHTS: Aleshia Brevard's life story is a tale of broken marriages, B-movie roles, a stint as a *Playboy* bunny, and the pursuit of a career in theatre. It is also the story of how a young man from a religious family in rural Tennessee decided to castrate himself on a kitchen table after years of feeling that he could not honestly live as the gender into which he had been born. The transformation of Alfred Crenshaw to Aleshia Brevard is only the beginning of her story for social acceptance and finally self acceptance, a story that ends with Brevard setting aside celebrity and enjoying life as "one of the little old ladies out tending their roses."

In her life as a boy, Aleshia was known as Buddy Crenshaw, the son of a Tennessee farmer. Brevard remembers that she never felt comfortable being identified as a boy, that being addressed as a boy felt improper. She moved to San Francisco in her early twenties to work in drag, although state laws at the time prohibited men from dressing as women in public. In order to appear as a woman offstage—to look like the person she felt she was—she had to be biologically female. In 1960 she convinced a veterinarian to tell her how to neuter her cat, then used the instructions, with the help of her lifelong friend Stormy, to remove her testicles (a procedure which was then unlawful for a surgeon). When Stormy had to leave the room and vomit during the procedure, Brevard sat up and finished the job herself. In 1962 she was able to have a surgeon complete the transformation, and subsequently had her birth certificate and name changed to reflect her new identity.

A central insight Brevard achieved early in her life as a woman was that femininity was not as freeing as she had hoped. Eric Nuzum, in the *Cleveland Free Times,* wrote, "Much to her surprise, Brevard realized that life as a 'sissy' man was preferable to that of an attractive young woman." The reasonably lucrative career of a drag performer was no longer an option, and Brevard faced the struggle of being a single woman in the early 1960s. Brevard later commented that Nusum misinterpreted her statements. "Life as a woman might not have been what I anticipated it would be," she wrote, "but it was a far sight better than the half-life I'd lived before." Her greatest successes as an actress include a role in the Don Knotts film *The Love God,* regular appearances on TV's *Red Skelton Show,* and the role of Tex on the soap opera *One Life to Live.* Brevard relates in her book the realization that what looked like a life of adoration and glamour was really a life of dependence. Nuzum wrote, "[Brevard] did star in several forgettable movies . . . but eventually found—like many women of her generation—that the easiest way to support herself was as someone's wife."

She was married three times, had a series of abusive boyfriends, and fended off advances from her co-stars, including Andy Griffith and Anthony Newley. In most cases, none of the men ever knew Aleshia had been born a man. Brevard embraced feminism in the 1970s and found an ally in her mother in her ongoing quest to accept herself and her history. In the *Village Voice,* Michael Musto wrote, "Brevard's multiple layers of self-loathing ultimately became even more oppressive than her heels and false lashes, but her loving mother . . . kept her so grounded she might as well have been in flats and glasses. It was when the men finally stopped clutching at her that Brevard found her self-respect." In an interview for the *Temple University Press Web site,* Brevard said of her relationships with men, "I was not being honest, even with myself. I was trying to be the woman my mate wanted me to be. By trying to live up to someone else's fantasy, I lost myself. I know a lot of married women who are still making that sad mistake."

Brevard published her biography as a host of transsexual stories were released. Reviewers have suggested that what distinguishes Brevard's story is her engaging humor and her intelligence. A reviewer for *Publishers Weekly* said that *The Woman I Was Not Born to Be* "adds an entertaining curve to the growing body of literature-academic, scientific, theoretical and literary-on transgender experience, without the self-pity or sentimentality found in many such memoirs." Musto called the book "a cut above" the usual transsexual memoir, noting Brevard's "serious discourse about the restraining roles society makes us play and an intelligent grasp of queer, transsexual, and feminist

history." Brevard continues to write about gender and sexuality from her home in California.

Brevard told *CA:* "My life in film, television, and especially on the dinner-theatre stage, pushed me into my first attempts at writing. I was writing for the stage until my father's death, January 15, 1996. Then, searching for cathartic release from my early transsexual experiences, having had transitional surgery in 1952, I began what became *The Woman I Was Not Born to Be.* With this venture the writing process was to trot down memory lane with my fingers flying on the keyboard trying to keep pace. I had no thought to editing. That came later when Temple University Press pressured me to trim my prose. The real work then began and I discovered joy in the process of telling my story."

BIOGRAPHICAL AND CRITICAL SOURCES:

PERIODICALS

Advocate, March 27, 2002, Etelka Lehoczky, "The Country Girl," p. 65.
Lambda Book Report, February, 2001, review of *The Woman I Was Not Born to Be,* p. 30.
Library Journal, April 15, 2001, Aaron Jason, review of *The Woman I Was Not Born to Be,* p. 30.
Publishers Weekly, November 20, 2000, review of *The Woman I Was Not Born to Be,* p. 53.
Wilson Quarterly, spring, 2001, Amy Bloom, "A Transsexual Journey," p. 121.

OTHER

Cleveland Free Times Online, http://www.freetimes. com/ (June 12, 2002), Eric Nuzum, "Enjoy Being a Girl? One of the Country's First Transsexuals on the Quest for Self."
NTAC Web site, http://www.ntac.org/ (June 12, 2002), Michael Musto, review of *The Woman I Was Not Born to Be,* from the *Village Voice.*
Sex in the Twentieth Century (television news segment), American Broadcasting System (ABC).
SFBG Web site, http://www.sfbg.com/ (June 20, 2001), Charles Anders, "Tranny Tales: A Whirlwind Tour of Transsexual Life Stories."

Temple University Press Web site, http://www.temple. edu/tempress/ (June 12, 2002), interview with Aleshia Brevard.

*   *   *

BRINK, Gijsbert van den
   See van den BRINK, Gijsbert

*   *   *

BRISSENDEN, Connie
   See BRISSENDEN, Constance

*   *   *

BRISSENDEN, Constance 1947-
   (Connie Brissenden)

PERSONAL: Born January 13, 1947, in Kingston, Ontario, Canada; daughter of Barry S. and Margaret Brissenden; companion of Larry Loyie (a writer). *Education:* University of Guelph, B.A., 1969; University of Alberta, M.A., 1972. *Religion:* Buddhist (Soka Gakkai International). *Hobbies and other interests:* Teaching creative writing.

ADDRESSES: Home—Vancouver, British Columbia, Canada. *Agent*—c/o Author Mail, Formac Publishing Co. Ltd., 5502 Atlantic St., Halifax, Nova Scotia, Canada B3H 1G4. *E-mail*—livingtradition@telus.net.

CAREER: Freelance writer. Expo '86, managing editor; Coast Mountain Bus Co., staff member, 1989-99, acting manager of corporate communications, 1999-2001, also creator of Transit History Wall. Simon Fraser University, Burnaby, British Columbia, Canada, teacher of corporate writing courses.

AWARDS, HONORS: Silver Pen Award and Gold Quill Award, International Association of Business Communicators, both 1986, both for work with Expo '86; Dalton Pen Communications Award, 2001, for Transit History Wall.

WRITINGS:

AS CONNIE BRISSENDEN

(Editor) *Now in Paperback: Six Canadian Plays of the 1970s,* Fineglow Plays (Toronto, Ontario, Canada), 1973.

(Editor) *The Factory Lab Anthology* (plays), Talonbooks (Vancouver, British Columbia, Canada), 1974.

(Editor) *West Coast Plays,* New Play Centre (Vancouver, British Columbia, Canada), 1975.

(Editor) *Carol Bolt* ("Playwrights in Profile" series), Playwrights Co-op (Toronto, Ontario, Canada), 1976.

Info to Go: For Women on the Go, Young Women's Christian Association (Vancouver, British Columbia, Canada), 1989.

Triple-O: The White Spot Story, Opus, 1993.

Whistler and the Sea to Sky Country, Altitude Publishing (Vancouver, British Columbia, Canada), 1995.

A Portrait of Vancouver, Altitude Publishing (Vancouver, British Columbia, Canada), 1995, abridged edition, 1996.

(Author of text) *Vancouver and the Lower Mainland from the Air,* photographs by Russ Heinl, Whitecap Books (New York, NY), 1999.

Colorguide to Vancouver and Whistler, James Lorimer, 2000.

(Editor) *Vancouver and Victoria,* photographs by Hamid Attie, Formac Publishing (Halifax, Nova Scotia, Canada), 2001.

Frommer's Portable Guide to Whistler, 2002.

(With Larry Loyie) *As Long as the Rivers Flow* (juvenile), Groundwood Books (Toronto, Ontario, Canada), 2002.

Contributor to books, including *The Greater Vancouver Book,* Linkman Press, 1997; and *DK Eyewitness Travel Guide to the Pacific Northwest,* 2003. Contributor of numerous articles to magazines and newspapers, including Toronto *Globe & Mail, Maclean's, Toronto Calendar, Western Living, BC Business, Personal Finance, BC Woman, Georgia Strait,* and *Chinese-Canadian.*

WORK IN PROGRESS: Two children's books; research on photographs of residential school life and on the life of Pauline Johnson.

BROWN, Lloyd L(ouis) 1913-2003

OBITUARY NOTICE—See index for *CA* sketch: Born April 3, 1913, in St. Paul, MN; died April 1, 2003, in New York, NY. Journalist and author. Brown is most remembered for his work with Paul Robeson and for editing the journal *New Masses.* He started his career in journalism before World War II, writing about such subjects as the antifascist movement in Europe. During the war he served in the U.S. Army Air Force, rising to the rank of staff sergeant. He then became editor of the leftist journal *New Masses,* which published the works of such famous writers as Langston Hughes, Richard Wright, and Ralph Ellison; from 1948 to 1952 he was managing editor of *Masses and Mainstream.* In the 1950s he helped his friend Robeson, an actor and equal rights activist, with the Harlem newspaper *Freedom.* Robeson's 1958 autobiography, *Here I Stand,* was edited by Brown, and in 1996 Brown published the biography *The Young Paul Robeson: On My Journey Now.* Brown also wrote fiction, including a 1951 novel titled *Iron City.*

OBITUARIES AND OTHER SOURCES:

BOOKS

Writers Directory, 18th edition, St. James Press (Detroit, MI), 2003.

PERIODICALS

Chicago Tribune, April 17, 2003, section 3, p. 14.
Los Angeles Times, April 15, 2003, p. B11.
New York Times, April 14, 2003, p. A21.
Washington Post, April 16, 2003, p. B6.

C

CADDEL, Richard (Ivo) 1949-2003

OBITUARY NOTICE—See index for *CA* sketch: Born July 13, 1949, in Bedford, England; died of leukemia April 1, 2003, in Durham, England. Editor, publisher, librarian, and author. Caddel was a poet and founder of poetry imprint Pig Press. He received a B.A. from the University of Newcastle on Tyne in 1971, after which he also studied library science at Newcastle Polytechnic for a year. His first job was as a reader in music—and later history and English—at Newcastle University; he then began a library career at the University of Durham, where he was senior library assistant from 1972 to 1986. At the same time he began library work, he started Pig Press with his wife, Ann. Pig Press published the works of such poets as Robert Creeley and Basil Bunting, the later of whose verses Caddel would later edit in several collections, including *Basil Bunting: Uncollected Poems* (1991) and *The Complete Poems/Basil Bunting* (1994). Caddel's work on these collections, along with his creation of the Basil Bunting Poetry Centre in 1988, is considered by many to have been important in keeping an interest in Bunting's writings alive. Caddel himself was a fairly prolific poet whose works, critics have noted, show the influence of such writers as Bunting, Ezra Pound, and William Carlos Williams. His first collection, *Heron* (1973), was followed by almost a dozen other poetry books. Caddel continued to write and direct Pig Press while earning an income at the University of Durham, becoming an assistant librarian there in 1986 and director of the Basil Bunting Poetry Centre in 1988. Some of his important verse collections during this time include *Sweet Cicely: New and Selected Poems* (1983; second edition, 1988), and *Uncertain Times* (1990). More recent verse works include *Ground* (1994), *Larksong Signal* (1997), and *Underwriter* (1999). Prose books by Caddel include *Deadly Sins* (1984) and *Quiet Music of Words: Richard Caddel in Conversation with Anthony Flowers* (2001), and his many edited works include *Pete Laver: Offcomers* (1985), *Sharp Study and Long Toil: Essays on Basil Bunting* (1995), and *Other: British and Irish Poetry since 1970* (1999), which he edited with Peter Quartermain. After the accidental death in 1995 of his son, Tom, Caddel's poems became understandably marked by his grief over this loss. Later, when he was diagnosed with leukemia in 1999, he decided to close Pig Press, and in 2000 he resigned from the staff of Durham University Library. However, he continued to do poetry readings, traveling widely, and directed the Basil Bunting Poetry Centre until his death. His last poetry collection, *Magpie Woods: Selected Poems*, was published in 2002.

OBITUARIES AND OTHER SOURCES:

BOOKS

Writers Directory, 18th edition, St. James Press (Detroit, MI), 2003.

PERIODICALS

Independent (London, England), April 11, 2003, p. 20.
Times (London, England), May 13, 2003, p. 31.

CAMPOY, F. Isabel (Coronado) 1946-

PERSONAL: Born June 25, 1946, in Alicante, Spain; daughter of Juan Diego Campoy (a professor of English) and Maria Coronado Guerro (a homemaker). *Ethnicity:* "Hispanic." *Education:* Universidad Complutense, Madrid, B.A. and M.A. (English philology); Reading University, M.A. (dialectology); doctoral studies in applied linguistics at University of California, Los Angeles. *Politics:* "A defender of justice and peace." *Hobbies and other interests:* Painting, collecting art, observing children and nature.

ADDRESSES: Home—10 Walnut St., Mill Valley, CA 94941. *Office*—38 Miller Ave., No. 181, Mill Valley, CA 94941. *E-mail*—fisabelcampoy@yahoo.com.

CAREER: Poet, playwright, storyteller, and editor. Mangold & Santillana Publishing, Madrid, Spain, editor, 1971-78; Houghton, Mifflin, Boston, MA, senior acquisitions editor, 1981-93; freelance writer and lecturer on educational and multicultural matters. Transformative Education Services, president. Member of board of directors, Children's Book Council, 1998—, and San Francisco Public Library Foundation, 1997—.

MEMBER: National Council of Teachers of English, International Reading Association, CABE, NABE, Association of Spanish Professionals in the U.S.A. (president, 1994-96), various national and regional bilingual education associations.

AWARDS, HONORS: Fulbright scholar, 1979-81; Friends and Foundation of San Francisco Public Library Laureate Award, 2003.

WRITINGS:

FOR CHILDREN; WITH ALMA FLOR ADA

Tablado de Doña Rosita/Curtain's Up, Santillana USA Publishing (Miami, FL), 2001.

¡Feliz cumpleaños, Caperucita Roja!/Happy Birthday, Little Red Riding Hood! (bilingual edition), illustrated by Ana López Escrivá, Alfaguara (Miami, FL), 2002.

El nuevo hogar de los siete cabritos/The New Home of the Seven Billy Goats, illustrated by Viví Escrivá, Alfaguara (Miami, FL), 2002.

A New Job for Pérez the Mouse/Ratoncito Perez, Cartero, illustrated by Sandra López Escrivá, Alfaguara (Miami, FL), 2002.

One, Two, Three, Who Can It Be?/Uno, dos, tres: ¡Dime quién es!, illustrated by Viví Escrivá, Alfaguara (Miami, FL), 2002.

On the Wings of the Condor/En alas del condor, Alfaguara (Miami, FL), 2002.

Eyes of the Jaguar/Ojos del jaguar, Alfaguara (Miami, FL), 2002.

The Quetzal's Journey/Vuelo del quetzal, illustrated by Felipe Davalos, Santillana USA Publishing (Miami, FL), 2002.

Friends from A to Z: A Glossary of the Hispanic World/Amigos de la A a la Z: Un alfabeto del mundo hispánico, Santillana USA Publishing (Miami, FL), 2002.

(Adaptor) *Rosa Raposa,* illustrated by Ariane Dewey and Jose Aruego, Harcourt (New York, NY), 2002.

(Compiler) *Pío peep!: Traditional Spanish Nursery Rhymes* (bilingual edition), illustrated by Vivi Escriva, English adaptations by Alice Schertle, HarperCollins (New York, NY), 2003.

Also translator of children's books into Spanish, including works by Louis Ehlert, Gary Soto, Kathleen Krull, and Gerald McDermott.

Works also published in Spanish translation.

"GATEWAYS TO THE SUN" SERIES; WITH ALMA FLOR ADA

Smiles/Sonrisas (biographies of Pablo Picasso, Gabriela Mistral, and Benito Juarez), Alfaguara (Miami, FL), 1998.

Steps/Pasos (biographies of Rita Moreno, Fernando Botero, and Evelyn Cisneros), Alfaguara (Miami, FL), 1998.

Voices/Voces (biographies of Luis Valdez, Judith F. Baca, and Carlos J. Finlay), Alfaguara (Miami, FL), 1998.

Paths/Caminos (biographies of José Marti, Frida Kahlo, and Cesar Chavez), Alfaguara (Miami, FL), 1998.

Yo/I Am, Santillana USA Publishing (Miami, FL), 1999.

Rimas/Rhymes, Santillana USA Publishing (Miami, FL), 1999.

Poemas/Poems, Santillana USA Publishing (Miami, FL), 1999.

Palabras/Words, Santillana USA Publishing (Miami, FL), 1999.

Mis relatos/My Stories, Santillana USA Publishing (Miami, FL), 1999.

Mis recuerdos/My Memories, Santillana USA Publishing (Miami, FL), 1999.

Mambru, Santillana USA Publishing (Miami, FL), 1999.

Letras, Santillana USA Publishing (Miami, FL), 1999.

Lapices/Pencils, Santillana USA Publishing (Miami, FL), 1999.

Crayones/Crayons, Santillana USA Publishing (Miami, FL), 1999.

Colores/Colors, Santillana USA Publishing (Miami, FL), 1999.

Así soy/This Is Me, Santillana USA Publishing (Miami, FL), 1999.

Acuarela, Santillana USA Publishing (Miami, FL), 1999.

Blue and Green/Azul y Verde, Alfaguara (Miami, FL), 2000.

Brush and Paint/Brocha y pinchel, Alfaguara (Miami, FL), 2000.

Artist's Easel/Caballete, Alfaguara (Miami, FL), 2000.

Canvas and Paper/Lienzo y Papel, Alfaguara (Miami, FL), 2000.

(Selector) *Dreaming Fish/Pimpón* (poetry), Alfaguara (Miami, FL), 2000.

(Selector) *Laughing Crocodiles/Antón Pirulero* (poetry), Alfaguara (Miami, FL), 2000.

(Selector) *Singing Horse/Mambrú* (poetry), Alfaguara (Miami, FL), 2000.

(Selector and contributor) *Flying Dragon/ Chuchurumbé* (poetry), Alfaguara (Miami, FL), 2000.

Series published in Spanish translation as "Colleccion Puertas al Sol."

POETRY; IN SPANISH; WITH ALMA FLOR ADA

Gorrión, Gorrión, Harcourt School Publishers (Orlando, FL), 1996.

El verde limón, Harcourt School Publishers (Orlando, FL), 1996.

La rama azul, Harcourt School Publishers (Orlando, FL), 1996.

Nuevo día, Harcourt School Publishers (Orlando, FL), 1996.

Huertos de coral, Harcourt School Publishers (Orlando, FL), 1996.

Ríos de lava, Harcourt School Publishers (Orlando, FL), 1996.

Dulce es la sal, Harcourt School Publishers (Orlando, FL), 1996.

Canta la letra, illustrated by Ulises Wensell, Del Sol (Westlake, OH), 1998, with music by Suni Paz, 2003.

Caracolí, illustrated by Ulises Wensell, Del Sol (Westlake, OH), 1998, with music by Suni Paz, 2003.

Con ton y son, illustrated by Ulises Wensell, Del Sol (Westlake, OH), 1998, with music by Suni Paz, 2003.

Corre al coro, illustrated by Ulises Wensell, Del Sol (Westlake, OH), 1998, with music by Suni Paz, 2003.

Do, re, mi, ¡sí, sí! illustrated by Ulises Wensell, Del Sol (Westlake, OH), 1998, with music by Suni Paz, 2003.

El camino de tu risa, illustrated by Ulises Wensell, Del Sol (Westlake, OH), 1998, with music by Suni Paz, 2003.

El son de sol, illustrated by Ulises Wensell, Del Sol (Westlake, OH), 1998, with music by Suni Paz, 2003.

Qué rica la ronda! illustrated by Ulises Wensell, Del Sol (Westlake, OH), 1998, with music by Suni Paz, 2003.

Sigue la música, illustrated by Ulises Wensell, Del Sol (Westlake, OH), 1998, with music by Suni Paz, 2003.

PLAYS; WITH ALMA FLOR ADA

Primer Acto, Harcourt School Publishers (Orlando, FL), 1996.

Risas y aplausos, Harcourt School Publishers (Orlando, FL), 1996.

Escenas y alegrías, Harcourt School Publishers (Orlando, FL), 1996.

Actores y flores, Harcourt School Publishers (Orlando, FL), 1996.

Saludos al público, Harcourt School Publishers (Orlando, FL), 1996.

Ensayo general, Harcourt School Publishers (Orlando, FL), 1996.

Acto final, Harcourt School Publishers (Orlando, FL), 1996.

Rat-a-Tat, Alfaguara (Miami, FL), 2000, published as *Rat-a-Tat Cat,* Santillana USA Publishing (Miami, FL), 2002.

Roll 'n' Roll, Alfaguara (Miami, FL), 2000, published as *Roll 'n Role,* Santillana USA Publishing (Miami, FL), 2002.

Top Hat, Alfaguara (Miami, FL), 2000.

Curtains Up! Alfaguara (Miami, FL), 2000.

Works published in Spanish translation.

IN SPANISH

Quieres que to cuente? Harcourt School Publishers (Orlando, FL), 1995.

En un lugar muy lejano, Harcourt School Publishers (Orlando, FL), 1995.

Erase que se era, Harcourt School Publishers (Orlando, FL), 1995.

Y fueron felices, Harcourt School Publishers (Orlando, FL), 1995.

Y colorín colorado, Harcourt School Publishers (Orlando, FL), 1995.

Así pasaron muchos años, Harcourt School Publishers (Orlando, FL), 1995.

(With Alma Flor Ada) *Sigue la palabra,* Harcourt School Publishers (Orlando, FL), 1995.

(With Alma Flor Ada) *Imágenes del pasado,* Harcourt School Publishers (Orlando, FL), 1995.

(With Alma Flor Ada) *Ecos de pasado,* Harcourt School Publishers (Orlando, FL), 1995.

(With Alma Flor Ada; and lyricist) *Música amiga* (anthology of Hispanic folklore; includes tapes and teacher's guide), ten volumes, Del Sol (Westlake, OH), 1996-98.

(With Alma Flor Ada) *Una semilla de luz,* illustrated by Felipe Dávalos, Santillana/UNICEF (Madrid, Spain), 2000.

Also coauthor, with Alma Flor Ada, of Spanish language-arts programs *Cielo abierto, Vamos de fiesta!* and *Trofeos,* Harcourt School Publishers (Orlando, FL), 1997, and of English-as-a-second-language programs.

TRANSLATOR; WITH ALMA FLOR ADA

Lois Ehlert, *Plumas para almorzar* (translation of *Feathers for Lunch*), illustrated by the author, Harcourt (San Diego, CA), 1996.

Lois Ehlert, *A sembrar sopa de verduras* (translation of *Growing Vegetable Soup*), illustrated by the author, Harcourt (San Diego, CA), 1996.

Gary Soto, *¿Que montón de tamales!* (translation of *Too Many Tamales!*), illustrated by Ed Martinez, PaperStar (New York, NY), 1996.

Ellen Stoll Walsh, *Salta y brinc,* (translation of *Hop Jump*), Harcourt (San Diego, CA), 1996.

Henry Horenstein, *Béisobol en los barrios,* Harcourt (New York, NY), 1997.

Mem Fox, *Quienquiera que seas* (translation of *Whoever You Are*), illustrated by Leslie Staub, Harcourt (San Diego, CA), 2002.

Gerald McDermott, *Zomo el conejo: un cuento de Africa occidental* (translation of *Zomo the Rabbit*), illustrated by the author, Harcourt (San Diego, CA), 2002.

Peter Golenbock, *Compañeros de equipo* (translation of *Teammates*), illustrated by Paul Bacon, Harcourt (San Diego, CA), 2002.

Lois Ehlert, *Día de mercado* (translation of *Market Day*), illustrated by the author, Harcourt (San Diego, CA), 2003.

FOR ADULTS

(With Alma Flor Ada) *Home School Interaction with Culturally or Language-diverse Families,* Del Sol (Westlake, OH), 1998.

(With Alma Flor Ada) *Ayudando a nuestros hijos* (title means "Helping Our Children"), Del Sol (Westlake, OH), 1998.

(With Alma Flor Ada) *Comprehensive Language Arts,* Del Sol (Westlake, OH), 1998.

(With Alma Flor Ada) *Effective English Acquisition for Academic Success,* Del Sol (Westlake, OH), 1998.

(With Alma Flor Ada and Rosalma Zubizarreta) *Authors in the Classroom: A Transformative Education Process,* Allyn & Bacon (Boston, MA), 2003.

WORK IN PROGRESS: A nonfiction collection for ages five to eleven.

SIDELIGHTS: F. Isabel Campoy is the prolific author of bilingual materials for children of Hispanic heritage. Plays, poems, educational materials, picture books, biographies, and easy-readers all have issued from Campoy's fertile imagination, most of these works coauthored by Alma Flor Ada. In addition to stand-alone books, the collaborators have produced a number of book series, and several of their works have been included in the "Coleccion Puertas al Sol" series designed to introduce young readers to Hispanic culture. Their *Música amiga* anthology, published beginning in 1996, encompasses ten volumes of Hispanic folklore, along with original lyrics by Campoy, while other books, such as *Happy Birthday, Little Red Riding Hood!* "combine the charm of traditional tales with the surprise of the unexpected," according to *Booklist* reviewer Isabel Schon.

Books by Campoy and Ada that are part of the "Gateways to the Sun" series include the art books *Blue and Green* and *Brush and Paper,* as well as a four-book series of biographies of notable Hispanic men and woman titled *Smiles, Steps, Voices,* and *Paths.* Profiling such diverse individuals as artist Frida Kahlo, labor activist Cesar Chavez, and actress Rita Moreno, these books "briefly tell about the lives and achievements" of their subjects, according to *Booklist* reviewer Schon, who praised the entire series as "a very appealing introduction" to Spanish-language culture.

In addition to her works with Ada, Campoy has authored the picture book *Rosa Raposa.* The book contains three stories adapted from Spanish trickster tales that take readers into the Amazon rain forest. In "A Cry for Help," "A Strong North Wind," and "The Green Dress" the clever little fox Rosa Raposa manages to outwit a hungry and bullying jaguar. While noting that the stories are "rather flat" in their narration, a *Publishers Weekly* contributor nonetheless praised *Rosa Raposa* for its lively watercolor illustrations. Julie Cummins was more enthusiastic in her *Booklist* review, noting that *Rosa Raposa* features a "well-paced text" that, with the rhyming conclusion to each story, "will make for lively read-alouds." Calling the book "delightful," *School Library Journal* contributor Judith Constantinides added that Campoy's stories do much to promote "the idea that brains are better than brawn."

Campoy told *CA:* "I was born by the Mediterranean Sea in a town called Alicante, an ideal vacation place in Spain both for national and international tourists, so during my childhood I was always in contact with people coming and going—family and friends from all over the world.

"That, and the fact that my father was a professor of English and wanted his children to become proficient in as many languages as possible, provided me with a great desire to travel and be in touch with other cultures very early on. My favorite books as a chid were always full of adventure, from the medieval chivalric romances and the pirates of Sandocán to *Treasure Island, The Adventures of Tom Sawyer,* and *Alice's Adventures in Wonderland.* But perhaps my favorite of all times is *The Little Prince* by Antoine de Sainte-Exupéry.

"My curiosity for all things far and different was nurtured by my father's vast collection of *National Geographic* magazines that covered one side of our hallway from floor to ceiling, with copies that went back as far as 1924. Each picture was a promise of a new adventure, and I started writing about them in a huge accounting book my brother and I shared: on his end, the names of soccer players and winning teams; on mine, the products of my fertile imagination. My first published story was about a snowman. I was eleven, and I had never seen snow.

"At age sixteen, after a hard time convincing my mother and many competitive examinations, I won a scholarship as an exchange student to Trenton, Michigan. Finally, that winter, I saw snow—almost daily! I have the impression that I have been traveling ever since.

"In my twenties I crossed Europe and in Greece I fell in love with mythology. Years later I wrote down many legends of the Hispanic world.

"Morocco, Egypt, and Turkey were countries that fascinated me and inspired my research into the Arabic contributions to the history of Spain and Latin America.

"Whether in Asia or Micronesia, Africa or the Middle East, I have always found reason to admire other cultures and reflect on them. Perhaps that is why I write about Hispanic art, artists, theatre, poetry, and folklore: In the process of looking at other cultures, I discovered the beauty and richness of my own."

See sketch on Alma Flor Ada for more information.

BIOGRAPHICAL AND CRITICAL SOURCES:

PERIODICALS

Booklist, August, 2000, p. 2154; February 15, 2002, Isabel Schon, review of *Happy Birthday, Little Red Riding Hood!* and *The New Home of the Seven Billy Goats,* p. 1022; September 1, 2002, Julie Cummins, review of *Rosa Raposa,* p. 136.

Kirkus Reviews, August 15, 2002, review of *Rosa Raposa,* p. 1219.

Publishers Weekly, September 9, 2002, review of *Rosa Raposa,* p. 66.

School Library Journal, September, 2002, Judith Constantinides, review of *Rosa Raposa,* p. 181.

ONLINE

F. Isabel Campoy Web site, http://www.isabelcampoy. com (May 5, 2003).

OTHER

Path to My Word (videotape), Del Sol (Westlake, OH).

*   *   *

CANDLER, Warren A(kin) 1857-1941

PERSONAL: Born August 23, 1857, near Villa Rica, GA; died of bronchial pneumonia, September 25, 1941, in Atlanta, GA; son of Samuel Charles (a farmer and merchant) and Martha (Beale; some sources cite maiden name as Beall) Candler; married Sarah Antoinette Curtright (some sources cite maiden name as Cartwright), November 21, 1877; children: Annie Florence, John Curtright, Warren Akin, Emory, Samuel Charles. *Education:* Emory College (now University), graduated (with honors), 1875.

CAREER: Minister of North Georgia Conference, Methodist Episcopal Church, South, beginning c. 1875; Methodist Episcopal bishop, 1898-1934. Emory University, Atlanta, GA, president, 1888-98, chancellor, 1914-22. Ecumenical Methodist Conference, delegate, 1891; missionary in Cuba, beginning 1898, and Mexico, 1903-10; supervisor of missionaries in the Far East, including Korea. Vanderbilt University, served as member of board of trustees; Paine College, founding member of board of trustees, 1884-c. 1909.

AWARDS, HONORS: Candler School of Theology named in Candler's honor at Emory University; a college in Havana, Cuba, and a hospital in Savannah, GA, were also named for Candler.

WRITINGS:

The History of Sunday Schools, Phillips & Hunt (New York, NY), 1880.

Christus Auctor: A Manual of Christian Evidences, Barbee & Smith (Nashville, TN), 1900.

Great Revivals and the Great Republic, Publishing House of the Methodist Episcopal Church, South (Nashville, TN), 1904.

Wesley and His Work; or, Methodism and Missions: A Volume of Addresses, Publishing House of the Methodist Episcopal Church, South (Nashville, TN), 1912.

Practical Studies in the Fourth Gospel, two volumes, Publishing House of the Methodist Episcopal Church, South (Nashville, TN), 1914.

The Kingdom of God's Dear Son, Publishing House of the Methodist Episcopal Church, South (Nashville, TN), 1921.

Wit and Wisdom of Warren Akin Candler, edited by Elam Franklin Dempsey, Publishing House of the Methodist Episcopal Church, South (Nashville, TN), 1922.

Life of Thomas Coke, Publishing House of the Methodist Episcopal Church, South (Nashville, TN), 1923.

The Feast of the Family on the Birthday of the King, Cokesbury Press (Nashville, TN), 1923.

Current Comments on Timely Topics, Cokesbury Press (Nashville, TN), 1926.

The Christ and the Creed, Cokesbury Press (Nashville, TN), 1927.

Bishop Charles Butts Galloway: A Prince of Preachers and a Christian Statesman, Cokesbury Press (Nashville, TN), 1927.

Easter Meditations, Cokesbury Press (Nashville, TN), 1930.

Young J. Allen, "the Man Who Seeded China," Cokesbury Press (Nashville, TN), 1931.

Author of *Georgia's Educational Work: What It Has Been, What It Should Be,* and *"Hammond's History" Corrected, Etc.,* Foote & Davies (Atlanta, GA). Assistant editor, *Christian Advocate,* beginning 1886. Some of Candler's writings have been published in Spanish.

Candler's papers are stored in Asa Griggs Candler Library, Emory University, Atlanta, GA.

BIOGRAPHICAL AND CRITICAL SOURCES:

BOOKS

Pierce, Alfred Mann, *Giant against the Sky: The Life of Warren Akin Candler,* Abingdon-Cokesbury (New York, NY), 1948.*

*   *   *

CAPPO, Nan Willard 1955-

PERSONAL: Born March 5, 1955, in Traverse City, MI; daughter of Gradon F. (a chemical company executive) and Ellen (a nurse; maiden name, Connor) Willard; married Dirk F. Cappo (a financial consultant), 1983; children: Ellen, Emily, Mark. *Ethnicity:* "Caucasian." *Education:* University of Notre Dame, B.A., 1977; University of Pittsburgh, M.B.A., 1981; Wayne State University, M.A., 2003. *Religion:* Roman Catholic. *Hobbies and other interests:* Reading, movies, international politics.

ADDRESSES: Home—Farmington, MI. *Agent*—Edite Kroll Literary Agency, 12 Grayhurst Park, Portland, ME 04102. *E-mail*—nancap@attglobal.net.

CAREER: Novelist, 2000—. IBM marketing representative, 1982-87; Oakland Community College, English teacher, 2002—; leader of various writing workshops; public speaker. Odyssey of the Mind, coach, 1991-99.

MEMBER: Society of Children's Book Writers and Illustrators, Detroit Women Writers (chair of writers' conference, 2002).

AWARDS, HONORS: Judy Blume Contemporary Novel-in-Progress grant, Society of Children's Book Writers and Illustrators, 1992; nomination, Edgar Award for best young-adult mystery, 2003, for *Cheating Lessons.*

WRITINGS:

Cheating Lessons (young adult novel), Simon & Schuster (New York, NY), 2002.

WORK IN PROGRESS: Natalie Wishbone, a young-adult novel.

SIDELIGHTS: Nan Willard Cappo told *CA:* "I always thought I'd be a writer someday, but until I quit my corporate job to stay home with my children, I never wrote fiction. Fortunately, a lifetime of reading had taught me more than I knew. The plot for *Cheating Lessons* came from my love of English literature, from coaching school teams in national competitions, and from my fascination with the difficulty most people, including me, have being honest all the time. As I wrote, the characters in the story began to remind me of people I knew. I changed their height and coloring to avoid libel charges and disinheritance. Bernadette is a bit like me at sixteen (though her memory is much better), and almost as smart as she thinks she is.

"My favorite review is the one in *Horn Book,* which calls Bernadette 'an adolescent who gains . . . friends when she learns to be a little less critical and who, while losing her naive confidence in adults, refreshingly maintains confidence in herself.' Bernadette's new tolerance for other people, now that she's seen how easy it is to do bad things for good reasons, is one of the things I like best about the book. Who doesn't face those temptations? Who doesn't wish the people you love could be a bit more lovable? But teenagers seem to like the scene where she hides in her teacher's closet while he takes off his shirt. Go figure.

"I have three teenagers of my own who supply me with plenty of material. Recently I began teaching college English, so my students, too, give me more ideas than they suspect. The best advice I have for young writers is to read like a writer. Try to figure out how authors did what they did, and then attempt the same thing, using your own material, of course. I pore over books by Anne Tyler and Jane Austen and Francine Prose—stories about things that matter, like courage and love and clever conversation. Some of my favorite writers for children are Anne Fine, Katherine Paterson, Nancy Farmer, Lynne Rae Perkins, and J. K. Rowling. For me, reading books I wish I'd written and trying to crack the code remains the best writing instruction in the world."

BIOGRAPHICAL AND CRITICAL SOURCES:

PERIODICALS

Horn Book, March-April, 2002, Jennifer M. Brabander, review of *Cheating Lessons,* p. 209.
Publishers Weekly, January 7, 2002, review of *Cheating Lessons,* p. 65.
School Library Journal, March, 2002, Susan Riley, review of *Cheating Lessons,* p. 226.
Teacher, May 1, 2002, review of *Cheating Lessons.*

*   *   *

CARMAN, Judith E. 1940-

PERSONAL: Born December 4, 1940, in Mayfield, KY; daughter of Roscoe Vernon (an automobile mechanic) and Mary Jewell (a homemaker; maiden name, Caldwell) Carman. *Ethnicity:* "Caucasian." *Education:* Attended Murray State Teacher's College (now Murray State University), 1958-61; George Peabody College (now Vanderbilt University), B.Mus., 1963, M.Mus., 1965; attended Stätliche Höchschule für Musik, Cologne, Germany, 1965-66; University of Iowa, D.M.A., 1973; University of Houston, postdoctoral study, 1989-90. *Politics:* Liberal. *Religion:* Episcopalian. *Hobbies and other interests:* Reading, cycling, camping, yoga, cooking.

ADDRESSES: Home and office—1404 Wood Hollow, No. 8805, Houston, TX 77057-1617. *E-mail*—jecarman@earthlink.net.

CAREER: Shenandoah College and Conservatory of Music, Winchester, VA, instructor in music, 1966-69; Central Michigan University, Mount Pleasant, assistant professor of voice, 1973-74; Lansing Community College, Lansing, MI, instructor in voice, 1974-78; Houston Baptist University, Houston, TX, adjunct instructor in voice, diction, and vocal literature, 1978-79; private voice instructor in Houston, 1979—. Texas Southern University, adjunct professor, 1992-97. Trinity Summer Opera Theater, director, 1983-93; Yoga for Singers, teacher, 1999—.

MEMBER: National Association of Teachers of Singing (chair of committee on American song, 1975-76; president of Greater Houston chapter, 1983-85, 1998-2000).

WRITINGS:

(Editor and contributor) *Art-Song in the United States: An Annotated Bibliography,* National Association of Teachers of Singing, 1976, 3rd edition published as *Art Song in the United States, 1759-1999: An Annotated Bibliography,* Scarecrow Press (Lanham, MD), 2001.

Author of "Music Reviews," a regular column in *NATS Journal of Singing,* 1997—. Contributor to music journals.

WORK IN PROGRESS: Research on yoga and singing as natural partners; a historical survey of art song in the United States.

SIDELIGHTS: Judith E. Carman told *CA:* "My fascination with the written word began as soon as I learned to read, and I have been a lifelong reader. Books were my constant companions throughout my public school years, and the topic of the first research paper I ever wrote was the invention and development of the art of writing itself. In college I enjoyed writing papers, and occasionally a professor would suggest that I submit a paper for publication. However, my primary activity was music, and I did not consider myself a writer, or even particularly creative.

"My first publication other than my doctoral dissertation was an extensively annotated bibliography of art songs by American composers, which two colleagues and I researched and compiled as a teaching reference for the use of studio voice teachers. I discovered that I could write fairly easily about music, but for a number of years I did not write at all. In 1996 I read Julia Cameron's *The Artist's Way* and began writing whatever came to mind each morning. It was this exercise that kindled my desire to write as a creative outlet. That same year I was invited to take over the 'Music Reviews' column for the *NATS Journal of Singing* as an adjunct activity to editing the third edition of the American art song bibliography. At the same time, I was developing a yoga class specifically for singers and did quite a lot of instructional writing for that project, which I have recently written up as a journal article.

"Most of my writing to date has been instructional, descriptive, or scholarly in my professional field of vocal music. As I write more, my interest in poetry and fiction grows. The process of writing—the appearance of words on a blank page from my mind through my own hand—is very much like the process of singing—the phenomenon of audible melody from the music in the mind sounding through the voice. Both are creations born from my own center—writing perhaps even more than singing, because in singing I interpret the creation of someone else, whereas in writing the ideas and words are my own.

"At this point in my writing career, I have more to look forward to than back upon, and I anticipate enjoying writing for many years to come. I also hope that whatever works see the light of publication will bring information, insight, or inspiration to others."

*   *   *

CARROLL, Benajah Harvey 1843-1914

PERSONAL: Born December 27, 1843, in Carrolton, MS; died November 11, 1914, in Fort Worth, TX; son of Benajah (a farmer and preacher) and Mary Eliza (Mallard) Carroll; married Ellen Virginia Bell, c. 1866. *Education:* Baylor University, A.B.

CAREER: Ordained minister of Southern Baptist Convention, c. 1866; pastor of Baptist churches in Burleson County and McLennan County, TX, c. 1866-70; pastor of Baptist church in Waco, TX, beginning 1870; Baylor University, Waco, TX, instructor in Bible and theology, 1872-c. 1908, founder of Baylor

Theological Seminary, 1905; Southwestern Baptist Theological Seminary, Fort Worth TX, president, 1908-14. Worked as a schoolteacher in McLennan County. Also active with Texas Baptist Convention. *Military service:* Texas Rangers, served prior to 1862. Confederate Army, 1862-65.

WRITINGS:

Sermons and Life-Sketch of B. H. Carroll, compiled by J. B. Cranfill, American Baptist Publications Society (Philadelphia, PA), 1895.

The Bible Doctrine of Repentance, Baptist Book Concern (Louisville, KY), 1897.

The Genesis of American Anti-Missionism, Baptist Book Concern (Louisville, KY), 1902.

Baptists and Their Doctrines, Fleming H. Revell (New York, NY), 1913.

Evangelistic Sermons, 1913.

Daniel and the Inter-Biblical Period, edited by J. B. Cranfill, Fleming H. Revell (New York, NY), 1915.

Galatians, Romans, Philippians, Philemon, edited by J. B. Cranfill, Fleming H. Revell (New York, NY), 1916.

Colossians, edited by J. B. Cranfill, Fleming H. Revell (New York, NY), 1917.

Inspiration of the Bible, Fleming H. Revell (New York, NY), 1930.

Studies in Genesis, edited by Prince Emanuel Burroughs, Broadman Press (Nashville, TN), 1937.

The Ten Commandments, Broadman Press (Nashville, TN), 1938.

The Holy Spirit: Comprising a Discussion of the Paraclete, the Other Self of Jesus, and Other Phases of the Work of the Spirit of God, edited by J. B. Cranfill and Joseph Wade Crowder, Zondervan Publishing House (Grand Rapids, MI), 1939.

Christ and His Church, edited by J. B. Cranfill and Joseph Wade Crowder, Helms Printing (Dallas, TX), 1940.

(With John Albert Broadus) *Saved to Serve: Comprising Appealing and Vital Messages on the Duties of Christians to Give of Their Time, Thought, and Means to God,* edited by J. B. Cranfill and Joseph Wade Crowder, Helms Printing (Dallas, TX), 1941.

The Book of Revelation, edited by J. B. Cranfill, Broadman Press (Nashville, TN), 1943.

The Books of Exodus and Leviticus, edited by J. B. Cranfill, Broadman Press (Nashville, TN), 1943.

The Hebrew Monarchy, edited by J. B. Cranfill, Broadman Press (Nashville, TN), 1943.

The Pastoral Epistles of Paul and I and II Peter, Jude, I, II, and III John, edited by J. B. Cranfill, Broadman Press (Nashville, TN), 1943.

An Interpretation of the English Bible, edited by J. B. Cranfill, seventeen volumes, Broadman Press (Nashville, TN), 1943-48.

BIOGRAPHICAL AND CRITICAL SOURCES:

BOOKS

Cranfill, J. B., compiler, *Sermons and Life-Sketch of B. H. Carroll,* American Baptist Publications Society (Philadelphia, PA), 1895.*

*   *   *

CARTER, Merri Sue 1964-

PERSONAL: Born November 16, 1964, in Columbus, OH; daughter of William E. (a research geodesist) and Marilyn (a contract officer; maiden name, Johnson) Carter; married James H. Clark III (an engineer), April 26, 1996; children: Wyatt Evan Clark, Holly Mae Clark. *Ethnicity:* "Caucasian." *Education:* University of Maryland, B.S., 1986; University of Maryland University College, M.S., 1999. *Hobbies and other interests:* Playing with her children, reading, needlework.

ADDRESSES: Home—4009 Stonewall Ave., Fairfax, VA 22032. *Office*—U.S. Naval Observatory, 3450 Massachusetts Ave., Washington, DC 20392. *E-mail*—msc@maia.usno.navy.mil.

CAREER: Astronomer. U.S. Naval Observatory, Washington, DC, astronomer, 1996—. Director of World Data Center A for the Rotation of the Earth.

MEMBER: American Geophysical Union.

WRITINGS:

(With father, Bill Carter) *Latitude: How American Astronomers Solved the Mystery of Variation,* Naval Institute Press (Annapolis, MD), 2002.

Author of scientific papers; contributor to *American National Biography.*

WORK IN PROGRESS: Research on the polar motion and variations in Earth rotation; research on the history of contributions made to the U.S. Naval Observatory by women.

SIDELIGHTS: Astronomer Merri Sue Carter wrote *Latitude: How American Astronomers Solved the Mystery of Variation* with her research geodesist father, Bill Carter. It is a history of the breakthrough discovery that established the United States as a player in the global scientific community.

The European community was stunned when, in 1891, Boston actuary Seth Carlo Chandler, Jr. developed a model—the "Chandler Wobble"—that explained oscillations in latitude, a problem that European scientists had attempted for decades to solve. Chandler had been able to develop his observational skills based on his early training, unimpeded by theories of celestial mechanics, of which he knew little. The United States had fallen behind in the field of science since the founding of the independent nation, but another American stepped forward to complete the model. Simon Newcomb confirmed Chandler's discovery, reconciled it with the current theory, and made it understandable.

This was a defining moment in America's advancement toward space-age technology, including global positioning satellite (GPS) systems, and it was all because of the perseverance of an untrained scientist and his inexpensive instrument. Chandler's granddaughter provided his papers and correspondence, allowing the authors to personalize the story of this scientific discovery, one which is written in a manner that is clear to the reader with an interest in science. *Booklist* contributer Bryce Christensen wrote that "readers who thrill to the unlikely triumphs of amateurs will greatly enjoy the compelling story of Seth Carlo Chandler, Jr." A *Kirkus Reviews* contributor commented on the "windows of opportunity for the nonspecialist to become acquainted with physical properties of Earth, including the revolution of Earth's pole, fluidity, elasticity, centrifugal force, and periodicity." The reviewer also noted that for those who understand it, the science explains why personal GPS units may occasionally need to be recalibrated.

Carter expanded more on how the idea for the book came to be, telling *CA:* "A quarter of a century ago, Bill Carter was shocked to learn that many of his colleagues used the term 'Chandler Wobble' in their everyday work, but had no idea who Chandler was or how he had discovered the wobble. Over the next decade, Bill authored papers for scientific journals and presented talks at scientific conferences to inform his colleagues about the remarkable work of Seth Carlo Chandler, Jr."

When Carter began her career at the U.S. Naval Obervatory (USNO), she developed an interest in the early history of the USNO, especially the contributions women had made, and began documenting these women's work in a series of talks and papers. Her research on earth rotation and the history of the USNO naturally led her to an interest in the internationally acclaimed work of Simon Newcomb, who had spent his entire career as a Navy Professor of Mathematics at the USNO and the Nautical Almanac Office. In 1994 Bill and Merri Sue were invited by the National Academy of Sciences to correct nearly a century of neglect by writing Chandler's biographical memoirs. "This work grew from a short article to a longer, but restricted, work," added Carter. "We wanted to expand on that and tell a more complete story in a way that the general audience would enjoy."

BIOGRAPHICAL AND CRITICAL SOURCES:

PERIODICALS

Booklist, September 1, 2002, Bryce Christensen, review of *Latitude: How American Astronomers Solved the Mystery of Variation,* p. 32.
Kirkus Reviews, September 1, 2002, review of *Latitude,* p. 1276.

*　　*　　*

CARVER, Caroline

PERSONAL: Born in London, England; daughter of a race-car driver and a jet pilot. *Hobbies and other interests:* Long-distance car rallies.

ADDRESSES: Agent—Elizabeth Wright, Darley Anderson Literary Agency, 11 Eustace Rd., London SW6 1JB, England. *E-mail*—caroline@carolinecarver.co.uk.

CAREER: Competition driver and writer.

MEMBER: Crime Writers' Association, Royal Geographic Society.

AWARDS, HONORS: New Writer Award, Crime Writers' Association, 1999, for *Blood Junction.*

WRITINGS:

Blood Junction, Orion Books (London, England), 2001, Mysterious Press (New York, NY), 2002.
Dead Heat, Orion Books (London, England), 2003.

WORK IN PROGRESS: Another India Kane thriller, to be published by Orion in 2004.

SIDELIGHTS: Caroline Carver is a London-born rally driver and writer whose mother set the Australian land speed record in 1957, and whose father was a jet fighter pilot. Adventure is in Carver's blood, witnessed by her record-setting competitions. Her first was the London-to-Saigon Motoring Challenge, a sixty-three-day, 12,500-mile drive made by Carver and her female codriver. When they reached Saigon, the team donated both the funds they had raised and their car to Save the Children. In 1998 Carver drove from London to Capetown, South Africa, and in 2001 she drove the Inca Trail, a 14,000-mile, fifty-five-day rally. She crossed South America with another female driver named Caroline.

Between the first and last of these trips, Carver began her writing career, first with travel articles, and then with her thriller *Blood Junction,* set in the Australian outback and featuring Sydney journalist India Kane. *Times Literary Supplement* contributor Heather O'Donoghue called the novel's opening "gripping."

In *Blood Junction* India travels to Cooinda because a journalist friend, Lauren, says she has discovered one of India's relatives. After India arrives, both Lauren and a policeman are murdered, and she is charged with the homicides. Her bail is posted by an unknown benefactor, and she is freed to pursue the real killers. Meanwhile, India discovers a fifty-year-old crime and the massacre of an Aboriginal family, and also learns of global conspiracies, a new biological weapon, and a suspect institute that supposedly tests cosmetics, as well as more about her own heritage. As she delves into the secrets of Cooinda, she is helped by Polly, an Aboriginal girl, and by Whitelaw, the police officer with whom she has a relationship.

A *Publishers Weekly* reviewer wrote that Carver "vividly renders the harsh Australian outback and candidly and effectively presents Australia's shameful treatment of 'Abos' (Aboriginals)." *Library Journal's* Jane Jorgenson felt that Carver "deftly evokes the claustrophobic feeling of a nineteenth-century Western frontier town." *Booklist's* Bill Ott noted that "this could be the start of something special."

Dead Heat, Carver's second novel, is set in Northern Queensland and features Georgia Parish. Her third is to be another India Kane mystery.

Carver told *CA:* "Writing thrillers is right up my street, not just because of my love of adventure, but because I've been scared witless a few times and known exactly how it feels!

"I started my first thriller, *Blood Junction,* when I saw an article on the stolen generation in Australia, where during the 1950s, over a hundred thousand Aboriginal children were forcibly taken from their families and adopted by whites. Most of these children were mixed race, with paler skin than their siblings, and several things struck me about this. There was the spectre of genocide, to 'breed' the Aborigines white. There was the struggle of the stolen child being brought up in an alien world. And what of the parents of these stolen children? What would happen if a whole Aboriginal family went missing today? Who would take up their cause?

"The more I delved, the more possibilities appeared. I'd wanted a setting that would excite me and hopefully a reader too, and the harshness of the Australian outback seemed to fit the bill nicely. I'd stayed on a sheep station in the outback ten years previously and quickly dug out my photographs to remind me of the dry heat, the interminable flies, sand clogging the back of my throat. I am also interested in how a character reacts when they're in a strange place and caught in events beyond their control. Being a lover of wilderness, I like to use the setting almost as another character."

BIOGRAPHICAL AND CRITICAL SOURCES:

PERIODICALS

Booklist, August, 2002, Bill Ott, review of *Blood Junction,* p. 1929.

Kirkus Reviews, July 1, 2002, review of *Blood Junction,* p. 919.

Library Journal, August, 2002, Jane Jorgenson, review of *Blood Junction,* p. 140.

Publishers Weekly, August 5, 2002, review of *Blood Junction,* p. 55.

Times Literary Supplement, Heather O'Donoghue, review of *Blood Junction,* p. 23.

ONLINE

Caroline Carver Home Page, http://www.caroline carver.com (February 14, 2003).

* * *

CATHY, S. Truett 1921-

PERSONAL: Born 1921, in Eatonton, GA; married; wife's name Jeannette; three children; ten grandchildren. *Religion:* Baptist. *Hobbies and other interests:* Motorcycling.

ADDRESSES: Office—Chick-fil-A Inc., 5200 Buffington Rd., Atlanta, GA 30349.

CAREER: Dwarf House Restaurant, Hapeville, GA, owner-operator, 1946—; Chick-fil-A Inc., president, 1946—; Clayton Fixtures Inc., Forest Park, GA, principal, 1980—. *Military service:* U.S. Army, 1944-46.

MEMBER: Pi Kappa Alpha, Iota Upsilon chapter (Georgia Southern University).

AWARDS, HONORS: Outstanding Business Leader award, Northwood University, 1988; Silver Plate Award, National Restaurant Association, 1988; Horatio Alger Distinguished American Award, 1989; Most Admired CEO designation, *Business Atlanta,* 1990;

designated Executive of the Year, University of Georgia, 1990; Pioneer of the Year designation, *Nation's Restaurant News,* 1991; National Commitment to Business Excellence in Foster Care honor, National Foster Parent Association.

WRITINGS:

It's Easier to Succeed than Fail, Thomas Nelson (Nashville, TN), 1989.
Eat Mor Chikin: Inspire More People, Looking Glass Books (Decatur, GA), 2002.
(With Ken Blanchard) *The Generosity Factor: Discover the Joy of Giving Your Time, Talent, and Treasure,* Zondervan (Grand Rapids, MI), 2002.

SIDELIGHTS: S. Truett Cathy is the founder and president of a fast-food chain specializing in chicken sandwiches, Chick-fil-A. The success of the company came about despite Cathy's insistence on choosing spiritual principles over business principles: none of the company's operations open on Sunday, and none are franchised to the individual operators, whose initial investment seems like chicken feed compared to the franchise fees of similar restaurants. With little advertising, the company has risen to third, behind Kentucky Fried Chicken and Copeland's, in the fast-food chicken business. Cathy's three books each focus on the challenge of living spiritual values in business life, bolstered by the credibility of Cathy's own success in doing so.

Cathy won the famous Horatio Alger Award in 1989, a prize recognizing Americans whose perseverance and determination allow them to rise from poverty and other hardships. Cathy grew up during the Great Depression of the 1930s, while his mother supported the family by running a boarding house in Eatonton, Georgia. Cathy soon caught the entrepreneurial spirit, selling Coca-Cola on the front lawn for spare change, then moving on to newspapers and books, and then to insurance. Cathy never attended college: after serving in the Army during World War II from 1944 to 1946, he opened a restaurant with his brother Ben Cathy. The Dwarf House, located near Atlanta, was a success for the brothers, but Cathy became the sole proprietor in 1947 when Ben died in a plane crash. The Dwarf House kitchen developed the quick-cooked boneless chicken breast that would become the Chick-fil-A

sandwich. In 1967 Cathy opened a separate location in Atlanta's Greenbriar Mall to sell the sandwich, and Chick-fil-A restaurants were born.

Chick-fil-A's sales quadrupled between 1977 and 1981, causing other businesses to take notice of Cathy's unusual approach. "The Food Business is a divine business," he once told *Forbes* reporter Barbara Rudolph. "Waiting on people is like a ministry." In addition to closing his restaurants on Sunday, Cathy asked Chick-fil-A employees to attend a half-hour devotional each week, and included a sermon from a minister at the grand opening of each new operation. At that point, Cathy had 180 stores, and Rudolph questioned whether he could compete and grow under the current business model. By the time Cathy was winning awards for corporate leadership in the 1990s, he had proven he could: Chick-fil-A units were numbering above 430, and by 2002 Cathy had 1,040 restaurants in the United States. In addition, Chick-fil-A has long maintained the highest employee retention rates in the industry, which Cathy attributes to his Sundays-off policy and a strong ethos of loyalty in the company.

Cathy wrote his first book about his success in 1989, *It's Easier to Succeed than Fail.* Reviewer Michael Schrader, writing for *Nation's Restaurant News,* said, "Cathy's advice is simple: Set goals, associate with winners, work hard." The book also emphasizes how Cathy's Christian faith provided the foundation of his methods, and motivated him to help others. Rev. Charles Carter of the First Baptist Church in Jonesboro, Georgia, told reporter D. M. Levine in *Nation's Restaurant News,* "No one will ever know how many young people Truett has helped along the way. . . . He helps them with family problems, medical bills, clothing costs, and college expenses." Cathy has also made that a centerpiece of his business model, charging operators seeking to open a new restaurant only $5,000 to start, in contrast to the hundreds of thousands in cash franchisees pay to start in other fast-food chains. Cathy said to Levine, "We'll provide the bread and water for you and your family, and we won't take your life savings. In return, all we ask is a real strong commitment." Chick-fil-A employees have also been able to earn scholarships since 1973; as of 1991 7,000 employees had done so. In 1984 Cathy launched the WinShape Centre Foundation (for "shaping winners"), which sponsors a scholarship program jointly with Berry College, Camp WinShape, and WinShape Foster

Care. Within ten years the foundation had given more than ten million dollars in scholarships.

In 2002 Cathy again took on the role of the author, publishing two books discussing his business principles. In *Eat Mor Chikin: Inspire More People,* Cathy tells the story of the growth of Chick-fil-A and the WinShape Foundation, challenging readers to follow in his path by putting people first. At the time his book appeared in 2002, Cathy was also asked to appear before the U.S. Congress, where he addressed the House Subcommittee on Commerce, Trade, and Consumer Protection. In a 2002 interview with Sarah Smith Hamaker for *Restaurants USA Online,* Cathy said the committee "wanted to know how you can operate a business honestly, and they asked me to talk about putting people before profits." Cathy described his business practices according to the five steps outlined in the book: "climb with care and confidence, create a 'loyalty effect,' never lose a customer, put principles and people ahead of profits, and close on Sundays." Cathy's other 2002 publication, *The Generosity Factor: Discover the Joy of Giving Your Time, Talent, and Treasure* which is coauthored with Ken Blanchard, makes a similar point in a different style. The book is a parable of the Broker and the Executive, as the Broker strives to understand how the Executive leads and succeeds by giving to others. A reviewer for *Publishers Weekly* wrote that "while the characters in this little parable . . . are more stereotypical than archetypal, the values presented are first-rate." A reviewer for *Bookpage* said that the principles of *The Generosity Factor* "can inspire success in the workplace and in the heart."

As of 2002, Cathy had expanded Chick-fil-A to thirty-four states, successfully bringing his fast-food chain beyond its Southern base. In *Restaurants USA Online* Cathy said the company remained committed to corporate responsibility: "We have a responsibility to our employees to give them abilities and securities. We ask them to invest a good part of their life in our restaurant and we need to give them something back."

BIOGRAPHICAL AND CRITICAL SOURCES:

PERIODICALS

Bookpage, July, 2002, review of *The Generosity Factor,* p. 21.
Business Atlanta, November, 1990, Faye McDonald Smith, "Vision and Integrity," pp. 28-34.

Forbes, June 4, 1984, Barbara Rudolph, "Never on Sunday," pp. 176-77.
Nation's Restaurant News, January 1, 1986, D. M. Levine, "Old-Time Religion Guides Chick-fil-A; Bible Sets Tone for Cathy," pp. 1-2; September 25, 1989, Michael S. Schraeder, review of *It's Easier to Succeed Than Fail,* p. 109; June 17, 1991, Charles Bernstein, "MUFSO Pioneer: Chick-fil-A Founder Cathy," pp. 1-2; October 21, 1991, Peter O. Keegan, "Industry Lauds Cathy as Pioneer of the Year," pp. 1-2.
Publishers Weekly, July 15, 2002, "Cultivating Virtue," p. 71.
Restaurant Business, May 1, 1992, Shelley Wolson, "Never on Sunday," pp. 110-11.
Restaurants & Institutions, July 22, 1992, Nancy Ross Ryan, "The Scoop on Chicken: S. Truett Cathy," p. 52.

ONLINE

Northwood University Web site, http://www.northwood.edu/ (October 15, 2002), Cathy's acceptance speech as Outstanding Business Leader of 1988.
Pi Kappa Alpha Web site, http://www.pka.com/ (October 15, 2002), "Hard Work and High Principles: Truett Cathy Embodies the Virtues of PiKA."
Restaurants USA Online, http://www.restaurant.org/ (October 15, 2002), Sarah Smith Hamaker, "Doing Business the Chick-fil-A Way."
Zondervan Web site, http://www.zondervan.com/ (October 15, 2002).*

* * *

CHAFFIN, J. Thomas 1952-
(Tom Chaffin)

PERSONAL: Born November 21, 1952, in Atlanta, GA; son of James T. and Martha B. Chaffin; married Lena Margareta Larsson, August 13, 1988. *Education:* Georgia State University, B.A. (English), 1977; New York University, M.A. (American civilization), 1982; Emory University, Ph.D. (U.S. history), 1995. *Politics:* Democrat. *Hobbies and other interests:* Hiking, backpacking, birdwatching.

ADDRESSES: Office—Department of History, Bowden Hall, Emory University, Atlanta, GA 30322. *E-mail*—jchaffi@emory.edu.

CAREER: *Esquire,* New York, NY, researcher, 1980-81; freelance writer, 1981-85; Pacific News Service, San Francisco, CA, correspondent,1983-86; Emory University, 1996—, director of Oral History Project, 1996—, lecturer, 2001—. Taught at California State University, Hayward, and the University of Georgia.

AWARDS, HONORS: Mellon fellow, Huntington Library, San Marino, CA, 1998-99.

WRITINGS:

AS TOM CHAFFIN

Fatal Glory: Narcisco López and the First Clandestine U.S. War against Cuba, University Press of Virginia (Charlottesville, VA), 1996.
Pathfinder: John Charles Frémont and the Course of American Empire, Hill and Wang (New York, NY), 2002.

Contributor to periodicals, including *Nation, New York Times, Washington Post, National Geographic Adventure, Outside,* and *Harper's.*

SIDELIGHTS: Tom Chaffin's interests—history as an academic subject and appreciation of a good story as a journalist—led him to write *Fatal Glory: Narcisco López and the First Clandestine U.S. War against Cuba.*

López was a Venezuelan who rose through the Spanish ranks to become an influential figure in colonial Cuba. After falling out of favor with the Spaniards and organizing a failed uprising against Cuba's Spanish regime, López fled to the United States. There between 1848 and 1851—initially in Washington and New York and later in New Orleans and Savannah, Georgia—he organized four clandestine expeditionary "filibuster" armies bent on invading Cuba and bringing it into the United States as three new slave states. Presidents Zachary Taylor and, later, Millard Fillmore both opposed López's efforts, and the federal government eventually used everything from Neutrality Act prosecutions to presidential proclamations to the U.S. Navy to oppose López. Two of his armies were thwarted before they could leave U.S. waters. Two, however, reached Cuba and engaged the island's Spanish garrison. The final landing, in August 1851, ended in a rout, and López himself was later publicly garroted in Havana.

Laurie Johnston noted in the *Journal of Latin American Studies* that although López is often dismissed by historians as being a servant of Southern planters, Chaffin argues that he "actually represented a cross-section of U.S. society, and that he spoke for what Chaffin describes as a republican and expansionist nationalism then competing in the United States with another form of nationalism, opposed to slavery." Howard Jones wrote in *Civil War History* that López "emerges as an American patriot who sought Cuba as part of the 'Young America' fever of the turbulent 1850s."

Ralph Lee Woodward, Jr. noted in *Louisiana History* that these invasions have been previously covered, particularly in the three-volume history written by Cuban Herminio Portell Vilá. Woodward continued by saying that Chaffin "makes a valuable contribution with this volume not so much by his description of the invasions themselves, but rather by his detailed description of the intrigues and behind-the-scenes maneuvering that surrounded these expeditions in the United States."

Pathfinder: John Charles Frémont and the Course of American Empire is Chaffin's biography of a figure whose life is closely linked to various aspects of American history, including Western exploration and settlement, the displacement of the American Indians, the Mexican-American War, and the U.S. Civil War. Frémont's three federally financed exploring expeditions of the American West during the 1840s, Chaffin writes, covered far more ground and generated far more data than Lewis and Clark's earlier, single transcontinental expedition. During Frémont's third federal expedition, bending to military purposes, he became the nominal leader of the U.S. conquest of California, which wrested California from Mexico. In 1856, as the Republican party's first presidential candidate, he made an unsuccessful run for the White House against Democrat James Buchanan. He later served as a major general for the Union Army during the Civil War, and was an investor in various mining and railroad enterprises.

Frémont was also accused of crimes, self-promotion, and lying, and his enemies were quick to point out that his father was a French homewrecker. Chaffin notes that Frémont's bookkeeping records for his mining and railroad ventures were so inexact that they verged on fraud. He had powerful enemies, including philosopher Josiah Royce, General Stephen Watts Kearny, and Frank Blair, and Abraham Lincoln removed him from his Civil War command. *Library Journal*'s Charles K. Piehl commented that Chaffin "sees his subject as tragic, used and ultimately pushed aside by a nation that had become larger than this larger-than-life man."

A *Kirkus Reviews* contributor wrote that Chaffin "takes pains to show what in Frémont's record was of his own making, and what was laid at his door by enemies." A *Publishers Weekly* reviewer called *Pathfinder* a "superb biography. . . . There's something here for every history buff." *Booklist*'s Margaret Flanagan commented that Chaffin's portrait "vivifies the extraordinary life story of an often controversial—but undeniably significant—American hero."

BIOGRAPHICAL AND CRITICAL SOURCES:

PERIODICALS

Booklist, November 1, 2002, Margaret Flanagan, review of *Pathfinder: John Charles Frémont and the Course of American Empire,* p. 470.
Boston Globe, December 5, 2002, Scott W. Helman, review of *Pathfinder.*
Choice, June, 2003, P. D. Travis, review of *Pathfinder.*
Civil War History, December, 1997, Howard Jones, review of *Fatal Glory: Narciso López and the First Clandestine U.S. War against Cuba,* p. 345.
Hispanic American Historical Review, November, 1997, Robert L. Paquette, review of *Fatal Glory,* p. 715.
History, spring, 1997, Frank A. Gerome, review of *Fatal Glory,* p. 114.
Journal of American History, September, 1997, John H. Schroeder, review of *Fatal Glory,* p. 663.
Journal of Latin American Studies, May, 1998, Laurie Johnston, review of *Fatal Glory,* p. 419.
Journal of Military History, July, 1997, Kinley Brauer, review of *Fatal Glory,* p. 618.
Journal of Southern History, February, 1998, Mary Seaton Dix, review of *Fatal Glory,* p. 131.
Journal of the Early Republic, fall, 1997, Dean Fafoutis, review of *Fatal Glory,* p. 550.

Kirkus Reviews, September 1, 2002, review of *Pathfinder,* pp. 1276-1277.
Library Journal, November 15, 2002, Charles K. Piehl, review of *Pathfinder,* p. 79.
Lingua Franca, July/August, 2001.
Louisiana History, spring, 1998, Ralph Lee Woodward, Jr., review of *Fatal Glory.*
Mississippi Quarterly, spring, 1998, Felix V. Matos Rodriguez, review of *Fatal Glory,* p. 363.
Publishers Weekly, September 23, 2002, review of *Pathfinder,* p. 61.
San Francisco Chronicle Book Review, December 13, 2002, David Kipen, review of *Pathfinder.*
Washington Post, January 5, 2003, Robert Wilson, review of *Pathfinder.*

ONLINE

Emory University Report Online, http://www.emory.edu/Emory Report/ (January, 1997), Stacey Jones, review of *Fatal Glory.*

*   *   *

CHAFFIN, Tom
  See CHAFFIN, J. Thomas

*   *   *

CHAMBERS, Stephen M. 1980-

PERSONAL: Born November 25, 1980, in Louisville, KY. *Education:* University of Chicago, B.A. (history), 2002.

ADDRESSES: Agent—Peter Rubie, Peter Rubie Literary Agency, 240 West 35th St., Suite 500, New York, NY 10001. *E-mail*—schambers@sff.net.

CAREER: Writer.

WRITINGS:

Hope's End, Tor (New York, NY), 2001.
Hope's War, Tor (New York, NY), 2002.

SIDELIGHTS: Stephen M. Chambers drafted his first novel, *Hope's End,* when he was a junior in high school; not surprisingly, his protagonist, Vel, is sixteen, approximately the same age as Chambers when he began the book. The story is set in a future that boasts little technology and where the act of owning a book carries the death penalty. The agrarian city of Hope is located on the planet Hera. The society of people originally from Earth is ruled by a totalitarian church and an executive council, and the city suffers attacks from aliens known as the "Frill," who live in underground tunnels, and a disease called the "Pox." Into this world Vel is born to a family of peasants, and in order to make his way, he becomes a hustler, then a political activist.

Alan Cheuse noted in Chicago's *Tribune Books* that before the end of the story is reached, Vel "will have suffered numerous skirmishes with the police, the soldiers of the church, and strange and murderous giant bugs, worked a computer by powering it with his own blood, and generally turned the planet upside down." A *Publishers Weekly* reviewer noted that Blakes, the DNA clone of British poet William Blake that was stored as artificial intelligence inside an old computer in a successful twenty-first-century experiment, is "worshipped as the 'great man' in a way that recalls Ayn Rand. . . . The book remains Vel's story, though it dangles such mysteries and paradoxes before the reader."

In reviewing the book for *Leo* online, Paul Kopasz called Vel "part Luke Skywalker, part Jesse James, and part Holden Caulfield," and said that Chambers "has affected a blending of the science-fiction and sword-and-sorcery genres that indeed does justice to both." Eva Wojcik-Obert both reviewed the book and interviewed Chambers for *Fantastica Daily* online and said that he "does a grand job of sucking us into his grubby city of suspicion, hunger, and conspiracy while hinting at deeper darker corners farther away in the depths of long-lost technology and science."

In the sequel, *Hope's War,,* Vel has killed Justice Hillor, head of the Council, and at the urging of Denon, the head of the Church who plans on exercising his own power through the boy, Vel agrees to serve as king of Hope, but then turns to Blakes for guidance, feeling that he is the only one he can trust. Gerald Jonas wrote in the *New York Times Book Review* that "the model for the narrative would seem to be one of those video games whose object is to kill as many people as possible in the shortest amount of time."

Hope is blanketed by continual snows, food is in short supply, King Vel learns of his connection to the red-eyed Frills that live beneath the city, and Blakes exercises a Nazi-like reign of terror on the people of Hope. A *Publishers Weekly* contributor called *Hope's War* a "solid sequel" and said that Chambers's "compelling dissection of good and evil will keep thoughtful readers involved."

Chambers told *CA:* "As a high school student I was extremely lucky to meet a literary agent, Peter Rubie, at a writers' conference in Kentucky, and just before graduating from high school, I sold two novels to Tor Books.

"I get extremely irritable if I go too long without writing, though my wife—we have been together since I was seventeen (1997) and were married this year (2002)—might suggest that transcends any creative outlet. I cannot go for more than a month without a major writing project.

"As a kid, I wrote copious amounts of horrible material, until eventually it became publishable. Currently (winter, 2002), I am living in Paris with my wife and our two cats and no knowledge of the French language.

About his major influences Chambers said, "I would say the writing of Orson Scott Card and an array of other science fiction/fantasy authors piqued my interest in the field early. Comic books—by Alan Moore and Neil Gaiman—are some of my favorite bits of literature, as well. I love Woody Allen films, *Star Wars,* and I have roughly eighty percent of *The Big Lebowski* committed to memory.

"Generally, I create some kind of outline in a notebook, with many question marks and doodles, until eventually I physically must write the story and put it out of its misery. Every time, I envision the beginning, the middle, and end of the novel: then I go to work. Generally, a rough draft takes a few months, then I spend another few months hammering at that rough draft, until I'm satisfied with it.

"The one thing I learned studying history at the University of Chicago is that I actually know next to nothing, which, I suppose, is a crucial $120,000 lesson.

Still, I am fascinated with history, though I don't have the patience to pursue it to the next level; at a certain point, it's all argument, which can be disconcerting for people in a society who are trained to memorize 1776 and the Magna Carta. I think history is 'the' subject, and I am endlessly frustrated when it's seen as pointless or irrelevant.

"Writing is lonely, hard work that does not usually pay particularly well, if at all, but I intend to keep at it to the end of my days. Not because I want to; I'd go mad if I didn't."

BIOGRAPHICAL AND CRITICAL SOURCES:

PERIODICALS

Chicago Tribune Books, August 19, 2001, Alan Cheuse, review of *Hope's End,* p. 2.
Kirkus Reviews, June 15, 2001, review of *Hope's End,* p. 837; July 1, 2002, review of *Hope's War,* p. 923.
Library Journal, August, 2001, Jackie Cassada, review of *Hope's End,* p. 171; August, 2002, Jackie Cassada, review of *Hope's War, p. 152.*
New York Times Book Review, October 13, 2002, Gerald Jonas, review of *Hope's War,* p. 29.
Publishers Weekly, July 16, 2001, review of *Hope's End,* p. 163; July 15, 2002, review of *Hope's War,* p. 60.

ONLINE

BookBrowser, http://www.bookbrowser.com/ (August 6, 2002), Harriet Klausner, review of *Hope's War.*
Fantastica Daily, http://www.mervius.com/ (October 15, 2002), Eva Wojcik-Obert, review of *Hope's End,* interview with Chambers.
Leo, http://www.louisville.net/ (September 12, 2001), Paul Kopasz, review of *Hope's End.*
Stephen Chambers Home Page, http://www.sff.net/people/schambers (December 20, 2002).

*   *   *

CHANNING, William Ellery, II 1817-1901

PERSONAL: Born November 29, 1817, in Boston, MA; died December 23, 1901; married Ellen Fuller, 1841; children: five. *Education:* Attended Harvard University.

CAREER: Poet; former employee of *New Bedford Mercury* and the *New York Tribune.*

WRITINGS:

Poems, Little, Brown (Boston, MA), 1843.
Poems: Second Series, Munroe (Boston, MA), 1847.
Conversations in Rome: Between an Artist, a Catholic, and a Critic, Crosby & Nichols (Boston, MA), 1847,
The Woodman, and Other Poems, Munroe (Boston, MA), 1849.
Near Home (poems), 1858.
The Wanderer, a Colloquial Poem, Osgood (Boston, MA), 1871.
Thoreau: The Poet-Naturalist (biography), Roberts (Boston, MA), 1873.
Eliot: A Poem, Cupples, Upham (Boston, MA), 1885.
John Brown, and the Heroes of Harper's Ferry, a Poem, Cupples, Upham (Boston, MA), 1886.
Poems of Sixty-Four Years, edited by F. B. Sanborn, J. H. Bentley (Philadelphia, PA), 1902.
The Collected Poems, edited by Walter Harding, Scholars' Facsimiles & Reprints (Gainesville, FL), 1967.

SIDELIGHTS: A poet of late nineteenth-century America, William Ellery Channing II—the nephew of noted clergyman Rev. William Ellery Channing—was born into a well-connected Boston family. It was expected that the young Ellery would follow in the footsteps of his uncle or his father, who was dean of the Harvard Medical School. But life held a different path for the young man, who put in a semester at Harvard before leaving the academic life behind.

Channing pursued the life of a farmer until 1840, when he took up newspaper work in Cincinnati, Ohio. There he met his future wife, Ellen Fuller; the newlyweds settled in Concord, Massachusetts, where Channing became friends with some of the most influential writers of the day: Ralph Waldo Emerson, Nathaniel Hawthorne, and Thoreau. Emerson printed some of Channing's early poetry in the *Dial,* a Transcendentalist publication. But writing poetry did not bring in much revenue for the family, to the consternation of Channing wife, who was the mother of five children. Still, Channing insisted on living what Joel Myerson called in a *Dictionary of Literary Biography* entry "his easy-going life" in letters.

While his poems did not bring him distinction—he "promised more than he delivered," wrote Myerson—Channing gained a reputation as an early biographer of Thoreau. While Channing's *Thoreau: The Poet-Naturalist* is "factually inaccurate," according to Myerson, still it is "the best extended study by a contemporary." Indeed, it was Channing's "genuine friendships" with Emerson and Thoreau that gave meaning to the life of the would-be poet, "and his conversations with these men also helped fill and affect their lives."

BIOGRAPHICAL AND CRITICAL SOURCES:

BOOKS

Dictionary of Literary Biography, Volume 1: *The American Renaissance in New England,* Gale (Detroit, MI), 1978.*

*   *   *

CHAPMAN, James B(laine) 1884-1947

PERSONAL: Born August 30, 1884, in Yale, IL; died February 30, 1947, in Indian Lake, MI; married Maud Frederick, c. 1903 (died 1940); married Louise Robinson, c. 1942. *Education:* Arkansas Holiness College, graduated, 1910; Texas Holiness University, A.B., 1912, B.D., 1913.

CAREER: Preacher in Oklahoma, beginning c. 1900; ordained minister of Independent Holiness Church, c. 1903; evangelistic preacher, 1903-05; pastor of Independent Holiness church in Durant, OK, beginning 1905; pastor of Holiness church in Vilonia, AR, 1908-10; Arkansas Holiness College, president, 1910-11; Texas Holiness University (also known as Peniel University), teacher, 1912-13, president, 1913-18; pastor of Holiness church in Bethany, OK, and evangelist preacher. Holiness Church of Christ, founding member, 1905, president of Texas-Oklahoma Council, 1907; Church of the Nazarene, founding member, 1908-46, general superintendent, 1928-46.

WRITINGS:

Some Estimates of Life, Nazarene Publishing House (Kansas City, MO), 1920.
A History of the Church of the Nazarene, Nazarene Publishing House (Kansas City, MO), 1926.

Christian Men in a Modern World, Nazarene Publishing House (Kansas City, MO), 1942.
Religion and Everyday Life, Beacon Hill Press (Kansas City, MO), 1945.
Chapman's Choice Outlines and Illustrations, Zondervan Publishing House (Grand Rapids, MI), 1947.
A Day in the Lord's Court, Beacon Hill Press (Kansas City, MO), 1948.
Let the Winds Blow, Beacon Hill Press (Kansas City, MO), 1957.

Herald of Holiness, associate editor, 1921-22, editor, beginning 1922; founder, *Preacher's,* 1926.

BIOGRAPHICAL AND CRITICAL SOURCES:

BOOKS

Wiseman, Neil B., editor, *Two Men of Destiny: Second-Generation Leaders in the Nazarene Movement,* Beacon Hill Press (Kansas City, MO), 1983.*

*   *   *

CHARLTON, Hilda 1910(?)-1988

PERSONAL: Born c. 1910, in London, England; immigrated to United States, c. 1914; died January 29, 1988, in New York, NY. *Education:* Studied Hinduism in India, c. 1947-50.

CAREER: Professional dancer, beginning c. 1928; dancer and dance teacher in San Francisco, CA, until c. 1945; dancer in India, beginning 1947; teacher of Eastern metaphysics, beginning 1965.

WRITINGS:

The New Sun, Golden Quest (Woodstock, NY), 1989.
Saints Alive, Golden Quest (Woodstock, NY), 1989.
Hell-bent for Heaven: The Autobiography of Hilda Charlton, Golden Quest (Woodstock, NY), 1990.
Pioneers of the Soul: The Last Teachings of Hilda Charlton, Golden Quest (Woodstock, NY), 1992.

Author of a column in *New Sun.*

BIOGRAPHICAL AND CRITICAL SOURCES:

BOOKS

Charlton, Hilda, *Hell-bent for Heaven: The Autobiography of Hilda Charlton,* Golden Quest (Woodstock, NY), 1990.*

*   *   *

CHINMAYANANDA, Swami 1916-1993

PERSONAL: Born Sri Balakrishna Menon, May, 1916, in India; name changed, 1943; died following a heart attack August 13, 1993, in San Diego, CA; father, a jurist. *Education:* University of Madras, graduated, 1939; University of Lucknow, graduate degree; studied yoga and Hinduism with masters.

CAREER: Worked as a journalist in New Delhi, India; began monastic life, 1943; teacher, beginning 1951; international lecturer, beginning 1965; Chinmaya Mission West, founder, 1975. Founder of Sandeepany Sadhanalaya, Bombay, India, Tapovan Kuti, in the Himalaya Mountains, and Sandeepany West, in northern California. Activist with Indian independence movement in the 1940s. Lecturer at U.S. universities.

WRITINGS:

Discourses on Mundakopanishad, [New Delhi, India], 1953.

Discourses on Isavasyopanishad at the Upanishad Gyana Yagna, edited by Sree Damodaran Nair, [Palghat, India], 1954.

(Editor and translator) *Discourses on Taittiriya Upanishad* (in English and Sanskrit), Chinmaya Publication Trust (Madras, India), 1962.

(Editor and translator) *Discourses on Kathopanishad* (in English and Sanskrit), Chinmaya Publication Trust (Madras, India), c. 1963.

(Editor and translator) *Discourses on Mandukya Upanishad with Gaudapada's Karika,* Chinmaya Publication Trust (Madras, India), c. 1966.

The Sreemad-Bhagawad-Geeta: The Art of Right Action, 3rd edition, four volumes, Central Chinmaya Mission Trust (Bombay, India), 1967, published as *Sreemad Bhagawad Geeta,* three volumes, Chinmaya Publications Trust (Madras, India), 1969-71.

Kindle Life (includes *The Art of Living*), Chinmaya Publications Trust (Madras, India), c. 1969.

Love-Divine (Narada Bhakti Sutra): The Highest Art of Making Love to the Lord of the Heart; Discourses, Chinmaya Publications Trust (Madras, India), 1970.

Talks on Sankara's Vivekachoodamani: Text with Translation and Commentary (in English and Sanskrit), two volumes, Central Chinmaya Mission Trust (Bombay, India), c. 1970.

Ashtavakra Geeta: With Word-Meaning and Elaborate Commentaries on Each Verse (in English and Sanskrit), Chinmaya Publications Trust (Madras, India), 1972, revised edition published as *Discourses on Ashtavakra Geeta: Original Upanisad Text in Devanagari with Transliteration in Roman Letters, Word-for-Word Meaning in Text Order with Translation and Commentary,* Central Chinmaya Mission Trust (Bombay, India), 1997.

Discourses on Aitareya Upanishad, Chinmaya Publications Trust (Madras, India), 1972.

Discourses in Prasnopanishad, Chinmaya Publications Trust (Madras, India), 1974.

The Art of Man-Making: Talks on the Bhagavad Geeta, Central Chinmaya Mission Trust (Calcutta, India), 1975.

The Holy Geeta, Central Chinmaya Mission Trust (Bombay, India), c. 1976.

Discourses on Isavasya Upanishad, revised edition, Chinmaya Publications Trust (Madras, India), 1977.

(Editor) *Discourses on Kaivalyopanishad,* Chinmaya Publications Trust (Madras, India), 1978.

Meditation and Life, Central Chinmaya Mission Trust (Bombay, India), 1980, Chinmaya Publications West (Piercy, CA), 1992.

My Trek through Uttarkhand, Indian Books Centre (Delhi, India), 1982.

A Manual for Self-Unfoldment, 6th edition, Central Chinmaya Mission Trust (Bombay, India), 1985, new edition published as *Self-Unfoldment,* Chinmaya Publications (Piercy, CA), 1992.

On Wings and Wheels: A Dialogue on Moral Conflict, Central Chinmaya Mission Trust (Bombay, India), 1991.

(With others) *Beyond Ego,* Chinmaya Publications (Piercy, CA), 1998.

(With others) *The Journey Called Life,* Chinmaya Publications (Piercy, CA), 2001.

Contributor to periodicals.*

CLIFFORD, Barry 1945-

PERSONAL: Born May 30, 1945 in Hyannis, MA; son of Robert and Shirley Clifford; children: Barry Jr., Jenny, Brandon. *Education:* Western State College, B.A., 1969.

ADDRESSES: Office—c/o Expedition Whydah, 16 Macmillan Wharf, Box 493, Provincetown, MA. *Agent*—Nat Sobel, Sobel-Weber Associates, 146 East Nineteenth St., New York, NY 10003.

CAREER: Underwater explorer, shipwreck surveyor, and founder of Expedition *Whydah* Sea Lab and Learning Center, Provincetown, MA. Worked variously as a lifeguard, gym teacher, and construction worker. *Exhibitions:* : *Whydah* artifacts exhibited at Pilgrim Monument and Provincetown Museum, Provincetown, MA, 1990-95, City Arts Center, Edinburgh, Scotland, 1995-96, Explorer's Hall of the National Geographic Society, 1999, Ubersee Museum Bremen, Germany, and Boston State House Museum, Boston, MA.

MEMBER: Explorer's Club.

WRITINGS:

(With Peter Turchi) *The Pirate Prince: Discovering the Priceless Treasure of the Sunken "Whydah,"* Simon and Schuster (New York, NY), 1993.
(With Paul Perry) *The Black Ship: The Quest to Recover an English Pirate Ship and Its Lost Treasure,* Headline (London, England), 1999.
(With Paul Perry) *Expedition Whydah: : The Story of the World's First Excavation of a Pirate Treasure Ship and the Man Who Found Her,* HarperCollins (New York, NY), 1999.
The Pirate Hunters: The Discovery of a Lost Fleet That Changed History, Cliff Street Books (New York, NY), 2001.
The Lost Fleet: The Discovery of a Sunken Armada from the Golden Age of Piracy, HarperCollins (New York, NY), 2002.
Return to Treasure Island, HarperCollins (New York, NY), 2003.

Author of monthly column for *Sport-Diver* magazine. Contributor to periodicals, including *Parade Magazine* and *Art and Antiques.*

SIDELIGHTS: Barry Clifford holds the distinction of having discovered and recovered the remains of the *Whydah,* the first authenticated pirate ship located in U.S. waters. In 1996 Clifford established the Expedition *Whydah* Sea Lab and Learning Center to educate the public and display the objects he retrieved from the ship, which was located in 1984. The author has, since then, been involved in numerous other ship discoveries, and investigations of archaeological sites. Some of his other projects have resulted in the retrieval of material connected to the Boston Tea Party from Boston Harbor. His organization has been involved in the successful identification and recovery of ships and airplanes in Lake Michigan, Lake Washington and the Solomon Islands. Historically significant ships have also been discovered from New York's East River by the author and his crew.

Clifford's efforts have not been confined exclusively to the United States. His search teams have assisted in explorations in Egypt's Valley of the Kings and have aided in the discovery of tombs of the sons of the pharaoh Ramses. In conjunction with researchers from Cornell University, one of Clifford's underwater survey teams in Greece found the classical-era city of Eliki. The Las Aves reef expedition, off the coast of Venezuela, shed light on European colonial aspirations in the Americas and contributed to the understanding of the early history of piracy and pirate culture. In 2000 Clifford and his underwater archaeological survey team discovered the remains of the *Adventure Galley,* flagship of the infamous pirate William Kidd, together with other pirate ship wrecks off the coast of Madagascar. Although Clifford's work has not been without some controversy, the Federal Advisory Council on Historic Preservation and other regulatory agencies have praised his efforts.

The Pirate Prince: Discovering the Priceless Treasure of the Sunken "Whydah" was Clifford's first book and was co-authored with Peter Turchi. The general location of the *Whydah* was common knowledge in the Cape Cod community, as were stories of the sunken treasure. The captain of the *Whydah,* Black Sam Bellamy, was said to have been en route to visit his mistress, Maria Hallett, when his ship was destroyed in a violent storm off the coast of Massachusetts on April 26, 1717. Of the 146 crew members, only two survived. The appeal of this story never lost its hold on Clifford, and in 1982, fortified with a permit granting exclusive search rights from the Commonwealth of Massachusetts, he began to organize the expedition that would result in the location and verification of this legendary ship. The wreck, found beneath twenty feet of water, yielded over 100,000 artifacts. Among the recovered items were such things as coins, a cannonball, and even a leg bone with shoe intact. The drama of the situation was amplified by an endless parade of obstacles, including bad weather and the machinations of rival searchers. The attention of the media to a colorful crew, which included John F. Kennedy, Jr., and the police chief of Aspen, Colorado, did nothing to detract from the glamour of the effort. Logistical issues covered in the book include the complexities of financing, legal questions relating to salvage rights and the technological challenges of an undersea search. A reviewer in *Booklist* praised the effectiveness of the combination of pirate lore with the realities of contemporary treasure-hunting. The text is supplemented with sixteen black-and-white photos.

Expedition Whydah: The Story of the World's First Excavation of a Pirate Treasure Ship and the Man Who Found Her was written by Clifford with Paul Perry. In this book the authors expand on some of the material presented in *The Pirate Prince*, notably Clifford's search for funding and the protracted legal wrangling between the salvage team and the Commonwealth of Massachusetts over the ownership of the *Whydah* materials. The author's involvement in these expeditions goes beyond the mapping and retrieval of the ship's contents, however. The book was praised by a *Kirkus* reviewer for the enrichment the biographical information on Black Sam Bellamy provided to the story. Clifford has become a recognized authority on pirate history and culture and it is this material that receives most of the critical acclaim in *Expedition Whydah*.

In 1997-98 Clifford and his underwater team began the exploration and mapping of the 1678 wreck of a French flotilla on the Las Aves reef, off the coast of Venezuela. A reviewer of *The Lost Fleet: The Discovery of a Sunken Armada from the Golden Age of Piracy* in *Booklist* notes that Clifford gives a good account of the political circumstances of the time and their historical impact. The French were attempting to establish a strong position in the New World. The French fleet, accompanied by a group of hired privateers and pirates, pursued a group of rival Dutch vessels in the same area. Not knowing the waters well, the French were lured into a trap by the Dutch, and crashed on the Las Aves reef. This disaster, with its huge loss of life and cargo, signaled the end of the possibility of a powerful French presence in the Americas. Clifford argues that the willingness of the British and French to hire privateers, or independent seamen with ships, to haul cargo led directly to the privateers' recognition of opportunities for enrichment through the plunder of rich trading vessels. In *The Lost Fleet,* the author devotes a substantial amount of the book to stories of the most notorious pirates' lives and the culture that grew from this activity. Critics have praised Clifford for writing knowledgeably about international politics that influenced the situation and also about the circumstances that gave rise to the establishment of the pirates as a substantial force on the seas. This historical treatment is combined with the tales of mapping and exploration.

BIOGRAPHICAL AND CRITICAL SOURCES:

PERIODICALS

Booklist, August, 1993, Alice Joyce, review of *The Pirate Prince: Discovering the Priceless Treasure of the Sunken "Whydah,"* p. 2034; May 15, 1999, Brendan Dowling, review of *Expedition Whydah: The Story of the World's First Excavation of a Pirate Treasure Ship and the Man Who Found Her,* p. 1663; July, 2002, Gavin Quinn, review of *The Lost Fleet: The Discovery of a Sunken Armada from the Golden Age of Piracy,* p. 1817.

Boston Magazine, May, 1986, Carol Farash, "A Tale of Two Explorers," p. 22; May, 1989, Seth Rolbein, "Glittering Prizes," p. 87.

Christian Science Monitor, November 5, 1998, David Mutch, "Pirate Ship Treasures Plucked from the Sea," p. 13.

Kirkus Reviews, May 15, 1993, review of *The Pirate Prince,* p. 636; May 15, 1999, review of *Expedition Whydah,* p. 769; May 15, 2002, review of *The Lost Fleet,* p. 714.

Library Journal, June 1, 1993, John Kenny, review of *The Pirate Prince,* p. 150; August, 2002, Robert C. Jones, review of *The Lost Fleet,* p.115.

National Geographic World, May, 1999, Donovan Webster, "Pirates of the Whydah"; April, 2000, Michael Burgan, "Lost and Found Treasures," p. 19.

New York Times, February 27, 1983, "Massachusetts Permits Diving for Pirate Ship," p. 24; July 27, 1984, "Wreck off Cape Cod May Contain Private

Treasure," p. B10; January 8, 1985, "Coins from Sea Might Solve a Pirate Mystery," p. 7; September 26, 1985, William G. Blair, "1780 Gold Ship Reported Found in East River," p. 12; November 1, 1985, Matthew L. Wald, "Bell Provides Identification of Pirate Ship for First Time," p. A1; May 7, 1986, Eric Pace, "Diver to Begin an East River Treasure Hunt," p. 17; October 26, 1986, "1717 Wreck of Galleon off Cape Yields Treasure and Hints at Pirates' Lives," p. 50; May 19, 1987, Matthew Wald, "Massachusetts' Claim to Pirate Ship Is Denied," p. A. 29; August 9, 1987, "About That Gold in the East River," p. 42; December 13, 1988, Susan Diesenhouse, "Court Awards Salvager Rights to Pirate Ship," p. A14; December 18, 1988, "Boston Harbor Is Mined for Historic Tea," p. 22; March 11, 1997, William J. Broad, "Archaeologists Revise Portrait of Buccaneers as Monsters," p. B7; July 26, 1998, William J. Broad, "Searchers Say They Have Found Elusive Hull of Pirate Ship," pp. 14, 18; February 22, 2000, William J. Broad, "Seeking Pirate Treasure: Captain Kidd's Sunken Ship," p. D1.

People Weekly, August 22, 1983, Michael Ryan, "Barry Clifford's Zany Crew—Including JFK, Jr.—Prove That Way down Deep, They're Gold Diggers," p. 26; May 22, 2000, Alec Foege, "Sunken Dream: Barry Clifford Has Found Captain Kidd's Long-Lost Pirate Ship—Maybe," p. 169.

Publishers Weekly, May 31, 1993, review of *The Pirate Prince,* p. 34; July 1, 2002, review of *The Lost Fleet,* p. 70.

Time, August 11, 1986, Jamie Murphy, "Down into the Deep: Using High Tech to Explore the Lost Treasures of the Seas," p. 48.

Wall Street Journal, August 13, 1999, Stuart Ferguson, review of *Expedition Whydah,* p. W6.

Yankee, March, 1984, James Dodson, "Not the Best of Times for Barry Clifford," p. 76.

ONLINE

Adventure Inc., http://www.adventureinc.net/ (November 22, 2002).

Fern Canyon Press Web site, http://ferncanyonpress. com/ (February 11, 2003).

Treasures of the Expedition Whydah, http://www. whydah.com/ (February 11, 2003).

Western State College Web site, http://www.western. edu/ (January 2, 2003).

COBURN, Louis 1915-2003

OBITUARY NOTICE—See index for *CA* sketch: Born August 13, 1915, in New York, NY; died January 31, 2003. Librarian, educator, and author. Coburn was a former library-science professor at Queens College of the City University of New York. He received his B.A. and M.S. in education from City College of the City University of New York in 1936 and 1941 respectively; he also earned a B.L.S. from Columbia University in 1938. In 1942 he joined the U.S. Army Air Forces as a cryptographic security officer, becoming a first lieutenant. After the war he continued to work as a high-school library teacher in the Bronx, where he had started his career back in 1938. Then, beginning in 1956, he taught in Jamaica, New York. Coburn joined the faculty at Queens College in 1963, where he was an assistant professor in library science from 1963 to 1973, and an associate professor from 1974 to 1979. He was the author of three books: *Case Studies in School Library Administration* (1968), *Library Media-Center Problems: Case Studies* (1973), and *Classroom and Field: The Internship in American Library Education* (1980).

OBITUARIES AND OTHER SOURCES:

PERIODICALS

American Libraries, May, 2003, p. 67.

* * *

COFFIN, Howard 1942-

PERSONAL: Born 1942, in Woodstock, VT. *Hobbies and other interests:* History, particularly U.S. Civil War history.

ADDRESSES: Home—Montpelier, VT. *Agent*—c/o Author Mail, Countryman Press, P.O. Box 748, Woodstock, VT 05091.

CAREER: Public relations consultant, writer, lecturer, and tour guide. Former press secretary to U.S. Senator James Jeffords; U.S. senate appointee, National Civil War Sites advisory committee; board member, Association for the Preservation of Civil War Sites. Rutland Herald, Rutland, VT, reporter; *Christian Science Monitor,* correspondent; University of Vermont, news director; public information position at Dartmouth College. *Military service:* Second Armored Division, Vietnam War.

WRITINGS:

UVM: A Special Place, photography by Sanders Milens, Donning (Virginia Beach, VA), 1990.

Full Duty: Vermonters in the Civil War, Countryman Press (Woodstock, VT), 1993.

Nine Months to Gettysburg: Stannard's Vermonters and the Repulse of Pickett's Charge, Countryman Press (Woodstock, VT), 1997.

The Battered Stars: One State's Civil War Ordeal during Grant's Overland Campaign, Countryman Press (Woodstock, VT), 2002.

(With James Jeffords and Yvonne Daley) *An Independent Man: Adventures of a Public Servant,* Simon & Schuster (New York, NY), 2003.

SIDELIGHTS: As a sixth-generation Vermonter with two great grandfathers having served with Vermont regiments during the U.S. Civil War, and having himself served in Vietnam, Howard Coffin's background gives him a solid intellectual and emotional foundation for his historic nonfiction works detailing Vermont's participation in the Civil War. As a committed Civil War historian, Coffin has been highly instrumental in protecting Civil War battlefields from development and was appointed by the U.S. Senate to the National Civil War Sites Advisory Committee. Coffin also lectures and gives tours of historic battlefield sites.

Coffin's interest in the Civil War stems from his childhood. Often, he heard the stories of one of his great grandfathers, Elba Jillson, a Vermont farmer and Union soldier who fought in the Battle at Fair Oaks near Petersburg. However, Coffin didn't see his first Civil War battlefield until 1966 when, as a National Guardsman attending summer camp at Fort A. P. Hill he talked a bunkmate into taking him to the battlefields. He recalled in an interview with Lawrence Beimiller in the *Chronicle of Higher Education:* "Outside Fredericksburg, in farm country, was this little Salem

Church, which still had bullet holes in it. I was hooked. I've been back to the battlefields every year since . . . but I've watched the progression—today Salem Church sits on an acre of ground surrounded by shopping malls. I finally decided I ought to try do to do something. I felt I owed it to the battlefields, and to those who fought there." Having been a political reporter for the Rutland *Herald,* Coffin had contacts. He called his local representative and, a month later, the Vermont General Assembly introduced—and ultimately passed—a resolution calling on Congress and the president to protect the historic sites.

Coffin's first book, *Full Duty: Vermonters in the Civil War,* is firmly based on research and emulates state-oriented Civil War volumes of a century ago. It provides background information on the Vermonters who became part of almost every major battle in the eastern states. While detailing vivid accounts of those battles, Coffin does not fail to include the experiences of those Vermonters who became prisoners of war, nor those at home who were raided by Confederate guerrillas stationed across the Canadian border.

Nine Months to Gettysburg: The Vermonters Who Broke Pickett's Charge is a stirring documentary of the Vermont Second Brigade, which held a key position at Gettysburg and, according to a 1863 *New York Times* article published soon after the Fourth-of-July battle, "did more than any other body of men to gain the triumph which decided the fate of the Union." These men were "citizen soldiers," young recruits from isolated Vermont farms who answered Lincoln's call in 1862 for 300,000 nine-month volunteers: 32,549 Vermonters answered the call, 5,224 of whom lost their lives as a result. Of the book, Tim Mudgett, writing for *New England Quarterly,* said: "Coffin has mined a wealth of soldiers' letters at the Vermont Historical Society and the University of Vermont. Since the book is based on quotations from soldiers' letters, the men get a chance to tell their story firsthand, and therefore the reader never loses sight of what war was like for the common soldier."

Again, in *The Battered Stars: One State's Civil War Ordeal during Grant's Overland Campaign,* Coffin uses first-hand information gleaned from diaries, letters, and family correspondence newly unearthed and never before published to tell the extraordinary story of the unique role played by Vermont troops during

General Grant's overland campaign. Of the book, John Carver Edwards wrote in *Library Journal*, "Coffin . . . weaves together stories of the participating military units, outlines the overall campaign, and gives voice to several hundred personalities on the battlefield and back home." Summarizing the book for Dartmouth Bookstore, a critic commented that it is a "new and unique contribution . . . the story of the home front, taking us behind the lines to dozens of small towns in Vermont to show how the great battles of the Civil War affected the lives of ordinary citizens."

BIOGRAPHICAL AND CRITICAL SOURCES:

PERIODICALS

Booklist, December 15, 1993, Roland Green, review of *Full Duty: Vermonters in the Civil War,* p. 735.

Chronicle of Higher Education, September 6, 1989, Lawrence Beimiller, "A Vermonter's Civil-War Campaign: Saving Imperiled Battlefields," p. A3.

Kirkus Reviews, November 1, 2002, review of *An Independent Man: Adventures of a Public Servant,* p. 1590.

Library Journal, October 1, 1997, Stephen G. Weisner, review of *Nine Months to Gettysburg: The Vermonters Who Broke Pickett's Charge,* p. 98; April, 2002, John Carver Edwards, review of *The Battered Stars: One State's Civil War Ordeal during Grant's Overland Campaign,* p. 123.

New England Quarterly, September, 1998, Tim Mudgett, review of *Nine Months to Gettysburg,* pp. 509-512.

Publishers Weekly, January 13, 2003, review of *An Independent Man: Adventures of a Public Servant,* p. 48.

ONLINE

Dartmouth Bookstore Web site, http://www.dartbook. com/ (May 31, 2002), brief author biography and review of *The Battered Stars.**

*   *   *

COLDIRON, A. E. B. 1959-

PERSONAL: Born 1959, in Greensboro, NC. *Education:* University of Virginia, Ph.D., 1996.

ADDRESSES: Office—Department of English, Louisiana State University, Baton Rouge, LA 70803. *E-mail*—acoldiron@lsu.edu.

CAREER: Louisiana State University, Baton Rouge, professor of English and comparative literature, 1998—.

MEMBER: Modern Language Association of America, Renaissance Society of America, Southeast Renaissance Conference.

AWARDS, HONORS: Fellow, National Endowment for the Humanities, 1998-99; Folger fellow, 1999; regents' research grants, 2000-01.

WRITINGS:

Canon, Period, and the Poetry of Charles of Orleans, University of Michigan Press (Ann Arbor, MI), 2000.

Contributor to books, including *Charles d'Orleans in England,* Boydell & Brewer, 2000. Contributor to periodicals, including *Comparative Literature, JEGP,* and *Translation and Literature.*

WORK IN PROGRESS: Between Caxton and Tottel: Verse Translation from French, 1476-1557, publication by University of Michigan Press (Ann Arbor, MI) expected in 2005.

*   *   *

COLE, Bernard D. 1943-

PERSONAL: Born October 13, 1943, in Neptune, NJ; son of Harry and Mildred (Ohlberg) Cole; married Carla Conn, January 4, 1969; children: Jennifer Anne, Marissa Elizabeth. *Education:* University of North Carolina, A.B., 1965; University of Washington, Seattle, M.P.A., 1972; Auburn University, Ph.D., 1978.

ADDRESSES: Office—National War College, Fort Lesley J. McNair, Washington, DC 20319-5078. *E-mail*—coleb@ndu.edu.

CAREER: U.S. Navy, career officer, including service in Vietnam, 1965-95, retiring as captain; National War College, Washington, DC, professor, 1995—.

MEMBER: International Institute for Strategic Studies, Organization of American Historians, Historians Society.

AWARDS, HONORS: Military: Three Legions of Merit, three Meritorious Service medals, three Presidential Unit citations, Meritorious Unit Commendation, Combat Action Medal, Overseas Deployment Medal, Vietnamese Presidential Unit Commendation. *Other:* John Lyman Book Award, North American Society for Oceanic History, 1982, for *Gunboats and Marines: The United States Navy in China, 1925-1928.*

WRITINGS:

Gunboats and Marines: The United States Navy in China, 1925-1928, University of Delaware Press (Newark, DE), 1983.
The Great Wall at Sea: China's Navy Enters the Twenty-first Century, Naval Institute Press (Annapolis, MD), 2001.

Contributor of articles and reviews to periodicals, including *Naval War College Review* and *Journal of Military History.*

WORK IN PROGRESS: Research on Chinese national-security affairs.

BIOGRAPHICAL AND CRITICAL SOURCES:

PERIODICALS

Choice, May, 2002, H. Nelsen, review of *The Great Wall at Sea: China's Navy Enters the Twenty-first Century,* p. 1658.
Journal of American History, December, 1983, William R. Braisted, review of *Gunboats and Marines: The United States Navy in China, 1925-1928,* p. 709.
Journal of Military History, April, 2002, Edward J. Marolda, review of *The Great Wall at Sea,* p. 643.

*   *   *

COLE, Jean Murray 1927-

PERSONAL: Born November 7, 1927, in Brantford, Ontario, Canada; daughter of Alexander A. (a journalist) and Gwendoline (a journalist; maiden name, Rivers) Murray; married Alfred O. C. Cole, June 15,

1950 (died October 21, 1996); children: Sally Cole Huberman, Leslie Cole Crump, Ian M. C., Alan D. C., Catherine Cole Wood, Emily. *Ethnicity:* "Mixed—fur trade ancestry." *Education:* Attended University of Toronto and University of Western Ontario. *Religion:* Anglican. *Hobbies and other interests:* Museology.

ADDRESSES: Home and office—2473 Cameron Line, R.R. 3, Indian River, Ontario, Canada K0L 2B0. *E-mail*—hutchisonhouse@nexicom.com.

CAREER: Journalist. *Brantford Expositor,* Brantford, Ontario, Canada, reporter, 1945-46; *London Free Press,* London, Ontario, feature writer, 1947-49; Maclean Hunter Publishing Co., feature writer and assistant editor of *Canadian Homes and Gardens,* 1949-51; freelance writer and editor, 1951—. Parks Canada, member of Trent-Severn Waterway advisory committee; member of Christ Church Community Museum board; executive of Friends of the Bata Library. Hutchison House Museum, past chair of management board; past chair of Peterborough County Public Library Board and Lake Ontario Regional Library Board; past board member of Canadian Canoe Museum, TV Ontario Council, and Lang Pioneer Village.

MEMBER: Ontario Historical Society (first vice president), Peterborough Historical Society (member of board of directors; past chair).

AWARDS, HONORS: Canada Council awards, 1969, 1970; Heritage Canada Communications Award, Local Histories Award from Canadian Historical Association, and Local Histories Award from Ontario Historical Society (with others), all 1976, all for *Illustrated Historical Atlas of Peterborough County, 1825-1875;* Civic Award of Merit, City of Peterborough, Ontario, Canada, 1980; award from Social Sciences and Humanities Research Council of Canada, 1982; volunteer service awards, Ontario Ministry of Citizenship and Culture, 1985, 1988, 1996, 2001; Millennium Award for Leadership in the Arts Community, County of Peterborough, 2000.

WRITINGS:

(Editor, with Alfred O. C. Cole and J. W. Deyman) *Illustrated Historical Atlas of Peterborough County, 1825-1875,* [Peterborough, Ontario, Canada], 1975.

Exile in the Wilderness: The Biography of HBC Chief Factor Archibald McDonald, 1790-1853, University of Washington Press (Seattle, WA), 1979.

(Editor, with Alfred O. C. Cole) *Kawartha Heritage; Proceedings of the Kawartha Conference, 1981,* Peterborough Historical Atlas Foundation (Peterborough, Ontario, Canada), 1981.

(Editor) Catharine Parr, *The Old Doctor,* Hutchinson House Museum (Peterborough, Ontario, Canada), 1985.

(Editor) *The Peterborough Hydraulic Lift Lock,* [Peterborough, Ontario, Canada], 1987.

The Loon Calls: A History of the Township of Chandos, 1989.

Origins: The History of Dummer Township, 1993.

South Monaghan: The Garden of Eden, 1998.

(Editor) *This Blessed Wilderness: Archibald McDonald's Letters from the Columbia, 1822-44,* University of British Columbia Press (Vancouver, British Columbia, Canada), 2001.

Author of booklets on local history topics. Contributor to books, including *Nastawgan: The Canadian North by Canoe and Snowshoe,* [Toronto, Ontario, Canada], 1985. Contributor to magazines and newspapers, including *Canadian Historical Review, Canadian Collector, Canadian Forum, British Columbia Historical News, Idaho Yesterdays,* and *Journal of Canadian Studies.*

WORK IN PROGRESS: Editing the diaries of a World War I nursing sister in Egypt and the diaries of Sandford Fleming; research for museum exhibits.

BIOGRAPHICAL AND CRITICAL SOURCES:

PERIODICALS

Oregon Historical Quarterly, winter, 2001, W. A. Sloan, review of *This Blessed Wilderness: Archibald McDonald's Letters from the Columbia, 1822-44,* p. 534.

*   *   *

CONDELL, Bruce 1941-

PERSONAL: Born April 5, 1941, in London, England; son of Stanley Morrow (a certified public accountant) and Margaret (MacGregor) Condell; married Nicole Roth, June 8, 1968. *Ethnicity:* "European." *Education:*

Queen's College, B.S., 1963. *Politics:* Conservative. *Religion:* Church of Scotland. *Hobbies and other interests:* Computers, photography, cuisine, wines, collecting books, baroque music.

ADDRESSES: Home—P.O. Box 9, F-04280 Cereste, France; fax: 0033-490-751-412. *E-mail*—bruce. condell@wanadoo.fr.

CAREER: British Broadcasting Corp., London, England, assistant editor, 1963-64; Vickers Industries Group, London, marketing executive, 1965-70; H. Clarkson Group, London, director of sales and purchases for Air Division, 1970-73; First Chicago Leasing, London, large engine leasing manager, 1973-74; Cessna Aircraft Co., Frankfurt, Germany, sales manager for Western Europe, 1974-76; Pilatus-Örlikon Group, Zurich, Switzerland, vice director for Asia, 1976-84; independent marketing consultant, 1984—. Clients include Finnish State Industrial Group, Alava S.A. Switzerland, and Farsound Group.

MEMBER: Masons, East Sussex Foxhounds, Lansdowne Club, Singapore Club, Royal Malaysia Polo Club, Bangkok Club.

WRITINGS:

(Editor and translator, with David T. Zabecki) *On the German Art of War: Truppenfürung,* Lynne Rienner Publishers (Boulder, CO), 2001.

WORK IN PROGRESS: Research on "army operations doctrine."

*   *   *

CONIL, Jean 1917-2003

OBITUARY NOTICE—See index for *CA* sketch: Born August 28, 1917, in Fontenay-le-Comte, France; died April 18, 2003, in England. Chef and author. Conil was a renowned chef whose life mission was to improve the cuisine of his adopted country, England. Descending from a long line of chefs who had cooked for such historical figures as Louis XVI and Napoleon III, Conil was educated at Stanislas College in Paris and trained under famed chef Auguste Escoffier. He found his way to London after fleeing the Germans in 1940. Joining the British Royal Navy, he served as a chef and cooked for an admiral. After the war, Conil found work at the Savoy Hotel in London. In 1950 he became senior chef and senior manager at the catering company Fortnum & Mason. His disgust for English cooking inspired his crusade to teach the British how to cook. Toward this end, he wrote 110 cookbooks, founded the International Academy of Chefs de Cuisine in 1949, was the founder and president of the Society of Master Chefs in 1982, was principal of the Academy of Gastronomy, and was one of the first chefs to host his own televised cooking show with *Café Continental,* which aired in the early 1960s. Conil was also catering director for the Atheneum Court Hotel in London from 1955 to 1958, senior catering manager for the Hurlingham Club in London from 1962 to 1964, and food and cookery lecturer at Hendo College of Hotel Administration during the late 1960s. His last position was with the London Arts Club, where he was executive chef until his retirement. During his lifetime, Conil never shied away from controversy and was famous for his frankness. He claimed that the British are extraordinarily wasteful with their food, accused almost all kitchen chefs in England of being alcoholics, and roundly criticized the food offered by Britain's major supermarket chains. Some of Conil's many books include *Haute Cuisine* (1953), *The Epicurean Book* (1961), *Passion for Food* (1991), and *Jean Conil's Food Encyclopedia* (1996). In addition to his cookbook writing, Conil was cookery correspondent for the London *Sunday Times,* contributed regularly to the *Daily Telegraph,* and was editor of *Look and Cook* magazine.

OBITUARIES AND OTHER SOURCES:

PERIODICALS

Los Angeles Times, May 4, 2003, p. B17.
New York Times, May 4, 2003, p. A34.
Times (London), May 22, 2003.

COOPER, Stephen 1949-

PERSONAL: Born October 11, 1949, in Los Angeles, CA; married Janet Stawisky, 1982; children: Daniel, Elizabeth. *Education:* University of California—Los Angeles, B.A., 1971; University of California—Irvine, M.F.A., 1984; University of Southern California, Ph.D., 1991.

ADDRESSES: Home—Los Angeles, CA. *Office*—California State University—Long Beach, 1250 Bellflower Blvd., Long Beach, CA 90840. *E-mail*—spcooper@csulb.edu.

CAREER: California State University, Long Beach, professor of English, 1984—.

AWARDS, HONORS: National Endowment for the Arts creative writing fellowship, 1991; Distinguished Faculty Scholarly and Creative Achievement Award, California State University, Long Beach, 2003.

WRITINGS:

(Editor) *Perspectives on John Huston,* G. K. Hall (New York, NY), 1994.
(Coeditor, with David Fine) *John Fante: A Critical Gathering,* Fairleigh Dickinson University Press (Madison, NJ), 1999.
Full of Life: A Biography of John Fante, North Point Press (New York, NY), 2000.
(Editor) John Fante, *The Big Hunger: Stories, 1932-1959,* Black Sparrow Press (Santa Rosa, CA), 2000.
(Editor) *The John Fante Reader,* William Morrow (New York, NY), 2002.

Contributor of short stories, articles, and essays to periodicals, including *Threepenny Review, Southwest Review, American Fiction, Hot Type, PEN Syndicated Fiction Project, Critic, Film Quarterly, Keats-Shelley Journal, Literature and Psychology, Flannery O' Connor Bulletin, Los Angeles in Fiction,* and *Los Angeles Times.*

Author's work has been translated into French and Italian.

WORK IN PROGRESS: Los Angelesque (stories); a novel.

SIDELIGHTS: Stephen Cooper is a professor of English at California State University, Long Beach. In 1991 he won a National Endowment of the Arts creative writing fellowship for his short stories. He has also published articles on literature, film, and culture, along with several books.

Cooper edited *Perspectives on John Huston,* in which he provides an analysis of the work of film director John Huston. Included are fifteen essays by authors espousing different viewpoints on Huston. Cooper also provides his own essay on Huston's film *The Maltese Falcon.* A *Films in Review* contributor called the book a "marvelous compilation."

Cooper's *Full of Life: A Biography of John Fante* is the first biography written about legendary novelist and screenwriter John Fante. Cooper first became interested in Fante shortly after graduating from the University of California, Los Angeles, but did not write the biography until twenty-five years later. Fante is known more for his novels than his screenplays. One of his greatest novels *Ask the Dust,* published in 1939, traces the tragicomic experiences of struggling young writer Arturo Bandini in Depression-era Los Angeles. Fante himself was an Italian American who came to Los Angeles from Colorado when he was twenty. He worked at odd jobs and wrote in the evenings. Soon after beginning to publish his stories he got a job as a contract screenwriter for Warner Bros. For the next few years his writing life was divided between serious fiction and hack work for various Hollywood studios. Cooper portrays not only Fante's career and lasting achievements, but also his dark side: gambling, womanizing, drinking, and violence. A *Publishers Weekly* contributor noted, "Cooper seamlessly pieces together every detail of Fante's life. . . . [and] makes a convincing case for Fante's placement on the mantel of the greats." Both the biography and and Cooper's edition of the *John Fante Reader* were named by the *Los Angeles Times* among the best books of the year.

Cooper told *CA:* "When I was in my early twenties I stumbled upon John Fante's masterpiece, *Ask the Dust.* The novel had been out of print for over thirty years, but I was so stunned by its beauties that I looked up Fante in *Contemporary Authors* and then I wrote him a unabashed fan letter. Incredibly, he wrote back: 'Writing is a great joy but the profession of writing is horrible. I wish you all the good luck in the world.' As I note at the end of my life of Fante, I have felt his wish with me all these years."

BIOGRAPHICAL AND CRITICAL SOURCES:

PERIODICALS

Films in Review, November, 1994, review of "Perspectives on John Huston," p. 70.
Historical Journal of Film, Radio, and Television, August, 1995, Nevena Dakovic, review of *Perspectives on John Huston,* p. 446.
Library Journal, April 1, 2000, Morris Hounion, review of *Full of Life: A Biography of John Fante,* p. 101.
Publishers Weekly, March 20, 2000, review of *Full of Life,* p. 78.

ONLINE

Canongate Books Web site, http://www.canongate.net/ (December 19, 2001).

*   *   *

CORNISH, Louis Craig 1870-1950

PERSONAL: Born April 18, 1870, in New Bedford, MA; died January 6, 1950, in Orlando, FL; son of Aaron and Frances W. (Hawkins) Cornish. *Education:* Harvard University, B.A., 1893, M.A., 1899.

CAREER: Secretary to an Episcopal bishop in Massachusetts, 1894-98; ordained Unitarian minister, c. 1899; pastor of Unitarian church in Hingham, MA, 1900-15; American Unitarian Association, staff secretary-at-large, 1915-27, president, 1927-37; international traveler to develop Unitarian networks worldwide, beginning 1937.

WRITINGS:

Transylvania in 1922, Beacon Press (Boston, MA), 1923.

The Religious Minorities in Transylvania, Beacon Press (Boston, MA), 1925.

Work and Dreams and the Wide Horizon, Beacon Press (Boston, MA), 1937.

The Philippines Calling, Dorrance and Co. (Philadelphia, PA), 1942.

Transylvania: The Land beyond the Forest, Dorrance and Co. (Philadelphia, PA), 1947.

Also author of "The Settlement of Hingham, Massachusetts," Rockwell & Churchill Press (Boston, MA), 1911.

BIOGRAPHICAL AND CRITICAL SOURCES:

BOOKS

Religious Leaders of America, 2nd edition, Gale (Detroit, MI), 1999.*

*   *   *

COTTAM, Francis 1957-

PERSONAL: Born 1957, in Liverpool, England.

ADDRESSES: Agent—Charles Walker, PFD, Drury House, 34-43 Russell Street, London WC2B 5HA, England.

CAREER: Journalist.

AWARDS, HONORS: W. H. Smith, Literature Award for *The Fire Fighter,* 2002.

WRITINGS:

The Fire Fighter, Chatto and Windus (London, England), 2001, St. Martin's Press (New York, NY), 2002.

SIDELIGHTS: Journalist Francis Cottam's first book, *The Fire Fighter,* recreates the terror of London in 1940 during World War II. The book is set in the middle of nightly air-raids and mayhem.

Amid London's depressing reality, the hero of the book is Jack Finlay, an artilleryman called home from Africa to work for British intelligence. His new job is to protect possible targets from the Germans. Because of his history as a fireman, his shady past is overlooked in favor of safeguarding five buildings in London. As he struggles to protect the buildings, however, he finds his murky, Liverpool history under scrutiny, after all. Meanwhile, a love story develops. The German godchild of his wartime military boss, Rebecca Lange, is a mysterious beauty who, David Horspool noted in his *Times Literary Supplement* review, Finlay predictably falls for. The love plot thickens to include an Irishman from Rebecca's past, with whom Finlay must fight for her affections.

Horspool appreciated Cottam's depiction of World War II London, and pointed out that even after the Allies' victory, the characters keep their somber outlook. But he also noted that the central characters detract from the more exciting background of the story. By focusing on Finlay, a thin, empty character, and, even worse, on the shallowly "mysterious" Rebecca, "Cottam robs the novel of much of its impact," Horspool commented. A *Publishers Weekly* reviewer also felt that Cottam spends too much time on his protagonists' personal lives, but suggested that, given Cottam's atmosphere creation and action scenes, readers can look forward to Cottam's future work.

BIOGRAPHICAL AND CRITICAL SOURCES:

PERIODICALS

Kirkus Reviews, May 15, 2002, review of *The Fire Fighter,* p. 680.

Library Journal, June 1, 2002, review of *The Fire Fighter,* p. 194.

Publishers Weekly, July 22, 2002, review of *The Fire Fighter,* p. 159.

Times Literary Supplement, April 13, 2001, David Horspool, review of *The Fire Fighter,* p. 23.*

CRAIG, Emma
    See DUNCAN, Alice

*   *   *

CROXTON, (Charles) Derek 1969-

PERSONAL: Born January 2, 1969, in Fairfax, VA; son of Robert Donald and Brenda (Weakley) Croxton; married June 15, 1991; wife's name Tanya Alison; children: Alexander. *Ethnicity:* "Caucasian." *Education:* University of Virginia, B.A., 1990, M.A., 1991; University of Illinois, Ph.D., 1996.

ADDRESSES: Home—26744 Golfview St., Dearborn Heights, MI 48127. *E-mail*—croxton3@hotpop.com.

CAREER: Instructor in history at Columbus State College, 1998, Modonna University, and 1999, Ohio State University, 1999. Yale University, New Haven, CT, visiting assistant in research in Department of History, 1994-95; presenter at conferences.

AWARDS, HONORS: MacArthur Foundation fellowship and history department fellowship, University of Illinois/ Program for Arms Control, Disarmament, and International Security, 1991-92; Smith-Richardson fellowship, Yale University, 1995-96; Mershon Center postdoctoral fellow, Ohio State University, 1997-99.

WRITINGS:

Peacemaking in Early Modern Europe: Cardinal Mazarin and the Congress of Westphalia, 1643-1648, Susquehanna University Press (Selinsgrove, NJ), 1999.
(With Anuschka Tischer) *The Peace of Westphalia: A Historical Dictionary,* Greenwood Press (Westport, CT), 2002.

Contributor of articles and reviews to periodicals, including *Journal of Military History, International History Review, Essays in History,* and *Sixteenth Century Journal.*

BIOGRAPHICAL AND CRITICAL SOURCES:

PERIODICALS

English Journal, June, 2003, David Parrott, review of *The Peace of Westphalia: A Historical Dictionary,* pp. 792-793.

D

DANIELE, Graciela 1939-

PERSONAL: Born December 8, 1939, in Buenos Aires, Argentina; immigrated to United States, 1963; daughter of Raul and Rosa (Almoina) Daniele; married Jules Fisher (a lighting designer). *Education:* Teatro Colon, Buenos Aires, Argentina, degree in art.

ADDRESSES: Agent—Howard Rosenstone, Rosenstone/Wender, 3 East 48th St., 4th floor, New York, NY, 10017.

CAREER: Dancer, director, and choreographer. Choreographer of stage productions, including *Yerma,* Greenwich Mews Theatre, New York, NY, 1971; (assistant to choreographer) *So Long, 174th Street,* Harkness Theatre, New York, NY, 1976; *Joseph and the Amazing Technicolor Dreamcoat,* Brooklyn Academy of Music Opera House, Brooklyn, NY, 1976-77; *A Lady Needs a Change,* Manhattan Theatre Club, New York, NY, 1978; *Twelfth Night; or, What You Will,* American Shakespeare Theatre, Stratford, CT, 1978; *The Most Happy Fella,* Majestic Theatre, New York, NY, 1979; *Girls, Girls, Girls,* New York Shakespeare Festival (NYSF), 1980; *Alice in Concert,* NYSF, 1980-81; *The Pirates of Penzance,* NYSF, 1980, Uris Theatre, New York, NY, 1981; *A Midsummer Night's Dream,* NYSF, 1982; *Zorba,* U.S. cities, 1983; *The Rink,* Martin Beck Theatre, New York, NY, 1984; *America's Sweetheart,* Hartford Stage Company, Hartford, CT, 1984-85; *The Mystery of Edwin Drood,* NYSF, 1985; *The Knife,* NYSF, 1987; (and director) *Tango Apasionado,* Westbeth Theatre Center, New York, NY, 1987; (and director) *Dangerous Games,*

Nederlander Theatre, New York, NY, 1989; (and director) *In a Pig's Valise,* Second Stage, New York, NY, 1989; (and director) *Once on This Island,* Playwrights Horizons, New York, NY, 1990; *Snowball,* Hartford, CT, 1991; *The Goodbye Girl,* Marquis Theatre, New York, NY, 1993; (and director) *Chronicle of a Death Foretold,* Plymouth Theatre, New York, NY, 1995; *Ragtime,* Ford Center for the Performing Arts, New York, NY, 1998-2000; (and director) *A New Brain,* Mitzi E. Newhouse Theatre, New York, NY, 1998; (and director) *Annie Get Your Gun,* Marquis Theatre, New York, NY, 1999-2001; (and director) *Marie Christine,* Vivian Beaumont Theatre, New York, NY, 1999-2000; and (and director) *My Favorite Broadway: The Love Songs,* City Center Theatre, New York, NY, 2000. Also choreographed *Naughty Marietta,* for New York Opera; *Die Fledermaus,* for Boston Opera Company, Boston, MA; and a Miliken industrial show. Worked on ballets for Ballet Hispanico of New York, 1989-91. Other theatre work includes musical staging, *A History of the American Film,* ANTA Theatre, New York, NY, 1978; production supervisor, *Rendezvous with Romance,* Joyce Theatre, New York, NY, 1989; and movement consultant, *Elaine Stritch at Liberty,* Neil Simon Theatre, New York, NY, 2002.

Director of stage productions, including *Falsetto Land,* Hartford Stage, 1991; and *Marcet of the Falsettos,* Hartford Stage, 1991. Appeared in stage productions, including *What Makes Sammy Run?* Broadway, 1964; (as Faith) *Here's Where I Belong,* Billy Rose Theatre, New York, NY, 1968; (as Clancy's employee) *Promises, Promises,* Shubert Theatre, New York, NY, 1968-69; (as Claire) *Coco,* Mark Hellinger Theatre, New York, NY, 1969-70; (as dancer) *Oklahoma!* New York State Theatre, New York, NY, 1969; (as Mariposa) *El*

Maleficio de la Mariposa, Puerto Rican Traveling Theatre, New York, NY, 1970; (as young Vanessa) *Follies,* Winter Garden Theatre, New York, NY, 1971; and (as Hunyak) *Chicago,* Forty-sixth Street Theatre, New York, NY, 1975. Also danced with Opera Ballet of Nice, before 1964.

Choreographer of films, including *The Pirates of Penzance,* Universal, 1983; *Haunted Honeymoon,* Orion, 1986; *Driving Me Crazy,* First Run Features, 1988; *Bullets over Broadway,* Miramax, 1994; *Mighty Aphrodite,* Miramax/Buena Vista, 1995; and *Everyone Says I Love You,* Miramax, 1996. Also provided additional choreography for *Naked Tango,* New Line Cinema, 1990. Choreographer of television programs "The Most Happy Fella," *Great Performances* (special), Public Broadcasting System (PBS), 1980; and *Mirrors* (movie), National Broadcasting Company (NBC), 1985. Appeared in television program "On the Move: The Central Ballet of China," *Great Performances* (special), PBS, 1988.

AWARDS, HONORS: Raul Julia Founders Award, Hispanic Organization of Latin Actors, 2002.

WRITINGS:

PLAYS

(With Jim Lewis) *Tango Apasionado,* based on stories by Jorge Luis Borges, produced at West Beth Theater, New York, NY, 1987.
(With Jim Lewis) *Dangerous Games,* produced at the Nederlander Theatre, New York, NY, 1989.
(With Jim Lewis) *Chronicle of a Death Foretold,* adapted from Gabriel García Márquez's novella of the same name, first produced at Plymouth Theatre, New York, NY, 1995.

Also provided Spanish lyrics for musical *Working,* performed on Broadway, 1978.

SIDELIGHTS: Argentinian dancer Graciela Daniele has made a name for herself as a Broadway choreographer since coming to New York in 1964. Although most of her work has involved choreographing shows written by other people, Daniele drew on the stories of two South American writers, Jorge Luis Borges and

Gabriel García Márquez, to create her own musical dance productions in the shows *Tango Apasionato* and *Chronicle of a Death Foretold.* The latter production, an adaptation of Márquez's novel of the same name, tells the story of a man who is about to be murdered. Everyone in his small town knows that he is about to be murdered, but because he is suspected of seducing a virgin, no one does anything to stop it. However, it is not at all clear that this man, named Santiago, actually is the one who deflowered the girl. Although Márquez's book largely explores the story from the side of the men involved, Daniele expands on Márquez's story to explore the thoughts and feelings of the town's women as well.

Chronicle of a Death Foretold and Daniele's other original works were not commercial successes, which Daniele finds frustrating. Noting that many of the current Broadway hits are revivals of older shows, she told Randy Gener of *American Theatre:* "It's important to see great shows of the past, like going to the Metropolitan Museum of Art to see classic paintings. But where would we be if we didn't have galleries for the modern painter? . . . Why do we want the safety of not being engaged intellectually and emotionally but just superficially entertained? Why can't dance be a part of that, rather than a form of entertainment only?"

BIOGRAPHICAL AND CRITICAL SOURCES:

BOOKS

Ganzl, Kurt, *Encyclopaedia of Musical Theatre,* second edition, Schirmer Books (New York, NY), 2001.
Notable Hispanic American Women, Book 1, Gale (Detroit, MI), 1992.

PERIODICALS

American Theatre, April, 1996, Randy Gener, review of *Chronicle of a Death Foretold,* pp. 12-17; May, 2002, "Awards & Prized," p. 9; April, 2003, Randy Gener, "Body Heat: Five American Director-Choreographers Break down the Steps That Lead to Sex, Love, Intimacy, and Erotic Tensions," pp. 32-36.

Back Stage, January 1, 1993, Phyllis Goldman, review of *Ballet Hispanico,* p. 24; February 4, 1994, Jerry Tallmer, review of *Hello Again,* pp. 1-2; February 11, 1994, Larry S. Ledford, review of *Hello Again,* p. 44; June 16, 1995, Ira J. Bilowit, review of *Chronicle of a Death Foretold,* pp. 32-33; March 15, 1996, David Sheward, review of *Dancing on Her Knees,* p. 60; November 2, 1990, David Sheward, review of *Once on This Island,* p. 45; January 25, 1991, Phyllis Goldman, review of *Ballet Hispanico,* p. 24; March 19, 1999, David A. Rosenberg, review of *Annie Get Your Gun,* p. 44; January 18, 2002, "HOLA Honors Riviera, Lopez, Daniele, and Sanchez," p. 48.

Dance Magazine, September, 1999, Rose Eichenbaum, "Faces in Dance: Graciela Daniele," p. 64.

Entertainment Weekly, March 12, 1999, Jess Cagle, review of *Annie Get Your Gun,* p. 58.

Nation, November 20, 1989, Thomas M. Disch, review of *Dangerous Games,* pp. 611-612; June 11, 1990, Thomas M. Disch, review of *Once on This Island,* p. 834.

National Review, December 31, 1990, Eva Resnikova, review of *Once on This Island,* p. 49.

New Leader, July 17, 1995; December 13, 1999, Stefan Kanfer, review of *Marie Christine,* p. 38.

New Republic, November 11, 1996, Stanley Kauffmann, review of *Everyone Says I Love You,* pp. 40-41.

New York, November 23, 1987, John Simon, review of *Tango Apasionado,* pp. 115-116; July 10, 1995, John Simon, review of *Chronicle of a Death Foretold,* p. 52.

New Yorker, December 21, 1987, Arlene Croce, review of *Tango Apasionado,* pp. 103-104.

New York Times, Moira Hodgson, "She Put *Pirates* on Its Toes," p. D6; November 1, 1987, Leslie Bennetts, review of *Tango Apasionado,* p. H5; November 10, 1987, Mel Gussow, review of *Tango Apasionado,* p. C15; October 15, 1989, Marilyn Stasio, review of *Dangerous Games,* p. H5; October 20, 1989, Frank Rich, review of *Dangerous Games,* p. B3; June 11, 1995, William Harris, review of *Chronicle of a Death Foretold,* p. H4; June 16, 1995, Vincent Canby, review of *Chronicle of a Death Foretold,* p. B1.

Nuestro, August-September, 1981, Maria Pallais, "Graciela Daniele: The Very Model of a Modern Made Choreographer," pp. 63-64.

Time, June 12, 1989, William A. Henry III, "Once Outposts, Now Landmarks," p. 72; October 21, 1991, William A. Henry III, review of *The Snow Ball,* p. 94; June 10, 1995, Brad Leithauser, review of *Chronicle of a Death Foretold,* p. 61; March 15, 1999, Richard Zoglin, review of *Annie Get Your Gun,* p. 86; December 13, 1999, Richard Zoglin, review of *Marie Christine,* p. 102.

Variety, June 19, 1995, Jeremy Gerard, review of *Chronicle of a Death Foretold,* p. 86; June 22, 1998, Charles Isherwood, review of *A New Brain,* p. 63; January 18, 1999, Chris Jones, review of *Annie Get Your Gun,* p. 140; October 23, 2000, Robert L. Daniels, review of *My Favorite Broadway: The Love Songs,* p. 62; March 31, 2003, Charles Isherwood, review of *Elegies,* pp. 39-40.

ONLINE

Dancer Jazz, http://dance.arts.uci.edu/ (April, 1998), Bob Boross, "Graciela Daniele and the Need for Jazz Dance Technique."*

* * *

DE BÚRCA, Gráinne 1966-

PERSONAL: Born 1966. *Education:* Attended University College, Dublin, and University of Michigan, Ann Arbor.

ADDRESSES: Office—European University Institute, Department of Law, Villa Schifanoia-Via Boccaccio, 121 Florence, Italy. *E-mail*—grainne.deburca@iue.it.

CAREER: Lawyer and author. Law Reform Commission, research assistant, beginning 1988; Somerville College, Oxford, Oxford, England, lecturer in law, beginning 1989, fellow, beginning 1990; European University Institute, professor of European law; Columbia Law School, visiting professor.

WRITINGS:

(With Paul Craig) *EC Law: Text, Cases, and Materials,* Clarendon Press (Oxford, England), 1995, 3rd edition published as *EU Law: Text, Cases, and Materials,* Oxford University Press (New York, NY), 2002.

(Editor, with Paul Craig) *The Evolution of EU Law,* Oxford University Press (New York, NY), 1999.

(Editor, with J. H. H. Weiler) *The European Court of Justice,* Oxford University Press (New York, NY), 2001.

(Editor, with Joanne Scott) *Constitutional Change in the EU: From Uniformity to Flexibility?* Hart Publishers (Oxford, England), 2000.

The Constitutional Limits of EU Action (Collected Courses of the Academy of European Law), Oxford University Press (New York, NY), 2003.

SIDELIGHTS: A lawyer, academic, and writer, Gráinne De Búrca has developed a notable expertise in the field of international law, particularly as it relates to the European Community (EC). With Paul Craig, she published *EC Law: Text, Cases, and Materials* in 1995, as a textbook for undergraduates in need of a one-volume treatment of this complex subject. *European Law Review* contributor Sarah Mercer commended it "as an excellent and innovative book. The incorporation of cases and materials with a substantial and argued text has resulted in a work that should enthuse students and teachers of EC law alike and make the reading of so lengthy and substantial a textbook a pleasure." In addition to covering the basics of EC law, the authors explored the tensions between the Court of Justice and the European Commission, and the Court of Justice and national courts. They also explore other relevant factors, such as the economics of competition law and the U.S. position on antitrust regulation. "This is a massive book," wrote Malcolm Jarvis in the *Modern Law Review.* "Its size, scope and depth combine to ensure that it immediately takes its place amongst the leading one-volume works on European Community law."

De Búrca and Craig followed up a few years later with a second edition, retitled *EU Law: Text, Cases, and Materials* "partly because the EC is in fact contained within the EU [European Union], but more specifically because . . . it is becoming increasing difficult and unhelpful . . . to assert such a clear distinction between the law of the Community and the law of the Union more generally," in the words of the authors. As such, and because of certain developments since *EC Law* was published, this is a substantially revised edition, and in fact somewhat smaller than the previous edition. "This has been achieved by a judicious slimming down of the text throughout and has allowed, in particular, sufficient space for a new sec-

tion on the Treaty of Amsterdam . . . treatment of state liability . . . and for a new chapter on Capital and Economic and Monetary union. Generally, therefore, revision of the text has been successful," wrote Peter Kunzlik in the *Cambridge Law Journal.* "The authors explore the meaning of EU concepts at a depth few others have attempted, and are always conscious of the different linguistic formulations that can be applied," concluded a *New Law Journal* reviewer. A third edition was published in 2003.

The contributors in *The Evolution of European Union Law,* edited by De Búrca and Craig, cover cases and institutions, but move beyond them to explore profound theoretical issues involved in EU law. The book "poses more questions than it has answers for, but the answers it suggests are crucial, seminal and riveting to anyone interested in why a nation or a corporate body has a constitution," wrote *Contemporary Review* contributor Michael L. Nash. The questions concern the proper mix of national and international sovereignty, the proper weight to give ethnic minorities, and the fundamental legitimacy of the whole system. The book "both provides an invaluable source of detailed information concerning EU law and institutions, while at the same time making a major contribution to current theoretical debates," concluded Lisa Busch in the *International and Comparative Law Quarterly.*

In *Constitutional Change in the EU: From Uniformity to Flexibility?* De Búrca and coeditor Joanne Scott bring together a number of essays on the future of the EU, particularly the tension between the current "uniformity" of legal concepts and a rising demand for "flexibility" as it grows to accommodate more disparate nations. "These lawyers demonstrate a sure grasp of the politics and the complex dynamics of European integration, and thus provide a valuable contribution to the long-running debate over the constitutional nature of the strange hybrid that is the EU," concluded *International Affairs* contributor William Wallace.

BIOGRAPHICAL AND CRITICAL SOURCES:

PERIODICALS

Cambridge Law Journal, March, 2000, Paul Kunzlik, review of *EU Law: Text, Cases, and Materials,* 2nd edition, p. 223.

Contemporary Review, December, 1999, Michael L. Nash, review of *Law and the European Union,* p. 322.

International Affairs, January, 2001, William Wallace, review of *Constitutional Change in the EU: From Uniformity to Flexibility?* p. 218.

International and Comparative Law Quarterly, October, 2001, Lisa Busch, review of *The Evolution of EU Law,* p. 1005.

Modern Law Review, September, 1996, Malcolm Jarvis, review of *EU Law: Text, Cases, and Materials,* 2nd edition, p. 768.

New Law Journal, February, 1999, review of *EU Law: Text, Cases, and Materials,* 2nd edition, p. 300.

*   *   *

DeLANCEY, Kiki 1959-

PERSONAL: Born 1959, in Cambridge, OH; married; children. *Education:* B.A. (political science and English).

ADDRESSES: Agent—c/o Author Mail, Sarabande Books, 2234 Dundee Road, Suite 200, Louisville, KY 40205.

CAREER: Former executive vice president of Marietta Coal Company; writer and investment manager.

WRITINGS:

Coal Miner's Holiday (stories), Sarabande Books (Louisville, KY), 2002.

Contributor to literary magazines.

WORK IN PROGRESS: A novel and a collection of stories.

SIDELIGHTS: Kiki DeLancey grew up in Cambridge, Ohio, the fifth of six children in a coal-mining family. DeLancey worked for fifteen years in that industry, first as a permit clerk and, much later, as the executive vice president of a coal company. She contributed to literary magazines for years before completing her first short story collection, *Coal Miner's Holiday.*

The book's eighteen stories, seven of which were previously published, are set in coal-mining towns from West Virginia to Tennessee, and they take place in a broad range of time, from the Great Depression to present day. In one, a woman washes the bodies of her four small children as they die from a mysterious fever. In another, the town sheriff, who has quit smoking, is so angered by a friend who lights up in a no-smoking area that he shoots him in the knees.

A *Publishers Weekly* reviewer wrote that despite some occasional "didactic, expository" writing in DeLancey's collection, "in the strongest stories, there is an immense, riveting power in the author's oblique, repetitive sentences." The tales reflect the day-to-day realities of miners who struggle to survive across the Great Appalachian Coal Basin, including those who die early deaths from diseases such as black lung. Significantly, the "holiday" of the title refers to layoffs, common in communities where there is no assurance of steady work.

A *Kirkus Reviews* contributor wrote that DeLancey "gives a gritty, real, and sexually charged rendering of life in hardscrabble towns all along the Ohio River." These are towns in which teen girls do whatever is necessary to make their lives secure, and where marriage vows are easily broken.

William Ferguson commented in the *New York Times Book Review* that some of DeLancey's stories "are remarkable for their laconic approach to brutality." Among these is "I Loved the Squire," in which the simple-minded narrator, who has murdered a woman for her money, doesn't make the connection between what he has done and the job of the lawman he admires. *Booklist*'s Carol Haggas called DeLancey "A natural talent, untrained and unfettered by convention."

BIOGRAPHICAL AND CRITICAL SOURCES:

PERIODICALS

Bloomsbury Review, July-August, 2002, Jeff Biggers, review of *Coal Miner's Holiday.*

Booklist, April 1, 2002, Carol Haggas, review of *Coal Miner's Holiday,* p. 1303.

Kirkus Reviews, April 15, 2002, review of *Coal Miner's Holiday,* p. 526.

New York Times Book Review, July 14, 2002, William Ferguson, review of *Coal Miner's Holiday,* p. 20.

Publishers Weekly, April 22, 2002, review of *Coal Miner's Holiday,* p. 50.

ONLINE

Kiki DeLancey Home Page, http://www.kikidelancey. com (February 4, 2003).*

*   *   *

Di PRISCO, Joseph 1950-

PERSONAL: Born 1950, in New York, NY; married Patricia James (a photographer). *Education:* Syracuse University, A.B. (summa cum laude), 1972; University of California—Berkeley, Ph.D., 1986.

ADDRESSES: Home—Northern CA. *Agent*—Elizabeth Trupin-Pulli, JET Literary Associates, 4519 Cherrybark Ct., Sarasota, FL 34241.

CAREER: Educator, writer, and poet. Saint Mary's College High School, instructor, 1972-73; Bentley School, instructor, 1973-75; University of California—Berkeley, instructor, 1980-86; San Francisco University High School, San Francisco, CA, instructor, 1986-94; University of California—Berkeley Extension, instructor, 1989-91; Saint Mary's College High School, instructor, 1994-96. Redwood Day School, Oakland, CA, trustee, 2001—; California Shakespeare Festival, Berkeley, trustee, 2001—.

AWARDS, HONORS: Poetry prizes, *Poetry Northwest,* 1976, 1977; John Atherton poetry fellowship, Middlebury College, 1982; Culpepper grant, 1990; Council for Basic Education fellowship, 1992; Dorothy Brunsman Poetry Prize, 2000; two Eisner prizes, Irving Prize, Academy of American Poets Prize, and James Phelan fellowship in poetry, all University of California—Berkeley.

WRITINGS:

Wit's End (poems), University of Missouri Press (Columbia, MO), 1975.

Confessions of Brother Eli (novel), MacAdam/Cage (San Francisco, CA), 2000.

(With Michael Riera) *Field Guide to the American Teenager: Appreciating the Teenager You Live With,* Perseus Publishing (Cambridge, MA), 2000.

Poems in Which, Bear Star Press (Cohasset, CA), 2000.

Sun City (novel), MacAdam/Cage (San Francisco, CA), 2002.

(With Michael Riera) *Right from Wrong,* Perseus Publishing (Cambridge, MA), 2002.

Contributor of poetry to journals, including *Threepenny Review, Midwest Quarterly, Prairie Schooner,* and *Berkeley Poetry Review,* and of essays and reviews to periodicals, including *New York Times, San Francisco Examiner, San Francisco Review of Books,* and *San Francisco Chronicle.*

SIDELIGHTS: Joseph Di Prisco's first book of poetry, *Wit's End,* is a collection that includes many themes, from the traditional to drug use. Some of the longer poems, called "essays," tend to be more reflective. A *Choice* reviewer considered them "perhaps the best work in the volume." Di Prisco's poems appeared in journals for more than two decades before he collected many of them in his second volume, *Poems in Which.*

Di Prisco, a long-time teacher of high school students, wrote *Field Guide to the American Teenager: Appreciating the Teenager You Live With* with fellow teacher Michael Riera, author of *Surviving High School.* By using anecdotes and conversations with teens, the authors address problems that include violence, drugs, sexual activity, drinking and driving, and eating disorders. The theme that is evident throughout is that parents should influence rather than control their teen's life and that teens should be loved, trusted, and guided.

In the introduction, the authors say that "Sometimes with our teenagers we get more information than we want, and sometimes we get less information than we need. The same is true with these narratives. The art of parenting begins with knowing how to read kids in between the lines of their lives. Teenagers don't fall in love, or grieve, or smoke, or play soccer in a vacuum. We only know what these experiences mean for them, and for us, when we grasp them in the context of their tribulations, aspirations, and dreams. Their decisions and choices, their weaknesses and strengths, are interconnected."

A *Publishers Weekly* contributor remarked that Di Prisco and Riera "have a solid grasp on what makes adolescents tick" and felt the book is "invaluable for parents facing this challenging time in their child's life." "This excellent work is to be thoroughly read, reread, and thought about," commented Linda Beck in *Library Journal*.

A *Publishers Weekly* reviewer wrote that in *Confessions of Brother Eli*, Di Prisco's debut novel, he "serves up a parochial world peopled by the unwashed, the unpromising, and the uninterested." The protagonist, Brother Eli, teaches English at a Catholic prep school near San Francisco that has never produced a student outstanding enough to get into one of the "better" colleges or universities. Brother Eli is himself a less-than-perfect role model, a smoker and an overeater and drinker who steals food from the cafeteria and wine from the rectory. The big man's life changes when transfer student Nadette Nevers shows up in his classroom, a super-bright girl who presents the kind of challenge not offered by his other students. His choice is whether or not he should accept that challenge.

J. Uschuk noted at *Tucson Weekly* online that the novel "fairly sparkles with humor that ranges from sophisticated to slapstick. . . . And yet, it's not only that. This is a novel that draws the readers in and becomes a serious meditation almost before you can put it down." Uschuk observed that in the last third of the book, "the novel becomes an elegant elegy for opportunities lost."

Sun City was called "red-hot at the start" by a *Kirkus Reviews* writer. This novel is about the blackjack players and card counters who try to beat the odds in Las Vegas, and in this tale, also in South Africa. Dolly Leone is a gambler who is beaten for failing to pay what he owes his bookie, and who is looking for a way to raise funds. An old gambling friend wrote a book about their escapades, at Dolly's suggestion, and Dolly revives the unpublished manuscript to promote it as his own writing. But the story contains little flattery about Dolly and exposes personal details of their lives that he wouldn't want made public. The story-within-a-story also follows the romance between the manuscript's creator, Valentino "Schoolboy" Comfort, and Tess, also known as the Teaser, as well as describing crime and terrorism from Las Vegas to Africa. A *Publishers Weekly* contributor described *Sun City* as a "noirish gambling novel."

BIOGRAPHICAL AND CRITICAL SOURCES:

PERIODICALS

Booklist, June 1, 2002, Bill Ott, review of *Sun City*, p. 1690.
Choice, October, 1976, review of *Wit's End*, pp. 978-979.
Kirkus Reviews, May 15, 2002, review of *Sun City*, p. 681.
Library Journal, June 1, 1976, Lynn Emanuel, review of *Wit's End*, p. 1291; September 15, 2000, Linda Beck, review of *Field Guide to the American Teenager: Appreciating the Teenager You Live With*, p. 99.
North American Review, spring, 1977, review of *Wit's End*.
Publishers Weekly, August 7, 2000, review of *Field Guide to the American Teenager*, p. 91; October 9, 2000, review of *Confessions of Brother Eli*, p. 75; June 3, 2002, review of *Sun City*, p. 62.

ONLINE

Tucson Weekly Online, http://www.tucsonweekly.com/ (October 11, 2001), J. Uschuk, review of *Confessions of Brother Eli*.*

*   *   *

DOBKOWSKI, Michael N. 1947-

PERSONAL: Born May 10, 1947, in Germany; naturalized U.S. citizen; son of Monik and Bronia (Kalt) Dobkowski; married Karen Gabe (a speech pathologist); children: Jessica, Jonathan, Tamar. *Ethnicity:* "Jewish." *Education:* New York University, B.A. (with honors), 1969, M.A., 1971, Ph.D. (with distinction), 1976.

ADDRESSES: Home—65 Parkwood Ave., Rochester, NY 14620. *Office*—Department of Religious Studies, Hobart and William Smith Colleges, Geneva, NY 14456. *E-mail*—dobkowski@hws.edu.

CAREER: Herbert H. Lehman College of the City University of New York, lecturer in American history, 1973-74; Upsala College, East Orange, NJ, lecturer in modern Jewish history, 1974-75; Research Foundation for Jewish Immigration, senior research fellow, 1975-76; Hobart and William Smith Colleges, Geneva, NY, assistant professor, 1976-82, associate professor, 1982-88, professor of religious studies, 1988—, department chair, 1992-95. Kean College of New Jersey, lecturer, 1975; University of Rochester, visiting assistant professor, 1979; Wroxton College, member of Goldner Holocaust Symposium, 1996, 1998, 2000, 2002; guest speaker at other institutions, including Bloomsburg State College, Rider College, Siena College, Virginia Commonwealth University, and Duquesne University. Hillel School of Rochester, chair of education committee, 1986-92, vice president of board of directors, 1987-89, president of board of trustees, 1992-94; Holocaust Commission of Rochester, chair, 1994-98; Ora Academy of Rochester, vice president, 1998-2002.

MEMBER: Phi Beta Kappa.

AWARDS, HONORS: Grants from Memorial Foundation for Jewish Culture, 1974-75, and National Endowment for the Humanities, 1977-78; fellow of Institute for the Teaching of the Post-Biblical Foundations of Western Civilization, Jewish Theological Seminary, 1979.

WRITINGS:

The Tarnished Dream: The Basis of American Anti-Semitism, Greenwood Press (Westport, CT), 1979.

The Politics of Indifference: A Documentary History of Holocaust Victims in America, University Press of America (Washington, DC), 1982.

(With Isidor Wallimann) *Toward the Holocaust: The Social and Economic Collapse of the Weimar Republic,* Greenwood Press (Westport, CT), 1983.

Jewish-American Voluntary Organizations, Greenwood Press (Westport, CT), 1986.

(With Isidor Wallimann) *Genocide and the Modern Age: Etiology and Case Studies of Mass Death,* Greenwood Press (Westport, CT), 1987.

(With Peter Beckman, Steven Lee, and others) *The Nuclear Predicament: An Introduction,* Prentice-Hall (Englewood Cliffs, NJ), 1988, revised edition, 1991.

(Editor, with Isidor Wallimann) *Radical Perspectives on the Rise of Fascism in Germany, 1919-1945,* Monthly Review Press (New York, NY), 1989.

(Editor, with Isidor Wallimann, and contributor) *Genocide in Our Time,* Pierian Press (Ann Arbor, MI), 1992.

(With Barbara Lovenheim) *A Family among Families: A History of the Jewish Home of Rochester,* Jewish Home Foundation (Rochester, NY), 1998.

(Editor, with Isidor Wallimann, and contributor) *The Coming Age of Scarcity: Preventing Mass Death and Genocide in the Twenty-first Century,* Syracuse University Press (Syracuse, NY), 1998, second edition published as *On the Edge of Scarcity: Environment, Resources, Population, Sustainability, and Conflict,* 2002.

(With Peter Beckman, Steven Lee, and Paul Crumlish) *The Nuclear Predicament: Nuclear Weapons in the Twenty-first Century,* Prentice-Hall (Tappan, NJ), 2000.

Contributor to books, including *Germany and America: Essays on Problems of International Relations and Immigration,* edited by Hans L. Trefousse, Brooklyn College Press (Brooklyn, NY), 1980; *Approaches to Modern Judaism,* edited by Marc Lee Raphael, Scholars Press (Chico, CA), 1983; *Persistent Prejudice,* edited by Herbert Hirsch and Jack D. Spiro, George Mason University Press (Fairfax, VA), 1988; and *Frontiers of Jewish Thought,* edited by Steven T. Katz, B'nai B'rith Books (Washington, DC), 1992. Contributor of articles and reviews to periodicals, including *American Quarterly, Markman Review, Studies in History and Society, Journal of Jewish Music and Liturgy, Judaism, Keeping Posted, Patterns of Prejudice,* and *Dimensions.* Coeditor of research annuals *Research in Inequality and Social Conflict,* 1989, 1992, and *Research in Social Movements, Conflicts, and Change,* 1993-98.

WORK IN PROGRESS: *Covered Mirrors,* a Holocaust-era novel.

BIOGRAPHICAL AND CRITICAL SOURCES:

PERIODICALS

Annals of the American Academy of Political and Social Science, July, 1980, David H. Rosenbloom, review of *The Tarnished Dream,* p. 274.

Journal of American Ethnic History, spring, 1989, Henry L. Feingold, review of *Jewish-American Voluntary Organizations,* p. 178.

Journal of Environmental Education, summer, 1999, Jeffrey Salmon, review of *The Coming Age of Scarcity: Preventing Mass Death and Genocide in the Twenty-first Century,* p. 42.

Monthly Review, November, 1991, Lukin Robinson, review of *Radical Perspectives on the Rise of Fascism in Germany, 1919-1945,* p. 43.

* * *

DOBSON, Frank E. 1952-

PERSONAL: Born July 3, 1952, in Buffalo, NY; son of Frank Everette (a steelworker) and Willa Mae Banks (a homemaker, domestic, and factory worker) Dobson; married Marla High (divorced); married Dioncia Coffey (an administrator), July 27, 1991; children: Jasmin Nicole. *Ethnicity:* "African American." *Education:* State University of New York at Buffalo, B.A., 1973; University of Nevada, M.A., 1975; Bowling Green State University, Ph.D. (English), 1985. *Hobbies and other interests:* "Weight lifting, music, travel, spirituality."

ADDRESSES: Office—Department of English, Wright State University, Dayton, OH 45435. *E-mail*—frank. dobson@wright.edu.

CAREER: Ohio University Academic Administration Center, assistant director, 1979-81; Lafayette College Prep Program, director, 1981-84; Wright State University, Dayton, OH, director of Bolinga Cultural Center, 1984-90, associate professor of English, 1994—; Shippensburg University, Shippensburg, PA, college administrator, 1990-91; Indiana University, Indianapolis, assistant professor of English, 1991-94. Affiliated with Antioch Writers Workshop.

MEMBER: Associated Writing Programs, Popular Culture Society.

AWARDS, HONORS: Hurston-Head Fiction Award, Chicago State University, 1994; Master Artists Award, Montgomery County, OH, 1996.

WRITINGS:

The Race Is Not Given, Sterlinghouse (Pittsburgh, PA), 1999.

Contributor of a short story and poetry to *Warpland* and *Shooting Star Review.* Contributor of nonfiction to various periodicals, including *Public Voices; contributor to books, including Contemporary African American Novelists* and *Dictionary of Literary Biography.*

WORK IN PROGRESS: Of Men and Masks, a short-story collection; *Climbing,* a novel.

SIDELIGHTS: Frank E. Dobson told *CA:* "I am a black, working-class college professor who was born and raised in Buffalo, New York. The themes within my creative work center around the quest for identity, particularly, how to live one's life on one's own terms. For me, the negotiation of this is mental, physical, and spiritual. And my protagonists/characters have to try to work this out, given all of the baggage (failures and even crippling successes) that they carry."

* * *

DOLLERY, Brian E(dward) 1952-

PERSONAL: Born September 2, 1952, in Port Elizabeth, Cape Province, South Africa; son of Edward Percy and Joan Livingstone (Pote) Dollery; married Therese Anne Burton, May 8, 1999. *Ethnicity:* "Anglo-Saxon." *Education:* Rhodes University, B.A., 1973, B.A. (with honors), 1974. *Politics:* "Liberal Party." *Religion:* Anglican. *Hobbies and other interests:* Cricket, rugby, karaoke.

ADDRESSES: Home—41 Gordon St., Armidale, New South Wales 2350, Australia. *Office*—Department of Economics, University of New England, Armidale, New South Wales 2351, Australia. *E-mail*—bdollery@ metz.une.edu.au.

CAREER: Educator and economist. Rhodes University, Grahamstown, South Africa, professor, 1978-87; University of New England, Armidale, New South Wales, Australia, professor of economics, 1988—. East Carolina State University, professor, 1985; Creighton University, professor, 1991; Yokohama National University, professor, 2002.

MEMBER: Economic Society of Australia, Economic Society of South Africa, American Economic Association.

WRITINGS:

(Editor with Philip A. Black) *Leading Issues in South African Microeconomics: Selected Readings,* Southern Book Publishers, 1992.

(Editor, with Neil Marshall) *Australian Local Government: Reform and Renewal,* Macmillan (South Melbourne, Australia), 1997.

(With Joe Wallis) *Market Failure, Government Failure, Leadership, and Public Policy,* St. Martin's Press (New York, NY), 1999.

The Political Economy of Local Government: Leadership, Reform, and Market Failures, Edward Elgar Publishing (Northampton, MA), 2001.

The Political Economy of the Voluntary Sector, Edward Elgar Publishing (Northampton, MA), 2002.

Contributor to periodicals, including *Applied Economics, Public Administration, World Development, Economic Record, International Journal of Social Economics, Public Budgeting and Finance,* and *Public Productivity and Management Review.*

BIOGRAPHICAL AND CRITICAL SOURCES:

PERIODICALS

Australian Journal of Political Science, March, 1998, John Power, review of *Australian Local Government: Reform and Renewal,* p. 137.

*   *   *

DORSEY, Tim 1961-

PERSONAL: Born 1961, in IN; married; children: two daughters. *Education:* Auburn University, B.S., 1983.

ADDRESSES: Home—Tampa, FL. *Agent*—c/o Author Mail, HarperCollins, 10 East 53rd Street, 7th Floor, New York, NY 10022. *E-mail*—tad2561@yahoo.com.

CAREER: Alabama Journal, Montgomery, police and courts reporter, 1983-87; *Tampa Tribune,* Tampa, FL, general assignment reporter, copy-desk editor, political reporter, 1987-94, night metro editor, night news coordinator, 1994-99.

WRITINGS:

"SERGE STORMS" SERIES

Florida Roadkill: A Novel, Morrow (New York, NY), 1999.

Hammerhead Ranch Motel: A Novel, Morrow (New York, NY), 2000.

Orange Crush: A Novel, Morrow (New York, NY), 2001.

Triggerfish Twist: A Novel, Morrow (New York, NY), 2002.

The Stingray Shuffle: A Novel, Morrow (New York, NY), 2003.

SIDELIGHTS: Tim Dorsey worked as a reporter, editor and news coordinator before becoming a full-time author. His novels are set in Florida, where he lives.

Dorsey's debut novel, *Florida Roadkill* tells the story of Serge Storms and his sidekick, Coleman, two con men. Sharon, a con woman and addict, secretly videotapes dentist Dr. Veale in the back room of a strip club. In order to keep Serge and Coleman quiet about the secret tape, Veale agrees to having his hands, which are insured for five million dollars, injured. Coleman and Serge want the insurance money, which Veale hides in the car of two men who leave the club not knowing about the money. What results is a chase through the state of Florida by the two con men and others looking to get rich quick. "Dorsey's wicked sense of humor and astounding knowledge of Florida's history and legends add levity and local color to this dark tale," noted *Library Journal* contributor Thomas L. Kilpatrick.

Serge is back in Dorsey's second novel, *Hammerhead Ranch Motel.* Serge is still searching for the five million dollars he was first after in *Florida Roadkill.* Serge and his new partner Lenny Lippowicz track the money and believe it is with the owner of the Hammerhead Ranch Motel. Serge and Lenny rent a room and wait for the perfect opportunity to nab the money. While they wait they meet the strange guests that are staying at the motel. *Mystery Net* contributor Anya R. Weber claimed, "Dorsey soars to glorious heights on the wings of his own absurdity."

Dorsey's third novel, *Orange Crush,* deals with Florida politics. Florida's governorship is between Marlon Conrad and Gomer Tatum. Something snaps in Conrad, and he takes off on a crazy election tour in a bright orange, second-hand Winnebago. Along the way Conrad meets some interesting people, including Serge. Opponent Tatum soon follows Conrad and eventually challenges him to a wrestling match that will decide who the next governor will be. "If 200-proof satire is your drink of choice, Dorsey is the guy you want behind the bar," concluded *Booklist* contributor Bill Ott.

In *Triggerfish Twist* Serge, Coleman, and Sharon are living on Triggerfish Lane in Tampa, Florida. Jim Davenport and his family move to Triggerfish Lane when Jim accepts a transfer from Wisconsin. Jim is a quiet man who doesn't like to argue or fight with anyone. He moved to the wrong street, however, if he was searching for peace and quiet. His neighbors include drug users, psychotics, and other sleazy people. Serge tries to protect Jim and his family from the other neighbors. *Book Reporter* contributor Joe Hartlaub praised, "With *Triggerfish Twist*, Dorsey has transformed himself from an author to be enjoyed to an artist whose next book will be anticipated with as much fervor as this one will be enjoyed."

Dorsey's fifth "Serge Storms" novel, *The Stingray Shuffle*, still finds Serge on the trail of the elusive five million dollars from *Florida Roadkill*. But now others, including Russian gangsters masquerading as Latinos, join the hunt. *Booklist*'s David Pitt called the novel "a brilliantly constructed romp."

BIOGRAPHICAL AND CRITICAL SOURCES:

PERIODICALS

Booklist, April 15, 1999, George Needham, review of *Florida Roadkill*, p. 1471; May 15, 2000, George Needham, review of *Hammerhead Ranch Motel*, p. 1733; May 1, 2001, Bill Ott and Brad Hooper, review of *Florida Roadkill*, p. 1603; May 1, 2001, Bill Ott, review of *Orange Crush*, p. 1630; February 15, 2003, David Pitt, review of *The Stingray Shuffle*, p. 1053.

Kirkus Reviews, June 1, 1999, review of *Florida Roadkill*, p. 817; May 15, 2001, review of *Orange Crush*, p. 680; March 1, 2002, review of *Triggerfish Twist*, p. 290; December 1, 2002, review of *The Stingray Shuffle*, p. 1735.

Library Journal, June 15, 1999, Thomas L. Kilpatrick, review of *Florida Roadkill*, p. 105; June 15, 2000, Thomas L. Kilpatrick, review of *Hammerhead Ranch Motel*, p. 112; June 15, 2001, Thomas L. Kilpatrick, review of *Orange Crush*, p. 102.

Publishers Weekly, July 5, 1999, review of *Florida Roadkill*, p. 58; August 30, 1999, Judy Quinn, "*Roadkill* the Rage in Florida," p. 23; July 31, 2000, review of *Hammerhead Ranch Motel*, p. 70; July 9, 2001, p. 49; March 1, 2002, review of *Triggerfish Twist*, p. 37; January 6, 2003, review of *The Stingray Shuffle*, p. 42.

ONLINE

Alabama Bound Web site, http://www.alabamabound. org/ (August 29, 2002), "Tim Dorsey."

Book Page, http://www.bookpage.com/ (August 29, 2002), review of *Florida Roadkill*.

Book Reporter, http://www.bookreporter.com/ (August 29, 2002), reviews of *Orange Crush* and *Triggerfish Twist*.

Books 'n' Bytes, http://www.booksnbytes.com/ (August 29, 2002), Harriet Klausner, review of *Florida Roadkill* and *Hammerhead Ranch Motel*.

Fire and Water, http://www.fireandwater.com/ (August 29, 2002), review of *Hammerhead Ranch Motel* and interview with Dorsey.

HarperCollins Web site, http://www.harpercollins.com/ (August 29, 2002).

Murder on Miami Beach Web site, http://www. murderonmiamibeach.com/ (August 29, 2002), review of *Orange Crush, Hammerhead Ranch Motel*, and *Florida Roadkill*.

Mystery Net, http://www.mysterynet.com/ (August 29, 2002), Anya R. Weber, review of *Hammerhead Ranch Motel*.

New York Times on the Web, http://www.nytimes.com/ (August 27, 2002).

Tim Dorsey Web site, http://www.timdorsey.com (August 29, 2002).*

*   *   *

DRAYSON, Nicholas 1954-

PERSONAL: Born 1954, in England; immigrated to Australia, 1982. *Education:* University of New South Wales, B.S., M.S., Ph.D.

ADDRESSES: Agent—c/o Author Mail, W. W. Norton & Co., 500 Fifth Ave., New York, NY 10110-0017.

CAREER: Writer, naturalist, and house painter. Former curator at Australian National Museum, Canberra, Australia.

WRITINGS:

Wildlife: Australia's Flora and Fauna Gently Observed, illustrated by Bruce Goold, Collins (Sydney, Australia), 1988.
Confessing a Murder, W. W. Norton (New York, NY), 2002.

Columnist for *Good Weekend* and *Australian Women's Weekly.* Contributor to periodicals, including *Australian Geographic.*

SIDELIGHTS: Nicholas Drayson's first book is a naturalist's observation of his adopted home of Australia. Drayson was living in Kenya in 1998 and 1999 when he wrote his second, a novel titled *Confessing a Murder,* which *Booklist*'s Michael Spinella commented "juxtaposes the dark nature of humanity with the exciting discoveries made about nature and the world."

Drayson begins *Confessing a Murder* by describing a manuscript that was found in Holland in 1988, the author of which becomes the narrator of the story. The narrator describes his life in England from a South Seas island that is threatened by volcanic activity. He first left England for Australia, where he became involved in trade, then as his financial success permitted, he traveled to the more remote areas in the Java Sea. He is a collector of beetles, a fascination he shared with his close school friend, Charles Darwin. The manuscript relates that after he shared his theory of biological evolution with Darwin and Wallace, who barely knew each other, they each raced to publish it as their own.

Mick Imlah wrote in the *Times Literary Supplement* that "the best things in the book, and they form a large part of it, are its descriptions of the plants, insects, and animals of the island's creation, one parallel to, but separate from, that of our knowledge. . . . There is something like poetry, or philosophy made animate, in the more remarkable of the invented forms."

The island is to the narrator what the Galapagos were to Darwin, filled with strange and unusual plants and peculiar animals, including beetles whose males and females breed without meeting and a small frog, the male of which is almost whollcy comprised of testicles. The narrator is a Robinson Crusoe of sorts, exploring the island with a young assistant. His ultimate goal is to find the Golden Scarab beetle, and as he searches, he names and classifies all the forms of life he discovers, knowing that he will never receive credit for his work.

Imlah wrote, "Ignorant and incurious of his origins, parentless, childless, alone, barren, old, homosexual; his work stolen from him, his world doomed by the volcano at its heart, his story and experience folding into nothing, he is multiply denied posterity. Except, of course, for this fluky, fictional survival."

Lewis Wolfe reviewed the novel for *Sydney Scope* online, saying that the narrator "is arrogant and not altogether likeable at times, but engagingly brilliant and possessed of a flowing, personal style." About Drayson, he wrote that he "has a scientific mind but also a keen eye for beauty and the many metaphors within nature itself."

A *Kirkus Reviews* contributor called *Confessing a Murder* "an intelligent, gripping, and vivid adventure: Drayson writes in an exceptionally self-assured tone that perfectly captures the spirit of the nineteenth century."

BIOGRAPHICAL AND CRITICAL SOURCES:

PERIODICALS

Booklist, April 15, 2002, Michael Spinella, review of *Confessing a Murder,* p. 1381.
Kirkus Reviews, March 1, 2002, review of *Confessing a Murder,* p. 276.
Publishers Weekly, May 13, 2002, review of *Confessing a Murder,* p. 53.
Times Literary Supplement, May 10, 2002, Mick Imlah, review of *Confessing a Murder,* p. 26.

ONLINE

Sydney Scope, http://www.sydneyscope.com.au (January 2, 2003), Lewis Wolfe, review of *Confessing a Murder.**

* * *

DUDEK, Louis 1918-2001

OBITUARY NOTICE—See index for *CA* sketch: Born February 6, 1918, in Montreal, Quebec, Canada; died of heart failure March 22, 2001, in Montreal, Quebec, Canada. Educator and author. Dudek was a Canadian modernist poet who was also a cofounder of Contact Press. A graduate of McGill University, where he received his bachelor's degree in 1939, he also earned a Ph.D. from Columbia University in 1951. His teaching career began at City College (now of the City University of New York) where he was an English instructor from 1946 to 1951. He then returned to his alma mater, joining the faculty as an assistant professor, becoming a full professor in 1969, and being named Greenshields Professor of English in 1972; he retired in 1984. While at McGill, Dudek accomplished a great deal to help up-and-coming poets, including publishing their verses in his literary magazine, *Delta,* and founding Contact Press with fellow poets Raymond Souster and Irving Layton. The publishing company was considered a leader in Canadian poetry publishing during the 1950s and 1960s. Dudek was also the editor of the "McGill Poetry Series," beginning in 1951, which helped poets such as Leonard Cohen get their start. As for his own writing, Dudek wrote over a dozen poetry collections, published several literary studies, and edited a number of books as well. His verse collections include *East of the City* (1946); *The Transparent Sea* (1956); *Atlantis* (1967), which was later published as *Poems from Atlantis* (1980); *Continuation I* (1981); *Zembla's Rocks* (1986); *Continuation II* (1990); *Small Perfect Things* (1991); *A Last Stand* (1995); *The Caged Tiger* (1997); and *The Poetry of Louis Dudek: Definitive Edition* (1998). His many nonfiction works include *Notebooks, 1960-1994* (1994), *The Birth of Reason* (1994), *1941* (1996), and *Reality Games* (1998).

OBITUARIES AND OTHER SOURCES:

BOOKS

Contemporary Poets, seventh edition, St. James Press (Detroit, MI), 2001.
Writers Directory, 18th edition, St. James Press (Detroit, MI), 2003.

PERIODICALS

Globe and Mail (Toronto, Ontario, Canada), March 22, 2001; May 2, 2001.
Maclean's, April 2, 2001, p. 18.

* * *

DUNCAN, Alice 1945-
(Emma Craig, Jon Sharpe, Rachel Wilson)

PERSONAL: Born November 29, 1945, in Pasadena, CA; daughter of Elbert H. (an electrician) and Wilma (a secretary; maiden name, Wilson) Duncan; married John Strathmann, 1964 (divorced, 1971); children: Anne, Robin. *Ethnicity:* "Caucasian." *Education:* Attended Pasadena City College. *Politics:* Democrat. *Religion:* United Methodist. *Hobbies and other interests:* Cooking, gardening, dachshunds.

ADDRESSES: Home—P.O. Box 2507, Roswell, NM 88202. *Agent*—Linda M. Kruger, Fogelman Literary Agency, 1717 Greenville Ave., Suite 712, Dallas, TX 75231. *E-mail*—aduncan@lookingglass.net.

CAREER: Author. Performed as a folk dancer; member of Zena, a Balkan women's choir.

MEMBER: Romance Writers of America, Authors Guild.

AWARDS, HONORS: Holt Medallion, Virginia Romance Writers of America, 1995, for *One Bright Morning;* KISS awards, *Romantic Times* Book Club, 2001, for *Cowboy for Hire,* and 2002, for *Bicycle Built for Two.*

WRITINGS:

One Bright Morning, HarperMonogram (New York, NY), 1995.
Texas Lonesome, HarperMonogram (New York, NY), 1996.
Wild Dream, Dell (New York, NY), 1997.
Secret Hearts, Dell (New York, NY), 1998.

"DREAM MAKER" SERIES

Cowboy for Hire, Zebra (New York, NY), 2001.
Beauty and the Brain, Zebra (New York, NY), 2001.
Her Leading Man, Zebra (New York, NY), 2001.
The Miner's Daughter, Zebra (New York, NY), 2001.

"CHICAGO WORLD'S FAIR" SERIES

Coming up Roses, Zebra (New York, NY), 2002.
Just North of Bliss, Zebra (New York, NY), 2002.
A Bicycle Built for Two, Zebra (New York, NY), 2002.

"SPIRITS" SERIES

Strong Spirits, Zebra Historical Romance (New York, NY), 2003.
Fine Spirits, Zebra Historical Romance (New York, NY), 2003.

AS RACHEL WILSON

Sweet Charity, Jove Books (New York, NY), 1997.
Restless Spirits, Jove Books (New York, NY), 1998.
Heaven's Promise, Jove Books (New York, NY), 1998.
Bittersweet Summer, Jove Books (New York, NY), 1999.
My Wild Irish Rose, Jove Books (New York, NY), 2000.
Heaven Sent, Jove Books (New York, NY), 2001.

AS EMMA CRAIG

Rosamunda's Revenge, Leisure Books (New York, NY), 1997.
Christmas Pie, Leisure Books (New York, NY), 1997.
Enchanted Christmas, Love Spell Books (New York, NY), 1998.
A Gentle Magic, Leisure Books (New York, NY), 1999.
A Gambler's Magic, Love Spell Books (New York, NY), 2000.
Cooking up Trouble, Love Spell Books (New York, NY), 2000.
Gabriel's Fate, Dorchester Publishing (New York, NY), 2001.

"TRAILSMAN" SERIES; AS JON SHARPE

Pecos Belle Brigade, Signet (New York, NY), 1999.
California Crusader, Signet (New York, NY), 2000.

Contributor to anthologies, including *The Magic of Christmas,* Love Spell Books (New York, NY), 1998, and *Winter Wonderland,* Love Spell Books (New York, NY), 1999.

SIDELIGHTS: Alice Duncan writes romance fiction under her own name and using the pen names Rachel Wilson, Emma Craig, and Jon Sharpe. Her stories feature various places and time periods, with many set during the Victorian era.

Duncan's *Bittersweet Summer* is set in 1895 New York, and involves feuding families, the Rakes and the Crowfoots. The latter built a splendid pre-Revolutionary castle that has fallen into disrepair, a condition current owner Genevieve Crowfoot is unable to remedy due to lack of funds. Tobias Rakes returns from fighting the tribes of North Dakota to an inherited fortune, more than enough money to buy the castle, which he does, and he hires Genevieve to be his housekeeper. This displeases Granny Crowfoot, the resident ghost, who is not only forced to see the family estate fall into the hands of the enemy, but also to watch Genevieve fall under Tobias's spell.

My Wild Irish Rose finds a destitute Rose Larkin and her Aunt Kate traveling from New York to Dublin after the death of Rose's father. Rose would be willing to marry well into a respectable, if boring life, but Kate, who did so but always envied her brother's wild ways, wants Rose to enjoy a bit of adventure before she settles down. Rose attracts the wrong kinds of men, who want to involve her in the wrong kinds of adventures, except for Cullen O'Banyon, who looks out for her safety and becomes smitten with her. Her objection to Cullen is that he works with horses, an occupation she associates with her father's footloose ways. Carol Carter, who reviewed the book for *Under the Covers* online, wrote that the story "focuses on the belief that the grass is greener on the other side, and the author takes it a step farther to give a glimpse of what it's like when you get there."

Carter also reviewed *Cooking up Trouble,* which she called "a fun tale that will bring back memories of Rumpelstiltskin." Heather Mahaffey is the daughter of an Irishman who delights in telling tall tales about the accomplishments of his children. When wealthy rancher Philippe St. Pierre, who has just moved to the New Mexico Territory, says he is looking for a cook, the father brags about Heather's abilities in the kitchen. Over a chorus of protests from everyone who knows her, Philippe hires the beautiful, but untalented, Heather. But Heather gets help in the form of D. A. Bologh, a stranger who appears from out of nowhere, and who seems to possess magical powers that result in elaborate and delicious dishes. *Romance Reader*'s Diana Burrell called the story "a classic tale of man selling his soul to the devil."

Duncan wrote a number of books that focus on the film industry. The first, *Cowboy for Hire,* is set in 1905. Meredith McGuire wrote in a review for *Romance Reader* that "it's always refreshing to discover an author who believes 'history' did not end in 1899. Too, early motion pictures provide a fascinating array of romantic possibilities." In this novel, Charlie Fox, a cowboy who works on an ostrich ranch, is offered the opportunity to play a villain in a Western film. Charlie is suspicious, but decides it could finance his escape from the big birds and enable him to buy some cattle. In real life, however, Charlie becomes the hero of costar Amy Wilkes who is being seduced by a wealthy actor who dangles a prime role to entice her.

Beauty and the Brain features a beautiful actress who admires intelligence, and an intelligent college graduate who masks his. It is 1907, and director Martin Tafft is shooting a film titled *Indian Love Song.* Handsome Colin Peters is hired to check the facts portrayed in the film, but, for the most part, his advice is ignored. He is growing more and more fond of the film's star, Brenda Fitzpatrick, who although attracted to him, feels that someone as smart as Colin could never find an actress attractive. Colin finds it hard to believe that the beautiful actress could fall for a brainy type like him.

In *Her Leading Man,* Tafft is directing a thriller and has cast Christina Mayhew in the starring role. Christina is a suffragette who is performing to finance her dream of becoming a doctor. She falls in love with Tafft, but his ethics get in the way of forming a relationship with his leading lady. *The Miner's Daughter* continues the theme and finds Tafft shooting a film in an old mine, which he thought to be abandoned but which seems to harbor dangerous elements that threaten the crew and the mine's actual owner.

Duncan wrote a series of books set at the 1893 World Columbian Exposition in Chicago (Chicago World's Fair). The first of these is *Coming up Roses,* in which Rose Ellen Gilhooley, who was transformed by Buffalo Bill Cody into a star in his Wild West Show, is pursued by a newspaperman. In *A Bicycle Built for Two* Alex English, one of the exposition's organizers, attempts to banish fortune teller Kate Finney from the grounds. His cold heart melts, however, when he learns that Kate is telling fortunes to support her family, including her dying mother. Kate lets her guard down, and Alex into her life, when he shows signs of being human.

Just North of Bliss finds nanny Rowena Belle teaching Southern-style manners to two young boys in a New York family. When she accompanies them to the World's Fair, she is spotted by Win, the official fair photographer and an aggressive Yankee who has a difficult time convincing her to pose for him. *Booklist*'s Maria Hatton called the novel a "detailed, lively, and entertaining escapade."

BIOGRAPHICAL AND CRITICAL SOURCES:

PERIODICALS

Booklist, May 1, 2002, Maria Hatton, review of *Just North of Bliss,* p. 1512; October 1, 2002, Maria Hatton, review of *A Bicycle Built for Two,* p. 305.
Library Journal, February 15, 2002, John Charles, review of *Coming up Roses,* p. 129.
Publishers Weekly, April 1, 2002, review of *Just North of Bliss,* p. 59.

ONLINE

All about Romance, http://www.likesbooks.com/ (January 2, 2003), Mary Sophia Novak, review of *Cooking up Trouble,* Ellen D. Micheletti, review of *My Wild Irish Rose,* Jane Jorgenson, review of *Beauty and the Brain,* Jennifer Keirans, review of *Her Leading Man.*
Romance Reader, http://www.theromancereader.com/ (January 2, 2003), Cathy Sova, review of *Bittersweet Summer,* Diana Burrell, review of *Cooking up Trouble,* Meredith McGuire, review of *Cowboy for Hire.*

Under the Covers, http://www.silcom.com/~manatee/ (January 28, 1997), Carmel Vivier, review of *Sweet Charity;* (January 11, 1999) Linda Hurst, review of *Bittersweet Summer;* (January 20, 1999) Lisa Wong, review of *Heaven's Promise;* (May 24, 2000, Holly E. Price, review of *Gabriel's Fate;* (February 19, 2001) Carol Carter, review of *Cooking up Trouble* and *My Wild Irish Rose.**

* * *

DURBIN, William 1951-

PERSONAL: Born February 17, 1951, in Minneapolis, MN; son of Charles (a barber) and Dona (a bookkeeper) Durbin; married October 14, 1971; wife's name Barbara (a teacher); children: Jessica Durbin Froehle, Reid. *Education:* St. Cloud State University, B.S., 1973; Middlebury College, M.A. 1987. *Hobbies and other interests:* Golf, canoeing.

ADDRESSES: Home and office—2287 Birch Pt. Rd., Tower, MN 55790. *Agent*—Barbara Markowitz, 1505 Hill Dr., Los Angeles, CA 90041. *E-mail*—Bill@williamdurbin.com.

CAREER: Writer and educator. Teacher of English in Minnesota public schools, grades four through college, including at Cook High School; speaker at writing conferences and at schools and libraries.

MEMBER: National Education Association, Society of Children's Book Writers and Illustrators, Children's Literature Network.

AWARDS, HONORS: Great Lakes Booksellers Association Book Award, Minnesota Book Award, Bank Street College Children's Book of the Year, and New York Public Library Books for the Teen-Age selection, all 1998; New River Press Poetry Competition finalist; Lake Superior Contemporary Writer's Series winner.

WRITINGS:

The Broken Blade, Delacorte (New York, NY), 1997.
Tiger Woods (biography; "Golf Legends" and "Black Americans of Achievement" series), Chelsea House (Philadelphia, PA), 1998.

Arnold Palmer (biography; "Golf Legends" series), Chelsea House (Philadelphia, PA), 1998.
Wintering (sequel to *The Broken Blade*), Delacorte (New York, NY), 1999.
The Song of Sampo Lake, Wendy Lamb Books (New York, NY), 2002.
Blackwater Ben, Wendy Lamb Books (New York, NY), 2003.

Contributor of poems, essays, and short stories to periodicals, including *English Journal, Great River Review, Milkweed Chronicle, Confrontation, North American Mentor, Canadian Author and Bookman, Boys Life, Loonfeather, Modern Haiku, Nebraska Language Arts Bulletin, Breadloaf News,* and *NCTE.*

Durbin's books have been translated into several languages, including Italian, and have been produced in Braille editions.

"MY NAME IS AMERICA" SERIES

The Journal of Sean Sullivan, a Transcontinental Railroad Worker: Nebraska and Points West, 1867, Scholastic (New York, NY), 1999.
The Journal of Otto Peltonen, a Finnish Immigrant: Hibbing Minnesota, 1905, Scholastic (New York, NY), 2000.
The Journal of C. J. Jackson, a Dust Bowl Migrant: Oklahoma to California, 1935, Scholastic (New York, NY), 2002.

ADAPTATIONS: The Broken Blade was adapted as a cartoon serial published in *Boys' Life* magazine.

WORK IN PROGRESS: The Darkest Evening, scheduled for publication by Scholastic in 2004.

SIDELIGHTS: Making his home on the shores of Minnesota's Lake Vermilion, author and teacher William Durbin shares his enthusiasm and interests in history, golf, and canoeing in the pages of his books for young readers. In addition to biographies of golfing greats Tiger Woods and Arnold Palmer, he has penned a number of works of historical fiction that have been praised by reviewers.

Born in Minneapolis, Minnesota in 1951, Durbin attended St. Cloud University before earning his master's degree at Middlebury College and spending a year at Lincoln College, Oxford on a scholarship from the school's Bread Loaf School of English. Trained as a teacher, he worked for decades as a teacher and mentor to writers at Bread Loaf as well as for those students participating in writing projects sponsored by the National Council of Teachers of English. He was inspired to begin writing for young adults after speaking to author Gary Paulson during the award-winning young-adult writer's workshop appearance at Durbin's wife's school.

Durbin's first book, 1997's *The Broken Blade,* was inspired by his interest in the French *voyageur* fur traders who canoed the waters of the northern Midwest and Canada during the eighteenth and early nineteenth centuries. In the book, which takes place in 1800, Pierre LaPage's father supports his family as an oarsman for the North West Fur Company on the long, heavy voyageur canoes used by fur traders to transport pelts out of northern Canada. When his father is unable to make the trip after severing his thumb in an accident, thirteen-year-old Pierre leaves school, determined to take his place on the 1,200-mile trip from Montreal to Grand Portage that requires incredible physical strength and fortitude. Noting that Durbin fills the novel with action and describes in vivid detail the events that "transform . . . Pierre from classroom-softened boy to hard-muscled man," a *Bulletin of the Center for Children's Books* contributor Elizabeth Bush added that *The Broken Blade* "should appeal to reluctant readers as well as adventure buffs." Dubbing the book "an impressive coming-of-age tale," a *Kirkus* reviewer added that "readers will embrace . . . [Pierre's] path to true bravery, strength of character, and self-reliance."

Wintering, which Durbin published in 1999, finds Pierre once again leaving his home in Montreal and heading north into the Canadian wilds, this time to work at the fur company's winter camp where he learns how to survive the region's brutal conditions with help from the native Ojibwa people. Dealing with the death of two close friends, as well as with the hardships of daily life, allow for a continuation of the coming-of-age theme, according to *Booklist* contributor Susan Dove Lempke, who noted that Durbin's use of period journals and diaries "gives the novel an authentic feel but doesn't overshadow the unfolding story of Pierre's growth and maturation." Dubbing *Wintering* an "engaging sequel," a *Kirkus* reviewer praised the novel as "well-written and atmospheric,"

and packed with "plenty of facts" about how the Native Americans of the Great Lakes region lived.

Durbin has produced several works of historical fiction for Scholastic's "My Name Is America" series. In *The Journal of Sean Sullivan, a Transcontinental Railroad Worker,* he recounts the experiences of a fifteen-year-old Irish immigrant who works alongside his father on the Transcontinental Railroad in 1867. Traveling from state to state across the western territory, Sean writes of conflicts between the railroad and the Plains Indians cowboys, discrimination suffered by Chinese laborers, and extensive financial corruption, creating a narrative that "focuses on historic details to bring the Old West vibrantly alive," according to *Booklist* reviewer Roger Leslie, who dubbed *The Journal of Sean Sullivan* "a rollicking, atmospheric journey" into the past.

The Journal of Otto Peltonen, a Finnish Immigrant takes place in 1905 as fifteen-year-old Otto sails from Finland to America with his mother and sisters to join his father in the iron-rich lands of Minnesota. Working as a miner, Otto finds himself caught up in the early union movement, and joins other workers in a fight for safe working and living conditions in the company-owned shantytowns of Minnesota's Mesabi Iron range. "Historical notes and authentic photos round out this captivating, dramatic view of the past," maintained Leslie in his *Booklist* review. Durbin's third contribution to the "My Name Is America" series, *The Journal of C. J. Jackson, a Dust Bowl Migrant,* focuses on a thirteen year old forced to abandon the family farm during the devastating drought of the late 1920s that forced many Midwest farming families into lives of poverty as migrant workers. Noting that the novel would provide young readers with a good introduction to John Steinbeck's *The Grapes of Wrath, School Library Journal* contributor Ronni Krasnow added that *The Journal of C. J. Jackson* features a "likeable protagonist" and "effectively conveys the plight of Dust Bowl families."

Durbin's stand-alone historical novel *The Song of Sampo Lake* takes place at the turn of the twentieth century, as a Finnish farming family makes their new home in the author's home state of Minnesota. Matti, whose achievements are constantly overshadowed in the eyes of his father by those of his older brother, works as a store clerk and teaches English at the local one-room schoolhouse in addition to working on the family farm. Other works of historical fiction include *Blackwater Ben,* published in 2003.

In addition to writing and teaching, Durbin lectures to school and library groups as well as at writing conferences, and focuses his talk on topics such as how to begin a narrative, how to get published, writing and researching historical fiction, generating ideas through wordplay, and overcoming writers' block.

BIOGRAPHICAL AND CRITICAL SOURCES:

PERIODICALS

Booklist, February 15, 1999, Susan Dove Lempke, review of *Wintering,* p. 1061; October 15, 1999, Roger Leslie, review of *The Journal of Sean Sullivan, a Transcontinental Railroad Worker,* p. 428; October 1, 2000, Roger Leslie, review of *The Journal of Otto Peltonen, a Finnish Immigrant,* p. 332.

Bulletin of the Center for Children's Books, February, 1997, Elizabeth A. Bush, review of *The Broken Blade,* pp. 203-204; April, 1999, Elaine. A. Bearden, review of *Wintering,* p. 276.

Faces, January 2002, review of *The Journal of Otto Peltonen,* p. 46.

Kirkus Reviews, November 15, 1996, review of *The Broken Blade,* p. 1688; December 1, 1998, review of *Wintering,* pp. 1732-1733; October 1, 2000, review of *The Journal of Otto Peltonen,* pp. 1421-1422.

Kliatt, May, 2001, Deane A. Beverly, review of *Wintering,* p. 18.

St. Paul Pioneer Press (St. Paul, MN), November 2, 2000, Mary Ann Grossman, "Fictional Diary Mines the Tumultuous History of the Iron Range."

School Library Journal, September, 2000, Ronni Krasnow, review of *The Journal of C. J. Jackson, a Dust Bowl Migrant,* p. 220.

Voice of Youth Advocates, August, 2000, Nancy Zachary, review of *Tiger Woods,* pp. 202-203; December, 2000, Cindy Lombardo, review of *The Journal of Otto Peltonen,* p. 348.

ONLINE

William Durbin Web site, http://www.williamdurbin. com (May 8, 2003).

DUTKA, June 1943-

PERSONAL: Born June 7, 1943, in Winnipeg, Manitoba, Canada; daughter of Michael Philip and Olga (Andrusyshen) Dutka. *Ethnicity:* "Ukrainian." *Education:* University of Manitoba, B.A., 1964; University of British Columbia, B.L.S., 1966. *Religion:* Ukrainian Catholic.

ADDRESSES: Home—Winnipeg, Manitoba, Canada. *Agent*—c/o Author Mail, Canadian Institute of Ukrainian Studies Press, Department of Slavic Languages and Literature, University of Toronto, 1 Spadina Cres., Room 109, Toronto, Ontario, Canada M5S 2J5.

CAREER: University of Manitoba, Winnipeg, Manitoba, Canada, reference librarian at Elizabeth Dafoe Library, 1966-68, government publications librarian, 1968-69, head of government publications section, 1969-95, libraries' development officer, 1995-98, senior scholar, 1999-2001, librarian emeritus, 2001—. Ukrainian Cultural and Educational Centre, member of board of directors, 1978-81.

MEMBER: Canadian Library Association, Canadian Association of University Teachers, Manitoba Library Association, Gilbert and Society of Winnipeg (member of board of directors, 2002—), Ukrainian Catholic Women's League of Canada, Alumni Association of the University of Manitoba, Friends of the University of Manitoba Libraries.

WRITINGS:

The Grace of Passing: Constantine H. Andrusyshen, the Odyssey of a Slavist, Canadian Institute of Ukrainian Studies Press (Toronto, Ontario, Canada), 2000.

Contributor to books, including *Extraordinary Ordinary Women: Manitoba Women and Their Stories,* edited by Colleen Armstrong, Manitoba Clubs of the Canadian Federation of University Women (Manitoba, Canada), 2000. Contributor of articles and reviews to library journals and other periodicals, including *Canadian Home Economics Journal.*

WORK IN PROGRESS: A book tracing the 100-year history of St. Nicholas Church, the oldest Ukrainian Catholic church in Winnipeg.

SIDELIGHTS: June Dutka told *CA:* "The result of my research and writing, *The Grace of Passing: Constantine H. Andrusyshen, the Odyssey of a Slavist,* fulfills my wish to recreate the main phases of the life and writings of Dr. Constantine Andrusyshen (1907-1983), because he had never written anything autobiographical. Through interviews with his colleagues, former students, and family members, it was interesting for me to gain insight into the social, spiritual, and cultural environment in which he grew up.

"Throughout my story, I attempted to illustrate the high value that immigrants who came to Canada during the early 1900s placed on education. Andrusyshen's chief legacy, the *Ukrainian-English Dictionary,* continues to be popular years after his death. At the time of his death in 1983, Andrusyshen was well known in Canada and abroad as a translator and lexicographer. He was recognized as a key figure in the establishment of Slavic studies in Canadian universities."

BIOGRAPHICAL AND CRITICAL SOURCES:

PERIODICALS

Manitoba History, autumn-winter, 2002-03, James Kominowski, review of *The Grace of Passing: Constantine H. Andrusyshen, the Odyssey of a Slavist.*

*   *   *

DWYER, Michael J(oseph) 1953-

PERSONAL: Born April 3, 1953, in Botwood, Newfoundland, Canada; son of Leo (a master mariner) and Kathleen (Burke) Dwyer; married Beulah B. Freake, 1976; children: Mark, Michelle. *Education:* Attended Memorial University of Newfoundland. *Religion:* Roman Catholic. *Hobbies and other interests:* Outdoor activities (hunting, fishing), karate (black belt).

ADDRESSES: Home—P.O. Box 855, Lewisporte, Newfoundland, Canada A0G 3A0. *E-mail*—dwyer.m@ nf.sympatico.ca.

CAREER: Writer. Also works as truck driver; formerly worked as an official Canadian river guardian.

MEMBER: Newfoundland Karate Association.

WRITINGS:

Over the Side, Mickey: A Sealer's First-Hand Account of the Newfoundland Seal Hunt, Nimbus Publishing (Halifax, Nova Scotia, Canada), 1998.
Sea of Heartbreak: An Extraordinary Account of a Newfoundland Fishing Voyage, Key Porter Books (Toronto, Ontario, Canada), 2001.

Contributor of short stories to periodicals, including *Eastern Woods and Waters* and *Newfoundland Sportsman.*

WORK IN PROGRESS: Gotta Run, a book about trucking.

SIDELIGHTS: Michael J. Dwyer told *CA:* "First of all, writing is not my career. It is more of a pastime. Primarily I make a living driving semi-trucks. I spend some of the in-between time writing.

"I first took writing seriously in 1985 when I was employed by the federal department of fisheries and oceans as a river guardian. My job included writing out information pertaining to poaching violations in which I was involved. This was turned over to Gilmore, the crown prosecutor, for prosecution. The crown prosecutor once said to me, 'Michael, you write out excellent information. Once I have read it, there is not a shadow of doubt in my mind as to what happened.' As fate should have it, five years later I had occasion to charge my fisheries boss with fisheries violations. When I confided in the crown prosecutor, he said, 'Michael, if you feel you are getting the [lousy] end of the stick, write things down. Journals are admissible as evidence in court. The faintest ink is brighter than the sharpest memory, and never put in writing what you don't want the whole world to read.' I took his advice seriously and, although I have received the [lousy] end of the stick to date, I have also accumulated 10,000 pages of my written words.

"I choose to write about what I am involved in. When I went sealing in 1998, my journal went along and I kept a day-to-day record. After the expedition was over and I was recovering from a serious case of cellulitis, I decided to write about the expedition for my own cleansing and peace of mind. When I put the last period onto the first draft, I felt cleansed and relieved, and lucky to be alive. Safety for the sealers was important to me, so to get the message out hopefully to improve safety conditions aboard sealing ships (that haven't changed much for the better since the 1800s), I decided to send the draft to a publisher. Of the three I contacted, Nimbus Publishing of Halifax thought it was a good story. I was thrilled, to say the least, and I am still grateful.

"In April, 1999, a film crew from Focus Television in Germany came to Newfoundland to interview me. I hired a boat for them, and they interviewed me while standing on a floating ice pan with the lighthouse on Surgeon's Cove Head, Exploits Island, beaming in the background. Jurgen, the producer, said that it was the most enjoyable assignment he ever undertook, and the awesome beauty of the grounded iceberg that we circled and filmed took his breath away. The twenty-minute film was shown on German television, but I never heard anything about it or viewed the documentary.

"My writing process involved my journals, both current and old. I find that just to write a little can focus my mind on the events about which I am writing. First, I blurt it all out without considering punctuation, paragraphs, or spelling. When that is on the computer screen, I walk away and think about it for a time. Then I correct the mistakes and add things that I have thought about or add things that I think about as I go along. Then I print it. It is that moment that I like because, regardless of what it is like, I have it in my hand and it's saved on my computer. I sit with a pencil and try to edit. Then I let it sit. A few days later I will compute the corrections and additions and start something else.

"I suggest to anyone, if he/she lives through any kind of interesting event, to write things down. If you have the nucleus of a good story, a good editor will see it. Together you can write a good story that will sell. A good editor is as important to a wanna-be writer as a producer is to a wanna-be movie star. You find good editors at publishing firms, and there are plenty of publishing firms, so don't give up. Even if it doesn't get off the ground, for sure your grandchildren will find it interesting. Maybe they will get it published for you."

BIOGRAPHICAL AND CRITICAL SOURCES:

PERIODICALS

Chronicle Herald (Halifax, Nova Scotia, Canada), May 27, 2001, Bruce Erskine, review of *Sea of Heartbreak: An Extraordinary Account of a Newfoundland Fishing Voyage.*

Downhomer, July 1, 2001, John Crane, review of *Sea of Heartbreak,* p. 102.

New Brunswick Reader, June 23, 2001, Kate Rutherford, review of *Sea of Heartbreak.*

Pilot (Lewisporte, Newfoundland, Canada), November 18, 1998, Linda Skinner, review of *Over the Side, Mickey: A Sealer's First-Hand Account of the Newfoundland Seal Hunt,* p. 3.

Western Star, November 18, 1998, Pamela Gill, review of *Over the Side, Mickey,* p. 17.

E

EDLER, Richard (Bruce) 1943-2002

PERSONAL: Born November 23, 1943, in Chicago, IL; died of a heart attack February 16, 2002, in Palos Verdes, CA; son of Francis and Kathryn (Merryweather) Edler; married; wife's name, Kitty; children: Mark (died 1992), Rick. *Education:* University of Iowa, B.A. (English), 1965, M.B.A., 1969.

CAREER: General Electric, Schenectady, NY, copywriter, 1965-67; Procter & Gamble, Cincinnati, OH, brand manager, 1969-74; Ketchum Communications, San Francisco, CA, senior vice president, 1974-81; Doyle Dane Bernbach, Los Angeles, CA, president, 1981—; R. B. Edler & Company, Los Angeles, founder and president.

WRITINGS:

If I Knew Then What I Know Now: CEOs and Other Smart Executives Share Wisdom They Wish They'd Been Told Twenty-five Years Ago, G. P. Putnam's (New York, NY), 1995.

Author of *Into the Valley and out Again.*

SIDELIGHTS: Richard Edler's *If I Knew Then What I Know Now: CEOs and Other Smart Executives Share Wisdom They Wish They'd Been Told Twenty-five Years Ago* contains advice on business and life from many top business leaders in entertainment, advertising, politics, television, religion, publishing, and other areas. A *Publishers Weekly* contributor noted, "This conversationally written book would make a fine gift for an ambitious and philosophical friend."

BIOGRAPHICAL AND CRITICAL SOURCES:

PERIODICALS

Publishers Weekly, November 6, 1995, review of *If I Knew Then What I Know Now: CEOs and Other Smart Executives Share Wisdom They Wish They'd Been Told Twenty-five Years Ago,* p. 77.
Sales & Marketing Management, April, 1996, Brian Silverman, review of *If I Knew Then What I Know Now,* p. 93.
South Florida Business Journal, March 30, 2001, review of *If I Knew Then What I Know Now,* p. 8.

OBITUARIES:

PERIODICALS

Adweek Western Advertising News, February 25, 2002, Rebecca Flass, "Ad Veteran Edler Dies," p. 6.
Los Angeles Times, February 26, 2002, Elaine Woo, "Richard B. Edler, 68; Ad Industry Leader Helped Bereaved Parents," p. B11.*

*   *   *

EDWARD, John

PERSONAL: Born John Maggee, Jr., in Long Island, NY; son of John (a police officer) and Perinda Magee; married; wife's name, Sandra. *Education:* Degree in public administration and health-care administration.

ADDRESSES: Office—P.O. Box 383, Huntington, NY 11743; fax: 631-547-6775. *E-mail*—jecustomsvc@aol.com.

CAREER: Psychic medium and writer. Worked as a laboratory blood technician, ballroom dance instructor, and in hospital management; host of syndicated television series *Crossing over with John Edward,* beginning 2000; guest on television programs, including *Life Afterlife,* Home Box Office (HBO), 1999. Producer of audio series *Developing Your Own Psychic Powers.*

WRITINGS:

One Last Time: A Psychic Medium Speaks to Those We Have Loved and Lost, Berkley Books (New York, NY), 1998.
What If God Were the Sun? (novel), Jodere Group (San Diego, CA), 2000.
Crossing Over: The Stories behind the Stories, Jodere Group (San Diego, CA), 2001.

ADAPTATIONS: Crossing Over was adapted for audio.

SIDELIGHTS: John Edward has written about his life in both *One Last Time: A Psychic Medium Speaks to Those We Have Loved and Lost* and *Crossing Over: The Stories behind the Stories.* The latter is based on his experiences in producing the syndicated television series *Crossing Over with John Edward.*

Born on Long Island, New York, Edward claimed he was an ordinary child, except for the fact that he had out-of-body experiences and visions of dead relatives he had never met, and could predict visitors and phone calls before they occurred. His mother was a believer in the paranormal and held group meetings in their home. It was through his mother's salons that he met Lydia Clar in 1985, a psychic who mentored the boy she felt had special gifts. Edward first read palms and tarot cards, and worked in a laboratory and as a ballroom dance instructor. He learned to dance at Arthur Murray from his wife, Sandra, who taught there. Edward established a career in hospital management, where he remained until his work as a psychic developed into a full-time job.

An *Entertainment Weekly* contributor wrote that "psychics certainly aren't new, but Edward has mainstreamed readings with his regular-Joe approach. . . .

His unique delivery aside, however, Edward's readings are similar to the ones psychics have been giving since Nostradamus. He gets information 'seeing, hearing, and feeling energy,' and though his details are sometimes fuzzy, he nearly always concludes with a clear message of forgiveness or love from the dearly departed. Thus, skeptics have been dissecting his routine . . . just as they have since Nostradamus." The writer noted that skeptics "commonly accuse of Edward of relying on a classic technique called cold reading: using a host of assumptions, generalizations, and subtle manipulations to lead someone into thinking you are 'hitting' many of their private memories. . . . Edward insists he's fine with people not believing in communicating with the dead, but he's insulted when they call him a fraud."

One Last Time is Edward's memoir of how he accepted his power and acted on it to help the living communicate with the dead. He explains how the spirits communicate to him through sounds, voices, smells, tastes, images, sensations, and symbolism. A *Publishers Weekly* contributor wrote that Edward "offers an intriguing collection of anecdotes that may not convince the cynical but that can both comfort and fascinate the merely skeptical."

Crossing Over is also a memoir in which Edward talks about specific experiences, what motivates him, and the rough spots he had to overcome in his career. *Salon.com* contributor Shari Waxman reviewed the book and wrote that Edward "is more than a psychic medium: he is also a master statistician. The smoke and mirrors behind his self-processed ability to communicate with the dead is a simple application of the laws of probability. Basically, if you keep trying something whose results are independent, your odds of getting your desired result increase."

Waxman pointed out that the book includes descriptions of Edward's more notable readings. "The careful plucking of successes from a mass of attempts is a technique used in Edward's television show as well. The creation of each half-hour episode requires six hours of taping. Do the math. Yet it works. I prefer to believe Edward's fans are not unintelligent, but simply in need of something to believe in, to feel good about, or to relieve the anxiety of what cannot be controlled. If he is fulfilling these needs, then in some ways, his gig is legit."

Entertainment Weekly contributor Noah Robischon noted that Gary Schwartz, founder of the Human

Energy Systems Laboratory and a Harvard-trained psychologist "found that mediums attempting to communicate with the dead were accurate more often than control subjects. And Edward is sure enough of his own abilities to brush off his detractors. Confidence, by the way, is one of the true hallmarks of a successful psychic."

But many are believers. Edward began by working at psychic fairs and developed a following of people who requested private readings. He appeared on radio shows on both coasts, and his television show first aired on the Sci Fi Channel in 2000. It was quickly syndicated and distributed on both sides of the Atlantic. He has appeared on many nationally televised shows, including *Entertainment Tonight Dateline,* and *Larry King,* and, in addition to his own very successful stage appearances and sold-out seminars, Edward's books and instructional tapes do very well. His waiting list for private readings became so long, that he was forced to stop taking names.

Edward, who lost his own mother to cancer, writes about such a loss in his novel, *What If God Were the Sun?* Timothy Callahan has a large, loving Italian-American family watched over by his mother, who is dying of cancer. As she deteriorates, he reflects on the existence of a welcoming afterlife where she will be reunited with loved ones. Sharon Galligar Chance reviewed the book for *BookBrowser* online, saying that "Edward's main point is to pass along the message of letting the important people in your life know that you are there for them in this lifetime. He offers a comforting message that love can bridge even death. . . . I was personally touched by this sensitive story."

BIOGRAPHICAL AND CRITICAL SOURCES:

BOOKS

Edward, John, *Crossing Over: The Stories behind the Stories,* Jodere Group (San Diego, CA), 2001.
Edward, John, *One Last Time: A Psychic Medium Speaks to Those We Have Loved and Lost,* Berkley Books (New York, NY), 1998.

PERIODICALS

Entertainment Weekly, September 14, 2001, "Tomb Reader," p. 57; September 21, 2001, Noah Robischon, "Dead End? TV Psychic John Edward claims That He Can Communicate with the Dead."

John Edward Home Page, http://www.johnedward.net (March 24, 2003).
People, May 6, 2002, Tom Gliatto, Natasha Stoynoff, "Medium Rare: Skeptics Howl, but TV Psychic John Edward Says He Hears Dead People," p. 85.
Publishers Weekly, November 16, 1998, review of *One Last Time: A Psychic Medium Speaks to Those We Have Loved and Lost,* p. 63.
Skeptical Inquirer, November, 2001, Joe Nickell, "John Edward: Hustling the Bereaved," p. 19.
Teen People, March 1, 2002, "The Great Communicator" (interview), p. 76.
Time, March 5, 2001, Leon Jaroff, "Talking to the Dead," p. 52.

ONLINE

BookBrowser, http://www.bookbrowser.com/ (May 11, 2002), Sharon Galligar Chance, review of *What If God Were the Sun?*
Salon.com, http://www.salon.com/ (June 13, 2002), Shari Waxman, review of *Crossing Over: The Stories behind the Stories.*
Sci Fi, http://www.scifi.com/ (January 2, 2003).*

*   *   *

EDWARDS, Gwynne

PERSONAL: Male. *Hobbies and other interests:* Spanish cinema, seventeenth-and twentieth-century Spanish theatre.

ADDRESSES: Agent—c/o Author's Mail, Oxford University Press, Great Clarerdon St., Oxford OX2 6DP, England.

CAREER: Writer.

MEMBER: Association of Hispanists of Great Britain and Northern Ireland, Anales de la Litertura Espanola (member, advisory board), Romance Studies (member, advisory board), Liverpool Monographs in Hispanic Literature (member, advisory board).

WRITINGS:

(Editor) Pedro Calderon de la Barca, *Los cabellos de Absalon,* Pergamon Press (Oxford, England), 1973.

The Prison and the Labyrinth: Studies in Tragedy, University of Wales Press (Cardiff, Wales), 1978.

The Discreet Art of Luis Bunuel: A Reading of His Films, Marion Boyars (London, England), 1982.

Dramatists in Perspective: Spanish Theatre in the Twentieth Century, St. Martin's Press (New York, NY), 1985.

(Translator) Tirso de Molina, *The Trickster of Seville and the Stone Guest,* Aris and Phillips (Warminster, England), 1986.

(Translator with Peter Luke) Federico Garcia Lorca, *Three Plays,* Methuen (London, England), 1987.

Lorca: The Theatre beneath the Sand, Marion Boyars (London, England), 1987.

(Translator) Francisco Ors, Sastre, Jaime Salom, Antonio Vallejo, *Burning the Curtain: Four Revolutionary Spanish Plays* (contains *Contradance, Tragic Prelude, Two Sides to Dr. Valmy's Story,* and *Almost a Goddess*) Marion Boyars (London, England), 1995.

Indecent Exposures: Bunuel, Saura, Erice, and Almodovar, Marion Boyars (London, England), 1995.

(Translator) Federico Garcia Lorca, *Blood Wedding,* Methuen (London, England), 1997.

(Translator) Lope de Vega, *Fuenta Ovejuna; The Knight from Olmedo; Punishment without Revenge,* Oxford University Press (Oxford, England), 1999.

(With Ken Haas) *Flamenco!* Thames and Hudson (New York, NY), 2000.

Almodovar: Labyrinths of Passion, Peter Owen (London, England), 2001.

SIDELIGHTS: Gwynne Edwards is a research professor, an author, and a scholar of Spanish theatre and film. In addition to translating many Spanish playwrights such as Federico Garcia Lorca, Lope de Vega, and Tirso de Molina into English, he has also published numerous critical books on Spanish theatre and film in general. Outside of the academic world, Edwards frequently lends his expertise to theatre productions.

The author began his varied career in 1973 editing the Pedro Calderon play, *Los cabellos de Absalon.* He published *The Prison and the Labyrinth: Studies in Tragedy* in 1978, a study of six Calderon plays that examines the role of chance in the lives of the plays' heroes and heroines. Edwards observes that seeming accidents result in large complications for Calderon's characters, while their actions play a somewhat lesser role. One reviewer writing for Choice commented,

"Both major and minor characters are closely studied through the dramatic action and dialogue to show the interplay of human nature (or identity) and chance or accident in bringing about the labyrinth/prison that ensnares the tragic individual(s)." Melveena McKendrick, writing about the book for *Modern Language Review,* noted, "I cannot . . . see that Dr. Edwards's book makes anything but a very positive contribution to Calderon studies."

Edwards' next work, *The Discreet Art of Luis Bunuel: A Reading of His Films,* published in 1982, provides biographical information on the acclaimed Spanish film director and surrealist Luis Bunuel and discusses thematic elements in Bunuel's oeuvre.

Dramatists in Perspective: Spanish Theatre in the Twentieth Century, published in 1985, provides overviews of a series of Spanish playwrights and their work. The book asserts that such dramatists as Lorca, Buero Vallejo, Sastre, Valle-Inclan, and Alberti chose to turn away from the commercial theatre and follow a more European model. Joan T. Cain, reviewing the book for *World Literature Today,* observed, "Edwards has achieved his stated goal. My only criticism is that at times he seems to be straining to attain it; the result is one of unnecessary repetition." However, a reviewer in *Choice* wrote, "Edwards' clearly written text offers a highly informative introduction to a national theater remarkably little studied in the English-speaking world."

Edwards' next two publications were translations. The first was Tirso de Molina's *The Trickster of Seville and The Stone Guest* 1986, and the second, *Three Plays* (1987), which includes Federico Garcia Lorca's *Blood Wedding, Dona Rosita the Spinster,* and *Yerma.*

Lorca: The Theatre beneath the Sand, published in 1987, includes detailed descriptions and discussions of the entire body of Lorca's work. The book describes Lorca's political views as well as his biography, illustrating how his personal experiences influenced his theatrical writings. A childhood fascination with marionettes provided lifelong inspiration. Although a reviewer writing for *Choice* claimed, "In fact, Edwards leans rather heavily on Lima, Nadal, and other critics for his own analytical observations," Edward F. Stanton in an article for *World Literature Today* explained, "Yet this book is so scrupulously composed that it will be useful to anyone who opens its covers, especially to those interested in staging Lorca's plays."

Published in 1995, *Burning the Curtain: Four Revolutionary Spanish Plays* features translations of Francisco Ors' *Contradance,* Jaime Salom's *Almost a Goddess,* Sastre's *Tragic Prelude,* and Antonio Vallejo's *Two Sides to Dr. Valmy's Story.* Edwards' fifth book, released the same year, *Indecent Exposures: Bunuel, Saura, Erice, and Almodovar,* surveys the lives of four celebrated filmmakers.

Gwynne drafted a second translation of Lorca's *Blood Wedding* in 1997 and, two years later, completed translation of three Lope de Vega's plays, *Fuenta Ovejuna; The Knight from Olmedo; Punishment without Revenge.*

Appearing in 2000, *Flamenco!* describes the history of the fiery Spanish flamenco dance and provides information on the various cultures that influenced the dance's changing face over several centuries. Patricia Griggs, contributing a review to *American Music Teacher,* commended, "This book would appeal to the connoisseur and the aficionado of flamenco history and music."

Edwards' next effort, *Almodovar: Labyrinths of Passion,* discusses each film produced by Spanish director and Academy Award winner Pedro Almodovar. Films *Tie Me up, Tie Me Down!, Women on the Verge of a Nervous Breakdown,* and *Flower of My Secret* are discussed. The book provides samples of Spanish reviews of Almodovar's films as well as behind-the-scenes stories concerning budgets, film plots, and thematic discussions. The book also provides a biography of the artist. In a review for *Library Journal,* Adriana Lopez noted, "A handy filmography, bibliography, and index make this book an important, up-to-date study for both devotees and newcomers to Almodovar's over-the-top dramas."

Edwards, a research professor at the University of Wales, has been involved in many professional translations. He continues to assist in actual stage productions.

BIOGRAPHICAL AND CRITICAL SOURCES:

PERIODICALS

American Music Teacher, June, 2001, Patricia Griggs, review of *Flamenco!* p. 108.

Choice, November, 1985, S. L. Gaggi, review of *Dramatists in Perspective: Spanish Theatre in the Twentieth Century,* p. 460; April, 1981, review of *Lorca: The Theatre beneath the Sand,* p. 1106; September, 1979, review of *The Prison and the Labyrinth: Studies in Tragedy,* p. 843.

Library Journal, March 15, 2002, Adriana Lopez, review of *Almodovar: Labyrinths of Passion,* p. 82.

Modern Language Review, October, 1980, Melveena McKendrick, review of *The Prison and the Labyrinth: Studies in Tragedy,* p. 916.

World Literature Today, 1981, Edward F. Stanton, review of *Lorca: The Theatre beneath the Sand,* p. 439; 1987, Joan T. Cain, review of *Dramatists in Perspective: Spanish Theatre in the Twentieth Century,* p. 255.*

*   *   *

ELLIS, Stephen 1953-

PERSONAL: Born June 13, 1953, in Nottingham, England; son of Derek Hugh John and Hilda Mary (Kingscote). *Education:* Oxford University, B.A., 1975, Ph.D., 1981.

ADDRESSES: Office—Afrika-Studiecentrum, Leiden University, P.O. Box 9555, 2300 RB Leiden, Netherlands.

CAREER: Amnesty International, London, England, researcher 1982-86; *Africa Confidential,* London, editor, 1986-91; Afrika-Studiecentrum, Leiden, Netherlands, director, 1991-94, senior researcher, 1994—.

WRITINGS:

The Rising of the Red Shawls: A Revolt in Madagascar, 1895-1899, Cambridge University Press (Cambridge, England), 1985.

(With Tsepo Sechaba) *Comrades against Apartheid: The ANC and the South African Communist Party in Exile,* Indiana University Press (Bloomington, IN), 1992.

(Editor) *Africa Now: People, Policies, and Institutions,* Heinemann (Portsmouth, NH), 1996.

(With Jean-François Bayart and Beatrice Hibou) *The Criminalization of the State in Africa,* Indiana University Press (Bloomington, IN), 1999.

The Mask of Anarchy: The Destruction of Liberia and the Religious Dimension of an African Civil War, New York University Press (New York, NY), 1999.

SIDELIGHTS: Stephen Ellis is a researcher and historian who has made the political struggles of African nations the center of his studies since the early 1980s. In books examining political uprisings in Madagascar, South Africa, Liberia, and other African countries, Ellis has made his career as an expert on modern African history and contemporary African politics.

Ellis's first study of African resistance movements is *The Rising of the Red Shawls: A Revolt in Madagascar, 1895-1899,* from 1985. Drawing from research in Madagascar as well as France and Britain, Ellis examines the late nineteenth-century insurrection against French colonizers in Madagascar, focusing on the unusual and disorganized character of the revolt itself. Ellis's first book was considered by many reviewers to be a valuable contribution to the study of this complicated event. In *Choice,* reviewer N. R. Bennett called *The Rising of the Red Shawls* "the most sophisticated English-language account yet published" on the subject. In the *American Historical Review,* Edward I. Steinhart said that Ellis's deft handling of the controversial relationship between the Merina kingdom and the French government "stands out as a high point of the book."

In his next work Ellis moved to a different time and place, studying the relationship between the African National Congress (ANC) and the South African Communist Party (SACP) in the 1992 book *Comrades against Apartheid: The ANC and the South African Communist Party in Exile.* Outlawed in the 1950s, the SACP was forced into hiding, working through other organizations. Ellis portrays the SACP acting in secrecy to gain total control of the ANC, and challenged in this aim by competing ethnic factions within the ANC as well as policies against non-African participation. Writing in *Foreign Affairs,* Gail M. Gerhart called the book "the most original contribution in a decade" on the subject of South African politics. Discussing Ellis's interpretation of the SACP's influ-

ence in the struggle against apartheid, *Choice* reviewer S. Mozaffar wrote that Ellis's account is "indispensable," providing a more complex and nuanced picture of the internal strife within the organizations than earlier histories had accomplished. By contrast, in the *New Statesman and Society,* reviewer Victoria Brittain maintained that Ellis's book is seriously marred by his "relentlessly hostile" portrait of the SACP.

Ellis also contributed to two publications in the growing body of African studies. In 1996 Ellis edited *Africa Now: People, Policies, Institutions,* a collection of essays by African scholars, many of which had never appeared before in English. Reviewing the book for the *Journal of Modern African Studies,* Richard J. Payne characterized *Africa Now* as a useful and informative text for students and for "politicians and decision-makers in both the public and private sectors, as well as people in business and workers in non-governmental organizations." Ellis provided a conclusion to the collection. Ellis also contributed to Jean-François Bayard's *Criminalization of the State in Africa* of 1999, collaborating in parts and providing a chapter on South Africa. The authors argue that African governments have become by their nature criminal, a controversial and difficult-to-establish thesis. Reviewer Eghosa E. Osaghae, writing in the *International Journal of African Historical Studies* suggested that like others of Bayart's works, *Criminalization of the State in Africa* betrays a paternalistic and racist approach to African studies. Osaghae criticized "the falsehood and veiled racism" of Bayart's analysis, but also said that Ellis's work on South Africa is distinct from Bayart's in its emphasis on "economic decline, forces of liberalization, and globalization" as important factors in the failure of certain African governments.

In his 1999 book *The Mask of Anarchy* Ellis narrows his focus to the state of Liberia and the civil war of 1989-97, providing both a history of the complicated event and an analysis of the role religion and beliefs about the supernatural played in the war. Western observers were generally horrified at the news of war and of video releases detailing gruesome human sacrifice and cannibalism at the center of the political conflict; stereotypes about primitive rural tribes and devil worship confounded most efforts at understanding. Ellis's study attempts to clarify the connection between religion and politics. Christopher Clapham, in the *Times Literary Supplement,* concluded that, in the context Ellis described, the cannibalistic practices of Liberian warriors "become readily comprehensible as means by which young soldiers, escaping from the constraints placed on the exercise of spiritual power in pre-war society, sought to garner this power in their own right." By contrast, Adewale Maja-Pearce, in the *London Review of Books,* criticized Ellis for portraying cannibalism and other practices as "illustrious and time-honoured indigenous traditions." On the whole, however, several reviewers called Ellis's history of the conflict a valuable contribution to a vexing problem. Charles Piot, writing for the *Journal of the Royal Anthropological Institute,* called the book "fascinating and provocative," Maja-Pearce described *The Mask of Anarchy* as "meticulously detailed," and Paul Richards, in the *Journal of African History,* said Ellis's history was "reliable." Clapham wrote that Ellis's analysis in *The Mask of Anarchy* "has profound implications not just for Liberia but for a much broader understanding of African politics."

BIOGRAPHICAL AND CRITICAL SOURCES:

PERIODICALS

Africa, summer, 2000, Donal B. Cruise O'Brien, review of *The Mask of Anarchy,* p. 520.
American Historical Review, 1986, Edward I. Steinhart, review of *The Rising of the Red Shawls,* pp. 972-973.
British Book News, June, 1985, Richard Brown, review of *The Rising of the Red Shawls,* p. 378.
Choice, February, 1986, N. R. Bennett, review of *The Rising of the Red Shawls,* p. 910; June, 1992, S. Mozaffar, review of *Comrades against Apartheid,* pp. 1606-1607.
Economist, August 7, 1999, "First Bad, Now Worse," p. 72; March 18, 2000, "The Spirits of War," p. 6.
Foreign Affairs, 1992, Gail M. Gerhart, review of *Comrades against Apartheid,* pp. 218-219.
International Affairs, April, 1996, Alex de Waal, review of *Africa Now,* p. 415; April, 1999, Patrick Chabal, review of *The Criminalization of the State in Africa,* pp. 441-443.
International Journal of African Historical Studies, spring/summer, 1999, Eghosa E. Osaghae, review of *The Criminalization of the State in Africa,* pp. 465-466.
Journal of African History, May, 1994, Maynard Swanson, review of *Comrades against Apartheid,*

pp. 331-332; January, 2001, Paul Richards, "'Witches,' 'Cannibals,' and War in Liberia," p. 167.
Journal of Economic Literature, September, 1996, review of *Africa Now,* pp. 1487-1488.
Journal of Modern African Studies, September, 1997, Richard J. Payne, review of *Africa Now,* pp. 519-20; September, 1999, John A. Wiseman, review of *The Criminalization of the State in Africa,* pp. 560-562.
Journal of the Royal Anthropological Institute, December, 2000, Charles Piot, review of *The Mask of Anarchy,* p. 745.
London Review of Books, July 25, 2002, Adewale Maja-Pearce, "Feed the Charm," pp. 23-26.
New Statesman and Society, March 6, 1992, Victoria Brittain, "Secret History," pp. 45-56.
Times Literary Supplement, June 7, 1985, review of *The Rising of the Red Shawls,* p. 632; March 17, 2000, Christopher Clapham, "Modern War and Ancient Powers," p. 30f.*

*   *   *

EMMETT, Rita

PERSONAL: Born April 12, in Chicago, IL; daughter of Tom Dorney (a businessman) and Helen Fischer (a waitress); married Bruce Karder (news video editor), May 21, 1994; children: Robb, Kerry Emmett. *Ethnicity:* "Irish, Ukrainian." *Education:* Northeastern Illinois University, B.A. (English, psychology); National Louis University, M.S. (adult education), 1985. *Religion:* Christian. *Hobbies and other interests:* Travel, writing, family, friends.

ADDRESSES: Home—2331 Eastview Dr., Des Plaines, IL 60018. *Agent*—Jane Jordan Browne, Multimedia Product Development, 410 S. Michigan Ave., Chicago, IL 60605. *E-mail*—Remmett412@aol.com.

CAREER: Author and lecturer. Leyden Family Service, Franklin Park, IL, public relations, 1977-95; Emmett Enterprises, Inc., Des Plaines, IL, professional speaker, 1995—.

MEMBER: Chicago Speakers Alliance, National Speakers Association, New Century Club, American Society of Training and Development, Professional Communicator's Roundtable, Off-Campus Writer's Workshop.

WRITINGS:

The Procrastinator's Handbook: Mastering the Art of Doing It Now, Walker (New York, NY), 2000.
The Procrastinating Child: A Handbook for Adults to Help Children Stop Putting Things Off, Walker and Company (New York, NY), 2002.

SIDELIGHTS: Rita Emmett describes herself as a "recovering procrastinator," and it is this experience that forms the foundation for her books. She has had a long career as an educator and in public relations. Emmett earned a license to teach Parent Effectiveness Training and has certification for Systematic Training for Effectiveness Training. She has been involved for several years in parenting seminars through a social service agency in the Chicago area. Motivated by a job offer that required a bachelor's degree; she abandoned her habit of procrastination and got a B.A. from Northeastern Illinois University in English and psychology. In 1985 she was awarded a master's degree in adult education from Louis National University. She is regarded as an effective public speaker and often conducts seminars on procrastination for various organizations. Her clients include: Big Brothers/Big Sisters, the American Lung Association, and Lucent Technologies.

Emmett's first book, *The Procrastinator's Handbook: Mastering the Art of Doing It Now,* grew out of her own experience with procrastination. In an interview published in the *Seattle Times,* she described chronic procrastination as a behavioral problem rather than a character defect. Procrastination as a stress-producing behavior is described in some detail. Unattended it can result in financial, emotional, and physical stress for the individual and have a correspondingly negative effect on the environment. Emmett argues that procrastination often takes hold as a response to an uninteresting or intimidating project, feelings of being overwhelmed and fear not only of failure but also of success. The author takes a practical approach to bringing about the desired behavioral change, spending a minimal amount of ink on the psychological explanations for chronic procrastination. She has many positive suggestions for attacking those jobs that are so often delayed. Approaching these activities in a structured manner, so that the task is broken down into manageable segments is emphasized. She uses a humorous, gentle tone and recommends rewarding

oneself after the successful completion of an unappealing task. The light and unintimidating style is sustained by chapter headings such as "Clutter Busters," "Fears That Stop You Cold", and "How to Make Boring Jobs More Enjoyable". The book has been praised for the author's common sense approach to ending the paralysis of procrastination. The reviews have been positive.

Emmett, through her work as a parent effectiveness trainer, is familiar with the obstacles parents face when trying to help a child overcome an unproductive habit. In *The Procrastinating Child: A Handbook for Adults to Help Children Stop Putting Things Off,* she addresses problems frequently faced by parents. The author, as in her previous book, uses a friendly approach to assist parents in understanding why children procrastinate. In a review of the book in *Publishers Weekly* Emmett was praised for making the observation that schools almost never include time-management skills in the curriculum. In addition to this, children are often confused and afraid to make mistakes. With these factors in mind, the author makes suggestions designed to divide tasks into manageable segments, teaching techniques of task and time management. Each chapter ends with a helpful summary. This book is a contribution to Emmett's work in the area of teaching parenting skills. In *The Procrastinating Child,* parents and children are offered the means to change a bad habit into something efficient and productive.

BIOGRAPHICAL AND CRITICAL SOURCES:

PERIODICALS

Booklist, September 1, 2002, Vanessa Bush, review of *The Procrastinating Child: A Handbook for Adults to Help Children Stop Putting Things Off,* p. 35.
Christian Science Monitor, October 4, 2000, Jennifer Wolcott, review of *The Procrastinator's Handbook: Mastering the Art of Doing It Now,* p. 16.
Health Science, spring, 2001, review of *The Procrastinator's Handbook,* p. 33.
Publishers Weekly, August 21, 2000, review of *The Procrastinator's Handbook,* p. 66; August 5, 2002, review of *The Procrastinating Child,* p. 70.
Seattle Times, September 28, 2000, Mark Rahner, review of *The Procrastinator's Handbook,* p. G1; November 5, 2002, Stephanie Dunnewind, review of *The Procrastinating Child,* p. E4.
Time, September 23, 2002, Carole Buia, review of *The Procrastinating Child,* p. 83.

ONLINE

Rita Emmett Home Page, http://www.ritaemmett.com (December 17, 2002).

*   *   *

ENGELBERG, Stephen 1958-

PERSONAL: Born 1958. *Education:* Attended Princeton University.

ADDRESSES: Office—Managing Editor, *The Oregonian,* 1320 Soutwest Broadway, Portland, OR 97201. *E-mail*—sengelberg@news.Oregonian.com.

CAREER: Journalist. *New York Times,* New York, NY, reporter and editor; *Oregonian,* Portland, OR, currently managing editor.

AWARDS, HONORS: Pulitzer Prize for explanatory journalism (with Adam Bryant and Matthew L. Wald of the *New York Times),* 1996, for coverage of deficient safety regulation of commuter air traffic.

WRITINGS:

(With Judith Miller and William Broad) *Germs: Biological Weapons and America's Secret War,* Simon and Schuster (New York, NY), 2001.

SIDELIGHTS: Stephen Engelberg is a Pulitzer Prize-winning journalist who has covered critical news stories for the *New York Times* over several decades. In both his role as a reporter and later as an editor, he has been involved in most major national stories that have affected the United States and the world. In the 1980s, he covered the Iran-Contra Affair. In the 1990s, as the *New York Times* bureau chief in Warsaw, Poland, he reported on the outbreak of war in Yugoslavia. Later in that same decade, he investigated, among other things, the failings of the Immigration and Naturalization Service and President Clinton's Whitewater case. Not only did he win a Pulitzer Prize for his investigation of the safety defects in commuter air traffic, but as editor, he also led several teams of reporters who went on to win Pulitzers of their own. These stories included coverage of drug rings in Mexico and American transfers of high technology to China. The rise of Osama bin Laden's al Qaeda network was another significant subject that he and his team of reporters researched for over five years in an attempt to understand the origins of Islamic terrorism. In 2001, before the destruction of the World Trade Center buildings and the delivery of deadly anthrax spores to several prominent locations in the United States, Engelberg, together with two of his colleagues, wrote a book about the threat of biological warfare.

Not many books captured as much public attention as Engelberg's work *Germs: Biological Weapons and America's Secret War* did in the days immediately following September 11, 2001. Long reviews in many of the major U.S. magazines attest to the concern that the book aroused. The book covers not only the threat of biological warfare but also the United States' involvement in the development of such weapons.

Biological weaponry was ironically borne from scientific discoveries meant to promote good health and thus prevent premature death. These discoveries began with Robert Koch and Louis Pasteur's accomplishments during the nineteenth century, which proved the theory that germs cause disease. In 1905 Koch won the Nobel Prize in medicine, and it was also Koch who first described the life cycle of what is now known as anthrax. During warfare in the 1930s and 1940s, Japan dropped crude anthrax bombs in Manchuria; when Japan surrendered, the United States granted immunity from war-crime convictions to several high-ranking Japanese officers in exchange for information on biological weapons. Thus, the threat of biological warfare was begun.

In 1942 the United States began a full-fledged development program of anthrax, which would be capable of producing one million to one million and a half four-pound anthrax bombs per month by 1944. The war ended before the actual production began. However, during the cold war of the 1950s, the United States again considered the mass production of anthrax, to be used as a weapon against the Soviet Union. Due to the fact that scientists could not prove the effectiveness of such a weapon, the plan was again dropped. However, new tests were made on different types of infectious germs. The U.S. military reportedly used conscientious objectors and animals to test their theories.

In the 1960s Cuba became the imagined target for the United States for possible biological warfare; but when President Richard Nixon came into office in 1969, he ordered a review of the military's biological and chemical weapons programs. Six months later Nixon issued a memorandum that called for a renunciation of all such programs. In a quote reprinted in Matthew Meselson's *New York Review* report, Nixon stated: "Mankind already carries in its hands too many of the seed of its own destruction." In 1993, a total ban of all biological weapons was imposed by the international Chemical Weapons Convention, approved by 174 countries, excluding Egypt, Iraq, North Korea, Lebanon, Libya, and Syria, to name a few.

Engelberg's book *Germs,* wrote Thomas R. Eddlem for the *New American,* "serves as a helpful and well-written primer on the 20th-century history of biological weapons." Eddlem also believed that the authors of this book should be commended for "almost anticipating the post-September 11th terrorist world," since *Germs* was actually in book stores before the terrorist attacks in New York City and Washington, DC. Engelberg and his coauthors, wrote Eddlem, also made it known that there were "non-state terrorist—mentioning Osama bin Laden by name," who were in possession of biological weapons.

Michael Massing, in the *Nation,* also noted the timeliness of the publication of *Germs.* However, he was a little more critical of the ironic twist of events. Although he wrote: Engelberg and his coauthors have "contributed some sharp stories about the lax security in Russia's remaining labs and about America's lack of preparedness for dealing with a biological attack," Massing was concerned that continuing coverage of these stories by reporters could possible be tainted by their also having a book to promote. "They face the constant temptation of covering events [for the newspaper] in a way that promotes their book." The authors, according to Massing might, for instance, "get locked into pushing a particular story line and relying on a fixed set of sources." Howard Markel, of *Harper's* took a different stance by stating that Engelberg and his coauthors of *Germs* "have ably assembled cold, hard epidemiological facts that cannot be refuted." Markel also described *Germs* as being as much an "inspirational" work of scientific progress as much as it is a book of "'cautionary tales.'"

BIOGRAPHICAL AND CRITICAL SOURCES:

PERIODICALS

Atlantic Monthly, December, 2001, Bruce Hoffman, "One-Alarm Fire," review of *Germs: Biological Weapons and America's Secret War,* p. 137.

Commentary, December, 2001, Frederick W. Kagan, review of *Germs: Biological Weapons and America's Secret War,* pp. 67-68.

Ecologist, December 2001, Gard Binney, review of *Germs: Biological Weapons and America's Secret War,* pp. 75-76.

Harper's, March, 2002, Howard Markel, review of *Germs: Biological Weapons and America's Secret War,* pp. 65-70.

Nation, December 17, 2002, Michael Massing, "Where Germs Rule," p. 7.

New American, January 14, 2002, Thomas R. Eddlem, review of *Germs: Biological Weapons and America's Secret War,* pp. 25-26.

New York Law Journal, November 2, 2001, Howard Goldman, review of *Germs: Biological Weapons and America's Secret War,* p. 2.

New York Review, December 20, 2001, Matthew Meselson, "Bioterror: What Can Be Done?", pp. 38-41.

Smithsonian, December 2001, Eliot Marshall, review of *Germs: Biological Weapons and America's Secret War,* p. 111.

Washington Post, October 21, 2001, "Touch of Evil", p. T05.*

*   *   *

ENKELIS, Liane 1948-

PERSONAL: Born 1948; married Richard Enkelis (an attorney). *Education:* University of Southern California, B.A. (journalism).

ADDRESSES: Office—1785 East Washington Blvd., #96, Pasadena, CA 91104; fax: 626-798-7070. *E-mail*—liane@lianeenkelis.com.

CAREER: Photojournalist. Taught photojournalism at San Jose State University.

WRITINGS:

(With others) *On Our Own Terms: Portraits of Women Business Leaders,* Berrett-Koehler (San Francisco, CA), 1995.
On Being One Hundred: Thirty-one Centenarians Share Their Extraordinary Lives and Wisdom, Prima (Roseville, CA), 2000.

Contributor to publications, including *Business Week, Forbes, Smithsonian, U.S. News & World Report, New York Times Magazine, Time, Black Enterprise, Islands, Americana, Technology Review, Electronic Business Today,* and publications of the National Geographic Society.

SIDELIGHTS: Liane Enkelis, whose photographs have graced the covers of national magazines, includes among her clients leading publications and corporations. Enkelis's photographs are also featured in books, including *On Our Own Terms: Portraits of Women Business Leaders.* The subjects are fifteen women presidents and CEOs whose companies have annual revenues of at least $10 million, and they reveal how they made it to the top, in spite of gender bias, and how they learned to balance work with family. They represent a cross-section with regard to age, ethnicity, geographical location, and experience, with some being leaders of nonprofits. The idea for the volume began with Enkelis, who in photographing corporate officers realized that very few of the portraits she was taking were of women. The team that produced the book eventually included Karen Olson, a graphic designer, and Marion Lewenstein, an editor.

Profiled are Wilma Mankiller, principal chief of the Cherokee Nation, who heads a government and tribal businesses. Kathy Taggares sold everything she owned and cashed in her life insurance to start a food processing business that became a nearly $30 million operation. At the age of thirteen, the woman who now runs K. T.'s Kitchens in Glendale sold her 4-H project Black Angus steers, then used the money to pay the rent on her parents' house.

Several of the women are immigrants, including Josie Natori, who founded the lingerie and accessories business that bears her name. Dian Owen became chairman of the board of Owen Health Care of Houston, overseeing more than 2,000 employees and $320 million in revenues.

Jacqueline Stanfield reviewed *On Our Own Terms* in the *Social Sciences Journal,* saying that it "is an excellent example of teamwork and collaboration, and how these 'feminine' attributes can result in a successful project." Don Kazak, who reviewed the volume in the *Palo Alto Weekly,* wrote that readers, "especially students, can use these stories to realize that while there is a glass ceiling in corporate America, it can be broken by women who have the right combination of talent, drive, an eye for details, and an instinct for making the right choices."

Enkelis photographed people over one hundred years old in black and white for her *On Being One Hundred: Thirty-one Centenarians Share Their Extraordinary Lives and Wisdom.* The book includes people who fought World War II and others who survived the Holocaust. Theodore J. Young helped design the Jefferson Memorial in Washington, D.C., while Cora Luchetti is a survivor of the 1906 San Francisco earthquake. Frederica Sagor Mass was a screenwriter for silent films, and Louise Scott danced at the Apollo Theater in Harlem. All have passed through the history of the twentieth century. John Swain wrote in *Zoomers* online that "we can be deeply inspired and guided by these amazing individuals."

BIOGRAPHICAL AND CRITICAL SOURCES:

PERIODICALS

Library Journal, December, 1995, Sue McKimm, review of *On Our Own Terms: Portraits of Women Business Leaders,* p. 122.
Palo Alto Weekly, January 3, 1996, Don Kazak, review of *On Our Own Terms.*
Publishers Weekly, October 23, 1995, review of *On Our Own Terms,* p. 64.
Social Science Journal, April, 1997, Jacqueline Stanfield, review of *On Our Own Terms,* p. 259.

ONLINE

Liane Enkelis Home Page, http://www.lianenkelis.com (March 25, 2003).
Zoomers, http://www.thorn.home.sonic.net/zoomersmagazine/ (January 2, 2003), John Swain, review of *On Being 100: Thirty-One Centenarians Share Their Extraordinary Lives and Wisdom.* *

EPSTEIN, Leslie 1938-

PERSONAL: Born May 4, 1938, in Los Angeles, CA; son of Philip (a screenwriter) and Lillian (Targen) Epstein; married Ilene Gradman, November 1, 1969; children: Anya, Paul and Theo (twins). *Education:* Yale University, B.A., 1960, graduate study, 1963-65, D.F.A., 1967; Oxford University, diploma, 1962; University of California, Los Angeles, M.A., 1963.

ADDRESSES: Office—Creative Writing Program, College of Arts and Sciences, Boston University, 236 Bay State Rd., Boston, MA 02215. *Agent*—Lane Zachary, Zachary/Shuster/Harmsworth Agency, 1776 Broadway, Ste. 1405, New York, NY 10019.

CAREER: Queens College of the City University of New York, Flushing, lecturer, 1965-67, assistant professor, 1968-70, associate professor, 1970-75, professor of English, beginning 1976; Boston University, Boston, MA, currently director of creative writing program.

MEMBER: International PEN.

AWARDS, HONORS: Rhodes scholarship, 1960-62; National Endowment for the Arts grant, 1972; Fulbright fellowship, Council for International Exchange of Scholars, 1972-73; CAPS grant, 1976-77; Guggenheim fellowship, John Simon Guggenheim Memorial Foundation, 1977-78; Most Distinguished Work of Fiction nomination, National Book Critics' Circle, 1979, and notable book citation, American Library Association, 1980, both for *King of the Jews: A Novel of the Holocaust.*

WRITINGS:

NOVELS

P. D. Kimerakov, Little, Brown (Boston, MA), 1975.
King of the Jews: A Novel of the Holocaust, Coward (New York, NY), 1979, reprinted, Handsel Books (New York, NY), 2003.
Regina, Coward (New York, NY), 1982.
Pinto and Sons, Houghton (Boston, MA), 1990.

Leslie Epstein

Pandaemonium, St. Martin's Press (New York, NY), 1997.
San Remo Drive: A Novel from Memory, Handsel Books (New York, NY), 2003.

SHORT STORY COLLECTIONS

The Steinway Quintet Plus Four, Little, Brown (Boston, MA), 1976.
Goldkorn Tales, Dutton (New York, NY), 1985, published as *Goldkorn Tales: Three Novellas,* with a new foreword by Frederick Busch and a new preface by Epstein, Southern Methodist University Press (Dallas, TX), 1998.
Ice Fire Water: A Leib Goldkorn Cocktail, Norton (New York, NY), 1999.

Also contributor of stories, articles, and reviews to periodicals, including *Atlantic Monthly, Esquire, Nation, Antaeus, Playboy,* and *Antioch Review.*

SIDELIGHTS: "If writers got gold stars for the risks they took, Leslie Epstein would get a handful," Katha Pollitt wrote in the *New York Times Book Review.* Epstein's fiction tackles weighty themes with light humor. His first novel, *P. D. Kimerakov,* is a satire of cold war tensions between the now-defunct Soviet Union and the United States. In a piece for the *New York Times Book Review,* David Bromwich praised the skillful characterizations and elegant style found in *P. D. Kimerakov,* but found the humor somewhat forced. But, Bromwich noted, "this defect may be a sign of Leslie Epstein's honesty: he cannot hide the essential grimness of this particular corner of history." The reviewer concluded that while Epstein's tone is at odds with his subject, "one senses in him what is rare enough at any time: the presence of a sly, appealing, grave and humorous talent."

Epstein's next book was a collection of short fiction, *The Steinway Quintet Plus Four.* The humor in the title story comes through the voice of its narrator, Lieb Goldkorn. Called "a truly enchanting character" by *New York Times* contributor Michiko Kakutani, Goldkorn personifies the dignified Jewish culture that once inhabited New York City's Lower East Side. He is the pianist in a quintet that plays in the Steinway Restaurant "once a favorite haunt of [actress] Sarah Bernhardt and [Nobel prize-winning physicist Albert] Einstein, but now the lonely relic of a vanished Jewish community," according to Pollitt. Epstein contrasts that faded culture with New York's contemporary atmosphere of violence when two young street toughs, armed and high on drugs, terrorize the Steinway Restaurant and hold its customers and employees hostage for a ridiculous ransom. Throughout the ordeal, Goldkorn remains "at once shrewd and wide-eyed, . . . the perpetual optimist," Pollitt wrote. Her review highlighted the story's deft humor, but Kakutani emphasized that the author makes a powerful statement on his deeper theme as well: "In its juxtaposition of Old World culture and contemporary violence, [*The Steinway Quintet* is] an organic and wholly complete work of art."

Lieb Goldkorn is also featured in two more recent story collections, *Goldkorn Tales* and *Ice Fire Water: A Leib Goldkorn Cocktail.* Kakutani deemed the former volume an "energetic, densely patterned" work, one which illuminates "revenge and forgiveness and the stunning tricks that life can play on its victims." In *Ice Fire Water* Epstein takes on the Holocaust, in what

Houston Chronicle reviewer Harvey Grossinger called a "profuse, digressive and meticulously crafted" book which is "an uncompromising philosophical meditation that conjoins a universal human catastrophe with individual misfortune in order to comprehend the unthinkable and demoralizing horrors of history." By *Ice Fire Water* Goldkorn is in his nineties, but his libido seems to be unflagging. He reminisces about his attempted Holocaust-era romances with Olympic figure skater-turned-movie star Sonja Henie, swimmer-turned-movie star Esther Williams, and Brazilian movie star Carmen Miranda, and about the operetta, *A Jewish Girl in the Persian Court,* that he was trying to get produced during those years. In the present day, Goldkorn is still striving to seduce women, including real-life *New York Times* book reviewer Michiko Kakutani. "Beneath the masterful linguistic and critical performance," a reviewer commented in *Publishers Weekly,* "Epstein slyly plants speculations about survivors' accountability, the responsibility of memory and the relativity of taboo." Epstein has said that he plans to write yet another book about Goldkorn someday, one in which he estimates the character to be about one hundred and four.

Epstein's most controversial work has been his 1979 novel *King of the Jews.* In it he examines the role that some European Jews played in betraying their own people to the Nazis. The story focuses on the leader of the Judenrat, or governing council of elders, in the ghetto of a Polish industrial city. The Nazis ordered the establishment of Judenrat to control the population that they had forced into the ghettos; the councils' duties eventually included drawing up lists of passengers for the trains to the death camps. Forced to choose between their people and the Nazis, Judenrat leaders knew that if they did not supply the required quotas for the trains, the entire ghetto might be destroyed in one stroke. The ambiguity of this position led at least one Judenrat leader to take his own life. Until *King of the Jews* was published, "no work of fiction [had] opened up so fully the unbearable moral dilemma in which the Judenrat members found themselves, governing with a pistol at their heads, administering the processes of death, corrupted of course by their awful power, yet trying to preserve life when there was no real way to preserve it," Robert Alter wrote in the *New York Times Book Review.*

Epstein's protagonist in *King of the Jews* is based on Mordecai Chaim Rumkowski, the real-life elder of the ghetto in Lodz, Poland. Rumkowski remains notorious for having relished the power of his position. Like him, the fictional Isaiah Chaim Trumpelman eagerly volunteers for the position of council elder. Then he exploits his privileges, riding in a limousine or on a white stallion and even having his picture printed on the currency and stamps used in the ghetto. Many critics praised Epstein's characterization of Trumpelman for its depth. The man is depicted in larger-than-life style as someone who enjoys his role; yet Epstein also shows the elder's apparently real concern for orphans, his uncertainties, and the rationalizations that allow him to continue in his position. For example, when the grisly destination of the trains is made clear to him, he justifies his cooperation with the Nazis by saying that by sending ten Jews away, he is saving one hundred others. He even begins to think of himself as a savior "the King of the Jews."

Washington Post Book World contributor Michael Kernan noted the author's original approach to his material: "Writing in the manner of the old Jewish storytellers, Epstein dares to be funny. It is the mordant humor that has always been the visible rage of those who are forbidden to show their rage." Kernan concludes that *King of the Jews* "may prove the most successful of all" novels about the Holocaust "because it manages, incredibly, to place the experience in the context of written Jewish tradition." Other reviewers, however, thought that any attempt to find humor in the Holocaust was offensive. But Epstein told *Atlantic Monthly* interviewer Daniel Smith that his novel is an accurate depiction of life in the ghetto. "In *King of the Jews* there are dozens of jokes. I don't think I made up a single one. I made up the humor of the book, but not the formal jokes. They were all taken from Jewish sources on the spot, like Ringelbaum," an inhabitant of the Warsaw ghetto who buried cans full of records about daily life there which were discovered after the war.

Taking place in the nineteenth century, Epstein's fourth novel, *Pinto and Sons*, relates the quixotic tale of Adolph Pinto, a Hungarian Jew who has immigrated to the United States to study at Harvard Medical School. After a botched experiment involving the newly discovered anesthetic ether, Pinto is expelled from Harvard. He travels to the American West, where his adventures include adopting and raising a Native American as his son, educating a tribe of Indians in mathematics and poetry, mining for gold, and attempt-

ing to discover a cure for rabies. Despite Pinto's good intentions, one catastrophe after another besets him. According to Michiko Kakutani, writing in the *New York Times,* Epstein is using "his hero's dilemmas to examine large historical and moral questions," namely, the inability of science and reason to solve basic human problems, the tendency of large man-made schemes to go awry, and the failed promised of the American dream as embodied in the frontier. Although Kakutani praises Epstein's "verbal exuberance" and his "gift for invention," she found *Pinto and Sons* "ultimately a disappointment," lacking the "moral resonance" of *King of the Jews* and sending the reader on an arbitrary "roller-coaster ride" where expectations are raised and then dashed. On the other hand, John Crowley of the *New York Times* wrote that that *Pinto and Sons,* despite being too long, "is a fantastic epic of the heroic age of applied science, a fit book to put on the shelf with the great tall tales of American expansion."

Epstein's fifth novel, *Pandaemonium,* returns to the era of *King of the Jews,* the late 1930s and early 1940s, and again deals, though in less-direct fashion, with the Holocaust. It is a complex and multi-charactered book, narrated in part by a fictionalized version of Jewish actor Peter Lorre and in part by a fictionalized version of Hollywood gossip columnist Louella Parsons. The title of the book is drawn from seventeenth-century poet John Milton's *Paradise Lost,* in which Pandaemonium is the capital of Hell, where Satan's fallen angels gather. David Freeman, writing in the *New York Times Book Review,* described the novel as "an exuberant mixture of high art and low comedy . . . a big, funny and bold book that is a virtual catalog of literary, historical, theatrical and cinematic devices and references." The action of *Pandaemonium* opens in Salzberg, Austria, in 1938, where director Rudolph Von Beckmann is staging an outdoor production of the classic Greek drama *Antigone.* International star Magdalena Mezaray will play the title role. Magda, a fictional creation of Epstein's, is reminiscent of both Greta Garbo and Marlene Dietrich and plays opposite male lead Peter Lorre. Lorre, who has been trapped in Hollywood in a series of mediocre films based on the exploits of the fictional Japanese detective Mr. Moto, sees this as a major career opportunity. Unfortunately, Hitler invades Austria before the production can be launched. Lorre, because he is Jewish, is soon displaced to a minor role. Magda is forced to become Hitler's consort. Von Beckman is eventually exposed as Jewish himself—the "Von" is assumed—and is sent to an internment camp. The action of the novel switches to Hollywood where Lorre, once again playing Mr. Moto for Granite Studios, futilely pursues his co-star and becomes increasingly dependent on cocaine. Fictionalized versions of real Hollywood personalties abound in the narrative and fictional events—Lorre's attempted suicide, the decapitation of Victor Granite, the kidnaping of Granite's daughter—occur in what Richard Bernstein in the New York Times Book Review refers to as "dizzying succession." "Von" Beckman turns up in Hollywood and, through a series of machinations, takes over production of *Mr. Moto Wins His Spurs.* Casting the newly liberated Magda opposite Lorre, Beckman transforms the movie into a kind of *Antigone* set in the Old West. Filming proceeds in the Nevada desert in the ghost town of Pandaemonium, where Beckman becomes a mini-Hitler himself, turning the town into an armed camp and ruling the production with a fascist hand. Epstein portrays the Hollywood power structure as fascist in nature, and is highly critical of the failure of Hollywood's Jewish community to respond to the Holocaust in any meaningful way.

Freeman said of *Pandaemonium:* "There is lunatic comedy here as well as moral seriousness. Epstein blends these disparate forces with considerable panache. . . . While I was there, in Pandaemonium, I didn't want to be anywhere else." Carolyn See, writing in the *Washington Post,* described Epstein as a writer who is "thoughtful, edgy, bitter, acute." She contends that in *Pandaemonium,* as in much of his other work, he is "concerned with illuminating and defining the Jewish experience in this century. . . . He's saying things that will not necessarily conform to the popular or politically correct view of life as we know it."

In 2003 Epstein published *San Remo Drive: A Novel from Memory,* which is based very closely on Epstein's own family life. The narrator is Richard Jacobi, who in the 1940s and 1950s is a boy of about Epstein's age. Jacobi is the son of a director/producer who bears a striking resemblance to Epstein's father, a famous screenwriter. The first four chapters of the book are set between 1948 and 1960; in them Jacobi's family suffers humiliation and the loss of their home on San Remo Drive when Jacobi's father is accused of being a Communist and, soon after, dies in a car crash. The remainder of the family learns to cope with life without him, and Jacobi and his brother, Barton,

become adults. In this section, "Epstein conjures up Southern California in the '50s with an abundance of deftly observed and deeply evocative details," Jonathan Kirsch wrote in the *Los Angeles Times.* The second half of the book is set in the present; in it, Donna Seaman wrote in *Booklist,* Epstein "muses eloquenty on the profound impact childhood memories have on both art and life." In the *New York Times,* critic Elizabeth Frank praised the novel, writing, "Losing and finding, [Epstein] shows us love between fathers and sons as the most powerful and enduring in life, capable of transcending death, time, folly, and a Hollywood childhood. In doing so he has given us, along with F. Scott Fitzgerald's *Last Tycoon,* Budd Schulberg's *What Makes Sammy Run?,* and his own *Pandaemonium,* one of the four best Hollywood novels ever written."

AUTOBIOGRAPHICAL ESSAY:

Leslie Epstein contributed the following autobiographical essay to *CA:*

I was born in 1938, in May, the same month Germans began sending Jews to Dachau. Germans? Jews? Dachau? I saw the light in Los Angeles, and for all I know the nurses in St. Vincent's wore the starched headgear of nuns. One of my earliest memories has to do with that sort of mix-up. I must have been four at the time, maybe five, and was sitting with my playmates around the edge of the Holmby Avenue pond, waiting for tadpoles to turn into frogs. The topic for the day seemed to be religion. At any rate, one of these contemporaries turned to me and said, "What are you?" Here was a stumper. All of the possible answers—a boy, a human, a first-grader—were common knowledge. While I stalled and stammered, one of the others took over:

"I know what I am! I'm a Catholic!"

That rang a bell. An historical tolling. Over a half-century before, and close to a century ago now, my grandfather had stood in line at Ellis Island, wondering how he could translate the family name—Shabilian, one way, Chablian if you're in the fancy mood—into acceptable English. Just in front an immigrant was declaring, *Mine name it is Epstein!* My grandfather, no dummy, piped up, "Epstein! That's my name, too!" Now, on the far side of the continent, his grandson provided the echo:

"Catholic! That's it! That's what I am!"

I must nonetheless have had my doubts, which I brought home that night. That's when I first heard the odd-sounding words, *Jewish, Jew.* "It's what you are," my mother informed me. "Tell your friends tomorrow."

The next afternoon, while the polliwogs battered their blunt heads against the stones of the pond, that is what I blithely proceeded to do. I do not think that, almost fifty years later, I exaggerate the whirlwind of mockery and scorn that erupted about me. I can hear the laughter, see the pointing fingers, still. What horrified my companions, and thrilled them, too, was not so much the news that I was a Jew—surely they knew no more about the meaning of the word than I—as the fact that I had dared to switch sides at all. "Religion changer!" That was the cry. "He changed his religion!" *Vanderbilt:* what if the gentleman, the greenhorn, ahead of my grandfather had said that magic name? Or Astor? Or Belmont even? What then?

From that day to this, the word *Jew,* especially in the mouth of a Gentile, has remained for me highly charged, with the ability to deliver something like an electric shock—rather the way the touch of a sacred totem might be dangerous to a Trobriand Islander, or the image of God forbidden, awesome, to the devout of my own tribe. The irony is, I doubt whether, through the first decade of my life, I heard the word mentioned within my family at all. In this my parents, the son and daughter of Yiddish-speaking immigrants, were not atypical. The second generation, emancipated, educated, was as often as not hellbent on sparing the third the kind of orthodox regime they had had to undergo themselves. Still, I imagine the situation of my brother and myself lies beyond the norm. For we were brought up less in the faith of our, than the founding, fathers: that is to say, as Deists, children of the Enlightenment, worshipers before the idol of FDR.

This minimifidianism sprang in part from the fact that our parents had settled in California while still in their twenties. Eastern shrubs in western climes. More decisive, I think, was the reason they'd made the move. Phil, my father, followed his identical twin brother, Julie, to Hollywood, where both began (and Julie yet continues) distinguished screenwriting careers. Now the figure of the Jew, on celluloid, had undergone any number of vicissitudes (my source on the subject is Patricia Erens's *The Jew in American Cinema*); but by the advent of the talkies, particularly with *The Jazz Singer* and *Abie's Irish Rose,* the puddle

The author's uncle (left) and father, screenwriters Julius and Philip Epstein, at Warner Brothers, 1944

in the melting pot, the stuffing in the American dream had pretty much taken on, at least insofar as the Jews were concerned, permanent shape. In the latter film, for instance, Abie Levy and Rosemary Murphy have to undergo three different marriage ceremonies, Episcopal, Jewish, and Catholic. As Erens points out, the title that introduces World War I reads like this:

> So in they went to that baptism of fire and
>   thunder—Catholics, Hebrews, Protestants
> alike . . .
>   Newsboys and college boys—aristocrats and
> immigrants—all
>   classes—all creeds—all Americans.

Moreover, one can easily determine, by the treatment of the descending generations in this film, from the bearded, accented and quite money-minded grandparents on, the ingredients for this Yankee stew: acculturation, assimilation, intermarriage; followed by blondness, blandness, and final effacement. These last three traits are meant always to apply to the third generation. Thus *Abie's Irish Rose* comes to a close with the birth of something like a genetic miracle—twins: Patrick, the lad; the girl, Rebecca. Once established, the movies rarely deviated from this recipe, which Erens calls "the tradition of casting Jewish actors as parents and Gentile-looking actors as their children." The point I wish to make is that my brother Ricky and I were firmly a part of that tradition.

Make no mistake: my father and uncle were proud of their Jewishness. Hank Greenberg and Sid Luckman were two figures followed with special attentiveness in the Holmby Hills. Indeed, Julie and Phil wrote the script not only for *Casablanca* (whose first word is "refugees"), but for what I believe is the *only* wartime film that dealt with domestic anti-Semitism. That, of course, is *Mr. Skeffington,* about which the Office of War Information complained, "This portrayal on the screen of prejudice against the representative of an American minority group is extremely ill-advised." Moreover, it should be pointed out that Jews of a certain stripe—the American Jewish Committee, for instance, or the Anti-Defamation League—have, from the days of Griffith's *Intolerance,* through *Gentleman's Agreement* and beyond, been no less zealous than government bureaucrats in trying to expunge the image of the Jew from the screen. Ostrich-ism, not ostracism.

In this atmosphere, is it surprising the real-life children of the film community should suffer the same fate as the Rebeccas and Patricks their parents had created? That my brother and I should, in a sense, be acted by, or inhabited by, Gentiles? Or that, since the word *Jew* had been banished from American popular culture from the beginning to the end of World War II ("If you bring out a Jew in film, you're in trouble": Louis B. Mayer), it might for the duration disappear from the households of those engaged on that particular front? Remember, the success of *The Jazz Singer,* whose theme was the repudiation of anything resembling ethnicity, turned Warner Brothers into a major studio: the Epstein twins had been writing for Jack ("See that you get a good clean-cut American type for Jacobs") Warner pretty much from the start of their careers. How could Julie and Phil, busily creating the American dream in a film like *Yankee Doodle Dandy* (don't look for their names in the titles, they gave the credit to a needy friend), not allow their own children to become part of that great national audience of upturned, white, anonymous faces? Would not we, no less than Paul Muni (né Weisenfreund) or Edward G. Robinson (Manny Goldenberg of yore) or John Garfield (another Julie—Garfinkle), become transformed? "People are gonna find out you're a Jew sooner or later," said Warner to Garfield, "but better later."

Meanwhile, the lives of the Deists went on. The great ceremony of the year was Christmas. I never lit a Chanukah candle in my life until, mumbling the words of a phonetic prayer, I held the match for my own daughter, my own twin boys. The Chanukah miracle is pretty small potatoes compared to the star in the heavens, the wise men and their gifts, the manger filled with awestruck animals, and finally the birth of the little halo-headed fellow before whom all fall to their knees. Rest assured that when all this was acted out for me, year after year, by the students of the public schools of California (I may well have donned a beard myself, and gripped what might have been a shepherd's crook or wise man's staff: either that, or I am once again adopting the guise—*that's what I am!*—of my friends), the *J*-word was never mentioned.

What most sticks in my mind, however, is the Christmas trees: giant firs, mighty spruces, whose stars—emblematic of the supernova over Bethlehem—grazed our eleven-foot ceilings. There were red balls and silver cataracts of tinsel and strings of winking lights—all strung by the black maid and butler the previous night. Mary and Arthur were there the next morning, too: she, to receive her woolen sweater; he, his briar pipe. Of course my brother and I were frantic with greed, whipped up by weeks of unintelligible hymns (*myrrh,* for instance, or *roundyon* from "Silent Night," or the Three Kings' *orientare*), by the mesmerizing lights and smell of the tree itself, and the sea of packages beneath it—and perhaps above all by the prospect of the rarest of all Epstein phenomena: the sight of our parents, in dressing gowns, with coffee cups, downstairs before the UCLA chimes struck noon.

Hold onto your hats: there was Easter. too. Not a celebration. No ham dinner. No parade. But there was no lack of symbols of rebirth and resurrection: the ones we dyed in pale pastels, the ones we hid under the cushions of the couch, or others, pure chocolate, that we gobbled down. The eggs I remember best were large enough to have been laid by dinosaurs, covered with frosted sugar, with a window at the smaller end. Through this we could see a sylvan scene: bunnies in the grass, squirrels in the trees, and birds suspended in a sky as perpetually blue as the one that arched over the city of the angels. Aside from Christmas and Easter, which created a special sort of pressure, there were ordinary Sundays, when it was my habit to lie late in bed, listening to the radio. More than once, twisting the dial between a boy's piping voice, "I'm Buster Brown! I live in a Shoe! *Arf! Arf!* That's my dog, Tyge; he lives in there, too!" and the genie's growl, "Hold on tight, little master!" I'd linger at a gospel station. At which point Mary would appear at my bedroom door. "That's right," she'd declare, with a broad smile. "You going to be blessed!" She was at least more subtle than the All-American rabbi in *Abie's Irish Rose,* whose words to a dying soldier the sharp-eyed Ms. Erens quotes as follows:

*Have no fear, my son. We travel many roads,
but we all come at last to the Father.*

Let's make a crucial distinction. Muni Weisenfreund turning into Paul Muni is one thing. Saul of Tarsus becoming Saint Paul is quite another. Everyone knows what happened after the local priest gave his Easter sermon. Those are not chocolate eggs the peasants of Europe have been hunting these hundreds of years. The Jews who were rounded up the month I was born would have gone free, just as the millions who were soon to be gassed in ovens or shot at the edge of ditches, would have been spared if Constantine the Great—*religion changer!*—had not seen a flaming cross in the sky: that is, if Christianity had remained, as I dearly wish it had, a minor sect and not become a major heresy. Nonetheless, those performances at Brentwood and Canyon Elementary had done their work. How appealing to a child those dumb donkeys! Those cows of papier-mâché! The mumbo jumbo of *inexcelsisdeo!* Few films have moved me as deeply as Pasolini's *Gospel According to Saint Matthew,* which I sat through twice in a row, weeping at the figure of Jesus, the babe in the grade-school manger, broken now on the cross.

*

Inconceivable that the whole of the Second World War could go by without leaving a trace. Nor did it. But the truth is that for us, in California, in sunshine, the conflict was more a matter of Japanese than Germans and Jews. I doubt very much whether I noticed when the Orientals in nursery school and kindergarten disappeared. Almost certainly I paid no heed when the same fate befell the old gardener who smoothed our flower beds with his bamboo rake. Odds are I was too distracted by the exciting talk of submarines off the coast, or bombs falling by parachute over Seattle.

There was never any question that the threat to us would come, as it already had at Pearl Harbor, from the Pacific. I can still remember the barrage balloons,

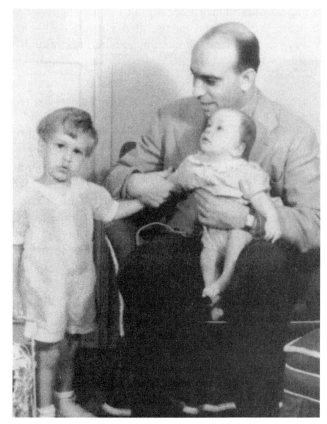

Leslie, with his father holding his brother, Ricky, about 1941

like plump brown eggs, tied off the local beaches. My brother—aged what? Three? Four?—saw them from the end of Santa Monica Pier, and began to whimper. A trick of perspective, the sharp sea air, the taut lines gathered on buoys or barges, made it seem that these fat blimps, a mile offshore, were street-corner balloons. "Want one! Want one!" Ricky cried, stamping his feet, throwing himself onto the planks of the dock. For the loss of this toy he would not be consoled.

Throughout the house on Holmby, half-smoked cigarettes, my mother's Chesterfields, bobbed in the waters of the toilet bowls. Sitting ducks, they were, for my stream of urine, which would sooner or later burst the zig-zagging hulls, sending thousands of tiny brown crewmen over the side, to drown next to their floundering transports. Even after the war, when we moved to a yet larger house on San Remo Drive, my fantasies remained fixed upon the Far East. And on nautical warfare. We'd purchased a surplus life raft, yellow rubber on the sides, blue on the bottom, which was initially, thrillingly, inflated by yanking a lever on a tube of gas. In this vessel, on the smooth waters of our swimming pool, I floated for hours. Through the windless afternoon. Under a pitiless sun. The downed airman. With a metal mirror, also surplus, I signaled every passing plane whose silhouette did not resemble that of a Zero.

Naturally my imaginative life was shaped by the movies. The jump from the cartoon festivals I attended each Saturday at the Bruin theater to the war films showing everywhere else seemed a normal progression, just as the cartoons themselves were an innate part of the animism of a child's world. If a discarded pair of pants could become, in the dim light of one's bedroom, a slumbering crocodile, or a breeze in the curtain a masked intruder, then there was little to wonder at when barnyard animals, creatures of instinct much like ourselves, began to dress up, sing like Jimmy Cricket, or scheme for a piece of cheese. Also: murder each other, poleax their enemies, chop them to smithereens, or flatten them, under the wheel of a steamroller, as thin as a dime. All victims, it seemed, had nine lives. No death was unresurrected. It was this, I suppose, along with the white-hat, black-hat morality of the westerns, with their thousands of expendable Indians, that eased the transition to *Winged Victory* and *Pride of the Marines*. Now the enemy were mowed down like ducks, or blown, as Tom was by Jerry and Jerry by Tom, sky high. *Yankee Doodle Mouse.* 1943.

The early immersion in cartoons may help explain why, since I probably saw as many movies about the war in Europe as I did about the fighting in Asia, my attention remained firmly fixed upon the Pacific Theater. The Germans in movies were simply too adult, real smoothies like Conrad Veidt, witty, cunning, prone to understatement and reserve. Even the Prussian stereotypes, the smooth-shaved head, curled lip, and glinting monocle of a Preminger or von Stroheim, possessed a kind of refined sadism worlds removed from the clear-cut cruelty of a mouse handing a cat a sizzling bomb.

There was no problem of reticence in the movies that dealt with the war in the Pacific. Here the violence was full bore. More crucial, the enemy, like the Indians, were a different race—no, almost a different species, like the talking animals we already knew. Indeed, when these short, comical characters—yellow-skinned, buck-toothed, bespectacled—did speak, they had something of the stammer of Porky, or Woody's cackle, or the juicy lisp of Daffy Duck. Thus the most

forceful images of war remained, for me, those of death marches, jungle patrols, palm trees bent under withering fire, and kamikaze pilots with blank faces and free-flowing scarves.

What made such pleasure possible was the certainty that nothing I saw was real. I was, remember, a Hollywood child. Towering over the lot at Twentieth Century-Fox was a huge outdoor sky, painted so much like the real one, white clouds against a background of startling blue, that whenever we drove by I had to look twice to see which was which. The decisive moment came when I visited a sound lot, probably at Warners, where a pilot, one of our boys, was trapped inside his burning plane. A cross section of the fuselage rested on sawhorses; the actor's legs protruded beneath it, standing firm on the floor. Also on the floor, flat on their backs, were two civilians, one with a flame-throwing torch, the other with a plain wooden stick. *Action!* shouted the director. At once the pilot began to beat on the inside of his cockpit. The torch shot gobs of fire in front of the white linen background. And the fellow with the stick banged at the fuselage, so that, bucking, shaking, it seemed about to break apart. Finally the pilot managed to pry off his canopy and thrust his head into the wind-machine's gale. *Cut!*

The ambiguity of both that Magritte sky and desperate scene, indeed the tranquil unreality of the war itself: all that concluded one afternoon at Holmby Park. What I remember is my father running pellmell down the avenue, snatching me off the playground swing, and then dashing back up the hill toward our house. "The war is over!" he shouted. Either that, or, "The president is dead!" I have a scar, hardly visible now, under my lip, from the time I fell off that very swing. Possibly it's that catastrophe I recall—the same sense of urgency, the same excitement, the elation at flying along in my father's arms—and not Roosevelt's death, or the bomb-burst that brought the war to an end.

Not long afterwards we moved to the house with the swimming pool. Already my missing schoolmates—the plump, pleasant James Wada, was one—were starting to return. So did our gardener: or someone like him, arriving like a comical fireman in an old truck covered with hoses and ladders and tools. He tended lawns set with cork trees and fig vines and eucalyptus. The property was surrounded by lemon groves, which perfumed the air and filled it, two or three times a year, with canary-colored light. We weren't the first movie people in the neighborhood: Joseph Cotten's place was catercorner, on Montana, and a block or two over, toward Amalfi, were Linda Darnell, Lou Costello, and Virginia Bruce. Down the hill, our school bus made a loop into Mandeville Canyon to drop off the son of Robert Mitchum. Not the first film folk, then: but among the first Jews. For when the former owner of our house, Mary Astor, changed her name, it wasn't from Manny or Muni but the proper Lucille. The Gentile who disguised himself as Phil Green in *Gentleman's Agreement* was none other than our neighbor, Gregory Peck. The closest we came to a refugee was the sight of Thomas Mann, walking his dog along San Remo Drive. The Epsteins were the pioneers.

That meant my friends had such names as Warren and Sandy and Tim and John. We used to build forts together, ride our bikes through the polo fields, and use our Whammos to shoot blue jays and pepper the cars on Sunset Boulevard with the hard round pellets that grew on the stands of cypress above. We also camped out on each other's lawns. The smear of stars in the Milky Way is the prime text for Deists. All is order, beauty, design. The ticking of the master clock. Yet our gaze, once we closed the flap of our pup tents, was lower. In the new sport of masturbation one kept score by palpable results. A drop. A dollop. At one such tourney, the champion posed in our flashlight beams, his member bent at the angle of a fly rod fighting a trout. At precisely the midway point in twentieth-century America, the rest of us, the slow pokes, saw that something was amiss. Uncircumcised. Here was a rip, a rent, in the universal design. From this common sight I drew a skewed lesson. I may have been in the immediate majority, hygienic as any in the crowd. Yet I knew as gospel that the one who had been torn from the true course of nature was not he, the victor, our pubescent pal, but I.

Which is to say that, over time, we discovered differences. This was palmy Pacific Palisades: no crosses were burned in yards, no swastikas were scratched on lampposts. In our half-wilderness—polo ponies in the fields below, and, above, hills covered with yucca, prowled by bobcats—there were not even lamps. Why, quail sang in our hedges and stood on the lawns! The bus for Ralph Waldo Emerson Junior High School picked us up at a vacant lot on Sunset near Amalfi. Wheat seemed to be growing in it, and fiddle-heads that tasted like licorice. One morning I arrived

to find that the usual allegiances had shifted. My friends greeted me by throwing clods of dirt, sending me back to the wrong side of the boulevard. They arched their bomblets over the traffic. Their cry was "Kike! Go Home! Kike! Kike!"

Now this was not, in the words of the old transcendentalist, the shot heard round the world. Certainly the incident was a far cry from the kind of warfare the Epstein boys had engaged in, circa 1921, on the Lower East Side. There, you had to battle your way, against the Irish, against the Italians, just to get to the end of the block. On the other hand, while my schoolmates had never learned Emerson's pretty rhyme—

Nor knowest thou what argument
Thy life to thy neighbor's creed has lent—

I knew what a kike was. *Not,* as in Salinger's story, something that goes up in the air. Thus I went home, as commanded, from which sanctuary Arthur drove me to school in the Buick.

Once a year farflung branches of the family gathered for the Passover Seder at my grandfather's house in Santa Monica—a time warp away, hyperspace distant, from Bialystok. "Say, der!" we called it, gazing with some dismay at these strange, gawky relations, mole-covered, all thumbs. The only cousins who counted were Jimmy and Lizzie, who, since they were Julie's children, and Julie and Phil—bald from their college days, two eggs in a carton, peas in a pod—were identical twins, were therefore my genetic half-brother and sister, Jim (later a starter at Stanford) and I made a point of throwing the football around the backyard and bowling over the pale kinfolk as if they had been candlepins. During the ceremony itself, which droned on forever, Jim and I would sit at the far end of the table, arm wrestling amidst the lit candles, the bowls of hot soup, the plates of (here is a title for a novel, or a memoir like this) *Bitter Herbs.* The empty chair, we were told, the untouched glass of wine, were not for yet more distant cousins, missing in Europe, unheard from since the start of the war, but for Elijah, who was fed by ravens and departed the earth in a chariot of fire.

That was the extent of my religious knowledge. Not once had I set foot in a synagogue, or been exposed to so much as a page of the Bible. I knew more about gospel music—*You going to be blessed*—and Christmas Hymns—*Glo-or-i-a-a, or-or-i-a-a, or-or-i-a-a, oria!*—than I did about the songs concerning grasshoppers and boils that my relatives chanted while thrusting their fingers into the sweet, red wine. Barmitzvahed? Perish the thought! Yet the idea must have occurred to someone, because, for perhaps three weeks in a row, I found myself in a Sunday school class of glum Jews whose dogma was so reformed in nature as to hardly differ from that of Franklin and Jefferson and the other founders. About this trial I remember little. Bad food, for one thing. And a distinctly dubious rabbi. My fellow sufferers seemed unlikely to be interested either in the fortunes of the Hollywood Stars—not the film colony, but our Triple-A franchise—or pup tent pleasures. Before I left, or, more likely, was asked to leave (the issue being my habit of roller-skating between the pews of the temple), I did pick up the fragment, the refrain, of one new song: *Zoom-golly-golly-golly,* so went the nonsense syllables, *Zoom-golly-golly!* Then I zoomed off myself, on my eight little wheels, back to the rhapsodies of secular life: "Sha-boom!" and "Gee (love that girl)," by the Four Crows.

*

"I got ice cream! Every flavor! Chocolate! Coffee! Vanilla! Strawberry! Lamb chop!" That speech, from a little Cub Scout play, was the first line I can remember writing. I suppose it was in the cards I would try my hand at the craft. Phil and Julie, unique among studio employees, did their writing at home. Once, Jack Warner cracked down about this, pointing out that their contract called for them to be at work on the lot by 9:00 a.m., just as bank presidents had to. "Then tell a bank president to finish the script," said one or the other of the twins, and drove off the premises. It wasn't long before Warner had another such fit, demanding that the boys, as they were habitually called, show up at the stipulated hour. They did, and at the end of the day sent over the typescript. The next morning Warner called them in and began to shout about how this was the worst scene he'd read in his life. "How is this possible?" asked the first twin. Concluded the second, "It was written at nine." So it was that I'd often lie upstairs, on the carpet, outside the closed library door. From the other side I'd hear a muffled voice—maybe Julie's: *yattita-yattita-yattita,* it would declaim, with rising inflection; then another voice, let's say Phil's, would respond, *yattita-yattita-yattita!* Then both would break out together, indistinguishably, in their crystal-shattering laugh. It seemed an attractive way to live one's life.

Still and all I don't think I wrote a story until my first year at University High. What I remember of it, more than three and a half decades later, is a public plaza, a milling crowd, a feeling of excitement, anticipation. There is, in the description of the square, the clothing, the mustachioed faces, something of a South American flavor. The snatches of dialogue, while not Spanish, must have been accented somehow. Buenos Aires, then. There was no real plot, only the waiting, the crush of numbers, the electric expectation. Finally, when the tension was as great as a fourteen-year-old could make it, that is, when all the upturned faces had turned in the direction of the tall brick building, when all eyes were focused upon the high balcony that jutted out over the square, the closed doors of the palace open. A small figure, unprepossessing, clean-shaven save for his mustache, and dressed in plain uniform, moves into the open. A sudden hush falls over the crowd. The man, not young, aged in fact sixty-three, steps forward. He leans over the balcony's wrought-iron rail. Then, suddenly, he stands upright and raises his right hand in the air. A great wave of sound, long suppressed, breaks from the crowd. It is half a sigh, half a shout. *"Viva!"* That is the cry. *"Viva,* Hitler!"

Where on earth, or at any rate in California, with its blue skies, from which the sun shone in winter at much the same angle it did in July, did this vision of evil incarnate come from? Had I, after all, noted something hidden, unspoken in those wartime films? Or heard a few whispered remarks around the Seder table? Or seen, in newspapers, a blurred early image of what would later become such familiar photos: bulldozers at work on piles of bodies; heaps of spectacles, sheared hair, shoes; wraithlike figures in striped pajamas; the lamp shades, the ovens, the showers, the ditches? The answer is no, and no, and no. Rather, an answer of yes would be superfluous here. The truth is I had always known—in the same way that one knows, from childhood on, the laws of gravitation. What goes up must come down. From childhood? I might have been born with an innate grasp of the fate of the Jews. What a person learns later, the facts of physics, the formulas about the mass of objects and the square of their distance, only confirms what he carries within like the weight of his bones. Hints, bushings, inflections, a glance: these pass from Jew to Jew, and from child to child, by a kind of psychic osmosis. So it was that history passed molecule by molecule through the membrane that held me apart from my fellows, and apart from a world long denied.

That's not the end of the story. Indeed, there was a second piece of fiction written for that same freshman class. The time, the present: that is, 1953. The place: the American Southwest. We see an old man, a prospector perhaps, a desert rat, dragging his way across the alkali flats. He pulls his burro behind him. The plot, hazily remembered, involves the way he had tricked everyone into thinking he had left the area, when in fact he had no intention of quitting the spot. It may be he was about to make his big strike. Or might have remained from cussedness alone. In any case the ending goes something like this. As the man and beast turn eastward, away from the setting sun, the sky lights up in a fireball, which grows larger and larger, lighting up the white sands, the tall cacti, the quartz hills, brighter than any day.

I mention this tale not because its subject, like that of its companion piece, was, for the frosh squad, so portentous, but because it indicates that in matters of war and peace my gaze was still out over the Pacific. How could it be anywhere else? The year before we had exploded a hydrogen bomb on the atoll of Eniwetok, and now the Russians had replied in kind. The weapon that had leveled Hiroshima, and killed a hundred thousand Japanese, served as a mere trigger, a kind of spark, for these giant explosions. The very air, it was thought, might catch fire. At University High we drilled for the moment the bomb would fall. There were three levels of strategy. The first, which assumed we had something like an hour's notice, involved a brisk march through the hallways and down the stairs to the fallout shelter in the boys' locker room. Not much different than a fire-drill, really, except that instead of milling outside we waited for the all-clear with our backs against the green metal doors. An imminent attack was indicated by a pattern of bells. The teacher lowered the blinds against flying glass while the students filed into the hall: silent, we were, in the dim light, the endless corridors. But the maneuver we practiced over and over occurred when there was to be no warning at all. A student might be in the middle of a recitation, *Tomorrow and tomorrow and tomorrow* from *Macbeth,* when suddenly, from nowhere, the teacher would bark out the word, "Drop!" There would be a rustle, a rumble—falling books, falling bodies, a

flutter of paper—as we hurled ourselves under our desks. We tucked our heads into our laps and clutched our knees, like the little crustaceans, the tightly coiled sow bugs, we unearthed from our lawns. The main thing, the great thing, was not to look out the windows. The light would blind us. It would fry the whites of our eyes.

Silent in the hallways, silent in the nation at large. Dumbstruck. Numb. This is how my brother and I entered the fifties. Ricky had already taken the measure of this world: he knew an illusion, a veil of Maya, when he saw one. Hence he drew inward, toward the realm of the spirit. That is to say, he drifted yet further toward the East—specifically toward the gardens and incense clouds and priests of Vedanta. I am certain that Ricky's sudden, but lifelong, interest in Karma, the way one's actions determine his destiny in past and future incarnations, the hope of rebirth on a higher plane, the dream of final release from the endless round of being—that all this was precipitated by the death of our father in 1952.

Even then we did not enter a synagogue. What rabbi could hope to match the vision of Nirvana preached by the followers of Vivekananda? Or compete with the scenes—Alec Guinness scrambling down the Eiffel Tower, clutching his ill-gotten gains—in the movie we attended instead of the funeral? A comedy, no less. There might be an echo, in our laughter that afternoon, of the afternoons at the Bruin. No death, to a child, is irrevocable. Cartoon critters pop up living and breathing. Why not our father, in the guise of his identical twin? Retake. Double exposure. Remember, though, that at the end of *The Lavender Hill Mob* Guinness is punished for his thievery and led off in chains. The doctrine of Karma is no less strict than the Hollywood Production Code. Our crime, those hours distracted, the glee, may yet lead to a lower form of existence—as Republicans, say, or reptiles—in the incarnation to come.

I cannot say whether Ricky was aware of the Holocaust, or, if he was, whether the knowledge had anything to do with his withdrawal. I do think that what little the country had discovered—in newsreels, mostly—about the destruction of the Jews of Europe, and the consequent erasure of those same mental traces, may have had no small part to play in the symptoms of paranoia, the deep, dumb shock, that characterized the decade. I do not mean to say the national hysteria had more to do with denial of the Holocaust than apprehension about the role of the Soviet Union in Europe and its testing of the same kinds of weapons we had already used. But those quick glimpses on the Movietone screen were not altogether ineradicable. That they left a mark could be determined from the kinds of comments people allowed themselves at the time. "How could these things happen in *Germany?*" was the most common remark. So clean. So enlightened. So civilized. Now we know better. It was the very modernity of German culture, its mastery of technology and the means of mass communication, that made it, with its glorification of violence, its infatuation with death, not our century's aberration, but its paradigm. Hence the chill that fell over the land. All the values of modern life had been given an ironic twist, a mocking echo. Belief in cleanliness? Here were bars of human soap. The quest for light? Here were lamp shades of human skin. What we feared in the fifties was not only communism, it was ourselves.

Throughout the nation, of course, the fear of fascism and the Yellow Peril had long since been replaced by that of the Red Menace. The hysteria was greatest in Hollywood, which, as Adolphe Menjou told the Committee, "is one of the main centers of Communism in America." If I had been older, and less sheltered, I might have found an example of resistance, one full of insouciance and dash, within my own family. When, in the late forties, Jack Warner testified before the House Un-American Activities Committee he produced a ludicrous list of subversives, largely consisting of those with whom he had contractual disputes. It included Philip G. and Julius J. Epstein, Roosevelt Democrats, on the grounds that they always seemed to be on the side of the underdog. Little wonder, then, that when Martin Dies took over the Committee he should send them a two-part questionnaire. The first question was, "Have you ever been a member of a subversive organization?" The second was, "What was that organization?" To part one the boys dutifully answered, "Yes." To part two they wrote, "Warner Brothers."

But I, no less than Ricky, or the country, joined the ranks of the silent, the stunned. After my quick start in the freshman year at high school, I withdrew. That is to say, I did not write any more stories, or playlets, or imaginative prose of any kind, until my undergraduate years in New Haven were drawing to a close. Why

not? While the answer is complex, I think it fair to state that in the course of the decade I was, all unwittingly, willy-nilly, coming to a decision: when I was ready to write, it would be as a Jew; or, better, when I was a Jew, I would be ready to write. There was, however, a long way to go.

Among the newsreel pictures in my own mental gallery—wasn't there a crowing rooster in the old Pathé titles, much like the roaring lion in MGM's?—are shots of crowds dancing about piles of burning books and young, grinning soldiers cutting the beards of learned men. These images, together with what I soon read about the music the Nazis banned from their concert halls and the paintings they mocked in their exhibition of degenerate art, convinced me that the war against the Jews was in some measure a war against the nature of the Jewish mind. Absurd, I know, to claim that by exterminating the Jews the Germans were in fact attempting to eliminate Jewish art: but it is far from senseless to claim that the oppressors had come to identify the Jews with some quality of imagination, and in creating a world without one they were attempting to confirm that it was possible to live without the other.

In a sense the Third Reich had no choice. An aesthetic of Blood and Kitsch must, by its very nature, try to undo that embodied in Abraham and Isaac: that is, imaginative reenactment, the metaphorical power of words, the inseparable link between act and consequence, and the symbolic prohibition of human sacrifice. Specifically, what fascism repudiates in the ancient tale is the power of faith, the recognition of limits, and trust in the word of God. Enter the Jews. It was they who took the greatest imaginative leap of all, that of comprehending, out of nothingness, an empty whirlwind, the glare of a burning bush, the "I am that I am." In spite of much backsliding, in spite of having been warned by a jealous God (in a commandment they have rebelled against ever since) not to make likenesses, those people have continued that "repetition in the finite mind of the eternal act of creation" that Coleridge defined as the essence of imagination. In an age when such faith was no longer tenable, when the supreme fiction—which is that we matter—became a rebuke to the countervailing belief—which was that everything is possible—then those finite minds, with their dream of the infinite, had to be eliminated.

These are the thoughts, or half-thoughts, I entertain now. The lesson I drew at the time, however, was little more than the proven adage: hard to be a Jew. And dangerous, as well. Once, in the mid-fifties, traveling back to California for summer vacation, I found myself on a New Orleans bus. A pleasant-looking lady leaned forward from the seat behind. "See that? See him there?" she asked, pointing out the window to where a motorcycle policeman sat on his machine, hidden behind a billboard. I nodded. The belle of the south lowered her voice. "The Jews put him there!" Now I knew how Gregory Peck felt, but—the Jew as Gentile, not the Gentile as Jew—in reverse. He had a swell speech for the occasion. I held my peace. A smile sufficed, and a nod.

Nonetheless, within me the ice was breaking. For one thing I had wheels. The friends with whom I cruised Hollywood Boulevard in the latest model of the Buick turned out—to my surprise: no, to my shock—to have names like Alan and Robbie and David and Dick. Similarly, the books I was reading, and the stories in the *New Yorker,* were written by fellows like Norman and Saul and Bernard and, soon enough, Philip. Not to mention J.D. I saw new kinds of movies: *Night and Fog, The Diary of Anne Frank,* and, best of all, Renoir's *La Règle du Jeu.*

*

So beneath the calm surface much was in turmoil. The symptom was this: no matter what situation I found myself in, I moved to the verge, the very edge. More to the point, having already been thrown out of the Jewish temple, I now proceeded to get myself banished from the citadels of Christendom. First was the Webb School, where I'd been sent, with several dozen other products of broken or unhappy homes, two years after my father's death. "With the cross of Jeee-suus," these were the words I mouthed in compulsory chapel, "going on beeeforrre!"

"What's this?" asked one of the preppies, as the turnips were plopped on his plate.

"The week's profit," sweetly said I.

Gone. Rusticated. Dismissed. Expelled. In the land of the *goyim,* however, what is done may, through contrition, repentance, and a good deal of breast-beating, be undone. The suspension lasted only three days.

Playing tennis at Webb School, 1955

Perhaps my goal was not so much to draw the wrath of the Christians as to bask in their forgiveness. Better a prodigal son than no son at all. A more likely explanation is that, at loose ends, in limbo, I was pushing myself toward becoming that marginal figure, the wisecracking Jew.

Then the scene shifted. Off I went to college in the cold, cloudy East. My instructions from Uncle Julie were as follows: when in New Haven buy an overcoat at Fenn-Feinstein; when in New York, eat the free rolls at Ratner's. There I was, a freshman again, at Second Avenue and Fifth. My coat, three sizes too large, was reddish-brown, with hairs sticking out of the lining. On my head, a snappy hat. Round my neck a Lux et Veritas tie. After studying the menu I raised a finger to the waiter. "I'm not electric," he said, hobbling by. A quarter of an hour later a second old man shuffled over.

"What's this *ma-ma-li-ga?*" I inquired.

Said he: "Not for you."

At about the same time I first met my maternal grandparents, who lived off the Boardwalk in Atlantic City. What drew me to them, through the last half of the fifties, and into the sixties too, was the way the aged couple clung together, whereas my own family had always gone their separate ways. A dead cigar in his lips, Herman would bicycle through the streets of the black ghetto, collecting rent. Our favorite restaurant—Clara, bedridden, was not to know—was a place that fried up forbidden crab cakes. Once I was at their shabby flat watching the evening news. "Nixon!" Herman said, grabbing his nose. "P! U!"

The waiter was right. Not for me. Not yet. It was still the era of the deaf and dumb. But things were soon to change. One afternoon at Yale, where the quota for those of the Mosaic persuasion was ten and 1/2 percent, I was standing on High Street when the mayor came out of Fenn-Feinstein and stepped into the barber shop next door. "What's the mayor doing?" asked my current straight man, as His Honor emerged from the doorway and moved toward the entrance to Barrie Shoes.

"Wednesday. 2:00 p.m.," I replied, not quite *sotto voce*. "Collection time."

We were, remember, still in the fifties. The next thing I knew I had been thrust up against the side of a car, had handed over my wallet, and been told to be at the dean's office the next morning at 10:00 a.m. By eleven, I was no longer a Son of Eli. Historians may yet come to note that this injustice, together with the response it provoked, represented the true birth pangs of the counterculture. I did not, as demanded, return to California. I spent a pleasant fortnight in nearby Hamden, strolling to the campus each evening to be interviewed by various senior societies: Manuscript, Elihu, Scroll & Key. Meanwhile, enough of a flap had developed—beginning with mimeographed notes on bulletin boards and ending with an interesting call from the *New Haven Register*—to bring about my reinstatement. Thus did the balance of power between the student and administrative bodies begin to tip. Some years later, after my years at the Drama School, the quota had been abandoned, Bobby Seale was camped on the New Haven Green, and the knock on the Elihu door was answered by—her blouse unbuttoned, a babe at her breast—a co-ed. *Après moi, le déluge.*

Oxford, or "Oggsford," as my coreligionist Meyer Wolfsheim is made in *The Great Gatsby* to call it, proved a tougher nut to crack. What do you do with people who, when asked to pass the salt, say, "Sorry!?" My boorish crowd used to hang out in the taverns and try, with comments on the weather and the bangers

and the temperature of the beer, to drive the locals out. The low point (or pinnacle, depending) of this campaign occurred in the dining hall of my college, Merton (a place so stuck in the mud that its library, as old as Bologna's, turned down the gift of T. S. Eliot's manuscripts because he was not yet dead). Let me paint the scene. On the floor are a series of long tables, upon which sit pots of marmalade made from the very oranges Richard the Lionhearted sent back from Seville. Huddled on long benches are the undergraduates, shoveling down peas and gruel. On a platform, perpendicular to the masses, the Dons are drawn up at high table. The crystal, the flatware, shine. The chef, a Frenchman, has made a *poulet en papillote*. Even down in the pit, we can hear the puff of the little paper bags as they are punctured by the professors' tines. Time for the savory. The Dons tilt back their heads, dangling asparagus spears over their open mouths. But what's this? A stir on the floor? Where the Americans sit? In the Jewry? Indeed, at the moment, friend Fried, out of New Jersey, is about to be sconced.

> "Sconce," says the OED. "At Oxford, a fine of a tankard of ale or the like, imposed by undergraduates on one of their number for some breach of customary rule when dining in hall."

The first infraction, 1650, was for "absence from prayers." Fried's folly, however, was making a serious remark, since the aforesaid rule forbade any conversation about one's studies, about politics, or anything that might be construed as an idea. That left the girls at Saint Hilda's and cricket. No sooner had Fried made his point about Marxist dialectics than gleeful cackle broke out among the Brits. Instantly a waiter appeared, sporting the usual bloodshot cheeks and bushy mustache. In his arms he held the foaming chalice that untold numbers of Merton men—including, surely, the animated Eliot—had raised to their lips. Fried, deep in his argument, paid no mind. The ruddy waiter—in his white apron he looked the kosher butcher—tapped him on the shoulder and held up, with a grin and a wink, the tankard. Fried whirled round.

"What am I supposed to do with this?" he asked, as if unaware that custom dictated he drink down the contents and order an equal portion for all those at table. "Shove it up your ass?"

Immense silence. Everything—the Dons with their buttery spears, the students balancing peas on their knives, the thunderstruck waiter—was as frozen, as still as the twelfth-century fly caught in the marmalade amber. Then, as if a howitzer had been fired, a sudden recoil. The students shrank away on every side, their hands to their mouths. "Oh!" they cried. "Oh, God!" Meanwhile Fried had turned back to his interlocutor, out of California, and together they resumed their argument about the merits of Marx and Freud, a sort of mental arm wrestling not much different from that at the end of the Seder table.

Clearly if Fried was not rusticated for this, I had my work cut out for me. To make a long story short I found myself on the telephone with the head of my department, Dame Helen Gardner. I fear that in so many words I told her that she ought to deposit her Anglo-Saxon riddles and Middle English charms (how to get honey from honeybees, for example, or cows out of bogs) where my compatriot had suggested placing the tankard of ale. Then, having resigned the major, I packed my bags, determined to leave the university at the start of the next term.

The two best things about an Oxford education are the length of the vacations and the relative proximity of the Mediterranean Sea. I'd already been to Greece, Spain, Italy, and Southern France. Now, on a broken-down freighter, the *Athenai,* I chugged right across the greasy, gray waters. Easy enough in the lurching bowels of this vessel to imagine that you were your own grandparents, storm-tossed, debating whether it was permitted to survive on a scrap of pork. Never mind that this journey lasted only two days, and that the welcoming landmark was not the Statue of Liberty but the golden dome of the Bahai temple, high above the harbor at Haifa.

What happened to me in Israel was at once common enough, and most bizarre. Instantaneously, virtually on the docks, the wall between myself and the world, that membrane, dissolved. Before my eyes hustled Jewish porters, policemen, soldiers and sharpies and sellers of pretzels. Osmosis cannot take place, nor can one live on the margin, or be expelled, when there are Jews in solution inside and out. The idea that I had grown up with—that the very word *Jew* was awesome, sacred, terrible, not to be thought of, never mentioned— became ludicrous on these shores swarming with the usual run of big shots and bums. What made Israel so appealing to many Jews like me (and so repugnant to the zealots of Crown Heights and the Mea Shearim) was the promise of the ordinary, the prospect of the

mundane. Only in the Holy Land could the Jews escape being a holy people.

The impact of that part of my trip (the fact that I now kept track of Sandy Koufax on his way to mowing down 269 of the *goyim*) was altogether banal. But there were eerier forces at work, and they involved the history of the Germans and Jews. Of course I visited the memorial at Yad Vashem and the smaller museum, with its cases of torn scrolls and striped pajamas, on Mount Zion. At the center of everything, dominating each day, was the spectacle of a well-guarded German, Eichmann, pleading for his life before a court of his former victims. What was odd about these things was that I saw them in the company of someone who belonged to the last generation of Germans to feel, if not guilt, then more than a twinge of shame. This was Katrin, an architect from Munich, whom I had met aboard the *Athenai.* Everything you need to know about her background may be inferred from the fact that the name on her passport read Karen and had been changed by her parents to avoid what became, in the Third Reich, the most fashionable Aryan moniker.

Our relationship ("Don't tell Clara" was Herman's reaction upon hearing the news) was to last five years. When it ended I met—and was eventually to marry—a young woman who had also been a passenger on the *Athenai,* just one week before Katrin and I. That we had both suffered seasickness on that old Greek tub and had quite likely rubbed elbows in one museum or the other was but one of a series of near misses. Here was an image in a flawed mirror: an identical twin herself, and not the offspring of identical twins; a mother dead in childhood instead of a father; years on the beaches of Florida instead of California; Christmas celebrated, but without servants, carols, trees.

*

All this had to be sorted out in the future. At present fate had more tricks in store. My plans to leave Oxford were suddenly abandoned when Khrushchev put up the Berlin Wall. Waiting for me in England was a letter from my draft board stating that I would be inducted the moment I set foot on native soil. "Agriculture": that was the first degree-granting program listed in the University Bulletin, which I'd dashed the mile to the Bodleian to read in only a little over the landmark 3:59.4 that Roger Bannister, my fellow Oxonian, had set a few years before. *Better boot camp,* I decided. *Better Berlin.* The bulletin's second entry was "Anthropology." The wise guy set out to talk his way back into yet another institution of learning. *Dip. Anthro. Oxon* reads my laconic degree.

But it was the beast in man I studied, while pretending to solve the kinship system among the Nuer. Nor was it the wall in Berlin that occupied me, but the one the Berliners had erected in the streets of Warsaw. In brief, I spent my second year in Oxford reading everything I could about the Holocaust, including the story of the Elder of the Lodz Ghetto—one paragraph in Gerald Reitlinger's important book *The Final Solution.* I turned down that page in my mind. When I wasn't reading, I was writing. The subject, at last, was myself.

This story, my first as an adult, was called "The Bad Jew," and in it the title character—a cool Californian, aloof from the faith of his fathers, unmoved by the traces of the Holocaust he sees about him—is nursed through an illness by two aged survivors. While recovering he comes across a long letter from one child in a death camp to another. The key passage deals with the time the writer, Jacob, gave way to despair and attempted to smother himself beneath a pile of dirt in Bergen-Belsen. He is foiled, first, by the sensation of an earthworm moving up his leg, and then by the fear that the slightest movement on his part will crush that little creature. The right thing to do, he realizes, both for himself and the Jews, is simply to wait. At this point a shift occurs in the tone of the story. The burden of irony, of detachment, is shifted from my alter-ego to the survivor, the mother of the dead Jacob. The crisis takes place when, on a bus trip across the desert, she turns in disgust from a group of dark-skinned Sephardim and says to the hero, "*Schvartzers!* Look at them! *Schvartzers!*" The Angelino, while no angel, is no longer the bad Jew.

The story has never been published. While it was making the rounds I returned full circle, to the sunshine, to the Pacific, in order to study Theater Arts at UCLA. Even then I sensed I owed this much to that city and those climes: if I had grown up there as a Jewish child, that is, if there had been nothing to search for, no vacuum to fill, I would never have become a Jewish adult. Now Ricky and I lived in an empty flat on Fountain Avenue. He burned his incense in one room. I wrote in another. The year sped quickly by. I was jogging with a friend, my old pal Alan, when the

Cuban Missile Crisis was at its worst: no way to fast talk my way out of that one. Koufax, I noted, was on his way to winning 25 games and striking out 306. Marilyn Monroe died, and so did Pope John.

Adolf Eichmann, of course, had already been hanged. In the course of that year the work that affected me most was Hannah Arendt's account of his trial. What so angered her critics—her claim that the Jewish leadership in Europe had been so compromised, so woeful, that the Jews themselves would have been better if they had had no self-government at all, and had merely run—seemed to me then, as it does now, so obvious as to be almost a truism. How on earth could things have been worse? The second half of her thesis, concerning the banality of the Obersturmbann-fuehrer, and of evil in general, was not welcome news either. Clearly her readers, Jews and Gentiles, were more comfortable thinking of Eichmann and Himmler and Goebbels and the rest as either subhuman, or superhuman, monsters, beasts, psychopaths, and not as human beings much like themselves. What struck me most about her argument—that evil was a kind of thoughtlessness, a shallowness, an inability to realize what one is doing, a remoteness from reality, and, above all, a denial of one's connectedness to others—was how much radical wickedness resembled a defect, and perhaps a disease, of imagination.

That malady, whose symptom, a stunned silence, was as prevalent in the sixties as in the fifties, could only be healed by the writers and poets whose special responsibility was to show the world what those plain men had done. As Arendt maintained, only those who have the imagination to recognize what they share with the force of evil—in her words, "the shame of being human . . . the inescapable guilt of the human race"—can fight against it. And only that fight, it seemed to me, that fearlessness, could give meaning to the suffering of the Jewish people and, in that narrow sense, bring the millions of dead back to life.

Grandiose thoughts, granted. I cannot claim to have entertained them, or worked them through, at the time. But it was partly under Arendt's spell that I spent the academic year writing a play. It doesn't take a prophet to guess the subject. An Ivy Leaguer, living abroad, first initial L., falls in love with a German heroine, first initial K. In spite of some humor ("An American Jew is someone who thinks a *shiksa* is an electric razor"), this is a tortured piece of work, haunted ("I

Yale graduation photo, 1960

have the feeling, when I think of Europe, of what happened here, that I ought to be dead") by the destruction of the Jews. Somehow, it won a large prize, the Samuel Goldwyn Award, and persuaded Yale to let me in yet again—this time to the School of Drama.

The award ceremony provided a kind of Hollywood ending. Certainly it drew many loose ends together, completing a kind of cycle. Goldwyn (né Goldfish) was the producer of one of my father's last films. Uncle Julie was in the audience. So was his ten-year-old son, Philip, named for his identical twin. Jimmy and Liz, grown-up, were in the auditorium, too. Alfred Hitchcock, for the Christians, gave a speech and handed over the prize. Thus did the film industry, which had played such a large role in making my childhood *Judenrein,* now bestow upon me—and for a play so Jewish it would make *Abie's Irish Rose* look like a crowd-pleaser at Oberammergau—its imprimatur.

Still, there were no happy endings. Katrin was in Munich, recovering from a recurrence of tuberculosis she had contracted during the war. I was already preparing for my trip to the East. Little did I know I would not return—at least not for more than a few days at a time—to the West Coast again. "Include me out": that

is not just a wacky Goldwynism. It is a description, canny to the point of genius, of the lives that Jews lived on the screen, and beneath the white clouds and peacock blue of the painted sky.

*

But I was back for good beneath the changeable vault of the East. I spent two years at the Drama School, feigning sore throats so I would not have to act in my own plays. None of these works had a Jewish theme or Jewish characters. It may or may not be a coincidence that this time I was not expelled. Immediately after completing my residency I started work at Queens College, where I was to remain for the next thirteen years. Apart from my marriage and the birth of my three children, two significant things happened during those years: I came to love the city that the Reverend Jackson quite accurately called Hymietown; and I began to write fiction. This work, on its own, it seemed, willy-nilly, veered back to what appears to be my natural subject. The first story dealt with an article from the newspapers—a Yeshiva playground under attack by a group of blacks; the second was about an exiled Romanian who had spent his entire life attempting to prove that Mozart was a Jew. Because both were immediately accepted for publication I wrote others. It was momentum, then, that drew me from the theater, though I have never stopped staging plays, sometimes of full chapter length, inside of most of what I've written since.

I finished my first novel under the thatched roof of a house in Holland, where I was teaching on a Fulbright. I can easily remember lifting, or half-lifting, its last words from what I recalled of *Little Dorrit:* ". . . they passed up and out of the courtyard itself, into the sky, like dandelions blown over the domes and towers and hot busy people of Moscow." Then I walked into our little Dutch garden and looked up at the real sky, which in the late afternoon was half pink, half blue, as if stitched like a flag down the middle. A writer isn't likely to forget such a moment—or the one, some months later, back in my windowless Queens College cubicle, when my agent called to say that an editor had accepted *P. D. Kimerakov* for publication. Here's a rarity: I've had the same agent, Lois Wallace, and the same editor, Joe Kanon, through thick and thin ever since.

For my next project I gathered five of my published stories into a book, *The Steinway Quintet Plus Four.*

The only class I ever had in writing fiction occurred when Joe, his two assistants, and I sat late one night with the manuscript all about us, scissoring out paragraphs, crossing off passages, pasting, rearranging, and smearing with pizza sauce some eighty thousand words I had always assumed to be sacred. Even then I was beginning to think about my second novel. For some reason I found myself going back to the battered Reitlinger volume (I have it, in pieces, still), which fell open to that same page 63 I had turned down in the winter of 1961-62: "At Lodz, however, the Germans chose a president in October, 1939, who suited their purposes for nearly five years. Mordechai Chaim Rumkowski . . ."

For the next year I spent every day at the YIVO Institute for Jewish Research, Fifth Avenue and 86th Street, reading everything I could about this man. The library itself was on the second floor of what must have once been a mansion, and the requested books came up the dumb waiter inside the librarian's flowered purse. The oddest, and in retrospect most frightening, aspect of this year was the way my heart, instead of skipping a beat, or stopping, at these accounts of misery and woe, pumped merrily along, essentially undeflected. I think I must have sensed soon after I began my research that if I were to get through such material at all, to say nothing of being able to think about it and shape it, I would have to draw a psychic shutter between myself and these tales of the fate of the Jews. Thus I sat through long winter months, wrapped in my overcoat, calmly, callously reading.

Finally, one day in spring, I looked up from my text. Sunlight shone from the west, lighting up the window box. The top of the trees in the park had already started to bud. *I'm going to be punished for this,* I thought. *I'm going to have nightmares.* Then I dropped my eyes to the book. In it a German officer was putting his ear to the side of a bus in which Jews were being gassed. "Just like in a synagogue," he says, of the wailing from within; and that, word for word, is how I recorded the line in my notebook and the novel to come.

There were no nightmares. I started work on my book, not looking back. "In the winter of 1918-1919, on a day when the wind was blowing, I. C. Trumpleman arrived in our town." Wait a minute! Who's talking here? Why so jaunty? So homey? So familiar? I stopped.

With wife, Ilene, about 1983

More solemnly I started again. Before I was done with page 1, I'd described another window box, "through which you can see clouds and birds and the lemon-colored lozenge of the Polish sun." Worse still! That "you," as if the speaker felt he could just come up and drop his hand on your shoulder; that sun like a cough drop. What nerve, what cockiness! Again I halted. High seriousness I wanted—not high spirits. Yet no matter which way I turned it, the material kept coming out in a tone so lighthearted and glad-to-be-alive—so much that of the reader's friend—that I had no choice but to surrender to it.

What, then, of the punishment I'd as much as promised myself? The nightmares that never came? One has only to wait. True, it did seem for a time there might be no price to pay at all. *King of the Jews* was more successful than I had dared hope: nominated for awards, translated into many foreign languages, still in print after more than a decade, it has come to look like a classic book on the Holocaust. The trouble started when, just before publication, I moved to Boston and began work on my next novel. It proved almost impossible to write. Everywhere I looked in this new manuscript I saw pain and death: amputations, autopsies, disinterments, acts of torture; whole armies crossed rivers, like Caesar's men, on the backs of their fallen comrades. I realized that all the horror I had kept from the pages of my Holocaust novel was now returning, as if in a reflex of revenge. Thousands of missing corpses were pressing round.

Clearly enough, I'd been made the butt of a joke, of an ironical trick I'd played on myself. It was as if I'd made a pact with my emotions not to feel, not to respond, but had forgotten about what might happen when the pact came to an end. This was the working out of one of the great archetypes of the culture, the bargain whose deepest meaning is never grasped by the bargainer: the man who asks for immortality but neglects to request perpetual youth; the figure who puts on a mask he can't remove; or a version of "The Sorcerer's Apprentice," in which the very powers sought for—to animate, to imagine, to control— become the source, through sheer repetition, of one's own demise.

Over the course of the next decade I continued my work on *Pinto and Sons.* Twice I came to a complete halt and wrote, rather quickly, two other books of fiction—*Regina,* a novel, that deals most explicitly with my interest in drama; and *Goldkorn Tales,* three novellas about Leib Goldkorn, the character of whom I am most fond. Always and ever I returned to the recalcitrant story of Adolph Pinto, and his adventures in the new world. Why was his tale so difficult to tell, and so filled with horrors? Part of the explanation is simplicity itself: the terms of the writing game had changed. The attention given to *King of the Jews* would now be refocused on me. My next large book had to be as good as the one that had come before. I was self-conscious, self-critical, in a way I had not yet experienced. But this is a happy hurdle, really, and one that any real writer (that is, an author who has more than one good book in him, just as a genius is someone with two great ideas) is only too eager to jump.

Nor do I think the emotional censorship I practiced at YIVO could by itself account for this large-scale return of what I believe is called the repressed. When, at what other time, had I purposefully turned my back on my feelings? Recall, if you will, the day after my father's death, when Ricky and I laughed our heads off at *The Lavender Hill Mob.* What kind of bargain, I wonder, was I making in my thirteen-year-old mind when I said I did not wish to attend the funeral? First, probably, that my refusal would not be allowed; the far-off beginnings of the ironical joke may lie here—in the way halfhearted words are taken at full value. Or perhaps this: if I ignored the proof of my father's death, he might return to us (remember those cartoon characters with nine lives?) in the guise of his identical twin. What were those gold statuettes that Alec Guinness had in his suitcase? Miniature Eiffel Towers? Or Oscars? My father's Academy Award?

Mother, Lillian, and stepfather, Erwin Gelsey, about 1980

"No Dancing on the Graves of the Dead!" That is the slogan of the young resistance fighters in *King of the Jews.* They're warning the residents of the ghetto not to go to a play (*Macbeth,* as it happens) while their people suffer. Was this meant to be a flag waved in my own direction? For going to the movies on the day my father was buried? For writing a novel about these millions of victims, in some sense ancestors too? For my laughter on both occasions? For the voice of that narrator, our jaunty friend? One would have to be a resistance fighter in a different, Freudian sense to untangle these knotty questions, though no less heroic for that.

It didn't take heroism, only grit and stubbornness, to complete *Pinto and Sons*—well over eight hundred pages in the first draft. Time, the one true critic, will determine whether the ten-year effort was misplaced. I can say this: the book only began to move, the logjam to break, when I overcame my written-in-stone objections to allowing any Jewish element into its pages. By the time I was done, my immigrant, a long-nosed and high-minded Austro-Hungarian, had taken over title and text. In a sense the writing of this book was a recapitulation of the journey I had taken from a *Judenrein* childhood to the discovery of the Jew.

And next? Well, as yet another Hebraic gentleman says at the end of *Regina,* "Lots of things, in my opinion, have got to be a secret." Not that one isn't allowed a couple of clues. Because the new book will be set in Hollywood, and in the forties, we again come round full circle. Who knows? Maybe Julie will be in

"En Famille: Anya, Paul, and Theo"

it, and Phil. Certainly there will be some of the characters, the emigrés and refugees, I glimpsed as a youth. Not to mention the writers and actors and agents who hung round our pool. The war will be in the background. Up front, the city, and the busy workings of its chief industry. And everywhere, of course, the flat, unchanging sunlight, the blue of the real and brush-stroked sky. During the task—and for how many years?—I won't budge from my study at Brookline, Massachusetts. The wings of the imagination are, for me, the best way home.

POSTSCRIPT

Leslie Epstein contributed the following update to *CA* in 2003:

The last words in the previous installment of what is clearly turning out to be an ongoing saga were, "The wings of the imagination are, for me, the best way home." What strikes me forcefully now, a decade and more later, is how fiercely those wings have been beating since. For home—that is to say, the literal house of my childhood on San Remo Drive and those who lived in it, my father and mother and brother, together with our various black servants; the swimming pool in the back yard, the lemon groves and the smell of the lemons, the cork trees, the little music alcove with its Capehart and 78-rpm records, the white pillars looming in front; and the more figurative home of the most western state and the faith of the fathers—is something that I now know has always been lurking in my work and which, at the turn of the millennium, asserted in undeniable ways its claim.

But if California and Judaism—or at any rate Jews—and the movie business together constituted a flame that this writerly moth circled and re-circled, it is a fact that the insect always veered away, apparently in fear of singeing those aforementioned wings. In other words, the memories of childhood were so efficiently repressed that they could only be expressed in sublimated form. Thus, throughout my career the past in general became the genre of history; the sorrows of childhood were transformed preposterously into the sufferings of the Jews; and my gaze was deflected from youth and adolescence toward aged figures who, however peppy, had one foot and maybe a calf and a thigh in the grave.

I have written earlier how I turned my back on Judaism, forsook family, and fled California; and how, *for that very reason,* Jews and Jewishness on the one hand and family, films, and California on the other became the entwined themes of my work (though the use of that word, *entwined,* suggests yet another theme, twins). I've often wondered: if I had not rejected religion and home, would either have played a role in my fiction? Indeed, would I have become a writer at all? I'll risk repetition: if I had had a religious life as a child, would I have attempted to fill what is cornily called a spiritual vacuum as an adult; if I'd remained on the shores of the Pacific, how could I constantly imagine making my return?

The first overt signs of the movement back appeared in the novel *Pinto and Sons.* There, a Jewish emigrant, thinking to return to his home in middle Europe to fight in the revolutionary wars of 1848, ends up in gold rush California by mistake. And if the role of the Jews had to be played by painted Indians, there was nonetheless a clear enough reference to a suffering people that was about to be exterminated by a technologically superior but morally dimmed society. If I am present anywhere, I suspect it is not so much in the figure of Adolph Pinto but in his "sons," the Modoc boys, ever precocious, who love learning and speak exclusively in the words and intonations of Robert Burns.In my next book, *Pandaemonium,* the approach to my own boyhood is more explicit still. Again, the movement is from Europe to California, but the journey is from necessity and not in error. Further, it is not only to my native state that all the characters come, but the Los Angeles of my infancy and boyhood and youth, the city of the film industry into which I had been born. What's this? These two bald writers? Cracking jokes, pulling pranks, and writing a new film for the narrator, Peter Lorre? Yep, it's the Epstein twins, Phil and Julie, who serve as a kind of Greek chorus throughout the drama.

(Parenthetically, have readers noticed how often my work contains plays within novels? *Antigone,* of course, in *Pandaemonium; Macbeth* in *King of the Jews; Othello* in *Goldkorn Tales; The Seagull* in *Regina? Not to mention Aïda* and *The Life of Louis Pasteur,* and all the other movies in *Ice Fire Water.* Is this because I was trained as a playwright, actually wrote plays, and so pay this tribute after having somehow taken a wrong turn into fiction? Or is it an indirect struggle with, and tribute to, my father and uncle, who of course wrote plays and screenplays all their lives?)

I didn't dawdle, as is my wont, over *Pandaemonium,* because I wanted Uncle Julie, already well into his eighties, to see himself in the book, which contains, in addition to every practical joke he and his brother pulled on Jack Warner, his practical wisdom as well. For example, when I told him how, at the banquet Warner gave for the premiere of *Midsummer Night's Dream,* he arranged for embossed medallions of himself and Shakespeare to be printed on the cover of the brochure, Julie said, "And neither one of them ever heard of the other." That made it into the novel, and so did this: I told Julie that I was going to recreate the famous moment at which he and Phil solved the riddle of the ending of *Casablanca* by turning to each other and simultaneously shouting, "Round up the usual suspects!" I mentioned to my uncle that while in reality that occurred in a Buick stopped at the red light at Beverly Glen and Sunset, I was going to move it to the Warners' sound stage and have Jack Warner present. "Fine," he answered, "but have Jack stand there and say, 'Huh? Round them up for what?'"

So there for all the world to see were two vital members of my family. Where, if anywhere, was I? Crouched, hidden in, and divided between, the two narrators, I suppose. Was Peter Lorre, with his wild ambitions for high art and his entrapment in an endless series of Mister Moto films, a commentary on my own academic and literary pretensions, while at bottom all I really wanted to do was write like my dad for the movies? I wouldn't go so far as to claim that the character of Louella Parsons was a Jungian anima, or shadow, of her creator; but her bottomless vulgarity, vindictiveness, and perpetual sniping is just what one

would expect of someone locked out of a community that she believed she deserved to inherit as her birthright.

The idea of a divided author, split between aspects of his characters, is perhaps clearer in my next book, *Ice Fire Water: A Leib Goldkorn Cocktail.* Yet again we have the sea change from Europe to Los Angeles; this time the traveler is our old friend, Leib Goldkorn, who because of a dyslexic French telegraphic boy (the telegram was actually meant for Korngold, the famous composer), ends up in Hollywood, writing music for Darryl Zanuck. Here I am to be found both in the youthful Leib, dizzyingly entangled in the world of glamorous Hollywood, filled with stars and starlets; and in the aged, solitary Jew, toilet bound, "Hustler," and much else, in hand, a figure I fear I am rapidly coming to resemble.

With my ninth book, *San Remo Drive: A Novel from Memory,* the process—half denial, half sublimation—came to an end. Perhaps I was forced to stop writing about aged, suffering Jews because all too clearly I was becoming just such a figure myself. All I know for certain is that in the midst of writing the usual kind of historical novel—subject: the Jews in Rome before and during the Second World War—I found myself pulling down the first volume of my Random House Proust and reading the famous words that described how Marcel used to fall asleep. It seemed a crazy thing to do. After all, I'd read through the unadorned Scott Moncrieff translation forty years earlier, lying in the guest room of my Uncle Julie's house with a thermometer in my mouth for what I suspect was a Proustian, couvadian fever. Then I read Kilmartin's touch-up in the early nineties. Why should Dobbin once more plod these same pages? But plod I did, two pages a night, every night. No, in truth there has been no plodding. I enjoyed, and enjoy still, the simultaneous commitment of five minutes and five years. Each night, like a box of Godivas on my pillow, rests the clothbound book. It is not a bad idea, I have come to understand, to keep a bedtime appointment with a noble mind; it has the power to purify even the most wasted day.

One morning, about a month after I had started reading *A la recherche du temps perdu,* I sat down at my desk and, after the usual Talmudic fiddling with the sports pages, started to write. What emerged on the legal pad had nothing to do with the novel that was already under way. In that work my narrator had arrived in Rome just in time to witness the triumphal parade of Mussolini's army and the spectacle of the vanquished Ethiopians being led through that same Arch of Titus that had been erected to celebrate the defeat of the Jews. What I saw before me now was a teenager in a Buick convertible driving along the Pacific Coast Highway with a woman trying to protect her blowing hair and another adolescent who had his arms around the family spaniel to make sure it would not jump from the car. A double take. Why, that fellow driving resembled me! Wasn't that my mother looking into her compact mirror? The curly blond hair, the blue, glittering eyes, and, yes, the gap in his teeth when he smiled: that was my brother. We were driving to Malibu to meet the man who wanted to marry my mother.

I put down my Pelikan pen. Where had these people come from? I had written the paragraph in a kind of trance. But I was not so dazed as not to understand why I had somnambulistically pulled down the volume of Proust. I needed Marcel's courage and Marcel's example. If *he* could write about how he would wait in literal breathlessness for his mother's good night kiss, perhaps I could depict my own past with its equivocal caress.

I finished the first story, and then a second and started a third. I began to see that a novel might be under way. By then I understood that there was another reason I had sought out Proust, one inextricably bound up with the passage of time. When Marcel returns to Parisian society after a hiatus of many years, he encounters his old friends at the Princesse de Guermantes. He hardly recognizes them. Trembling, they are, and pale, the women bent as if their dresses had already become entangled in their tombstones, their heads drooping in a trajectory, the momentum of whose parabolas nothing will be able to check. Even the tremor on their lips seems to him a last prayer. I, too, had recently returned to the neighborhood in which I'd grown up and saw once again the generation of actors and actresses, the writers and agents, who had so dazzled me once with their wit, beauty, and bright spirits. There they were, huddled at the edges of the Palisades, as at the end of a continent, over which a wind was blowing them—like pumice stone dolls, as Marcel puts it—unrelenting down.

As Marcel puts it. That is the purpose of literature: to organize our experience, to prefigure it, and to provide

both the recognition of, and consolation for, the fact that we ourselves are growing old. I sensed that Proust, or my memory of Proust buried in that final volume, had helped me deal with the shock of what awaited me each time I returned to the West.

*

But I could not know that a greater shock lay just ahead. Midway through that third story, while working on a scene in which the boy who resembles me wraps a towel about the woman who resembles my mother after she has emerged shivering from an all too familiar pool, the telephone rang. My actual mother had had a heart attack, a bad one, out of the blue. I arrived at her bedside the next day. She was up, she was chipper, she wanted her glasses to read the *New Yorker;* but a second attack two days later tore a hole in that already damaged muscle, and the blood swished back and forth for a few hours, until she, I think to her own surprise, slipped away. Three days later Uncle Julie died too. We held one funeral. We held the other. Again the survivors appeared before me, though this time I did not give a thought to the glamorous lives they had led: these were just ladies from my mother's bridge group, and other ladies and gentlemen from the Plato Society, for which to the end my mother had been writing a paper on the Ottoman Turks.

I returned to my home in the East. Old newspapers, old letters, students and students' stories. Also waiting was the yellow pad, similar to the one I am writing on now, and the abandoned sentence: my mother's double, in her white bathing cap, her bathing costume, blue-lipped from the cold. My Pelikan was waiting too. Proust could no longer help me. I was alone in the room. Somewhere Matisse has written that the great thing about art is that no matter what happens to the painter, whatever the interruptions or vicissitudes of his life, the daffodil or the patch of sunlight is still waiting utterly unchanged, so that he can make it complete. I picked up my pen. I finished the scene. I finished the story. I do not believe anyone can find that moment—I cannot find it myself—at which I was forced to suspend the sentence. All is seamless. With those words, and with these, I console myself.

I'd like to add, if I may, another thought or two. This, from Freud, is the epigraph at the start of *San Remo Drive:*

The Epstein family today: Paul, Leslie, Anya, Ilene, and Theo

E.T.A. Hoffman used to explain the wealth of imaginative figures that offered themselves to him for his stories by the quickly changing pictures and impressions he had received during a journey of of some weeks in a post-chaise, while still a babe at his mother's breast.

It seems crazy to assert that the whole of a writer's imaginative life can spring from such a source. And yet, think of the scene: the horse, the shine of sweat on its rump, the smell of that sweat, the crack of the whip, the sound of the hooves over cobblestones, the light winking through the leaves of the trees, the faces of those standing at the side of the road, and, above all, the mother's arms, the mother's breast—suddenly, what Hoffman asserted is not so unlikely after all.

I have a similar memory, my first. This is how the figure who (no splitting, no disguises) represents me in the novel describes it to those attending his mother's funeral:

> "My first memory is of a rowboat," I told the mourners. And so it was. I was I think little more than one year old. My mother and I were in a lake. I think it was at MacArthur Park. I think it was a Sunday. My evidence for that was the colored funny papers that the man in the boat held before his lips, like a guide using a megaphone. Was that Norman? Fooling around to divert us? Or was it some stranger? Were there even multi-colored comics in 1939? In all likelihood Lotte was pregnant;

thus it is not beyond all possibility that I could feel my brother moving as she pressed me against her. Nothing was certain, save for the green grass, the blue sky, the white clouds, and the undeniable fact that my mother was holding me in her arms; and what I told all her friends was that for the whole course of my life she had held me, and was doing so still. (*San Remo Drive: A Novel from Memory*)

Why was that distant experience available to me as a fiction writer now in his sixties? I think because, lodged in my adolescent memory, there was a second rowboat, the one in which—or so I was convinced— that man who wanted to marry my mother rowed me well off the Malibu shore in order to kill me. *San Remo Drive* is filled with such doubling, echoing memories. The day after my mother's funeral I went back to that house I mentioned earlier, the one with the lemon groves, 1341 San Remo Drive. The elderly woman who let me in turned out to be the young bride we had sold it to a half century before. Inside, I thought I recognized our dinner table. I thought I recognized our credenza. "Yes," said Miss Havisham, "and there is your mother's baby grand. We haven't changed a thing." She led me through the living room to the bar, and the little room where we used to play music. She threw open a pair of cabinet doors: there was our antique Capehart and the 78-rpm records, the show tunes and Rachmaninoff concertos that I used to sneak downstairs and conduct at night. Here again were two experiences: an old one and a new one, a doubled memory, the house that was eternally mine and the one that this stranger was only renting.

Think of Uncle Julie's funeral; it, too, resembled that party at the Princesse des Guermantes'. The gathered figures from my childhood were at one and the same time young and old, present and past. The key thing in making any memory available to imagination, and perhaps to art, is not only that it is doubled (and heavy, often, with an Oedipal atmosphere), but that it makes us aware of the passage of time and hence of our own mortality. All of my life seemed now open to me, as it had not been before, and as it may not be again. Here is another quote from Freud; it too could be the epigraph not only for *San Remo Drive* but for all my work:

> What a child has experience and not understood by the age of two he may never again remember, except in his dreams.

My books have been just such dreams.

BIOGRAPHICAL AND CRITICAL SOURCES:

BOOKS

Contemporary Literary Criticism, Volume 27, Gale (Detroit, MI), 1984.

PERIODICALS

Atlantic Monthly, October 20, 1999, Daniel Smith, interview with Epstein.

Best Sellers, August, 1975.

Booklist, October 15, 1999, Donna Seaman, review of *Ice Fire Water: A Leib Goldkorn Cocktail,* p. 417; May 15, 2003, Donna Seaman, review of *San Remo Drive: A Novel from Memory,* p. 1644.

Boston Globe, October 26, 1990, p. A19.

Boston Herald, May 13, 1997, James Verniere, review of *Pandaemonium,* p. 33.

Boston Magazine, November, 1982, Lee Grove, interview with Epstein, pp. 107-114; May, 1985, Lee Grove, review of *Goldkorn Tales,* pp. 98-99.

Buffalo News (Buffalo, NY), August 17, 1997, Mark Shechner, review of *Pandaemonium,* p. F8.

Chicago Tribune, November 18, 1990, section 14, p. 6.

Commentary, May, 1979.

Harper's Magazine, August, 1985, "Atrocity and Imagination," pp. 13-16.

Houston Chronicle (Houston, TX), February 13, 2000, Harvey Grossinger, review of *Ice Fire Water,* p. 14.

Kirkus Reviews, April 15, 2003, review of *San Remo Drive,* pp. 554-555.

Library Journal, October 15, 1982, review of *Regina,* p. 2002; April 15, 1985, Herman Elstein, review of *Goldkorn Tales,* p. 85; October 1, 1990, Elise Chase, review of *Pinto and Sons,* p. 115; April 15, 1997, David Dodd, review of *Pandaemonium,* p. 117; September 15, 1999, Marc A. Kloszewski, review of *Ice Fire Water,* p. 114; May 1, 2003, Jim Dwyer, review of *San Remo Drive,* pp. 154-155.

Los Angeles Times, February 17, 1983, Elizabeth Wheeler, review of *Regina,* p. 30; December 14, 1997, Jeremy Larner, review of *Pandaemonium,* p. 4; June 15, 2003, Jonathan Kirsch, review of *San Remo Drive,* p. R2.

Los Angeles Times Book Review, February 17, 1983; April 23, 1985; November 22, 1990, p. E14; June 8, 1997, p. 4.

New Republic, March 10, 1979.

Newsweek, January 29, 1979.

New York Times, February 7, 1979; April 3, 1985, Michiko Kakutani, review of *Goldkorn Tales,* p. 19; November 16, 1990, Michiko Kakutani, review of *Pinto and Sons,* p. B4; June 2, 1997, Richard Bernstein, review of *Pandaemonium,* p. B7; June 12, 2003, Dinitia Smith, review of *San Remo Drive,* p. E1; July 20, 2003, Elizabeth Frank, "You'll Never Have to Leave," p. 10.

New York Times Book Review, August 10, 1975; December 12, 1976; February 4, 1979; May 5, 1979; February 28, 1980, review of *King of the Jews,* p. 47; October 10, 1982; November 21, 1982, George Stade, review of *Regina,* p. 12; December 5, 1982, review of *Regina,* p. 46; January 1, 1984, review of *Regina,* p. 32; April 7, 1985, David Evanier, review of *Goldkorn Tales,* p. 8; May 11, 1986, review of *King of the Jews,* p. 42; December 7, 1986, Patricia T. O'Connor, review of *King of the Jews,* p. 84; November 4, 1990, John Crowley, review of *Pinto and Sons,* and Judith Shulevitz, interview with Epstein, p. 3; June 22, 1997, David Freeman, review of *Pandaemonium,* p. 6; October 31, 1999, D. T. Max, review of *Ice Fire Water,* p. 15.

Present Tense, summer, 1985, Gerald Jonas, review of *Goldkorn Tales,* pp. 62-63.

Publishers Weekly, January 8, 1979; March 1, 1985, review of *Goldkorn Tales,* p. 69; September 7, 1990, Sybil Steinberg, review of *Pinto and Sons,* p. 75; March 24, 1997, review of *Pandaemonium,* pp. 59-50; August 23, 1999, review of *Ice Fire Water,* p. 47.

St. Louis Post-Dispatch (St. Louis, MO), August 17, 1997, Dale Singer, review of *Pandaemonium,* p. 5C.

San Francisco Chronicle, December 2, 1990, p. 5.

Saturday Review, March 31, 1979.

Seattle Post-Intelligencer, June 4, 1997, review of *Pandaemonium,* p. C2.

Tribune Books (Chicago, IL), February 25, 1979.

Village Voice, February 19, 1979; January 18, 1983.

Washington Post, March 11, 1979; January 1, 1983; March 20, 1985; November 25, 1990, p. 9; May 30, 1997, p. B2.

Yale Review, October, 1979.

ONLINE

Boston University Web site, http://www.bu.edu/ (June 28, 2003).

Boston Phoenix Online, http://www.bostonphoenix. com/ (June 28, 2003), Michael Bronski, review of *San Remo Drive.*

*   *   *

ERNE, Lukas (Christian) 1968-

PERSONAL: Born January 19, 1968, in Zurich, Switzerland; married. *Education:* Attended University of Exeter, 1989-90; University of Lausanne, licence en lettres, 1993; Lincoln College, Oxford, M.St., 1995; University of Geneva, Ph.D., 1998.

ADDRESSES: Office—Department of English, Faculty of Letters, University of Geneva, Uni Bastions, CH-1211 Geneva 4, Switzerland; fax: +41-22-320-04-97. *E-mail*—lukas.erne@lettres.unige.ch.

CAREER: University of Geneva, Geneva, Switzerland, member of English faculty, 1997—.

AWARDS, HONORS: Andrew W. Mellon fellow, Huntington Library, San Marino, CA, 1997-98; Swiss National Science Foundation scholar, Washington, DC, 2000-01; Myra and Charlton Hinman fellow, Folger Shakespeare Library, 2002.

WRITINGS:

(Editor, with Guillemette Bolens, and contributor) *The Limits of Textuality,* Gunter Narr (Tübingen, Germany), 2000.
Beyond the "Spanish Tragedy": A Study of the Works of Thomas Kyd, Manchester University Press (Manchester, England), 2001.
Shakespeare as Literary Dramatist, Cambridge University Press (Cambridge, England), 2003.

Contributor to books, including *Renaissance Papers 2001,* edited by Thomas Hester, Boydell & Brewer (Cambridge, England), 2002. Contributor of articles and reviews to periodicals, including *English Literary Renaissance, Essays in Criticism, Shakespeare Quarterly, Theatre Research International,* and *English Studies.*

WORK IN PROGRESS: Editing *The First Quarto of Romeo and Juliet,* for Cambridge University Press (Cambridge, England); editing *Textual Performances: The Modern Reproduction of Shakespeare's Drama,* with M. J. Kidnie.

*   *   *

ESKIN, Blake 1970-

PERSONAL: Born November 15, 1970, in New York, NY.

ADDRESSES: Agent—Writers House, 21 West 26th St., New York, NY 10010.

CAREER: Writer and editor. *Forward,* arts editor.

WRITINGS:

(Compiler) *The Book of Political Lists: From the Editors of George Magazine,* Villard (New York, NY), 1997.
A Life in Pieces: The Making and Unmaking of Binjamin Wilkomirski, W. W. Norton (New York, NY), 2002.

Contributor to periodicals, including the *New Yorker New York Times Washington Post* (magazine), and *Newsday;* contributor to *This American Life,* National Public Radio.

SIDELIGHTS: Writer and editor Blake Eskin compiled *The Book of Political Lists: From the Editors of George Magazine,* a book of trivia that includes Thomas Jefferson's twelve rules of conduct, facts about the U.S. government's special-interest spending, and the most notable Congressional filibusters. Other lists in the book are: "The Dumbest Things Ever Said on the Floor of Congress," "The Ten Biggest Bribes," and "Presidents with Ancestors Who Came over on the Mayflower." In the *Virginia Quarterly Review,* a contributor called the book an "entertaining and informative book that could sit proudly on any coffee table or commode."

Eskin's second book, *A Life in Pieces: The Making and Unmaking of Binjamin Wilkomirski,* tells the story of literary fraud, as well as Eskin's personal involvement with the subject. Binjamin Wilkomirski had published, in Germany, a 1995 memoir called *Fragments,* which purportedly recounted the author's survival of Nazi concentration camps, specifically, Auschwitz and Majdanek. The music teacher and clarinet maker claimed he was smuggled into Switzerland as a child, where a family then took him from an orphanage and raised him as a Christian. When, in his fifties, Wilkomirski said he remembered bits and pieces of those years, friends and mental health professionals urged him to write his account.

Critics hailed the book as an instant classic of Holocaust literature, and it won prizes internationally. Even before its publication, however, a Swiss journalist approached its publisher with concerns as to its authenticity. When it became available in English in the United States, in 1996, Eskin informed his mother; her family, named Wilkomirski, came from Riga, Latvia, and she was eager to learn more of their heritage. So when Wilkomirski toured the States in 1997, well funded, to speak to survivor groups, Holocaust researchers, and the media, Eskin's family invited the author to attend a reunion. He did, but the bloodlines failed to be clearly established and Eskin began to have his own suspicions.

In 1998 Swiss writer Daniel Ganzfried, the son of an Auschwitz survivor, wrote an article that revealed that Wilkomirski was not Jewish and had not been born in Latvia, as he had claimed. He had instead been named Bruno by his mother, Yvonne Grosjean, a poor unmarried Swiss factory worker who placed him with foster families when she could no longer support him, and who eventually gave him up for good. He was adopted in 1957 by the Doessekkers, a Zurich doctor and his wife.

Even as the hoax was confirmed over the following year, so many people and groups had accepted his story that there was resistance to withdrawing the book from publication. Many people viewed the account as an accurate portrayal of a child's view of the horrors of the period, despite revelations about its evident fabrication. Also, supporters felt that some inconsistencies in Wilkomirski's story could be explained by the fact that he had been only three or four at the time he claimed to be in the camps. In addition, survivors feared that if Wilkomirski's story proved false, their own would lose credibility. As a result, a significant contingent refused to believe that it was a hoax, but in 2002, DNA tests confirmed conclusively that it was.

Wilkomirski did suffer as a child, but in a different way: by being shuffled from foster home to foster home. In the *Spectator,* Theo Richmond wrote, in regard to *A Life in Pieces,* that "There is much to be said for Eskin's proposition that the man's emotional distress was genuine, and that he took the Holocaust as a metaphor for his own real traumas as a child."

Library Journal reviewer Frederic Krome, meanwhile, called Eskin's book "a cautionary tale about the role of memory in historical investigation." Maurice Walsh wrote in *New Statesman* that the book "is a triumph of the necessity of thinking and feeling at the same time."

Jonathan Lear wrote in the *New York Times Book Review* that *A Life in Pieces* "is much more than an exposé. It is a telling account of our culture's love affair with the victim" and "shows in bold relief . . . how the culture was ready to fall in love with this myth."

In an online review for the *Houston Chronicle,* Harvey Grossinger wrote that Eskin's "unprejudiced and mesmerizing account is an amalgam of disoriented family history and the history of the mass of European Jews during the war. It's a detective story, a penetrating study of violated trust and incredulous quackery, and a validation of Eskin's tireless efforts as a skeptical reporter to track down the truth. It is also a deeply reflective meditation on the credibility and value of individual testimony."

BIOGRAPHICAL AND CRITICAL SOURCES:

PERIODICALS

Booklist, May 15, 1998, Bonnie Smothers, review of *The Book of Political Lists: From the Editors of George Magazine,* p. 1569; February 1, 2002, Vanessa Bush, review of *A Life in Pieces: The Making and Unmaking of Binjamin Wilkomirski,* p. 916.

Bookseller, February 8, 2002, Benedicte Page, review of *A Life in Pieces,* p. 31.

Foreign Affairs, May-June, 2002, Stanley Hoffman, review of *A Life in Pieces.*

Library Journal, January, 2002, Frederic Krome, review of *A Life in Pieces,* p. 122.

New Statesman, May 20, 2002, Maurice Walsh, review of *A Life in Pieces,* p. 54.

Newsweek International, March 25, 2002, Caille Millner, review of *A Life in Pieces,* p. 4.

New York, February 4, 2002, Ben Kaplan, review of *A Life in Pieces,* p. 82.

New Yorker, February 4, 2002, review of *A Life in Pieces,* p. 81.

New York Times Book Review, February 24, 2002, Jonathan Lear, review of *A Life in Pieces,* p. 22.

Publishers Weekly, December 24, 2002, Michael Bronski, "PW Talks with Blake Eskin," p. 54.

Spectator, April 27, 2002, Theo Richmond, review of *A Life in Pieces,* p. 39.

Times Literary Supplement, May 17, 2002, Elaine Glaser, review of *A Life in Pieces,* p. 33.

Virginia Quarterly Review, autumn, 1998, review of *The Book of Political Lists: From the Editors of George Magazine,* p. 140.

Wall Street Journal, February 5, 2002, Tom Gross, review of *A Life in Pieces,* p. A16.

Wilson Quarterly, summer, 2002, Paul Maliszewski, review of *A Life in Pieces,* p. 109.

ONLINE

Houston Chronicle, http://www.chron.com/ (July 19, 2002), Harvey Grossinger, review of *A Life in Pieces.*

F

FIELD, (William) Todd 1964-

PERSONAL: Born February 24, 1964, in Pomona, CA; married Serena Rathbun, July 25, 1987; children: three, including Alida P. (daughter). *Education:* Attended Southern Oregon State University; American Film Institute, M.F.A., 1995.

ADDRESSES: Home—ME. *Agent*—Endeavor Talent Agency, 9701 Wilshire Blvd., 10th Floor, Beverly Hills, CA 90212.

CAREER: Actor, producer, director, photographer, and jazz musician. Actor in films, including (as crooner) *Radio Days,* 1987; (as bellhop) *The Allnighter,* Universal, 1987; (as David Schreiner) *Gross Anatomy* (also known as *A Cut Above*), Buena Vista, 1989; (as Robert Wilson) *Fat Man and Little Boy* (also known as *Shadowmakers*), Paramount, 1989; (as Anthony Glenn) *Eye of the Eagle 2: Inside the Enemy* (also known as *KIA*), 1989; (as Johnson) *Full Fathom Five,* Concorde, 1990; (as Todd Brand) *Back to Back,* Concorde, 1990; (as Cecil) *Queens Logic,* Seven Arts, 1991; (as Richard) *The End of Innocence,* Skouras Pictures, 1991; (as The Dog) *The Dog,* 1992; (as Mike McCaslin) *Ruby in Paradise,* October Films, 1993; (as Duane) *Sleep with Me,* Metro-Goldwyn-Mayer (MGM), 1994; (as Tim "Beltzer" Lewis) *Twister,* Warner Bros., 1996; (as Frank) *Walking and Talking,* Miramax, 1996; (as Chase) *Farmer and Chase,* Arrow Releasing, 1997; (as Jimmy Warzniak) *Broken Vessels,* Unapix Entertainment, 1998; (as Nick Nightingale) *Eyes Wide Shut,* Warner Bros., 1999; (as Todd Hackett) *The Haunting,* DreamWorks Distribution, L.L.C., 1999; (as Thad Davis) *Net Worth,* Curb Entertainment, 2000; (as Mr. Walsh) *New Port South,* Buena Vista, 2000; (as Toretti) *Beyond City Limits* (also known as *Rip It Off*), 2002; and (as Dr. Bell) *Alphawave,* 2002.

Actor in television series, including (as Andres Johansson) *Lance et compte* (also known as *Cogne et gagne* and *He Shoots, He Scores*), 1986; (as Kevin Davis) *Take Five,* Columbia Broadcasting System (CBS), 1987; (as Ray "Rake" Monroe) *Danger Theatre,* 1993; and (as David Caselli) *Once and Again,* American Broadcasting Company (ABC), 1999-2000. Actor in made-for-television movies, including (as Neil Barton/Adriano Pabrizi) *Student Exchange,* ABC, 1987; (as David Yates) *Jonathan Stone: Threat of Innocence* (also known as *Frame Up*), National Broadcasting Company (NBC), 1994; (as Bob Younger) *Frank and Jesse,* Home Box Office (HBO), 1994; and (as Donovan Miller/Austin Walker) *Stranger than Fiction,* Cinemax, 1999. Played Jason in television special *Lookwell,* Disney Channel, 1991. Guest star on television series, including *Roseanne, Tales from the Crypt,* and *Chicago Hope.*

Director of films, including *Too Romantic* (short film), Mercury Film, 1992; (with Alex Vlacos) *The Dog,* 1992; (also additional camera operator) *When I Was a Boy* (short film), 1993; *Delivering* (short film), 1993; (also camera operator) *Nonnie and Alex,* Sundance Channel, 1995; and (also producer and camera operator) *In the Bedroom,* Miramax, 2001. Also additional boom operator, *The Rapture,* Fine Line, 1991, and coproducer, *Broken Vessels,* 1998. Directed episodes of television series *Once and Again,* ABC, 1999-2001. Author of musical scores for films *Nowhere to Run,* Concorde, 1989; *The Dog,* 1992; *Ruby in Paradise,* October Films, 1993; and *Broken Vessels,* Unapix Entertainment, 1998, and songs for film *Gross Anatomy,* 1989.

AWARDS, HONORS: Special Jury award, Sundance Film Festival, best film prize, Aspen Film Festival, and special citation, Academy of Television Arts and Sciences, all for *Nonnie and Alex;* best film award, Los Angeles Film Critics Association, best first film award, New York Film Critics' Circle, and Academy Award nominations for best picture and best screenplay based on material previously produced or published, Academy of Motion Picture Arts and Sciences, all 2001, all for *In the Bedroom;* Satyajit Ray Award, Satyajit Ray Foundation, 2001; Franklin J. Schaffner Alumni Medal, American Film Institute, 2002.

WRITINGS:

SCREENPLAYS; SHORT FILMS, UNLESS OTHERWISE NOTED

(And director) *Too Romantic,* Mercury Film, 1992.
When I Was a Boy, Mercury Film, 1993.
Delivering, based on a short story by Andre Dubus, Mercury Film, 1993.
(With Richard Festinger; and director) *In the Bedroom* (feature film), based on the short story "Killings" by Andre Dubus, Miramax, 2001.

SIDELIGHTS: Todd Field, an actor possibly best known for his role as the piano player in director Stanley Kubrick's film *Eyes Wide Shut,* became one of Hollywood's hottest new writer/directors with the release of *In the Bedroom,* a film based on a short story by author Andre Dubus. (Field counts both Kubrick and Dubus among his mentors; tragically, both died during the production of *In the Bedroom.*) "I don't mind telling you that *In the Bedroom* didn't make me cry. It made me weep," reviewer Bob Ivry wrote in the *Record.* "Mature filmgoers with a hunger for an emotionally satisfying cinematic meal . . . will no doubt find *In the Bedroom* a work of virtuosity."

Set in a small town in coastal Maine, *In the Bedroom* examines the grief of two parents, Matt and Ruth Fowler (played by Oscar-winning actress Sissy Spacek and British actor Tom Wilkinson), after their young adult son Frank is brutally murdered by the estranged husband of an older woman, Natalie (played by Oscar-winning actress Marissa Tomei) with whom the young man had been having an affair. Because the killer is from a rich and powerful family in their small town, he is soon set free on bail, and instead of being tried for murder he is only going to be tried for manslaughter, which carries a sentence of around five years. This eats away at Matt and Ruth, and their search for a way to deal both with their grief and with this miscarriage of justice forms the heart of the film.

In the Bedroom was a labor of love for Field: it was made in his home town—the house where he, his wife, and their three children live when they are not in Los Angeles was even used as the setting for one scene—his wife and Spacek did a portion of the set designing, and Field handled a camera himself on some of the shots. "My hair has turned gray on this; I've lost fifteen pounds. I'm in debt up to my ears and I haven't worked [as an actor] in two years!," Field told David Ansen of *Newsweek.* But the result, most critics said, was stunning. Bob Longino of the *Atlanta Journal-Constitution* dubbed it "the most heartbreaking movie of the year—and easily one of the best," while reviewer Anthony Quinn of the London *Independent* noted that "Field has pulled off something here I thought no American film-maker would ever manage again: he makes violence feel genuinely shocking." Nigel Andrews of the London *Financial Times* declared: "I cannot remember a better film about the shock of loss."

BIOGRAPHICAL AND CRITICAL SOURCES:

PERIODICALS

Albuquerque Tribune (Albuquerque, NM), March 22, 2002, Jeff Commings, "Field Finds Himself Finding Favor as a Multi-hatted Man," p. C5.
America, March 4, 2002, Richard A. Blake, review of *In the Bedroom,* p. 23.
Atlanta Journal-Constitution, December 25, 2001, Bob Longino, review of *In the Bedroom,* p. C11; August 11, 2002, Bob Longino, review of *In the Bedroom,* p. L8.
Back Stage, December 21, 2001, David Sheward, "Crix Have *Bedroom* Eyes: Drama Only Frontrunner in Year-End Prizes," pp. 8-9.
Christian Century, February 13, 2002, Phil Christman, review of *In the Bedroom,* pp. 47-48.

Commonweal, January 11, 2002, Rand Richards Cooper, review of *In the Bedroom,* p. 19.

Cosmopolitan, October, 1993, Guy Flatley, review of *Ruby in Paradise,* p. 26.

Film Journal International, September, 2001, Kevin Lally, review of *In the Bedroom,* p. 51.

Financial Times (London, England), January 24, 2002, Nigel Andrews, review of *In the Bedroom,* p. 14.

Guardian (London, England), January 16, 2002, Howard Feinstein, interview with Field, p. 13; January 25, 2002, Peter Bradshaw, review of *In the Bedroom,* p. 12; March 1, 2002, David Lodge, review of *In the Bedroom,* p. 8.

Harper's Bazaar, October, 2001, Catherine Hong, interview with Field, pp. 161-162.

Independent (London, England), January 11, 2002, Matthew Sweet, interview with Field, p. S12; January 25, 2002, Anthony Quinn, review of *In the Bedroom,* p. 10.

Independent Sunday (London, England), January 27, 2002, Jonathan Romney, review of *In the Bedroom,* p. 9.

Insight on the News, December 17, 2001, Rex Roberts, review of *In the Bedroom,* pp. 32-33.

Knight Ridder/Tribune News Service, December 24, 2001, Bruce Newman, "Todd Field Makes a Splash with Directorial Debut *In the Bedroom,*" p. K1420; August 20, 2002, Randy Myers, "*In the Bedroom* Director Todd Field Did It His Way," p. K2586.

Los Angeles Times, November 23, 2001, Kenneth Turan, review of *In the Bedroom,* p. F2; December 16, 2001, Susan King, "*Bedroom* Is Top Pick of L.A. Film Critics," p. B3; March 13, 2002, "Secrets of a Mysterious Trade," p. E2.

National Catholic Reporter, November 12, 1993, Joseph Cunneen, review of *Ruby in Paradise,* p. 16; January 25, 2002, Joseph Cunneen, review of *In the Bedroom,* pp. 14-15.

New Republic, December 17, 2001, Stanley Kauffmann, review of *In the Bedroom,* p. 28.

Newsweek, August 5, 1996, Karen Schoemer, review of *Walking and Talking,* p. 73; December 3, 2001, David Ansen, review of *In the Bedroom,* p. 72; January 21, 2002, Jeff Giles and David Ansen, "Break on Through to the Oscar Side: Two Hot Talents Reach Critical Mass," p. 50.

New Yorker, November 26, 2001, David Denby, review of *In the Bedroom,* pp. 121-123.

New York Post, November 23, 2001, review of *In the Bedroom,* p. 46; December 14, 2001, "New York Film Critics Pick *Drive* and *Bedroom,*" p. 58.

New York Times, July 2, 1999, Steven Holden, review of *Broken Vessels,* p. B12; November 18, 2001, Laura Winters, review of *In the Bedroom,* p. AR15; November 23, 2001, Stephen Holden, review of *In the Bedroom,* p. E25; August 9, 2002, Peter M. Nichols, review of *In the Bedroom,* p. E26.

Observer (London, England), January 13, 2002, Demetrios Matheou, interview with Field, p. R7; January 27, 2002, Philip French, review of *In the Bedroom,* p. 7.

People, November 1, 1993, Leah Rozen, review of *Ruby in Paradise,* p. 16; December 3, 2001, review of *In the Bedroom,* p. 33.

Premiere, December, 2001, Glenn Kenny, review of *In the Bedroom,* p. 91.

Record (Bergen County, NJ), November 23, 2001, Bob Ivry, review of *In the Bedroom,* p. 3.

Rolling Stone, December 6, 2001, Peter Travers, review of *In the Bedroom,* pp. 155-156.

San Francisco Chronicle, December 23, 2001, Carla Meyer, interview with Field, p. 27; December 25, 2001, Edward Guthmann, review of *In the Bedroom,* p. D1; August 16, 2002, Edward Guthmann, review of *In the Bedroom,* p. D10.

Seattle Times, December 24, 2001, Moira Macdonald, "His Field Is behind the Camera," p. C4.

Sight and Sound, January, 2002, Charlotte O'Sullivan, review of *In the Bedroom,* pp. 44-45; February, 2002, Demetrios Matheou, interview with Field, p. 10.

Time, December 24, 2001, Richard Schickel, review of *In the Bedroom,* p. 79.

TV Guide, April 23, 1994, Myles Callum, review of *Ruby in Paradise,* p. 38.

US Weekly, November 26, 2001, Andrew Johnston, review of *In the Bedroom,* p. 72.

Variety, April 8, 1987, review of *Take Five,* p. 66; December 2, 1987, review of *Student Exchange,* p. 68; October 25, 1989, review of *Gross Anatomy,* pp. 29-30; February 8, 1993, Todd McCarthy, review of *Ruby in Paradise,* p. 75; October 16, 1995, Dennis Harvey, review of *Farmer and Chase,* p. 97; January 26, 1996, Todd McCarthy, review of *Walking and Talking,* pp. 64-65; April 27, 1998, Leonard Klady, review of *Broken Vessels,* p. 60; January 29, 2001, Todd McCarthy, review of *In the Bedroom,* p. 43.

Wall Street Journal, August 20, 1999, Carrie Dolan, review of *Broken Vessels,* p. W4; November 23, 2001, Joe Morgenstern, review of *In the Bedroom,* p. W1.

ONLINE

BBC News, http://news.bbc.co.uk/ (November 19, 2001), Rebecca Thomas, review of *In the Bedroom.*

MovieMaker Magazine, http://www.moviemaker.com/ (April 26, 2003), Paula Schwartz, "The Circus Comes to Town: Todd Field Talks about Shooting *In the Bedroom* on the Coast of Maine."*

*   *   *

FITZGERALD, Liv 1950-

PERSONAL: Born January 24, 1950, in Detroit, MI; daughter of Gerald Thomas (a police officer) and Ida Fitzgerald; married Paul M. Detweiler, June 8, 1969 (divorced, May, 1987); children: Brian, Keith. *Education:* Eastern Michigan University, B.S., 1986, M.A., 1988; Wayne State University, Ph.D., 1996.

ADDRESSES: Agent—c/o F.A.C.T. Publishing, P.O. Box 6124, Marietta, GA 30065. *E-mail*—livfitz gerald@msn.com.

CAREER: Hair and Co., Brighton, MI, owner, manager, and public relations representative, 1974-84; National Institute for Burn Medicine, Ann Arbor, MI, trainer and public speaker, 1985-87; General Motors Corp., Detroit, MI, writer of instructional videotapes, 1987-88; Oakland Livingston Human Service Agency, Pontiac, MI, training and public relations representative, 1988-91; Federal Reserve Bank, Detroit, trainer, 1992-94; Fitzgerald Applied Communication Training, Marietta, GA, owner, 1998—, and publisher of F.A. C.T. Publishing. Georgia State University, instructor, 1997—. Public speaker, including appearances at Women's Fest, Michigan Institute for Educational Management, Livingston Intermediate Educational Management, Single Place, and Single Point.

WRITINGS:

Visualization and Brainstorming: An Exploration, 1996.
Typical Thoughts, Triumphant Results: A Five-Step Strategy for Mastering Your Potential, F.A.C.T. Publishing (Marietta, GA), 2001.

Author of home workshop and tape series, including "Lose Weight with Visualization" and "Reduce Stress with Visualization."

WORK IN PROGRESS: A book on mastering business potential with communication and visualization.

SIDELIGHTS: Liv Fitzgerald told *CA:* "Mastering our personal and professional potential has captivated my attention, and it is the focus of my writing. I studied communication and visualization for my doctoral dissertation and have continued researching their effects in my professional practice. When combined, communication and visualization create an explosive technique for attaining potential. In my seminars I've helped thousands of people learn this technique to lost weight, stop smoking, and reduce stress. On a professional basis, my seminars help managers inspire excellence in their staff.

"With communication we learn to take small steps toward our goals. One woman I know lamented that she wanted to write a book but couldn't find the time to write 300 pages. I can't find the time to do that, either, but I can write one page at a time—small steps. The small steps necessary for reaching our potential are creating correct thoughts, creating correct behaviors, and developing a plan of action. When asked, most people agree that these steps are necessary for attaining goals, yet too often we skip the steps! Then we're stunned when we are in the same position where we were last year and the year before that.

"Communication is a prerequisite to effective visualization. Most of us are under the misguided impression that to simply imagine what you want is visualizing. To the contrary, visualization has specific steps that must be learned and practiced. In addition to the three steps mentioned above, visualization has a relaxation component, and when mentally rehearsing you must be 'associated.' Being associated means imagining your day as if you are actually doing the behaviors you desire, in contrast to watching yourself as if you were watching a movie. Visualization is a mental practice that aligns the conscious and subconscious mind. We can think of the conscious and subconscious as our 'two selves.' These two selves work under two different sets of rules: the conscious mind is critical, its job is to protect you. So when you want to try something new, it reminds you that you might get hurt, or you've tried this before and failed, or any other negative aspect. The subconscious mind is open and accepting of new ideas. It doesn't know the difference between real and imagined experiences. So, if you mentally practice a behavior you desire, the subconscious simply accepts it as real. Eventually, if you keep practicing, the conscious mind gives up being critical and starts performing the behavior the way you mentally practiced it.

"*Typical Thoughts, Triumphant Results: A Five-Step Strategy for Mastering Your Potential* is the only, up-to-date, self-help book on communication and visualization. I wrote the book because there are no other sources available to describe this technique, and because the technique works!"

*   *   *

FRASER, Marian Botsford 1948-

PERSONAL: Born 1948; divorced; children: one. *Education:* Attended Kirkland Lake Collegiate and Vocational Institute, 1960-65; University of Western Ontario, B.A. (English and philosophy), 1969; Victoria University, New Zealand, M.A. (English literature); University of British Columbia, A.B.D., 1976-82.

ADDRESSES: Home—Toronto, Ontario, Canada. *Agent*—Jackie Kaiser, Westwood Creative Artists, 94 Harbord Street, Toronto, Ontario M5S 1G6, Canada. *E-mail*—sola@marianbotsfordfraser.ca.

CAREER: Warner Bros., London, England, transportation research/writing, 1969-72; Pacific Films, New Zealand, assistant film editor, 1973-74; Radio New Zealand, script editor, 1975-76; freelance critic, New Zealand, 1973-76; New Zealand Bookworld, book review editor, 1975-76; CBC Stereo, host of *Testament,* 1983-85, interviewer, 1984-88; The Knowledge Network, writer, host, 1986-88; CBC Radio, *Ideas* program, documentary producer, 1982-95, script editor, 1989-92; Arctic Council Panel, Ottawa, Ontario, Canada, coordinator, editor, writer, 1992-98; Inuit Tapirisat of Canada, speechwriter, 1992-98; freelance editing, writing, speechwriting, documentary-making, 1992-98. Communicati ons strategy work for CARE Canada, Health Canada, Saugeen First Nation, and Canadian Policy Research Networks.

AWARDS, HONORS: Nonfiction grant, Canadian Council, 1992; grants, Ontario Arts Council, 1997-2001.

WRITINGS:

Walking the Line: Travels along the Canadian/ American Border, Douglas & McIntyre (Toronto, Ontario, Canada), 1989.
Solitaire: The Intimate Lives of Single Women, Macfarlane, Walter & Ross (Toronto, Ontario, Canada), 2001.

Contributor to *Globe and Mail, Toronto Life,* and *Financial Post.* Contributor to *Writing Home: A PEN Canada Anthology.*

WORK IN PROGRESS: A collection of linked short stories.

SIDELIGHTS: Marian Botsford Fraser is a freelance writer, broadcaster, and critic. She is a contributor to *Globe and Mail, Toronto Life, Elm Street,* and the *Financial Post,* and has been a regular contributor to CBC Radio.

Fraser traveled along the United States-Canadian border. along the way she visited towns, met people, and viewed the scenery. In *Walking the Line: Travels along the Canadian/American Border,* Fraser provides information on what she saw, interviews with the locals, and her own feelings and impressions.

There are more than four million single women in Canada between the ages of twenty and ninety. Being one of those four million, Fraser wanted to learn more about single women in Canada, and to do so she set out on a three-year journey across the country. She interviewed 150 single women of different ages. *Solitare: The Intimate Lives of Single Women* was the result. *Quill & Quire* contributor Jenefer Curtis called the work "A book that offers some of the most frank, fascinating, and amusing writing for women and by women to hit the mainstream press in a long while."

BIOGRAPHICAL AND CRITICAL SOURCES:

PERIODICALS

Books in Canada, March, 1990, review of *Walking the Line: Travels along the Canadian/American Border,* p. 18; May, 2002, Jana Prikryl, "Women Wanter about Love," pp. 12-13.

Canadian Geographic, June, 1990, Arthur Charity, review of *Walking the Line,* p. 78.

Chatelaine, February, 2002, "Going Solo," p. 20.

Library Journal, March 15, 1990, Mary Hemmings, review of *Walking the Line,* p. 106.

Maclean's, February 18, 2002, "Suddenly Single," p. 31.

Quill & Quire, November, 2001, Jenefer Curtis, review of *Solitaire: The Intimate Lives of Single Women,* p. 27.

ONLINE

Marian Botsford Fraser Web site, http://www.marianbotsfordfraser.ca (August 31, 2002).

McFarlane, Walter & Ross Web site, http://www.mwandr.com/ (August 31, 2002), "Marian Botsford Fraser."

Montreal Mirror Online, http://www.montrealmirror.com/ (August 31, 2002), Juliet Waters, "Single Blithe Female."*

* * *

FRIEDMAN, Robert I. 1950-2002

PERSONAL: Born 1950; died of heart failure caused by a rare blood disease July 2, 2002, in New York, NY; married Christine Dugas (a business journalist). *Education:* University of Colorado, B.A. (African and Middle Eastern studies); attended American University, Beirut; University of Wisconsin, M.A. (journalism).

CAREER: Investigative journalist. Worked on a defense plant assembly line, late 1960s. *Village Voice,* New York, NY, contributing editor.

AWARDS, HONORS: Alicia Patterson fellowship, 1987. An award in Friedman's name was established by the Fund for Investigative Journalism, Washington, DC.

WRITINGS:

The False Prophet: Rabbi Meir Kahane: From FBI Informant to Knesset Member, Lawrence Hill Books (Brooklyn, NY), 1990.

Zealots for Zion: Inside Israel's West Bank Settlement Movement, Rutgers University Press (New Brunswick, NJ), 1994.

Red Mafiya: How the Russian Mob Has Invaded America, Little, Brown (Boston, MA), 2000.

Contributor to publications, including *Village Voice, Nation, New York Review of Books, New Yorker, Vanity Fair, Details, New York Times,* and *New York.*

SIDELIGHTS: Robert I. Friedman was an investigative journalist who is perhaps best known for delving into the workings of the Russian mob in the United States, which resulted in threats to his life. His own contacts spanned the globe, and he worked in relative anonymity until 1999, when he was credited with uncovering the information that led to national headlines alleging that the Russian mob had set up a $10 billion money-laundering scheme through the Bank of New York.

Friedman grew up in Denver, Colorado, and worked on an assembly line while taking classes at the University of Colorado. He took time off to travel and audited courses at American University in Beirut, Lebanon and stayed in a red-light district where he was the only Jew living among members of the Palestinian Liberation Organization (PLO). In October 1973, he volunteered to work on a kibbutz in Israel while the men fought the Yom Kippur War.

Upton Sinclair's 1906 *The Jungle* was Friedman's inspiration. Freedman once said, "I wanted to be a writer and bring down the bastions of power that caused common people so much suffering. That's what I thought in eleventh grade. I guess I never grew up. I still feel that way."

Friedman was known for his attention to detail and attribution in his controversial and volatile reporting. The *New York Times* allowed him to break news on the op-ed page, and in 1987, a grant allowed him to report on the radical Jewish right, whose hope it was to establish a Greater Israel on the West Bank and the Gaza Strip.

Friedman, who was of Russian-Jewish heritage, sometimes alienated other Jews for his criticism of figures like Meir Kahane, the founder of the Jewish

Defense League. *Nation* reviewer Michael Rosenthal called his biography, *The False Prophet: Rabbi Meir Kahane: From FBI Informant to Knesset Member*, "a devastating, thoroughly convincing account of the career . . . of a world-class fraud, megalomaniac, and vicious bigot who rose to prominence—and a seat in the Knesset in 1984—by exploiting the basest fears of Jews both here and in Israel. A genius in the marketing of racial and religious hatred, Kahane demonstrates what implacable ambition unsullied by any trace of decency or morality can do for you if only you are serious."

Friedman notes that Kahane was fired from his first and only job as a rabbi and then became an informant for the Federal Bureau of Investigation (FBI). He used a pseudonym, Michael King, and spent the 1960s infiltrating left-wing peace groups, lobbying for the Vietnam War, and reporting on various organizations, including the Black Panthers and other Black Nationalist groups in which the FBI was interested. He achieved greater public recognition when he founded the militant Jewish Defense League (JDL) in 1968.

"Capitalizing on the racial tensions of the late 1960s, the JDL purported to be ready to defend innocent Jews from the alleged anti-Semitism stemming from the increasingly militant black civil rights movement," wrote Rosenthal. "In fact, it never defended anybody from anything, except perhaps Kahane from his creditors. In providing Kahane a platform from which to spout his politics of hate and fear, it enabled him to galvanize the anxieties of thousands of Jews into pouring millions of dollars into an organization whose real mission was not their protection but the selling of Meir Kahane." Friedman notes that many of the contributors would never admit to their support.

Kahane became a hero to the Jewish right of New York and was in league with mob boss Joseph Columbo, who showed up in court and paid Kahane's bail of $25,000. In 1971, Kahane left for Israel after being indicted for manufacturing weapons, where he coined his slogan, "Every Jew a .22," as he called for the expulsion of Arabs from Israel and the Occupied Territories.

Rosenthal concluded by saying that Friedman "negotiates the miasma of Kahane's life with both admirable restraint and a compelling urgency, exposing his cyni-

cism, his dishonesty, his untroubled racism. He examines as well the human wreckage spawned by Kahane's fanaticism—altogether, a grim and unforgiving portrait of a man who has always feasted on confrontation."

Zealots for Zion: Inside Israel's West Bank Settlement Movement followed. *Tikkun* reviewer Rita E. Hauser wrote that "the details and color that Friedman provides about the agenda of the messianic Jewish settlers in the West Bank and Gaza will surely deepen the foreboding that often grips supporters of a truly democratic Israel. Above all else, Friedman documents the extent to which Israeli political figures have used the settler movement for their own purposes."

Friedman had moved in mob circles for years, including for his reportage on the Cosa Nostra, and his connections helped him infiltrate the Russian mob early in the 1990s, after the cold war had ended. Russians with criminal records had taken refuge in the United States during the 1970s when Russia, under pressure from the U.S. government, allowed Jews to emigrate. Russia took advantage of this opportunity to rid itself of thousands of jailed criminals on an unsuspecting United States.

Friedman never gave away his informants, who continually fed him information because they trusted him. In a 1993 *Vanity Fair* article, he wrote about Marat Balagula and others in the Russian Jewish mob that were based in Brighton Beach on the Brooklyn shore and who were loosely connected to the Italian mob. Balagula was eventually convicted of evading taxes owed the federal government from the sale millions of gallons of gasoline.

Through the 1990s, Friedman broke other stories on various operations and figures, including Semion Mogilevich—whose network is the "Red Mafiya" of the title. A Ukranian Jew who was linked to prostitution, drugs, nuclear arms trafficking, and the New York money laundering scheme, Mogilevich employed a sophisticated staff that used modern technology to extend his operations around the world. Friedman drew on interviews and data contained in classified documents to expose the various schemes, and the FBI contacted Friedman and suggested that he and his wife go into hiding when death threats were made. They did, for just a week, then returned to New York City.

Friedman's reporting on the Russian mob culminated with his book, *Red Mafiya: How the Russian Mob Has Invaded America,* in which he documents the corruption that has flourished since the end of the cold war, resulting in a "criminal colossus that has surpassed the Colombian cartels, the Japanese Yakuzas, the Chinese triads, and the Italian Mafia in wealth and weaponry." Friedman lists the schemes of dozens of Russian crime syndicates operating in the United States, including Medicare fraud, theft, stock scams, money laundering, and their activities in business and real estate. He writes of deals in which helicopters and a submarine were sold to Colombian drug lords and how the Russian mob is expanding into Africa and Australia.

In reviewing *Red Mafiya* for the *New York Review of Books,* Raymond Bonner wrote that Friedman's prose "sometimes makes it sound like a sequel to *Pulp Fiction.*" *Washington Post Book World*'s Peter H. Stone said Friedman "does a first-rate job of showing why FBI director Louis Freeh has said that the Russian mob poses an 'immense' threat."

In 1996 Friedman was on assignment in Bombay to investigate how political corruption and sexual slavery were contributing to the AIDS epidemic. Upon returning to the States, he experienced flu-like symptoms that were the first signs of a rare, incurable blood disease that eventually damaged his heart to such an extent that it not support him past the age of fifty-one. *Nation* contributor and friend Julian Epstein wrote: "Robbie was the real thing: a courageous reporter who, operating freelance, made headlines exposing how the thuggish and greedy, in all their guises as politicians, bankers, revolutionaries, and mobsters, were preying on the weak."

BIOGRAPHICAL AND CRITICAL SOURCES:

PERIODICALS

American Journalism Review, January, 2000, Sherry Ricchiardi, "The Best Investigative Reporter You've Never Heard Of," p. 44.
Journal of Church and State, autumn, 1993, Louis Gordon, review of *The False Prophet: Rabbi Meir Kahane: From FBI Informant to Knesset Member,* p. 916.

Middle East Journal, spring, 1991, Dennis King, review of *The False Prophet,* p. 354.
Nation, October 29, 1990, Michael Rosenthal, review of *The False Prophet,* p. 494.
New Leader, December 14, 1992, Yehudah Mirsky, review of *Zealots for Zion: Inside Israel's West Bank Settlement Movement,* p. 13.
New York Review of Books, October 25, 1990, Arthur Hertzberg, review of *The False Prophet,* pp. 41-47; November 16, 2000, Raymond Bonner, review of *Red Mafiya: How the Russian Mob Has Invaded America,* pp. 52-55.
New York Times Book Review, May 13, 1990, Robert Leiter, review of *The False Prophet,* p. 18; January 10, 1993, Peter Grose, review of *Zealots for Zion,* p. 21.
Oral History Review, winter, 1995, Sherna Berger Gluck, review of *Zealots for Zion,* p. 115.
Publishers Weekly, February 9, 1990, Genevieve Stuttaford, review of *The False Prophet,* p. 54; October 12, 1992, review of *Zealots for Zion,* p. 58; May 8, 2000, review of *Red Mafiya,* p. 216.
Tikkun, September-October, 1990, Milton Viorst, review of *The False Prophet,* p. 86; March-April, 1993, Rita E. Hauser, review of *Zealots for Zion,* p. 65.
Times Literary Supplement, August 24, 1990, Patrick Seale, review of *The False Prophet,* p. 890.
Washington Post Book World, July 16, 2000, Peter H. Stone, review of *Red Mafiya,* p. 9.

ONLINE

Flak, http://www.flakmag.com/ (January 3, 2003), Ben Welch, review of *Red Mafiya.*
Salon.com, http://www.salon.com/ (May 18, 2000), Mark Schone, review of *Red Mafiya.*

OBITUARIES:

PERIODICALS

American Journalism Review, September, 2002, p. 10.
Nation, August 5, 2002, p. 4.
Washington Post, July 9, 2002, p. B7.

ONLINE

Freedom Forum Web site, http://www.freedomforum. org/ (July 16, 2002).*

FUERST, Jeffrey B. 1956-

PERSONAL: Born February 17, 1956, in Paterson, NJ; son of Joel (a business executive and college professor) and Paulette (a teacher and librarian) Fuerst; married Marjorie Siegel (an attorney), October 2, 1988; children: Jacob, Alexa. *Education:* Oberlin College, B.A., 1978; Brooklyn College of the City University of New York, M.F.A., 1983. *Hobbies and other interests:* Cooking, tennis, reading, travel, cultural events.

ADDRESSES: Home—95 Fairmont Ave., Hastings-on-Hudson, NY 10706. *E-mail*—jbfuerst@cs.com; jeff 1st@optonline.com.

CAREER: Phoenix Theater, worked as literary assistant; Medicine Show Theater Ensemble, worked as booking manager, publicist, and grant writer; script analyst for National Playwrights Conference and Eugene O'Neill Festival; American Stage Festival, Milford, NH, assistant artistic director, 1979-81; Nederlander Television and Film Productions, writer and literary manager, 1983-84; Museum of Television and Radio, associate curator, 1984-89; freelance writer and television producer, 1989-91; *Zillions: Consumer Report for Kids* (magazine and Internet Web site), writer and editor, 1990-2001; freelance writer and editor, 2002—. Consumers Union, educational programs editor, 2001-02. Creator of interactive quiz series *Kat Man Doo Asks You, Guess What?, The Bob Show,* and *Movie Mania with 2-XL,* 1987-88. Inter-Village Continuing Education Program, member of advisory board, 2002—. State University of New York—Westchester, adjunct instructor in television writing; workshop presenter for schools, libraries, and community organizations; teacher of writing classes; public speaker; judge of writing competitions. National Couch Potato Olympix, creator, producer, and commissioner.

MEMBER: Society of Children's Book Writers and Illustrators.

AWARDS, HONORS: Distinguished Achievement Awards, Association of Educational Publishers, 1992, 1998.

WRITINGS:

Greetings from Nowheresville! (humor), Scott, Foresman (Glenview, IL), 1999.
When in Rome (fiction), Scott, Foresman (Glenview, IL), 1999.

Pound Pals (fantasy), Scott, Foresman (Glenview, IL), 1999.
Hot Gobs: The Art of Glassblowing, Scott, Foresman (Glenview, IL), 1999.
The Iditarod: Dogsled Race across Alaska, Wright Group (San Diego, CA), 2000.
Inside a Radio Station, McGraw-Hill (New York, NY), 2001.
African-American Cowboys: A True Tale of the Old West, Celebration Press (Parsippany, NJ), 2002.
The Kids' Baseball Workout: How to Get in Shape and Improve Your Game, illustrated by Anne Canevari Green, Millbrook Press (Brookfield, CT), 2002.
Funhouse Mirrors and Optic Tricks, Four Corners/Pearson Learning (Parsippany, NJ), 2003.
Explore the World: Earth Science Experiments, Four Corners/Pearson Learning (Parsippany, NJ), 2003.

PLAYS; FOR CHILDREN

The Perfessers (original skits and adaptations from children's literature), produced in Oberlin, OH, 1975.
It's a Dog's Life (based on the book *The Farmer Giles of Ham* by J. R. R. Tolkien), produced in Milford, NH, 1981.
Dr. Seuss on the Loose (based on the stories of Dr. Seuss), produced in Milford, NH, 1981.
What a Vacation! Celebration Press (Parsippany, NJ), 2002.
The Substitute Tooth Fairy, produced, 2003.

PLAYS; FOR ADULTS

Never up, Never In, produced in Bloomington, IL, 1978.
The Imaginary Unit, produced in Oberlin, OH, 1978.
Boys Will Be Boys, produced in New York, NY, 1979.
The Plot beneath the Plot, produced in New York, NY, 1980.
Larry and His Old Lady, produced in New York, NY, 1981.
Wading for Cousteau, produced in New York, NY, 1983.
Beginner's Luck, produced in New York, NY, 1986.

OTHER

(With others; and associate producer) *Milton Berle: Mr. Television* (documentary television special), WNYC-Television, 1985.

D. J. Kat's Christmas Party (television special), Fox, 1990.

Kids-TV (educational television series), Showtime, 1990.

(With others; and producer) *Guide to New York City Housing Courts* (educational film), New York City Bar Association, 1990.

Contributor of articles and television reviews to periodicals, including *Scholastic Search, Writer's Digest, Animation, Cooking Light, Hartford Monthly, Instructor, Manhattan Spirit, Newsday,* and *Video Review.* Contributor to Internet Web sites, including *Nestle's Kids Corner* and *Juniornet.*

WORK IN PROGRESS: *Attack of the Googolplex: A Lone Integer Math Adventure;* a musical play; a pilot for an animated cartoon series designed to "make learning math fun by spoofing super-hero comics and movie conventions."

SIDELIGHTS: Jeffrey B. Fuerst told *CA:* "I like to make learning stuff fun. Whenever possible I try to infuse my nonfiction with humor. I call this the '3E' approach because my goal is to engage, entertain, educate. It is my hope that after kids read my work they will be inspired to go out and learn more on their own.

"I'm also a big believer in doing. When people say to me, 'Gee, I always wanted to be a writer' or 'Gee, I wish I could write,' I say don't think about it, just do it. Put the words on paper or the computer screen, or talk into a tape recorder. Don't be afraid to create. Go with it. Say what you want to say. It's always easier to crumple up paper or hit the delete button afterwards. The editing comes later in the writing process.

"After you write something, let it sit for awhile. Then look at it again. Read it aloud to yourself. Don't ask for too many opinions because in the long run, yours is the only one that really matters. You can listen to others, but trust yourself, and be willing to revise, revise, then revise some more. If it matters to you, you'll keep going, and you won't be afraid to work at it.

"I keep notebooks of ideas and have many projects in different stages of development at all times. I keep my projects in different folders and add to them as notions strike me, as character traits and plot points become apparent. As the stories or projects begin to take shape, I write a plot outline. The outline, or treatment, can go on for pages. When I think I know what the story is, I'll type up my notes and create a computer file. Then the hard work begins of actually writing. But it is also the fun work—invigorating. My favorite part is when characters start talking to each other. Even though I am their creator, it is as if I no longer exist except as a conduit for their thoughts, actions, reactions, feeling.

"I'm usually at my computer by nine o'clock in the morning on weekdays, just like someone with a 'real' job. This discipline I learned from having a staff writing job at a magazine for many years."

BIOGRAPHICAL AND CRITICAL SOURCES:

PERIODICALS

Booklist, September 1, 2002, Marta Segal Block, review of *The Kids' Baseball Workout: A Fun Way to Get in Shape and Improve Your Game,* p. 129.

School Library Journal, July, 2002, Blair Christolon, review of *The Kids' Baseball Workout,* p. 106.

ONLINE

J. B. Fuerst Web site, http://www.jbfuerst.com (April 21, 2003).

G

GAFFNEY, Patricia

PERSONAL: Born in Tampa, FL; daughter of Jim (a lawyer) and Joem (a homemaker) Gaffney. *Ethnicity:* "Irish American." *Education:* Marymount College, B.A. (English and philosophy); studied at Royal Holloway College, London and George Washington University; University of North Carolina, Chapel Hill, M.A. (education).

ADDRESSES: Agent—c/o Author Mail, 7th Floor, HarperCollins Publishers, 10 East 53rd Street, New York, NY 10022.

CAREER: Novelist. English teacher, East Mecklenburg High School, Charlotte, NC; worked variously as a freelance photographer and court reporter.

AWARDS, HONORS: Romance Writers of America Golden Heart awardm 1989, for *Sweet Treason.*

WRITINGS:

Sweet Treason, Dorchester Publishing (New York, NY), 1989.
Fortune's Lady, Dorchester Publishing (New York, NY), 1989.
Thief of Hearts, Dorchester Publishing (New York, NY), 1990.
Lily, Dorchester Publishing (New York, NY), 1991.
Another Eden, Dorchester Publishing (New York, NY), 1992.

Sweet Everlasting, Topaz (New York, NY), 1993.
Crooked Hearts, Topaz (New York, NY), 1994.
To Love and to Cherish (first novel in "Wyckerley" trilogy), Topaz Publishing (New York, NY), 1995.
To Have and to Hold (second novel in "Wyckerley" trilogy), Topaz Publishing (New York, NY) 1995.
Forever and Ever (second novel in "Wyckerley" trilogy), Topaz Publishing (New York, NY), 1996.
Outlaw in Paradise, Wheeler Publishing (Rockland, MA), 1997.
Wild at Heart, Topaz Publishing (New York, NY), 1997.
The Saving Graces, HarperCollins (New York, NY), 1999.
Circle of Three, HarperCollins (New York, NY), 2000.
Flight Lessons, HarperCollins (New York, NY), 2002.

WORK IN PROGRESS: Working on a new novel.

SIDELIGHTS: Patricia Gaffney grew up in the Washington, D.C. area. Her father was a government lawyer, and upon graduating from college, Gaffney thought she might enjoy being a court reporter. The job had just the right amount of passivity, a quality that suited her personality. She could sit around and record what was happening in other people's lives. However, the writing she was required to do was very disciplined. There was no room for creativity. In 1984, after discovering a lump in her breast and convinced that she did not have much time left to live, she asked herself what she most wanted to do with the rest of her life. In response to this question, she convinced her husband to move with her to a quiet country house, where she could do what she loves to do most: write fiction.

Gaffney's first five books were written in the romance genre. The first one, 1989's *Sweet Treason,* is about a young Scottish woman who becomes intrigued by her enemy and captor, an English officer. Though most of Gaffney's fans claim that this is not her best work, the book did win Gaffney the Romance Writers of America's Golden Heart Award for best new work. That same year, Gaffney also wrote *Fortune's Lady,* another story with espionage as a major theme. This time the response to the novel was more positive: Gaffney's confidence with the genre began to take shape and her characters were more fully fleshed out and crisp. Gaffney also created a strong sexual tension that critics and readers enjoyed. *Fortune's Lady* was a finalist for the Rita Award.

1990's *Thief of Hearts,* according to some critics, set an example of what a good romance novel is all about. Rounding up the first set of novels is the dark Gothic tale, *Lily,* which was nominated as best English historical romance by *Romantic Times; Another Eden,* a tale set in New York during the 1890s, also was nominated for an award, this time the best Victorian historical romance by *Romantic Times.*

In 1993 Gaffney changed publishers. She wrote another series of romance books for Penguin USA, including the "Wyckerley" trilogy of *To Love and to Cherish, To Have and to Hold,* and *Forever and Ever.* These novels are set in Victorian England, and the first follows the sad details of Anne Verlaine as she suffers through a bad marriage. The heroine of the second is Rachel, who has been imprisoned for ten years for the murder of her husband. She is not given the death sentence because some of her husband's cruelties become known. She must, however, find a patron after she is released from jail. Thus enters the potential lover. The third novel in the set revolves around the lives of Sophie and Connor, through which Gaffney discusses the social issues women in the Victorian era had to face. This is a "touching story," wrote a reviewer for *Publishers Weekly,* which ends "with love winning over pride and ambition."

After completing this series, Gaffney began to feel restless about the romance theme. She wanted to continue writing fiction, but she wanted it to relate more to her own life. Toward this end, Gaffney wrote 1999's *Saving Graces,* a book that enjoyed a stay on the *New York Times* bestseller list. This is a story very close to home for Gaffney, as she tells of the trials of

four women, all battling cancer. Gaffney herself has belonged to such a group for several years, and one of the women in her group died. *Saving Graces* tells the story of that experience. Summing up the novel, Gaffney calls it a story about love, friendship, trust, and commitment among women. In a review posted on the *Romance Reader* Web site, a reviewer also commented that *Saving Graces* is also part comedy, "one of those rare novels that can make a reader grin while being slowly twisted into knots inside." A *Publishers Weekly* reviewer described it as "a variation on the theme of women's solidarity and bravery."

Gaffney explores the relationship between mother and daughter in her novel *Circle of Three.* The story actually involves three generations: daughter, mother, and grandmother. The matriarch of the trio, Dana, is modeled on the author's own mother, Gaffney reported in an interview posted on the Web site *Crescent Blues,* especially in terms of "her southernness, her bluntness, her absolute certainty she knows what's best for her daughter—well, for everybody—and her constant and unconditional love.". In *Circle of Three,* Gaffney has each of the three female protagonists take turns telling their story in alternating chapters, which Patty Englemann for *Booklist* found "added dimension to this poignant story of growing up and growing old."

The main protagonist in 2002's *Flight Lessons* is Anna Catalano, a thirty-something woman who returns home for a short spell to mend her relationship with her Aunt Rose, who runs the family restaurant. Although the women in this story are a niece and aunt, Gaffney admits it really is a mother-daughter relationship in disguise; the core story is about two women who really love one another but must fight their way through a lot of emotional baggage in order to renew their relationship. In an interview posted on the *HarperCollins* Web site Gaffney stated: "Anna has to learn to forgive Rose for an ancient betrayal; Rose has to learn to forgive Anna for being self-righteous, intolerant, and pretty much a blockhead."

BIOGRAPHICAL AND CRITICAL SOURCES:

PERIODICALS

Booklist, April 15, 1999, Nancy Pearl, review of *The Saving Graces,* p. 1452; May 15, 2000, Patty Engelmann, review of *Circle of Three,* p. 1700; January 1, 2002, Whitney Scott, review of *Circle of Three,* p. 987.

Library Journal, August 1997, Kristin Ramsdell, review of *Outlaw in Paradise,* p. 66; April 15, 1999, Jodi L. Israel, review of *The Saving Graces,* p. 143; June 1, 2000, Jodi L. Israel, review of *Circle of Three,* p. 196.

Publishers Weekly, September 15, 1989, review of *Fortune's Lady,* p. 114; June 21, 1993, review of *Sweet Everlasting,* p. 99; March 7, 1994, review of *Crooked Hearts,* p. 66; July 24, 1995, review of *To Have and to Hold,* p. 58; March 11, 1996, review of *Forever and Ever,* p. 57; June 30, 1997, review of *Outlaw in Paradise,* p. 74; May 24, 1999, review of *The Saving Graces,* p. 63; August 2, 1999, Judy Quinn, "Amazing 'Grace', " review of *The Saving Graces,* p. 20; May 29, 2000, review of *Circle of Three,* p. 51.

ONLINE

Crescent Blues, http://www.crescentblues.com/ (April 9, 2002), "Patricia Gaffney: Swimming in the Mainstream" (interview).

HarperCollins Web site, http://www.harpercollins.com/ (January 11, 2003), interview with Gaffney.

Romance Reader, http://www.theromacereader.com/ (May 7, 2002), Cathy Sova, review of *The Saving Graces;* Linda Mowery, review of *Circle of Three.**

*   *   *

GARDNER, Scot 1968-

PERSONAL: Born August 16, 1968, in Melbourne, Victoria, Australia; son of James (a drafter) and Joan (a diversional therapist; maiden name, Sloan) Gardner; married Robyn Grant (a natural therapist), June 2, 1995; children: Jennifer Ellen, Michelle Anne, Bryce James. *Ethnicity:* "Australian." *Education:* Holmsglen Tafe, gardening certificate, 1990; Melbourne School of Massage and Physical Culture, therapeutic massage certificate, 1997; Victorian School of Hypnotic Science, postgraduate diploma in psychotherapy, 1999. *Politics:* "Greens." *Religion:* "Pantheist." *Hobbies and other interests:* Nature photography, camping, riding mountain bikes, sailing, flying aircraft, stone sculpture, "building with earth."

ADDRESSES: Home—Yinnar South, Victoria, Australia. *Office*—Karijan Enterprises, P.O. Box 8, Churchill, Victoria 3842, Australia. *Agent*—Pippa Mas-son, Curtis Brown Australia, P.O. Box 19, Paddington, New South Wales 2021, Australia. *E-mail*—scot@scotgardner.com.

CAREER: Morwell City Council, Morwell, Victoria, Australia, apprentice gardener, 1986-90; self-employed landscape gardener in Morwell, 1990-97; self-employed therapeutic masseur in Morwell, 1997-2000; freelance writer, 2000—. Victorian Writers' Centre, member, 2002—.

MEMBER: Australian Society of Authors.

WRITINGS:

One Dead Seagull (young-adult fiction), Pan Macmillan Australia (Sydney, Australia), 2001.
White Ute Dreaming (young-adult fiction), Pan Macmillan Australia (Sydney, Australia), 2002.
Burning Eddy (young-adultfiction), Pan Macmillan Australia (Sydney, Australia), 2003.

Contributor to *Earth Garden.*

WORK IN PROGRESS: The Other Madonna, young-adult fiction, for Pan Macmillan Australia, completion expected in 2004; *The Legend of Kevin the Plumber,* general fiction, for Pan Macmillan Australia, 2005; *The Chainsaw Prince,* general fiction, for Pan Macmillan Australia, 2006.

SIDELIGHTS: Australian author Scott Gardner's *One Dead Seagull,* which Helen Purdie of *Magpies* called a "promising first novel," focuses on two boys who go head-to-head with some school bullies while coming to terms with personal tragedy, problems at school and at home, and confusing situations involving the opposite sex. As Gardner noted on his Web site: "I wrote parts of *One Dead Seagull* at Tarra Bulga National Park. Parts of the sequel, [*White Utne Dreaming,*] were written by gaslight in the Outback. The tools of the trade are simple—for me it's a pen and paper for the first draft then I take all the papers and stuff them into my computer. The technicians at Compaq said that 'damage caused by inserting hand-written manuscripts into a CD drive is not covered under warranty.'" As a result—and fortunately for fans of his books—Gardner has since learned how to type.

BIOGRAPHICAL AND CRITICAL SOURCES:

PERIODICALS

Magpies, July, 2001, Helen Purdie, review of *One Dead Seagull,* p. 39.

ONLINE

Officious Scot Gardner Home Page, http://members. datafast.net.au/gmob/essgee (March 10, 2003).

*   *   *

GAYLORD, Edward Lewis 1919-2003

OBITUARY NOTICE—See index for *CA* sketch: Born May 28, 1919, in Oklahoma City, OK; died from complication due to pancreatic cancer April 27, 2003, in Oklahoma City, OK. Publisher and business executive. Gaylord was the former publisher and editor of the *Oklahoman* who also built a multimedia empire. His father, E. K. Gaylord, had been publisher and editor of the paper before him, and the younger Gaylord followed in his father's footsteps. He began working at the paper when he was in high school before attending Stanford University, where he earned a bachelor's degree in 1941. He earned an M.B.A. from Harvard University after that. With the onset of World War II, Gaylord left school to serve in the U.S. Army. When he returned, he went back to work at his father's newspaper, working his way up the ranks and holding several offices, including assistant general manager, executive vice president, director, and treasurer. When his father died in 1974, Gaylord took over as editor and publisher of the *Oklahoman.* Seeking to diversify the Oklahoma Publishing Co., which owned the paper, he set out to expand into television and established the Gaylord Production Co. in Los Angeles. This company went on to produce such television staples as *Hee Haw* and *The Glen Campbell Show* during the 1970s. Gaylord continued to show his interest in country music by purchasing Opryland in 1983, the Opryland Music Group, Opryland Hotel, and Opryland Theme Park, as well as the television networks Country Music Television and the Nashville Network. In 1991 he also headed Gaylord Entertainment in Nashville. Other business concerns included

television stations in Florida, Texas, New Mexico, and Oregon, as well as oil and gas interests with his company Publisher's Petroleum, a real estate company, and shares of sports teams, such as the Texas Rangers, San Antonio Spurs, and Nashville Predators. In the 1990s, Gaylord turned the presidency of Oklahoma Publishing over to his son, and he also sold his television networks. Ten days before his death, he resigned as publisher and editor of the *Oklahoman.*

OBITUARIES AND OTHER SOURCES:

PERIODICALS

Chicago Tribune, April 29, 2003, section 1, p. 11.
Los Angeles Times, April 30, 2003, p. B11.
New York Times, April 29, 2003, p. A27.
Washington Post, April 29, 2003, p. B6.

*   *   *

GELLERMAN, Saul W(illiam) 1929-2003

OBITUARY NOTICE—See index for *CA* sketch: Born January 8, 1929, in Brooklyn, NY; died of complications from heart surgery March 26, 2003, in Cleveland, OH. Psychologist, educator, consultant, and author. Gellerman used his psychology background as a business management consultant and author of books that often dealt with the issue of how to effectively manage employees. He earned his master's degree from the University of Missouri in 1950 and, after serving in the U.S. Army Medical Service Corps during the conflict in Korea, a Ph.D. from the University of Pennsylvania in 1956. During the late 1950s he was director of psychological services for Personnel Laboratory, Inc., in New York City, followed by employment with International Business Machines as a personnel research associate and then manager of personnel research. In 1967 he opened his own business consulting firm, Gellerman Consulting, Inc., which he headed until 1984. Gellerman then switched to teaching, and was a professor and dean of management for the University of Dallas in Irving from 1984 to 1999. At the time of his death he was teaching on-line business school graduate courses for Rushmore University. Supplementing this work with books about management, Gellerman published fifteen works, including *The Management of Human Relations* (1966), *Behavioral Science in Management* (1974), *Motivating Superior Performance* (1994), and *How to Manage a Motivation Machine* (2000).

OBITUARIES AND OTHER SOURCES:

PERIODICALS

New York Times, April 20, 2003, p. A17.

*   *   *

GEOGHEGAN, Adrienne 1962-

PERSONAL: Born March 4, 1962, in Dublin, Ireland; daughter of Noel and Marie (Woods) Haughney; married Ken Geoghegan, September 26, 1981 (divorced, 2001); married Mark Neiland (a photographer), May 17, 2002. *Education:* Kingston University, B.A. (graphic design/illustration; first class honours), 1993.

ADDRESSES: Home and office—4 Provost Row, Palantine Square, Arbour Hill, Dublin 7, Ireland. *Agent*—Eunice McMullen, Low Ibbotsholme Cottage, Off Brick Lane, Troutbeck Bridge, Windemere, Cumbria LA23 IHV, England. *E-mail*—addieg@gofree.indigo.ie.

CAREER: Illustrator and writer. Dublin Institute of Technology, College of Marketing and Design, Dublin, Ireland, part-time lecturer, 1996—. *Exhibitions:* Solo exhibitions at Beint & Beint Gallery, London, England, 1993; TOSCA, Dublin, Ireland, 2000; and Linenhall Arts Centre, Castlebar, County Mayo, Ireland, 2000. Group exhibitions include Illustration '90, Riverside Centre, Dublin, 1990; Macmillan Prize Exhibition, Royal College of Art, London, 1992; Just Art '92, Crypt Gallery, London, 1992; Barbican Awards Show, Barbican Gallery, London, 1993; Images 19, Mall Galleries, London, 1994; Great Illustrations, The Ark, Dublin, 1997; and Celebrity Art Auction, Bank of Ireland Arts Centre, Dublin, 1997.

MEMBER: Association of Artists in Ireland, Illustrators Guild of Ireland.

AWARDS, HONORS: Just Art '92 exhibition winner, 1992; award from Barbican Awards Show, 1993; Irish Copyright Licensing Agency Award, for best illustrated children's book, 1996, for *Dogs Don't Wear Glasses;* Norway Arts Council ArtFlight award, 1997.

WRITINGS:

PICTURE BOOKS

Six Perfectly Different Pigs, illustrated by Elisabeth Moseng, Hazar (London, England), 1993, Gareth Stevens (Milwaukee, WI), 1994.
(With John Cotton) *Oscar the Dog and Friends* (poetry), Longman (London, England), 1994.
(With Wendy Body and Ann Jungman) *Sally and the Booted Puss and Other Stories,* Longman (London, England), 1994.
(And illustrator) *Dogs Don't Wear Glasses,* Magi Publications (London, England), 1995, Crocodile Books (New York, NY), 1996.
There's a Wardrobe in My Monster! illustrated by Adrian Johnson, Carolrhoda Books (Minneapolis, MN), 1999.
Who Needs Pockets, Hippo (London, England), 2000.
All Your Own Teeth, illustrated by Cathy Gale, Bloomsbury (London, England), 2001, Dial (New York, NY), 2002.

ILLUSTRATOR; "READ-ON BEGINNER BOOKS" SERIES BY WENDY BODY

When the Toy Shop Shuts, Longman (London, England), 1994, Sundance Press (Littleton, MA), 1997.
Our Play, Longman (London, England), 1994, Sundance Press (Littleton, MA), 1997.
The Toy Shop, Longman (London, England), 1994, Sundance Press (Littleton, MA), 1997.
In the Toy Shop, Longman (London, England), 1994, Sundance Press (Littleton, MA), 1997.
Special Friends, Longman (London, England), 1994, Sundance Press (Littleton, MA), 1997.
Can You Do This? Longman (London, England), 1994, Sundance Press (Littleton, MA), 1997.
Who Am I? Longman (London, England), 1994, Sundance Press (Littleton, MA), 1997.
In the Box, Longman (London, England), 1994, Sundance (Littleton, MA), 1997.

I'm Red, Longman (London, England), 1994, Sundance (Littleton, MA), 1997.

I Like Green, Longman (London, England), 1994, Sundance (Littleton, MA), 1997.

I Want a Red Ball, Longman (London, England), 1994, Sundance (Littleton, MA), 1997.

Where Is the Snake? Longman (London, England), 1994, Sundance (Littleton, MA), 1997.

Where Is My Ball? Longman (London, England), 1994, Sundance (Littleton, MA), 1997.

Our Play, Longman (London, England), 1994, Sundance (Littleton, MA), 1997.

I Don't Want That! Longman (London, England), 1994, Sundance (Littleton, MA), 1997.

What's That? Longman (London, England), 1994, Sundance (Littleton, MA), 1997.

I Can Make You Red, Longman (London, England), 1994, Sundance (Littleton, MA), 1997.

Come In! Longman (London, England), 1994, Sundance (Littleton, MA), 1997.

I Want to Be, Longman (London, England), 1994, Sundance Press (Littleton, MA), 1997.

Can I Play? Longman (London, England), 1994, Sundance Press (Littleton, MA), 1997.

Where Do You Live? Longman (London, England), 1997, Sundance Press (Littleton, MA), 1998.

What Are You Making? Longman (London, England), 1997, Sundance Press (Littleton, MA), 1998.

I Don't Want to Do That, Longman (London, England), 1997, Sundance Press (Littleton, MA), 1998.

It Wasn't Me! Longman (London, England), 1997, Sundance Press (Littleton, MA), 1998.

I Like to Play, Longman (London, England), 1997, Sundance Press (Littleton, MA), 1998.

What Do I Want? Longman (London, England), 1997, Sundance Press (Littleton, MA), 1998.

Can You Make a Bird? Longman (London, England), 1997, Sundance Press (Littleton, MA), 1998.

But Where Is Jake? Longman (London, England), 1997, Sundance Press (Littleton, MA), 1998.

I Want That! Longman (London, England), 1997, Sundance Press (Littleton, MA), 1998.

Come and Play, Longman (London, England), 1997, Sundance Press (Littleton, MA), 1998.

I Like You, Longman (London, England), 1997, Sundance Press (Littleton, MA), 1998.

What's in the Box? Longman (London, England), 1997, Sundance Press (Littleton, MA), 1998.

I Live Here, Longman (London, England), 1997, Sundance Press (Littleton, MA), 1998.

Where Is My Snake? Longman (London, England), 1997, Sundance Press (Littleton, MA), 1998.

This Is Megan, Longman (London, England), 1997, Sundance Press (Littleton, MA), 1998.

Megan Went to Bed, Longman (London, England), 1997, Sundance Press (Littleton, MA), 1999.

One Duck, Two Ducks . . . , Longman London, England), 1997, Sundance Press (Littleton, MA), 1999.

In the Backyard, Longman (London, England), 1997, Sundance Press (Littleton, MA), 1999.

I Like Red, Longman (London, England), 1997, Sundance Press (Littleton, MA), 1999.

It's Time for Bed, Longman (London, England), 1997, Sundance Press (Littleton, MA), 1999.

In the Garden, Longman (London, England), 1997.

One and One Make Two, Longman (London, England), 1997, Sundance Press (Littleton, MA), 1999.

Is She with You? Longman (London, England), 1997, Sundance Press (Littleton, MA), 1999.

Did You Do That? Longman (London, England), 1997, Sundance Press (Littleton, MA), 1999.

Let's Make a Cake, Longman (London, England), 1997, Sundance Press (Littleton, MA), 1999.

One for You, Longman (London, England), 1997, Sundance Press (Littleton, MA), 1999.

Let's Play with My Dog, Longman (London, England), 1997, Sundance Press (Littleton, MA), 1999.

I Do, Too! Longman (London, England), 1997, Sundance Press (Littleton, MA), 1999.

Jake's Poem, Longman (London, England), 1997, Sundance Press (Littleton, MA), 1999.

ILLUSTRATOR; OTHER

Tony Bradman, *Pushchair Polly,* Picture Ladybird (Loughborough, England), 1996.

Tessa Krailing, *The Battle of Waterloo Road,* Oxford University Press (Oxford, England), 2001.

Contributor of illustrations to periodicals, including London *Guardian, Economist, Irish Times,* and Dublin *Independent.*

ADAPTATIONS: The characters from Geoghegan's *Dogs Don't Wear Glasses* were used in a televison advertizing campaign for Jacob's Kimberly Mikado biscuits, 1999.

SIDELIGHTS: Irish illustrator and author Adrienne Geoghegan has seen success on both sides of the Atlantic, creating artwork for newspapers and book publishers in Dublin, London, and Massachusetts and exhibiting her work at group and solo art shows. From 1994 to 1997 she illustrated the "Read-on Beginner Books" series by Wendy Body, which numbers some forty books, each made up of eight pages of rudimentary text. Beginning in the mid-1990s Geoghegan began authoring her own picture-book texts, one of which, *Dogs Don't Wear Glasses,* she also illustrated. A hallmark of Geoghegan's work is humor, which a *Kirkus* reviewer, in an appraisal of *Dogs Don't Wear Glasses,* described as "satisfying silliness." The humor in *Dogs Don't Wear Glasses* lies in the actions of the visually imparied Nanny Needles, who has a number of accidents but blames them on her dog Seymour. Finally, thinking that Seymour cannot see well, she buys him glasses. At home Granny puts the glasses on herself, to see how they look, and discovers how much better she can see. Geoghegan's "bright and lively" crayon with watercolor-wash illustrations earned the praise of *Booklist* contributor Carolyn Phelan, although they were deemed "awkward" by a critic in *Publishers Weekly.*

The picture book *There's a Wardrobe in My Monster!,* which Sue Sherif of *School Library Journal* called "predictable but fun," revolves around the antics of Martha's new pet, a small green fellow who eats only wood. As the monster grows, its appetite increases until it has literally eaten a wardrobe. Finally, in this "romp of a tale to read aloud," to quote a *Kirkus* critic, Martha is forced by the monster's voracious appetite to return it to the pet shop for an exchange. *There's a Wardrobe in My Monster!* is a "quirky take on a tried-and-true pet story," concluded a *Publishers Weekly* contributor.

In the same vein of dry humor is Geoghegan's *All Your Own Teeth,* about would-be painter Stewart, who rather than realize he has no talent, searches for the perfect model from among the animals of the jungle. After rudely turning down an elephant, cheetah, giraffe, and hippopotamus who have answered his advertizement for a "Hansum wild animal" with his "own teeth and nice big smile," Stewart meets a crocodile. Stewart thinks the crocodile is just right and the crocodile, thinking Stewart is just right, gobbles up the nasty boy, a climax that *Booklist*'s Connie Fletcher thought might make this "rollicking morality tale" too intense for very young listeners. On the other hand, a critic for *Kirkus Reviews* predicted that "children will chuckle over this archly-delivered cautionary tale."

Wendy Lukehart pointed out the work's "alliteration and letter play," dubbing the tale "perfectly preposterous" in her *School Library Journal* review, and in *Publishers Weekly* a contributor summed up *All Your Own Teeth* as an "odd but visually enticing parable."

BIOGRAPHICAL AND CRITICAL SOURCES:

PERIODICALS

Booklist, April 1, 1996, Carolyn Phelan, review of *Dogs Don't Wear Glasses,* p. 1371; March 1, 2002, Connie Fletcher, review of *All Your Own Teeth,* p. 1141.

Kirkus Reviews, April 1, 1996, review of *Dogs Don't Wear Glasses,* p. 529; September 15, 1999, review of *There's a Wardrobe in My Monster!* pp. 1499-1500; February 1, 2002, review of *All Your Own Teeth,* p. 181.

Publishers Weekly, March 4, 1996, review of *Dogs Don't Wear Glasses,* p. 64; August 16, 1999, review of *There's a Wardrobe in My Monster!* p. 82; December 24, 2001, review of *All Your Own Teeth,* pp. 63-64.

School Library Journal, January, 1995, Patricia Pearl Dole, review of *Six Perfectly Different Pigs,* p. 86; May, 1996, Susan Garland, review of *Dogs Don't Wear Glasses,* p. 91; November, 1999, Sue Sherif, review of *There's a Wardrobe in My Monster!* p. 116; April, 2002, Wendy Lukehart, review of *All Your Own Teeth,* p. 110.*

*   *   *

GLAZER, Amihai 1950-

PERSONAL: Born March 22, 1950, in Haifa, Israel; U.S. citizen; married Debra Goodman, August 22, 1976; children: Danielle. *Education:* Cornell University, B.A., 1974; Yale University, Ph.D., 1978.

ADDRESSES: Home—12 Urey Ct., Irvine, CA 92612. *Office*—Department of Economics, University of California—Irvine, Irvine, CA 92697. *E-mail*—aglazer@uci.edu.

CAREER: University of California—Irvine, professor of economics, 1979—. Carnegie-Mellon University, Pittsburgh, PA, visiting professor, 1991-92.

WRITINGS:

(With Jack Hirchleifer) *Price Theory and Applications,* 5th edition, Prentice-Hall (Englewood Cliffs, NJ), 1992.

Why Government Succeeds and Why It Fails, Harvard University Press (Cambridge, MA), 2001.

BIOGRAPHICAL AND CRITICAL SOURCES:

PERIODICALS

Booklist, April 1, 2001, Mary Carroll, review of *Why Government Succeeds and Why It Fails,* p. 1433.

Journal of Political Analysis and Management, spring, 2002, Laurence E. Lynn, Jr., review of *Why Government Succeeds and Why It Fails,* p. 314.

Political Science Quarterly, spring, 2003, Hugh Heclo, "What Government Can Do," p. 138.

*   *   *

GLENN, Susan A(nita) 1950-

PERSONAL: Born March 8, 1950, in Los Angeles, CA; daughter of Norman and Rhoda Glenn; married James Gregory, 1980; children: Rachel. *Ethnicity:* "Jewish." *Education:* San Diego State University, B.A. (cum laude), 1973; University of California, San Diego, M.A., 1975; University of California, Berkeley, Ph.D. (history), 1983.

ADDRESSES: Office—University of Washington, Department of History, Box 353560, Seattle, WA 98195. *E-mail*—glenns@u.washington.edu.

CAREER: Educator and historian. Visiting assistant professor at Scripps College and Claremont College, 1983-85; North Carolina State University, assistant professor of history, 1985-88; University of California, Berkeley, visiting associate professor of history, 1991-92; University of Texas at Austin, assistant professor, 1988-91, associate professor of history, 1991-93; University of Washington, Seattle, associate professor, 1993-99, professor of history, 1999—, member of faculty of Jewish studies program at Jackson School of International Studies, and adjunct professor of women's studies. Member of advisory board, Jewish Women's Archive (documentation project, 2000—).

MEMBER: American Jewish Historical Society (member of academic council, 2000—), Organization of American Historians, American Historical Association, American Studies Association, Association for Jewish Studies.

AWARDS, HONORS: National Endowment for the Humanities (NEH) research fellowship, 1985; American Council of Learned Societies fellowship, 1986; Joan Kelly Memorial Prize, American Historical Association, 1991, for *Daughters of the Shtetl;* Davis Humanities Institute on Constructions of Gender fellow, University of California, Davis, 1992-93; NEH fellowship for university teachers, 1996-97; Keller Fund Research Award, University of Washington, 1994, 1995, 1997; Royalty Research Fund scholar, University of Washington, 1998; Constance Rourke Prize, American Studies Association, 1999, for article "Give an Imitation of Me: Vaudeville Mimics and the Play of the Self."

WRITINGS:

Daughters of the Shtetl: Life and Labor in the Immigrant Generation, Cornell University Press (Ithaca, NY), 1990.

Female Spectacle: The Theatrical Roots of Modern Feminism, Harvard University Press (Cambridge, MA), 2000.

Contributor to periodicals, including *American Quarterly* and *Reviews in American History;* contributor of book reviews to *American Historical Review, Nation, Journal of American Ethnic History, Journal of Social History, Journal of American History,* and *Southwestern Historical Quarterly.*

WORK IN PROGRESS: Research for *Jewish Self-Fashioning: The Paradoxes of Assimilation,* a examination of themes of invisibility and hyper-visibility in the individual and institutional strategies of Jewish self-fashioning from the early twentieth century to the present; and *The Lynching of Leo Frank: A Brief History with Documents.*

GOLDINGAY, John (Edgar) 1942-

PERSONAL: Born June 20, 1942, in Birmingham, England; son of Edgar Charles and Ada Irene (Horton) Goldingay; married Ann Elizabeth Wilson, August 28, 1967; children: Steven, Mark. *Ethnicity:* "Caucasian." *Education:* Keble College, Oxford, B.A.; University of Nottingham, Ph.D.; Archbishop of Canterbury at Lambeth, D.D. *Politics:* Socialist. *Religion:* Episcopalian *Hobbies and other interests:* The Old Testament, blues, jazz, and rock music.

ADDRESSES: Home—111 South Orange Blvd., Apt. 108, Pasadena, CA 91105; fax: 626-584-5251. *Office*—Fuller Theological Seminary, 135 North Oakland Ave., Pasadena, CA 91182 *E-mail*—johngold@fuller. edu.

CAREER: Theologian, clergyman, educator, and writer. Ordained Church of England minister, 1966; Christ Church, Finchley, London, England, parish minister, 1966-69; St. John's College, Nottingham, England, lecturer, 1970-97, principal, 1988-97; Fuller Theological Seminary, Pasadena, CA, David Allan Hubbard Professor of Old Testament, 1997—. Associate minister at Christ Church, Chilwell, Nottingham, 1970-86, All Souls, Radford, Nottingham, 1986-97, and St. Barnabas, Pasadena, 2002—; Council of the Church's Ministry among the Jews, chair, 1991-96.

MEMBER: Society for Old Testament Study, Society of Biblical Literature.

WRITINGS:

Authority and Ministry (booklet; "Grove Books on Ministry and Worship" series), Grove Books (Bramcote, England), 1976.
How to Read the Bible, Oliphants (London, England), 1977.
Songs from a Strange Land ("The Bible Speaks Today" series), InterVarsity Press (Downers Grove, IL), 1978.
Approaches to Old Testament Interpretation ("Issues in Contemporary Theology" series), InterVarsity Press (Downers Grove, IL), 1981, revised edition, 1990.

Theological Diversity and the Authority of the Old Testament (revision of 1983 dissertation), W. B. Eerdmans (Grand Rapids, MI), 1987.
Daniel ("Word Biblical Themes" series), Word Publishing (Dallas, TX), 1989.
(Editor and contributor) *Signs, Wonders, and Healing,* InterVarsity Press (Leicester, England), 1989.
Models for Scripture, W. B. Eerdmans (Grand Rapids, MI), 1994.
Models for Interpretation of Scripture, W. B. Eerdmans (Grand Rapids, MI), 1995.
(Editor and contributor) *Atonement Today,* SPCK (London, England), 1995.
After Eating the Apricot, Paternoster (Carlisle, England), 1996.
To the Usual Suspects, Paternoster (Carlisle, England), 1998.
Men Behaving Badly, Paternoster (Carlisle, England), 2000.
Isaiah ("New International Biblical Commentary" series), Hendrickson Publishers (Peabody, MA), 2001.
Walk On: Life, Loss, Trust, and Other Realities, Baker Academic (Grand Rapids, MI), 2002.
God's Prophet, God's Servant: A Study in Jeremiah and Isaiah 40-55 (revised edition), Clements (Toronto, Ontario, Canada), 2002.

Contributor to and reviewer for periodicals and religious journals, including *Journal of Biblical Literature, Church Times, Journal of Semitic Studies, Journal of Theological Studies, Biblical Theology Bulletin, Missionary Studies Bulletin, Churchman,* and *Catholic Biblical Quarterly;* work represented in books by others, including *Reading the Hebrew Bible for a New Millennium,* edited by W. Kim and others, Trinity (Harrisburg, PA), 2000; *Covenant Theology,* edited by M. J. Cartledge and D. Mills, Paternoster (Carlisle, England), 2001; and *The New Dictionary of Pastoral Studies,* edited by Wesley Carr and others, Eerdmans (Grand Rapids, MI), 2002.

WORK IN PROGRESS: Research into Old Testament theology and the Psalms.

SIDELIGHTS: John Goldingay served as a clergyman and educator in his native England for three decades before taking the position of professor at Fuller Theological Seminary in Pasadena, California. He has written a number of books, including one of his first, a small volume titled *How to Read the Bible,* which he based on the *Good News Bible.* Goldingay places New Testament writings according to the categories of the Old Testament, feeling that the Old Testament describes the problem and how it had to be solved, and noting that the New Testament "saw the question to which Jesus was the answer." *Times Educational Supplement* contributor Ronald Lunt praised Goldingay's "bright and lively style."

Goldingay's more recent titles include *Models for Scripture,* in which he "presents a doctrine of Scripture by revisiting the traditional categories of tradition, inspiration, authority, canon, inerrancy, and revelation," noted Harry T. Fleddermann in *Theological Studies.* "These categories," continued Fleddermann, "often form battlegrounds that sharply divide conservative and liberal Christians, and widely differing view points surface in the present discussion. Rather than abandon the traditional categories, Goldingay seeks to heal them by bringing them under the framework of models."

The four models within which Goldingay demonstrates the functions of scripture in the Christian community are titled "Scripture as Witnessing Tradition," "Scripture as Authoritative Canon," "Scripture as Inspired Word," and "Scripture as Experienced Revelation." Fleddermann noted the strengths of the work, including the thirty-page bibliography, and pointed out that Goldingay "dialogues with a wide range of contemporary scholars" and "tries to stay close to the text of the Bible." Fleddermann continued, saying that "although his primary audience is the academic community, he also demonstrates a pastoral concern for how a doctrine of Scripture can influence the life of the churches."

Theology Today's A. K. M. Adam wrote that Goldingay's "aim is to show that the entrenched positions in the authority debate all diminish the richness and vitality of the Bible's relation to church and to lay an alternate, less polemically charged foundation for approaching issues of authority." Adam concluded by saying that Goldingay "has put together a sensible contribution to a vexatious dispute; whether as a model for supporters or a foil for antagonists, Goldingay's proposal enriches the discussion of biblical authority."

Jack Dean Kingsbury reviewed *Models for Scripture* in *Interpretation,* saying that Goldingay "has read mas-

sively in his field of expertise, and his book is a gold mine of both historical and theological information. It also reads well."

In Goldingay's companion book, *Models for Interpretation of Scripture,* he notes that God spoke to the spiritual leaders "in many and various ways" and added that the interpretation of the Bible "requires a variety of hermeneutical approaches, corresponding to the variety in types of texts." In reviewing the volume in *Theology Today,* Bernhard W. Anderson noted that Goldingay identifies four models, which Anderson noted are "(1) scriptural narrative (story or history); (2) norms for behavior (Torah, authoritative canon); (3) inspired word (prophecy); and (4) reflection on experienced revelation (for example, Psalms, Wisdom, Apocalypse). These four forms correspond broadly to 'four modes of utterance': law, prophecy, wisdom, and gospel."

Joel B. Green wrote in *Journal of Biblical Literature* that "Goldingay's discussion takes up the variety of methods current in the biblical studies marketplace. His presentation is not serialized, however, or piecemeal. Major critical approaches are thoughtfully discussed in light of their champions and detractors, and links to other approaches are repeatedly made."

In *Walk On: Life, Loss, Trust, and Other Realities* Goldingay considers the basics of leading a Christian life. Here he incorporates references to popular music and his own personal experiences, including his wife's battle with multiple sclerosis, with approaches to spiritual questions. A *Publishers Weekly* contributor called the volume a "theologically and biblically sound book."

BIOGRAPHICAL AND CRITICAL SOURCES:

PERIODICALS

Catholic Biblical Quarterly, April, 1990, Don C. Benjamin, review of *Theological Diversity and the Authority of the Old Testament,* p. 318; July, 1996, J. Terence Forestell, review of *Models for Scripture,* p. 547.
Interpretation, October, 1996, Jack Dean Kingsbury, review of *Models for Scripture,* p. 434.

Journal of Biblical Literature, winter, 1997, Joel B. Green, review of *Models for Interpretation of Scripture,* pp. 721-722.

Publishers Weekly, July 1, 2002, review of *Walk On: Life, Loss, Trust, and Other Realities,* p. 73.

Theological Studies, March, 1996, Harry T. Fleddermann, review of *Models for Scripture,* p. 141.

Theology Today, January, 1996, A. K. M. Adam, review of *Models for Scripture,* pp. 525-526, 528; January, 1997, Bernhard W. Anderson, review of *Models for Interpretation of Scripture,* pp. 544, 546.

Times Educational Supplement, March 24, 1978, Ronald Lunt, review of *How to Read the Bible,* p. 22.

*   *   *

GOLDSTONE, Richard J. 1938-

PERSONAL: Born October 26, 1938, in Boksburg, South Africa; married Noleen Behrman, 1962; children: Glenda, Nicole. *Education:* University of Witwatersrand, South Africa, B.A., LL.B. (cum laude), 1962.

ADDRESSES: Office—Constitutional Court, Private Bag X32, Braamfontein 2017, South Africa.

CAREER: Jurist. Johannesburg Bar, South Africa, advocate, 1962-76; senior counsel, 1976-80; Transvaal Supreme Court, judge, 1980-89, Appellate Division, judge, 1989-94; Constitutional Court of South Africa, justice, 1994—. Commission of Inquiry Regarding Public Violence and Intimidation, chair, 1991-94; United Nations International Criminal Tribunals for the former Yugoslavia and Rwanda, chief prosecutor, 1994-96. National Institute of Crime Prevention and the Rehabilitation of Offenders, president, 1985-2000. Chair, Standing Advisory Committee of Company Law, Valencia Declaration, 1998, International Independent Inquiry on Kosovo, 1999-2001, International Task Force on Terrorism, 2001—, Bradlow Foundation, and Human Rights Institute of South Africa; chancellor, University of the Witwatersrand; president, World ORT.

MEMBER: American Academy of Arts and Sciences.

AWARDS, HONORS: International Human Rights Award, American Bar Association, 1994; honorary doctorates of law from universities of Cape Town, Witwatersrand, Natal, Notre Dame, Glasgow, and Calgary, and from Hebrew University, Jerusalem, Maryland University College, Wilfred Laurier University, Catholic University of Brabant, and Emory University; honorary benchee of Inner Temple, London; honorary fellow, St. Johns College, Cambridge; honorary member, Association of the Bar of New York. Fellow, Weatherhead Centre for International Affairs of Harvard University.

WRITINGS:

For Humanity: Reflections of a War Crimes Investigator, Yale University Press (New Haven, CT), 2000.

SIDELIGHTS: South African judge Richard J. Goldstone has been involved in the promotion of human rights throughout his career. Goldstone grew up in a very conservative suburb of Johannesburg; by law, his community was for whites only, but his liberal parents objected to the racist policies of the South African government. Goldstone was also deeply influenced by his maternal grandfather, who encouraged his interest in law. He told Sudarsan Raghavan in the *Los Angeles Times,* "I hadn't any doubts since the age of four about entering the legal profession. I spent a lot of my childhood with [my grandfather]."

As a college student at the University of Witwatersrand, Goldstone exposed a member of the South African secret police, who had been sent to spy on a student group agitating against the official policy of apartheid, the forced separation of racial groups. Goldstone secretly taped a conversation with the spy. The tape was later used as evidence to dismiss the national police commissioner.

After passing the Johannesburg Bar, Goldstone ran a commercial law firm before being appointed a judge in 1980. As a justice, he became known for his sympathy toward human-rights lawyers, political prisoners, and anti-apartheid activists, and he refused to be swayed by government policies he believed were wrong.

His career as an investigator and judge of cases involving political violence began in 1981, when he was chosen to head a commission that investigated crimes that occurred after the fall of apartheid in 1991 and before South Africa's first democratic elections in 1995.

Goldstone has been a justice of the Constitutional Court of South Africa since 1994, and has also chaired the Commission of Inquiry Regarding the Prevention of Public Violence and Intimidation in that country. In addition, he was chief prosecutor of the United Nations International Criminal Tribunals, which considered war crimes in the former Yugoslavia and Rwanda. He was chair of the International Independent Inquiry on Kosovo, and since 2001 has been chair of the International Task Force on Terrorism.

In *For Humanity: Reflections of a War Crimes Investigator* Goldstone describes his involvement in the transition of South Africa from an apartheid state to a democracy, and tells why he was chosen to head a commission that investigated crimes during the transition. He also discusses his work as chief prosecutor for United Nations Tribunals, considering both the legal issues of the tribunals and his personal feelings and experiences. He advocates for the establishment of a permanent international criminal justice system that would be "sufficiently empowered to cause would-be war criminals to reconsider their ambitions, knowing that they might otherwise be hunted for the rest of their days and eventually be brought to justice." In the *New York Times,* Chuck Sudette wrote that the book is an important reminder "that if our world is to become more globalized and humane, governments, including our own, must keep step by prosecuting war criminals."

BIOGRAPHICAL AND CRITICAL SOURCES:

PERIODICALS

Ethics and International Affairs, April, 2001, Dorothy V. Jones, review of *For Humanity: Reflections of a War Crimes Investigator,* p. 212.
Global Governance, January-March, 2002, James P. Sewell, review of *For Humanity,* p. 119.
Los Angeles Times, March 14, 1995, Sudarsan Raghavan, profile of Goldstone, p. H5.
New Republic, January 29, 2001, Tzvetan Todorov, review of *For Humanity,* p. 29.

New York Times, July 9, 1994, Paul Lewis, "South African Judge Is to Prosecute War Criminals," p. 2.
Publishers Weekly, August 7, 2000, review of *For Humanity,* p. 86.
Times Literary Supplement, November 9, 2001, Anthony Dworkin, review of *For Humanity,* p. 11.*

*   *   *

GORIN, Natalio 1940-

PERSONAL: Born April 21, 1940, in Buenos Aires, Argentina; son of Aaron and Matilde (Schapchuk) Gorin; married Carola Flora Kurman, March 30, 1969; children: Pablo, Veronica. *Education:* Escuela Superior de Periodismo Deportive-Curso, diploma, 1963. *Religion:* Jewish. *Hobbies and other interests:* Music.

ADDRESSES: Home—Honorio Pueyrredon 1552, No. 9A, Buenos Aires, Argentina 1414. *E-mail*—gorin@ciudad.com.ar.

CAREER: Journalist. *Grafico* (magazine), Buenos Aires, Argentina, sports journalist and director, 1979-97. World Cup USA, assessor, 1994.

WRITINGS:

(With Hugo Gatti) *Mis veinte años en el futbol,* Atlantida, 1984.
(Coauthor) *Astor Piazzolla: A Memoir* (interviews with Piazzolla), translated by Fernando Gonzalez, Timber Press (Portland, OR), 2001.

WORK IN PROGRESS: A history of Argentinian soccer.

*   *   *

GRAVEL, François 1951-

PERSONAL: Born October 4, 1951, in Montreal, Quebec, Canada; son of Gérard and Martine (Robillard) Gravel; married Murielle Grégoire, October 28, 1971; children: Elise, Simon. *Education:* University of Quebec.

ADDRESSES: Agent—c/o Author Mail, Cormorant Books, R.R. 1, Dunvegan, Ontario KOC 1J0, Canada. *E-mail*—francois.gravel@cstjean.qc.ca.

CAREER: CEGEP, Saint-Jean-sur-Richelieu, Montreal, Quebec, Canada, professor of economics, 1975—.

MEMBER: Writers Union of Quebec.

AWARDS, HONORS: Mr. Christie's Book Award, 1990, for *Mr. Zamboni's Dream Machine*.

WRITINGS:

La note de passage: roman, Boréal Express (Montreal, Quebec, Canada), 1985.

L'effet Summerhill, Boréal (Montreal, Quebec, Canada), 1988.

La zamboni, Boréal Express (Montreal, Quebec, Canada), 1990, translated by Sarah Cummins published as *Mr. Zamboni's Dream Machine,* James Lorimer (Toronto, Ontario, Canada), 1992.

Les Black Stones vous reviendront dans quelques, Editions Québec Amérique (Montreal, Quebec, Canada), 1991.

Felicity's Fool, translated by Sheila Fischman, Cormorant Books (Dunvegan, Ontario, Canada), 1992.

Klonk, ou, comment se débarasser des adolescents: roman, illustrations by Pierre Pratt, Amerique Jeunesse (Boucherville, Quebec, Canada), 1993.

Ostende: roman, Editions Québec Amérique (Montreal, Quebec, Canada), 1994, translated by Sheila Fischman, Cormorant Books (Dunvegan, Ontario, Canada), 1996.

Miss Septembre, Editions Québec Amérique (Montreal, Quebec, Canada), 1996, translation by Sheila Fishman published as *Miss September: A Novel,* Cormorant Books (Montreal, Quebec, Canada), 1998.

Vingt et un tableaux (et quelques craies), Editions Québec Amérique (Montreal, Quebec, Canada), 1998.

Fillion et frères, Editions Québec Amérique (Montreal, Quebec, Canada), 2000.

L'ete de la moustache, illustrated by Anatoli Burcev, Bookbird, 2001.

A Good Life, translated by Sheila Fischman, Cormorant Books (Toronto, Ontario, Canada), 2001.

Je ne comprends pas tout, Editions Québec Amérique (Montreal, Quebec, Canada), 2002.

Author of *Waiting for Jasmine,* translated by Sheila Fischman; *My Life as a Crow,* translated by Sheila Fischman; and *Benito,* Lester & Orpen Dennys.

SIDELIGHTS: Canadian François Gravel is a professor of economics as well as an author of both adult and children's books. In his 1992 novel *Felicity's Fool,* a French-Canadian doctor removes and studies the brains of dead patients at the psychiatric hospital where he is employed. Through studying these brains he hopes to find the answer to what makes people happy.

In *Ostend* Jean François learns about life and death during the 1960s and 1970s. As a young boy Jean sees the deaths of President Kennedy and his killer Lee Harvey Oswald. At this time he starts to believe that it would be best to die young and famous. As teenagers, Jean and his friends reject all things that depict normal middle-class life, including marriage and living in the suburbs. But the deaths of people Jean admires, including Jimi Hendrix, Salvador Allende, and John Lennon, and then Jean's own father, wakes him up, and he realizes what is important in life. *Quill & Quire* contributor Tony Burgess noted, "Gravel makes his narrator a complex and difficult person to like, telling an exhilarating and important story."

In *Miss Semptember,* Lieutenant Brodeur is sent to investigate a bank robbery. The suspect is Genevieve, a twenty-two-year-old exotic dancer. She buys a dry-cleaning business in order to launder the money. As Brodeur investigates the crime, Brodeur and Genevieve begin to fall in love with each other. *Canadian Book Review Annual* contributor Sarah Robertson praised, "There isn't a wasted word in this exquisitely crafted tale."

In his children's book *Mr. Zamboni's Dream Machine,* Gravel tells the story of Daniel, a young boy who lives to play on his hockey team. His father, a divorced parent, is always telling Daniel how to play and what he did wrong in the game. One day Mr. Zamboni invites Daniel into his Zamboni machine. Inside the machine Daniel sees a movie in which he is the hero. Daniel learns to be more understanding of his father and, after watching the movie, the reasons why his father criticizes him. *Canadian Materials* contributor Norma Charles claimed, "A quick, satisfying read."

In his children's book *My Life as a Crow,* Gravel tells the story of a young boy who turns into a crow. The boy, a good student and son, must travel five blocks to school. Along the way he encounters bullies and an old lady with a mean dog. The boy is upset with the people he encounters and out of frustration shoots a sling shot at some crows. He hits one and is immediately sorry and attempts to fix the crow's broken wing. The crow talks to the boy and tells him how great the life of a crow is. The crow tells him of a witch who can turn him into a crow. After the boy is turned into a crow he learns that life was much better as a boy. *Canadian Materials* contributor Dave Jenkinson called *My Life as a Crow* "a fun read which imaginatively revisits the adage concerning the grass being greener."

BIOGRAPHICAL AND CRITICAL SOURCES:

PERIODICALS

Books in Canada, May, 2002, "The Not-So-Simple Good Life," p. 11.
Canadian Book Review Annual, 1998, Sarah Robertson, review of *Miss September: A Novel,* p. 184.
Canadian Literature, winter, 1992, Diane Watson, "Secrets," pp. 185-186; summer, 1993, Jill Lebihan, "Pain and Disorder," p. 113; summer, 1999, Ulrich Teucher, "Probabilities of Life," p. 205; spring, 2001, Susan Knutson, "Landmark Translations from Literary Quebec," pp. 147-148.
Canadian Materials, May, 1993, Norma Charles, review of *Mr. Zamboni's Dream Machine,* p. 94.
Quill & Quire, July, 1992, Jane Aspinall, "Pursuit of Happiness," p. 41; April, 1993, Annette Goldsmith, review of *Mr. Zamboni's Dream Machine,* p. 32; December, 1993, Ken Setterington, "Grand Travels," p. 34; October, 1996, Tony Burgess, review of *Ostend,* p. 41.
University of Toronto Quarterly, winter, 1999, Jane Koustas, "Translations," pp. 104-114.

ONLINE

Canadian Materials Online, http://www.umanitoba.ca/cm/ (September 3, 2002), David Jenkinson, review of *My Life as a Crow.**

GREEN, Terence M(ichael) 1947-

PERSONAL: Born February 2, 1947, in Toronto, Ontario, Canada; son of Thomas and Margaret (Radey) Green; married Merle Casci, September 2, 1994; children: Conor, Owen, Daniel. *Education:* University of Toronto, B.A., 1967, B.Ed., 1973; University College, Dublin, M.A., 1972.

ADDRESSES: Home—Toronto, Canada. *Agent*—Shawna McCarthy, The McCarthy Agency, 7 Allen St., Rumson, NJ 07760.

CAREER: Novelist and author of short fiction. East York Collegiate Institute, Toronto, Ontario, Canada, English teacher, 1968-99. Mohawk College, Hamilton, Ontario, writer-in-residence, 2003. Juror for Philip K. Dick Award, 1995, and for Sunburst Award, 2003.

MEMBER: Science Fiction Writers of America, Writers' Union of Canada.

AWARDS, HONORS: Recipient of Canada Council grants, Ontario Arts Council grants, and Toronto Arts Council grants; participant in Harborfront Festival of Authors; five-time finalist for the Aurora Award; two-time World Fantasy Award finalist.

WRITINGS:

The Woman Who Is the Midnight Wind (short stories), Pottersfield Press (Porters Lake, Nova Scotia, Canada), 1987.
Barking Dogs (novel), St. Martin's Press (New York, NY), 1988.
Children of the Rainbow (novel), McClelland & Stewart (Toronto, Ontario, Canada), 1992.
Shadow of Ashland (novel), Tor/Forge (New York, NY), 1996.
Blue Limbo (novel), Tor (New York, NY), 1997.
A Witness to Life (novel), Tom Doherty Associates (New York, NY), 1999.
St. Patrick's Bed (novel), Tom Doherty Associates (New York, NY), 2001.

Contributor of short stories, articles, interviews, reviews, and poetry to periodicals, including *Globe and Mail, Books in Canada, Quarry, Magazine of*

Terence M. Green

Fantasy and Science Fiction, Isaac Asimov's SF Magazine, Twilight Zone, Unearth, Thrust, SF Review, SF Chronicle, Poetry Toronto, and *Leisure Ways.* Contributor to anthologies, including *Northern Stars, Northern Frights, Ark of Ice, Dark Visions, Conversations with Robertson Davies, Tesseracts, The Writer's Voice 2, Over the Edge, Crossing the Line,* and *Aurora: New Canadian Writing.*

WORK IN PROGRESS: The Man Who Disappeared, a novel.

SIDELIGHTS: Canadian science-fiction writer Terence M. Green has been praised throughout his career for his quiet, restrained style. A *Science Fiction Chronicle* reviewer, discussing Green's first collection of stories, *The Woman Who Is the Midnight Wind,* theorized that such a style, however worthy, would not establish the author's fame until a substantial body of work had been built up. The reviewer further stated that while not yet widely known, Green's writing "is extraordinary and indicates a great talent masquerading as simplicity." Reviewer Joel Yanofsky wrote in *Books in Canada,* "it's Green's restrained and understated prose style that makes his fiction work." Yanofsky approved

of the fact that the short stories in Green's collection deal with universal human emotions as much as with the trappings of science-fiction. In some of the stories, for instance, futuristic technology allows characters to speak with their dead relatives; Green uses this scenario to explore the emotional ramifications of such communication. "Green's vision of the future," Yanofsky asserted, "is of a world, not unlike our own, that has progressed too much and gotten too smart for the people who inhabit it."

Green's first novel, *Barking Dogs,* is a futuristic, violent thriller. The novel's hero is police officer Mitch Helwig of the Canadian city of Toronto, Ontario, who takes revenge on criminals after his partner is murdered. The cop's equipment includes a kind of portable super-lie-detector called a "barking dog." Reviewers in both *Maclean's* and *Books in Canada* compared the tale with "Rambo" movies, while *Books in Canada's* Douglas Hill observed that "the dialogue is snappy and sharp-edged."

More favorably received was Green's 1992 novel, *Children of the Rainbow,* a time-travel novel that centers on a character named Fletcher Christian IV—a descendant of the hero of the classic book *Mutiny on the Bounty* by Charles Nordhoff and James Norman Hall. The plot focuses on a hypothetical New Inca Church in the 2070s that is run by a leader who discovers a way to send people one hundred years back in time. This device allows Green to move his narrative through different historical periods—from the Norfolk Island penal colony in 1835 to French nuclear tests in 1972. While *Quill and Quire* reviewer R. John Hayes accused *Children of the Rainbow* of being too clever, he noted that Green "draws his characters very well and manages the frequent temporal shifts, which might have been disconcerting, brilliantly." Barbara Canfield, analyzing the novel as suitable for ages fourteen and up in *Canadian Materials,* approved of the Greenpeace aspect of the plot, and of the book in general; a *Science Fiction Chronicle* reviewer found it "a very quiet, introspective work." In *Canadian Forum,* Douglas Barbour called Green "very good at showing the psychological disruption the time shifts create in his two central characters" and singled out the long conversations between twenty-first-century Fletcher Christian IV and the nineteenth-century penal colony commandant as the best parts of the book, capturing "perfectly the intelligent incomprehension of [the commandant]." *Books in Canada* contributor John Degen labeled *Children of the Rainbow* "gracefully and authoritatively written . . . a questioning novel, a book that wonders as much about the lessons of our past as about our possible future." In an afterword to the novel, Green himself said, "writing *Children of the Rainbow* gave me the opportunity to revisit the magic of the stories of my youth. Everyone should be so lucky."

Four years after the release of *Children of the Rainbow,* Green produced the novel *Shadow of Ashland.* The story is set in Ashland, Kentucky, a town that was also the setting of a story in *The Woman Who Is the Midnight Wind.* In the novel, protagonist Leo Nolan takes up his mother's deathbed request to find her long-lost brother Jack. Letters from Jack written in 1934 have mysteriously been arriving in the mail; Leo not only traces them back to Ashland, Jack's old stomping ground, but finds himself in the year 1934, mixed up in a crime hatched by Jack. In the *New York Times Book Review,* Malachy Duffy regretted a "clumsy" subplot, but deemed the work an overall success because of the author's "dedication to exploring its underlying themes of redemption, resolution and homecoming." George Needham, in *Booklist,* was still more enthusiastic, declaring, "This is a jewel of a novel, sensitively told and filled with fascinating characters."

With *Blue Limbo* Green returns to the style of the futuristic thriller, and to hero Mitch Helwig. Out to avenge the murder of his partner—and a murder attempt on his own life and his captain's—Helwig finds himself on suspension from the police force—"a rogue cop," according to a *Publishers Weekly* contributor. Coinciding with Helwig's violent mission is a twenty-first-century medical breakthrough, a technique known as "Blue Limbo," used for reviving the recently deceased back to consciousness. "What separates Green's thrillers from conventional ones is his concern for the emotional lives of his characters," commented Douglas Barbour in the Edmonton *Journal.* In *Publishers Weekly,* a reviewer described *Blue Limbo* as "a high tech action cop thriller, albeit one sensitively drawn." Barbour concluded in the *Journal* that the novel "is a solid entertainment, with more than a bit of heart."

A Witness to Life follows one of the characters only mentioned in *Shadow of Ashland.* Green told *CA* that both novels "use as their starting points real people

and incidents in my own family. (In *Shadow of Ashland,* a major character, Jack Radey, is the real name of an uncle of mine who disappeared in the 1930s"; *A Witness to Life,* which had previously been titled *The Redemption of Martin Radey,* "is based on the life of my maternal grandfather, whose name is in fact Martin Radey. They illustrate my growing interest in exploring the intricacies of family in fiction, a kind of blend of genealogy, drama, mythologizing, and personal resolution."

Leo Nolan and his family reappear in *St. Patrick's Bed,* another sequel to *Shadow of Ashland.* The theme of the novel is the complexity of father-son relationships. In late 1990s Toronto, Leo and his stepson Adam become involved in a search for Adam's birth father, who had abandoned him before Adam was born. This endeavor prompts Leo to think not only about his own father and grandfather, but about his own paternal role. Whitney Scott in *Booklist* found the novel full of "a tender regard for ordinary pathos and for quiet truths" that a lesser talent might have made overly melodramatic.

AUTOBIOGRAPHICAL ESSAY:

Terence M. Green contributed the following autobiographical essay to *CA:*

Our own lives start long before we're born. Millions of years of genetic encoding funnel down into our great-grandparents, then grandparents, finally parents.

I wrote those words. You can find them near the beginning of Chapter Six, in my 2001 novel, *St. Patrick's Bed.* Casting about for a beginning to this essay, I realized that I'd already turned much of this soil, distilling many of my thoughts and feelings about family throughout my own stories. People have asked me about my fiction: did it happen like that? My answer, usually: no . . . but it is all true. Fact, fiction, fact, fiction.

Born in Toronto's Irish Cabbagetown in 1904, the oldest of five children who lived—Thomas Green, my father, entered the work world in 1918, where he toiled for fifty-one years until retirement in 1969. The majority of that time he spent doing blue-collar work in the

The author's parents, Thomas and Margaret Green, Toronto, 1930

circulation departments of two Toronto newspapers: the *Globe and Mail* (twenty-three years) and the *Toronto Star* (seventeen years).

He was a part-time professional musician. At the beginning he played banjo, later strummed guitar in various groups and orchestras around southern Ontario, and finally, by the time I had arrived, demonstrated a rather rare versatility by morphing into a trombone player in the Royal Canadian Artillery band. I remember the mellow slide sounds as he practiced in the basement. I remember him marching and playing in the annual Santa Claus parade. When he died in 1995, in the top drawer of his dresser, in a plastic case, I found a small metal plaque with his name engraved on it. It stated that he was a Life Member of the Toronto Musicians Association, Local 149 A.F. of M.

On November 30th, 1929—one month after the stock market crash that signaled the Great Depression—my father, two days shy of his twenty-fifth birthday, married twenty-year-old Margaret Radey, my mother—also born in Toronto—in a wedding whose strange timing would be clarified by the arrival in May of 1930 of my oldest sister, Anne. She was the first of five surviving (as in his own family) children born during the nineteen-year span from 1930 to 1949, in a marriage that would last almost fifty-four years—until my mother's death in 1984—defying its hurried,

unpromising origins. Ron was born in 1932, Judy 1939. My younger brother and I were the late family: February 2, 1947 for me; Dennis, 1949.

Dennis and I were postwar babies—a distinct unit, raised as a pair—far removed from Anne and Ron. Even Judy, our other sister, born in 1939, was virtually a decade older. Dennis and I, then, were the children of older parents, with all that that entails—an experience, in hindsight, mostly positive.

In the three-bedroom, semidetached house in North Toronto, purchased in 1929, there was always family around—uncles, aunts, cousins, added to brothers, sisters, and grandparents. This was the crowded scene into which I made a late arrival. Both sides of my family were Catholics who had emigrated from Ireland (counties Kerry, Cork, Dublin, Offaly, Limerick) and settled in and around Toronto and southern Ontario in the mid-1800s. My father's mother, Nanny (Annie Sutton), then the family matriarch, born in 1885, also lived with us until her death in 1974. After Anne, Ron, and Judy left and got married, Dennis and I squeezed into bunk beds, sharing the smallest bedroom.

So my mother was thirty-seven, my father forty-two when I was born, the fourth of five—three boys and two girls. Nanny, the sole grandparent still alive, was sixty-one, widowed for five years. Dennis was still two years in the future. But Anne (seventeen), Ron (fourteen), and Judy (eight) were all in the house, as was Jacquie (nineteen), my cousin who lived with us. We were seven—soon to be eight—in what I have already explained was a modest three-bedroom house. Privacy was nonexistent. Noise was everywhere.

A disjointed collage of memories from the first few years . . . Climbing out of the crib in my parents' bedroom. Stepping on a bee and being stung on the foot at the summer cottages at Port Dover, on Lake Erie. Dennis and I sitting in metal washtubs in the backyard in summer. Hollyhocks and peonies at the back of the house. The feel and smell of the Insulbrick on the garage and back porch. The forest fire in Disney's *Bambi*. Riding the streetcar with my mother to shop at Eaton's and Simpson's in downtown Toronto. Seeing *Annie Get Your Gun* at the Tivoli theatre—where Nanny worked behind the candy counter—in 1950 (age three) and not understanding the title, thinking I would get a gun there. *The Du-*

Terence (left) and brother Dennis, c. 1951

rango Kid serials, yo-yo demonstrations, Debbie Reynolds singing "Abba Dabba Honeymoon" in *Two Weeks with Love* at the Fairlawn theatre, with my big sister, Judy, on Saturday afternoons. Being taken to swim in the Rouge River by Uncle Jim and Anna Mae, the sudden realization that I was under water, being pulled out by a lifeguard. The squeaking door of *Inner Sanctum* from the radio in the living room. My mother reading *Peter and the Wolf* and the Golden Book *Tawny Scrawny Lion* to me on Nanny's bed—where I slept until well into grade one after moving from the crib in my parents' room. Watching my mother cry when she found out her father (whom I don't remember) had died, Christmas Day, 1950.

Where does a writer come from? What are the seminal signs? I don't know. I have been asked at least twice that I can recall, "How did you get into it?"—as if one "got into it" somehow. I shake my head, realizing that I did not get into it, but rather, it got into me. I have

come to believe that you just are a writer or you are not. It is a vocation, a passion. It chooses you.

There was no kindergarten at St. Monica's School when I started in 1952, so I went right into grade one—a room with the green letter cards atop the blackboards, wooden desks with metal legs and tops that lifted. I'm not sure how it came to be, but I could read before I knew it, and Sister Rosemary would sit me on a chair at the front of the room to read to the class—that is, until one day I told her that I didn't want to do it. I was too shy. After that, she didn't ask any more. Perhaps this was the beginning: books, reading, preferring to remain in the background.

I don't know how old I was, but the first non-illustrated book-length story I remember reading by myself was a "Bobbsey Twins" volume that was in one of the two built-in bookcases in our living room on Maxwell Avenue. One afternoon, trying to occupy a bored child, my mother suggested I try it. I finished it before dinner, amazed to have read so much, equally amazed to have understood and enjoyed such a long story on my own. There followed the introduction (by my mother) of Thornton W. Burgess's animal books: *Reddy the Fox, Prickly Porky the Porcupine, Bowser the Hound,* and company. She bought me my own hardcovers. And thus it began—the love affair with books, encouraged and abetted by my mother, entwined with a natural bent toward reading that emerged in that first year of school.

For the first two grades I had five-and-six-year-old confidence and poise. I was doing okay—more than okay. I liked school, was popular with my classmates and teachers. And in a Catholic school, we studied our catechism, and like James Joyce before me, I too was terrified of going to hell at much too early an age. (And again, like Joyce, this was a bit of heritage that I refrained from passing on to my own children.)

They skipped me past grade three, directly into grade four, and this is where it changed. As proud (and bewildered) as I was at this sudden shift in status, my peers were gone. I found myself the youngest and smallest in my new class, and until I finished grade eight and got into high school, I never regained that early poise and confidence that had been my initial experience. Throughout grades four to eight—age seven to twelve—my academic achievement leveled

The author (far right) with father and brother Dennis, fishing near Bancroft, Ontario, c. 1955

and I became a quiet, withdrawn student, unable to compete with the bigger boys in sports or interact socially with my female classmates. This is when my brother Dennis—two years younger—and I were the closest. In many ways, I changed from being a participant to being an observer. My grade six/seven teacher, Miss Gettings, wrote on one of my report cards, "Terry is a dreamer."

Some of my fondest memories of this period revolve around two-and three-week summer vacations near Bancroft, Ontario, fishing and swimming in cottage country some 160 miles northeast of Toronto on the Canadian shield. It was the only time we seemed to be a nuclear family: Mom and Dad, Dennis and me. These cottages and times were genuine idylls. Dennis and I fished, played, swam together. We were good company for each other. It was on Bow Lake and Weslemkoon Lake that I began skin diving and snorkeling, which would lead to a later small interest in scuba diving. I saw my father enjoy himself, felt him radiate a pleasure and patience while with us and while fishing that was seldom evident at home. Fishing suited him. It was a way for us to spend time together, doing something that interested us all. And I saw my mother enjoy all of us enjoying ourselves.

This was the 1950s. Television was a novelty, limited in what it could deliver. Video games and computers were concoctions that even science-fiction writers hadn't dreamed up. I read and collected Superman and Batman comic books when they were a dime apiece. Somewhere in the middle of all this, in grade five (age eight or nine), I discovered the "Hardy Boys" books and their clones: Tom Swift Jr., Rick Brant science

adventure stories, etc. My mother, aware of my passion, continued to feed books to me. I loved them, devoured them. Having finished high school and even having attended the Ontario College of Art after graduation, Mom was the educated one in the family. My father, though, lacking the same polish (never having attended high school), was, nevertheless, no slouch. Both my parents were readers. They always had a book on the go.

*

I've pondered autobiographical notes by other writers who mention having been raised on classics and surrounded by Literature in their formative years. It wasn't like that in my house. There were books—they were revered—but they weren't part of The Canon. They were whatever was popular, whatever caught their fancy. Historical novels abounded. My father also read Jules Verne, Thomas B. Costain, loved James Michener's books; *True* and *Argosy* magazines were by his bedside. Mom read *Pageant of the Popes* by John Farrow (several times, I believe; I still have the paperback of hers—copyrighted 1949—among my own books), *Lives of the Saints*—and of course, Michener (*Hawaii* was read more than once as well). Mom introduced me to Edgar Rice Burroughs's "Tarzan" novels, which she herself had read as a child—buying the Grosset and Dunlap hardcovers for me—eight of which I still have. At age twelve I took out my first science-fiction novel from the now-defunct St. Clement's Branch of the Toronto Public Library System—*Islands in the Sky*, by Arthur C. Clarke. This led me to Clarke's nonfiction, including his scuba-diving books, like *The Reefs of Taprobane*, as well as Robert A. Heinlein's juveniles.

Reading, apparently, kept my family sane. Books were our getaway. We read as omnivores, without guidance or discrimination, taking whatever roads we stumbled upon. I've mentioned my first reading experience with the "Bobbsey Twins" books. These comprised a series that was the brainchild of Edward Stratemeyer, whose syndicate also produced the "The Hardy Boys," "Rick Brant," "Tom Swift Jr.," and "Nancy Drew" books. I didn't know it at the time, but these books (along with Burroughs's "Tarzan" books) were unavailable in libraries, dismissed by the literary custodians of the day who looked down their collective noses at such formulaic, work-for-hire fiction. There were no such authors as Franklin W. Dixon, John Blaine, Victor

Appleton. They were three of the many house names under which the Stratemeyer Syndicate published more than a hundred different series, spanning more than seventy-five years.

Since everybody I know admits to having read "Hardy Boys" or "Nancy Drew" books—and sales statistics confirm their staggering popularity—arguably, for my generation, Stratemeyer is the most influential person in the history of children's literature. I never understood the fear and concerns of librarians about letting young people read these books, since their heroes and heroines were teens (usually) of exceptional moral character, engaged in exciting adventures, and they made books appealing and reading an exhilarating experience—something librarians and teachers and parents still have trouble doing. As evidence of their beneficence, I offer myself.

From age twelve to seventeen, I attended St. Michael's College School in Toronto, a private Catholic institution of about a thousand boys. I did much growing up there—in every way. When I entered at age twelve, I was five feet two; I shot up about a foot over the next two years—to my present lanky stature—regaining some of my self-confidence in the process. A part of my father emerged in me as I played trumpet in the school band for five years, ending up as the concert master in my last year. I made friends and began to think of myself as a good student again. In short, I was glad to leave grade school and St. Monica's behind.

But what part of the author was groomed there? I try to understand it myself. I have vivid memories of two pieces I wrote for Mr. Reddall in grade-nine English. One was a description of ducks swimming out onto a lake through the reeds, which he read aloud to the class as an example of good description. Another was a small story I wrote that he asked me to write out neatly and submit to a school magazine that was being published—which they didn't take, I recall, but that seemed secondary to his praise. In grade ten, Mr. Warden had us write a short story. He read mine aloud to the class and graded it a ten out of ten. My grade thirteen (we had such things in Ontario then) teacher, Fr. Sheedy, told me I had beautiful sentence structure, and thought I should consider journalism.

These things seem important now only because, out of the vast detritus of memories that clog all our minds, I can recall them. Clearly, I was doing something that

Terence and Dennis, Toronto, 1958

stood out, no matter how immature; and just as clearly, the praise was a necessary catalyst—something not lost on me when I began my own teaching career in 1968.

During that time, from 1959 to 1964, I read voraciously, but fastened on science fiction and fantasy, devouring all I came across. At the beginning I read novels in the Winston Science Fiction series—books like *The Star Seekers*, by Milton Lesser, and *Mists of Dawn*, by Chad Oliver. These were hardcover novels that cost $2.75 each, that came in colorful dust jackets, and included vivid endpaper illustrations by Alex Schomburg. On a bookshelf in my basement, I still have seven of these novels. Later, I added the paperbacks of Heinlein, Bradbury, Dick, Simak, Walter Miller, Jr., plus a host of authors so obscure that their books can't even qualify as collector's items (Jack Sharkey, Jerry Sohl). Part of me had slid sideways into another world, a world in which I found great pleasure.

High school English class was a revelation to me. Being assigned a book to read was something that had never happened in my years at St. Monica's. Here, at last, was some direction, some discussion of what I was reading. It was a breath of fresh air. Books that I recall discovering, fondly, in classes: *Oliver Twist, Prester John, Huckleberry Finn, Mutiny on the Bounty, The Catcher in the Rye, The Old Man and the Sea, Cry, the Beloved Country,* and I even enjoyed and responded to *Hamlet.* These were indeed, new worlds.

And part of me was a typical Canadian teenage boy. I loved hockey and baseball, played them enthusiastically and often, if not too well. To this day, I am an avid hockey and baseball enthusiast, seeing sport as an enriching and interesting aspect of life.

My years at St. Mike's were positive. It was a good school. I still have friends from those years.

I entered University of Toronto in 1964, at age seventeen (much too young), and studied general arts, majoring in English. When forced to select a one-year physical education elective, I chose skin and scuba diving. To this day, though, my scuba experience has been confined to the university's pool. Three years later, in 1967, age twenty (again, much too young), I graduated with a B.A.

The one-year program to become a high school teacher at what was then called the College of Education in Toronto was next on the agenda. I wanted to teach English. In September, 1968, at age twenty-one, I found myself doing just that: teaching English in Toronto's East York Collegiate Institute—suddenly, a full-time professional, tossed unceremoniously into a career that would—with interruptions—span thirty-one years.

This thing about being much too young had become a refrain. And it was not over. I was married in December, 1968, shortly before my twenty-second birthday, to the young woman a year younger than myself that I had met only that summer, who would become my first wife. She was a grade school teacher. The whirlwind seemed in keeping with my strange, accelerated journey into adulthood.

I taught at East York C.I. for two years, an amazingly full experience, both exhausting and exhilarating, then resigned, going back to University of Toronto full-

Age 21, at East York Collegiate Institute, 1968

time at age twenty-three in 1970. Teaching books had made me want to know even more about them. I took more English courses, targeting graduate school. As the year progressed, one course rose above the others for me, and I found a new obsession: Irish writers. Yeats, Joyce, Synge, Beckett. I applied and was accepted into the M.A. program in Anglo-Irish Studies at University College, Dublin, in the National University of Ireland, and in September, 1971, my wife Penny and I were off on the grand adventure. She enrolled in the one-year diploma course for teachers of the deaf at the university, giving both of us who had leapt into adulthood too fast another crack at being young.

It was a great year. But great years cost money, and this one was no exception. Neither of us had any requisite family fortune, and our savings were running out fast. The goal was to make it to the end of the school year as best we could, and in a cold-water flat, without central heating, in quasi-poverty, we more or less managed it. We spent a few days in the west of Ireland, and saw Kerry, Galway, Sligo—stunning landscapes which imprinted themselves indelibly on my psyche. In the spring of 1972, broke, I wrote and applied for my old job back at East York C.I. in Toronto (I've often thought of it as coming home on my hands and knees), and they rehired me. Economic determinism had always been with me, and was to be a significant feature of my life as a writer in the future. This was, though, perhaps its rudest awakening. I was learning the compromise with reality.

We returned to Toronto and were back at the front of classrooms in September, 1972. I taught at East York for two more years, until 1974, when, restless, curious, still young (always), I took a job in a more rural area. From 1974 to 1976, I taught English at Bayside Secondary School, just outside Belleville, Ontario, while Penny worked at the local school for the deaf.

*

It was during this period that I began to actually write. I'd always known that I would write—even back when I was reading those "Hardy Boys" novels in grade school. I longed to be able to create the books that gave me so much pleasure. For reasons both practical and irrational, though, I had managed to delay it as long as possible. There were no more excuses. It was time to try.

This is a daunting time for a writer: the beginning. There is no way to measure the possibility of success. In contrast, what one is sure of is that there is, indeed, quite a high probability of failure. No one I know likes to fail. So this is it, the test, the initial, serious rudimentary scribblings.

I sold the first piece I wrote. In 1975, I received a check for $35 for a thirty-five-hundred-word article, an overview of the work of one of my favorite writers, Philip K. Dick. It appeared in the May 1976 issue of *Science Fiction Review*. With that money, I bought an old oak office desk at a local auction, painstakingly stripped the black enamel paint from it, and used it for writing. I sold it in 2001, twenty-six years later, for $40, attesting clearly to the wild money and vast profits of the writing game.

In spite of university degrees in literature and five years' experience teaching English, when it came time to write, I had fallen back on my old love of fantastic literature. There followed other critical pieces on the field, then the necessary foray into fiction: the short story. I wrote my first, "Japanese Tea," during this period, which finally saw publication in the 1979 anthology *Alien Worlds*. Set in a high school of the near future, it posited an educational dystopia which exaggerated much of the path down which it all seemed to be sliding. Written in 1975, it was mildly prescient, mentioning mass killings in schools in 1997 and 1998. The Columbine horror occurred in 1999.

Ever restless, I lasted only two years working and living in the Belleville area before I realized that I was in the wrong place. We both missed Toronto. Nervously, I let it be known back at my old school—East York C.I.—that I was on the move again, and amazingly—and thankfully—they hired me for an incredible third time. So I returned to both Toronto and East York in 1976, at age twenty-nine, and for the next twenty-three years, even though I employed various ruses to interrupt my tenure there, I was careful not to resign again. I figured I'd definitely run out my string.

At thirty years of age, I was on the threshold of one of the moments that define who we are and what we will become. In 1977 Penny became pregnant. It was intentional. When we found out there would be twins, I was sky-high with anticipation. But when the actual births came round, they needed to be induced, and on March 7, 1978, suddenly, everything went wrong. Foetal distress, an emergency Caesarean. Two boys were born. One of them lived only twenty-four hours. The other, Conor, is a healthy twenty-five years of age as I write this in 2003.

I had been sailing along on gloriously smooth waters. Overnight, the wind was taken out of my sails. Values shifted, my eyes opened in new ways. I had the best and the worst of life simultaneously. There were no words. When things settled, I was a father, the most profound role I would play.

A year later, I wrote a small, twenty-two-hundred-word story called "Of Children in the Foliage." It was set on another planet. It tells the story, in first person, of a father who has one of his twin sons die at birth, and the otherworldly way in which the lost twin lives in a limbo world. It was published in the mainstream Doubleday anthology, *Aurora: New Canadian Writing 1979*. When editor Morris Wolfe called me on the phone to discuss a few minor editorial sentence changes, I mentioned to him that I had been pleasantly surprised that he had accepted it, suggesting that he probably didn't get many SF stories submitted. He flattered and surprised me with his response: "Oh, I get lots of science fiction stories." Then he paused. "But nothing like this."

As catharsis, I had gone inside, written the truth, from pain, had produced something different. It had transcended its genre. The lesson was learned.

Between 1981 and 1985 there were more stories, ostensibly science fiction and fantasy, published in such places as *Isaac Asimov's Science Fiction Magazine,* and the venerable *Magazine of Fantasy and Science Fiction,* American digest periodicals which to this day still publish the best the field has to offer. When ten of my tales were eventually collected in the volume *The Woman Who Is the Midnight Wind* (1987), a reviewer for *Books in Canada* wrote: "[Green's] new collection of short stories is simply good fiction."

Reading habits changed, grew. I admired Steinbeck, Updike, Vanderhaeghe, Carver, Malamud—mainstream writers. I learned writing from reading, and I still do. The more widely I read, the more perspective I gained on what constituted good, lasting fiction, and felt the urge to try to create it expand.

A novel beckoned. By 1983, I had been in and out of the classroom for fifteen years—half a career. I was caught between the desire to write and the need to make a living, frustrated by the constraints of a regular job, yet fully aware of the folly of tossing it away. I was thirty-six years old, not a kid living in a garret. My second son, Owen, had arrived back on February 16, 1981—I had a wife and two children, bills to pay, more to come. And yet. . . . How could I live with myself if I didn't try? Things can die inside you, can lie there withering.

I bit the bullet, took the plunge, opted to teach half-time. For half the money, I taught mornings only, wrote at home in the afternoons in an office I built in my garage. Between 1983 and 1985 I produced my first novel, *Barking Dogs,* a near-future police thriller set in Toronto, complete with infallible lie detectors (the Barking Dogs of the title). When it was published by St. Martin's Press of New York in 1988, Margaret

Cannon, the Toronto *Globe and Mail*'s mystery reviewer, concluded—perceptively, I felt—that "the SF touches of Toronto in the very near future are really nice and the invention of the Barking Dog is terrific, but the truth is that Green doesn't need them. This story of nice people under immense pressure is good enough to keep the reader riveted to the last paragraph." Once again, although labeled and marketed as SF, the suggestion was that the ideas were subordinate to the characters and their plights, something not necessarily a hallmark of the genre—something in which I took pride.

Nineteen eighty-five was a landmark year for another reason. After seventeen years and two children, my marriage washed up on the shore. To outsiders, these things seem like they happen overnight, but they never do. In fact, I'm still not sure what happened or how it happened, but it wouldn't be wrong to say that it all stemmed from our rather hasty marriage in our callow youth, and had been heading—not quickly, but more like molasses—in this direction all that time. In hindsight, perhaps the real wonder is that it didn't end sooner. Along with the death of my mother on March 14, 1984, perhaps the desire to go sideways into a writing life instead of continuing the conservative, middle-class path of career teacher was the other catalyst that brought things to a boil. Penny told me that she had changed, but I had not, which was as probable as any other conclusion I have been able to draw. I believe these things have a momentum that is undefinable, and analyzing them often provides answers too simplistic.

But with two small children, the sudden fracture in my life was almost unbearable. Conor was seven, Owen four. I could never have imagined this happening to my family, to them, yet there it was. I moved out. It almost killed me.

*

In October, 1985, I rented a small studio apartment— five hundred square feet—on the third floor of a house on Heath Street East in Toronto. I took virtually nothing with me, left everything behind. The only things I wanted were my sons. Over the next months, amidst pain and anger, I began building a new life, from the ground up. Joint custody of my boys was all I really wanted—that, and the chance to start again. At first, I found a mattress in the basement of the house in which I was living, cleaned it up, and slept on it. When my boys began to stay overnight, I bought myself a large piece of foam and slept in a sleeping bag on it, ceding the mattress to them. After six months, I bought a waterbed—it being the only bed of any size that I could get up the winding stairs to my third-floor apartment. Curiously, to this day, I still have it.

I arranged to have my sons half-time, fourteen of every twenty-eight days, an arrangement that lasted virtually until they entered university. Now, in 2003, Conor is twenty-five, finished school, and has a place of his own. Owen is twenty-two, in the middle of college, and has lived with me full-time for the past two years—since his mother moved to take a job in Kingston, Ontario. But I'm getting ahead of myself. . . .

I mentioned the death of my mother in March of 1984. I don't know if I can do justice to the impact this had on me, and continues to have on me to this day. Like the death of my son, six years earlier, it changed everything, again. Hers was a life that I could see had been shortchanged. Her mother had died when she was sixteen. Her father had remarried a year-and-a-half later, been smitten with his new, younger wife, and ignored his two children (my mother and her brother, Jack, two years younger), who ended up living mostly with relatives. Four years later, age twenty, she was pregnant, married, and was to be a mother before she turned twenty-one. Her only sibling, Jack, had a falling-out with their father, left Canada for the United States to look for work circa 1932, sent my mother—his sister—a handful of cards and letters home, then disappeared around 1935, never to be heard from again. My mother had been abandoned, ended up in the Green clan, and made what she could of her life by having her own family. But there was always a wistfulness, a sense of something missing that even her children could pick up. I know too, now, how much of my life I spent just trying to please my mother, how much I wanted to make her happy, how happy it made me when she was happy.

When my mother died in March of 1984, in a trunk at the foot of her bed I found the letters and cards that her brother Jack had sent her back in the 1930s. She had kept them for fifty years. They were from Toledo; Detroit; Bucyrus, Ohio; and Ashland, Kentucky. I imagined his trail into the heart of America in the Dodge Roadster he mentioned in his letters. There was

a tone of warmth and confidence in the writing that was at odds with his disappearance.

After her death, in the summer of 1984—a year before my own marriage was to collapse—we took a family car trip to visit Joe and Pam Zarantonello, a couple we had met on my year in Ireland back in 1971-72. Joe, an American who had taken the same degree that I had, was now teaching school in Bardstown, Kentucky. While there, among other things, he showed me the Trappist monastery at Gethsemani, where Thomas Merton had lived and was now buried. On our way home to Toronto, we detoured to Ashland, Kentucky, the source of one of Jack's last letters. I spent a day there, trying to imagine his brief stay in that small city of thirty-thousand on the Ohio River. And a story began percolating, forming, slowly.

Six months later, in January of 1985, the letters from Jack to my mother still sitting like stones inside me, in the office of my renovated garage I wrote a nine-thousand word novelet called "Ashland, Kentucky." It's the story of a man whose mother is dying, who wants to see her lost brother who disappeared into the States fifty years earlier. The son tries to find him and fails and his mother dies. Then letters start showing up at the family home in Toronto in 1984, from the lost brother to his sister, postmarked 1934. The son travels to the source of the last letter, Ashland, Kentucky, to see what's going on. He ends up in 1934, meeting with his uncle.

The fiction was both biography and autobiography, yet neither. It was both fantastic fiction as well as of the here-and-now. In short, I didn't know what it was. Neither did anyone else. Published originally in the November 1985 issue of *Isaac Asimov's Science Fiction Magazine,* and subsequently collected in anthologies *Tesseracts* and *Northern Frights,* it became my most popular piece of short fiction. As had been the case with "Of Children in the Foliage," it was written from the heart, and apparently, it showed. Once again, I had taken personal experience and transmuted it into fantastic form.

But back to my new world in that tiny, third-floor apartment. . . . It was during my time there that Merle entered my life. In 2003, eighteen years later, she is my wife. The passion of our relationship was overwhelming in its initial stages, and even though

The author and wife Merle on their wedding day, September 1994, Graceland Wedding Chapel, Las Vegas

she was a University of Toronto graduate—our first date was at that institution's eminent Hart House—the fact that I was fourteen years older than she gave us some cause to think of it as something magical that might disappear. But it did not.

Perhaps the dedication in my 1992 novel *Children of the Rainbow* says it best: "For Merle, who healed me with love, words are not enough." (Speaking of *Children of the Rainbow.* . . . Most of it was written in that tiny third-floor apartment during a 1986-87 leave-of-absence from my teaching position. In hindsight, it mirrors much of my psychological state at the time, with themes of displacement in time and space abounding). By 1988, I had a financial settlement attached to my separation (I wasn't officially divorced until 1990), and Merle and I took a plunge and purchased a house together, forging new bonds.

We bought a big, old, three-storey semidetached home in downtown Toronto. It needed never-ending work. It was still being renovated fourteen years later when we finally left it. But it seemed like a castle after the five-hundred-square-foot apartment of the previous two-and-a-half years. Besides the two of us and my sons half-time, we made our living arrangement even more unusual by adding one more person. My father, who had been living in a senior citizens' apartment since 1985, came to live with us.

The house on Brooklyn Avenue served us all well. My father had his own space and contributed financially. But his real contribution was just being there. I liked that my sons had the chance to interact with him, to

get to know him. He felt needed. As much as he occasionally drove me crazy, and as much as I could never have envisioned living with him again after so many years, it was, simply, the right thing to do. He and I had both mellowed.

He moved in with us in the spring of 1988, age eighty-three. He left us when he died, spring, 1995, age ninety. As a result, I never felt about his death the same sense of unfairness that surrounded my mother's. Closure is an overused word, but sometimes it comes closest.

In 1991-92 I was awarded a sabbatical leave, with partial salary, from the East York Board of Education to study and create a computerized writing class that could serve as a prototype for the board. Among other things, it involved taking a course called "Computers and Writing" at the Harvard Graduate School of Education, so I rented a room in a house in Cambridge, Massachusetts, and commuted back and forth from Toronto to Boston during the spring of 1992. It was a fine year, and at the same time I managed to complete a first draft of the novel *Blue Limbo*—a sequel to my 1988 novel, *Barking Dogs*—something I had been working on sporadically since 1989.

In *Blue Limbo,* the main character, Mitch Helwig, has seen his marriage collapse, and has moved to a small third-floor apartment. His father, eighty-four-year-old Paul Helwig, is living in the same Toronto senior citizens' apartment complex in which my own father resided from 1985 to 1988. The "blue limbo" device of the title is a device of the near future that enables people to keep loved ones "alive" for a period of up to four weeks after they have "died."

So I'd done it again: life and death, autobiography, personal turmoil, a shroud of the fantastic hovering over it all.

But it didn't find a publisher immediately. The reasons for this are integral to the business side of writing, rather than the quality of the work—a situation more common than casual observers might suspect. St. Martin's Press had dropped its SF&F line, and Canadian publisher McClelland & Stewart, who published *Children of the Rainbow* in 1992, declined to make an offer on it. *Rainbow* had not secured an

American copublisher, and had, therefore, not sold the number of books they had hoped. So I did what writers do. I put it "in the drawer" for the time being and moved on.

In early 1992, I began expanding my 1985 story, "Ashland, Kentucky." I revisited my mother's 1984 death and the shadowy disappearance of her brother, Jack, back in the 1930s. The story still haunted me, and there was more to tell. And I had been encouraged by reviewers and casual commentators that I "had something" in this tale.

By summer, 1992, I had about a hundred pages of a draft written. In September, I put it aside to resume normal family life. Back in the classroom after my sabbatical, the novel languished until May of 1993, when I applied for and received a Canada Council travel grant to go to Ashland, Kentucky for a weekend of research. The trip was invaluable. Walking its streets, eating in its restaurants, sitting in the library there, the story came more sharply into focus, and there was much revision upon my return to Toronto.

Once home, I was dealt an unexpected blow. My brother, Ron, sixty years old, married father of four grown boys, collapsed and died at work. The sobering effect of this went deeper than I had ever understood it could. No one saw it coming, and like my mother's death, we all knew Ron had been cheated out of much of life. In my father's eyes at the funeral, I saw his own world being taken from him in ways too profound to articulate.

That summer, life continued. The novel grew another hundred pages or so, but by September, I had put it aside once again to return to teaching. It sat until summer of 1994. But it grew vividly in my head during that fall, winter, and spring. I heard the characters talking, knew what awaited them, felt nuances grow, made notes. The main character, Leo Nolan, would begin his quest for his mother's brother, Jack, in 1984 Toronto, pursue him to Ashland, Kentucky, where he would spend nine days with him in 1934 Kentucky, and return, changed, to 1984 Toronto. Fantasy? Time travel? Magic realism? I didn't know. In July and August of 1994, I wrote steadily, finishing, finally, the little book that had gestated in stages for ten years.

As an unwitting climax to the book's completion, on the Labor Day weekend, 1994—more than six years after buying the house together and establishing our unique, generational family—Merle and I, along with her mother and my two sons (now thirteen and sixteen years of age) flew to Las Vegas, where we were married in the Graceland Wedding Chapel. Her mother was her matron of honor, my sons were my best men. Elvis gave the bride away, and sang for us after the ceremony. It was like going to city hall, only more fun—and as much as one might find it difficult to believe, we were pleasantly surprised by the sensitivity and taste exhibited by the folks who clearly understood how to stage this ritual of rituals. The honeymoon—such as it was with our extended family—was at the MGM Grand, and we were back home by Monday evening. Tuesday, life resumed, and once again, I was teaching.

The uniqueness of the year continued: a month later, at a Friday evening Toronto launch for *Northern Stars: The Anthology of Canadian Science Fiction*—which contained my story "The Woman Who Is the Midnight Wind"—I met David Hartwell, editor of the anthology and an editor with Tor Books in New York. Tor, the world's leading publisher of science fiction and fantasy, is one of the imprints employed by Tom Doherty Associates, itself owned and distributed by St. Martin's Press from New York's historic flatiron building. Learning that I had just completed a novel, he asked to see it. I contacted Shawna McCarthy, my American agent, and she submitted *Ashland, Kentucky* to him the following Monday. Within six weeks, we had a deal. By Christmas, the contracts were signed. The long road into and out of Ashland seemed to be coming to an end. But as always, another beckoned.

In October, before the *Ashland* publishing agreement was finalized, my father fell ill with pneumonia. Mild dementia followed. It was the beginning of the end. After ninety years of pretty good health, he plummeted like a stone. But for those around him, the next six months trickled by. In the spring, a second bout of pneumonia ensued. He died on April 15, 1995. I describe his death and his life as best I can in my 2001 novel, *St. Patrick's Bed,* another of the books he never got to see that feature him and my mother and so much of our family on their covers.

At Tom Doherty Associates in New York, *Ashland, Kentucky* was morphing into *Shadow of Ashland*. Still in its editorial and production stages, enthusiasm for it spread throughout the publishing house over the next few months. They massed behind it aggressively,

With sons Conor and Owen, San Antonio, 1997

deciding to publish it in a small hardcover format. The original 1930s' letters from Jack to my mother, along with personal family photographs from the era, were arranged into a stunningly attractive wraparound jacket. Aligned with this was the decision—after much discussion about what exactly it was that they had in hand—to use their mainstream imprint, Forge, on the book's spine, instead of the Tor imprint that denoted primarily SF&F—an attempt to reach a larger, broader readership.

With anticipation for *Ashland* high, in August, 1995 editor David Hartwell purchased *Blue Limbo,* which appeared—risen from "the drawer"—as a Tor hardcover in January, 1997.

On a roll, Merle and I took our first vacation together alone longer than a weekend in almost ten years. At the end of August, 1995, without my sons Conor and Owen (now seventeen and fourteen), without my father (who had died that spring) to be concerned about, we left for a week in Scotland. The World Science-Fiction Convention was in Glasgow that year, and using it as an opportunity to combine business matters (publishers, editors, agents, writers, fans, all congregate) with pleasure, we reveled in three days in Glasgow, followed by four glorious days in the Scottish highlands. In my memory, this break symbolizes the start of the life that flowered as a result of *Shadow of Ashland.*

Thirty thousand hardcovers were published in March, 1996, and the little book has continued to grow. In the years since, it has been: optioned as a feature film six

times; a finalist as best novel for both the 1997 World Fantasy Award and the Aurora Award (Canada) in 1997 and 1998; the subject of numerous book-club discussion groups; required reading on several university English courses (including ENG 237, University of Toronto); published in both mass market paperback and larger trade paperback; and most recently, broadcast on more than four hundred stations across Canada by CBC Radio in ten fifteen-minute segments, twice daily, during two weeks in November and December of 2002.

The book had exceeded all my initial modest expectations. In 1996-97, I took another unpaid leave from my teaching position and wrote the prequel, *A Witness to Life,* the story of Jack's father, Martin Radey, and his life in and around Toronto from 1880 to 1950. Told from the point of view of a dead man revisiting the critical junctures and events of his life, once again, the elements of biography, autobiography, and fiction tumbled together into an alloy with a fantastic capstone. Published in 1999 as a Forge Book from Tom Doherty Associates, it was, like *Shadow of Ashland,* a best novel finalist for the 2000 World Fantasy Award.

For a writer, things experienced and noted along the way do indeed become potential fodder for stories. Earlier, aware of its place in my future fiction, I mentioned my 1984 visit to the Abbey of Gethsemani, the Trappist monastery near Bardstown, Kentucky, final resting spot of the monk Thomas Merton. In the ensuing years, I read much Merton, coming to see him as, arguably, the premier spiritual guru of the twentieth century. Anything but a saint, flawed and human, anti-institutional, with more than fifty volumes of meditations and a host of posthumous writings (following his accidental death at age fifty-three, in 1968), he flirted with Zen, Chuang Tzu, Blake, Bob Dylan, and jazz and everything else of cultural import that caught his fancy. His philosophy permeates *A Witness to Life* ("a monk has nothing to tell you except that if you dare to enter the solitude of your own heart, you can go beyond death, even in this life, and be a witness to life"), and near the end of the novel, in 1948, Martin Radey meets him in the garden of Gethsemani.

Everything goes into a book.

*

An overnight success after almost twenty-five years of writing, in 1999, at age fifty-two, I retired from my position as English teacher at Toronto's East York Collegiate Institute, a career begun thirty-one years earlier. Teaching had been everything it should be: rewarding, frustrating, enriching, draining, broadening, constraining, keeping me in touch with everyday life and my finger on the pulse of education. It had provided the best of friends and a social world I wouldn't have missed. There are students who still keep in touch. But I was finally a full-time writer, and it felt good.

Relaxed, in September I enjoyed the open-ended vista of my solitary pursuit and began my new book. Novels have a way of growing into something not completely foreseen when they are started, and this is part of the mystery of creation. Every day brings something new. I am now fairly certain that all serious fiction—all fiction that is not merely a job—is a personal reinterpretation of the writer's existence during the time the fiction is written, accounting for the transmutation through the months and years of writing. The first working title was *No Other Son.* By the beginning of 2000, it was *Turning of Bones.* When it was finished, in June of 2000, *St. Patrick's Bed* had emerged. It was the sequel to *Shadow of Ashland,* set eleven years later, in 1995.

November 1999 found me driving from Toronto to Dayton, Ohio to research that city, much as I had Ashland years earlier. There was another missing relative there, but not the narrator's. This time it was his stepson's father, and traveling with Leo Nolan was the ghost of his own father, who, as told on the first page, had died on April 15, 1995. I was writing about my father, using fiction, cradling the tale, once again, in the soft fold of the fantastic.

In May, Merle and I left for one week in the west of Ireland. A critical, climactic scene in the novel was to be set atop a mountain in Galway that had a pilgrimage site atop it: St. Patrick's Well and Bed. I had written the scene using memory of my time there on my previous visits (1971, 1997), and had a slew of research books and material surrounding my desk, but I wasn't satisfied. I had to see it for myself, know what the wind felt like, smell the air. And Merle was pregnant.

Clearly, things had been transpiring in the background. Merle and I had been trying to have a child of our own since our 1994 marriage. For the first while, we

Terence and Merle, San Francisco, 1998

approached the matter casually, figuring it would surprise us pleasantly when it happened, and we fully expected it at any time. Nothing happened. For people entering the baby arena, we were running out of time. When we finally got around to visiting a doctor, we learned that there were complications, mostly due to our ages, which needed attention.

Ah persistence, ah faith! In March, 2000, Merle phoned me from her work to tell me she was pregnant. At my computer, I clicked on "Save," sat back, smiled. Like the novel on the screen in front of me that had grown and shifted, the world was changing profoundly as I breathed in and out, alone in my office. Daniel Casci Green arrived November 19, 2000. A miracle. I was fifty-three, Merle thirty-nine. His big brothers were nineteen and twenty-two. My generational family was continuing. My mother and father would have been thrilled.

St. Patrick's Bed, another Forge book from Tom Doherty Associates, encompassing my father and the mysterious roads to Daniel's arrival, was launched in Toronto on October 30, 2001. With my three sons present, along with extended family and hosts of friends and well-wishers, I had no reason to be

The author with son Daniel, 2002

anything but happy, and happy I was. In many ways, the novel was the end of one stage and the beginning of another, both in terms of my books and my personal life. With a new baby in the house, the writing began to slow to a crawl, then stalled completely for a while. I did not mind. I had a new future, a new life.

For the first year, Merle was home from her job, even extending her leave. When she returned to work in September, 2001, my new position began in earnest. I was a stay-at-home father. As I write this, in May of 2003, I am fifty-six. Daniel is two-and-a-half. My days are simple, demanding, often exhausting, but always rewarding. Daniel's big brother, Owen, is twenty-two, working full-time, but planning to return to college in the fall. He has lived with us for the past two years now. Conor, big brother number two, is twenty-five, has his own apartment, his own life. The glass has never been so full.

Today, I wrote some of this essay in the morning, fed and dressed Daniel, watched him play in the backyard while I did the dishes, then trundled him off to the supermarket to get some dinner for later. We stopped off at Home Depot on the way and bought one of those peanut-halogen bulbs needed for under the kitchen cabinets. "How would you like a donut?" I asked him.

"I think so."

We coasted through the drive-through at Tim Hortons. In the parking lot, in the front seat I read the newspaper and drank a coffee. I passed bits of the chocolate dip donut back to him in his rear car-seat. Suddenly: quiet.

I punched in Merle's work number on my cell phone. "He's asleep." For us, this is news to be shared, smiled about, discussed, analyzed.

He's on our bed as I write this, in slumberland. I can hear Owen showering in the basement, getting ready for his afternoon-evening shift. In the backyard, through the window of my office, it is flowering season: lilacs, maples, oaks, even dandelions.

How did all this happen?

Of course, things will change. I will be back. In September, 2003, I assume the post of writer-in-residence at Hamilton, Ontario's Mohawk College; in anticipation of my absence, Daniel is on a waiting list for day-care at Merle's work for two days a week. It's something he needs—getting out more into the big world of other kids, socializing, learning new things. I'm looking forward to the variation too.

And even as I spend my days in domestic routine, comforted always by the thought that I am helping my family move ahead to whatever comes next, I am writing in my head, working on the next book, making notes in stolen time, clarifying what it is I want to say, constructing a story in which to say it, realizing the scope and breadth and value of my own parents' achievement, wanting to honor them by continuing what I see as a valid life.

BIOGRAPHICAL AND CRITICAL SOURCES:

PERIODICALS

Booklist, February 1, 1996, p. 917; April 1, 1999, Deborah Rysso, review of *A Witness to Life,* p. 1385; September 1, 2001, Whitney Scott, review of *St. Patrick's Bed,* p. 50.

Books in Canada, June-July 1987, pp. 18-19; June-July 1988, p. 35; summer 1992, p. 52.

Canadian Forum, July/August 1992, p. 30.

Canadian Materials, September 1992, p. 220.

Journal (Edmonton, Alberta, Canada), August 11, 1996, p. C6; January 11, 1997; February 23, 1997, p. D5.

Maclean's, June 27, 1988, p. 53.

Magazine of Fantasy and Science Fiction, May, 2002, Charles De Lint, review of *St. Patrick's Bed,* p. 28.

New York Times Book Review, September 15, 1996, p. 30.

Publishers Weekly, December 30, 1996; February 8, 1999, review of *A Witness to Life,* p. 193.

Quill and Quire, May 1992, p. 23.

Science Fiction Chronicle, February 1988, pp. 43-44; October 1992, p. 33.

OTHER

Terence M. Green Home Page, http://www.tmgreen. com (August 21, 2002).

*   *   *

GREENHILL, Basil (Jack) 1920-2003

OBITUARY NOTICE—See index for *CA* sketch: Born February 26, 1920, in Weston-super-Mare, England; died April 8, 2003, in St. Dominick, Cornwall, England. Greenhill is best remembered as the director of the National Maritime Museum in London from 1967 to 1983. His love of ships began in the 1930s, at a time when there were still some commercial use of sailing ships in Cornwall, where he lived. In university he studied economics, politics, and philosophy at Bristol University, but his education was interrupted after two years by World War II. During the war, he served in the Royal Navy's Air Branch, achieving the rank of lieutenant. He then returned to university, completing a B.A. in 1946; much later in life, his alma mater awarded him a Ph.D. in 1981 based on the merits of his published work. Greenhill then went to work for the Diplomatic Service, and was assigned to posts in Pakistan, New York, Tokyo, Geneva, and Ottawa. He left diplomatic service in 1967, when he became the third director of the National Maritime Museum. As director, Greenhill worked to gain the museum international prominence as he expanded its focus from British history to include all types of maritime history from around the world. He lectured extensively on the subject of maritime history, writing and editing about three dozen books on the subject, many with his second wife, historian Ann Giffard. Among these works are *The Merchant Sailing Ship* (1970), *Archaeology of the Boat* (1976), *The Life and Death of the Sailing Ship* (1981), and *The First Atlantic Liners:*

Seamanship in the Age of Paddle Wheel, Sail, and Screw (1997). His *Westcountrymen in Prince Edward's Isle* (1967) was later adapted as an award-winning film. Throughout his life, Greenhill was widely sought after for his expertise. He was trustee of the Royal Naval Museum during the 1970s and early 1980s, founded and chaired international conferences, and chaired the SS *Great Britain* project, as well as being chairman of maritime historical studies for Exeter University, beginning in 1985. His many post-retirement activities also included work as governor of Dulwich College and chair of Dulwich Picture Gallery. For his accomplishments, Greenhill receive many honors, including the 1980 Order of the White Rose from Finland, and honorary doctorates from Plymouth and Hull universities in 1996 and 2002 respectively. He was named companion of St. Michael and St. George in 1967 and of the Bath in 1981.

OBITUARIES AND OTHER SOURCES:

BOOKS

Writers Directory, 18th edition, Gale (Detroit, MI), 2003.

PERIODICALS

Independent (London, England), April 22, 2003, p. 18.
Times (London, England), April 15, 2003, p. 34.

*   *   *

GREGORY, Jill

PERSONAL: Born in Chicago, IL; married; children: one daughter. *Education:* University of Illinois, B.A.

ADDRESSES: Agent—c/o Random House, 1745 Broadway, New York, NY 10019. *E-mail*—jillygreg@ aol.com.

CAREER: Novelist.

AWARDS, HONORS: Romantic Times Lifetime Achievement Award for Excellence; Romantic Times Reviewer's Choice Award for Best Western Historical Romance, for *Never Love a Cowboy* and *Cold Night, Warm Stranger.*

WRITINGS:

To Distant Shores, Ace (New York, NY), 1979.

The Wayward Heart, Ace (New York, NY), 1982.

Promise Me the Dawn, Berkley (New York, NY), 1984.

My True and Tender Love, Berkley (New York, NY), 1985.

Moonlit Obsession, Jove (New York, NY), 1986.

Looking-Glass Years, Jove (New York, NY), 1987.

Always You, Dell (New York, NY), 1992.

Cherished, Dell (New York, NY), 1992.

When the Heart Beckons, Dell (New York, NY), 1995.

Just This Once, Dell (New York, NY), 1997.

Never Love a Cowboy, Dell (New York, NY), 1998.

(With Nora Roberts, Ruth Ryan Langan, and Marianne Willman) *Once upon a Castle,* Jove (New York, NY), 1998.

(With Nora Roberts, Ruth Ryan Langan, and Marianne Willman) *Once upon a Star,* Jove (New York, NY) 1999.

Cold Night, Warm Stranger, Dell (New York, NY), 1999.

Rough Wrangler, Tender Kisses, Dell (New York, NY), 2000.

(With Nora Roberts, Ruth Ryan Langan, and Marianne Willman) *Once upon a Dream,* Jove (New York, NY), 2000.

Once an Outlaw, Dell (New York, NY), 2001.

(With Nora Roberts, Ruth Ryan Langan, and Marianne Willman) *Once upon a Rose,* Jove (New York, NY), 2001.

SIDELIGHTS: Jill Gregory is a prolific author of romances who often writes stories set in the Old West. In *Always You,* Melora Deanne returns to her family ranch in Wyoming after her father's unexpected death, and falls in love with Wyatt Holden, a prominent figure in the town. The night before their wedding, she is abducted by a man who claims he is the real Wyatt Holden. He wants to expose her fiancée as an imposter and a murderer. He says her fiancé's real name is Rafe Campbell, and that he is a con artist.

Melora is worried about the welfare of her little sister, Jinx, who is crippled and who is now left alone back at the ranch. She tries to get her abductor to let her go, but without success. Eventually, though, she begins to fall in love with her abductor, and decides to help him, thus placing herself in danger—and inadvertently almost ruining his chances to expose the imposter.

Just This Once stars Josephine Cooper, who flees her abusive outlaw husband, stealing his loot as she goes. She is hoping to go to England to find her long-lost family. When an Englishman, Ethan Savage, catches her picking his pocket, he decides to use her to get what he wants. He blackmails her into marrying him, because a provision in his father's will states that he must marry in order to inherit. He does not want to marry, but decides it will be a nice joke on his dead father if he marries a criminal simply to satisfy the will. After they marry, though, they fall in love and want to lead a respectable life. This dream is nearly shattered when Josephine's criminal past catches up with her, and Ethan must prove that she is worthy of being his wife.

Never Love a Cowboy tells the story of Emma Malloy, a smart, sharp-tongued woman who was educated in the East but is now returning to her father's ranch. She finds that the old family feud against the nearby Garrettsons has only gotten worse during her absence: Beau Garrettson is found dead, shot in the back, on her family's land. However, another Garrettson, Tucker, is deeply attracted to Emma, and she returns his interest. They get into deeper trouble as the feud progresses, encompassing a bank robbery, cattle poisoning, and an ambush. They have been wary of their feelings for each other, but now decide to fully experience their love. They realize that if they are going to have a lifelong relationship, they must end their families' feud.

In *Cold Night, Warm Stranger,* Maura Jane Reed is at the mercy of her brothers, who make her a slave, doing cooking and cleaning for their family hotel, and won't let any suitors come near her. However, the brothers can't be home all the time, and one winter night when they're away, gunfighter Quinn Lassiter arrives at the hotel. Maura, who has never been alone with a man before, is quickly seduced. Quinn disappears, but when Maura later finds that she is pregnant, she runs away from her brothers, searching for Quinn. She tracks him to his ranch, where he acts honorably and marries her. Luckily, they fall in love once they are married. Meanwhile, Maura's brothers have lost a secret stash of gems, and they believe Maura stole this fortune when she ran away, and they are tracking her, ready to demand its return.

In *Once an Outlaw,* Emily Spoon's uncle wins a ranch in a card game and she is happy, confident that her family will end their outlaw days and settle down, so that she can have a stable home and family. However, the local sheriff, Clint Barclay, doesn't believe the Spoon Gang will ever settle down, and he harasses them. Emily, who is falling in love with him, has to find a way to convince him, but he is torn between his love for her and his loyalty to the law.

BIOGRAPHICAL AND CRITICAL SOURCES:

PERIODICALS

Booklist, July, 1999, review of *Cold Night, Warm Stranger,* p. 1929; November 15, 2000, Megan Kalan, review of *Once an Outlaw,* p. 559.

Kirkus Reviews, February 1, 1984, review of *Promise Me the Dawn,* p. 99; March 1, 1985, review of *My True and Tender Love,* p. 189; January 1, 1982, review of *The Wayward Heart,* p. 24; February 1, 1984, review of *Promise Me the Dawn,* p. 99.

Publishers Weekly, November 19, 1979, review of *To Distant Shores,* p. 77; January 29, 1982, review of *The Wayward Heart,* p. 64; March 2, 1984, review of *Promise Me the Dawn,* p. 87; March 15, 1985, review of *My True and Tender Love,* p. 114; March 28, 1986, review of *Moonlit Obsession,* p. 55; October 9, 1987, review of *Looking-Glass Years,* p. 82; February 3, 1992, review of *Cherished,* p. 76; March 2, 1994, review of *Promise Me the Dawn,* p. 87; February 26, 1996, review of *Always You,* p. 100; July 26, 1999, review of *Cold Night, Warm Stranger,* p. 88; November 12, 2001, review of *Once an Outlaw,* p. 42.

Romance Reader, July 21, 1999, Ann McGuire, review of *Cold Night, Warm Stranger,* p. 246.

West Coast Review of Books, January, 1980, Henry Zorich, review of *To Distant Shores,* p. 51; July, 1984, Suzy Nelson, review of *Promise Me the Dawn,* p. 42; September, 1985, Henry Zorich, review of *Promise Me the Dawn,* p. 32.

ONLINE

Jill Gregory Web site, http://members.aol.com/jillygreg (August 14, 2002).

Romance Reader, http://www.theromancereader.com/ (August 14, 2002), review of *Once an Outlaw.**

GROOM, Nick 1966-

PERSONAL: Born February 19, 1966, in Northampton, England. *Education:* Oxford University, M.A., D.Phil. *Hobbies and other interests:* "Wine, beer, and song (especially of Merrie England)."

ADDRESSES: Office—Department of English, University of Bristol, 3/5 Woodland Rd., Bristol BS8 1TB, England. *Agent*—David Godwin Associates, 55 Monmouth St., London WC2H 9DG, England. *E-mail*—nickgroom@totalise.co.uk; or david@davidgodwin associates.co.uk.

CAREER: Educator, writer, and editor. University of Bristol, Bristol, England, senior lecturer in post-medieval literature. Visiting professor, Stanford University, 2000, and University of Chicago, 2001.

MEMBER: Thomas Chatterton Society (secretary).

WRITINGS:

(Editor) *Narratives of Forgery* (volume one; "Angelaki" series), A. Rowe (London, England), 1994.
(Editor) *The Plays of William Shakespeare* (originally published, 1778-80), twelve volumes, Routledge (London, England), 1995.
Percy's "Reliques of Ancient English Poetry," three volumes, Routledge (London, England), 1997.
Richard Wentworth's Thinking Aloud (companion book to touring exhibition), Hayward Gallery (London, England), 1998.
The Making of Percy's Reliques ("Oxford English Monographs" series), Oxford University Press (New York, NY), 1999.
(Editor and contributor) *Thomas Chatterton and Romantic Culture,* St. Martin's Press (New York, NY), 1999.
(Editor and author of introduction) *The Bloody Register* ("Subcultures and Subversions" series; originally published 1764), four volumes, Routledge (London, England), 1999.
Introducing Shakespeare, edited by Richard Appignanesi, illustrated by Piero, Icon (Cambridge, England), 2001.
The Forger's Shadow: How Forgery Changed the Course of Literature, Picador (London, England), 2002.
(Editor) *Thomas Chatterson: Selected Poems,* Cider Press (Cheltenham, England), 2003.

Work represented in books, including *Early Romantics: Perspectives in British Poetry from Pope to Wordsworth,* edited by Thomas Woodman, Macmillan, 1998, and *Companion to Literature from Milton to Blake,* edited by David Womersley, Blackwell's, 2000; contributor to periodicals, including *Notes and Queries, Times Higher Education Supplement* and *Erotic Review;* reviewer for periodicals, including *Times Higher Education Supplement, Popular Music and Society, Times Literary Supplement,* and *Independent.*

WORK IN PROGRESS: A critical edition of Thomas Percy's *Reliques of Ancient English Poetry* for University of Exeter Press, 2004-05, a selected edition of Percy's *Reliques* for English Folk Dance and Song Society, and compiling and co-editing *The Arthurian Texts of the Percy Folio.*

SIDELIGHTS: British professor Nick Groom teaches courses on Shakespeare, eighteenth-century poetry, contemporary writing, and popular culture. His own writings cross these lines and go beyond to fiction. Among his undertakings is the most recent version, since Henry Wheatley's in 1889, of Bishop Thomas Percy's *Reliques of Ancient English Poetry,* first published in 1765. Landeg White wrote in the *Times Literary Supplement* that Groom's edition "should restore *Reliques* to their rightful place in Romantic criticism after a long period in which references to Percy have become somewhat formal and perfunctory."

The Making of Percy's Reliques is the first critical study of Percy's twelve-year effort which began with his rescue of a seventeenth-century collection, the pages of which were being used by a maid to light the fire in the Shropshire house of Percy's friend Humphrey Pitt. Percy solicited contributions from the collections of others through a huge volume of correspondence and borrowed so many books from friends and acquaintances that they were often transported by wagon.

Brean S. Hammond said in *Review of English Studies* that "with the painstaking labour of love, Groom shows how Percy worked with Shenstone and an ever-widening circle of scholars to cull the beauties from the seventeenth-century folio manuscript of songs and ballads that he retrieved from a Salopian parlour-grate in 1753, and to combine them with ballads already collected by Selden and Pepys available in the Pepys Library in Cambridge and with yet others that existed in a wide range of archival and printed sources."

William Bernard McCarthy noted in *Essays in Criticism* that "carried to the Continent and there devoured by the critic Herder and the poets Schiller, Heine, and Goethe, the *Reliques* inspired the Romantic transformation of poetry in Germany. Back home in England it ushered in the first great age of British folkloric and philological studies, and it inspired a whole series of poets—Wordsworth and Coleridge, Blake, Keats, Scott, Tennyson, Rossetti, and Yeats."

Percy made changes up until the last minute before publication as he tried to bring order to the vast collection. The volumes were printed over a period of more than two years by James Dodsley, and Percy's collaborator, William Shenstone, died before the project was completed. "Groom's microbibliographical analysis . . . is extraordinarily detailed, yet lucid and entertaining," wrote Katherine Turner in a review of *The Making of Percy's Reliques* for the *Times Literary Supplement.*

Groom edited *Thomas Chatterton and Romantic Culture,* the first collection of essays on Thomas Chatterton (1752-1770), the young poet who died of either suicide or a drug overdose and who was celebrated by such literary figures as Coleridge, Wordsworth, Keats, and Shelley even though they knew he was a forger. Chatterton invented a fifteenth-century monk named Thomas Rowley, then wrote all of the prose and poetry attributed to Rowley that was supposedly found in a chest in a Bristol church. John Mullan wrote in the *Times Literary Supplement* that "Chatterton became what Nick Groom calls 'a Romantic icon' because his forgery was taken to be creativity, a doomed but brilliant revolt against polite codes of taste. . . . This mostly excellent collection only touches on what is wonderful in what the whelp wrote."

Introducing Shakespeare is a cartoon-version of the Bard's works and influence. Characters include such figures as Johnson, Coleridge, Keats, and Goethe, but also the unexpected, such as Freud, Oscar Wilde, and P. T. Barnum. Virginia Woolf makes an appearance in a reference to feminist criticism, and each critic and topic is commented on by a cloaked figure who at the end reveals himself to be Shakespeare.

Paul Ellis wrote in the *Times Literary Supplement* that in *The Forger's Shadow: How Forgery Changed the Course of Literature* Groom paints such plagiarists and counterfeiters as Chatterton and James Macpherson—the latter who borrowed from Celtic history and myth for his *Fragments* by "Ossian"—"as Promethean figures who have lost their rightful place in literary history." Ellis said the book "investigates brilliantly the peculiar qualities of Romantic poetry's relations with literary forgery. Groom presents this encounter as a delicate, extra-legal and triumphantly creative negotiation between forgery, authenticity, inspiration, and authorship. It is his knowledgeable enthusiasm, nostalgia even, for the time when forgery demanded a sophisticated understanding of authenticity that makes his book so rewarding. Refreshingly humanist and carefully researched, *The Forger's Shadow* is the most entertaining, erudite, and authoritative book on literary forgery to date."

Groom told *CA:* "Pleasure, a passion for the value of poetry and lost traditions, academic demands, and money" are his motivations for writing. He is influenced by "the daemon, old books, library archives, English folk music, beer, wine, and good conversation." Groom noted that he is inspired to write on the subjects he does by "neglect of the English tradition," and that he writes "from before breakfast until after dinner; then I need a drink. Rewriting and revision is the key to good writing."

BIOGRAPHICAL AND CRITICAL SOURCES:

PERIODICALS

Albion, summer, 2001, Robert S. Thomson, review of *The Making of Percy's Reliques,* pp. 319-320.
Choice, March, 2000, D. L. Heyck, review of *Thomas Chatterton and Romantic Culture,* pp. 1303-1304.
Essays in Criticism, April, 2001, William Bernard McCarthy, review of *The Making of Percy's Reliques,* pp. 260-269.
London Review of Books, September 20, 2001, Jonathan Lamb, review of *Thomas Chatterton and Romantic Culture,* pp. 32-33.
Review of English Studies, February, 2001, Brean S. Hammond, review of *The Making of Percy's Reliques,* pp. 120-121.
Times Educational Supplement, October 19, 2001, Rex Gibson, review of *Introducing Shakespeare,* p. 22.
Times Higher Education Supplement, May 26, 2000, John Sutherland, review of *The Making of Percy's Reliques* and *Thomas Chatterton and Romantic Culture,* p. 27.

Times Literary Supplement, June 27, 1997, Landeg White, review of *Percy's "Reliques of Ancient English Poetry,"* p. 24; November 26, 1999, Katherine Turner, review of *The Making of Percy's Reliques,* p. 28; March 9, 2001, John Mullan, review of *Thomas Chatterton and Romantic Culture,* p. 25; April 26, 2002, Paul Ellis, review of *The Forger's Shadow: How Forgery Changed the Course of Literature,* p. 36.

ONLINE

Guardian Unlimited, http://www.books.guardian.co.uk/ (June 6, 2002), Terry Eagleton, review of *The Forger's Shadow: How Forgery Changed the Course of Literature.*

*   *   *

GUNDLE, Stephen 1956-

PERSONAL: Born 1956. *Education:* University of Liverpool, B.A.; State University of New York at Binghamton, M.A.; Cambridge University, Ph.D..

ADDRESSES: Agent—c/o Author Mail, Duke University Press, Box 90660, Durham, NC 27708-0660. *E-mail*—s.gundle@rhul.ac.uk.

CAREER: Royal Holloway College, University of London, senior lecturer and head of the department of Italian.

WRITINGS:

(Editor, with Simon Parker) *The New Italian Republic: From the Fall of the Berlin Wall to Berlusconi,* Routledge (New York, NY), 2000.
I comunisti italiani tra Hollywood e Mosca, 1995, translated as *Between Hollywood and Moscow: The Italian Communists and the Challenge of Mass Culture, 1943-1991,* Duke University Press (Durham, NC), 2000.

WORK IN PROGRESS: Collaborating with David Forgacs and Marcella Filippa on a study of mass culture and national identity in Italy between the years 1936-54; working on books about glamour and about feminine beauty and national identity in nineteenth- and twentieth-century Italy.

SIDELIGHTS: British educator Stephen Gundle has published several books dealing with the Italian political and social world. As the senior lecturer and head of the department of Italian at Royal Holloway College, University of London, Gundle has a number of research interests, including twentieth-century Italian cultural and political history. He also teaches courses on Italian cinema, television, and the mass media, as well as fashion and design. Two of Gundle's books have been published in English, including *The New Italian Republic: From the Fall of the Berlin Wall to Berlusconi,* which he coedited with Simon Parker. The book contains more than twenty essays, written by a variety of British political scientists and historians, dealing with how the Italian political landscape was dramatically transformed during the early 1990s. In addition, Gundle authored *Between Hollywood and Moscow: The Italian Communists and the Challenge of Mass Culture, 1943-1991,* an in-depth study of the Italian Communist Party's rise and fall in the years following World War II. Both books were published in the United States in 2000.

In *The New Italian Republic* Gundle and Parker collect and edit the work of twenty-two authors who specialize in Italian politics. Each essay examines the dramatic events, between 1991 and 1994, which led to the fall from power of two political parties: the Christian Democrats and Italian Communist Party. Up until the early 1990s, the two parties had dominated Italian politics for nearly fifty years. In their place, the Italian people elected a number of different parties, including the neo-fascist MSI and the Forza Italia, which was led by Italian media baron Silvio Berlusconi. Each of the authors discusses a different aspect of the monumental shift, and most agree that it signaled a crisis in Italy's democratic process. However, none of the essayists believe the changes amount to a revolution. "The essays in this volume are almost all clearly written, and will be readily accessible to students as well as specialists," wrote Christopher Duggan, who reviewed the book for *Political Studies.* Duggan went on to refer to the work as an "excellent collection of essays." S. Z. Koff of *Choice* also lauded the book. "The editors have assembled a very knowledgeable group of contributors," Koff wrote. James Newell, writing for *West European Politics,* felt the work is especially beneficial to students. Newell called it "a convenient and authoritative introduction to recent developments in contemporary Italian politics."

Originally published in Italian in 1995, *Between Hollywood and Moscow* also won the praise of literary critics. In this work Gundle reviews the legacy of the Italian Communist Party (PCI), which came to power in the aftermath of World War II and dissolved itself in 1991. As Gundle points out, the PCI was probably the most successful communist party in the Western world, and "the last great left-wing subculture in Western Europe." However, the party faced many challenges to maintain its rule, and much of the book focuses on these challenges. Drawing from his extensive research of PCI archives, Gundle discusses how the party dealt with the tremendous success of capitalism in Italy, due largely to increased consumerism, as well as a major influx of American culture. Gundle surmises that the party's downfall was a result of its inability to understand mass culture. For this, he largely blames the PCI's rigid party structure. Several literary critics felt *Between Hollywood and Moscow* would further the understanding of why the PCI collapsed. "The book is an original contribution to knowledge based on a prodigious amount of research," wrote Stephen Hellman of the *International History Review.* "The interpretive framework and the treatment of specific historical details are wholly persuasive." Hellman called the effort a "superb study." Likewise, Chiarella Esposito, who reviewed the book for *History: Review of New Books,* referred to it as "a comprehensive and sound study."

BIOGRAPHICAL AND CRITICAL SOURCES:

PERIODICALS

Choice, October, 1996, p. 354; September, 2001, p. 200.
History: Review of New Books, fall, 2002, p. 21.
International History Review, March, 2002, pp. 193-195.
Political Studies, September, 1997, pp. 815-816.
Times Literary Supplement, February 8, 2002, p. 31.
West European Politics, January, 1997, pp. 255-256.

ONLINE

Duke University Press Web site, http://www.dukeu press.edu/ (August 1, 2002).
Royal Holloway College Web site, http://www.rhul.ac. uk/Italian (August 1, 2002), "Stephen Gundle."*

GUTIÉRREZ, Pedro Juan 1950-

PERSONAL: Born 1950.

ADDRESSES: Home—Havana, Cuba. *Agent*—c/o Author Mail, Farrar, Straus & Giroux, 19 Union Square W, New York, NY 10001.

CAREER: Author and magazine journalist.

WRITINGS:

Espléndidos peces plateados, Nueva Géneration (Buenos Aires, Argentina), 1996
Nada que hacer, Anagrama (Barcelona, Spain), 1998.
Trilogía sucia de la Habana, Anagrama (Barcelona, Spain), 1998, translation by Natasha Wimmer published as *Dirty Havana Trilogy,* Farrar, Straus & Giroux (New York, NY), 2001.
El rey de la Habana, Anagrama (Barcelona, Spain), 1999.
Animal tropical, Anagrama (Barcelona, Spain), 2000.
Melancolía de los leones, Ediciones Unioón (Havana, Cuba), 2000.
El insaciable hombre araña, Anagrama (Barcelona, Spain), 2002.

SIDELIGHTS: Dirty Havana Trilogy, Cuban writer and poet Pedro Juan Gutiérrez's debut novel, is set in the "special period" that followed the collapse of the Soviet Union and the end of its huge subsidies to the Cuban government. The regime was left in shambles: there were dramatic shortages of all the basic necessities; food, drinking water, medicine, and decent housing were almost nonexistent. What drives the book and its characters is the day-to-day grind of survival, by any means at all, and enough sex to forget the despair of it all. "I was getting used to lots of new things in my life," the novel's protagonist, Pedro, says, "getting used to poverty, to taking things in stride. I was training to be less ambitious, because if I didn't, I wouldn't make it." It has been fifty years since the triumph of the Cuban Revolution, and the only maxim left standing is "you can't let down your guard."

Gutiérrez's alter ego in this frankly autobiographical novel is a down-and-out dropout living in downtown Havana. He was once a radio journalist with a wife and kids who wrote propaganda for the government. After going from odd job to odder job, including a stint distributing human livers to restaurants (he is told they are pigs' livers), he lives the hustler's life. He lives on the roof of a dilapidated building on the Malecon and cruises for the European sex tourists who are arriving in droves. "It's been years since I expected anything, anything at all, of women, or of friends, or even myself, of anyone," Pedro says.

In the background is the continuing clandestine exodus to Miami of thousands of potential refugees, who set themselves adrift in the Straits of Florida hoping to make it on rafts of truck tires, oil drums and palm trunks. They leave the island, and no one knows for certain if they make it or not.

Gutiérrez writes in a brutally honest style, in the tradition of Genet, Bukowski and Miller. The despair he sees around him is somehow transformed into a primal joy of living. The theme of the book is moral, as well as physical, survival. Like Miller and Genet, Gutiérrez explores these larger issues of morality, religion and government through sex. As Taro Greenfeld wrote in the *New York Times,* "What Gutiérrez, who lives in Havana, shares with that gritty crowd is the ability to evoke sensory experience in his prose and to use the immediacy of that description to make sense of a world that simply doesn't make sense. What motivates a man in an imploding society like 1990's Cuba? The promise of good sex, Gutiérrez knows, will keep a man going far longer than a regular paycheck or a balanced diet."

Despite the vitality of the sex and the exotic setting of decaying Havana, *Dirty Havana Trilogy* is a sad book full of characters at the ends of their ropes. As Roger Kaplan commented in the *National Review,* "It does not say everything, or perhaps not even most things, about Cuba today. But it is probably the most honest depiction of life under Castro to have emerged in recent years."

BIOGRAPHICAL AND CRITICAL SOURCES:

BOOKS

Gutiérrez, Pedro Juan, *Trilogía sucia de la Habana,* Anagrama (Barcelona, Spain), 1998, translation by Natasha Wimmer published as *Dirty Havana Trilogy,* Farrar, Straus & Giroux (New York, NY), 2001.

PERIODICALS

Daily Telegraph (London, England), April 28, 2001, Andrew Biswell, review of *Dirty Havana Trilogy.*

Guardian (London, England), April 14, 2001, Jonathan Glancey, review of *Dirty Havana Trilogy*, p. 10.

Library Journal, November 1, 2000, Lawrence Olszewski, review of *Dirty Havana Trilogy,* p. 133.

National Review, April 30, 2001, Roger Kaplan, review of *Dirty Havana Trilogy.*

New York Times, February 5, 2001, Richard Bernstein, review of *Dirty Havana Trilogy,* p. E7.

New York Times Book Review, March 25, 2001, Karl Taro Greenfeld, review of *Dirty Havana Trilogy,* p. 13.

Publishers Weekly, October 16, 2000, review of *Dirty Havana Trilogy,* p. 46.

ONLINE

BookBrowser, http://bookbrowser.com/ (December 2, 2001), Harriet Klausner, review of *Dirty Havana Trilogy.**

*   *   *

GUTTENPLAN, Samuel 1944-

PERSONAL: Born July 26, 1944, in New York, NY; son of Julius (a statistician) and Helen (a librarian) Guttenplan; married Jennifer Jutsen (a lawyer), June 30, 1995. *Education:* City College of New York, B.A., 1965; Oxford University, Ph.D., 1976. *Religion:* Jewish.

ADDRESSES: Office—Philosophy Department, Birkbeck College, University of London, Malet St., London WC1E 7HX, England. *E-mail*—s.guttenplan@bbk.ac.uk.

CAREER: Educator and philosopher. City College of New York, lecturer in philosophy, 1966-71; Birkbeck College, University of London, London, England, reader in philosophy, 1976—.

MEMBER: Phi Beta Kappa.

WRITINGS:

(Editor) *Mind and Language,* Clarendon Press (Oxford, England), 1975.

(With Martin Tamny) *Logic: A Comprehensive Introduction,* Basic Books (New York, NY), 1978.

The Languages of Logic: An Introduction, Blackwell (Oxford, England), 1987.

(Editor) *The Companion to the Philosophy of Mind,* Blackwell (Oxford, England), 1994.

Mind's Landscape: An Introduction to the Philosophy of Mind, Blackwell Publishers (Malden, MA), 2000.

(Editor with Jennifer Hornsby and Christopher Janaway) *Reading Philosophy: Selected Texts with a Method for Beginners,* Blackwell Publishers (Malden, MA), 2002.

Executive editor of interdisciplinary journal *Mind and Language.*

WORK IN PROGRESS: Objects of Metaphor.

SIDELIGHTS: Samuel Guttenplan is a reader in philosophy at Birkbeck College at the University of London, and serves as executive editor of the interdisciplinary journal *Mind and Language.* Philosophy of mind and language have been Guttenplan's primary areas of scholarly endeavor; however, he also has a strong interest in moral philosophy. The book *Objects of Metaphor* was also in the works in 2003, after which Guttenplan planned to turn his attention to issues of moral conflict as it is experienced by individuals, societies, and groups.

Mind and Language, published in 1975, collects the Wolfson College Lectures presented at Oxford University in 1974. The lecturers are among the most eminent philosphers who have contributed to the field of language and mind, including G. E. M. Anscombe, Peter Geach, W. V. Quine, Donald Davidson, D. Follesdal, and Michael Dummett. Guttenplan arranges and presents the articles in this volume. P. F. Strawson, in his *Times Literary Supplement* review, credited Guttenplan for a job skillfully done. Elsewhere, critical reviews suggested that the book is suited to well-grounded graduate students and professional philosophers.

A Companion to the Philosophy of Mind, edited by Guttenplan, is part of the "Blackwell Companion to Philosophy" series. Critics have remarked that this volume is not aimed at the uninitiated; however, the editor provides a clear and lengthy introduction to issues in philosophy of mind that will serve well any reader with some background in philosophy. The emphasis is contemporary rather than historical. For example, no scholars earlier than Wittgenstein are listed. Avoiding the dictionary format, the book, with fewer than one hundred articles, is a broad overview of the current concerns of scholars working in the field. Included are discussions of neural networks as well as the nature of semantics. In his review in *New Scientist* David Concar praised Guttenplan for the depth and breadth of the book stating that, "Here scholarly entries on the nature of semantics and the human imagination lie cheek-by-jowl with hard-nosed expositions of neural-network type models of perception. And helping you to find out who thinks what and why are a dozen or so self-profiles penned by heavy weights such as Noam Chomsky, Daniel Dennett and Jerry Fodor." The majority of the entries are listed by subject. Some topics are covered in more than one article, the purpose being to offer a balanced view. Extensive bibliographies have been included. The book has been well received and is considered by many to be an indispensable item in any philosophy reference collection.

Many critics consider *Mind's Landscape: An Introduction to the Philosophy of Mind* as an enlargement of Guttenplan's introduction to *A Companion to the Philosophy of Mind.* The author's stated goal is to provide a narrative account of the development of the understanding of mind. The landscape metaphor is used to structure the book and each section is composed of separate chapters. Brendan O'Sullivan, in his review in *Philosophical Quarterly,* described the material covered in the sections in the following way: 'Surveying the Territory,' the first section, describes mental phenomena. 'Digging Deeper' examines selected mental concepts, such as conscious experience. 'Bedrock,' the third section, addresses the mind-body problem, or the connection between the physical and the mental. O'Sullivan went on to praise the author for his restrained use of jargon, using specialized terms only as needed. This book has been praised consistently for its lucid, well-organized approach to a complex and abstract subject.

Guttenplan told *CA:* "My writing is partly intended as a contribution to the teaching of philosophy and partly to expose my ideas to the criticism of others in this field."

BIOGRAPHICAL AND CRITICAL SOURCES:

PERIODICALS

American Reference Books Annual, 1996, Mark Cyzyk, review of *A Companion to the Philosophy of Mind,* p. 609.
Choice, May, 1976, review of *Mind and Language,* p. 381; September, 1995, J. White, review of *A Companion to the Philosophy of Mind,* p. 136; April, 2001, M. R. Hebert, review of *Mind's Landscape: An Introduction to the Philosophy of Mind,* p. 1475.
New Scientist, March 11, 1995, David Concar, review of *A Companion to the Philosophy of Mind,* p. 45.
Philosophical Quarterly, January, 2002, Brendan O'Sullivan, review of *Mind's Landscape,* pp. 126-128.
Review of Metaphysics, December, 1976, review of *Mind and Language,* p. 342.
Times Literary Supplement, November 21, 1975, P. F. Strawson, review of *Mind and Language,* p. 1383; April 21, 1995, review of *A Companion to the Philosophy of Mind,* p. 28; April 12, 2002, Sean Crawford, review of *Mind's Landscape,* p. 29.

ONLINE

Birkbeck College Web site, http://www.bbk.ac.uk/ (September 3, 2002), "Samuel Guttenplan."

*   *   *

GUYTON, Arthur C(lifton) 1919-2003

OBITUARY NOTICE—See index for *CA* sketch: Born September 8, 1919, in Oxford, MS; died in a car accident April 3, 2003, near Jackson, MS. Physician, educator, and author. Guyton did groundbreaking work in the area of hypertension and his first textbook has become a standard in medical schools. After earning his bachelor's degree from the University of Mississippi in 1939 and his medical degree from Harvard University in 1943, Guyton contracted polio in 1946 and suffered from paralysis in his left upper arm and shoulder and in his right leg. Nevertheless, he managed to enjoy a successful academic career and gained some fame as the father of ten Harvard graduates. He began his teaching career at the University of Tennessee in 1947, but spent the rest of his years as a professor at the University of Mississippi. Beginning as an associate professor of pharmacology there from 1947 to 1948, he served as professor and chairman of the department of physiology and biophysics from 1948 to 1989, when he was made professor emeritus. Guyton's first book, *Textbook of Medical Physiology* (1956), was written by him for his students because other textbooks available at the time did not suit his course. The book is notable as one of the few medical texts still in use—the tenth edition was published in 2000—that was written by a single author. But Guyton was also highly respected for his studies in hypertension, and he is credited with discovering that it is the kidneys, and not the heart, that is primarily responsible for regulating blood pressure in the body; he also showed that heart rate is determined not so much by the heart but by how the body senses how much oxygen is needed in its body tissues. Over the course of his career, he wrote, co-wrote, or edited over a dozen books, including *Circulatory Physiology: Cardiac Output and Its Regulation* (1963; second edition, 1984), *Arterial Pressure and Hypertension* (1980), and the second edition of *Basic Neuroscience: Anatomy and Physiology* (1991).

OBITUARIES AND OTHER SOURCES:

PERIODICALS

Los Angeles Times, April 17, 2003, p. B13.
New York Times, April 14, 2003, p. A21.
Washington Post, April 7, 2003, p. B6.

H

HAAS, Ernst B(ernard) 1924-2003

OBITUARY NOTICE—See index for *CA* sketch: Born March 31, 1924, in Frankfurt, Germany; died March 6, 2003, in Berkeley, CA. Educator and author. Haas was an expert on international relations who wrote influential books on the subject. He emigrated to the United States from Germany in 1938, attending the University of Chicago for a year before serving in U.S. Army Military Intelligence during World War II. After the war, he attended Columbia University, where he earned his Ph.D. in 1952. He joined the University of California at Berkeley as an instructor in 1951, becoming a full professor of political science in 1962 and being named Robson Research Professor of Government in 1974, as well as directing the university's Institute for International Studies from 1969 to 1973. He retired in 1999, while still teaching courses and conducting research thereafter. As an expert on foreign relations, Haas also worked as a consultant to the State Department during the 1960s, as well as for the United Nations in 1980. Haas's books were often concerned with the unification of nations and with the role of international organizations in the world. His most influential book on the subject is the forward-looking *The Uniting of Europe* (1958); he was also the author or editor of over a dozen other books, including *Beyond the Nation-State: Functionalism and International Organization* (1964), *Human Rights and International Action: The Case of Freedom of Association* (1970), *When Knowledge Is Power: Three Models of Change in International Organizations* (1990), and *Nationalism, Liberalism, and Progress* (1997).

OBITUARIES AND OTHER SOURCES:

PERIODICALS

San Francisco Chronicle, March 13, 2003, p. A20.

ONLINE

UC Berkeley News Online, http://www.berkeley.edu/news/ (April 11, 2003).

*   *   *

HAGUE, Nora

PERSONAL: Female. *Education:* New York University, M.F.A.

ADDRESSES: Home—New York, NY. *Agent*—c/o Author Mail, William Morrow, 10 East 53rd Street, New York, NY 10022.

CAREER: Novelist.

WRITINGS:

Letters from an Age of Reason, William Morrow (New York, NY), 2001.

WORK IN PROGRESS: A second novel.

SIDELIGHTS: Nora Hague's first novel, *Letters from an Age of Reason,* is set in the 1860s. It is the story of two young people living very different lives. Sixteen-year-old Arabella Leeds comes from a wealthy New York family. Aubrey Paxton, a young colored man, is a house servant in New Orleans. When the U.S. Civil War begins Aubrey escapes to New York with plans to board a ship heading for Europe. Once in New York he meets Arabella, and they soon fall in love, which may cause trouble for them both. *Library Journal* contributor Cynthia Johnson stated, "Well-developed secondary characters and subplots make this debut novel difficult to put down."

BIOGRAPHICAL AND CRITICAL SOURCES:

PERIODICALS

Booklist, July, 2001, Beth Warrell, review of *Letters from an Age of Reason,* p. 1950.
Library Journal, October 15, 2001, Cynthia Johnson, review of *Letters from an Age of Reason,* p. 106.
Publishers Weekly, August 6, 2001, review of *Letters from an Age of Reason,* p. 60.
Washington Post, November 28, 2001, Elizabeth Ward, review of *Letters from an Age of Reason,* p. C8.

ONLINE

HarperCollins Web site, http://www.harpercollins.com/ (May 14, 2002).
Simon & Schuster Australia Web site, http://www.simonsays.com/ (January 13, 2002).*

*   *   *

HALKIN, Hillel 1939-

PERSONAL: Born 1939, in New York, NY; immigrated to Israel, 1970; son of Abraham Halkin (a Judaic scholar). *Education:* Attended Columbia University.

ADDRESSES: Agent—c/o Author Mail, Houghton Mifflin, 222 Berkeley Street, Boston, MA 02116.

CAREER: Writer, translator, and journalist.

WRITINGS:

Letters to an American Jewish Friend: A Zionist's Polemic, Jewish Publication Society of America (Philadelphia, PA), 1977.
(With Hans G. Kahn) *Luck and Chutzpah: Against All Odds,* Gefen Publishing House (Jerusalem, Israel), 1997.
Across the Sabbath River: In Search of a Lost Tribe of Israel, Houghton Mifflin (Boston, MA), 2002.

TRANSLATOR

Uri Orlev, *The Lead Soldiers,* Taplinger Publishing Co. (New York, NY), 1980.
A. B. Yehoshua, *A Late Divorce,* Doubleday (New York, NY), 1984.
Uri Orlev, *The Island on Bird Street,* Houghton Mifflin (Boston, MA), 1984.
Yehuda Amichai, *The World Is a Room,* Jewish Publication Society of America (Philadelphia, PA), 1984.
Amos Oz, *A Perfect Peace,* Harcourt Brace Jovanovich (New York, NY), 1985.
(And author of afterword) Shmuel Yosef Agnon, *A Simple Story,* Schocken Books (New York, NY), 1985, reprinted ("Library of Modern Jewish Literature" series), Syracuse University Press (Syracuse, NY), 2000.
(And author of introduction) Sholem Aleichem, *Tevye the Dairyman* and *The Railroad Stories* ("Library of Yiddish Classics" series), Schocken Books (New York, NY), 1987.
Shulamith Hareven, *The Miracle Hater,* North Point Press (San Francisco, CA), 1988.
Tamar Bergman, *The Boy from over There* (juvenile), Houghton Mifflin (Boston, MA), 1988.
A. B. Yehoshua, *Five Seasons,* Collins (London, England), 1989.
Jewish Folktales, edited by Pinhas Sadeh, Doubleday (New York, NY), 1989.
Shulamith Hareven, *Prophet,* North Point Press (San Francisco, CA), 1990.
Meir Shalev, *The Blue Mountain,* Aaron Asher/HarperCollins (New York, NY), 1991.
Uri Orlev, *The Man from the Other Side,* Houghton Mifflin (Boston, MA), 1991.

Matti Golan, *With Friends like You: What Israelis Really Think about American Jews,* Free Press (New York, NY), 1992.

A. B. Yehoshua, *Mr. Mani,* Doubleday (New York, NY), 1992.

Uri Orlev, *Lydia, Queen of Palestine,* Houghton Mifflin (Boston, MA), 1993.

Nava Semel, *Flying Lessons,* Simon and Schuster Books for Young Readers (New York, NY), 1995.

Uri Orlev, *The Lady with the Hat,* Houghton Mifflin (Boston, MA), 1995.

S. Y. Abramovitsch, *Tale of Mendele the Book Peddler: Fishke the Lame and Benjamin the Third,* edited by Dan Miron and Ken Frieden, Schocken Books (New York, NY), c. 1996.

Shulamith Hareven, *Thirst: The Desert Trilogy,* Mercury House (San Francisco, CA), 1996.

Roman Frister, *The Cap: The Price of a Life,* Grove Press (New York, NY), 1999.

Samuel ha-Nagid, *Grand Things to Write a Poem on: A Verse Autobiography,* Gefen Publishing House (Jerusalem, Israel), 2000.

(And author of introduction) Sholem Aleichem, *The Letters of Menakhem-Mendl* and *Sheyne-Sheyndl and Motl, the Cantor's Son* ("New Yiddish Library" series), Yale University Press (New Haven, CT), 2002.

SIDELIGHTS: Hillel Halkin, a journalist and a writer, was born in New York City on the Upper West Side. He attended Columbia University, moved to Israel as a young man, and established himself by way of his seamless translations, from Hebrew and Yiddish to English, of a great many important writers, including Amos Oz, Uri Orlev, and A. B. Yehoshua. Halkin is also the author of several books, including *Letters to an American Jewish Friend: A Zionist's Polemic.* He wrote the 1977 volume several years after relocating to Zichron Ya'akov, a small town on Mount Carmel, far from the bustle of Tel Aviv and historic Jerusalem.

The American-Jewish friend of the title is a fabrication. The book consists of letters Halkin wrote, as well as brief responses from the fictional friend who has returned to the United States, critical of what he found in Israel. Amos Elon wrote in the *New York Times Book Review* that Halkin "in effect argues with himself—harangues might be a better word—and sorts out his feelings about Israel, its politics and culture and above all about what he sees as the ultimate question of Jewish life today: Is it possible for a Jew today to live as a Jew anywhere but in Israel?"

Halkin sees Jewish life vanishing everywhere in the diaspora, including in America. He writes that in order for an Israeli Jew to talk to a diaspora Jew, the conversation must begin with the question of why the latter doesn't come home. Halkin not only criticizes Jewish life away from Israel, but says that Israel itself is in need of more of a "Jewish soul." Elon called *Letters to an American Friend* "a polemic, blazing with passion and inventiveness and good humor, a *cri de coeur* impelled by a fury of conviction, the existential statement of a solitary man. Therein lies its power and peculiar charm, even for those who may disagree with it."

A *Publishers Weekly* reviewer called another Halkin book, *Across the Sabbath River: In Search of a Lost Tribe of Israel,* "a captivating tale that is part travelogue, part ethnography, part cultural treasure hunt." The book is Halkin's account of his journey with Rabbi Eliahu Avichail, head of an organization called Amishav: My People Returneth. On their expedition to China and Tibet, Halkin and Avichail encounter a group of people, the B'nai Menashe, who lived in northeast India, along the borders of Burma and Bangladesh.

These people claim to be the descendants of the Manasseh, one of the ten tribes exiled from Israel by Assyrian king Shalmaneser in the eighth century B.C. The group is made up of the Kuki, a Tibetan-Burmese group living in northeast India, and several others nearby, particularly the Mizo and the Chin. As of the book's publication, approximately ten percent of the 5,000 people living in the Indian states of Manipur and Mizoram had moved to Israel, where they continued their fight for recognition and immigration rights. Those still in India pray in newly built synagogues, recite Hebrew prayers, and formerly petitioned the United Nations to recognize their status as a lost tribe.

On Halkin's first trip, he was under contract with the *New Yorker* for an article that was never published. But his interest took him back to the region, and using local translators, he collected clues that might legitimize the Manasseh's claims. He discovered a song about the Red Sea and compared their tribal practices with rituals in Judaism. The Mizo's god was called Za or Ya, possibly a version of Yahweh, and baby boys were ceremoniously circumcised when they were eight days old.

Richard Bernstein wrote in the *New York Times Book Review* that Halkin "finds some of the most active purveyors of the lost-tribe idea to be little more than charlatans, and for many of its pages, *Across the Sabbath River* is more a tale of desperate identity search than it is about real lost tribes."

Just as Halkin was about to pack up and leave the region, he met Khuplam Lenthang, a doctor who had spent most of his life conducting ethnographic research and documenting folk tales, which he had collected into a book titled *The Wonderful Genealogical Tales of the Kuki-Chin-Mizo.* Bernstein noted that this provided Halkin with "strong evidence of old religious practices and terms that seemed unexplainable except by recourse to a lost-tribes theory. But let Mr. Halkin himself provide the persuasive and closely examined details, which come at the end of a book that has many delights, a variegated cast of characters and a conclusion stimulating many thoughts about the persistence of ancient behavior and belief."

Sandee Brawarsky wrote in *Jewish Week* that "Halkin writes beautifully, whether describing the misty landscapes, the passions of the Kuki-Chin-Mizo peoples or the humorous moments of cultural displacement. Readers will find an appealing guide in him. Even those who remain skeptical can't help being struck by his conclusions."

Halkin planned to return to the region with a team from the University of Arizona and the Haifa Technion to conduct genetic testing. He told Brawarsky, "In my opinion, the empirical evidence in my book is so strong that I would continue to believe, even if the DNA evidence were negative."

BIOGRAPHICAL AND CRITICAL SOURCES:

PERIODICALS

Forward, August 16, 2002, Alana Newhouse, review of *Across the Sabbath River: In Search of a Lost Tribe of Israel.*

Jewish Week, August 9, 2002, Sandee Brawarsky, review of *Across the Sabbath River.*

Kirkus Reviews, June 15, 2002, review of *Across the Sabbath River,* p. 855.

New York Times Book Review, August 28, 1977, Amos Elon, review of *Letters to an American Jewish Friend: A Zionist's Polemic,* p. 9; September 18, 2002, Richard Bernstein, review of *Across the Sabbath River.*

Publishers Weekly, July 22, 2002, review of *Across the Sabbath River,* p. 175.*

*　　　*　　　*

HAMILTON, Denise 1959-

PERSONAL: Born 1959, in Los Angeles, CA; married; children: two. *Education:* Loyola Marymount University, B.A., 1981; California State University, M.A., 1987.

ADDRESSES: Home—Glendale, CA. *Agent*—Georges Borchardt Inc., 136, 14th Fl., 57th St., New York, NY 10022. *E-mail*—denise@denisehamilton.com

CAREER: Freelance journalist. *Los Angeles Times,* staff writer; New York University's Institute for War, Peace, and Reporting, consultant.

MEMBER: Silverlake Fiction Writer's Workshop; Mystery Writers of America; Sisters in Crime; PEN West; Crime Writers International; LA Press Club.

AWARDS, HONORS: Fulbright Scholar; Edgar Award nomination, 2001, for *The Jasmine Trade;* LA Press Club awards in feature writing and business writing.

WRITINGS:

The Jasmine Trade: A Novel of Suspense Introducing Eve Diamond, Scribner (New York, NY), 2001.
Sugar Skull, Scribner (New York, NY), 2003.
Last Lullaby, Scribner (New York, NY), 2004.

Contributor to *Los Angeles Times, Wired, Cosmopolitan, Der Spiegel,* and *New York Times.*

SIDELIGHTS: Denise Hamilton worked as a reporter for the *Los Angeles Times* for ten years. During her time there Hamilton reported on the fall of communism in Eastern Europe, the break-up of the Soviet Union, Japan's youth movements, and news from the suburbs of Los Angeles. She is a freelance journalist and has continued to write for the *Los Angeles Times,* as well as for *Wired, Cosmopolitan, Der Spiegel,* and the *New Times.*

In her first novel, *The Jasmine Trade: A Novel of Suspense Introducing Eve Diamond,* Hamilton used her experiences as a *Los Angeles Times* reporter. In the book, *Los Angeles Times* reporter Eve Diamond is covering the story of seventeen-year-old engaged woman Marina Chang, who was murdered during a hijacking at a suburban mall. As she investigates the murder Eve discovers the world of the parachute kids, Asian kids who live by themselves in luxurious mansions while their parents run businesses in Japan and China. Eve enters the world of the parachute kids and finds dangers in the form of gangs, murder, and prostitution rings. *Los Angeles Magazine* contributor Roberto Ito praised *The Jasmine Trade* for containing "all the plot twists and creepy characters one would expect from an L.A. noir thriller." "In addition to a gripping story and keen observations about contemporary Los Angeles, she also offers an undeniably winning narrator," noted a *Publishers Weekly* contributor of Hamilton.

BIOGRAPHICAL AND CRITICAL SOURCES:

PERIODICALS

Booklist, May 15, 2001, Stephanie Zvirin, review of *The Jasmine Trade: A Novel of Suspense Introducing Eve Diamond,* p. 1736.
Kirkus Reviews, January 15, 2003, review of *Sugar Skull,* p. 114.
Library Journal, January, 2003, review of *Sugar Skull,* p. 164.
Los Angeles Times, August, 2001, Robert Ito, review of *The Jasmine Trade,* p. 108.
New York Times Book Review, August 5, 2001, Marilyn Stasio, review of *The Jasmine Trade.*
Publishers Weekly, July 2, 2001, review of *The Jasmine Trade,* p. 53.

ONLINE

Books 'n' Bytes, http://www.booksnbytes.com/ (September 3, 2002), Harriet Klausner, review of *The Jasmine Trade.*

Denise Hamilton Web site, http://www.denisehamilton. com (September 3, 2002), "Denise Hamilton, Author Biography."
Mystery Reader, http://www.mysteryreader.com/ (September 3, 2002), Cathy Sova, "Denise Hamilton"; Andy Plonka, review of *The Jasmine Trade.*

*   *   *

HAMILTON, Ron 1948-

PERSONAL: Native-American name, Ki-ke-in; born 1948, in Aswinis, Barkley Sound, British Columbia, Canada. *Education:* University of British Columbia, B.A., 1992.

ADDRESSES: Home—Port Alberni, British Columbia, Canada. *Office*—Department of Art, Malaspina College, 900 Fifth St., Nanaimo, British Columbia, Canada V9R 5S5.

CAREER: Graphic artist, carver, painter, illustrator, printmaker, and jewelry designer, sometimes under the name Ki-ke-in. British Columbia Provincial Museum, Victoria, British Columbia, Canada, apprentice to carver Henry Hunt, 1971; Malaspina College, teacher of Northwest Coast art, 1995—. Nuu-chah-nulth Tribal Council, interviewer and researcher. Also worked as fisherman, drafter, dancer, composer, and drummer. *Exhibitions:* Work represented in solo and group exhibitions at Royal British Columbia Museum, Vancouver Art Gallery, Port Alberni Museum, British Museum, London, England, National Museum of Ethnology, Osaka, Japan, and elsewhere in British Columbia.

WRITINGS:

We Sing to the Universe: Poems, [Vancouver, British Columbia, Canada], 1994.

Contributor to periodicals, including *British Columbia Studies.*

BIOGRAPHICAL AND CRITICAL SOURCES:

BOOKS

Halpin, Marjorie, editor, *Ki-ke-in: The Drawings,* University of British Columbia Press (Vancouver, British Columbia, Canada), 1997.
St. James Guide to Native North-American Artists, St. James Press (Detroit, MI), 1998, pp. 287-288.*

HANCOCK, Karen 1953-

PERSONAL: Born 1953, in Pasadena, CA; married; children: a son. *Education:* University of Arizona, B.S. (biology and wildlife biology). *Religion:* Christian. *Hobbies and other interests:* Painting watercolors, tennis, reading.

ADDRESSES: Home—Tucson, AZ. *Agent*—c/o Bethany House Publishers, 11400 Hampshire Ave., South Minneapolis, MN 55438. *E-mail*—kmhancock@kmhancock.com.

CAREER: Novelist. Has worked as a manager of stables; Steward Observatory, Tucson, AZ, artist; University of Arizona Biology Department, animal keeper.

WRITINGS:

Arena, Bethany House Publishers (Minneapolis, MN), 2002.
The Light of Eidon, (first novel in "Legends of the Guardian King" series), Bethany House Publishers (Minneapolis, MN), 2003.

SIDELIGHTS: Although Karen Hancock completed a Western novel while still in high school and worked on a science-fiction tale, she did not have a book published until her son had graduated from high school and was off to college. Her return to writing is linked to an incident that occurred when Hancock herself was still a university student. She attended a meeting in which the Christian creation version of the origin of humans was discussed, as was the theory of evolution. At the time, Hancock supported the evolution theory. By the time the meeting was over, she had a new-found interest in evangelical Christianity. Years later, after complaining to her husband about a popular novel, he suggested she write one herself. In response, Hancock began work on *Arena,* a science-fiction allegory of Christianity.

According to Hancock, she became interested in writing a science-fiction Christian allegory when she first saw the film *Star Wars* in the late 1970s. She recognized certain parallels between the film's themes—good versus evil and "the Force," for example—and

biblical Christianity. "There is a real strong savior motif," she told Marcia Z. Nelson in an interview for *Publishers Weekly.* "Science fiction and fantasy are among the best media for conveying spiritual truth. . . . I don't think we have to say 'Christ' and the typical words, but the truth has to be there."

Arena focuses on Callie Hayes, a frustrated artist who works for minimum wage in a research laboratory and is full of fear and disillusionment. After volunteering for a psychology experiment, she finds herself faced with life-and-death adventure in a strange, alien world. Thrown into the "Arena" with only a backpack filled with unfamiliar objects and a manual (which represents the *Bible*), Callie must find the way home or be trapped there for the rest of her life. Along the way, she falls in love with Pierce Andrews, and the two battle their way through the many obstacles in their path, including mutant "Trogs," disgusting creatures who rape and eat their victims. Integral to the plot are a few cryptic words that are part of the plan the "Benefactor" has established to help guide Callie to her escape.

Arena received praise from critics like *Booklist* reviewer John Mort, who wrote that Hancock's "landscapes and alien creatues sing themselves to life." Mort also noted that the author's "theological argument, while certainly Christian, is quite subtle." A reviewer for *Publishers Weekly* commented that Hancock's book "is an excellent—though edgy—contribution" to the Christian science-fiction novel market, in which, unlike many Christian science-fiction books, "characters struggle believably with sexual feelings and passion." In her review for *Library Journal,* Melanie C. Duncan called *Arena* a "classic in the making for the modern era."

BIOGRAPHICAL AND CRITICAL SOURCES:

PERIODICALS

Booklist, April 15, 2002, John Mort, review of *The Arena,* p. 1380.
Library Journal, April 1, 2002, Melanie C. Duncan, review of *The Arena,* p. 86.
Publishers Weekly, April 15, 2002, review of *The Arena,* p. 46; June 17, 2002, Marcia Z. Nelson, "In Profile: Top Novelists in the Category Talk About Their Worth" (interview), p. S23.

Karen Hancock Home Page, http://www.kmhancock. com (March, 2003).

*   *   *

HANNAH, Leslie 1947-

PERSONAL: Born June 15, 1947, in Oldham, Lancashire, England; son of Arthur and Marie (Lancashire) Hannah; married Nuala Barbara Zahedieh, 1984 (divorced, 1998). *Education:* St. John's and Nuffield College, Oxford, M.A., Ph.D., D.Phil.

ADDRESSES: Office—Ashridge Business School, Berkhamsted, Hertfordshire HP4 1NS, England.

CAREER: St. John's College, Oxford University, Oxford, England, junior resident fellow, 1969-73; University of Essex, lecturer in economics, 1973-75; Emmanuel College, Cambridge, fellow and financial tutor, 1976-78; London School of Economics, London, England, business history unit director, 1978-88, professor of business history, 1982-97, pro-director, 1995-97, acting director, 1996-97; NRG London Reinsurance, director, 1986-93; London Econs Ltd., 1991—; City University Business School, dean, 1997-2000; Ashridge Business School, Berkhamsted England, chief executive, 2000—; Institute of Management Consultancy, independent director. Harvard University, visiting professor, 1984-85.

MEMBER: Association of Business Schools (board member).

WRITINGS:

(Editor) *Management Strategy and Business Development: An Historical and Comparative Study,* Macmillan (London, England), 1976.
The Rise of the Corporate Economy, Methuen (London, England), 1976.
The Rise of the Corporate Economy: The British Experience, foreword by Alfred D. Chandler, Johns Hopkins University Press (Baltimore, MD), 1976.

(With J. A. Kay) *Concentration in Modern Industry: Theory, Measurement, and the U.K. Experience,* Macmillan (London, England), 1977.
Electricity before Nationalisation: A Study of the Development of the Electricity Supply Industry in Britain to 1948, Macmillan (London, England), 1979.
Engineers, Managers, and Politicians: The First Fifteen Years of Nationalised Electricity Supply in Britain, Johns Hopkins University Press (Baltimore, MD), 1982.
Inventing Retirement: The Development of Occupational Pensions in Britain, Cambridge University Press (New York, NY), 1986.
(Editor) *Pension Asset Management: An International Perspective,* R. D. Irwin, 1988.
(With Margaret Ackrill) *Barclays: The Business of Banking, 1690-1996,* Cambridge University Press (New York, NY), 2001.

SIDELIGHTS: Leslie Hannah is the chief executive of Ashridge Business School and independent director of the Institute of Management Consultancy. His research interests include economics and business history. *British Book News* contributor David Fanning called Hannah "one of Britain's leading business historians."

In *The Rise of the Corporate Economy: The British Experience* Hannah provides a history of the development of industrial corporations in the United Kingdom between 1880 and 1973. He discusses why and how there was a change in Great Britain from small businesses to large monopolizing corporations. "Readable and convincing, the fascination of this study owes much to its rare and elegant blend of well-researched historical narrative and effective, yet unobtrusive, economic analysis," noted Peter L. Payne in *Business History Review.*

In *Inventing Retirement: The Development of Occupational Pensions in Britain* Hannah discusses the evolvement of occupational pensions in the United Kingdom. He provides a history of how pensions began and how they have changed over the years. *Business History Review* contributor Steven A. Sass praised the work as "a brilliant piece of work that deserves a wide audience among readers of this journal."

BIOGRAPHICAL AND CRITICAL SOURCES:

PERIODICALS

American Historical Review, December, 1977, Donald N. McCloskey, review of *The Rise of the Corporate Economy: The British Experience,* pp. 1258-1259.

British Book News, August, 1986, David Tanning, review of *Inventing Retirement: The Development of Occupational Pensions in Britain,* p. 461.

Business History Review, winter, 1977, Peter L. Payne, review of *The Rise of the Corporate Economy,* pp. 506-507; summer, 1984, Richard B. Du Boff, review of *Engineers, Managers, and Politicians: The First Fifteen Years of Nationalised Electricity Supply in Britain,* pp. 282-283; summer, 1987, Steven A. Sass, review of *Inventing Retirement,* p. 351.

Choice, May, 1977, review of *The Rise of the Corporate Economy,* p. 100; January, 1979, review of *Concentration in Modern Industry: Theory, Measurement, and the U.K. Experience,* p. 1543.

Economist, July 16, 1977, review of *Concentration in Modern Industry,* pp. 126-127.

English Historical Review, October, 1980, Barry Supple, review of *Electricity before Nationalisation: A Study of the Development of the Electricity Supply Industry in Britain to 1948,* pp. 939-941.

History: Reviews of New Books, August, 1979, review of *Electricity before Nationalisation,* pp. 197-198.

Journal of Economic History, September, 1978, James H. Soltow, review of *Concentration in Modern Industry,* pp. 776-778.

Journal of Economic Literature, March, 1987, review of *Inventing Retirement,* p. 244.

Journal of Modern History, December, 1980, S. G. Checkland, review of *Electricity before Nationalisation,* pp. 692-694.

Journal of Political Economy, December, 1978, Leonard W. Weiss, review of *Concentration in Modern Industry,* pp. 1162-1164.

Journal of Social History, spring, 1987, W. Andrew Achenbaum, review of *Inventing Retirement,* pp. 650-651.

Library Journal, February 15, 1977, Ted Samore, review of *The Rise of the Corporate Economy,* p. 484.

ONLINE

Cambridge University Press Web site, http://us.cambridge.org/ (September 3, 2002).*

HARKNESS, Margaret (Elise) 1854-1923
(John Law)

PERSONAL: Born February 28, 1854, at Upton-on-Severn, Worcestershire, England; died October 10, 1923, in Florence, Italy; daughter of Robert (an Anglican priest) and Jane Waugh Law Harkness. *Politics:* Socialist.

CAREER: Nurse trainee, 1877-81; journalist and freelance writer, 1881-1921.

MEMBER: Social Democratic Federation; Labour Party.

WRITINGS:

Assyrian Life and History ("By-paths of Bible Knowledge" no. 2), Religious Tract Society (London, England), 1883.

Egyptian Life and History according to the Monuments ("By-paths of Bible Knowledge" no. 6), Religious Tract Society (London, England), 1884.

Out of Work, Swan Sonnenschein (London, England), 1888, with introduction by Bernadette Kirwan, Dee (Chicago, IL), 1990.

A Manchester Shirtmaker: A Realistic Story of To-day, Authors' Cooperative Publishing (London, England), 1890.

AS JOHN LAW

A City Girl: A Realistic Story, Garland (London, England), 1884.

Tempted London: Young Men, Hodder & Stoughton (London, England), 1888.

Toilers in London: or Inquiries concerning Female Labour in the Metropolis, Hodder & Stoughton (London, England), 1889.

Captain Lobe: A Story of the Salvation Army, Hodder & Stoughton (London, England), 1889, published as *In Darkest London: A New and Popular Edition of Captain Lobe, A Story of the Salvation Army,* Reeves (London, England), 1891, published as *Captain Lobe,* Hodder & Stoughton, 1915.

Imperial Credit, Vardon & Pritchard (Adelaide, Australia), 1899.

George Eastmont: Wanderer, Burns & Oates (London, England), 1905.

Glimpses of Hidden India, Thacker, Spink (Calcutta, India), 1909, revised as *Indian Snapshots: A Bird's-Eye View of India from the Days of the Saib Company to the Present Time,* 1912.

Modern Hyderabad (Deccan), Thacker, Spink (Calcutta, India), 1914.

The Horoscope, Thacker, Spink (Calcutta, India), 1915.

A Curate's Promise: A Story of Three Weeks, September 14-October 5, 1917, Hodder & Stoughton (London, England), 1921.

Contributed to *Nineteenth Century, Justice, Pall Mall Gazette, New Review, Woman's Herald,* and *Fortnightly Review.*

SIDELIGHTS: Margaret Harkness—or John Law, as she called herself in print—is best known for her socially radical fiction of the late nineteenth century. Her empathetic portrayal of impoverished women's lives stands her apart from such like-minded writers as George Gissing, George Bernard Shaw, and Rudyard Kipling. As Eileen Sypher suggested in *Dictionary of Literary Biography:* "Harkness' novels are important because they offer the student of turn-of-the-[twentieth-]century England a different perspective than that found in the writing of better known authors. . . . Not only are her novels among the few of the period to record the impact of socialist ideas on the working class, but they also provide a portrait of women both in the social movement and in slum life." Harkness's fiction chronicles the radical movement from a female perspective, and reveals how socialism was constructed in her day.

Harkness's family, according to a writer in *The Feminist Companion to Literature in English,* was "clerical and conventional," and much of Harkness' work seems reactive to her parents' strictness. Herfather, Robert Harkness, was an Anglican priest, and her mother, Jane Waugh Law Harkness, had aristocratic ties. Beatrice Potter, with whom Harkness was close early in her life, was Harkness's second cousin. As Sypher explained, however: "Potter's letters provide a portrait of Harkness in her early youth as restless and given to depression and in her twenties and thirties as ambitious and hysterical—but this portrait of Harkness as a neurotic is supplied by Potter, and no confirmation has been found."

Aiding others was Harkness's calling. She tried nursing, but gave that up to pursue journalism and writing in London. Once there, Harkness became deeply involved with the suffering of East End slum residents. She explained this in *Imperial Credit,* writing how, after her father's 1886 death, she "determined to do something to lessen the miseries of those who to-day have neither land nor money." Harkness sacrificed herself while trying to help the destitute; in 1887, her friend Olive Schreiner wrote to Havelock Ellis: "Maggie has no money and she came thinking I would support her." Soon after her father's death Harkness inherited a sizable estate, but still appeared to have been desperate to help more of London's poor, remaining poor herself.

Possibly in an effort to support herself, Harkness began to write popular novels under the name John Law. Sypher wrote: "She might have chosen the name because Law was her mother's maiden name, signaling her developing feminism, although it might have been chosen for John Law of Lauriston, a seventeenth-century French eccentric whose economic theories are seen by some as foreshadowing modern state socialism." Regardless, the novels did well enough to help Harkness financially—and perhaps help Harkness' middle-class readers understand urban hardship.

In the first of these novels, *A City Girl: A Realistic Story,* Harkness tells of Nellie, an apparently illegitimate child who works as a seamstress. Nellie is engaged, but nonetheless falls for a genteel married man, Arthur. When Arthur impregnates Nellie, she decides to raise her baby alone amid neighbors' ostracism. She manages, with the Salvation Army's help, but the baby dies anyway. Arthur finally finds Nellie again, and with the Salvation Army's guidance, he marries her.

Realistic detail bolsters the novel's pat, sentimental ending. Friedrich Engels praised the novel's truthfulness of presentation, though he found it "not quite realistic enough." The novel attempts to forge understanding between middle-class readers and poor people, whom Harkness represents. The resolution between middle-class Arthur and lower-class Nellie offers political as well as emotional overtones.

Harkness's best-known novel, *Captain Lobe,* again trumpets the Salvation Army. The book's "slum saviours" tour a hellish underworld of poverty, overpopulation, filth and despair. Within this world, women provide much hope; as Sypher suggested: "The novel particularly shows the strength of women . . . [who] occasionally form female subcultures, as strong women support weaker ones." *A Manchester Shirtmaker: A Realistic Story of To-day* depicts the problems powerful women endure. Harkness considers the pain of Mary Dillon, a widow who must sell her means of support in order to feed her starving infant. Unable to continue to feed the baby, she kills it with opium rather than have it starve to death. When a psychiatrist attempts to help Mary, she commits suicide.

Though many Harkness novels appear to offer conservative, not revolutionary resolutions, she appealed to her middle-class audience for immediate sympathy for the working class. Harkness's novels never preached revolution, but rather exposed poverty to those who might help immediately.

Late in Harkness's career, she abandoned radicalism, claiming she was "got at, abused and misunderstood by the people who call themselves socialist." She complains in *Imperial Credit:* "Birth, sex, and temperament have prevented me from coming forward openly among those who are fighting in the labor ranks." Following this break, Harkness wrote a few novels, mostly dealing with the beauty of pre-Empire India.

Harkness's perspective, which her socialist contemporaries marginalized, enhances the study of radical writing in England. Her novels realistically display the urban poor, but insist on idealizing the connection between the middle and lower classes. Her novels imagine women broken by economic forces even as they advocate women's power as the only possible salvation for the underprivileged.

BIOGRAPHICAL AND CRITICAL SOURCES:

BOOKS

Dictionary of Literary Biography, Volume 197: *Late-Victorian and Edwardian British Novelists, Second Series,* Gale (Detroit, MI), 1999.
Feminist Companion to Literature in English, Yale University Press (New Haven, CT), 1990.

PERIODICALS

Turn-of-the-Century Women, winter, 1984, pp. 12-26.*

*   *   *

HAVELIN, Kate 1961-

PERSONAL: Born January 23, 1961, in Bryn Mawr, PA; daughter of Dudley W. (a banker) and Marie (a nurse; maiden name, Doherty) Havelin; married Leo Timmons (an Internet director), June 30, 1990; children: Max Timmons, William Havelin. *Ethnicity:* "Caucasian." *Education:* Macalester College, B.A., 1983. *Politics:* "Liberal progressive." *Hobbies and other interests:* Running, including marathons, reading, travel, politics.

ADDRESSES: Home and office—2028 Ashland Ave., St. Paul, MN 55104. *E-mail*—khavelin@aol.com.

CAREER: KTCA-TV, St. Paul, MN, administrative assistant, 1983-84; *Forum,* Fargo, ND, copy editor, 1984-85; WCCO-TV, Minneapolis, MN, producer, 1985-96; freelance writer, 1996—. Professional Editors Network, co-coordinator. Million Mom March, board member of Twin Cities chapter.

WRITINGS:

Imagine You Are a Secret Service Agent, Imaginarium (Edina, MN), 1999.
Imagine You Are an ER Doctor, Abdo Publishing (Edina, MN), 1999.
Assertiveness: How Can I Say What I Mean? LifeMatters (Mankato, MN), 2000.
Child Abuse: Why Do My Parents Hit Me? LifeMatters (Mankato, MN), 2000.
Dating: What Is a Healthy Relationship? LifeMatters (Mankato, MN), 2000.
Family Violence: My Parents Hurt Each Other! LifeMatters (Mankato, MN), 2000.
Incest: Why Am I Afraid to Tell? LifeMatters (Mankato, MN), 2000.
Parents: "They're Driving Me Crazy!" LifeMatters (Mankato, MN), 2000.

Peer Pressure: How Can I Say No? LifeMatters (Mankato, MN), 2000.

Sexual Harassment: "This Doesn't Feel Right!" Life-Matters (Mankato, MN), 2000.

Queen Elizabeth I, Lerner Publishing Group (Minneapolis, MN), 2002.

Andrew Johnson, Lerner Publishing Group (Minneapolis, MN), in press.

Ulysses S. Grant, for Lerner Publishing Group (Minneapolis, MN), in press.

WORK IN PROGRESS: John Tyler, Lerner Publishing Group (Minneapolis, MN), 2005.

SIDELIGHTS: Kate Havelin told *CA:* "I grew up in a family that loved reading and history. My mom's idea of a great vacation was visiting presidents' homes, and growing up in the Philadelphia area meant I had lots of lively historic places to visit close to home. So it's probably no surprise that I've ended up writing biographies of presidents and other historical figures.

"In college, I majored in anthropology and am still interested in different cultures and countries. I love to travel, to read, to run, and to spend time with my family."

BIOGRAPHICAL AND CRITICAL SOURCES:

PERIODICALS

School Library Journal, February, 2000, Katie O'Dell, review of *Parents: "They're Driving Me Crazy!"* p. 130; May, 2000, Sally Bates Goodroe, review of *Child Abuse: Why Do My Parents Hit Me?* and *Family Violence: My Parents Hurt Each Other!* p. 182; July, 2002, Kathleen Simonetta, review of *Queen Elizabeth I,* p. 136.

*   *   *

HAYDEN, G. Miki 1944-

PERSONAL: Born 1944.

ADDRESSES: Agent—c/o Author Mail, Jona Books, Box 336, Bedford, IN 47421. *E-mail*—gmh222222@ aol.com.

CAREER: Writer. Has also worked as a book reviewer, first reader for literary agents and periodicals, book doctor, writing teacher, and freelance writer.

MEMBER: Mystery Writers of America,

WRITINGS:

By Reason of Insanity, Free Range Press (New York, NY), 1998.

Pacific Empire, Jona Books (Bedford, IN), 1998

Writing the Mystery: A Start-to-Finish Guide for Novice and Professional, Intrigue Press (Philadelphia, PA), 2001.

Contributor of short stories to numerous genre magazines, including *Murderous Intent Mystery Magazine, Whispering Willows, Futures, Nefarious, Tale Spinner, Kracked Mirror Mysteries, Keen Science Fiction, Unholy Orders, Spaceways Weekly, Star Anthology, Galactic Citizen, Lost Worlds, Romantic Bower, True Romance,* and *True Love.* Contributor of short stories to anthologies.

WORK IN PROGRESS: A sequel to *By Reason of Insanity.*

SIDELIGHTS: G. Miki Hayden is the author of two novels, *Pacific Empire* and *By Reason of Insanity. Pacific Empire* is an alternative history novel based on the premise "What if Japan had not lost World War II?" Covering the period of time from the 1930s to the 1980s, the novel features the family of Japanese Baron Shimazo. Shimazo, along with other Japanese leaders, is attempting to retain Japan's hold on its shaky Pacific Empire. The story is presented in nine parts, featuring Shimazo's sons, wives, lovers, children, and crewmates as they move through the decades of alternative events. In the *New York Times,* Gerald Jonas praised Hayden's ability to convincingly present a world that never existed, as well as her depiction of vibrant characters. He also noted that some of the book's "finest moments" involve the clash of Japanese tradition with the rapidly changing world of the twentieth century.

In *By Reason of Insanity* Hayden tells the story of psychiatrist Dennis Astin, who is also his small town's medical examiner, and his quest to determine who murdered a young woman found dead in a local park. Astin is convinced that someone he knows is the killer, but at the same time, he begins to question his own sanity. Although Dan Swearingen wrote in *Book-browser* that the setting of the book is "drab," he noted that in this novel, the characters provide color and texture, and that he did not figure out the murderer's identity until late in the book.

Hayden's *Writing the Mystery: A Start-to-Finish Guide for Novice and Professional* provides down-to-earth advice for aspiring mystery writers. In accessible, everyday language, Hayden explains the ins and outs of plotting, characterization, suspense, editing, agents, and publication. She also provides helpful exercises that allow writers to practice what they've learned, and interviews with well-known mystery writers such as Elmore Leonard, Laura Lippmann, and Rick Riordan. A *Publishers Weekly* writer noted that this volume would be helpful to both aspiring writers and experienced writers who want to move up in the genre.

In addition to writing fiction and nonfiction, Hayden has worked as a book reviewer, feature writer, and columnist for various mystery magazines. She has also worked as a first reader for literary agents and for various publications, including *Alfred Hitchcock's Mystery Magazine, Ellery Queen's Mystery Magazine, Asimov's Science Fiction,* and *Analog Science Fiction.* Hayden is also a teacher of online courses for Writer's Online Workshop.

BIOGRAPHICAL AND CRITICAL SOURCES:

PERIODICALS

Library Journal, August, 2001, Lisa J. Cihlar, review of *Writing the Mystery,* p. 125.
New York Times Book Review, April 12, 1998, Gerald Jonas, review of *Pacific Empire,* p. 20.
Publishers Weekly, August 6, 2001, review of *Writing the Mystery,* p. 81.

ONLINE

Bookbrowser, http://bookbrowser.com/ (July 23, 2002), Dan Swearingen, review of *By Reason of Insanity.*
Writers Online Workshops, http://www.writersonline workshops.com/ (July 23, 2002).*

HEATON, Patricia 1958-

PERSONAL: Born March 4, 1958, in Bay Village, OH; daughter of Chuck (a sports writer) and Pat Heaton; married second husband, David Hunt (an actor and producer), 1992; children: Sam, John, Joseph, Daniel. *Education:* Ohio State University, B.A. (theater), 1980; studied acting under William Esper in New York. *Religion:* Christian.

ADDRESSES: Agent—International Creative Management, 8942 Wilshire Blvd., Beverly Hills, CA 90211.

CAREER: Actress, producer, and author. Appearances in television series include *Room for Two,* American Broadcast Company (ABC), 1992-93, *Someone like Me,* (National Broadcasting Corporation (NBC), 1994, *Women of the House,* Columbia Broadcast Company (CBS), 1995, and *Everybody Loves Raymond,* CBS, 1996—. Episodic television appearances include *Alien Nation,* 1989, *thirtysomething,* ABC, 1990, *Everybody Loves Raymond* (in the role of Young Marie), CBS, 1997. Television movie appearances include *Shattered Dreams: The Charlotte Fedders Story,* CBS, 1990, *Miracle in the Woods,* CBS, 1997, and *A Town without Christmas,* CBS, 2001. Film appearances include *Beethoven,* Universal, 1992, *Memoirs of an Invisible Man,* Warner Bros., 1992, *The New Age,* Warner Bros., 1994, and *Space Jam,* Warner Bros., 1996. Stage appearances include *The Johnstown Vindicator,* Harold Clurman Theatre, New York City, 1987, *Don't Get God Started,* Longacre Theatre, New York City, 1987-88, and (and producer) *The Johnstown Vindicator,* Los Angeles, CA, 1989.

AWARDS, HONORS: Emmy Award for Outstanding Lead Actress (Comedy), 2000, 2001; Viewers for Quality Television awards for Best Actress in a Quality Comedy Series, 1999, 2000.

WRITINGS:

Motherhood to Hollywood: How to Get a Job like Mine, Villard Books (New York, NY), 2002.

SIDELIGHTS: Patricia Heaton is best known for her role as Debra Barone, the lead female character in the television comedy series *Everybody Loves Raymond.*

Her interest in acting developed during her college years. The actress's father, Chuck Heaton, a sports columnist, had always been an important influence in her life, to the extent that Heaton assumed that she, too, would be a journalist. However, she chose the theater as her major course of study, and in 1980 earned a B.A. in theater from Ohio State University. After her graduation, a move to New York led to a succession of jobs, including waiting tables and, for a time, copy editing for the magazine *People Weekly.* Heaton's career has included television, films, and off-Broadway theater in New York. *Memoirs of an Invisible Man, Space Jam,* and *Beethoven* are among her film credits. The actress has also been a frequent guest on such talk shows as *The Late Show with David Letterman* and *Oprah.* She lives and works in Los Angeles.

Motherhood to Hollywood: How to Get a Job like Mine, was published in 2002 by Villard Books. The book is divided into three sections named for the cities she lived in at different periods in her life. It is a collection of brief essays on topics ranging from marriage, motherhood, and show business to celebrity life, plastic surgery, and psychotherapy. Heaton has made the point in interviews that her book is really not an autobiography, but rather a series of humorous and pointed pieces on modern life. A review of the book in *Kirkus* praised it as "an upbeat memoir that doesn't obsess about the rough times but instead is beguilingly sensible and wise about what's important: the author's family, faith, and craft." In her reflections on motherhood she speaks frankly about the loss of her own mother at age twelve and the pressures of modern parenthood. The critical reception has been positive, as has been the response of the general readership. The book has been praised for its expression of warmth and candor, and above all, for its humor.

BIOGRAPHICAL AND CRITICAL SOURCES:

BOOKS

Contemporary Theatre, Film, and Television, Volume 27, Gale (Detroit, MI), 2000.

PERIODICALS

Entertainment Weekly, December 18, 1992, Alan Carter, review of *Room for Two,* p. 13; January 13, 1995, Ken Tucker, review of *Women of the House,* p. 42; April 11, 1997, Bruce Fretts, review of *Everybody Loves Raymond,* p. 67; November 28, 1997, Bruce Fretts, review of *Everybody Loves Raymond,* p. 44; September 27, 2002, review of *Motherhood to Hollywood: How to Get a Job like Mine,* p. 80.

Hollywood Reporter, August 20, 2001, p. 2; November 5, 2001, p. 35; December 13, 2001, Michael R. Farkash, review of *A Town without Christmas,* p. 14.

Inside Media, April 15, 1992, Ed Martin, review of *Room for Two,* p. 60.

Kirkus Reviews, August 1, 2002, review of *Motherhood to Hollywood,* p. 1095.

People Weekly, March 23, 1992, David Hiltbrand, review of *Room for Two,* p. 17; November 9, 1992, Shelley Levitt, review of *Room for Two,* p. 93; April 25, 1994, David Hiltbrand, review of *Someone like Me,* p. 13; January 9, 1995, David Hiltbrand, review of *Women of the House,* p. 15; June 8, 1998, review of *Everybody Loves Raymond,* p. 31; November 23, 1998, p. 101; November 28, 2000, p. 52; December 10, 2001, review of *Motherhood to Hollywood,* p. 19.

Publishers Weekly, August 5, 2002, review of *Motherhood to Hollywood,* p. 66.

ONLINE

CNN.com, http://www.cnn.com/ (December 12, 2002).

Entertainment Tonight Online, http://www.etonline.com/ (December 13, 2002).

Patricia Heaton Online, http://www.particiaheatononline.com (November 11, 2002).*

*   *   *

HEENAN, David A. 1940-

PERSONAL: Born 1940. *Education:* College of William and Mary, A.B., 1961; Columbia University, M.B.A., 1966; University of Pennsylvania, Wharton School, Ph.D., 1972.

ADDRESSES: Agent—c/o Caroline O'Connell, Caroline O'Connell Communications 11275 La Maida St., Suite 200, North Hollywood, CA 91601-4514. *E-mail*—dh@double-lives.com.

CAREER: Author and businessman. Caltex Oil Corporation, New York, NY, assistant to the director, 1966, sales manager, Sydney, Australia, 1967-68; McKinsey & Co., New York, associate, 1969; First National City Bank, New York, director of human resources, 1969-72; Citicorp, New York, 1972-75; University of Hawaii, vice president for academic affairs, 1975-82; Theodore H. Davies and Co., Ltd., Honolulu, chairman of the board, chief executive officer, and president, board of directors, 1982—; trustee for estate of James Campbell. Maui Land & Pineapple Co. Inc., chairman, 2003. *Military service:* U.S. Marine Corps, captain, 1961-65.

WRITINGS:

Multinational Management of Human Resources: A Systems Approach, Bureau of Business Research, University of Texas (Austin, TX), 1975.

(With Howard V. Perlmutter) *Multinational Organization Development,* Addison-Wesley (Reading, MA), 1979.

The Re-United States of America: An Action Agenda for Improving Business, Government, and Labor Relations, Addison-Wesley (Reading, MA), 1983.

The New Corporate Frontier: The Big Move to Small Town, USA, McGraw-Hill (New York, NY), 1991.

(With Warren Bennis) *Co-Leaders: The Power of Great Partnerships,* John Wiley (New York, NY), 1999.

Double Lives: Crafting Your Life of Work and Passion for Untold Success, Davies-Black Publishers (Palo Alto), 2002.

SIDELIGHTS: David A. Heenan has distinguished himself in the academic world and in business. He has written steadily throughout his professional life, with titles that include *Multinational Management of Human Resources: A Systems Approach* and *Double Lives: Crafting Your Life of Work and Passion for Untold Success.* Over the years, Heenan has focused on defining styles of leadership and the characteristics of successful leaders, as well as identifying techniques that enable people to work together more productively. Quality of life issues have also been among his concerns. He has addressed this topic in two books, *Double Lives* and *The New Corporate Frontier: The Big Move to Small Town, USA.*

In *Co-Leaders: The Power of Great Partnerships* Heenan and coauthor Warren Bennis argue that the future belongs not to solitary leaders, but to those individuals willing to work with a partner. As a reviewer in *Publishers Weekly* pointed out, the form this partnership often takes is that of one very visible individual who is working in tandem with someone else of equal capability, but who maintains a significantly lower public profile. Heenan and Bennis's book presents a detailed look at successful leadership partnerships, defining the different styles and the elements that lead to their productivity. Examples are not drawn exclusively from the business world. Figures from politics, sports, and literature are also included. The authors employ an historical approach, looking at leadership from ancient Crete up to and including contemporary times. By examining the lives of people who have occupied a secondary, but crucial role, Heenan and Bennis show how and why this arrangement can produce beneficial results. Although most of the attention is paid to the value of shared leadership at the highest level, the authors suggest that shared responsibility at all levels of an organization produces the most desirable result. Critics responded positively to the ideas and arguments offered in *Co-Leaders.*

The New Corporate Frontier describes the late-twentieth-century trend of large businesses relocating to smaller towns. In 1960 130 of the *Fortune* 500 companies were located in New York; by 1990 that figure had fallen to only forty-three. Chicago and other large cities showed similar decreases. The new, desirable business locations are in parts of the country that are not within commuting distance to large cities. Larger corporations are generally relocating to small cities, suburbs and business enclaves set in rural areas. These areas offer lower business costs, in the form of tax relief, cheaper labor and occupancy fees. Jan Hawn commented in a review in *Government Finance Review* that employees have the advantage of better schools, homes, jobs, decreased crime, and a slower pace of life. Heenan expresses some concern for the effects of this trend on urban life and challenged the reader to think about the future of the large cities. He is, however, an advocate of the move away from the cities, and has found a receptive audience among city council members, urban planners and economic development experts. Ten guideposts based on the success of these new communities are described, as well as clear advice to CEO's contemplating such a change. The book was lauded for its thoughtful look at an important trend.

Double Lives is concerned with quality of life, but in a more personal way than *The New Corporate Frontier.*

This book moves away from strictly business and organizational interests and enters the realm of philosophy and psychology. In approaching this topic, however, Heenan maintains his straightforward approach, complete with useful checklists. *Double Lives* asserts that it is important to live a life of clear meaning and purpose. While recognizing the necessity of taking care of life's requirements, he argues for the importance of finding deep satisfaction through the pursuit of a personal interest. Profiled are such people as James Wolfensohn, Winston Churchill, and Sally Ride, all people with strong avocations that brought them an additional sense of fulfillment. In her review in *Booklist*, Mary Whaley pointed out that Heenan includes a list of twenty items aimed at keeping the individual focused and able to achieve the desired goal. The list includes the value of learning from failure, avoidance of procrastination, and the necessity of defining success.

BIOGRAPHICAL AND CRITICAL SOURCES:

PERIODICALS

Booklist, August, 2002, Mary Whaley, review of *Double Lives: Crafting Your Life of Work and Passion for Untold Success*, p. 1890.

Business Credit, October, 1991, Cindy Tursman, review of *The New Corporate Frontier: The Big Move to Small Town, USA*, p. 35.

Business Horizons, June, 1983, Calvin Reynolds, review of *The Re-United States of America: An Action Agenda for Improving Business, Government, and Labor Relations*, pp. 81-83.

Business Week, September 30, 1991, Bruce Hager, review of *The New Corporate Frontier*, p. 10.

Choice, December, 1991, R. A. Beauregard, review of *The New Corporate Frontier*, p. 634.

Forbes, September 16, 1991, James Cook, review of *The New Corporate Frontier*, p. 56; September 16, 2002, Caspar W. Weinberger, review of *Double Lives*, p. 37.

Government Finance Review, December, 1992, Jan Hawn, review of *The New Corporate Frontier*, p. 44.

HR Magazine, July, 1999, Jeanine Brannon, review of *Co-Leaders: The Power of Great Partnerships*, p. 150.

Journal of Business Strategy, September, 1999, Bristol Lane Voss, review of *Co-Leaders*, p. 45.

National Review, June 10, 1983, George Viksnins, review of *The Re-United States of America*, p. 708.

New York Times Book Review, December, 26, 1982, Paul Lewis, review of *The Re-United States of America*, p. 9.

Publishers Weekly, February 22, 1999, review of *Co-Leaders*, p. 80; June 17, 2002, review of *Double Lives*, p. 56.

Wall Street Review of Books, summer, 1984, Michael M. Kurth, review of *The Re-United States of America*, pp. 184-186.*

* * *

HEFFERNAN, Deborah Daw 1952-

PERSONAL: Born 1952; married; husband's name, Jack; children: five. *Education:* Attended Georgetown University and Harvard Graduate School of Education.

ADDRESSES: Home—ME. *Agent*—c/o Author Mail, Simon & Schuster, 1230 Avenue of the Americas, New York, NY 10020.

CAREER: Writer. École d'Humanité, Switzerland, teacher; Boston University, Boston, MA, associate dean of program in artisanry; vice president of corporate-training enterprise, Boston, 1983-97; freelance writer.

WRITINGS:

An Arrow through the Heart: One Woman's Story of Life, Love, and Surviving a Near-Fatal Heart Attack, Free Press (New York, NY), 2002.

SIDELIGHTS: Writer Deborah Daw Heffernan earned degrees from Georgetown University and the Harvard Graduate School of Education before moving on to a career as an executive. In May of 1997, Heffernan was a healthy forty-four-year-old woman; she had been happily married since 1989 to her husband Jack, who was thirteen years older than she and who had five grown children. However, during a yoga class, she suffered a massive—and nearly fatal—heart attack. In *An Arrow through the Heart: One Woman's Story of*

Becoming Whole After a Heart Attack, Heffernan describes her life before and after the heart attack, and examines the changes it brought to her life.

Before the heart attack, Heffernan was a nonsmoker and healthy eater with no family history of heart disease: she had no way of knowing she was at risk. She had a high-pressure position as a corporate training executive. When the heart attack hit, Heffernan was fortunate to be close to a hospital in Cambridge, Massachusetts, and to receive prompt care from rescue workers, who transported her to the hospital for an emergency bypass operation. Physicians implanted a defibrillator—a device that regulates heart beats—in her chest, and this allowed her to survive.

The ensuing period of lengthy recovery changed Heffernan's life. Her relationship with her husband grew even stronger, as he became her temporary caregiver. In order to help her heal, they moved from Cambridge to a vacation home in Maine. Jack's grown children, who had formerly been distant from their father's new wife, became closer to her as she spent more time with them, and she also became closer to her sisters. Gradually, she became stronger, walking in the Maine woods, taking up yoga again. Through her experience she learned that, despite her physically healthy lifestyle, she had been under stress for decades as a result of her career choices and her family background. Although Heffernan's continuing health was by no means assured—doctors told her that she might need a transplant in the future—she was able to find great peace and happiness in her new life.

A *Booklist* reviewer called the book "absorbing" and in *Publishers Weekly,* a reviewer commented that it is an "insightful and openly emotional account" of a life-changing experience. A *Kirkus Reviews* writer called it "an arresting story" and praised Heffernan's mingling of medical facts with her inner journey. In a newsletter for the Massachusetts General Hospital, where Heffernan was treated, she wrote that this mingling was her intent: "More than half a million woman die each year from heart disease. . . . I wrote *An Arrow through the Heart* to ambush women with critical information disguised as a good read, rather than letting heart disease ambush them as it did me."

BIOGRAPHICAL AND CRITICAL SOURCES:

PERIODICALS

Booklist, April 15, 2002, review of *An Arrow through the Heart,* p. 1365.

Kirkus Reviews, March 15, 2002, review of *An Arrow through the Heart,* p. 382.

Publishers Weekly, April 15, 2002, review of *An Arrow through the Heart,* p. 51.

ONLINE

MGH Hotline Online, http://www.mgh.Harvard.edu/ (May 24, 2002), review of *An Arrow through the Heart.*

SimonSays.com, http://www.simonsays.com/ (July 23, 2002).*

*   *   *

HEIM, Bruno Bernhard 1911-2003

OBITUARY NOTICE—See index for *CA* sketch: Born March 5, 1911, in Olten, Switzerland; died March 18, 2003, in Olten, Switzerland. Priest and author. Heim is best remembered for his twelve-year role as the pope's representative in England, but he was also a noted expert on heraldry. Educated in Rome and Switzerland, he earned a Ph.D. in 1934 from St. Thomas University, a B.D. in 1937 from the University of Fribourg, a Dr. Jr.Can. in 1946 from Gregorian University, and a degree from the Pontifical Diplomatic Academy in 1947. He was ordained a priest in the Roman Catholic church in 1938, whereupon he served in parishes in Arbon and Basle, Switzerland. During World War II he was chief chaplain for Italian and Polish military internees in the Emmental. One of the first non-Italians to be trained for diplomatic service in the church, in 1947 Heim was a secretary to Archbishop Angelo Roncalli in Paris before working directly for Pope John XXII, serving in the nunciatures in Vienna, Austria, and Bonn, Germany, during the 1950s. After being promoted to Archbishop of Xanthos in 1961, Heim was assigned to be a delegate and then pro-nuncio for Scandinavia until 1969. The next four years were spent in Cairo, Egypt, as pro-nuncio. In 1973 he was made fifth apostolic delegate to Great Britain, where he remained until 1985. While in England, Heim played an important role in appointing bishops there and helped to smooth out relations between England and Rome, especially during the Falkland Islands War. He was made apostolic pro-nuncio to the Court of St. James in 1982, the first priest to be so named since the Reformation. In addition to his work in the church,

Heim designed coats of arms for four popes as an authority on ecclesiastical heraldry and was the author of such books on the subject as *Heraldry in the Catholic Church: Its Origin* (1978) and *Or and Argent* (1994).

OBITUARIES AND OTHER SOURCES:

PERIODICALS

Independent (London, England), March 26, 2003, p. 20.
Times (London, England), March 25, 2003, p. 34.

*　　*　　*

HEKER, Liliana 1943-

PERSONAL: Born 1943, in Buenos Aires, Argentina.

ADDRESSES: Agent—c/o Author Mail, Coach House Press, 401 Huron St., Toronto, Ontario, Canada M5S 2G5.

CAREER: Writer. Director of literary magazines *Escarabajo de Oro* and *Ornitorrinco* (title means "Platypus").

WRITINGS:

Los que vieron la zarza (title means "The Ones That Saw the Zarza"), J. Alvarez (Buenos Aires, Argentina), 1966.
Acuario (title means "Aquarium"), Centro Editor de América Latina (Buenos Aires, Argentina), 1972.
Un resplandor que se apagó en el mundo (novel; title means "A Brightness That Was Put out in the World"), Sudamericana (Buenos Aires, Argentina), 1977.
(Editor) *Diálogos sobre la vida y la muerte* (title means "Dialogues on the Life and the Death"), Grupo Editor de Buenos Aires (Buenos Aires, Argentina), 1980.
Zona de clivaje (novel; title means "Zone of Clivaje"), Legasa (Buenos Aires, Argentina), 1987.

Los bordes de lo real (stories; title means "The Edges of the Real Thing"), Alfaguara (Buenos Aires, Argentina), 1991.
The Stolen Party: And Other Stories ("Passport Books" series), translation by Alberto Manguel, Coach House Press (Toronto, Ontario, Canada), 1994.
El fin de la historia (title means "The End of History"), Alfaguara (Buenos Aires, Argentina), 1996.
Las hermanas de Shakespeare (essays; title means "The Sisters of Shakespeare"), Alfaguara (Buenos Aires, Argentina), 1999.
La crueldad de la vida (title means "The Cruelty of Life"), Alfaguara (Buenos Aires, Argentina), 2001.

SIDELIGHTS: Liliana Heker is an Argentine novelist and short-story writer who is also responsible for the success of two literary magazines that feature the writings of her region. Rather than fleeing Argentina during the period of military dictatorship that prevailed from the 1960s through 1982, she remained to edit and publish literary contributions.

Heker's work has been translated into many languages, and her collection *The Stolen Party: And Other Stories,* was translated into English as part of Coach House Press's "Passport Books" series. It contains six stories from three untranslated collections and feature mostly young, intelligent female characters who question the meaning of their lives. In the opening story a young girl comes to the realization that her beauty will not guarantee success, nor will it last forever. A male computer programmer is flung into an alternate world in the Kafkaesque "Family Life." The girl of the title story, the daughter of a maid, attends the birthday party of the employer's daughter, thinking she is an honored guest. What she discovers is that she has just begun her own training in servitude.

A *Kirkus Reviews* contributor noted that Heker is "a writer concerned with the role of artists in society." *Quill & Quire*'s Andi Curtis wrote that *The Stolen Party* "highlights Heker's sparse prose and her keen eye for bypassable, but potent, details."

BIOGRAPHICAL AND CRITICAL SOURCES:

PERIODICALS

Kirkus Reviews, May 1, 1994, review of *The Stolen Party: And Other Stories,* p. 577.
Quill & Quire, June, 1994, Andi Curtis, review of *The Stolen Party,* p. 43.*

HELDMANN, Richard Bernard 1857-1915
  (Richard Marsh)

PERSONAL: Born June 1, 1857 in Butler, OH; died August 9, 1915; married Matilda Dieterich, 1885.

CAREER: Novelist, c. 1895-1915; also worked as a journalist.

WRITINGS:

UNDER PSEUDONYM RICHARD MARSH

The Beetle, Skeffington, 1895, Putnam (New York, NY), 1917, reprinted, Arno Press (New York, NY), 1976.

The Crime and the Criminal, Ward, Lock (New York, NY), 1897.

Tom Ossington's Ghost, 1898, 1931.

Marvels and Mysteries, Methuen (London, England), 1900.

Ada Vernham, Actress, L. C. Page & Co. (Boston, MA), 1900.

The Seen and the Unseen, Methuen (London, England), 1900.

Both Sides of the Veil, Methuen (London, England), 1901.

The Twickenham Peerage, 1902.

Between the Dark and the Daylight, 1902.

A Metamorphosis, Methuen (London, England), 1903.

The Death Whistle, 1903.

Garnered, Methuen (London, England), 1904.

A Duel, Methuen (London, England), 1904.

The Marquis of Putney, Methuen (London, England), 1905.

In the Service of Love, Methuen (London, England), 1906.

The Romance of a Maid of Honor, Long, 1907.

The Girl and the Miracle, Methuen (London, England), 1907.

Who Killed Lady Poynder? D. Appleton (New York, NY), 1907.

The Coward behind the Curtain, 1908.

The Surprising Husband, 1908.

A Royal Indiscretion, 1909.

A Spoiler of Men, Chatto (London, England), 1911.

Judith Lee, 1912.

Justice Suspended, Chatto (London, England).

The Great Temptation, T. F. Unwin (London, England), 1916.

Also author of other novels, including *Justice Suspended.*

SIDELIGHTS: Although he authored over two dozen adventure/romance novels and short-story collections, Richard Marsh—the pen name of Richard Bernard Heldmann—is perhaps best remembered as the author of the late-Victorian horror novel *The Beetle,* published in 1897. *The Beetle* tells the story of the efforts by the members of an Egyptian religious sect to use the powers of "a strange female figure that turns periodically into a large beetle," explained a contributor to the *Penguin Encyclopedia of Horror and the Supernatural.* "It is similar in structure to [Bram] Stoker's *Dracula,*" the contributor continued, "telling its story by the use of extracts from various characters' journals." *The Beetle* won for its author a significant amount of popularity, and the volume remained in print for almost seventy years.

In addition to *The Beetle,* Marsh composed a number of other horror works. His collections *The Seen and the Unseen* (1900), *Marvels and Mysteries* (1900), and *Between the Dark and the Daylight* (1902) contain stories that are, according to the *Penguin Encyclopedia of Horror and the Supernatural* contributor, "worthy of the researcher's time." In addition, the author penned at least three more gothic horror novels: *Tom Ossington's Ghost* (1898), *The Death Whistle* (1903), and *A Spoiler of Men* (1911). Marsh died in 1915.

BIOGRAPHICAL AND CRITICAL SOURCES:

BOOKS

Penguin Encyclopedia of Horror and the Supernatural, Viking Penguin (New York, NY), 1986.*

*   *   *

HENRI, Noble
  See WYNORSKI, Jim

HENRY, Noble
    See WYNORSKI, Jim

                    *   *   *

HEUVEL, Jon Vanden
    See VANDEN HEUVEL, Jon

                    *   *   *

HOLLANDER, Xaviera 1943-

PERSONAL: Born Xaviera de Vries, 1943, in Indonesia; daughter of Mick and Germaine de Vries; married Frank Allen (divorced).

ADDRESSES: Agent—c/o Regan Books, HarperCollins Publishers, 10 East 53rd St., New York, NY 10022. *E-mail*—xaviera@xavierahollander.com.

CAREER: Secretary, copy writer, prostitute, brothel keeper, author, and magazine columnist.

MEMBER: Speakers Academy of Rotterdam.

WRITINGS:

(With Robin Moore and Yvonne Dunleavy) *The Happy Hooker,* Bell Publishing (New York, NY), 1972.
Xaviera's Supersex: Her Personal Techniques for Total Lovemaking, illustrated by Robert Baxter, New American Library (New York, NY), 1976.
Xaviera's Magic Mushrooms, New English Library (Sevenoaks, Kent, England), 1981.
Fiesta of the Flesh (novel), Panther (London, England), 1984.
The Kiss of the Serpent (novel), Grafton (London, England), 1987.
Yours Fatally (novel), Grafton (London, England), 1987.
Child No More (memoir), Regan Books, (New York, NY), 2002.

SIDELIGHTS: Xaviera Hollander began her career as a secretary and after working for some time as a prostitute, she achieved notoriety in the 1970s as the madam of one of New York City's most exclusive brothels. It was also in 1972 that her first book, *The Happy Hooker,* was published. Hollander's testimony before the Knapp Commission revealed that she was making payoffs to New York City police. Not long after this revelation, she had to leave the United States, the official reason being an expired visa. Her next home was in Canada. During her stay there, she married Frank Allen, an antiques dealer. Canada denied her permanent-residence status, and upon learning this, Hollander left, although Allen stayed in Canada. Hollander now resides in Amsterdam and Marbella, Spain. She has written a sex-advice column titled "Call Me Madam," which has run in *Penthouse* magazine for thirty years. She also has five books to her credit. Hollander's most recent publication, *Child No More,* is a memoir of her early life with her parents in Indonesia and the Netherlands. She has retired from prostitution.

The Happy Hooker is Hollander's story of her time as a prostitute and madam in New York City. It is a frank account of her relationships with her clients, her philosophy of work, and various sex techniques. The beginning of the book is devoted to her early years with her parents, describing the rivalry between her and her mother for her father's attention and a description of the openness about sexual anatomy within the family. *The Happy Hooker* has recently been reissued to coincide with the publication of Hollander's memoir, *Child No More.*

In addition to her nonfiction writing, Hollander has also penned novels, including *Fiesta of the Flesh, The Kiss of the Serpent,* and *Yours Fatally.* They are considered to be erotica, and set in contemporary times. They have received little critical attention.

Child No More recounts Hollander's early life and the relationships she had with her two loving but volatile parents. The book opens and closes with her mother, Germaine, a beautiful model of French and German heritage. Germaine and Hollander's father, Mick, had a whirlwind romance and married quickly. They made their lives in Indonesia, where Mick had a medical practice. Xaviera was born during World War II and shortly after her birth the family was interned in a camp by the Japanese army. Their suffering was great, but all three survived. Reviewers commented on the frankly erotic nature of the author's early experiences with her father, and wondered why, in her memoir,

Hollander fails to explain why she chose a profession in the sex industry.

BIOGRAPHICAL AND CRITICAL SOURCES:

PERIODICALS

Book, July-August, 2002, Jerry Tallmer, review of *Child No More,* p. 16.
Books and Bookmen, August, 1973, Raymond Durgnat, review of *The Happy Hooker,* pp. 48-51.
Kirkus Reviews, April 15, 2002, review of *Child No More,* p. 545.
Newsweek, November 10, 1980, review of *The Happy Hooker,* pp. 20-21.
Publishers Weekly, May 20, 2002, review of *Child No More,* p. 58

ONLINE

Xaviera Hollander Web site, http://www.xaviera-theatre.com (September 3, 2002).*

* * *

HOLMES, Frederic L(awrence) 1932-2003

OBITUARY NOTICE—See index for *CA* sketch: Born February 6, 1932, in Cincinnati, OH; died of stomach cancer March 27, 2003, in New Haven, CT. Educator and author. Holmes was an authority on the history of medicine and science. After earning a B.S. from the Massachusetts Institute of Technology in 1954, he went on to receive his Ph.D. from Harvard University in 1962. He then returned to MIT as an assistant professor of humanities and history of science for two years. This was followed by eight years at Yale University. From 1972 to 1979 he was a professor in the same disciplines at the University of Western Ontario before going back to Yale. He spent the rest of his career there and played an important role in reestablishing Yale's doctoral program in the history of medicine. Holmes himself was a highly regarded expert in the field whose meticulous research into the processes by which scientists developed their theories and made their discoveries led to landmark books such as the two-volume *Hans Krebs* (1991, 1993), *Lavoisier*

and the Chemistry of Life (1985), *Meselson, Stahl, and the Replication of DNA: A History of the Most Beautiful Experiment in Biology* (2001), and *Reworking the Bench: Research Notebooks in the History of Sciences* (2003), the last which he edited with Jürgen Renn and Hans-Jörg Rheinberger. Holmes gathered his data not only from interviews and trips to the library, but also by analyzing laboratory notebooks to reconstruct scientists' thought processes. He published ten books in all before his death, the last of which, completed just at before his death, being a study on geneticist Seymour Benzer.

OBITUARIES AND OTHER SOURCES:

PERIODICALS

New York Times, April 7, 2003, p. A21.
Washington Post, April 10, 2003, p. B8.

* * *

HOLTBY, Robert Tinsley 1921-2003

OBITUARY NOTICE—See index for *CA* sketch: Born February 25, 1921, in Thornton-le-Dale, England; died March 13, 2003, in Malton, North Yorkshire, England. Priest and author. Holtby was a former director of education for the Church of England and Dean of Chichester cathedral. He earned M.A. degrees from St. Edmund Hall, Oxford, and King's College, Cambridge, in 1946 and 1948 respectively, followed by a B.D. in 1957. Ordained a minister in the Church of England in 1946, he was a curate in Pocklington for two years before becoming a chaplain in the British Armed Forces, serving with the 14/20 Hussars at Catterick, and later in Singapore. Returning to England, he became a chaplain and assistant master of private boys' secondary schools in Malvern and Oxford during the 1950s. From 1959 to 1967 he was canon residentiary and diocesan director of education in Carlisle. This was followed by a decade with the Church of England's Board of Education, for which he was general secretary of the National Society for Promoting Religious Education, beginning in 1967, and secretary of the General Synod Board of Education, beginning in 1974. By the time he became dean of Chichester in 1977, his concern for and experience in education had been well established. While at Chichester, Holtby did much to improve and revive programs in education there, while also raising funds to repair the cathedral's organ and collapsing spire, and increased community awareness of the cathedral in general. He retired as dean emeritus in 1989. Holtby was the author of several books, including *Carlisle Cathedral* (1971), *Chichester Cathedral* (1980), *Robert Wright Stopford* (1988), *Bishop William Otter* (1989), *Eric Milner-White, Dean of York* (1991), and *The Minister School, York* (1994).

OBITUARIES AND OTHER SOURCES:

BOOKS

Writers Directory, 18th edition, St. James Press (Detroit, MI), 2003.

PERIODICALS

Independent (London, England), April 9, 2003, p. 16.
Times (London, England), March 20, 2003.

*   *   *

HREBEJK, Jan 1967-

PERSONAL: Born June 27, 1967, in Prague, Czechoslovakia (now Czech Republic). *Education:* Film Academy of Prague (FAMU), graduated, 1991.

ADDRESSES: Agent—Total HelpArt T.H.A., Studio Barrandov, Kříženeckého nám. 322, 153 52 Praha (Prague) 5, Czech Republic.

CAREER: Director, actor, producer, and writer. Director of films, including (and producer) *Co vsechno chcete vedet o sexu a bojite se to prozit* (also known as *Everything You Always Wanted to Know about Sex but Were Afraid to Experience*), 1988; *L.P. 1948* (also known as *1948 A.D.*), 1989; *Nedelejte nic, pokud k tomu nemate vazny duvod* (also known as *You Do Nothing Because You've Got No Good Reason*), 1990; *Sakali leta* (also known as *Big Beat*), 1993; *Ceská soda,* 1998; *Pelísky* (also known as *Cosy Dens*), 1999;

Musíme si pomáhat (also known as *Divided We Fall*), 2000; and *Obsluhoval jsem anglického krále* (also known as *I Served the King of England*), 2002. Actor in films, including *Silaci,* 1991; (as Woody) *Septej* (also known as *Whisper*), 1996; and *Rok dábla* (also known as *Year of the Devil*), 2002. Director of stage productions, including *Dangerous Relationships, Bullets over Broadway,* and *Amadeus,* all at Pod Palmovkou Theater. Director of television programs *Dobrocinny vecírek* (also known as *Charity Benefit*), 1992; *Jak se zije zpevnemu svedomi naroda, Zivot spevaka a skladatele Vladimira Miskia,* and *Kde padaji hvezdy* (miniseries; also known as *Where Stars Fall*), all 1996; and *60* (series), 1998; worked on television series *Bachelors,* 1997.

AWARDS, HONORS: Czech Lions award for best director and best film, 1993, for *Big Beat;* critics prize, Karlovy Vary Film Festival, 1999, for *Cosy Dens;* Academy Award nomination for best foreign-language film) Academy of Motion Picture Arts and Sciences, Golden Kingfisher prize, and Don Quixote Jury Prize, Nove Mesto's Barrel of Laughs audience award, Kristian award for best drama, FIPRESCI award, Cottbus Film Festival of Young East-European Cinema award, and most popular film designation, Vancouver Film Festival, all 2000, and Palm Springs International Film Festival audience award, Febiofest film columnists and critics award, Czech Lions award for best film and best director, and most popular feature film, Sydney Film Festival, all 2001, all all for *Divided We Fall.*

WRITINGS:

Patosání (poetry), Mladá fronta (Prague, Czech Republic), 1990.
(With Petr Jarchovsky) *Pejme písen dokola* (also known as *Let's Sing a Song* and *Let's Sing All Around;* television screenplay), 1990.
Jak se zije zpevnemu svedomi naroda (television screenplay), 1996.
Zivot spevaka a skladatele Vladimira Misika (television screenplay), 1996.

Also the author of four one-act plays written for the theatre group "Ordinary Loves."

SIDELIGHTS: To American audiences, Czech filmmaker Jan Hrebejk is probably best known for directing *Divided We Fall* (*Musíme si pomáhat*), a film about a Czech couple who is trying to hide a Jewish refugee in their apartment in Nazi-occupied Czechoslovakia, despite the fact that a local collaborationist is obsessed with the wife and keeps dropping by at inopportune times. This film won awards at film festivals around the world and was often favorably compared to Roberto Benigni's 1997 Holocaust movie *Life Is Beautiful.* "Hrebejk has made one of the best films of the year," Evan Williams wrote in the *Weekend Australian.*

Hrebejk also achieved global recognition for an earlier film, *Pelísky* (also known as *Cosy Dens*). This film, shot just prior to *Divided We Fall,* uses the same crew. Both films were also written by the same man, Hrebejk's former high-school and film-academy classmate Petr Jarchovsky. *Cosy Dens* is set in the late 1960s, during a brief period of liberalization known as the Prague Spring. The story is told from the points of view of two families with teenage children who live in the same Prague apartment building. One family is in favor of communism, one is against it, but both children are united in their desire for Westernized products like rock and roll. *Cozy Dens* became one of the highest-grossing Czech feature films of all time; about ten percent of the population of the Czech Republic saw the film in theaters. Hrebejk and Jarchovsky also collaborated on *Sakali leta.* "Sakali leta," which translates as "Big Beat," is the name for a Czech type of rock music. This film tells the story of rock and roll's Czech debut at the end of the 1950s. *Big Beat* won Hrebejk and Jarchovsky several awards.

BIOGRAPHICAL AND CRITICAL SOURCES:

BOOKS

Contemporary Theatre, Film, and Television, Volume 34, Gale (Detroit, MI), 2001.

PERIODICALS

Atlanta Journal-Constitution, September 21, 2001, Eleanor Ringel Gillespie, review of *Divided We Fall,* p. P1.
Buffalo News (Buffalo, NY), July 27, 2001, Jan Sandberg, review of *Divided We Fall,* p. G4.
Entertainment Weekly, June 22, 2001, Lisa Schwartzbaum, review of *Divided We Fall,* p. 63; August 10, 2001, Gillian Flynn, review of *Divided We Fall,* p. 30.
Financial Times, May 30, 2002, Nigel Andrews, review of *Divided We Fall,* p. 18.
Guardian (London, England), May 24, 2002, Kate Connolly, "Hate Thy Neighbor: Czech Director Han Hrebejk's Oscar-nominated *Divided We Fall* Tells of His Compatriots' Opportunism, Cowardice, and Treachery under Nazi Rule," p. 10.
Independent (London, England), Anthony Quinn, review of *Divided We Fall,* p. 10.
Journal News (Westchester, NY), June 7, 2001, Marshall Fine, review of *Divided We Fall,* p. 9G.
Knight Ridder/Tribune News Service, July 19, 2001, Desmond Ryan, review of *Divided We Fall,* p. K3594; August 2, 2001, Jane Sumner, review of *Divided We Fall,* p. K0923.
Library Journal, February 15, 2002, Jeff T. Dick, review of *Divided We Fall,* p. 192.
Los Angeles Times, June 8, 2001, Kenneth Turan, review of *Divided We Fall,* p. F6.
National Catholic Reporter, July 27, 2001, Joseph Cunneen, review of *Divided We Fall,* p. 14.
New Republic, June 18, 2001, Stanley Kauffmann, review of *Divided We Fall,* p. 26.
New York, June 11, 2001, Peter Rainer, review of *Divided We Fall,* pp. 54-55.
New York Observer, June 18, 2001, Andrew Sarris, review of *Divided We Fall,* p. 19.
New York Times, June 8, 2001, A. O. Scott, review of *Divided We Fall,* p. B16; June 10, 2001, Peter S. Green, "First Prague, Then the World: With an Eye for Profits and a Nod to Hollywood, a New Generation of Czechs Seeks a Wider Market," p. AR13; July 18, 2001, Josephine Schmidt, "Filming the Comic and the Absurd in Czech History," p. B2.
People, June 18, 2001, Leah Rozen, review of *Divided We Fall,* p. 31.
Record (Bergen County, NJ), June 8, 2001, Laurence Chollet, review of *Divided We Fall,* p. 7.
San Francisco Chronicle, June 15, 2001, Bob Graham, review of *Divided We Fall,* p. C3.
Scotsman (Edinburgh, Scotland), June 13, 2002, Andrew Eaton, review of *Divided We Fall,* p. 10.
Seattle Post-Intelligencer, June 29, 2001, Sean Axmaker, review of *Divided We Fall,* p. 30.
Star-Ledger (Newark, NJ), June 9, 2001, Bob Campbell, review of *Divided We Fall,* p. 23.
Time, July 23, 2001, Richard Schickel, review of *Divided We Fall,* p. 70.
Time International, September 3, 2001, Richard Schickel, review of *Divided We Fall,* p. 71.

Variety, November 1, 1999, Ken Eisner, review of *Cosy Dens,* p. 91; September 18, 2000, Eddie Cockrell, review of *Divided We Fall,* p. 40; July 9, 2001, "Auds United about Hrebejk's 'Divided,'" p. 38.

Wall Street Journal, June 8, 2001, Joe Morgenstern, review of *Divided We Fall,* p. W1.

Weekend Australian, December 15, 2001, Evan Williams, review of *Divided We Fall,* p. R19.

Winston-Salem Journal (Winston-Salem, NC), August 10, 2001, Mark Burger, review of *Divided We Fall.*

ONLINE

Czech Center New York Web site, http://www.czechcenter.com/ (February 25, 2003), review of *Divided We Fall.*

Czech Television Web site, http://www.czech-tv.cz/ (February 25, 2003), interview with Hrebejk and Petr Jarchovsky.

International Thessaloniki Film Festival Web site, http://www.filmfestival.gr/ (February 25, 2003), profile of Hrebejk.

Kamera.co.uk, http://www.kamera.co.uk/ (February 25, 2003), Nicci Tucker, "A Quick Chat with Jan Hrebejk."

Magic Lantern Web site, http://www.magiclanternpr.com/ (March 4, 2003).

Sofia International Film Festival Web site, http://www.cinema.bg/ (February 25, 2003).*

*   *   *

HSU, Feng-Hsiung 1959-

PERSONAL: Born 1959, in Taiwan; immigrated to United States, 1985. *Education:* Earned a degree in electrical engineering in Taiwan; Carnegie Mellon University, Ph.D., 1989.

ADDRESSES: Office—Hewlett-Packard, Western Research Laboratory, 1501 Page Mill Road, MS 1251, Bldg. 5U, Palo Alto, CA 94304.

CAREER: Computer scientist. T. J. Watson Research Center, International Business Machines (IBM), architect and chip designer; Hewlett-Packard Western Research Lab, Palo Alto, CA, Compaq research scientist.

AWARDS, HONORS: Fredkin Intermediate Prize, 1988; Mephisto Award, 1990; Grace M. Hopper Award, 1991, for contributions in architecture and algorithms for chess machines.

WRITINGS:

Behind Deep Blue: Building the Computer That Defeated the World Chess Champion, Princeton University Press (Princeton, New Jersey), 2002.

SIDELIGHTS: Hsu Feng-Hsiung began a computer chess project as a graduate student at Carnegie Mellon University in 1985. More than two decades later, his project settled the man versus machine debate. Deep Blue, the computer he refined during his time with International Business Machines (IBM), defeated chess master Garry Kasparov in 1997 in a six-game match. Kasparov had defeated Deep Blue in 1996, losing only one of six games. Hsu relates the history of the project from its beginnings in his *Behind Deep Blue: Building the Computer That Defeated the World Chess Champion. Library Journal*'s Joe J. Accardi called it "an intelligent, well-written account of a milestone in the history of computer science."

Hsu immigrated to the United States from Taiwan in 1982 to study at Carnegie Mellon University, where he began his development of the artificial intelligence system that would later be named Deep Blue. Hsu was asked by Dr. Hans Berliner to assist with his Hitech project, which had produced the most sophisticated chess-playing machine to date, but which still fell short of the mark. *Computer User* reviewer James Mathewson wrote that "by 1989, his solution—a computer chess program on a single chip—had eclipsed Berliner's life's work." Hsu was joined by team member Murray Campbell in 1986, and Joe Hoane in 1991, after Hsu and Campbell moved to IBM. The team later grew to include Jerry Brody and C. J. Tan.

A *Kirkus Reviews* contributor noted that Hsu "insists that this was not a case of John Henry versus the steam engine; instead, it was man-as-toolmaker defeating man-as-performer."

In the book Hsu admits that he is not a strong chess player, and, in fact, his favorite game is Go. In designing Deep Blue, he and his team were assisted by a number of grandmasters. During the match with Kasparov, Hsu made the physical moves indicated by Deep Blue, but when Kasparov asked him for Deep Blue's perspective of a game, he notes that he was unable to do so on the same level as Kasparov and the computer. In an open letter posted on *Week in Chess* online, Web site of the London Chess Center, Hsu noted that Kasparov publicly asked for a rematch on several occasions. Hsu "spent a small personal fortune to get the right to the chess chip." His real reason was to answer Kasparov's challenge, but it didn't happen, first because of hesitation by potential sponsors, then because Kasparov decided against playing the new computer in a title match.

Hsu wrote that "the computer chess world had treated us well, and the chess world had been kind to us. There was some apprehension in the chess world when we arrived on the scene. . . . I think I can say fairly that Deep Blue did not destroy chess. There was perhaps even a mini boom in chess popularity as a result of the Deep Blue matches." Hsu said, "We owed greatly our success to computer chess pioneers before us. Finally, I have to give my thanks to Kasparov himself. . . . The two Deep Blue matches were the most exciting experiences in my life, and Kasparov, our worthy opponent, played the central role in the experiences."

Elizabeth Armstrong reviewed *Behind Deep Blue* in *Christian Science Monitor,* saying that "although he is not a writer and English is not his first language, Hsu's enthusiasm and expertise allow him to ease into the role of storyteller, and his personal narrative is colored with details that make, surprisingly, for a thrilling page-turner."

John Derbyshire wrote in the *New York Sun* that Hsu "got my attention and kept it . . . bringing this strange story to life with a fluent, modest style, some side excursions into academic politics, a dash of wit, and riveting accounts of the games—and the gamesmanship—that led up to the May 1997 victory. . . . I finished *Behind Deep Blue* heartened and uplifted at the astonishing things the dedicated human mind can accomplish."

BIOGRAPHICAL AND CRITICAL SOURCES:

PERIODICALS

Booklist, October 15, 2002, Gilbert Taylor, review of *Behind Deep Blue: Building the Computer That Defeated the World Chess Champion,* p. 364.

Christian Science Monitor, November 14, 2002, Elizabeth Armstrong, review of *Behind Deep Blue.*
Computer, February, 2003, Michael J. Lutz, review of *Behind Deep Blue,* p. 82.
Computer User, February, 2003, James Mathewson, review of *Behind Deep Blue,* p. 22.
Kirkus Reviews, September 1, 2002, review of *Behind Deep Blue,* p. 1282.
Library Journal, November 15, 2002, Joe J. Accardi, review of *Behind Deep Blue,* p. 93.
Los Angeles Times Book Review, November 20, 2002, Anthony Day, review of *Behind Deep Blue,* p. E-8.

ONLINE

IBM Research Web site, http://www.research.ibm.com/ (January 6, 2003), biographical information, interview.
New York Sun Online, http://olimu.com/ (October 16, 2002), John Derbyshire, review of *Behind Deep Blue.*
Week in Chess (London Chess Center), http://www.chesscenter.com/ (January 6, 2003), "Open Letter from Feng-Hsiung Hsu."*

*   *   *

HULME, George 1930-

PERSONAL: Born September 25, 1930, in London, England; son of Wilfred (an engineer) and Ethel (a homemaker) Hulme; married Shirley O'Neill, 1958 (marriage ended, 1978); married Jean Butterworth, March 26, 1986; children: (first marriage) Susan, Graeme. *Education:* University of London, B.Sc. (with honors), 1950. *Religion:* Methodist.

ADDRESSES: Home—Willowbank, 1 London Rd., Old Basing, Hampshire RG24 7JE, England; fax: +44-1256-844305. *E-mail*—george.willowbank@btinternet.com.

CAREER: Acorn Anodising Co. Ltd. (metal finisher), London, England, assistant chief chemist, 1954-60; writer and editor, 1960-70; Technical Indexes Ltd. (publisher), Ascot, England, executive editor, 1970-89; IME Ltd. (library software producer), London, project manager, 1989-96; writer, 1996—. Chartered chemist. *Military service:* Royal Air Force, flying officer in Education Branch, 1952-55.

MEMBER: Institute of Information Scientists, Count Basie Society.

AWARDS, HONORS: Meritorious Service Award, Referees Association, for services to association football referees.

WRITINGS:

Mel Tormé: A Chronicle of His Recordings, Books, and Films, McFarland and Co. (Jefferson, NC), 2000.

Writer and director of technical film *Tin Nickel Plating,* 1964. Contributor of discographies, articles, and photographs to periodicals, including *Discophile, Matrix, Jazz Journal, Jazz Monthly,* and *Coda.* Editor, *Matrix,* 1959-77; assistant editor, *Tin and Its Uses,* 1960-66.

WORK IN PROGRESS: A biography of Bobby Hackett; research on various jazz artists.

SIDELIGHTS: George Hulme told *CA:* "My primary motivation for writing is a desire to see full and accurate information on the recording activities of jazz and popular song performers. In my writing process, first I gather information and listen to recordings. Then I make a draft of the information in chronological order. Finally I write the text. Most of it is written 'in my head' before I commit anything to paper. I am inspired by my admiration for the quality of the performances of the musicians who are my subjects."

*   *   *

HULTGREN, Arland J(ohn) 1939-

PERSONAL: Born July 17, 1939, in Muskegon, MI; son of Arnold E. and Ina (Wold) Hultgren; married Carole Ruth Benander, June 26, 1965; children: Peter A., Stephen J., Kristina E. Hultgren Fredrick. *Ethnicity:* "Caucasian." *Education:* Augustana College, Rock Island, IL, B.A. (magna cum laude), 1961; University of Michigan, M.A., 1963; Lutheran School of Theology at Chicago, M.Div. (summa cum laude), 1965; Union Theological Seminary, Th.D., 1971; postdoctoral study at Cambridge University, 1984-85, and University of Uppsala, 1990-91. *Religion:* Lutheran.

ADDRESSES: Home—609 Ryan Ave. W., Roseville, MN 55113. *Office*—Luther Seminary, 2481 Como Ave., St. Paul, MN 55108; fax: 651-641-3345. *E-mail*—ahultgren@luthersem.edu.

CAREER: Ordained minister of Evangelical Lutheran Church in America, 1966; Augustana College, Rock Island, IL, instructor in religion, 1963-65; pastoral assistant at Lutheran church in Tenafly, NJ, 1965-66, assistant pastor, 1966-68; Wagner College, Staten Island, NY, instructor, 1969-71, assistant professor, 1971-75, associate professor of religious studies, 1975-77, teacher in study program in Bregenz, Austria, 1972-73; Luther Theological Seminary, St. Paul, MN, associate professor, 1977-82; Lutheran Northwestern Theological Seminary, St. Paul, associate professor, 1982-86, professor of New Testament, 1986-94; Luther Seminary, St. Paul, professor of New Testament, 1994—. Supply pastor for a Lutheran church in Staten Island, NY, 1975; pastor of Lutheran church in Minneapolis, MN, 1979-80. Guest lecturer at educational institutions, including University of Uppsala, University of Glasgow, University of Aberdeen, and University of St. Andrews; public speaker. Evangelical Lutheran Church in America, member of planning committee for Convocation of Teaching Theologians, 1998-2002; National Council of Churches of Christ in the USA, member of Faith and Order Commission, 2001—. Gustavus Adolphus College, member of board of trustees, 1990-99; University of Minnesota, member of Campus Ministry Council, 1994-97.

MEMBER: Society of Biblical Literature, Studiorum Novi Testamenti Societas, Augustana Heritage Association (member of board of directors, 2000—), Phi Beta Kappa.

AWARDS, HONORS: Saints and Reformers Award, Lutherans Concerned (Twin Cities), 1994; Outstanding Alumni Achievement Award, Augustana College, 1996.

WRITINGS:

The Year of Matthew: Advent-Christmas-Epiphany, Augsburg Publishing House (Minneapolis, MN), 1977.

Jesus and His Adversaries: The Form and Function of the Conflict Stories in the Synoptic Tradition, Augsburg Publishing House (Minneapolis, MN), 1979.

1, 2 Timothy, Titus, Augsburg Publishing House (Minneapolis, MN), 1984.

Paul's Gospel and Mission: The Outlook from His Letter to the Romans, Fortress Press (Philadelphia, PA), 1985.

Christ and His Benefits: Christology and Redemption in the New Testament, Fortress Press (Philadelphia, PA), 1987.

New Testament Christology: A Critical Assessment and Annotated Bibliography, Greenwood Press (Westport, CT), 1988.

Advent-Christmas: Proclamation 4, Fortress Press (Minneapolis, MN), 1989.

(Editor, with Barbara Hall, and contributor) *Christ and His Communities: Essays in Honor of Reginald H. Fuller,* Forward Movement Publications (Cincinnati, OH), 1990.

(Editor, with Donald H. Juel and Jack D. Kingsbury) *All Things New: Essays in Honor of Roy A. Harrisville,* Luther Seminary (St. Paul, MN), 1992.

The Rise of Normative Christianity, Fortress Press (Minneapolis, MN), 1994.

(Editor, with Steven A. Haggmark) *The Earliest Christian Heretics: Readings from Their Opponents,* Fortress Press (Minneapolis, MN), 1996.

(Editor, with Vance L. Eckstrom, and contributor) *The Augustana Heritage: Recollections, Perspectives, and Prospects,* Augustana Heritage Association (Chicago, IL), 1999.

The Parables of Jesus: A Commentary, William B. Eerdmans Publishing (Grand Rapids, MI), 2000.

Author of pamphlets. Creator of audiovisual presentations. Contributor to books, including *Studies in Lutheran Hermeneutics,* edited by John Reumann, Fortress Press (Philadelphia, PA), 1979; *A Primer on Prayer,* edited by Paul R. Sponheim, Fortress Press, 1988; *A Reforming Church: Gift and Task; Essays from a Free Conference,* edited by Charles P. Lutz, Kirk House (Minneapolis, MN), 1995; *The Quest for Jesus and the Christian Faith,* edited by Frederick J. Gaiser, Luther Seminary (St. Paul, MN), 1997; and *The Last Things: Biblical and Theological Perspectives on Eschatology,* edited by Carl E. Braaten and Robert W. Jenson, William B. Eerdmans (Grand Rapids, MI), 2002. Contributor of articles and reviews to periodicals, including *Bible Translator, Lutheran*

Quarterly, Journal of Biblical Literature, Interpretation, Novum Testamentum, New Testament Studies, Lutheran Forum, Lectionary Homiletics, Pro Ecclesia, and *Horizons in Biblical Theology. Word and World,* editor, 1981-88, chair of editorial board, 1996-2002; member of editorial board, *Dialog,* 1979—.

WORK IN PROGRESS: Romans, for William B. Eerdmans (Grand Rapids, MI).

SIDELIGHTS: Arland J. Hultgren told *CA:* "Throughout my career as a biblical scholar, I have sensed a continuing need for writing that is both responsible to the subject matter—meeting the highest critical and scholarly standards—and accessible to a wide range of readers. In every field of scholarly endeavor there is a wide gap between what the scholars themselves know and think and what the general public knows and thinks. That is certainly the case in the study of religion.

"In an increasingly pluralistic world it is particularly incumbent upon specialists in every religious tradition to communicate between themselves and with the general public. Too often religion is understood in terms of deeply held private opinions and emotions. But religion is also a public expression of traditions and values that are shared among adherents in communities of belief and action. In the case of Christianity, Judaism, and Islam there are shared texts and traditions that have had, and continue to have, powerful affects and consequences for both mutual respect and controversies. The study of the basic texts—collected within the Bible in its Hebrew, Christian, and Islamic versions—will go on apace with or without the work of biblical scholars. But scholars have a particular role and responsibility to play in the enterprise and, hopefully, can promote mutual understanding and respect. The biblical scholar therefore has a very public, indeed humanistic, function in a religiously diverse and pluralistic world.

"My work is primarily that of a seminary teacher, educating persons for ministry in the church. The writing that I do actually serves the church more than the general public. But that too is essential for the good of the church and society at large. Churches and their members are served best when the riches of modern biblical scholarship are made available to them. I enjoy writing, even though it does not come easily, and it is a special joy to receive comments from persons who have found my books and articles helpful."

HUME, Christine 1968-

PERSONAL: Born May 21, 1968, in Fairbanks, AK; married Eric Elshtain (a poet), April 30, 1994. *Education:* Pennsylvania State University, B.A., 1990; Columbia University, M.F.A., 1993; University of Denver, Ph.D., 2000.

ADDRESSES: Home—5532 South Shore Dr., No. 7E, Chicago, IL 60637. *E-mail*—chume@titan.iwu.edu.

CAREER: High school teacher of English and humanities, New York, NY, 1993-94; Aims Community College, Greeley, CO, instructor in English and humanities at Greeley and Loveland campuses, 1994-96; University of Denver, Denver, CO, instructor in English, 1996-99; Illinois Wesleyan University, Bloomington, visiting assistant professor of English, 2000-01. Colorado State University, instructor, 1995-96; School of the Art Institute of Chicago, visiting poet, 2000. Gives readings from her works.

MEMBER: Modern Language Association of America, Small Press Distribution, Associated Writing Programs.

AWARDS, HONORS: Writers at Work Award and fellowship, Park City, UT, 1995; Academy of American Poetry Award and Colorado fellowship, 1997; fellow, Rocky Mountain Women's Institute, 1997-98; grant from Colorado Council on the Arts, 1998-99; fellow, Fine Arts Work Center, Provincetown, MA, 1998-99; Helene Wurlitzer Foundation residency in Taos, NM, 2000; Barnard New Women Poets Prize, 2000, for *Musca Domestica.*

WRITINGS:

Musca Domestica (poems), Beacon Press (Boston, MA), 2000.
(Contributor) Claudia Rankine, editor, *Poets in the Twenty-first Century,* Wesleyan University Press (Hanover, NH), 2001.

Work represented in anthologies, including *Best of Writers at Work,* edited by W. Scott Olsen, Pecan Grove Press (San Antonio, TX), 1995; *Anthology of Magazine Verse,* edited by Alan Pater, Monitor Book (Palm Springs, CA), 1996; *Best American Poetry 1997,*

edited by James Tate, Scribner (New York, NY), 1997; and *American Writing: The Next Generation,* edited by Jerry Costanzo, Carnegie-Mellon University Press (Pittsburgh, PA), 2000. Contributor of poems, articles, and reviews to periodicals, including *Denver Review, Epoch, New American Writing, Boston Review, New Republic,* and *Sonora Review. Denver Quarterly,* began as assistant editor, became associate editor, 1996-99.

WORK IN PROGRESS: Fata Morgana Alaska, a collection of poems, short prose, and twelve-second plays.*

*   *   *

HUNNINGS, Vicky 1947-

PERSONAL: Born October 29, 1947, in Rushville, Indiana.; son Robert and Gladys (Rouse) Hunnings; divorced; children: Philip Bradley. *Education:* Nursing degree; postgraduate training as a nurse practioner. *Religion:* Presbyterian *Hobbies and other interests:* Reading, writing.

ADDRESSES: Home—Hilton Head Island, SC. *Agent*—c/o Avalon Books, 160 Madison Ave., 5th Floor, New York, NY 10016. *E-mail*—islanderv@aol.com.

CAREER: Author and nurse. Cardiac and intensive care nurse and family nurse practitioner in Indiana until 1981; nurse in South Carolina, 1981-98.

MEMBER: Sisters in Crime, Island Writer's Network.

AWARDS, HONORS: Hilton Head Monthly award for fiction, 2000.

WRITINGS:

The Bride Wore Blood, Avalon Books (New York, NY), 2002.
Death on a Cellular Level, Avalon Books (New York, NY), 2003.

Contributor of articles to professional journals.

WORK IN PROGRESS: Third book in the "Shark Morgan" series, *Murder 101.*

SIDELIGHTS: Mystery author Vicky Hunnings enjoyed a long and active career in medicine before becoming an author. She spent her early years in Indiana where, as a nurse she worked with cardiac and intensive-care patients. She has also been involved in reproductive health. In 1974 she was one of the first nurses in the country trained as a nurse practitioner. After graduation she established the first rural health clinic in Indiana staffed by a nurse practitioner where she did family practice for seven years. In 1981 Hunnings and her family moved to Hilton Head Island in South Carolina, where she continued her work in medicine until 1998. Her fiction writing began with her retirement from medicine, but was not a completely new activity, as she had written articles on various aspects of nursing for journals and other professional publications. She joined a writers' group in South Carolina and thus, began her move into the mystery genre. Her debut novel, *The Bride Wore Blood,* was published in 2002 by Avalon Books. The second book in the series, *Death on a Cellular Level,* was released in August 2003.

Set in the Hilton Head area, *The Bride Wore Blood* is the first book in a series. Hunnings's novel begins with a dramatic murder in a small community, as businessman Marcus DeSilva is shot dead on the steps of the church on his wedding day. Nothing about the incident is clear: was it an accidental shooting by a careless hunter or a premeditated murder? An array of motivated suspects keeps the detectives busy, as does a growing romantic interest between the new widow and Shark Morgan, the chief detective on the case. In a review of the novel in the *Beaufort Gazette,* Keith Wells remarked that this is more than a mystery, it is also a study of love that is believable and full of complexity. Critics have noted the well-drawn nature of the characters' relationships and the skillful unfolding of the plot. A second work featuring Shark Morgan, *Death on a Cellular Level,* was issued in 2003.

BIOGRAPHICAL AND CRITICAL SOURCES:

PERIODICALS

Beaufort Gazette, September 17, 2002, Keith Wells, review of *The Bride Wore Blood.*

Booklist, August, 2002, Sue O'Brien, review of *The Bride Wore Blood,* p. 1931.
Library Journal, August, 2002, Rex Klett, review of *The Bride Wore Blood,* p. 150.

ONLINE

Avalon Books Web site, http://www.avalonbooks.com/ (December 16, 2002), "Vicky Hunnings."
Palladium-Item Online (Richmond, IN), http://www.pal-item.com/ (December 12, 2002), "Vicky Hunnings."
Vicky Hunnings Home Page, http://www.vicky hunnings.com (December 12, 2002).

*   *   *

HUNT, Wayne Henry
    See HUNT, Wolf Robe

*   *   *

HUNT, Wolf Robe 1905-1977

PERSONAL: Also known as Wayne Henry Hunt; alternate Native American name, Kewa; born October 14, 1905, in Acoma Pueblo, New Mexico Territory (now New Mexico); died December 10, 1977. *Education:* Attended University of Chicago; studied with Carl Redin and Frank Von der Laucken.

CAREER: Painter and jewelry designer. Operator of various galleries in Oklahoma, beginning 1937; dancer, dance interpreter, and leader of a dance troupe. Also lecturer and writer. *Exhibitions:* Work represented in solo and group shows, including exhibitions at Philbrook Museum of Art, Heard Museum, American Indian Exposition of 1935, U.S. Department of the Interior, and Mayfest International Festival.

AWARDS, HONORS: Named Oklahoma Indian of the Year, Council of American Indians, 1973; Waite Phillips Trophy, Philbrook Museum of Art, 1974.

WRITINGS:

(With Helen Rushmore; and illustrator) *The Dancing Horses of Acoma, and Other Acoma Indian Stories* (juvenile), World Publishing (Cleveland, OH), 1963.

BIOGRAPHICAL AND CRITICAL SOURCES:

BOOKS

St. James Guide to Native North American Artists, St. James Press (Detroit, MI), 1998, pp. 248-249.

PERIODICALS

Tulsa World, May 5, 1977; December 10, 1977.*

* * *

HUNTER, Karen 1945-

PERSONAL: Born 1945. *Education:* Attended Drew University, B.A. (English literature).

ADDRESSES: Office—New York Daily News, 450 West 33rd St., New York, NY 10001. *E-mail*—khuntercolumn@aol.com.

CAREER: Writer and journalist. Legal Outreach, New York, NY, instructor; began as a sports writer for *Daily News,* New York, 1988, then became a staff reporter, business writer, and entertainment writer.

New York University, New York, NY, instructor, 1996-98; Hunter College of the City University of New York, visiting assistant professor, 2002—.

AWARDS, HONORS: Pulitzer Prize (as part of *Daily News* editorial team), 1999, for best editorial writing; National Association of Black Journalists award, for series on rap music; awards from Associated Press, Deadline Club, and Sigma Delta Chi.

WRITINGS:

(With L. L. Cool J.) *I Make My Own Rules,* St. Martin's Press (New York, NY), 1997.
(With Queen Latifah) *Ladies First: Revelations of a Strong Woman,* William Morrow (New York, NY), 1999.
(With Mason Betha) *Revelations: There's a Light after the Lime,* Pocket Books (New York, NY), 2001.
(With Al Sharpton) *Al on America,* Dafina (New York, NY), 2002.
(With Wendy Williams) *Wendy's Got the Heat,* Atria Books (New York, NY), 2003.

SIDELIGHTS: Karen Hunter is a journalist and the first black woman to write a news column for the *New York Daily News.* Hunter collaborated with a number of celebrities in writing their books, including entertainer Queen Latifah. In *Ladies First: Revelations of a Strong Woman,* the actress and rapper recalls her difficult childhood, rise to stardom, personal losses, and addictions. She relates how her faith in God and the support of family and friends helped her turn her life around. A *Publishers Weekly* contributor called the book "less a biography than a motivational tract." Ginger Schwartz wrote in *School Library Journal* that *Ladies First* "will inspire and motivate young women of any background to discover who they are."

Hunter's collaboration with the Reverend Al Sharpton produced *Al on America,* published at the time Sharpton announced his candidacy for the 2004 Democratic presidential race. *Black Issues Book Review* contributor E. Assata Wright commented that "like every other book in this category, *Al on America* is long on political platitudes and short on realistic public policy. Throughout the book, the reverend proudly flaunts his old-school brand of liberalism. Although he steers clear of specific campaign promises, he endorses a number of broad principles that come straight from the most marginalized corners of the Democratic Party."

Sharpton describes how he was groomed by his mentors, Adam Clayton Powell, Jr., Jesse Jackson, and James Browne. The book details what Sharpton considers his successes and his failures, the latter including his support of Tawana Brawley, who in 1987 claimed she had been raped by a gang of white men, a charge that was later proved to be a hoax. Sharpton comes across as the controversial figure he is, a supporter of the Million-Man March, a man who, he says, was tricked by Yasser Arafat into shaking hands for a photo op, a man who served three months in jail for protesting the U.S. Navy's bombing exercises in Vieques, Puerto Rico, and a man who, in this book, alleges that former President Bill Clinton duped black Americans.

"For those who have tracked Sharpton's evolution over the years, it is almost endearing to watch him struggle to adjust to middle age and the middle class," wrote Adam Nagourney in the *New York Times Book Review*. "There is Sharpton, the father of teenage girls, lamenting the depravity of the kids today. . . . And there is Sharpton, embarking on his presidential campaign and sounding like a presidential candidate, right down to lists of policy proposals. We are not, thankfully, talking *Earth in the Balance* here, but if you ever wanted to find out what Sharpton thinks about globalization, you'll find it in this book." *Booklist*'s Vernon Ford felt that "readers interested in politics and this controversial figure will enjoy reading Sharpton's own views on his platform."

BIOGRAPHICAL AND CRITICAL SOURCES:

PERIODICALS

Black Issues Book Review, November-December, 2002, E. Assata Wright, review of *Al on America,* p. 49.

Booklist, January 1, 1999, Mike Tribby, review of *Ladies First: Revelations of a Strong Woman,* p. 798; October 15, 2002, Vernon Ford, review of *Al on America,* p. 384.

Chicago Tribune, October 16, 2002, Clarence Page, review of *Al on America.*

Kirkus Reviews, September 1, 2002, review of *Al on America,* p. 1290.

New York Times Book Review, December 1, 2002, Adam Nagourney, review of *Al on America,* p. 29.

Publishers Weekly, December 14, 1998, review of *Ladies First,* p. 69; August 26, 2002, review of *Al on America,* p. 54.

School Library Journal, May, 1999, Ginger J. Schwartz, review of *Ladies First,* p. 161.

Washington Times, November 15, 2002, Deborah Simmons, review of *Al on America.*

ONLINE

National Review Online, http://www.nationalreview.com/ (October 8, 2002), Rod Dreher, review of *Al on America.*

New York Observer Online, http://www.observer.com/ (January 6, 2003), Baz Dreisinger, review of *Al on America.*

I

IQBAL, Muhammad 1877-1938

PERSONAL: Born November 9, 1877, in Sialkot, Punjab, India; died April 21, 1938, in Lahore, Pakistan. *Education:* Government College, Lahore, degree in philosophy, 1899; attended Trinity College, Cambridge, 1905; studied law in London; University of Munich, Ph.D. (philosophy), 1907. *Religion:* Islam.

CAREER: Poet, essayist, and philosopher. Elected to Punjab legislature, 1926; Muslim League, president, 1930, lobbied for separate Muslim state in northwest India; lawyer in private practice in Lahore. Government College, Lahore, lecturer in history and philosophy.

AWARDS, HONORS: Knighted in 1922.

WRITINGS:

The Development of Metaphysics in Iran, 1908.
Asrar-i khudi, 1915, published as *The Secrets of the Self,* 1920.
Rumuz-i-bekhudi, 1918, published as *The Mysteries of Selflessness,* 1953.
A Voice from the East: The Urdu Poetry of Iqbal, 1922.
Payam-i-mashriq, 1923, published as *The Tulip of Sinai,* 1947.
Bang-i-dara, 1924, published as *Complaint and Answer,* 1955.
Zabur-i ajam, 1927, published as *Persian Psalms,* 1948.
The Reconstruction of Religious Thought in Islam, 1934.

Javid-namah, 1932, published as *The Pilgrimage of Eternity,* 1961 and *Javid-Nama,* 1966.
Bal-i Jibril, 1936.
Pas cha bayad kard ay aqwam-i sharq, 1936.
Musafir, 1936.
Zarb-i kalim, 1937.
Armaghan-i hijaz, 1938.
Urdu Poems from Iqbal, 1955.
Islam and Ahmadism, Academy, Islamic Research & Publications (Lucknow, Pakistan), 1974.

SIDELIGHTS: Muhammad Iqbal, born to a staunchly Muslim family, was known as much for his politics as for his poetry and philosophy. Iqbal, with professional interests spanning from teaching to law and politics, is considered Pakistan's spiritual founder. As an *Encyclopedia of World Biography* writer said: "His statement in his presidential address that the 'final destiny' of Indian Moslems was to have a 'consolidated Northwest Indian Moslem state' is regarded as one of the earliest expressions of the idea of Pakistan." Iqbal, however, argued not for a separate nation, but for an independent state within India. Though better known for his politics, his philosophical reflections on the self, often expressed in his poetry, have been equally influential.

Iqbal attended Government College, Lahore, earning his degree in philosophy in 1899. He taught there after his graduation, experimenting with poetry he wrote in Urdu. Here, he began to gain literary and academic admiration for spiritual, songlike poetry that frequently expresses a fervent Indian nationalism. His politics changed considerably, however, after studying for his doctorate at Cambridge University in England. Between 1905 and 1908 he studied the philosophies of such influential Western thinkers as Friedrich Nietzsche and Henri Bergson, simultaneously admiring their ideas while disdaining their Western culture for its self-indulgence. He traveled throughout Europe, visiting German universities in particular, closely studying the works of prominent intellectuals. Rejecting nationalism as fundamentally Western, Iqbal embraced Islam as the Muslim solution in India.

Iqbal, viewing Islam as central to uniting Muslims regardless of boundaries, drew rebuke for viewing everything in terms of East and West. Yusuf Ali lectured in *Essays by Divers Hands* in 1938: "The contrast between the East and the West, much to the spiritual and moral disadvantage of the West, is almost an obsession in Iqbal. It colours his views on many questions, social, political, and economic." In Iqbal's first collection of Urdu poems, *Bang-i dara,* he cautions Indians about Western governance and law. His readership reflected this polarity. Muslim and non-Muslim readers in India knew Iqbal best for his poetry, while Western audiences studied his prose in such works as *The Development of Metaphysics in Persia* and *The Reconstruction of Religious Thought in Islam.*

The ideas Iqbal adopted while in England emerge in several of his longer poems, particularly *Asrar-i Khudi* and *Rumuz-i-Bekhudi.* For Iqbal to appeal to a wider readership both inside and outside India, he wrote these poems in Persian and not in his standard Urdu. Both poems underscore the absolute necessity of self-development, through which the individual would eventually achieve perfection. Much to Iqbal's dismay, critics often compared his "Perfect Man" concept to Nietzsche's exploration of the Superman. Iqbal's theory, however, incorporated religion whereas Nietzsche's society is godless.

Iqbal, while attacking Western decadence, also criticized the mystic approach to Islam as practiced in India and believed that without an overhaul, Muslims would continue to deteriorate politically. Iqbal, calling for Muslim self-determination, believed individual growth benefited society as well. Greed and material pursuit, however, deteriorated the self. Iqbal also believed religion shaped statehood to a greater degree than geography or ethnicity. Muslim activism, he said, was good for society. Ali also proclaimed in his 1938 lecture: "Courage, Power, Action are the Ideals [Iqbal] would point to. Swiftness, forcefulness, unflinching assertion of Personality are the watchwords which he would din into the ears of a lethargic world."

Iqbal became a more public character, earning recognition for his poetic and philosophical works. In 1922 he was knighted for his literary contributions. Turning increasingly toward politics, he was elected to the Punjab legislature and became president of the Muslim League. During his presidential address to the league, he called for a separate Muslim state in northwest India and he emphasizes this in his major English work, *The Reconstruction of Religious Thought in Islam.* These ideas resonated deeply within India in the early twentieth century. As one writer in the *Encyclopedia of World Literature in the Twentieth Century* said: "His message of self-reliance and Islamic activism both shaped and reflected the Indian nationalist movement during the 1920s and 1930s, especially for Muslims, who look upon him even today as their leading intellectual figure of the 20th century."

Iqbal became more convinced the Hindu majority would swallow up Muslims in India were the country to gain independence from Great Britain. He began to publicly support Mohammad Ali Jinnah as the most appropriate leader of India's Muslims. Later, Iqbal returned to his native language, Urdu, and wrote the collection of poems, *Bal-i Jibril* in 1935, followed by *Zarb-i Kalim. Bal-i Jibril* contains much of his best-known poetry, although critics said the collection lacks the power and passion of his earlier works. Nonetheless, he still draws acclaim as a great Persian poet, as well as the most famous poet of the twentieth century among Urdu speakers in India and Pakistan.

BIOGRAPHICAL AND CRITICAL SOURCES:

BOOKS

Bausani, Alessandro, *Crescent and Green: A Miscellany of Writings on Pakistan,* Cassell & Company (London, England), 1955, pp. 131-141.
Encyclopedia of World Biography, Gale (Detroit, MI), 1998.
Encyclopedia of World Literature in the Twentieth Century, St. James Press (Detroit, MI), 1999.
Forster, E. M., *Two Cheers for Democracy,* Harcourt Brace Jovanovich, Inc., 1951, pp. 288-291.

Hasan, Masudul, *Life of Iqbal: General Account of His Life,* Ferozsons (Lahore, Pakistan), 1978.

Hasan, Mumtaz, *Tribute to Iqbal,* Iqbal Academy Pakistan (Lahore, Pakistan), 1982.

Hussain, Riaz, *The Politics of Iqbal: A Study of His Political Thoughts and Actions,* Islamic Book Service (Lahore, Pakistan), 1977.

Iqbal, Muhammad, *Mementos of Iqbal,* All-Pakistan Islamic Education Congress (Lahore, Pakistan), 1976.

Malik, Hafeez, *Iqbal: Poet-Philosopher of Pakistan,* Columbia University Press (New York, NY), 1971.

Munawwar, Muhammad, *Iqbal: Poet-Philosopher of Islam,* Islamic Book Foundation (Lahore, Pakistan), 1982.

Qadir, Abdul, *Iqbal: The Great Poet of Islam,* Sang-e-Meel Publications (Lahore, Pakistan), 1975.

Singh, Iqbal, *The Ardent Pilgrim: An Introduction to the Life and Work of Mohammed Iqbal,* Longmans, Green (New York, NY), 1951.

Tributes to Iqbal, Sangemeel Publications (Lahore, Pakistan), 1977.

Twentieth-Century Literary Criticism, Volume 28, Gale (Detroit, MI), 1988.

Vahid, Syed Abdul, *Iqbal: His Art and Thought,* John Murray (London, England), 1959.

Zakaria, Rafiq, *Iqbal: The Poet and the Politician,* Viking (New York, NY), 1993.

PERIODICALS

Asian Review, April, 1961, Ya'acob Tunku, "Homage to Iqbal," pp. 199-200.

Essays by Divers Hands, 1940, A. Yusuf Ali, "Doctrine of Human Personality in Iqbal's Poetry," pp. 89-105.

Hibbert Journal, July, 1958, R. Harré, "Iqbal: A Reformer of Islamic Philosophy," pp. 333-339.

Indian P.E.N., February, 1975, Gurbachan Singh Talib, "Iqbal's Poetic Achievement: An Estimate," pp. 6-9.

Religious Studies, September, 1982, Mohammed Maruf, "Allama Iqbal on 'Immortality,'" pp. 373-378; September, 1983, Mohammed Maruf, "Iqbal's Concept of God: An Appraisal," pp. 375-383.

Review of Metaphysics, June, 1956, Robert Whittemore, "Iqbal's Pantheism," pp. 681-699.

Times Literary Supplement, March 15, 1934, "Islam and the Modern World," p. 178.*

ISENBERG, Jane Frances 1940-

PERSONAL: Born August 27, 1940, in Paterson, NJ; daughter of Hymen and Marian Alma (Spitz) Siegendorf; married Donald Windham Isenberg, August 19, 1962 (died June 1985); married Phil Thompkins; children: Rachel, Daniel. *Education:* Vassar College, B.A. (English), 1962; Southern Connecticut State College, M.A. (English), 1971; New York University, Ph.D. (applied linguistics), 1993.

ADDRESSES: Agent—c/o Author Mail, HarperCollins Publishers, 10 East 53rd Street, New York, NY 10022.

CAREER: James Hillhouse High School, New Haven, CT, teacher, 1962-69; South Central Community College, New Haven, CT, teacher, 1969-77; Outreach Program Human Resources Administration, New Haven, director, 1976-77; Goddard College, Plainfield, VT, teacher, 1975-77; English Hudson Country Community College, Jersey City, NJ, associate professor, 1979—. Yale University, teacher, 1977, 1978; Stevens Institute of Technology, Hoboken, NJ, teacher, 1982. Member, board of trustees of Jewish Family and Counseling Services, Bayonne, NJ, 1994—; Hudson School, Hoboken, NJ, 1979-89; and Stevens Cooperative School, Hoboken, 1978-84.

MEMBER: Modern Language Association, National Council of Teachers of English, Hudson County Community College Professional Association, Hudson Reading Council, Language Educators Applying Reflection Now, New Jersey Education Association, New Jersey Reading Association, New York Metropolitan Association for Developmental Education; New York State TESOL.

AWARDS, HONORS: James N. Britton Award, National Council of Teachers of English, 1994.

WRITINGS:

Going by the Book: The Role of Popular Classroom Chronicles in the Professional Development of Teachers, Bergin and Garvey (Westport, CT), 1994.

The M Word, Avon (New York, NY), 1999.
Death in a Hot Flash, Avon (New York, NY), 2000.
Mood Swings to Murder, Avon (New York, NY), 2000.
Midlife Can Be Murder, Avon (New York, NY), 2001.
Out of Hormone's Way, Avon (New York, NY), 2002.

WORK IN PROGRESS: "The Proof Is in the Patch," a mini-mystery to be published in the anthology *Motherhood Is Murder.* Also a sixth "Bel Barret" mystery in which a fellow professor is murdered.

SIDELIGHTS: Jane Frances Isenberg has enjoyed a long career in teaching. She has taught on both the high school and the community-college level in several different states. She has also written several books, all of them containing reflections of her professional teaching career. Her first book, *Going by the Book,* is a memoir of her teaching experiences when she was fresh out of college. Her subsequent books have stretched the truth of her experience, however. Although Isenberg calls on her experiences of teaching community-college students in this second series of books, they are purely creations of her imagination. They are all murder mysteries in which Bel Barrett, a menopausal professor of English, has a knack for solving crimes.

In 1962 Isenberg had just graduated from Vassar and had accepted a job as an English teacher at a local high school in urban New Haven, Connecticut. Her first years of teaching were both difficult and rewarding, and Isenberg was glad to have books written by other teachers who had similar experiences. These works acted as mentors for her, and she devotes a chapter to each in *Going by the Book.* These influential books include *Teacher,* by Sylvia Ashton-Warner; *Up the down Staircase,* by Bel Kaufman; *To Sir, with Love,* by E. R. Braithwaite; *How Children Fail,* by John Holt; and *Thirty-six Children,* by Herbert Kohl.

In addition, Isenberg shares her own classroom experiences: her fears, her doubts, and frustrations as well as her reflections after having re-read these same books many years later as a veteran teacher. Some of the concepts that helped her the most were Ashton-Warner's suggestion that rigid planning is not necessarily a key to success. From Braithwaite, she learned to become aware of racism. Holt taught her to take time to get to know her students in order to understand why they might not be doing so well in the classroom.

She was inspired to become an educational activist after reading Kohl. Despite the fact that Bonnie Ericson, in an *English Journal* review of *Going by the Book,* did not concur with all of Isenberg's conclusions, she highly recommended the book to all teachers because "teacher narrative authors serve a vital role as change agents."

In a more entertaining vein, Isenberg has also written several mystery novels. Her protagonist sleuth Bel Barrett, who, according to Isenberg on her Web site, has "never been able to resist an underdog in distress" and thus often finds herself involved in solving murders. Isenberg has made her female protagonist a fifty-something who is out-of-the-closet menopausal. When asked by Julia P. Allen, in a interview for the online publication *A Friend Indeed,* why she made her female lead so obviously menopausal, Isenberg replied that sometimes she and her friends want to see women in literature with whom they can identify. "The passage that is midlife is significant, and to ignore it or pretend it is not happening is as ludicrous as ignoring adolescence in a teenager." She went on to add: "Midlife is certainly not unspeakable in reality and it should not be so in fiction."

Each of the five mysteries have titles that not only insinuate murder but also symptoms of menopause. In the first, 1999's *The M Word,* college president Altagracia Garcia drops dead at a school function after eating some of the food offered at the affair. A culinary student is the accused murderer, but Bel Barrett cannot accept this. When the student asks Bel to help him, she cannot resist, even when in the midst of the investigation she discovers that someone is trying to kill her.

In *Death in a Hot Flash* Bel agrees to teach writing to a class of future undertakers. One night her co-teacher, Vinny the undertaker, does not show up. Bel later finds out that he has been murdered and once again become involved in finding the killer. *Mood Swings to Murder,* also published in 2000, and covers the death of a Frank Sinatra wannabe. Bel is distracted by an adult son who returns to live at home and an adult daughter who comes home pregnant. However, this will not stop her from solving the crime.

Midlife Can Be Murder finds Bel involved in what some people are trying to claim was an accident at an indoor rock-climbing wall. However, former student

Ashley Roberts believes it was murder. Bel becomes more involved that she wants as she uncovers corporate espionage and some unethical practices at a new Internet company. In 2002 Isenberg's *Out of Hormone's Way* was published. A *Publishers Weekly* reviewer stated that in this novel watching Bel deal with some very interesting personal problems is "nearly as compelling as watching her unravel the mystery. In this book, one of Bel's students is murdered while out on a kayaking trip that Bel is overseeing."

On her Web site, Isenberg commented on her protagonist, Bel Barrett. Is Bel her alter ego? Isenberg maintained that Bel is both her and not her. Some of Bel's strengths, Isenberg stated, are reflections of some of her strongest female friends. Her weaknesses, however, Isenberg identified with. "Her vices," Isenberg added, like "overworking, over worrying, and over eating, are mine alone."

BIOGRAPHICAL AND CRITICAL SOURCES:

PERIODICALS

English Journal, March, 1995, Bonnie Ericson, review of *Going by the Book,* pp. 83-84.
Publishers Weekly, August 5, 2002, review of *Out of Hormone's Way,* pp. 57-58.

ONLINE

A Friend Indeed, http://www.afriendindeed.ca/ (December 9, 2002), Julia P. Allen, "A Conversation with Jane Isenberg."
Jane Isenberg Web site,, http:www.janeisenberg.com (December 9, 2002).*

*   *   *

ISHII, Sogo 1957-

PERSONAL: Born Toshihiro Ishii, January 15, 1957, in Hakata, Fukuoka Prefecture, Japan.

ADDRESSES: Agent—c/o Suncent CinemaWorks, 1-12-9 6th Floor Hiratsuka, Shinagawa-ku, Tokyo 142-0051, Japan; fax: +81-3-5749-2341.

CAREER: Director, screenwriter, and punk musician. Director of films, including *Koko dai panikku* (also known as *Panic High School* and *Panic in High School*), 1978; *Totsugeki! Hakata Gurentai* (also known as *Charge! Hooligans of Hakata*), 1978; *Hachijyu-Hachi-Man Bun no Ichi no Kodoku* (also known as *Solitude of One Divided by 880,000*), 1978; *Hashiru,* 1979; *Kuruizaki sanda rodo* (also known as *Crazy Thunder Road*), Toei, 1980; *Anarchy '80 Ishin* (promotional film for the punk band Anarchy), 1981; *Shuffle,* 1981; *Bakuretsu toshi* (also known as *Burst City*), 1982; *Stop Jap* (music video for the punk band The Stalin), 1982; *Norikoto: Toriaezu no Taiwa No. 1,* 1982; *Ajia no gyakushu* (also known as *Asia Strikes Back;* concert video for the punk band Sogo Ishii and the Bacillus Army), 1983; *Gyakufunsha kazoku* (also known as *The Crazy Family*), 1984; *Isseifubi Sepia: Genzai Ga Suki Desu* (title means "Isseifubi Sepia: We Love the Present"; music video for the pop band Isseifubi Sepia), 1984; *The Roosterz: Paranoic Live* (concert video for the punk band The Roosterz), 1984; *The Stalin: For Never, Last Live Zessan Kaisanchu* (concert video for the punk band The Stalin), 1984; *1/2 Mensch* (also known as *1/2 Man* and *Hanbun ningen;* film of the 1985 Japanese tour of the German noise band Einstürzende Neubauten), 1986; *Shiatsu Oja* (also known as *The Master of Shiatsu*), KSS Inc., 1989; *Private 8mm Film Live Diary 81-86,* 1989; *J-Movie Wars: Tokyo Blood* (made-for-television movie), 1992; (and editor, with Hiroshi Matsuo) *Enjeru dasuto* (also known as *Angel Dust*), 1994; *Mizu no naka no hachigatsu* (also known as *August in the Water*), 1995; *Yume no ginga* (also known as *Labyrinth of Dreams,* 1997; *Gojoe senki* (also known as *Gojoe* and *Gojo reisen ki*), 2000; and *Electric Dragon 80,000 V,* Suncent CinemaWorks, 2000. Member of the punk band Sogo Ishii and the Bacillus Army, with Toshiyuki "Kiku" Shibayama, c.1983, and of the noise band Mach 1.67, with Tadanobu Asano and Masatoshi Nagase, c. late 1990s—. Sogo Ishii and the Bacillus Army released one album, *Asia Strikes Back.*

WRITINGS:

SCREENPLAYS; ALSO DIRECTOR

Shuffle, based on the manga *Run* by Katsuhiro Otomo, 1981.
Gyakufunsha kazoku (also known as *The Crazy Family*), 1984.

1/2 Mensch (also known as *1/2 Man* and *Hanbun nin-gen*; film of 1985 Japanese tour of German noise band Einstürzende Neubauten), 1986.

(With Yorozu Ikuta) *Enjeru Dasuto* (also known as *Angel Dust*), 1994.

Mizu no naka no hachigatsu (also known as *August in the Water*), 1995.

Yume no ginga (also known as *Labyrinth of Dreams*), based on a novel by Kyusaku Yumeno, 1997.

Gojoe senki (also known as *Gojoe* and *Gojoe reisen ki*), Sento Takenori and Suncent CinemaWorks, 2000.

Electric Dragon 80,000 V, Suncent CinemaWorks, 2000.

SIDELIGHTS: Japanese writer and director Sogo Ishii is famous for his ability to mix his two loves, punk music and film, to create imaginative, energetic pieces of art. As a teenager in the 1970s, Ishii was part of the punk rock revolution that was then underway in his native northern Kyushu; he took up film directing as a college student in Tokyo. While in college, Ishii used equipment borrowed from his university to make numerous shorts and the feature-length films *Panic High School* and *Crazy Thunder Road.* These films "inevitably carried Ishii's affinity with the punk scene on their sleeves, featuring the struggles of misfits and underdogs against established society," Tom Mes explained on *Midnight Eye. Crazy Thunder Road,* Ishii's graduation project, was so impressive that a major studio bought it and distributed it to theaters across Japan.

After graduating, Ishii made films about the punk scene, like the notable *Burst City,* and also made concert and promotional films for Japan's hottest punk bands, including Anarchy and The Stalin. Ishii later moved into more conventional films, such as the thriller *Angel Dust* about a serial murderer who operates in the crowded, rush-hour Tokyo subways, but with Ishii's more recent film *Electric Dragon 80,000 V* he returned to his punk roots. This film has been described as "a wild ride" and "heavy duty craziness," by David Rooney of *Variety* and Rob Ferraz of *Exclaim!,* respectively. The film's protagonist, Dragon Eye Morrison, developed dragon-like powers after being electrocuted as a child. His nemesis, Thunderbolt Buddha, was struck by lightning as a child, and his electrical experience has also left him deeply changed. In the film's climactic scene, which, Rooney noted, like the rest of the film is "cut at breakneck speed and shot with convulsive, multiangle dexterity," the two fight for dominance on the rooftops of Tokyo.

BIOGRAPHICAL AND CRITICAL SOURCES:

BOOKS

Contemporary Theatre, Film, and Television, Volume 35, Gale (Detroit, MI), 2001.

Singer, Michael, editor, *Michael Singer's Film Directors,* ninth international edition, Lone Eagle Publishing (Los Angeles, CA), 1992.

PERIODICALS

Independent (London, England), January 7, 1999, Anthony Quinn, review of *Angel Dust,* p. 9.

New Statesman, February 21, 1986, John Coleman, review of *The Crazy Family,* p. 30.

New York Times, February 11, 1986, Janet Maslin, review of *The Crazy Family,* p. 26; January 24, 1997, Stephen Holden, review of *Angel Dust,* p. B20; June 13, 1997, Peter M. Nichols, review of *Angel Dust,* p. B16.

Progressive, March, 1986, Michael H. Seitz, review of *The Crazy Family,* p. 40.

Star-Ledger (Newark, NJ), January 30, 1997, Bob Campbell, review of *Angel Dust,* p. 63.

Variety, March 6, 1985, review of *Gyakufunsha kasoku,* p. 249; March 5, 2001, David Rooney, review of *Electric Dragon 80,000 V,* p. 46.

ONLINE

Exclaim!, http://www.exclaim.ca/ (September 21, 2001), Rob Ferraz, review of *Electric Dragon 80,000 V.*

Midnight Eye, http://www.midnighteye.com/ (April 11, 2003), Tom Mes, "The Concert Films of Sogo Ishii."*

*   *   *

ISRAEL-CURLEY, Marcia

PERSONAL: Born in NY; married Larry Israel (an aeronautical engineer), 1947 (died 1991); married Jim Curley, December 28, 1995; children: (first marriage) Judy, Jane. *Politics:* Republican.

ADDRESSES: Agent—c/o Overlook Press, One Overlook Drive, Woodstock, NY 12498.

CAREER: Author, model, bookkeeper, buyer, and entrepreneur; University of Southern California, adjunct professor. President Ronald Reagan's Committee for Small and Minority Business Ownership, chair; Yale Cancer Center, member of board of directors; Cedars-Sinai Medical Center, member of board of directors.

AWARDS, HONORS: Named *Los Angeles Times* Woman of the Year, 1964; University of Southern California Entrepreneur Award, 1983; decorated by U.S. Navy and by the government of France.

WRITINGS:

Defying the Odds: Sharing the Lessons I Learned as a Pioneer Entrepreneur, Overlook Press (Woodstock, NY), 2002.

SIDELIGHTS: The life of Marcia Israel-Curley is a modern-day rag-to-riches story. She was born into poverty, graduated from high school at age fifteen, found work in New York City, then moved to Los Angeles, and after many decades of hard work, found herself the owner of 104 fashion stores. Along the way, she won many awards for her efforts, and in 2002 she wrote a book, *Defying the Odds: Sharing the Lessons I Learned as a Pioneer Entrepreneur,* that fills in all the details of her illustrious career.

Israel-Curley was born on a farm outside New York City. When her father abandoned his family, he left his wife with no means of caring for herself and her four daughters. For awhile, Israel-Curley's mother was dependent on the generosity of members of her extended family and other sources of charity. She was an enterprising woman, however, and soon moved her family to New York City, where she took a job as a janitor. Meanwhile, her daughter excelled at school, especially in business courses, and after graduating from high school Israel-Curley found a job as a part time model and bookkeeper. Several years later she was courted by a Hollywood movie studio and a friend encouraged her to go to Los Angeles in order to pursue a career as an actress—a career that Israel-Curley eventually turned down. Instead, she became a buyer for Mayson's, a Los Angeles department store.

Defying the Odds is an autobiographical account of Israel-Curley's climb to fame, a rise that culminated in being named Entrepreneur of the Year by the University of Southern California, an experience that Israel-Curley has referred to as one of the biggest highlights of her life. The entrepreneur aspect of the story begins modestly in the late 1940s. Israel-Curley was looking for a place she could call her own. She had always wanted to own a store. With her background in fashion and merchandising, she thought she had a sense of what customers were looking for. The only storefront she could afford at that time, was a tiny retail space next to a movie theatre on Whittier Boulevard in East Los Angeles—not one of the more glamorous areas of town. However, she took it and named the store Judy's, for two reasons: she admired the actress Judy Garland and the store was so narrow, only seven feet wide, that the sign in front could only hold six characters. The name Judy's fit just right.

Judy's was a specialty store, one of the first of its kind. The merchandise targeted young women who were looking for clothes that were markedly different from the things that their mothers were wearing. Although this kind of store prevails in most shopping districts today, in the late 1940s, it was a novelty. The store was a hit. Israel-Curley had taken a gamble and won. In the *Beverly Hills Courier* online, Connie Martinson described the interior of the early store: "The walls became like an art gallery of clothes, where customers could visualize the mix and match before their eyes." The store became more than just a place to buy cool clothes. It also became a gathering place. Young women often brought their boyfriends with them, making an event out of the shopping excursion.

Judy's stores eventually expanded as Israel-Curley opened shops in California malls. Major American publications such as *Women's Wear Daily,* the *New York Times,* and the *Wall Street Journal* ran frequent stories on the business and the entrepreneur behind the Judy's stores. Israel-Curley was making more than a fashion statement. She was quickly becoming a role model for all small businesses. A reporter for *News Max* online described Israel-Curley's story as that of "a businesswoman with vision and an uncompromising work ethic who let nothing stand in her way."

Israel-Curley had her share of challenges. As a *Publishers Weekly* reviewer pointed out, the author "opens her memoir with her doctor telling her the tumor in her lymph nodes is malignant." This horrifying event was the stimulus for Israel-Curley to write her autobiography. She wanted to record the exciting adventure she had lived. A few years later, she lost her husband to cancer. This inspired her to give a major portion of her profits to charity, including a very generous gift to the Yale Cancer Center, which has a laboratory named in her honor.

She grew her business to the point where she had two thousand employees. Then, in 1989, Israel-Curley sold all her stores to Law's Knitting Company, a firm with roots in Hong Kong. She was later asked by the dean of the business school at the University of Southern California to teach a class on business. The dean saw to it that she was tutored for two and one half years and then given the title of adjunct professor. Israel-Curley's business experience, her courage, and her innovative spirit more than made up for the lack of a college degree. The dean had heard her speak the night she accepted the university's award as Entrepreneur of the Year. He told her later that his students needed to hear what she had to say.

When asked by a writer for *Westside Life* online why she wrote her book, Israel-Curley replied: "I realized [upon learning that I had cancer] that all the things I learned building a business in a man's world, without a formal business education, would be lost. All the experiences of growth, relations with the employees, customers and vendors would be gone." A *Kirkus Reviews* writer summed it up nicely: "Israel-Curley was a rare bird, and it paid off handsomely."

BIOGRAPHICAL AND CRITICAL SOURCES:

PERIODICALS

Booklist, November 1, 2002, Barbara Jacobs, *Defying the Odds: Sharing the Lessons I Learned as a Pioneer Entrepreneur,* pp. 458-459.
Kirkus Reviews, August 15, 2002, *Defying the Odds: Sharing the Lessons I Learned as a Pioneer Entrepreneur,* p. 1197.
Publishers Weekly, September 2, 2002, review of *Defying the Odds: Sharing the Lessons I Learned as a Pioneer Entrepreneur,* p. 66.

ONLINE

Beverly Hills Courier Online, http://www.thebeverly hillscourier.com/ (December 9, 2002), Connie Martinson, review of *Defying the Odds: Sharing the Lessons I Learned as a Pioneer Entrepreneur.*

News Max Online, http://www.newsmax.com/ (January 12, 2003), *Defying the Odds: Sharing the Lessons I Learned as a Pioneer Entrepreneur.*
Westside Life Online, http://www.westsidelife.com/ (January 12, 2003), Martha Singer, "The Mother of All Specialty Stores" (interview).*

*   *   *

IWASAKI, Mineko 1949-

PERSONAL: Born 1949, in Kyoto, Japan.

ADDRESSES: Agent—c/o Atria Books, Simon & Schuster Publicity Dept., 1230 Avenue of the Americas, New York, NY 10020.

CAREER: Geisha and author.

WRITINGS:

Geisha, a Life, Atria Books (New York, NY), 2002.

SIDELIGHTS: Mystery surrounds the world of the Japanese geisha, both in Japan as well as in other countries of the world. The veil of mystery is part of the illusion necessary for the practicing geisha, but some of that mystery is caused by misunderstandings. Mineko Iwasaki, in writing her memoir *Geisha, a Life,* tries to illuminate the profession to which she dedicated almost three decades of her life, retiring from her role while she was at the height of her career and considered one of the most famous of all geishas.

American literary views of the geisha range from John Patrick's dramatization of *Teahouse of the August Moon,* published in 1954, to Arthur Golden's 1997 book *Memoirs of a Geisha.* However, until Iwasaki wrote her memoirs, no one in the three-hundred-year history of the profession had ever read an account of the life of a geisha from inside that secretive world. The world of the geisha is constrained by many ancient rules. One of them is the rule of silence; that is, geishas are told that they should never reveal the details of their lives to the outside world. However, Iwasaki became frustrated by the public misunderstanding of her profession, and after retiring from her role as geisha and entering the twentieth-century, she set out to clear the misconceptions. The result, stated a *Kirkus Reviews* writer, provides a "valuable look at a little-known world."

Iwasaki entered into the world of the geisha when she was only five years old. She looked upon her early entry as a privilege and honor. It was something she knew she wanted to do since she was only three. She was subsequently adopted by the Iwasaki family and became heir and successor to the Iwasaki geisha house when she was ten. From the age of five until she was fifteen, she was trained in stylized movements, from the way to use a fan to how to walk, a style of short steps that make the geisha appear to be floating. She also studied dance, music, and the traditional and intricate details of the Japanese tea ceremony. She was also trained in how to carry on a conversation with her customers, which she claims were predominately men, but occasionally women.

At the age of twenty, she "turned her collar," or went through a rite of passage, from *geiko*, or "woman of art," to *maiko*, or "woman of dance." Iwasaki vehemently states that women in her profession are not prostitutes or courtesans. Rather, she says, her training was more aligned to that of a ballerina, concert pianist, or opera singer.

Iwasaki's life was filled with constant practices and rehearsals. Once she was ready to debut, her life did not become much easier, as she frequently had to attend eight to ten banquets a night, performing for her guests. She would get out of bed at dawn to begin her rehearsals, then later to wash and dress, both elaborate ritualistic undertakings, and would not return from the banquets until early the next morning. She also appeared at public events a few times a year. These were annual dance programs that were very spectacular and drew audiences from all over the world. As Rosemary Sayer, writing for the *Asian Review of Books* online put it, in many ways "the life of a geisha is really one of a highly trained actress performing on a stage."

It has been reported that during the 1960s, at the height of her career, Iwasaki was earning about $500,000 a year; her picture adorned everything in Japan from calendars to shopping bags. Prince Charles, President Gerald Ford, and Henry Kissinger were among her guests. On a more personal level, some of her kimonos are said to have cost $5,000 and weighed more than forty pounds. Since Iwasaki only weighed ninety pounds, carrying the kimono on her small body was a feat in itself.

In a review for *Time: Asia* online, Alyssa Kolsky wrote that she found Iwasaki's book "alluring." Kolsky was captivated by the details of "the day-to-day minutiae of one of the world's most fascinating, secretive and oldest professions." Although Iwasaki loved her profession, at the age f twenty-nine she decided to retire. At heart a feminist of sorts, she fought to make changes in the ancient profession. She wanted geishas to have more control over the money they earned. She also wanted the women to have more access to education outside of the profession and claims that the life of a geisha is too sheltered from the modern world. When she was twenty-one she knew nothing about money and did not know how to use the simplest electronic appliance. When she retired, she thought that she would open a beauty parlor. Instead, she met a man who would soon become her husband, a traditional Japanese painter. Today, she enjoys being a mother.

The result of Iwasaki's willingness to open at least some of the doors of her world makes her book, according to Oscar Johnson from the *Asian Reporter,* "a read as pleasant as it is informative." However, a *Publishers Weekly* reviewer found Iwasaki's literary stance a bit too objective and likened it somewhat to the profession of the geisha. The reader becomes like a customer, stated the reviewer, "looking at a beautiful, elegant woman who speaks fluidly and well, but with never a vulnerable moment."

BIOGRAPHICAL AND CRITICAL SOURCES:

PERIODICALS

Asian Reporter, October 15-21, 2002, Oscar Johnson, "A Real Geisha Memoir", p. 15.
Kirkus Reviews, August 15, 2002, review of *Geisha, a Life,* p. 1198.
Publishers Weekly, September 9, 2002, review of *Geisha, a Life,* p. 56.

ONLINE

Asian Review of Books Online, http://www.asian reviewofbooks.com/ (December 19, 2002), Rosemary Sayer, review of *Geisha, a Life.*
Time: Asia Online, http://www.time.com/time/asia/ (January 13, 2002), Alyssa Kolsky, "Real Geisha, Real Story."*

J

JACKSON, Mick 1960-

PERSONAL: Born 1960, in Great Harwood, Lancashire, England; son of Robert (a foundry supplies company owner) and Kathleen (a librarian) Jackson. *Education:* Dartington College of Arts, B.A. (theatre studies), 1983; University of East Anglia, M.A. (creative writing), 1992. *Hobbies and other interests:* "Bee-keeping, running, collecting junk."

ADDRESSES: Home—Brighton, England. *Agent*—Derek Johns, A. P. Watt Ltd., 20 John Street, London WC1N 2DR, England.

CAREER: Author, screenwriter, and filmmaker. Singer/ songwriter with bands Dancing with the Dog, Screaming Abdabs, and Dinner Ladies. Directed short documentary *The Pylon People,* short dramas *Pieces of the Moon* and *The Walberswick Detectives,*, and BBC documentary about pylon painters titled *Silvering Up.*

AWARDS, HONORS: Royal Society of Authors' First Novel Award, Booker Prize shortlist, and Whitbread First Novel Award, all 1997, all for *The Underground Man.*

WRITINGS:

The Underground Man, William Morrow (New York, NY), 1997.
Five Boys, William Morrow (New York, NY), 2001.

WORK IN PROGRESS: A collection of short stories for children, a variety of screenplays, and a third novel.

SIDELIGHTS: Upon graduating from Dartington College of Arts in England, Mick Jackson founded a music group and toured under a variety of band names such as Dancing with the Dog, the Screaming Abdabs, and the Dinner Ladies. He was the singer for the band and also wrote the lyrics. He played at concerts throughout the United Kingdom until his fellow musicians told him that his song lyrics were turning into short stories. From that point, Jackson quit the music circuit and tried his hand at writing fiction. He submitted some of his stories to the prestigious University of East Anglia, renowned for its creative writing program, and after his second attempt, he was accepted. His first published novel proved to those who supported his entrance to the university to be well worth their confidence, as Jackson's *The Underground Man* went on to be shortlisted for the coveted Booker Prize.

The Underground Man is a fictionalized account of a real person, William John Cavendish-Bentinck-Scott, the fifth duke of Portland, an eccentric man who lived in the mid-nineteenth century. The duke lived at Welbeck Abbey in Nottinghamshire, where he built a lavish system of subterranean tunnels, famous in Great Britain although the public has never seen them. The tunnels are long, and some of them are very wide— large enough for two carriages to fit side by side. Jackson's account of the duke's life is based, in part, on very limited actual recorded details, a larger portion on popular stories about the duke's eccentricities, and to a greater extent on Jackson's own imagination.

Jackson writes his novel in the form of a journal, as if the duke had kept a recorded history of his own psychological descent. This journal begins with a collection of incidents, which Mary Ellen Quinn for *Booklist* found, make the duke appear "to be nothing more than a harmless crackpot," at certain points of the story, but then, unfortunately, the journal entries grow "more disturbing" as the story works its way to the conclusion. The story reflects on the duke's "often hilarious hypochondria, his bright if useless observations . . . and his inevitable descent into madness," wrote Erik Burns for the *New York Times Book Review.*

Although the peculiar attributes of the duke's personality might keep the reader interested in this story, it is the intrigue that some reviewers found more fascinating. According to David Horspool, for the *Times Literary Supplement,* "Jackson's purpose in writing this story is to give his readers an insight into the workings of the Duke's mind." "Searching motivates the book," wrote Horspool, "from the Duke's reflections about the ways things work to the eventual unearthing of repressed memories and loss." At times, Jackson makes the duke appear amusing. At other times, the author makes his protagonist appear vulnerable. The mood of the novel becomes darker and darker as it moves along the erratic lifeline of this troubled man, until, as Horspool stated, the "shocking and gruesome" conclusion is reached. Lawrence Rungren, for *Library Journal* referred to Jackson's first novel as "a subdued, though peculiarly compelling, tale."

Five Boys, published in 2001, is Jackson's second novel, which *Times Literary Supplement*'s Jonathan Keates described as "a work of striking originality, refreshingly unconcerned with emulating an established mode or idiom and triumphantly indifferent to stylistic influences." Both the story, which concerns a close-knit group of boys who live in England during World War II, and the style in which Jackson tells it are original. Through the novel, Jackson explores the life of the inhabitants of a small British village which has been largely deserted by the most able and disciplined men. Left behind are the wives and mothers, the old and frail men, and the children, who soon discover a new sense of freedom because their fathers are gone and their mothers are distracted by worry. Additional children have been sent to the village to get away from the threat of attack on the larger cities in the United Kingdom. The story is a reflection on how the war affected the villagers, with special atten-

tion paid to the boys who were too young to be sent to battle and now suddenly find themselves bonding with one another in a series of adventures.

The experimental form of Jackson's writing—Jackson loosely ties his story together in a series of separate vignettes—has been described in a variety of ways. Joanne Wilkinson, for *Booklist,* referred to *Five Boys* as a "vivid, episodic novel" with a "quirky cast of characters." Meanwhile, a *Publishers Weekly* reviewer called Jackson's book "an integrated collection of seriocomic short stories" and also stated that the creative form demonstrates "Jackson's writerly skill and imagination." On the other hand, William Skidelsky, writing for the *New Statesman,* found that *Five Boys,* like Jackson's first novel, "contains many bold, unconventional ideas, and is probably worth reading just for these." Skidelsky, however, questioned if *Five Boys* could really be classified as a novel because it lacks a "sustained focus." He believed that Jackson tried to pack too much information into his stories. Possibly, Skidelsky considered, Jackson's purpose in doing so is "to build up an authentically holistic picture of village life." Finally, there was the point of view of a *Kirkus Reviews* writer, who concluded that *Five Boys* is "destined to move and please all but the meanest of souls."

BIOGRAPHICAL AND CRITICAL SOURCES:

PERIODICALS

Booklist, June 1, 1997, Mary Ellen Quinn, review of *The Underground Man,* p. 1658; June 1, 2002, Joanne Wilkinson, review of *Five Boys,* p. 1684.

Kirkus Reviews, April 1, 2002, review of *Five Boys,* p. 443.

Library Journal, June 1, 1997, Lawrence Rungren, review of *The Underground Man,* p. 148.

New Statesman, September 3, 2001, William Skidelsky, review of *Five Boys,* p. 39.

New York Times Book Review, July 20, 1997, Erik Burns, "Brain Surgery Made Easy," review of *The Underground Man,* p. 20; June 23, 2002, Tom Shone, "The Sting," review of *Five Boys,* p. 25.

Publishers Weekly, May 5, 1997, review of *The Underground Man,* p. 199; May 13, 2002, review of *Five Boys,* pp. 49-50.

Times Literary Supplement, January 31, 1997, David Horspool, "Subterranean Melancholy," review of *The Underground Man,* p. 21; September 7, 2001, Jonathan Keates, "Fun on the Home Front", review of *Five Boys,* p. 9.

ONLINE

Mick Jackson Home Page, http://www.mickjackson. com (August 2003).

*   *   *

JACKSON, Shelley 1963-

PERSONAL: Born 1963, in the Philippines; immigrated to United States; naturalized U.S. citizen. *Education:* Stanford University, A.B.; Brown University, M.F.A.

ADDRESSES: Home—New York, NY. *Agent*—c/o Author Mail, Random House, 299 Park Ave., New York, NY 10171-0002. *E-mail*—shelley@drizzle.com.

CAREER: Writer and illustrator.

WRITINGS:

Patchwork Girl, by Mary/Shelly & herself (hypertext novel), Eastgate Systems, 1995.
(Illustrator) *The Old Woman and the Wave* (juvenile), DK Ink (New York, NY), 1998.
(Illustrator) *Sophia, the Alchemist's Dog* (juvenile), DK Ink (New York, NY), 2000.
The Melancholy of Anatomy (short stories), Anchor (New York, NY), 2002.

CHILDREN'S BOOKS; AS ILLUSTRATOR

Nancy Farmer, *Do You Know Me?* Orchard Books (New York, NY), 1993.
Rebecca C. Jones, *Great Aunt Martha,* Dutton Children's Books (New York, NY), 1995.
Cynthia DeFelice, *Willy's Silly Grandma,* Orchard Books (New York, NY), 1997.
Kim Siegelson, *Escape South,* Golden Books (New York, NY), 2000.

Contributor to periodicals, including *Grand Street* and *Kenyon Review.*

SIDELIGHTS: Shelley Jackson creates fiction rife with base imagery and characters exhibiting disturbing behavior. Her works include *Patchwork Girl, by Mary/ Shelley & herself,* a hypertext novel that has drawn comparisons to Mary Shelley's *Frankenstein.* In Jackson's novel, Mary Shelley has actually fashioned a female creature similar to the gruesome male monstrosity featured in her own novel. But Shelley's female creation, fashioned—like the creature in *Frankenstein*—from various body parts, becomes obsessed with her creator and tracks her to America. During one notable episode in Jackson's tale, the ungainly female creation loses control of her various parts and is compelled to reassemble herself.

The Melancholy of Anatomy is a collection of short stories that Judith Rosen, writing in *Publishers Weekly,* deemed full of "corporeal fantasies." The collection includes "Eggs," wherein a middle-aged woman secretes—from one of her tear ducts—an egg that grows as large as a boulder; "Sperm," and "Nerve," in which a deranged individual reaps nerve fibers and fashions them into hats. Susan Salter Reynolds, writing in the *Los Angeles Times Book Review,* proclaimed *The Melancholy of Anatomy* "subversive," and a *Publishers Weekly* reviewer, while contending that Jackson's stories are "laboriously executed," conceded that they are also "cleverly imagined."

Jackson is also an illustrator and writer of children's books. In 1998 she produced *The Old Woman and the Wave,* in which an irritable old woman discovers the magical properties of a huge wave that has hovered over her home for some time. Lisa Shea, writing in the *New York Times Book Review,* proclaimed the tale "wistful, wishful," and a reviewer in the *Bulletin of the Center for Children's Books* described Jackson's book as a "modern fable." The latter critic acknowledged Jackson's illustrations as "surrealistic collage paintings . . . with splashes of color and myriads of shapes and viewpoints." Jackson is also the illustrator and author of *Sophia, the Alchemist's Dog,* in which a dog discovers the alchemical potion for creating gold.

In addition to both illustrating and writing children's books, Jackson has provided artwork to books by other storytellers. In 1993 she served as illustrator of Nancy Farmer's *Do You Know Me?* which recounts the culture clash that ensues when a family in Zimbabwe hosts an uncle from Mozambique. "Universal themes . . . are central to this novel," declared Lyn

Miller-Lachmann in *School Library Journal.* Lois F. Anderson reported in *Horn Book* that *Do You Know Me?* "manages to deal with serious issues and . . . provoke laughter." A *Publishers Weekly* reviewer, meanwhile, affirmed that "Jackson's spirited . . . illustrations exhibit a distinctive personality."

Jackson also supplied illustration for Rebecca C. Jones's *Great Aunt Martha,* wherein a girl sees her playtime options limited as a consequence of a relative's visit. Jody McCoy, writing in *School Library Journal,* noted Jackson's "lively illustrations," and Martha V. Parravano, in her *Horn Book* analysis, remarked on the "strong, stylized illustrations that successfully play with perspective." Further praise came from a *Publishers Weekly* critic who declared that "Jackson's illustrations are marked by vibrant colors and varied perspectives."

Cynthia DeFelice's *Willy's Silly Grandma* impressed Nancy Vasilakis, who wrote in *Horn Book* about Jackson's "bold ink and crayon vignettes." A *Publishers Weekly* critic stated that Jackson's artwork "impressively manages to both scare and comfort."

BIOGRAPHICAL AND CRITICAL SOURCES:

PERIODICALS

Booklist, April 1, 1993, Janice Del Negro, review of *Do You Know Me?* p. 143; May 15, 1998, Susan Dove Lempke, review of *The Old Woman and the Wave,* p. 1633; February 15, 2001, Hazel Rochman, review of *Escape South,* p. 1153.

Bulletin of the Center for Children's Books, March, 1998, review of *The Old Woman and the Wave,* p. 247.

Horn Book, September-October, 1993, Lois F. Anderson, review of *Do You Know Me?;* September-October, 1995, Martha V. Parravano, review of *Great Aunt Martha;* May-June, 1997, Nancy Vasilakis, review of *Willy's Silly Grandma.*

Los Angeles Times Book Review, April 28, 2002, Susan Salter Reynolds, "Discoveries."

New York Times Book Review, September 20, 1998, Lisa Shea, review of *The Old Woman and the Wave,* p. 33.

Publishers Weekly, March 15, 1993, review of *Do You Know Me?;* June 26, 1995, review of *Great Aunt Martha;* February 24, 1997, review of *Willy's Silly*

Grandma, p. 89; January 19, 1998, review of *The Old Woman and the Wave,* p. 377; February 4, 2002, Judith Rosen, "Hip-Lit 101"; February 18, 2002, review of *The Melancholy of Anatomy,* p. 71.

School Library Journal, April, 1993, Lyn Miller-Lachmann, review of *Do You Know Me?* p. 118; July, 1995, Jody McCoy, review of *Great Aunt Martha,* p. 64.

ONLINE

Shelley Jackson Web site, http://www.ineradicablestain. com (May 9, 2003).*

*   *   *

JACQUES, Elliott 1917-2003

OBITUARY NOTICE—See index for *CA* sketch: Born January 18, 1917, in Toronto, Ontario, Canada; died of an infection that damaged his heart March 8, 2003, in Gloucester, MA. Psychoanalyst, consultant, and author. Jacques was a behavioral scientist who is most often remembered for coining and defining the term "midlife crisis," which has since become an accepted theory among psychologists. A bright scholar at a young age, Jacques completed his B.A. degree from the University of Toronto when he was only eighteen. He earned a master's the next year, followed by a medical degree from Johns Hopkins University in 1940 and a Ph.D. in social relations from Harvard University in 1942, just as the United States was entering World War II. His military service involved an assignment in the Canadian Army Medical Corps, where he rose to the rank of major. After the war, he worked for the Tavistock Institute of Human Relations in London, where he became involved in a study of worker relations at the Glacier Metal Co. Here he learned how blue-collar workers were paid hourly wages while supervisors were salaried, and he formulated a theory that salaries should depend on how involved and time-consuming project responsibilities were and how much planning they required. Therefore, it was justified and equitable that someone performing a menial task that could be completed in a few hours or days should be paid less than a manager who might be planning strategies that take years to come to fruition. Jacques's theory was accepted and implemented at only a few factories and businesses, however, while it drew criticism from some experts who viewed it as elitist. Jacques's theories were later published in his first book, *The Changing Culture of a Factory* (1951). After becoming a certified psychoanalyst in 1951, Jacques went into private practice and was a consultant to the Department of Health and Social Security in England from 1952 to 1979. As he approached middle age, he observed changes in his mood that led him to research the emotional and psychological effects of middle age. He concluded that all people go through, in one way or another, a "midlife crisis" during which they try to recapture their youth as their awareness of their impending mortality becomes more enhanced. The idea that human beings continue to go through stages of development even after reaching adulthood was a new one among psychologists and psychiatrists, and quickly became a subject of intense interest in the field. Toward the end of his career, Jacques was a professor at Brunel University, Uxbridge, where from 1965 to 1971 he headed the School of Social Sciences, and from 1970 to 1986 was director of the Institute of Social and Organizational Studies. Beginning in 1979, he also worked as a consultant to the U.S. Army. He published nineteen books during his lifetime, including *Work, Creativity, and Social Justice* (1970), *Free Enterprise, Fair Employment* (1982), and *The Life and Behavior of Living Organisms: A General Theory* (2002).

OBITUARIES AND OTHER SOURCES:

BOOKS

Writers Directory, 18th edition, St. James Press (Detroit, MI), 2003.

PERIODICALS

Chicago Tribune, March 24, 2003, section 2, p. 11.
Los Angeles Times, March 23, 2003, p. B17.
New York Times, March 17, 2003, p. A23.
Times (London, England), March 26, 2003, p. 32.
Washington Post, March 24, 2003, p. B5.

*   *   *

JAFFE, Michele (Sharon)

PERSONAL: Female. *Education:* Harvard University, B.A., 1991, Ph.D., 1998.

ADDRESSES: Home—Las Vegas, NV. *Agent*—c/o Author Mail, Random House, 1745 Broadway, New York, NY 10019.

CAREER: Huntington Library, San Marino, CA, staff member; Harvard University, Cambridge, MA, instructor in Shakespeare.

WRITINGS:

The Story of O: Prostitutes and Other Good-for-Nothings in the Renaissance, Harvard University Press (Cambridge, MA), 1999.

ROMANCE NOVELS

The Stargazer, Pocket Books (New York, NY), 1999.
The Water Nymph, Pocket Books (New York, NY), 2000.
Lady Killer, Ballantine Books (New York, NY), 2002.
Secret Admirer, Ballantine Books (New York, NY), 2002.
Bad Girl, Ballantine Books (New York, NY), 2003.
Lover Boy, Ballantine Books (New York, NY), 2004.

SIDELIGHTS: Michele Jaffe left her job in academics to pursue a career as a romance novelist. In an online interview with *Beatrice Interview* Jaffe claims about her career change, "It first started when it became startlingly clear that I didn't want to be an academic. But I loved doing research, I loved what I was studying, and I wanted another outlet for the fascinating facts that I was finding, the interesting people I was meeting in my research." Jaffe earned her Ph.D. in the comparative literature of the Renaissance, and her novels are set in that time period. Jaffe's novels are part of a series that features six male cousins.

Jaffe's first novel *The Stargazer* is set in Venice. Bianca Salva stumbles across the body of Isabella Bellochio, who was stabbed with a dagger belonging to aristocrat Ian Foscari. Ian, upon receiving a note from Isabella, goes to see her. He walks in just as Bianca pulls the dagger out of the body, and assumes that Bianca is the killer. Ian decides to bring Bianca to his castle and gives her one week to prove her innocence. As a cover-up he tells everyone that she is his fiancee, which will please his family since they want him to be married. Bianca, the daughter of a doctor, agrees as long as she can perform an autopsy. As Bianca and Ian work to find the true murderer they fall passionately in love. *Booklist* contributor Patty Engelmann concluded, "Jaffe's characters are intriguing, and the plot's many twists and turns are wonderfully entertaining."

Jaffe's second novel, *The Water Nymph,* is set in England during the reign of Queen Elizabeth I. Grispin Foscari, the earl of Sandal, is dismissed from his position on Queen Elizabeth's secret service after being accused of treason. He has two weeks to uncover the person who is making the accusations. During his investigation, Crispin meets Sophie Champion, a businesswoman who is investigating the suspicious death of her father. Their paths cross numerous times and they develop a mutual admiration and love for each other. "Fast-paced historical fiction fairly crackling with passion and suspense," praised Margaret Flanagan in a *Booklist* review.

Secret Admirer is set in London, England, in the late 1500s. Lady Tuesday Arlington finds that painting the scenes of her deathly nightmares helps her deal with them. But when her husband is murdered her paintings incriminate her as the killer. Investigating the murder is Lawrence Pickering. As he investigates, he begins to believe that Lady Tuesday is not the real killer and falls in love with her. At the same time the murderer sets his sights on Pickering. *Romantic Times* contributor Kathe Robin claimed, "Jaffe creates a masterful and highly suspenseful mystery with enough red herrings and stunning surprises to keep any fan enthralled."

Jaffe's novel *Lady Killer* is also set in London, England, in the late 1500s. Miles Loredon killed the vampire of London three years ago in front of numerous witnesses. But detective Lady Clio Thornton finds the body of a woman who appears to have died of a vampire bite. Clio approaches Miles, who is to be married to her cousin, with her findings. Clio and Miles work to solve the case, but along the way they fall in love. *Romantic Times* contributor Kathe Robin commented, "a compelling, hard-to-put-down read."

BIOGRAPHICAL AND CRITICAL SOURCES:

PERIODICALS

Booklist, May 1, 1999, Patty Engelmann, review of *The Stargazer,* p. 1581; June 1, 2000, Margaret Flanagan, review of *The Water Nymph,* p. 1857.

Kirkus Reviews, April 15, 2000, review of *The Water Nymph,* p. 511.

Library Journal, May 1, 1999, Kim Uden Rutter, review of *The Stargazer,* p. 110; October 1, 1999, review of *The Stargazer,* p. 51; May 15, 2000, Kim Uden Rutter, review of *The Water Nymph,* p. 125.

Publishers Weekly, June 7, 1999, review of *The Stargazer,* p. 71; May 1, 2000, review of *The Water Nymph,* p. 50; May 20, 2002, review of *Lady Killer* and *Secret Admirer,* p. 53.

Renaissance Quarterly, autumn, 2000, David Marsh, review of *The Story of O: Prostitutes and Other Good-for-Nothings in the Renaissance,* p. 906.

Seventeenth-Century News, fall, 2000, Edward H. Thompson, review of *The Story of O,* pp. 232-235.

ONLINE

All about Romance, http://www.likesbooks.com/ (September 5, 2002), Colleen McMahon, review of *The Stargazer;* Blythe Barnhill, review of *The Water Nymph;* Jennifer Keirans, review of *Lady Killer.*

Beatrice Interview, http://www.beatrice.com/ (September 5, 2002), "Michele Jaffe."

Book Browser, http://www.bookbrowser.com/ (September 5, 2002), Harriet Klausner, review of *The Water Nymph;* Harriet Klausner, review of *Lady Killer* and *Secret Admirer.*

Escape to Romance, http://www.escapetoromance.com/ (September 5, 2002), Darlene Howard, review of *Lady Killer* and *Secret Admirer.*

Michele Jaffe Web site, http://www.michelejaffe.com/ (September 5, 2002).

Romance Reader, http://www.theromancereader.com/ (September 5, 2002), Cathy Sova, review of *The Stargazer.*

Romantic Times, http://www.romantictimes.com/ (September 5, 2002), Kathryn Falk, review of *The Stargazer;* Kathe Robin, review of *The Stargazer;* Kathe Robin, review of *The Water Nymph;* Kathe Robin, review of *Secret Admirer;* Kathe Robin, review of *Lady Killer.*

Simon & Schuster Web site, http://www.simonsays.com/ (September 5, 2002), "Michele Jaffe."*

*   *   *

JAGO, Lucy 1968(?)-

PERSONAL: Born c. 1968; children: one. *Education:* King's College, Cambridge, double first class honors degree; Courtauld Institute, M.A.

ADDRESSES: Home—Dorset, England. *Agent*—c/o Author Mail, Random House, 1745 Broadway, New York, NY 10019. *E-mail*—info@lucyjago.com.

CAREER: Worked as documentary producer for British Broadcasting Channel and Channel 4 in England.

WRITINGS:

The Northern Lights, Knopf (New York, NY), 2001.

Regular contributor to newspapers and magazines.

WORK IN PROGRESS: A book set in the Gobi desert.

SIDELIGHTS: Lucy Jago, now a regular contributor to newspapers and magazines, is a former documentary producer for the British Broadcasting Channel (BBC) and Channel 4. While making a documentary about the sun for the BBC, Jago discovered the story behind the northern lights and the scientist who was able to correctly explain their origin.

Jago's first book, *The Northern Lights,* is a biography of Norwegian scientist Kristian Birkeland (1867-1917). Birkeland was the first scientist to discover the correct explanation behind the northern lights. Through scientific observations and experiments, Birkeland theorized that the northern lights were a result of electrically charged particles from the sun hitting the earth's upper atmosphere. His theory was scoffed at by British scientists, but accepted by others; it was proven to be correct after his death.

In *The Northern Lights* Jago examines Birkeland's dangerous expeditions and experiments which led to his theory on the origin of the northern lights. She also gives details about his other works, which include sixty patents for fertilizers, an electro-magnetic gun, and other inventions. Not only does Jago detail Birkeland's work, she also discusses his personal life, including his childhood, family, romantic life, idiosyncrasies, and mental health. "Instead of a stiff, scholarly biography, British journalist Jago has written a poignantly human story filled with minute, extensively researched details," noted Gloria Maxwell in a *Library Journal* review. *Booklist* contributor Donna Seaman concluded, "Jago's lucid and captivating blend of biography, physics, and cultural history adds a vital chapter to the annals of science and finally gives Birkeland his due."

BIOGRAPHICAL AND CRITICAL SOURCES:

PERIODICALS

Booklist, September 1, 2001, Donna Seaman, review of *The Northern Lights,* p. 27; January 1, 2002, Barbara Baskin, review of *The Northern Lights,* p. 876.
Economist, June 16, 2001, "Atmospheric Stuff; Understanding the Sky; Weather Patterns," p. 2.
Harper's Magazine, November, 2001, Guy Davenport, review of *The Northern Lights,* p. 73.
Library Journal, November 1, 2001, Gloria Maxwell, review of *The Northern Lights,* p. 129.
New York Times Book Review, October 21, 2001, Annette Kobak, "Running Outside in Pajamas."
Publishers Weekly, August 13, 2001, review of *The Northern Lights,* p. 296.
World and I, March, 2002, Alv Egeland, "A Brilliant, yet Mysterious Scientist," p. 256.

ONLINE

Austin Chronicle Online, http://www.austinchronicle.com/ (September 5, 2002), Ana Hanks, review of *The Northern Lights.*
Book Browse, http://www.bookbrowse.com/ (September 5, 2002), "A Conversation with Lucy Jago, author of *The Northern Lights,*"
Decatur Daily Online, http://www.decaturdaily.com/ (September 5, 2002), David L. Roop, "Kristian Birkeland and the Story of the Northern Lights."
Guardian Unlimited, http://books.guardian.co.uk/ (September 5, 2002), Chris Lavers, "Light Fantastic."
Lucy Jago Web site, http://www.lucyjago.com (September 5, 2002).
Nonfiction Reviews, http://www.nonfictionreviews.com/ (September 5, 2002), Rob Hardy, "Fascinating Biography Lights Up the Skies."
Random House Web site, http://www.randomhouse.com/ (September 5, 2002), "Lucy Jago."
Rhode Island College Web site, http://www.ric.edu/ (September 5, 2002), Jonathan Dore, review of *The Northern Lights.**

*   *   *

JAPRISOT, Sébastien
See ROSSI, Jean-Baptiste

JOHNSON, D(avid) Gale 1916-2003

OBITUARY NOTICE—See index for *CA* sketch: Born July 10, 1916, in Vinton, IA; died of pneumonia related to Amyotrophic Lateral Sclerosis (Lou Gehrig's disease) April 13, 2003, in Northampton, MA (one source says Amherst, MA). Economist, educator, and author. Johnson was a renowned expert in the area of agricultural economics who also took an interest in the economies of communist China and the Soviet Union. He was a graduate of Iowa State University, where he received his B.S. in 1938 and a Ph.D. in 1945. His master's degree was earned at the University of Wisconsin in 1939, and he also attended graduate school at the University of Chicago. His teaching career began at Iowa State, where he was a research associate and then assistant professor of agricultural economics in the early 1940s. But Johnson spent the rest of his career at the University of Chicago, where he taught for many decades, becoming a professor emeritus in 1986. At Chicago he also served as dean from 1960 to 1970 and was chair of the economics department from 1971 to 1975 and from 1980 to 1984. In 1975 he was vice president and dean of faculties, and from 1976 to 1980 he held the office of provost. Johnson, who spent his childhood growing up on a farm, was renowned for his work in agricultural economics, and he did groundbreaking work in areas such as farm employment and commodities pricing. His interest in agriculture led him to study the economics of farming not only in the United States but also as it applied to Russian and Chinese economics. Consequently, Johnson was made director of the Center for East Asian Studies from 1994 to 1998. His ideas were published in dozens of books, including *Agricultural Price Policy and International Trade* (1954), *Farm Commodity Programs: An Opportunity for Change* (1973), *Progress of Economic Reform in the People's Republic of China,* (1982), and *The Economics of Agriculture* (1996).

OBITUARIES AND OTHER SOURCES:

BOOKS

Writers Directory, 18th edition, St. James Press (Detroit, MI), 2003.

PERIODICALS

Chicago Tribune, April 17, 2003, Section 3, p. 13.
New York Times, April 17, 2003, p. C13.

JOHNSON, Kij 1960-

PERSONAL: Born January 20, 1960, in Harlan, IA; daughter of David P. (a pastor) and Elizabeth (a librarian and bookstore owner) Johnson; married Chris McKitterick (a writer and university faculty member), July 4, 1999. *Ethnicity:* "Norwegian." *Education:* St. Olaf College, B.A. (ancient British history), 1982. *Hobbies and other interests:* history, origami.

ADDRESSES: Home—2110 Elmwood, Lawrence, KS 66046. *Office*—Department of English, Wescoe Hall, University of Kansas, Lawrence, KS 66045. *E-mail*—kijo@msn.com.

CAREER: Writer and editor. Tor Books, New York, NY, managing editor, 1990-92; Dark Horse Comics, Milwaukie, OR, collections editor, 1992-94; Wizards of the Coast, Renton, WA, managing editor, creative director, research and development, 1995-2000; MIcrosoft, Redmond, WA, contracted project director, Microsoft Reader E-Book Project; University of Kansas, Lawrence, associate director of the Center for the Study of Science Fiction, 2001—. Final judge for Theodore A. Sturgeon Award, with James Gunn and Frederik Pohl, 1997—.

MEMBER: Science Fiction Writers of America, Science Fiction Research Association, International Association for the Fantastic in the Arts.

AWARDS, HONORS: Theodore A. Sturgeon Award for best short story of the year, Center for the Study of Science Fiction, 1995, for "Fox Magic"; Crawford Award for best new fantasist of the year, International Association for the Fantastic in the Arts, 2001.

WRITINGS:

(With Greg Cox) *Dragon's Honor* ("Star Trek: The Next Generation" series), Pocket Books (New York, NY), 1996.
The Fox Woman, Tor Books (New York, NY), 2000.
Tales for the Long Rains (e-book short-story collection), Scorpius Digital, 2001.
Fudoki, Tor Books (New York, NY), 2003.

Contributor of short stories to science-fiction and fantasy periodicals, including *Amazing Stories, Analog, Duelist, Realms of Fantasy,* and *Fantasy and Science Fiction.*

WORK IN PROGRESS: A third book set in Heian Japan (with the fox woman and Fudoki) for Tor Books; two-book "Kylen" series, set in enlightenment England and Turkey.

SIDELIGHTS: Kij Johnson cowrote one installment of the *Star Trek: The Next Generation* series, then her fantasy, *The Fox Woman,* the first novel in a projected three-book series. The story is an expansion of Johnson's award-winning "Fox Magic," which is based on a ninth-century Japanese fairy tale. Kaya no Yoshifuji is a nobleman who retreats to his country estate with his wife, Shikujo, and his young son after failing to secure a court position. There he is seen by Kitsune, a young fox who falls in love with him and uses magic to transform herself into a human.

The story, which *Booklist* reviewer Sally Estes considered "haunting," unfolds through the journals of the three main characters and follows the seasons. Its use of poetry and traditional lore drew particular praise. A *Publishers Weekly* writer called the book "A meditation on poetry, ritual, and humanity" and a "literate, magical, and occasionally grotesque love story." In *Locus,* Faren Miller hailed the novel as a "moving examination of passion and the gaining of hard-won knowledge," concluding that the story "entirely escapes the constraints of standard fairy tales . . . to stand entirely on its own as a celebration of that far from mundane thing we call life."

Johnson told *CA:* "I find myself especially influenced by nonfiction writings, particularly diaries, journals, and letters of Fanny Burney and Lady Mary Wortley Montagu; the Monogatari and diaries of Heian and Kamakura-era Japanese noblewomen; Samuel Pepys's diaries; and Gilbert White's natural history of Selborne. I can't read much fiction when I'm writing, since it starts to flavor my work, but I will turn to Jane Austen, Daniel Defoe, and Patrick O'Brian. If they change my writing, so much the better for me."

BIOGRAPHICAL AND CRITICAL SOURCES:

PERIODICALS

Booklist, January 1, 2000, Sally Estes, review of *The Fox Woman,* p. 887.
Kliatt, May, 1996, Hugh M. Flick, Jr., review of *Dragon's Honor,* p. 18.
Library Journal, January, 2000, Jackie Cassada, review of *The Fox Woman,* p. 167.
Locus January, 2000, Faren Miller, review of *The Fox Woman,* p. 25.
Magazine of Fantasy and Science Fiction, January, 2000, Charles De Lint, review of *The Fox Woman,* p. 36.
Publishers Weekly, December 20, 1999, review of *The Fox Woman,* p. 60.

ONLINE

Kij Johnson Home Page, http://www.sff.net/people/kij-johnson (November 29, 2002).
Kij Johnson Online Journal, http://www.livejournal.com (August 21, 2003).
Speculon, http://www.speculon.com/ (January, 2001), Trent Walters, interview with Johnson.

* * *

JOHNSON, Patricia E. 1951-

PERSONAL: Born February 22, 1951; married, 1989; children: one. *Education:* Earlham College, B.A., 1973; University of Minnesota, Ph.D., 1985.

ADDRESSES: Office—W356 Olmsted Building, School of Humanities, Pennsylvania State University, Harrisburg, Middletown, PA 17057. *E-mail*—pejl@psu.edu.

CAREER: University of Alabama, Huntsville, assistant professor, 1985-89; Pennsylvania State University, Harrisburg, associate professor of literature and humanities, 1989—.

MEMBER: Modern Language Association.

AWARDS, HONORS: University of Minnesota fellowship.

WRITINGS:

Hidden Hands: Working-Class Women and Victorian Social-Problem Fiction, Ohio University Press (Athens, OH), 2001.

Contributor of articles to periodicals, including *Mosaic, Studies in the Novel,* and *Victorians Institute Journal.*

SIDELIGHTS: Patricia E. Johnson is an associate professor of literature and humanities at Pennsylvania State University. She has written articles on authors Charles Dickens, Charlotte Brontë, and George Eliot that have appeared in periodicals including *Mosaic, Studies in the Novel,* and *Victorians Institute Journal.*

In her first book, *Hidden Hands: Working-Class Women and Victorian Social-Problem Fiction,* Johnson analyzes the role working women played during the industrial revolution. A large number of women worked in order to support the family when the father figure could not provide enough wages. Working women were not seen in a positive way, however, because they went against the beliefs of how women should act during the Victorian era. As a result, working women were not represented in novels published during that time, or if they were included, then they were represented in a negative manner. "Johnson's prose is lucid and her readings plausible," noted M. E. Burstein in a *Choice* review.

BIOGRAPHICAL AND CRITICAL SOURCES:

PERIODICALS

Choice, February, 2002, M. E. Burstein, review of *Hidden Hands: Working-Class Women and Victorian Social-Problem Fiction,* p. 1048.
English Literature in Transition 1880-1920, spring, 2002, Emily Clark, review of *Hidden Hands,* p. 254.
Times Literary Supplement, May 10, 2002, Sara Hudston, review of *Hidden Hands,* p. 31.

ONLINE

Ohio University Press Web site, http://www.ohiou.edu/ (September 5, 2002).
University of Southern California Web site, http://www.usc.edu/ (September 5, 2002).*

JOHNSON, Sandra E.

PERSONAL: Born in Frankfurt, Germany.

ADDRESSES: Agent—c/o St. Martin's Press, 175 Fifth Ave., New York, NY 10010. *E-mail*—sandrajohnson@ msn.com

CAREER: Freelance writer and columnist.

WRITINGS:

Standing on Holy Ground: A Triumph over Hate Crime in the Deep South, St. Martin's Press (New York, NY), 2002.

Contributor of newspaper column to *State* (South Carolina's largest newspaper); contributor of articles to periodicals, including *Washington Post, Transitions Abroad,* and *Columbia Metropolitan.*

WORK IN PROGRESS: A novel with the working title *Soul Catch a Fire.*

SIDELIGHTS: Sandra E. Johnson was born in Frankfurt, Germany, the daughter of a military father. When she was one year old her family moved back to the United States, where Johnson currently lives in South Carolina. Her family's roots are in the South and the topic of her first published book confronts the issues of racism and hate crimes as witnessed by the African-American community in the South.

Standing on Holy Ground: A Battle against Hate Crime in the Deep South was born from a magazine article Johnson wrote that was slated to be published by one of Johnson's favorite magazines until the editor decided against it at the last minute. The reason: Too many similar articles had been recently published by other magazines on the same topic. Although Johnson was disappointed by the rejection, she maintained confidence in her account, knowing that the whole story behind the rash of church burnings and other hate crimes in the South had not truly been told. Her belief in her story lead her to extend the it into a full-length book, for which she subsequently found a publisher.

Standing on Holy Ground relates the account of how, in January 1985, Ammie Murray and Barbara Simmons organized the refurbishing of St. John Baptist Church in Dixiana, South Carolina, after it had been desecrated by vandals. The two women—one black, the other white—had been friends before the vandalism occurred, but over the course of their thirteen-year venture of trying to save the church, their friendship had deepened. The church was attacked several times, and at one point, the graveyard was even dug up, the graves violated, and evidence of satanic rituals was left behind. In 1995 the church suffered its worst offence when someone burned it to the ground.

The efforts of Murray and Simmon were often criticized by people in their community, and their lives were threatened for their attempts to save the church. However, the confidence and spiritual strength of their commitment kept their project alive. In the end, their story received nationwide publicity, and people from all over began offering their assistance.

As it turned out, St. John's was only the first church to be torched in the South during the 1980s and 1990s; and Johnson broadens the scope of her book to include information on the successful lawsuit brought against the Ku Klux Klan by two other Southern churches. As a *Publishers Weekly* reviewer noted: "By the end, the book becomes a stimulating whodunit and courtroom drama."

The strength and commitment of Murray and Simmon won the hearts of many people in their community, who eventually supported the women's efforts. Murray and Simmon proved themselves through their own continued efforts as they withstood personal attacks against them, verbal abuse, and other pressures that would not shake them from their goal. As Cathleen Medwick for *O* wrote: Johnson's book "shows how faith, love, and sheer bullheadedness may lose battle after battle against racism—and still win the war."

Karen Sandlin Silverman in *Library Journal,* called Johnson's book a "gripping page-turner" and commended the author for telling such a "compelling" story, while a *Kirkus Reviews* writer referred to *Standing on Holy Ground* as a confident report that "delves without blinking into the depths of human depravity and emerges with an inspiring story."

BIOGRAPHICAL AND CRITICAL SOURCES:

PERIODICALS

Kirkus Reviews, March 1, 2002, review of *Standing on Holy Ground,* p. 310.
Library Journal, April 1, 2002, Daren Sandlin Silverman, review of *Standing on Holy Ground,* p. 126.
O, June, 2002, review of *Standing on Holy Ground,* p. 158.
Publishers Weekly, April 15, 2002, review of *Standing on Holy Ground,* p. 53.*

* * *

JOLLY, W(illiam) P(ercy) 1922-2003

OBITUARY NOTICE—See index for *CA* sketch: Born December 2, 1922, in Plymouth, England; died March 28, 2003. Engineer, educator, and author. Jolly was an electrical engineer who also wrote several well-received biographies. He studied at Plymouth College before leaving school for a time to be a dockyard worker and Civil Service clerk. He then returned to school, attending Exeter College until the beginning of World War II. He joined the Royal Navy and became a Special Branch radar officer. When the war was over, he was able to return to Exeter, where he earned a B.Sc. in physics in 1949. Jolly then embarked on a teaching career, first at the now-defunct Royal Naval College, where he was a lecturer and then professor of physics and electrical engineering until 1969, and then at King's College, London, where he spent the next twenty years as a visiting professor of electronics and electrical engineering. His early writings, such as *Physics for Electrical Engineers* (1961; second edition, 1970) and *Low Noise Electronics* (1967), concerned his area of study. His work *Marconi: A Biography* (1972) was therefore not a surprising stretch. His next biography, *Sir Oliver Lodge: Psychical Researcher and Scientist* (1974), is about the radio inventor's predecessor. Jolly also wrote a biography about industrialist William Hesketh Lever and a popular book about a famous zoo pachyderm, *Jumbo* (1976). Later, he wrote business books, but the last project he was working on at the time of his death was a fictionalized story about Queen Henrietta Maria's court dwarf, Sir Jeffrey Hudson. Besides his published work, Jolly was also notable for being the cofounder of a software company that designed an educational virtual physics laboratory.

OBITUARIES AND OTHER SOURCES:

BOOKS

Writers Directory, 12th edition, St. James Press (Detroit, MI), 1996.

PERIODICALS

Times (London, England), May 16, 2003, p. 43.

*   *   *

JONES, Aubrey 1911-2003

OBITUARY NOTICE—See index for *CA* sketch: Born November 20, 1911, in Merthyr Tydfil, Wales (one source says Pen-y-darren, Glamorgan, Wales); died April 10, 2003, in Westhampnett, West Sussex, England. Politician, journalist, businessman, and author. Jones was a conservative member of Parliament during the 1950s and 1960s who became known for his perceptive vision of the future, but whose initiatives to make changes in government were often blocked by opponents. A graduate of the London School of Economics, where he was a first-class graduate in 1933 and won the Gladstone Memorial Prize, Jones worked for the League of Nations before joining the London *Times* as a sub-editor on foreign affairs. When World War II started, he served in military intelligence in England and the Middle East until 1946. His first forays into politics were two unsuccessful attempts in 1945 and again 1946 to run for office. Barring this, he took a job with the Iron and Steel Federation, where he remained until 1955. His prospects in politics saw the light in 1950, when he won the seat to

Hall Green, Birmingham. From 1955 to 1957 he was minister of fuel and power, and from 1957 to 1959 he was minister of supply. According to Jones, however, his happiest post came after he resigned from Parliament in 1965 and became chair of the National Board for Prices and Incomes from 1965 to 1970. While a member of Parliament, Jones's philosophy was that government should be highly involved in the course of the economy, and he objected to Tory notions of a free economy, a stand that was in marked contrast to his other conservative party colleagues. Eventually, this conflict in philosophies led him to switch to the Liberal Party in 1981. His later career was occupied by chairing companies such as Laporte Industries and Cornhill Insurance; during the 1960s and 1970s, he was also director of Guest, Keen & Nettlefolds Steel Company, Courtaulds Ltd., and Black & Decker. He was an adviser for the Nigerian Public Service Review Commission from 1973 to 1974, the Iranian government from 1974 to 1978, and Plessey Ltd. from 1978 to 1980. Jones was also president of the Oxford Energy Policy Club from 1976 to 1988. He was the author of several books about the economy and politics, including *The Pendulum of Politics* (1946), *The New Inflation: The Politics of Prices and Incomes* (1973), and *Britain's Economy: The Roots of Stagnation* (1985).

OBITUARIES AND OTHER SOURCES:

PERIODICALS

Guardian (London, England), April 12, 2003, p. 25.
Independent (London, England), April 21, 2003, p. 16.
Times (London, England), April 17, 2003, p. 37.

*   *   *

JOY, Thomas Alfred 1904-2003

OBITUARY NOTICE—See index for *CA* sketch: Born December 30, 1904, in Oxford, England; died April 15, 2003, in Twickenham, Middlesex, England. Bookseller and author. Joy was well known in England as the former book manager at Harrod's and managing director of Hatchards. Born to a family of limited means, he went to private school at Bedford House with the help of a choral scholarship. He left school at the age of fourteen to work at the Bodleian Library. Finding library work not to his taste, he became an indentured apprentice for the university booksellers J. Thornton & Son, where, except for a year as head of mail orders for A. & F. Denny booksellers in London in 1926, he remained until 1935. Joy joined Harrod's as manager of its circulating library in 1935 and was manager of the book department from 1942 to 1946. He then spent the next twenty years at Army and Navy Stores in London, where he managed the book department, was founder of its library service, and worked as deputy managing director from 1956 to 1965. From 1965 to 1985 he was managing director for Hatchards Limited, helping to make the struggling company profitable again. Joy was an expert on books of Asian interest and, although on first impression he could seem pompous and unapproachable, proved himself to always be kind and eager to help his patrons, some of which included members of the royal family. He was the author of several books about bookselling, including *Bookselling* (1953) and *The Bookselling Business* (1974), as well as the memoir *Mostly Joy* (1971).

OBITUARIES AND OTHER SOURCES:

BOOKS

Writers Directory, 12th edition, St. James Press (Detroit, MI), 1996.

PERIODICALS

Independent (London, England), May 2, 2003, p. 22.
Times (London, England), May 3, 2003, p. 43.

K

KANAN, Sean 1966-

PERSONAL: Born Sean Perelman, November 2, 1966, in Cleveland, OH; son of Dale (a jewelry chain-store owner) and Michele (a real-estate agent) Perelman; married Athena Ubach, September 26, 1999. *Education:* Attended Boston University; University of California—Los Angeles, B.A.

ADDRESSES: Office—c/o *The Bold and the Beautiful,* 7800 Beverly Blvd., Los Angeles, CA 90036. *Agent*—Independent Management Group, 6380 Wilshire Blvd., Suite 1010, Los Angeles, CA 90048.

CAREER: Actor, producer, and screenwriter. Owner of Kanan/Hammerschlag Productions. Actor in films, including (as John Robbins) *Hide and Go Shriek,* New Star Entertainment, 1988; (as Mike Barnes) *The Karate Kid III,* Columbia, 1989; (as Jeffrey) *Rich Girl,* Studio Three Film Corp., 1990; (and producer) *Oasis Café* (short film), 1994; *The Fear: Halloween Night,* 1999; (as Jay) *The Chaos Factor,* PM Entertainment Group, Inc., 2000; *Chump Change,* 2000; (as Don) *Crash Point Zero* (also known as *Extreme Limits*), New City Releasing, 2000; (as Julian March; and producer) *March,* 2001; (as Alex Patterson; and executive producer) *Chasing Holden,* Christopher Eberts Productions, 2001; and (as Craig) *Ten Attitudes,* 2001.

Actor in television series, including (as Gregg Parker) *The Outsiders,* Fox, 1990; *Wild Palms* (miniseries), 1993; (as Alan "A. J." Quartermain, Jr. #7) *General Hospital,* American Broadcasting Companies (ABC), 1993-97; (as Jude Cavanaugh) *Sunset Beach,* National Broadcasting Company (NBC), 1999; and (as Deacon Sharp) *The Bold and the Beautiful,* Columbia Broadcasting System (CBS), 2000—. Actor in made-for-television movies, including (as Jeff Sorrento) *Perry Mason: The Cast of the Maligned Mobster,* NBC, 1991; and (as Mark Stratton) *Perry Mason: The Case of the Killer Kiss,* 1993. Celebrity contestant on two Cancun-based episodes of *Search Party,* E! Network, 2000; guest star on numerous television series. Actor in stage productions, including *Irish Coffee,* Burbage Theater, Los Angeles, CA, and (as Austin; and producer) *True West,* Zephyr Theater, Los Angeles. Also does stand-up comedy; Father's (bar), Boston, MA, bouncer.

AWARDS, HONORS: Golden Boomerang award for best couple in daytime television (with Adrienne Frantz), for *The Bold and the Beautiful.*

WRITINGS:

(With others; and producer) *Oasis Café* (short film), 1994.
(And co-executive producer) *Chasing Holden* (screenplay), Christopher Eberts Productions, 2001.

SIDELIGHTS: Sean Kanan, screenwriter for the film *Chasing Holden,* got his first big break as an actor when he was cast as the villain in the 1989 film *Karate Kid III.* Although the role nearly killed him—he developed severe internal bleeding after performing twenty takes of a stunt that required him to land hard on his stomach—it helped to propel him into long-term roles on the popular soap operas *General Hospital* and *The Bold and the Beautiful.*

In addition to acting, Kanan has been involved in writing and producing films since 1994, when the short film *Oasis Café* was released. Kanan's first feature-length film, *Chasing Holden,* was released in 2001. This film, which is loosely based on Kanan's own experiences in boarding school, is about the teenage son of the governor of New York. The boy, Neil, is sent to a boarding school by his father because the man is too busy running New York to take proper care of his troubled son. At the school, Neil meets a young woman named T. J., with whom he runs away to New York to try to meet J. D. Salinger, the author of the novel *Catcher in the Rye.* Neil wants to meet Salinger because he sees strong parallels between his own life and the life of Holden Caulfield, the runaway teenage protagonist of *Catcher in the Rye,* but as the movie progresses the audience is forced to wonder if Neil's interest in Salinger and *Catcher in the Rye* is a healthy way of searching for meaning in his own life, or if it is a dangerous obsession.

BIOGRAPHICAL AND CRITICAL SOURCES:

BOOKS

Contemporary Theatre, Film, and Television, Volume 38, Gale (Detroit, MI), 2002.

PERIODICALS

Entertainment Weekly, October 21, 1994, Alan Carter, interview with Kanan, p. 54.
Interview, July, 1989, Firooz Zahedi, "Reel Villains," pp. 62-65.
People, July 17, 1989, Margot Dougherty, "Critically Injured in Filming, *Karate Kid* Bad Boy Sean Kanan Rallies to Fight to the Finish," pp. 51-52.
Soap Opera Digest, August 31, 1993; October 24, 2000.
Soap Opera Magazine, December 28, 1993.
Soap Opera Update, April 20, 1993.
Soap Opera Weekly, September 28, 1993; August 24, 1999.
Soap World, May, 2001.

Teen Magazine, July, 1989, Michele Schooler, "Teens They're Talking About," pp. 42-43; September, 1990, "Kids with a Cause: A Look at Some Young Stars Making a Difference in the World Today," pp. 84-85; May, 1991, review of *Rich Girl,* pp. 62-63.
TV Guide, June 21, 1997, Michael Logan, "Shake-up at the *Hospital,*" p. 34.
Variety, June 10, 1991, review of *Rich Girl,* p. 61.

ONLINE

Bikkit.com, http://www.bikkit.com/ (April 28, 2003), review of *Chasing Holden.*
CBS Daytime, http://www.cbs.com/ (April 24, 2003), "Sean Kanan Speaks Out."
Movie Chicks, http://www.themoviechicks.com/ (April 28, 2003), review of *Chasing Holden.*
Sean Kanan Home Page, http://www.seankanan.com (April 24, 2003).
Soap Central, http://www.soapcentral.com/ (April 24, 2003), "Sean Kanan."*

*   *   *

KEATING, Edward M. 1925-2003

OBITUARY NOTICE—See index for *CA* sketch: Born April 17, 1925, in New York, NY; died of pneumonia April 2, 2003, in Palo Alto, CA. Publisher, attorney, educator, and author. Keating is remembered as the founder of the left-wing magazine *Ramparts.* An attorney by training, he earned his law degree from Stanford University in 1950 after serving in the U.S. Navy for three years. He practiced law for four years before becoming a businessman, exploring various business options, including real estate. Raised in a Protestant family, Keating converted to Catholicism in his late twenties, and this eventually led to his founding in 1962 of *Ramparts,* which was originally intended to be a quarterly Catholic magazine for writers and intellectuals. Soon, however, it became noted as a left-wing monthly periodical with a circulation of 400,000. Keating's stand against the Vietnam War and strong pro-civil rights ideas made the magazine a leading voice for what was called the New Left. He had great sympathy for even the most radical African Americans, including the Black Panthers, hiring Eldridge Cleaver, author of *Soul on Ice,* straight out of prison and publishing the writings of John Howard Griffin, among other black writers. Within the pages of *Ramparts* could also be found contributions by such authors as Susan Sontag and Seymour Hersh. When *Ramparts* was taken over by new investors in 1967, Keating was dismissed from his own magazine, which continued on only until 1975. He subsequently abandoned Catholicism for agnosticism and made an unsuccessful bid for Congress. Next, he plunged into anti-war activism, was chair of the West Coast Committee to End the War in Vietnam, and resumed practicing law. Typically, he defended underdogs such as Black Panther leader Huey Newton. An account of this experience was published in his *Free Huey!: The True Story of the Trial of Huey P. Newton for Murder* (1971). Keating was also the author of two other books, *The Scandal of Silence* (1965) and the novella *The Broken Bough: The Solution to the Riddle of Man* (1975), as well as a number of short stories.

OBITUARIES AND OTHER SOURCES:

PERIODICALS

Los Angeles Times, April 12, 2003, p. B19.
New York Times, April 12, 2003, p. A20.

*　　*　　*

KEITH, (G.) Stuart 1931-2003

OBITUARY NOTICE—See index for *CA* sketch: Born September 4, 1931, in Clothall, Hertfordshire, England; died of a heart attack February 13, 2003, on the island of Chuuk, Micronesia. Ornithologist and author. Keith was a world-renowned bird expert and cofounder of the American Birding Association. He attended Marlborough College before serving in the King's Own Scottish Borderers during the Korean War. After the war, he earned a master's degree in classics from Oxford University. Being practical-minded, Keith began his career working in finance, but his love of birds led him to quit in 1958 and take a job as a research associate in the department of ornithology at the American Museum of Natural History in New York City. He was still on staff there at the time of his death. His income mostly came from writing and lecturing about birds, and he used this money for his travels around the world, often leading field trips to places such as Africa, Costa Rica, the Far East, and New Zealand. A cofounder of the American Birding Association in 1968, Keith became the group's president in 1970 and was active on its board until 1990. He also cowrote *The Collins Bird Guide: A Photographic Guide to the Birds of Britain and Europe* (1980) and coedited the seven-volume *The Birds of Africa* (1980—), the last volume of which was in progress at his death. During the course of his life, Keith identified over 6,500 birds on his "lifelist," a record topped only by Phoebe Snetsinger in 1999. He was in Micronesia on a birding expedition when he had a fatal heart attack just after spotting a new bird species for his lifelist.

OBITUARIES AND OTHER SOURCES:

PERIODICALS

Independent (London, England), March 21, 2003, p. 22.
New York Times, March 8, 2003, p. B7.
Times (London, England), April 5, 2003, p. 46.

*　　*　　*

KELLEY, Joanna (Elizabeth) 1910-2003

OBITUARY NOTICE—See index for *CA* sketch: Born May 23, 1910, in Muree, India (now in Pakistan); died April 12, 2003, in London, England. Prison director and author. Kelley was a former governor of Holloway Prison, where she was known for making reforms in how women prisoners are treated. She studied economics at Girton College, Cambridge, where she received a B.A. in 1931, before attending the Sorbonne and earning a diplôme pour étrangers in 1932. Working at the Department of Pre-History at the Musée de l'Homme in Paris, France, she was forced to return to England following the German invasion of France. During the first part of World War II Kelley was a youth club leader for her local YWCA, and then, from 1942 to 1947, was a welfare officer in Bath. She next took up a career working at women's prisons, serving as assistant governor at Holloway Prison from 1947 to 1952, as governor of Askham Grange Prison until 1959, and then returning to Holloway Prison from 1959 to 1966. Having a deep concern for the inmates at her prisons, she believed that incarcerated women should be given as much help as possible to prepare them for productive lives after their release. Toward this end, as assistant director of prisons for women from 1967 to 1974 she tried to organize prisons in a way where the inmates could live in family-like groups, but bureaucracy often stood in the way of making her plans a complete success. She outlined her ideas on prison management in two books: *When the Gates Shut* (1967) and *Who Casts the First Stone?* (1978). Her work did not go unrecognized; Kelley was names to the Order of the Council of St. George's House from 1971 to 1977, and was a member of the Redundant Churches Committee from 1974 to 1979 and of the Scott Holland Trust from 1978 to 1986. She also was a continuing sponsor of the YWCA.

OBITUARIES AND OTHER SOURCES:

PERIODICALS

Guardian (London, England), May 2, 2003, p. 31.
Independent, (London, England), May 6, 2003, p. 16.
Times (London, England), April 22, 2003, p. 28.

* * *

KELLEY, Robin D. G. 1962-

PERSONAL: Born March 14, 1962; daughter of Ananda Sattwa; married Diedra Harris-Kelley (an artist); children: Elleza. *Ethnicity:* "African American." *Education:* California State University at Long Beach, B.A., 1983; University of California, Los Angeles, M.A. (African history), 1985, Ph.D. (U.S. history), 1987. *Hobbies and other interests:* "Playing piano."

ADDRESSES: Agent—Mary Evans Inc., 242 East Fifth St., New York, NY 10003.

CAREER: Southeastern Massachusetts University, professor of history; Emory University, Philadelphia, PA, professor of history; University of Michigan, Ann Arbor, professor of history; New York University, New York, NY, professor of history and Africana studies, 1994—; Brooklyn College, scholar-in-residence, 2001-02.

AWARDS, HONORS: Southern Historical Association's Francis Butler Simkins Prize, and Organization of American Historians Elliot Rudwick Prize, both 1991, both for *Hammer and Hoe;* National Conference of Black Political Scientists, Outstanding Book Award for *Race Rebels,* 1995; *Village Voice* best book designation, 1997, for *Yo' Mama's Dysfunktional!: Fighting the Culture Wars in Urban America;* New York Public Library's Outstanding Book for the Teen Age, 1997, for *Into the Fire;* History Book Club and *Choice* Outstanding Academic title, 2000, for *To Make Our World Anew.*

WRITINGS:

Hammer and Hoe: Alabama Communists during the Great Depression, University of North Carolina Press (Chapel Hill, NC), 1990.
Race Rebels: Culture, Politics, and the Black Working Class, Free Press (New York, NY), 1994.
Into the Fire—African Americans since 1970, Oxford University Press (New York, NY), 1996.
(With Vincent Harding and Earl Lewis) *We Changed the World: African Americans, 1945-1970,* Oxford University Press (New York, NY), 1997.
Yo' Mama's Disfunktional!: Fighting the Culture Wars in Urban America, Beacon Press (Boston, MA), 1997.
(With Howard Zinn and Dana Frank) *Three Strikes: Miners, Musicians, Salesgirls, and the Fighting Spirit of Labor's Last Century,* Beacon Press (Boston MA), 2001.
Freedom Dreams: The Black Radical Imagination, Beacon Press (Boston, MA), 2002.

EDITOR

(With Sidney J. Lemelle) *Imagining Home: Class, Culture, and Nationalism in the African Diaspora,* Verso (New York, NY), 1994.
(With Earl Lewis) *The Young Oxford History of African Americans,* Oxford University Press (New York, NY), 1995.
(With Earl Lewis) *To Make Our World Anew: A History of African Americans,* Oxford University Press (New York, NY), 2000.

Contributor of articles to periodicals, including *New York Times* and *Chronicle of Higher Education.*

WORK IN PROGRESS: Writing a biography of jazz pianist and composer Thelonious Monk.

SIDELIGHTS: Robin D. G. Kelley, a professor of history and Africana studies at New York University, has spent a major portion of his life examining the lives of people who tried to change the world. He studied these people and the social movements in which they were involved as he attempted to discover a formula that might be the most effective in making much-needed transformations in society. In the course of his examination, however, Kelley was forced to conclude that it is hard to define the success of such social movements. Looking at them from the point of view of whether they were able to topple or transform the basic power base that had existed before the social movement, one would have to judge that most movements failed; but then, over the course of years, Kelley began to look at the movements in a different way. He studied the inspiration behind the radical factions, the "alternative visions and dreams that inspire new generations to continue to struggle for change." It is these visions, Kelley believes, that will inspire new concepts of freedom.

Kelley is often referred to as an accessible writer and lecturer. As Clayborne Carson described Kelley in the *Stanford Online Report,* "He's in the middle ground between social history and a kind of postmodern cultural analysis." In other words, not only is he easy to understand, Kelley is also as aware of cultural history as he is of current events. The major focus of his writing is on how people—black people in particular—have defined freedom and the ways in which to attain it. The history he writes is informed by what Kelley refers to as the ebb and flow of freedom. "I don't think there's going to be a moment when suddenly we're all going to get together and win," Kelley told Elaine Ray in the *Stanford Online Report.* "I think it's a constant battle."

Kelley's first book, 1990's *Hammer and Hoe,* relates the story of the relationship between the Communist Party in America and the black community through an emphasis on African Americans living in Alabama during the 1930s. "Alabama Communism in the 1930s," wrote Daniel Wright in a review of Kelley's book for the *Southern Humanities Review,* "resembled nothing so much as a great evangelical community of the harassed and disposed." The Communist Party was

the only source of inspiration for African Americans living in the Deep South, in states that saw frequent lynchings, beatings, and rampant disparities between the lives of its citizens based only on the color of their skin. In the North, African Americans were assisted by "divergent movements," Wright stated, such as "Socialism, the Wobblies, and communities of radical European immigrants." In Alabama, only the communists had the courage to defy the ruling "class terror." In his concluding remarks about *Hammer and Hoe,* Wright stated that Kelley's book is not only an outstanding account of "events and persons largely unknown to and unacknowledged by much of the world, but a passionate summons to readers to explore a militant past that in many unappreciated ways has shaped our present and assuredly will help determine our future." In another article in the *New York Review of Books,* George M. Fredrickson pointed out that Kelley's book provides "revisionist post-cold war scholarship" that is unlike the more popular political rhetoric regarding the Communist Party in the United States, showing that "the Party did not merely project Soviet influence onto the American domestic scene but was also helping to organize grass-roots movements that embodied the beliefs, needs, and aspirations of the people who took part in them."

Race Rebels: Culture, Politics, and the Black Working Class is a collection of eight essays that cover a wide range of topics, from Jim Crow laws and their effects on black workers in the South to contemporary rappers in Los Angeles. In these essays, according to Bruce Nelson for the *Journal of Southern History,* "Kelley challenges traditional interpretations of the black working class." Kelley's beliefs run contrary to the easily accepted myth that blacks are lazy. As Nelson found in Kelley's writing, "the black working class has had good reason to develop an antiwork ethic." They were, after all, doing the most difficult and most disgusting work in the labor force with the least reward for their efforts. In retaliation against these challenging working conditions, many African Americans rebelled. These rebellions took various forms, as quoted from Kelley's book by Eric Lott in the *Village Voice Literary Supplement:* "from foot-dragging to sabotage, theft at the workplace to absenteeism, cursing to graffiti." Kelley's interpretations, according to David Rouse, writing for *Booklist* contain "a bold premise" that will most certainly "provoke controversy."

In 1997 Kelley published *Yo' Mama's Disfunktional!: Fighting the Culture Wars in Urban America,* in which, according to Salim Muwakkil in the *Washington Post Book World,* Kelley argues against the often accepted "culturalist views of conservatives" that the "behavior of the urban poor explains their poverty." The conservative view of people living in urban ghettos, Kelley states in his book, is that they are imbued with errant cultural values, and that explains their actions as well as the reasons why they are so economically devastated.

Kelley continues his exploration of black culture and social movements in his 2002 publication *Freedom Dreams: The Black Radical Imagination,* which has gained the most critical attention of all his books. In it, Kelley discusses what he calls the Marvelous, a concept his mother taught him. It is a way of seeing beauty in the world, which in turn inspires the imagination. "This parental gift," wrote Lisa Kennedy, in the *Village Voice,* has provided Kelley with an understanding of the "wild current of freedom" that weaves through the lives and philosophies of "black cultural prophets and community visionaries, poetic renegades and musical rebels" whose lives Kelley studies in his book. In *Freedom Dreams* Kelley unearths the inner core of beliefs from a variety of black radical thinkers, which include Paul Robeson, Jayne Cortez, and Richard Wright. Borrowing concepts from all of his subjects, Kelley puts together a philosophy of his own, one influenced by the concepts of surrealism as espoused by Aimé Cesaire, who believed in the power of the unfettered imagination. *Freedom Dreams* concluded Laura Ciolkowski in the *New York Times Book Review* is a "bold and provocative celebration of the black radical imagination."

Kelley told *CA:* "I write primarily to effect change. I hope my work helps readers think critically about the world we've inherited and inspire some to participate in movements for social change. For this reason being politically involved is important for my own work. It always enriches my writing, forcing me to be clear and accessible. However, my latest project, a biography of Thelonious Monk, is less a product of politics and social movements than a labor of love."

BIOGRAPHICAL AND CRITICAL SOURCES:

PERIODICALS

American Prospect, January 1, 2002, Cowie Jefferson, review of *Three Strikes: Miners, Musicians, Salesgirls, and the Fighting Spirit of Labor's Last Century,* pp. 41-44.

American Visions, February, 1996, Dale Edwyna Smith, review of *Race Rebels: Culture, Politics, and the Black Working Class,* p. 34.

Black Issues in Higher Education, January 8, 1998, D. Kamili Anderson, review of *Yo' Mama's Disfunktional!: Fighting the Culture Wars in Urban America,* pp. 37-38.

Booklist, October 15, 1994, David Rouse, review of *Race Rebels,* p. 382; February 15, 1996, Hazel Rochman, review of *Into the Fire: African Americans since 1970,* p. 999; October 15, 1997, Mary Carrol, review of *Yo' Mama's Disfunktional!,* p. 367; June 1, 2002, Vernon Ford, review of *Freedom Dreams: The Black Radical Imagination,* p. 1652.

Choice, April, 1991, R. D. Ward, review of *Hammer and Hoe: Alabama Communists during the Great Depression,* pp. 1370-1371.

Civil Rights Journal, fall, 2000, review of *To Make Our World Anew: A History of African Americans,* p. 62.

Journal of African History, January, 1996, Wilson J. Moses, review of *Imagining Home: Class, Culture, and Nationalism in the African Diaspora,* pp. 128-129.

Journal of American Ethnic History, fall, 1997, Donald R. Wright, review of *Imagining Home: Class,* pp. 71-75; fall, 1998, Emory J. Tolbert, review of *Race Rebels,* pp. 103-108.

Journal of Southern History, February, 1996, Bruce Nelson, review of *Race Rebels,* pp. 171-172; August, 2002, Charles Pete Banner-Haley, review of *To Make Our World Anew,* p. 669.

Library Journal, October 1, 1997, Ellen Gilbert, review of *Yo' Mama's Disfunktional!* p. 106; May 1, 2000, Edward G. McCormack, review of *To Make Our World Anew,* p. 134.

Monthly Review, February, 1996, Paul Buhle, review of *Race Rebelss,* pp. 41-48.

Nation, June 24, 1991, Jon Wiener, review of *Hammer and Hoe,* pp. 854-856.

New York Times Book Review, June 8, 1995, George M. Fredrickson, review of *Hammer and Hoe,* pp. 33-35, 38-39; June 23, 2002, Laura Ciolkowski, review of *Freedom Dreams: The Radical Black Imagination,* p. 21.

Publishers Weekly, September 26, 1994, review of *Race Rebels,* p. 48; April 24, 2000, review of *To Make Our World Anew: A History of African Americans,* p. 76; July 16, 2001, review of *Three Strikes,* p. 173.

Southern Humanities Review, Spring, 1992, Daniel Wright, review of *Hammer and Hoe,* pp. 172-73.

Village Voice, July 5, 2002, Lisa Kennedy, "Love and Bullets", review of *Freedom Dreams.*

Village Voice Literary Supplement, February, 1996, Eric Lott, review of *Race Rebels,* pp. 12-14.

Washington Post Book World, November 30, 1997, Salim Muwakkil, review of *Yo' Mama's Disfunktional!;* spring, 2002, Steve Early, review of *Three Strikes,* p. 157.

ONLINE

Stanford Online Report, http://www.Stanford.edu/dept. news/ (July 29, 1998), Elaine Ray, "Robin Kelley Brings Grass-roots Movements to History's Grand Narrative."

*   *   *

KERR, E(laine) Katherine 1942-

PERSONAL: Born April 20, 1942, in Indianapolis, IN; daughter of John Francis (a physician) and Beatrice Mae (Westfall) Kerr; married James Joseph Mapes (a hypnotist, producer, and actor), May 31, 1980 (divorced, 1986).

ADDRESSES: Agent—Silver, Massetti & Szatmary, 145 West 45th Street, Suite 1204, New York, NY 10036. *E-mail*—ekath@ekatherinekerr.com.

CAREER: Actress, writer, and teacher. Actress in stage productions (under the name Elaine Kerr), including (as chorus leader and Cassandra) *The Trojan Women,* Off-Broadway, 1963; (as Kay) *Oh, Kay,* Buffalo, NY, 1967; (as Ellen) *Luv,* New Orleans, LA, 1970; (as Rosalind) *As You Like It,* New Orleans, 1970; (as Lucy Brown) *The Threepenny Opera,* New Orleans, 1970; (as Blanche DuBois) *A Streetcar Named Desire,* New Orleans, 1970; (as Dee Jacobson) *No Place to Be Somebody,* Morosco Theatre, New York, NY, 1971; (as Letitia) *The Contrast,* Eastside Playhouse, New York, 1972; (as Melanie) *Boo Hoo,* Playwrights Horisons Theatre, New York, 1972; (as Sabina) *The Skin of Our Teeth,* Seattle, WA, 1973; *A Streetcar Named Desire,* St. James Theatre, New York, 1973; *Mert and Phil,* New York Shakespeare Festival, 1974; (as Sparky Snyder) *In Honored Memory of Ted and Sparky,* Universal Relevance Group Enterprises, National

Theatre (U.R.G.E.N.T.), New York, 1974; (as Valerie) *The Pornographer's Daughter,* Manhattan Theatre Club, New York, 1975; and (as Cecil) *Juno's Swans,* PAF Playhouse, Huntington, NY, 1978.

Actress in stage productions (under the name E. Katherine Kerr), including (as Ellen, Mrs. Saunders, and Betty) *Cloud 9,* Lucille Lortel Theatre, New York, 1981; (as Nell) *Passion,* Longacre Theatre, New York, then London, both 1983; *Laughing Wild,* Playwrights Horizons Theatre, 1987 and 2003; *Urban Blight,* Manhattan Theatre Club, 1988; *The Fourth Wall,* Westport, CT, 1992; *Unfinished Stories,* New York Theatre Workshop, New York, 1994; and *The Credeaux Canvas,* Playwrights Horizon, 2001. Also appeared at Pennsylvania State Theatre Festival in (as Rosalind) *As You Like It,* (as Gwendolyn) *Ernest in Love,* and (as Blanche Cook) *Night Watch;* at the Alliance Theatre in Atlanta, GA, in (as Miss Gilchrist) *The Hostage,* (as Rita Marimba) *Marathon 33,* (as Beatrice) *Much Ado about Nothing,* (as Jenny Diver) *The Threepenny Opera,* and (as Viola) *Twelfth Night;* at the Arena Stage in Washington, DC, in (as Ellen) *Exhibition* and (as Amy) *Porch;* has also appeared in *Scenes from American Life* and *Search for Signs of Intelligent Life;* also appeared at McCarter Theatre, Princeton, NJ, 1975-76. Toured (as Toby Laundau) with *Gingerbread Lady.*

Actress in films, including (as Harry's wife) *Tattoo,* Twentieth Century-Fox, 1981; (as Irene Furman) *Power,* Metro-Goldwyn-Mayer (MGM), 1983; (as analyst) *Lovesick,* Warner Bros., 1983; (as Gilda Schultz) *Silkwood,* Twentieth Century-Fox, 1983; (as Lucille Haxby) *Reuben, Reuben,* Twentieth Century-Fox, 1983; (as Mary Lee Ochs) *Children of a Lesser God,* Paramount, 1986; (as Grace Komisky) *Suspect,* TriStar, 1987; (as Adelle Phillips) *Three o'Clock High,* 1987; (as judge) *The Devil's Advocate,* Warner Bros., 1997; (under the name Katherine Kerr; as Candace) *Next Stop Wonderland,* Miramax, 1998; (as Gertrude) *The Imposters,* Fox Searchlight, 1998; (as attorney general) *The Siege,* Twentieth Century-Fox, 1998; and (as Harriet Tolliver) *Songcatcher,* Trimark, 2000.

Actress in television programs, including (as Marguerite) *Ryan's Hope,* American Broadcasting Companies, Inc. (ABC); (as kidnapper) *Shady Hill Kidnapping,* Public Broadcasting Service, 1982; *Abby, My Love,* Columbia Broadcasting System (CBS), 1991; (as Mrs. Elizabeth Avery Waring) *Separate But Equal* (miniseries), ABC, 1991; (as Mrs. Parmore) *The Buccaneers* (miniseries), (PBS), 1995; (as Judge Stockton) *The Prosecutors* (made-for-television movie), National Broadcasting Company (NBC), 1996; and (as Cecilia) *Cupid & Cate* (made-for-television movie), 2000. Guest star on *Law & Order,* NBC.

New York University and Playwright's Horizons, both New York, NY, instructor (advanced scene study); former instructor at the 42nd Street Collective and Sarah Lawrence College; leads other acting classes and workshops in NY and CT.

MEMBER: Actors' Equity Association, Screen Actors Guild, American Federation of Television and Radio Artists, Dramatists Guild.

AWARDS, HONORS: Obie Award and Villager Award, for *Cloud 9.*

WRITINGS:

Juno's Swans (produced in Huntington, NY, 1978, then Second Stage, New York, NY, 1985), Dramatists Play Service (New York, NY), 1998.
The Four Principles: A Guide for Living from Authentic Acting, 2003.

Contributor to *Urban Blight,* produced at Manhattan Theatre Club, New York, NY, 1988. Author of the one-woman show *On the Zip-Line* and of an unbroadcast television adaptation of *Juno's Swans.*

SIDELIGHTS: E. Katherine Kerr has been a notable presence on American stages for several decades. Although she is best known for her theatrical performances, Kerr is also a writer. She is the author of several plays and of the book *The Four Principles: A Guide for Living from Authentic Acting,* which is based on acting workshops Kerr has led for many years.

Kerr's best-known play may be *Juno's Swans,* which was first performed in 1978 but remains popular enough that the script was reprinted in 1998. The play is about a woman named Cary who lives in a tiny apartment on the Upper West Side of Manhattan while attempting to break into acting. Her ex-boyfriend, a songwriter whose current project is a musical adapta-

tion of the Shakespearean play *As You Like It,* also lives in Cary's one-room apartment some of the time. Then Cary's sister Cecilia appears on Cary's doorstep, after leaving her husband and two children in California, and moves in with them as well. Cecilia, formerly a traditional, conservative housewife, does not fit in well with Cary and her ex-boyfriend's bohemian life at first, but eventually, after a few crises, the three all learn to get along, and Cary and her ex-boyfriend's Broadway dreams are realized.

BIOGRAPHICAL AND CRITICAL SOURCES:

BOOKS

Contemporary Theatre, Film, and Television, Volume 34, Gale (Detroit, MI), 2001.

PERIODICALS

Back Stage, February 12, 1982, Judy Thrall, "Women Playwright Upsurge: Gain Stronghold on Stage," pp. 39-40; June 10, 1983, Michael Sommers, review of *Passion,* p. 87; March 18, 1994, Amy Hersh, "How Performers Stay at Their Peak," pp. 29-33; July 6, 2001, Michael Lazan, review of *The Credeaux Canvas,* p. 40.
Los Angeles Times, January 6, 1984, Clarke Taylor, "Kerr Keeps an Eye out for Bigger Roles," p. 1.
Nation, June 27, 1981, Richard Gilman, review of *Cloud 9,* pp. 802-803.
New Leader, June 13, 1983, Leo Sauvage, review of *Passion,* pp. 19-20.
New Republic, June 27, 1983, Robert Brustein, review of *Passion,* p. 24; January 30, 1984, Stanley Kauffmann, review of *Reuben, Reuben,* pp. 26-27.
Newsweek, June 6, 1983, Jack Kroll, review of *Passion,* p. 90; January 2, 1984, David Ansen, review of *Reuben, Reuben,* p. 58; October 26, 1987, David Ansen, review of *Suspect,* p. 86.
New York, May 30, 1983, John Simon, review of *Passion,* pp. 74-75; June 10, 1985, John Simon, review of *Juno's Swans,* p. 93; November 23, 1987, John Simon, review of *Laughing Wild,* p. 117; March 7, 1994, John Simon, review of *Unfinished Stories,* pp. 66-67.
New Yorker, June 1, 1981, Edith Oliver, review of *Cloud 9,* p. 124; May 23, 1983, Brendan Gill, review of *Passion,* p. 103; November 23, 1987,

Edith Oliver, review of *Laughing Wild,* p. 153; March 14, 1994, Nancy Franklin, review of *Unfinished Stories,* p. 89.

New York Times, May 31, 1981, Walter Kerr, review of *Cloud 9,* p. D3; August 7, 1981, Carol Lawson, "Chaplin Is Subject of a Second Planned Musical," p. 15; December 19, 1983, Vincent Candy, review of *Reuben, Reuben,* p. 21; May 29, 1985, Frank Rich, review of *Juno's Swans,* p. 22; November 12, 1987, Frank Rich, review of *Laughing Wild,* p. 22; February 27, 1994, Vincent Canby, review of *Unfinished Stories,* p. H10.

People, November 9, 1987, Ralph Novak, review of *Suspect,* p. 14.

Time, May 30, 1983, T. E. Kalem, review of *Passion,* p. 85.

Variety, November 18, 1987, review of *Laughing Wild,* p. 98; July 29, 1988, review of *Urban Blight,* p. 67; August 24, 1992, Markland Taylor, review of *The Fourth Wall,* p. 69.

Wall Street Journal, July 24, 1981, Edwin Wilson, review of *Cloud 9,* p. 21; June 10, 1983, Edwin Wilson, review of *Passion,* pp. 27, 31.

ONLINE

E. Katherine Kerr Home Page, http://ekatherinekerr. com (February 25, 2003).

Guide to World Drama, http://www.4-wall.com/ (February 25, 2003), summary of *Juno's Swans.**

* * *

KIRK, G(eoffrey) S(tephen) 1921-2003

OBITUARY NOTICE—See index for *CA* sketch: Born December 3, 1921, in Nottingham, England; died March 10, 2003, in Rake, West Sussex, England. Educator and author. Kirk was a scholar of Greek who was a longtime professor at Cambridge University. He received his education at Clare College, Cambridge, attending classes only a year before joining the British Royal Navy. Because he had learned some modern Greek, he was sent to that country, where he helped with the Greek resistance against the Germans and received a Distinguished Service Cross. After the war, Kirk completed a master's degree at Cambridge in 1948 and a D.Litt. in 1965. His career as an educator began when he joined the Cambridge staff as a

research fellow in 1946; he later became Regius Professor of Greek and fellow of Trinity College in 1974. This long association with Cambridge was interrupted by five years at Yale University from 1965 to 1970, and two years at the University of Bristol in the early 1970s. He retired from Cambridge as professor emeritus in 1982. During his career, Kirk edited and wrote a number of scholarly books on classic Greek literature, including *Heraclitus: The Cosmic Fragments* (1952), *The Songs of Homer* (1962), *Homer and the Oral Tradition* (1977), and two of the six volumes of *The Iliad: A Commentary* (1985, 1990), for which he was also the series' general editor. In 1997 he published his memoir of his early life in the Navy and Cambridge titled *Toward the Aegean Sea.*

OBITUARIES AND OTHER SOURCES:

BOOKS

Writers Directory, 18th edition, St. James Press (Detroit, MI), 2003.

PERIODICALS

Independent (London, England), March 19, 2003, p. 20.

Times (London, England), March 24, 2003, p. 28.

* * *

KUHN, Wolfgang Erasmus 1914-2003

OBITUARY NOTICE—See index for *CA* sketch: Born April 12, 1914, in Leipzig, Germany; died March 10, 2003, in Stanford, CA. Educator, musician, and author. Kuhn was known as the co-creator of a computerized system of music instruction. After immigrating with his family to America from Germany, he attended college at the University of Illinois, where he earned a B.Mus. in 1936, a master's in 1943, and a doctorate in music education in 1953. Kuhn also taught at his alma mater from 1943 to 1955, followed by three years as associate professor of music at the University of Colorado at Boulder. At both universities he was head of the music education department. In 1958 he joined the faculty at Stanford, where he was in charge of both the Department of Music and the School of Education. Kuhn was an advocate of the Suzuki method of teaching music and held summer workshops using Suzuki's instruction principles. Later, he teamed up with Paul Lorton, Jr., to develop computer software called the *MusicMaster.* Released in 1982, it used an Apple II-Plus to help students learn to play by ear. Not long after this accomplishment, Kuhn retired from Stanford. During his career he published several books on music instruction, including *Principles of String Class Teaching* (1957), *Instrumental Music: Principles and Methods of Instruction* (1962; second edition, 1970), and *The Strings* (1967).

OBITUARIES AND OTHER SOURCES:

PERIODICALS

Los Angeles Times, March 23, 2003, p. B16.

ONLINE

Stanford Report Online, http://www.stanford.edu/dept/ news/report/ (March 19, 2003).

*   *   *

KURKOV, Andrei 1961-

PERSONAL: Born 1961, in St. Petersburg, USSR (now Russia). *Education:* Attended Kieve Foreign Language Institute.

ADDRESSES: *Home*—Kiev, Russia. *Agent*—c/o Author Mail, Farrar, Straus & Giroux, 19 Union Square West, New York, NY 1003.

CAREER: Novelist, children's author, and screenwriter. Worked as a warden at Odessa Prison while serving in the military; worked as a journalist and film cameraman.

AWARDS, HONORS: Independent Foreign Fiction Prize finalist, Arts Council of England, 2002.

WRITINGS:

Death and the Penguin, translated by George Bird, Farrar, Straus & Giroux (New York, NY), 2001.

Also author of three other novels, four children's books and several screenplays in Russian.

SIDELIGHTS: *Death and the Penguin* is the first novel by Ukrainian author Andrey Kurkov to be translated into English. Ostensibly a mystery, the book is actually a satirical look at life in post-Soviet Ukraine, with all of its corruption and its crumbling institutions. According to Ken Kalfus in the *New York Times,* while the novel "strains to succeed as a existential thriller, it does offer a striking portrait of post-Soviet alienation."

Set in the city of Kiev, the novel concerns the grim life of a man named Viktor, a lonely writer who adopts a penguin from a down-and-out zoo which can no longer care for its animals. The penguin, whom he names Mischa, serves as a kind of alter ego for Viktor since both are lonely residents of a world gone awry. Viktor abandons his literary ambitions when he gets a job writing advance obituaries for a newspaper dominated by Ukrainian Mafia figures. Viktor's suspicions are awakened when, one by one, the people whose obituaries he has written begin to die mysteriously.

Viktor is befriended by another character named Mischa (whom he dubs "Mischa non-penguin"), an associate of his editor and a single parent with a four-year-old daughter, Sonya. One night Mischa (the friend) leaves Sonya with Viktor, asking that he care for her. The nanny he hires, Nina, soon becomes involved with Viktor, but the two do not fall in love. Meanwhile, Viktor's job description has come to include attendance, with the penguin, at the funerals of all the people whose obituaries he has written.

When the penguin Mischa becomes ill, in what Gabriele Annan in the *London Review of Books* called "the surreal element . . . readers expect from a Ukrainian novel," he receives a heart transplant from a boy who has been killed in an auto accident. The doctors soon advise that Mischa be sent to Antarctica to recover. In the meantime, Viktor loses his job and, fearing for his life since his own obituary has been written, takes Mischa's ticket and goes to Antarctica himself.

Critics seemed both amused and intrigued by the bizarre plot and characters of Kurkov's novel. Kalfus said that "Kurkov writes with a light, deadpan tone in a style reminiscent of Donald Barthelme." He noted that the book is a "Hitchcockian" story "whose absurdities are meant to provoke Kurkov's readers to strive for something beyond mere endurance." In the *Sunday Telegraph,* Christopher Tayler wrote that *Death and the Penguin* is "part fable, part thriller and part political satire—one which paints a bleak picture of life in post-Communist Ukraine." Annan called attention to the "implausibilities" in the novel, but complimented Kurkov "for the sense of Kiev that it evokes: an agreeable city—more modern than one might imagine—only with black splodges of mafialand sprinkled over its map." Moreover, Annan said, "Kurkov writes about relationships which are friendly without being warm, let alone passionate; and they have an unexpected, quite unforeseeable matter-of-fact charm."

In a review in the *Times Literary Supplement,* Joanna Griffiths wrote that "the simple fabular style suggests a Russian-language tradition of horrors told ingenuously, as in the works of Daniil Kharms." Kurkov, she continued, "has written a successfully brooding novel, which creates an enduring sense of dismay and strangeness."

BIOGRAPHICAL AND CRITICAL SOURCES:

PERIODICALS

Booklist, August, 2001, Bill Ott, review of *Death and the Penguin,* p. 2087.

Kirkus Reviews, August 15, 2001, review of *Death and the Penguin,* p. 1153.

London Review of Books, June 7, 2001, Gabriele Annan, "Two Mishas and Two Sergeys," p. 34.

New York Times, November 11, 2001, Ken Kalfus, "Open Season," p. 8L.

Spectator, May 5, 2001, John de Falbe, review of *Death and the Penguin,* p. 37.

Sunday Telegraph (London, England), June 17, 2001, Christopher Tayler, "A Man and His Bird."

Times (London, England) *Literary Supplement,* May 4, 2001, Joanna Griffiths, "Pining for the Antarctic," p. 23.*

KUSUGAK, Michael (Arvaarluk) 1948-

PERSONAL: Born April 27, 1948, in Repulse Bay, Northwest Territories, Canada; married; four sons. *Ethnicity:* "Inuit." *Education:* University of Saskatchewan, B.A. (English literature).

ADDRESSES: Home—P.O. Box 572, Rankin Inlet, Nunavut, Canada X0C 0G0. *E-mail*—mkusugak@ arctic.ca.

CAREER: Storyteller and author of books for children. Worked as a civil servant in Canada for fifteen years; Arctic College, director of community programs. Member, National Library of Canada advisory board and Rankin Inlet Library board. Lecturer at schools and libraries; storyteller at festivals and other venues, including Kaleidoscope 6, Calgary, Alberta, 1996, Young People's Theatre, Toronto, Ontario, 1997, Wordfest, 1998, and Sunshine Coast Festival of the Written Arts, Sechelt, British Columbia, 2003.

AWARDS, HONORS: Ruth Schwartz Children's Book Award, 1994, for *Northern Lights: The Soccer Trails.*

WRITINGS:

(With Robert Munsch) *A Promise Is a Promise,* illustrated by Vladyana Langer Krykorka, Firefly Books (New York, NY), 1988.

Baseball Bats for Christmas, illustrated by Vladyana Langer Krykorka, Firefly Books (New York, NY), 1990.

Hide and Sneak, illustrated by Vladyana Langer Krykorka, Firefly Books (New York, NY), 1992.

Northern Lights: The Soccer Trails, illustrated by Vladyana Langer Krykorka, Firefly Books (New York, NY), 1993.

My Arctic 1, 2, 3, illustrated by Vladyana Langer Krykorka, Annick Press (Willowdale, Ontario, Canada), 1996.

Arctic Stories, illustrated by Vladyana Langer Krykorka, Firefly Books (New York, NY), 1998.

Who Wants Rocks? Firefly Books (New York, NY), 1999.

A Promise Is a Promise has been anthologized in *Munschworks 3: The Third Munsch Treasury,* Firefly Books (New York, NY), 2000, and *The Munchworks Grand Treasury,* Annick Press (Willowdale, Ontario, Canada), 2001.

ADAPTATIONS: Northern Lights: The Soccer Trails was adapted as a CD-ROM, Discis Knowledge Research (Toronto, Ontario, Canada), 1995.

SIDELIGHTS: Michael Kusugak is a Canadian author who has broadened the spectrum of children's literature through his contribution of stories focusing on his Inuit heritage. Many of his titles, among them *Hide and Sneak, Baseball Bats for Christmas* and the short-story collection *Arctic Tales,* engage early elementary-grade readers with their crisp prose and unique subject matter. Reviewing *Baseball Bats for Christmas,* Kenneth Oppel remarked in *Quill & Quire* that Kusugak's "first-person narration is warm, energetic, and wonderfully humorous" as he tells the story of growing up in an Inuit fishing village.

Kusugak grew up in the small village of Repulse Bay, in Canada's Northwest Territories, and inherited his love of storytelling from his grandmother. As a child he spoke only Inuit, the language of his family, and his memories of those years, in which he lived in sod houses and igloos and traveled by dog team, has served as the basis of much of his fiction for young readers. By the time Kusugak was a teen the old Inuit way of life had gradually slipped away. He became one of the first Inuit in his region to graduate from a high school, a goal that required him to leave his home and become a boarding student during the school year. After college, although he worked for the Canadian government and for a local university, he always remained tied to his cultural roots and to Canada's Arctic region. As Jon C. Stott explained in an essay in *St. James Guide to Children's Writers,* "Kusugak set about to create stories that would combine elements of the old and modern worlds, would appeal to his own people as well as to larger audiences and would catch the attention of children who were primarily interested in television and video games."

Written with coauthor Robert Munsch, whom Kusugak met when Munsch appearing at a northern Canada school assembly, Kusugak's first published book, *A Promise Is a Promise,* is based on a childhood memory of going ice fishing. In the story, an Inuit girl named Allashua decides to disobey her parents' wishes and go fishing alone, but falls through the ice and is trapped by the Qallupilluit—creatures who dwell beneath the frozen sea. Released on her word that she will return to the Qallupilluit with her brothers and

sisters, Allashua tricks the sea beasts with help from her mother. André Gagnon praised the story in his *Canadian Materials* review, commending its "suspense, magical moments, and . . . most satisfying ending." *A Promise Is a Promise* has been included in several anthologies of Munsch's stories.

Allashua returns in *Hide and Sneak,* and again gets herself into trouble with a magical being. This time the being is a Ijiraq, a small impish man who lures the young girl from her home but is thwarted in his kidnaping attempt when Allashua finds help from another source. Calling *Hide and Sneak* "a triumph," *Canadian Children's Literature* reviewer Stan Atherton praised Kusugak's preteen heroine as "credible, open, imaginative, and even slightly rebellious," while a *Bloomsbury Review* contributor dubbed the story "charming."

Kusugak's short story collection *Arctic Stories* was published in 1999 and also features a young female protagonist. Agatha is the focus of the three tales included, all of which are take place during the late 1950s in a village along the Hudson Bay. Encounters with a U.S. Navy blimp and a large raven, as well as her adventures during her first year at boarding school, are recounted by Kusugak with what a *Publishers Weekly* contributor characterized as "clarity and dry humor." John Peters added in *Booklist* that *Arctic Tales* is a "combination of recognizable characters and exotic locale [that] will transport young readers effortlessly."

Also for novice readers, *Who Wants Rocks?* tells the story of Little Mountain, which exists in the Arctic region and leads a quiet life. With the coming of the Yukon gold rush, Little Mountain must contend with a strange man named Old Joe, who is determined to disrupt the mountain's surface and the creatures and plants making Little Mountain their home in his search for gold. Finally, Joe realizes that the true treasure lies elsewhere, and determines to make his home atop Little Mountain and enjoy the hillside's natural beauty. Praising the story as a good read-aloud choice due to its focus on environmental themes, Patty Lawlor commended *Who Wants Rocks?* in *Quill & Quire* for its "short sentences and simple, carefully worded descriptions" and noted that Kusugak recounts his tale in "traditional storytelling style."

In addition to writing stories, which he does in a shed next to his house, Kusugak enjoys telling his tales aloud to young listeners in much the same way that his grandmother used to tell stories to him. With only a single piece of string with which to bring to life his animal characters, he performs at schools and libraries around Canada, and in 1997 was featured on stage at Toronto's Young People's Theatre.

BIOGRAPHICAL AND CRITICAL SOURCES:

BOOKS

Jones, Raymond E., and Jon C. Stott, *Canadian Children's Books: A Critical Guide to Authors and Illustrators,* Oxford University Press (Toronto, Canada), 2000.
St. James Guide to Children's Writers, 5th edition, St. James Press (Detroit, MI), 1999, p. 615.

PERIODICALS

Bloomsbury Review, September, 1992, review of *Hide and Sneak* p. 21.
Booklist, November 1, 1998, John Peters, review of *Arctic Stories,* p. 503.
Books in Canada, summer, 1992, Rhea Tregebov, review of *Hide and Sneak,* p. 36.
Canadian Children's Literature, Volume 72, 1993, Stan Atherton, review of *Hide and Sneak,* p. 84.
Canadian Materials, November, 1988, André Gagnon, review of *A Promise Is a Promise.*

Children's Book News, winter, 1999, Jeffrey Canton, review of *Arctic Stories,* p. 23.
Horn Book, May-June, 1991, Sarah Ellis, review of *Baseball Bats for Christmas,* pp. 366-368.
Publishers Weekly, November 30, 1998, review of *Arctic Stories,* p. 71.
Quill & Quire, October, 1990, Kenneth Oppel, review of *Baseball Bats for Christmas,* p. 14; February, 1991, Peter Cumming, "Inuit Writer Kusugak Thrives in Two Worlds," pp. 21, 23; March, 1992, Sarah Ellis, review of *Hide and Sneak,* p. 65; September, 1993, Linda Granfield, review of *Northern Lights: The Soccer Trails,* p. 67; September, 1999, Patty Lawlor, review of *Who Wants Rocks?* p, 69.
School Librarian, autumn, 1999, Jane Doonan, review of *Arctic Stories,* p. 145.
School Library Journal, February, 1989, Reva Pitch Margolis, review of *A Promise Is a Promise,* p. 74; September, 1995, LaVonne Sanborn, "Storyteller: Michael Arvaarluk Kusugak," p. 154; May, 1997, Roz Goodman, review of *My Arctic 1, 2, 3,* pp. 120-121; March, 1999, Mollie Bynum, review of *Arctic Stories,* p. 177.

ONLINE

Annick Press Web site, http://www.annickpress.com/ (March 12, 2003), "Michael Kusugak."
Michael Kusugak Web site, http://www.michael kusugak.com (March 12, 2003).*

L

LAFFAN, Kevin (Barry) 1922-2003
(Kevin Barry)

OBITUARY NOTICE—See index for *CA* sketch: Born May 24, 1922, in Reading, Berkshire, England; died March 11, 2003, in London, England. Author. Laffan was a playwright and television scriptwriter best known for creating the popular British soap opera *Emmerdale Farm.* He began his career as an actor and during the early 1950s was artistic director for the Everyman Theatre in Reading, England. He then started writing stage plays under the name Kevin Barry, including *Ginger Bred* (1951), *The Strip-Tease Murder* (1955), *Winner Takes All* (1956), and *First Innocent* (1957). As he became more successful, he reverted to his real name for his play writing and found success with his comedy *It's a Two-Foot-Six-Inches-above-the-Ground World* (1970), which he adapted into a movie in 1972. By the 1960s and 1970s, he was also building a reputation for his television writing, including the programs *Bud* (1963), *Castle Haven* (1969), and *Decision to Burn* (1971). Asked to write a series about a farming family, Laffan created *Emmerdale Farm* in 1972. He wrote for the series until 1985, when he became the show's consultant; it was renamed *Emmerdale* in 1989 as the show gained popularity and began to shift attention away from the farm and focus on relationships among the townspeople. Laffan's other successful series at this time was *Beryl's Lot,* which aired during the 1970s. He continued writing into the 1980s—including the sitcom 1980 *I Thought You'd Gone*—and contributed episodes to other television series into the 1990s. Laffan's first novel, *Virgins Are in Short Supply,* was published in 2001.

OBITUARIES AND OTHER SOURCES:

BOOKS

Contemporary Dramatists, sixth edition, St. James Press (Detroit, MI), 1999.
Writers Directory, 18th edition, St. James Press (Detroit, MI), 2003.

PERIODICALS

Guardian (London, England), March 20, 2003.
Independent (London, England), March 15, 2003, p. 20.
Scotsman (Edinburgh, Scotland), March 21, 2003.
Times (London, England), March 27, 2003.

*   *   *

LAJER-BURCHARTH, Ewa

PERSONAL: Female. Education: Institute of Art History, University of Warsaw, Poland, M.A.; City University of New York, Ph.D.

ADDRESSES: Office—Department of History of Art and Architecture, Harvard University, Cambridge, MA 02138. *E-mail*—burchart@fas.harvard.edu.

CAREER: Harvard University, Cambridge, MA, Harris K. Weston Associate Professor of History of Art and Architecture.

MEMBER: Association of Art Historians

AWARDS, HONORS: John Simon Guggenheim Memorial Foundation fellowship, 2000.

WRITINGS:

Necklines: The Art of Jacques-Louis David after the Terror, Yale University Press (New Haven, CT), 1999.

Other writings include *Counter-Monuments,* 1987. Also contributor to academic journals in art history and feminist studies.

SIDELIGHTS: Ewa Lajer-Bucharth is a Harvard University professor who specializes in eighteenth-and nineteenth-century contemporary art, feminism, and critical theory. She is recognized for writing *Necklines: The Art of Jacques-Louis David after the Terror,* a book about the work of a noted French artist between 1794 and 1800. Nicholas Mirzoeff reviewed the work for the *College Art Association Web site,* noting: "She presents David as an artist struggling with trauma and loss that he often represented in terms of gender and gender ambiguity. Hers is a David for our time, a man desperately searcing for Prozac avant la lettre." Lajer-Burcharth discusses the "unresolved tension" the artist had within his body and connects it to popular prints, medical literature, fashion and pyschoanalysis. The result, Mirzoeff concludes, will change many perceptions of David's work.

BIOGRAPHICAL AND CRITICAL SOURCES:

PERIODICALS

Afterimage, May, 1987, review of *Counter-Monuments,* p. 5.
New York Review of Books, May 25, 2000, P. N. Furbank review of *Necklines: The Art of Jacques-Louis David after the Terror.*
Publishers Weekly, September 27, 1999, review of *Necklines,* p. 86.

ONLINE

College Art Association Web site, http://www.caa reviews.org/ (September 13, 2003).
Barnes and Noble Web site, http://barnesandnoble. com/ (April 12, 2000).*

LAMB, Simon

PERSONAL: Male.

ADDRESSES: Office—St. Anne's College, Oxford University, Oxford OX2 6HS, England. *E-mail*—simon.lamb@earth.ox.ac.uk.

CAREER: Professor and author. St. Anne's College, Oxford, Oxford, England, lecturer in earth sciences.

AWARDS, HONORS: St. Anne's College fellowship; Best Books for Junior High and High School Readers designation, *Science Books and Film Online,* 1999, for *Earth Story.*

WRITINGS:

(With David Singington) *Earth Story: The Shaping of Our World,* Princeton University Press (Princeton, NJ), 1998.

Contributor to scientific journals, such as *Earth and Planetary Science Letters* and *Nature.*

ADAPTATIONS: Earth Story was adapted to an eight-part documentary mini-series by the British Broadcasting Corporation.

SIDELIGHTS: Simon Lamb is a lecturer and a fellow of St. Anne's College, Oxford and the author, with David Singington, of *Earth Story: The Shaping of Our World.* The volume is the companion book to an eight-part British Broadcasting Corporation (BBC) series that aired beginning in September of 1998. Gloria Maxwell, in *Library Journal,* called the book "a noteworthy addition to any library." The authors explore how our planet was formed, the connection between volcanoes and the creation of continents, the causes of ice ages, and the effects of mountains on climate. They show how seemingly unrelated earthquakes, glaciers, volcanoes, and weather are very connected. Earth is a complex, balanced system because of its unique atmosphere that sustains liquid water. To date, no other planet has been discovered to contain the geological activity of Earth. The book covers the geology of Mars and Venus and the evolution of the solar system.

Lamb and Sington demonstrate with photographs, illustrations, and graphics how Earth's layers of crust, mantle, and outer and inner cores are continually changing. They discuss how, through cracks in mid-ocean ridges, new surfaces emerge and how the resulting heated waters create currents that impact weather. Plate tectonics are linked to the geological activity of Earth, and geological activity was crucial to the beginning of life on the planet and to its continuing evolution. The authors demonstrate how the balance of tectonic plates, atmosphere, water, and living organisms has sustained Earth as a living planet for nearly four billion years. *Booklist* reviewer Gilbert Taylor wrote that in describing how plate tectonics became the accepted theory in explaining the history of the Earth, the authors "offer a splendidly concise presentation." A *Publishers Weekly* reviewer called *Earth Story* a "compelling and accessible account."

Lamb's research as a professor includes work on the deformation process in the Peruvian Andes. He also has supervised students studying geological formations in the Andes.

BIOGRAPHICAL AND CRITICAL SOURCES:

PERIODICALS

Booklist, September 1, 1998, p. 45.
Library Journal, October 15, 1998, pp. 93-94.
Publishers Weekly, August 17, 1998, p. 60.

ONLINE

Science Books and Film Online, http://www.sbfonline.com/ (September 14, 2003).*

*   *   *

LANGDON, Danny G. 1938-

PERSONAL: Born November 16, 1938, in Twin Falls, ID; son of Lambert (a scrap iron dealer) and Marion (a scrap iron dealer; maiden name, Smith) Langdon; married Patricia O'Hara (marriage ended); married Kathleen Whiteside, December 29, 1991; children:

(first marriage) Lisa, Kimberly. *Ethnicity:* "Caucasian." *Education:* University of Idaho, B.S. Ed. (chemistry), 1961; University of Missouri, M.Ed. (secondary administration), 1962; attended New York University, 1964-65, University of Pennsylvania, 1972, and Georgetown University, 1976. *Politics:* Independent. *Religion:* Roman Catholic. *Hobbies and other interests:* Biking, basketball.

ADDRESSES: Home and office—1330 Stanford St., Suite D, Santa Monica, CA 90404; fax: 310-829-3457. *E-mail*—parformi@aol.com.

CAREER: Business consultant and author. U.S. Peace Corps, teacher in Harar, Ethiopia, 1962-64; Job Corps Center, Pleasanton, CA, instructor and supervisor, 1965-67; Central Programmed Teaching, Palo Alto, CA, manager, 1967-69; American College of Life Underwriters, Bryn Mawr, PA, director of instructional design, 1969-79; Morrison Knudsen Corporation, Boise, ID, director of corporate training, 1979-90; International Technology Corporation, Torrance, CA, director of quality management, 1990-93; Performance International (consultants in business performance improvement), Santa Monica, CA, president, 1993—. Head of Loaves and Fishes Food Drive for Santa Monica church.

MEMBER: National Society for Performance and Improvement (international president, 1989-90).

AWARDS, HONORS: Awards for Outstanding New Systematic Approach, and Outstanding Performance Aid, National Society for Performance and Instruction.

WRITINGS:

Interactive Instructional Designs for Individualized Learning, Educational Technology Publications (Englewood Cliffs, NJ), 1973.
The New Language of Work, HRD Press, 1995.
(Editor, with Kathleen Whiteside) *Intervention Resource Guide: Fifty Performance Improvement Tools,* Jossey-Bass (San Francisco, CA), 1999.
Aligning Performance: Improving Performance in People, Systems, and Organizations, Jossey Bass (San Francisco, CA), 1999.

Series editor and contributor, "Instructional Design Library," 40 volumes, Educational Technology Publications, 1978-80.

BIOGRAPHICAL AND CRITICAL SOURCES:

ONLINE

Performance International Web site, http://www.performanceinternational.com/ (August 9, 2003).

*   *   *

LARAQUE, Paul 1920-
(Jacques Lenoir)

PERSONAL: Born September 21, 1920, in Haiti; son of Franck H. (a merchant) and Clarisse (a homemaker; maiden name, Leger) Laraque; married Marcelle Rene-Louis, 1951 (died, 1998); children: Max, Serge, Danielle. *Ethnicity:* "Black." *Education:* Earned bachelor's degree in Port au Prince, Haiti, 1938; attended military academy in Port au Prince, 1939-41; Fordham University, M.A., 1960. *Politics:* Marxist.

ADDRESSES: Home—43-36 Robinson St., Apt. 6C, Flushing, NY 11355.

CAREER: Haitian Army and Police, career military officer, 1939-60; manager of car-parking service, New York, NY, 1961-65; Fordham Preparatory School, Bronx, NY, teacher of French, 1966-86. Active in organizations opposed to Duvalier dictatorship in Haiti, 1960-86.

MEMBER: Association of Haitian Writers Abroad (secretary general, 1979-86).

AWARDS, HONORS: Casa de las Américas Prize for poetry, 1979.

WRITINGS:

Ce qui demeure (poetry), postscript by André Breton, illustrated by Davertige, Éditions Nouvelle Optique (Montreal, Quebec, Canada), 1973.

Fistibal (poetry), Éditions Nouvelle Optique (Montreal, Quebec, Canada), 1974.

Les armes quotidiennes [and] Poésie quotidienne, Casa de las Américas (Havana, Cuba), 1979.

Sòlda mawon, Haitian Book Center (Flushing, NY), 1987.

Le vieux nègre el l'exil, Silex (Paris, France), 1988.

Liberty Drum: Selected Poems, Azul Editions (Washington, DC), 1995.

(Editor, with Jack Hirschman) *Open Gate: An Anthology of Haitian Creole Poetry,* translated by Hirschman and Boadiba, Curbstone Press (Willimantic, CT), 2001.

Lespwa (poetry), Editions Mémoire (Port au Prince, Haiti), 2001.

Author of poetry collections published in French or French Creole. Contributor to periodicals, sometimes under pseudonym Jacques Lenoir.

SIDELIGHTS: Paul Laraque told *CA:* "My inspiration comes, first of all, from my desire to share my feelings and ideas with others, especially my wife, who symbolized love in my life."

BIOGRAPHICAL AND CRITICAL SOURCES:

PERIODICALS

Publishers Weekly, December 17, 2001, review of *Open Gate: An Anthology of Haitian Creole Poetry,* p. 88.

World Literature Today, spring, 2002, Chris Waters, review of *Open Gate,* p. 129.

*   *   *

LAW, John
See HARKNESS, Margaret Elise

*   *   *

LAWSON, Mary 1946-

PERSONAL: Born 1946, in Blackwell, Ontario, Canada; married; husband's name, Richard; children: sons. *Education:* McGill University, B.S., 1968.

ADDRESSES: Home—Surrey, England. *Agent*—c/o Author Mail, A.A. Knopf, One Toronto Street, Unit 300, Toronto, Ontario M5C 2V6, Canada.

CAREER: Worked in a steel research lab, London, England.

WRITINGS:

(Editor) *While You Wait: A Guide to the Opportunities for Students, between Leaving School and Continuing Further Education,* Careers Research and Advisory Centre (Cambridge, England), 1974.
Crow Lake, A.A. Knopf Canada (Toronto, Ontario, Canada), 2002.

SIDELIGHTS: Mary Lawson's debut novel, *Crow Lake,* began as a short story she wrote in the 1980s. *Crow Lake* is set in a small, quiet town of the same name in Northern Ontario, where Lawson spent much of her childhood. Kate Morrison's parents were killed when a logging truck hit their car. Desperate to keep their family together, her older brother Luke, then just nineteen, gave up his college education to raise his three younger siblings, which included seventeen-year-old Matt, Kate, then seven, and baby Bo. Luke wants Matt, the smartest one, to be the first of the siblings to go to college, but he isn't interested. Kate ends up being the first and earns a degree in zoology. Years later Kate works as a professor far away from Crow Lake. She feels guilty about her success and the opportunities her brothers missed out on because of her. Kate hasn't been back to see her siblings in years and feels distant from them all. When invited back for her nephew's birthday party Kate starts to think back to her childhood and realizes there is something she must confront back at Crow Lake. *Book Browser* contributor Maureen O'Connor noted, "Storytelling involves so much: characters, setting, plot, language, structure. And Mary Lawson has excelled in all of these." *January Magazine* contributor Margaret Gunning concluded, "Let us rejoice in the discovery of this subtle, graceful, late-blooming talent."

BIOGRAPHICAL AND CRITICAL SOURCES:

PERIODICALS

Booklist, January 1, 2002, Danise Hoover, review of *Crow Lake,* p. 811.
Chatelaine, April, 2002, "Ripple Effect," p. 28.

Kirkus Reviews, December 15, 2001, review of *Crow Lake,* p. 1706.
Library Journal, February 15, 2002, Beth E. Anderson, review of *Crow Lake,* p. 178.
Maclean's, July 1, 2002, Brian Bethune, "Unforgotten Country: New Canadian Fiction Still Draws from a Past Quickly Fading into Myth," p. 84.
New York Times Book Review, March 31, 2002, Janet Burroway, "The Girl She Left Behind."
Spectator, April 6, 2002, Nicolette Jones, "A Child's Book of True Crime," p. 35.

ONLINE

Book Browser, http://www.bookbrowser.com/ (September 5, 2002), Maureen O'Connor, review of *Crow Lake.*
Book Page, http://www.bookpage.com/ (September 5, 2002), Amy Scribner, "Canadian Writer Spins a Lyrical Debut."
Book Reporter, http://www.bookreporter.com/ (September 5, 2002), Kathy Weissman, review of *Crow Lake.*
January Magazine, http://www.januarymagazine.com/ (September 5, 2002), Margaret Gunning, "In Praise of Late Bloomers."
Random House of Canada Web site, http://www.randomhouse.ca/ (September 5, 2002).*

* * *

LEE, Michael 1946-

PERSONAL: Born 1946. *Education:* Miami-Dade Junior College, A.A. (journalism); University of Massachusetts, Dartmouth, B.A.; Emerson College, M.F.A. (writing).

ADDRESSES: Office—c/o Cape Cod Voice, 56 Main Street, P.O.B. 156, Orleans, MA 02653. *E-mail*—mlee@capecodvoice.com.

CAREER: Journalist and author of fiction. *Miami Magazine,* editor; *Cape Codder,* columnist; *Cape Cod Voice,* senior editor; freelance writer. Worked variously as a deep-sea diver, cook, shell fisherman, construction worker, shrimp peeler, and teacher. *Military service:* U.S. Marine Corps; stationed at Khe Sanh, Vietnam.

WRITINGS:

Paradise Dance, Leapfrog Press (Wellfleet, MA), 2002.

Short stories have appeared in *Yale Review, Potpourri, Writer's Digest, Northeast Magazine, Boston Herald*, and *Fantasy & Science Fiction Magazine*. Contributor of articles to *Stars and Stripes, Framingham News, Cape Cod Times*, and *Cape Codder*.

SIDELIGHTS: Over the years, Michael Lee has seen the world through the eyes of a soldier and cook, a writer and fisherman, a deep-sea diver and teacher. From these different positions in life, he has gained a broad vision of life. It is from this vantage point that he is able to understand and write stories about a wide range of personalities—people from various walks of life. He has read his short stories to New England audiences and published some of his writing in a number of literary publications over the past two decades. It was not, however, until 2002 that he brought together some of his best work to create the collection *Paradise Dance*, which a *Kirkus Reviews* writer proclaimed a "Solid work from a writer who should have been recognized long ago."

The stories in *Paradise Dance* are about the people of fictional Albright, Massachusetts, a mill town that has lost its focus. Time is all that the people of the town have left, and most of that time is spent in recalling the past. Lee's stories look deeply into what is left of the townspeople's lives. These people are quite ordinary, which makes them also universal. They are the backbone of the village: the mechanics, small business owners, teachers, waitresses, war vets, and local musicians. Their stories are set in the cemetery, the bars, the bedrooms, the golf course, and in the hospital. Their stories are imbued with themes of about abandoned hope and lost illusions. However, Lee's characters have not yet given up.

Lee's writing has been compared to that of short story writer Raymond Carver for its focus on the concerns of everyday people and for its barebones presentation. As a *Publishers Weekly* reviewer put it: "Lee offers a heady blend of compassion, razor-sharp wit, and well-honed storytelling skills." The stories range from serious issues to those that flirt with comedy. On the more solemn side is the story "Koza Nights," about a war veteran who is blackmailed by a fellow soldier, a man who knows that the vet murdered a prostitute while both men were on tour in Vietnam. In contrast, Lee offers his "Another Wonder of the World," in which he relates the details of a far-flung dream of several cohorts who meet at the local bar and plan the creation of an X-rated miniature golf course.

Most of Lee's characters are men who are not afraid to admit their weaknesses. Although Faye A. Chadwell for *Library Journal* admitted that the overall tone of Lee's stories are "decidedly masculine," she concluded that readers will in no way "succumb to a testosterone overdose." The stories are tough but the characters are sensitive. The people who live in Albright might be flawed, but as most reviewers have found, that just makes them all the more real.

BIOGRAPHICAL AND CRITICAL SOURCES:

PERIODICALS

Kirkus Reviews, June 1, 2002, review of *Paradise Dance*, p. 759.
Library Journal, October 1, 2002, Faye A. Chadwell, review of *Paradise Dance*, p. 130.
Publishers Weekly, July 29, 2002, review of *Paradise Dance*, p. 54.*

*   *   *

LEE, Wen Ho 1940-

PERSONAL: Born 1940, in Taiwan; married. *Hobbies and other interests:* Fishing, cooking, gardening.

ADDRESSES: Home—Los Alamos, NM. *Agent*—c/o Author Mail, Hyperion Books, 77 West 66th Street, 11th Floor, New York, NY 10023.

CAREER: Los Alamos National Laboratory, Los Alamos, NM, former computer scientist.

WRITINGS:

(With Helen Zia) *My Country versus Me: The First-Hand Account by the Los Alamos Scientist Who Was Falsely Accused of Being a Spy*, Hyperion (New York NY), 2001.

SIDELIGHTS: Lee Wen Ho is a former computer scientist for the Los Alamos National Laboratory, which helps develop U.S. defense strategies and helps protect defense secrets. In 1999, Lee was accused of espionage. The U.S. government believed he was giving classified information about the U.S. nuclear program to China, specifically the design information for the W-88 nuclear warhead. In total Lee was accused of fifty-nine different charges, and spent 277 days in jail, a majority of the time shackled and in solitary confinement, while on trial for the charges. In truth, the U.S. government did not have solid evidence to convict Lee of his charges. On September 13, 2000, Lee bargained with prosecutors and agreed to plead guilty to one of the fifty-nine charges, which was misuse of classified materials, in order to be set free from jail.

In *My Country versus Me: The First-Hand Account by the Los Alamos Scientist Who Was Falsely Accused of Being a Spy,* Lee and Helen Zia tell his story about being accused of espionage, his work at the Los Alamos National Laboratory, his time in jail, how the FBI invaded his and his family's privacy, how the media played into his arrest, his innocence, and how his life has changed because of the experience. "The story of Wen Ho Lee is really about how a bureaucracy run amok can steamroll the average citizen," noted a *Conservative Monitor* contributor. *Book Loons* contributor Marian Powell claimed, "This is a very frightening book, showing how easily someone can become a target."

BIOGRAPHICAL AND CRITICAL SOURCES:

PERIODICALS

American Scientist, July-August, 2002, Wolfgang K. H. Panofsky, "A Spy or Not a Spy, That Was the Question," p. 371.
Business Week, February 4, 2002, "The Making of a Scapegoat," p. 17.
Economist, February 9, 2002, "Trade Secrets; Nuclear Espionage."
Entertainment Weekly, December 1, 2000, p. 90.
Nation, October 23, 2000, Robert Scheer, "No Defense," p. 11; April 15, 2002, Dusanka Miscevic and Peter Kwong, "The China Syndrome," p. 25.

New York Times Book Review, February 17, 2002, Joseph E. Persico, "Life under Suspicion."
Publishers Weekly, November 20, 2000, John F. Baker, "Dr. Lee of Los Alamos to Tell All," p. 14; March 4, 2002, review of *My Country versus Me: The First-Hand Account by the Los Alamos Scientist Who Was Falsely Accused of Being a Spy,* p. 42.
Times Literary Supplement, April 26, 2002, Ernest R. May, "Was Vanity the Spur?" p. 8.

ONLINE

Asian Reporter Online, http://www.asianreporter.com/ (September 5, 2002), Jeff Wenger, "Wen Ho Lee and America."
Book Loons, http://www.bookloons.com/ (September 5, 2002), Marian Powell, review of *My Country versus Me.*
Conservative Monitor, http://www.conservative monitor.com/ (September 5, 2002), review of *My Country versus Me.*
FindLaw's Legal Commentary, http://writ.news. findlaw.com/ (September 5, 2002), Mark S. Zaid, "A Tale of Espionage or a Government Witch Hunt?"
Hyperion Books Web site, http://www.hyperionbooks. com/ (September 5, 2002).
People's Daily Onlne, http://english.peopledaily.com/ (September 5, 2002), "Wen Ho Lee Says US Targets Him Due to Race."
Race Relations, http://racerelations.about.com/ (September 5, 2002), review of *My Country versus Me.*
Salon.com, http://www.salon.com/ (September 5, 2002), Eric Boehlert, "The Spy Who Wasn't."*

*   *   *

LENOIR, Jacques
See LARAQUE, Paul

*   *   *

LERNER, Motti 1949-

PERSONAL: Born September 16, 1949, in Zichron Yaakov, Israel; son of Arie and Dvora Lerner; married December 13, 1983; wife's name Tamar; children: Noam, Matan, Avigail. *Education:* Attended Hebrew

University, Jerusalem, 1967-76. Studied theater at various workshops throughout London, and with San Francisco Dancers Workshop.

ADDRESSES: Office—5 Massada St., P.O. Box 4305, Ramat Hasharon 47290 Israel. *E-mail*—motti@macam. ac.il.

CAREER: Maduga Experimental Theater, Jerusalem, Israel, writer and director, 1978-79; Khan Theater, Jerusalem, dramaturge and director, 1978-84; freelance playwright and screenwriter, Israel, 1984—; Kibbuts College Drama School, Tel Aviv, Israel, instructor in dramatic writing, 1984—. Centre for Postgraduate Hebrew Studies, Oxford, England, writer-in-residence, 1992; Beit Lessin Theatre, Tel Aviv, dramaturge, 1993-96; Duke University, visiting professor, 1997; Tel Aviv University, instructor in political playwrighting, 1997—; University of Iowa, International Writing Program resident, 2000. *Military service:* Israel Defense Forces, 1970-73.

AWARDS, HONORS: Best Children's Play of the Year award (Israel), 1981, for *The Princess and the Hobo;* Best Play of the Year award (Israel), 1985, for *Kastner;* Prime Minister of Israel Award for Writers, 1994; Best T.V. Drama award (Israel), 1995, for *Kastner's Trial.*

WRITINGS:

The Princess and the Hobo (children's play), produced by Jerusalem Khan Theatre, 1980.
Kastner, produced in Tel Aviv, Israel, 1985.
Pangs of the Messiah, produced in Tel Aviv, Israel, 1987.
Paula (a monodrama), produced in Tel Aviv, Israel, 1987.
Exile in Jerusalem (originally titled *Else*), produced in Tel Aviv, Israel, 1990; produced in London, England, 1992; produced in New York, NY, 1998.
The Donkey of Oz (children's comedy), produced in Ramat Gan, 1993.
Loves at Bitania (television drama), Israeli Television, 1993.
Kastner's Trial (three-part television drama), Israeli Television, 1994.
Pollard, produced in Tel Aviv, Israel, 1995.

Autumn, produced in Tel Aviv, Israel, 1996; produced in New York, NY, 1996.
Bus 300 (five-part television drama), by Israeli Television, 1997.
EGOZ (three-part television drama), Israeli Television, 1998.
The Murder of Isaac, produced in Heilbronn, Germany, 1999.
The Institute (twelve-part television drama), Israeli Television, 2001.
Battle in Jerusalem (three-part television drama), Israeli Television, 2002.
Silent Sirens (television film), Israeli Television, 2002.
Hard Love, produced in Haifa, Israel, 2003.

Lerner's work has been translated into English and German.

WORK IN PROGRESS: Passing the Love of Women, inspired by a short story by I. Bashevis Singer, 2004 production in Israel and Washington, DC.

SIDELIGHTS: Motti Lerner is an Israeli playwright and screenwriter whose political works have been translated into several languages. Lerner's topics—always about the Jewish community and Israeli identity—include the Holocaust, Zionism, terrorism, and a few biographies. His controversial work has been the target of censorship, though he has also been the recipient of various literary awards.

One of Lerner's most talked-about works is the drama *Kastner,* in which the author recreates the events that occurred in Budapest during the summer of 1944, when Germans used Jews to extort large sums of money from their community in return for false promises to slow down the flow of deportation trains. Dr. Rudolf Kastner was a German-educated Budapest attorney who was chosen as a liaison; he met with high-ranking Nazi officials on a regular basis.

Kastner's role was an important one. He collaborated with the Nazis by keeping silent about the true nature of the death camps, and betrayed his people by supplying their persecutors with Jewish underground activity. Kastner disagreed with the tactics used by the Nazis, but he never revealed what he knew. Nor did he leave Hungary, despite having numerous opportunities to do so. He and his family remained there until

January, 1945, trying to save the few remaining Jews. In fact, Kastner's behavior did manage to save some Jews, but ultimately, his decision to work with the Nazis was seen as a betrayal of the highest magnitude. Therein lies the controversy explored in Lerner's play.

Lerner presents Kastner as a tireless fighter who seeks only to help others survive. Postwar critics condemn Kastner's silence regarding Auschwitz and the other death camps as his most serious crime. But Lerner wants people to see Kastner's decision as being one of calculated risk, if not admirable. Kastner eventually defended Eichmann and other Nazis. He was charged with collaborating with the enemy, acquitted at trial, and then murdered at his home by a right-wing nationalist.

In *Modern Judaism* Michael Taub discussed Lerner and Joshua Sobol, another noteworthy Israeli dramatist, noting: "What these playwrights ask of their audience is that, in addition to admiring the supreme sacrifices made under fire, a fresh look be taken at the contributions that the less 'heroic' Jewish figures made to Jewish survival."

Another Lerner piece, *Pollard,* is a political drama based on the scandal created by the Israeli intelligence service that hired an American Jew employed by the U.S. Navy to spy for Israel. Jonathan Pollard was convicted in 1987 of selling military secrets to Israeli agents. The Zionist pled guilty but argued he was not a traitor, because Israel was an American ally. That line of reasoning did not hold up and Pollard was sentenced to life in an American prison; he continues to be denied parole.

What makes *Pollard* controversial is the sentence given Pollard and Lerner's depiction of how it came to happen. Some members of the Jewish community found the sentence too harsh and saw in it anti-Semitic bias. These people were afraid to publicly speak out, however, for fear of a backlash. The Israeli government called the event a minor intelligence blunder. Lerner, however, portrays Pollard as a victim who is refused asylum at the Israeli embassy in Washington. With nowhere else to go, Pollard is forced into capture by American agents. In other words, Lerner suggests that Pollard was given up to the FBI by top-ranking Israeli government officials, possibly the prime minister himself.

"While the play has not led to Pollard's release or changed the government's official line about the incident, it did challenge the myth that Israel, with its superior army and intelligence agencies, would be able and willing to save Jews regardless of who they were or where they lived," explained Taub.

Lerner teaches advanced playwriting and political playwrighting at the Kibbutz College Drama School in Tel Aviv and Tel Aviv University, respectively.

BIOGRAPHICAL AND CRITICAL SOURCES:

PERIODICALS

Modern Judaism, May, 1997, Michael Taub, "The Challenge to Popular Myth and Conventions in Recent Israeli Drama," pp. 133-62.

ONLINE

Tel Aviv University Web site, http://www.tau.ac.il/ (April 24, 2002).

* * *

LEVERITT, Mara

PERSONAL: Female.

ADDRESSES: Office—Arkansas Times, P.O. Box 34010, Little Rock, AR 72203.

CAREER: Contributing editor and columnist for *Arkansas Times.*

AWARDS, HONORS: Has received numerous awards for investigative journalism.

WRITINGS:

NONFICTION; JOURNALISM

The Boys on the Tracks: Death, Denial, and a Mother's Crusade to Bring Her Son's Killers to Justice, Thomas Dunne Books/St. Martin's Press (New York, NY), 1999.

WORK IN PROGRESS: A nonfiction book about a triple murder in West Memphis.

SIDELIGHTS: Journalist Mara Leveritt is a contributing editor and columnist for the *Arkansas Times.* In 1999 she published *The Boys on the Tracks: Death, Denial, and a Mother's Crusade to Bring Her Son's Killers to Justice,* the story of the deaths of two teenagers, Don Henry and Kevin Ives, who were both run over by a train near Little Rock, Arkansas. Initially ruled a suicide, the case was later described as an accident after authorities ruled that the boys had been smoking marijuana and had passed out on the train tracks where they were subsequently killed.

Linda Ives, mother of Kevin, fought for years to expose what she believed to be a cover-up, and to discover the truth about what happened to her son that fateful night of August 23, 1987. On *Idmedia.com,* she wrote: "In August 1987, the body of my 17-year-old son, Kevin, who had been murdered, was left on a railroad track near our home to be dismembered by an oncoming train. His best friend, also murdered, was placed on the track beside him. The mutilation was a savage attempt to destroy evidence of the murders. Other futile attempts to thwart an investigation quickly followed—first in our county, then in our state, and finally during federal investigations. Even now . . . the FBI refuses to open its files on this case."

Investigative journalist Leveritt became interested in the story, as she explained in an interview with *NewsMax.com:* "It was a bizarre story from the very first. It remains bizarre to this day. I learned a long time ago that criminal investigations are supposed to follow certain procedures. If those procedures are followed the investigation moves along in an orderly and logical fashion." "The more I learned about this investigation," she continued, "the less logic in it I saw. It followed a crooked path that led in many strange directions. The further I looked at this case the more curious I became. So I devoted several years to looking as far down that crooked path as I could."

The result of those years of investigation was Leveritt's 1999 work *The Boys on the Tracks.* In the work Leveritt "draws no conclusions," wrote a *Publishers Weekly* critic. "She merely fleshes out the context and explores all the leads in all their various directions."

One of these directions involves President Bill Clinton, his mother Virginia Kelley, and Arkansas state medical examiner Fahmy Malak. Leveritt argues that Kelley, an anesthetist at a local hospital, was involved in the deaths of two patients and that Malak covered up her responsibility. Malak was the man who ruled the boys' deaths were caused by marijuana. The bodies of both boys were exhumed and an independent pathologist ruled there was evidence to suggest the boys were indeed murdered. Clinton, then governor of Arkansas, refused to remove Malak from office despite the public outcry. Malak eventually resigned after he received a job offer from Clinton associate Jocelyn Elders at the State Health Department. Clinton has denied any role in the case.

Critics were mixed in their assessment of the work. "If this Arkansas murder tale weren't a true-crime thriller by an established investigative journalist, it would be too crazy, complicated and bizarre to believe," wrote a *Publishers Weekly* critic. The critic faulted Leveritt for exploring too many conspiracy-type theories, arguing that what is chilling becomes "merely fantastical." Patrick Petit in *Library Journal* concluded: Leveritt "handles a mountain of details well and succeeds in making this convoluted story reasonably understandable. However, her intimation, in the epilog, of an ongoing, largescale conspiracy is open to question."

"This story deserves serious mainstream interest," Leveritt commented in her interview on *NewsMax.com.* "And I am a serious journalist. So I tried to be cautious in this book and not get into things about which we do not have definitive information." She continued: "I was dismayed to run into some of the same walls that have blocked others seeking information on these matters. The Department of Justice has erected these walls to hide what should be public information. At the same time, I am proud of what I was able to discover and report about these dark affairs." Leveritt's investigative work has made her a respected authority for those who are critical or skeptical of the U.S. war on drugs.

BIOGRAPHICAL AND CRITICAL SOURCES:

PERIODICALS

Library Journal, October 1, 1999, Patrick Petit, review of *The Boys on the Tracks: Death, Denial, and a Mother's Crusade to Bring Her Son's Killers to Justice,* p. 112.
Publishers Weekly, October 25, 1999, review of *The Boys on the Tracks,* p. 61.

ONLINE

Idmedia, http://www.idmedia.com/ (February 3, 2000).

Konformist, http://www.CIA-Drugs.org/ (February 3, 2002).

NewsMax, http://www.newsmax.com/ (February 3, 2000), interview with Leveritt.*

*   *   *

LEVINE, Rick

PERSONAL: Male

ADDRESSES: Office—Word of Mouth, 4750 Walnut St., Suite 100, Boulder, CO 80301. *E-mail*—rick. levine@levinesquared.com; or rick@WordofMouth. com.

CAREER: Mancala, Inc., Boulder, CO, president; Word of Mouth, Boulder, co-founder. Sun Microsystems, Palo Alto, CA, former web architect. Previously worked in film, video, and videodisk production; worked for NCR COMTEN, Control Data's PLATO system group.

AWARDS, HONORS: "InnoThink Award," Management General, for *The Cluetrain Manifesto.*

WRITINGS:

(With Christopher Locke, Doc Searle, and David Weinberger) *The Cluetrain Manifesto: The End of Business as Usual,* Perseus Books (New York, NY), 2000.

SIDELIGHTS: In 1999 Rick Levine, along with three other marketing consultants and journalists, wrote a manifesto which surfaced on the Internet. The manifesto, in ninety-five theses, illustrates a marketing strategy directed at communicating with, instead of manipulating, the customer. Through the original manifesto and the publication of its printed sequel, *The Cluetrain Manifesto,* Levine, a Web architect and entrepreneur, rose to the status of a guru of Internet business.

Though extremely popular on the Web, *The Cluetrain Manifesto* met with mixed reviews from critics when its authors elaborated on their ninety-five theses in print. "Bold and irreverent to the point of being smart-alecky, the Manifesto makes a fun, thought-provoking read," wrote Wade Roush in *Technology Review.* A *Publishers Weekly* reviewer commended the quartet of authors for wanting "nothing less than to change the way the world does business," but though they make "solid, clever points that reveal fundamental flaws," they neglect to mention companies succeeding in their market strategy, gloss over instructions for implementing their business plan, and assume that "everyone in upper management . . . is a dolt." However, Andy Cohen, writing for *Sales & Marketing Management,* found none of these faults, celebrating the "frank language and . . . irreverent tone." He concluded, "Forget what you've already read; this book is different."

Building on the success of the book, Levine and his associates co-founded Word of Mouth, an online network of local consumer-opinion Web sites. The service allows consumers to exchange opinions on local merchants and services. It is being co-branded with newspapers like the *Denver Post* and the *Minneapolis-St. Paul Star Tribune.* On writenews.com, Nick Rogosienski predicted that Word of Mouth will help businesses stay focused on their customers. "The Word of Mouth service will open up a new and efficient channel for local businesses to listen to their customers and interact with them," Rogosienski said.

BIOGRAPHICAL AND CRITICAL SOURCES:

PERIODICALS

Publishers Weekly, January 24, 2000, review of *The Cluetrain Manifesto,* p. 305.

Sales & Marketing Management, February, 2000, Andy Cohen, "February Must-Reads," p. 22.

Technology Review, March, 2000, Wade Roush, "Manifestly Clueless," p. 108.

Fast Company, March 2000, Katharine Mieszkowski, "Clued In? Sign On!"

ONLINE

Cluetrain Manifesto Web site, http://www.cluetrain. com/ (1999).

WriteNews.com, http://www.writenews.com/ (August 28, 2003).*

LILBURN, Tim 1950-

PERSONAL: Born 1950, in Regina, Saskatchewan, Canada; *Education:* University of Regina, Campion College, B.A. (education); Luther College, M.A. (philosophy).

ADDRESSES: Office—St. Peter's College, RPO Box 40, Muenster, Saskatchewan S0K 2Y0, Canada; St. Thomas More College, University of Saskatchewan, 1437 College Drive, Saskatoon, Saskatchewan, S7N 0W6, Canada.

CAREER: Teacher, poet, and essayist. Member of faculty at University of Saskatchewan, St. Thomas More College, Saskatoon, Saskatchewan, Canada, and St. Peter's College, Muenster, Saskatchewan. Former writer-in-residence, University of Alberta, Regina Public Library, University of Western Ontario, and St. Mary's University, Halifax, Canada. Has taught at Sage Hill Writing Experience, Banff School of Fine Arts, and in West Africa, and has lectured in China.

AWARDS, HONORS: Canada Governor-General's Award shortlist, 1990, for *Tourist to Ecstasy;* Canadian Authors Association Award for Poetry for *Moosewood Sandhills;* Saskatchewan Nonfiction Award for *Living in the World as if It Were Home;* Saskatchewan Book of the Year Award for *To the River.*

WRITINGS:

Names of God (poems), 1986.
Tourist to Ecstasy, 1989.
Moosewood Sandhills: Poems, McClelland & Stewart (Toronto, Ontario, Canada), 1994.
(Editor) *Poetry and Knowing: Speculative Essays and Interviews,* Quarry Press (Kingston, Ontario, Canada), 1995.
To the River, (poems) McClelland & Stewart (Toronto, Ontario, Canada), 1999.
Living in the World as If It Were Home, (essays), Cormorant Books (Dunvegan, Ontario), 1999.
(With Erica Grimm-Vance) *Imagining the Sacred: The Fruitful Alliance between Gospel and Art,* Campion College, University of Regina (Regina, Saskatchewan, Canada), 2002.

(Editor and contributor) *Thinking and Singing: Poetry and the Practice of Philosophy,* Cormorant Books (Toronto, Canada), 2002.

Works also published in anthologies *Twentieth Century Poetry and Poetics* and *A Matter of Spirit: Recovery of the Sacred in Contemporary Canadian Poetry.*

SIDELIGHTS: In 1990 Tim Lilburn was shortlisted for Canada's Governor General's Poetry award for his second book, *Tourist to Ecstasy.* While Lilburn did not win the award, Michael Williamson believed he should have. In *Canadian Forum,* Williamson commented that, of the three books nominated, "One . . . has more than international appeal, it has universal appeal. It's the one by that guy hugging the goat on the back cover, and his name is Tim Lilburn." Nearly ten years later, on the *St. Peter's College Web site,* a reviewer for Lilburn's *Living in the World as If It Were Home,* wrote, "Fortunate the student who has a teacher of the calibre of Tim Lilburn. It may well be that the first-year college students are not ready to work their way through these essays unaided, but for some of us who have experience in the school of life, and are at a point of looking for meaning, this book might point in the right direction."

Jacqueline Dumas, writing in *Confluence,* also commented on Lilburn's collection of essays and paid particular attention to the philosophy contained therein: that is, the idea that sophisticated writing is a dichotomy, drawing us into the world while simultaneously working to alienate us from it. Lilburn wrote, "Language's quickness to overcome the conflict between person and the world, its inadvertence to the extreme difficulty of this, its solicitude for the homeless mind, causes it to reduce being utterly to its names. . . . language unhurt by wonder, confects a union between self and the world that seems right, the summation of yearning, but that in fact asserts this separation with fresh force by making what it is vanish in caricature. Poetry is the rearing in language of a desire whose end lies beyond language."

Writing for *Canadian Book Review Annual,* Bert Almon referred to Lilburn as an "excellent contemplative poet"; Thomas M.F. Gerry, in the same publication, called him "a contemporary of Gerald Manley Hopkins." Marnie Parsons, writing for the *University of Toronto Quarterly,* found Lilburn's work "so encyclopedic, so *full,* that I feel my smallness before it," and Iain Higgins explained in *Books in Canada* that "Lilburn offers the untaking, undoing activity of contemplation . . . crucial exemplars for him are the occasionally zen-like Desert Fathers of the early Christian Church and such practitioners of negative theology as Simone Weil and the anonymous author of 'The Cloud of Unknowing.'"

Lilburn, born and raised in Saskatchewan, worked in Nigeria, West Africa, before farming and studying for more than eight years with the Jesuits (Society of Jesus). His acclaimed writings embody his "negative way" of contemplating the universe—that is, pursuing the holy not through what is known but through what is unknown and unknowable. He explores the unknowableness of spirituality by becoming assimilated into the natural world. In *Moosewood Sandhills,* a collection of poetry, Lilburn wrote, "I am seduced by the shapeliness/of the failure of knowledge." To write the collection, Lilburn took himself into an isolated spot in the Saskatchewan woodland, living among the tussocky sandhills on the banks of the Saskatchewan River for a time. Here, he dug a root cellar, grew subsistence crops, slept under the stars in a coyote burrow, and watched. In his book, he writes: "looking with care and desire seemed like a political act. . . . You could hold your beautiful gaze like a hand out to the world, say/'here, pup,' and it'd come." Regarding this poetry collection, George Woodcock, writing for *Quill & Quire,* stated, "What the poems represent is the experience of going into the wilderness . . . to witness nature spiritualized through privation and solitude. . . . A strange, wonderful book, to be absorbed rather than described, as one absorbs books of devotion."

Reviewing *To the River* in *Quill & Quire,* Tim Bowling called Lilburn's work so intense that "reviewing it seems almost like an interruption of someone at prayer." Again, for this book of poems, Lilburn draws from the natural world on the banks of the Saskatchewan River. Bowling notes that, while the book contains fourteen poems, they can be read together as "one long, connected celebration of physical detail, seasonal change, and the ways in which the Earth can lead us deeper and deeper into a fuller appreciation of our lives."

Parsons explained that the poems in *To the River* are virtually songs of praise, stemming from Lilburn's experience with poetic traditions in Nigeria while also

reminiscent of Roman Catholic monastic traditions, particularly the "negative way." Dennis Lee, in his foreword to *Living in the World as If It Were Home,* identifies connections between Lilburn's works and those of Hector de Saint-Denys-Garneau, Robert Bringhurst, Thomas Merton, Gary Snyder, and John of the Cross. Noting these comparisons, Parsons wrote, "But while such sympathies are strong, Lee continues, 'Lilburn is his own man, and there's no need to strain for comparisons.' Lee is right; no one else has quite Lilburn's spit and crackle, his linguistic gumption, his irreverent reverence. Lilburn *is* his own man, and the prairie he writes towards could be no one else's."

BIOGRAPHICAL AND CRITICAL SOURCES:

PERIODICALS

Books in Canada, May, 1987, Margaret Avison, review of *Names of God,* p. 23; summer 1994, Brian Bartlett, review of *Moosewood Sandhills,* p. 43; June-July, 2002, Iain Higgins, review of *Living in the World as If It Were Home,* p. 26.

Canadian Book Review Annual, 1995, Thomas M.F. Gerry, review of *Moosewood Sandhills,* p. 219; 1995, Bert Almon, review of *Poetry and Knowing,* p. 262; 1999, Patrick Colgan, review of *Living in the World as If It Were Home,* p. 257.

Canadian Forum, July, 1990, Michael Williamson, review of *Tourist to Ecstasy,* p. 27; April, 1999, Maggie Helwig, review of *To the River,* p. 40.

Quill & Quire, April, 1994, George Woodcock, review of *Moosewood Sandhills,* p. 27; April, 1999, Tim Bowling, review of *To the River,* p. 29.

University of Toronto Quarterly, winter, 2000, Marnie Parsons, review of *To the River* and *Living in the World as If It Were Home,* p. 208.

ONLINE

Confluence Online, http://confluence.athabascau.ca/ (October 19, 2002), Jacqueline Dumas, "Issues of Othering and Translating Experience in Western Canadian Writing."

St. Peter's Community Web site, http://www.stpeters. sk.ca/ (October 19, 2002), review of *Living in the World as If It Were Home.**

LIPPENS, Ronnie L. G. 1962-

PERSONAL: Born September 3, 1962; citizenship, Belgian; married Kathleen Vandenberghe, 1985. *Education:* University of Louvain, Kand., 1984; University of Ghent, license, 1986, Ph.D., 1998.

ADDRESSES: Office—Department of Criminology, University of Keele, Keele, Staffordshire ST5 5BG, England.

CAREER: University of Keele, Keele, England, lecturer in criminology.

WRITINGS:

Grenze(n)loze Kriminologie: spreken, subjektiviteit, radikale demokratie en de hypermoderne evaporatie van de kritische kriminologie (1975-1995), Academia Press (Ghent, Belgium), 1998.
Chaohybrids: Five Uneasy Peaces, University Press of America (Lanham, MD), 2000.

Contributor to scholarly journals, including *Social Justice.*

WORK IN PROGRESS: White Jungles, on peace and justice.

SIDELIGHTS: Ronnie L. G. Lippens told *CA:* "My book in Dutch is on critical criminology. *Chaohybrids: Five Uneasy Peaces* is on the ambivalence of twenty-first-century life. I am also writing essays on crime and social justice; imageries of law, peace, and justice; crime, ethics and (dis)organization; and organization and the imaginary.

"I have come to realize that we are damned if we do, and damned if we don't. Try to be a nihilist these days, I often sigh. Even that will prove to be an unattainable—an impossible—goal. But then, this is what keeps me going and writing."

                      *   *   *

LIPPINCOTT, Gertrude (Lawton) 1913-1996

PERSONAL: Born June 29, 1913, in St. Paul, MN; died June 2, 1996; married Benjamin Evans Lippincott (died 1989), 1934. *Education:* Attended University of Chicago; studied dance with Marion Van Tuyl; University of Minnesota, B.A. (magna cum laude),

1935; attended Bennington School of Dance, summers 1937-38; attended Martha Graham studio, 1939; New York University, M.A., 1943.

CAREER: Modern Dance Center, Minneapolis, MN, founder, 1937, dancer, 1937-42; Mt. Holyoke College, South Hadley, MA, assistant professor of dance, 1943-46; presented solo and group dance concerts, 1946-66; Minneapolis YWCA Studio Dance Group, Minneapolis, MN, founder and director, 1949-57; Mills College, assistant dance professor, 1953; University of Minnesota adjunct professor of theatre, 1965-72. Toured with dance partner Robert Moulton, 1949-64; Dance Repertory Group, Minneapolis, founder; Committee on Research in Dance (later Congress on Research in Dance), founder, 1965; dance lecturer.

AWARDS, HONORS: Ninety-second Street YM-YWHA, audition award, 1944, and choreographic awards, 1948, 1949; Copper Foot Award, Wayne State University, 1964; Heritage Award, AAPHERD National Conference, 1973; Distinguished Teachers Award, American Dance Guild, 1974; Founding Fellow Award, National Council for the Arts in Education; National Retired Teachers Award, American Dance Guild; Distinguished Service to Dance in the Twin Cities, Minneapolis Jewish Community Center, 1979; Outstanding Achievement Award, University of Minnesota, 1982.

WRITINGS:

Aesthetics and the Dance: A Study of Some Problems in Dance Theory Presented for the Dancer, [New York, NY], 1943.
Dance Production: Music, Costumes, Staging, Decor, Lighting, Photography, Make-up, Planning, and Rehearsing, American Association for Health, Physical Education, and Recreation (Washington, DC), 1956.

Contributor to *Dance Observer, Dance, Focus on Dance, Dance Scope, Journal of Art and Art Criticism, Creative Dance Journal, Impulse,* and *Journal of Health, Physical Education, Recreation, and Dance.*

SIDELIGHTS: Dancer, choreographer, and instructor Gertrude Lippincott was nationally known, but she was especially influential in the Midwest. A Minnesota native, Lippincott founded the Modern Dance Center in Minneapolis, the first modern dance group and school in the area, in 1937. It was also one of the first dance groups in the United States to include people of color. She also founded other Minnesota dance companies, including the Modern Dance Group, the Studio Dance Group, the Dance Trio, the Dance Repertory Group, and the Dance Duo. Over the period of her career she gave 107 concerts in twenty-one states plus Washington, D.C. Lippincott was also an instructor and lecturer in dance, and instructed seventy-two master classes in twenty-two states, in over 250 colleges and universities. *Star Tribune* contributor Amy Woods, quoted Judith Brin Ingber, who worked with Lippincott at *Dance* magazine, "She was really inspiring to performers and educators in the dance world. She was a remarkable dance doctor."

BIOGRAPHICAL AND CRITICAL SOURCES:

PERIODICALS

Star Tribune, June 7, 1996, Amy Woods, "Modern Dance Pioneer Gertrude Lippincott Dies at 82," p. 6B.

ONLINE

Minnesota Historical Society, http://www.mnhs.org/ (April 12, 2002), "Gertrude Lawton Lippincott: An Inventory of Her Papers at the Minnesota Historical Society."*

*   *   *

LITT, Jacquelyn S. 1958-

PERSONAL: Born May 5, 1958, in New York, NY. *Education:* William Smith College, B.A., 1980; University of Pennsylvania, M.A., 1983, Ph.D., 1988.

ADDRESSES: Office—Department of Sociology, Iowa State University, Ames, IA 50011.

CAREER: Allegheny College, Meadville, PA, assistant professor of sociology, 1987-95, chairperson of women's studies, 1987-90 and 1993-94; Iowa State University, Ames, assistant professor of sociology and women's studies, 1995—, member of board of directors of "We Can" Learning Community, 1999—. Guest lecturer at educational institutions, including University of Lancaster, 2000. ACCESS, Ames, member of board of directors, 1996-99; Children with Dyslexia Scholarship Fund, vice president, 1997—. Consultant to North Central Center for Rural Development.

AWARDS, HONORS: Woodrow Wilson fellow, 1985; award from William T. Grant Foundation, 1990.

WRITINGS:

Medicalized Motherhood: Perspectives from the Lives of African-American and Jewish Women, Rutgers University Press (New Brunswick, NJ), 2000.

Contributor to books, including *Private Risks and Public Dangers,* Avebury Press (London, England), 1992. Contributor of articles and reviews to periodicals, including *Race, Gender, and Class, Sociological Quarterly, Health Care for Women International, Gender and Society, Research in the Sociology of Health Care,* and *Journal of Consumer Affairs.**

*   *   *

LITTLE, Linda 1959-

PERSONAL: Born 1959. *Education:* Attended Queen's and Memorial universities.

ADDRESSES: Home—River John, Nova Scotia, Canada. *Agent*—c/o Author Mail, Goose Lane Editions, 469 King Street, Fredericton, New Brunswick, Canada E3B 1E5.

CAREER: Novelist and author of short fiction. Nova Scotia Museum, tour guide.

AWARDS, HONORS: Cunard First Book Award, and shortlists for Dartmouth Book Award for Fiction, and Thomas Head Raddall Atlantic Fiction Award, all 2002, all for *Strong Hollow.*

WRITINGS:

Strong Hollow: A Novel, Goose Lane (Fredericton, New Brunswick, Canada), 2001.

Short stories have appeared in literary journals and anthologies including *Descent, Antigonish Review,* and *Journey Prize Anthology,* 1999.

WORK IN PROGRESS: A second novel with the working title *The Railbed Silences.*

SIDELIGHTS: Linda Little's short stories have appeared in literary journals and anthologies. Her first novel, *Strong Hollow,* is set in the backwoods of Nova Scotia, Canada. At the age of nineteen Jackson Bigley, a shy, quiet young man, finds his alcoholic father dead in a ditch. When all the Bigley children come home for the funeral, Jackson can't stand the arguing that continually occurs. As a result, he leaves the family home and builds a cabin in the woods. He makes a meager living by bootlegging and half the time he is drunk to drown out the pain he feels inside. He meets a young fiddler named Ian and begins a love affair with him, which is Jackson's first homosexual experience. Ian gets Jackson to open up and brings out the best in him. When Ian leaves him, Jackson misses his fiddle music, which leads Jackson to his new profession of fiddle making. Soon Jackson's fiddles gain in popularity and he moves away from the backwoods to the city of Halifax. "The strength of *Strong Hollow* is Little's development of her characters. They are intricate and believable," noted James W. Ridout in a *Lambda Book Report* review.

BIOGRAPHICAL AND CRITICAL SOURCES:

PERIODICALS

Lambda Book Report, October, 2001, James W. Ridout, review of *Strong Hollow,* p. 20.
Quill & Quire, April, 2001, Stephanie Domet, review of *Strong Hollow,* p. 31.

ONLINE

Great West, http://www.greatwest.ca/ (September 5, 2002), Amy Dunn Moscoso, review of *Strong Hollow.**

LLEWELLYN, Claire 1954-

PERSONAL: Born 1954, in Great Britain; married, 1979; children: one daughter, one son.

ADDRESSES: Home and office—27 North Road Ave., Hertford, Hertfordshire SG14 2BT, England.

CAREER: Longman Publishers, London, England, editor, 1978-84; Macdonald Children's Books, London, commissioning editor, 1984—. Writer of children's books.

AWARDS, HONORS: Times Educational Supplement Junior Information Book Award, 1992, for *My First Book of Time.*

WRITINGS:

My First Book of Time, illustrated by Julie Carpenter, photographs by Paul Bricknell, Dorling Kindersley (New York, NY), 1992.
Trucks, illustrated by Nicholas Hewetson, F. Watts (New York, NY), 1995.
Disguises and Surprises, Candlewick Press (Cambridge, MA), 1996.
Wild, Wet, and Windy: The Weather—from Tornadoes to Lightning, Candlewick Press (Cambridge, MA), 1997.
The DK Picture Encyclopedia, Dorling Kindersley (New York, NY), 1997.
Our Planet Earth, Scholastic (New York, NY), 1997.
Cities, illustrated by Roger Stewart, Heinemann Interactive Library (Des Plaines, IL), 1998.
The Encyclopedia of Awesome Animals, illustrated by Chris Shields, Copper Beech Books (Brookfield, CT), 1998.
Animal Atlas, World Book (Chicago, IL), 1998.
The Best Book of Bugs, illustrated by Chris Forsey and others, Kingfisher (New York, NY), 1998.
The Big Book of Bones: An Introduction to Skeletons, Peter Bedrick Books (New York, NY), 1998.
The Earth Is like a Roundabout: A First Look at Night and Day, illustrated by Anthony Lewis, Macdonald Young Books (London, England), 1999.
The Best Book of Sharks, illustrated by Ray Grinaway and Roger Stewart, Kingfisher (New York, NY), 1999.

The Big Book of Mummies: All about Preserved Bodies from Long Ago, Peter Bedrick Books (Lincolnwood, IL), 2001, published as *The Complete Book of Mummies,* Wayland (London, England), 2001.

Kid's Survival Handbook, Scholastic (New York, NY), 2001.

Slugs and Snails, F. Watts (London, England), 2001.

Reptiles, Kingisher (New York, NY), 2002.

Who's Who in the Bible, Kingisher (New York, NY), 2002.

The Best Ears in the World (fiction), Smart Apple Media (North Mankato, MN), 2002.

Saints and Angels, Kingfisher (New York, NY), 2003.

The Sea, Smart Apple Media (North Mankato, IL), 2003.

Butterfly, illustrated by Simon Mendez, NorthWord Press (Chanhassen, MN), 2003.

Frog, illustrated by Simon Mendez, NorthWord Press (Chanhassen, MN), 2003.

The Moon, Smart Apple Media (North Mankato, IL), 2003.

Duck, illustrated by Simon Mendez, NorthWord Press (Chanhassen, MN), 2004.

Tree, illustrated by Simon Mendez, NorthWord Press (Chanhassen, MN), 2004.

Llewellyn's books have been translated into several languages, including Hebrew and Spanish.

"TAKE ONE" SERIES

Changing Clothes, Simon & Schuster (New York, NY), 1990.

Growing Food, Simon & Schuster (New York, NY), 1990.

Under the Sea, Simon & Schuster (New York, NY), 1990.

In the Air, Simon & Schuster (New York, NY), 1990.

Rubbish Simon & Schuster (New York, NY), 1990.

Bridges, Simon & Schuster (New York, NY), 1990.

Winter, Simon & Schuster (New York, NY), 1991.

Spring, Simon & Schuster (New York, NY), 1991.

Summer, Simon & Schuster (New York, NY), 1991.

Autumn, Simon & Schuster (New York, NY), 1991.

"FIRST LOOK" SERIES

First Look at Clothes, Gareth Stevens Children's Books (Milwaukee, WI), 1991.

First Look in the Air, Gareth Stevens Children's Books (Milwaukee, WI), 1991.

First Look at Growing Food, Gareth Stevens Children's Books (Milwaukee, WI), 1991.

First Look under the Sea, Gareth Stevens Children's Books (Milwaukee, WI), 1991.

"MIGHTY MACHINES" SERIES

Tractor, Dorling Kindersley (New York, NY), 1995.

Truck, Dorling Kindersley (New York, NY), 1995.

"WHY DO WE HAVE" SERIES

Day and Night, illustrated by Anthony Lewis, Barron's (Hauppauge, NY), 1995.

Rivers and Seas, illustrated by Anthony Lewis, Barron's (Hauppauge, NY), 1995.

Rocks and Mountains, illustrated by Anthony Lewis, Barron's (Hauppauge, NY), 1995.

Wind and Rain, illustrated by Anthony Lewis, Barron's (Hauppauge, NY), 1995.

Towns and Cities, illustrated by Anthony Lewis, Rigby Interactive Library (Crystal Lake, IL), 1997.

Deserts and Rainforests, illustrated by Anthony Lewis, Rigby Interactive Library (Crystal Lake, IL), 1997.

"I DIDN'T KNOW THAT" SERIES

Some Birds Hang upside Down: And Other Amazing Facts about Birds, illustrated by Chris Shields and Jo Moore, Copper Beech Books (Brookfield, CT), 1997.

Some Bugs Glow in the Dark: And Other Amazing Facts about Insects, illustrated by Mike Taylor, Rob Shone, and Jo Moore, Copper Beech Books (Brookfield, CT), 1997.

Some Snakes Spit Poison: And Other Amazing Facts about Snakes, illustrated by Francis Phillipps, Copper Beech Books (Brookfield, CT), 1997.

Spiders Have Fangs: And Other Amazing Facts about Arachnids, illustrated by Mike Taylor and Christopher J. Turnbull, Copper Beech Books (Brookfield, CT), 1997.

Sharks Keep Losing Their Teeth: And Other Amazing Facts about Sharks, Copper Beech Books (Brookfield, CT), 1998.

Some Plants Grow in Midair: And Other Amazing Facts about the Rainforest, illustrated by Mike Taylor and Christopher J. Turnbull, Copper Beech Books (Brookfield, CT), 1998.

Chimps Use Tools: And Other Amazing Facts about Animals, illustrated by Chris Shields and Jo Moore, Copper Beech Books (Brookfield, CT), 1999.

Only Some Big Cats Can Roar: And Other Amazing Facts about Cats, illustrated by Peter Barrett and others, Copper Beech Books (Brookfield, CT), 1999.

"WHAT'S FOR LUNCH" SERIES

Milk, Children's Press (New York, NY), 1998.
Peanuts, Children's Press (New York, NY), 1998.
Potatoes, Children's Press (New York, NY), 1998.
Chocolate, Children's Press (New York, NY), 1998.
Bread, Children's Press (New York, NY), 1998.
Eggs, Children's Press (New York, NY), 1999.
Oranges, Children's Press (New York, NY), 1999.
Peas, Children's Press (New York, NY), 1999.

"GEOGRAPHY STARTS" SERIES

Caves, Heinemann Library (Chicago, IL), 2000.
Coral Reefs, Heinemann Library (Chicago, IL), 2000.
Geysers, Heinemann Library (Chicago, IL), 2000.
Glaciers, Heinemann Library (Chicago, IL), 2000.
Islands, Heinemann Library (Chicago, IL), 2000.
Volcanoes, Heinemann Library (Chicago, IL), 2000.

The "Geography Starts" series was published as the "What Are . . ." series, Heinemann First Library (London, England), 2001.

"THE FACTS ABOUT" SERIES

Arthritis, illustrated by Tom Connell, Smart Apple Media (North Mankato, MN), 2001.
Diabetes, illustrated by Tom Connell, Smart Apple Media (North Mankato, MN), 2001.
Epilepsy, illustrated by Tom Connell, Smart Apple Media (North Mankato, MN), 2001.

"MATERIAL WORLD" SERIES

Plastic, F. Watts (New York, NY), 2002.
Rubber, F. Watts (New York, NY), 2002.
Silk, F. Watts (New York, NY), 2002.

Wood, F. Watts (New York, NY), 2002.
Concrete, F. Watts (New York, NY), 2002.
Glass, F. Watts (New York, NY), 2002.
Metal, F. Watts (New York, NY), 2002.
Paper, F. Watts (New York, NY), 2002.

"LETS RECYCLE" SERIES

Save Energy, Chrysalis Education (North Mankato, IL), 2003.
Stop Water Waste, Chrysalis Education (North Mankato, IL), 2003.
Fight Air Pollution, Chrysalis Education (North Mankato, MN), 2003.
Let's Recycle, Chrysalis Education (North Mankato, IL), 2003.
Protect Natural Habitats, Chrysalis Education (North Mankato, IL), 2003.

SIDELIGHTS: Claire Llewellyn is a prolific author of juvenile nonfiction whose books have been incorporated into numerous book series that, while originating in the author's native England, have also been released in the United States. One of her first books, *My First Book of Time,* was highly praised by reviewers for its enthusiastic and clear explanation of time zones, seasons, fractions, and the history of timepieces. Dubbing it "comprehensive" in its scope, a *Publishers Weekly* contributor noted of *My First Book of Time* that Llewellyn covers the material "in exhaustive but never overwhelming detail." Other books by Llewellyn include *The Big Book of Mummies: All about Preserved Bodies from Long Ago, Our Planet Earth,* and *Some Plants Grow in Midair: and Other Amazing Facts about Rain Forests,* and she has also utilized her organizational and research skills as well as her attention to detail to produce *The Encyclopedia of Awesome Animals* and *Animal Atlas.*

Some of Llewellyn's most popular books are included in the multi-author "I Didn't Know That" series, published in the United States by Copper Beech Books. One of the first series installments, *Some Snakes Spit Poison: and Other Amazing Facts about Snakes,* was described by *Science Books and Films* reviewer Edna DeManche as an "action-packed" "attention getter" of a book. In a text that speaks to kids in their own language, Llewellyn presents information on a variety of snakes, and adds quizzes and games to make the learning experience complete. Packed with information on everything from how spiders evolved, make webs, hunt, and communicate with each other, *Spiders Have Fangs: And Other Amazing Facts about Arachnids* is "loaded with fascinating facts and colorful drawings" that serve as a "fine starting point . . . for further learning," according to *School Library Journal* contributor Anne Chapman Callaghan. And in *Some Plants Grow in Midair,* the rainforest environment is described, along with information regarding its importance to the Earth's ecological health. Not only plants and animals, but also the human inhabitants of the Amazon region are discussed in a book that *School Library Journal* reviewer Ann G. Brouse dubbed "fresh and exciting." Each volume in the "I Didn't Know That" series contains an index, glossary, and projects, and is illustrated with drawings that afford curious readers the chance to explore in search of hidden objects.

Llewellyn covers a broad range of topics in her writing, and while most of them involve the world of plants and animals, some books, such as the three volumes in the "The Facts About" series, delve into medical matters. In the series installment titled *Diabetes* she describes in what *School Librarian* contributor James Donnelly termed "careful, unsentimental" terms, the causes, symptoms, and methods of treating the disease. Geared toward elementary-age children, each book in the series features a child who deals with the covered disease—other volumes deal with asthma, arthritis, and epilepsy—and the text relates their childlike concerns over their medical condition. Praising the series as "thorough and positive," Elizabeth Schleuther noted in her *Books for Keeps* review that Llewellyn mixes her clear, informative text with photographs, graphics, glossary, and information sidebars. Noting that the series will provide "reassurance to those who live with the condition" and also inform friends and family of a loved one's condition, Tom Deveson praised Llewellyn's "The Facts About" books for "perform[ing] a useful informative task without sentimentality and with laudable directness."

While most of Llewellyn's books for young researchers are organized into multi-volume series, several of her books serve as one-volume resources containing a wealth of detail on a single subject. In 2001's *The Big Book of Mummies*—published in England as *The Complete Book of Mummies*—Llewellyn discusses burial practices dating from 4,000 years ago in many different cultures, and explains why the study of mum-

mies is so crucial to our understanding of the past. Noting that the book "lives up to its title," *School Librarian* reviewer Michael Kirby praised *The Big Book of Mummies* for its clear text, exemplary illustrations, and its graphically detailed description of Egyptian embalming rites. In fact, according to somewhat squeamish *Times Educational Supplement* contributor Paul Noble, "it is just too complete"; although Noble was deterred by the book's "revealing" photographs, he nonetheless agreed that *The Big Book of Mummies* is "a fine book."

Other single-volume books include *The Best Book of Bugs* a compendium of insects that a *Kirkus Reviews* contributor described as a "radiantly illustrated" introduction to every bug from ants and bees to spiders and worms. Part of the Scholastic "First Encyclopedia" series, *Our Planet Earth* is organized in a topical format, providing readers with information regarding the Earth's surface, evolution, and life forms. Praising the book's short, "easy to understand" entries, *School Library Journal* reviewer Peg Glisson cited the volume as "an enjoyable browsing book," while in her appraisal for *American Reference Books Annual* Janet Hilbun noted that *Our Planet Earth* "has value as an overview" for budding Earth scientists.

BIOGRAPHICAL AND CRITICAL SOURCES:

PERIODICALS

American Reference Book Annual, Volume 30, 1999, Janet Hilbun, review of *Our Planet Earth,* pp. 417-418.

Appraisal, winter, 1999, Helen James and Leonard Garigliano, review of *Some Plants Grow in Midair,* pp. 53-54; spring, 2000, Barbara C. Sotto and Melvin S. Kaufman, review of *Chimps Use Tools,* pp. 150-151.

Booklist, October 15, 1991, p. 441; December 1, 1996, Hazel Rochman, review of *Disguises and Surprises,* p. 658; February 1, 1998, review of *Our Planet Earth,* p. 941; September 1, 19998, Karen Hutt, review of *The Big Book of Bones,* p. 116.

Books for Keeps, January, 1998, Ted Percy, review of *Wild, Wet, and Windy,* p. 19; November, 1999, Marget Mallett, review of *The Earth Is like a Roundabout,* p. 24; September, 2001, Elizabeth Schleuther, review of *The Facts about Epilepsy,* p. 26.

Bulletin of the Center for Children's Books, July, 1992, p. 299.

Horn Book, July, 1992, p. 468.

Junior Bookshelf, June, 1992, pp. 112-113; December, 1996, review of *Disguises and Surprises,* p. 254.

Kirkus Reviews, May 1, 1992, p. 613; June 1, 1997, review of *Some Snakes Spit Poison,* p. 876; March 15, 1998, review of *The Best Book of Bugs,* pp. 406-607.

Magpies, July, 1995, review of *Truck,* pp. 33-34.

Publishers Weekly, May 4, 1992, review of *My First Book of Time,* p. 55; May 20, 2002, review of *The Kid's Survival Guide,* p. 69.

School Librarian, August, 1995, Alasdair Campbell, review of *Truck* p. 104; November, 1997, p. 205; spring, 1999, John Feltwell, review of *Animal Atlas,* p. 40; summer, 2001, Michael Kirby, review of *The Complete Book of Mummies,* p. 95; winter, 2001, James Donnelly, review of *The Facts about Diabetes,* p. 218; spring, 2002, Joyce Banks, review of *Slugs and Snails,* p. 19, and Shirley Paice, review of *Epilepsy,* p. 51.

School Library Journal, August, 1992, p. 152; February, 1998, Peg Glisson, review of *Our Planet Earth,* p. 138; August, 1995, John Peters, review of *How Things Work,* p. 168; February, 1997, Lisa Wu Stowe, review of *Disguises and Surprises,* p. 93; September, 1997, Jeffrey A. French, review of *Some Bugs Glow in the Dark* and Kathy Piehl, review of *Deserts and Rainforests,* p. 204; March, 1998, Ann Chapman Callaghan, review of *Spiders Have Fangs,* p. 197; July, 1998, Karen Wehner, review of *The Best Book of Bugs,* p. 89, and Christine A. Moesch, review of *The Big Book of Bones,* p. 108; August, 1998, Ann G. Brouse, review of *Some Plants Grow in Midair,* p. 178; September, 1998, Eldon Younce, review of *Potatoes,* p. 193.

Science Books and Film October, 1995, James R. Hanley, review of *Tractor,* pp. 214-215; October, 1997, Edna DeManche, review of *Some Snakes Spit Poison,* p. 210; August, 1998, Katharine C. Payne, review of *Sharks Keep Losing Their Teeth,* p. 177; May, 2001, review of *Some Plants Grow in Midair,* p. 98.

Teaching Children Mathematics, September, 1994, David J. Whitin, review of *My First Book of Time,* p. 44.

Times Educational Supplement, April 6, 2001, Paul Noble, review of *The Complete Book of Mummies,* p. 22; April 13, 2001, review of "What Are" series, p. 22; November 16, 2001, Tom Deveson, review of "Facts About" series, p. 22.*

LOCKWOOD, Lewis 1930-

PERSONAL: Born December 16, 1930, in New York, NY; son of Gerald and Madeline (Wartell) Lewis; married Doris Hoffman, December 26, 1953; children: Alison, Daniel. *Education:* Queens College, B.A., 1952; Princeton University, M.F.A., 1955, Ph.D., 1960.

ADDRESSES: Office—Harvard University, Music Building, 201S, Cambridge, MA 02138. *Agent*—c/o W. W. Norton, 500 Fifth Avenue, New York, NY 10110. *E-mail*—llockw@fas.Harvard.edu.

CAREER: Princeton University, Princeton, NJ, music professor, 1958-80; Harvard University, Cambridge, MA, music professor, 1980-90; International Beethoven Festival-Conference, co-director. *Military service:* U.S. Seventh Army Symphony, cellist, 1957-58.

MEMBER: American Academy of Arts and Sciences, member, 1984—; American Musicological Society, president, 1987-88.

AWARDS, HONORS: Fulbright Award for study in Italy, 1955-56; National Endowment for Humanities, Senior Fellow, 1973-74, 1984-85; Guggenheim fellowship, 1977-78; Einstein Award, 1971; Kindeley Award, 1985; Universita degli Studi in Ferrara, honorary doctorate, 1991; ASCAP-Deems Taylor Award, for *Beethoven: Studies in the Creative Process,* 1993; nominated for Pulitzer Prize for Biography, 2003.

WRITINGS:

MUSICOLOGY

The Counter-Reformation and the Sacred Music of Vincenzo Ruffo, Princeton University Press (Princeton, NJ), 1960.

Music in Renaissance Ferrara, 1400-1505: The Creation of a Musical Center in the Fifteenth Century, Harvard University Press (Cambridge, MA), 1984.

Beethoven: Studies in the Creative Process, Harvard University Press (Cambridge, MA), 1992.

Beethoven: The Music and the Life, Norton (New York, NY), 2002.

AS EDITOR

Pope Marcellus Mass: An Authoritative Score, Backgrounds and Sources, History and Analysis, Views and Comments, Norton (New York, NY), 1975.

(With Phyllis Benjamin) *Beethoven Essays: Studies in Honor of Elliot Forbes*, Harvard University Department of Music (Cambridge, MA), 1984.

(With Edward Roesner) *Essays in Musicology: A Tribute to Alvin Johnson*, American Musicological Society (Philadelphia, PA), 1990.

(With Christopher Reynolds and James Webster) *Beethoven Forum 1*, University of Nebraska Press (Lincoln, NE), 1992.

(With James Webster) *Beethoven Forum 4*, University of Nebraska Press (Lincoln, NE), 1996.

(With James Webster) *Beethoven Forum 5*, University of Nebraska Press (Lincoln, NE), 1996.

(With Christopher Reynolds and Elaine R. Sisman) *Beethoven Forum 7*, University of Nebraska Press (Lincoln, NE), 1999.

SIDELIGHTS: Lewis Lockwood, professor emeritus at Harvard University, is a renowned musicologist and a leading scholar on the life and music of Beethoven. In the course of over four decades of teaching music at both Princeton and Harvard universities, Lockwood has written and edited several noted books that critics have praised for their clarity and, as stated by a *Kirkus* reviewer, for Lockwood's "remarkable ability to describe music in words."

As an authority on Beethoven, Lockwood has written several important books as well as editing many collections of essays concerning the German composer. Scholarship on Beethoven is extensive, and, as Denis Matthews in his critique of Lockwood's *Beethoven Essays: Studies in Honor of Elliot Forbes*, 1984, for the *Times Literary Supplement*, pointed out: "It may surprise many readers that there are still a number of untapped, or untabulated, sources of information about the most copiously documented of all composers." This may or may not be the case, but as critics are quick to demonstrate, due to Lockwood's keen insights and detailed research, new facts and observations about Beethoven's life and work continue to come to the surface, shining new light upon the great master. In this particular collection, Lockwood honors the scholarship of his own teacher, Elliot Forbes, also a scholar on the works of Beethoven. Forbes is noted

for having revised Alexander Wheelock Thayer's *Life of Beethoven,* another classic study. In reference to Lockwood's *Beethoven Essays,* Richard Kramer for the publication *Notes* commented that this collection offered a "broad spectrum of views and voice" and that readers "who delight in bold juxtapositions will find much pleasure here."

Lockwood has also edited a series of published forums on Beethoven, beginning with his *Beethoven Forum 1* published in 1992. In this first collection, readers will find ten articles and one review written by the leading scholars of Beethoven. Commenting on this collection, M. N. Cheng, writing for *Choice* described the book as "thought-provoking and provocative." The works on which the contributors focus include Beethoven's Sonata Op. 110, Quartet Op. 130, "Waldstein Sonata," and his Ninth Symphony, among others. *Beethoven Forum 4,* 1996, is a bit more conservative, according to reviewer Daniel K. L. Chua, writing for *Music and Letters,* but the collection remains enjoyable. Chua wrote: "For those who wish to sit back and enjoy some good editing, solid scholarship and beautiful typography . . . *Beethoven Forum 4* will not disappoint." Included in this collection are essays on Beethoven's third movement of the "Pastoral Symphony," and analysis of his "Tempest Sonata", as well as an exploration by William Rothstein on Beethoven's metrical ambiguity.

In 1992 Lockwood authored the book *Beethoven: Studies in the Creative Process,* which *Times Literary Supplement* reviewer Paul Griffiths called "a collection of masterly essays." Particularly enjoyable for Charles Rosen, writing for the *New York Review of Books,* is Lockwood's study of Beethoven's "Eroica Symphony", for which Lockwood's work, according to Rosen, went "farther than any other work I know to show how Beethoven mapped out and controlled a large-scale form." Lockwood's narrative on Beethoven's creative process also includes a close look at the mundane details of living that plague the composer, pulling him away, time after time, from his writing. These details include the physical torment of having to hand-write his compositions, as well as Beethoven's publishers not being able to fully appreciate the extreme efforts and significance of Beethoven's insistence in lack of printing errors in the final texts.

Of particular interest to Paul Driver of the *London Review of Books* was Lockwood's "dazzling though demanding analysis of the autograph first movement of the Opus 69 Cello Sonata." This work is one of the few of Beethoven's autograph pieces that have survived intact. Driver complimented Lockwood's reproduction of this work by stating: "His decipherment of the manuscript is a diplomatic . . . triumph," and "his ability to interpret the result, to follow Beethoven's moment-by-moment creative track seems at times miraculous."

In 2002 Lockwood presented yet another study of Beethoven in his *Beethoven: The Music and the Life*, which a writer for *Kirkus Reviews* called "an outstanding new survey of the great composer's life and works." In this study, Lockwood looks at the three different phases of Beethoven's creative life, with an emphasis on Beethoven's musical development. Concerning the music, a reviewer for *Publishers Weekly* observed, that Lockwood had "many fine insights." This reviewer noted specifically Lockwood's examination of Beethoven's "very conscious and determined development of his skills." Beethoven's early period was heavily influenced by Wolfgang Amadeus Mozart (1756-1791) and the later works of Franz Joseph Haydn (1732-1809). During his early years, Beethoven gladly took on the role of being the "next Mozart." It was in his middle years, though, that Beethoven began branching out, moving away from the old style and trying to create his own. He became more creative as he searched for new musical forms and harmonies. It was during these middle years that he wrote many of his piano sonatas and symphonies. The third period of his development took on a more romantic bent, and his pieces became grander in scope. *Library Journal*'s Timothy J. McGee praised Lockwood's study, which "offers a new and authoritative interpretation of a prodigiously gifted and complex man and artist."

Beethoven: The Music and the Life also contains a historic perspective, as Lockwood demonstrates how the French Revolution and Napoleon's rise to power affected Beethoven's work. There is also a discussion of the aesthetic and philosophical influences that were popular during Beethoven's time. By relying on the composer's autograph manuscripts and his sketchbooks, Lockwood also provides insights into Beethoven's compositional methods. All-important compositions are discussed, but not in a voice that is too technical to be appreciated only by other musicologists. Most reviewers have found that Lockwood has written a very accessible book for any one interested in Beethoven.

BIOGRAPHICAL AND CRITICAL SOURCES:

BOOKS

Owens, Jessie Ann and Anthony M. Cummings, editors, *Music in Renaissance Cities and Courts: Studies in Honor of Lewis Lockwood*, Harmonie Park Press (Warren, MI), 1997.

PERIODICALS

American Historical Review, December, 1985, Charles L. Stinger, review of *Music in Renaissance Ferrara 1400-1505: The Creating of a Musical Centre in the Fifteenth Century*, pp. 1227-1228.
Booklist, October 15, 2002, Alan Hirsch, review of *Beethoven: The Music and the Life*, p. 375.
Choice, July, 1985, A. G. Spiro, review of *Music in Renaissance Ferrara, 1400-1505: The Creation of a Musical Center in the Fifteen Century.*, p. 1643; April, 1993, M. N. H. Cheng, review of *Beethoven Forum 1*, p. 1322.
Journal of Modern History, September, 1986,Charles M. Rosenberg, review of *Music in Renaissance Ferrara 1400-1505*, pp. 740-742.
Kirkus Reviews, August 15, 2002, review of *Beethoven: The Music and the Life*, p. 1199.
Library Journal, September 15, 2002, Timothy J. McGee, review of *Beethoven: The Music and the Life*, p. 64.
London Review of Books, April 8, 1993, Paul Driver, review of *Beethoven: Studies in the Creative Process*, pp. 22-23.
Music and Letters, August, 1993, Nicholas Marston, review of *Beethoven: Studies in the Creative Process*, pp. 446-448; February, 1994, F. W. Sternfeld, review of *Beethoven Forum 1*, pp. 92-94; August, 1997, Daniel K. L. Chua, review of *Beethoven Forum 4*, pp. 431-432; August, 2001, Barry Cooper, review of *Beethoven Forum 7*, pp. 456-459.
New York Review of Books, June 23, 1994, Charles Rosen, review of *Beethoven: Studies in the Creative Process*, pp. 55-62.
New York Times, November 24, 2002, James R. Oestreich, review of *Beethoven: The Music and the Life*, p. 33.
Notes, December, 1971, Denis Stevens, review of *The Counter-Reformation and the Masses of Vincenzo Ruffo*, pp. 217-220; June, 1986, Richard Kramer,

review of *Beethoven Essays: Studies in Honor of Elliot Forbes,* pp. 773-775; September, 1993, Ellen S. Beebe, review of *Essays in Musicology: A Tribute to Alvin Johnson,* pp. 120-122; December, 1993, Geoffrey Block, review of *Beethoven: Studies in the Creative Process,* pp. 571-573; March, 1994, Geoffrey Block, review of *Beethoven Forum 1,* pp. 959-961; June, 2000, James Parsons, review of *Beethoven Forum 7,* p. 944.

Publishers Weekly, August 26, 2002, review of *Beethoven: The Music and the Life,* p. 52.

Times Literary Supplement, April 12, 1985, Denis Stevens, review of *Music in Renaissance Ferrara 1400-1505,* p. 415; June 14, 1985, Denis Matthews, review of *Beethoven Essays: Studies in Honor of Elliot Forbes,* p. 670; November 13, 1992, Paul Griffiths, review of *Beethoven: Studies in the Creative Process,* pp.8-9.*

* * *

LONERGAN, Kenneth 1963(?)-

PERSONAL: Born c. 1963, in New York, NY; son of a doctor and a psychiatrist. *Education:* New York University, B.A.

ADDRESSES: Home—New York, NY. *Agent*—c/o Author Mail, Vintage Books, Random House, 1745 Broadway, New York, NY 10019.

CAREER: Playwright, screenwriter, and director. Member, Naked Angels Theater Company.

AWARDS, HONORS: Sundance Film Festival Grand Jury prize and Waldo Salt Screenwriting Award, 2000, National Society of Film Critics award for best screenplay, and Oscar and Golden Globe nominations for best original screenplay, all 2000, all for *You Can Count on Me.*

WRITINGS:

The Rennings Children (one-act play), produced at the Circle Repertory Co. New York, NY, 1982.

This Is Our Youth (two-act play; produced off Broadway 1996; produced at London, England, 2002), Overlook Press (Woodstock, NY), 2000.

Analyze This (screenplay), Warner Bros., 1999.

The Adventures of Rocky and Bullwinkle (motion picture screenplay), Universal, 2000.

The Waverly Gallery (two-act play; produced at Promenade Theatre, New York, NY, 2000), Grove Press (New York, NY), 2000.

Lobby Hero (two-act play; produced in New York, NY, 2001; produced in London, England, 2002), Grove Press (New York, NY), 2001.

(And director) *You Can Count On Me* (screenplay; produced by Paramount Classics, 2000), Vintage Books (New York, NY), 2002.

(Rewrites, with others) *Gangs of New York* (screenplay), Miramax, 2002.

Also author of plays *The Lost Army* and *Betrayal by Everyone* (one-act).

WORK IN PROGRESS: Screenplay adaptations of *The Once and Future King* by T. H. White, and *Time and Again,* by Jack Finney.

SIDELIGHTS: Kenneth Lonergan began writing in the ninth grade at Walden School, a private school in Manhattan, when his drama teacher asked him to collaborate on a play. This experience led him to graduate from the playwriting program at New York University. While still an undergraduate, his first play, *The Rennings Children,* was chosen for the Young Playwright's Festival of 1982. Following graduation, he began work as a speechwriter at the Environmental Protection Agency, as well as writing industrial shows for clients such as Weight Watchers and Fuji Film. All the while, he continued his theatrical writing, participating in readings and workshops with the Naked Angels off-Broadway theater troupe.

Lonergan's mother and stepfather are psychiatrists and his father is a retired doctor and medical researcher. According to Peter Marks in a *New York Times* article, the influence of their professions can be seen in many of his works: In The *Rennings Children* Lonergan, who has a brother, half-brother, and several step-siblings, explores the relationship between a teenage boy committed to a psychiatric institution after being involved in an automobile accident that killed his best friend, and the boy's young married sister, who tries in vain to prevent her brother's mental disintegration. Likewise in the analytical vein, Lonergan's screenplay *Analyze This,* which became a successful motion picture starring Robert deNiro and Billy Crystal, is the story of a Mafia don suffering anxiety attacks who enters psychotherapy.

Marks commented: "[Lonergan's] family's deep therapeutic connections no doubt also help to account for the acute distillation of human behavior and revelatory exactitude of language in his work." Marks also quoted film and theater director, Scott Elliott, of the New Group Off Broadway company that premiered *This Is Our Youth:* "He's an ultrarealist," said Elliott. "It's the same way he is when you talk to him. You sort of get everything. There are no masks. There is a true emotional resonance that I think makes his plays bigger than they seem."

This Is Our Youth was expanded from Lonergan's one-act play *Betrayal by Everyone,* which gained attention during the 1993 festival of short plays at the Met Theater in New York. The play, which Pamela Renner described in *American Theatre* as an "ascerbic comedy about two boy-men taking cover from the adult world," has a cast of three and takes place entirely in an Upper West Side apartment. It is the 1980s, and the apartment belongs to twenty-two-year-old Dennis, son of an affluent Upper West Side family and college dropout who prefers to deal drugs than end up like his elitist parents. In the same vein, Warren, a sensitive youth of eighteen, quits college, stuffs childhood memorabilia and $15,000 stolen from his parents into a sack, and is ultimately granted refuge by the dominating, verbally abusive, and cruel Dennis. The story follows their resistance to the inevitable transition into adulthood. "They have enough unfocused angst to claim membership in the Holden Caulfield Hall of Arrested Development," wrote Renner. The girl of Warren's dreams, Jessica, plays devil's advocate, and introduces the locus to Lonergan's play: that aging inevitably produces self-forgetting because, in the growing-up process, one becomes a different person. "It's a testament to Lonergan's slyness and restraint as a writer that one comes to care powerfully about this hapless Warren—who has a way of reminding you instinctively how much the empty spaces inside your heart ached at this age."

The Waverly Gallery, perhaps Lonergan's most autobiographical work, resembles Tennessee Williams' *The Glass Menagerie* in that it is a "memory" play. It follows the experience of his grandmother from the perspective of a grandson as she descends by degrees into Alzheimer's disease. While the play received good reviews in general, Charles Isherwood, writing for *Variety,* commented: "The life trauma being depicted has an inherent pathos, and in Lonergan's hands, no small amount of comic potential. And yet, while Lonergran mines his subject with delicacy and wit, he runs out of dramatic ore well before the evening's end." While the play received positive critical acclaim in general, it never attained commercial success.

Lobby Hero landed on the top-ten list in *Best Plays of 2001-2002.* Toby Young, in his review for *Spectator,* wrote: "*Lobby Hero* is a fantastic play but I'd be hard pushed to say why. You can tell it's good because, within about five minutes, any sense you have of being a member of the audience, sitting down and watching a group of actors perform on stage, has vanished. . . . In what amounts to an out-of-body experience, you're totally absorbed in what's going on." Set in the foyer of a middle-income Manhattan apartment building in the middle of the night, the play follows an easy-going doorman in his late twenties, his not-so-easy-going supervisor, and an overbearing cop and his rookie female partner. The characters quickly find themselves involved in a complicated situation involving homicide, sexual assault, and perjury. Young said: "Lonergan is particularly good, both here and in *This Is Our Youth,* at showing how good intentions can be undermined by unconscious desires. Few of his characters are capable of resisting their own malignant impulses."

Lonergan's screenwriting assignments include the gangland comedy *Analyze This,* which became a successful motion picture, and—as a writer-for-hire—*The Adventures of Rocky and Bullwinkle.* Following hot on that film's tail was *You Can Count on Me,* an award-winning film. Not only did Lonergan write the screenplay, he was also director and a supporting actor. Of the movie, which had its genesis as a one-act stage play, Lisa Schwarzbaum commented in *Entertainment Weekly:* "Characters talk to one another in this beautiful compassionate, articulate domestic drama" that tells the story of Sammy and Terry, orphaned siblings who found different ways of adapting to their situation. Sammy, while raising her eight-year-old son in the upstate New York family home, lives a life of habit and excessive control. Terry, who buries his grief by refusing to commit anywhere to anyone and leaves behind him a wake of disaster, suddenly appears at Sammy's in need of money. "The unexpected attachment he forms with his nephew rattles his sister so much," wrote Schwarzbaum, "that she's shaken out of complacency. . . . [The movie] is so delicate and low-keyed a drama of deep feelings that it hinges all the more crucially on dramatic subtlety."

In *Back Stage West* Jamie Painter Young noted that Lonergan decided the only way the movie script would retain its essence was if he directed it. Even so, realizing the production company had ultimate say in the editing process he called successful film-making friend Martin Scorsese—whom he felt confident would respect him as a director—to produce the film. Scorsese accepted the invitation, and ultimately found little that needed to be changed. "As much as Lonergan enjoyed the challenge of directing his first film," commented Young, "he admitted that his primary love remains writing."

Lonegan's play *Lobby Hero* attests to that, as does the fact that—as a screenwriter-for-hire—he is in much demand. He wrote *The Lost Army* for Scorsese's company, and was hired for on-the-set rewrites in Rome, Italy, for Scorsese's ambitious *Gangs of New York.* Lonergan planned to produce screenplay adaptations of *The Once and Future King* by T. H. White and *Time and Again* by Jack Finney.

BIOGRAPHICAL AND CRITICAL SOURCES:

PERIODICALS

America, December 9, 2000, Richard A. Blake, review of *You Can Count on Me,* p. 22.

American Theatre, January, 1999, Pamela Renner, review of *This Is Our Youth,* p. 54.

Back Stage West, November, 2000, Jamie Painter Young, "In the Driver's Seat," p. 18; February 28, 2002, T.H. McCulloh, review of *Lobby Hero,* p. 23.

Christian Century, December 13, 2000, review of *You Can Count on Me,* p. 1307.

Entertainment Weekly, November 17, 2000, Lisa Schwarzbaum, "Upstate of Grace: A Brother and Sister Are Reunited in the Home Where They Were Orphaned as Children in *You Can Count on Me,*" p. 92.

Hollywood Reporter, February 27, 2002, Ed Kaufman, review of *Lobby Hero;* April 30, 2002, Bill Hagerty, review of *Lobby Hero,* p. 22.

Interview, November, 2000, Graham Fuller, review of *You Can Count on Me,* p. 106.

Los Angeles Magazine, December, 2000, James Greenberg, review of *You Can Count on Me,* p. 96.

National Review, December 4, 2000, John Simon, review of *This Is Our Youth.*

New Republic, April 5, 1999, Stanley Kauffmann, review of *Analyze This,* p. 28; June 28, 1999, Robert Brustein, review of *You Can Count on Me,* p. 36.

New York Times, March 12, 2001, Peter Marks, "Artist at Work, Kenneth Lonergan, Finding the Drama in Real Life," p. E1.

Spectator, April 6, 2002, Toby Young, review of *This Is Our Youth,* p. 38; April 20, 2002, Toby Young, review of *Lobby Hero,* p. 47.

Time, November 27, 2000, Richard Schickel, review of *You Can Count on Me,* p. 92.

Variety, November 9, 1998, Charles Isherwood, review of *This Is Our Youth,* p. 40; February 7, 2000, Emanuel Levy, review of *You Can Count on Me,* p. 52; March 27, 2000, Charles Isherwood, review of *The Waverly Gallery,* p. 33; July 10, 2000, Joe Leydon, review of *The Adventures of Rocky and Bullwinkle,* p. 20; January 8, 2001, Claude Brodesser, "Playwright Embraces Director's Reins," p. S17; March 19, 2001, Christopher Isherwood, review of *Lobby Hero,* p. 40; April 1, 2002, Matt Wolf, review of *This Is Our Youth,* p. 40.

ONLINE

Hollywood.com Web site, http://www.hollywood.com/ (June 5, 2002), "Kenneth Lonergan."

indieWIRE, http://www.indiwire.com/ (June 5, 2002), Andrea Meyer, "Interview: You Can Count on Kenneth Lonergan."*

*   *   *

LONGSTRETH, W(illiam) Thacher 1920-2003

OBITUARY NOTICE—See index for *CA* sketch: Born November 4, 1920, in Haverford, PA; died of a pulmonary embolism April 11, 2003, in Florida. Businessman, politician, and author. Longstreth was a former Philadelphia councilman and mayoral candidate. Graduating from Princeton University in 1941, he served in the U.S. Navy from 1942 to 1946 in the South Pacific theater and was awarded two bronze stars. Returning home, he embarked on a career in advertising, selling advertising for *Life* magazine until 1953, when he became vice president at the Geare-Marston Advertising Agency, followed by a similar stint at Aitkin-Kynett Advertising Agency, where he worked until 1964. Elected to the Greater Philadelphia City Council that year, he became president and chief executive officer and was reelected five times. Longstreth also ran for mayor of the city twice but was defeated both times. During his later years, he worked in various business posts, including as vice-chair of Winchell Co. and Packard Press. Longstreth will best be remembered in Philadelphia for his bow tie and wisecracking antics at city council meet-

ings, about which he wrote in his memoir, *Main Line WASP* (1990).

OBITUARIES AND OTHER SOURCES:

BOOKS

Writers Directory, 13th edition, St. James Press (Detroit, MI), 1997.

PERIODICALS

Chicago Tribune, April 12, 2003, section 2, p. 11.
New York Times, April 12, 2003, p. A20.

M

MA, Jian 1953-

PERSONAL: Born 1953, in Quingdao, China.

ADDRESSES: Home—London, England. *Agent*—c/o Author Mail, Pantheon Books, Knopf Publishing Group, 299 Park Ave., New York, NY 10171-0002.

CAREER: Painter, writer, poet, and photographer.

WRITINGS:

Red Dust: A Path through China, translated from the Chinese by Flora Drew, Pantheon Books (New York, NY), 2001.

SIDELIGHTS: Until 1983 Chinese writer Ma Jian was a photographer in the propaganda department of the Chinese government. Six years after the death of Mao Zedong and the end of the Cultural Revolution, the backlash of the opening of China's economy took the form of repression of all political dissent.

Ma was also a painter, a writer, and a poet who let his disaffection be known by wearing jeans, growing his hair long, and hanging out with like-minded intellectuals to discuss politics, art, and literature. This aroused censure from his section heads, who asked him to write a "self-criticism" for the Campaign against Spiritual Pollution. This was followed by a series of disciplinary sessions and the breakup of his marriage. Ma responded to these circumstances by illegally leaving his job and taking to the road to discover the China outside the walls of his native Beijing. Before buying a ticket for Urumqi and the Chinese "Wild West," Ma took Buddhist vows.

As a dropout, a fugitive from the police, and a Buddhist in search of enlightenment, Ma spent the next three years wandering China, armed only with a notebook, a camera, a change of clothes and Whitman's *Leaves of Grass.* He made himself fake letters of recommendation and paid his way by writing articles, painting pictures, giving an occasional lecture, or passing himself off as a fortuneteller, hair dresser, toothpaste seller, or sofa-maker. For part of his travels he slept and ate free of charge with the help of a network of dissident poets and artists, but for the most part Ma relied upon his own resources to survive in the most distant parts of China.

Ma often abandoned public transportation and sojourned in small villages and mud houses in Gansu, staying with Kazak nomads in a tent, crossing the desert to reach the Qinghai lake or finding a route though the jungle to see the Li people of Hainan Island. Once or twice, he lost his way and came close to death.

"Red dust" is a Buddhist term for the veil of materialism that keeps a man from enlightenment. Throughout his memoir *Red Dust: A Path through China,* Ma attempts to lift this veil of illusion in order to find himself and the real China. But it is a voyage of disappointment, disgust, and disorientation. Rural China is medieval, almost primitive, in its cruelty and backwardness. Urban China is overcrowded and reeking of jealousy, body odor, and corrupt politics. "When a man's spirit is in chains," writes Ma, "he loses all respect for nature."

At the end of his journey Ma wearied of the road. "I need to live in big cities that have hospitals, bookshops and women," he writes. Shortly after returning to Beijing, he moved to Hong Kong and then on to London.

Frank Dikötter, in the *Times Literary Supplement*, commented that "Ma Jian has an undeniable talent for bringing China to life, from the primeval jungle, with a canopy resembling a deserted cathedral, to the moths glowing under the dirty ceiling light of a cramped room filled with sweating bodies. *Red Dust* . . . [provides] an unforgettable sense of what it is like to live in China since the death of Mao." Jonathan Spence, in *The Search for Modern China*, wrote that "In this skillfully constructed, picaresque memoir, Ma Jian takes us on an absorbing tour of the emotional, intellectual and sexual travails of China's Beat generation in the early 1980s. *Red Dust* is full of surprising insights into the China that emerged, for better or worse, after the death of Mao."

BIOGRAPHICAL AND CRITICAL SOURCES:

BOOKS

Ma Jian, *Red Dust*, translated from the Chinese by Flora Drew, Pantheon Books (New York, NY), 2001.
Spence, Jonathan, *The Search for Modern China*, Norton (New York, NY), 2001.

PERIODICALS

Booklist, December 1,2001, Allen Weakland, review of *Red Dust: A Path through China*, p. 626.
Geographical, July, 2001, Anna Sansom, review of *Red Dust*, p. 80.
Guardian, (London, England), June 10, 2001, Phillip Marsden, review of *Red Dust*, p. 6.
Kirkus Review, September 15, 2001, review of *Red Dust*, p. 1340.
New York Times, November 4, 2001, Barbara Crossette, review of *Red Dust*, p. 37.

Observer, June 1, 2001, Philip Marsden, review of *Red Dust*.
Times Literary Supplement, July 27, 2001, Frank Dikötter, review of *Red Dust*, p. 6.
Washington Post, November 4, 2001, Andrew J. Nathan, review of *Red Dust*, p.T13.*

*   *   *

MACDONALD, Hector (R.) 1973-

PERSONAL: Born April 2, 1973, in Nairobi, Kenya. *Education:* Oxford University, B.A., 1995; INSEAD, M.B.A., 1999.

ADDRESSES: Home—London, England. *Agent*—Conville & Walsh, 2 Ganton St., London W1F 7QL, England. *E-mail*—mail@hectormacdonald.com.

CAREER: English teacher in northeastern Brazil; strategy consultant. Writer.

WRITINGS:

The Mind Game, Ballantine Books (New York, NY), 2001.
The Hummingbird Saint, Michael Joseph (London, England), 2003.

Contributor to *Girls' Night Out/Boys' Night In*, HarperCollins (New York, NY), 2001.

SIDELIGHTS: Hector Macdonald grew up in Kenya and was a student at Oxford University. His debut novel, *The Mind Game*, is set in both places. *Booklist* contributor Julia Glynn claimed, "Macdonald's debut novel is a tale of intrigue and intimate game playing." *Publishers Weekly* contributor noted, "First-time novelist Macdonald delivers twists and turns with the ease of an old pro in this brainy, exotic suspense thriller."

BIOGRAPHICAL AND CRITICAL SOURCES:

PERIODICALS

Booklist, November 15, 2000, Julia Glynn, review of *The Mind Game*.

Library Journal, November 15, 2000, Linda M. G. Katz, review of *The Mind Game,* p. 96.

Publishers Weekly, February 19, 2001, review of *The Mind Game,* p. 70.

Times Literary Supplement, February 2, 2001, Keith Miller, "Messing with the Head," p. 22.

ONLINE

Book Browser, http://www.bookbrowser.com/ (September 5, 2002), Harriet Klausner, review of *The Mind Game.*

Complete Review, http://www.complete-review.com/ (September 5, 2002), review of *The Mind Game.*

Hector Macdonald Web site, http://www. hectormacdonald.com (December 26, 2002).

iVenus, http://www.ivenus.com/ (September 5, 2002), Marius Silke, review of *The Mind Game.*

Murder out There, http://www.murderoutthere.com/ (September 5, 2002), Kerry J. Schooley, review of *The Mind Game.*

New York Times on the Web, http://www.nytimes.com/ (August 28, 2002), Emily White, review of *The Mind Game.*

Penguin UK Web site, http://www.penguin.co.uk/ (September 5, 2002).

*   *   *

MacDONALD, Scott 1942-

PERSONAL: Born October 10, 1942, in Easton, PA. *Education:* DePauw University, B.A., 1964; University of Florida, M.A., 1966, Ph.D., 1970.

ADDRESSES: Home—5 Sherman Street, New Hartford, NY 13413. *Office*—Department of English & Film, Utica College, 1600 Burrstone Road, Utica, NY 13502.

CAREER: Critic and educator. University of Florida, Gainesville, assistant professor of humanities, 1969-70; Utica College, New York, NY, began as assistant professor, became professor emeritus of English and film studies, 1971—. Visiting professor, media arts, University of Tucson, Tucson, AZ, 2000. Guest curator of exhibit *Frames of Mind: Recent Filmmaking in Central New York,* at Munson-Williams-Proctor Institute, Utica, 1986.

WRITINGS:

(Editor) *Critical essays on Erskine Caldwell,* G. K. Hall (Boston, MA), 1981.

A Critical Cinema: Interviews with Independent Filmmakers, three volumes, University of California Press (Berkeley, CA), 1988-1998.

Avant-Garde Film: Motion Studies, Cambridge University Press (New York, NY), 1993.

(Editor) *Screen Writings: Scripts and Texts by Independent Filmmakers,* University of California Press (Berkeley, CA), 1995.

The Garden in the Machine: A Field Guide to Independent Films about Place, University of California Press (Berkeley, CA), 2001.

(Editor) *Cinema 16: Documents toward a History of the Film Society,* Temple University Press (Philadelphia, PA), 2002.

Articles have been published in numerous journals, including *Quarterly Review of Film Studies, Arts & Cinema,* and *Afterimage.*

SIDELIGHTS: Scott MacDonald's special interest lies in researching avant-garde filmmakers. In an article for the *Tucson Weekly,* Mari Wadsworth quoted MacDonald: "I've never liked the term avant-garde. It sounds like the avant-garde gets there first, and then everybody else follows. That's true sometimes, but just as often Hollywood gets there first, and then the avant-garde satirizes it."

While MacDonald was visiting professor at the University of Arizona, he conducted a series of free lectures titled "American Place in American Avant-Garde Film," a series, Wadsworth noted, "aimed at those who may have previously assumed avant-garde is French for 'I don't get it.'" MacDonald acknowledged that, while he loves all kinds of film, he believes avant-garde requires special attention. "No matter how good [avant-garde] cinema is," he commented, "it doesn't get in front of audiences. Consequently, it doesn't get rented much, so prints aren't struck . . . so it's a bit like nature itself. It's endangered."

To that end, his publications focus on the film genre and its creators. For the first installment of his three-volume *A Critical Cinema: Interviews with Independent Filmmakers* MacDonald interviewed "critical" filmmakers Hollis Frampton, Larry Gottenheim, Robert Huot, Taka Iimura, Babette Magolte, and Diana Barrie. *A Critical Cinema 2* consists of interviews with nineteen independent filmmakers, including Michael Snow, Robert Beer, and Bruce Baillie. He also focuses much of this second volume on women filmmakers, including Yoko Ono, who discusses her early work with the dadaist Fluxus group and joint projects with husband John Lennon. *A Critical Cinema 3* expands the scope of the previous two volumes by treating independent filmmaking on an international and multiethnic level. Interviews include Armenian filmmaker Arthur Peleshian, Mani Kaul of India, Nick Deocampo of the Philippines, and British filmmaker Sally Potter. Neal Baker, commented in *Library Journal:* "The filmmakers in these volumes strive to create new kinds of imagery, narratives, and audiences that challenge Hollywood norms." A reviewer for *Publishers Weekly* wrote: "MacDonald is a near-ideal interviewer—well informed, concise and unobtrusive—and his subjects are good talkers. The filmographies and bibliographies included here are especially welcome."

Of *Avant-Garde Film: Motion Studies,* M. Yacowar and Emily Carr commented in *Choice,* "At last! A work on avant-garde film that is not as confounding as the films. . . . He succeeds in his aim to show how this challenging and unfamiliar cinema can enliven even conventional film viewing." The book contains fifteen short chapters, each headed with the name of one filmmaker and one of that filmmaker's works, then studies that particular work in relation to other works by the same artist. For example, the chapter, "Su Friedrich: *The Ties That Bind*" also contains extensive remarks on *Sink or Swim* by the same artist. William Wees noted in *Film Quarterly* that MacDonald examines "the ways avant-garde filmmakers use serial organization—a kind of temporal grid—and, in most cases, long takes as well, to 'focus attention—an almost meditative level of attention—on subject matter normally ignored or marginalized by massentertainment films.'"

The Garden in the Machine is a far-reaching and original work focusing on place, especially American place, represented in literature, art, photography, and moving images. In particular, MacDonald analyses mainstream and alternative movies and their representation of landscape and nature. He garnered the title of his book from *The Machine in the Garden,* a famous book by Leo Marx, and explained to Wadsworth the opposing premises of the two books and how Marx depicts nineteenth-century American as an Eden into which rolls the locomotive. "He talks about trying to come to terms with the industrial revolution and what you would rather think of as a kind of dying, natural space. My premise is that a century later, as Americans, we're dealing with basically the same issue. But the whole country is a continental machine, and what we're looking for are the little moments of garden—not just physical garden, but what a garden means—in that machine."

MacDonald continued, "This is part of the premise, too, that when you go into a movie theater you're inside a machine. There's a machine in a room, and you turn out these machines (lights) and you turn on a machine (projector) and sound is going on. You're in an electronic, mechanical space, looking at a natural thing. And yet, seeing nature in a movie theater can re-alert you to reality."

An article on the *University of California Press Web site* quoted author Patricia Zimmerman as saying: *The Garden in the Machine* "is MacDonald's magnum opus: it represents a deep immersion in and advocacy for independent, experimental cinema." Scott Slovic also commented on the same Web site: "This is a brilliant study—learned, authoritative, and often eloquent. One reads this book with astonishment at the wealth of thoughtful and playful and provocative work that has occurred in this medium—and astonishment too that most scholars of environmental literature and nature in the visual arts have had minimal contact with independent film and video."

BIOGRAPHICAL AND CRITICAL SOURCES:

PERIODICALS

American Studies International, October, 1998, James Deutsch, review of *A Critical Cinema 3: Interviews with Independent Filmmakers,* p. 87.

Choice, September, 1993, M. Yacowar and Emily Carr, review of *Avant-Garde Film: Motion Studies,* p. 134.

Film Quarterly, spring, 1994, William C. Wees, review of *Avant-Garde Film,* p. 51.

Films in Review, September, 1995, review of *Screen Writings: Scripts and Texts by Independent Filmmakers,* P. 68.

Journalism Quarterly, winter, 1989, review of *A Critical Cinema: Interviews with Independent Filmmakers,* p. 1021.

Library Journal, February 1, 1998, Neal Baker, review of *A Critical Cinema 3,* p. 88.

Publishers Weekly, August 31, 1992, review of *A Critical Cinema 2: Interviews with Independent Filmmakers,* p. 70.

Sight and Sound, October 1993, Ian Christie, review of *Avant-Garde Film,* p. 34.

Videomaker, April, 1999, Joe McCleskey, review of *A Critical Cinema 3,* p. 13.

ONLINE

Tuscon Weekly Online, http://www.tucsonweekly.com/ (September 23, 2002), Mari Wadsworth, "Manifest West: A Series of Films from the Avant-Garde Breathe New Life into the Old West."

University of California Web site, http://www.ucpress. edu/ (June 5, 2002).*

* * *

MACHTAN, Lothar 1949-

PERSONAL: Born 1949. *Education:* Received Ph.D., 1978.

ADDRESSES: Office—Institut für Geschichte, Universität Bremen, Postfach 33 04 40, 28334 Bremen, Germany.

CAREER: Bremen University, Bremen, Germany, associate professor of modern and current history.

WRITINGS:

(With Deitrich Milles) *Die Klassensymbiose von Junkertum und Bourgeoisie,* Ullstein (Frankfurt am Main, Germany), 1980.

Streiks im frühen deutschen Kaiserreich, Campus (New York, NY), 1983.

(Editor) *Bismarcks Sozialstaat: Beiträge zur Geschichte der Sozialpolitik und zur sozialpolitischen Geschichtsschreibung,* Campus (New York, NY), 1994.

Bismarck und der deutsche National-Mythos, Temmen (Bremen, Germany), 1994.

(Editor) *Mut zur Moral: aus der privaten Korrespondenz des Gesellschaftsreformers Theodor Lohmann,* Temmen (Bremen, Germany), 1995.

Der Gesellschaftsreformer Theodor Lohman, in: Festschrift für H. J. Steinberg, 1995.

Bismarcks Tod und Deutschlands Tränen: Reportage einer Tragödie, Goldmann, 1998.

Hitlers Geheimnis. Das Doppelleben eines Diktators, Alexander Fest (Berlin, Germany), 2001, translation by John Brownjohn published as *The Hidden Hitler,* Basic Books (New York, NY), 2001.

(With Peter Weidisch) *Bismarck und die politische Kultur in Deutschland,* Petersburg, 2002.

SIDELIGHTS: Lothar Machtan, an associate professor of history at Bremen University, has been well known as an historian in his native Germany for many years, but only recently has his work been translated into English. His first book to be translated is a controversial study of Nazi dictator Adolf Hitler's alleged homosexuality, titled *The Hidden Hitler.*

The Hidden Hitler is "an impressively researched and fascinating study that raises provocative questions on a score of subjects," Gabriel Rotello declared in the *Advocate.* Although the evidence is patchy, since gays were rarely out of the closet during Hitler's lifetime and Hitler himself had many of the records relating to his youth destroyed, Machtan has found evidence of homosexual relationships dating back to Hitler's stay in Vienna, where he moved when he was nineteen, and throughout his time in the German Army during World War I and his early years in politics. Machtan also speculates that the massacre of German leadership that happened on June 30, 1934, may have been motivated in part by Hitler's desire to permanently silence old friends who knew of his homosexuality and wanted to blackmail him with it. Despite the difficulties in finding firm proof about Hitler's past, "Machtan is able to provide evidence for his assertions as well as a nuanced and readable study of Hitler's sexuality," Barbara Walden wrote in *Library Journal.*

BIOGRAPHICAL AND CRITICAL SOURCES:

PERIODICALS

Advocate, November 20, 2001, Charles Kaiser, review of *The Hidden Hitler,* pp. 73-75; December 25, 2001, Gabriel Rotello, review of *The Hidden Hitler,* p. 72.

Booklist, November 1, 2001, Brad Hooper, review of *The Hidden Hitler,* pp. 442.

Gay & Lesbian Review Worldwide, January-February, 2002, David Williams, review of *The Hidden Hitler,* p. 41.

History Today, November, 2001, Richard Bessel, review of *The Hidden Hitler,* p. S4.

Insight on the News, February 25, 2002, Nathaniel S. Lehrman, review of *The Hidden Hitler,* pp. 44-45.

Library Journal, January, 2002, Barbara Walden, review of *The Hidden Hitler,* p. 116.

New York Review of Books, February 28, 2002, Gordon A. Craig, review of *The Hidden Hitler,* pp. 24-27.

New York Times Book Review, December 16, 2001, Walter Reich, review of *The Hidden Hitler,* p. 6.

Times Literary Supplement, January 11, 2002, Anson Rabinbach, review of *The Hidden Hitler,* p. 10.

U.S. News & World Report, October 29, 2001, Andrew Curry, review of *The Hidden Hitler,* p. 8.

Washington Post, November 25, 2001, Geoffrey Giles, review of *The Hidden Hitler,* p. T04.

ONLINE

Institut für Geschichte, http://www.ifg.uni-bremen.de/ (December 3, 2002).

Salon.com, http://www.salon.com/ (January 14, 2002), Allen Barra, review of *The Hidden Hitler.**

*   *   *

MAGEE, John
    See EDWARD, John

*   *   *

MALROUX, Claire

PERSONAL: Born in Albi, France.

ADDRESSES: Home—Paris, France, and Cabourg. *Agent*—c/o Author Mail, Sheep Meadow Press/University Press of New England, 23 South Main St., Hanover, NH 03755.

CAREER: Poet and translator.

AWARDS, HONORS: Prix Maurice Edgar Coindreau, 1990, for translation of *Poemes,* by Emily Dickinson; Grand Prix National for translation, 1995; French Legion of Honor award for translations.

WRITINGS:

Edge (poems), translated by Marilyn Hacker, Wake Forest University Press (Winston-Salem, NC), 1996.

Soleil de jadis: recit poeme, preface by d'Alain Borer, Castor Astral (Bordeaux, France), 1998, translated by Marilyn Hacker as *A Long Gone Sun: A Poem,* Sheep Meadow Press (Riverdale-on-Hudson, NY), 2000.

Author of two books of poetry, *Aires* and *Entre nous et la lumiere.* Contributor of poetry to *Antioch Review, Prairie Schooner, International Quarterly, Luna, New England Review, Field, Boulevard, TriQuarterly,* and *New Yorker.*

SIDELIGHTS: Claire Malroux is a French poet as well as a translator. She has translated from English to French the works of poets such as Derek Walcott, Emily Dickinson, and Emily Brontë.

Her 1998 work, *A Long Gone Sun,* is a poem in which Malroux tells of her childhood in France during World War II and her father's involvement in the French Resistance, which ultimately lead to his death in a Nazi concentration camp. *Edge* is a collection of Malroux's poems taken from two of her previous books of poetry, *Aires* and *Entre nous et la lumiere,* and also a handful of new poems. *Prairie Schooner* contributor Eleanor M. Hamilton noted that "Malroux's poetry is a mirror she reaches through in search of what lies behind it," and also added: "I find her poems stimulating and freeing."

BIOGRAPHICAL AND CRITICAL SOURCES:

PERIODICALS

Prairie Schooner, winter, 1998, Eleanor M. Hamilton, review of *Edge,* pp. 193-195.

Publishers Weekly, January 22, 2001, review of *A Long Gone Sun,* p. 321.

World Literature Today, winter, 1997, Bruce King, review of *Edge,* p. 114.

ONLINE

CC Access, http://www.ccaccess.net/ (April 3, 2002), "Claire Malroux."

French Culture Web site, http://www.frenchculture.org/ (August 23, 2001), review of *A Long Gone Sun.*

Humanite, http://www.humanite.presse.fr/ (August 23, 2001), "Claire Malroux, Traductrice de Poesie: un acte d'amour avec le texte."

Ploughshares Online, http://www.pshares.org/ (August 23, 2001), "Claire Malroux."

Poetry Daily, http://www.poems.com/ (August 23, 2001), "Claire Malroux."

Sweet Briar College Web site, http://www.sbc.edu/ (August 23, 2001), "The Sweet Briar Seminars 1999-2000: International Writers, Marilyn Hacker and Claire Malroux."

University Press of New England Web site, http://www.dartmouth.edu/ (August 23, 2001).*

* * *

MANFREDI, Valerio Massimo 1943-

PERSONAL: Born 1943; married; children: two.

ADDRESSES: Home—Near Bologna, Italy. *Agent*—c/o Author Mail, Mondadori, Segreteria Letteraria, 20090 Segrate M1, Italy.

CAREER: University of Milan, Milan, Italy, professor of classical archeology.

AWARDS, HONORS: Man of the Year award, American Biographical Institute, 1999.

WRITINGS:

Anabasi/Senofonte, Rusconi (Milan, Italy), 1980.

Petra e le città morte della Siria, Instituto geografico de Agnostini (Novara, Italy), 1983.

Palladion: romanzo A. Mondadori (Milan, Italy), 1985.

Lo scudo di Talos, A. Mondadori (Milan, Italy), 1988.

L'oracolo, A. Mondadori (Milan, Italy), 1990.

Mare greco: eroi ed esploratori nel Mediterraneo antico, A. Mondadori (Milan, Italy), 1992.

(With Luigi Malnati) *Gli Etruschi in Val Padna,* Saggiatore (Milan, Italy), 1991.

Le Isole Fortunate: topografia di un mito, "L'Erma" di Bretschneider (Rome, Italy), 1993-95.

Le paludi di Hesperia, A. Mondadori (Milan, Italy), 1994.

(With Giorgio Celli and Francesco Guccini) *Storie d'inverno* (stories), A. Mondadori (Milan, Italy), 1994.

Tesori dal buio: le inchieste del colonnello, Editalia (Rome, Italy), 1994.

(With Maurizio Baroni) *Platea in piedi: manifesti e dati statistici del italiano/Italian Cinema—Posters and Statistical Data,* Bolelli (Bologna, Italy), 1995-1999.

(With Lorenzo Braccesi) *I Greci d'Occidente,* A. Mondadori (Milan, Italy), 1996.

La torre della solitudine, A. Mondadori (Milan, Italy), 1996.

Aléxandros, A. Mondadori (Milan, Italy), 1998, translation by Iain Halliday published in three volumes as *Alexander: Child of a Dream, Alexander: The Sands of Ammon,* and *Alexander: The Ends of the Earth,* Macmillan (New York, NY), 2001.

Il faraone delle sabbie, A. Mondadori (Milan, Italy), 1998.

(With Veceslas Kruta) *I celti in Italia,* A. Mondadori (Milan, Italy), 1999.

Akropolis: la grande epopea di Atene, A. Mondadori (Milan, Italy), 2000.

Manfredi's books have been translated into several languages, including Spanish, French, German, Greek, and Russian.

ADAPTATIONS: The "Alexander" trilogy was adapted as an audiobook and movie rights bought by Hollywood studio.

WORK IN PROGRESS: A movie screenplay of the "Alexander" trilogy.

SIDELIGHTS: For his colorful personality and infectious love of adventure, Italian archeologist and author Valerio Massimo Manfredi is known as the "Indiana

Jones of Italian archeology." In addition to his numerous topographical studies of archeological sites, Manfredi has penned the best-selling "Alexander" trilogy: *Alexander: Child of a Dream, Alexander: The Sands of Ammon,* and *Alexander: The Ends of the Earth.* Selling over three million copies world-wide, the trilogy was optioned for a movie, for which Manfredi planned to write the screenplay.

Manfredi has long enjoyed a good story, as he told *Times* reporter James Christopher: "I grew up in a small village where the only opportunity for adventure was the beggars who turned up in the bitter cold during winter. We would give them shelter in the barn and these nomads would tell splendid stories." As a professor of archeology at the University of Milan, Manfredi was asked to serve as a consultant for a crew making a German documentary film about Alexander the Great, the ancient king of Macedonia known for his exploits in battle. This experience prompted Manfredi to write his own biography of the great man.

Working in an isolated house without amenities high in the Alps, Manfredi often used music to get in the right mood for the episode to be told. "I worked for fourteen months straight, nine or ten hours a day, no vacation, no Sundays, just full immersion," Manfredi recalled to *Bookseller* interviewer Benedicte Page. "At the end I was exhausted, and of course the book was not perfect, but it was full of emotions—I was totally involved in the world." The world of Alexander, that is, which Manfredi recreated in his mind from the numerous bits of information he amassed as a scholar of the classical world. Manfredi portrays Alexander's boyhood as the son of Philip of Macedon and his queen, Olympias. As well as a military education, Alexander received an intellectual education at the hands of Aristotle. At age nineteen, Alexander took over the kingship after his father was murdered, and he began his famous campaigns to conquer the known world.

Critics noted the authenticity of Manfredi's portrayal of the ancient world. *Books* reviewer Fred Newman praised Manfredi for his attention to detail, stating, "His detailed knowledge of the ancient world has been skilfully woven into the fabric of *Alexander.*" So too, Christopher remarked, "What distinguishes Manfredi's trilogy is the spicy authenticity of his scenarios: the food, clothes, songs, swear words, characters, and provenance of the prostitutes sets pulses racing. Even the dialogue has been shrimped from the plays and comedies of the time."

According to several critics, the trilogy contains some flaws, however. In a review of the audiobook version for the London *Times,* Sue Townsend commented that the "prose is purple at times," and in *Publishers Weekly* a reviewer remarked that, although Manfredi "balances the action and characterization that brings Alexander and Memnon to life," he omits potentially interesting personality details and the writing style is rather flat. *Times Literary Supplement*'s Emily Wilson noted that though Manfredi has "tried hard to be true to the historical and literary sources, . . . there are some odd scholarly slips." She felt, moreover, that the "novels come alive only in the battle scenes." Despite any perceived flaws, Karen Robinson of the London *Times* described the three-volume tale as "gripping stuff."

BIOGRAPHICAL AND CRITICAL SOURCES:

PERIODICALS

Bookseller, August 17, 2001, Benedicte Page, "Manfredi the Conqueror," p. 38.
Books Magazine, spring, 2001, Fred Newman, "Fear and Loathing in Ancient Greece," pp. 14-15.
Publishers Weekly, March 4, 2002, review of *Alexander: The Sands of Ammon,* pp. 58-59.
Times (London, England), August 8, 2001, James Christopher, "Alexander's Bigtime Fans," p. 22; March 2, 2002, Sue Townsend, review of *Alexander: Child of a Dream* (audiobook), p. 17; March 3, 2002, Karen Robinson, review of *Alexander: Child of a Dream* (audiobook), p. 45.
Times Literary Supplement, February 8, 2002, "Superman in Sandals," p. 23.*

*   *   *

MANNING, Maurice 1966-

PERSONAL: Born 1966, in Lexington, KY. *Education:* Earlham College, B.A., 1988; University of Kentucky, M.A., 1996; University of Alabama, M.F.A., 1999. *Politics:* Independent. *Religion:* Protestant.

ADDRESSES: Office—De Pauw University, 313 South Locust St., Greencastle, IN 46135-0037. *E-mail*—mmanning@depauw.edu.

CAREER: Poet. De Pauw University, Greencastle, IN, assistant professor of English.

MEMBER: Academy of American Poets.

AWARDS, HONORS: Provincetown, MA, Fine Arts Work Center fellowship; Yale Younger Poets Series honor, 2000, for *Lawrence Booth's Book of Visions.*

WRITINGS:

Lawrence Booth's Book of Visions, Yale University Press (New Haven, CT), 2001.
A Companion for Owls, Harcourt (New York, NY), 2004.

Contributor of poetry to periodicals, including *Green Mountains Review, Hayden's Ferry Review, Sonora Review, Shenandoah, Southern Review, Spoon River Poetry Review,* and *New Yorker.*

SIDELIGHTS: Maurice Manning is an assistant professor of English at De Pauw University in Greencastle, Indiana. Manning was born and raised in Kentucky, and often writes about the land and culture of his home. He has written since childhood, and was inspired by his two grandmothers, three great grandmothers, and one great-great grandmother to remember and tell stories. He told Brandon Sokol in *TheDePauw. com,* "My older relatives kept the past alive for me by telling stories, particularly my grandmothers." Although he was always interested in writing, he did not consider pursuing it as a career until he was almost done with his undergraduate degree. "The whole concept of art is hard to see as a practical venture; it doesn't make money."

Manning's poetry has appeared in *Green Mountains Review, Hayden's Ferry Review, Sonora Review, Shenandoah, Southern Review, Spoon River Poetry Review,* and *New Yorker* as well as in the collection *Lawrence Booth's Book of Visions.* He has held a fellowship to the Fine Arts Work Center in Provincetown, Massachussetts, and is a winner of the Yale Series of Younger Poets competition.

W. S. Merwin, who selected Manning's *Lawrence Booth's Book of Visions* for the Yale award, commented, "The writing's unfaltering audacity is equaled by its content, and the result is an outstanding collection, still more astonishing for a first book; the achievement of a fresh and brilliant talent." In *Webdelsol* online, Gunnar Benediktsson described the collection as "fascinating" and noted that "the book is at the very least a miracle of structure." He also wrote, "The language is rich and densely flavorful, and Manning's work will recommend itself highly to those readers who are interested in experiments with the lyric form."

BIOGRAPHICAL AND CRITICAL SOURCES:

PERIODICALS

Library Journal, November 15, 2001, review of *Lawrence Booth's Book of Visions,* p. 71.
New York Times Book Review, August 19, 2001, Dwight Garner, review of *Lawrence Booth's Book of Visions,* p. 17.
Poetry, July, 2001, p. 241; May, 2002, John Taylor, review of *Lawrence Booth's Book of Visions,* p. 99.
Publishers Weekly, July 23, 2001, review of *Lawrence Booth's Book of Visions,* p. 70.

ONLINE

Academy of American Poets Web site, http://www.poets.org/ (July 24, 2002).
TheDePauw.com, http://www.thedepauw.com/ (October 20, 2000), Brandon Sokol, "Manning Wins Poetry Award."
Webdelsol.com, http://www.webdelsol.com/ (July 24, 2002), Gunnar Benediktsson, review of *Lawrence Booth's Book of Visions.*

*   *   *

MANUEL, Frank Edward 1910-2003

OBITUARY NOTICE—See index for *CA* sketch: Born September 12, 1910, in Boston, MA; died April 23, 2003, in Boston, MA. Historian, educator, and author. Manuel considered himself an intellectual historian, and was best known for his books about philosophy and utopian ideals. Educated at Harvard University, where he earned his Ph.D. in 1933, he also studied at the École des Hautes Études Politiques et Sociales in Paris. Returning to Harvard, he was a member of the history department staff before World War II. During the war he was an intelligence officer and French interpreter; a wartime accident cost him a leg that had to be amputated. He later wrote about his war experiences in his 2000 memoir, *Scenes from the End: The Last Days of World War II in Europe.* After working for the National Defense Commission and the Office of Price Administration as a researcher and administrator, Manuel resumed his career in academia at what is now Case Western University. From 1949 to 1965 he was professor of history and moral psychology at Brandeis University. He then taught at New York University for eleven years before returning to Brandeis in 1977, retiring as professor emeritus in 1986. Manuel was fascinated by the history of ideas, and one of his best-known works is *Utopian Thought in the Western World* (1979), cowritten with his wife, which won the American Book Award. He also wrote three books about Isaac Newton, and other works about philosophy, religion, and science, including *The Age of Reason* (1951), *Shapes of Philosophical History* (1965), *The Changing of the Gods* (1983), and *A Requiem for Karl Marx* (1995). Furthermore, Manuel was the editor of such books as *Utopias and Utopian Thought* (1966) and *French Utopias: An Anthology of Ideal Societies* (1966), which he also translated.

OBITUARIES AND OTHER SOURCES:

PERIODICALS

Boston Globe, April 24, 2003, p. C16.
New York Times, May 4, 2003, p. A35.

* * *

MARKS, Jeffrey 1960-

PERSONAL: Born October 8, 1960, in Georgetown, OH; son of Gerald (a production engineer), and Barbara (an optician; maiden name, Cummins) Marks; married V. L. Shaefer, July 7, 1990 (divorced). *Education:* Miami University, B.S., 1983; Xavier University, M.B.A., 1986. *Politics:* Democrat. *Religion:* Methodist. *Hobbies and other interests:* Collecting antiques, tae kwon do.

ADDRESSES: Home—5470 Asbury Lake, #27, Cincinnatti, OH 45247. *E-mail*—jeffmarks@aol.com.

CAREER: General Electric, Cincinnati, OH, systems analyst, 1983-99; Tech Decisions, staff writer, 1999-2001; freelance writer, 1999—.

MEMBER: Mystery Writers of America, Sisters in Crime.

AWARDS, HONORS: Barnes and Noble award, 1997, for "Talked to Death"; Anthony Award, 2001.

WRITINGS:

(Editor) *Canine Crimes,* Ballantine Books (New York, NY), 1998.
(Editor) *Canine Christmas,* Ballantine Books (New York, NY), 1999.
(Editor) *Magnolias and Mayhem,* Silver Dagger Mysteries (Johnson City, TN), 2000.
Who Was That Lady?: Craig Rice: The Queen of Screwball Mystery, Delphi Books (Lee's Summit, MO), 2001.
The Ambush of My Name, Silver Dagger Mysteries (Johnson City, TN), 2001.
(Editor) Craig Rice, *Murder, Mystery, and Malone,* Crippen and Landru (Norfolk, VA), 2002.
Intent to Sell: Marketing the Genre Novel, Deadly Alibi Press, 2002.
A Good Soldier, Silver Dagger Mysteries (Johnson City, TN), 2003.
Atomic Renaissance: Women Mystery Writers of the 1940s and 1950s, Delphi Books (Lee's Summit, MO), 2003.
Criminal Appetites, Silver Dagger Mysteries (Johnson City, TN), 2003.
Some Hidden Thunder, Silver Dagger Mysteries (Johnson City, TN), 2004.

Contributor of short stories to periodicals.

SIDELIGHTS: When Jeffrey Marks was twelve years old, he read a collection of mystery writer Agatha Christie's short stories, *The Underdog and Other Stories.* By the time he was sixteen he had read all of Christie's numerous mysteries and had begun collecting first editions of mysteries.

Marks worked on his high school and college newspapers, and began working as a freelance writer. His first book-length work was a profile of mystery writer Craig Rice, *Who Was That Lady? Craig Rice: The Queen of Screwball Mysteries.* Craig Rice was the pseudonym of Georgina Craig Rice, known for her comedic mysteries as well as for the tragedy of her life. Abandoned by her parents, Craig Rice became an alcoholic and had a series of abusive marriages before dying early at age forty-nine. In *Publishers Weekly,* a reviewer praised Marks's dedication to depicting Craig Rice's life.

He followed this with his first mystery novel, *The Ambush of My Name.* Set in Georgetown, Ohio, in the fall after the end of the U.S. Civil War, it stars Ulysses S. Grant, who is returning to his boyhood home. Grant expects to be greeted with parades and fanfare, but instead finds a body in his hotel room. Evidence indicates that the murder is connected to the assassination of Abraham Lincoln. In addition, the corpse has Confederate money in its pockets, and Grant finds out that Confederates are nearby. Grant investigates the crime, and finds out that he is not welcomed by everyone in town; someone is trying to turn his homecoming into a trap, and also sabotage his running in the impending presidential election.

Marks's second book, *A Good Soldier,* also stars Grant. Grant travels with his family to Bethel, Ohio, to visit friends he knew from his time at West Point. He is startled to find that, in a time of great poverty and need, they are mysteriously rich; further mystery ensues when he finds that people in the town are dying at an alarming rate. Grant must solve the mystery of the money in order to prevent further deaths in the town.

Canine Crimes, edited by Marks, is a collection of short mystery stories featuring dogs that help solve the crimes, and Marks's anthology *Canine Christmas* is a collection of mystery stories set during the Christmas season that also feature four-legged sleuths.

Marks told *CA:* "I've always wanted to be a writer, from the time that I could put pen to paper. Since then, it's been my dream, and I count myself lucky to have gotten this far in my chosen field. I write mysteries because I have loved them since I was a child. I write about Ulysses Grant as I am from the same home town as he is."

BIOGRAPHICAL AND CRITICAL SOURCES:

PERIODICALS

Booklist, May 15, 2002, David Platt, review of *Murder, Mystery, and Malone,* p. 1580.
Kirkus Reviews, April 1, 2002, p. 458.
Publishers Weekly, March 26, 2001, review of *Who Was That Lady?: Craig Rice: The Queen of Screwball Mystery,* p. 84; May 14, 2001, review of *The Ambush of My Name,* p. 57.

ONLINE

Jeffrey Marks Web site, http://www.jeffreymarks.com (July 24, 2002).

*   *   *

MARSH, Richard
See HELDMANN, Richard Bernard

*   *   *

MARSHALL, Andrew 1967-

PERSONAL: Born 1967.

ADDRESSES: Home—Bangkok, Thailand. *Agent*—c/o Author's Mail, Counterpoint/Perseus Press, 387 Park Avenue South, New York, NY 10016.

CAREER: Writer. *Daily Telegraph,* London, England, features editor and writer beginning 1988; freelancer in post-revolutionary Romania and Albania, then deputy-editor for Tokyo's leading English-language magazine; *British Esquire,* chief correspondent.

WRITINGS:

(With David E. Kaplan) *The Cult at the End of the World: The Terrifying Story of the Aum Doomsday Cult, from the Subways of Tokyo to the Nuclear Arsenals of Russia,* Crown Publishers (New York, NY), 1996.

The Trouser People, Counterpoint Press (Washington, DC), 2002, published as *The Trouser People: The Quest for the Victorian Footballer Who Made Burma Play the Empire's Game,* [London, England,] 2002.

SIDELIGHTS: Andrew Marshall, a Bangkok-based journalist who has traveled throughout Asia on assignments since 1993, set out to explore Burma after immersing himself for five years in the diaries of Sir George Scott, a Scottish-born adventurer and war correspondent. Scott arrived in Burma in 1875 and helped establish British colonial rule by photographing and mapping Burma's remote and previously uncharted jungle at its eastern border with China. He also introduced soccer to the country by organizing the first game at a Rangoon university, between the native peoples and their English oppressors, and wrote a book titled *The Burman,* which was originally published in 1882 and is still in print. The sarong-wearing locals nicknamed their English oppressors "Trouser People," a name Marshall applies to the brutal military dictatorship and drug lords that have oppressed the country since the early 1960s, and which became the title of the book that recounts his own daring trek through Burma.

Fascinated by Scott's adventures, Marshall, under the guise of a tourist, traced Scott's route from Rangoon to the now-forlorn and decrepit royal capital, Mandalay, and then into the remote tribal lands, where he encountered a village of headhunters. Brian Bennett, writing for *Time Asia,* commented that "Marshall uses the tale of Scott's travels and football's rise as the architecture for a witty account of life in today's diverse and suppressed Burma." Lucian W. Pye, meanwhile, reviewing *The Trouser People* for *Foreign Affairs Magazine,* wrote, "Marshall suggests that life today in Burma may be no better than it was one hundred years ago."

The book—the British edition of which is subtitled *The Quest for the Victorian Footballer who Made Burma Play the Empire's Game*—is part travel guide and part journalism. Will Buckley wrote in the London *Observer* that "reading Marshall is like being locked in a youth hostel . . . with a new age Canadian. . . . 'Ironies' are 'bitter', 'admiration' is 'sneaking' and the 'obvious' is 'blinding'. And that's only the prologue. . . . It cannot be doubted that Marshall, in

his bid to 'out-Scott Scott', has been brave to travel to the less charted parts of Burma, and he is at all times worthy. But nothing very amazing happens." Similarly, a contributor to *Complete Review* online commented: "Marshall doesn't seem very sure what he wants *The Trouser People* to be. . . . Marshall does offer . . . a striking portrait of a horrendous regime. It is not a well-laid out indictment—just bits and pieces, with Scott and football mixed in to keep things confused—but perhaps it will help open some readers' eyes to the plight of this sad, forgotten country."

In contrast, Bertil Lintner wrote in *Asia Pacific Media Services Limited* that *The Trouser People* "towers above all other contemporary ooks on Burma—whether they be travelogues, biographies or scholarly texts trying to explain the complexities of the country's tangled politics. Marshall's book is personal without being egocentric, beautifully written, and tells us more about Burma's past and present troubles than most academic writings." Bennett concluded his review of the book by stating that "Marshall gives us a rare glimpse into the jukes and jibes . . . of Burma's mysterious balance of power."

Marshall's earlier book, *The Cult at the End of the World: The Incredible Story of Aum,* coauthored with David E. Kaplan, plumbs what Wendy Cavenett called, in her online review for *Between the Lines,* "the deepest underworld in existence—where life is sacrificed and the will of hope abolished." This is the world of Japan's Aum Shinrikyo cult, or the Aum Supreme Truth, a wealthy religious sect with more than 10,000 followers in Japan alone, headed by self-proclaimed messiah and former con-artist Shoko Asahara. Cult members consisted primarily of young, well-educated, highly skilled professionals who left their careers to follow Asahara.

In 1995 cult members released bags of toxic chemicals into Tokyo's subway system, killing twelve people and injuring thousands more. The cult also forged ties with Japan's mafia and KGB veterans in an attempt to obtain nuclear weapons from Russia, and explored Australia's outback for uranium. Cavenett remarked, "It's ultra-real reality, frightening in its impact and disastrous if one thinks of what could have been if the cult was able to continue its master plan of Armageddon. . . . The pain of [the book's] authors . . . reaches from each page in a desperate attempt to inform of the degree of persecution and dictatorship suffered under the guise of a religious cult." A *Publishers Weekly* contributor commented, "A superb job of reporting, this account unfolds like a scary cyberpunk thriller presaging a new era of high-tech terrorism, and it brings the cult into sharper focus."

BIOGRAPHICAL AND CRITICAL SOURCES:

PERIODICALS

Kirkus Reviews, December 15, 2001, review of *The Trouser People,* p. 1741.

Publishers Weekly, June 10, 1996, review of *The Cult at the End of the World: The Incredible Story of Aum,* p. 82; November 12, 2001, review of *The Trouser People,* p. 44.

Spectator, February 16, 2002, Philip Glazebrook, review of *The Trouser People,* p. 39.

Time International, March 11, 2002, Brian Bennett, "Power Plays: In Search of Burmese Football's Footprints," p. 52.

ONLINE

Asia Pacific Media Services Limited Web site, http://www.asiapacificms.com/ (October 19, 2002), Bertil Lintner, review of *The Trouser People.*

Between the Lines, http://www.thei.aust.com/ (October 19, 2002), Wendy Cavenett, review of *The Cult at the End of the World.*

City Pages Online, http://citypages.com/ (October 19, 2002), Tricia Cornell, review of *The Trouser People.*

Complete Review, http://www.complete-review.com/ (October 19, 2002), review of *The Trouser People.*

Counterpoint Press Web site, http://www.counterpointpress.com/ (October 19, 2002).

Foreign Affairs Online, http://www.foreignaffairs.org/ (October 19, 2002), Lucian W. Pye, review of *The Trouser People.*

Guardian Unlimited, http://books.guardian.co.uk/ January 20, 2002, (October 19, 2002), William Buckley, "When the Empire Was Caught with Its Trousers Down."

Time Asia Online, http://time.com/ (October 19, 2002), Brian Bennett, review of *The Trouser People.**

MARSHALL, June 1947-

PERSONAL: Born June 2, 1947, in Saõ Paolo, Brazil; U.S. citizen; daughter of William G. (an architect and builder) and Adele (in business) Marshall; married Steven Kingsley; children: Anna Werrin, Sarah Sockett. *Ethnicity:* "Caucasian." *Education:* University of Pittsburgh, M.A. (English literature), 1971. *Politics:* Independent. *Hobbies and other interests:* Teaching group fitness, web site usability topics.

ADDRESSES: Office—31 Franklin Turnpike, Waldwick, NJ 07463; fax: 815-550-4364. *E-mail*—june marshall@home.com.

CAREER: High school English teacher, 1971-83; B. Flower and Sun Honey Co., Frenchtown, NJ, owner, 1983-87; American Telephone and Telegraph, Basking Ridge, NJ, speechwriter, human-factors engineer, and Web master, 1987-2000; writer. Shop owner in Ocean City, MD, 1979-82; worked as actress in off-off-Broadway productions and as a handwriting analyst; Web-site design consultant.

WRITINGS:

The Dirty Seven: Ladies Beware: Who They Are, What They Do; Hint: It's Not Love! Newmedia Publishing (Waldwick, NJ), 2001.

Booby Trapped: Me Beware! The Dirty Seven Sisters: A Dating Guide for the Twenty-first Century, Mewmedia Publishing (Waldwick, NJ), 2003.

WORK IN PROGRESS: The Second Marshall Plan: Making the World Safe for Love and Happiness.

*   *   *

MARTELL, Dominic
See REAVES, Sam

*   *   *

MARTIN, Jesse 1981-

PERSONAL: Born 1981, in Munich, Germany.

ADDRESSES: Home—Melbourne, Australia. *Agent*—c/o Author's Mail, Allen & Unwin, PO Box 8500, St. Leonards, 1590, New South Wales, Australia.

CAREER: Sailor and author. Ambassador to youth outreach organizations, including Reach Youth and Young Endeavor program.

WRITINGS:

(With Ed Gannon) *Lionheart: A Journey of the Human Spirit,* Allen & Unwin (St. Leonards, New South Wales, Australia), 2000.

ADAPTATIONS: A television documentary, *Lionheart: The Jesse Martin Story,* aired in Australia in 2000.

WORK IN PROGRESS: A proposed television documentary series focusing on Martin's 2002-2004 round-the-world sailing expedition.

SIDELIGHTS: On October 31, 1999, seventeen-year-old schoolboy Jesse Martin left Melbourne, Victoria, Australia, in a thirty-four-foot sailboat, the *Ariel of Lionheart,* on a solo Southern Hemisphere circumnavigation of the globe. He arrived home 328 days later, having never resorted to using the yacht's engine. Just weeks after Martin's eighteenth birthday, a huge crowd cheered as he pulled into Melbourne harbor, having just become the youngest person to make an uninterrupted, unassisted, solo journey around the world.

Martin kept a journal throughout his trip and he recounts his experience in the book *Lionheart: A Journey of the Human Spirit,* which sold more than 100,000 copies in Martin's native Australia. In *Chimes* Mandy Suhr quoted Martin on writing the book: "The process wasn't fun. I had to look into myself and ask a lot of questions." Reviewing the book for *School Library Journal,* Vicki Reutter called it "conversational in tone and unsparingly honest, revealing [Martin's] insecurities as well as a quick wit." A contributor for *Kirkus Reviews* wrote: "The rapid narrative is peppered with Martin's journal entries, which reveal the remarkable teen's complexity. . . . A tribute to the spirit of adventure, akin to Robin Lee Graham's *Dove.*"

Martin was born in Munich, Germany, while his parents were traveling through Europe in a kombi van, and he was reared in the Daintree Rainforest in North Queensland, Australia. He backpacked with his mother and younger brother, Beau, through Southeast Asia at the age of eleven; learned to sail at the age of fourteen while on a three-month catamaran trip from Melbourne to Cape York with his father and brother; and kayaked in Papua New Guinea with Beau a year later. "I've never been one to live a conventional life," said Martin in an interview with *Habitat Australia,* "and I've always been a dreamer. For me, this trip is a lifelong dream come true. I'm a born adventurer." The 27,000-nautical-mile adventure was for him the culmination of years of dreaming.

In February 2002 Martin set off on another adventure. This time, he, his brother, and two friends left Melbourne on a two-year journey in their fifty-four-foot old-style cutter yacht *Kijana* (Swahili for "young people"). Their planned journey took them up the Queensland Coast to Kimberley in northern Western Australia, to Indonesia's Spice Islands, Sri Lanka, India, across Africa through Kenya and the Congo to Venezuela and the United States, then to the Caribbean, the Galapagos Islands, Ecuador, Chile, Easter Island, Pitcairn and Tahiti in French Polynesia, to Samoa, PNG in Micronesia, and other stops determined along the way. "The Journey of *Kijana* is a unique exploration of environmental and cultural aspects of different countries throughout the world; integral to this journey is a commitment to education and the environment," announced the *Kijana Web site.* With digital cameras, the crew recorded their experiences with the intention of creating a television documentary series; meanwhile computers allowed the crew to create an interactive, online, "global classroom" that could be accessed by children around the world.

BIOGRAPHICAL AND CRITICAL SOURCES:

PERIODICALS

Kirkus Reviews, February 1, 2002, review of *Lionheart: A Journey of the Human Spirit,* p. 163.
Know Your World Extra, April 26, 2002, Suzanne I. Barchers, "Sailing into the Record Books; A Teen Braves the Seas—Alone—for Nearly a Year," p. 12.
Publishers Weekly, January 28, 2002, "Land Ho!," p. 215.
Ruminator Review, summer 2002, Eleise Jones, "Choose Your Own Adventure," p. 25.
School Library Journal, May 2002, Vicki Reutter, review of *Lionheart,* p. 173.

ONLINE

Calvin College Web site, http://www-stu.calvin.edu/ (October 19, 2002), Mandy Suhr, "Australian Teenager Sails Solo around the World."

Kijana Web site, http://www.kijana.net/ (January 4, 2003), "The Journey of Kijana: A Celebration of Youth, Discovery and the Spirit Within Us All."

National Geographic Web site, http://www. nationalgeographic.com.au/ (October 19, 2002).

SailNet Web site, http://www.sailnet.com/ (October 19, 2002), "Jesse Martin Interview."

Teen Newsweek Web site, http://stacks.msnbc.com/ (October 19, 2002), "The Young Man and the Sea" (interview).*

*   *   *

MASSEY, Sujata 1964-

PERSONAL: Born 1964, in Sussex, England; married Tony Massey (a U.S. Navy medical officer); children: Pia. *Education:* Johns Hopkins University, graduated 1986.

ADDRESSES: Home—Baltimore, MD. *Agent*—c/o Author Mail, HarperCollins, 10 East 53rd Street, 7th Floor, New York, NY 10022. *E-mail*—sujata&atdot; or ix.netcom.com.

CAREER: Writer. *Baltimore Evening Sun,* journalist; freelance writer, 1997—.

AWARDS, HONORS: Malice Domestic unpublished writers grant, 1996, and Agatha Award for Best First Novel, 1998, both for *The Salaryman's Wife.*

WRITINGS:

The Salaryman's Wife, HarperCollins (New York, NY), 1997.

Zen Attitude, HarperCollins (New York, NY), 1998.

The Flower Master, HarperCollins (New York, NY), 1999.

The Floating Girl, HarperCollins (New York, NY), 2000.

The Bride's Kimono, HarperCollins (New York, NY), 2001.

The Samurai's Daughter, HarperCollins (New York, NY), 2003.

SIDELIGHTS: Sujata Massey was born in Sussex, England in 1964, the daughter of a father from India and a mother from Germany. When she was five years old, her parents immigrated to the United States. Massey grew up in Philadelphia, Pennsylvania, Berkeley, California, and St. Paul, Minnesota, but never became totally Americanized because her family often returned to England; she remains a citizen of the United Kingdom, but is a legal resident of the United States.

Massey graduated from Johns Hopkins University in Baltimore, Maryland, in 1986, and worked as a journalist for the *Baltimore Evening Sun* newspaper. Eventually she met Tony Massey, a U.S. Navy medical officer, and they eventually married. Tony Massey was eventually posted to Japan, and they moved there in 1991, returning to the United States in 1993.

While in Japan, Massey became fascinated with Japanese culture and history. She united this interest with her love of mystery novels to write mysteries with Japanese characters. For her first novel, she won a grant from Malice Domestic, a mystery writers' organization, to complete the work, and soon after signed a contract with HarperCollins to write more novels. Both *The Salaryman's Wife* and *Zen Attitude* star sleuth Rei Shimura; they did so well that Massey followed them with more "Rei Shimura" mysteries.

Shimura, like Massey, is a multicultural woman; born in California to a Japanese father and an American mother, she speaks Japanese well and can almost pass for Japanese when she needs to. At her Web site, Massey noted, "The most important similarity I share with my sleuth is confusion over cultural identity." Rei is torn between her two cultures, enjoying Japanese art and aesthetics, but also enjoying the freedom she has as an American woman.

In *The Flower Master,* Rei is living in Tokyo, working as an antiques dealer. When her aunt, who is a master of traditional Japanese flower arranging, or *ikebana,* tells her she should enroll in a flower-arranging class, Rei does so, and finds that the battles over aesthetics at the school soon escalate into violence. A master teacher is stabbed to death with gardening shears, and Rei's aunt is suspected of the murder. Rei must clear her name, and find the real murderer. In the *New York Times Book Review* Marilyn Stasio wrote that Massey carefully observes Japanese customs, and that she brings a "fresh perspective" to her depiction of Japanese culture. In the *Washington Post Book World*, Paul Skenazy commented that Massey "provides us with a wonderfully detailed tour of Japan, and of *ikebana*."

In 2000 Massey and Tony adopted a daughter, Pia, who was born in South India. Massey stayed in India with Pia from December, 1998, through February, 1999. Although she was under contract at the time to complete her novel *The Floating Girl*, she was unable to travel with a laptop computer because she had too much baby equipment. She took discs with her to India and worked on computers whenever she could find one available.

While in India, a computer virus erased half of the novel she was working on, but she had printed out much of her material. When she returned to Baltimore with Pia, Tony typed all of these pages into their home computer, and it took Massey five more months to complete the novel. She wrote in her Web page, "Now I'm happy to report having a baby has not slowed me down too much as a writer." She writes during her daughter's naps, and hires a babysitter occasionally when she needs more time.

The Floating Girl explores the Japanese love of cartoon characters. Rei finds a comic that illustrates a murder, and the murder later happens. Rei must find the comic's artist, as well as the murderer. In *Publishers Weekly*, a reviewer praised Massey for depicting a part of Tokyo that tourists never see, and called the book an "accomplished murder mystery."

In *The Bride's Kimono* Shimura must transport a valuable kimono to a museum exhibit in Washington, D.C. En route, she meets a Japanese office worker who is heading to a mall to shop for her wedding. This woman disappears in the mall, and Rei must investigate her murder. The victim is initially identified as Rei, but when Shimura is found alive, she runs into further trouble when the police accuse her of running a prostitution ring. Romantic entanglements, as well as family issues, complicate the story. In *Publishers Weekly*, a reviewer praised Massey's use of romantic suspense as well as her detailed understanding of Japanese and American culture. In the *Washington Post Book World*, Patrick Anderson wrote that Shimura, "sexy, breezy, and smart, holds our interest even as the novel veers off in unexpected directions."

Massey writes at her home in Baltimore, but travels to Japan for about a month each year to check on her settings and soak up Japanese culture. She wrote on her Web site, "I always return to Baltimore five pounds lighter and lugging a suitcase jammed with antique textiles, photographs of my travels, and notes for the next book." She also gave advice to aspiring writers, "I rewrote my first book more than fifty times before submitting it to an agent. There is something to be said for not proceeding until you are as polished as you can be."

BIOGRAPHICAL AND CRITICAL SOURCES:

PERIODICALS

Booklist, April 15, 1999, review of *The Flower Master,* p. 1482; May 1, 2000, Jenny McLarin, review of *The Floating Girl,* p. 1622; May 1, 2001, Merle Jacob, review of *The Flower Master,* p. 1607; August, 2001, Jenny McLarin, review of *The Bride's Kimono,* p. 2098; February 15, 2003, Jenny McLarin, review of *The Samurai's Daughter,* p. 1055.

Kirkus Reviews, August 1, 2001, review of *The Bride's Kimono,* p. 1071; January 15, 2003, review of *The Samurai's Daughter,* p. 114.

Library Journal, April 15, 1999, Francine Fialkoff, review of *The Flower Master,* p. 149; April 1, 2000, Dean Jones, review of *The Flower Master,* p. 160; February 15, 2003, Jackie Cassada, review of *The Samurai's Daughter,* p. 173.

New York Times Book Review, May 2, 1999, Marilyn Stasio, review of *The Flower Master,* p. 28.

People, November 17, 1997, p. 43.

Publishers Weekly, April 13, 1998, review of *Zen Attitude,* p. 72; April 5, 1999, review of *The Flower Master,* p. 225; April 17, 2000, review of *The Floating Girl,* p. 54; August 6, 2001, review of *The Bride's Kimono,* p. 66; February 24, 2003, review of *The Samurai's Daughter,* p. 56.

Washington Post Book World, October 10, 1999, Paul Skenazy, review of *The Flower Master,* p. 13; October 14, 2001, Patrick Anderson, review of *The Bride's Kimono,* p. 13.

ONLINE

Sujata Massey Web site, http://www.interbridge.com/sujata (July 24, 2002).
Writers Write, http://www.writerswrite.com/ (October, 1998), interview with Massey.*

* * *

MATTHEW, Kathryn I. 1950-

PERSONAL: Born October 21, 1950, in Oakland, CA; daughter of Robert E. (in U.S. Marine Corps) and Evelyn (Hymel) Ingraham; married Millard E. Matthew, Jr. (an attorney), January 4, 1972; children: Joshua Neil, Benjamin Bradley. *Ethnicity:* "White." *Education:* University of New Orleans, B.A., 1972, M.Ed., 1988; University of Houston, Ed.D., 1995. *Hobbies and other interests:* Reading, sewing.

ADDRESSES: Home—Texas. *Agent*—c/o Author Mail, Neal-Schuman Publishers, Inc., 100 Varick St., New York, NY 10013. *E-mail*—kmatthew@pdq.net.

CAREER: Teacher and technology specialist for public schools in Luling, LA, 1988-89, and Alief, TX, 1992-94; Louisiana Tech University, Ruston, associate professor, 1995-2002.

MEMBER: International Reading Association, International Society for Technology in Education, Society for Technology and Teacher Education.

AWARDS, HONORS: Award for best reading-language arts software, Society for Technology and Teacher Education, 1994.

WRITINGS:

(With Jerry Willis and Elizabeth Stephens) *Technology, Reading, and Language Arts,* Allyn & Bacon (Boston, MA), 1996.

(With Joy L. Lowe) *Neal-Schuman Guide to Recommended Children's Books and Media for Use with Every Elementary Subject,* Neal-Schuman Publishers (New York, NY), 2002.
Colonial America in Literature for Youth: A Guide and Resource Book, Scarecrow Press (Metuchen, NJ), 2002.
(With Kimberly Kimbell-Lopez) *Reading Comprehension: Books and Strategies for the Elementary Curriculum,* Scarecrow Press (Metuchen, NJ), 2003.
(With Joy L. Lowe) *Neal-Schuman Guide to Celebrations and Holidays around the World,* Neal-Schuman Publishers (New York, NY), 2003.

Member of editorial review board, *Journal of Computing in Education,* 1998-2002.

SIDELIGHTS: Kathryn I. Matthew told *CA:* "My coauthors and I rely on our public school teaching experiences for ideas for our books. As we write we talk with librarians and classroom teachers. We spend time in classrooms and libraries working with students, teachers, and librarians to assure that our books are useful resources."

BIOGRAPHICAL AND CRITICAL SOURCES:

PERIODICALS

Language Arts, February, 1997, Linda McMillen, Sherrel Shanahan, Kathleen Dows, Joyce Macphee, and Jennifer Hester, "Technology, Reading, and Language Arts," p. 138.
School Library Journal, April, 2002, Mary Lankford, review of *Neal-Schuman Guide to Recommended Children's Books and Media for Use with Every Elementary Subject,* p. 191.

* * *

McCAFFERY, Edward J. 1958-

PERSONAL: Born 1958. *Education:* Yale University, B.A. (summa cum laude), 1980; Harvard Law School, J.D. (Magna cum laude), 1985; University of Southern California, M.A., 1994.

ADDRESSES: Office—University of Southern California Law School, 699 Exposition Boulevard, Los Angeles, CA 90089. *E-mail*—emccaffe@law.usc.edu.

CAREER: Educator and author. Admitted to the Bar of the State of California, 1986; New Jersey Supreme Court, law clerk to Chief Justice Robert N. Wilentz, 1985-86; Tichell, Maltzman, Mark, Bass, Ohleyer & Mishel, associate attorney, 1986-89; Golden Gate University, lecturer, 1988-89; University of Southern California Law School, assistant professor, 1989-91, associate professor, 1991-94; professor, 1994-98; Maurice Jones, Jr. professor of law, 1998—. Yale Law School, visiting professor, 1993-94; California Institute of Technology, visiting professor, 1994—. University of Southern California Institute on Federal Taxation planning committee, executive director and chair, 1997—; University of Southern California—Caltech Center for the Study of Law and Politics, director.

MEMBER: American Economic Association, National Tax Association, Phi Beta Kappa, Phi Kappa Phi.

WRITINGS:

Taxing Women, University of Chicago Press (Chicago, IL), 1997.
Fair Not Flat: How to Make the Tax System Better and Simpler, University of Chicago Press (Chicago, IL), 2002.

Contributor to numerous books, including *Behavioral Economics and the Law,* edited by Cass R. Sunstein, 2000; *Encyclopedia of the American Constitution,* 2nd edition, edited by Leonard W. Levy and Kenneth L. Karst, 2000; and *Gender and American Politics: Women, Men, and the Political Process,* Jyl Josephson and Sue Tolleson-Rinehart, editors, 2000.

Contributor to numerous magazines and journals, including *Political Research Quarterly, National Tax Association Proceedings, National Tax Journal, Chapman Law Review, Women's Law Journal,* and *Philosophy and Public Affairs.*

WORK IN PROGRESS: A New Undertaking of Property, for University of Chicago Press; book chapters and journal articles.

SIDELIGHTS: With a solid background in law, politics, and economics, Edward J. McCaffery is well-equipped to write—as he does—on such topics as death taxes, capital-gains taxes, pain and suffering damages, wealth-transfer taxation, election reform, and a plethora of related topics. He has also given testimony before the U.S. Senate Committee on Finance regarding estate tax, and the House Committee on Small Business's Subcommittee on Tax and Finance and Exports regarding death-tax reform. His books *Taxing Women,* and *Fair not Flat: How to Make the Tax System Better and Simpler* have been widely reviewed and critically acclaimed, even by those not necessarily agreeing with all his analyzes, philosophies, or suggested reforms.

Of *Taxing Women,* a reviewer for *Publishers Weekly* wrote, "Any contemporary woman who believes that strides toward gender equality are reflected in the tax laws of the U.S. should read this book." Analyzing Newt Gingrich's "Contract with America" and the Christian Coalition's "Contract with the American Family," McCaffery argues that these social contracts have a specific political agenda which, simplistically put, is to keep women out of the workforce and at home with their families. Because the major elements of the tax system were instituted during an era when traditional family structures were the norm, tax laws rewarded the single-earner household, particularly one in which the woman was the stay-at-home-mom and homemaker and the man the breadwinner.

"The passage of time brought about some major changes in the status of women in the family and society," commented Rafat Fazeli in *Signs.* "However, the tax system remained virtually unchanged in its gender orientation. In reality, the rigidity of the tax system and its underdeveloped gender structure became a barrier to a richer and deeper equality." Briefly summarizing McCaffery's perspective, Michael McCrary wrote for *Journal of Women's History,* "However, the effects of the tax code for women vary depending on a family's income. Poor women are rewarded for being single parents, while women from affluent families are rewarded for remaining out of the labor force altogether. In contrast, middle-income women must choose between highly taxed, paid work or full-time homemaking with a subsequent rise in husbands' hours of work to compensate."

McCaffery uses statistics, charts, and personal anecdotes to support his theory as to why women are kept on the margins of economic life. He notes how the joint filing system considers women "secondary earners" that places them in their husband's usually higher tax bracket. "The average working wife in a middle-or upper-income household sees two-thirds of her salary lost to taxes and work-related expenses," writes McCaffery in his book, providing examples of women who could no longer afford to work once child-care costs were factored in. And he astutely points out that staying at home is a no-win situation, particularly devastating for older divorced women with little work experience, no pension, and no accumulation of social security benefits during their unemployed, married years. McCrary commented: "Arguing that the status quo is unacceptable, McCaffery identifies partial solutions to reduce gender inequality in taxation policies. These include separate filing for married couples, increased child care deductions, and tax breaks rather than penalties for spouses earning the lower of the two incomes (typically women)."

Fair Not Flat provides what Norm Hutcherson referred to in *Library Journal* as "an accessible and effective analysis of the present federal income tax and estate- and gift-tax system and proposes an innovative approach that would replace both with a consistent progressive consumption tax." McCaffery's basic premise is to tax spending instead of taxing income and savings. Bruce Bartlett wrote in the *Wall Street Journal:* "McCaffery believes that the rich are undertaxed on what they spend. Since unrealized capital gains are never taxed and because borrowing is not taxed as income, the wealthy can live lavishly, waste money on luxuries, shamelessly flaunt their wealth and pay few taxes."

Bartlett continued, "By contrast those in the middle class, struggling to save a few dollars for retirement or a child's education, are taxed mercilessly." There are income and payroll taxes and, when they can save, taxes on interest earned. McCaffery's solution—tax spending. A family of four, for example, would pay no taxes on their first $20,000 of expenditures, then 15 percent on the next $60,000. In addition, the relatively few families who spend more than $80,000 a year would be subject to a supplemental tax. In addition, necessities would be taxed less than ordinary and luxury items. "To be sure, Bill Gates could still escape taxation by saving all his money. But then he would have to live in the style of an ordinary American. . . .

On the other hand, if people want to borrow, splurge and live for today, they should pay a tax penalty for doing so."

McCaffery's plan would also eliminate death and estate taxes, because—obviously—dead people don't spend. Their heirs would therefore pay taxes, according to the prorated scale, as they spent their inheritance. And best of all, noted the author of the book's synopsis for the University of Chicago Press, "most Americans would not have to fill out tax returns."

BIOGRAPHICAL AND CRITICAL SOURCES:

PERIODICALS

Antioch Review, spring, 1998, Susan McCabe, review of *Taxing Women,* p. 241.

Booklist, May 1, 1997, Mary Carroll, review of *Taxing Women,* p. 1465.

Independent Review, summer, 1998, Eugenia F. Toma, review of *Taxing Women,* p. 136.

Journal of Women's History, winter, 2000, Michael McCrary, review of *Taxing Women,* p. 219.

Library Journal, March 15, 2002, Norm Hutcherson, review of *Fair Not Flat: How to Make the Tax System Better and Simpler,* p. 91.

National Tax Journal, December, 1997, Michael J. McIntyre, review of *Taxing Women,* pp. 819-826.

Publishers Weekly, March 10, 1997, review of *Taxing Women,* p. 57.

Signs, winter, 2002, Rafat Fazeli, review of *Taxing Women,* p. 569.

Wall Street Journal, April 10, 2002, Bruce Bartlett, review of *Fair Not Flat,* p. D12.

ONLINE

University of Chicago Press Web site, http://www. press.uchicago.edu/ (June 5, 2002).*

*   *   *

McCANLESS, Christel Ludewig 1939-

PERSONAL: Born November 20, 1939, in Peenemünde, Germany; naturalized U.S. citizen; daughter of Hermann R. R. (a missile and space engineer) and Emmy (a homemaker; maiden name, Jaglitz) Ludewig; married George F. McCanless, Jr., July 11, 1963;

children: Katherine W. *Education:* University of Montevallo, B.A., 1961; University of North Carolina, M.S.L.S., 1966. *Religion:* Protestant. *Hobbies and other interests:* Swimming, sailing, travel, colored-pencil drawings.

ADDRESSES: Home and office—3218 Panorama Dr. SE, Huntsville, AL 35801-1110. *E-mail*—christel@hiwaay.net.

CAREER: University of Alabama in Huntsville, library director, 1963-68, bookstore consultant, 1968-76; Huntsville-Madison County Public Library, Huntsville, consultant, 1975-78; *Huntsville Times,* consultant, 1985-89; Alabama Library Exchange, Huntsville, consultant, 1991-99; Huntsville Museum of Art, consultant, 1999-2000. Member of board of directors, Burrit Museum and Park and Friends of the Huntsville-Madison County Public Library; member of Fabergé Arts Foundation and WLRH-Radio.

MEMBER: Art Librarians Association of North America, Alabama Library Association, Alabama Museum Association, Huntsville Literary Association (member of board of directors), Monte Sano Civic Association (member of board of directors), Beta Phi Mu, Mu Alpha Theta.

AWARDS, HONORS: Library Volunteer Award, Huntsville Museum of Art, 1999.

WRITINGS:

Fabergé and His Works: An Annotated Bibliography of the First Century of His Art, Scarecrow Press (Lanham, MD), 1994.
(With Will Lowes) *Fabergé Eggs: A Retrospective Encyclopedia,* Scarecrow Press (Lanham, MD), 2001.

WORK IN PROGRESS: The Lowes and McCanless Index to Fabergé at Auction, 1934-2000, with Will Lowes, a database.

SIDELIGHTS: Christel Ludewig McCanless told *CA:* "I became interested in the art of Fabergé in the late 1960s when I read Robert K. Massie's book, *Nicholas and Alexandra,* and Morton Shulman's book, *Anyone Can Make a Million.* Massie's book gives the historical details of tsarist Russia in which the decorative art of the Russian court jeweler to the tsars, Peter Carl Fabergé, flourished. Shulman's book discussed how one 'can make a million' in collecting art objects. As a practicing librarian, I began collecting pieces of paper; that is, books and journals, which mentioned Fabergé and his art.

"In the early 1990s a friend suggested I organize my boxes of paper. On a dare I submitted a proposal to three publishers, and the first one, Scarecrow Press, was interested in my manuscript for publication within three months. But to compile an annotated bibliography from scratch took three years. A tremendous network of fellow Fabergé enthusiasts developed, and to this day I depend heavily on these folks to alert me to new discoveries in this exciting art history venue.

"After the publication of my bibliography, Will Lowes of Adelaide, Australia, contacted me and soon a collaborative effort began. The one-volume encyclopedia *Fabergé Eggs: A Retrospective Encyclopedia* is our first joint effort. Because we are in two different continents in the world and in different time zones (Will is sixteen-and-a-half hours ahead of me), all our work is done by e-mail, fax machine, FedEx, and infrequently via phone and snail mail. Because of computers it has been possible to do this kind of long-distance scholarship within the last five years. One special treat from this joint venture has been that Will and I have met twice in the United States and have traveled with a Fabergé scholar to modern St. Petersburg, once the Mecca of tsarist Russia, Fabergé, and his 500 artisans.

"Our current project is a descriptive database of over 18,500 Fabergé objects which have been in the auctions worldwide between 1934 and the present. It can be searched by the name of the decorative object, date of the auction, work master, inscriptions, historical data, et cetera.

"The rewards of this writing project have been a deeper understanding and appreciation of the decorative arts, travel to museums and libraries worldwide, and exciting friends."

McCART, Joyce 1936-

PERSONAL: Born May 24, 1936, in Montreal, Quebec, Canada; daughter of Stan (an electrical contractor) and Gladys (a schoolteacher; maiden name, Walsh; later surname Dunning) Cassidy; married Peter McCart (a scientist and photographer), June 30, 1956; children: Susan, Peter. *Ethnicity:* "White, Anglo-Saxon Protestant." *Education:* Simon Fraser University, B.A.; University of Calgary, B.Ed. *Politics:* Conservative. *Hobbies and other interests:* Reading, dog training.

ADDRESSES: Office—Aquatic Environments Ltd., Box 7B, Spruce View, Alberta, Canada T0M 1V0. *E-mail*—pmcca102@aol.com.

CAREER: Aquatic Environments Ltd. (biological consulting firm), Spruce View, Alberta, Canada, cofounder and co-owner, c. 1973—. Southern Alberta Institute of Technology, teacher of technical writing; freelance technical editor and writer. Sheep farmer, 1973-96.

WRITINGS:

The First R: A Basic Course in Reading for Children, Lyndenhall Learning Systems (Spruce View, Alberta, Canada), 1985.
(With husband, Peter McCart) *On the Road with David Thompson,* Fifth House Publishers (Calgary, Alberta, Canada), 2000.

Contributor to periodicals. Founding editor, *Sheep Canada,* 1975-77.

WORK IN PROGRESS: A book about the travels of the Palliser Expedition, 1857-60, with Peter McCart.

SIDELIGHTS: Joyce McCart told *CA:* "I was born in Montreal and raised in North Vancouver. My husband Peter was born and raised in Vancouver. We were married while he was still a sophomore at the University of Oregon, and over the next fifteen years we moved from Oregon to Wisconsin to northern British Columbia to Vancouver, working at any jobs we could find to keep us (and our two children) in school. By 1970 Peter had a Ph.D. in marine biology, and I had a B.A.

in philosophy and English. (When I started that degree, I was a secretary with a high school diploma; when I finished it, I was a secretary with a B.A.)

"By 1973 we were living on the prairies, where we incorporated a biological consulting firm to assess the effects of industrial development on fish populations. Peter was the scientist and I was secretary, bookkeeper, librarian, and general factotum. With the semi-mutinous help of two teenagers, we raised horses and sheep and a few chickens. Within Canada, the company's projects—and Peter's travels—ranged from Newfoundland to British Columbia to the Northwest Territories, and outside Canada, from Alaska to Siberia.

"In 1975 we founded Canada's first national sheep magazine, which started life in a garage on the farm. I edited the magazine and wrote most of the copy for two-and-a-half years, then sold it for a dollar and went back to school. A B.Ed. in secondary English, coupled with a few sample copies of *Sheep Canada,* landed me a job teaching technical writing at the Southern Alberta Institute of Technology. Later I picked up two courses in technical writing at schools of engineering in New York and Washington, then freelanced for a while as a technical editor.

"By the early 1980s our children were off on their own. We started dismantling the offices, labs, and field operations of the company, reducing it to a size we could handle ourselves. In 1985, theorizing that 200 sheep would be less trouble than one employee, we decided to get serious about sheep production. We set up a genetic selection program and lambed every four months for eleven years. Peter built corrals, hauled feed, out-muscled recalcitrant rams, and continued consulting to finance our sheep habit. I slept in the lambing barn, computerized the records, and wrote the occasional article for American sheep magazines. We did pretty well—sold breeding stock into Wisconsin and Texas and half the provinces of Canada. In 1996, worn out, we sold the whole flock to a producer in Quebec.

"By the late 1990s we were semi-retired, and we decided our next project had to be a book. Our first notion was a book on fisheries (write what you know, they say) and to that end, we made a trip to visit the scientists stationed at Flathead Lake in Montana. It was there we first ran across]the path of early nineteenth-century Canadian explorer and fur trader&;sqb; David Thompson, and for the next three years we followed his trail. Peter drove thousands of miles, took hundreds of photographs, and analyzed dozens of forestry maps, county maps, and road maps. The interpretation of all the information we gathered was a joint effort, but I wrote most of the text, making use, of course, of the techniques of technical writing."

BIOGRAPHICAL AND CRITICAL SOURCES:

PERIODICALS

BC Historical News, fall, 2001, R. J. Welwood, review of *On the Road with David Thompson,* p. 37.
Times-Colonist (Victoria, British Columbia, Canada), Dave Obee, review of *On the Road with David Thompson.*
Toronto Star, February 17, 2001, Michael Hanlon, review of *On the Road with David Thompson,* p. L26.

*   *   *

McCOOL, Charles 1964-

PERSONAL: Born August 2, 1964, in Madrid, Spain; U.S. citizen; mother's name, Joanne Els McCool; married Julie Bingham; children: Katie, Andy. *Education:* University of Southern California, B.S., 1985. *Hobbies and other interests:* Genealogy, travel.

ADDRESSES: Agent—Hawk Ridge Press, P.O. Box 2755, Reston, VA 20195-0755; fax: 508-256-7671. *E-mail*—CharlesMcCool@usa.com.

CAREER: Software developer for various companies in California and Virginia, 1985-99; travel consultant and writer, 1990—.

WRITINGS:

Winning the Airfare Game: Save Money and Stress on Every Flight, Hawk Ridge Press (Reston, VA), 2001.

WORK IN PROGRESS: Winning the Travel Game.

McCRACKEN, Linda D. 1950-

PERSONAL: Born February 6, 1950, in Yakima, WA; daughter of Clifford (a mechanic) and Clara June (a fruit industry worker; maiden name, Townsend) Huebner; married Coy McCracken, March 11, 1974. *Ethnicity:* "White." *Education:* Attended Oregon State University, 1968-71; Central Washington University, B.S., 1974. *Hobbies and other interests:* Reading, camping, travel.

ADDRESSES: Home—102 North 53rd Ave., Yakima, WA 98908. *Office*—Yakima Valley Regional Library, 102 North Third St., Yakima, WA 98901. *E-mail*—lmccracken@yvrl.org.

CAREER: Yakima Valley Regional Library, Yakima, WA, library assistant, 1974-81, supervisor in reserve department, 1981-91, adult services manager, 1991—. Yakima Literacy Coalition, president, 2000-02.

MEMBER: American Library Association, Public Library Association, Pacific Northwest Library Association, Washington Library Association.

WRITINGS:

(With Lynne Zeiher) *The Library Book Cart Precision Drill Team Manual,* McFarland and Co. (Jefferson, NC), 2002.

Contributor to library journals.

WORK IN PROGRESS: Research on the coalition-building process, and on team-building and marketing library services to the community.

SIDELIGHTS: Linda D. McCracken told *CA:* "As funding became more critical for our library, we began to look for new ways to promote our services to our communities. Forming a book cart drill team was an inexpensive, fun way for us to do that. One small article in an administrative journal led to a longer article in the *U*N*A*B*A*S*H*E*D Librarian,* which caught the eye of Robert Franklin at McFarland & Co. Publishing. He proposed a book and I began writing. As I wrote, I tried to keep in mind the audience that I was writing for, and the fact that we wanted the tone of the book to be casual and upbeat. That helped to focus and select the information that would be included. I have always dreamed of writing mysteries but have never really attempted it. To have a nonfiction book actually published was beyond my expectations. Despite the fact that I found writing to be hard work, I may now be inspired to take a chance with a mystery."

BIOGRAPHICAL AND CRITICAL SOURCES:

PERIODICALS

American Libraries, February, 2002, Cathleen Bourdon, review of *The Library Book Cart Precision Drill Team Manual,* p. 64.

Booklist, March 1, 2002, Patricia Hogan, review of *The Library Book Cart Precision Drill Team Manual,* p. 1177.

*   *   *

McKEON, Doug(las Jude) 1966-

PERSONAL: Born June 10, 1966, in Pompton Plains, NJ; son of Richard F. (a stock broker) and Irene Anne (a teacher; maiden name, Kisla) McKeon.

ADDRESSES: Agent—c/o Porchlight Entertainment, 11777 Mississippi Ave., Los Angeles, CA 90025.

CAREER: Actor in films, including (as Robbie) *Uncle Joe Shannon,* United Artists, 1979; (as Frank Strelzyk) *Night Crossing,* Buena Vista, 1981; (as Billy Ray) *On Golden Pond,* Universal, 1981; (as Jonathan Bellah) *Mischief,* Twentieth Century-Fox, 1985; (as Ben Aitken) *Turnaround,* 1986; *Deadly Illusion,* 1989; (as Billy Coleman) *Where the Red Fern Grows: Part 2,* 1992; (as patron) *Kounterfeit* (also known as *Money Crush*), Live Entertainment, 1996; (as the typist) *The Empty Mirror,* Lions Gate Films, 1997; (as Barney) *Courting Courtney,* Broken Twigs Productions, 1997; and (as Breem) *Critical Mass,* 2000.

Actor in made-for-television movies, including (as Dirk) *The Silent Eye,* National Broadcasting Company (NBC), 1974; (as Timmy) *Tell Me My Name,* NBC,

1977; (as Peter) *Daddy, I Don't Like It Like This,* Columbia Broadcasting System (CBS), 1978; (as Michael) *The Comeback Kid,* American Broadcasting Companies (ABC), 1980; (as Scott Cameron) *Desperate Lives,* CBS, 1982; (as Harry Woodward) *An Innocent Love* (also known as *One Starry Night*), CBS, 1982; (as Ray "Boom Boom" Mancini) *Heart of a Champion: The Ray Mancini Story,* 1985; (as Lonnie) *Breaking Home Ties,* 1987; (as therapist) *Without Consent* (also known as *Tell Laura I Love Her* and *Trapped and Deceived*), ABC, 1994; (as chief of the boat) *Sub Down,* USA Network, 1997; and (as flight surgeon #2) *Rocket's Red Glare* (also known as *The Mercury Project*), 2000.

Actor in television series, including (as Timmy Ferraday #1) *The Edge of Night,* ABC, 1975-76; and (as Max Sutter) *Big Shamus, Little Shamus,* CBS, 1979. Actor in television miniseries, including (as Phillip Wendell) *Centennial,* NBC, 1978; (as Marc Schreuder) *At Mother's Request,* CBS, 1987; and (as Joe Allen) *From the Earth to the Moon,* Home Box Office (HBO), 1998. Appeared on *Battle of the Network Stars XVIII* (television special) as CBS team member.

Actor in stage productions, including (as Tommy) *Dandelion Wine,* Broadway, 1974; (as Leon) *Truckwood,* Broadway, 1974; and (as Eugene) *Brighton Beach Memoirs,* Neil Simon Theatre, New York, 1983.

AWARDS, HONORS: Golden Globe nomination for *Uncle Joe Shannon.*

WRITINGS:

(And director) *The Boys of Sunset Ridge,* Porchlight Entertainment (Los Angeles, CA), 2001.

Also author and director of the film *The Gang's All Here.*

SIDELIGHTS: Doug McKeon was one of the biggest child stars of the 1970s and early 1980s. He earned a Golden Globe nomination at a mere twelve years of age, for his work on the film *Uncle Joe Shannon,* and the same year he co-starred opposite well-known actor Brian Dennehy in the television series *Big Shamus,*

Little Shamus. McKeon's best-known role was as Jane Fonda's son in the 1981 film *On Golden Pond,* which starred Henry Fonda and Katherine Hepburn.

McKeon continues to act as an adult, and has also written and directed a film, *The Boys of Sunset Ridge.* This movie covers sixty years in the lives of four boyhood friends, played by actors Ronny Cox, Burt Young, John Heard, and Pat Morita, who meet every year at the Sunset Ridge Country Club to play a game of golf and catch up on each other's lives.

BIOGRAPHICAL AND CRITICAL SOURCES:

PERIODICALS

CoEvolution Quarterly, winter, 1981, Sheila Benson, review of *On Golden Pond,* p. 122.

Fifty Plus, December, 1981, Judith Crist, review of *On Golden Pond,* p. 55; February, 1982, Judith Crist, review of *Night Crossing,* p. 58.

Los Angeles Magazine, March, 1985, Merrill Shindler, review of *Mischief,* p. 40.

Maclean's, December 21, 1981, Lawrence O'Toole, review of *On Golden Pond,* pp. 47-48.

Newsweek, November 30, 1981, David Ansen, review of *On Golden Pond,* p. 105.

New York, December 7, 1981, David Denby, review of *On Golden Pond,* pp. 156-157; November 30, 1987, John Leonard, review of *Breaking Home Ties,* pp. 74-75.

New Yorker, December 7, 1981, Pauline Kael, review of *On Golden Pond,* pp. 198-202.

People, December 21, 1981, review of *On Golden Pond,* p. 14; March 22, 1982, Lee Wohlfert-Wihlborg, "He May Be the Smallest Fish in *Golden Pond,* but Doug McKeon Is Making a Big Splash," pp. 67-68; February 25, 1985, Ralph Novak, review of *Mischief,* p. 12; January 5, 1987, Jeff Jarvis, review of *At Mother's Request,* p. 9; November 30, 1987, Jeff Jarvis, review of *Breaking Home Ties,* p. 17.

Seattle Times, May 14, 1999, John Hartl, review of *The Empty Mirror,* p. D12.

Seventeen, January, 1982, Edwin Miller, "Teen-age Actor Doug McKeon Looks like a Disney Character, Acts like a Trooper," p. 72; March, 1982, Edwin Miller, review of *On Golden Pond,* p. 105.

Time, November 16, 1981, Richard Schickel, review of *On Golden Pond,* pp. 112-114; January 5, 1987, Richard Zoglin, review of *At Mother's Request,* p. 78.

Variety, February 6, 1985, review of *Mischief,* p. 19; May 8, 1985, review of *The Heart of a Champion: The Ray Mancini Story,* p. 158; January 21, 1987, review of *At Mother's Request,* p. 171; December 2, 1987, review of *Breaking Home Ties,* p. 68; October 10, 1994, Tony Scott, review of *Without Consent,* p. 44.

Wilson Library Bulletin, February, 1982, Judith Trojan, review of *On Golden Pond,* pp. 455-456.

ONLINE

Moviesite, http://www.moviesite.co.za/ (March 11, 2003).

Porchlight Entertainment Web site, http://www.porchlight.com/ (March 11, 2003).*

*　　*　　*

McKINNON, Ray 1961(?)-

PERSONAL: Born c. 1961, in Adel, GA; married Lisa Blount (an actress). *Education:* Attended Valdosta State University, 1981.

ADDRESSES: Agent—Judy Schoen & Associates, 606 North Larchmont Blvd., Suite 309, Los Angeles, CA 90004.

CAREER: Actor and screenwriter; co-owner, with Lisa Blount, of Ginny Mule Pictures. Actor in films, including (as trooper number one) *Driving Miss Daisy,* Warner Bros., 1989; (as cub reporter) *Tune in Tomorrow . . .* (also known as *Aunt Julia and the Scriptwriter*), 1990; (as Harmon) *Livin' Large!* (also known as *The Tapes of Dexter Jackson*), Samuel Goldwyn, 1991; (as David Hinton) *Bugsy,* TriStar Pictures, 1991; (as Frank) *The Gun in Betty Lou's Handbag,* Buena Vista, 1992; (as Lawyer Webb) *Sommersby,* Warner Bros., 1993; (as Bradley) *A Perfect World,* Warner Bros., 1993; (as Deputy Norris Ridgewick) *Needful Things,* Columbia, 1993; (as FIDO White), *Apollo 13,* Universal, 1995; (as Dale) *The Net,* Sony Pictures Entertainment, 1995; (as Charlie Cool, Jr.) *The Grass Harp,* Fine Line, 1995; (as Nathaniel Rollins) *Goodbye Lover,* Warner Bros., 1999; (as Harry Lehman) *This Is Harry Lehman,* 1999; (as Vernon T.

Waldrip) *O Brother, Where Art Thou?*, Buena Vista, 2000; (as title role) *The Accountant*, Ginny Mule Pictures, 2000; and (as Craig) *The Pickets*, 2002.

Actor in made-for-television movies, including (as Lyle's father) *Murder in Mississippi*, Arts and Entertainment (A&E), 1990; (as Ken Mott) *Rising Son*, Turner Network Television (TNT), 1990; (as Stuart Troxel) *Web of Deceit*, USA Network, 1990; (as man with basketball) *When Will I Be Loved?* National Broadcasting Company (NBC), 1990; (as Carol Bonner) *Paris Trout*, Home Box Office (HBO), 1991; (as Ben Harper) *Night of the Hunter*, American Broadcasting Companies (ABC), 1991; (as Bob Cheshire) *In the Line of Duty: Manhunt in the Dakotas* (also known as *In the Line of Duty: The Twilight Murders* and *Midnight Murders*), NBC, 1991; (as Dr. Nyland) *In Sickness and in Health* (also known as *Hearts on Fire*), Columbia Broadcasting System (CBS), 1992; (as Les) *Taking Back My Life: The Nancy Ziegenmeyer Story*, CBS, 1992; (as Victor) *Indecency*, USA Network, 1992; (as Deputy Joe Pritchard) *Roswell: The U.F.O. Cover-up*, Showtime, 1994; (as Buddy Rivers) *Moment of Truth: Caught in the Crossfire*, NBC, 1994; (as Steve Sweetzer) *Forgotten Sins*, ABC, 1996; (as shanty man with gun) *William Faulkner's Old Man*, CBS, 1997; *The Price of a Broken Heart*, Lifetime, 1999; and (as C. B.) *The Badge*, Starz, 2002.

Actor in television miniseries, including (as Lee Bob) *The Gambler Returns: The Luck of the Draw*, NBC, 1991; (as Charlie Campion) *Steven King's The Stand*, ABC, 1994; (as Will Benteen) *Scarlet*, CBS, 1994; and (as Long Bill Coleman) *Larry McMurtry's Dead Man's Walk*, ABC, 1996. Played Sheriff Rick in television series *Rocky Times*, 2000. Actor in television pilots, including (as Jordan McNeil) *The Last Best Place*, PBS, 1996; and (as senator) *Grapefruit Moon*, ABC, 1998. Guest star in television shows, including *In the Heat of the Night*, *Designing Women*, and *John Grisham's The Client*.

AWARDS, HONORS: Southeastern Media Makers Award and best narrative short, Atlanta Film and Video Festival, 2001, and Academy Award for best live action short film, Academy of Motion Picture Arts and Sciences, 2002, all for *The Accountant;* named best local filmmaker, Creative Loafing Atlanta, 2001.

WRITINGS:

(And director, actor, and co-producer) *The Accountant* (screenplay), Ginny Mule Pictures, 2000.

Also author of three as yet unproduced feature length screenplays.

SIDELIGHTS: Georgia native Ray McKinnon won an Academy Award for his very first film, *The Accountant*. McKinnon not only wrote this independent film, but also directed it, acted in it, and co-produced it, with his wife, accomplished actress Lisa Blount, with whom he owns his own production company, Ginny Mule Pictures.

The Accountant is "a darkly-comic analysis of an incarcerated Southern culture" set on a struggling fifth-generation family farm in Georgia, Morgan Miller wrote in a review for *FilmThreat.com*. The farm is owned by David O'Dell, played by Atlanta native Eddie King. His brother, Tommy O'Dell, is played by Walton Coggins, a Hollywood actor and Ginny Mule Pictures' resident producer. The two brothers hire an accountant—played by McKinnon—to help them figure out how to save the farm. This accountant, a dusty, hard-drinking, chain-smoking man who drives a 1935 Chevy pickup truck, is paranoid and full of conspiracy theories, mostly about how the rest of the country is out to destroy the Southern way of life. His suggestions for saving the farm include murdering Mrs. O'Dell for the life insurance money. This dark tale is "worthy of Flannery O'Connor," Curt Holman wrote on *Creative Loafing Atlanta* online.

BIOGRAPHICAL AND CRITICAL SOURCES:

BOOKS

Contemporary Theatre, Film, and Television, Volume 33, Gale (Detroit, MI), 2001.

PERIODICALS

Record (Bergen County, NJ), April 16, 1999, Roger Ebert, review of *Goodbye, Lover*, p. 40.
Sight and Sound, October, 1995, John Harkness, review of *The Net*, pp. 55-56.
Variety, May 6, 1991, review of *Night of the Hunter*, p. 338.

ONLINE

Animal Actors, http://www.animal-actors.com/ (February 3, 2003), text of McKinnon and Blount's Oscar acceptance speech.

Creative Loafing Atlanta, http://atlanta.creativeloafing.com/ (April 17, 2002), Curt Holman, review of *The Accountant.*

Film Threat, http://www.filmthreat.com/ (January 31, 2001), Morgan Miller, review of *The Accountant.*

Georgia, You Get the Picture, http://www.georgia.org/ (March 16, 2003), review of *The Accountant.*

Ginny Mule Pictures, http://www.ginnymule.com (March 16, 2003).

MSN Entertainment, http://entertainment.msn.com/ (February 3, 2003), review of *The Badge.*

Valdosta State University Spectator Online, http://www.valdosta.edu/ (March 16, 2003), Jason Howell, "VSU Alum Scores an Oscar."*

*   *   *

McNALLY, John (Raymond) 1965-

PERSONAL: Born November 8, 1965, in Oak Lawn, IL; son of Robert (a roofer) and Margie (a factory worker; maiden name Triplett) McNally; married Amy Knox Brown (a writer). *Education:* Southern Illinois University, B.A., 1987; University of Iowa, M.F.A., 1989; University of Nebraska, Ph.D., 1999.

ADDRESSES: Office—Wake Forest University, English Department, P.O. Box 7387, Reynolda Station, Winston-Salem, NC 27109. *E-mail*—mcnalljr@wfu.edu; fiction101@aol.com.

CAREER: Writer and educator. University of South Florida, Tampa, visiting assistant professor, 2000-01; George Washington University, Washington D.C., visiting writer, 2001-02; Wake Forest University, Winston-Salem, NC, assistant professor of English, 2002—.

AWARDS, HONORS: University of Iowa Writers Workshop James Michener fellowship, 1991-92; Wisconsin Institute for Creative Writing Djerassi fiction fellowship, 1998-99; Bread Loaf Writers' Conference Margaret Bridgman scholarship, 1999; University of Iowa John Simmons short-fiction award, 2000, and Nebraska Book Award, 2001, both for *Troublemakers;* George Washington University Jenny McKean Moore fellowship, 2001-02.

WRITINGS:

(Editor) *High Infidelity: Twenty-five Great Short Stories about Adultery by Some of Our Best Contemporary Authors,* William Morrow (New York, NY), 1997.

Troublemakers (short story collection) University of Iowa Press (Iowa City, IA), 2000.

(Editor) *The Student Body: Short Stories about College Students and Professors,* University of Wisconsin Press (Madison, WI), 2001.

(Editor) *Humor Me: An Anthology of Humor by Writers of Color,* University of Iowa Press (Iowa City, IA), 2002.

(Editor and author of introduction) *Bottom of the Ninth: Great Contemporary Baseball Short Stories,* Southern Illinois University Press (Carbondale, IL), 2003.

The Book of Ralph, Free Press (New York, NY), 2004.

Contributor of fiction and nonfiction to magazines and anthologies, including *With Love and Squalor: Fourteen Writers Respond to the Work of J. D. Salinger,* (Broadway Books, 2001); *The Iowa Award: The Best Stories, 1991-2000,* edited by Frank Conroy, 2001; *Open City, Chelsea, North American Review, New England Review, Florida Review, Idaho Review, Punk Planet, Colorado Review,* and *Columbia.*

WORK IN PROGRESS: A novel and a collection of short stories.

SIDELIGHTS: John McNally's first fiction collection, *Troublemakers,* consists of ten short stories and a novella about lower-middle-class men and boys driven to what Rob Thomas called in his review for the *Capital Times,* "desperate acts. . . . usually hilarious, or at least head-scratchingly bizarre. Even if you've never waited in a dry reservoir for an imaginary Styx concert, played in an 'air band,' or tried to sell a trunkload of bootleg Tootsie Rolls to get out of a jam, you'll recognize the human impulses behind them." Three stories are connected: "The Vomitorium," "Smoke," and "The Grand Illusion," and take place in the 1970s on Chicago's southwest side. Hank, the narrator, is a good kid at heart who hangs out with Ralph, "a juvenile delinquent so loopy," according to Thomas, "that his anti-social ways are almost endearing." In fact, several of McNally's narrators bear a similar relationship to the other characters in the stories. Although personally involved, they are the ones watching with what Thomas called "a look of mingled awe and disdain on their faces. . . . *Troublemakers* confirms McNally's status as a major and exciting new talent."

As editor of four collections of short stories, McNally has received equally enthusiastic reviews. In *High Infidelity: Twenty-four Great Short Stories about Adultery by Some of Our Best Contemporary Authors,* McNally chose stories by well-known authors such as John Updike, Bharati Mukherjee, Margaret Atwood, and T. Coraghessan Boyle, to name just a few, as well as some less-seasoned but talented ones. All the stories are about forbidden relationships. In his introduction, McNally writes: "Adultery, I suspect, has been with us since the dawn of man. I wouldn't be at all surprised to learn of hieroglyphics on cave walls documenting infidelities and indiscretions, sketched by some woebegone or cuckolded Cro-Magnon," then mentions many infamous infidelities throughout history. Mark Graham noted in his review for *Rocky Mountain News* that McNally gathered these stories from "major and obscure magazines and anthologies, so it is unlikely that any reader will have read many of them." Beginning his story, Russell Banks writes: "By the time I was nineteen years old I had broken all but three of the Ten Commandments. I had made no graven image, had killed no one, and had not committed adultery." He then proceeds to reveal how he broke the latter.

Humor Me: An Anthology of Humor by Writers of Color grew from McNally's frustrations while preparing a course on humor in American literature and found almost no representation of minority writers. This representative work encompasses different genres such as poetry, cartoons, drama, and fiction. McNally notes that not all those represented identify themselves as humorists; that race is not the central theme; and that the role of humor is broadly represented, flowing around such universals as ambition, ladder-climbing,

and sex. A reviewer for *Publishers Weekly* commented: "Given McNally's multigenre approach, the lack of bigger names here—cartoonist Aaron McGruder (*The Boondocks*) comes immediately to mind—make this book feel like an academic exercise, despite McNally's best intentions."

The title of *The Student Body: Short Stories about College Students and Professors* is self-explanatory. In his introduction, McNally writes: "University campuses, small and large, are treasure-troves of material for fiction writers." And in this collection are stories by a diverse group of authors such as Stephen King, Thisbe Nissen, Marly Swick, and Ron Carlson. The book is divided into two sections, one from the students' perspectives, the other from the educators'. Kristine Huntley commented in *Booklist:* "In [Richard] Russo's gracefully told tale, a 70-year-old nun joins an advanced creative writing class and uses her story to tell the tale of her life, which is as rife with subtext as any novel. . . . [Dan] Chaon and Amy Knox Brown weigh in with stories of fraternity brothers, Gillian Kendall writes of a professor's deeply buried passion for her student, and Tom Whalen's attractive female student wanders through a myriad of lecherous professors. This excellent collection captures both the passion and isolation in academia."

BIOGRAPHICAL AND CRITICAL SOURCES:

PERIODICALS

Booklist, July, 1997, Donna Seaman, review of *High Infidelity: Twenty-four Great Short Stories about Adultery by Some of Our Best Contemporary Authors,* p. 1796; September 15, 2001, Kristine Huntley, review of *The Student Body: Stories about College Students and Professors,* p. 197.
Capital Times (Madison, WI), October 13, 2000, Rob Thomas, "Creating Chaos Is Hilarious Fun in Bizarre Tales of *Troublemakers,*" p. 9A.
Library Journal, March 15, 2002, A. J. Anderson, review of *Humor Me: An Anthology of Humor by Writers of Color,* p. 81.
People Weekly, August 18, 1997, Francine Prose, review of *High Infidelity,* p. 40.
Publishers Weekly, September 11, 2000, review of *Troublemakers,* p. 66; February 11, 2002, review of *Humor Me,* p. 169.

Rocky Mountain News (Denver, CO), July 27, 1997, Mark Graham, "Anthology Gives Adultery Its Due," p. 2E.

School Library Journal, March, 2001, Emily Lloyd, review of *Troublemakers,* p. 282.

ONLINE

Creighton University Nebraska Center for Writers Web site, http://mockingbird.creighton.edu/ (July 16, 2002), "What the Critics Say about John McNally."

University of Wisconsin Press Web site, http://www.wisc.edu/ (July 16, 2002), "Contemporary Short Stories about College Life, by Famed Writers and Rising Stars."

*   *   *

MEIER, August 1923-2003

OBITUARY NOTICE—See index for *CA* sketch: Born April 30, 1923, in New York, NY; died from a progressive neurological disorder March 19, 2003, in New York, NY. Educator and author. Meier was an expert on African-American intellectual thought during the civil rights movement. He was a graduate of Oberlin College, where he earned an A.B. in 1945, after which he worked as an assistant professor at Tougalloo College in Mississippi until 1949. That year, he receives his master's degree from Columbia University, where he also earned a Ph.D. in 1957. During the 1950s and early 1960s Meier taught history at Fisk University and Morgan State College; then, from 1964 to 1967 he was a history professor at Roosevelt University in Chicago. In 1967 he joined the faculty at Kent State University, where he would remain until his retirement in 1993. Although he was not an African American himself, Meier wrote so fairly about important figures such as Frederick Douglas and W. E. B. Du Bois that he was sometimes mistaken for being black by those who read his work. Of the books he wrote and edited, the one that is often considered his most significant was also his first, *Negro Thought in America, 1880-1915* (1963). He also edited *Black Nationalism in America* (1970), and wrote *Black Detroit and the Rise of the U.A.W.* (1979) and *A White Scholar and the Black Community, 1945-1965* (1992), among other books.

OBITUARIES AND OTHER SOURCES:

BOOKS

Martin, Waldo E., and Patricia Sullivan, editors, *Civil Rights in the United States,* Macmillan Reference (New York, NY), 2000.

PERIODICALS

Los Angeles Times, March 27, 2003, p. B17.
New York Times, March 25, 2003, p. A17.

*   *   *

MESSINGER, Sheldon L(eopold) 1925-2003

OBITUARY NOTICE—See index for *CA* sketch: Born August 26, 1925, in Chicago, IL; died of cancer March 6, 2003, in Berkeley, CA. Educator and author. Messinger was an expert in criminology who was a longtime faculty member of the University of California at Berkeley. A World War II veteran who was in the U.S. Army infantry, he completed a Ph.B. at the University of Chicago in 1947, followed by an A.B. in 1951, an M.A. in 1953, and a Ph.D. in 1969, all at the University of California at Los Angeles. He began his academic career as an instructor at Princeton in 1956, followed by a year at the Center for Advanced Study in the Behavioral Sciences in Stanford, California. He then moved to the University of California at Berkeley, where he was vice chair of the Center for the Study of Law and Society during the 1960s, becoming a full professor in 1970. He was named Elizabeth J. Boalt Professor of Law in 1988, became a professor of law emeritus in 1991, and was professor of the graduate school from 1995 to 1997. Messinger was the coauthor of several books, including *Civil Justice and the Poor* (1967), and was coeditor of *The State of the University: Authority and Change* (1970).

OBITUARIES AND OTHER SOURCES:

PERIODICALS

San Francisco Chronicle, March 20, 2003, p. A19.

MILLER, Paul 1906-1991

PERSONAL: Born September 28, 1906, in Diamond, MO; died of cardiac arrest August 21, 1991, in West Palm Beach, FL; son of James (a minister) and Clara (Ranne) Miller; married Louise Johnson, 1933; children: Jean, Ranne, Paul, Jr., Kenper. *Education:* Attended Oklahoma A & M (now Oklahoma State University), B.A. (journalism), 1933.

CAREER: Pawhuska Daily Journal, Pawhuska, OK, reporter, then city editor, c. 1921-24; *Okemah Daily Leader,* Okemah, OK, editor, beginning 1926; writer for papers in Stillwater, Guthrie, and Norman, OK, c. 1926-30; Associated Press, night rewrite man in Columbus, OH, beginning 1932, worked in bureaus in New York, NY, Kansas City, MO, bureau chief in Salt Lake City, UT, 1936, in charge of operations in Pennsylvania, 1937-41, assistant general manager in New York, NY, 1941-43, Washington bureau chief, 1943-47, president/chairman, 1963-77. Gannett Corporation, Rochester, NY, executive assistant, 1947-49, publisher of *Rochester Times-Union,* 1949-51; *Rochester Democrat and Chronicle,* publisher, 1951, executive vice president, 1951-55, operating head, 1955-57, president, 1957-78. Member, Pulitzer Prize advisory board and American Press Institute of Columbia University advisory board (chair).

MEMBER: Boys Club of America (former national director), Society of Professional Journalists (honorary president), New York State Publishers Association (former president).

AWARDS, HONORS: Named one of five most influential U.S. newspaper executives, *U.S. News & World Report,* 1975, 1976, 1977; Syracuse University School of Journalism Distinguished Service Medal; University of Missouri medal for distinguished service to journalism.

WRITINGS:

China Opens the Door, Gannett (Rochester, NY), 1972.

SIDELIGHTS: Paul Miller is credited with building the Gannett Corporation into the largest newspaper chain in the United States. "That geographic breadth provided the company with a broad economic base that insulated its profits from regional downturns," Cecilia Friend wrote in *Dictionary of Literary Biography,* "It also gave it a national dimension lacking in the nineteen-paper, mostly upstate New York chain that Miller inherited from founder Frank E. Gannett in 1957." Before Gannett, Miller was chairman of the Associated Press.

Miller began his career with several small papers in his home state of Oklahoma. "Miller was a newsman first and foremost," Friend said, "even during the time he was the top executive at Gannett and the AP. He started as a reporter and never completely gave up that role, whether filing dispatches from around the world—including Berlin during the 1949 airlift and the Soviet Union, where he interviewed Nikita Khrushchev in 1962—or writing local columns for the Rochester, New York, paper that he edited."

In 1932 Miller left small-town journalism for the Associated Press (A.P.), the agency that supplies U.S. newspapers with access to world news and vice versa. He stayed with the A.P. for fifteen years, serving as editor and writer in a variety of positions across the United States, including Columbus, Ohio; New York City; Kansas City, Missouri; Salt Lake City, Utah; and Washington, D.C. In Washington, according to Friend, Miller demanded tighter leads to stories and more interpretive reporting. He also supported staff in disagreements with the home office and increased salaries. Miller became A.P. president in 1963, the only A.P. employee to do so. The news service changed the title of this part-time position to chairman in 1972. "Paul Miller was not just A.P.'s chairman. He was its champion, always challenging us to do better but never failing to hail a job well done," said Louis D. Boccardi, A.P. president and general manager, as quoted in the *Dictionary of Literary Biography.* "He had many interests and many successes but we always knew he loved the Associated Press."

In 1947, Miller left the A.P. to become executive assistant to Frank Gannett, president of the Gannett Company, and as such, Gannett's hand-picked successor o the family chain of New York state newspapers. The seventy-year-old Gannett left no doubt that he had hired Miller as his right-hand man, and when Gannett died Miller took charge. He continued Gannett's policy of purchasing papers in small towns with little competition, but expanded the policy far beyond New

York state. When Miller retired in 1978, the corporation controlled seventy-eight papers in thirty states, including Hawaii, the Virgin Islands and Guam, and could boast forty-four straight profitable quarters after going public in 1967.

"While some hailed the scope of Miller's vision, others scored it," Friend wrote. "He regularly felt the need to defend Gannett's acquisitions and strategy against criticism, including the charge that large chains that operate monopolies in one-newspaper cities stifle diversity, the foundation of press freedom."

Oklahoma State University named its journalism and broadcasting building in honor of Miller, and offers a Paul Miller Scholarship Fund. Since 1986 the Gannett Foundation has offered Paul Miller Washington reporting fellowships for journalists.

BIOGRAPHICAL AND CRITICAL SOURCES:

BOOKS

Dictionary of Literary Biography, Volume 127: *American Newspaper Publishers, 1950-1990,* Gale (Detroit, MI), 1993.

ONLINE

Oklahoma State University Web site, http://www.library.okstate.edu/ (November 11, 1998), *The Paul Miller Collection.* *

*   *   *

MINNS, Susan 1839-1938

PERSONAL: Born August 21, 1839; died August 1, 1938; daughter of Constant Freeman Minns (translator and merchant) and Frances Ann Parker. *Hobbies and other interests:* Breeding silkworms.

CAREER: Collector of death memorabilia, 1850s-1922; silkworm breeder.

WRITINGS:

Book of the Silkworm: A Plea for the Cultivation of Silk and the Silkworm in the United States, National Americana Society (New York, NY), 1929.

SIDELIGHTS: Susan Minns is best known for her lifelong pursuit of death. She collected representations of death—particularly books and prints depicting the danse macabre—for about seventy years, and during the first two decades of the twentieth century she even converted a portion of her house into a death gallery. There she displayed poison cups, prints, prayers for and invitations to funeral services, death notices, bills of mortality, and illuminated texts.

Minns' family had a printing background. Her father, Constant Freeman Minns, was a translator and her grandfather, Thomas Minns, was a publisher of the *Massachusetts Mercury* and was printer to the Massachusetts legislature.

Minns credited her fascination with morbidity as steming from an early interest in woodcuts. "As a child I was given books illustrated by [Alexander] Anderson, [Thomas] Bewick, Birket Foster, [Carl August] Richter and others. I was shown how woodcuts were printed and even tried my hand at blocks," she once wrote, as quoted in the *Dictionary of Literary Biography.* "So that quite early I began to buy anything that had a woodcut." Soon, death in its many forms appealed to her. According to a *Dictionary of Literary Biography* critic, Minns read Francis Douce's *The Dance of Death Exhibited in Elegant Engravings on Wood, with a Dissertation on the Several Representations of That Subject.* Inspired, she studied *Recherches historiques et littéraires sur les danses des morts et sur l'origine des cartes à four,* by Gabriel Peignot; *Literatur der Todtentänze,* by H. F. Massman; and *Essai historique, philosophique et pittoresque sur les danses des morts,* by E. H. Langlois.

Minns began to concentrate exclusively on representations of death, particularly anthropomorphizing representations. Her primary fascinating, apparently, was *ars moriendi,* those texts and images that counseled people to prepare for death. She also collected some remarkable prints and texts over seventy years.

She purchased a copy of the 1490 edition of Guy Marchant's *Danse macabre,* the earliest known book depicting the dance of death. She also found a 1568 edition of *La grande danse macabre des homes & des femes hystoriee et augmentee de beaulx dictz en Latin,* as well as other editions of these texts. The *danse macabre* was central to each; as the *Dictionary of Literary Biography* writer explained: "The Dance of Death was a procession of all ranks and orders of society. Hierarchically arranged, each person was shown in his or her encounter with Death, who took the form of a skeleton."

Minns also collected *horae,* or books of hours, illuminated prayer and meditation books. Inside, one might find pictures of death, or prayers, or descriptions of related preparations. The *Dictionary of Literary Biography* critic wrote: "The subject matter included death and burial scenes, the raising of Lazarus, and various depictions of Death Triumphant, Death as the Grim Reaper with his scythe, Death on a coffin, Death carrying a coffin, Death seated on an open tomb, Death riding an ox, Death on horseback, as well as the Dance of Death." In Minns' collection, death approaches the living in many forms: in Pierre Michault's *La dance des aveugles* death is a blind guide; in Sebastian Brand's *Stultifera Navis* death charts the water. In Hans Holbein's *Les simulachres et historiees faces de la mortes* each human "type" is imagined interacting with death in a particular way.

Minns sold her memories of death in 1922, at the American Art Association in New York. "I have had the pleasure of collecting," she said. "Let others have the same." Her collection, however, inspired little interest, despite its aesthetic value. Minns had donated $12,500 to the Committee for the Restoration of Louvain, earmarked for the purchase of her own collection, but the entire sale produced only $5,500 more than that. As the *Dictionary of Literary Biography* critic said: "she was in effect the chief buyer at her own sale." Few shared Minns' taste for skeletons, swinging dark capes, and little persons hiding desperately from the inevitable.

After taking up silkworm breeding, she wrote a tract, *Book of the Silkworm,* but again found little public interest.

BIOGRAPHICAL AND CRITICAL SOURCES:

BOOKS

Dictionary of Literary Biography, Volume 140: *American Book Collectors and Bibliographers,* Gale (Detroit, MI), 1994, pp. 159-164.

PERIODICALS

Descant, Volume 22, 1991-92, p. 87.*

*   *   *

MOLESKI, Martin X. 1952-

PERSONAL: Born August 21, 1952, in Allegany, NY; son of Desmond D. (a physician) and Ruth (Gabriel) Moleski. *Education:* Boston College, B.A., 1973; Fordham University, M.A., 1977; Catholic University of America, Ph.D., 1991. *Politics:* "Pro-life." *Religion:* Roman Catholic. *Hobbies and other interests:* Radio-controlled airplanes, NASCAR auto racing.

ADDRESSES: Home and office—Canisius College, 2001 Main St., Buffalo, NY 14208. *E-mail*—moleski@canisius.edu.

CAREER: Ordained Roman Catholic priest of the Society of Jesus (Jesuits; S.J.), 1973—; high school teacher in New York, NY, 1976-78; Le Moyne College, Syracuse, NY, assistant professor of religious studies, 1988-90; Canisius College, Buffalo, NY, associate professor of religious studies, 1990—.

MEMBER: American Academy of Religion, Polanyi Society.

WRITINGS:

Personal Catholicism: The Theological Epistemologies of John Henry Newman and Michael Polanyi, Catholic University of America Press (Washington, DC), 2000.

WORK IN PROGRESS: A biography of Michael Polanyi; research on theological epistemology.

SIDELIGHTS: Martin X. Moleski told *CA:* "The Enlightenment idea of an idea—clear, distinct, propositional, atomic, unchanging, and undeniable—coupled with a model of reason derived from mathematics and the physical sciences—rigid, formal, demonstrative, and explicit—has reached a dead end because there is so much more to life than we can put into words. I seek to develop the post-critical vision of John Henry Newman and Michael Polanyi. Because neither thoughts nor things can be fully articulated, we always see more than we can say and know more than we can tell. This is a modest, realistic appraisal of knowing. We know enough to know how little we know."

BIOGRAPHICAL AND CRITICAL SOURCES:

ONLINE

Martin X. Moleski Web site, http://www2.canisius.edu/˜moleski (August 10, 2003).

*　　*　　*

MOLLEUR, (Michael B.) Joseph 1962-

PERSONAL: Born August 7, 1962, in North Adams, MA; son of Michael J. and Theresa A. (Marcil) Molleur; married Linda M. May, December 5, 1992. *Education:* Grinnell College, B.A., 1984; Episcopal Divinity School, M.A., 1995; Boston College, Ph.D., 1999. *Religion:* Episcopalian. *Hobbies and other interests:* Collecting stamps (first-day covers).

ADDRESSES: Home—606 Third Ave. S., Mount Vernon, IA 52314. *Office*—Department of Religion, Cornell College, 600 First St. W., Mount Vernon, IA 52314. *E-mail*—jmolleur@cornellcollege.edu.

CAREER: Boston College, Chestnut Hill, MA, member of Jewish-Christian-Muslim Interfaith Trialogue, 1996-2001, postdoctoral fellow in theology, 1999-2001; Cornell College, Mount Vernon, IA, assistant professor of religion, 2001—.

MEMBER: American Academy of Religion, College Theology Society, Society of Anglican and Lutheran Theologians, Phi Beta Kappa.

WRITINGS:

Divergent Traditions, Converging Faiths: Troeltsch, Comparative Theology, and the Conversation with Hinduism, Peter Lang Publishing (New York, NY), 2000.

WORK IN PROGRESS: Research on the Christian theology of religions and religious pluralism.

*　　*　　*

MOREY, James H. 1961-

PERSONAL: Born May 5, 1961, in Ohio; son of John H. (a college president and professor) and Arlene T. (a nurse) Morey; married May, 1999; wife's name Barbara (in real estate); children: Aidan, Catherine. *Ethnicity:* "White." *Education:* Hamilton College, A.B., 1983; Cornell University, M.A., 1987, Ph.D., 1990. *Religion:* Episcopalian.

ADDRESSES: Office—Department of English, Emory University, Atlanta, GA 30322. *E-mail*—jmorey@emory.edu.

CAREER: Texas Tech University, Lubbock, assistant professor, 1990-94; Emory University, Atlanta, GA, associate professor of English, 1994—.

MEMBER: Fulbright Alumni Association, Phi Beta Kappa.

AWARDS, HONORS: Fulbright fellow.

WRITINGS:

Book and Verse: A Guide to Middle-English Biblical Literature, University of Illinois Press (Urbana, IL), 2000.

BIOGRAPHICAL AND CRITICAL SOURCES:

PERIODICALS

Choice, October, 2000, C. S. Cox, review of *Book and Verse: A Guide to Middle-English Biblical Literature,* p. 331.
Christianity and Literature, winter, 2001, David C. Fowler, review of *Book and Verse,* p. 343.
Review of English Studies, May, 2001, H. L. Spencer, review of *Book and Verse,* p. 249.

*   *   *

MOYNIHAN, Daniel P(atrick) 1927-2003

OBITUARY NOTICE—See index for *CA* sketch: Born March 16, 1927, in Tulsa, OK; died from complications after suffering a ruptured appendix March 26, 2003, in Washington, DC. Politician, educator, and author. Moynihan was a neoconservative Democrat who was a former U.S. senator for New York, ambassador to India, and a presidential advisor. He served as a gunnery officer in the U.S. Navy from 1944 to 1947, after which he completed a B.A. from Tufts University and an M.A. in 1949 and Ph.D. in 1961 from the Fletcher School of Law and Diplomacy. His entrance into politics began in the 1950s when he was an assistant to the governor of New York's secretary, but he moved toward an academic career when he joined Syracuse University as the director of the New York State Government Research Project in 1959, followed by a year as an assistant professor of political science. During the early 1960s he returned to government, working in several assistant roles in the U.S. Department of Labor. After an unsuccessful run for president of the New York City Council in 1965 and working in the mayoral campaign for Abraham Beame, Moynihan once again returned to academia as a fellow at Wesleyan University. He then spent ten years at the Massachusetts Institute of Technology, where he directed the Joint Center for Urban Studies from 1966 to 1969 before becoming a professor of government in 1972. He was concurrently a professor at Harvard University, where he taught at the Kennedy School of Government. From 1969 to 1970 he also was a U.S. government advisor on urban affairs, and from 1973 to 1975 was an ambassador to India; this was followed by a year as an ambassador to the United Nations. In 1977 Moynihan was elected to the U.S. Senate for his state of New York, winning reelection several times before he retired in 2000. While serving in the senate he earned a reputation as a "neoconservative" Democrat who demonstrated both an earnest concern for the poor and a strong, conservative stand against the Soviet Union. His other concerns included what he saw as a crisis in the dissolution of the traditional American family and the decay of urban centers; he also advocated changes in welfare and Social Security to benefit the underprivileged. The year he retired, President Bill Clinton awarded him the Medal of Freedom for his public service. Even after he retired, Moynihan continued to work for politicians on both the Democratic and Republican sides; he campaigned for his replacement in the senate, Hilary Clinton, and worked on President George W. Bush's Social Security commission. In addition to his active political service, Moynihan was also the author of almost two dozen books, including *The Assault on Poverty* (1965), *The Politics of Guaranteed Income: The Nixon Administration and the Family Assistance Plan* (1973), *Family and a Nation: The Godkin Lectures, Harvard University* (1986), and *Secrecy: The American Experience* (1998).

OBITUARIES AND OTHER SOURCES:

BOOKS

Barone, Michael, and Grant Ujifusa, *The Almanac of American Politics,* National Journal (Washington, DC), 1999.
Congressional Directory. 106th Congress, 1999-2000, United States Government Printing Office (Washington, DC), 1999.
Writers Directory, 18th edition, St. James Press (Detroit, MI), 2003.

PERIODICALS

Chicago Tribune, March 27, 2003, section 1, p. 9.
Los Angeles Times, March 27, 2003, p. B16.
New York Times, March 27, 2003, pp. A1, A22.
Times (London, England), March 28, 2003.
Washington Post, March 27, 2003, pp. A1, A6.

*   *   *

MURHALL, J(acqueline) J(ane) 1964-

PERSONAL: Born April 22, 1964, in London, England; daughter of Colin and Gwendoline (Goodwin) Murhall; partner of Michael Toumey (an actor, director, and playwright); children: Saoirse Ruby Murhall-Toumey.

Education: Reigate School of Art and Design, degree in design. *Hobbies and other interests:* Reading, theatre, cinema, traveling, music, eating, dogs.

ADDRESSES: Home—London, England. *Agent*—c/o Author Mail, Hodder Children's Books, 338 Euston Road, London NW1 3BH, England; and c/o Author Mail, Bloomsbury Children's Books, 38 Soho Square, London W1D 3HB, England.

CAREER: Author of children's books. Worked for Virgin Records, London, England; former jewelry salesperson and dealer in vintage clothes from the 1950s and 1960s. Has appeared on television and radio programs in England, and at numerous writers' festivals. Became an ambassador for Reading Is Fundamental U.K., 2000.

AWARDS, HONORS: Series winner of a British Academy of Film and Television Arts award and two prestigious awards from "Cartoons on the Bay" animation festival (Italy).

WRITINGS:

Eddie and the Swine Family, illustrated by Tony Blundell, HarperCollins (London, England), 1994.
Stinkerbell, illustrated by Tony Blundell, Bloomsbury (London, England), 1996.
Stinkerbell and the Fridge Fairies, illustrated by Tony Blundell, Bloomsbury (London, England), 1997.

Author of episode "You're My Hero" for Collingwood O'Hare animated television program *Eddie and the Bear,* CITV, 2002.

"MAGNIFICENT MISFITS" SERIES; ILLUSTRATED BY ELEANOR TAYLOR

The Great Mistake, Bloomsbury (London, England), 1998.
The Ghastly Ride, Bloomsbury (London, England), 1998.
Ride Again, Bloomsbury (London, England), 1998.
The Terrible Toddler, Bloomsbury (London, England), 1998.

Series has been translated into Italian.

"STAR PETS" SERIES; ILLUSTRATED BY ELEANOR TAYLOR

On Stage, Hodder Wayland (London, England), 1999.
Make It Big, Hodder Wayland (London, England), 1999.
On TV, Hodder Wayland (London, England), 1999.
In the Spotlight, Hodder Wayland (London, England), 1999.

"ST. MISBEHAVIOURS" SERIES; ILLUSTRATED BY MARTIN REMPHRY

Disco Inferno, Hodder Children's Books (London, England), 2001.
Roman Around, Hodder Children's Books (London, England), 2001.
Go Wild! Hodder Children's Books (London, England), 2001.
No Surrender, Hodder Children's Books (London, England), 2001.

Series has been translated into Polish.

"HORSE FORCE" SERIES; ILLUSTRATED BY GARY SWIFT

Smash and Grab Squirrels, Hodder Children's Books (London, England), 2002.
Stick 'em Up, Bunny, Hodder Children's Books (London, England), 2002.
Riddle of a Rich Rat, Hodder Children's Books (London, England), 2002.

WORK IN PROGRESS: A novel for adults; a novel for teenage girls; a book series for six to ten year olds.

SIDELIGHTS: Design-school graduate J. J. Murhall worked as a vintage clothing dealer before deciding to make the break and begin a writing career in 1990. With the popularity of her first book, 1994's *Eddie and the Swine Family,* her success as a children's author was assured, and she has gone on to publish many other titles, all which contain her irreverent humor and energetic, likeable characters. *Stinkerbell,* which Murhall published in 1996, features a dirty, ill-tempered fairy who lives in a garbage can and has to contend with a group of Elvis-lookalike goblins that are even more ill-tempered than she is. Describing

Murhall's bewinged protagonist as a "punk fairy," a *Books for Keeps* contributor praised *Stinkerbell* as a "short and spicy book" that would captivate pre-teen readers.

Born in London in 1964, Murhall grew up reading books by Roald Dahl and C. S. Lewis, among others. She attended the city's Reigate School of Art and Design, where she earned a degree in surface decoration and three-dimensional design. After graduation, she traveled in Europe, at one point paying her way as a jewelry salesperson on a beach in the south of France. Returning to London, she worked for Virgin Records, then decided to start her own business selling clothing from the 1950s and 1960s in a market stall on London's trendy Portobello Road. Although Murhall had lots of ideas for books spinning around in her head, she never had the time to stop and write them down. Finally, in 1988 with the birth of her daughter, she found herself at home with some free time. *Eddie and the Swine Family* was the result, and HarperCollins publishers quickly snapped it up.

Eddie and the Swine Family is told from the point of view of the family's youngest member, who, despite his age, is left in charge of his less responsible siblings when his parents are away from home. Eddie is destined for life as a "astropig" according to his doting mother, while his sister idles away her time with dreams of soap-opera stardom and his brother plans small-scale criminal activities. Praising the book's "rich mixture of characters," a *Junior Bookshelf* contributor praised *Eddie and the Swine Family* as a humorous book that leads readers on a "bizarre journey" in a pizza delivery truck as Eddie thwarts his brother's latest criminal romp and helps his siblings make "at least part of their dreams come true."

Other books by Murhall include a sequel to *Stinkerbell,* titled *Stinkerbell and the Fridge Fairies.* Content to live in her grubby dustbin, Stinkerbell is not bad at heart, and is forced to come to the aid of a group of fridge-dwelling fairies when the dastardly goblin family—the Gobs—become too much to handle. Despite expressing some reservations about having "such a scruffy . . . thing as Stinkerbell as a role model" *School Librarian* reviewer Audrey Laski found *Stinkerbell and the Fridge Fairies* to be "great fun." Murhall has also penned a number of book series for older readers. In *Go Wild!* part of her "St. Misbehaviours" series, Students at St. Saviour's School find their

highly unconventional school threatened with closure and must come to the aid of their teachers when an undercover inspector from the "Department of Unnecessary Buildings" poses as a geography teacher in order to find reasons to close the building down. Praising Murhall's "firm storyline" good choice of vocabulary, Joan Nellist noted in her *School Librarian* review that despite being painted as quirky, "teachers are drawn quite sympathetically" and that *Go Wild!* would find many fans among reluctant readers.

Making her home in London with her partner, actor, director, and playwright Michael Toumey, and daughter Saoirse Ruby—a "major fashion fiend"—Murhall cites her favorite pastime as writing. She told *CA:* "I still love clothes and even though I don't sell them anymore I do continue to buy them avidly. I'm also a big music fan and listen to all types. I like going to the cinema, restaurants, and the occasional club to watch live bands play."

Regarding her work habits, Murhall told *CA:* "I get up about 8:00 a.m. After three or four cups of coffee I finally start writing about 9:30 a.m. I try to write until about 1:00 p.m. and break for lunch. I then continue to write from about 2:00 p.m. until 6:00 p.m.

"I do sound like I am very disciplined, which obviously you do have to be in order to ever get anything written. However I, like a lot of writers I'm sure, will always find excuses not to sit down and actually make a start. Especially if I am about to embark on something new! Reasons can range from: 'The dog needs *another* walk' to 'Oh look. There's an episode of *The Loveboat* on TV this morning. I wonder if that's the original 1970s version that's really brilliantly bad and tacky! I might just have to watch it!'"

Murhall offered this advice to aspiring writers: "Read, read, read all the time. Write, write, write whenever you can. Believe in and care about the characters that you create and your readers will too. Don't waste time watching tacky 1970 television programmes!"

BIOGRAPHICAL AND CRITICAL SOURCES:

PERIODICALS

Books for Keeps, July, 1996, review of *Stinkerbell,* p. 7.

Junior Bookshelf, August, 1994, review of *Eddie and the Swine Family,* p. 138.

School Librarian, spring, 1998, Audrey Laski, review of *Stinkerbell and the Fridge Fairies,* pp. 35-36; spring, 2002, Joan Nellist, review of *Go Wild!* pp. 33-34.

ONLINE

Bloomsbury Magazine Online, http://www.bloomsbury magazine.com/ (February 12, 2003), "Jacqui Murhall."

N

NAGL-DOCEKAL, Herta 1944-

PERSONAL: Born May 29, 1944, in Wels, Austria; daughter of Friedrich (an engineer) and Anna (a homemaker; maiden name, Kirchmayr) Docekal; married Ludwig Nagl (a university professor), April 10, 1970. *Education:* University of Vienna, Ph.D., 1967.

ADDRESSES: Home—82 Weimarerstrasse, A-1190 Vienna, Austria. *Office*—Department of Philosophy, University of Vienna, Universitätsstrasse 7, A-1010 Vienna, Austria; fax: +431-4277-47492. *E-mail*—herta.nagl@univie.ac.at.

CAREER: University of Vienna, Vienna, Austria, currently professor of philosophy. Millersville University, adjunct professor, 1980; visiting professor at University of Utrecht, 1990-91, University of Frankfurt, 1991-92, University of Konstanz, 1993, Free University of Berlin, 1994-95, and University of Innsbruck, 2000-01; University of Calgary, visiting scholar, 1999.

MEMBER: Fédération Internationale des Sociétés de Philosophy, International Association of Women Philosophers (member of board of directors, 1989-96), Internationale Hegel-Vereinigung, Internationale Hegel-Gesellschaft, Internationalen Vereinigung für Rechts-und Sozialphilosophie (Austrian section), European Forum Alpbach, Austrian Academy of Sciences, Austrian Society for Philosophy (vice president, 1996-98), Society for Women in Philosophy, Institute of Human Sciences (Vienna; member of board of directors, 1993—), Kulturwissenschaftliches Institut am Wissenschaftszentrum Nordrhein-Westfalen (member of board of directors, 1998—), Allgemeine Gesellschaft für Philosophie in Deutschland (member of board of directors, 1994-2000).

AWARDS, HONORS: Förderungspreis, City of Vienna, Austria, 1983; Käthe Leichter prize, State of Austria, 1997.

WRITINGS:

IN ENGLISH TRANSLATION

(Editor, with Cornelia Klinger, and contributor) *Continental Philosophy in Feminist Perspective: Rereading the Canon in German,* Pennsylvania State University Press (University Park, PA), 2000.

Feministische Philosophie: Ergebnisse, Probleme, Perspektiven, S. Fischer (Frankfurt am Main, Germany), 2000, 2nd edition, 2001, translation published as *Feminist Philosophy,* Westview Press (Boulder, CO), 2003.

Contributor to books, including *Biopolitics: The Politics of the Body, Race, and Nature,* edited by Agnes Heller and Sonja Puntscher Riekmann, Avebury (Aldershot, England), 1995; *The Philosophy of Hans-Georg Gadamer,* edited by Lewis Edwin Hahn, Open Court (Chicago, IL), 1997; *Feminist Interpretations of Immanuel Kant,* edited by Robin May Schott, Pennsylvania State University Press (University Park, PA), 1998; *A Companion to Feminist Philosophy,* edited by Alison M. Jaggar and Iris M. Young, Blackwell (Oxford, England), 1998; and *Rethinking Modernity:*

Philosophy, Values, Gender, edited by Yvanka B. Raynova, Institut für Axiologische Forschung (Vienna, Austria), 2002. Contributor to periodicals, including *Philosophy and Social Criticism* and *Hypatia.* Member of editorial board, *Ethical Theory and Moral Practice: International Forum, Transactions of the Royal Society of Canada,* and *European Journal of Women's Studies.*

IN GERMAN

Ernst von Lasaulx: Ein Beitrag zur Kritik des organischen Geschichtsbefriffs, Aschendorff (Münster, Germany), 1970.

Die Objektivität der Geschichtswissenschaft: Systematische Untersuchungen zum wissenschaftlichen Status der Historie, Oldenbourg (Vienna, Austria), 1982.

(Editor) *Überlieferung und Aufgabe: Festschrift für Erich Heintel zum siebzigsten Geburtstag,* Braumueller (Vienna, Austria), 1982.

(Editor, with Franz M. Wimmer, and contributor) *Neue Ansätze in der Geschichtswissenschaft,* Verband der wissenschaftlichen Gesellschaften Österreichs (Vienna, Austria), 1984.

(Editor, with Helmuth Vetter, and contributor) *Tod des Subjekts?* Oldenbourg (Vienna, Austria), 1987.

(Editor and contributor) *Ludwig Wittgenstein und die Philosophie des 20. Jahrhunderts,* Miscellanea Bulgarica (Vienna, Austria), 1989.

(Editor and contributor) *Feministische Philosophie,* Oldenbourg (Vienna, Austria), 1990.

(Editor, with Herlinde Pauer-Studer) *Denken der Geschlechterdifferenz,* Wiener Frauenverlag (Vienna, Austria), 1990.

(Editor, with Franz M. Wimmer, and contributor) *Postkoloniales Philosophieren: Afrika,* Oldenbourg (Vienna, Austria), 1992.

(Editor, with Herlinde Pauer-Studer, and contributor) *Jenseits der Geschlechtermoral: Beiträge zur feministischen Ethik,* S. Fischer (Frankfurt am Main, Germany), 1993.

(Editor) *Der Sinn des Historischen: Geschichtsphilosophische Debatten,* M. Fischer (Frankfurt am Main, Germany), 1996.

(Editor, with Herlinde Pauer-Studer, and contributor) *Politische Theorie: Differenz und Lebensqualität: Beiträge zur feministischen politischen Philosophie,* Suhrkamp (Frankfurt am Main, Germany), 1996.

(Editor, with Herlinde Pauer-Studer, and contributor) *Freiheit, Gleichheit und Autonomie,* Oldenbourg (Vienna, Austria), 2002.

Coeditor of book series published in Germany and Austria. Contributor to books. Contributor to scholarly journals. Coeditor or member of editorial board of various German-language periodicals.

WORK IN PROGRESS: Research on contemporary philosophy of history.

*   *   *

NORRIS, Robert S(tandish) 1943-

PERSONAL: Born July 21, 1943, in Beloit, WI; son of Robert S. (an engineer and chemist) and Betty (a homemaker; maiden name, Hilberg) Norris; married, 1970: wife's name, Andrea, (divorced, 1977); married Myriam Zigrand (an artist), June 20, 1980. *Education:* Syracuse University, B.A., 1965; New York University, M.A., 1971, Ph.D., 1976.

ADDRESSES: Home—3158 Rolling Rd., Edgewater, MD 21037. *Office*—Natural Resources Defense Council, 1200 New York Ave. NW, Suite 400, Washington, DC 20005. *E-mail*—rnorris@nrdc.org.

CAREER: Miami University, Oxford, OH, and Luxembourg, adjunct assistant professor, 1977-80; Center for Defense Information, Washington, DC, research analyst, 1981-84; Natural Resources Defense Council, Washington, DC, senior research associate, director of Nuclear Weapons Databook Project, 1984—.

MEMBER: Cosmos Club.

AWARDS, HONORS: James C. Healey Award for best dissertation in the arts, New York University, 1976.

WRITINGS:

(Editor, with others) *Nuclear Weapons Databook,* Natural Resources Defense Council (Washington, DC), Volume 1: *U.S. Nuclear Forces and Capabilities,* 1984, Volume 2: *U.S. Nuclear Warhead Production,* 1987, Volume 3: *U.S. Nuclear Warhead Facility Profiles,* 1987, Volume 4, *Soviet Nuclear Weapons,* Ballinger Publishing Co. (Cambridge,

MA), 1989, Volume 5: *British, French, and Chinese Nuclear Weapons,* Westview Press (Boulder, CO), 1994.

(With Thomas B. Cochran and Oleg A. Bukharin) *Making the Russian Bomb: From Stalin to Yeltsin,* Westview Press (Boulder, CO), 1995.

(With others) *Atomic Audit: The Costs and Consequences of U.S. Nuclear Weapons since 1940,* Brookings Institution Press (Washington, DC), 1998.

Racing for the Bomb: General Leslie R. Groves, the Manhattan Project's Indispensable Man, Steerforth Press (South Royalton, VT), 2002.

Author of publications of the Natural Resources Defense Council; coauthor of entry on nuclear weapons for *Encyclopedia Britannica,* 1990; contributor to periodicals, including *Bulletin of the Atomic Scientists.*

WORK IN PROGRESS: Research of nuclear history and the cold war.

SIDELIGHTS: Robert S. Norris taught political philosophy until 1981, when he moved to Washington, D.C., only to find there were no academic jobs available. He took a position with the Center for Defense Information, a liberal think tank, and three years later he became a nuclear weapons analyst with the Natural Resources Defense Council (NRDC). Norris monitors global nuclear weapon stockpiles and is often quoted by government officials and the and media who rely on the accuracy of Norris's figures. Norris coauthored an entry for the *Encyclopedia Britannica* that drew comment in the *New York Times.* In an interview with *National Journal* writer David C. Morrison, Norris said, "I felt a terrible responsibility. Generations of schoolchildren would be plagiarizing my article for years to come, so I really wanted to get it right." Morrison wrote that Norris "has solidified a reputation as one of Washington's top atomic 'bean counters.'"

As director of the NRDC's "Nuclear Weapons Databook" Project, Norris coedited the series of books that was produced, including the third volume, *U.S. Nuclear Warhead Facility Profiles,* which reviews facilities in the United States nuclear warhead complex, including those whose main purpose is research and others used for weapons development.

Each facility is listed, along with address, telephone numbers, mission, history, staff, and budget. The volume also contains maps, figures, and photographs. Included are entries for Los Alamos, Rocky Flats, Oak Ridge National Laboratory, Argonne National Laboratory, the Hanford Reservation, Sandia National Laboratories, the Pantex plant, and others. Writing in the *Journal of Peace Research,* Magne Barth felt that this volume is closely connected to the previous volume, which covers U.S. nuclear warhead production and which also contains a glossary that this volume lacks. "However," said Barth, "with its masses of information and references, this databook is indispensable."

The fifth volume is titled *British, French, and Chinese Nuclear Weapons. Choice* contributor M. J. Smith, Jr., wrote that it "continues the project design of providing current and accurate information." The volume begins with a chapter titled "Lesser Nuclear Weapons States," and then continues with two chapters on each of the title countries—one covering the history and production of weapons and the other noting capabilities. The volume includes tables and figures and three indexes that note the nuclear testing carried out in each of the countries.

Orbis reviewer Bruce D. Berkowitz wrote that this volume "provides insights beyond its current objectives." Berkowitz felt that in covering the development of the "medium" nuclear powers, assumptions about future nuclear powers can be drawn. Berkowitz continued, saying that "many analysts and political leaders were surprised by the Iraqi and North Korean programs because they were thinking of future proliferation in terms of the very expensive and difficult-to-conceal U.S. and Soviet nuclear-weapons programs. The United States and Soviet Union employed a huge infrastructure . . . partly because they were the first nuclear powers and could not know in advance the most efficient way to structure a weapons program, partly because their military plans required thousands of nuclear warheads, and partly because both powers had deep pockets. Future nuclear-weapons programs are far more likely to resemble those operated by the British, French, and Chinese."

"Nor do medium nuclear powers require the level of sophistication built into U.S. nuclear weapons," continued Berkowitz. Whereas the United States designs nearly all of its weapons for specific delivery systems, medium powers favor generic designs that can be used in multiple systems. Berkowitz also noted that this volume "provides insight into what is easy and what is difficult in building bombs—an important lesson for detecting and preventing proliferation."

British, French, and Chinese Nuclear Weapons documents the early relationship between the United States and Britain that ended with the British spy scandals, beginning with the Fuchs case, and the Atomic Energy Act of 1946, which halted the transfer of nuclear knowledge from the United States. During the 1950s, the United States and Britain resumed a cooperative relationship in the development of nuclear weapons. Chuck Hansen wrote in *Bulletin of the Atomic Scientists* that "the history of the British nuclear weapons program includes the most comprehensive collection of photos and specifications of British warheads and nuclear tests ever assembled in one publication; by itself it is worth the cost of the book."

The French lost their testing ground when Algeria became independent in 1962 and experienced a long delay for lack of a program director, but by the 1990s, the French had stockpiled 500 warheads. Hansen noted that although the United States was at first opposed to the growth of France's nuclear program, in the 1970s, with the approval of President Richard Nixon and national security advisor Henry Kissinger, an exchange of information took place that helped the lagging progress of the French. "This program, kept from Congress and the American public until 1985," wrote Hansen, "used 'negative guidance' to allow the transfer of restricted data without technically violating the Atomic Energy Act."

The Chinese progressed from atomic to thermonuclear weapons in under three years, accelerated by China's deteriorating relationship with the Soviets, who had initially helped them create their weapons; China ultimately targeted their former benefactor. Hansen concluded by saying, "I highly recommend Volume Five as a comprehensive source for the mechanics—and politics—of nuclear weapons proliferation."

Foreign Affairs writer Eliot A. Cohen called this entry in the series "an excellent reference work that combines a great deal of information with thoughtful analysis." Bert Chapman commented in *American Reference Books Annual* that it "is a useful chronicle of historical and ongoing nuclear weapons development in these important nations."

Norris is one of the authors of *Atomic Audit: The Costs and Consequences of U.S. Nuclear Weapons since 1940,* which tracks costs through 1996. The authors estimate that in 1996 dollars, the United States spent $5.28 trillion, or nearly thirty percent of all military spending, to build nuclear weapons, deploy and target them, and control and defend them. Other costs included in this figure were spent for dismantling, managing nuclear waste, remediating the environment, compensating victims, and protecting secrets. The total cost is exceeded only by non-nuclear national defense ($13.2 trillion), and Social Security ($7.9 trillion), and averaged $98 billion per year, or eleven percent of all government expenditures.

Although much of the data has been lost, classified, or undocumented, the accounting provided by this volume demonstrates the huge expense the nuclear program has imposed on the American taxpayer. The book notes that for more than fifty years, the government failed to ensure that the money spent on the nuclear weapons programs was allocated efficiently. In a 1993 U.S. General Accounting Office (GAO) report evaluating the Reagan administration's modernization program, the GAO concluded that during the 1980s, the Defense Department had a tendency to "overstate threats to our weapons systems, to understate the performance of mature systems, to overstate the expected performance of upgrades, and to understate the expected costs of those upgrades."

John Mendelsohn reviewed *Atomic Audit* in *Issues in Science and Technology.* Mendelsohn wrote that "the book is replete with examples of how, in the heat of the confrontation, common sense often fell prey to presidential politics (the Star Wars debates), bureaucratic advocacy (nuclear-powered aircraft), or scientific arrogance (human radiation experiments). The authors also make clear the risks that the United States runs by continuing to believe that its security is enhanced by deploying more nuclear weapons. And, thanks to *Atomic Audit,* we now have the data to show that the nuclear weapons infrastructure is a substantially more expensive enterprise than many had believed." The authors state that although the pressures of the Cold War realistically placed cost second after national security, "there is no justification today for continued inattention" to expenditures.

In the final chapter of *Atomic Audit* recommendations are made. Among them is a suggestion that the president should take a more active role in nuclear policy and that he should prepare and submit an annual report with his yearly budget that would provide costs of the government's nuclear-weapons programs. Congress is urged to take a larger role in developing a strategic plan of how weapons would be used, as well as overseeing the costs of the programs.

"Inconvenient realities have a way of being overlooked when politics are involved," noted Mendelsohn, who noted that although Congress did pass legislation establishing a nuclear testing moratorium and prevented the Reagan administration from disabling the Anti-Ballistic Missile Treaty, "as a body it has very limited ability to adumbrate nuclear strategy or determine what constitutes deterrence." Mendelsohn concluded by calling *Atomic Audit* "a splendid one-stop reference, great ammunition for the never-ending battle with the forces of nuclear darkness."

Library Journal's Daniel K. Blewett said that in writing *Racing for the Bomb: General Leslie R. Groves, the Manhattan Project's Indispensable Man,* Norris "uses his expertise to good effect." A *Kirkus Reviews* contributor called it "an overly detailed but useful biography of an unacknowledged founding father of the nuclear era."

Although much has been written about the scientists of the Manhattan Project, it was Groves (1896-1970) who managed construction and formulated procedures, and who ultimately shared in the responsibility for dropping the atomic bomb on Japan. He was a West Point graduate and career officer in the Army Corps of Engineers when he was selected in 1942, after completing the construction of the Pentagon. It was his task to coordinate scientists, construction crews, military and civilian officials, and others in bringing the task of the Manhattan Project to fruition, which he did in just over 1,000 days in a time of scare materials and limited resources. The procedures and practices established by Groves have had a lasting effect on national security policy.

In order to obtain enough fissionable uranium for the Los Alamos-based project, Groves arranged for the construction and operation of facilities in Oak Ridge, Tennessee and Hanford, Washington, and he established the Air Force unit that would deliver the bombs. "General Groves planned the project, ran his own construction, his own science, his own army, his own

State Department, and his own Treasury Department," declared one of his aides after the war was over. He gave clearance to J. Robert Oppenheimer, lead scientist on the project, even though he had been associated with communists, a decision Groves said he never regretted. Groves was resented by many of the scientists, officers, and politicians who found him offensive and opposed the strict control and secrecy he maintained in the performance of his task.

"Groves emerged from the war a hero," wrote Daniel J. Kevles in the *New York Times Book Review,* "but his reputation and influence rapidly declined. During the battle over postwar control of atomic energy, scientists and journalists hauled him over the coals for his power-hungry and autocratic ways, making him symbolic of the reasons for not ceding control of nuclear affairs to the military." In 1948, Dwight Eisenhower, then chief of staff, severely criticized Groves, and three days later, Groves announced his retirement at age fifty-one. He took a position with Remington Rand in Connecticut, and when he died in 1970, he was buried in Arlington National Cemetery. Groves had written *Now It Can Be Told* in 1962, his story of the Manhattan Project, but Norris offers a complete biography, drawing on a study by historian Stanley Goldberg, who died while working on it.

Norris had access to the large collection of papers left by Groves, as well as to military records and personal accounts. Kevles concluded by saying that "the result is an authoritative biography that is important for its illuminating account of both the man and his crucial role in the race for the bomb."

BIOGRAPHICAL AND CRITICAL SOURCES:

PERIODICALS

American Reference Books Annual, 1995, Bert Chapman, review of *Nuclear Weapons Databook,* Volume 5: *British, French, and Chinese Nuclear Weapons,* p. 309.

Bulletin of the Atomic Scientists, July-August, 1994, Chuck Hansen, review of *British, French, and Chinese Nuclear Weapons,* p. 54.

Choice, November, 1994, M. J. Smith, Jr., review of *British, French, and Chinese Nuclear Weapons,* p. 434.

Environment, November, 1988, Magne Barth, review of *Nuclear Weapons Databook,* Volume 3: *U.S. Nuclear Warhead Facility Profiles,* p. 26.

Foreign Affairs, July-August, 1994, Eliot A. Cohen, review of *British, French, and Chinese Nuclear Weapons,* p. 166.

Issues in Science and Technology, winter, 1998, John Mendelsohn, review of *Atomic Audit: The Costs and Consequences of U.S. Nuclear Weapons since 1940,* p. 92.

Journal of Peace Research, November, 1989, Magne Barth, review of *U.S. Nuclear Warhead Facility Profiles,* pp. 433-434.

Kirkus Reviews, February 1, 2002, review of *Racing for the Bomb: General Leslie R. Groves, the Manhattan Project's Indispensable Man,* p. 165.

Library Journal, April 1, 2002, Daniel K. Blewett, review of *Racing for the Bomb,* p. 120.

National Journal, February 15, 1992, David C. Morrison, "A Bean Counter Who Knows His Beans," p. 402.

New York Times, January 3, 1990, William J. Broad, "Spy's Role in Soviet H-Bomb Now Discounted," p. A1.

New York Times Book Review, June 30, 2002, Daniel J. Kevles, review of *Racing for the Bomb.*

OnEarth, summer, 2002, review of *Racing for the Bomb,* p. 44.

Orbis, spring, 1995, Bruce D. Berkowitz, review of *British, French, and Chinese Nuclear Weapons,* p. 279.

Scientific American, September, 1994, Philip Morrison, review of *British, French, and Chinese Nuclear Weapons,* p. 109.

O-P

OSBORNE, Adam 1939-2003

OBITUARY NOTICE—See index for *CA* sketch: Born March 6, 1939, in Bangkok, Thailand; died March 18, 2003, in Kodiakanal, India. Entrepreneur and author. Osborne is best remembered as the inventor of the portable Osborne-1 computer, which was an industry sensation in 1981. Born in India to English parents, he moved to England as a teenager and earned a B.S. in chemical engineering in 1961 from the University of Birmingham. This was followed by a master's degree in 1966 from the University of Delaware and a Ph.D. in 1967. He used his education to get a job at Shell Oil in California, but his interest in computing led him to found Adam Osborne & Associates, a publishing company that published works about computers, in 1970. He sold this venture in 1981 to McGraw-Hill, a year after he had already founded Osborne Computer Corp. His creation of the Osborne-1 was popular because, weighing in at only twenty-three pounds, it was the first portable PC on the market. Although it had certain limitations, including a small five-inch screen, it including word processing and spreadsheet software that was sufficient for most business people's needs. Sales at first were strong, but when Osborne announced an upgraded version of his computer—the Executive—before it was ready for sale, customers stopped buying the Osborne-1 to wait for the new model. Unfortunately, this resulted in a huge inventory backlog that devastated the company, which went bankrupt in 1983. Next, Osborne founded Paperback Software International, which sold inexpensive software products; but a lawsuit with Lotus Development in 1987 led to Osborne leaving the company in 1990. Finally, in 1992, he founded one more company, Noetics Software, which aimed to develop state-of-

the-art technology such as neural networks. Later that same year, however, Osborne's worsening health compelled him to moved to India to live with his sister. Osborne wrote about his experiences with Osborne Computer in his 1994 memoir, *Hypergrowth: The Rise and Fall of Osborne Computer Corporation.* He was also the author of *Running Wild: The Next Industrial Revolution* (1979) and numerous computer programming guides.

OBITUARIES AND OTHER SOURCES:

PERIODICALS

Los Angeles Times, March 25, 2003, p. B11.
New York Times, March 26, 2003, p. C13.
Times (London, England), March 28, 2003, p. 42.
Washington Post, March 30, 2003, p. C10.

*   *   *

OWEN, Douglas David Roy 1922-2003

OBITUARY NOTICE—See index for *CA* sketch: Born November 17, 1922, in Norton, Suffolk, England; died March 15, 2003. Educator and author. Owen was an authority on medieval French and Arthurian studies. After serving as a navigation officer in the Royal Air Force, he attended the University of Nottingham briefly before transferring to St. Catharine's College, Cambridge, where he completed his Ph.D. in 1955. By that time, he was already a lecturer at the University of St. Andrews, where he would eventually become a professor of French in 1972, retiring in 1988. At St. Andrews he was also the founding editor of the *Forum for Modern Language Studies,* which had the unique distinction of being sued over copyright infringement by an Amsterdam pornography publication that used a similar title. Much more importantly than this strange controversy, however, was Owen's work as a translator and editor of medieval French literature, and as an author of books such as *The Evolution of the Grail Legend* (1968), *The Legend of Roland: A Pageant of the Middle Ages,* (1973), and *Noble Lovers* (1975). He was, furthermore, praised for his translation *The Song of Roland: The Oxford Text* (1972) and *The Romances of Chrétien de Troyes* (1985). Owen's last publications included *Eleanor of Aquitaine: Queen and Legend* (1993), *William the Lion: Kingship and Culture, 1143-1214* (1997), and his translation *The Romance of Reynard the Fox* (1994).

OBITUARIES AND OTHER SOURCES:

BOOKS

Writers Directory, 18th edition, St. James Press (Detroit, MI), 2003.

PERIODICALS

Times (London, England), March 26, 2003, p. 33.

*　　*　　*

PATEMAN, Roy 1935-

PERSONAL: Born August 15, 1935, in Leicester, England; son of Harry (a printer) and Elsie (a seamstress; maiden name, Pearson) Pateman; married Carole Bennett, February 27, 1960. *Ethnicity:* "White." *Education:* University of Nottingham, B.Sc., 1958; University of Reading, M.Phil., 1971. *Politics:* Democratic Socialist. *Religion:* Zen Buddhist. *Hobbies and other interests:* Opera, fitness, wine, books.

ADDRESSES: Home—Turin, Italy. *Agent*—c/o Author Mail, University Press of America, 15200 NBN Way, P.O. Box 191, Building B, Blue Ridge Summit, PA 17214-0191. *E-mail*—roypateman@msn.com.

CAREER: Economics teacher at schools in Oxfordshire, England, 1961-69; National Farmers' Union, London, England, lobbyist and economist, 1969-72; University of Sydney, Sydney, Australia, tutor in politics, 1972-89; University of California—Los Angeles, professor of politics, 1990-2002; retired. Also taught at Princeton University. Workers' Educational Association, Sydney, president, 1980-82; Eritrean Relief Association, chair, 1980-89. *Military service:* British Army Intelligence Corps, 1958-61. British Army Reserve, 1961-64.

MEMBER: Eritrean Studies Association (chair, 1998-2000), Wagner Society of New York.

WRITINGS:

Eritrea: Even the Stones Are Burning, Red Sea Press, 1990, 2nd edition, 1997.
Chaos and Dancing Star: Wagner's Politics, Wagner's Legacy, University Press of America (Blue Ridge Summit, PA), 2002.
(With Lyda Favali) *Blood, Land, and Sex: Legal and Political Pluralism in Eritrea,* Indiana University Press (Bloomington, IN), 2003.
Residual Uncertainty: Trying to Avoid Intelligence and Policy Mistakes in the Modern World, University Press of America (Lanham, MD), 2003.

Author of scholarly articles.

WORK IN PROGRESS: Empty Lands, Empty Titles, with Lyda Favali; research for a literary biography of Ben Traven.

SIDELIGHTS: Roy Pateman told *CA:* "I seem always to have been scribbling if I have not been reading. In 1951, at the age of fifteen, I thought that I would start a list of every book I read to the finish. Anthony Powell once wrote that he wished he had [done the same]. Unlike Powell, more than fifty years later I am still adding to my list. I reached the 3,000 mark early this year, and over the years I expanded the categories of my list to include cinema (1,750 films since 1961), theater, and opera, and finally gardens, stately homes, exhibitions, and art galleries. I also keep a short list of the finest talks I have heard—the most memorable remains one by Eduardo Mondlane, the leader of the

Mozambique liberation movement FRELIMO, speaking in Oxford in the 1960s. Later I started a short, exclusive list of my most loved wines (top of the list, Australian Henschke Hill of Grace, 1961) and restaurants (the Manoir a Quatre Saisons in Oxfordshire).

"While I may seem to be extraordinarily eclectic in my literary interests and writing, many of my books were at the back of my mind for many years. *Chaos and Dancing Star: Wagner's Politics, Wagner's Legacy* grew from my interest in opera—encouraged from the earliest age by musical parents—and in anarchism—through reading and activism in the 1960s and 1970s. I have always been fascinated by quotations and aphorisms and collected apt political examples for many years. Eventually I put some order into them and found many very appropriate to the life of my favorite composer, and a man I consider the most creative to have lived. The main reason I wrote it is that I hadn't found a satisfactory account of Wagner's complex politics and the legacy he bequeathed to many brilliant men and women. Having a Jewish grandmother also spurred me to come to terms with Wagner's gross anti-Semitism.

"My first book, *Eritrea: Even the Stones Are Burning,* came about because of my active involvement in liberation politics and as chair of a major Australian organization, the Eritrean Relief Association, in the 1980s. I visited Eritrea several times during its thirty-year struggle for independence, was enormously impressed by the people and country, and looked around for an adequate account of why the Eritreans had fought so long and how they seemed to be winning in spite of considerable odds against them. I didn't find one, so I set about writing articles that were eventually edited rigorously and put into a book. Here I am reminded of one of my first loves as a writer, who said when he wanted to read a book, he wrote one. The first edition of my book was launched providentially just as Eritrea had finally beaten the Ethiopians, and the second edition came out after five years after it became a sovereign state. Both editions have almost sold out, so I am writing two further chapters to go into a third edition. Political conditions no longer look as promising in Eritrea, so I expect to be working on this book for the rest of my life!

"The book *Blood, Land, and Sex: Legal and Political Pluralism in Eritrea* was written with my intimate friend and companion, the Italian lawyer Lyda Favali.

It started life when she translated one of my articles so eloquently that I wanted the cooperation to continue. In the course of her doctoral research, she had collected a large number of Italian documents dealing with state, traditional, and religious law in the colony of Eritrea in the nineteenth and twentieth centuries. These documents had been gathering dust for years and were virtually unknown to the non-Italian-reading scholar. We translated them, and during some extended field work found that traditional and religious laws were very much alive in Eritrea. We are very excited to have breathed new life into a very important area and hope it will appeal to lawyers, historians, anthropologists, and political scientists, among other readers.

"Another book, published in 2003, is *Residual Uncertainty: Trying to Avoid Intelligence and Policy Mistakes in the Modern World.* My interest in intelligence and security matters dates back to my army days, when I spent two very formative years in Kenya, dabbling in counterintelligence. During the past twenty-five years most of my income came from teaching classes in international relations and comparative politics at universities. One of my most successful courses was an investigation of the importance of intelligence in the formulation and execution of foreign policy (often with unfortunate consequences). The book ranges wider than the usual discussion of Central Intelligence Agency covert action to deal with the work of our allies and the opposition since the end of World War II. One modest aim is to assist our masters in avoiding more disasters.

"I have a number of other books planned. With my coworker Lyda I hope next to write a broad comparative study of 'Terra Nullius,' the doctrine of empty lands that has been used by settler regimes from the United States, Australia, South Africa, Russia, and Israel, to name only five, to justify their expropriation and exploitation of land from indigenous inhabitants or weaker actors.

"Coming from a working-class background, I am fond of proletarian writers, and Ben Traven has fascinated me for thirty years. While in Australia I wrote a long review of his life and work, and I want to expand this into a full-scale monograph. I will use the format of my Wagner book. Part One will be an examination of the influences on Traven as a man and writer. Part Two will be a full account of his politics through an examination of his life, activity, and writing. Part

Three, which will be the longest, will look at how Traven has influenced the life and work of a number of socialist, nationalist, and anarchist writers, activists, and artists.

"After this I hope to write a short monograph on two of my forebears: Isabella (Bella) Pateman, a significant actress in Edwardian times (and, like so many, reputed to have been a mistress of Edward VII), and Izzy Bon, the well-known Jewish comic of the music halls in the 1930s and 1940s. Finally I trust I will be spared to write a self-indulgent autobiography. I have two alternative titles: *Opera: Its Part in My Downfall* or *I Shouldn't Have Stopped Running.*"

BIOGRAPHICAL AND CRITICAL SOURCES:

PERIODICALS

Opera News, October, 2002, Robert Croan, review of *Chaos and Dancing Star: Wagner's Politics, Wagner's Legacy,* p. 88.

*   *   *

PATTIE, Donald L. 1933-

PERSONAL: Born November 22, 1933, in Volt, MT; son of LuLu Marie Pattie (a schoolteacher; later surname Thompson); married Elke Sibbele; children: Kevin, Chris, Christopher. *Education:* Concordia College, B.A.; Montana State University, M.A.T.; University of Montana, Ph.D.

ADDRESSES: Home—10404 114th Ave., Edmonton, Alberta, Canada T5G 0K9. *E-mail*—donpatt@nait.ab.ca.

CAREER: Northern Alberta Institute of Technology, Edmonton, Alberta, Canada, staff member and participant in expeditions, 1973-2000, lecturer, 1989-99. *Military service:* U.S. Army 22nd Infantry, 1956-61.

WRITINGS:

(With Robert S. Hoffman) *A Guide to Montana Mammals: Identification, Habitat, Distribution, and Abundance,* University of Montana (Missoula, MT), 1968.

Mammals of Alberta, Lone Pine Publishing (Edmonton, Alberta, Canada), 1999.
Rocky Mountain Mammals, Lone Pine Publishing (Edmonton, Alberta, Canada), 2000.
Horticultural Support for Zookeepers, Northern Alberta Institute of Technology (Edmonton, Alberta, Canada), 2000.
Communications for Zookeepers, Northern Alberta Institute of Technology (Edmonton, Alberta, Canada), 2000.
Animal Breeding and Behavior, Northern Alberta Institute of Technology (Edmonton, Alberta, Canada), 2000.
Mammals of British Columbia, Lone Pine Publishing (Edmonton, Alberta, Canada), 2001.

WORK IN PROGRESS: Basic Biology for Zookeepers.

SIDELIGHTS: Donald Pattie told *CA:* "My writing is generated by a perceived educational need. All is nonfiction designed to assist others in learning about the creatures with which we share this world. Thirty years of experience in the polar areas, working in areas related to natural history, have provided the experience on which some of my writing is based."

*   *   *

PECHEFSKY, Rebecca

PERSONAL: Born in New York, NY.; married Erik Ryding. *Education:* Degrees from Columbia University, Queens College, and City University of New York Graduate Center.

ADDRESSES: Home—Brooklyn, NY. *Agent*—c/o Author Mail, Yale University Press, P.O. Box 209040, New Haven, CT 06520-9040. *E-mail*—rpechefsky@aol.com.

CAREER: Harpsichordist, biographer, and writer. Performer at venues such as Weill Hall, Lincoln Center's Bruno Walter Auditorium, Brooklyn Museum, and Donnell Library; participant in Arkansas Music Festival, Aston Magna Academy, and American Festival of Microtonal Music. Brooklyn Baroque, founding member.

WRITINGS:

(With husband, Erik Ryding) *Bruno Walter: A World
    Elsewhere,* Yale University Press (New Haven,
    CT), 2001.

SIDELIGHTS: Rebecca Pechefsky and Erik Ryding,
husband-and-wife authors of *Bruno Walter: A World
Elsewhere,* demonstrate in their biography that "Bruno
Walter was one of the twentieth century's most
important and influential conductors," wrote Scott
Warfield in *Notes.* Pechefsky, a professional harpsichordist, and Ryding, the manager of catalog development at Sony Classical, "have written a detailed, well-
documented biography of a respected musician whose
career as a conductor was long and successful," wrote
George Jochnowitz in *Midstream. Bruno Walter: A
World Elsewhere* is the first biography of the conductor in English and the second in any language, noted
Allan Keiler in *New York Review of Books.* Ryding
and Pechefsky "argue that the absence of any serious
study of Walter's career in English since the publication of his autobiography in 1946 'is extraordinary . . .
given the wealth of primary sources available, which
could furnish material for a study many times the
length of the current volume.' In view of Walter's pre-
eminence as a conductor during the first half of the
twentieth century," Keiler wrote, "one can hardly
disagree with them."

Born Bruno Schlesinger in New York, New York,
Walter began his career as a piano prodigy but turned
to conducting "after attending a concert directed by
Hans von Bulow, and a performance of *Tristan and
Isolde* opened his ears to the music of Richard Wagner
and other progressive composers," Warfield wrote.
Debuting as a conductor in 1894 at the age of
seventeen, Walter led a performance of the light opera
Der Waffenschmied to positive, even enthusiastic
reviews. "A few days later, he conducted an emergency
performance of the same work," Jochnowitz noted.
"The original cast was not available for this unscheduled performance. Two of the singers who were called
in at the last minute hadn't sung their roles in years.
One of the reviews was quite hostile. Then another
newspaper came to Schlesinger's defense. Controversy
may be an even better source of publicity than praise.
At the age of seventeen, Schlesinger had achieved
fame and success."

After serving briefly as composer Gustav Mahler's assistant in Hamburg, Walter accepted a position at the
Stadttheater in Breslau. "The offer came, however,

with the condition that he change his name, because
'Schlesinger' was so common in that region of
Poland," Warfield wrote. Or perhaps, Jochnowitz
noted, "the director of the Stadttheater thought the
name Schlesinger sounded too Jewish. Bruno was not
happy about changing his name, but he gave in to
pressure; he remained Bruno Walter ever since."

"By nature mild-mannered, soft-spoken, benign, Bruno
Walter was not caught up in controversy or touched
by scandal," Keiler remarked, "nor did he have the
kind of charisma or eccentricity that encourages
worshipful followers or cult-like defenders, even
among connoisseurs. In rehearsal Walter would plead
and cajole, holding out with unyielding stubbornness
for what he wanted, but he would never raise his voice
to insult musicians." To Keiler, "it is no surprise that
fellow musicians, singers, and instrumentalists with
whom he collaborated praised him with great
affection."

Pechefsky and Ryding trace Walter's career through
his early career at the Stadttheater through a series of
similar positions, until he went to Vienna in 1901 to
serve as Mahler's second-in-command at the Hofoper.
"When Mahler left for New York in 1907, Walter took
his place," Warfield wrote.

Walter became Generalmusik-direktor in Munich in
1913, and "over the next nine years he contributed to
a glorious musical era in that city's history," Warfield
remarked. He accepted many invitations to guest
conduct, including his American debut in 1923. Walter
was, at first, able to remain outside of Germany's
political problems in the 1920s, but as the Nazis gained
power, Walter was forced from venue to venue until
he finally came to the United States in 1939. There
Walter was associated with the Metropolitan Opera,
the New York Philharmonic, and other major
orchestras. A series of now legendary recordings for
Columbia Records "crowned his career," Warfield
wrote.

Pechefsky and Ryding "describe all of this and much
more in *Bruno Walter: A World Elsewhere,*" Warfield
commented. "In addition to quoting liberally from the
conductor's autobiography, his published letters, and
other obvious sources, these authors are the first to
make use of the Bruno Walter Papers (New York
Public Library for the Performing Arts), a collection

with over seven thousand letters." Warfield noted that "Their dedication to verifying statements and authenticating facts is evident in the mere handful of endnotes that discuss a few unresolved details or conflicting accounts of minor events." Even accounting for extensive citations from primary sources, Pechefsky and Ryding "have woven it all into a highly readable narrative that is accessible to a broad audience."

Alan Hirsch, writing in *Booklist,* noted that Ryding and Pechefsky "illuminate the honorable and ethical man that he was as well as his interpretive approaches as one of the best-loved conductors of the twentieth century." Timothy J. McGee, writing in *Library Journal,* remarked that "The biography is deservedly full of praise for its talented subject, but the authors do not hide his faults or suppress the less favorable reviews or criticisms he received during a brilliant career."

Although he achieved great success as a conductor, Walter's personal life "was filled with disappointment and tragedy," Jochnowiz commented. "The fact that his compositions are unknown was one source of sadness. Another was his lovelife. He remained married to his wife Elsa for almost 44 years until she died in 1945, but loved a different woman, the singer Delia Reinhardt. He was deeply grieved when he had to flee Germany and then Austria after Hitler took over. Worst of all, his younger daughter, Gretel, fell in love with baritone Ezio Pinza and was murdered by her jealous husband, a man named Robert Neppach, who then killed himself."

Despite the strongly positive reaction to *Bruno Walter: A World Elsewhere,* Keiler noted a few flaws in the book. "I have the impression, and it is nothing more, that Ryding and Pechefsky, in their timely and welcome biography, are not as admiring of Walter as they are respectful, even in awe, of his long and impressive career. Indeed, what they give us is not so much a well-rounded biography of Walter the man and artist as a steady, evenhanded chronicle of Walter's career," Keiler wrote. Although they worked directly with primary sources and interviewed more than sixty people who knew or worked with Walter, "these sources do not leave a strong enough mark on the narrative, especially with regard to Walter's private and family life." In addition, Keiler notes that "The authors have painstakingly documented [Walter's] reception by critics and other musicians through the years, but they have not given us the kind of detailed reassess-

ment of his art that one should expect from so serious and dedicated a biography, nor do they provide enough of a guide to his many recordings."

Despite any shortcomings, "Ryding and Pechefsky have written a fine account of Walter's life," Warfield remarked, "and it will be all the more useful if their readers seek out Walter's recordings to hear what prompted its writing."

BIOGRAPHICAL AND CRITICAL SOURCES:

PERIODICALS

Biography, fall, 2001, Michelle Krisel, review of *Bruno Walter: A World Elsewhere,* p. 1008.
Booklist, April 1, 2001, Alan Hirsch, review of *Bruno Walter: A World Elsewhere,* p. 1441.
Library Journal, March 1, 2001, review of *Bruno Walter: A World Elsewhere,* p. 96.
Midstream, July, 2001, George Jochnowitz, review of *Bruno Walter: A World Elsewhere,* p. 44.
New York Review of Books, February 14, 2002, Allan Keiler, review of *Bruno Walter: A World Elsewhere,* p. 35.
Notes, December, 2001, Scott Warfield, review of *Bruno Walter: A World Elsewhere,* pp. 385-386.
Wall Street Journal, August 16, 2001, Harvey Sachs, review of *Bruno Walter: A World Elsewhere,* p. A12.

ONLINE

Houston Chronicle Online, http://www.chron.com (May 8, 2002), Lynwood Abram, review of *Bruno Walter: A World Elsewhere.*
Rebecca Pechefsky, Harpsichordist, http://www. harpsichord.ws.futuresite.register.com/ (May 8, 2002).*

*   *   *

PEIRCE, Penney 1949-

PERSONAL: Born August 11, 1949, in Audubon, NJ; daughter of Millard O. (an engineer and corporate president) and Ruth (an architect and artist; maiden name, Martin) Peirce. *Education:* California Institute of the Arts, B.F.A., 1973.

ADDRESSES: Home—12 Grande Vista, Novato, CA 94947. *E-mail*—pennpeirce@aol.com.

CAREER: Novato, CA, counselor, trainer, 1977—.

WRITINGS:

The Intuitive Way: A Guide to Living from Inner Wisdom, Beyond Words, 1997.
Dreams for Dummies, HungryMinds, 2000.
The Present Moment: A Daybook of Clarity and Intuition, Contemporary Books, 2000.

WORK IN PROGRESS: Research on demystification of dying process; accepting one's destiny; soul mates; numerology; becoming a visionary.

SIDELIGHTS: Penney Peirce told *CA:* "I am a lecturer, counselor, and trainer specializing in intuition development, 'skillful perception,' and dream work. I have worked throughout the United States, Japan, and Europe since 1977 as a coach to business executives, psychologists, scientists, other trainers, and those on a spiritual path. My work synthesizes diverse cultural and spiritual worldviews with many years' experience in business as a corporate art director. I attempt to blend an understanding of natural laws with a designer's skill in structural patterning, and try to present complex ideas in a common sense, easy-to-understand way."

*   *   *

PELIN, Elin 1877-1949

PERSONAL: Born Kimitur Ivanov Stoyanov, July 18, 1877, in Baylovo, Sofia District, Bulgaria; died December 3, 1949, in Sofia, Bulgaria; son of Ivan (an educator) and Tota Stoyanov; married Stefana; children: Elka, Boyan.

CAREER: Teacher in Baylovo, 1896-99; freelance writer, 1899-1903; University Library, 1903; National Library, 1908; staff editor of periodicals *Slunchogled,* 1909, *Veselushka,* 1908-10, *Chavche,* 1913-14, *Svetulka,* 1920-32, *Puteka,* 1933-34, and *Septemyriyche,*

1945-49. Curator of Ivan Vazov Museum, 1926-44. *Wartime service:* Editor of *Voenni izvestiva* ("Military News") and *Otechestvo* ("Fatherland") in World War I.

MEMBER: Union of Writers (chairman, 1940), Bulgarian Academy of Sciences.

WRITINGS:

Razkazi (title means "Stories"), 2 volumes, St. Atanasov (Sofia, Bulgaria), 1904.
Pepel ot tsigarite mi (title means "Ashes from My Cigarettes"), (Sofia, Bulgaria), 1905.
Ot prozoretsa (title means "From the Window"), Ya. Yakimov (Sofia, Bulgaria), 1906.
Kitka za yunaka: Razkazi (title means "A Wreath for the Hero"), (Sofia, Bulgaria), 1917.
Pizho i Pendo: Khumoristichni stikhove, razkazi i dialozi na shopski dialect (title means "Pizho and Pendo"), Knigoizdatelstvo na bulgarskite pisateli, (Sofia, Bulgaria), 1917.
Gori Tilileyski: Prikazki za detsa, naredeni v stikhou, Khemus (Sofia, Bulgaria), 1919.
Sladkodumna baba: Narodni prikazki, Paskalev (Sofia, Bulgaria), 1919.
Svatbata na Chervenushko: Vesela istoriya v stikhove za detsa, Paskalev (Sofia, Bulgaria), 1924.
Tsar Shishko: Prikazki v stikhove, Ministerstvo na narodnata prosveta (Sofia, Bulgaria), 1925.
Pravdata I krivdata: Narodni prikazki, Khemus (Sofia, Bulgaria), 1927.
Pesnichki (title means "Little Songs"), Ministerstvo na narodnoto prosveshtenie (Sofia, Bulgaria), 1927.
Zemya: Povest (title means "Land"), Ministerstvo na narodnoto prosveshtenie (Sofia, Bulgaria), 1928.
Cherni rozi (title means "Black Roses"), T. F. Chipev (Sofia, Bulgaria), 1928.
Tri babi, Khemus (Sofia, Bulgaria), 1930.
Potocheta bistri: Stikhove za detsa (title means "Clear Brooks"), Ministerstvo na narodnoto prosveshtenie (Sofia, Bulgaria), 1931.
Yan Bibiyan: Neveroyatnite priklyucheniya na edno khlape (title means "Yan Bibiyan: The Unbelievable Adventures of One Kid"), Khemus (Sofia, Bulgaria), 1933.
Yan Bibiyan na lunata (title means "Yan Bibiyan on the Moon"), Khemus (Sofia, Bulgaria), 1934.
Az, ti, toy: Mili rodni kartinki (title means "I, You, He"), Khemus (Sofia, Bulgaria), 1936.

Pod manastirskata loza (title means "In the Monastery Arbor"), Khemus (Sofia, Bulgaria), 1936.

Dyadovata rukavichka, Khemus (Sofia, Bulgaria), 1937.

Zlatni lyulki: Stikhove za detsa, Grazhdanin (Sofia, Bulgaria), 1938.

Suchineniya (title means "Works"), 5 volumes, edited by Todor Borov, Khemus (Sofia, Bulgaria), 1938-1942.

Kumcho Vulcho I Kuma Lisa: Stsenirana prikazka, Khemus (Sofia, Bulgaria), 1939.

Shturche-svirche: Veseli stikhcheta za momicheta I momcheta (title means "Little Cricket-Little Musician"), Khemus (Sofia, Bulgaria), 1940.

Geratsite: Povest, Khemus (Sofia, Bulgaria), 1943.

Strashen vulk: Prikazki v stikhove, Khemus (Sofia, Bulgaria), 1944.

Subrani suchneniya, 10 volumes, edited by Todor Borov and others, Bulgarski pisatel (Sofia, Bulgaria), 1958-1959.

EDITIONS IN ENGLISH:

Short Stories, Foreign Languages Press (Sofia, Bulgaria), 1965.

Short Stories, edited by Mercia Macdermot, translated by Maguerite Alexieva, Foreign Languages Press (Sofia, Bulgaria), 1972.

Bag Boys, Sofia Press (Sofia, Bulgaria), 1975.

SIDELIGHTS: Elin Pelin is best known for his jovial short fiction, in which he uses disarmingly simple stories to communicate complex ideas about Bulgarian culture. His charmingly direct fiction resonates with children. Though he also edited several children's journals, his is readable at many levels. His stories of rural life in western Bulgaria, the so-called "shop" where Pelin was raised, earned him the moniker "the bard of rural misery."

Pelin's parents were education advocates in the village of Baylovo in the Sofia district of Bulgaria. Pelin's father, one of the few literate men in Baylovo, ran the local school out of his basement. From his own meager income, Pelin's father even began to develop the town library. But Pelin was more dreamer than student; he alone among the seven Stoyanov siblings failed to finish high school.

After teaching briefly and traveling through Europe, Pelin went to work at the university library. World War I intervened, and Pelin began to edit the military newspapers *Voenni izvestiya* and *Otechestvo.* By 1926 Pelin had resettled in Sofia as director of the Ivan Vazov Museum, which provided support for him, his wife and their two children. In his free time he edited such literary journals as *Slunchogled, Veselushka, Chavche, Svetulka, Puteka* and *Septemvriyche.*

Pelin wrote jokingly of events in western Bulgaria, in a literate, homespun tone. Frequently sidetracked in his attempts to write novels, he wrote mostly short stories. His two-volume collection *Razkazi* comprises forty-one stories and a novelette in which readers have discerned Pelin's first mature work. Lyubomira Parpulova-Gribble wrote in *Dictionary of Literary Biography,* "Typically the quality of Elin Pelin's first mature works is as high as that of the later ones. In the prehistory of nearly every one of his stories—early and late—there is a real event that set his imagination in motion. The action takes place in the country, and the main characters are simple people (peasants, village teachers, priests, and monks). An element of humor or satire is usually present."

For example, in "Napast bozhiya," a local priest and a schoolteacher clash over scientific versus religious perspectives while amid a diphtheria epidemic. In "Proletna izmama," a white spot in the green distance of the fields, which he believes to be a woman's white handkerchief, seduces a monk.

Despite Pelin's soft tone, his works were often politically and philosophically deep. In "Proletna izmama," for example, the monk's fascination with the white spot suggests how the seductions of the outside world are often concocted in one's mind; the story obliquely comments on the foolishness of censorship where evil is in the beholder's eye. In the stories from *Pod manastirskata loza,* too, Pelin uses folk tales and saints' lives to offer a new mode of Christianity that is not edged with violence. By setting conflicts between the religious and the "scientific" life in small villages of the rural shop, Pelin subtly argues for community harmony over ideology.

Pelin, combining humor and folk tales with realism, is a precursor to such Bulgarian writers as Yordan Radichkov. Critics considered Pelin's work delightful to children and suggestive to adults.

BIOGRAPHICAL AND CRITICAL SOURCES:

BOOKS

Dictionary of Literary Biography, Volume 147: *South Slavic Writers before World War II,* Gale (Detroit, MI), 1995, pp. 54-60.
Encyclopedia of World Literature in the Twentieth Century, St. James Press (Detroit, MI), 1999, p. 22.*

*   *   *

POLSON, John 1965-

PERSONAL: Born September 6, 1965, in Sydney, New South Wales, Australia; son of Ron (a jazz singer) and Marie Francis (a piano player) Polson; engaged to Amanda Harding (a casting director).

ADDRESSES: Agent—Robyn Gardiner, RGM Associates, P.O. Box 128, Surry Hills, New South Wales 2010, Australia.

CAREER: Actor, director, producer, and screenwriter. Actor in films, including (as Leo Hawkins) *For Love Alone,* 1986; (as Brian Day) *Call Me Mr. Brown,* 1986; (as Tony) *Tender Hooks,* 1989; (as Cyril) *Candy Regentag* (also known as *Kiss the Night*), 1989; (as Private Jimmy Fenton) *Prisoners of the Sun* (also known as *Blood Oath*), Skouras Pictures, 1990; (as Billy) *Raw Nerve,* 1990; (as Tony) *Dangerous Game,* 1991; (as Greg) *The Sum of Us,* Hallmark Home Entertainment, 1994; (as Frank) *What's Going on, Frank?* 1994; (as Tom) *Sirens,* Columbia Tristar, 1994; (as Stan) *Gino,* 1994; (as Johnny Peterson) *Stitched,* 1995; (as Nick) *Back of Beyond,* Live Entertainment, 1995; (as Jonah) *Idiot Box,* Alta Films, 1996; (as Glenn Sprague) *The Boys* (also known as *Down under Boys*), Axiom Films, 1997; and (as Billy Baird) *Mission: Impossible II,* Paramount, 2000.

Actor in made-for-television movies, including (as Deejay Saxophone) *Shout! The Story of Johnny O'Keefe,* 1985; *More Winners: The Journey* (also known as *Touch the Sun: The Journey*), 1990; and (as Richard Turner) *Kangaroo Palace,* 1997. Actor in television miniseries, including (as Serge) *Vietnam,* 1986; (as George Forster) *Captain James Cook,* 1987; and (as Kevin) *Dadah is Death,* Columbia Broadcasting System (CBS), 1988. Actor in television series *Embassy,* 1990.

Director of films, including *What's Going On, Frank?* 1994; *Siam Sunset,* 1999; *Swimfan,* 2002; and *Fear Itself,* 2003. Founder, Tropicana Film Festival.

AWARDS, HONORS: Critics' Week Audience award, Cannes Film Festival, 1999, for *Siam Sunset.*

WRITINGS:

SCREENPLAYS

(And producer and director) *What's Going on, Frank?* (short film), 1994.
(With Howard Roughan and Michael Douglas; and director) *The up and Comer,* Further Films, forthcoming.

SIDELIGHTS: Australian screenwriter John Polson is best known for directing such hit films as *Swimfan* and for starting the Tropicana Short Film Festival, universally referred to as "Tropfest." Tropfest started in 1993, with two hundred people jammed around one television at the Tropicana Café in Sydney to screen a short film which Polson had directed; ten years later, 150,000 people in six cities across Australia watched sixteen short films, each a maximum of seven minutes long, which were selected from the several hundred films submitted.

Polson is also an actor. Among his more notable roles are Russell Crowe's gay lover in *The Sum of Us* and a helicopter pilot in *Mission: Impossible 2,* which starred Tom Cruise. Polson collaborated with Michael Douglas, who produced *Swimfan,* to write his first feature-length screenplay, for the film *Up and Comer.* Based on the novel by Howard Roughan—who also helped to write the screenplay—*Up and Comer* is a dark comedy about a successful New York lawyer who suddenly finds himself being blackmailed by an old school friend.

Through acting with so many Hollywood stars, Polson made many powerful friends in Hollywood, among them Crowe, Cruise, and Douglas, who have helped

Polson to get his own films made and distributed. (Crowe has also been instrumental in bringing Tropfest up to its current level of size and success.) But, Polson told an interviewer from *Age,* "I don't think of it as networking. I like people. That's me. . . . I'll go to a party and realize that I haven't spoken to anybody who can do anything for me. The other night I went out to dinner with all these big-time film-makers. I ended up speaking to the driver of one of the actors."

BIOGRAPHICAL AND CRITICAL SOURCES:

PERIODICALS

Age (Melbourne, Victoria, Australia), October 8, 2002, "In the Deep End: Director John Polson."

Australian (Sydney, New South Wales, Australia), September 10, 2002, Sophie Tedmanson, "Mr. Tropfest Fans U.S. Box-Office Fire," p. 3; February 24, 2003, Jane Albert and Sophie Tedmanson, "Tropfest Awash with Stars and Crowe Flies In," p. 3.

Daily Telegraph (Surry Hills, New South Wales, Australia), September 14, 2002, Freya Grant, "John Knows More than Great Friends," p. 33.

Film Journal International, October, 2002, Kevin Lally, review of *Swimfan,* p. 86.

Hollywood Reporter, September 6, 2002, David Hunter, review of *Swimfan,* pp. 13-14.

Independent (London, England), November 10, 2000, review of *Siam Sunset,* p. 11.

Los Angeles Times, September 6, 2002, Manohla Dargis, review of *Swimfan,* p. F11.

Maclean's, April 3, 1995, Brian D. Johnson, review of *The Sum of Us,* p. 67.

New York Times, October 28, 1988, John J. O'Connor, review of *Dadah Is Death,* pp. 22, C34; March 8, 1995, Janet Maslin, review of *The Sum of Us,* pp. B4, C19; September 6, 2002, Stephen Holden, review of *Swimfan,* pp. B11, E13; September 13, 2002, Peter M. Nichols, review of *Swimfan,* pp. B8, E8.

People, October 31, 1988, Jeff Jarvis, review of *Dadah Is Dead,* pp. 19-20; August 5, 1991, Ralph Novak, review of *Prisoners of the Sun,* pp. 16-17; March 27, 1995, Joanne Kaufman, review of *The Sum of Us,* p. 17.

San Francisco Chronicle, September 9, 2002, Jonathan Curiel, review of *Swimfan,* p. D2.

Sight and Sound, November, 1998, Richard Falcon, review of *The Boys,* p. 43; December, 2000, Claire Monk, review of *Siam Sunset,* pp. 54-55.

Sunday Mail (Brisbane, Australia), September 22, 2002, Paul Fischer, "In the Swim," p. 68.

Sun-Herald (Sydney, New South Wales, Australia), September 16, 2002, John Polson, "My Week as the World's Hottest Film Director."

Sydney Morning Herald (Sydney, New South Wales, Australia), August 15, 2002, Garry Maddox, "Polson Sticks to Straw Dogs Formula"; August 18, 2002, Jennifer Hansen, "Big Pond Splash," p. 106.

Time International, May 11, 1998, review of *Darkness of the Soul,* p. 64.

Variety, February 23, 1998, David Stratton, review of *The Boys,* pp. 78-79.

Who Weekly, February, 2002, Craig Henderson, interview with Polson.

ONLINE

BigPond, http://www.bigpond.com/ (March 11, 2003), "Telestra BigPond Chat: John Polson."

*   *   *

POWELL, Kenneth 1947-

PERSONAL: Born 1947.

ADDRESSES: Office—c/o Twentieth Century Society, 70 Cowcross Street, London EC1M 6E3, England. *Agent*—c/o Author Mail, Merrell Publishers Ltd., 42 Southwark St., London SE1 1UN, England.

CAREER: Architecture critic, journalist, and author. *Daily Telegraph,* architecture correspondent.

MEMBER: Twentieth Century Society.

AWARDS, HONORS: Royal Institute of British Architects, honorary fellow.

WRITINGS:

The Fall of Zion: Northern Chapel Architecture and its Future (photography by Keith Parkinson), Save Britain's Heritage (London, England), 1980.

(With Celia de la Hay) *Churches: A Question of Conversion,* Save Britain's Heritage (London, England), 1987.

(Editor) *London,* Academy Editions (London, England) 1993.

Stansted: Norman Foster and the Architecture of Flight, Fourth Estate (London, England), 1992.

Lloyd's Building: Richard Rogers Partnership, Phaidon Press (London, England), 1994.

Edward Cullinan Architects, Academy Editions (London, England), 1995.

Grand Central Terminal: Warren and Wetmore, Phaidon Press (London, England), 1996.

(Author of introduction) *John Lyall, Contexts and Catalysts,* Arca Edizioni (Milan, Italy), 1999.

Architecture Reborn: Converting Old Buildings for New Uses, Rizzoli (New York, NY), 1999.

Richard Rogers Complete Works, Phaidon Press (London, England), Volume 1, 1999, Volume 2, 2001.

The Jubilee Line Extension, foreword by Roland Paoletti, Laurence King Publishing (London, England), 2000.

City Transformed: Urban Architecture at the Beginning of the Twenty-first Century, Laurence King (London, England), 2000.

Modern House Today, photographs by Nick Dawe, Black Dog (London, England), 2001.

John McAslan, Thames & Hudson (London, England), 2000.

New London Architecture, Merrell Publishers (London, England), 2001.

Will Alsop, Laurence King (London, England), 2001.

(Editor) *Collaborations: The Architecture of Ahrends, Burton, and Koralek,* Birkhauser Architectural, 2002.

New Architecture in Britain, Merrell Publishers (London, England), 2003.

Contributor to *The New Office,* by Francis Duffy, Conrad Octopus (London, England), 1997, and *The National Portrait Gallery: An Architectural History,* with Graham Hulme, Brian Buchanan, photographs by John Goto.

SIDELIGHTS: Kenneth Powell is an architecture critic and journalist. His many books on English architecture include studies of England's most prominent architects, Norman Foster and Richard Rogers. His works range from in-depth analyses of major structures in London, considered by many to be the architectural capital of the world, to new uses for old structures, to international urban design precepts, to the impact of modern practitioners on the house of the twenty-first century.

Peter Kaufman, in *Library Journal,* noted that Powell's introduction in *New London Architecture* is targeted primarily to an English, and particularly London, audience, which places it "out of the ken of modern American readers." The book is a glossy pictorial survey of modern architecture in London, both recent and proposed, and covers a diverse range of structures, including bridges, subway stations, entertainment centers, and museums. It combines critical texts, photographs, and plans of more than one hundred projects combining to create a radical renaissance of this urban landscape.

Architecture Reborn: Converting Old Buildings for New Uses considers forty-four conversion projects in various locations, primarily in North America, Eastern and Western Europe, Australia, and Japan. Organized into three broad categories—museums, living and working, and leisure and learning—the review includes important projects by internationally renowned designers. Powell's documentation includes descriptive essays, floor plans, what was salvageable and what was not, and project credits. D. P. Doordan's review in *Choice* praised Powell's work here, considering the lack of a bibliography to be its only drawback.

Paul Glassman, reviewing *City Transformed: Urban Architecture at the Beginning of the Twenty-first Century,* noted that Powell believes that, to be successful, city architecture requires solid urban-design precepts. Glassman wrote: "Powell . . . has assembled an international selection of 25 urban design projects from the 1990s. Summarizing urban design over the last century, the introductory essay includes stimulating observations amid a few puzzling generalizations on the political, economic, and aesthetic dimensions of the modern city." The book's four major sections address issues of healing, extending, motion, and culture, providing several examples of each.

In a 228-page paperback, *Modern House Today,* Powell combines documentary records and photographs as he discusses the effects of modern architects such as Lubetkin, Gropius, Fry, and Mendelsohn on the modern house. At the other end of the spectrum is a two-volume set, *Richard Rogers, Complete Works.*

Volume 1 of this set was described by Jain Borden in *Building Design* as "a monumental affair. It hits the table with a massive thud factor . . . an authoritative guide to every building and project of note from 1961 to 1988." This is a comprehensive overview of major projects in chronological order, aided by illustrations and four essays from Powell. Commenting on the essays, Borden wrote: "Powell is particularly good on biographic detail. . . . Powell is careful to go beyond the surface of events, identifying the role of less well known characters. . . . The book is full of these kinds of details, and very nice they are too."

BIOGRAPHICAL AND CRITICAL SOURCES:

PERIODICALS

Building Design, November 12, 1999, Jain Borden, review of *Richard Rogers, Complete Works,* Volume 1, p. 20.
Choice, November, 1999, D. P. Doordan, review of *Architecture Reborn: Converting Old Buildings for New Uses,* p. 527.
Design, July, 1992, Tim Ostler, review of *Stansted: Normal Foster and the Architecture of Flight,* p. 53.
Interiors, June, 1999, Eve M. Kahn, review of *Architecture Reborn,* p. 124.
Library Journal, January 1, 2002, Paul Glassman, review of *City Transformed: Urban Architecture at the Beginning of the Twenty-first Century,* p. 100; April 1, 2002, Peter Kaufman, review of *New London Architecture,* p. 104.*

*   *   *

PRATT, William K. 1937-

PERSONAL: Born June 24, 1937, in Kankakee, IL; son of Kenneth Alvin and Helen Louise Pratt; married; wife's name Barbara (marriage ended); married; second wife's name Rochelle S.; children: Kathleen Ann, Carolyn Lee Pratt Konecki, Christine Maree Pratt Jorgenson, Michael Thomas. *Ethnicity:* "White." *Education:* Bradley University, B.S., 1959; University of Southern California, M.S.E.E., 1961, Ph.D., 1965. *Politics:* Republican. *Religion:* Roman Catholic.

ADDRESSES: Home—8 Almendra Lane, Los Altos, CA 94022. *Office*—Photon Dynamics, Inc., 17 Great Oaks Blvd., San Jose, CA 95119; fax: 650-948-5757. *E-mail*—pratt@pixelsoft.com.

CAREER: Hughes Aircraft Co., member of technical staff, 1959-65; University of Southern California, Los Angeles, professor of electrical engineering, 1965-79, and founder and director of Image Processing Institute; Compression Labs, Inc., senior vice president, 1979-81; Vicom Systems, Inc., founder, chair, chief executive officer, and chief technical officer, 1981-88; Sun Microsystems, Inc., director of multimedia and imaging technology, 1988-94; Pixelsoft, Inc., founder and president, 1993—. Photon Dynamics, Inc., chief technical officer, 1996—; Image Enhancement Systems, Inc., member of technology advisory board, 1997; holder of patents for television coder, computer simulator, facsimile coder, image coder, two-dimensional convolution processor, and flat-panel defect detector; consultant to numerous corporations, including Aerojet-General, Bendix, Ford Aerospace, International Business Machines Corp., and Silicon Graphics. Massachusetts Institute of Technology, visiting assistant professor, 1969; University of Paris, visiting scientist and visiting professor, 1977-78.

MEMBER: Institute of Electrical and Electronic Engineers (senior member).

AWARDS, HONORS: Guggenheim fellow in France, 1977; named Albert Rose Electronic Imager of the Year, 1988.

WRITINGS:

Laser Communication Systems, Wiley Publishing Group (New York, NY), 1969.
Digital Image Processing, Wiley Publishing Group (New York, NY), 1969, 3rd edition, 2001.
(Editor) *Image Transmission Techniques,* Academic Press (New York, NY), 1979.
(Editor with Ronald B. Arps) *Image Processing and Interchange: Implementation and Systems* (conference proceedings), Society for Imaging Science and Technology (Bellingham, WA), 1992.
PIKS Foundation C Programmer's Guide, Prentice-Hall (Englewood Cliffs, NJ), 1995.
XIL: An Imaging Foundation Library, Manning Publications (Englewood Cliffs, NJ), 1996.

Contributor to books, including *Computer Techniques in Image Processing,* Academic Press (New York, NY), 1970; contributor of numerous articles to periodicals.

SIDELIGHTS: William K. Pratt told *CA:* "I have worked in two technological areas: laser communications and digital image processing. In the field of laser communications, I developed the basic concepts of laser modulation and detection processes. I was responsible for the discovery of the transform image coding concept, which is the basis of the JPEG and MPEG image coding standards. I also invented a facsimile coding system and a means of high-speed image convolution.

"I am the chief technology officer for software at Photon Dynamics, Inc., a leading supplier of image processing equipment for industrial inspection applications in the display industry. I am also the founder of PixelSoft, Inc., which has developed and marketed image processing software based upon the International Standards Organization Programmer's Imaging Kernel System (PIKS) application program interface."

*   *   *

PRIDGEN, Allen 1943-

PERSONAL: Born October 16, 1943, in Portsmouth, VA; son of Rufus Allen and Lois (a postal employee; later surname, Barnes) Pridgen; married May 28, 1983; wife's name Linda; children: Nathaniel. *Ethnicity:* "Caucasian." *Education:* University of North Carolina—Chapel Hill, A.B., 1965; East Carolina University, M.A., 1968; Florida State University, Ph.D., 1975. *Religion:* Roman Catholic.

ADDRESSES: Home—208 Haldane Dr., Southern Pines, NC 28387-7512. *E-mail*—apridgen@pinehurst.net.

CAREER: Richard Bland College—William and Mary, Petersburg, VA, assistant professor of English, 1971-76; Chowan College, Murfreesboro, NC, professor of English, 1978-87; Virginia Intermont College, Bristol, professor of English and program coordinator, 1987-2001; retired. Methodist College, Fayetteville, NC, assistant professor, 1978; National Humanities Center, visitor, 1993, 1995; University of North Carolina—Chapel Hill, visiting scholar, 1996, 1997, 1998. Southern Humanities Council, member.

MEMBER: American Literature Association, College English Association, Society for the Study of Southern Literature, Christianity and Literature Association, South Atlantic Modern Language Association.

AWARDS, HONORS: Appalachian College Association Mellon grant, 1994, Mellon fellow, 1996, 1997, 1998.

WRITINGS:

Walker Percy's Sacramental Landscapes: The Search in the Desert, Susquehanna University Press (Susquehanna, PA), 2001.

Contributor of articles and reviews to periodicals, including *Mississippi Quarterly, Renascence, Virginian-Pilot,* and *Southern Quarterly.*

WORK IN PROGRESS: Research on Walker Percy and James Lee Burke.

*   *   *

PUGH, Geoff(rey) 1953-

PERSONAL: Born May 12, 1953, in Exeter, England. *Education:* London University, M.Sc. (economics); Kent University, Ph.D. *Religion:* Christian.

ADDRESSES: Home—9 Richmond Rd., Wakefield WF1 3LA, England. *E-mail*—gpugh@rmond.demon.co.uk.

CAREER: Staffordshire University, Stafford, England, principal lecturer in economics, 1993—. Birmingham University, Institute for German Studies, external research associate.

WRITINGS:

(Editor with Chris Cook) *Sources in European History,* Volume I: *The European Left,* Volume II: *Diplomacy and International Affairs,* Volume III: *War and Resistance,* Facts on File (New York, NY), 1987-1991.

(With Thomas Lange) *The Economics of German Unification: An Introduction,* Edward Elgar (Northampton, MA), 1998.

Contributor to periodicals, including *International Journal of Manpower* and *Financial Management.*

WORK IN PROGRESS: The German Social Market Economy: Culture and Performance.

*   *   *

PULLEN, John James 1913-2003

OBITUARY NOTICE—See index for *CA* sketch: Born December 17, 1913, in Amity, ME; died February 25, 2003, in Brunswick, ME. Journalist, advertising executive, and author. Pullen is best remembered for his historical writings about Union Army General Joshua Chamberlain. After earning a bachelor's degree from Colby College in 1935, he worked as a reporter for the *Daily Kennebec Journal* in Maine and then for Baker Advertising in Hartford, Connecticut. When World War II began, he enlisted in the army and became an artillery captain. After the war, he returned to advertising, this time with N. W. Ayer & Son in Philadelphia, where he was promoted to vice president and executive director of the copy department in 1958. He left advertising in 1965 to focus on his writing career. Pullen's first published book, *The Twentieth Maine: A Volunteer Regiment in the Civil War* (1957), brought the all-but-forgotten story of Joshua Chamberlain and his heroic acts at the Battle of Gettysburg back to public attention; he wrote about Chamberlain again in *Joshua Chamberlain: A Hero's Life and Legacy* (1999). Pullen was also the author of several other books on American history and biography, including *A Shower of Stars: The Medal of Honor and the 27th Maine* (1966) and *Comic Relief: The Life and Laughter of Artemus Ward, 1834-1867* (1983).

OBITUARIES AND OTHER SOURCES:

PERIODICALS

Boston Globe, February 27, 2003, p. C14.
Los Angeles Times, March 1, 2003, p. B21.

*   *   *

PUSHKIN, Dave
See PUSHKIN, David B.

PUSHKIN, David B. 1963-
(Dave Pushkin)

PERSONAL: Born March 21, 1963, in New York, NY. *Education:* Excelsior College, B.S., 1984; University of South Florida, M.A., 1986; Pennsylvania State University, Ph.D., 1995.

ADDRESSES: Home—204 Tenth St., No. 114, Jersey City, NJ 07302. *Office*—Department of Chemistry and Physical Science, Pace University, New York, NY 10038. *E-mail*—dpushkin@pace.edu.

CAREER: Educator and chemist. E-Z-EM, Inc., Westbury, NJ, quality control chemist, 1983-84; Hillsborough Community College, Tampa, FL, teacher of chemistry and algebra and tutor at Leaning Center, 1985; teacher of science and algebra at a private high school in Tampa-Davis Island, FL, 1985-86, and a Roman Catholic high school in St. Petersburg, FL, 1987-88; Ohio State University, Columbus, visiting fellow in mathematics, 1988; James A. Haley Veterans Administration Hospital, Tampa, research chemist, 1988-89; physics and chemistry teacher at a high school in Bradenton, FL, 1989-93; Pennsylvania State University, University Park, academic fellow and instructor in physics and science education, 1993-95; College Misericordia, Dallas, PA, visiting assistant professor of physics, 1995-96; Montclair State University, Upper Montclair, NJ, assistant professor of chemistry and science education, 1996-98; Wilmington College of Delaware, New Castle, assistant professor of educational research, 1999-2001; Pace University, New York, NY, adjunct assistant professor, 2002—. St. Petersburg Junior College, adjunct instructor, 1987-88; University of Medicine and Dentistry of New Jersey, adjunct instructor, 1999; William Paterson University, visiting assistant professor, 1999; Brooklyn College of the City University of New York, adjunct assistant professor, 1999, 2002—; Saint Leo University, adjunct professor, 2002—; guest lecturer at other institutions, including King's College, London, American University, University of Massachusetts—Boston, McGill University, Wayne State University, University of Calgary, Memorial University of Newfoundland, and University of Moncton. City of Bradenton, wastewater consultant to Department of Public Works, 1990-91.

MEMBER: International Cultural Research Network, European Science Education Research Association, European Association for Research on Learning and

Instruction, American Chemical Society, National Association for Research in Science Teaching, National Science Teachers Association, American Educational Research Association, Association for the Education of Teachers in Science, Society of College Science Teachers, Association for the Study of Higher Education.

WRITINGS:

(Under name Dave Pushkin) *Teacher Training: A Reference Handbook,* American Bibliographic Center-Clio Press (Santa Barbara, CA), 2001.

Contributor to books, including *Unauthorized Methods: Strategies for Critical Teaching,* edited by J. Kincheloe and S. Steinberg, Routledge (New York, NY), 1998; *The Post-Formal Reader: Cognition and Education,* edited by J. Kincheloe, S. Steinberg, and P. H. Hinchey, Falmer Press (New York, NY), 1999; *Standards and Schooling in the United States: An Encyclopedia,* edited by J. L. Kincheloe and D. Weil, American Bibliographical Center-Clio Press (Santa Barbara, CA), 2001; and *(Post) Modern Science*

(Education): Propositions and Alternative Paths, edited by J. Weaver, M. Morris, and P. Appelbaum, Peter Lang Publishers (New York, NY), 2001. Contributor to academic journals, including *Science Education, Journal of Chemical Education, Association of Women in Science, Physics Essays, Physics Teacher, Journal of Chemical Education,* and *Journal of Research in Science Teaching.* Member of editorial committee, *Journal of College Science Teaching;* member of editorial board, *History of Intellectual Culture.*

WORK IN PROGRESS: You Tell Me It's the Institution . . . You Better Free Your Mind Instead: Challenging the Paradigm of Stasis (tentative title), for Kluwer; *The Threat of Thinking: Challenging the Paradigm of Punitive Pedagogy* (tentative title), for Kluwer; *The "Dime a Dozen" Teacher: Systematic Devaluation of Educators; Dial "M" for Mental Mediocrity: Critical Thinking in Reverse; Chemistry and Physics for the Critical Mind; Our Concerns, Our Questions: A Collection of Essays of Educators' Experiences;* research on critical thinking in chemistry and physics at the university level.

R

REAVES, Sam 1954-
(Dominic Martell)

PERSONAL: Born 1954; married; children: one daughter.

ADDRESSES: Agent—c/o Author Mail, Carroll & Graf, 19 West 21st Street New York, NY 10010.

CAREER: Mystery writer, teacher, and translator.

WRITINGS:

A Long, Cold Fall, Putnam (New York, NY), 1991.
Fear Will Do It, Putnam (New York, NY), 1992.
Bury It Deep, Putnam (New York, NY), 1993.
Get What's Coming, Putnam (New York, NY), 1995.
Dooley's Back, Carroll & Graf (New York, NY), 2002.

AS DOMINIC MARTELL

Lying, Crying Dying, Carroll & Graf (New York, NY), 2002.
The Republic of the Night, Carroll & Graf (New York, NY), 2002.

SIDELIGHTS: Although he has traveled throughout Latin America and the Middle East and lived for a time in Europe, Sam Reaves has spent most of his life in and around Chicago, where his "Cooper MacLeish" mysteries are set. Introduced in *A Long, Cold Fall,* "a solid first novel for those who like their tough guys philosophical," in the words of a *Kirkus Reviews* contributor, MacLeish is a Vietnam vet and cabdriver who must rescue the teenage son of an old flame after she apparently commits suicide. "The book's smashing start . . . establishes character and milieu with whiplash speed," according to *Los Angeles Times* reviewer Charles Champlin, and before long MacLeish is caught up in a dangerous world trying to protect a sometimes sullen teenager, who may well be his own son, from determined and vicious killers. "Cooper doesn't have the stomach for violence. He just can't help attracting it. And that's about as good a definition of a hero as you get in this genre," concluded *New York Times* reviewer Marilyn Stasio.

Cooper MacLeish returns in *Fear Will Do It,* this time with a new girlfriend, Diana, who has a few secrets she has kept from MacLeish. When Tommy, an old acquaintance of hers, uses her in a dangerous plot to blackmail a local porn king, MacLeish, "an alluring blend of kinetic force and intellectual hesitation," according to *Booklist* reviewer Peter Robinson, once again finds himself drawn into a deadly game. Pretty soon, Tommy is dead, and Diana is in mortal peril. "Intricate plotting, careful characterization, and well-drawn surroundings add to the excitement," noted *Library Journal* reviewer Rex Klett. "Cooper manages to be both scared and tough. Excellent escapist fare," wrote a *Kirkus Reviews* contributor. According to a *Publishers Weekly* reviewer, "Reaves develops a story that is far more satisfying than its seamy, ordinary ingredients would indicate."

In *Bury It Deep,* friend and reporter Mel Moreland lands MacLeish in the middle of big trouble, this time in the form of thuggish teamsters and corrupt politicos. When Mel ignores a macabre warning—the murder of his cat—to stay away from a story he's pursuing, he enlists the help of a reluctant Cooper. Soon the two of them are pursuing leads and reluctant witnesses through the back alleys of Chicago, "the perfect setting for plot credibility," in the words of *Library Journal* reviewer Rex Klett. An assortment of high-priced lawyers, powerbrokers, and a mayoral candidate round out the unsavory cast of characters. "With so many sleazeballs running around loose, you'll be positively relieved by the bloody final holocaust," a *Kirkus Reviews* contributor concluded.

"Cooper's fourth adventure is as smooth and tough as all the others," wrote a *Kirkus Reviews* contributor about *Get What's Coming.* "The man's doing his bit to make the streets of Chicago a little safer—and a lot more interesting." This time out, MacLeish is married and working as a driver for a real-estate tycoon named Regis Swanson. It is a relatively safe job, despite Swanson's ties to some union heavies, at least until a drug dealer steals a million dollars from his employers, and throws the blame on Swanson's son Nate. When Nate is murdered, Cooper decides to help his employer catch the killers, and he uncovers a tangled layer of corruption. "This tightly plotted tale offers sizzling dialogue," according to *Booklist* reviewer Wes Lukowsky. A *Publishers Weekly* reviewer called it the "best of Reaves's strong series about Chicago existential scholar-cabbie Cooper MacLeish."

In 2002 Reaves introduced a new hero to the streets of Chicago in *Dooley's Back.* Frank Dooley is a police officer who fled Chicago after killing the man who raped and murdered his wife, but got off on a technicality. When he returns, he finds that his victim's case remains unsolved and his sympathetic former colleagues seem content to leave it that way. Soon, he finds himself on the track of another killer, this time a mobster named Spanos who has murdered Dooley's old partner, Roy Ferguson. Determined to get the killer, but without repeating his previous vigilantism, Dooley sets out to trap Spanos into a confession that will put him away. For a *Publishers Weekly* reviewer, "neither alienated ex-copper Frank Dooley nor his adventures matches Reaves's previous efforts." A *Kirkus Reviews* contributor found that "Canny noirist Reaves . . . keeps the action lean and mean until that far-fetched, impossibly elaborate sting turns it soft and fuzzy at the end." *Deadly Pleasures* online reviewer

Russ Isabella was considerably more impressed: "Lean and mean prose, a story fueled by adrenaline and desperation to set things right, fine writing, perfect pacing-this one has everything to feed the need for the rush of a great read."

BIOGRAPHICAL AND CRITICAL SOURCES:

PERIODICALS

Booklist, February 15, 1992, Peter Robinson, review of *Fear Will Do It,* p. 1091; March 15, 1995, Wes Lukowsky, review of *Get What's Coming,* p. 1312.
Kirkus Reviews, December 1, 1990, review of *A Long, Cold Fall,* p. 1643; January 15, 1992, review of *Fear Will Do It,* p. 80; June 15, 1993, review of *Bury It Deep,* p. 755; March 15, 1995, review of *Get What's Coming,* p. 347; August 1, 2002, review of *Dooley's Back,* p. 1082.
Library Journal, March 1, 1992, Rex Klett, review of *Fear Will Do It,* p. 123; August, 1993, Rex Klett, review of *Bury It Deep,* p. 158.
Los Angeles Times, February 10, 1991, Charles Champlin, review of *A Long, Cold Fall,* p. 9.
New York Times, February 24, 1991, Marilyn Stasio, review of *A Long, Cold Fall,* p. 31.
Publishers Weekly, January 27, 1992, review of *Fear Will Do It,* p. 91; February 27, 1995, review of *Get What's Coming,* p. 89; August 5, 2002, review of *Dooley's Back,* p. 55.

ONLINE

Deadly Pleasures Online, http://www.deadlypleasures. com/ (December 10, 2002), Russ Isabella, review of *Dooley's Back.*

*   *   *

RHEIMS, Maurice 1910-2003

OBITUARY NOTICE—See index for *CA* sketch: Born January 4, 1910, in Versailles, France; died March 6, 2003, in Paris, France. Auctioneer and author. Rheims was a well-known fine-art auctioneer in France who also wrote books about art, as well as fiction. Educated at the Louvre and the Sorbonne, he began dealing in fine art as a teenager and had steady business as an auctioneer in Paris from 1935 to 1972, a career interrupted only by World War II. Because he was Jewish, he was imprisoned by the Nazis and scheduled to be executed. Intervention from an influential friend of his father's allowed Rheims to escape this fate, however, and he joined the French Resistance. Later, he fled to Algiers, where he fought with a regiment of Free French paratroopers; his war service earned him a Croix de Guerre and Médaille de la Résistance. After the war, he returned to his auctioning career, becoming particularly expert at the art of the period from 1880 to 1910. Later in his life, he was a vice president of the administrative council of the National Library, beginning in 1983, and president of the prix Vasari, beginning in 1986, as well as serving as president of the Cultural Development Fund for the Foundation of France. Rheims published over twenty nonfiction works during his career, including several books on art such as *L'objet 1900* (1964) and *La vie d'artist* (1970), the latter of which received the 1970 prix Broquette-Gonin from the Académie Française. He also completed eight works of fiction, one of which, *Le saint-office* (1983), won a grand prize for black humor. Rheims was also praised for his *Dictionnaire des mots sauvages* (1969), a collection of arcane and bizarre words. For his accomplishments, Rheims was made a member of the Académie Française in 1976 and was named a commander of the French Legion of Honor in 1979.

OBITUARIES AND OTHER SOURCES:

PERIODICALS

Independent (London, England), March 10, 2003, p. 16.

*   *   *

ROLEFF, Tamara L. 1959-

PERSONAL: Born November 27, 1959, in Council Bluffs, IA; daughter of Richard A. Fahey (an engineer) and Linda E. Schoenrock (an attorney); married Keith W. Roleff (a U.S. Marine Corps officer), March 17, 1984. *Education:* Iowa State University, B.S., 1981. *Hobbies and other interests:* Golden retrievers, travel.

ADDRESSES: Office—Greenhaven Press, 10911 Technology Place, San Diego, CA 92127. *E-mail*—orchids59@hotmail.com.

CAREER: Author and editor. Worked as a newspaper "Lifestyles" editor in New Bern, NC, 1991-93; Greenhaven Press, San Diego, CA, book editor, 1995—; nonfiction author.

AWARDS, HONORS: Invited to enter *Inner City Poverty* for 2002 Harry Chapin Media Award, sponsored by World Hunger Year.

WRITINGS:

Hate Groups ("Opposing Viewpoints Digest" series), Greenhaven Press (San Diego, CA), 2001.

EDITOR

The Atom Bomb ("Turning Points in World History" series), Greenhaven Press (San Diego, CA), 2000.
Sex ("Teen Decisions" series), Greenhaven Press (San Diego, CA), 2001.
America under Attack: Primary Sources, Lucent (San Diego, CA), 2002.
Inner-City Poverty ("Contemporary Issues Companion" series), Greenhaven Press (San Diego, CA), 2003.

EDITOR; "OPPOSING VIEWPOINTS" SERIES

The Homeless, Greenhaven Press (San Diego, CA), 1995.
The Legal System, Greenhaven Press (San Diego, CA), 1996.
Abortion, revised edition, Greenhaven Press (San Diego, CA), 1997.
(With others) *Gun Control,* Greenhaven Press (San Diego, CA), 1997.
(With others) *Global Warming,* Greenhaven Press (San Diego, CA), 1997.
Sexual Violence, Greenhaven Press (San Diego, CA), 1997.
AIDS, Greenhaven Press (San Diego, CA), 1997, third edition, 2003.

Biomedical Ethics, Greenhaven Press (San Diego, CA), 1998.

Suicide, Greenhaven Press (San Diego, CA), 1998.

Tobacco and Smoking, Greenhaven Press (San Diego, CA), 1998.

Immigration, Greenhaven Press (San Diego, CA), 1998, second edition, 2003.

War, Greenhaven Press (San Diego, CA), 1999.

(With others) *Hate Groups,* Greenhaven Press (San Diego, CA), 1999.

Civil Liberties, Greenhaven Press (San Diego, CA), 1999.

Pollution, Greenhaven Press (San Diego, CA), 2000.

Mental Illness, Greenhaven Press (San Diego, CA), 2000.

Crime and Criminals, Greenhaven Press (San Diego, CA), 2000.

Domestic Violence, Greenhaven Press (San Diego, CA), 2000.

Teen Sexuality, Greenhaven Press (San Diego, CA), 2001.

Censorship, Greenhaven Press (San Diego, CA), 2002.

(With others) *Extremist Groups,* Greenhaven Press (San Diego, CA), 2001.

Criminal Justice, Greenhaven Press (San Diego, CA), 2002.

EDITOR; "HISTORY FIRSTHAND" SERIES

The Vietnam War, Greenhaven Press (San Diego, CA), 2002.

The Holocaust: Death Camps, Greenhaven Press (San Diego, CA), 2002.

The World Trade Center, Greenhaven Press (San Diego, CA), 2003.

The American Frontier, Greenhaven Press (San Diego, CA), 2003.

Oklahoma City Bombing, Greenhaven Press (San Diego, CA), forthcoming.

EDITOR; "AT ISSUE" SERIES

Business Ethics, Greenhaven Press (San Diego, CA), 1996.

Gay Marriage, Greenhaven Press (San Diego, CA), 1998.

Sex Education, Greenhaven Press (San Diego, CA), 1999.

Guns and Crime, Greenhaven Press (San Diego, CA), 2000.

Teen Suicide, Greenhaven Press (San Diego, CA), 2000.

Teen Sex, Greenhaven Press (San Diego, CA), 2001.

Satanism, Greenhaven Press (San Diego, CA), 2001.

What Encourages Gang Behavior? Greenhaven Press (San Diego, CA), 2002.

Police Corruption, Greenhaven Press (San Diego, CA), 2003.

EDITOR; "CURRENT CONTROVERSIES" SERIES

Genetics and Intelligence, Greenhaven Press (San Diego, CA), 1996.

Gay Rights, Greenhaven Press (San Diego, CA), 1997.

(With others) *Marriage and Divorce,* Greenhaven Press (San Diego, CA), 1997.

Native American Rights, Greenhaven Press (San Diego, CA), 1998.

The Rights of Animals, Greenhaven Press (San Diego, CA), 1999.

Police Brutality, Greenhaven Press (San Diego, CA), 1999.

Hate Crimes, Greenhaven Press (San Diego, CA), 2001.

EDITOR; "FACT OR FICTION" SERIES

Alien Abductions, Greenhaven Press (San Diego, CA), 2003.

Black Magic and Witches, Greenhaven Press (San Diego, CA), 2003.

Psychics, Greenhaven Press (San Diego, CA), 2003.

EDITOR; "CONTEMPORARY ISSUES COMPANION" SERIES

Extraterrestrial Life, Greenhaven Press (San Diego, CA), 2001.

Inner-City Poverty, Greenhaven Press (San Diego, CA), 2003.

WORK IN PROGRESS: War on Drugs ("Opposing Viewpoints" series).

SIDELIGHTS: Tamara L. Roleff is a book editor and author who specializes in nonfiction titles. In her job for Greenhaven Press, she has contributed edited titles to several book series, among them Greenhaven's "Opposing Viewpoints," "History Firsthand," and "Current Controversies," which has allowed Roleff to research a number of hotly debated social issues. In her books for the "Current Controversies" series, for instance, she has edited the titles *Gay Rights, Native-American Rights,* and *Genetics and Intelligence.* Praising *Gay Rights* in her *School Library Journal* review, Sue A. Norkeliunas cited both the "well-selected articles" and "extensive list" of sources cited for students to contact, and praised the book as "an ideal research tool for short assignments" due to its "balanced coverage of emotional topics."

Most of Roleff's books are contained in the "Opposing Viewpoints" books, which *Kliatt* reviewer Claire Rosser praised as an "excellent" series that provides a "wonderful" opportunity for high school students to "improve . . . critical thinking skills." For titles such as *Suicide, Global Warming, Sex Education,* and *Civil Liberties,* Roleff assembles a number of essays representing a diverse selection of views on the topic, as well as illustrations, a list of relevant organizations, and bibliographies for use in more in-depth study. In *Suicide,* an extensively revised version of a 1992 work, Roleff includes Pope John Paul II, physician Thomas Quill, and others, who debate issues such as whether suicide is a personal right, the reason for escalating suicide among adolescents, and the legalities of assisted suicide. *Hate Groups* includes essays authored by U.S. Senator Orin Hatch, David Kopel, U.S. Supreme Court Justice Thomas Scalia, and former president Bill Clinton that present several sides of the freedom-of-speech issues surrounding the treatment of hate crimes and the social effects of hate-group activity, providing both high school and college students with "excellent source material for debates or class discussion." Background material is presented by Roleff in what *Booklist* contributor Randy Meyer characterized as a "crisp, journalistic" style that "combines anecdotes and facts," as well as documents such as the Bill of Rights, relevant legislation, and actual hate-group propaganda pieces. In *Global Warming* maps and charts are included, along with contradictory views regarding whether the Earth's ecosystem is being threatened by industrialization and the destruction of the Amazonian rainforests. Information regarding the issue of global warming is presented in what R. M. Ferguson described in *Choice* as an "antagonistic format" in which the viewpoints of "well-known and articulate commentators, leading professionals, and . . . ordinary observers" are presented. As Rosser

noted in a review of *Global Warming* and several other series installments for *Kliatt:* The "Opposing Viewpoints" series allows students to see that "issues have to be argued in a democracy, that compromise is probably the outcome of any legislation, and that it is important to be informed because policy affects us all."

Roleff told *CA:* "When I went to college, my intention was to become a veterinarian. It wasn't long, however, before I discovered that I was baffled by organic chemistry, a requirement I needed to fulfil if I was to become a vet. I drifted along in school until forced to declare a major in my junior year. I had taken a lot of English literature classes, as I loved to read, and so I decided to major in English.

"After graduating, I didn't have a clue what I was going to do with my degree. I found out employers were not at all anxious to hire me simply because I had a college degree in English. I finally got a job entering orders for a mail-order printing company; I did proofreading for them as well, then customer service. After four years, I decided I needed to do something new in my life, so I tried to get a job in advertising. I ended up writing copy for another mail-order company that sold stamps and coins and collectibles. This was a great job for two years until the company had to lay off employees—including me.

"Then I started working for newspapers writing stories, and from there I got a job editing the 'Lifestyles' section of a small-town paper in North Carolina—my husband is in the military, so we moved around a lot. Just as I was getting tired of the deadlines of working for a newspaper, we moved to Okinawa, Japan for a year. I took the year off and thought about what I wanted to do, and I decided I wanted to become an editor for a book publisher. I was lucky enough to move to San Diego, California, which had a couple of publishing companies, and I got a job at one of them, where I've worked since. Book editors are expected to complete their books in eight weeks—or less! We learn a lot about our topic, and it's always interesting. It's definitely the best job I've ever had. When my husband's job forced us to move away from San Diego, I was lucky enough to be able to continue working for the same company on a freelance basis."

BIOGRAPHICAL AND CRITICAL SOURCES:

PERIODICALS

Booklist, January 1-15, 1997, Sally Estes, review of *Abortion,* p. 828; January 1, 1997, Sally Estes, review of *Abortion*, p. 828; April 1, 1997, Frances Estes, review of *Gay Rights*, p. 1321; July, 1997, F. Bradburn, review of *Sexual Violence*, p. 1810; November 1, 1997, Anne O'Malley, review of *Suicide*, p. 461; February 15, 1998, F. Bradburn, review of *AIDS*, p. 993; May 1, 1998, Roger Leslie, review of *Gay Marriage*, p. 1508; February 1, 1999, Karen Hutt, review of *Police Brutality*, p. 969; May 15, 1999, R. Leslie, review of *Sex Education*, October 15, 1999, Roger Leslie, review of *The Rights of Animals*, p. 428; February 1, 2000, Roger Leslie, review of *Crime and Criminals*, p. 1013; November 15, 2000, Shelle Rosenfeld, review of *Domestic Violence*, p. 627; January 1, 2001, Roger Leslie, review of *Mental Illness*, p. 936; February 15, 2001, Roger Leslie, review of *Hate Crimes*, p. 1126; September 15, 2001, Roger Leslie, review of *Extremist Groups*, p. 214; January 1, 2002, Randy Meyer, review of *Hate Groups*, p. 838; April 1, 2002, Roger Leslie, review of *Censorship*, p. 1315; May 15, 2002, R. Leslie, review of *Satanism*, p. 1590; November 1, 2002, Roger Leslie, review of *America under Attack: Primary Sources*, p. 483.

Book Report, March, 1999, Anitra Gordon, review of *Civil Liberties* and *Hate Groups*, p. 85; March-April, 2002, Mary Hofmann, review of *Teen Sex* p. 62.

Catholic Library World, March, 1999, Michael Dialessi, review of *Hate Groups* and *Civil Liberties*, p. 56.

Choice, February, 1998, R. M. Ferguson, review of *Global Warming*, p. 1028.

History: Review of New Books, winter, 2001, Thomas W. Judd, review of *The Atom Bomb*, p. 54.

Kliatt, May, 1996, Shelley A. Glantz, review of *Business Ethics*, p. 28; July, 1996, p. 32; March, 1997, Claire Rosser, review of *Abortion* and *Censorship*, p. 30; September, Rita M. Fontinha, review of *Marriage and Divorce*, p. 33; January, 1998, review of *AIDS*, p. 28; January, 1999, Claire Rosser, review of *Hate Groups*, p. 28; May, 1999, Claire Rosser, review of *Sex Education*, p. 39; September, 1999, Rosser, review of *The Rights of Animals*, p. 38.

School Library Journal, February, 1997, Sue A. Norkeliunas, review of *Gay Rights*, p. 124; January, 1998, Sylvia V. Meisner, review of *Suicide*, p. 130; March, 1998, Darcy Schild, review of *Native American Rights*, p. 241; July, 1998, Edward Sullivan, review of *Gay Marriage*, p. 111; February, 2001, Katie O'Dell, review of *Teenage Sexuality*,

p. 138; March, 2001, Marilyn Heath, review of *Hate Crimes*, p. 276; December, 2001, Pat Scales, review of *Censorship*, p. 156; March, 2002, Paula J. LaRue, review of *The Holocaust: Death Camps*, pp. 256-257; June, 2002, Edward Sullivan, "Teens and Sex," p. 160; July, 2002, Ann G. Brouse, review of *Satanism*, p. 141; September, 2002, Wendy Lukehart, review of *America under Attack: Primary Sources*, p. 251; February, 2003, Libby K. White, review of *Inner-City Poverty*, p. 168.

Teaching History, spring, 2002, Brian Boland, review of *The Atom Bomb*, p. 53.

Voice of Youth Advocates, June, 1996, Mary Jo Peltier, review of *The Homeless*, p. 117; December, 1996, Ann Welton, review of *Genetics and Intelligence*, pp. 286-287; June, 1999, Cindy Lombardo, review of *Civil Liberties*, p. 130.

*   *   *

ROSSI, Jean Baptiste 1931-2003
(Sébastien Japrisot)

OBITUARY NOTICE—See index for *CA* sketch: Born July 4, 1931, in Marseille, France; died March 4, 2003, in Vichy, France. Film director and author. Rossi was a popular French crime novelist best known under his pseudonym, Sébastien Japrisot. After attending—and being thrown out of—a Jesuit college, he went on to study philosophy at the Sorbonne. However, he was more interested in writing than studying, so he dropped out of university and completed his first novel, *Les mal partis* (1948), under his real name when he was only seventeen years old. The erotic plot concerning the forbidden love between a nun and a fourteen-year-old boy caused a scandal, but sold very well, being translated in 1950 as *The False Start* and again two years later as *Awakening*. With this initial success, Rossi was asked to translate J. D. Salinger's *The Catcher in the Rye*, which he did as *L'attrappe-coeur*. Rossi then set out to write a series of police procedurals under his pseudonym, beginning with *Compartiment tueurs* (1962) and *Piège pour Cendrillon* (1962), the latter of which won the Grand Prix de la Littérature Policiére. He also won the 1966 Prix d'Honneur for *La dame dans l'auto avec les lunettes et un fusil* (1966), later translated as *The Lady in the Car with Glasses and a Gun* and also adapted as a film. Rossi spent more time making films during the 1970s than writing, but his *L'été meurtrier* (1978), one of only two books he published in the 1970s, is often considered his masterpiece. Although his later books are often thought of as having a slower pace than his initial crime stories, works such as *Un long dimanche de fiançailles* (1991), translated as *A Very Long Engagement* (1994), and *Le passager de la plui* (1992), translated as *Rider in the Rain* (1999), were still met with critical praise. Considered a worthy successor to French writer Georges Simonon, Rossi will remain one of the most acclaimed novelists of police procedurals of the twentieth century.

OBITUARIES AND OTHER SOURCES:

PERIODICALS

Los Angeles Times, March 26, 2003, p. B10.
Times (London, England), March 20, 2003.

*   *   *

ROY CHOUDHURY, Malay 1939-

PERSONAL: Born October 29, 1939 in Patna, Bihar, India; son of Ranjit (a photographer and painter) and Amita (Bandyopadhyay) Roy Choudhury; married Shalila Mukherjee, 1968; children: Anushree (daughter), Jitendra (son). *Education:* Bihar National College, B.A. (honors), 1958; Patna University, M.A., 1960.

ADDRESSES: Office—166A, Raipur Road, Second Floor, Letterbox Para, Naktala, Kolkata 700047, West Bengal, India. *E-mail*—malayroychoudhury@yahoo. co.in.

CAREER: Poet and novelist, c. 1961—. Has worked as a clerk, an inspector of banks in Patna, an agricultural analyst in Lucknow, as rural investigator in Bombay (now Mumbai), and as rural development facilitator at Calcutta (now Kolkata), all in India. Editorial advisor to Haowa49 Publishers, beginning 1991.

WRITINGS:

Marxbader Uttaradhikar (nonfiction), Shakti Publications (Kolkata, India), 1962.
Shoytaner Mukh (collected poems), Krittibas Prakashani (Kolkata. India), 1963.

Malay Roy Choudhury

Amimangsita (book-length poem), Zebra Publications (Kolkata, India), 1965.
Stark Electric Jesus (book-length poem), Tribal Press (Washington, DC), 1966.
Jakham (book-length poem), Zebra Publications (Kolkata, India), 1966.
Hungry Andoloner Kavyadarshan (manifesto), Debi Roy (Howrah, India), 1965.
Hungryalist Manifestoes/Ishtahar Sankalan (collection of manifestoes), Mahadiganta (Kolkata, India), 1986.
Kobita Sankalan (collected poems), Mahadiganta (Kolkata, India), 1986.
Medhar Batanukul Ghungur (collected poems), Mahadiganta (Kolkata, India), 1987.
Hattali (English-Bangla bilingual poem), Mahadiganta (Kolkata, India), 1989.
Selected Poems, Writers Workshop (Kolkata, India), 1989.
Dubjaley Jetuku Prashwas (novel), Haowa49 Publishers (Kolkata, India), 1994.
Hungry Kimvadanti (memoir), Dey Books (Kolkata, India), 1994.

Chitkarsamagra (poems), Kabita Pakshik (Kolkata, India), 1995.

Chhatrakhan (poems), Kabitirtha (Kolkata, India), 1995.

Postmodernism (nonfiction), Haowa49 Publishers (Kolkata, India), 1995.

(Translator) *Allen Ginsberg's Kaddish,* Kabitirtha (Kolkata, India), 1995.

Bhennogalpo (short-story collection), Dibaratrir Kavya (Kolkata, India), 1996.

Jalanjali (novel), Raktakarabi (Kolkata, India), 1996.

(Translator) *Tristan Tzara's Poems,* Kalimati (Jamshedpur, India), 1996.

(Translator) *Allen Ginsberg's Howl and Other Poems,* Kabita Pakshik (Kolkata, India), 1996.

Ja Lagbey Bolben (poems), Kourab Prakashani (Jamshedpur, India), 1996.

(Translator) *Jean Cocteau's Crucifixion,* Kabita Pakshik (Kolkata, India), 1996.

(Translator) *Blaise Cendrar's Trans Siberian Express,* Amritalok Prakashani (Midnapore, India), 1997.

(Translator) *Willian Blake's Marriage of Heaven and Hell,* Grafitti (Kolkata, India), 1998.

Natoksamagra (collection of *Illot, Hibakusha,* and *Napungpung*) Kabitirtha (Kolkata, India), 1998.

A (deconstruction of twenty-three poems), Kabita Pakshik (Kolkata, India), 1998.

Naamgandho (novel), Sahana (Dhaka, Bangladesh), 1999.

(Translator) *Autobiography of Paul Gaugin,* Grafitti (Kolkata, India), 1999.

Jean Arthur Rimbaud (criticism), Kabitirtha (Kolkata, India), 1999.

Allen Ginsberg (includes correspondence), Kabitirtha (Kolkata, India), 2000.

Atmadhwangser Sahasrabda (poems), edited by Rabindra Guha, Grafitti (Kolkata, India), 2000.

Surrealism/Paravastavbad (nonfiction), Ebong Prakashani (Kolkata, India), 1997.

Adhunikatar Biruddhey Kathavatra (non-fiction), Kabita Pakshik (Kolkata, India), 1999.

Hungryalist Interviews, edited by Ajit Ray, Mahadiganta (Kolkata, India), 1999.

Matantar (nonfiction), Ataeb Prakashani (Kolkata, India), 2000.

Postmodern Kalkhando O Bangalir Patan (nonfiction), Khanan (Nagpur, India), 2000.

Uttorouponibeshik Postmodernism (nonfiction), Bakpratima (Mahishadal, India), 2001.

Salvador Dali, based on Dali's *The Secret Life of Salvador Dali,* Grafitti (Kolkata, India), 2001.

Ei Adham Oi Adham (novel), Kabitirtha (Kolkata, India), 2001.

Postmodern Bangla Poetry 2001: An Overview (nonfiction), Haowa49 Publishers (Kolkata, India), 2001.

Postmodern Bangla Short Stories 2001: An Overview (non-fiction), Haowa49 Publishers (Kolkata, India), 2001.

(Translator) Tristan Tzara, *Dada Manifestoes,* Grafitti (Kolkata, India), 2002.

Nakhadanta (novel), Haowa49 Publishers (Kolkata, India), 2002.

Kounaper Luchimangso (collected poems), Kobita Campus (Howrah), 2003.

Postmodern Jibanananda (nonfiction), Grafitti (Kolkata, India), 2003.

Postmodern Bangla Poetry 2003: An Overview (nonfiction), Haowa49 Publishers (Kolkata, India), 2003.

Postmodern Bangla Short Stories 2003: An Overview (nonfiction), Haowa49 Publishers (Kolkata, India), 2003.

Editor of publications, including *Hungryalist Bulletins,* 1961-65; and *Zebra Literary Magazine,* 1966-67. Roy Choudhury's papers are archived at the Hungry Generation Archive, Northwestern University Library, Evanston, IL; Hungryalist Bulletins Archive, Bangla Academy, Dhaka, Bangladesh; and Hungry Movement Archive, Little Magazine Library, Kolkata, India.

ADAPTATIONS: Illot was adapted as a play, which was first staged at Agartala, India by the Tripura Group, 1971.

SIDELIGHTS: Poet Malay Roy Choudhury writes both in Bangla—one of the many native languages of South Asia—and English. One of the founders of the Hungryalist literary movement, Roy Choudhury has been sought out by such notable writers as Mexican Nobel prize winner Octavio Paz, American poet Allen Ginsberg, and Nicaraguan poet and priest Ernesto Cardenal. In addition to being a poet, Roy Choudhury is also a novelist, essayist, dramatist, short-story writer, translator, critic, interviewer, thinker, philosopher, recitationist, rural development facilitator, and cook.

In *Intrepid,* Carl Weissner wrote of Roy Choudhury's ancestral hometown: "Calcutta, in its sheer overwhelming hypertrophy and with its all-pervasive smell of resignation, apathy and corruption, certainly provides some of the reasons why the first rebel avantagardist call-to-arms was sounded right there." Spearheaded by Roy Choudhury, the Hungryalist movement soon spread to neighboring states and countries. Professor Howard McCord, who met Roy Choudhury during a visit to Kolkata, succinctly traced his emergence in *City Lights Journal 3:* "Roy Choudhury, a Bengali poet, has been a central figure in the Hungry Generation's attack on the Indian cultural establishment since the movement began in the early 1960's." He wrote, "I believe the movement is autochthonous and stems from the profound dislocations of Indian life," and added that, "acid, destructive, morbid, nihilistic, outrageous, mad, hallucinatory, shrill—these characterize the terrifying and cleansing visions that the Hungryalists insist Indian literature must endure if it is ever to be vital again." In *Sunday Searchlight* Subhash Chandra Sarkar discussed Roy Choudhury's work, portraying him as "a poet wounded by society itself where values are confused if not wholly inverted."

The publication of Roy Choudhury's collection of poems *Medhar Batanukul Ghungur* saw extreme critical responses, possibly because its author had by this time been accepted as a poet to reckon with by both the rightist and leftist media. While in *Guerilla* Arun Banik castigated his poems as "militant activism in poetic space," Ranjan Bandopadhyay in *Pratikshan* claimed that "the poems failed to become the ultimate religion of man." However, in *Amritalok*, critic Nilanjan Chattopadhyay wrote that "the poems change the constructs of our experience," whereas in *Lekhak Samavesh*, Dipankar Datta wrote that "the texts have earned fire-eyes of a jail breaker and made available flashing weaponary to the next generation of poets." In 2002 Ratan Biswas published a special commemorative issue of *Ahabkaal*, celebrating forty years of the Hungryalist movement, compiling together reviews for and against Roy Choudhury's poems written during past four decades.

Since the publication of the postcolonial trilogy, comprising *Dubjaley Jetuku Prashwas, Jalanjali,* and *Naamgandho,* Roy Choudhury has been best known for this nightmare-like work, which is flooded with hundreds of characters in a multilinear, polycentric, and indeterminant textual design in the format of the Hindu epic *Mahabharata.* This was noticed by Tapodhir Bhattacharya, who termed the trilogy a "rebel-

lious counter discourse" in his essay in *The Individual Malay Roy Choudhury.* In the same book, Satyajit Bandopadhyay termed the trilogy a "real-time post-Independence socio-political nightmare." The trilogy depicts the ascent of degeneration in stages, starting with an institution that issues fresh bank notes and destroys soiled ones, then a predominantly agricultural district in the Bihar region, and ultimately the state of West Bengal, India, where a large segment of the population is rootless due to the partition of the British colony of India into the two separate nations of India and Pakistan (which later split into Pakistan and Bangladesh) after independence in 1947. In Roy Choudhury's trilogy, each individual—even the most socially insignificant—resists the monster of degeneration, destruction and decay.

During the period when Roy Choudhury was writing essays on various aspects of postcolonialism, he told Sudakshina Chattopadhyay in an interview for *Sumana* magazine that his intention to write novels emanated from a strong conviction to do away with the literary canons imposed by the British through university syllabi, which were still in use. His novel *Ei Adham Oi Adham* has a central character who dies in the very first paragraph. The narrator of the story, the nine-year-old-brother of the dead hero, comes to know from the discussions of the crowd that his elder brother was actually purchased from a prostitute as an infant. In this gloomy scenario, the narrator is stationed in his own world of hilarious fancy, which is occasionally interrupted by a subaltern linguistic discourse of the economically depressed neighborhood in which his extended family of twenty members lives. Biswajit Sen has called the novel "a diasporic vision of narrative originality" in his essay in *The Individual Malay Roy Choudhury.* On *Bahirbanga.com*, Arun Chakraborty called *Ei Adham Oi Adham* "the outsider Bangla speaker's inner-diasporic novel."

Roy Choudhury's novel *Nakhadanta* is segmented into seven sections which are actually pages lifted out of his own diary revealing seven different dates in his life. Within the seven-day narrative he has placed seven short stories relating to the gradual decimation of the jute industry around Kolkata, these stories based on real-life incidents that took place around those dates. In an interview with Shyamal Shill of *Kabiswar,* Roy Choudhury informed his readers that he borrowed the idea of seven-segmentation from the Hindu epic *Ramayana.* Each short story is self-contained, but the plight of the jute industry, the laborers, and the jute cultivators interlink each of the story. The first story deals with the nauseatingly violent murder of an innocent laborer named Kangal Chamar while in police custody. The presence of the dead laborer pervades the other stories, implanted as a juxtopposite to the intellectual diary of a thinker. Shishir Dey in his review in *Sahitya Setu* wrote that the novel contained "too much brainstorming for the common reader." However, Dhurjati Chanda in *Ahabkaal* magazine hailed Roy Choudhury as "a prose architect comparable to great Bangla novelists such as Satinath Bhaduri, Amiyabhushan Majumder, Kamal Kumar Majumdar and Subimal Basak."

Though Roy Choudhury has ventured into genres other than poetry, he continues to write poems "in order to decanonise and denarrativise them," as Santanu Bandopadhyay wrote in *The Individual Malay Roy Choudhury*. As Ajit Ray explained in *Shahar*, in view of Roy Choudhury's command over the genres of poetry, novel, short story, drama, and essay, branding the author in a specific slot is well nigh impossible. It has been argued that for his contribution to Bangla language and literature through the Hungryalist movement, Roy Choudhury has created the same sort of space as Stefan Mallarmé has for symbolism, Tristan Tzara for dadaism, Ezra Pound for imagism, and Andre Breton for surrealism.

After the publication of his *Hungryalist Interviews,* twenty interviews given by Roy Choudhury remained to be anthologized. These interviews map the changes his authorial self has undergone during the late twentieth century. He has said that, "with emphasis on periphery, the foci of my narrative thoughts have shifted to micro-territory of characters, a territory which remains increasingly plagued by neo-colonial ills: economic disorder, social malaise, political scams, criminal as politician, pockets of terrorists, government corruption, influx of famished Bangladeshi Muslim families, repression by state and political party apparatus, digitalization of individuals as voter, indifference and apathy of public service institutions, etc." He has said that his fictions are "nomadic in their peregrinatory outreach," and that his "nonmimetic narrative modes are fashioned in such a way that they can create social and conceptual spaces within which the problematiques of meaning assume socio-political as well as ethnico-cultural significance."

Justifying changes in his poetry dating from the Hungryalist literary upsurge in the 1960s, Roy Choudhury

once said that, "we are far removed from the past as we live and get continuously constructed by Bangla language. My poems are bound to get loaded with my experience and psycho-linguist insights which make them multi-exit, open-ended with a disturbed narrative, wherein the Indian universe, summoned up by a poem, is grounded in its own textuality, incorporating polyphonic voices and carnivalesque styles which dissociates itself from the decorous colonial hierarchy which had some sort of concealed presence during the Hungryalist literary movement." He has further said that, "my poems, by sheer acceleration of imageries and sprinkling of broken-mirror pieces, aspire to create multiple centres of interest, and an ethical awareness in diversity. Humans are first and foremost ethical beings, irrespective of what they have done, are doing, and would do to this beautiful world."

AUTOBIOGRAPHICAL ESSAY:

Malay Roy Choudhury contributed the following autobiographical essay to *CA*:

1

I don't know when I was born. Ma didn't ever go to school and Dad learned his alphabet late.

Eyes closed, holding a tiny steel chisel between forefinger and thumb for cutting my nails, she'd reminisce of a devastating earthquake in Bihar when she lost her pet blackbuck and swan couple. I was born during a lagoon-coloured autumn at Patna in the Prince of Wales Hospital, five or maybe five-and-a-half years after the earthquake that demolished the hutment Dad with five brothers and family lived in. I was called Fauna at home though formally named Malay because the Hindu zodiac indicated *M* on the day of my first rice ritual.

Dad consulted the Hindu almanac, deciding on a holy date at the time of my admission to kindergarten at Saint Joseph's convent, in order to convince the Irish doe-eyed nun of the fact of my birth on October 29, 1939. Ma contested this date till she died of an enlarged heart in 1982, as she thought I was born on a Friday on the eleventh day of the month of *Kartika* with the help of metal forceps nurses used to pull me out of her body, for my legs had come out first.

A devout Brahmin, revelling in his puritanic logic, Dad insisted a Hindu Aryan was born on the date of his sacred thread ceremony and that we were descen-

"Grandfather in 1931. The photograph is from his own mobile firm, Studio Bengal, established in 1886 at Calcutta."

dents of Bidyadhar Roy, the great zemindar who sold Sutanuti Gobindapur Kolikata villages for a meagre three hundred rupees to the firangi Job Charnok of East India Company, which became the joie de vivre called Calcutta. Dad wished to stay there when young but lived instead 550 kilometers away at Patna, the seat of the Buddhist emperor Asoka during 264-223 B.C.E.

Dad told us about his dad who was a great painter and wanderer, who moved from one maharajah's fort to another maharani's castle with a palette always wet, dragging his caravan of half-a-dozen sons and a daughter from Rangoon to Colombo to Kabul to Cooch-Behar, drawing portraits of Indian kings, nabobs, and their shoals of queens. Granpa was Luxminarayan. His sons Promod, Sushil, Ranjit, Anil, Sunil, and Biswanath. His daughter, Kamala. Ranjit is my dad.

The sudden death of the grand old man forced his survivors at Patna, an alien land for them, to eke out

collective bread, hawking any damn thing that could be purchased and sold, settling as a last resort on photography, which clicked.

Despite Granpa's adventures, Dad cocooned in an orthodox seed: a vegetarian, devoted to a 333 million pantheon, fasting on the eleventh day of the lunar fortnight, mantras at lunch and dinner, a change of sacred thread once a month, no eating cereals cooked by untouchable castes, a daily mustard-oil bath in cold water.

Granma—Apurbamayee—lived alone at Uttarpara, a suburb twenty kilometers away from Calcutta across the Hooghly River, in an ancestral edifice in ruins habitated by hundreds of wild pigeons and bats, with incorrigible weeds shooting off a miasma of tentacles from the salt-eroded, moss-eaten clay bricks. Here she roamed with a torn napkin around her skinny waist, dried teats dangling on her topless bust. Her companions were single-room tenants using the same toilet and a couple of black cows she milked with her own hands for a living. There were guava and starapple trees, creepers unable to bear gourds—ashgourds, bottlegourds—festooned precariously overhead.

After Granny's death in December 1964, Uttarpara looked deserted except for strange tenants. Seven years later when the roof of a ground-floor room crashed down it became haunted, as Cousin Puti, Uncle Sunil's daughter, unroped the noose of a heifer and hung herself from an exposed wooden beam of the ceiling to be discovered in the night chill by someone who took her to be a flying ghost. Puti was in love with a Marxist revolutionary killed in an encounter.

The brothers had shifted to a double-storied brick house in Bakharganj at Patna after the earthquake, constructed in instalments by Uncle Promod, each brother and his family in a room with a common bath and toilet and water fetched in buckets from a roadside tap. We had a ten-foot-by-ten-foot room facing west on the first floor, a cot beneath which belongings were kept, a packing box used as bookshelf cum table, and a wall-to-wall wire for hanging clothes. Bakharganj was a Hindi-speaking slum area; hoochers and gamblers had their nights, no neighbours' children went to school, women in veils kneaded dungcakes for fuel. Nobody knew of toothbrush paste, we brushed our teeth with fresh coal ash powder using our forefingers.

Uncle Promod's daughters, Sabu and Dhabu, were married before my birth, prompting him to purchase a male infant from a Punjabi prostitute whom he didn't legally adopt and couldn't decide what to do with as the boy grew up to become a ruffian and mugger at fifteen, exhibiting unabashed scorn for everything Bengali to deculturise himself. I was in complete awe of the fearful respect he generated in neighbours. Buro, as he was called, had a country-made revolver spinning on his forefinger. One day he allowed me to shoot at a sitting popinjay—I got my thumb bruised.

I remember Buro brought a whore home with him secretly, double his age, and the thud of the wooden bolt woke up an aunt whose midnight yell pulled out adults and children from their rooms, an event sufficient to provoke Dad and my uncles to dismantle the Bakharganj establishment. In 1953 we shifted out to the locality of Dariapur.

Buro had a sad death. Aunt Nanda, his foster mother, on advice from some sannyasin, devised an enchantment potion made of herbs, fed to him weekly with his food, resulting in slow poisoning. He grew weak and dropped dead. Aunt Nanda wailed uncontrollably over his corpse.

Uncle Promod worked as a preserver of paintings at Patna Museum. I visited it on Saturdays for hours to become a part of ancient and prehistoric mysteries amid granite *apsaras,* Egyptian mummies, fossilised monsters, going back home with him on his bicycle, the only movable asset of the household, cleaned and oiled in turns by the children. I learned cycling on it and in 1956 Dad purchased a bike for me, enabling me to learn by heart the town's alleys and joints.

Uncle Promod loved picnics. On holidays our entire clan of twenty would go out to cook and eat by a slim stream or in a mango orchard or near a wellspring on the outskirts. I carried a book, any book, even a schoolbook, searching for the insect, bird, tree, or grains described therein. Sometimes other Bengali acquaintances were invited to join the picnics, probably as an effort to overcome alienation from mainstream Bengal. One of the ladies would burst out singing, invariably a Hindu religious song, as film songs were taboo and Rabindranath Tagore songs considered un-Hindu.

Since Uncle Promod didn't have a son when he died—in 1966 during an election campaign for an obscure candidate—I performed the rituals by setting fire to the funeral pyre on which lay his cold body embalmed by me with clarified butter. He was a fat man who turned to ashes in two hours in a yelling blaze that licked the horizon on the other side of Ganges River. Satish Ghoshal, our family priest, directed me to collect a few bones from the ashes, which I immersed in the river. This was my first encounter with the beyond, a plight Satish Ghoshal sermoned not to give importance to as it happened when you came to burn or bury the dead!

A couple of years later Aunt Nanda died of burn injuries she received when her cooking stove exploded. But Sabu and Dhabu, scared of my property claims for the last rites performed, sued each other for Uncle Promod's Bakharganj house as well as the assets of their father-in-law, who was the same for both, since they had married two brothers. I used to visit their sylvan house during 1948-50 to play with my nieces Manju, Jaya, and Madhuri in their sprawling garden.

2

As any venture Uncle Sushil embarked upon was a flop, he joined my father at the photography shop on Main Road that shifted later to Dariapur in 1953 when Dad purchased a 1,300-square-foot house. I have recollections of him as a snuff-inhaling afternoon dreamer, customers constantly knocking at his mental absence after his wife died of tuberculosis, leaving behind daughters Dolly and Monu, who flunked school and had to be looked after by Ma. Dolly was packed off in a negotiated marriage I couldn't attend. Monu decided to marry a local non-Brahmin Hindi-speaking boy whom Uncle Sushil didn't approve of, so the responsibility of solemnising the marriage in a Shiva temple befell me. I went attired in a pink dhoti and yellow shawl with collyrium in my eyes and performed priest-directed rituals I was not conversant with. Uncle Sushil died in 1968 of a hernia he was too shy to get treatment for, on the day of my marriage.

Anil, the brother next to Dad, had a photo studio at Uttarpara at the time of his negotiated marriage with Omiya, a school-educated lady who was already in love with a guy living in the erstwhile French colony of Pondicherry. She continued the relationship despite her marriage, provoking Uncle Anil to abandon his shop and become a recluse. I thought he was nuts when he, along with daughters Shubhra and Rakhi and wife, came down to live with us at Uncle Promod's Bakharganj house in 1947. Aunt Omiya didn't give a damn for Uncle Anil. She took a teacher's job in a grammar school and introduced newspaper reading in the family, creating in us a fascination for her. Among the children she had a strange soft spot for me though I should have drawn her hatred as I resembled Uncle Anil. The daughters were not good at studies; the elder was packed off to boarding school at Mayapur, run by Iskcon, to get rid of her array of boyfriends. She married one, a gambler, then came back divorced, remarried a non-Brahmin, and disappeared. Panicked, Aunt got the second one married to a doctor. Both Aunt and Uncle died of cancer; Omiya had one teat operated upon, Anil's nose had become cauliflower shaped. They stayed on at the Bakharganj house, occupied the room vacated by us in 1953, husband and wife not talking to each other, a menage of dissent with a window opening inside.

Unhappy with his three daughters and three sons, Uncle Sunil, who had a catering job on the Eastern Railway, broke our eating taboo by inducting varieties of forbidden food into the menu for the children, depending on items knocked off from pantry cars. His daughter Puti committed suicide, the eldest son, Khoka, eloped and married the non-Brahmin tutor of his brothers, the second daughter married a boy of the washerman caste, the younger sons flunked school and tried to start a broiler farm in the gloomy rooms of Uttarpara that made the fowls sick and mad. Uncle Sunil died on the day after I met him in February 1989, in unbound glee that he was on the verge of getting out of the mess his incorrect decisions had created.

The youngest of the brothers, Biswanath, who was childless, got himself gifted a small piece of land from Granny that Dad claimed he had purchased for her. Aunt Kuchi used to have religious fits diagnosed by doctors as depression when she was in the Bakharganj establishment. Their prayer for a child at sundry temples spawned in them an insight for having a temple of their own for attracting the gullible, which included my dad also, who thought both his sons had out-Hindued themselves with their way of life and thinking. In 1986 he went to Kotrong to live at Uncle Biswanath's ashram, indicated in brochures printed by Uncle as the place visited by Saint Ramakrishna of Dakshineshwar, though there was a pond forty years earlier at the place marked as the saint's seat in which I had waded in knickers and netted small fish and snails.

Dad's only sister, Kamala, lived in a single-room tenement at Ahiritola in Calcutta, adjacent to the red-light tourist spot Sonagachi. The room had a two-tiered bed for her eight children, seven of whom quit school to be found always on either of the tiers doing nothing by her husband, who would come back from his office every evening high on Goddess Kali brand rice liquor whistling a nineteenth-century tune, alerting neighbours to his drunkenness. It being the only place to stay during a visit to Calcutta, the floor of the room meant for guests was also where we sat and ate steamed rice, pigeon pea pulse, and shrimp fried in mustard oil served on brass plates. The toilet was slippery, without doors, and I used to keep coughing to notify my presence to any intruder. Aunt Kamala became blind yet continued her cooking routine believing, as she told me, the blindness was for having seen six toes on a woman's feet during a full moon. Her husband was found in a pool of blood on a summer morning in 1967 when he had nightwalked off a terrace during one of his spells; the remains of his body were scraped from the asphalt into a loincloth bundle for the postmortem.

3

Ma was in charge of cooking at Bakharganj, which she did for twenty persons on two coal ovens made of clay placed on the kitchen floor. Through day and night she sat there beside a large wooden box containing spices stored in phials of used medicine and cereals in tin cannisters bought out of a collective fund. She would detect sudden shortages while cooking and haul me up from studies for an immediate purchase in the smallest quantity, which I'd procure in a jiffy to enable her to complete the dish. She loved to apply vermillion on her parted hair twice a day. And her favourite dish was *dhoka*—asafoetida-flavoured cakes of steamed and grinded chick-pea. Unlike Dad she was a nonvegetarian, mainly a fish eater.

Spice pastes were prepared on a stone grinder by our part-time servant Sheonanni, on whose back I climbed while he swayed to and fro pulping turmeric, chilli, ginger, cumin, onion, coriander, garlic, and spearmint for an hour or two in the evening.

Each of my uncles had his own time for lunch and dinner when he ate alone, served by his wife, whereas the children and ladies ate together each on a small

The author's parents, Ranjit and Amita, on their first wedding anniversary

piece of mat sitting crosslegged, except for Sundays, which was a meat-eating day, when lunch was late. We ate goat meat or at the most mutton, since chicken, duck, cow, buffalo, rabbit, deer, frog, horse, pig, and turtle meat were prohibited, which later we relished at cheap roadside restaurants when we grew up and accumulated some pocket money. Even some fish like eel and flounder were taboo. Ma never went beyond goat meat though she cooked fowl for us after we shifted to Dariapur.

4

My brother Samir, about five years my elder, was the first individual in our family to complete school and college, as he was sent to our maternal uncle's place in Panihati for studying at Calcutta when Dad decided to keep him culturally uncorrupt. He studied science at City College, joined Satyajit Ray's drama group, Har-

bola, and started frequenting joints visited by the reigning Bengali poets of the thirties, about whom he talked to us in bated breath, often brandishing books of verse written in a Bengali diction foreign to our tongue; not even Aunt Omiya used such words while talking to her guests.

Panihati was a boat ride across the river Hooghly, where I was sent during vacation to keep in touch with Bengal as well as to improve my health. The maternal uncles were comparatively richer and educated, had a radio, read the English newspaper the *Statesman,* a status symbol, talked among themselves sometimes in English, and were interested in political developments.

Ma was called Bhulti at Panihati and Amita at Patna. Once while we were crossing the river on the ferry boat, I remember she jumped out into the deep water, presented us with her memory of cross-current swimming, and came out with tiny transparent crablings crawling down her uncoiffured hair. Every time she went to the bank to withdraw her savings, she misspelt Amita in her labouriously practiced signature. Ma was scared of pox inoculation, locking herself up in the lavatory whenever the municipal doctor arrived for the annual prick.

In 1948 I was withdrawn from Saint Joseph's convent and admitted to the Bengali-medium Ram Mohan Roy Seminary, a Brahmo Samaj school, primarily, I learned later, because Dad came to know we were having a prayer class every day at the Gothic cathedral of the convent, meeting with folded hands Jesus Christ in agony in flowing Italian marble surrounded by azure-tipped candle flickers. He didn't have a high opinion about Brahmos though, as the sect had been advocating against idol worshipping. But this might have been the source of my religious pacifism. I don't consider myself an apostate or atheist and may probably define myself as vaguely Hindu without much to do with religious rituals, gods, and goddesses.

Saint Joseph's convent to Ram Mohan Roy Seminary was an unhealing journey of cultural hiatus for me, cause of the schism that still invades my poems; doe-eyed nuns carrying a bleeding Jesus made of soft marble through the bazaars of Patna float in my dreams even at this age.

Ram Mohan Roy Seminary, a three-kilometer walk every day, sun or rain, had boys and girls of the same lower middle-class milieu as that of mine to whom I

Malay as a child, 1941

was embarrassed to divulge my fleabag residential area considered infested by criminals, deterring classmates to visit me at home. I was not allowed to mix up with the boys of my locality as Dad thought they were lumpens. I didn't have personal friends for long and learned to adjust to my loneliness, Samir always at Panihati, Buro away with the ruffians, other cousins very junior to me. Sari-clad girl students were there in my class but the mystery seized me late. I can remember only three girls with effort: Hashi, Juthika, and Bijoya, presumably because of their colourful attire.

Lack of a cricket bat of my own didn't give me much scope to have a place in the school games and I couldn't do well in football either because of a weak physique, so I found my way into the library and reading room, the lady librarian chaperoning my interest to school editions of Homer, Edmund Spenser, Miguel de Cervantes, Shakespeare, Voltaire, and a Sanskrit classics compendium, finding finally in the last year of my school text writings of six persons who changed the condition of my loneliness: George Gordon Byron, William Wordsworth, Samuel Taylor Coleridge, Percy

Bysshe Shelley, John Keats, and Alfred, Lord Tennyson. Except for Tagore, the Bengali poets in the text had only moral sermons to deliver whereas Hindi poets talked about the greatness of the creator in a never-changing rhythm.

In the final years of school I made friendships with three boys who were themselves unable to make friends, Subarna, Barin, and Tarun. Subarna couldn't afford to have a cricket uniform, white shirt and pants, and was removed from the team. Barin was a myopic. Tarun a short and weak boy who talked little. We sat at the shore of the Ganges River, talked about whatever we knew, pooled resources to see Sunday-morning movies, ate at cheap restaurants, and roamed about from camp to camp during the three-day festival of the goddess Durga. Barin had a good voice, sang Tagore and Atulprasad songs at the riverbank. For three days during the Durgapuja festival, Subarna wore saffron, white, and green shirts stitched out of the silk national flag supplied to his father's office each year by the state government.

Overreading strained my eyesight. I got specs in 1952, the year of my sacred thread ceremony when our family priest gave me a mantra of the goddess Gayatri. My head was shaved and I wore a saffron dhoti. I was required to perform *puja* twice a day, observe celibacy, eat only vegetarian dishes, no cereals, on the eleventh day of the moon, no talking while eating, no eating out, and the sacred thread continuously on my left shoulder. I tried for a couple of weeks, gave up thereafter.

Performancewise I was average at high school, completed in 1954. Then I left home with Tarun, hitchhiking to Calcutta on an illegal truck carrying old and sickly goats for slaughter. As interstate carriage of goats was prohibited by road transport, we feigned ourselves shepherds and herded the goats on the roadside grasslands, heigh-hoing them at the border checkpost into West Bengal where the empty truck was waiting after showing documents at the crossing. We took baths at a village well in a bucketful of cold water. At sundown, stopping at a Punjabi *dhaba,* we ate handmade bread fried in sheep lard, pickled onion, and liquor made of *mahua*—my first taste of an intoxicant. The driver bargained with a suburban whore, went with her into the paddy field under a neap-tide eroded moon while we fought phantoms inside the dim-lit truck.

During 1954-60 we made several such forays in bus, train, steamer, or jeep, visiting Allahabad, Jhansi, Ranchi, Kanpur, a hundred to a thousand kilometers from Patna. Tarun died early of leukemia.

My first two years in college were a real academic disaster. At school I had studied physics, chemistry, biology, mathematics, history, geography, along with Sanskrit, Hindi, Bengali, and English. At college, on Samir's advice, I opted for economics, political science, and mathematics, with Hindi, Bengali, and English; I found interest in none, devoting most of my time at various libraries of the town gobbling up the history of literature of various languages, history of art, philosophy, and the lives of poets; Western and Eastern names started reeling in my brain. For a time I joined the infantry division of the National Cadet Corps and practiced rifle shooting, but I was finding myself unsolvable, rootless, obscure, anonymous. My exam results were weepable.

In 1956 I got admitted in B.A. honours economics, regular subjects being English, Bengali, Hindi, and politics. An exclusive room was at my disposal now, a table and chair, a bed, and three *almirahs* on the wall for books on the first floor at the Dariapur house; the complete ground floor was used as a photo studio by Dad; Ma's cooking exercises reduced now to courses for only three persons.

Alone in my room I felt despair for no known reason and attempted in March 1956 to get a few crystals of potassium ferricyanide from the downstairs photo studio used for making sepia prints. The emotion withered on its own. To keep me absorbed Ma purchased a gramophone and some records.

In my B.A. honours class I met a bespectacled Nepali woman made of snow. Bhuban Mohini Rana was from the royal family and always kept me at a commoner's distance, never allowing me to touch her queenly complexion. The other woman I was in trouble with was Shubhra Ray, of whom I do not prefer to talk.

The years 1957-58 were the period of my introduction to Bengali poetry in a big way. I stumbled upon Bengali poet Madhusudan Dutt, who exemplified moral violence in his epic work *Murder of Meghnad* in such deft rhyming that he proved somewhat curative for me—a stunning perceptual accuracy that instilled purpose. There was something beyond experience in him I became enamoured to. I hero-worshipped him, read the turbulent story of his life, allowed my scanty beard and moustache to grow like his.

5

My memory of India's liberation movement is strewn with opaque scenes of Ma waving a tricolour in a crowd of ladies, horsemen ploughing through a procession, a fat lady donating her bangles to Gandhi under a green canopy, a leader in a marigold garland, and a burned junk of a 1942 van on a road crippled with monsoon weeds. When the British quit in 1947 I was eight years old, a student of Saint Joseph's convent.

Dad had no respect for Gandhi, did not forgive Jawaharlal Nehru, who he insisted was responsible for the partition and eventual plight of the Bengalis. He appreciated Hitler and highly esteemed Subhas Chandra Bose, the nationalist leader. Other uncles also didn't have much political knowledge. A Bengali newspaper I started reading was subscribed to when we went to live in Dariapur.

Prepartition communal riots I do remember: burning hutments, religious howls, shrieks, mutilated bodies seen through a peephole, vultures in the sky, groups being chased, army patrols, caravans proceeding toward nowhere. One day when Aunt Nanda was hospitalised for a tumor operation, Gandhi was murdered. I learned of it in the evening sitting inside mosquito netting and completing classwork, as Uncle Promod told everybody in a hushed voice.

Not until 1957 was I able to get out of the political confusion of our family and allow the formation of my own ideas and views, clashing then with Dad and the other uncles. Samir's progressive and liberal leanings had been worrying them for quite some time.

At the Dariapur residence Uncle Biswanath had presented to me a white puppy with brown patches, which turned out to be a country dog as it grew up. I named him Robert Lingchipula, caricaturing a British name. The dog ate spicy leftovers, became hairless, and died after six years.

Since we had a lot of space at Dariapur, Uncle Promod started an amateur drama group staging nonpolitical works, mainly Hindu mythologies; rehearsals of silky goddesses or woolly monsters barged into my study in gargling voices, characters in beards of jute with wooden swords and tin crowns delivered dialogues in nineteenth-century textbook Bengali occasionally interrupted by a sudden spurt of harmonium followed by a line of a song.

I never heard Dad singing or humming. Ma did a little bit of one line. Uncle Promod, who exuded a sort of holiday gaiety, had a clarinet he took out once in a while but never played a full tune. Aunt Kuchi knew some imitation of *bharat natyam.* That's all. My indulgence in music had to wait. Samir, before he left for studies at Calcutta, sang "Toofan Mail," a Hindi pop song of early movies; that's the name of a fast train of those days.

Whenever Ma and Dad went to Uttarpara, I'd go to the railroad station a few hours in advance, occupy a berth in a compartment attachable to the train, and keep a space for them so that they could join me a few minutes prior to departure. That was the lowest class we travelled in. My first train travelling was inside a compartment full of luggage, no space to drop a pin, myself hoisted throughout the night on a gunny-bag from which fresh potatoes peeped out.

6

The result of a B.A. in honours economics turned out quite good, making it easier to get admitted for an M.A. in the same subject at Patna University, where in the beginning of 1959 I got a glimpse of Toynbee, Marx, and Spengler. Pages of their books had been removed in several places with the help of a blade in the copies available at the university library. I went to other libraries, took notes, revelling in Spenglerian prophecy taking off from celebrations of decentralisation espoused by Bakunin, Kropotkin, Godwin, and wrote a hundred-page postmodernist treatise, *The Marxist Heritage.* For the moral vacuum laid bare, the printed book gave me shivers. I got all the copies dunked in gasoline and set them on fire, allowing Spengler to haunt me all along.

My journey into realms of poetry had started by literally setting intellectual bridges ablaze. Around the end of 1959 I had been scribbling in my notebook, trying to shape up a few poems.

"With my first specs in a photograph by Uncle Biswanath"

Samir got a Fisheries Officer's job, posted at Chaibasa, a tiny hilly township of tribals surrounded by green sal, sesame, and teak trees splashed in spring with scarlet splendour of kapok and kino flowers. He was staying in a thatched hut on a hillock touching the moon. Distant cool nights flickered in the villages below amid the sweet aroma of handpounded tribal rice, roasted pig, faint drumbeats, sparkling laughter of Santhal women. During the day, fowls fought each other with knives tied to legs, a tribal gambling sport, and overloaded rickety buses passed by. I visited Chaibasa during vacation, and again after completing my M.A., the results of which were exemplary in view of my preparations. The caste factor didn't allow me to top the batch.

Involved with Bela, one of eight daughters of a local gentleman straight from Emily Brontë fiction, Samir married; I thought it better to keep myself out of the reach of the ladies.

After my disastrous start as an author I indiscriminately stormed through whatever works I could lay my hands on: Rimbaud, Poe, Baudelaire, Apollinaire, Pound,

Eliot, Rilke, Mallarmé, Mayakovsky, Lorca. Surrealism thrilled me. I could imagine myself on the streets of Paris, Madrid, or Moscow with a young André Breton or Jean Cocteau. Samir brought for me from Calcutta collections of Jibanananda Das, Bishnu Dey, Buddhadev Bose, Premendra Mitra, Samar Sen, Amiya Chakraborty, and Sudhindra Dutta, as well as little magazines run by mentors of various groups.

From the notebooks I maintained Samir copied a couple of poems and got them printed in *Krillibas* in 1959, for which I feel embarrassed even now as I wanted to do something historical, an entry with a bang, an event to remember in literary history.

My perception of Bengali poetry was that it had a place in the sun, notwithstanding its treatment in Western media as a language of a handful. A Nobel Prize to Tagore was the last glory fifty years back. I wondered about the limitations of Bengali not being talked about in international literature as French, German, Italian, Spanish, Russian, and Portuguese were. No doubt the Indian government was spending millions for sponsoring Hindi, which was not my mother tongue; something had to be done in Bengali literature itself, I felt.

I found editors of literary magazines were not conversant with international writing standards, read very little, detested the avant-garde, had contempt for experiments in prose and poetry. Bengali novels thrived on the market of half-literate ladies. Poems were time servers, filling up spaces for which no ads could be procured. Bearded gentries in *kurta* pyjamas stitched of handloom cloth with dirty slingbags passed for poets, even the films invariably depicted them in such fixed attire. The entire corpus after Tagore had been a soft option for the creative writer, articulated in a language not spoken in a common Bengali household. Most of the poets till then were from upper caste, that is, Brahmin or Kayastha from urban areas.

I knew I could do nothing alone. I didn't have money. I didn't have access to reputed periodicals. I didn't have a group. I didn't have a mentor or a sponsor. I didn't know any writers or poets in Calcutta.

I found a queer name in a little magazine in early 1961, Mr. Haradhon Dhara, traced him out in a notorious slum at Howrah near Calcutta, winding my way through a stinky buffaloshit lane onto a hay-roofed mud-tiled clay hut with small cane windows nibbled by termites. In the middle of the room lay a high, squeaky antique bed beneath which were stacked magazines gathering dust. Further magazines were sprawled around with no room to move about except for a folding chair offered to me. Debi Roy, which was Dhara's pen name, had worked as an errand boy in a pedestrian restaurant, as a taxi washer, didn't have any knowledge of world literature, had written a few poems rejected by reputed magazines, belonged to a very low caste, and couldn't speak English well. Could be a genuine anchorman, I felt.

We sat together on the clay verandah beside heaps of gourdseeds and pondsnails, I gradually explaining my views of unleashing a literary movement to be called "Hungryalism." I had concentrated on the word *Hungry* from Chaucer's prophetic line "In the sowre Hungry tyme" with a Spenglerian perspective of the assimilation of cultures and ultimate decline thereof in view of the overwhelming infiltration of an alien ethos into Bengali culture. Hungryalism was a postmodern idea, not a philosophy but rather the apotheosis of self-expression, which accepted contradictions as a part of the human condition. Not a theory.

Debi Roy was happy with the coinage from a different perspective, as he thought Hungryalism suited the economic nightmare of a postpartition society suffering from unemployment, shortages of food and clothing, inhuman living conditions of the human individual, hunger of body and soul, mind and being, essence and existence, matter and spirit, known and unknown.

It was decided to print one-page handouts initially, when and as money permitted, for distribution, bringing gradually within our fold likeminded poets, writers, and artists as a beginning of a multicentered formlessness pervading all diversity where the individual was whole and the whole was individual. We should have sufficient activists to launch a cultural avalanche, we felt.

In April 1961 I got a job in the Reserve Bank of India with a monthly salary of one hundred seventy rupees (ten dollars) which required me to write owners' names on gilt-edged bonds. I wrote a piece on poetry printed on a foolscap paper and arranged for its distribution as the first *Hungryalist* bulletin in November 1961 in the Albert Hall Coffee House on Calcutta's College Street across from Presidency College.

7

The effect of the first bulletin was stunning as it started a swelling of the ranks and provoked editorials and literary headlines in newspapers and periodicals. The *Hungryalist*—later *Hungrealist*—bulletin went from five pages to twenty pages, quarto to scroll size, woodcut-designed cover to offset, black and blue prints to handpaint.

Between 1961 and 1965 about a hundred bulletins were released by participants, of which nine are preserved by Sandip Dutta in the archives of the Little Magazine Library and Research Centre. Poets, authors, and artists who had joined the movement are Subimal Basak, Rabindra Guha, Sankar Sen, Arupratan Basu, Basudeb Dasgupta, Asok Chatterjee, Pradip Choudhuri, Benoy Majumdar, Amit Sen, Amrita Tanay Gupta, Sayad Mustafa Siraj, Bhanu Chatterjee, Utpal Kumar Basu, Tridib Mitra, Phalguni Ray, Satindra Bhowmik, Shambhu Rakshit, Tapan Das, Sandipan Chatterjee, Anil Karanjai, Subhas Ghosh, Karuna Nidhan, Ramananda Chatterjee, Subo Acharja, Saileswar Ghose, Debasis Banerjee, Sukumar Mitra, Mihir Pal, Arani Basu, and Arunesh Ghosh.

I had drafted the manifestoes on poetry, prose, politics, and religion for the Hungryalist movement, reprinted in *Kultchur* Volume 15, edited by Lita Hornick, and *Salted Feathers,* Volumes 8/9, edited by Dick Bakken and Lee Altman.

Actually I personally didn't know all the Hungryalists as it was Debi Roy and later Subimal Basak who did the organisational work. I knew the authors, however, who came to be known as the major Hungry writers and was in correspondence with them: Debi Roy, Saileswar Ghose, Subimal Basak, Pradip Choudhuri, Subo Acharja, Subhas Ghosh, Tridib Mitra, Phalguni Ray, and Arunesh Ghosh. Later Phalguni died from drugs, Tridib gave up writing, and Subo joined a religious sect. Funny to note, a police informer by the name of Pabitra Ballabh had infiltrated the movement keeping a tab on us; we didn't even notice till he himself spilled the beans.

Until 1963 I visited Calcutta frequently, staying at Uttanpara, Ahiritola, Debi's place, or in Subimal Basak's uncle's goldsmith shop, which did not have a window, ceiling fan, or lavatory, compelling me to go to the nearby Sealdah railroad station, where I used the toilets of arriving long-distance trains. We slept on the cement floor using old magazines wrapped in our shirts for pillows. The shop had a castor-oil lamp that Subimal made use of at night for drafting his novel *Chhatamatha,* written in the dialect of horsecart pullers of Dhaka. Subimal was beaten up in December 1963 at the entrance of the Albert Hall Coffee House by a group of status quoists hostile to our movement.

There were other strange happenings too. A couple of presses refused to print *Hungryalist* bulletins; Pradip Choudhuri was expelled from Visva Bharati University, Santiniketan, for his association with the movement; Subhas Ghose was notified to vacate his apartment; Patiram book stall was threatened by a gang for selling the bulletin. Pressure kept on mounting. Refusal of auditoria led us to recite our poems at street corners, parks, cemeteries to the attention of growing crowds every day. The main theme of hostility to us centered round one single argument: that the movement was foreign inspired and against Bengali culture and literary tradition.

In fact all the major Hungryalists were from the lower middle class and came from outside Calcutta. Subimal and I came from Patna, Subo from Bishnupur, Pradip from Agartala, Debi from Howrah, Subhas and Saileswar from Balurghat. Almost all were first-generation literates. One researcher has argued that the breakdown of the extended family was one of the factors in promoting the Hungryalist movement.

The Indian press harped on the tune that the movement's origin should be traced to the Calcutta visit in the early sixties of Allen Ginsberg, Peter Orlovsky, Gary Snyder, and Joanne Snyder. How far that is correct is a matter of conjecture and serious research. I did meet Allen Ginsberg but not the other people; none of the Hungryalists met any of them.

Ginsberg had been to Samir's place at Chaibasa and stopped over for a few nights at Dariapur on his way to a Buddhist pilgrimage at Rajgir in the summer of 1963. Ginsberg was saintly. Dad took him to be Bishma from the Hindu epic *Mahabharata*. In 1985-86 I translated his *Howl* and *Kaddish* into Bengali. In the sixties I had translated some poems of Lorca, Neruda, and Artaud.

Karuna Nidhan, Malay Roy Choudhury, and Anil Karanjai on New Road, Kathmandu, 1966

All these three years from 1961 to 1963 I had been working on *Shoytaner Mukh,* a collection of my poems. Samir selected some of them for their ratiocinative abstraction and total effect in terms of sound and sight. Krittibas Publishers agreed to publish them. There were guarded critical reactions to the book at the time. The cover was based on a drawing made available by Margaret Randal, editor of *El Corno Emplumado,* who was in Buenos Aires at that time.

Exploiting Bengali etymology in the costume of a tyrant jester, I wrote a drama—*Illot*—assured of being staged by Nripen Saha of Gandharba. He retained the manuscript for a year then developed cold feet because of its political overtones. I got it published in the first issue of *Zebra* in 1966.

8

Karuna Nidhan and Anil Karanjai, painters, invited me to Banaras where hashish was available in plenty, the visiting hippies having passed on to them marijuana

and LSD. Subimal and I took a train to Banaras, stayed there for a few days on top of a garage in smoke and hallucination. All four of us made a trip to Kathmandu where we rented a wooden room with four mattresses made of hay. Basu Sasi of the Royal Nepal Academy took care of our food and drink. I loved *kachila,* made of uncooked buffalo flesh, pickled deer meat, and white rum *ela.* There was unrestricted hashish and opium to float in, cool temples to meditate in, and hilltops to recite poems from. I got rid of the taboos of my milieu but reared instead some lice on my skin and hair.

As my presence became known in the Nepali media, Parijat, Nepal's foremost woman poet of the sixties, sent me a word for poetry, drink, and dinner. She was exquisitely beautiful, reclining on a pillow on a floor mattress, without the black panthers Cleopatra had by her side. Serving super-strong homemade liquor in brass saucers, she removed her black woollen robe to show her polio-stricken, cream-coloured legs. I placed my hand on them. She kissed my forehead and informed me she was an admirer of my poems. It was my first literary award.

I attended a few poetry recitations in Kathmandu and met Nepali poets Puskar Lohani, Madan Rengbi, and Padam Sudas. Ramesh Srestha took me to his village, Basantpur, for lunch, flattened green rice soaked in curd, a terrific taste.

Karuna Nidhan and Anil Karanjai talked to the owner of Max Gallery, a black American lady, who arranged for an exhibition of their paintings not for sale. I wrote the brochure. On the concluding day the paintings were placed in one corner and set on fire. Oh, one of the foreign woman spectators cried like a child. Karuna and Anil consoled her. Karuna afterwards became a Maoist, Anil migrated to the United States.

I came back to Patna where Rajkamal, the poet and editor who had introduced Hindi readers to me, was hospitalised. He loved to play chess with me after a pethidine injection. In 1967 he died after a long stint of hospitalisation, monomania, and lack of writing.

9

On September 2, 1964, Sub-Inspector Kaiikinkar Das of the Calcutta Police lodged a complaint based on a copy of a *Hungryalist* bulletin—made available to him by Pabitra Ballabh, a poet—claiming that it came within the purview of Sections 120(B) and 292 of the Criminal Code and I should, along with other members of the movement, be prosecuted. Section 120(B) was for conspiracy against society and Section 292 for the sale, hire, distribution, public exhibition, and circulation of obscene writing.

On September 4, 1964, I was arrested by police officers S. M. Baron and Amal Mukherjee, handcuffed with a rope tied to my waist, and paraded on the streets of Patna. A posse of policemen searched the Dariapur house, broke open Ma and Dad's boxes, seized a large number of books, magazines, letters, manuscripts, and a typewriter, which were never to be returned.

I was incarcerated without food and water in a dark cell with crooks and criminals. The corner of the lockup was used as a toilet by inmates, the flow of urine and shit blocked by a tattered rug; rodents moved around in search of food crumbs and bugs crawled the walls. Through the night I stood like a statue of flesh and bone aside the crooks and criminals, who thought I was absurd. The next day I was taken to the local court on foot in handcuffs with a rope around my waist, together with the bunch of criminals, and released on a bail of ten thousand rupees (six hundred dollars) with orders to present myself at Calcutta Court, which I did. At Calcutta I was interrogated by a group of officials and my interview recorded.

The first thing that happened was I was kicked out of the bank job, making money scarce. Worse still, Granny died, so there was no place to stay at Calcutta.

I was not chargesheeted immediately; the police required me to report to them every alternate day. I felt depressed except for some letters of encouragement from Octavio Paz, Allen Ginsberg, Lawrence Ferlinghetti, and others, which were edited and published by Tridib Mitra in 1969. A lawyer, Satyen Banerjee, volunteered to defend me and intervened to stop my visits to police headquarters.

News of my persecution appeared in the November 4, 1964, issue of Time, City Lights Journal, and Evergreen Review. The Time report said the Hungryalist movement was a "growing band of young Bengalis with tigers in their tanks." I appealed to the Indian Committee for Cultural Freedom for help, but they did nothing. Its executive secretary, A. B. Shah, wrote me in January 1965 that he had met the police chief, who informed him that a number of citizens to whom Hungryalist writings had been made available wanted action against me. Dipak Majumdar, a poet of the fifties, initiated a signature campaign in my favour, got rebuffed by a senior editor, and gave a hasty retreat. Most of the writers in my group were avoiding me; I was feeling alone, tormented, frustrated, estranged, and abandoned.

I made a trip to Bishnupur, Subo Acharja's place; a devout Hindu by then, he reeled off incomprehensible metaphysics. Went to Mursidabad for a change, discovered a cobra snake atop the mosquito-net roof. I was on the verge of breaking down. Hindi author Sharad Deora wrote The College Street Messiah, a novel based on me and our time.

On May 3, 1965, I was chargesheeted under Section 292 of the Criminal Code for my poem Stark Electric Jesus in the court of the presidency magistrate, Mr. Amal Mitra. Commissioned by Bonnie Crown of Asia Foundation, this poem was reprinted in City Lights Journal no. 3 with an essay on the subject by Professor Howard McCord. It was also published separately in the United States in 1965-66 in three ditto editions by Tribal Press with a verifax cover showing the sorcerer of the Trois Frères. The poem is included in my Selected Poems, published by Writers Workshop, Calcutta, in 1989. It is a poem of mourning based on speech rhythms.

The legal battle went on for twenty-to-thirty minutes every week; the prosecution produced witnesses to prove it was my poem, written and circulated by me, seized from my custody, and that it was obscene. Only Pabitra Ballabh testified that it was vulgar and that he had seen me distributing it. Defense witnesses were Sunil Gangopadhyay, poet and novelist; Jyotirmoy Dutta, critic and editor; Tarun Sanyal, professor; and Satrajit Dutta, psychiatrist.

Sunil, in cross-examination, told the court that he had read the poem several times and would read it out loud if the court permitted it. Stark Electric Jesus was a beautiful poem, he said, the expression of an important poet. Tarun said his students had liked the poem, that it was a piece of creative art. Jyotirmoy testified that it was an experimental poem and not at all immoral and obscene. Satrajit said there was no question of inflaming passion or depraving the mind of a reader.

The judge, Amal Mitra, in his ten-page verdict on December 28, 1965, found me guilty, directed me to pay a fine of 200 rupees (fifteen dollars) or be imprisoned for one month, and gave orders for the destruction of all copies of the issue. It being the maximum penalty, the judge did not permit me to appeal to the High Court. I filed a revision petition at the High Court and started searching for a good criminal lawyer.

Stark Electric Jesus was the first condemned poem in Bengali literature. The judge did not rely on prosecution and defense testimony, but rather drafted his own piece of literary criticism, aware of its going down in our literary history, as evident from this last passage of his verdict:

> By no stretch of imagination can it be called, what has been argued, an artistic piece of erotic realism opening up new dimensions to contemporary Bengali literature or a kind of experimental piece of writing, but it appears to be a report of a repressed or a most perverted mind that is obsessed with sex in all its nakedness and thrives on, or revels in, utter vulgarity and profanity preoccupied with morbid erotism and promiscuity in all its naked ugliness and uncontrolled passion for the opposite sex. It transgresses public decency and morality substantially, rather at public decency and morality by its higher morbid erotic effect unredeemed by anything literary or artistic. It is an affront to current community standards, decency, and morality. The writing viewed separately and as a whole treats sex, that great motivating force in human life, in a manner that surpasses the permissible limits judged from our community standards, and as there is no redeeming social value or gain to society which can be said to preponderate, I must hold that the writing has failed to satisfy the time-honoured test. Therefore it has got to be stamped out.

10

Alhough *The Searchlight,* a daily newspaper, published a special supplement on the eve of my conviction, with a twenty-thousand-word essay by its editor, Subhas Chandra Sarker, life for me had become miserable all those six months. Living in a dark, damp, dilapidated room at Uttarpara, alone, shrinking, taking a bath once or twice a week in the Hooghly River to get rid of lice, eating at anybody's expense, begging around for money for the court, no editor agreeing to print my poems, in dwindling health, suffering harsh criticisms, and with dementia creeping in, I felt shattered. All these experiences I was putting bit by bit, being a slow writer, in *Jakham,* a long poem alternating sigh and shriek as I abandoned traditional metrics. It was translated by Carl Weissner in 1967, the German translator of William Burroughs, and reprinted by Joan Silva in *Network,* translated into Hindi by Kanchan Kumar.

Jyotirmoy Dutta introduced me to K. S. Roy, a barrister who had practised in London, and said top attorneys required big money. Professor Howard McCord had raised some money from three editions of *Stark Electric Jesus.* Carol Bergé organised a poetry reading at Saint Mark's Church, New York—by Paul Blackburn, Allen Hoffman, Clayton Eshleman, Armand Schwerrier, Carol Rubenstein, Gary Youree, Allen Planz, Ted Berrigan, Jerome Rothenberg, Bob Nichols, David Antin, Jackson MacLow—and remitted the collection. Special Indian issues of *Intrepid* by Allen De Loach, *Salted Feathers, Fact, San Francisco Earthquake, Imago, Where, Trace, Work, Iconolatre, Kiacto* were printed in the United states and the United Kingdom and the proceeds were sent to me. In Calcutta I got help only from Ashok Mitra and Kamal Kumar Majumdar. I also raised some loans and engaged the attorneys K. S. Roy, Mrigen Sen, Ananga Dhar, and A. K. Basu.

With my conviction most of the Hungryalists started deserting me; it was not possible to hold them together. Debi and Saileshwar, Subo and Ramananda, Subhas and Tridib developed a sort of George Oppen-Louis Zukofsky relationship, making it very difficult to carry on the group with me.

My attorneys were not sure when the case would come up for a hearing, maybe in six months, maybe in ten years. I had drifted around for food and shelter, voyeuring like a fool, depending on remittances from Dad and Samir, straying out to villages, unwanted at the residences of poets and editors, gloomy with plenty of time, when my ill health struck me. Subimal bought me a train ticket for Patna, which I reached in stupor and delirium; Ma weeped at my trauma, and I remained bedridden for a month. Tridib's letters were awaiting my recovery. He had written that Subhas, Saileshwar, Basudeb, Pradip, and Arunesh had launched a new group—keeping Subimal, Debi, and myself out—and that their magazine contained a vituperative attack on us. I felt sad. Phalguni came to Patna to meet me; I advised him never to come again. The doe-eyed nuns had returned in my dreams carrying Parijat's marble body, the candles were now replaced by castor oil lamps.

My ill health, Ma thought, might be due to drugs and sex, so she informed marriage agents to get me involved. The agents knew of my whereabouts and every now and then presented before me a nervous girl of marriageable age for my consent, I had to quarrel it out with Ma to stop the horrible affair.

Music was there to fall back upon as I came to know Robin Dutta, who drew me first into stories from Palestrina, Monteverdi, Purcell, Handel, Haydn, Berlioz, Franck and then to his discs and cassettes of compositions by Bach, Mozart, Beethoven, Schubert, Chopin, and Brahms, an engaging experience relieving my burden. Dad purchased for me a record player with a sitar recital disc of maestro Ravishankar and *thumri* of Bade Gulam Ali. Ferlinghetti sent me Ginsberg's reading of *Kaddish* and Ezra Pound reading his *Cantos,* which I listened to in the evenings. I had, on doctor's advice, stopped smoking except for a rolled tobacco once in a while.

Subimal's younger brother informed Dad that the hearing at the High Court was fixed for July 26, 1967. I didn't feel like going to Calcutta. The life I had spent there was horrifying; I shuddered at the thought. July 26 came and passed away. Subimal arrived after a week, smiling, with newspaper reports of my exoneration and a certified copy of the verdict of Justice T. P. Mukherji of the High Court castigating lower court judge Amal Mitra for his judicial blunder and the Calcutta police for their harassment.

I felt blank, gave Subimal whatever books, correspondence files he wanted, gave up meeting people, withdrew into my loneliness. My blankness continued. I was unable to write, no images flitted by, lines refused to be composed in my mind. I sat at the table

doing nothing, for weeks, for months, nervousness galloped, without a purpose; there was no request from any editor for my poems, no letter from anyone.

11

In the winter of 1968 I was introduced by Sulochna Naidu, a Telugu lady, to her bespectacled friend Shalila Mukherjee, a frail lady of peacock gait, a couple of schoolgirl tresses, deep eyes, and a voice shy enough to make me fumble for words as I controlled myself from placing my head on her lap and weeping. She had lost her mother when a baby; her father had left her with the maternal grandfather, never to return again.

On my first visit her uncle showed me eight rifles and double-barrel guns, the hides of predators he had hunted, and then whistled for his two pet Pomeranians, Suzie and Caesar. I got the message and obliquely told him to get in touch with Dad or Samir in case he felt uncomfortable about me. He did. Samir was hastily dispatched by Ma to descend to Nagpur, more than a thousand kilometers from Patna, for finalising any nuptial possibility.

I married Shalila on December 4, 1968, reciting fullthroated Sanskrit mantras I vaguely understood, prompted by a bearded priest in a saffron robe who had Old Testament-prophet looks, in front of crackling holy fire and smoke, angels, gods, friends, relatives, in a carnival of midnight glory and glamour. The marriage rituals regenerated my lust for life, Wordsworthian fullness, an inspiration to live that was robust. Shalila's cousin married an airport official the same night and the joint marriage created a sort of flutter in the sleepy town.

To avoid the funeral gloom at Patna, where Uncle Sushil had died on the day of my marriage—why such things happen to me I do not know—I made a stopover in Chaibasa at Samir's in-laws' place. I reached Patna to find visitors arriving to celebrate the bridal reception and bereave the dead, provoking Cousin Dolly, Uncle Sushil's daughter, to give me a piece of her mind in chewed verbiage.

I left Patna with Shalila for the tribal jungles of Palamau, four hundred kilometers away by train, in the grip of spring, with a whiff of blooming kino and

"Shalila in 1968. I took the photograph. In the background are flower plants in wood packing boxes on the roof of the Dariapur house."

kapok. We lunched there on coloured rice, barbecued meat, boiled snails, and a dash of liquor made of mahua, rejuvenating my lazy tendencies in pluralist happiness. Pangs of not being able to write were subsiding. Palamau was soothing. The wild elephants, however, didn't give us an audience during the fortnight we stayed.

We made a trip to Shimla by train in February 1969, experiencing the first snowfall I ever saw. Our luggage was placed on the bus top for traversing between Kalka and Shimla and covered with three inches of flakes by the time we stepped down into the knee-deep snow. Then we fetched up a hotel room and finished a full brandy. We didn't have sufficient clothes to go out in the snow, so we remained indoors for the period of our stay.

When we were back in Patna, George Dowden was there, in a saffron dhoti, with the flowing hair of a sannyasin. He was working on Ginsberg's bibliography. Shalila fed him some Indian dishes. I

felt a little embarrassed, with nothing to talk about, alienated from what was going on at Calcutta. He excluded me from his India memoirs.

Shalila introduced a Marathi dimension to our Bengali cuisine; we had a dining table now from her Nagpur job savings, curtains on the windows, flower-pots, stainless steel utensils in place of brass, a part-time maid.

Ma was free; she seized the opportunity to revive her interest in Hindu gods and goddesses she had forgotten after coming to Dariapur, sang holy songs in the evenings. Ma and Shalila enjoyed each other's pagan faith, solicited mantras from respective gurus, followed worship rituals. Ma's favourite god was Ganesha, a marble replica originally worshipped by Granny. Ma did abandon her Ganesha later and transferred her interest to stitching a *kantha,* a patchwork bedsheet for my daughter.

Dimple, as we called our daughter, born on September 5, 1969, got her name changed to Anushree fourteen years later when a film star named Dimple hit the screen. She introduced me to an infant's universe of wordless communication that I never knew so closely, her vocabulary growing sound by sound, deciphered by Ma and Dad in their new vocation of baby-sitting after Shalila went out to her job as an accounts assistant on a rickshaw. Annoyed with my impatience in teaching Anushree the English alphabet and numbers, she appointed a tutor.

On a day of cloudburst, driblets trickled down from the ceiling and entered the bookshelf, which had been shut for more than a year. I opened it to find corridors of hefty termites revelling through Sade's *Hundred-Twenty Days of Sodom* to Genet's *Our Lady of the Flowers.* I felt like weeping; my throat choked, I allowed the white ants to live and spread their colony. Why did I have this acquisitive streak? Since then I have been giving away books and magazines to others after I have read them. Lithe turning of water, Ezra Pound had written.

12

I got a bank officer's job in 1972, conducting credit utilisation studies and impact assessments in deep rural areas I had not been to earlier. I began to understand the life and living of cultivators and artisans. I loved the job. Now I could tell from afar whether a paddy stalk was wheat or barley, pulses of various plants, chillies or *rohu, katla* and *mrigel* fish in pond water; I acquainted myself with the daily life of a farmer's family, the ruthlessness of rural poverty, machinations of caste substratums, village violence, names of birds, herbs, shrubs, and trees I had not known, men and women ploughing, harvesting, threshing, levelling, jungle-clearing with their own hands. I thought of Whitman, Neruda, Mayakovsky, and the Bengali poets Jibanananda and Sukanta but was unable to write any line myself.

Talking to people was a part of my job—farmers, labourers, social servicemen, government officials, rural headmen, bankers, craftsmen—characters filtering through experience. Hundreds of thousands of kilometers I traversed from village to village—fifteen days a month—on train, steamer, boat, van, bus, horsecart, elephant, camel, bullock cart. Alone on a bed in a hotel or country house, I thought of poetry. I was barren.

Shalila bought me a Lambretta scooter on my birthday in 1973 (we started celebrating it after our marriage; Ma and Dad had not been aware of the custom). We drove into town Sunday evenings entertaining ourselves with Chinese dishes. I had become fond of rum and cola, given up smoking, gathered fat around my waist.

Our son, Bappa, was born on February 19, 1975, a caesarian.

Saint Joseph's convent, my first school (where I got Anushree, later Bappa, admitted), had expanded like a deep sea fish out of water: cement crawled to eat up violets, roses, marigolds, dahlias, chrysanthemums; doe-eyed nuns were replaced by serious-looking Keralites; children spilled out like mustard seeds from multistoried blocks onto grassless playgrounds; Saint Joseph's statue was full of crowshit. I visited the other school, Ram Mohan Roy Seminary, in ruins now, physically and ideologically, under a moneymaking buffoon of a principal, damn it.

The inevitable stroke in the winter of 1975: I pissed blood, my blood pressure shot up beyond limits, infarction of the heart, bedrest for two months, medi-

cines, medicines, oh, pain in my thought process, fear of death, but no poetry came to my mind. Editors and poet friends might have forgotten me.

13

My office, the Agricultural Refinance and Development Corporation, in the summer of 1979 transferred me to Lucknow, city of nabobs during the British raj, which saw to the decimation of the Moslem aristocracy. The town was far better than Patna. I couldn't get a house and stayed for some time with Abdul Karim, a Telugu-speaking Moslem agricultural economist, and afterwards with Prabhakara, an analyst who spoke the Kannada language, who prevented me from lapsing into disorder as I was damn scared of loneliness.

The office gave me a newly constructed bungalow across the Gomti River and adjacent to the Kukrail Crocodile Sanctuary in early 1980 when Shalila and the children joined me. I developed a lawn of Bermuda grass and a rose garden in the front; Shalila took care of a kitchen garden at the rear. I planted guava, jujube plum, banana, papaya, and horseradish, got the fruits, felt fantastic. On the gate we had multicoloured bougainvillea through the entire year spreading a soft carpet for visitors. I regained my health.

Being the Section in Charge of credit deployment for poverty-alleviation programmes, I found myself in a tension of human misery, unredeemable through post-Keynesian methods. World Bank minions, dizzy with imaginative success, looked like jokers doling out cookies to the dead and dying from their Tutankhamen gold masks, from poems of Francois Dufrene or Gil Wolman, from paintings by Mondrian or Kandinsky. This entire period from 1979 had been one of regaining helplessness for me. I was a drawing-room intellectual, nuts, retheorising frightening abstractions, suffering from an inexplicable sense of guilt capped with a secret gnawing anxiety of not being able to write, which aggravated my nervous system. I knew that only ten percent of people had the freedom to pursue happiness, the rest were nonpersons, invisible pariahs of our polity. There was nothing I could do, nothing.

Ma and Dad came to Lucknow to spend the winter of 1981 with us, Samir having shifted with his family to Patna. We enjoyed winter, sitting in wicker chairs placed on the lawn, dozing off during sunny, shaded afternoons, disturbed occasionally by a couple of grumbling doves nesting in the bougainvillea. Flocks of low-flying Russian white cranes glided towards Bharatpur Sanctuary a hundred kilometers away, parrots nibbled ripe guava; there were sparrows, swifts, woodpeckers, mynahs, bitterns, thrushes, buntings, cuckoos, falconets, larks, kites, orioles, storks, warbiers visiting the garden, and the insects, frogs, butterflies of endless creations, and earthworms and lizards. It was a long way from Bakharganj days.

As the astrologers had predicted Dad would die first, Ma didn't reveal the severe arthritis she was suffering from, detected when her legs swelled, but not before wrong medicines prescribed by a physician led to a massive heart attack, hospitalisation, and death two days after the 1982 Diwali festival of lights. Samir rushed from Patna in response to my telegram, told me and Shalila we had neglected Ma. She was cremated on a funeral pyre the next morning on the banks of the Gomti River, turned into ashes from which I collected a small shining piece of bone and kept it in my purse. I remained in ritual mourning for thirteen days in a single piece of loincloth, barefoot, without shaving or combing my hair, at the end of which I shaved my head, took a bath in the Ganges, and fed Brahmins.

Ma had been in a coma for two days, cut off from us, in her suffering, oxygen pipe in nostrils, eyes closed, soundless. Where was she!

Personal loss is the exact description of the depressive void created by her absence. I brooded in blank anguish and aching insight; no death had absorbed me earlier. A few months later, returning from the office, I found myself weeping one day in the busy market square of Lucknow, overwhelmed by a sudden feeling choking my throat.

I booked train tickets for Dad, Shalila, and the children, journeyed two nights to the temple towns of south India, stayed for a month, and returned confused, mystified, unsettled, words and images in a whirling chaos in me searching for an expansive flow of ideation. I wrote several love poems as they kept on coming, mailed them to Kamal Chakraborty, editor of *Kourab* who had been pestering me for poems during the last couple of years. Floodgates were sprung open.

"Brother Samir; Kamal Chakraborty, editor of **Kourab***; Dr. Uttam Das; Malay; and Bela, Samir's wife, on the eve of Honey's—Samir and Bela's daughter—marriage. They are in ceremonial dress. Calcutta, 1986"*

That spread the word. Poet and researcher Dr. Uttam Das with his wife, Malabika, visited us at Lucknow with the proposal for a book on the Hungryalist movement for which I made available all the material from Patna. His book appeared to stir a hornet's nest again, and I had to give several interviews clarifying my current thoughts on life and poetry, past and present. There was now a generation of poets who were not born or were infants when I was convicted for poetry, and they had their own image of me.

Uttam got the manifestoes and earlier poems collected and published in two volumes in 1985 and 1986, with covers designed by Charu Khan, turning them into avant-garde collectors' items. The manifesto collection was dedicated to Malabika, whose voice resembled Parijat's, and the poetry collection to Bhulti, my mother.

I reciprocated Dr. Das's consideration by a visit to his house and farm at Baruipur near Calcutta, a cool country greened with fruits, foliage, coconuts, and bamboos. Malabika, a teetotaler, cooked steamed prawns for me. I visited Debi Roy and his wife, Mala, and Subimal Basak; they had greyed and become old. Debi, now secretary of the Indian Writers Association, had purchased a flat and Subimal had constructed a double-decker house. Debi had become a prolific writer. Subimal had translated the Hindi author Premchand and published an *Anthology of Superstitions*.

On a request from Professor Sibnarayan Ray, a radical humanist thinker, I wrote a story for his periodical recounting the Hungryalist days, leading to an avalanche of special issues of *Godhuli Mone, Swakal, Uttarapath, Jiraffe, Pat her Panchali, Goddo Poddo Samvad, Atalantik,* etc., on the movement.

I was now experimenting for a post-Hungryalist, eugenic ethos in my poems, a diction to overcome the musical pattern of Bengali language, a possible perfection in timelessness, closeting myself in the back room when all had gone for work and school.

Prokash Karmaker, painter, who was in France for some years, suggested we bring out a one-page offset magazine with a drawing by him and a poem of mine on the theme of violence. Every month during 1985 and 1986 a sheet was published. These poems were collected, and publisher-poet Mrityunjay Sen of Mahadiganta Publishers brought out my book *Medhar Batanukul Ghungur* during the Calcutta Book Fair of 1987, with a cover designed by Jogen Choudhuri, head of the department of painting and sculpture, Visva Bharati University. The book was a great critical success.

14

Lucknow for me had become a small place now. I moved to Bombay as deputy manager in the National Bank for Agriculture and Rural Development, staying for some time in a house inside a mango orchard in Borivili, shifting later to a Santa Cruz apartment provided by office. I could have gone to Calcutta but didn't, feeling scared of the collectivised response and streamlined thinking of the city and remembering my experience of having lived in squalor, filth, and poverty there despite the fact that my great-great granpa once owned the city.

Coming to Bombay, I loved it: its fast life, Zoroastrians, Moslems, Goanese, Orthodox Marathis, Iranian restaurants, Gujarati jewellers, the Western cultural inroads, and, above all, the sea. I visited Nissim Ezekiel, the grand old man of Indian poetry in English, Adil Jussawala, and cute Charmayne D'Souza of Bombay's Poetry Circle, dubbed by Professor John O. Perry of Tufts University, Massachusetts, as below international standards.

I have wondered why Indian poetry should be judged by Western native norms. Why can't the editors and critics in the West have a feel of the soil of one's Swa-

Malay and Shalila in their Santa Cruz apartment in Bombay, 1989

hili, Nepali, or Bengali mother? And unless one gains a foothold in the U.S.A. and the U.K., international recognition remains a pipedream.

When Professor P. Lal of the Writers Workshop agreed to bring out my *Selected Poems* in English in 1989, designed by himself with a cotton loom sari cover, I saw the end of the tunnel. The translation is shabby but it certainly opens up the chance to work out my next ventures. Reviews have been wonderful.

Meanwhile, I have kept myself busy drafting my memoirs for Mizanur Rahaman's *Quarterly*—published in Dhaka, Bangladesh—going back in time, hazily remembering people and events, moments of joy and humiliation, breakdown and despair, challenges of loneliness, and Ma talking of Patna's devastating earthquake in which she lost her black-buck and swans, five years after which I was born.

(March 12, 1990)

POSTSCRIPT

Malay Roy Choudhury contributed the following update to *CA* in 2003:

Things have changed a lot during the last two decades, most visible being that I have grown a beard, salt-pepper by now, and look older after sustaining two heart attacks, one of them after undergoing angioplasty and stenting. I grew the beard not because I wanted to look like a philosopher, but just for camouflage during my job as a rural development investigator and facilitator when I was required to extensively tour India and meet farmers, weavers, artisans, landless labourers, fishermen, shepherds and such people living in villages who did not open up easily to an urban outsider's questionnaire. Since a portion of my name, *Choudhury,* would be found amongst Muslims, Hindus, and Sikhs throughout the country and I could speak English, Hindi, Bangla, and a little bit of Urdu, I could feign to become an insider or outsider as the situation demanded. Apart from the official information collated and processed during these visits, I started maintaining a personal corpus of people's experiences, incidents, vagaries faced, as well as the nightmares they encountered, with a secret idea that I have been nursing of writing a novel after I completed the assignment of Hungryalist movement memoirs in Mizanur Rahaman's *Quarterly,* which was named *Hungry Kimvadanti* and published as a hardbound book in 1994.

The beard proved to be a risky proposition as well, when Hindu-Muslim riots and terrorist bombing broke out in Mumbai (earstwhile Bombay) in the aftermath of the demolition of the disputed temple-mosque structure at Ayodhya. In Mumbai a bearded man ostensibly meant a Muslim. Violence and mayhem during the riot-week became so nerve-wracking that even some of my Muslim neighbours and colleagues shaved off their beards. I did not. I knew it would be a defeat. I disregarded everybody's advice and ventured out along with Shalila, attending to our normal routine, on to the streets of the city which were palpably tense. Mumbai came back to normalcy and I have my beard intact to this day. But strangely, looking back at my tenure at Lucknow, when I was serving as a member of the board of directors of the Faizabad Gramin Bank under whose jurisdiction the pilgrim township of Ay-

Daughter Anushree and son-in-law Prashant at their marriage ceremony, 1993

odhya is stationed, I do not remember anyone telling me that the structure was communally so relevant and sensitive. I had seen only one policeman dozing off his bored afternoon loneliness, who had asked me and the bank's managing director to remove our shoes, money purse, and waist belt before entering the precincts. Well, collective human happenstance may convert inorganic reality into organic imagination, without any rhyme or reason.

Since our Santa Cruz residential colony had enough parking space and adequate security, we borrowed some funds and added our savings to it to enable us to purchase a Fiat car (1990) after Shalila and I learned driving at an automobile school. Though we were able to drive the vehicle quite smoothly on Mumbai's busiest roads, both of us failed at the Road Transport officer's license awarding test, the reason for which was explained later by a tout, that for each license one has to pay a fixed bribe for a particular type of vehicle. We protested to the inchange of the automobile school and obtained our licenses. Visiting the sea every morning, to Chowpati, Marine Drive, Nariman Point, Juhu, and other shores in our car, all four of us, became sort of a daily fun-filled routine. Santa Cruz being a locality where severalHollywood film stars lived, we could see hourglass figures with pretty faces jogging on the shores in order to maintain their saleability. On holidays we went for long drives. My son, Bappa, now called Jitendra, did not go to an automobile school and learned to drive within a couple of days. Occasionally I resorted to drunk driving while returning from a friend's or relative's cocktail *hungama,* the neon signs and sodium lights of Mumbai streets blinking through the amazed windscreen. I met with an accident only once, while reversing the car, and the disfigured vehicle caused a sadness that quite surprised me, as this feeling was previously unknown; some sort of *de profundis.*

In one of my visits to Calcutta (now Kolkata) from Mumbai, I travelled to Kotrong to meet Dad who was staying with uncle Bishwanath for quite some time. Steeped in Hindu scriptures he looked quite lonely after Ma's death. That is the last time I met him as he went back to Patna to live with Samir, my elder brother, at our Dariapur residence, from where he used to write long sad letters to Shalila and to my daughter, Anushree. I learned of his death on October 8, 1991, when I was on tour to Bhubaneshwar and could reach Patna only after his cremation, as I had to pick up Shalila and the children from Mumbai. As a mark of respect to his departure, both Samir and I had to get our heads tonsured. I returned to Dariapur residence after a decade and found it desolate beyond recognition without Ma and Dad or my collection of books, emptied by Samir's cobrother Ranju Bhattacharja, who sold them to run his family, and with the huge framed photographs of Leo Tolstoy and Rabindranath Tagore absent from the walls of the room that was once my study and the originating station of the Hungryalist movement.

When I had met Dad at Kotrong he was quite annoyed with the Left Front government of West Bengal as the school books, which the administration had had written by historians, claimed that Job Charnok was the father of Calcutta. Dad claimed that it was our ancestors, the *Saborno Choudhurys,* who actually established the city, and advised me to trace out our ancestral lineage, which I did, as I had been toying with the idea of writing a childhood memoir with occasional flashbacks to antiquity, which every now and then used to be referred to during our poverty stricken Bakharganj days, possibly as a psychological safe heaven.

I researched and found out that our clan surname, Roy Choudhury, was bestowed on my warrior ancestor Lak-

shmikanta Gangopadhyay (1570-1649) by Emperor Jehangir of India when he defeated a few local rajahs backed by the Portugese armada. Lakshmikanta's grandfather Panchanan also was a warrior in Emperor Akbar's cavalry. Along with the title, Lakshmikanta was awarded revenue rights over several shoreline villages, sunderban forests, and water surfaces, which today is known as greater Calcutta. Since Lakshmikanta was a Saborno Brahmin, our clan, comprising about twenty thousand members spread throughout the world today, is known as Saborno Choudhurys. When Jehangir's discendants forced the clan to hand over the rights to East India Company in 1698, the Saborno Choudhurys lost their sheen and got decentered to eke out alternate sources of living. The Durgapuja festival, started by Lakshmikanta in 1610, is still celebrated every year in the remnant of his palace where the deed of transfer to the British was signed. I belong to the branch of Ratneshwar Roy Choudhury (1670-1718), great grandson of Lakshmikanta, who moved to the west of river Hooghly to establish Uttarpara township. My Granpa broke out of Uttarpara, became a roving traveller, and as a result of a chance meeting with English writer Rudyard Kipling's father, John Lockwood Kipling, curator of Lahore Museum (now in Pakistan), learned photography from him.

Dad would have been delighted to know that the Kolkata branch of Saborno Choudhurys sued the government of West Bengal at the High Court in 2002, and got the distorted history of Job Charnok removed from school books and all other records. While comparing our Patna clan with the Kolkata clan, I found myself and other members of Patna clan hybridised culturally due to the influences to which the family has happily exposed itself from Granpa's travelling days, a feature I have dealt with in my novel *Ei Adham Oi Adham* through the apparently incoherent discourse of a schoolkid whose childish discursive practices reveal that the precolonial-premodern self-definition of the adults around him had long been dispossessed, but the hybridised individual, collectively and singly, wants to repossess it which, however, does not exist. This novel, a risky proposition for a publisher, could be placed before readers only in 2001 when Utpal Bhattacharya of Kabitirtha Publishers was quite impressed with the strangeness of the narrative. Utpal had earlier published the second edition of my Hungryalist long poem *Jakham.*

For my daughter and son, though Mumbai proved to be far more crowded and fast compared to the leisurely city of Lucknow, they could get into and come out of jam-packed buses and sardine-tin trains quite easily, which initially appeared a bit difficult for me and Shalila. The Santa Cruz vegetable and fish market was so crowded that bodies were almost always pressed to each other, a physical experience I learned to bear with. Shalila could not, and found herself grumbling whenever she went for marketing. The parking lot was a kilometer away. Once when I was going to Anushree's Parle College, it was a quite dark early morning, she got down from the train at Parle station from the ladies compartment but I overshot the distance due to packed crowding in gent's compartment, and returned to find her laughing with friends on college steps as she outgrew me after coming to Mumbai. Both Anushree and Jitendra knew all the roads and routes of Mumbai much faster than we did.

Publication of Hungryalist memoirs in Mizanur Rahaman's *Quarterly* prompted editors of Bangladeshi magazines to seek for my collection of poems. *Medhar Batanukul Ghungur* contained poems written when I was at Lucknow. The poems I started writing at Mumbai took a completely different structural and dictional turn, not at all intentionally. I wrote a hundred-line poem called *Hattali* (Clapping), my last long poem. The bunch of poems I wrote while at Mumbai were published in two collections, *Chitkarsamagra* and *Chhatrakhan*. These poems are being called *adhunantika,* which, when translated, means postmodern; and not only mine, works of several other poets have been called *adhunantika.* After being told that my poems were postmodern, I started reading books on the subject, as well as on postcolonialism, postmarxism, poststructuralism, ecofeminism, and subaltern studies.

The knowledge proved quite helpful. Samir, my elder brother, had shifted his base to Kolkata in 1991 and established a publication venture under the banner of Haowa49 Publishers. He told me to start writing a novel, since on his return to Kolkata he was stunned to find that almost all dissenters have vanished, and writers were scared to write things which might be unpalatable to the political masters. I had not written a novel before. I did not want to write on the lines that mass or class novels were being written. Instead of beginning, middle, end technique with a few central characters, I started scribbling on paper sheets the actual life incidents of people I knew of, my university mates and Reserve Bank of India colleagues, their involvement in urban and rural micro level politics,

violence, single and collective sexual extravaganza, unethical practices, vagabondism etc., that I could recollect. I took two years to write a hundred pages, and then arranged the pages to give a semblance of sequence. I allowed six months' incubation time, and then worked on the final draft, naming the book *Dubjaley Jetuku Prashwas* (Saved Breath in Deep Waters). On its publication in 1994 it was hailed as outstanding by writers of such diverse opinion as Kartik Lahiri and Sayad Mustafa Siraj. A second edition was published by Avishkar Publishers.

I had to withdraw from my writing table for some time in 1992 as Shalila suddenly became sick; her feet and flesh below her eyes got swelled every now and then, and her underbelly started hardening. Clinical tests could not reveal her ailment. A specialist doctor anticipated kidney trouble, and his treatment, instead of curing, further worsened her condition. On enquiry we came to know of Dr. Shankari, a lady gynecologist who was considered to be an expert in female anatomy. She diagnosed the problem and referred Shalila to Dr. Bhalerao, surgeon in charge at Hinduja Hospital. Shalila had to undergo an operation spanning five hours. We learnt that during the caesarian operation at the time of Jitendra's birth, a touch of knife had inadvertently slashed the stomach wall, and intestines had come out and taken the shape of a ball which went on increasing in size over these years, collecting fat around itself. I did the cooking and ran the show till she recovered. I thanked Ma as well as the bangle seller at Dariapur who had taught me how to cook normal and special dishes.

*

Anushree was good at studies. She graduated in science, completed postgraduate work in marine biology, did a diploma in export-import management and a diploma in computer science. On August 21, 1993, she married herself to Prashant Dass, a gold medalist mechanical engineer and management postgraduate who was working with Times Bank. Prashant is quite handsome and smart. He is a Punjabi from Multan, now in Pakistan. Anushree also got a job at Tata Exports. They took an apartment in Virar about 50 km north of Santa Cruz. Shalila thought that Anushree might not be conversant with daily cooking and used to carry cooked food quite frequently to her office or her apartment, which I presume might have interfered with their convenience, as a result of which they

Son Jitendra's **upanayanam** *(sacred thread) ceremony in 1996*

shifted to new jobs at New Delhi. Anushree joined the Indian Express newspaper, gave up, joined a school for elite children, gave up, and decided to stay at home when Prashant purchased a house on the outskirts of Delhi. Since Jitendra's *upanayanam* (sacred thread) ceremony had not been performed till then, Prashant arranged for it at New Delhi Kali Bari temple, Jitendra being seriously religious compared to Anushree's staunch atheism.

After Anushree's marriage and departure for Delhi, Jitendra found himself somewhat lost and did not appear for his first-year graduation examination. My transfer from place to place and frequent change of his schools and friends might have affected somewhere deeper inside him. I got him admitted in Ahmadnagar Engineering College where he got hostel accommodation. Meanwhile I got transfer orders to Kolkata. Anushree in Delhi, Jitendra in Ahmadnagar, me at Kolkata, Shalila felt enough was enough, resigned from her Mumbai job, got our belongings packed and transported on a truck, booked the car by Indian Airlines flight to join me at Kolkata, where we had purchased a flat in 1988, unknowingly in a post-partition refugee locality, which gave us cultural nightmares, as we found out that the apparent Marxist bastion lived in sonic loudspeaker boom throughout the year in worshipping prehistoric idols of Shani, Shitala, Manasa, Kartika, Sankata, Vishwakarma, Jagaddhatri, and other gods and goddesses. People of the locality are so antiquated that curd, french chalk, and plaster of paris are not sold after sundown. Shalila says it is not West Bengal but Waste Bengal. The redeeming feature is that the vegetables and edible herbs in the local Bansdroni market are fresh from the field, and fishes swimming in tubs may be purchased just by identifying the ones the customer prefers.

I had earlier visited West Bengal for a few days to a few weeks on some assignments. Now I returned to the Saborno Choudhury homeland after twenty-five years to live the rest of my life, and found it changed beyond recognition. College Street, on which Subimal Basak was beaten up during Hungryalist movement by old-school writers, was now unwalkable due to hundreds of kiosks selling books. With the financial backing of a developer, a four-storied building had come up at uncle Bishwanath's Kotrong hutment. The Uttarpara villa, constructed by a Turkish architect three hundred years ago, was in complete ruins after uncle Sunil's death, with walls smithereened by tentacles of wild banyan trees. Sheathed swords, horse saddles, huge utensils, palm leaf scriptures, Persian books, etc., all had vanished. Uttarpara was a sylvan town in my childhood, now full of matchbox houses teaming with sweating people I do not know from where. The other side of the railroad, Makhla, was a sprawling green rice field to the horizon, even during Hungryalist movement days, now looked studded with matchbox houses and quarreling housewives. Hooghly River was no longer visible from Grand Trunk road as the shoreline was blocked by apartment houses. The famous Jaikrishna Library of Uttarpara, once lively with the presence of nineteenth century greats such as Michael Madhusudan Dutt, Rabindranath Tagore, Ishwarchandra Vidyasagar, Subhas Chandra Bose, Arabinda and Mary Carpenter, now looked desolate and ghostly. As it had happened with Patna after Dad's death, similarly I could feel my relations snapped with Uttarpara. Driving the car from Kolkata to Kotrong and Uttarpara required magical skills, as the roads were potholed, encroached upon by hawkers, crowded with loafers, and nobody bothered to obey traffic rules. It was a world apart from Mumbai, and I never dared to drive in Kolkata thereafter.

My Kolkata job of rural development facilitator was a glimmer amid depression. I was deputy general manager now, and the Officer's Association members had elected me the president of their union. I could now prepare my own program and visit any accessible village or town in West Bengal accompanied by one or two junior officers who performed the requisite official work. I mostly gossiped with people, observed their life style, marked their way of talking, discussed their sociopolitical problems and vocational rivalries, and collected snatches of their life. Since I could not go inside people's houses to talk to the womenfolk to ascertain their private problems, Shalila started accompanying me to collate this segment of the information, especially the state of affairs in the kitchen. During these forays also my beard performed the camouflaging well. Shalila was born and brought up in Maharashtra, which gave her way of talking an attractive distance that relieved her of acting her role. I collected a lot of information to toy with the idea of extending *Dubjaley Jetuku Prashwas* into a trilogy, augmenting the narrative panorama in stages.

Pradip Bhattacharya of Raktakarabi Publishers was impressed with *Dubjaley Jetuku Prashwas* and asked for a novel. I picked up a few characters from *Dubjaley* just for linkage, and shaped out several new characters without allowing any to hold the centre stage. I selected the most underdeveloped district of Bihar as a backdrop and shifted the narrative from urban to rural locales in order to destroy the then reigning aesthetic reality of Kolkata-centric fiction. Halfway through I shifted the narrative to West Bengal, journeying with secret Marxist insurgents comprised of untouchable caste people who actually were fighting an agrarian caste war. I named the book *Jalanjali* (Water Oblation). Prakash Karmakar lent a drawing for the cover. Pradip Bhattacharya did not get the book reviewed as he claimed that his market niche was sufficient to get all the copies absorbed.

During my stay at Lucknow I had translated Allen Ginsberg's *Howl and Other Poems* and *Kaddish* for two magazines. In view of Ginsberg's readership in West Bengal and Bangladesh, two publishers brought them out in book form. I also translated Jean Cocteau's long poem *Crucifixion,* a bunch of poems of Tristan Tzara, and William Blake's *Marriage of Heaven and Hell,* which I first got published in periodicals. From their small presses Prabhat Choudhury published *Crucifixion,* Kajal Sen published the Tzara poems, and Shubhankar Das published Blake's poem in book form. Bangla readers were not exposed to this side of the paradise, and all the translated books were sold out. At the response of readers to these translated works I traced out a translated copy of Blaise Cendrar's *Trans Siberian Express* from Subimal Basak's archive which was published in the 1960s in a *Hungryalist* bulletin, and requested Samiran Majumdar to reprint it in *Amritalok* magazine, which he did. He also brought it out in book form, but unfortunately most of the copies got charred due to the devastating fire which struck the Kolkata Book Fair that year. Another turnaround I created was in interviewing writers. I found out that most of the interviewers were asking only one-line ques-

tions. I introduced a different pattern so that the questions probe into the depth of the author's various works. I published interviews of Kedar Bhaduri, Dipankar Datta, Swadesh Sen, and Subimal Basak ranging up to seventy pages.

In August, 1996, one night while I was enquiring over the telephone about the condition of an officer who had met with an accident and was hospitalized in the morning, I sustained a heart attack, and while slumping down got my left ear slashed. Shalila was alert to put a couple of Sorbitrate tablets below my tongue, call for a cab, and get me admitted in the same hospital in which my colleague had been admitted in the morning. Shalila had held a kerchief on my profusely bleeding ear, which was stitched after I was shoved into the Intensive Care Unit, Shalila waiting outside throughout the night. Angiography revealed that some of my arteries were blocked, and in order to clear them, a balloon angioplasty was carried out and stenting done. In the process black patches developed on my right loin around which needles had been pricked, which, I came to know later, were not sterilized. The doctors might have panicked, and the heavy dose of drugs they administered caused severe arthritis.

It was a hell of an experience at the hospital. I found young doctors, instead of attending to patients, flirted during the day and slept during the night. Old patients wailing in pain were mimicked by menial staff. Since the hospital had a checkout time rule similar to hotels, dead bodies of patients were retained for a few additional hours to increase the stay by one more day. Clinical tests were carried out that were not required at all. One day the hospital employees went on lightning strike, and a few patients died in my block, from where I could hear the slogans being raised outside. Shalila had to run around for my early release. I got home with severe arthritis. Winter had set in, and taking off my sweater and shirt was possible only with the help of my son and daughter, who had come down to give moral and physical support to their mother. I had unbearable pains in my fingers and thought my writing career was over. Shalila had appointed a driver and took me every evening to the physiotherapist for exercise as well as a hot wax wash of my hands. But I developed a high fever which, the doctors of the same hospital I had been admitted to, failed to cure. Samir's cobrother Shanti Lahiri, also a poet—Samir has a museum of cobrothers—told him about Dr. T. K. Das who attended to only ten patients a day in the evening.

Right from ten o'clock in the morning Samir and my son queued up at the doctor's clinic to be examined at five o'clock in the evening when my turn came. In about six months; time the pains subsided, though I still suffer from joint pain every now and then when I am required to spend lot of time on the word processor. As a way out I have started drafting with a pen, which I get typed by a computer operator. I do not have an internet connection and visit cyber cafes once a fortnight to check my mails. My son also keeps a watch. However, the rest and recuperation proved beneficial for the fact that I could delve into the works of Theodor W. Adorno, Ludwig Wittgenstein, Michel Foucault, Jacques Lacan, Gayatri Chakravorty Spivak, Umberto Eco, Edward Said, and Homi Bhaba, which created a knowledge bank in me that I could draw upon while writing subsequent short stories and novels.

*

After my recovery, Jitendra went back to Ahmadnagar and Anushree to Delhi. The womenfolk in Anushree's in-laws place were annoyed with her because she could not bear a child till then. She had conceived twice but the gynaecologist got them aborted due to complications which further got her in-laws disgruntled. The third time, the baby boy died in her womb just a couple of days before delivery, and Shalila had to fly immediately to Delhi to handle Anushree's tension, and get the baby cremated, since her in-laws at that time were stationed at a remote place called Jajpur in Orissa. In view of her depression, and Prashant having been offered a lucrative executive job with Shell, they shifted to Mumbai. Prashant's father, Mr. Narayan Dass, died of coronary thrombosis at doctorless Jajpur.

I retired from the rural development facilitator's job in October, 1997. Since Shalila felt she was missing Mumbai, and Anushree had shifted to that city, we pooled our savings to purchase a one-room flat in Mumbai to enable Jitendra to use our flat in Kolkata to search for a job. Getting a job in West Bengal by someone not connected with the ruling party apparatus had become impossible during the last two decades. Moreover, postpartition refugee vandalism had led to the closure of almost all factories owned by ethnic West Bengalies. Factories owned by non-Bengalies had fled to other states. Whatever remained were stricken with lockout, strike, suspension of work, go-slow, complete standstill of the state called *bandh,*

daylong obstruction of roads and railway tracks called *avarodh,* mob encirclement of executives or officials called *gherao,* roughing up and mugging of doctors and professors called *prativad,* etc. No author dared to write fictions concerning such a doomed condition. Even if someone did he would not get a publisher. But in February, 2000, the day we arrived from Kolkata to our Mumbai flat, I sustained a heart attack again, which I survived only because the neighbors carried my unconscious body to a nearby heart clinic and the doctor administered two life saving injections. Shalila said, "Thank God we were not at Kolkata."

My novel *Naamgandho* ("Fragrant Name") was rejected by all the publishers I approached, even by Pradip Bhattacharya, who had published *Jalanjali.* Somehow Mizanur Rahaman came to know about it and arranged for publication of the book by Sahana Publishers of Dhaka, Bangladesh, in 1999. In India the book was published only this year, in April, 2003, by Haowa49 Publishers. During my illness, I had maintained a notebook, scribbling therein, in my spider handwriting, uncommon association of words to construct sentences, which I used in the fiction. For linkage, I had brought into *Naamgandho* a couple of characters from *Dubjaley Jetuku Prashwas* and *Jalanjali.* The narrative base of the fiction was the plight of potato farmers and corrupt practices of storing potatoes in cold storages set against the backdrop of village politics of power and pelf. I had collected actual events, incidents and life stories of innumerable individuals. I weaved them into some political dirt that is regularly printed in vernacular newspapers, clippings of which I had preserved in sufficient numbers. I was provoked to write the novel by the shocking fact that whenever there was overproduction of paddy, potato, or mango, a large number of farmers committed suicide, as they were unable to recover production costs to repay their loans to usurers! At the same time a large number of landless labourers, mostly lowest caste people and tribals, died of hunger as they had no purchasing power due to nil income! Some womenfolk had informed Shalila that whenever there was overproduction of farm produce, they would invariably hide bottles of pesticides to thwart suicide attempts of the menfolk. *Naamgandho* had a great reception among younger generation writers and critics both in Bangladesh and India.

There were, however, a lot of arguments for and against my post-Hungryalist poems both in the small press as well as in academic circles, mainly because I

The author with his granddaughter, Mihica, 2002

had done away with the inherent lyricism of Bangla language. The problem lay, I found out, not with my poems but with the teachers of Bangla in most of the schools, who got their job simply because they were ruling party members and functioned as vote canvassing machinary. Most of the teachers had poor academic records or they did not update themselves. I selected twenty-three of my poems, including *Stark Electric Jesus* (this poem pops up quite frequently on personal websites of poet-aspirants in various languages), which had faced obscenity charges during my Hungryalist trial, and deconstructed them myself. The furor against my poems died down. I named the book *A,* which is the first alphabet letter of Bangla and may be of all languages of the world. The pathetic state of Bangla teaching was discovered by me during my tours throughout West Bengal as rural development facilitator. I also found out that abolition of teaching English language in government schools had harmed readers in many ways. Students from Christian missionary schools only read English books. I took upon myself to write essays on various subjects, ideas, and personalities with which Bangla magazine readers were not conversant. I got them first published in small

press magazines. Half of the essays could be anthologised. About eighty published essays are yet to get bound in hard or paperback covers. I also introduced Bangla readers to Salvador Dali and Paul Gaugin's autobiographies as well as Tzara's Dada Manifestoes. Since Allen Ginsberg had stayed with my parents at Patna and I could trace out three of his letters from my pile of papers, on Utpal Bhattacharya's request, I wrote a book on him. On request I also wrote a book on Jean Arthur Rimbaud.

Samir took up the Herculean responsibility to get two hundred younge-generation poets and short-story writers of both India and Bangladesh translated into English, and anthologized. We were stunned by the absence of translators, which was the direct result of the abolition of English in both West Bengal and Bangladesh. My daughter, Anushree, who has been writing poems in English, and Samir's daughter, Drishadwati, a postgraduate in the language, came to our rescue for the poetry collections published in 2001 and 2003. For the short story anthology, the individual authors were requested to search for translators and get them translated, which delayed the project, but worked. This was the first time in the history of Bangla language that a massive translated corpus of poems and short stories were built up for foreign readers. Based on the poems and short stories submitted to the editors, I have written four *Overviews* in English which have already started stirring the English-knowing hornet's nests. Since this corpus was different from the earlier academic as well as regular kitch, I preferred for the word *adhunantika* coined by linguist Prabal Dasgupta of Hyderabad University. Since the expression *adhunantika* somewhat defines postmodern, postcolonial, subaltern, postmarxist, postlanguage etc discourses put together, I accepted the synonym *postmodern* for the benefit of non-Bangla readers.

Shalila and myself felt like visiting Lucknow in order to revive our fond memories. A friend arranged for our stay at the posh guest house of Bankers' Institute for Rural Development. On arrival I was amazed to see a changed Lucknow. When we were there, the Shias and Sunnies used to fight each other. In post-Ayodhya Lucknow, a strange distrust had developed in the city among Hindus and Muslims. The bungalow in which we had lived was a high-rise concrete structure now, my garden with all the trees completely wiped out. All the bangalows in the vicinity were now high-rises with a huge market complex teaming with people.

Other than crows not a single coloured bird or butterfly could be seen, which used to flock our garden. My son had requested for a couple of photographs of his St. Francis School, which too had become different, with iron barricades and new structures to prevent kidnapping of kids. I could not think of a plot of a novel based on Lucknow which I had nursed for some time, a fast narrative starting from the nabobs through British days to the present day multiparty rule. In such a short visit I could not make out the state of affairs of the Bangla-speaking people living there. In the case of present-day Patna, I know most of the Bangla-speaking people are fleeing to other states, since one has to take the law in his own hands if he wants to live in Patna.

After Prashant and Anushree shifted to Mumbai, Dr. Soonawala of Breach Candy Hospital took charge of Anushree. She delivered a healthy baby girl on November 21, 2001. We were with them at the hospital. They named her Mihica, a Sanskrit word meaning "dew drop." On her birth I realised that someone within me was waiting to be a grandfather, who wanted to play with a toddler, talk in incomprehensible baby language, and feel delighted to enjoy unexplainable ecstasy, a discursive space inhabited by William Blake, Jean Arthur Rimbaud, or Indian saint Chaitanyadev.

BIOGRAPHICAL AND CRITICAL SOURCES:

BOOKS

Murshid, A.M., and Arabinda Pradhan, editors, *The Individual Malay Roy Choudhury,* 2001.

PERIODICALS

Ahabkaal, winter, 2002, Dhurjati Chanda, review of *Nakhadanta.*
Amritalok, May, 1989, Nilanjan Chattopadhyay, review of *Medhar Batanukul Ghungur.*
Guerilla, July, 1990, Arun Banik, review of *Medhar Batanukul Ghungur.*
Intrepid, spring, 1968, review by Carl Weissner.
Kabiswar autumn, 2002, Shyamal Shill, interview with Roy Choudhury.
Lekhak Samavesh, January, 1990, Dipankar Datta, review of *Medhar Batanukul Ghungur.*

Pratikshan, December, 1988, Ranjan Bandopadhyay, review of *Medhar Batanukul Ghungur.*
Sahitya Setu, June, 2002, Shishir Dey, review of *Nakhadanta.*
Sunday Searchlight, Patna (Patna, India), December 25, 1966, review by Subhash Chandra Sarkar.

*   *   *

RYDING, Erik (S.) 1953-

PERSONAL: Born September 11, 1953; married Rebecca Pechefsky (a harpsichordist and author).

ADDRESSES: Home—Brooklyn, NY. *Agent*—c/o Author Mail, Yale University Press, P.O. Box 209040, New Haven, CT 06520-9040.

CAREER: Writer, biographer, editor, and recording producer. Carnegie Hall, currently managing editor.

AWARDS, HONORS: ASCAP-Deems Taylor Award, 2002, for *Bruno Walter: A World Elsewhere.*

WRITINGS:

In Harmony Framed: Musical Humanism, Thomas Campion, and the Two Daniels, Truman State University Press (Kirksville, MO), 1993.
(With wife, Rebecca Pechefsky) *Bruno Walter: A World Elsewhere,* Yale University Press (New Haven, CT), 2001.

SIDELIGHTS: Rebecca Pechefsky and Erik Ryding, husband-and-wife authors of *Bruno Walter: A World Elsewhere,* demonstrate in their biography that "Bruno Walter was one of the twentieth century's most important and influential conductors," wrote Scott Warfield in *Notes.* Pechefsky, a professional harpsichordist, and Ryding, managing editor at Carnegie Hall, "have written a detailed, well-documented biography of a respected musician whose career as a conductor was long and successful," wrote George Jochnowitz in *Midstream. Bruno Walter: A World Elsewhere* is the first biography of the conductor in English and the second in any language, noted Allan Keiler in *New York Review of Books.* Ryding and Pechefsky "argue that the absence of any serious study of Walter's career in English since the publication of his autobiography in 1946 'is extraordinary . . . given the wealth of primary sources available, which could furnish material for a study many times the length of the current volume.' In view of Walter's pre-eminence as a conductor during the first half of the twentieth century," Keiler wrote, "one can hardly disagree with them."

Born Bruno Schlesinger in Berlin, Germany, Walter began his career as a piano prodigy but turned to conducting "after attending a concert directed by Hans von Bülow, and a performance of *Tristan und Isolde* opened his ears to the music of Richard Wagner and other progressive composers," Warfield wrote. Debuting as a conductor in 1894 at the age of seventeen, Walter led a performance of the light opera *Der Waffenschmied* to positive, even enthusiastic reviews. "A few days later, he conducted an emergency performance of the same work," Jochnowitz noted. "The original cast was not available for this unscheduled performance. Two of the singers who were called in at the last minute hadn't sung their roles in years. One of the reviews was quite hostile. Then another newspaper came to Schlesinger's defense. Controversy may be an even better source of publicity than praise. At the age of seventeen, Schlesinger had achieved fame and success."

"In rehearsal Walter would plead and cajole, holding out with unyielding stubbornness for what he wanted, but he would never raise his voice to insult musicians." To Keiler, "it is no surprise that fellow musicians, singers, and instrumentalists with whom he collaborated praised him with great affection."

Pechefsky and Ryding trace Walter's career from his early career at the Stadttheater to a series of similar positions, until he went to Vienna in 1901 to serve as Mahler's second-in-command at the Hofoper where he conducted for the next eleven years.

Walter became Generalmusik direktor in Munich in 1913, and "over the next nine years he contributed to a glorious musical era in that city's history," Warfield remarked. He accepted many invitations to guest conduct, including his American debut in 1923. Walter was an early victim of national Socialist abuse, and as the Nazis gained power, he was forced from Germany,

Austria, and France, until he finally came to the United States in 1939. In the United States Walter associated with the Metropolitan Opera, the New York Philharmonic, and other major orchestras. A series of "now legendary recordings" for Columbia "crowned his career," Warfield wrote.

Pechefsky and Ryding "describe all of this and much more in *Bruno Walter: A World Elsewhere,*" Warfield commented. "In addition to quoting liberally from the conductor's autobiography, his published letters, and other obvious sources, these authors are the first to make use of the Bruno Walter Papers (New York Public Library for the Performing Arts), a collection with over seven thousand letters." Warfield noted that "Their dedication to verifying statements and authenticating facts is evident in the mere handful of endnotes that discuss a few unresolved details or conflicting accounts of minor events." Even accounting for extensive citations from primary sources, Pechefsky and Ryding "have woven it all into a highly readable narrative that is accessible to a broad audience."

Alan Hirsch, writing in *Booklist,* noted that Ryding and Pechefsky "illuminate the honorable and ethical man that he was as well as his interpretive approaches as one of the best-loved conductors of the twentieth century." Timothy J. McGee, writing in *Library Journal,* remarked that "The biography is deservedly full of praise for its talented subject, but the authors do not hide his faults or suppress the less favorable reviews or criticisms he received during a brilliant career."

"Ryding and Pechefsky have written a fine account of Walter's life," Warfield remarked, "and it will be all the more useful if their readers seek out Walter's recordings to hear what prompted its writing."

In his book *In Harmony Framed: Musical Humanism, Thomas Campion, and the Two Daniels,* Ryding examines the poetry of Thomas Campion and Samuel Daniel, the songs of Samuel's brother John Daniel, and musical settings of Renaissance poetry. "There is much that is useful in this work," wrote David Lindley in *Modern Language Review,* "but, equally, little that is in any way particularly novel. It is in many ways a synthesis of what has often been remarked of the poetry, music, and metrical speculations of its various subjects. Amiably and clearly written, the book would be useful to a student encountering the field for the first time, but the more experienced reader is unlikely to be startled into new awareness."

Although James A. Winn, writing in *Notes,* found the book "well informed and frequently informative, this monograph still bears the marks of its origins as a dissertation." To Winn, there is no doubt that "Erik Ryding writes well and has read widely," but even though he "produces an up-to-date narrative synthesis," it is "one too encyclopedic in method to allow much in the way of analysis." Winn felt that Ryding makes good choices of examples, but "the examples are too short and too scantily analyzed to have much impact." Lydia Hamessley, writing in *Sixteenth Century Journal,* observed that Ryding's "explanations are not untenable, and at times, they are compelling. The concern is that Ryding does not force these two poets into their 'proper' categories, but that he does not attempt a deeper analysis into how and why they stray from their places." Wilson also noted that Ryding has "Brought much labour and learning to his book in dealing with a complex and extensive topic," and felt that "English Renaissance scholars will not wish to ignore his account."

John Walter Hill, writing in *Renaissance Quarterly,* remarked that Ryding argues his points "most convincingly with respect to the poetry of Campion and Samuel Daniel, taking into account exceptions to his general observations and criticizing specific passages with erudition and sensitivity."

BIOGRAPHICAL AND CRITICAL SOURCES:

PERIODICALS

Booklist, April 1, 2001, Alan Hirsch, review of *Bruno Walter: A World Elsewhere,* p. 1441.

Boston Globe, August 16, 2001, Richard Buell, review of "Biography Hits All the Right Notes."

Commentary, July-August, 2001, Terry Teachout, "Bruno Walter's Way," pp. 54-58.

Irish Times, June 16, 2001, Vincent Deane, "Conductor of Another World," pp. 2-3.

Journal of the Lute Society of American, vol. 25, 1992, Daniel Fischlin, review of *In Harmony Framed: Musical Humanism, Thomas Campion, and the Two Daniels,* pp. 39-45.

Library Journal, March 1, 2001, Timothy J. McGee, review of *Bruno Walter: A World Elsewhere,* p. 96.

Midstream, July, 2001, George Jochnowitz, review of *Bruno Walter: A World Elsewhere,* p. 44.

Modern Language Review, April, 1995, David Lindley, review of *In Harmony Framed: Musical Humanism, Thomas Campion, and the Two Daniels,* p. 409.

Music & Letters, May, 1994, Christopher R. Wilson, review of *In Harmony Framed: Musical Humanism, Thomas Campion, and the Two Daniels,* pp. 260-261.

New York Review of Books, February 14, 2002, Allan Keiler, review of *Bruno Walter: A World Elsewhere,* pp. 35-38.

Notes, June, 1995, James A. Winn, review of *In Harmony Framed: Musical Humanism, Thomas Campion, and the Two Daniels,* pp. 1131-1132; December, 2001, Scott Warfield, review of *Bruno Walter: A World Elsewhere,* pp. 385-386.

Renaissance Quarterly, spring, 1995, John Walter Hill, review of *In Harmony Framed: Musical Humanism, Thomas Campion, and the Two Daniels,* p. 200.

Sixteenth Century Journal, winter, 1994, Lydia Hamessley, review of *In Harmony Framed: Musical Humanism, Thomas Campion, and the Two Daniels,* pp. 999-1003.

Sunday Telegraph, May 20, 2001, Noel Malcolm, "How to Conduct Oneself," p. 14.

Wall Street Journal, August 16, 2001, Harvey Sachs, "Gentle Autocrat, Formidable Interpreter, Revered Maestro," review of *Bruno Walter: A World Elsewhere,* p. A12.

ONLINE

Houston Chronicle Online, http://www.chron.com/ (May 9, 2002), Lynwood Abram, "Bruno Walter's Odyssey."

Yale University Press Web site, http://www.yale.edu/ (May 9, 2002).

S

SANFORD, John 1904-2003
(Julian L. Shapiro, John B. Sanford)

OBITUARY NOTICE—See index for *CA* sketch: Born May 31, 1904, in New York, NY; died of an aortic aneurism March 6, 2003, in Santa Barbara, CA. Author. Sanford was a critically acclaimed novelist who later created a unique blend of fiction, history, and autobiography in vignette collections. After attending Lafayette College for a year, he earned his LL.B. from Fordham University in 1927. A friend, author Nathanael West, inspired him to write, and after practicing law from 1928 to 1936 he finally abandoned it to become a full-time author. His first novels include *The Water Wheel* (1933), and, after legally changing his name from Shapiro to Sanford as prejudice against Jews grew, *The Old Man's Place* (1935), *Seventy Times Seven* (1939), and *The People from Heaven* (1943). His writing drew the attention of movie studios, and he signed a six-month contract with Paramount. But his wife, screenwriter Marguerite "Maggie" Roberts, encouraged him to continue writing novels instead. Unfortunately, Sanford's membership in the Communist Party not only put him on the blacklist of the House Un-American Activities Committee, but it also put a halt to his wife's film career. During the 1950s both writers were prevented from producing any work. By the 1960s, however, the blacklist restrictions eased and Sanford began to write again. He was tiring of novels, however, and instead began to focus on historical vignettes, assuming the voice of historical characters, both famous and ordinary, in pieces that blended fiction with history. *A More Goodly Country: A Personal History of America* (1975) was the first collection of these vignettes to be published. This was followed by such historical works as *View from This Wilderness: American Literature as History* (1977) and *To Feed Their Hopes: A Book of American Women* (1980). Later in his life, especially after his wife's death in 1989, Sanford focused on autobiography, publishing the acclaimed four-volume work *Scenes from the Life of an American Jew* (1985-91), *Maggie: A Love Story* (1993), and *A Palace of Silver* (2001), among other books. His *The Color of Air,* the first volume of his four-volume autobiography, won a PEN award.

OBITUARIES AND OTHER SOURCES:

PERIODICALS

Los Angeles Times, March 8, 2003, p. B20.
Washington Post, March 11, 2003, p. B7.

*   *   *

SANFORD, John B.
See SANFORD, John

*   *   *

SCHMITT, Peter 1958-

PERSONAL: Born December 2, 1958, in Miami, FL; son of W. Gordon (a food-processing plant owner) and Evelyn (a volunteer public television producer; maiden name, Vrdang) Schmitt. *Ethnicity:* "Caucasian." *Education:* Amherst College, B.A., 1980; University of Iowa, M.F.A., 1983.

ADDRESSES: Home—8101 Camino Real, C-420, Miami, FL 33143. *Office*—Department of English, University of Miami, Box 248145, Coral Gables, FL 33124. *E-mail*—profpschmitt@gateway.net.

CAREER: University of Miami, Coral Gables, FL, lecturer in English, 1986—.

MEMBER: Academy of American Poetry, Poetry Society of America, Association of Literary Scholars and Critics, Elizabeth Bishop Society.

AWARDS, HONORS: Discovery/*Nation* Prize for Poetry, 1988; Lavah Award, Academy of American Poets, 1991.

WRITINGS:

POETRY

Country Airport, Copper Beech Press (Providence, RI), 1989.
Hazard Duty, Copper Beech Press (Providence, RI), 1995.

WORK IN PROGRESS: A third collection of poems.

* * *

SCHOFIELD, Janet Ward 1946-

PERSONAL: Born May 8, 1946, in Newark, NJ; daughter of William Rankin, Jr. (a physician) and Sarah Ellis (a teacher) Ward; married Douglas Franklin Schofield, III, September 1, 1968; children: Alanya Lynn, Heather Ward, Emily Duncan. *Education:* Radcliffe College, B.A. (magna cum laude), 1968; Harvard University, M.A., 1969, Ph.D. 1972.

ADDRESSES: Home—319 Nottingham Circle, Pittsburgh, PA 15215. *Office*—Learning Research and Development Center, Room 517, University of Pittsburgh, Pittsburgh, PA 15238. *E-mail*—schof@vms.cis.pitt.edu.

CAREER: Spelman College, Atlanta, GA, instructor in psychology and sociology, 1969-70; Policy Research Division, Office of Economic Opportunity, Washington, DC, research psychologist, 1972-73; National Institute of Education, Washington, DC, research psychologist, 1973-74; University of Pittsburgh, associate professor, 1974-86, senior scientist, Learning Research and Development Center, 1981—, professor, Social Personality Program, department of psychology, 1986—. Speaker and consultant.

MEMBER: American Psychological Association (executive committee, 1993-96; council of representatives, 1993-96; publications committee, 1993-2000; fellows committee, 1995-2000), Society for the Psychological Study of Social Issues (fellows selection committee, 1991-93, Gordon Allport Intergroup Relations Prize committee, 1985), American Educational Research Association, Society for Experimental Social Psychology.

AWARDS, HONORS: Society for the Psychological Study of Social Issues Gordon Allport Intergroup Relations Prize, 1983, for *Black and White in School: Trust, Tension or Tolerance?;* honorary member Phi Eta Sigma, 1976, and Phi Beta Kappa.

WRITINGS:

Black and White in School: Trust, Tension, or Tolerance? Praeger (New York, NY), 1982, revised edition, Teachers College Press, (New York, NY), 1989.
Computers in Classroom Culture, Cambridge University Press (New York, NY), 1995.
Bringing the Internet to School: Lessons from an Urban District, Jossey-Bass (San Francisco, CA), 2002.

Work represented in many professional journals, including *Journal of Personality and Social Psychology, Journal of Educational Psychology* and *Social Psychology Quarterly.* Member of editorial board, *Sociology of Education,* 1986-89, *Social Psychology Quarterly,* 1982-85, and *Interactive Learning Environments,* 1990-93. Work represented in anthologies, including, *The Development of Children's Friendship,* edited by S. Asher and J. Gottman, Cambridge University Press, (New York, NY), 1981; and *Coopera-*

tion in Education, edited by S. Sharon, P. Hare, C. Webb, and R. Hertz Lazarowitz, Brigham Young University Press, (Provo, Utah), 1980.

SIDELIGHTS: Janet Ward Schofield's academic training, her varied experience in the Office of Economic Opportunity and the National Institute of Education, and her teaching and research have led her to produce significant work in sociology and education. While she has written books and scholarly papers, she has also reviewed and edited the work of her peers.

Black and White in School: Trust, Tension, and Tolerance?, first published in 1982 and later released in 1989 in a revised edition, is the result of a three-year study, sponsored by the National Institute of Education in the mid-1970s, of a desegregated middle school in a northern U.S. urban environment. The research team used observation, interviews, and field experiments to create a detailed portrait of the social dynamics of the school. Social relationships and interactions among black and white students were the particular focus of this study. Students in grades six, seven, and eight composed the population studied. Attention was given to external factors, including local politics and shifts in decisions made by the school board.

Scholars agreed that one of the study's most significant findings is that the students' interracial behavior changed more than their attitudes. It was suggested that the reason for this change was that students of different races came to know each other as individuals, rather than members of a group. The book implies that schools should promote programs that allow racially mixed student populations to get to know one another on a personal level. Changes in behavior rather than changes in attitude form the core of more realistic expectations. Included in the study are some observations on gender differences in interracial interactions. *Contemporary Psychology* reviewer John U. Ogbu called *Black and White in School* "an important contribution on desegregated schools and interracial relations."

In *Computers and Classroom Culture* Schofield describes the many ways—some of them unexpected—that computer technology has changed the learning environment. The data for this study was gathered during the 1985-86 and 1986-87 academic years at a large, public high school with a diverse enrollment.

Schofield directed a group of researchers as they conducted approximately 250 hours of interviews with students and faculty. Close to 400 hours of observation of the use of computers in class was recorded. Some of the more surprising findings of the study have to do with the expectations of administrators and teaching staff. At the outset, these two groups of adults expected that the arrival of computers in the classroom would totally transform the learning environment. They had not counted on the confusion and uncertainty that the computers brought along with them. Uninformed choices in the purchase of both hardware and software, added to poor teacher training with the new technology, were more than enough to create a climate of dissatisfaction and uncertainty in the classroom. Lack of regard for the classroom as a social environment which influences the way technology is used and, in turn, is also influenced by it, was a significant factor contributing to the initial lack of ease.

The study was built around four environments: a geometry class using a computer tutoring system, a business class emphasizing computer use, a computer-science class that included software design as part of the curriculum, and a lab available for use during the lunch break.

The author concludes that "the effect of computer usage is likely to depend on a plethora of factors including the kind of software used (e.g. drill and practice, simulations, networking, tutoring), the kind of students using the software, the social and physical context of computer use, and prior classroom practices."

Schofield and Ann L. Davidson produced a five-year study of the Networking for Education Testbed (NET), sponsored by the National Science Foundation. The focus of the study, *Bringing the Internet to School: Lessons from an Urban District,* is the use of the Internet in education. The researchers have cautioned against the unconsidered adoption of the Internet in a school's curriculum, suggesting that it is necessary to understand the effects of technology on a school's culture and the mirroring influence of the school on technology. Schofield and Davidson point out that the wealth of information and ideas available to students via the Internet can be more distracting than helpful. Teachers' twin concerns about losing control of the curriculum and the potential loss of authority are also factors in a changing learning environment. However, Schoefield and Davidson note that Internet use also brings with it some unexpected positive change in the classroom environment and in teacher-student relations.

BIOGRAPHICAL AND CRITICAL SOURCES:

PERIODICALS

Choice, April, 1983, review of *Black and White in School: Trust, Tension, or Tolerance?* p. 1185; July, 1996, G. H. Alexander, review of *Computers in Classroom Culture,* p. 1845.
Contemporary Psychology, May, 1984, John U. Ogbu, review of *Black and White in School: Trust, Tension, or Tolerance?* p. 373.
Library Journal, March 15, 2002, Scott Walter, review of *The Internet in School: Promise and Problems,* p. 92.
Publishers Weekly, February 4, 2002, review of *The Internet in School: Promise and Problems,* p. 70.
Social Science Computer Review, summer, 1998, Robert J. Buckley, review of *Computers in Classroom Culture,* p. 219.
Teachers College Record, winter, 1983, Nobuo K. Shimahara, review of *Black and White in School: Trust, Tension, or Tolerance?* p. 334; winter, 1996, Benjamin L. Bell, review of *Computers in Classroom Culture,* p. 346.

ONLINE

University of Pittsburgh Web site, http://www.pitt.edu/ (August 29, 2002), "Janet Ward Schofield."

*   *   *

SCHORR, Jonathan

PERSONAL: Male. *Education:* Graduate of Yale University; Mount S. Mary's College, teaching certificate. *Hobbies and other interests:* Skiing, cycling, outdoors.

ADDRESSES: Home—Oakland, CA. *Agent*—c/o Author Mail, Random House, 1745 Broadway New York, NY 10019. *E-mail*—jonathan@jonathanschorr. com.

CAREER: Writer. Former teacher and reporter for *Oakland Tribune,* Oakland, CA.

AWARDS, HONORS: Open Society Institute fellowship.

WRITINGS:

Hard Lessons: The Promise of an Inner-City Charter School, Ballantine Books (New York, NY), 2002.

Contributor to periodicals and Web sites, including the *New York Times, Los Angeles Times, Nation, Salon. com,* and *Education Week.*

SIDELIGHTS: Jonathan Schorr was first a teacher, then a journalist who writes about education. His articles have been published in prominent mainstream, educational, and progressive periodicals. Schorr's *Hard Lessons: The Promise of an Inner-City Charter School* studies the ongoing effort by teachers, parents, and the poor Oakland community in which E. C. Reems Academy is located to improve the education of their children.

Reems, one of more than 2,000 charter schools in the United States, was established in 1999 through the nonprofit School Futures. The children who made up the student body were so behind that some in the fourth and fifth grades couldn't write recognizable English. Even though the school's first year was difficult, with threats of being shut down because of the mishandling of paperwork, it survived, but it continued to struggle to educate students with low scores in a population with a large number of immigrants and homeless. In addition, lack of funds prevented the school from providing adequate tools and teaching materials.

Booklist's David Carr called Schorr "a warm and graceful writer" and the book "a story that measures out hope in teaspoons, and frustration by the cup."

Mother Jones contributor Blair Campbell wrote that Schorr's study of the charter school is unexpected, offering "vividly rendered heroes and villains, gripping plot twists, and a nail-biting climax."

Colman McCarthy, who reviewed *Hard Lessons* in the *Washington Post Book World,* wrote that the book demonstrates that those who are working to lift children out of poverty through education are "too often . . . not supported or appreciated—least of all by those who offer opinions about public school reform while putting their own children in private schools." McCarthy called Schorr "a partisan who wants charter schools to succeed."

BIOGRAPHICAL AND CRITICAL SOURCES:

PERIODICALS

Booklist, August, 2002, David Carr, review of *Hard Lessons: The Promise of an Inner-City Charter School,* p. 1898.
Mother Jones, September-October, 2002, Blair Campbell, review of *Hard Lessons.*
Publishers Weekly, June 3, 2002, review of *Hard Lessons,* p. 74.
Washington Post Book World, August 25, 2002, Colman McCarthy, review of *Hard Lessons,* p. 4.

ONLINE

Hard Lessons Home Page, http://www.hardlessons.com/ (February 28, 2003).

*   *   *

SCHROEDER, Karl 1962-

PERSONAL: Born September 4, 1962, in Brandon, Manitoba, Canada.

ADDRESSES: Agent—Donald Maass, Donald Maass Literary Agency, 160 West 95th St., Suite 1B, New York, NY 10025. *E-mail*—karlds@rogers.com.

CAREER: Writer. Taught continuing education courses in writing science fiction.

MEMBER: Science Fiction Writers of America, SF Canada (founding member; vice president, 1994-95; president, 1996-97).

AWARDS, HONORS: Context short story winner, 1989, for "Live Wire" (retitled "The Cold Convergence"); Aurora Award (with David Nickle), 1993, for "The Toy Mill."

WRITINGS:

A Mourning Place (play), produced in North York, 1993.
(With David Nickle) *The Claus Effect,* Tesseracts, 1997.
(With Cory Doctorow) *The Complete Idiot's Guide to Publishing Science Fiction,* Alpha Books (New York, NY), 2000.
Ventus, Tor (New York, NY), 2000.
Permanence, Tor (New York, NY), 2002.

Work represented in multiple "Tesseracts" anthologies. Contributor to periodicals, including *Figment, On Spec,* and *Cosmic Visions.*

SIDELIGHTS: Science fiction writer Karl Schroeder wrote his first novel, *The Claus Effect,* with David Nickle. It is an extension of their award-winning short story, "The Toy Mill," about Emily, a girl who works for Santa. In the novel, Emily is an adult with the security department of a big box store, and the plot includes bad elves, the military, and satellite weaponry.

The Complete Idiot's Guide to Publishing Science Fiction, which Schroeder cowrote with Cory Doctorow, introduces the genre, explains the ins and outs of sci fi conventions, and advises readers about how to get published. Ernest Lilley reviewed the book for *SFRevu* online, calling it "a really good book. It is full of good advice, cute graphics, and an appreciation of science fiction."

Lilley also reviewed Schroeder's *Ventus,* a novel the critic called "a fast paced and engaging epic adventure from start to finish and an excellent example of Arthur Clarke's rule that sufficiently advanced technology is indistinguishable from magic." The story is set on a remote colony planet that has been isolated by artificial intelligence, known as the Winds, which created an ideal environment for a human population but turned against settlers when they arrived, and ultimately refused to give up control. Every aspect of Ventus can be managed through imbedded technology, except for the humans who live in near-medieval conditions.

In reviewing the novel for *SF Site* online, Greg L. Johnson wrote that "The most clever idea is the glitch that prevents the Winds from operating as their designers intended. It is not only a technological puzzle, but also a philosophical one." Johnson noted that the fact that most of the novel's action occurs in a low-tech environment "plays to the book's artistic strength, a cast of characters who, if not all that complex, each have a definite personality of their own." The characters include young visionary Jordan Mason, cyborg Armiger, Desert Voice, and Calandria May, a freelance interstellar agent.

"Neatly illustrating Clarke's aphorism," wrote *Voice of Youth Advocates* reviewer Bill White, "the Winds manage the hierarchical orderings of molecules into objects and objects into processes; they are programmed to maintain the ecology of Ventus even in the face of human technology." A *Publishers Weekly* contributor stated that Schroeder's "first large-scale SF work . . . should greatly expand his reputation." *Analog Science Fiction and Fact*'s Tom Easton, meanwhile, called *Ventus* "a grand adventure with satisfyingly meaty content." Gerald Jonas, who reviewed *Ventus* in the *New York Times Book Review,* wrote that "the plotting is appropriately multifaceted, the characters surprisingly complex, the denouement—which may be termed post-Aristotelian—deeply satisfying."

A *Publishers Weekly* writer called Schroeder's *Permanence* "a complex, conceptually satisfying story of interstellar intrigue, cosmology, theology, and nanotechnology." In a *School Library Journal* review, Christine C. Menefee described the story's beginning as "reminiscent of classic Heinlein." The protagonist is Rue Cassels, a young woman who flees an abusive brother and finds herself faced with a cycler: a slow-moving, unmanned shuttle that she may claim as her own if she is able to board and navigate it. Cyclers had been used to keep connected the Halo worlds, between the brighter stars, before the struggling worlds suffered from crumbling economies and decay. Rue's mission is to use technology to reverse the trend, while others from the luminal worlds are intent on creating a powerful empire.

Lilley wrote that Schroeder "has created a terrific ensemble cast. . . . A manic-depressive cousin, a budding journalist, a resourceful female doctor, a member of the cycler cult, and a former cycler crewman. The characters are everything one needs to keep the story moving as the author unfolds greater themes and issues before us." *Booklist*'s Roberta Johnson, meanwhile, called *Permanence* "the best kind of coming-of-age tale, one that seizes the imagination and the emotions." Finally, a *Kirkus Reviews* contributor called the novel a "thoughtful, well-informed, insightful work, with a sharp yet subtle political subcontext, catapulting Schroeder into SF's front rank."

BIOGRAPHICAL AND CRITICAL SOURCES:

PERIODICALS

Analog Science Fiction and Fact, June, 2001, Tom Easton, review of *Ventus,* p. 133.
Booklist, April 15, 2001, Ray Olson, review of *Ventus,* p. 1543; April 15, 2002, Roberta Johnson, review of *Permanence,* p. 1390.
Kirkus Reviews, March 1, 2002, review of *Permanence,* p. 297.
Library Journal, December, 2000, Jackie Cassada, review of *Ventus,* p. 196.
New York Times Book Review, April 29, 2001, Gerald Jonas, review of *Ventus,* p. 18; June 3, 2001, review of *Ventus,* p. 31.
Publishers Weekly, November 27, 2000, review of *Ventus,* p. 59; April 15, 2002, review of *Permanence,* p.46.
School Library Journal, September 2002, Christine C. Menefee, review of *Permanence,* p. 257.
Voice of Youth Advocates, October, 2001, Bill White, review of *Ventus,* pp. 268-269.

ONLINE

Karl Schroeder Home Page, http://www.kschroeder.com/ (December 9, 2002).
Scifi.com, http://www.scifi.com/ (July 25, 2002), Paul Di Filippo, review of *Permanence.*
SFRevu, http://www.sfrevu.com/ (December 9, 2002), Ernest Lilley, reviews of *The Complete Idiot's Guide to Publishing Science Fiction, Ventus,* and *Permanence.*
SF Site, http://www.sfsite.com/ (July 25, 2002), Greg L. Johnson, review of *Ventus.*

*   *   *

SCHUTZ, Alfred 1899-1959

PERSONAL: Born April 13, 1899 in Vienna, Austria; immigrated to United States, 1938; died May 20, 1959, in New York, NY; son of Alfred and Johann (Fialla) Schütz; married Ilse Heim, 1926; children: two. *Edu-*

cation: University of Vienna, LL.D. (international law). *Hobbies and other interests:* Phenomenology.

CAREER: Reitler and Company (banking firm), employee, 1929-59. New School for Social Research, New York, NY, part-time instructor. *Philosophy and Phenomenological Research,* publisher. *Military service:* Served in Austrian army during World War I.

WRITINGS:

Sinnhafte Aufbau der sozialen Welt, J. Springer (Vienna, Austria), 1932, translation by George Walsh and Frederick Lehnert published as *The Phenomenology of the Social World,* Northwestern University Press (Evanston, IL), 1967.

On Phenomenology and Social Relations: Selected Writings, edited by Helmut R. Wagner, University of Chicago Press (Chicago, IL), 1970.

Reflections on the Problem of Relevance, edited by Richard M. Zaner, Yale University Press (New Haven, CT), 1970.

(With Thomas Luckmann) *Struckturen der Lebenswelt,* H. Luchterhand (Neuwied, Germany), 1975, translation by Richard M. Zaner and H. Tristram Engelhardt, Jr., published as *The Structures of the Life-World,* Northwestern University Press (Evanston, IL), 1973-1989.

Zur Theorie sozialen Handelns: E. Briefwechsel, Suhrkamp (Frankfurt am Main, Germany), 1977, translation published as *The Theory of Social Action: The Correspondence of Alfred Schutz and Talcott Parsons,* edited by Richard Grathoff, Indiana University Press (Bloomington, IN), 1978.

Lebensformen und Sinnstruktur, translation by Helmut R. Wagner published as *Life Forms and Meaning Structure,* Routledge & Kegan Paul (Boston, MA), 1982.

Collected Papers, four volumes, edited and introduced by Maurice Natanson, M. Nijhoff (Boston, MA), 1982-1996.

Alfred Schütz, Aron Gurwitsch: Briefwechsel, 1939-1959, W. Fink (Munich, Germany), 1985, translation by J. Claude Evans published as *Philosophers in Exile: The Correspondence of Alfred Schutz and Aron Gurwitsch, 1939-1959,* edited by Richard Grathoff, Indiana University Press (Bloomington, IL), 1989.

Copies of Schutz's papers are found in the Center for Advanced Research in Phenomenology at the Atlantic University, Boca Raton, Florida.

SIDELIGHTS: Viennese-American lawyer Alfred Schutz is considered one of the founders of phenomenology, that is, the study of structures of consciousness that enable a person to refer to objects outside of himself. The discipline was first named phenomenology in a publication by German philosopher Edmund Husserl in 1913. Later, other philosophers, including Schutz, following Husserl's lead, made variations in the discipline to reflect their own thinking on the subject.

Though influential, Schutz was not like other professional philosophers who occupied university teaching positions for a livelihood. While a student he was interested in literature, art, and music, but after serving in the Austrian army during World War I Schutz studied law and economics at the University of Vienna. He found a position as executive secretary of the Austrian Banker's Association and several years later joined the bank Reitler and Company. At the outset of World War II, when Germany invaded Austria, Schutz and his wife and two children escaped to Paris. Later they immigrated to New York City, where Schutz was able to retain his job with the same company, a post he held until his death.

During his after-work hours, Schutz delved into literature on the numerous theories being developed about human interactions. He read works by German sociologist Max Weber, French philosopher Henri-Louis Bergson, and German phenomenologist Edmund Husserl. Schutz began forming his own theories, synthesizing ideas and applying them to American society. In 1940 he created *Philosophy and Phenomenological Research,* a scholarly journal, and published a handful of works. For a time he lectured at the graduate school at the New School for Social Research in New York City.

BIOGRAPHICAL AND CRITICAL SOURCES:

BOOKS

Koev, Kolyo, editor, *Phenomenology as a Dialogue: Dedicated to the Ninetieth Anniversary of Alfred Schutz,* Critique and Humanism (Sofia, Bulgaria), 1990.

Natanson, Maurice, editor, *Phenomenology and Social Reality: Essays in Memory of Alfred Schutz,* Nijhoff (The Hague, Netherlands), 1970.

Wolff, Kurt H., editor, *Alfred Schutz: Appraisals and Developments,* Nijhoff (Boston, MA), 1984.

World of Sociology, Volume 2, Gale (Detroit, MI), 2001.

PERIODICALS

American Journal of Economics and Sociology, January, 1996, Nicolai Juul Foss, "Spontaneous Social Order: Economics and Schutzian Sociology," pp. 73-86.

Ethics, July, 1984, James Johnson, review of *Life Forms and Meaning Structures,* p. 729.

International Philosophical Quarterly, March, 1994, Meredith Williams, "Private States and Public Practices: Wittgenstein and Schutz and Intentionality," pp. 89-101.

Philosophy of the Social Sciences, December, 1994, Timothy M. Costelloe, "Schutz, Music, and Temporality: A Wittgensteinian Assessment," pp. 439-447.

Sociology, November, 2000, Austin Harrington, "Alfred Schutz and the 'Objectifying Attitude,'" p. 727.*

* * *

SCOTT, Andrew (Paul) 1947-

PERSONAL: Born November 26, 1947, in Swansea, Wales. *Education:* University of British Columbia, B.A. (with honors), 1969; University of New Brunswick, M.A., 1975.

ADDRESSES: Home—British Columbia, Canada. *Agent*—c/o Author Mail, Whitecap Books Ltd., 351 Lynn Ave., North Vancouver, British Columbia, Canada V7J 2C4. *E-mail*—andrewscott@dccnet.com.

CAREER: Freelance writer and photographer, 1971-80; *Western Living,* Vancouver, British Columbia, Canada, assistant editor, 1980, managing editor, 1980-81, editor, 1981-87; Seattle Northwest Publishing Co., Seattle, WA, publisher of *Alaska Airlines,* 1987-89; *Globe & Mail,* Toronto, Ontario, Canada, travel and homes editor for regional magazines *West, Toronto,* and *Montreal,* 1990, senior editor of *West,* 1991; freelance writer, editor, and photographer, 1991—.

Mysterious East, editor, 1969-75. Beneficial Income Tax Service, regional director in British Columbia and Alberta. Consumer Action League of Vancouver, consumer advocate; director of St. John River Project and New Brunswick Journalism Cooperative, 1969-75; New Brunswick Department of Education, audiovisual editor and script writer. Juror for National Magazine Awards, Western Magazine Awards, and other competitions.

MEMBER: Periodicals Writers Association of Canada, Sunshine Coast Conservation Association (member of board of directors).

AWARDS, HONORS: Western Magazine Awards, magazine of the year, 1985, 1986, and 1987, for *Western Living,* and 1991, for *West,* best travel article, 1986, gold award for best article from British Columbia, 1994, special award for editorial impact, 1994, and best science, technology, and medicine article, 1995; National Magazine Awards, magazine of the year, 1991, for *West,* and gold award for personal journalism, 1994; Canada Council grants, 1995, 2000; BC2000 Book Award, for *Secret Coastline: Journeys and Discoveries along B.C.'s Shores.*

WRITINGS:

(And photographer) *The Promise of Paradise: Utopian Communities in British Columbia,* Whitecap Books (North Vancouver, British Columbia, Canada), 1997.

(And photographer) *Secret Coastline: Journeys and Discoveries along B.C.'s Shores,* Whitecap Books (North Vancouver, British Columbia, Canada), 2000.

Contributor to books, including *Big New British Columbia Travel Guide, Greater Vancouver,* and *Encyclopedia of British Columbia.* Contributor of numerous articles and photographs to periodicals, including *Equinox, Discovery, Endless Vacation, Western Living, Beautiful British Columbia, Midwest Express, Westworld, Waters, Rail Traveller,* and *Toronto.*

BIOGRAPHICAL AND CRITICAL SOURCES:

PERIODICALS

Canadian Geographic, July, 2000, Shawn Blore, review of *Secret Coastline: Journeys and Discoveries along B.C.'s Shores,* p. 70.

SEYFFERT, Kenneth D. 1927-

PERSONAL: Born September 12, 1927, in Corsicana, TX; son of Walter Henry, Sr. and Maud (Knapp) Seyffert. *Ethnicity:* "Caucasian." *Education:* Attended Southern Methodist University and University of Texas—Austin. *Politics:* Democrat. *Hobbies and other interests:* Birdwatching.

ADDRESSES: Home—2206 South Lipscomb St., Amarillo, TX 79109.

CAREER: Illinois-California Express, Inc., Amarillo, TX, officer manager, 1950-84; writer. Texas Breeding Bird Atlas Project, regional director; Texas Bird Records Committee, past member.

MEMBER: National Audubon Society, Texas Ornithological Society (past vice president and member of board of directors), Texas Partners in Flight (regional director), Texas Panhandle Audubon Society (past president).

AWARDS, HONORS: Certificates of Recognition, U.S. Fish and Wildlife Service, 1997 and 2001, for outstanding contributions to America's natural and cultural resources; Certificate of Appreciation, Lone Star Legends, Texas Parks and Wildlife Department, 1999; Outstanding Volunteer Award, conservation category, Texas Audubon Society, 2000.

WRITINGS:

Birds of the Texas Panhandle: Their Status, Distribution, and History, illustrated by Carolyn Stallwitz, Texas A & M University Press (College Station, TX), 2001.

Contributor of articles to *Bulletin of the Oklahoma Ornithological Society* and *Bulletin of the Texas Ornithological Society.* Subregional editor, *North American Birds.*

SIDELIGHTS: Kenneth D. Seyffert told *CA:* "The Texas Panhandle is the least known and understood region of the state insofar as its bird life is concerned. My motivation in writing on its birds was to correct this deficiency. Not only was it my wish to write on the current status of the region's birds, but also I wanted to make known their histories, going back to the early and mid-nineteenth century. Material in archives is not readily accessible to the public."

*   *   *

SHAPIRO, Julian L.
     See SANFORD, John

*   *   *

SHARPE, Jon
     See DUNCAN, Alice

*   *   *

SHAW, Joseph Thompson 1874-1952

PERSONAL: Born May 8, 1874, in Gorham, ME; died August 1, 1952; son of Milton and Nellie Morse Shaw; married Hanna Muskova. *Education:* Bowdoin College, B.A., 1895.

CAREER: New York Globe, staff member, 1895; American Woolen Company, Boston, MA, secretary, 1890s-1900s, writer from 1904; American Relief Administration; *Saturday Evening Post,* story editor. Sidney A. Sanders Literary Agency (later Joseph T. Shaw Associates), owner, 1942-52. Member, national championship fencing team, 1916. *Military service:* U.S. Army; captain, and bayonet instructor during World War I.

MEMBER: Alpha Delta Phi.

WRITINGS:

From Wool to Cloth, Livermore and Knight (Providence, RI), 1904.
The Wool Trade of the United States: History of a Great Industry; Its Rise and Progress in Boston, Now the Second Market of the World, U.S. Government Printing Office (Washington, DC), 1909.

Spain of To-Day: A Narrative Guide to the Country of the Dons, with Suggestions for Travellers, Grafton (New York, NY), 1909.

Derelict, Knopf (New York, NY), 1930.

Danger Ahead, Mohawk (New York, NY), 1932.

Out of the Rough, Windward House (New York, NY), 1934.

Blood on the Curb, Dodge (New York, NY), 1936.

It Happened on the Lake, Dodd, Mead (New York, NY), 1937.

(Editor) *The Hard-boiled Omnibus: Early Stories from Black Mask,* Simon and Schuster (New York, NY), 1946.

(Editor) *Spurs West!* Permabooks (Garden City, NY), 1951.

Black Mask (magazine), editor and contributor, 1926-36.

SIDELIGHTS: Joseph T. Shaw developed a vigorous form of American storytelling while running *Black Mask,* the detective-fiction pulp magazine that delivered the hard-bitten, blunt tales of Dashiell Hammett and Raymond Chandler. "Although Shaw did not create the hard-boiled writing style . . . he was largely responsible for the success of this uniquely American genre," Garyn G. Roberts wrote in *Dictionary of Literary Biography.* Shaw respected detective fiction, which most editors regarded as nonsense, and from his respect grew a literary force.

Shaw's parents were of old New England stock; his paternal ancestor, Roger Shaw, had come to New England in the 1630s. Shaw attended Bowdoin College in Maine, where he practiced swordplay and editing: he starred on the school fencing team and edited the campus paper. Upon graduation, Shaw worked at the *New York Globe* and as a secretary and writer for the American Woolen Company. He competed on the 1916 national championship fencing team, earning a presidential medal. During these early years, Shaw's writing and editing were limited to such pedestrian fare as *From Wool to Cloth, The Wool Trade of the United States,* and *Spain of To-Day.*

Shaw was a bayonet instructor during World War I, rising to captain. He stayed in Europe after the war, distributing food to starving people in Czechoslovakia and Greece with President Hoover's American Relief Administration. By the time Shaw came home, though,

he wanted to get back to editing. He worked on stories at *Saturday Evening Post* before assuming the editorship of *Black Mask* in 1926. The magazine was no prize: it was called a pulp because of the cheap paper stock on which it was printed; its writers were considered hacks; its editors disowned it. Shaw thought he could make a success of it.

Black Mask, according to Roberts, "had been founded in 1920 by H. L. Mencken and George Jean Nathan; its content was described its subtitle, *An Illustrated Magazine of Detective, Mystery, Adventure, Romance, and Spiritualism.* Mencken and Nathan had started the magazine to help support their sophisticated literary periodical, *Smart Set.* . . . Mencken always despised the *Black Mask* . . . and neither his nor Nathan's name ever appeared on it." The magazine had a revolving door of editors. The journal was successful, but many considered it a sleazy piece of work.

Shaw began by looking through all the back issues and liked what he saw of Hammett's work. Hammett had begun his career by trying to publish in *Smart Set,* and had been shunted over to *Black Mask.* When Hammett had asked for a raise from two cents per word to three, the editors refused. Hammett had quit and gone into advertising, but Shaw wooed him back. Circulation climbed when he featured Hammett's stories.

Hammett's stories, as did much of *Black Mask* detective fiction, revealed a gritty world of cynicism and cunning. Shaw, seeing literary possibilities, encouraged stylish writers of it, such as Hammett, Chandler, Daly, Erle Stanley Gardner, and Lester Dent.

Shaw also directed art for the journal that rendered its rough-hewn edges chic, dangerous. Arthur Rodman Bowker, whose work Rogers called "bold" and "stylized," illustrated these stories exclusively. The sharp artwork nicely complemented the terse prose. Shaw also insisted on calling the magazine a "rough-paper book" rather than pulp, and spoke of the journal respectfully. He paid and treated his writers better. Dent recalled: "When you went into his office and talked with Shaw, you felt you were doing fiction that was powerful. You had a feeling of stature." Shaw also connected his authors with publishers and movie studios, helping to make detective fiction more lucrative and respectable.

He wrote in a 1932 editorial: "*Black Mask* is unique among fiction magazines, appealing to a wide group of readers ranging from those who like action fiction for action alone, where it is real and convincing, to the most discriminating readers in the professional classes. . . . While it is commonly classed as a detective fiction magazine, it has, with the help of its writers, created a new type of detective story which is now being recognized by book critics as inaugurating a new era of fiction dealing with crime and crime combatting."

Shaw was a better editor than writer. Chandler once said of Shaw's prose: "[It's about the deadliest writing I ever saw on a supposedly professional level.'" Shaw, however, had a golden talent for recognizing gifted writers, promoting them and advancing daring fiction. After he left *Black Mask* in 1936 over a salary dispute with the magazine's owners, Shaw became a literary agent. He also edited several successful collections of detective and western fiction before he died.

Shaw, who could sharpen stories, also had a vision for genre fiction. He recognized that writers such as Hammett and Chandler created realistic characters in dangerous situations, rather than complex crime puzzles. As Shaw wrote in the introduction to *The Hard-Boiled Omnibus:* "We . . . created a new type of detective story differing from . . . the cross-word puzzle sort, that is lacking deliberately all . . . human emotional values . . . .in this new pattern, character conflict is the main theme; the ensuing crime, or its threat, is incidental."

BIOGRAPHICAL AND CRITICAL SOURCES:

BOOKS

Dictionary of Literary Biography, Volume 137: *American Magazine Journalists, 1900-1960,* Gale (Detroit, MI), 1994, pp. 283-288.

Durham, Philip, *Down These Mean Streets a Man Must Go,* University of North Carolina Press (Chapel Hill, NC), 1963.

Goulart, Ron, *The Dime Detectives,* Mysterious Press (New York, NY), 1988.

Nolan, William F., editor, *The Black Mask Boys,* Morrow (New York, NY), 1985.

PERIODICALS

Clues, fall-winter, 1981, Dave Lewis, "The Backbone of *Black Mask,"* p. 117.*

SHELL, Ray

PERSONAL: Born in the United States; immigrated to Great Britain, 1978. *Education:* Attended Emerson College.

ADDRESSES: Agent—Nicki Stoddart, PFD, Drury House, 34-43 Russell Street, London WC2B 5HA, England.

CAREER: Actor and writer. Actor in stage productions, including *Ain't Misbehavin',* London, England, 1995; *Jesus Christ Superstar,* Barbican, London; *Mass Carib; Little Willies Jr.; Miss Saigon,* London's West End; *King; Hair; Children of Eden; Starlight Express,* Apollo Victoria Theatre, London; *Five Guys Named Moe; Sweeney Todd,* Holland Park Theatre, London; *Happy End,* Nottingham Playhouse, Nottingham; *Two Trains Running,* Tricycle Theatre, London; *Blues for Mr. Charlie,* Royal Exchange, Manchester; *Lion King,* London, England; *The Music of Andrew Lloyd Webber; Andrew Lloyd Webber, The Royal Albert Hall Celebration,* London, England, 1998; and *125th Street,* London, England, 2002. Actor in films, including (as Shake) *The Apple* (also known as *Star Rock*), Cannon Films, 1980; (as Jeff Kane) *Young Soul Rebels,* Ibero Films Internacional, S.A., 1991; (as Murray) *Velvet Goldmine,* Miramax, 1998; and *Andrew Lloyd Webber, the Royal Albert Hall Celebration,* PolyGram Video, 1998. Played Darbo in made-for-television movie *Pirate Prince,* 1993. Producer of audio recordings for Steve Williamson and Dark Secret; manager of pop group Damage.

WRITINGS:

Iced (novel; also see below), Random House (New York, NY), 1993.

Iced (play; based on novel of the same name), produced in London, England, 1998.

White Folks (musical), produced in London, England, 2002.

Also author (and director and producer) of plays *Flatshare, Frederick Avery Visits,* and *Street Angels.*

WORK IN PROGRESS: Tender, a novel.

SIDELIGHTS: Although best known as an actor, Ray Shell is also the author of a novel, *Iced,* and a play of the same name based on the novel. Both the novel and the play feature a forty-something black man's retrospective of how drugs led him to give up a promising future as a lawyer and to kill several people, including a two-month-old baby he threw from a roof while trying to extort money for the baby's safe return. In the play it is this last crime which sends the man, Cornelius Washington Jr., to prison, where the action opens. On stage, his reminisces are framed by conversations with the prison psychiatrist; the novel is structured as a diary. *Iced* the novel, as Benedict Nightingale wrote in the London *Times,* "reportedly became one of the most shoplifted books in publishing history," and the stage version was also praised by critics. "There is some magnificent prose on display" in the scenes of *Iced* where Washington describes what it feels like to be high: "sheer, cold and snapping off like vast shards from the face of an iceberg," Ian Shuttleworth wrote in the *Financial Times.*

BIOGRAPHICAL AND CRITICAL SOURCES:

BOOKS

Contemporary Theatre, Film, and Television, Volume 32, Gale (Detroit, MI), 2000.

PERIODICALS

Financial Times, January 27, 1998, review of *Iced,* p. 19.
New Statesman, October 22, 1993, Laurence O'Toole, review of *Iced,* p. 40.
New Yorker, July 18, 1994, review of *Iced,* p. 81.
Publishers Weekly, June 12, 1995, Paul Nathan, "From Seminar to Contract," p. 18.
Spectator, January 21, 1995, Sheridan Morley, review of *Ain't Misbehavin',* pp. 44-45.
Times Literary Supplement, November 5, 1993, Holly Eley, review of *Iced,* p. 19.
Variety, April 4, 1984, review of *Starlight Express,* p. 84.

ONLINE

125th Street Web site, http://www.125thstreet.co.uk/ (February 27, 2003), "Ray Shell."

Borkowski PR Web site, http://www.borkowski.co.uk/ (August 5, 2002), "125 Streets Ahead."
Fire and water, http://www.fireandwater.com/ (February 27, 2003), "Ray Shell."*

*   *   *

SHENNAN, Margaret 1933-

PERSONAL: Born 1933.

ADDRESSES: Agent—c/o Author's Mail, John Murry Publishing, 50 Albemarle Street, London W1S 4BD, England.

CAREER: Historian and educator.

WRITINGS:

The European Dynamic: Aspects of European Expansion, 1450-1715, A. and C. Black (London, England), 1976.
Missee, Kensal Press (Bourne End, England, 1986.
The Devil's Diagonal,, Swallow, 1990.
Teaching about Europe, Cassell (New York, NY), 1991.
The Rise of Brandenburg Prussia, Routledge (New York, NY), 1995.
Berthe Morisot, the First Lady of Impressionism, Sutton Publishers (Stroud, England), 1996.
Out in the Midday Sun: The British in Malaya, 1880-1960, John Murray (London, England), 2000.

SIDELIGHTS: Margaret Shennan has written several history books, ranging in topic from European expansionism to British colonialism in Malaya. Her *The Rise of Brandenburg Prussia* is a treatise on the Great Elector and his son, King Frederick I, and Frederick William I. In his review for *History Review,* Graham Darby wrote, "There is little here that cannot be found in work already published, but it is conveniently packaged in a single volume." Gerd Mischler wrote, "Shennan manages to tell her story in a logical and convincing way" in his review for *History: Journal of the Historical Association.*

Shennan's next book is a biography of Berthe Morisot, the model who sat for Edouard Manet's famous 1870 portrait, "Le Repose." The book is aptly titled *Berthe*

Morisot, the First Lady of Impressionism, and in it, Shennan depicts the life of Morisot as a painter. The reader is introduced not only to Morisot's career and its struggles, but also to the painter's politics, commitments, and loveless marriage. In a review of the book for the *Spectator,* Richard Shone commented, "Shennan is a most sympathetic biographer. . . . She delicately suggests the tensions and frustrations of Morisot's life, balancing her gaiety and melancholy, setting the sensuous self-absorption of the painter against the woman capable of sudden crushing, ironic phrases."

Out in the Midday Sun: The British in Malaya, 1880-1960 is one of Shennan's more recent works. A review in *Contemporary Review* praised the book, noting: "Here the great sweep of history is mingled with individual memories and stories to give us not only a well-researched history but a superb read." Shennan's presentation of the British experience in Malaya depicts a world that was, until the advent of World War I, primarily one of happiness and contentment. Her book covers the Japanese bombing of Singapore and the chaos that followed. Anthony Milner of the *Times Literary Supplement* wrote, "The conveying of the experience of the British themselves—including their sense of satisfaction, whether or not it was misplaced—is Margaret Shennan's purpose and achievement. No study I know of has been able to achieve an equally eloquent representation of the experience of the colonial subject."

BIOGRAPHICAL AND CRITICAL SOURCES:

PERIODICALS

Choice, October, 1997, M. Hamel-Schwulst, review of *Berthe Morisot, the First Lady of Impressionism,* p. 287.

Contemporary Review, October, 2000, review of *Out in the Midday Sun: The British in Malaya, 1880-1960,* p. 249.

History: Journal of the Historical Association, January, 1999, Gerd Mischler, review of *The Rise of Brandenburg Prussia,* p. 161.

History Review, December, 1996, Graham Darby, review of *The Rise of Brandenburg Prussia,* p. 51.

Journal of Common Market Studies, September, 1992, Linda Hantrais, review of *Teaching about Europe,* p. 369.

Spectator, June 3, 2000, Richard Shone, "On the Side of the Angels," p. 39.

Times Literary Supplement, April 12, 2002, Anthony Milner, "Gin Sling and Stengah," p. 26.*

*   *   *

SHILLING, Arthur 1941-1986

PERSONAL: Born 1941, in Rama Reserve, Ontario, Canada; died 1986. *Education:* Attended New School of Art and Ontario College of Art.

CAREER: Painter and drafter. *Exhibitions:* Participant in solo and group shows, including exhibitions at Gallery Indigena, Stratford, Ontario, Canada, Thunder Bay Art Gallery, Beckett Gallery, Joseph D. Carrier Gallery, and in Germany and England; work represented in permanent collections, including Canadian Museum of Civilization, Indian and Northern Affairs Canada, Royal Ontario Museum, McMichael Canadian Collection, and Sundance Gallery, Calgary, Alberta, Canada.

AWARDS, HONORS: Art Fund Award for aspiring young artists, *Globe and Mail,* 1962; Department of Indian and Northern Affairs scholarship, 1964; Centennial Medal, 1967; first prize for Canadian Indian Christmas card design.

WRITINGS:

The Ojibway Dream, Tundra Books (Montreal, Quebec, Canada), 1967.

BIOGRAPHICAL AND CRITICAL SOURCES:

BOOKS

St. James Guide to Native North American Artists, St. James Press (Detroit, MI), 1998, pp. 516-517.

PERIODICALS

Artwest, Volume 6, number 9, 1981, Karen Mills, "Arthur Shilling."

Atlantic Monthly, May, 1967, "Working in Solitude."
Tawow, Volume 7, number 1, 1980, "An Interview with Arthur Shilling."*

*   *   *

SHIVA, Vandana 1952-

PERSONAL: Born 1952, in India. *Education:* Punjab University, B.A., M.A.; Western Ontario University, Ph.D., 1979.

ADDRESSES: Agent—c/o Author Mail, Sage Publications, 2455 Teller Rd., Thousand Oaks, CA 91320. *E-mail*—vshiva@giasdl01.vsnl.net.in.

CAREER: Physicist and environmentalist. Indian Institute of Management, Bangalore, India, 1980; United Nations University, consultant, 1982; Research Foundation for Science, Technology, and Natural Resource Policy, Dehradun, India, 1990. Navdanya, founder.

AWARDS, HONORS: Global 500 Award, United Nations Environment Program, 1992; Earth Day International Award, 1993; Right Livelihood Award, 1994.

WRITINGS:

Forestry Crisis and Forestry Myths: A Critical Review of Tropical Forests: A Call for Action, World Rainforest Movement (Penang, Malaysia), 1987.
(With J. Bandyopadhyay) *Ecological Audit of Eucalyptus Cultivation,* Research Foundation for Science and Ecology (Dehra Dun, India), 1987.
Staying Alive: Women, Ecology, and Development, Zed Books (London, England), 1988.
The Violence of the Green Revolution: Ecological Degradation and Political Conflict in Punjab, Natraj Publishers (Dehra Dun, India), 1989, Zed Books (Atlantic Highlands, NJ), 1991.
(With J. Bandyopadhyay and others) *Ecology and the Politics of Survival: Conflicts over the Natural Resources in India,* United Nations University Press (New Delhi, India), 1991.
Biodiversity: Social and Ecological Perspectives, Zed Books (Atlantic Highlands, NJ), 1991.

(With Sunderlal Bahuguna and M. N. Buch) *Environment Crisis and Sustainable Development,* Natraj Publishers (Dehra Dun, India), 1992.
Toward Hope: An Ecological Approach to the Future, Indian National Trust for Art and Cultural Heritage (New Delhi, India), 1994.
(With V. M. Meher-Homji, N. D. Jayal, and Sahabat Alam Malaysia) *Forest Resources, Crisis, and Management,* Natraj Publishers (Dehra Dun, India), 1992.
Monocultures of the Mind: Perspectives on Biodiversity and Biotechnology, Zed Books (Atlantic Highlands, NJ), 1993.
(With Maria Mies) *Ecofeminism,* Zed Books (Atlantic Highlands, NJ), 1993.
(With Vanaja Ramprasad) *Cultivating Diversity: Biodiversity Conservation and the Politics of the Seed,* Nataraj Publishers (Dehra Dun, India), 1993.
Sustaining Diversity: Renewing Diversity and Balance through Conservation, Navadanya (New Delhi, India), 1994.
Biodiversity Conservation: Whose Resource? Whose Knowledge? Indian National Trust for Art and Cultural Heritage (New Delhi, India), 1994.
Neem, a User's Manual, Center for Indian Knowledge Systems/Research Foundation for Science, Technology, and Natural Resource Policy (New Delhi, India), 1995.
Captive Minds, Captive Lies: Essays on Ethical and Ecological Implications of Patents on Life, Research for Science, Technology, and Natural Resource Policy, 1995.
(With Padmini Krishnan and others) *The Seed Keepers,* Navdanya (New Delhi, India), 1995.
Biopolitics: A Feminist and Ecological Reader on Biotechnology Zed Books (Atlantic Highlands, NJ), 1995.
Towards Sustainable Aquaculture, Research Foundation for Science, Technology, and Natural Resource Policy (New Delhi, India), 1996.
Biopiracy: The Plunder of Nature and Knowledge, South End Press (Boston, MA), 1997.
(With Afsar H. Jafri and Gitanjali Bedi) *Ecological Costs of Economic Globalisation: the Indian Experience,* Research Foundation for Science, Technology, and Ecology (New Delhi, India), 1997.
The Enclosure and Recovery of the Commons: Biodiversity, Indigenous Knowledge, and Intellectual Property Rights, Research Foundation for Science, Technology, and Ecology (New Delhi, India), 1997.

(With Afsar H. Jafri and Shalini Bhutani) *Campaign against Biopiracy,* Research Foundation for Science, Technology, and Ecology (New Delhi, India), 1999.

Betting on Biodiversity: Why Genetic Engineering Will Not Feed the Hungry or Save the Planet, Research Foundation for Science, Technology, and Ecology (New Delhi, India), 1999.

Stolen Harvest: The Hijacking of the Global Food Supply, South End Press (Cambridge, MA), 2000.

(With Ashok Emani) *Climate Change, Deforestation, and the Orissa Super Cyclone: Ecological Costs of Globalisation,* Research Foundation for Science, Technology, and Ecology (New Delhi, India), 2000.

Seeds of Suicide: The Ecological and Human Costs of Globalisation of Agriculture, Research Foundation for Science, Technology, and Ecology (New Delhi, India), 2000.

Tomorrow's Biodiversity, Thames & Hudson (London, England), 2000.

(With Margaret Antony) *The Beedi Ban, Tobacco Monopolies, and the Myth of Labour: Deconstructing the Politics of Trade Sanctions,* Research Foundation for Science, Technology, and Ecology (New Delhi, India), 2000.

License to Kill: How the Unholy Trinity—The World Bank, the International Monetary Fund, and the World Trade Organization—Are Killing Livelihoods, Environment, and Democracy in India, Research Foundation for Science, Technology, and Ecology (New Delhi, India), 2000.

Patents: Myths and Reality, Penguin Books (New York, NY), 2001.

Protect or Plunder? Understanding Intellectual Property Rights, Zed Books (New York, NY), 2001.

Yoked to Death: Globalisation and Corporate Control of Agriculture, Research Foundation for Science, Technology, and Ecology (New Delhi, India), 2001.

Water Wars: Privatization, Pollution, and Profit, South End Press (Cambridge, MA), 2002.

(Editor) *Sustainable Agriculture and Food Security: The Impact of Globalisation,* Sage Publications (Thousand Oaks, CA), 2002.

India on Fire: The Lethal Mix of Free Trade, Famine and Fundamentalism in India, Seven Stories Press (Berkeley, CA), 2003.

SIDELIGHTS: Vandana Shiva is one of the youngest female scientists in the world to receive such a high degree of global recognition and prominence in as short a career as she has so far experienced. Well known as an environmentalist, feminist, and physicist, Shiva has taken up numerous global causes for which she has received many awards. A prolific author, she uses her published writings to explore and promote environmental conservation and biodiversity in tropical forests, particularly in her native India.

Shiva abandoned her country's nuclear energy program early in her career to devote herself to halting the global destruction of nature. "I was very lucky to have been born the daughter of a forester in India and to have grown up in the Himalayan forest," she told Judith Bizot of the *UNESCO Courier.* "Then I studied physics. . . . Then I went into nuclear physics, where I experienced massive disappointments. It was only when I was doing my master's degree that I realized how unthinking nuclear scientists were about the question of radiation hazards. . . . While I was groping my way . . . senior physicists would say, 'You don't need to know these things.' If science means to know, then I had no scientific training. So I went to Canada and enrolled on a foundations of physics program, where some of the basic questions about science that were troubling me were being asked."

Shiva has dedicated her career to battling the injustices and causes she cares about, and her bibliography reflects that. One issue in particular that has interested her is the Chipko women's movement, whose goal is to protect the environment. Shiva became involved with the movement after listening to and observing the women. In her *UNESCO Courier* interview, she explained, "It was their perceptions and their beliefs that were the really rich foundations of my knowledge of ecology. They offered me a new sensibility about relationships. . . . All my theory-building has come out of this nature-centered and woman-centered action. In my book *Staying Alive* I attempted to explain why my insights came from women who were considered ignorant and marginal, who were not given a platform of any kind by society."

Staying Alive: Women, Ecology, and Development was described as "a uniquely modern Green mixture of Hindu mythology, social disquiet, dry statistical tables and bouncy assaults on West 'male' science," by Alexandra Artley in her review for *Spectator.*

Shiva has found that her feminism and environmentalism are intimately linked, and her writing reflects that. "I think women are taking the lead today. . . . I believe that women in the North are also intimately linked to the environment. Even in the most advanced societies, women have been left to care for children, homes, and health. It's wrong to say that women are unproductive, that they don't work," she told Judith Bizot. "It is often said that women who stay home do not work, but in fact they work harder than anyone else." In addition to *Staying Alive,* some of her other titles are evidence of her belief that women are nature-centered: *Biopolitics: A Feminist and Ecological Reader on Biotechnology,* and *Ecofeminism.*

Other topics of interest and concern for Shiva are the green revolution, biodiversity, genetic engineering, and the sustainability of water. Her book on the last-mentioned topic is titled *Water Wars: Privatization, Pollution, and Profit.* In it she explores the relationship between sustainability and equal fair access. Shiva condemns the trend towards redefining water as a commodity and calls for a reckoning of the costs of modern development. Kerryn Higgs in the *Women's Review of Books* found value in the work. "This book makes an excellent starting point for anyone who wants to understand the forces driving water scarcity today and threatening its future supply."

For Shiva, contemporary society abuses its power. As she explained to Bizot: "Industrial society is the only one which believes that if you have the power to do something, you must do it. Indian philosophy is built on the concept that 'Yes, you might have the power, but it is important that you use your discrimination in the exercise of that power.'"

Biopiracy: The Plunder of Nature and Knowledge is one of Shiva's more recent titles. "Biopiracy" refers to the corporate practice of stealing germ plasm from nature and Earth-based cultures and turning it into a commercial commodity. The book takes an historical view of imperialism, and explores the issues of biopatents and intellectual property rights. In his review for *Canadian Book Review Annual,* Patrick Colgan wrote, "Shiva makes an eloquent plea for diversity, local freedom, and reconnecting elements of intrinsically holistic web. While her opinions are occasionally questionable . . . her arguments merit serious attention and constitute a stiff challenge to the paradigms within which the West deals with nature." Helen Forsey of *Canadian Forum* wrote, "I found myself totally caught up in Shiva's analysis. Not content with merely exposing and denouncing the corporate outrage

of biopiracy, she has pushed the political and philosophical envelopes on questions ranging from nonviolence to patriarchy, from the nature of knowledge and creativity to regional and ethnic separatism."

In addition to giving lectures, presenting papers, and writing, Shiva has established Navdanya, a movement in India calling for biodiversity conservation and farmers' rights.

BIOGRAPHICAL AND CRITICAL SOURCES:

BOOKS

Breton, Mary Joy, *Women Pioneers for the Environment.* Northeastern University Press (Boston, MA), 1998, pp. 210-218.
Notable Women Scientists. Gale (Detroit, MI), 1999, pp. 533-534.

PERIODICALS

Canadian Book Review Annual, 1997, Patrick Colgan, review of *Biopiracy: The Plunder of Nature and Knowledge,* p. 436.
Canadian Forum, April, 1998, Helen Forsey, "Stealing the Stuff of Life," pp. 42-43.
Choice, October, 1997, R. Seelke, review of *Biopiracy,* p. 318.
Journal of Asian Studies, November, 1993, Douglas E. Streusand, review of *The Violence of the Green Revolution: Third World Agriculture, Ecology, and Politics,* pp. 1042-1044.
New York Review of Books, June 21, 2001, Richard Lewontin, "Genes in the Food!" pp. 81-84.
Progressive, September, 1997, David Barsamian, interview with Vandana Shiva, pp. 36-39.
Signs, winter, 1997, Rhonda Roland Shearer, review of *Ecofeminism,* pp. 496-501.
Spectator, March 18, 1989, Alexandra Artley, "Bookman, Spare That Tree," pp. 23-25.
UNESCO Courier, December, 2001, "Vandana Shiva Talks to Judith Bizot," pp. 36-39.
Whole Earth Review, winter, 1995, Nathan Boone, review of *Staying Alive: Women, Ecology, and Development,* p. 20.
Women's Review of Books, June, 2002, Kerryn Higgs, "Running on Empty," pp. 6-7.

ONLINE

International Institute for Sustainable Development Web site, http://www.iisd.ca/ (June 1, 1996), "Vandana Shiva."

Tom Paine.com, http://www.tompaine.com/ (September 7, 2002), "Hoover Dam: Water Wars in the American West."

Weston A. Price Foundation Web site, http://www.westonaprice.org/ (September 7, 2002), Sally Fallon, review of "Stolen Harvest: The Hijacking of the Global Food Supply."

Zmag, http://www.zmag.org/bios/ (September 7, 2002), "Vandana Shiva.".*

* * *

SHOCKLEY, William (Bradford) 1910-1989

PERSONAL: Born February 13, 1910, in London, England; died of prostate cancer August 11, 1989, in Palo Alto, CA; son of William Hillman (an American mining engineer) and May (a mineral surveyor; maiden name, Bradford) Shockley; married Jean Alberta Baily, 1933 (divorced, 1955); married Emily I. Lanning (a psychiatric nurse); children (first marriage) Alison, William, Richard. *Education:* Attended University of California—Los Angeles; California Institute of Technology, B.A., 1932; Massachusetts Institute of Technology, Ph.D., 1936.

CAREER: Physicist. Bell Telephone Laboratories, Murray Hill, NJ, staff physicist, then director of research program on solid-state physics, 1945-54; U.S. Navy Anti-Submarine Warfare Operations Research Group, Columbia University, research director, 1942; U.S. Secretary of War, consultant, 1944-45; U.S. Department of Defense Weapons Systems Evaluation Group, director of research, 1954; California Institute of Technology, visiting professor, 1954-55; Shockley Semiconductor Laboratories, founder, 1955-65; Stanford University, Alexander M. Poniatoff Professor of Engineering and Applied Science, 1963-75, emeritus professor of electrical engineering, 1975-89.

AWARDS, HONORS: U.S. Medal of Merit, 1946; Morris E. Liebmann Award, Institute of Radio Engineers, 1951; Comstock Prize, National Academy of Sciences, 1954; Nobel Prize in Physics, 1956, for development of the transistor; Institute of Electrical and Electronics Gold Medal, 1972 and Medal of Honor, 1980; named to National Inventor's Hall of Fame, 1974.

WRITINGS:

Electrons and Holes in Semiconductors, with Applications to Transistor Electronics, Van Nostrand (New York, NY), 1950, reprinted, R. E. Kreiger Publishing Company (Huntington, NY), 1976.

(Editor, with others), *Imperfections in Nearly Perfect Crystals: Symposium Held at Pocono Manor, October 12-14, 1950,* John Wiley & Sons (New York, NY), 1952.

(With Walter A. Gong) *Mechanics,* Charles E. Merrill Books (Columbus, OH), 1966.

Shockley on Eugenics and Race: The Application of Science to the Solution of Human Problems, edited by Roger Pearson, preface by Arthur R. Jensen, Scott-Townsend Publishers (Washington, DC), 1992.

SIDELIGHTS: Physicist William Shockley shared the 1956 Nobel Prize in physics for his work in the development of the transistor. Shockley was also known for his controversial views on the genetic basis of intelligence, specifically his ideas that people of African descent have a genetically inferior mental capacity when compared with Caucasians. "This hypothesis became the subject of intense and acrimonious debate," wrote a biographer in *World of Sociology.*

Shockley was born in London, England, on February 13, 1910, to William and May Shockley. The Shockleys, Americans who were living in London on a business arrangement, returned to California in 1913. Shockley was home-schooled until the age of eight. His interest in physics developed early in his life, inspired partially by a neighbor who taught the subject at Stanford. His parents also encouraged his interests in science. After completing his secondary education at Palo Alto Military Academy and Hollywood High School, Shockley attended the University of California, Los Angeles for a year. Shockley completed his advanced education at California Institute of Technology, where he earned a bachelor's degree in physics in 1932, and the Massachusetts Institute of Technology, where he was awarded a Ph.D. in physics in 1936. His doctoral research in solid-state physics led to his interest in transistors.

Soon after receiving his Ph.D., Shockley went to work at the Bell Telephone Laboratories in Murray Hill, New Jersey. "Shockley's first assignment at Bell was the development of a new type of vacuum tube that would serve as an amplifier," wrote the *World of Sociology* biographer. "Soon he began to think of a radically new approach to the transmission of electrical signals using solid-state components rather than conventional vacuum tubes. By 1939, Shockley was experimenting with semiconducting materials to achieve that transition."

After serving as research director of the U.S. Navy's Anti-Submarine Warfare Operations Research Group at Columbia University from 1942 to 1945 and as a consultant to the U.S. Secretary of War from 1944 to 1945, Shockley returned to Bell Laboratories and assumed the position of director of its research program on solid-state physics. Together with John Bardeen, a theoretical physicist, and Walter Brattain, an experimental physicist, Shockley resumed study of semiconductors as a means of amplification.

"By 1947, Bardeen and Brattain had learned enough about semiconductors to make another attempt at building a device," commented the *World of Sociology* writer. "This time they were successful. Their device consisted of a piece of germanium with two gold contacts on one side and a tungsten contact on the opposite side. When an electrical current was fed into one of the gold contacts, it appeared in a greatly amplified form on the other side. The device was given the name transistor (for *trans*fer re*sistor*)."

Despite his earlier work on semiconductors that led to the transistor, "Bell Labs attorneys thought it would be wiser to exclude Shockley from that first patent because his work bore some similarity" to the work of Julius Lilienfild, who had done work on a similar transistor in the 1920s, noted a biographer in *Electronic Engineering Times*. Some believe that Shockley harbored anger at Bardeen and Brattain for the exclusion, yet all three later shared the Nobel Prize for the development of the transistor.

The transistor was announced in a brief article in the July 1, 1948 issue of the *New York Times*. "Few readers had the vaguest notion of the impact the fingernail-sized device would have on the world," the *World of Sociology* biographer remarked. "In a remarkable series of insights made over a few short weeks, he greatly extended the understanding of semiconductor materials and developed the underlying theory of another, much more robust amplifying device—a kind of sandwich made of a crystal with varying impurities added, which came to be known as the junction transistor," wrote Gordon E. Moore in *Time*. Shockley proposed a modification to Bardeen and Brattain's device, which worked much better than the previous point contact device. In 1956, Shockley shared the Nobel Prize for physics with Bardeen and Brattain for their development of the transistor.

"Shockley's invention had created a new industry, one that underlies all of modern electronics, from supercomputers to talking greeting cards," Moore observed. "Today, the world produces about as many transistors as it does printed characters in all the newspapers, books, magazines, and computer and electronic-copier pages combined." However, at the time of his death, Shockley thought his work in genetics was more important than the role he played in creating the $130 billion semiconductor industry.

Shockley left Bell Laboratories in 1954 (some sources say 1955), and served in various positions over the next decade, including research director for the Weapons Systems Evaluation Group of the Department of Defense and as a visiting professor at Caltech in 1954 and 1955. He founded Shockley Semiconductor Laboratories—later Shockley Transistor Corporation—in order to take commercial advantage of the transistor. Shockley Transistor was incorporated into Beckman Instruments, Inc., and then Clevite Transistor. The company went out of business in 1968.

In 1963 Shockley undertook a new career, one that would make him the target of considerable controversy. After accepting an appointment at Stanford University as its first Alexander M. Poniatoff Professor of Engineering and Applied Science, he developed an interest in genetics and the related origins of human intelligence. Shockley became particularly interested in the correlation between race and IQ. "Although he had no background in psychology, genetics, or any related field, Shockley began to read on these topics and formulate his own hypotheses," a *World of Sociology* biographer wrote. "Using data taken primarily from U.S. Army pre-induction IQ tests, Shockley came to the conclusion that the genetic component of a person's intelligence was based on racial heritage. He ignited further controversy with his suggestion that inferior individuals (those with IQ numbered below 100) be paid to undergo voluntary sterilization. The social implications of Shockley's theories were, and still are, profound."

Shockley's theories on the racial basis of intelligence branded him a racist, and he was barred from speaking on several university campuses. "With the same grit that carried him and his team of scientists past failure after failure to the transistor, he pursued a theory that the poor, especially blacks, inherit a genetic inferiority that an improved environment cannot overcome," remarked a writer in *U.S. News and World Report.* "He believed that black intelligence rises in proportion to a person's percentage of white blood." Shockley was frequently booed and heckled at his speaking engagements, but he held to his beliefs.

Shockley successfully sued the *Atlanta Constitution* for libel over an article comparing his voluntary sterilization proposal with Nazi genetic experiments. The jury found that Shockley had indeed been libeled, but awarded him $1 in compensation. "Unsparing in the application of his views, Shockley has described his three children as 'a significant regression' (though one has a physics Ph.D. and another graduated from Radcliffe), The fault of his less intelligent first wife, he suggests," wrote Richard Lacayo in *Time.* "His own genes he holds to be made of sterner stuff." At age seventy, Shockley "announced that he had made donations to a sperm bank established to spawn the offspring of Nobel-prizewinning men and highly intelligent women," Lacayo wrote.

"Those who knew him best described Shockley as a reserved man, independent, intellectually honest, direct, and with a sense of humor," wrote Victoria Tamborrino in *The Scribner Encyclopedia of American Lives.* "Scientifically, he was considered brilliant, perhaps even a genius. His brainchild, the transistor, is, arguably, the most important invention of the twentieth century. Certainly, it revolutionized computer technology, making computers smaller, cheaper, and more reliable. The transistor's use is virtually limitless in communication systems and other electronic devices as well."

As a result of his role in the development of the transistor, Tamborrino wrote, "Shockley made a significant contribution to mankind. Perhaps it is both unfortunate and fitting that his scientific accomplishments are often overshadowed by the memory of his racial views."

BIOGRAPHICAL AND CRITICAL SOURCES:

BOOKS

Asimov, Isaac, *Asimov's Biographical Encyclopedia of Science and Technology,* Avon (New York, NY), 1976.
Encyclopedia of World Biography, 2nd edition, Gale (Detroit, MI), 1998.
Garraty, John A., editor, *Encyclopedia of American Biography,* Harper & Row (New York, NY), 1974.
Garraty, John A. and Jerome L. Sternstein, *Encyclopedia of American Biography,* HarperCollins (New York, NY), 1996.
Hart, James D., *A Companion to California,* Oxford University Press (New York, NY), 1978,
Howat, Gerald, editor, *Who Did What,* Crown Publishers (New York, NY), 1974.
Leaders in Electronics, McGraw-Hill Book Company (New York, NY), 1979.
Lincoln Library of Social Studies, 8th edition, Frontier Press Co. (Columbus, OH), 1978.
McGraw-Hill Modern Scientists and Engineers, McGraw-Hill Book Company (New York, NY), 1980.
New York Times Biographical Series, Volume 20, University Microfilms International (Ann Arbor, MI), 1989.
Notable Scientists: From 1900 to the Present, Gale (Detroit, MI), 2001.
Palmisano, Joseph M., editor, *World of Sociology,* Gale (Detroit, MI), 2001.
Scribner Encyclopedia of American Lives, Volume 2: *1986-1990,* Charles Scribner's Sons (New York, NY), 1999.
World of Invention, 2nd edition, Gale (Detroit, MI), 1999.

PERIODICALS

America's Network, June 1, 1998, "Fathers of Invention," pp. 32-33.
Chicago Daily Law Bulletin, September 6, 1984, William E. Schmidt, "Race Genetics Focus of Trial," p. 3.

Datamation, September, 1982, "Thanks for the Memories," p. 27.

Editor & Publisher, September 29, 1984, "A Loss That's Really a Win," p. 15.

Electronic Business, December, 1997, Heidi Elliott, "Happy 50th," pp. 60-63.

Electronic Design, May 7, 2001, Steve Scrupski, "Just Diodes in Hi-Fi Amplifier," p. 48.

Electronic Engineering Times, October 20, 1997, "Leaving the Master," p. 58; January 10, 2000, "Industry Pioneers Inducted into Computer Electronics Hall of Fame," p. 122.

Jet, October 1, 1984, "Journalist Is Fined $1 in Shockley Libel Suit," p. 36.

Journal of Commerce and Commercial, August 2, 1983, Susan Bereitner, "Tiny Transistor Sparked Electronic Revolution," p. 3A.

Los Angeles Daily Journal, September 17, 1984, Adrienne Y. Welch, "Shockley wins Libel Lawsuit, but Georgia Jury Sets $1 Award," p. 3.

Los Angeles Times, April 1, 1984, Peter J. Boyer, "Libel Trial to Provide Forum for Shockley's Controversial Racial Theory," p. 18; September 5, 1984, Peter J. Boyer, "Shockley Race Theory Libel Trial Opens Today," p. 18; September 15, 1984, Peter J. Boyer, "Shockley Wins $1 in Libel Suit on Race Issue," p. 1; October 25, 1999, Ashley Dunn, "With Transistor, They Sparked a Revolution," P. U1.

National Law Journal, September 24, 1984, Michael Hirsley, "The Testing of a Theory about Race: A Question of Libel and Genes," p. 6; October 1, 1984, Michael Hirsley, "Jury Gives Physicist $1 for Libel," p. 8.

New York Times, September 6, 1984, William E. Schmidt, "Trial May focus on Race Genetics; Scientist Who Asserts Blacks are Inferior to Whites Sues Reporter in Libel Case," p. A16; September 15, 1984, "Shockley Wins $1 in Libel Suit," p. 8; August 4, 1985, "$1 Award to Shockley Upheld," p. 18.

Physics Today, December, 1997, "The Moses of Silicon Valley," p. 42.

San Jose Mercury News, July 15, 1998, "Silicon Valley Birthplace: William Shockley's Digs?"

Science '84, November, 1984, John Bardeen, "To a Solid State," p. 143.

Science Digest, June, 1985, Signe Hammer, "Stalking Intelligence: IQ Isn't the End of the Line; You Can Be Smarter," p. 30.

Time, January 3, 1983, Frederic Golden, "Big Dimwits and Little Geniuses," p. 30; September 24, 1984, Richard Lacayo, "A Theory Goes on Trial: In Atlanta, a Controversial Scientist Cries Libel and Wins $1," p. 62; March 29, 1999, Gordon E. Moore, "Solid-State Physicist," p. 160.

U.S. News & World Report, November 5, 1984, Alvin P. Sanoff, "Behind Wave of Libel Suits Hitting Nation's Press," pp. 53-54; August 28, 1989, "Dr. Shockley and Mr. Hyde," p. 16.

Wall Street Journal, September 17, 1984, "Shockley Wins Libel Suit, Gets $1 from Newspapers," p. 13E.

Washington Post, September 12, 1984, Art Harris, "The Shockley Suite: In Atlanta, Debating IQ Ideas Is a Libel Case," p. B1.

ONLINE

Nobel e-Museum, http://www.nobel.se/ (May 4, 2003), biography of William Shockley.

OBITUARIES:

PERIODICALS

Electronic Engineering Times, August 21, 1989, p. 4.
Electronic News, August 21, 1989, p. 20.
Los Angeles Times, August 14, 1989, p. 1.
Nature, September 21, 1989, p. 190.
New York Times, August 14, 1989, p. B15.
Physics Today, June, 1991, pp. 130-131.
Solid State Technology, September, 1989, p. 44.
Time, August 28, 1989, p. 61.*

*   *   *

SMITH, Alexander McCall 1948-

PERSONAL: Born 1948, in Southern Rhodesia (now Zimbabwe); married; children: two daughters. *Education:* Studied law in Scotland. *Hobbies and other interests:* Plays bassoon in Really Terrible Orchestra.

ADDRESSES: Agent—David Higham Associates, 5-8 Lower John St., Golden Square, London W1R 4HA, England.

CAREER: Professor of medical law at Edinburgh University. Taught law at University of Botswana; helped create a criminal code for Botswana. Human Genetics Commission of the United Kingdom (vice chairman), UNESCO (member, International Bioethics Commission).

WRITINGS:

NONFICTION

(Editor with Tony Carty) *Power and Manoeuvrability,* Q Press (Edinburgh, Scotland), 1978.

(With John Kenyon Mason) *Butterworths Medico-Legal Encyclopedia,* Butterworths (Boston, MA), 1987.

(Editor with Elaine Sutherland) *Family Rights: Family Law and Medical Advances,* Edinburgh University Press (Edinburgh, Scotland), 1990.

(With John Kenyon Mason) *Law and Medical Ethics,* third edition, Butterworths (Austin, TX), 1991.

(With Kwame Frimpong) *The Criminal Law of Botswana,* Juta (Cape Town), 1992.

(Editor with Michael A. Menlowe) *The Duty to Rescue: The Jurisprudence of Aid,* Dartmouth (Brookfield, VT), 1993.

(Editor with Colin Shapiro) *Forensic Aspects of Sleep,* Wiley (New York, NY), 1997.

(With Daniel W. Shuman) *Justice and the Prosecution of Old Crimes: Balancing Legal, Psychological, and Moral Concerns,* American Psychological Association (Washington, DC), 2000.

(With Alan Merry) *Errors, Medicine, and the Law,* Cambridge University Press (New York, NY), 2001.

FICTION

Children of Wax: African Folk Tales, Interlink Book (New York, NY), 1991.

Heavenly Date and Other Stories, Canongate (Edinburgh, Scotland), 1995.

Morality for Beautiful Girls, Anchor Books (New York, NY), 2002.

Tears of the Giraffe, Anchor Books (New York, NY), 2002.

The No. 1 Ladies' Detective Agency, Anchor Books (New York, NY), 2002.

The Kalahari Typing School for Men, Pantheon (New York, NY), 2003.

CHILDREN'S BOOKS

Film Boy, illustrated by Joanna Carey, Methuen (London, England), 1988.

Mike's Magic Seeds, illustrated by Kate Shannon, Young Corgi (London, England), 1988.

Suzy Magician, Young Corgi (London, England), 1990.

The Five Lost Aunts of Harriet Bean, Blackie (London, England), 1990.

The Popcorn Pirates, Scholastic Young Hippo (London, England), 1999.

Author of more than fifty books, including children's books such as *The White Hippo,* Hamish Hamilton; *The Perfect Hamburger,* Hamish Hamilton; *Akimbo and the Elephants,* Mammouth, *Marzipan Max,* Blackie; *The Ice-Cream Bicycle,* Viking Read Alone; *The Doughnut Ring,* Hamish Hamilton; *The Muscle Machine,* Hamish Hamilton; *Paddy and the Ratcatcher,* Heinemann; and *The Princess Trick,* Puffin.

ADAPTATIONS: The story "Children of Wax" was made into an animated film; other stories by Smith have been read on BBC Radio. Film rights to *The No. 1 Ladies' Detective Agency* have been sold.

WORK IN PROGRESS: Portuguese Irregular Verbs and *The Perfect Imperfect,* to be published by Polygon with a third volume, c. late 2003.

SIDELIGHTS: The diverse accomplishments of Alexander McCall Smith, include a distinguished career as a legal scholar and more recent fame as a best-selling novelist. A professor of medical law at Edinburgh University, Smith has published many works on medical ethics and criminal law. For example, he has written about the duty to rescue and the impact of medical advances on parental rights. Smith also had numerous books of fiction for young children and short-story collections in print before he published a series of detective stories set in Zimbabwe. The first installment, *The No. 1 Ladies' Detective Agency,* became a best-selling novel in the United States after it was popularized by word of mouth. Readers and critics have been charmed by the stories, which are more about relationships, customs, and informal justice than sleuthing.

Born and raised in the British colony of Southern Rhodesia (now Zimbabwe), Smith studied law in Edinburgh, Scotland. He then assisted in creating

Botswana's first law school, taught law at the University of Botswana, and wrote a criminal code for Botswana. Many years later, in 1992, he would publish *The Criminal Law of Botswana* with Kwame Frimpong. The book interested critics with its discussion of how the country's criminal law is unlike others in southern Africa and how it resembles the Queensland Criminal Code of 1899. Two reviewers regretted that the work is not more detailed: in the *Journal of African Law* Simon Coldham advised that the book is "designed primarily for students," while James S. Read said in the *International and Comparative Law Quarterly,* that the book provides "a short and selective introduction" to the subject.

Most of Smith's legal scholarship treats subjects relating to medical and criminal law issues. He served as co-editor and contributor for *Family Rights: Family Law and Medical Advances,* which contains seven essays about the legal and ethical implications of new medical capabilities that affect the creation of life as well as the extension of life. The essays consider the impact of laws on a family's ability to make their own medical decisions. McCall's contribution, "Is Anything Left of Parental Rights?," addresses the increased autonomy of children.

Reviews of *Family Rights* described the book as an in-depth treatment suitable for specialists and general readers. In the *Sydney Law Review* Belinda Bennett recommended it as "a very readable collection" that avoids jargon and explains the necessary medical and scientific terminology. Jenny L. Urwin said in the *Journal of Medical Ethics* that it provided "interesting and thoughtful analysis" on a previously neglected subject. The book's "interdisciplinary and comparative flavour" was noted in *Family Law* by Andrew Bainham, who also said, "The scholarship in this volume is, for the most part, as original as it is provocative and the two most impressive contributions are by the editors themselves." Writing for *Nature,* Andrew Grubb commented on the context of Smith's essay, saying, "Faced with this largely interventionist judicial attitude, it is left to Sandy McCall Smith to challenge its basis and to sound a note of caution."

In *The Duty to Rescue: The Jurisprudence of Aid* Smith helped compile essays that discuss the moral and sometimes legal duty to provide aid. The writings cover theoretical and philosophical concerns, the possible ways of putting theory into practice, and the state's duty to assist at-risk individuals. Reviewers said the work does a good job of addressing the diverse implications of making rescue a legal obligation. In a review for *Choice,* M. A. Foley called the book "rather comprehensive" and recommended it as a primary reference on the subject. In the *University of British Columbia Law Review* Mitchell McInnes commented that Smith's essay, "The Duty to Rescue and the Common Law," raises an interesting and incomplete point on the subject of how a legal requirement would impact the formation of individual moral intuition. Celia Wells recommended the volume and McCall's contributions in *Criminal Law Review.* She concluded, "This collection sweeps effortlessly across legal, jurisdictional, and philosophical boundaries posing on its way a series of fascinating questions and supplying some clues to the answers."

Smith is also a prolific fiction writer. His books for children reflect both Western and non-Western cultural influences, and are mostly written for new readers. One example showing Smith's African background is *The White Hippo,* a story set in Gambia about the unsuccessful efforts of villagers who want to protect an albino hippo from a white man claiming to be a photographer. In *The Perfect Hamburger,* an old man and a young boy join forces to try to save a family-run hamburger shop from being forced out of business by a chain restaurant.

The twenty-seven stories in *Children of Wax: African Folk Tales* are more suited for older children and storytellers. Smith collected the tales from old and young members of the Ndebele people of Zimbabwe. Featuring shape-changing animals and supernatural powers, they nevertheless contain realistic portrayals of hardship and danger. The stories often serve to condemn bad behaviors such as greed and unfounded trust and show that justice does not always follow wrongdoing. *Library Journal*'s Patricia Dooley warned that this is "emphatically not children's pabulum." In a review for *Choice,* P. Alden was not quite satisfied with the authenticity of Smith's retelling, but said that the stories are "engaging" and that some are notable for their depiction of Zimbabwean women. A *Kirkus Reviews* writer admired the collection for its "evocative, involving narratives that reveal much about the culture from which they spring."

The collection *Heavenly Date and Other Stories* is comprised of original stories by Smith that are international in scope. Among them, "Intimate Accounts" is set in a fictional world, "Bulawayo" happens in Southern Rhodesia, and others take place in Zurich, Lisbon, and Northern Queensland. The dark and funny pieces relate all kinds of strange dates, meetings, and exchanges between men and women. In a review for the *Times Literary Supplement,* Andrew Biswell made note of Smith's inventiveness, stylistic range, and the "remarkable absence of excess baggage" in the collection that he thought showed the influence of African oral story-telling.

Smith's inspiration for *The No. 1 Ladies' Detective Agency* and the protagonist Mma Precious Ramotswe was his admiration for the women of Africa, according to an interviewer in *Publishers Weekly.* The novel and subsequent books in the series—*Tears of the Giraffe, Morality for Beautiful Girls,* and *The Kalahari Typing School for Men*—are mostly about everyday life in Africa. The character of Mma Ramotswe is the dynamic central force behind these stories. A solidly built, divorced woman in her late thirties, she uses a tiny inheritance to start a detective agency. Her work takes place in the city of Gaborone and in cattle country near the Kalahari Desert. She deals mostly with family conflicts, including cheating husbands, and employer-employee troubles. Mma Ramotswe runs a threadbare operation, but she does have an assistant, Mma Makutsi, a secretarial college graduate who has lost better jobs to her prettier classmates. Another key figure is J. L. B. Matekoni, a mechanic who assists them and later becomes engaged to Mma Ramotswe. The bride-to-be is a rather unconventional detective, one who also serves as family counselor, comments on manners and the lack of them, and is less concerned with legally administered justice than with doing right by her clients.

Mma Ramotswe and Smith's novels about her have charmed reviewers, who have found the novels fresh, amusing, and affecting. In a *BookLoons* review, G. Hall described the first installment as "truly unique," explaining that "the best part of the book is, in fact, not the mysteries but the stories of Precious and her father." Mahinder Kingra of the *Baltimore City Paper* judged that in this "deceptively frivolous" novel there is "as honest and sympathetic a portrait of contemporary African life as [Nigerian writer Chinua] Achebe's." Kingra commented that the book is "one of those rare, unassuming novels that seems to contain all of life

within its pages, and affirms life in telling its story." Christine Jeffords noted in *Best Reviews* online that Smith "succeeds in giving his story a lilting, lyrical flavor that makes the reader feel almost as if she is listening to a story being spun by a native tale-teller." Comments on the first three novels by Anthony Daniels in the *Spectator* included the assessment "I know nothing else like them." Daniels credited Smith with an admirably simple writing style and the remarkable feat of "creating fictional characters who are decent, goodhearted but not in the least bit dull." And the critic advised that "for all their apparent simplicity, the Precious Ramotswe books are highly sophisticated."

When Alida Becker reviewed the first three books for the *New York Times,* dubbing Mma Ramotswe the "Miss Marple of Botswana," it dramatically increased public awareness of the series. As Becker noted, film rights for the series had already been sold to Anthony Minghella, director of *The English Patient.* In the *Wall Street Journal,* Matthew Gurewitsch found *The No. 1 Ladies' Detective Agency* to be no less than "one of the most entrancing literary treats of many a year." Gurewitsch exulted that Smith planned more stories about Mma Ramotswe and would be publishing a series of academic satires about a professor of Romance philology named Dr. Mortiz-Maria von Igelfeld.

BIOGRAPHICAL AND CRITICAL SOURCES:

PERIODICALS

Choice, February, 1992, P. Alden, review of *Children of Wax,* p. 903; July/August, 1994, M. A. Foley, review of *The Duty to Rescue,* p. 1792.

Criminal Law Review, January, 1996, Celia Wells, review of *The Duty to Rescue,* pp. 71-72.

Family Law, April, 1992, Andrew Bainham, review of *Family Rights,* p. 135.

International and Comparative Law Quarterly, July, 1993, review of *The Criminal Law of Botswana,* pp. 748-749.

Journal of African Law, autumn, 1992, Simon Coldham, review of *The Criminal Law of Botswana,* pp. 193-194.

Journal of Medical Ethics, June, 1992, Jenny L. Urwin, review of *Family Rights,* pp. 108-109.

Kirkus Reviews, June 15, 1991, review of *Children of Wax,* p. 793.

Library Journal, July, 1991, Patricia Dooley, review of *Children of Wax,* p. 106.

Nature, June 27, 1991, Andrew Grubb, review of *Family Rights,* p. 707.

New York Times Book Review, January 27, 2002, Alida Becker, "Miss Marple of Botswana," p. 12.

Publishers Weekly, July 22, 2002, Charlotte Abbott, "From Africa, with Love," p. 75.

Spectator, September 1, 2001, Anthony Daniels, "Something Really New out of Africa," pp. 36-37.

Sydney Law Review, June, 1992, Belinda Bennett, review of *Family Rights,* pp. 253-255.

Times Literary Supplement, November 3, 1995, Andrew Biswell, "Mr Self and Ms Ms," p. 25.

University of British Columbia Law Review, winter, 1994, Mitchell McInnes, review of *The Duty to Rescue,* pp. 201-204.

Wall Street Journal, September 4, 2002, Matthew Gurewitsch, "A Scholarly Scot Writes of African Intrigue," p. D8.

ONLINE

Baltimore City Paper Online, http://citypaper.com/ (September 5-11, 2001), Mahinder Kingra, review of *The No. 1 Ladies' Detective Agency.*

Best Reviews, http://thebestreviews.com/ (October 4, 2002), review of *The No. 1 Ladies' Detective Agency.*

BookLoons, http://bookloons.com/ (December 12, 2002), G. Hall, review of *The No. 1 Ladies' Detective Agency.**

*   *   *

SMITH, Suzanne E. 1964-

PERSONAL: Born August 19, 1964, in Detroit, MI; daughter of Gerald (an assembly line worker) and Caralee (Narden) Smith. *Education:* University of California—Los Angeles, B.A., 1986; Carnegie-Mellon University, M.A., 1988; Yale University, Ph.D. (American studies), 1996.

ADDRESSES: Office—Department of History and Art History, George Mason University, Fairfax, VA 22030-4444; fax: 703-993-1251. *E-mail*—smisuze@gmu.edu.

CAREER: George Mason University, Fairfax, VA, associate professor of history, 1995—. Contributor to public history projects, including "I'll Make Me a World: African-American Arts in the Twentieth Century"; contributor to television film *Rachel Carlson's Silent Spring,* Public Broadcast System.

MEMBER: American Studies Association, American Historical Association, Organization of American Historians.

AWARDS, HONORS: Gleason Music Book Awards, third prize, 2000, for *Dancing in the Street.*

WRITINGS:

Dancing in the Street: Motown and the Cultural Politics of Detroit, Harvard University Press (Cambridge, MA), 1999.

WORK IN PROGRESS: Research on black entrepreneurship.

BIOGRAPHICAL AND CRITICAL SOURCES:

PERIODICALS

American Quarterly, September, 2001, Steve Waksman, review of *Dancing in the Street: Motown and the Cultural Politics of Detroit,* p. 518.

American Studies, summer, 2001, Sherrie Tucker, review of *Dancing in the Street,* p. 171.

Billboard, March 18, 2000, Timothy White, review of *Dancing in the Street,* p. 3.

Black Issues Book Review, July, 2000, Tracy Roberts, review of *Dancing in the Street,* p. 37.

Booklist, December 15, 1999, Mike Tribby, review of *Dancing in the Street,* p. 750.

Journal of American History, June, 2001, Michael Bertrand, review of *Dancing in the Street,* p. 299.

Library Journal, December, 1999, David P. Szatmary, review of *Dancing in the Street,* p. 138.

Michigan Historical Review, fall, 2000, Kenneth J. Bindas, review of *Dancing in the Street,* p. 182.

Times Higher Education Supplement, October 20, 2000, John White, review of *Dancing in the Street,* p. 32.

*   *   *

SMITHSON, Peter (Denham) 1923-2003

OBITUARY NOTICE—See index for *CA* sketch: Born September 18, 1923, in Stockton-on-Tees, Durham, England; died of a heart attack March 3, 2003, in London, England. Architect, educator, and author. Along with his wife, Alison, Smithson was a noted British architect who became known for his New Brutalism style. He attended King's College, Durham, before the war interrupted his studies. During World War II, he fought in Burma and India; he then returned to university and completed a degree in architecture in 1947. After working in the Architects' Department for the London County Council for a year, he and his wife started a private architectural firm in 1950. Together, they competed to win a contract to rebuild the Coventry Cathedral. Though they lost this commission, they went on to design the Economist Building complex, which includes three structures arranged in an L-shaped complex. Completed in 1964, it is considered to be among their best works. In 1972 Smithson's reputation suffered with the Robin Hoods Gardens housing complex, which was criticized by many for having an "inhumane" feeling to it and was subjected to repeated vandalization. Later designs fared better, but were often seen as less unique than his earlier work. Nevertheless, Smithson remained respected for his ideas on architecture, and during the 1950s and 1960s he was a tutor at the Architectural Association School; beginning in 1976, he was also Banister Fletcher Professor of Architecture at University College in London. During the 1980s, he continued teaching at the University of Munich, the University of Barcelona, and the University of Delft. Later in their career, Smithson and his wife designed furniture for the Germany company Tecta, some of which was exhibited at galleries. The Smithsons published a number of books on architecture, including *The Euston Arch and the Growth of the London, Midland and*

Scottish Railway (1968), *Without Rhetoric: An Architectural Aesthetic, 1955-1972* (1973), *The Heroic Period of Modern Architecture* (1981), and *The Charged Void: Architecture* (2001). Smithson was also the sole author of *Bath: Walks within the Walls* (1971; revised, 1980). Smithson was working on a second volume to *The Charged Voice* when he died.

OBITUARIES AND OTHER SOURCES:

BOOKS

Johnson, Donald Leslie, and Donald Langmead, *Makers of Twentieth-Century Modern Architecture,* Greenwood Press (Westport, CT), 1997.

Writers Directory, 18th edition, St. James Press (Detroit, MI), 2003.

PERIODICALS

New York Times, March 7, 2003, p. C13.
Times (London, England), March 10, 2003.

*   *   *

SNYDER, Leslie Crocker 1942-

PERSONAL: Born March 8, 1942, in New York, NY; daughter of Lester (a professor) and Billie (a homemaker) Crocker; married Fred Snyder (an attorney and artist), 1968. *Education:* Radcliffe College, A.B. (with honors), 1962; Harvard Business School, certificate, 1963; Case Western Reserve Law School, J.D. (with honors), 1966, associate editor of law review.

ADDRESSES: Office—100 Centre St., New York, NY 10013. *Agent*—Suzanne Gluck, William Morris Agency, 1325 Avenue of the Americas, New York, NY 10019.

CAREER: Judge. Admitted to the Bar of New York State, 1966; Kaye, Scholer, Fierman, Hayes & Handler (law firm), New York, NY, associate, 1966-68; Manhattan district attorney's office, assistant district attorney, 1968-76, founder and chief of Sex Crimes Prosecution Bureau; General Chief of Trials, New York State Office of the Special Prosecutor, assistant attorney, 1976-79; in private practice, 1979-82; City of New York, deputy criminal justice coordinator and arson strike force coordinator, 1982-83, criminal court judge, 1983-86; New York State Supreme Court, First Judicial District, acting justice, 1986—. Served on various advisory boards and committees; lecturer.

AWARDS, HONORS: Women of Achievement award, *Mademoiselle,* 1974.

WRITINGS:

(With Tom Schachtman) *Twenty-five to Life: The Truth, the Whole Truth, and Nothing but the Truth,* Warner Books (New York, NY), 2002.

SIDELIGHTS: Leslie Crocker Snyder became the first female assistant district attorney in New York City's Homicide Bureau and the first female attorney in that city to try felonies. After hearing her first rape case, she was determined to make rape laws fairer to women, and in 1974, she established the first sex crimes division in the nation within the Manhattan district attorney's office. As a state Supreme Court judge, Snyder hears cases involving the most heinous crimes and is known for her tough sentencing, particularly of drug dealers. She shares her history with the criminal justice system in her memoir *Twenty-five to Life: The Truth, the Whole Truth, and Nothing but the Truth.*

Snyder is the daughter of a professor of eighteenth-century French philosophy, born in New York City but raised on university campuses, including those of the University of Virginia, Johns Hopkins, and the Sorbonne. She entered Radcliffe College at the age of sixteen on a full scholarship and graduated with honors. She spent a year at Harvard Business School, then enrolled in Case Western Reserve Law School, where she continued her education. In 1966, with her law degree in hand, she applied to New York City firms, and because her first name is gender-neutral, she was granted interviews that would lead to nothing when it was discovered that she was female.

Snyder joined the Manhattan district attorney's office in 1968, where District Attorney Frank Hogan, who was ruffled by the fact that Snyder was not married, suggested that she concentrate on consumer fraud cases. Hogan finally caved and assigned Snyder to homicide. In 1970 Snyder tried a robbery case in which two women had been raped. At that time, the law required that three things be proven before rape could be established: force, identity, and penetration. Snyder could prove the first two, but not the third, because the women's testimonies and the fact that semen had been found on their underwear were both inadmissible.

Outraged, Snyder worked to change the law, and did. She is also responsible for New York's rape-shield law, which disallows a victim's sexual history in a rape case. Nina Burleigh noted in a *New York* article that Snyder "has a classic seventies feminist's sympathy for the women she sees before her and freely admits to giving women involved in drug cases more lenient sentences, on the grounds that their macho boyfriends, brothers, and fathers have probably abused them. 'I know I have had the reputation of being pro-female,' she says. 'Certainly there are some queenpins, but a lot of these women are victims.'"

In 1976 Snyder left the district attorney's office to work on a special task force investigating police corruption. From 1979 to 1983 she returned to private practice. She reentered public service, first as a judge in criminal court, and then in 1986 for a ten-year term on the New York State Supreme Court. She was first appointed by Mayor Ed Koch and was reappointed in 1996 by Mayor Rudolph Giuliani. She took her place on the bench as the crack cocaine epidemic and its associated crime hit the streets.

Burleigh commented that Snyder "made some controversial law in the areas of search and seizure; one of her rulings, for example, denied defendants the names of the informants in certain search warrants if the informants have reason to fear for their safety. But that tightly reasoned ruling was upheld and is now precedent in New York. In a less clear-cut case, Snyder is now embroiled in a seven-year legal battle over her use of what's called a shadow counsel—a second attorney assigned secretly to a defendant who wants to cooperate with the government but doesn't want the original attorney to know." The shadow attorney is most often used in trials where the defendant's attorney is being paid for by organized crime, in cases where information transmitted back to the mob could endanger the defendant's family.

Snyder was interviewed for *BookPage* online by Edward Morris, who asked if it had been difficult for her to hand down her typically long sentences. She replied that "most of the cases in which I've given out these high sentences were for people who had been involved in multiple murders or murder and rape or multiple sex crimes, or they were the heads of drug gangs who'd delegated other people to kill or torture. So as the cases became more and more serious, it did become easier to hand out time of that kind."

The judge's tough stance and maximum sentences have resulted in threats to her life, beginning in 1988, when she was told that a drug lord had put out a hit on her. Since then, she has had around-the-clock police protection. Snyder and her husband never discuss their family, and the children, now grown, were also guarded while attending high school. The threats continue, but Snyder takes them in stride.

Bookreporter.com contributor Curtis Edmonds wrote that *Twenty-five to Life* "appropriately shows the dangers and the glories of a life on the bench in the riskiest of situations. It should remind all of us that our safety is largely due to the hard, unacknowledged work of the police and attorneys and judges who work in the criminal justice system, and that we owe them a debt of honor that we cannot easily repay."

BIOGRAPHICAL AND CRITICAL SOURCES:

BOOKS

Snyder, Leslie Crocker, and Tom Schachtman, *Twenty-five to Life: The Truth, the Whole Truth, and Nothing but the Truth,* Warner Books (New York, NY), 2002.

PERIODICALS

Booklist, September 15, 2002, Mary Frances Wilkens, review of *Twenty-five to Life: The Truth, the Whole Truth, and Nothing but the Truth,* p. 186.

Library Journal, September 1, 2002, Harry Charles, review of *Twenty-five to Life,* p. 195.

New York, March 30, 1998, Nina Burleigh, "Court of Appeal," p. 34.

New York Times, December 20, 2000, Katherine E. Finkelstein, "Hard-Liner in Pearls and Basic Black Robe," p. B2.

People, October 7, 2002, Patrick Rogers, "Tough Justice," p. 129.

Publishers Weekly, July 29, 2002, review of *Twenty-five to Life,* p. 63.

ONLINE

BookPage, http://www.bookpage.com/ (December 12, 2002), Edward Morris, "The Judge Takes the Stand" (interview).

Bookreporter, http://www.bookreporter.com/ (December 12, 2002), Curtis Edmonds, review of *Twenty-five to Life.**

*   *   *

ST. ANDREWS, B(onnie). A. 1950-

PERSONAL: Born July 18, 1950, in NY; child of Wally (a builder) and Anne (a designer) St. Andrews. *Ethnicity:* "French." *Education:* St. Lawrence University, B.A.; Syracuse University, Ph.D., 1980. *Hobbies and other interests:* The islands, currents, and events related to the St. Lawrence River.

ADDRESSES: Home—Syracuse, NY. *Office*—Center for Bioethics and Humanities, State University of New York—Upstate Medical University, 725 Irving Ave., Suite 406, Syracuse, NY 13210; fax: 315-464-5407. *E-mail*—standreb@upstate.edu.

CAREER: State University of New York—Upstate Medical University, Syracuse, professor, 1992-97, distinguished professor at Center for Bioethics and Humanities, 1997—. Kids-in-Art Program, founder; gives poetry readings.

MEMBER: Poetry Society of America, Poets and Writers, Associated Writing Programs, American Society for Bioethics and Humanities, Aurora for the Blind.

AWARDS, HONORS: Pushcart Prize nomination, 2002, for "Phenol"; grants from Merck Corp., Brown University, Canadian Embassy, and Yaddo Corp.

WRITINGS:

Forbidden Fruit: A Scholarly Study of the Relationship between Women and Knowledge in Doris Lessing, Selma Lagerlöf, Kate Chopin, Margaret Atwood, Whitston Press (Troy, NY), 1986.
Stealing the Light (poetry chapbook), University of Alabama (Tuscaloosa, AL), 19912.
The Healing Muse (poetry chapbook), Silverman Review Press (Syracuse, NY), 1999.

Contributor of poetry to anthologies, including *Nantucket: A Collection,* White Fish Press, 2001; contributor to journals, including *New Yorker, Paris Review, Gettysburg Review, Carolina Quarterly, Commonweal, Journal of General Internal Medicine, Midnight Mind, Journal of Genetic Counseling, Pharos,* and *Journal of the American Medical Association.* Editor, *Healing Muse* (journal).

WORK IN PROGRESS: The Last Farmhouse of Feeling, a poetry chapbook; *Pen among Scalpels,* a chapbook of medical poetry.

SIDELIGHTS: B. A. St. Andrews told *CA:* "Entering a medical university with a new-minted terminal degree in one hand and a sheaf of poems in the other, I was transported to a world of open-heart surgeries, 'do not resuscitates,' desiccated cats, neonatal intensive care units, electron microscopes, and magnetic-resonance imagers. I had found my strange way home to a place I'd never been before, leaving the illuminating questions of the liberal arts and entering the dubious certainties of medical sciences.

"Far from being separate, art and science, I discovered, are Siamese twins joined at the heart. They are two hands clapping. They are the recto and verso pages of one long and balanced book. My medical poems now appear in [medical journals and literary journals].

"My poetry moved from images of Nature to those of technology, from lacy tracery to tendon, sinew, musculature, and bone growing like jade inside a

mountain. Working with physicians, nurses, clinicians, technologists, therapists, patients, children with oncology opened the arteries of my creative life and saved rather than imperiled it.

"I began therapeutic poetry and art workshops for the hospitalized children; I started a journal of literature and graphic art for my diverse colleagues who participate in the world of healing. I invited closet writers to share their narratives of the courage and challenge each day provides in this medical university and its hospital.

"In my non-medical poems, I continue to explore mythic archetypes, the sea's profundity, the ineffable Beauty within the quotidian and commonplace. Through my medical poems and stories, I have tried to shed light on what Willa Cather correctly called 'the dark science'; of medicine. I hope my works praise the courage and compassion of patients and practitioners, of families and intimate strangers within the world of the Healers. And I hope I have helped to place the Arts back in the heart of that world."

*   *   *

STANKUS, Tony 1951-

PERSONAL: Born March 9, 1951, in Worcester, MA; son of Frank (a career army officer in Lithuania and Germany and a janitor in the United States) and Anna (an army telephone operator abroad and a homemaker in the United States; maiden name, Rauch) Stankus; married Jeanne Marie Yess, 1972 (divorced, 1975); married Mary Frances Doyle, 1978 (divorced, 2000); children: (second marriage) Andrew Francis (deceased), Peter Cornelius (deceased). *Ethnicity:* "Baltic-German." *Education:* College of the Holy Cross, B.A. (summa cum laude), 1973; University of Rhode Island, M.L.S., 1975. *Politics:* Republican. *Religion:* Roman Catholic. *Hobbies and other interests:* Movies, museums, vegetable gardening.

ADDRESSES: Office—Science Library, College of the Holy Cross, 1 College St., Box 30A, Worcester, MA 01610-2322; fax: 508-793-3530. *E-mail*—tstankus@holycross.edu.

CAREER: College of the Holy Cross, Worcester, MA, science librarian, 1974—. University of Rhode Island, adjunct professor, 1982—.

WRITINGS:

(Editor) *Scientific Journals: Issues in Library Selection and Management,* Haworth Press (Binghamton, NY), 1987.

(Editor) *Scientific Journals: Improving Library Collections through Analysis of Publishing Trends,* Haworth Press (Binghamton, NY), 1990.

(Editor and author of introduction) *Biographies of Scientists for Sci-Tech Libraries: Adding Faces to the Facts,* Haworth Press (Binghamton, NY), 1991.

Making Sense of Journals in the Life Sciences: From Specialty Origins to Contemporary Assortment, Haworth Press (Binghamton, NY), 1992.

Making Sense of Journals in the Physical Sciences: From Specialty Origins to Contemporary Assortment, Haworth Press (Binghamton, NY), 1992.

(Editor and contributor) *Science Librarianship at America's Liberal Arts Colleges: Working Librarians Tell Their Stories,* Haworth Press (Binghamton, NY), 1992.

(Editor and contributor) *Scientific and Clinical Literature for the Decade of the Brain,* Haworth Press (Binghamton, NY), 1993.

Special Format Serials and Issues: Annual Reviews of . . . , Advances in . . . , Symposia on . . . , Methods of . . . , Haworth Press (Binghamton, NY), 1996.

Electronic Expectations: Science Journals on the Web, Haworth Press (Binghamton, NY), 1999.

(Editor) *The Journals of the Century,* Haworth Press (Binghamton, NY), 2001.

Contributor to books, including *Creative Planning of Special Library Facilities,* edited by Ellis Mount, Haworth Press (Binghamton, NY), 1988. Author of columns "Alert Collector," in *Reference Quarterly,* 1988-96, and "Making Sense of Serials," in *Technicalities,* 1995—. Contributor to periodicals, including *Reference & User Services Quarterly, Serials Librarian, Library Resources and Technical Services, College and Research Libraries, Library Journal,* and *Library Trends.* Associate editor for submissions, *Science & Technology Libraries,* 1983—; member of editorial board for submissions, *Library Acquisitions: Practice and Theory,* 1991-93.

WORK IN PROGRESS: Research on "encroachments on freedom of scientists to choose their journal outlets by the 'LC' (Library Correctness) movement which favors only not-for-profit publishers approved of by certain library organizations"; investigating "the stability of reputational hierarchies of scientific journals given the growing developments in Web publishing and anti-capitalist sentiments among some librarians"; an analysis of "the degree to which foreign publishers take over American scientific publishing and to which American publications attract foreign submissions."

SIDELIGHTS: Tony Stankus told *CA:* "I write to try to resolve a love-hate triangle involving librarians in training to serve scientists, the scientists that those librarians will serve, and the publishers of the journals that librarians buy with great resentment to serve those scientists. This soap opera seems trivial to others until they realize that about a trillion dollars a year are involved worldwide.

"The overwhelming majority of students are initially educated in one of three undergraduate majors (history, English, or education) before enrolling in a graduate school of library and information science. There, the formative readings they are assigned to study and told to emulate later as future professional authors are often hopelessly full of facts yet surprisingly devoid of historical context, arduously readable at best, and embellished with all manner of seemingly sophisticated statistical foreplay and computer simulation in a vain attempt to ape the dubious distinction of resembling the depersonalized social science writing and thereby gain academic standing as full-fledged quantitative social scientists.

"This sideshow devalues the cumulative academic advantage and natural inclinations of the students, and it coincidentally scarcely impresses real scientists, who would really favor any training that would genuinely foster high quality, empathetic service. My approach is to take advantage of what the students are already accustomed to, and to explain science and the wants of scientists to these students by literate tutorial writing involving the very human, and sometimes humorous, stories of how given scientists, scientific fields, and scientific publications developed over time.

"I further try to explain that, while science librarians are indeed less well paid than science publishing professionals, at least part of this is due to the relatively greater risk-taking assumed by publishers who face far greater challenges through the possibility of poor market conditions, poor adherence to deadlines by their scientist authors and print suppliers or electronic infrastructure workers or technology, and the unforeseen personal consequences of larger corporate mergers and acquisitions over which publishing employees individually have little control. I try to remind librarians that, while it is often true that publishers get their manuscripts for free from university-based scientists, most university science libraries are effectively funded via overhead monies taken by university administrations from grants awarded to universities for the use of their scientists.

"Yet while both science publishing and science librarianship are both effectively derivative and dependent on the output of scientists, there is little evidence that the scientists are better served by becoming either their own publishers or librarians, particularly if the cost of this diversion of energy is doing less science or poorer science."

BIOGRAPHICAL AND CRITICAL SOURCES:

PERIODICALS

Wilson Library Bulletin, Volume 67, number 3, 1992, Robert Chadbourne, "Holy Cross Library Honors an Unlikely Hero," pp. 17, 98.

ONLINE

College of the Holy Cross Web site, http://www.holycross.edu/ (July 19, 2001), "Tony Stankus."

*　　*　　*

STANSFIELD, William D. 1930-

PERSONAL: Born February 7, 1930, in Los Angeles, CA; married; children: three. *Education:* California Polytechnic State College (now University), B.S., 1952, M.A., 1960; University of California—Davis, M.S., 1962, Ph.D., 1963.

ADDRESSES: Home—653 Stanford Dr., San Luis Obispo, CA 93405-1123. *E-mail*—wstansfi@calpoly.edu.

CAREER: High school teacher of vocational agriculture in Fortuna, CA, 1958-59; California Polytechnic State University, San Luis Obispo, faculty member in biological sciences, 1963-92, professor emeritus, 1992—. JBL Scientific (now Promega), technical services representative and consultant, 1998-99. *Military service:* U.S. Naval Reserve, line officer, 1953-67.

MEMBER: American Association for the Advancement of Science, National Center for Science Education, Sigma Xi.

WRITINGS:

Schaum's Theory and Problems of Genetics, McGraw-Hill (New York, NY), 1969, 4th edition (with Susan L. Elrod), 2002.
The Science of Evolution, Macmillan Publishing (New York, NY), 1977.
Serology and Immunology: A Clinical Approach, Macmillan Publishing (New York, NY), 1981.
(With Robert C. King) *A Dictionary of Genetics,* Oxford University Press (New York, NY), 1985, 6th edition, 2002.
(With Jaime S. Colomé and Raúl J. Cano) *Schaum's Outline of Theory and Problems of Molecular and Cell Biology,* McGraw-Hill (New York, NY), 1996.
Death of a Rat: Understandings and Appreciations of Science, Prometheus Books (Amherst, NY), 2000.

Contributor to encyclopedias. Contributor to periodicals, including *Journal of Heredity.*

WORK IN PROGRESS: Research on sheep blood groups, productivity, and reproduction; ovine twinning; Murine genetics and physiology; and Minoxodil and hair growth in mice.

SIDELIGHTS: William D. Stansfield told *CA:* "The seeds for writing *Death of a Rat: Understandings and Appreciations of Science* were sown as a consequence of my assignment to teach a graduate course in the history of biology. The book was planned to serve as an example of the kinds of questions and case histories suitable for analyses in such a class. However, I retired before it could be completed for the intended purpose.

Then I saw that such a book, with some revisions, might be of great interest and value to a broader audience of inquisitive minds in the general adult population. Critics of our educational system have challenged scientists to come out of their 'ivory towers' of research and academia to educate the general public about the importance of their work to society, how science should be done, and the roles a scientifically literate public can play in the advancement of science, as well as to encourage more youngsters to pursue careers in science. In retirement I decided to complete *Death of a Rat* as a contribution to those goals. Royalties from the book go to support the work of the National Center for Science Education.

"The subjects treated in *Death of a Rat* were selected primarily because of their relevance to public concerns about scientific issues such as fetal cell research, animal rights, scientific ethics, creation science, et cetera, and/or because of the innate human interest in stories such as how Mendelian genetics came to be outlawed in the USSR, the hoax of the Piltdown man, the squabble over the discovery of the human immunodeficiency virus (HIV), the 'hit list' of laboratories contaminated with the cultured cell line known as HeLa, and the cold fusion fiasco.

"Perhaps the person who provided the greatest inspiration for the writing of *Death of a Rat* was James Watson in *The Double Helix,* his book about the discovery of the structure of DNA. Watson had been warned by some of his friends that such a book would be too difficult for non-scientists to understand. How wrong that advice turned out to be! Not just anyone can write authoritatively for the general public as well as Watson has done, but scientists should not be deterred from attempting to do so."

BIOGRAPHICAL AND CRITICAL SOURCES:

PERIODICALS

Choice, May, 1998, Leo Miller, review of *A Dictionary of Genetics,* p. S2; March, 2001, N. Shrimpton, review of *Death of a Rat: Understandings and Appreciations of Science,* p. 1296.
Journal of Heredity, July-August, 1999, Joseph O. Falkinham III, review of *A Dictionary of Genetics,* p. 504.

Quarterly Review of Biology, March, 1998, Jules Elias, review of *A Dictionary of Genetics,* p. 71.
Skeptical Inquirer, January, 2001, Kendrick Frazier, review of *Death of a Rat,* p. 64.

*   *   *

STANTON, Arch
See WYNORSKI, Jim

*   *   *

STARR, Kenneth W(inston) 1946-

PERSONAL: Born July 21, 1946, in Vernon, TX; son of Willie D. (a minister) and Vannie Maude (Trimble) Starr; married Alice Jean Mendell (a public relations executive), August 23, 1970; children: Randall Postley, Carolyn Marie, Cynthia Anne. *Education:* Attended Harding College; George Washington University, B.A., 1968; Brown University, M.A., 1969; Duke University, J.D., 1973.

ADDRESSES: Home—McClean, VA. *Office*—Kirkland & Ellis, 655 15th St. NW, Ste. 1200, Washington, DC 20005.

CAREER: Admitted to the Bar of the State of California, 1973, State of Virginia, 1979, and District of Columbia, 1979; U.S. Court of Appeals, Fifth Circuit, Miami, FL, law clerk to Judge David Dyer, 1973-74; Gibson, Dunn & Crutcher, Los Angeles, CA, associate, 1974-75, partner, 1977-81; U.S. Supreme Court, Washington, DC, law clerk to Chief Justice Warren E. Burger, 1975-77; U.S. Dept. of Justice, Washington, DC, chief of staff to Attorney General William French Smith, 1981-83, solicitor general, 1989-93, independent counsel, 1994-99; U.S. Court of Appeals, Washington, DC, judge, c. 1980s; Kirkland & Ellis, Washington, partner, 1993. New York University, adjunct professor; George Mason University, visiting professor.

MEMBER: American Bar Foundation, American Bar Association, American Law Institute, American Judicature Society, Institute of Judicial Administration (president), Supreme Court Historical Society, Order of the Coif, Phi Delta Phi (Hughes chapter Man of the Year, 1973).

AWARDS, HONORS: Honorary law degrees from Hampden Sydney College, Shenandoah University, and Mitchell College; Attorney General's Award for Distinguished Service, 1993; American Values Award, U.S. Industrial Council, 1993; alumni awards from George Washington University and Duke University.

WRITINGS:

Referral from Independent Counsel Kenneth W. Starr in Conformity with the Requirements of Title 28, United States Code, Section 595(c): Communication from Kenneth W. Starr, Independent Counsel, Transmitting a Referral to the United States House of Representatives Filed in Conformity with the Requirements of Title 28, United States Code, Section 595(c) (called *The Starr Report;* includes appendices and supplemental materials), U.S. Government Printing Office (Washington, DC), 1998, published as *The Starr Report: The Evidence,* edited by Phil Kuntz, Pocket Books (New York, NY), 1998, published as *The Starr Report: The Findings of Independent Counsel Kenneth W. Starr on President Clinton and the Lewinsky Affair* ("Public Affairs Reports" series), with analysis by the staff of the *Washington Post,* Public Affairs (New York, NY), 1998.

First among Equals: The Supreme Court in American Life, Warner Books (New York, NY), 2002.

As Independent Counsel, author of other reports, including *Report on the Death of Vincent Foster, Jr.,* 1997.

ADAPTATIONS: The Starr Report: Substantial and Credible Information (sound recording, eight cassettes), narrated by David Ackroyd and Tracy Brooks Swope, commentary by Alan Dershowitz and Dean Erwin Chemerinsky, Dove Audio (Los Angeles, CA), 1998.

SIDELIGHTS: In 1994 Kenneth W. Starr was appointed independent counsel by Attorney General Janet Reno to investigate the Whitewater affair, an assignment that eventually led to a White House sex scandal and the impeachment of President Bill Clinton. Starr, who had served as a federal judge and solicitor general, replaced Robert B. Fiske, who had served for several months in investigating Clinton's activities

while he was governor of Arkansas, because many conservative Republicans felt Fiske was not tough enough. Starr reopened the case concerning the 230 acres known as Whitewater, but when he couldn't make a case against Clinton based on that business deal, he went after him on charges of sexual misconduct, particularly with a young White House intern named Monica Lewinsky. Ironically, when all the sordid facts came out, President Clinton's popularity ratings climbed, while the American public felt that Starr's investigation, which cost the American taxpayers more than forty million dollars, may have gone too far in invading the president's private life over activities that did not constitute a crime.

Starr was born in Vernon, Texas to a religious family, and his father was a Church of Christ minister who worked as a barber for extra money. The family moved to San Antonio when Starr was in grade school. While attending Harding College, a Christian school in Searcy, Arkansas, Starr sold bibles door-to-door to raise money for tuition, then transferred to George Washington University, where he was editor of the school paper. He continued his education at Brown University and Duke University Law School and landed two plum jobs right out of Duke. He first clerked for U.S. Court of Appeals Judge David Dyer in Miami, then spent two years clerking for Chief Justice of the U.S. Supreme Court Warren E. Burger.

While with the Washington law firm of Gibson, Dunn & Crutcher, Starr was approached by William French Smith, who asked him to serve as his chief of staff when President Ronald Reagan appointed Smith as his attorney general in 1981. This move led to Reagan's appointing Starr to the bench of the U.S. Court of Appeals, which he left in 1989 to become solicitor general under President George Bush. In this capacity, he represented the administration in front of the U.S. Supreme Court. His positions, though conservative—he was against legalized abortion—were not conservative enough to justify his appointment when a seat on the Supreme Court became vacant. Bush named David Souter, and when President Clinton was elected in 1992, Starr returned to private practice with the firm of Kirkland & Ellis.

In 1993 Starr became embroiled in his first sexual misconduct investigation when the Senate Ethics Committee asked him to look into allegations against Senator Bob Packwood. He also reopened the investigation into the death of White House counsel Vincent W. Foster, Jr., which was deemed a suicide, a conclusion Starr later let stand. When Starr was asked to replace Fiske, the law written in 1970 that had established the position of independent counsel was about to expire. President Clinton renewed it, and a month later, three federal judges assigned Whitewater to Starr. None of the people linked to Whitewater testified against either President Clinton or his wife, Hillary Rodham Clinton. Among the Clintons' friends and business partners who were convicted or entered pleas were Arkansas Governor Jim Guy Tucker, Webster Hubbell, a partner in Hillary Clinton's law firm and a former deputy attorney general, and Susan McDougal, and her husband Jim. Susan McDougal served twenty-one months on civil contempt charges, then published her account, titled *The Woman Who Wouldn't Talk*. McDougal contends in her book that she refused to testify before the Starr commission for fear that her words would be twisted and used against the Clintons. Jim McDougal, who cut a deal to lesson his jail time, died in prison.

A hornet's nest was stirred up when Paula Corbin Jones filed a sexual harassment suit against President Clinton. Although the case was eventually dropped, it was during this investigation that Monica Lewinsky's name first came up. Starr was relentless in trying to prove a sexual relationship between the president and the intern, although both denied his accusations. The truth became apparent when a number of recorded tapes made by Linda Tripp, with whom Lewinsky had worked at the Pentagon, indicated that President Clinton had asked Lewinsky to lie and cover up their affair.

It was Starr's tactics that undermined his investigation in the eyes of many. He confiscated bookstore receipts to see what Lewinsky had been reading and called on her mother to testify. And then there was the little blue dress, the one that was supposedly stained with presidential semen, an allegation that was never proven. In a show of indignation, Hillary Rodham Clinton accused Starr of leading a right-wing conspiracy against her husband.

On August 17, 1998, President Clinton testified before the grand jury and appeared on television to blast Starr and admit that he had an "inappropriate" relationship with Lewinsky. Even Clinton's supporters felt he had not adequately expressed genuine sorrow for his actions. When Starr's incendiary 454-page report was released on September 11, 1998, it listed eleven

grounds for impeachment, including allegations that the president had lied about the nature of his relationship with Lewinsky and had used his office and staff to cover up that relationship. *New York Review of Books* contributor Lars-Erik Nelson noted that "according to the transcript contained in Part 1 of the separately published appendix . . . even the grand jurors had misgivings about Starr's techniques." Michael Emmick, one of Starr's deputies, tried to end one day's proceedings but was challenged by a juror who wanted to hear more about January 16, the day Lewinsky was seized by Emmick, along with two FBI agents, who refused her request for an attorney, held her in a hotel room, and threatened her with jail time of twenty-seven years for perjury and other charges. In all, they detained and terrorized Lewinsky for eleven hours.

"And with that, the tables turned," wrote Nelson. "Starr joins Lewinsky and Clinton on the hot seat. Whereas Starr's *Referral to the House of Representatives* is the equivalent of an indictment—accusatory, one-sided, damning—the appendix to his report is far more ambiguous and perhaps more damaging to Starr than to the president. The appendix poses the question: Which is more outrageous to us—Clinton's sexual relationship with a twenty-one-year-old intern or Starr's use of the law to hound an elected president from office."

On October 2, the House released nearly 5,000 pages of additional material, including testimonies and transcripts. These three volumes represented thousands of hours of work and seemed by some disproportionate to the offense. On December 19, 1998, President Clinton was impeached by the House on two charges, obstructing justice and committing perjury before a federal grand jury, but the Senate declined to remove him from office. Starr returned to private practice and to teaching.

New Republic reviewer Cass R. Sunstein noted that "under Starr's leadership, the Office of Independent Counsel was overzealous, to say the very least. This came as a big surprise to those who knew Starr's earlier work, or who knew the man personally, because Starr's performance showed so little of the caution and the good judgement that previously marked his career. Since resigning as independent counsel, Starr has, in his writing and public statements, acted in the measured and responsible way that he did as a judge and a solicitor general."

First among Equals: The Supreme Court in American Life is Starr's account of the Rehnquist Court. He details rulings involving the Miranda law, flag burning, federalism, states' rights, freedom of speech, campaign finance, discrimination against homosexuals (the Boy Scout case), affirmative action, and *Roe v. Wade*. In an interview with a writer for *American Lawyer*, Starr said that his view is that the Rehnquist Court "follows a more traditional mode of constitutional interpretation than did the Warren Court."

Dennis J. Hutchinson, who reviewed the volume in the *New York Times Book Review*, questioned why Starr calls the Supreme Court *First among Equals*, "in what is otherwise a democratic government. Starr concedes that 'justices appointed for life' constitute 'the least accountable branch of government.' The Warren court constantly got it wrong, according to Starr. . . . The Burger court wasn't much better—fewer mistakes but one whopper, what he calls the 'unspeakably unacceptable' abortion decision. What vexes Starr, and all who grasp the theoretical nettle, is distinguishing between good and bad reasons where the constitutional language is at its most ambiguous." Hutchinson noted that "the debate over the proper role of the court has been acute for the last two generations, and quickened again when the 2000 presidential election was decided by a 5-4 vote in *Bush v. Gore*."

Book reviewer Terry Teachout wrote that Starr "uses his long experience to illuminate the inner workings of the most mysterious branch of government, as well as to elucidate his counterintuitive conviction that the current Court, for all its reputation as a hotbed of right-wing judicial activism, is in fact 'dedicated to stability, not change; moderation and incrementalism, not liberalism or progressivism,' and to assert that 'prudence and caution have characterized much of the work of this Court of lawyers, not politicians.'"

Andrew Musicus reviewed *First among Equals* for *Bookreporter.com*, commenting that Starr "has great respect for Justice Breyer's intellect and his ability to build consensus. Justice O'Connor is another favorite, who Starr called the 'most influential and powerful woman in America.' In the end, however, Starr's real favorite is the Court itself. *First among Equals* is his love letter to an institution he reveres. And this authoritative telling of some of its history adds greatly to the rich tapestry of Supreme Court literature."

BIOGRAPHICAL AND CRITICAL SOURCES:

BOOKS

Carville, James . . . *and the Horse He Rode in On: The People v. Kenneth Starr*, Simon & Schuster (New York, NY), 1998.

McDougal, Susan, and Pat Harris, *The Woman Who Wouldn't Talk*, introduction by Helen Thomas, Carroll & Graf Publishers (New York, NY), 2003.

Newsmakers 1998, Gale (Detroit, MI), 1998.

St. James Encyclopedia of Popular Culture, St. James Press (Detroit, MI), 2000.

Schmidt, Susan, and Michael Weisskopf, *Truth at Any Cost: Ken Starr and the Unmaking of Bill Clinton*, HarperCollins (New York, NY), 2000.

Wittes, Benjamin, *Starr: A Reassessment*, Yale University Press (New Haven, CT), 2002.

PERIODICALS

American Enterprise, January, 2000, John Meroney, interview with Starr, p. 18.

American Lawyer, June, 2000, "A Starr Is Reborn" (interview), p. 25.

American Prospect, December 16, 2002, Garrett Epps, review of *First among Equals: The Supreme Court in American Life*, p. 37.

Book, November-December, 2002, Terry Teachout, review of *First among Equals*, p. 77.

Business Week, October 21, 2002, Dan Carney, review of *First among Equals*, p. 26.

Kirkus Reviews, August 15, 2002, review of *First among Equals*, p. 1207.

National Review, December 31, 2002, Richard A. Epstein, review of *First among Equals*, p. 42.

New Republic, October 21, 2002, Cass R. Sunstein, review of *First among Equals*, p. 23.

New Statesman, October 2, 1998, Michael Bywater, review of *The Starr Report*, pp. 47-48.

New York Review of Books, November 5, 1998, Lars Erik Nelson, reviews of appendices to *The Starr Report*, pp. 8, 10.

New York Times Book Review, October 13, 2002, Dennis J. Hutchinson, review of *First among Equals*, p.14.

Observer (London, England), September 20, 1998, review of *The Starr Report*, p. 16.

People, February 16, 1998, Thomas Fields-Meyer, "The Inquisitor," p. 182.

Publishers Weekly, September 2, 2002, review of *First among Equals,* p. 68.

Time, December 28, 1998, Eric Pooley, Michael Weiss-skopf, "How Starr Sees It" (interview), p. 82.

ONLINE

Bookreporter.com, http://www.bookreporter.com/ (December 12, 2002), Andrew Musicus, review of *First among Equals.*

Charlotte Observe Onliner, http://www.charlotte.com/ (October 28, 2002), David W. Marston, review of *First among Equals.**

*   *   *

STEINBECK, Thomas

PERSONAL: Son of John (an author) and Gwyn Steinbeck; married Gail Knight. *Education:* Attended Chouinard Art Institute and University of California—Los Angeles.

ADDRESSES: Agent—c/o Author Mail, Random House, 1745 Broadway, New York, NY 10019.

CAREER: Writer. Worked as a cinematographer, photojournalist, and educator. Taught college-level courses in American literature, communication arts, and creative writing. National Steinbeck Center, board of trustees. *Military service:* U.S. Army; served one tour of duty as a soldier in Vietnam and another to cover that war as a photojournalist.

WRITINGS:

Down to a Soundless Sea (stories), Ballantine Books (New York, NY), 2002.

WORK IN PROGRESS: A novel.

SIDELIGHTS: Thomas Steinbeck is the son of novelist John Steinbeck, and John's second wife, Gwyn. He spent much of his life writing screenplays, articles, and documentaries and was a journalist in Vietnam. Steinbeck intended to publish his first volume privately, and copies were to be given as gifts to guests at a friend's inn. But when a draft of *Down to a Soundless Sea,* a collection of five short and two long stories, was circulated by his father's agents, Steinbeck was offered a two-book deal, the second to be a novel about a ranching family.

A *Kirkus Reviews* contributor called *Down to a Soundless Sea* "stories of subtle fantasy, with an open-ended feel." A *Publishers Weekly* reviewer remarked that "Steinbeck's naturalism and his accomplished voice make it clear that the family's literary legacy is in very good hands."

The stories of *Down to a Soundless Sea* "have a rhythm and tone apart from most contemporary writing," commented Regis Behe in a review for *PittsburghLIVE.com.* "Similar to the folk tales about Pecos Bill, Paul Bunyan and Babe the Blue Ox, and other mythic heroes of the era, Steinbeck's writing has a plain, simple, but specific voice."

The stories are set at the beginning of the twentieth century and take place on the Monterey Peninsula of California. They are stories that were told in the Steinbeck household, not only by Fa, their name for the senior Steinbeck, but by their aunts and uncles and others close to the family. Steinbeck did a great deal of research to find the authentic voices of that period.

His father's characters were the downtrodden, like the Joad family in *The Grapes of Wrath,* and John Steinbeck counted among his friends the farmers and boat captains of the region. The stories in this collection are sometimes set at sea, as in "The Blighted Cargo" and "Blind Luck." Others are stories of adventures across land, such as the longest, "Sing Fat and the Imperial Duchess of Woo," based on the adventures of an actual Chinese immigrant who slaved in the California gold mines before leaving to find his true destiny. Joe Hartlaub wrote in a *Bookreporter.com* review that this "tale of romance and traditional Chinese engagement between a young widow and a student apothecary is practically worth the price of admission in and of itself. . . . It is unfortunate that stories like this are so rarely written in these politically correct, supposedly liberated days; it makes the beauty of this one resonate all the more strongly."

Among the other stories is "The Wool Gatherer," in which the character of young John Steinbeck spots the mythical Big Sur bear. Hartlaub wrote that "The Night Guide" "is, perhaps, a tale of the supernatural, but more so it is the story of a quiet, but indestructible bond between mother and child, a fable and a history."

Sacramento Bee writer Will Evans interviewed Steinbeck, who said that his father was actually two people and that one "belongs as much to you as he does to me." Steinbeck said his father was "hysterically funny, very creative, very entertaining," a man who "could start a conversation with a parking meter." Steinberg noted that the best storyteller in the family was actually his mother. "But my father was very funny. He was very Dickensian. He would do all the parts—go into a falsetto for the women's voices and that kind of stuff. We were little and we just loved hearing stories, and some of them we'd call for again and again." Steinbeck was twenty-four when his famous father died.

Los Angeles Times writer Fred Alvarez was in a Santa Barbara bookstore for an appearance by Steinbeck. Alvarez noted Steinbeck's response to his newfound popularity at the age of fifty-eight. Steinbeck said, "I am as mystified as you are, believe me. My writing most of my life has been dedicated toward making a living, and I haven't had the luxury of saying, 'Oh, I think I'll write the great American novel.' The fact is, somebody in my family has already pulled it off, and I've got no desire to compete with that."

BIOGRAPHICAL AND CRITICAL SOURCES:

PERIODICALS

Book, November-December, 2002, Paul Evans, review of *Down to a Soundless Sea,* p. 82.
Bookseller, January 3, 2003, Benedicte Page, review of *Down to a Soundless Sea,* p. S26.
Kirkus Reviews, July 15, 2002, review of *Down to a Soundless Sea,* p. 991.
Los Angeles Times, October 21, 2002, Fred Alvarez, review of *Down to a Soundless Sea,* p. E11.
New York Times, November 7, 2002, Martin Arnold, review of *Down to a Soundless Sea,* p. E3.
Publishers Weekly, August 12, 2002, review of *Down to a Soundless Sea,* p. 273.

ONLINE

Bookreporter.com, http://www.bookreporter.com/ (December 12, 2002), Joe Hartlaub, review of *Down to a Soundless Sea.*
PittsburghLIVE.com, http://www.pittsburghlive.com/ October 20, 2002) Regis Behe, review of *Down to a Soundless Sea,*
Sacramento Bee Online, http://www.sacbee.com/ (October 10, 2002), Will Evans, interview with Steinbeck.*

*   *   *

STEINBERG, Jacques

PERSONAL: Married Sharon Weinstock (an attorney); children: two. *Education:* Graduate of Dartmouth College.

ADDRESSES: Agent—c/o Author Mail, Penguin Putnam, Inc. 375 Hudson St., New York, NY 10014.

CAREER: Journalist. *New York Times,* New York, NY, researcher in Washington, DC, beginning 1981, reporter in New York, NY, 1993-99, national education correspondent, beginning 1999.

AWARDS, HONORS: Fred M. Hechinger Grand Prize for Distinguished Education Reporting, Education Writers Association of America, 1998.

WRITINGS:

The Gatekeepers: Inside the Admissions Process of a Premier College, Viking (New York, NY), 2002.

SIDELIGHTS: Jacques Steinberg began his career with the *New York Times* as a researcher and assistant to long-time Washington columnist James (Scotty) Reston, and moved to New York in 1993 to cover a variety of beats. Beginning with the 1996-97 school year, Steinberg devoted more of his time to covering education when he spent much of that year inside a third-grade classroom and wrote about children's efforts to read. In 1999, Steinberg was made national education correspondent for the newspaper, and since then he has covered a broad range of issues, including bilingual education in California, school vouchers in Cleveland, Ohio, the for-profit Edison schools, shortages of teachers and principals nationwide, and the educational pressures facing American children.

Beginning in the fall of 1999, Steinberg spent eight months in the admissions office of Wesleyan University in Middletown, Connecticut. In his book *The Gatekeepers: Inside the Admissions Process of a Premier College* he follows the activities of admissions officer Ralph Figueroa and the application processes of six high school seniors seeking entry into the prestigious school. Most of the book covers the ten-week period during which Wesleyan admissions officers spend long hours reading applicant files, evaluating prospective students, and accepting the only one in ten of nearly 7,000 applicants who will be offered a place in the incoming class.

During this process, applicants who receive scores of "admit minus" or "deny plus" by two separate readers are resubmitted to the entire panel of officers, who then decide by majority vote. Steinberg notes that individual officers make their decisions based on scores, essays, accomplishments, affirmative action policies, and their individual values. While one officer might be more receptive to a student who has not experienced permanence, another might favor a student from a rural background. Children of college-educated parents are held to a higher standard than children from families unable to offer as many advantages.

Figueroa spends half the year promoting Wesleyan and the other half rejecting most of the applicants. A *Kirkus Reviews* contributor commented that "what shines through in the portrait of Figueroa and his colleagues is their utter commitment to a Herculean, if somewhat paradoxical task."

"What Steinberg discovered," noted Joanna Schultz in an online review for the *Pittsburgh Post-Gazette,* "was that although there is no single definition of merit, there is a great deal of thought, sensitivity, and nuance that goes into making each difficult decision." Schultz noted that Steinberg "explains clearly how and why Wesleyan searches for a perfect class rather than for perfect students. Like most private colleges and universities, it enrolls as diverse a student body as it

can on the theory that learning in such a community produces the kind of education effective in production citizens for our increasingly global society."

Steinberg reports on the six students, using their real names, scores, and situations. "With permission, Steinberg describes students like Becca Janol, an outstanding leader whose adolescent flirtation with a marijuana-laced brownie creates a nightmare for Ralph Figueroa and the admissions committee," wrote Shannon Bloomstran for *Bookreporter.com.* Janol wrote of her experience in her essay. Other students include Aggie Ramirez, whose grades had suffered because she concentrated on leadership activities, and Migizi Pesoneau, a Native American who overcame poor grades to attend a progressive experimental school in New Mexico. Steinberg also follows Julianna Bentes, a dancer being courted by many schools, and who scored a perfect 1600 on her SAT, and Jordan Goldman, an aspiring writer.

Steinberg waits, along with the six, not only for the decisions from Wesleyan, but also for those from other schools to which they have applied, like Brown, Goldman's first choice. Bloomstran concluded by saying that *The Gatekeepers* "provides a glimpse into the lives of some interesting, high-powered kids. It's a fascinating peek behind the curtain into a process that is sometimes unfair, sometimes fatiguing, but always compelling."

New York Times writer Patricia M. McDonough found one aspect of the book troubling. She said that Steinberg "is relatively silent on the inequity of most applicants' not having access to the kinds of school counselors he so richly describes." One of the applicants, Tiffany Wang, attended a public high school which, even though it was located in an affluent community, employed counselors who had too many responsibilities to afford students adequate advising time.

McDonough continued, saying that Steinberg "muses on Tiffany's choice not to talk about her passion for corresponding with death-row inmates and on whether it might have turned her rejection into an admission. I couldn't help wondering whether the college counselors at a private prep school might have coached her better on her essay topics and the messages thus conveyed. Morever, Mr. Steinberg uncritically accepts

Mr. Figueroa's derision of 'counselors for hire' and the suggestion that they 'massage' students' application essays. This struck me as unfair in a book that describes how prep school counselors confer with their seniors on their essays."

Christian Science Monitor reviewer John Budris wrote that "Steinberg's research into the fierce competition for the few coveted spots at elite colleges will stagger the uninitiated, but his epilogue serves as a balm for all the anxiety. The students he profiles ultimately thrive and mature—regardless of where each was accepted and eventually enrolled. That lesson alone makes bearable the long wait until the April envelope arrives."

BIOGRAPHICAL AND CRITICAL SOURCES:

PERIODICALS

Booklist, August, 2002, Vanessa Bush, review of *The Gatekeepers: Inside the Admissions Process of a Premier College,* p. 1899.
Business Week, September 23, 2002, William C. Symonds, review of *The Gatekeepers,* p.20.
Christian Science Monitor, December 10, 2002, John Budris, review of *The Gatekeepers.*
Kirkus Reviews, July 15, 2002, review of *The Gatekeepers,* p. 1018.
Newsweek, September 23, 2002, Barbara Kantrowitz, review of *The Gatekeepers,* p. 70.
New York Times, September 27, 2002, Patricia M. McDonough, review of *The Gatekeepers,* p. E37.
Publishers Weekly, July 29, 2002, review of *The Gatekeepers,* p. 64.

ONLINE

Bookreporter.com, http://www.bookreporter.com/ (December 12, 2002), Shannon Bloomstran, review of *The Gatekeepers.*
Gatekeepers Home Page, http://www.the-gatekeepers.com/ (March 4, 2003).
Pittsburgh Post-Gazette Online, http://www.post-gazette.com/ (September 15, 2002), Joanna Schultz, review of *The Gatekeepers.**

STEPHEN, Lily G(ebhardt) 1943-
(Lily Vallerey)

PERSONAL: Born December 19, 1943, in Dayton, OH; daughter of Gerald Leroy (a watchmaker, landscaper, and tree surgeon) and Mary Rosa (a homemaker; maiden name, Vezina) Gebhardt; married James Clinton Allison, December, 1961 (divorced, August, 1970); married Thomas Ray Hardman, 1977 (divorced, 1983); married Robert L. Stephen (a dentist), September, 1996; children: (second marriage) Derrick Ray. *Religion:* Tibetan Buddhist, Nyingma. *Hobbies and other interests:* Spirituality and mysticism, gardening, poetry writing.

ADDRESSES: Home—Mount Shasta, CA. *Agent*—c/o Author Mail, Blooming Rose Press, P.O. Box 1211, Mount Shasta, CA 96067-1211.

CAREER: Schlumberger Well Services, Houston, TX, secretary, 1966-68; freelance photographic model, Houston, TX, 1967-71; Cummings Advertising Agency, secretary and copywriter, 1969-71; Mercy Medical Center, Mount Shasta, CA, manager of communications, 1980-97.

MEMBER: Small Publishers Association of North America, Publishers Marketing Association.

WRITINGS:

The Tenth Muse: A Modern Myth (fiction; first volume of "Third Verse" trilogy), Blooming Rose Press (Mount Shasta, CA), 2001.

Also author of upublished work *From Seed to Shining Seed,* and of poetry. Some writings appear under pseudonym Lily Vallerey.

WORK IN PROGRESS: The Eleventh Hour, the second volume of the "Third Verse" trilogy, "a continuing story of adventure incorporating multi-dimensional concepts that interface physics with spirituality"; research on theoretical physics, the life work of David Bohm, and the language and culture of the Quechua Indians of Peru.

SIDELIGHTS: Lily G. Stephen told *CA:* "Since the age of four, when I began reading, the world of fiction lit up my life. From the time of birth until age twenty-one, I was governed by a restricted Christian sect, one that directed youth away from higher education into missionary work. Prior to my inner wake-up call, when it became clear there was a universe of spiritual realization I'd never been exposed to, I sought relief from austerity and dogma in abundant fictional works.

"By the late 1960s my horizons widened at the same time that unexpected changes entered in. It was suggested that I write to assist in understanding a way through change. I was surprised to find verses of poetry emerge on pages of the journal I began to keep.

"Fiction reading continued to be a source of inspiration, cycled with long periods of investigation of philosophy, mysticism, and spirituality, both through books and personal instruction from teachers. By 1977 I was ready to attempt the next step—to write a book-length fictional work certain to transport readers to higher levels of realization, a story having at its heart the concept presented in one of the most sublime schools of teaching called 'Dzogchen': that purity of mind is always present and needs only to be recognized.

"Throughout the twenty years I spent writing, rewriting, and rewriting *From Seed to Shining Seed,* I was assisted by memories of fiction writers who had left their marks, authors like Marie Corelli, Ayn Rand, and Anya Seton, to name a few. There is a long list of authors on the spiritual path whose works were influential. Foremost among them is Tenzin Gyatso, the fourteenth Dalai Lama. Others are John Blofeld, Ram Dass, Jack Kornfield, and Joseph Goldstein.

"Even though I ruthlessly pared down the final manuscripts, at 830 pages it was clearly too long for a debut novel. I shelved it for the time being, wrote poetry for a couple of years, studied writing techniques, and realized that quite a different story waited in the wings. The new story offered an initial obstacle: it hadn't made itself known to me yet. The twentieth century was winding down to its final days; that was when I invited the story in and resolved to be patient at a time when the world and our collective future had become infused with a sense of urgency in the form of a now-overused term, millennial madness.

"By the end of January, 2002, the story came through with the same urgency that had been in the air and provided a multi-layered, complex underpinning superbly suited to convey those uplifting, expansive wisdom-concepts I aspire to weave throughout my work.

"My writing process isn't according to formula or method. Forcing out dutiful daily pages doesn't work for me and isn't harmonious with the demands of my life. There are times when we digest, assimilate, and practically ferment experience and concept until what results is better for the passage of time. On the other hand, if a novel is in the works, there are times when there's no way around it—either the writing flows and all else takes a back seat, or else it may just be plain hard work to bridge those high spots.

"The labor as well as the soaring of creative spirit are incidental to the quest: that readers encounter in the 'Third Verse' trilogy a fresh view of the world that uplifts those conditioned by delusion and mired in personal suffering; that the vehicle of visionary fiction will help them to remember the wisdom they already know but have become disconnected from; that they will regain their cognizance of seamless unity with all beings and with the universe."

*　　*　　*

STEVENS, Mitchell L. 1966-

PERSONAL: Born May 26, 1966, in Iowa City, IA; son of Wendell C. (an anesthesiologist) and Lola C. (a homemaker) Stevens. *Ethnicity:* "White." *Education:* Macalester College, B.A. (magna cum laude), 1988; Northwestern University, M.A., Ph.D., 1996.

ADDRESSES: Office—Department of Sociology, Hamilton College, Clinton, NY 13323. *E-mail*—mstevens@hamilton.edu.

CAREER: Hamilton College, Clinton, NY, associate professor, 1996-2002, professor of sociology, 2002—.

MEMBER: American Sociological Association, Society for the Study of Social Problems.

AWARDS, HONORS: NAE/Spencer Foundation post-doctoral fellow, 1999-2000.

WRITINGS:

Kingdom of Children: Culture and Controversy in the Home-Schooling Movement, Princeton University Press (Princeton, NJ), 2001.

Contributor to journals, including *Work and Occupations Studies in Symbolic Interaction* and *Annual Review of Sociology.*

WORK IN PROGRESS: Research on the ethnography of college admissions.

*　　*　　*

SUTTON, Marilyn (Phyllis) 1944-

PERSONAL: Born June 21, 1944, in Sydney, Nova Scotia, Canada; daughter of William B. (in accounting) and Mary Phyllis O'Gorman Buckley; married Thomas C. Sutton, 1965; children: Stephen, Paul, Matthew, Meagan. *Education:* St. Michael's College, University of Toronto, B.A., 1965; Claremont Graduate University, M.A., 1969, Ph.D., 1973. *Hobbies and other interests:* The Outdoors, travel.

ADDRESSES: Office—California State University, Dominguez Hills, 1000 East Victoria, Carson, CA 90747; fax: 949-760-8393. *E-mail*—msutton@csudh. edu.

CAREER: California State University—Dominguez Hills, Carson, professor of English, 1973—. WASC SNR Commission, chair.

MEMBER: Modern Language Association, MAP.

WRITINGS:

(With Susan Galdieri, Wilcox) *Understanding Death and Dying,* Alfred Publishing (Port Washington, NY), 1977, 3rd edition, Mayfield (Palo Alto, CA), 1985.

(Editor) *Chaucer's Pardoner's Prologue and Tale: An Annotated Bibliography, 1900 to 1995,* University of Toronto Press (Toronto, Ontario, Canada), 2001.

*　　*　　*

SWANSON, Denise 1956-

PERSONAL: Born December 25, 1956, in IL; daughter of Ernest W. (a farmer and mechanic) and Marie (a police, fire, and emergency dispatcher; maiden name, Votta) Swanson; married David Stybr, January 26, 1980. *Ethnicity:* "Caucasian." *Education:* University of Illinois, Urbana, B.S., 1979; Governors State University, M.A., 1982. *Religion:* Roman Catholic. *Hobbies and other interests:* Travel, bridge, animals.

ADDRESSES: Office—PMB 107, 429 North Weber Rd., Romeoville, IL 60446. *Agent*—Laura Blake Peterson, Curtis Brown, 10 Astor Pl., New York, NY 10003-6935. *E-mail*—MsSleuth@aol.com.

CAREER: Young Men's Christian Association, Joliet, IL, counselor in anti-crime program, 1979-80; intern psychologist at public schools in Kankakee, IL, 1982-83; school psychologist in Prince George's County, MD, 1983-85, and in Illinois, 1986-90; Center Cass District 66, Downers Grove, IL, school psychologist, 1990—. Moraine Valley Community College, psychology instructor. Carillon Theater Guild, president, 1992-94.

MEMBER: National Association of School Psychologists, Sisters in Crime, Romance Writers of America, Illinois School Psychologists Association.

AWARDS, HONORS: Named school psychologist of the year, Prince George's County, MD, 1983-84; Reviewers' Choice Award, best first novel and best amateur sleuth series, both Independent Mystery Booksellers Association, 2000, for *Murder of a Small-Town Honey.*

WRITINGS:

"SCUMBLE RIVER MYSTERY" SERIES

Murder of a Small-Town Honey, Penguin Putnam (New York, NY), 2000.

Murder of a Sweet Old Lady, Penguin Putnam (New York, NY), 2001.

Murder of a Sleeping Beauty, Penguin Putnam (New York, NY), 2002.

Murder of a Snake in the Grass, Penguin Putnam (New York, NY), 2002.

Murder of a Barbie and Ken, Penguin Putnam (New York, NY), in press.

Work represented in anthologies, including *And the Dying Is Easy,* Penguin Putnam (New York, NY), 2001, and *Mayhem in the Midlands.*

SIDELIGHTS: Denise Swanson told *CA:* "As a school psychologist, I rarely have any closure in my work. Even when I do, it is often not the outcome I would like to see. As an author, I can right wrongs, punish the wicked, and avenge the deserving. As an author, I am able to have control.

"I've always been an avid reader since teaching myself at the age of three. Throughout the years I've been influenced by strong female writers, such as Louisa May Alcott, Jane Austen, and the Brontë sisters. More currently I admire mystery writers Carolyn G. Hart, Margaret Maron, and Earlene Fowler.

"I write every day, usually in the morning. I start my books by choosing a victim, a murderer, and a motive. Using a loose outline, I write a proposal or synopsis of the plot. From there I tend to write in order, starting with Chapter 1. I revise as I write and do one final revision before submitting the book to my editor.

"I am greatly inspired by my real-life experiences when I choose the material for my books. In my first book I was working in a rural community as a school psychologist and witnessed the division of the town over their annual fair. This animosity extended to the principal and mayor having a fist fight in the school parking lot. My second book was influenced by my grandmother's decline and death. At the time I realized she knew many family secrets that would go to the grave with her, and what a relief this would be to the people involved in them. My third book was influenced by a young girl telling me how much she disliked being made to compete, but how much her mother wanted her to continue."

BIOGRAPHICAL AND CRITICAL SOURCES:

ONLINE

Denise Swanson Web site, http://www.deniseswanson. com (July 4, 2003).

SWENSEN, Cole 1955-

PERSONAL: Born October 22, 1955, in San Francisco, CA. *Education:* San Francisco State University, B.A., 1980, M.A., 1983; University of California, A.B.D., 1992.

ADDRESSES: Office—P.O. Box 927, Fairfax, CA 94978.

CAREER: Poet. University of Denver, Denver, CO, teacher, 1996—. Worked variously as a translator, editor, copywriter, and teacher.

MEMBER: Marin Poetry Centre (president 1985-87).

AWARDS, HONORS: Marin Arts Council creative advancement grant, 1987; National Poetry Series award, 1987, for *New Math;* Shifting Foundation grant, 1989; New American Poetry Series award, 1995, for *Noon;* Iowa Poetry Prize, 1998, and San Francisco State Poetry Center Book Award, 1999, both for *Try.*

WRITINGS:

POETRY

It's Alive She Says, Floating Island Press (Point Reyes Station, CA), 1984.

New Math, William Morrow (New York, NY), 1988.

Park, Floating Island Publications (Point Reyes Station, CA), 1991.

Numen, Burning Deck Press (Providence, RI), 1995.

Noon, Sun and Moon Press (Los Angeles, CA), 1997.

Try, University of Iowa Press (Iowa City, IA), 1999.

Oh, Apogee Press (Berkeley, CA), 2000.

Such Rich Hour, University of Iowa Press (Iowa City, IA), 2001.

TRANSLATIONS

Pierre Alferi, *Natural Gaits,* Sun and Moon Press (Los Angeles, CA), 1995.

Oliver Cadiot, *Art Poetic,* Green Integer (Los Angeles, CA), 1999.

Jean Frèmon, *Island of the Dead,* Green Integer (Los Angeles, CA), 2002.

Pascale Monnier, *Bayart,* Duration Press (New York, NY), 2002.

OTHER

Contributor to periodicals, including *Chicago Review, American Poetry Review, Boston Book Review, Common Knowledge, Conjunctions, Grand Street, New American Writing,* and *Zzyzzyva.*

SIDELIGHTS: Poet Cole Swensen was born and raised near San Francisco, and has since lived in Santa Cruz, California, London, England, Paris, France, and Denver, Colorado, working as a translator, editor, copywriter, and teacher. She began teaching at an alternative high school while in her early twenties and has since taught in community colleges and universities. She began teaching full-time at the University of Denver in 1996 and is the author of several poetry collections.

In the *American Book Review,* Fred Muratori described Swensen's poetry in *New Math* as "a collection of deft, sleight-of-hand lyrics that teased images or ideas through unpredictably widening or shifting chains of association." A *Publishers Weekly* reviewer wrote that Swensen's lyrics in *New Math* are "elusive, obscure, nearly hallucinatory." A reviewer in *Publishers Weekly* called Swensen's collection *Such Rich Hour,* "a very long, fragment-strewn, philosophically-minded sequence."

On the *Denver University* Web site, Swensen described her teaching philosophy: "I stress writing as thinking—as thinking that creates new territory." She urges her students to create new material and revise it over and over, in the context of a workshop, so that they can hone their own critical abilities and will be able to see what could be improved in their work, and how to improve it. "Education is a process of expansion—expanding strategies as writers, expanding knowledge as scholars, expanding concerns as citizens. Every class should be a community in which students safely and certainly expand their worlds."

BIOGRAPHICAL AND CRITICAL SOURCES:

PERIODICALS

American Book Review, February, 1996, Fred Muratori, *The Cadence of Disclosure,* p. 21.
American Poet, spring, 2002, review of *Such Rich Hour,* p. 61.

Library Journal, June 1, 1988, Louis McKee, review of *New Math,* p. 116.
Literary Review, summer, 2001, Burton Raffel, review of *Try,* p. 791.
Publishers Weekly, April 1, 1988, review of *New Math,* p. 80; February 22, 1999, review of *Try,* p. 89; July 9, 2001, review of *Such Rich Hour,* p. 63.

ONLINE

Denver University Web site, http://www.du.edu/ (July 25, 2002).*

*   *   *

SWETNAM, Ford 1941-

PERSONAL: Born August 30, 1941, in Alexandria, VA; married; wife's name Susan H. (a teacher and writer). *Education:* Hamilton College, A.B., 1963; Cornell University, M.A., 1964, Ph.D., 1967.

ADDRESSES: Agent—C/O Blue Scarab Press, 243 South Eighth Avenue, Pocatello, ID 83201.

CAREER: Idaho State University, Pocatello, member of staff, 1976—. Pocatello Valley Fire Department, member.

WRITINGS:

(Editor with Richard Ardivger) *High Sky over All* (fiction anthology), Idaho State University (Pocatello, ID), 1990.
Another Tough Hop (poems), Walrus & Carpenter, 1992.
301 (poems), Redneck, 1995.
Ghostholders Know (poems), Blue Scarab Press (Pocatello, ID), 1999.

SIDELIGHTS: Ford Swetnam told *CA:* "I've almost always lived where rural economics or extractive economics are giving way to others or just being pinched out. There are a lot of stories there, and I try to let the people doing the living do the telling."

SYLVESTER, Harold

PERSONAL: Married Kathleen Dunn; children: Tracey, Harold. *Education:* Tulane University, degree in psychology, 1972.

ADDRESSES: Agent—United Talent Agency, 9560 Wilshire Blvd., Suite 500, Beverly Hills, CA 90212-2427.

CAREER: Actor and screenwriter. Worked at DePaul (psychiatric hospital) and New Orleans Free Southern Theatre, New Orleans, LA, c. 1972-74. Actor in films, including *Night of the Strangler,* 1972; (as Nathan Lee Morgan) *Sounder, Part 2,* Gamma III, 1976; (as first goon) *Alex and the Gypsy* (also known as *Love and Other Crimes*), 1976; (as doctor) *A Hero Ain't Nothin' but a Sandwich,* New World, 1978; (as D. C.) *Fast Break,* Columbia, 1979; (as Alvin Martin) *Inside Moves,* Associated, 1980; (as Perryman) *An Officer and a Gentleman,* Paramount, 1982; (as Johnson) *Uncommon Valor,* Paramount, 1983; (as Tanneran) *Vision Quest* (also known as *Crazy for You*), Warner Bros., 1985; (as Pete Blanchard) *Innerspace,* Warner Bros., 1987; (as Max Bryson) *Space Rage* (also known as *A Dollar a Day, Space Rage: Breakout on Prison Planet,* and *Trackers,*), Vestron, 1987; (as Brian Armstrong) *Hit List,* New Line Cinema, 1989; (as Frank) *Corrina, Corrina,* 1994; (as James Tyler) *The Sixth Man,* Buena Vista, 1997; (as Willie Reed) *Trippin',* October Films, 1999; and (as Stan Wade) *Missing Brendan,* 2003.

Actor in made-for-television movies, including (as Rider) *Richie Brockelman: The Missing 24 Hours,* National Broadcasting Company (NBC), 1978; (as Sergeant Johnson) *Uncommon Valor,* Columbia Broadcasting System (CBS), 1983; (as Granville) *Hearts of Steel,* 1986; (as Sam) *Double Your Pleasure* (also known as *The Reluctant Agent*), 1989; (as Oliver Jackson) *Angie, the Lieutenant,* American Broadcasting Companies (ABC), 1992; (as Art Regan) *In the Line of Duty: A Cop for the Killing* (also known as *A Cop for the Killing*), NBC, 1990; (as John Gilbert) *Line of Fire: The Morris Dees Story* (also known as *Blind Hate*), NBC, 1991; (as Lieutenant Paul Moret) *Love and Curses . . . And All That Jazz,* CBS, 1991; (as George Dunaway) *In the Deep Woods,* NBC, 1992; (as Lieutenant Jack Emery) *Someone She Knows,* Warner Bros. Television, 1994; and (as God) *What Wouldn't Jesus Do?* 2002.

Actor in television series, including (as Deputy Aaron Fairfax) *Walking Tall,* NBC, 1981; (as Agent Dwayne Thompson) *Today's F.B.I.,* ABC, 1981-82; (as Harry Dresden) *Mary,* CBS, 1985; (as Russell) *Shaky Ground,* Fox, 1992-93; (as Grill) *Married . . . with Children,* Fox, 1994-97; (as Colonel John Henchy) *The Army Show,* The WB, 1998; and (as Wendell Loman) *City of Angels,* CBS, 2000. Guest star on television series, including *Hill Street Blues, A Different World,* and *NYPD Blue.*

MEMBER: Academy of Motion Picture Arts and Sciences, John Anson Ford Theatre Foundation (board member), Urban League (board member), Tulane University President's Council.

WRITINGS:

(With others) *NYPD Blue* (television series), American Broadcasting Companies (ABC), 1993.

Passing Glory (made-for-television movie), Turner Network Television (TNT), 1999.

(And co-executive producer) *On Hallowed Ground: Streetball Champions of Rucker Park* (television special), Turner Network Television (TNT), 2000.

(And producer and story editor) *City of Angels* (television series), Columbia Broadcasting System (CBS), 2000.

SIDELIGHTS: Best known for his role as Al Bundy's coworker and friend "Griff" on the sitcom *Married . . . with Children,* Harold Sylvester has also had a productive career behind the camera. He has written for two television series, and has also written a movie, *Passing Glory,* which is based on his own life.

Sylvester grew up in a housing project in New Orleans, Louisiana. His parents were devout Catholics, and they sent Sylvester to an all-black, all-male Catholic high school, St. Augustine, where he became one of the stars of the basketball team. Since this was the mid-1960s and segregation was still in full force in Louisiana, the black schools played in one league and the white schools played in another. In 1965, when the St. Augustine Purple Knights were clearly the best black team in New Orleans, a local television sports commentator suggested that the top black team in the state should play the top white team, which happened to be a New Orleans Catholic school called Jesuit High. This historic game is the focus of Sylvester's film *Passing Glory.*

Passing Glory had an all-star team behind the cameras: basketball star Magic Johnson produced, and Steve James, who also directed the critically acclaimed film *Hoop Dreams,* directed. This is a "raw and passionate and exquisitely paced" film, Ray Richmond noted in a review for *Variety,* and Sylvester's script "features sprightly interaction and sharp dialogue, with lines like, 'Down here, "should" and "is" is a long way apart.'"

After that first integrated basketball game in the New Orleans Archdiocese, the black and white Catholic high schools started to play each other more often. In the next year's Catholic Youth Organization basketball tournament, which before 1965 had only included white schools, St. Augustine won and Sylvester was named Most Valuable Player. In 1968, on the strength of his basketball skills, Sylvester became the first African-American student ever to receive an athletic scholarship to Tulane University.

Originally, Sylvester had planned to study psychology, but when he took a psychodrama class and wound up playing a part in one of the theater department's productions because of it, "I fell in love with the whole process," Sylvester told Tulane University Magazine interviewer Jason Eness. After graduating in 1972, Sylvester worked in a mental hospital while acting with the New Orleans Free Southern Theatre in his free time. Then, in 1974 he auditioned for and got the lead role in the movie *Sounder II.* He moved to Los Angeles and has been working in Hollywood ever since.

Sylvester's son, Harold Jr., is following in his father's footsteps, at least as far as basketball is concerned: he was a walk-on player for the University of California—Los Angeles in the late 1990s.

BIOGRAPHICAL AND CRITICAL SOURCES:

BOOKS

Contemporary Theatre, Film, and Television, Volume 34, Gale (Detroit, MI), 2001.

Mapp, Edward, *Directory of Blacks in the Performing Arts,* second edition, Scarecrow Press (Metuchen, NJ), 1990.

PERIODICALS

Daily News (Los Angeles, CA), January 4, 1996, "Sylvester Warms Bench, but Lives Dream," p. S3.

Fresno Bee (Fresno, CA), September 13, 1998, review of *The Army Show,* p. H4.

Lansing State Journal (Lansing, MI), February 21, 1999, review of *Passing Glory,* p. E5.

Los Angeles Times, February 24, 1984, Robert Koehler, "Just a Case of the Blues," p. 13.

New Orleans Magazine, March, 1981, Joe Leydon, review of *Inside Moves,* pp. 36-37.

New Yorker, January 23, 1984, Pauline Kael, review of *Uncommon Valor,* pp. 91-93.

New York Times, February 20, 1999, William Mc-Donald, "Good Sports Matched against Bad Odds," p. B7.

People, November 26, 1990, David Hiltbrand, review of *In the Line of Duty,* pp. 9-10; December 21, 1992, David Hiltbrand, review of *Shaky Ground,* p. 14.

Record (Bergen County, NJ), May 13, 1999, review of *Trippin',* p. Y2.

Variety, December 14, 1992, Dominic Griffin, review of *Shaky Ground,* p. 48; February 15, 1999, Ray Richmond, review of *Passing Glory,* p. 49.

ONLINE

Black Collegian Online, http://www.black-collegian. com/ (March 11, 2003), Russell L. Stockard, Sr., "*Passing Glory*—Past History: 1965 Revisited."

Tulane University Magazine Online, http://www2. tulane.edu/ (March 11, 2003), Jason Eness, "Path to Glory: Harold Sylvester."

TV Tome, http://www.tvtome.com/ (March 11, 2003), "Harold Sylvester."*

T-V

TAGAWA, Cary-Hiroyuki 1950-

PERSONAL: Born September 27, 1950, in Tokyo, Japan; son of a member of the U.S. Army and a Japanese actress; married Sally Phillips; children: Calen, Brynne. *Education:* Attended the University of Southern California; exchange student in Japan.

ADDRESSES: Home—Kauai, HI. *Agent*—International Creative Management, 8942 Wilshire Blvd., Beverly Hills, CA 90211-1934.

CAREER: Actor in films, including *Big Trouble in Little China,* 1986; (as Toshi) *Armed Response* (also known as *Jade Jungle*), CineTel, 1986; (as Chang) *The Last Emperor,* Columbia, 1987; (as Lieutenant Lee) *Spellbinder,* Metro-Goldwyn-Mayer/United Artists (MGM/UA), 1988; (as Oriental man) *Twins,* Universal, 1988; (as Imperial Marine) *The Last Warrior* (also known as *Coastwatcher*), ITC Films, 1989; (as Kwang) *License to Kill* (also known as *License Revoked,* MGM/UA, 1989; (as Yoshida) *Showdown in Little Tokyo,* Warner Bros., 1991; (as Kai) *The Perfect Weapon,* Paramount, 1991; (as Mr. Sangha) *Kickboxer 2: The Road Back,* Trimark Pictures, 1991; (as El Japo) *American Me,* Universal, 1991; (as Angie-Liv) *Nemesis,* Imperial Entertainment, 1993; (as Eddie Sakamura) *Rising Sun,* Twentieth Century-Fox, 1993; (as Major Somchai) *Natural Causes,* Columbia TriStar Home Video, 1994; (as Kon Seki) *The Dangerous,* Orion Home Video, 1994; (as Kanzaki) *Picture Bride,* Miramax, 1995; (as Shang Tsung) *Mortal Kombat,* New Line Cinema, 1995; (as Victor Chow) *White Tiger,* Keystone Pictures, 1995; (as Kabai Sengh) *The Phan-*

tom, Paramount, 1996; (as Captain Jong) *Provocateur* (also known as *Agent Provocateur*), Via Appia Communications, 1996; (as Chang) *Danger Zone,* NuImage, 1996; (as Matsuyama) *American Dragons* (also known as *Double Edge*), Orion Home Video, 1997; (as Captain Hefter) *Top of the World* (also known as *Cold Cash* and *Showdown*), Warner Bros., 1997; (as David Deyo) *Vampires* (also known as *John Carpenter's Vampires*), Sony Pictures Entertainment, 1998; *Double Edge,* Orion, 1999; (as Zenhichi Miyamoto) *Snow Falling on Cedars,* Universal, 1999; (as Ruechang) *Bridge of Dragons,* 1999; (as Alex) *Fixations,* 1999; (as David Chan) *The Art of War,* Warner Bros., 2000; (as Chang) *The Ghost* (also known as *Code of the Dragon*), Regent Entertainment, 2000; (as Ross Kawaii) *Camp Ninja,* Brimstone Entertainment, 2000; (as Genda) *Pearl Harbor,* 2001; (as Krull) *Planet of the Apes,* 2001; and *Speedball: The Movie,* 2002.

Actor in made-for-television movies, including (as Mandarin Bailiff) *Star Trek: The Next Generation: Encounter at Farpoint,* 1987; (as Hugh Denny) *L.A. Takedown* (also known as *L.A. Crimewave* and *Made in L.A.*), National Broadcasting Company (NBC), 1989; *Murder in Paradise,* NBC, 1990; (as Thai Major) *Vestige of Honor,* Columbia Broadcasting System (CBS), 1990; *Not of This World,* CBS, 1991; (as Hashimoto) *Mission of the Shark: The Saga of the U.S.S. Indianapolis,* CBS, 1991; (as Heroshi Osato) *Raven: Return of the Black Dragons,* 1992; (as Prakit) *Day of Reckoning,* NBC, 1994; (as Vinh Moc) *Soldier Boyz,* Home Box Office (HBO), 1996; (as Johnny Tsunami) *Johnny Tsunami,* Disney Channel, 1999; (as Leong Cheng) *NetForce* (miniseries; also known as *Tom Clancy's Netforce*), American Broadcasting

Companies (ABC), 1999; (as Yang Roechang) *Bride of Dragons,* HBO, 1999; and (as Mason Sato) *Baywatch: Hawaiian Wedding,* 2003. Actor in television series, including (as Osato) *Raven,* 1992; (as Zylyn) *Space Rangers,* 1993; and (as Lt. A. J. Shimamura) *Nash Bridges,* 1996. Frequent guest star on *Space Rangers.* Before becoming an actor, worked as a limo driver, farmer, photojournalist, and in food service. Mu Hawaii Conservatory, president.

WRITINGS:

(With Derek Kim and Tony T. L. Young) *Camp Ninja* (screenplay), Brimstone Entertainment, 2000.

WORK IN PROGRESS: A comic book.

SIDELIGHTS: Japanese-American actor Cary-Hiroyuki Tagawa grew up on army bases in North Carolina, Louisiana, and Texas, and has appeared in numerous films since his 1986 screen debut. His first big break was playing a eunuch in the blockbuster epic history of China, *The Last Emperor.* Because of his ethnicity Tagawa is often type-cast as villains in martial arts-related films, but he also received a great deal of attention for his role as a Japanese businessman in *Rising Sun,* based on the novel by Michael Crichton. His other notable roles have included the warrior ape Krull in the 2001 remake of *Planet of the Apes,* Commander Minoru Genda in *Pearl Harbor,* and the villainous Shang Tsung in the film *Mortal Kombat.* Tagawa is also the author of one screenplay, *Camp Ninja.* He currently resides in Kauai, Hawaii with his wife and their two children. In addition to his theatrical works, Tagawa teaches acting classes and is developing his own style of martial arts, which involves focus, concentration, and balance rather than fighting. He has also designed his own clothing line, Mu, and is writing a futuristic comic book that examines the distinction between warriors and soldiers.

BIOGRAPHICAL AND CRITICAL SOURCES:

BOOKS

International Motion Picture Almanac, 1996 edition, Quigley Publishing (New York, NY), 1996.

PERIODICALS

Entertainment Weekly, January 8, 1993, Ken Tucker, review of *Space Rangers,* p. 46; September 10, 1993, James Earl Hardy, review of *Rising Sun,* p. 51; September 8, 1995, Lisa Schwarzbaum, review of *Mortal Kombat,* p. 54; December 11, 1998, review of *Double Edge,* p. 88.

Honolulu Advertiser, November 7, 2002, Wayne Harada, "Media Watch," p. E5.

Jet, September 11, 2000, review of *The Art of War,* p. 14.

Newsweek, August 2, 1993, David Ansen, review of *Rising Sun,* p. 55.

Pacific Business News, September 7, 2001, Debbie Sokei, "Actor Redirects Energy to Balance Business," p. 22.

People, August 2, 1993, Ralph Novak, review of *Rising Sun,* p. 17; September 4, 1995, Ralph Novak, review of *Mortal Kombat,* p. 20.

Record (Bergen County, NJ), August 25, 2000, Kirk Honeycutt, review of *The Art of War,* p. 4.

Rocky Mountain News (Denver, CO), June 7, 1996, Robert Denerstein, review of *The Phantom,* p. 6D.

Scotsman (Edinburgh, Scotland), December 7, 2000, review of *The Art of War,* p. 13.

Times Literary Supplement, August 24, 2001, Christopher Tayler, review of *Planet of the Apes,* p. 19.

Variety, January 4, 1993, Tom Bierbaum, review of *Space Rangers,* p. 50; March 25, 1996, John P. McCarthy, review of *Nash Bridges,* p. 30; June 10, 1996, Godfrey Cheshire, review of *The Phantom,* pp. 40-41; February 1, 1999, Laura Fries, review of *Tom Clancy's Netforce,* p. 29; August 21, 2000, Emanuel Levy, review of *The Art of War,* p. 15.

Video Review, February, 1992, George Mannes, review of *Showdown in Little Tokyo,* p. 78.

ONLINE

Fanboy Planet, http://www.fanboyplanet.com/ (March 11, 2003), Derek McCaw, "Interview with Cary-Hiroyuki Tagawa."

Hawaii 411, http://www.hawaii411.com/ (March 11, 2003), Derek Kim, "A 411 Inspirational Hollywood Story."

Official Cary-Hiroyuki Tagawa Web Site, http://www.ctagawa.com (March 11, 2003).*

TANHAM, George K(ilpatrick) 1922-2003

OBITUARY NOTICE—See index for *CA* sketch: Born February 23, 1922, in Englewood, NJ; died of congestive heart failure March 29, 2003, in VA. Educator, consultant, researcher, and author. Tanham was a trained historian who later became a consultant on military defense and third-world countries. After receiving his bachelor's from Princeton University in 1943, he served as a captain in the Seventh Armored Division, earning numerous medals for bravery, including the Purple Heart, the Air Medal, and two Silver Stars; the French government also gave him the Croix de Guerre avec Etoile d'Argent. He returned to America to earn his Ph.D. in history and political science from Stanford University, teaching military history as an associate professor at the California Institute of Technology in Pasadena from 1947 to 1955. He then joined the RAND Corporation as a staff member, rising to the rank of vice president and trustee in 1971. From 1971 to 1982 he was senior researcher at RAND, and worked as a consultant in Washington, D.C., beginning in 1987. Tanham became a respected authority on counter-insurgency warfare and was a member of the U.S. Department of Defense task force in Vietnam in 1961. He also served as U.S. representative on the Southeast Asia Treaty Organization study on countersubversion in 1961 and 1969 and was a minister at the U.S. Embassy in Bangkok, Thailand, from 1968 to 1970; the Thai government awarded him the Most Exalted Order of White Elephant for his work there. During the 1960s, Tanham became fascinated by India, and repeatedly made visits to that country. His interest in military strategy and third-world countries led to his writing several books, including *War without Guns: American Civilians in Rural Vietnam* (1966), *Trial in Thailand* (1974), *Securing India: Strategic Thought and Practice* (1996), and the cowritten work *Islam and Conflict Resolution: Theories and Practices* (1998).

OBITUARIES AND OTHER SOURCES:

BOOKS

Writers Directory, 18th edition, St. James Press (Detroit, MI), 2003.

PERIODICALS

Hindu, April 9, 2003.
Washington Post, April 6, 2003, p. C10.

TANNENBAUM, Robert 1915-2003

OBITUARY NOTICE—See index for *CA* sketch: Born June 29, 1915, in Cripple Creek, CO; died of congestive heart failure March 15, 2003, in Carmel, CA. Educator and author. Tannenbaum was a longtime business professor at the University of California, Los Angeles, who was best known for his research in business leadership. He earned an A.A. from Santa Ana Junior College in 1935 and an M.B.A. from the University of Chicago before working as an accounting instructor at what is now Oklahoma State University. He then taught business at the University of Chicago from 1940 to 1942. When World War II started, he enlisted in the U.S. Navy, serving in the South Pacific and attaining the rank of lieutenant. After the war, he returned to the University of Chicago. In 1948, he joined the faculty at UCLA as an assistant professor, becoming a professor of development of human systems in 1971 and retiring in 1977. After retirement, he continued to teach seminars and work as a consultant for several years. Tannenbaum became an influential figure in business research in the 1950s with his ideas about managing employees that were published in his *Harvard Business Review* article "How to Choose a Leadership Pattern." His work is credited with leading to such concepts as "sensitivity training" and "T-groups." Tannenbaum was the coauthor of *Leadership and Organization: A Behavioral Science Approach* (1961), and coeditor of *Human Systems Development* (1985).

OBITUARIES AND OTHER SOURCES:

PERIODICALS

Los Angeles Times, March 30, 2003, p. B19.
Washington Post, March 31, 2003, p. B7.

*   *   *

VAIZEY, Edward 1968-

PERSONAL: Born June 5, 1968. *Education:* Attended Merton College, Oxford and Oxford Inns of Court School of Law.

ADDRESSES: Agent—c/o Author Mail, Politico's Bookstore, 8 Artillery Row, London SW1P 1RZ England.

CAREER: Civil servant, consultant, and lawyer. Conservative Research Department, desk officer, 1989-91; barrister, 1993-96; Public Policy Unit, political consultant, 1996—; Regent's Park and Kensington North Association, associate treasurer.

WRITINGS:

(Editor, with Michael Gove and Nicholas Boles) *A Blue Tomorrow,* Politico's Pub. (London, England), 2001.

(Editor) *The Blue Book on Health,* Politco's Pub. (London, England), 2001.

(Editor, with Michael McManus) *The Blue Book on Transport,* Politico's Pub. (London, England), 2002.

SIDELIGHTS: Edward Vaizey, along with Michael Gove and Nicholas Boles, edited *A Blue Tomorrow,* a collection of political essays published in 2001. *A Blue Tomorrow* was put together after a slate of conservatives in the United Kingdom were defeated in 2001, their second loss in a row. The book begins with an introduction to the party's key problems, and puts much blame on traditional family ideals. The authors call for recognition of same-sex unions and a loosening of drug laws. Generally, the book points toward social libertarianism.

A Blue Tomorrow welds together a range of perspectives, all of which look at the party's troubles and try to figure out how to remedy them. The twenty-one essays discuss the party's perceived racism and homophobia, its aging population and the overall lack of women in its ranks. The book emphasizes culture and gender; contributor Jo-Anne Nadler urges readers to consider the meaning of social liberalism and contributor Aidan Rankin addresses the conservative party's lack of dogma, identifying this as a conservative strength. Simon Walters, in his review in the *Times Literary Supplement,* complimented the editors, calling them "three very sharp young Tories," but felt the book lacks substance in terms of issues like economic policy, health policy, foreign policy and Northern Ireland. A *Reformer* magazine reviewer called it a good book to read if "you want pages and pages on what is wrong with the Tory Party, followed by some 'radical' proposals on what should be done." Walters noted, overall, that "most of the twenty-one contributors have sensible and worthwhile things to say."

BIOGRAPHICAL AND CRITICAL SOURCES:

PERIODICALS

Reformer, spring, 2002, review of *A Blue Tomorrow.*
Times Literary Supplement, April 12, 2002, Simon Walters, review of *A Blue Tomorrow,* p. 28.

*   *   *

VALLEREY, Lily
    See STEPHEN, Lily G(ebhardt)

*   *   *

van den BRINK, Gijsbert 1963-

PERSONAL: Born May 15, 1963, in Utrecht, Netherlands; son of Tijs van den Brink (a minister) and Aaltje Esveld; married Gerie-Anne Blankensteijn, August 30, 1988; children: Bertha Aaltje Christina. *Education:* University of Utrecht, Ph.D. (theology), 1993. *Religion:* Protestant.

ADDRESSES: Home—Merellaan 9, 3722 Ak Bilthoven, Netherlands. *E-mail*—gudbrink@solcon.nl.

CAREER: Gröningen University, Gröningen, Netherlands, lecturer in philosophy of religion, 1992-95; University of Utrecht, Utrecht, Netherlands, lecturer in philosophy of religion, 1995-2001. Minister in Dutch Reformed Church.

WRITINGS:

(With H. J. van der Kwast) *Een kerk ging stuk: relaas van de breuk die optrad binnen de Gereformeerde Kerken (vrijgemaakt) in de jaren 1967-1974,* Buijten & Schipperheijn (Amsterdam, Netherlands), 1992.

(Coeditor) *Christian Faith and Philosophical Theology: Essays in Honour of Vincent Brümmer, Presented on the Occasion of the Twenty-fifth Anniversary of His Professorship,* Kok Pharos (Kampen, Netherlands), 1992.

Almighty God: A Study of the Doctrine of Divine Omnipotence, Kok Pharos (Kampen, Netherlands), 1993.

(Editor with Marcel Sarot) *Identity and Change in the Christian Tradition,* Peter Lang (New York, NY), 1999.

(Editor with Marcel Sarot) *Understanding the Attributes of God,* Peter Lang (New York, NY), 1999.

Op betrouwbare grond: over onstaan en gezag van het Nieuwe Testament, Barnabas (Heerenveen, Netherlands), 1999.

Oriëntatie in de filosofie: westerse wijsbegeerte in wisselwerking met geloof en theologie, Boekencentrum (Zoetermeer, Netherlands), 2000.

WORK IN PROGRESS: Research on the philosophy of science, and systematic theology.*

*   *   *

VANDEN HEUVEL, Jon 1963-

PERSONAL: Born September 28, 1963, in Appleton, WI; son of Ben and Priscilla Vanden Heuvel; married; wife's name Kathleen Grace; children: Benjamin. *Education:* Lawrence University, B.A., 1985; Columbia University, M.A., M.Phil., Ph.D., 1996.

ADDRESSES: Home—660 West End Ave., New York, NY 10024. *E-mail*—jon-vdh@hotmail.com.

CAREER: Credit Suisse First Boston, New York, NY, vice president, 1996-2001; Wit Soundview, London, England, director, 2001—. American Academy in Berlin, member of board of trustees.

MEMBER: American Historical Association, Council on Foreign Relations.

WRITINGS:

The Unfolding Lotus: East Asia's Changing Media, Media Studies Center, 1993.

Changing Patterns: Latin America's Vital Media, Media Studies Center, 1995.

A German Life in the Age of Revolution: Joseph Görres, 1776-1848, Catholic University of America Press (Washington, DC), 2001.

*   *   *

VICTOR, Ed(ward) 1939-

PERSONAL: Born September 9, 1939, in Queens, NY; son of Jack (a photography-equipment shop owner) and Lydia Victor; married Micheline Dinah Samuels, 1963 (divorced, 1970); married Carol Lois Ryan (a lawyer), 1980; children: (first marriage) Adam and Ivan; (second marriage) Ryan. *Education:* Dartmouth College, B.A. (summa cum laude), 1960; Pembroke College, Cambridge, M. Litt., 1963. *Religion:* Jewish. *Hobbies and other interests:* Golf, tennis, travel, opera.

ADDRESSES: Home—10 Cambridge Gate, Regent's Park, London NW1 4XJ, England. *Office*—6 Bayley St., Bedford Square, London WC1B 3HB, England.

CAREER: Osborne Press, 1963-64; Weidenfeld & Nicholson, London, England, 1964-67, began as book editor, became editorial director; Jonathan Cape Limited, London, editorial director, 1967-71; Alfred Knopf Incorporated, New York, NY, senior editor, 1973; John Farquharson Limited (literary agency), London, director, 1974-76; Ed Victor Limited (literary agency), London, founder and president, 1977—.

MEMBER: AIDS Crisis Trust (council member, 1986-98), Almeida Theater (vice chairman and director, 1994—), Arts Foundation (trustee, 1991—), Garrick Club, Beefsteak Club.

AWARDS, HONORS: Marshall Scholarship, 1961.

WRITINGS:

The Obvious Diet, Arcade Publishing (New York, NY), 2002.

SIDELIGHTS: Ed Victor, the London-based literary agent of some of the world's most successful writers—among them such luminaries as Jack Higgins,

Frederick Forsyth, and Erica Jong, and the literary estates of Graham Greene, Iris Murdoch, and Raymond Chandler—stepped into the limelight himself in 2001 when he wrote his first book. *The Obvious Diet* is a common-sense self-help guide for people who want to lose weight and maintain a healthy body image. Explaining his motives for writing the book, Victor told Geraldine Bell of the London *Observer* that he simply "wanted to see what it was like." However, Victor also confided, "I would like the book to sell a lot of copies. I didn't write it for the money, although it's always nice to make [it]."

According to Katy Guest of the London *Independent,* Victor "is known for the ruthless bargaining that has won seven-figure advances for his clients and reduced publishers to quivering wrecks." He learned to look out for himself growing up on the streets of New York, then sharpened his skills during the nine years he spent working in the book-publishing industry in London and New York.

Victor, the son of Russian-Jewish immigrants, was born in the Queens borough of New York City one week after World War II broke out in Europe. His father Jack ran a camera store, which provided the family with a comfortable lifestyle. However, living in an immigrant neighborhood, young Ed and his brother learned the value of hard work and getting ahead in life early on. Victor was ambitious, in addition to being an excellent student. "My parents were not literary, nor well educated, but they imbued me with a feeling that there was nothing I couldn't do. I grew up perceiving life as a long highway littered with green lights," Victor once told reporter Noreen Taylor of the London *Times.*

After completing high school, Victor went on to earn a bachelor of arts degree summa cum laude from Dartmouth College in 1960. He won a Marshall scholarship in 1961 and used the money to fund his graduate studies at Cambridge University in England, where he earned a master's degree in English literature in 1963. His thesis examined the role of the artist as hero in the works of novelists James Joyce, Henry James, George Moore, and George Gissing.

Victor had gone to Cambridge with a vague plan to teach at Harvard University one day. He told Noreen Taylor, "As a boy, I had this image of becoming an Ivy-League professor, wearing a tweed jacket with leather patches on the elbows, lecturing on Henry James, and driving an old car. Then I won a scholarship to Cambridge and the dream shattered. Those professors were largely sedentary, inward-looking people, not the kind of person I wanted to be."

His career plans having changed, Victor married an English woman, Micheline Samuels, and began looking for work in London. At the time, the city was at the epicenter of a great reawakening of British pop culture; it was the heyday of the Beatles, the Rolling Stones, Carnaby Street, psychedelia, mini-skirts, and hippie flower power. "When I came here, [this] was an austere, post-war society, a black-and-white movie. And then—boom—everything changed. This place became so vibrant, so sexy, so full of life—pop music, photographers—I mean it became really fun," Victor told Geraldine Bell of the *Observer.*

Although he had changed his mind about a career in academia, Victor remained captivated by the world of books and literature. He took an entry-level job with the Osborne Press, a subsidiary of the *Daily Express* newspaper. It was not long before he moved to Weidenfeld and Nicolson publishing house, serving as "a kind of editor and tea boy," he recalled for Geraldine Bell. At first, Victor worked on coffee table book projects, but before long he wanted to be involved with more serious content. When he happened to meet one of the company's owners, George Weidenfeld, in the men's room one day, Victor asked for a promotion.

After that Victor's career progressed quickly. Within three years, he was the company's editorial director. In 1967, he moved on to Jonathan Cape, another London publisher, where he remained for four years. When Victor's marriage ended in 1970, he left book publishing and collaborated with business partners to start a new arts and culture newspaper in London called *Ink.* Unfortunately for Victor, the venture was short-lived and folded after only a few issues. In his interview with Geraldine Bell, he called this the "first major failure" in his career.

In 1973 Victor returned home to New York for the first time in twelve years and went back to work as a senior editor with the Alfred Knopf publishing house. Around the same time, he met and fell in love with New York lawyer Carol Ryan. The pair took a year off to travel around the world. During the trip, Victor decided that he wanted to return to England, where he would be close to his two sons, and that the time had come to settle into a career and make some money. With this in mind, he took a job as a literary agent with London's John Farquharson agency in 1974.

Victor quickly showed a talent for his new line of work. He negotiated a $1.5-million deal for book and movie rights to a now forgotten novel called *The Four Hundred* by Stephen Shephard, a kind of Victorian-era version of the 1973 Oscar-winning con-man movie *The Sting.* This early success set the tone for Victor's career as a literary agent. By late 1976, he was doing so well that he left Farquharson and opened his own agency. "No one believed how frightened I was during those first months. I'd wake up at night in a sweat. I even did my own accounts so no one would be able to pull anything on me," he told Noreen Taylor.

Victor's diligence and hard work paid off. He went on to become one of the world's most high-profile and successful literary agents. He began dividing his time between homes in London and a summer home in the Hamptons, the exclusive ocean-side community in the New York suburb of Long Island.

Now semi-retired, Victor no longer seeks new clients and has turned the day-to-day operations of his agency over to his staff. He devotes himself to favored clients and other initiatives in which he is especially interested. One of these projects was his first book, *The Obvious Diet,* which was inspired by his own lifestyle. Although he is a tall man, Victor, like many people, has always had a tendency to put on weight if he is not careful in his eating habits. "I was getting fat, but—thanks to excellent tailoring—no one knew. After all, I do live it up," Victor told Noreen Taylor. "So I worked out a diet for myself, one so successful that I decided to write a book, to share my discoveries."

Victor reasoned that everyone knows what foods he or she should avoid and what weight-control measures will work best. With that in mind, he advocates a balanced approach to eating: limiting one's intake of high-calorie foods such as pasta, bread, and red meats; exercising moderation at the table; fasting one day per week; and enjoying one "treat day" per week when you can eat anything you like in small amounts. The book also includes recipes, and diet tips from some of Victor's celebrity friends, among them talk-show host Larry King and composer Andrew Lloyd Webber.

A *Publishers Weekly* reviewer wrote, "This diet book delivers exactly what the author promises: practical if unoriginal advice on starting and sticking to a diet from an ordinary person, not a professional." Geraldine Bell, writing in the *Observer* commented that Victor's diet plan involves working with a nutritionist, jumping into an exercise program, and "doesn't read as if it's pitched at mortals." When asked about this, Victor admitted, "[The book] is not written for the average person . . . I wrote it for people like me, who have a lot going on in their lives."

The Obvious Diet sold well enough that Victor was prompted to start a second book. It is about traveling tips, another subject area in which Victor has considerable personal experience.

BIOGRAPHICAL AND CRITICAL SOURCES:

PERIODICALS

Bookseller, October 19, 2001, "Secret Book," p. 12; December 7, 2001, William Boot, "You Either Read Hello! or You're in It," p. 27.

Daily Telegraph, February 1, 2002, Amanda Ursell, "I Saw I'd Lost 12 lbs.—I Burst into Tears"; April 17, 2002, Amanda Ursell, "How to Beat Diet Saboteurs."

Independent (London, England), November 22, 2001, Katy Guest, "Ed Victor—The Ed-Plan Diet," p. 7.

Library Journal, October 1, 2002, Susan B. Hagloch, review of *The Obvious Diet,* p. 121.

New York Post, July 30, 2002, "Diet dish—The Skinny on How Rich Stay So Thin," p. 38.

Observer (London, England), November 25, 2001, Geraldine Bell, "Ed's Slimline Tonic," p. R3; August 11, 2002, "The Browser," p. 19.

Publishers Weekly, July 1, 2001, "Health: The Obvious Diet," p. 50; December 10, 2001, "Talking of Ed Victor," p. 14.

Times (London, England), November 23, 2001, Noreen Taylor, "Victor's Slimline Tonic," p. S7; July 21, 2002, Jasper Gerard, "Tempted by the Obvious Diet: Atticus," p. 15.*

*   *   *

VICTOROFF, Jeffrey Ivan

PERSONAL: Born in the United States. *Education:* Attended University of Chicago; Case Western Reserve University, M.D., 1982. *Hobbies and other interests:* Hiking, bicycling, travel.

ADDRESSES: Office—Department of Neurology, Rancho Los Amigos National Rehabilitation Center, Keck School of Medicine, University of Southern California, 7601 East Imperial Highway, Downey, CA 90277.

CAREER: Medical doctor, 1982—; Keck School of Medicine, University of Southern California, associate professor of clinical neurology.

AWARDS, HONORS: Faculty Scholar Award from Alzheimer's Association.

WRITINGS:

The Wild Type, Crown Publishing (New York, NY), 1989.
Saving Your Brain: The Revolutionary Plan to Boost Brain Power, Improve Memory, and Protect Yourself against Alzheimer's, Bantam Books (New York, NY), 2002.

Contributor to various journals, including *Neurolgy, Archives of Neurolgy,* and *American Journal of Psychiatry.*

SIDELIGHTS: Following in the footsteps of Robin Cook, Somerset Maugham, and a long line of literary-minded medical doctors, University of Southern California neurologist and neuro-psychiatrist Jeff Victoroff is the author of a 1989 suspense novel and a 2002 medical self-help book that offers plain-language advice on how readers can avoid the ravages of Alzheimer's Disease.

After attending graduate school at the University of Chicago and earning his medical degree at Case Western Reserve University in Cleveland, Ohio, Victoroff completed his residency training in neurology and psychiatry at Harvard University. In his spare time, he liked to read, and having a vivid imagination, he decided to try writing a novel. The result was his first book, *The Wild Type.* Conceived in the late 1980s, it is a story about genetic engineering gone awry.

Set against the backdrop of the Maryland National Institute of Health where Victoroff once worked, the story's hero, Doctor Jason McCane, falls in love with fellow medical researcher Jennifer Darien and gets involved in a renegade military man's plot to replace humanity with a genetically engineered superspecies of his own creation. Reviewer Newgate Callendar of the *New York Times* described *The Wild Type* as "a mixture of the mad-scientist novel coupled with Tarzan of the Apes." In *School Library Journal,* reviewer Susan Penny wrote that "Victoroff has created characters and a setting . . . that will draw readers into the plot," and added: "Robin Cook fans will want to take note of this author's first novel." A *Publishers Weekly* reviewer expressed reservations about the credibility of the plot, but concluded that *The Wild Type* is "smoothly paced as it builds to an exciting conclusion."

Victoroff's second book, *Saving Your Brain: The Revolutionary Plan to Boost Brain Power, Improve Memory, and Protect Yourself against Alzheimer's,* is a product of his research into the effects of Aging-related Neurodegeneration of the Alzheimer's Type (ARNAT), the results of which he has also reported in various professional journals. Statistics indicate that ailments associated with aging-related brain degeneration are now the fourth most common cause of death in North America, and the rate is rising. In *Saving Your Brain,* Victoroff explains that most elderly people develop preconditions for the onset of ARNAT as part of the aging process and addresses why some people develop Alzheimer's and related diseases while others do not. A number of variables, including genetics, the environment, and diet, play a part in this phenomenon, and Victoroff offers some practical advice on how the average person can help keep his or her brain healthy by making some simple lifestyle changes. Among Victoroff'suggestions are eating a healthy diet, exercising both the body and the mind, reducing stress, controlling blood pressure and cholesterol, and reducing exposure to neurotoxins, especially aluminum, which is found in everything from deodorants to drinking water.

Natural Health reviewer Judy Bass wrote, "What's intriguing about this engaging book is its central argument, which is that brain deterioration is not inevitable." *Library Journal* reviewer Karen McNally credited *Saving Your Brain* for being an authoritative yet very readable look at "the evolution and function of the human brain and the many things that can damage the delicate balances that enable us to think and function." Writing in *Bookpage,* Albert L. Huebner praised Victoroff for making a complex subject accessible to the average reader. "His presentation is by no means dry, precisely because the science is so fascinating," Huebner wrote. Reviewer Susan Pickens of the *Decatur Daily* concluded, "The author clearly states that the book is not intended to substitute for the advice of a good, competent doctor, but is a tool to enable the individual to become a better partner with the doctor in making the best choices."

BIOGRAPHICAL AND CRITICAL SOURCES:

PERIODICALS

BookPage, July 2002, Albert L. Huebner, "The Aging Brain: Act Now So You Don't Lose Your Mind," p. 18.
Kirkus Reviews, December 1, 1988, review of *The Wild Type,* p. 1705.
Library Journal, July, 2002, Karen McNally, "The Memory Bible: An Innovative Strategy for Keeping Your Brain Young", p. 109.
Natural Health, August 2002, Judy Boot, "Discover the Way to True Satisfaction," pp. 90-91.
New York Times, May 7, 1989, Newgate Callendar, review of *The Wild Type,* p. 18.
Publishers Weekly, December 16, 1988, review of *The Wild Type,* p. 70; June 3, 2002, review of *Saving Your Brain,* p. 86.
School Library Journal, September 1989, Susan Penny, review of *The Wild Type,* pp. 284-285.

ONLINE

Decatur Daily Online, http://www.decaturdaily.com/ (July 28, 2002), Sandra Pickens, "How Your Brain Works and How to Keep It Working."*

*   *   *

VILLA, Dana R.

PERSONAL: Male. *Education:* Princeton University, Ph.D., 1987.

ADDRESSES: Office—Department of Political Science, University of California—Santa Barbara, CA 93106-9420. *E-mail*—villa@polsci.ucsb.edu.

CAREER: University of California—Santa Barbara, associate professor of political theory. Previously worked at Amherst College, Amherst, MA.

WRITINGS:

(Editor, with Austin Sarat) *Liberal Modernism and Democratic Individuality: George Kateb and the Practices of Politics,* Princeton University Press (Princeton, NJ), 1996.
Arendt and Heidegger: The Fate of the Political, Princeton University Press (Princeton, NJ), 1996.
Politics, Philosophy, Terror: Essays on the Thought of Hannah Arendt, Princeton University Press (Princeton, NJ), 1999.
(With Joke J. Hermsen) *The Judge and the Spectator: Hannah Arendt's Political Philosophy,* Peeters (Leuven, Belgium), 1999.
(Editor) *The Cambridge Companion to Hannah Arendt,* Cambridge University Press (New York, NY), 2000.
Socratic Citizenship, Princeton University Press (Princeton, NJ), 2001.

Contributor to journals and periodicals, including *Political Theory, Constellations, American Political Science Review,* and *Revue Internationale de Philosophie.*

SIDELIGHTS: Dana R. Villa, a career academic, has published books and articles focusing on the political theorists Hannah Arendt, George Kateb and Socrates. Villa works as an associate professor at the University of California—Santa Barbara's political science department. He teaches courses on political theory and the people who helped to create it.

His first published work was 1996's *Liberal Modernism and Democratic Individuality: George Kateb and the Practices of Politics,* which he edited with Austin Sarat. The book consists of a group of essays, in which critics, colleagues and friends of liberal thinker George Kateb analyze the political theories Kateb spent his lifetime creating. Editors Villa and Sarat include an introduction to Kateb's theories as well as an index. A reviewer for *Perspectives on Political Science* called the essays "uniformly interesting and often provocative."

Also in 1996, Villa wrote *Arendt and Heidegger: The Fate of the Political.* In this book, Villa focuses on three issues: Arendt's political action theory, the areas in which Arendt and Martin Heidegger, former lovers, converge, and the areas in which the two political theorists disagree. He argues that, generally, Arendt's philosophies grew mainly out of Heidegger's ideas. Villa includes views from Nietzsche and Aristotle, as well as other theorists who contributed to Arendt's political theories. "Finally a book about Arendt and Heidegger that one can read with intellectual benefit," commented Fred Dallmayr in *American Political Science Review.*

In his 1999 *Politics, Philosophy, Terror: Essays on the Thought of Hannah Arendt,* Villa examines Arendt's familiarity with Leo Strauss, Jürgen Habermas, Socrates, Nietzsche, and Heidegger. Villa writes that Arendt's experience of alienated and lonely people inspired her writing. This collection of nine essays addresses Arendt's ideas of evil and contend that her arguments don't excuse Holocaust participants as players in a play they couldn't control, but that they should be responsible for their sins. Villa argues that active citizenry best protects against evil, better than a focus on philosophy or morality. *Journal of Politics* reviewer Elizabeth Brake called the book "lucid, well-argued, and interesting,"

During the same year, Villa coauthored *The Judge and the Spectator: Hannah Arendt's Political Philosophy* with Joke J. Hermsen. This time, Arendt's political ideas and thinking are highlighted, focusing on some of the moral and philosophical questions from which she extracted her political theories.

In 2000, Villa edited *The Cambridge Companion to Hannah Arendt,* one in a series. The book is a group of fourteen articles organized into six topics: totalitarianism, political evil, political action and freedom, Arendt and the ancient thinkers, revolution, and philosophy. With a focus on the controversy of Arendt's political theories, Villa includes Arendt's critiques of democratic institutions and the relationship she saw between politics and philosophy, as well as a chronology of Arendt's life and a large bibliography. Some of the writings in this work are important additions to political theory, noted S. D. Jacobitti in a *Choice* review, and the book is, overall, "an outstanding group of new essays," he noted.

Villa broadens his subject in his 2001 book, *Socratic Citizenship.* In this work, Villa agrees with scholars' opinions that public life lacks civic involvement, and

argues that Socrates' ideas on politics are the base for the five political theorists in his book: Nietzsche, Max Weber, Arendt, Strauss, and J. S. Mill. Socratic politics, he says, are accessible to everyone. Villa contends that Socrates demonstrated how intellectuality and morality can work together, and that they, as a team, are important to politics. He reminds readers that Socrates stressed thinking and morals over political activism, patriotism and a strict adherence to law. *Choice* reviewer P. Coby noted that the book's chapters "bristle with insight," and commented that "Villa offers an exceptional book, well written and instructive at every point."

BIOGRAPHICAL AND CRITICAL SOURCES:

PERIODICALS

American Political Science Review, December, 1996, Fred Dallmayr, review of *Arendt and Heidegger: The Fate of the Political,* pp. 901-903; December, 1997, David Weinstein, review of *Liberal Modernism and Democratic Individuality,* p. 953.

Choice, September, 2001, S. D. Jacobitti, review of *The Cambridge Companion to Hannah Arendt,* p. 204; March, 2002, P. Coby, review of *Socratic Citizenship,* p. 1321.

Ethics, April, 1997, Mary G. Dietz, review of *Arendt and Heidegger,* p. 552; January, 2002, Mark A. Garnett, review of *Politics, Philosophy, Terror: Essays on the Thought of Hannah Arendt,* p. 409.

Journal of Politics, May, 2001, Elizabeth Brake, review of *Politics, Philosophy, Terror: Essays on the Thought of Hannah Arendt,* pp. 661-664.

Perspectives on Political Science, summer, 1997, review of *Liberal Modernism and Democratic Individuality: George Kateb and the Practices of Politics,* p. 184.

Review of Metaphysics, June, 1998, Tom Rockmore, review of *Arendt and Heidegger,* p. 966.*

* * *

VILLAGGIO, Paolo 1932-

PERSONAL: Born December 31, 1932, in Genoa, Liguria, Italy.

ADDRESSES: Agent—c/o Author Mail, Mondadori Libri, Via Mondadori 15, 37131 Verona, Italy.

CAREER: Actor, author and screenwriter. Actor in films, including *Mangiala* (also known as *Eat It*), 1968; (as Eddy) *I quattro del pater noster* (also known as *In the Name of the Father*), 1969; *Il terribile ispettore*, 1969; *Pensando a te*, Titanus, 1969; *La torta in cielo* (also known as *Cake in the Sky*), 1970; (as Thorz) *Brancaleone alle crociate* (also known as *Brancaleone at the Crusades*), Titanus, 1970; (as Agostino Antoniucci) *Senza famiglia, nullatenenti cercano affetto* (also known as *Without Family*), 1972; *Beati i ricchi*, 1972; (as Don Albino Moncalieri) *Che c'entriamano noi con la rivoluzione?* (also known as *What Am I Doing in the Middle of the Revolution?*), 1973; (as CIA agent) *Non toccare la donna bianca* (also known as *Don't Touch the White Woman!*), Video Search of Miami, 1974; (as Giovanni Bonfiglio) *Sistemo l'America e torno,* (also known as *Black Is Beautiful* and *I Fix America and Return*), 1974; (as Checco "Biancone" Coniglio/the pimp) *La mazurka del barone, della santa e del fico fiorone*, 1974; *Alla mia cara mamma nel giorno del suo compleanno*, 1974; (as Ugo Fantozzi) *Fantozzi* (also known as *White Collar Blues*), 1975; (as Dante Bompazzi) *Di che segno sei?* 1975; (as Robi) *Il Signore Robinson, monstruosa storia d'amore e d'avventure* (also known as *Mr. Robinson*), 1976; (as Schmidt) *Signore e signori, buonanotte* (also known as *Goodnight, Ladies and Gentlemen*), 1976; (as Gio Batta/Superman Italiano) *Quelle strane occasioni* (also known as *Strange Occasion*), 1976; (as Ugo Fantozzi) *Il secondo tragico Fantozzi*, 1976; *Tre tigri contro tre tigri* (also known as *Three Tigers against Three Tigers*), 1977; (as Guido) *Il belpaese*, 1977; (as Della Spignola) *Io tigro, tu tigri, egli tigra*, 1978; (as Kranz) *Professor Kranz tedesco di Germania*, Gold Film, 1978; (as Wilson/Arturo) *Dove vai in vacanza?* (also known as *Where Are You Going on Holiday?*), 1978; (as Rag. Arturo De Fanti) *Rag. Arturo de Fanti, bancario—precario* (also known as *The Precarious Bank Teller*), 1979; (as Dr. Jekyll) *Dottor Jekyll e gentile signora* (also known as *Dr. Jekyll Likes Them Hot* and *Jekyll Junior*), Video Search of Miami, 1979; (as Marchese di Forlipopoli) *La Locandiera* (also known as *Mirandolina*), 1980; (as Ugo Fantozzi) *Fantozzi contro tutti* (also known as *Fantozzi against the Wind*), 1980; (as Giandomenico Fracchia/la Belva Umana) *Fracchia la belva umana*, 1981; (as Don Pepe Alletto) *Il Turno*, 1981; *Pappa e ciccia*, 1982; (as Leo) *Bonnie e Clyde all'italiana* (also known as *Bonnie and Clyde Italian Style*), 1982; (as Paolo Coniglio) *Sogni mostruosamente proibiti*, 1983; (as Ugo Fantozzi) *Fantozzi subisce ancora*, 1983; (as Gino Sciaccaluga) *A tu per tu*, 1984; (as Ugo Fantozzi) *Superfantozzi*, 1985; (as Paolo Casarotti) *I Pompieri*, 1986; (as Giandomenico Fracchia) *Fracchia contro Dracula*, 1985; (as Robot) *Grandi Magazzini* (also known as *Department Store*), 1986; (as Dalmazio Siraghi) *Scuola di ladri—parte seconda*, 1987; *Roba di ricchi*, 1987; (as Gildo Morelli) *Rimini Rimini*, 1987; (as Paolo Casalotti) *Missione Eroica. I pompiere 2*, 1987; (as Ugo Maria Volpone) *Il Volpone* (also known as *The Big Fox*), 1988; (as Ugo Fantozzi) *Fantozzi va in pensione*, 1988; (as Doctor Zappi) *Come è dura l'avventura*, 1988; (as Gonella) *La voce della luna* (also known as *The Voice of the Moon*), 1989; (as Paolo Ciottoli) *Ho vinto la lotteria di Capodanno*, 1989; (as Ugo Fantozzi) *Fantozzi alla riscossa* (also known as *Fantozzi colpisce ancora*), 1990; (as Paolo) *Le comiche* (also known as *The Comics*), 1990; (as Paolo) *Le Comiche 2* (also known as *The Comics 2*), 1992; (as Marco Sperelli) *Io speriamo che me la cavo* (also known as *Ciao, Professore!* and *Me Let's Hope I Make It*), Miramax, 1993; (as Colonel Procolo) *Il segreto del bosco vecchio* (also known as *The Secret of the Old Woods*), 1993; (as Ugo Fantozzi) *Fantozzi in paradiso* (also known as *Fantozzi in Heaven*), 1993; *Le nuove comiche*, 1994; (as Dieci) *Cari fottutissimi amici* (also known as *Dear Goddamned Friends*), 1994; (as Billy Bolla) *Palla di neve* (also known as *Snowball*), 1995; (as Sergio Colombo) *Io no spik inglish*, 1995; (as Loris Bianchi) *Camerieri* (also known as *Waiters*), 1995; (as Ugo Fantozzi) *Fantozzi—Il ritorno*, Italian International Film, 1996; *Il caso Kappa* (also known as *The Strange Case of Mr. K*), 1996; (as Sergio Colombo) *Banzai*, Italian International Film, 1997; (as Gino) *Un bugiardo in paradiso*, Cecchi Gori Group, 1998; (as Gino) *Per motivi di famiglia*, 1998; (as Ugo Fantozzi) *Fantozzi 2000-la clonazione*, 1999; (as Guiseppe De Metrio) *Azzurro*, 2000; (as Doctor Cagnano) *Denti* (also known as *Teeth*), Cecchi Gori Distribuzione, 2000; (as Grossvater) *Heidi*, 2001; (as Gaio) *San Giovanni—L'apocalisse* (also known as *The Apocalypse*), 2002; and (as Don Eugenio) *Hermano*, 2003.

Actor in television programs, including *Sogni e bisogni* (miniseries), 1984; *Angelo di seconda classe* (series), 1999; (as Giovanni) *Carabinieri* (series), 2002; and (as Don Abbondio) *Renzo e Lucia* (made-for-television movie), 2003. Director of film *Fantozzi contro tutti*, 1980.

WRITINGS:

NOVELS

Fantozzi, Rizzoli (Milan, Italy), 1971.

Il secondo tragico libro di Fantozzi, Rizzoli (Milan, Italy), 1974.

Le lettere di Fantozzi, Rizzoli (Milan, Italy), 1976.

Fantozzi contro tutti, Rizzoli (Milan, Italy), 1979.

Fantozzi subisce ancora, Rizzoli (Milan, Italy), 1983.

Caro direttore, ci scrivo: Rag. Ugo Fantozzi: lettere del tragico ragioniere, Mondadori (Milan, Italy), 1993.

Fantozzi saluta e se ne va: le ultime lettere del rag. Ugo Fantozzi, Mondadori (Milan, Italy), 1994.

Vita, morte e miracoli di un pezzo di merda, Mondadori (Milan, Italy), 2002.

SCREENPLAYS

(With Franco Castellano, Sergio Corbucci, and Giuseppe Moccia) *Il Signor Robinson, mostruosa storia d'amore e d'avventure* also known as *Mr. Robinson*), 1976.

(With Leonardo Benvenuti, Piero De Bernardi, and Luciano Salce) *Il secondo tragico Fantozzi,* 1976.

(With Franco Castellano, Giuseppe Moccia, and Luciano Salce) *Il Belpaese,* 1977.

(With others) *Superfantozzi,* 1985.

(With Franco Marotta, Neri Parenti, and Laura Toscano) *Fracchia contro Dracula,* 1985.

(With others) *Fantozzi alla riscossa* (also known as *Fantozzi colpisce ancora*), 1990.

(With others) *Fantozzi in paradiso* (also known as *Fantozzi in Heaven*), 1993.

(With others) *Fantozzi—Il ritorno,* 1996.

ADAPTATIONS: Villaggio's novel *Fantozzi* was adapted into a screenplay by Leonardo Benvenuti, Piero de Bernardi, and Luciano Salce.

SIDELIGHTS: Italian comic actor Paolo Villaggio is best known for creating the character Ugo Fantozzi, a hapless, put-upon office worker. Fantozzi first appeared in a novel of the same name by Villaggio in 1971, and four years later, a low-budget film based on the novel and starring Villaggio as Fantozzi became a surprise hit and spawned an ongoing series. Throughout the Fantozzi films and novels, Fantozzi struggles against the myriad insults of life but never really overcomes them, giving the stories a biting sense of black humor.

BIOGRAPHICAL AND CRITICAL SOURCES:

BOOKS

Steward, John, *Italian Film: A Who's Who,* McFarland & Co. (Jefferson, NC), 1994.

PERIODICALS

Christian Science Monitor, February 2, 1995, David Sterritt, review of *Ciao, Professore!* p. 10.

New York Times, January 6, 1995, Caryn James, review of *Ciao, Professore!* pp. B10, D15.

Variety, December 3, 1980, review of *La locandiera,* p. 26; December 17, 1980, review of *Fantozzi contro tutti,* pp. 17-18; December 26, 1984, review of *A tu per tu,* p. 14; January 17, 2000, Deborah Young, review of *Fantozzi 2000: The Cloning,* p. 53; September 18, 2000, David Rooney, review of *Teeth,* p. 36.

ONLINE

Blockbuster.com, http://www.blockbuster.com/ (April 21, 2003), Clarke Fountain, review of *Fantozzi.*

ReelViews, http://movie-reviews.colossus.net/ (April 21, 2003), James Berardinelli, review of *Ciao, Professore!**

W-Z

WALKER, Theodore J. 1915-2003

OBITUARY NOTICE—See index for *CA* sketch: Born January 7, 1915, in Great Falls, MT; died of complications from a stroke February 28, 2003, in Seattle, WA. Biologist and author. Walker was a noted oceanographer and marine biologist who was best known for his research on whales, though he was interested in all types of wildlife. He received his B.A. from Montana State University in 1938, his M.S. from the University of Oklahoma in 1940, and, after serving in the U.S. Navy as a lieutenant during World War II, his Ph.D. from the University of Wisconsin—Madison in 1947. A research oceanographer with the renowned Scripps Institute of Oceanography from 1948 to 1971, Walker was also a naturalist for the U.S. Park Service for many years. He resigned from Scripps in order to live for seven months on Baranof Island in Alaska. Here he conducted research that was eventually published in his *Red Salmon, Brown Bear: The Story of an Alaskan Lake, Based on the Experiences of Dr. Theodore J. Walker* (1971), which was later adapted as the documentary *Alaskan Wilderness Lake,* a film that was nominated for the Oscar. Walker, who discovered that whales feed on plankton during their migrations, was also the author of *Whale Primer: With Special Attention to the California Gray Whale* (1962; revised edition, 1979), and of film scripts and article contributions to *National Geographic* magazine. He also served as a consultant for the Jacque Cousteau film *Desert Whale.*

OBITUARIES AND OTHER SOURCES:

PERIODICALS

Los Angeles Times, March 13, 2003, p. B15.
Seattle Post-Intelligencer, March 8, 2003, p. B4.

WARD, Lester Frank 1841-1913

PERSONAL: Born June 18, 1841 (some sources say 1839), in Joliet, IL; died April 18, 1913, in Washington, DC; son of Justus (a mechanic) and Silence (Rolph) Ward; married Elisabeth Carolyn Vought (deceased, 1872), married Rosamond Asenath Simons, March 6, 1873; children: one son (died in infancy). *Education:* Attended Susquehanna Collegiate Institute at Towanda, 1861-62; Columbia College (now George Washington University), A.B., 1869, LL.B, 1871, A.M., 1873.

CAREER: Paleontologist, sociologist, educator, and writer. U.S. Treasury Department, member of staff, 1865-81; U.S. Geological Survey, geologist, 1883-92, paleontologist, 1892-1906; Brown University, professor of sociology, 1906-13. *Military service:* Union Army, 1862-64; discharged due to wounds received at Chancellorsville.

MEMBER: Institut International de Sociologie (president, 1903), American Sociological Society (president, 1906-1907).

WRITINGS:

Haeckel's Genesis of Man; or, History of the Development of the Human Race, E. Stern & Co. (Philadelphia, PA), 1879.
Guide to the Flora of Washington and Vicinity, Government Printing Office (Washington, DC), 1881.

Incomplete Adaption as Illustrated by the History of Sex in Plants, [Philadelphia, PA], 1881.

Politico-Social Functions, [Philadelphia, PA], 1881.

Dynamic Sociology, D. Appleton and Company (New York, NY), 1883, reprinted, Greenwood Press (New York, NY), 1968.

Sketch of Paleobotany, Government Printing Office (Washington, DC), 1885.

Synopsis of the Flora of the Laramie Group, Government Printing Office (Washington, DC), 1886.

The Geological Distribution of Fossil Plants, 1888.

The Course of Biologic Evolution, [Washington, DC], 1890.

Neo-Darwinism and Neo-Lamarckism, Press of Gedney & Roberts (Washington, DC), 1891.

The Psychic Factors of Civilization, Ginn & Company (Boston, MA), 1893.

The Psychologic Basis of Social Economics, American Academy of Political and Social Science (Philadelphia, PA), 1893.

A Monistic Theory of Mind, [Chicago, IL], 1894.

Status of the Mind Problem, [Washington, DC], 1894.

The Political Ethics of Herbert Spencer, American Academy of Political and Social Science (Philadelphia, PA), 1894.

The Nomenclature Question, [New York, NY], 1895.

Outlines of Sociology, Macmillan (New York, NY), 1898.

Report on the Petrified Forests of Arizona, Government Printing Office (Washington, DC), 1900.

Pure Sociology, Macmillan (New York, NY), 1903, reprinted, A. M. Kelley (New York, NY), 1970.

(With James Quayle Dealey) *A Text-Book of Sociology,* Macmillan (New York, NY), 1905.

Status of the Mesozoic Floras of the United States, Government Printing Office (Washington, DC), 1905.

Lester Frank Ward, selected with an introduction by Israel Gerver, Crowell (New York, NY), 1963.

Glimpses of the Cosmos, edited by Emily Palmer Cape, G. P. Putnam's Sons (New York, NY), 1913-1918.

The Ward-Gumplowicz Correspondence: 1897-1913, translated and with an introduction by Aleksander Gella, Essay Press (New York, NY), 1971.

Applied Sociology, Arno Press (New York, NY), 1974.

Editor of *American Journal of Sociology.*

SIDELIGHTS: A U.S. Civil War veteran, autodidact, scientist, and sociologist, Lester Frank Ward "is one of American sociology's most colorful characters," it was stated in a biographical profile in *World of Sociology.*

Born in 1841 (some sources say 1839) in Joliet, Illinois, Ward was the youngest of ten children. His father, Justus, "was a mechanic of an inventive turn of mind," and his mother, Silence, was the "daughter of a clergyman," and "is said to have been a woman of scholarly tendencies and versatile accomplishments," according to James Quayle Dealey in the *Dictionary of American Biography.* Ward's early childhood was spent in Illinois and Iowa, "in close contact with nature under frontier conditions," Dealey remarked.

Early in life, Ward developed a keen appreciation for education. "He considered learning to be the chief mechanism for self-improvement and progress," it was noted in the *World of Sociology* profile. However, his family's working-class existence meant there was little opportunity or resources for a formal education. Ward's early "formal schooling was scrappy at best, and he was often required to contribute to the family income through part-time mill work or farm labor," wrote Wilfred M. McClay in *Society.* "Yet somehow Ward became fixed with an iron determination to better his lot in life and had a growing conviction that education was the key to such self-betterment." As part of this steadfast determination, Ward taught himself several subjects, including five classical languages and mathematics; his diary was written in French as a linguistic exercise.

"It is not hard to guess that Ward's ambition was powered by a burning desire to escape his hardscrabble origins," McClay remarked. "To put it mildly, he was not held back by attachment to family," having little or no affection toward his parents. Ward cared little for genealogy or family history, and to him, "nothing was more unpleasant than looking backward." Ward believed that his liberation from poverty and "a defining milieu he despised" would depend on "the firm resolution of Ward's own will," McClay remarked. "His task would require of him the single-minded strength of the self-made man, who could not take the time, or the risk, of backward glances. Whatever his view of individualism in the realm of social ideas, he was personally committed to an ethos of self-propelled equal opportunity, in which a man ought to get just as far in life as his abilities and his tenacity would take him—no less and no more," McClay wrote.

In 1861 Ward began the first of four terms at the Susquehanna Collegiate Institute in Towanda, Pennsylvania. "But in August of 1862 he found himself drifting without sufficient funds to continue his education," McClay wrote, "and so the twenty-one-year-old Ward finally enlisted as a private in the 141st Regiment of the Pennsylvania Volunteers." Ward was seriously wounded in combat during the Battle of Chancellorsville in May, 1963, and he was discharged in November, 1864.

Ward turned his attention toward government work in Washington, securing a clerkship at the Treasury Department, and remained in government service for the next forty years. His government employment allowed him to finally pursue a formal education, and he took night classes at Columbian College (now George Washington University), eventually earning A.B., LL.B, and A.M. degrees.

In 1875 Ward was invited to join a botanical survey in Utah and to prepare a paleobotanical collection for Philadelphia's 1876 Centennial Exposition. This work eventually led to Ward's employment with the U.S. Geological Survey in 1881. He was appointed geologist in 1883, and paleontologist in 1892. Ward contributed numerous papers and studies to the fields of the natural sciences while pursuing intellectual interests in biology, anthropology, psychology, and sociology.

Ward's professional exposure to science led him to the theories of August Comte and Charles Darwin, whose ideas he began incorporating into his sociological work. "Knowledge, he claimed, not only has the capacity to expand happiness but prevent crises as well," it was noted in the *World of Sociology* profile. "Ward concluded that disruptions, such as labor strikes and populist movements, could be prevented in the public were educated. Evolution, controlled through education, would eliminate uncontrolled social revolution. Ward began his first formal work in sociology with these ideas in mind."

That work, 1883's *Dynamic Sociology,* is considered among Ward's greatest contributions to the development of sociology. Written over fourteen years, *Dynamic Sociology* established Ward as the founder of the field of sociology. In *Dynamic Sociology* Ward conceived of "a world driven by social forces," it was stated in the *World of Sociology* profile. "Biological evolution was the conceptual fulcrum on which all social forces operate. Organic matter, Ward argued,

including the human mind, is shaped by centuries of progressive evolution. But human beings, through their intelligence, can understand the laws of nature and statistically use them. As the title of his book attests, society and social forces exist in reciprocal relationship."

In his sociological work, "Ward sought to give a strongly monistic and evolutionary interpretation to social development," Dealey remarked. Ward argued that "the human mind is a great factor in evolution," and that human intellect, "when rightly informed with scientific truth, enables the individual or the social group to plan intelligently for future development." Ward maintained his strong belief that education was the key to improvement of the self and of society, and advocated that the government eliminate harsh poverty and develop a broad national systems for education that would accommodate the genius on one hand and the more ordinary minds on the other.

Other of Ward's works, including *The Psychic Factors in Civilization, Pure Sociology,* and *Applied Sociology,* were "efforts to elaborate on the evolution of humanity," it was stated in the *World of Sociology* profile. The first of these books centered on psychic human development, whereas the other two focused on issues of societal growth and control.

Ward's work in sociology was so influential that he was elected president of the American Sociological Socity in 1906 and 1907, even though he did not hold an academic position at the time of his election. However, in 1906, Ward was appointed professor of sociology at Brown University, in large part because of his prodigious output and well-received writing. Ward died in Washington, D.C., on April 18, 1913.

BIOGRAPHICAL AND CRITICAL SOURCES:

BOOKS

Dictionary of American Biography, American Council of Learned Societies, 1928-1936.
Encyclopedia of World Biography, 2nd edition, Gale (Detroit, MI), 1998.
Garraty, John A., and Jerome L. Sternstein, editors, *Encyclopedia of American Biography,* HarperCollins (New York, NY), 1996.

Hart, James D., *Oxford Companion to American Literature,* 6th edition, Oxford University Press (New York, NY), 1995.

Herzberg, Max J., *The Reader's Encyclopedia of American Literature,* Thomas Y. Crowell Co. (New York, NY), 1962.

Johnson, Rossiter, editor, *The Twentieth Century Biographical Dictionary of Notable Americans,* Biographical Society (Boston, MA), 1904, reprinted, Gale (Detroit, MI), 1968.

Johnson, Thomas H., *The Oxford Companion to American History,* Oxford University Press (New York, NY), 1966.

Mitchell, G. Duncan, editor, *A Dictionary of Sociology,* Aldine Publishing Co. (Chicago, IL), 1968.

National Cyclopaedia of American Biography, Volume 13, James T. White & Co. (New York, NY), 1906, reprinted, University Microfilms (Ann Arbor, MI), 1967-1971.

Page, Charles Hunt, *Class and American Sociology: From Ward to Ross,* Octagon Books (New York, NY), 1964.

Palmisano, Joseph M., editor, *World of Sociology,* Gale (Detroit, MI), 2001.

Preston, Wheeler, *American Biographies,* Gale (Detroit, MI), 1974.

Scott, Clifford H., *Lester Frank Ward,* Twayne (Boston, MA), 1976.

Steele, Henry, editor, *Lester Ward and the Welfare State,* Bobbs-Merrill (Indianapolis, IN), 1967.

Wallace, W. Stewart, compiler, *A Dictionary of North American Authors Deceased before 1950,* Ryerson Press (Toronto, Ontario, Canada), 1951; reprinted, Gale (Detroit, MI), 1968.

Wilson, James Grant and John Fiske, editors, *Appleton's Cyclopaedia of American Biography,* D. Appleton & Co (New York, NY), 1888-1889, reprinted, Gale (Detroit, MI), 1968.

Wood Clement, *The Substance of the Sociology of Lester F. Ward,* The Vanguard Press (New York, NY), 1930.

PERIODICALS

Gender & Society, April, 1999, Barbara Finley, "Lester Frank Ward as Sociologist of Gender," p. 251.

Society, May-June, 1995, Wilfred M. McClay, "The Socialization of Desire," pp. 65-73.

ONLINE

Tri-County Genealogy & History Web Site, http://www.rootsweb.com/ (May 4, 2003), Guy Abell, "Lester Frank Ward: Bradford County's Aristotle."*

WARD, Stuart

PERSONAL: Married; wife's name, Lill; children: Oscar. *Education:* University of Queensland, B.A. (history); University of Sydney, Ph.D. *Hobbies and other interests:* Playing guitar.

ADDRESSES: Home—London, England. *Office*— Menzies Centre for Australian Studies, King's College, University of London, London WC2R 2LS, England.

CAREER: Professor and writer. Taught at European University Institute, Florence, Italy, and University of Southern Denmark; University of Greenland, visiting lecturer; Menzies Centre for Australian Studies at King's College, London, lecturer in history.

WRITINGS:

(Editor, with R. T. Griffiths) *Courting the Common Market,* 1996.

(Editor) *British Culture and the End of Empire,* Manchester University Press (New York, NY), 2001.

Australia and the British Embrace: The Demise of the Imperial Ideal, Melbourne University Press (Carlton, Victoria, Australia), 2001.

WORK IN PROGRESS: Discordant Communities; Australia, Britain, and the Integration of Europe, to be published by Melbourne University Press.

SIDELIGHTS: Stuart Ward, a history professor at the Menzies Centre for Australian Studies at King's College, London, is an academic whose writings have focused on British and Australian history. Ward grew up on the Queensland coast in Australia. He earned a B.A. in history from the University of Queensland and then went on to University of Sydney, where he earned his Ph.D. Fluent in several languages, Ward has taught at a variety of universities in Europe,, including the European University Institute in Florence, the University of Southern Denmark and King's College, London. He has also lectured at the University of Greenland.

Ward's book *Australia and the British Embrace: The Demise of the Imperial Ideal* takes a new look at the time when Australian culture no longer stemmed from being British. Ward challenges other accounts that claim earlier dates for this shift, according to John Ramsden in *Times Literary Supplement*. Instead, Ward argues that Britain, rather than Australia, initiated the separation of the two countries by not being forthright with Australia about its intentions for joining the European Economic Community in 1957. Although Britain did not join until 1973, Australia had already refocused its trade and foreign policy toward the Pacific.

Ward also edited and contributed to *British Culture and the End of Empire*. This book asserts that the effect of decolonisation was felt as strongly in Britain as it was in its colonies. Ward contends that the fall of the British empire shocked British popular culture.

BIOGRAPHICAL AND CRITICAL SOURCES:

PERIODICALS

History Today, November, 2001, Anne Pointer, review of *British Culture and the End of Empire*, p. 57.
Times Literary Supplement, May, 10, 2002, John Ramsden, review of *Australia and the British Embrace*, p. 13.*

*   *   *

WARE, Jim (Clark) 1953-

PERSONAL: Born May 31, 1953, in Los Angeles, CA; son of Morris C. (a lithographer) and Margie (Lawson) Ware; married Joan E. McClamont, 1975; children: Alison, Megan, Bridget, Ian, Brittany, Callum. *Education:* University of California-Los Angeles, B.A., 1976; Fuller Theological Seminary, M.A., 1979. *Religion:* "None—I'm a Christian." *Hobbies and other interests:* Folk and traditional music, especially Irish.

ADDRESSES: Home—1420 North Chestnut Street, Colorado Springs, CO 80907. *Office*—Focus on the Family, Colorado Springs, CO 80996. *Agent*—Chip MacGregor, Alive Communications, 7680 Goddard Street, Ste. 200, Colorado Springs, CO 80920. *E-mail*—oliver5930@aol.com.

CAREER: Author. First Presbyterian Church of Hollywood, Hollywood, CA, maintenance crew, 1974-86; Focus on the Family, Colorado Springs, CO, staff writer, 1986—.

WRITINGS:

Crazy Jacob (children's fiction), Bethany House (Minneapolis, MN), 2000.
Dangerous Dreams (children's fiction), Bethany House (Minneapolis, MN), 2001.
The Prophet's Kid (children's fiction), Bethany House (Minneapolis, MN), 2001.
(With Kurt Bruner) *Finding God in the Lord of the Rings* (inspirational), Tyndale House (Wheaton, IL), 2001.
The God of Fairy Tales, WaterBrook Press (Colorado Springs, CO), 2002.

WORK IN PROGRESS: Canyon Quest (fiction).

SIDELIGHTS: Jim Ware's love of story began as a young child. He read all the classics—*Tom Sawyer, Huckleberry Finn, King Arthur and His Knights of the Round Table, Robinson Crusoe, The Merry Adventures of Robin Hood*—as well as Greek and Norse myths retold by Padraic Colum. He also loved poetry and music, and—by the age of twelve, guitar in hand—established a band with some friends. In the late 1960s, their music style went from Lennon and McCartney to the spiritual sounds encompassed by the Jesus Movement.

After three years at California State University studying English and education, Ware's focus switched and he graduated from the University of California—Los Angeles with a degree in classics. Following his marriage, he entered Fuller Theological Seminary, specializing in Hebrew, Aramaic, and Ugaritic languages. After graduation, to support his growing family, he joined the maintenance crew at the First Presbyterian Church of Hollywood, where he also taught youth and adult Bible classes. In 1986 he became a staff writer with the multimedia Christian ministry Focus on the Family. When the organization moved to Colorado, Ware and his family moved with them.

It was in association with Focus on the Family that Ware authored his books. His love of story, of the Bible, of history, and—of course—of children, inspire his works. In the book *Crazy Jacob,* Jacob is possessed by demons, and his son, eleven-year-old Andrew, watches as Jesus drives the demons out and turns them into swine. Crystal Faris, in *School Library Journal,* commented that, while Evangelical Christian principles are apparent in the story, they are not overwhelming.

In *The Prophet's Kid,* Shub is the son of the prophet Isaiah. Tired of being the prophet's kid he and some rebellious friends sneak out to catch a glimpse of idol worship ceremonies and discover they are not all fun and games.

"*Finding God in the Lord of the Rings* has nearly twenty applications to the Christian lifestyle, all drawn directly from Tolkien's *Silmarillion, Hobbit,* and *Lord of the Rings,*" observed a reviewer for *Fool of a Took* Web site. Each chapter illustrates a concept from Tolkien's series, explains the Christian message behind the concept, then provides relevant Bible verses. "Most of the themes illustrated here . . . will already have been obvious to Christian readers with the intelligence needed to read through the entire trilogy," noted a *Publishers Weekly* reviewer. A reviewer for *The Prayer Foundation,* observed that Tolkien's "Lord of the Rings" series "grew out of the author's strong Christian faith. . . . As Kurt Bruner and Jim Ware show us, the stories of Tolkien's elves, dwarves, and hobbits is really our story—a compelling picture of an epic drama playing out on the stage of time."

BIOGRAPHICAL AND CRITICAL SOURCES:

PERIODICALS

Publishers Weekly, October 1, 2001, review of *Finding God in the Lord of the Rings,* p. 56.
School Library Journal, February 2001, Crystal Faris, review of *Crazy Jacob,* p. 106; February 2002, Elaine Fort Weischedel, review of *The Prophet's Kid,* p. 134.

ONLINE

Fool of a Took Web site, http://wwwfoolofatook.com/ (June 19, 2002), review of *Finding God in the Lord of the Rings.*
Prayer Foundation Web site, http://www.prayer foundation.org/ (June 19, 2002), review of *Finding God in the Lord of the Rings.*

WARNER, Jessica 1956-

PERSONAL: Born 1956, in Washington, DC; daughter of John Finney (reporter and editor for *New York Times*); married Reese Warner, 1991. *Education:* Princeton University, B.A. (magna cum laude), 1978; Yale University, M.Phil., 1981, Ph.D., 1991.

ADDRESSES: Office—Centre for Addiction and Mental Health, 33 Russell St., Toronto, Ontario, M5S 2S1, Canada. *E-mail*—Jessica_Warner@camh.net.

CAREER: University of Toronto, Toronto, Ontario, Canada, professor of history; Centre for Addiction and Mental Health, Toronto, research scientist.

AWARDS, HONORS: Fellowships from Yale University; grants from U.S. Department of Health and Human Services, 1997-2000, and Social Sciences and Humanities Research Council of Canada, 2000-2003.

WRITINGS:

Craze: Gin and Debauchery in an Age of Reason, Four Walls Eight Windows (New York, NY), 2002.

Contributor to journals, including *Albion, Journal of Family History, Addiction, Journal of Criminal Justice and Popular Culture, Journal of Social History, Globe and Mail, Social Science History, Contemporary Drug Problems,* and *American Journal of Public Health.*

WORK IN PROGRESS: A book set during the American Revolution.

SIDELIGHTS: Jessica Warner is the author of *Craze: Gin and Debauchery in an Age of Reason.* She noted on her Web site that she was a Medievalist who "somehow managed to convince a bunch of epidemiologists that they—and the U.S. government—needed to know why medieval people drank so much. I was never much with Latin, the language of true Medievalists, and so I naturally found myself drawn to texts written in English. But even sixteenth-century texts were hard going, and it was only a matter of time before I looked for something easier on the eyes, which in this case happened to be seventeenth-century sermons against drunkenness. From there it was a quick leap into the eighteenth century."

With grant money, Warner was able to spend four months in and around London, researching the history of the use of gin. Warner wrote the book in a lighter style but found the facts to be dark, especially those that show that addiction, then as now, affects the same set of people, and is addressed by politicians with the same sorts of pat answers and solutions to the problem.

What Warner shows is that from 1720 to 1751, cheap gin was the urban drug of choice. The working poor turned to it to numb them from the cold and their misery, and the more well-off looked down on the gin drinkers. But they also recognized that drunkenness tended to immobilize the masses, rendering them more docile and more likely to do the bidding of the government and their employers. Jonathan Yardley noted in *Washington Post Book World* that Warner "has chosen to tell the story of the gin craze largely in terms of class. . . . This places her squarely within academic orthodoxy . . . which for some time has been fixated on class as well as race and gender, but in this instance ideological fashion appears to agree with historical truth."

Gin had been invented by the Dutch, made by redistilling malt spirits with juniper berries. At one point, more than 7,000 licensed distillers served a London of 600,000, but street vendors turned out a "barely drinkable" liquor that was so strong that it sometimes turned deadly. Individuals in Warner's cast of characters play a role in commenting on the drink. Some of the most well-known figures include Samuel Johnson, Lord Chesterfield, Sir Robert Walpole, Daniel Defoe, Henry Fielding, and William Hogarth.

Parliament levied excise taxes on the sale of gin which ballooned by more than 1,000 percent between 1700 and 1771, and this way of raising money was popular with the ruling class, who also profited from the sale of the grain needed to make it. The working class, the gin drinkers, had no say in elections, and, therefore, they had no control over these levies. But the people ignored the taxes and laws restricting the sale of gin and continued to drink it, causing terrible health consequences. There were eight laws passed that both controlled and taxed gin through excise taxes and license fees, with the Gin Act of 1736 being the most restrictive. The poor took it as a challenge to their freedoms and continued to drink, and to hunt down the paid informers who turned them in. The 1743 act raised excise taxes, but reduced licensing fees and eliminated rewards to informers. There was a fear that the return of soldiers after the 1748 peace treaty in Europe would result in additional disruption, and the most restrictive legislation of all was passed. The craze ended not by law, but when jobs became more scarce and grain more expensive. The government banned its sale for distilling, limiting its use to food products.

Gin again became fashionable some eight decades later. "Once again, though," noted Alan Riding in the *New York Times Book Review,* "the real problem was not what people drank, but who did the drinking. In the quiet comfort of London clubs, gin could be tippled with impunity. But when the poor drank it to excess, they were viewed as a threat to society. Charles Dickens saw through this hypocrisy. 'Gin drinking is a great vice in England,' he wrote in the early 1830s, when he was still a journalist, 'but wretchedness and dirt are greater.'" Riding noted that Warner thinks along the same lines as Dickens. "Recalling the failure of many antidrug campaigns since the 1970s, she argues that we are 'too easily seduced by the notion that the complex problems that come with complex places boil down to a simple and single source, be it gin, heroin, or crack cocaine.'"

A *Kirkus Reviews* contributor who called *Craze* "a tart, acute inquiry," wrote that Warner "gives her savvy investigation a second, deeper dimension as a parable about drugs: why some take them and others worry when they do."

"The gin shop has given way to the crack house, but the anti-drug rhetoric sounds eerily familiar," commented D. J. Morel on the Web site of the *Seattle Times.* "It remains far easier for government to demonize drugs than do something about the squalid environments that encourage their use in the first place."

In a London *Guardian* review, Frances Wilson wrote of Warner's findings: "Arguing with great skill and wit that drug abuse is a symptom and not the cause of social problems, she is persuasive and compelling to a surprising degree. *Craze* stirs us into action rather than allowing us to feel, as do many historical accounts or several glasses of gin, comfortably distanced from the grim reality."

BIOGRAPHICAL AND CRITICAL SOURCES:

PERIODICALS

Guardian (London, England), March 1, 2003, Frances Wilson, review of *Craze: Gin and Debauchery in an Age of Reason.*
Kirkus Reviews, July 15, 2002, review of *Craze,* p. 1021.
Library Journal, October 1, 2002, Isabel Coates, review of *Craze,* p. 114.
New York Times Book Review, January 19, 2003, Alan Riding, review of *Craze,* p. 9.
Publishers Weekly, August 5, 2002, review of *Craze,* p. 62.
Washington Post Book World, October 24, 2002, Jonathan Yardley, review of *Craze,* p. 4.

ONLINE

Jessica Warner Web site, http://www.mothergin.com/ (March 8, 2003).
Seattle Times Online, http://www.seattletimes. nwsource.com/ (November 10, 2002), D. J. Morel, review of *Craze.*

*   *   *

WARREN, Scott S. 1957-

PERSONAL: Born August 22, 1957, in Wilmington, DE; son of R. Bruce and Nancy (a lab curator; maiden name, Hunter) Warren; married Beth Lamberson (a development director for public radio); children: Kathrine, Christopher. *Ethnicity:* "Anglo." *Education:* Utah State University, B.F.A. (photography), 1980. *Politics:* "Democratic." *Hobbies and other interests:* Hiking, bicycling, travel.

ADDRESSES: Office—P.O. Box 3512, Durango, CO 813026. *E-mail*—sswarren@frontier.net.

CAREER: Freelance photographer and writer, 1980—.

MEMBER: Society of Children's Book Writers and Illustrators.

AWARDS, HONORS: Alicia Patterson fellowship, 1998.

WRITINGS:

(Photographer) *Enemy Ancestors: The Anasazi World with a Guide to the Sites,* by Gary Matlock, Northland Press (Flagstaff, AZ), 1988.
(With wife, Beth Lamberson Warren) *Victorian Bonanza: Victorian Architecture of the Rocky Mountain West,* Northland Press (Flagstaff, AZ), 1989.
(And photographer) *The San Juan Skyway: A Colorado Driving Adventure,* Falcon Books (Helena, MT), 1990.
(And photographer) *Cities in the Sand,* Chronicle (San Francisco, CA), 1992, published as *Cities in the Sand: The Ancient Civilizations of the Southwest,* Skipping Stones, 1994.
(And photographer) *Exploring Colorado's Wild Areas,* Mountaineers Books (Seattle, WA), 1992.
One Hundred Years of Arizona, Mountaineers Books (Seattle, WA), 1993.
One Hundred Hikes in Arizona, Mountaineers Books (Seattle, WA), 1994.
Exploring Arizona's Wild Areas, Mountaineers Books (Seattle, WA), 1996, 2nd revised edition, 2002.
(And photographer) *Desert Dwellers: Native People of the American Southwest* Chronicle (San Francisco, CA), 1997.
One Hundred Classic Hikes in Colorado, Mountaineers Books (Seattle, WA), 2001.

Contributor to periodicals and newspapers, including *Audubon, National Geographic World, Newsweek, Smithsonian, Time, U.S. News and World Report, Outside, Washington Times,* and *Salt Lake Tribune.*

WORK IN PROGRESS: Photographs and video of people in Siberia and Cuba.

SIDELIGHTS: Freelance photographer and writer Scott S. Warren has carved out a successful career for himself capturing images of the Arizona and Colorado wilderness and of the ruins of the long-lost native civilizations of the American Southwest. He has worked often for *National Geographic World* and other well-known publications; however, it is as an author-photographer with a dozen books to his credit that

Warren is best known. "My interest in producing books stems from the fact that I have been a photographer for about as long as I can remember (since age twelve, actually)," he once commented. "I received a B.F.A. in photography in 1980 and shortly after decided that the printed page was the best medium for my work."

Warren was born in Delaware, but he grew up in Santa Fe, New Mexico, where his mother worked as a photographer. Her fascination with cameras rubbed off on her son, who majored in photography at Utah State University and attended the *National Geographic* photography workshop in Steamboat Springs, Colorado. Warren began shooting landscapes, but soon branched out into capturing images of human interest and travel destinations for various publications.

Warren's first two books were collaborative efforts. In 1988 he teamed with writer Gary Matlock on *Enemy Ancestors: The Anasazi World with a Guide to the Sites,* which chronicles the ancient history and culture of the Anasazi Indians, a tribe who lived during the period 200 B.C.-1300 A.D. in the area that is now part of the state of Arizona. An unnamed reviewer writing in *American West* observed that *Enemy Ancestors* "serves as an interpretive text and guide to well-known and little-known ruins. . . . Fine photographs accompany the text." In 1989 Warren and his wife Beth created *Victorian Bonanzas: Victorian Architecture of the Rocky Mountain West,* which an *American West* reviewer praised as "a delightful volume."

Warren has authored numerous other books, which can be loosely divided into two categories: travel guides and picture books which capture the essence of times and places little-known or forgotten. In the former category, the travel guides include *Exploring Colorado's Wild Areas, One Hundred Hikes in Arizona, Exploring Arizona's Wild Areas,* and *One Hundred Classic Hikes in Colorado.*

The reviews for *Exploring Colorado's Wild Areas* are typical of the critical reaction to Warren's tour guides. Assessing the book for *Bloomsbury Review,* Amanda Bailey noted, "this book breaks down the lesser-known regions of the Colorado wilderness with excellent detail." She went on to point out that "Rather than bring hordes of adventurous souls to the pristine wilderness areas of the state, author Scott S. Warren hopes to 'help disperse backcountry visitors more

evenly.'" Meanwhile, a reviewer for *Sierra* lauded the same book as "a thorough introduction to Colorado," one that provides "detailed trail descriptions, trailhead directions, and maps."

Among the second type of books on Warren's bibliography—those which chronicle times and places little-known or now forgotten—are *The San Juan Skyway: A Colorado Driving Adventure, Cities in the Sand: The Ancient Civilizations of the American Southwest, Desert Dwellers: Native People of the American Southwest,* and *Land of the Lost.*

Reviewing *Cities in the Sand* for *School Library Journal,* David N. Pauli commented, "The book is graced with attractive color photographs, many of them full-page," and as such it would be "a good resource for research and reports." Deborah Abbott of *Booklist* expressed a similar assessment, noting that "This in-depth look at the ancient cultures of the Anasazi, Hohokam, and Mogollon peoples of the Southwest provides student researchers with plenty to ponder."

School Library Journal reviewer Lisa Wu Stowe wrote that Warren's 1997 book *Desert Dwellers: Native People of the American Southwest* is "a good read for anyone interested in modern Indians." Writing in *Booklist,* Susan DeRonne commented that Warren "is careful to note how the tribes have integrated ancient traditions with twentieth-century life."

In 1997 Warren chanced to read a newspaper article about some Navajo students from Utah who were going on a six-week exchange visit to northwest Siberia, in northern Russia. Warren signed on to accompany the students as an adult supervisor. Upon his return home, he sold some of his photographs and an article he wrote about the experience to the *Salt Lake Tribune.* Warren was so intrigued by what he had seen in Siberia that he went back there seven more times on his own to take photos and gather information for articles and a book he was planning. He spent a total of twelve months in the Russian north, with financial support from an organization called the Blue Earth Alliance and a thirty-five-thousand-dollar Alicia Patterson fellowship. *Photo District News* reviewer Jane Gottlieb wrote that "In six visits to the Russian territory, Warren has documented what happens to a people isolated from the rest of the world."

Warren plans to spend more time in Siberia and to document how oil exploration in the region is about to forever change the sensitive environment and the lives and culture of the people who live there. Warren told Jane Gottlieb that he thinks about going back to Siberia. "I think about it all the time. I have as many friends there as anywhere else at this point."

BIOGRAPHICAL AND CRITICAL SOURCES:

PERIODICALS

American West, April, 1989, review of *Enemy Ancestors,* p. S7.

Bloomsbury Review, July-August, 2002, Amanda Bailey, review of *Exploring Colorado's Wild Areas,* p. 14.

Booklist, October 1, 1992, Deborah Abbot, review of *Cities in the Sand,* p. 325; September 1, 1997, Susan DeRonne, review of *Desert Dwellers: Native People of the American Southwest,* p. 121.

Horn Book Guide, July-December, 1997, review of *Desert Dwellers: Native People of the American Southwest,* p. 190.

Library Journal, April 15, 1994, Thomas K. Fry, review of *One Hundred Hikes in Arizona,* p. 100.

Photo District News, November 2001, Jane Gottlieb, "Land of the Lost," pp. 131-132.

School Arts, January 1994, Kent Anderson and David Baker, review of *Cities in the Sand,* p. 40.

School Library Journal, August 1992, David N. Pauli, review of *Cities in the Sand,* p. 176; October 1997, Lisa Wu Stowe, review of *Desert Dwellers: Native Peoples of the American Southwest,* p. 158.

Sierra, July, 1994, review of *Exploring Colorado's Wild Areas,* p. 83.

Skipping Stones, spring-summer 1994, review of *Cities in the Sand: The Ancient Civilizations of the Southwest,* p. 32.

*   *   *

WATSON, Brad

PERSONAL: Born in Meridian, MS. *Education:* Mississippi State University, B.A., 1978; University of Alabama, M.F.A., 1985.

ADDRESSES: Home—Pensacola, FL. *Office*—University of West Florida, 11000 University Parkway, Pensacola, FL 32514.

CAREER: Writer. Worked as a newspaper reporter in Alabama and Florida; University of Alabama, public relations department and lecturer; Harvard University, Cambridge, MA, Briggs-Copeland writer-in-residence and director of creative writing program; University of West Florida, Pensacola, teacher.

AWARDS, HONORS: Sue Kaufman Prize, American Academy of Arts and Letters, for *Last Days of the Dog-Men.*

WRITINGS:

Last Days of the Dog-Men (stories), W. W. Norton (New York, NY), 1996.

The Heaven of Mercury (novel), W. W. Norton (New York, NY), 2002.

Contributor to anthologies, including *Dog Stories,* University of Colorado Press (Boulder, CO), 1993, and *Walking on Water and Other Stories,* edited by Alan Wier, University of Alabama Press (Tuscaloosa, AL), 1996, and to literary journals, including *Black Warrior Review, Story,* and *Greensboro Review.*

SIDELIGHTS: While Brad Watson worked as a reporter for Gulf Coast newspapers, he spent his free time polishing his fiction, which included many short stories. Many of these are about dogs, inspired by an anecdote he heard while at a party. Apparently a woman had her lover's dog euthanized when she learned he was cheating on her. This was the first dog story Watson tucked away and one that he later adopted and expanded. Watson hadn't been published in any of the popular literary journals, but he persisted in sending out his work. He had sent many submissions to *Story,* before his "Seeing Eye" clicked. After it appeared in the journal, Watson was approached to publish his dog stories as a collection. In the year the award-winning *Last Days of the Dog-Men,* was published, he moved to Massachusetts to teach at Harvard University, a position that lasted several years before Watson returned to the South to teach at the University of West Florida.

In these stories, dogs are intrinsically connected to the lives of people. "Such a high concept sounds like the premise for comedy," wrote Gregory Feeley in *Wash-*

ington Post Book World, "and indeed several of Watson's stories are either droll or hilarious." All of these contemporary stories are set in the South, and the central theme is the failed relationships between men and women.

In a review for *BookPage* online, Alex Richardson called them "stories of human regret and sadness, of loss and lunacy, which a dog's presence somehow underscores."

In the title story, the narrator is a man who has always lived with dogs, and when his marriage and life in suburbia fail, he moves into a dilapidated farmhouse that he shares with other men and dogs. "Every detail is meaningful," wrote Irvin Malin in *Studies in Short Fiction.* "The narrator is displaced, separated from Lois; the other men who live in the same house are 'unbalanced,' 'off-center.' They are a 'little tilted'—unlike the dogs who don't have to worry about the significance of things." Malin called the collection "remarkable" and said it "heralds a brilliant career."

Infidelity is a frequent theme, as are cruelty and despair. "Actually, everyone in Mr. Watson's territory has a secret life," commented Tom De Haven in the *New York Times Book Review.* "Except of course, for the retrievers, mutts, collies, and bulldogs that never stray far from their mixed-up human companions."

Three of the eight stories are told from a woman's point of view, and two are about elderly women. In "Bill," eighty-seven-year-old Wilhelmina's husband is in a nursing home, and her even-more-frail poodle must be put down. Before she takes the dog on the final trip to the vet, she prepares him a sumptuous meal and serves it on her best china. De Haven called this "a terrific love story. . . . Written in crisp, rhythmic prose, Mr. Watson's work manages to avoid the showboating and fey self-esteem that infect so much contemporary short fiction. His men, women, and dogs—those wonderful dogs!—are superbly imagined. And in each and every story they come alive with honest, thrumming energy."

New York Times Book Review contributor Emily Hall called Watson's debut novel, *The Heaven of Mercury,* "Southern Gothic down to its core, with all the requisite grotesquerie, including corpse-reviving necro-

philia and families bound by hate and spite as much as they are by blood." The story is set in Mercury, Mississippi and spans most of a century, reflected on by narrator Finus Bates, over eighty and still editor of the town newspaper, and who also greets the day on the local radio station. Finus writes eloquent obituaries, and with each, he contemplates his connection with the diminishing number of Mercury's older residents. In writing his wife's, he notes that Avis's life had been a trial. And it had, because Finus had been in love with her best friend since 1916, when he saw Birdie doing a cartwheel nude at the swimming hole. He never pursued her though, and Birdie married Earl Urquhart, a violent man who was perpetually unfaithful to her, and who is the son of the repugnant funeral director. Finus never got over it, even though he and Avis eventually had a son, and on her deathbed, she told him that he had ruined her life. Other characters include Creasie, Birdie's housemaid, and Aunt Vish, a former slave and healer who a *Kirkus Reviews* contributor felt "Faulkner might have created," and who noted that "the real strength of the novel lies in its flexible structure, which allows us to overhear details of Mercury's overheated history as pieced together by several involved observers."

Scott Morris wrote in *National Review* that "what saves Finus and the others in the story may be described as the long view—the fact that most people amount to more in this life, for better and for worse, than they suppose; and furthermore, that death is a transition and not a terminus. The *Heaven of Mercury* cannot be understood without coming to terms with these ideas; they are much more than a backdrop, they are shimmering and omnipresent. And the artfulness with which Watson has spiritually supercharged the air his characters breathe is the primary reason this novel is exceptional."

As Finus nears the end of his life, he takes a trip down the Mississippi coast, where lying in the sand he is thrilled to see Monarch butterflies, newly arrived from South America. Watson writes that "they seemed to shiver under his rapt attention. He felt such an outpouring of love for them, he thought he could weep. They seemed hardly able to contain their delight that he was gazing upon their beautiful wings."

Morris commented that "a sinner like Finus knows that there is but one response to such a vision: gratitude. Readers will be thankful as well."

BIOGRAPHICAL AND CRITICAL SOURCES:

PERIODICALS

Boston Globe, November 17, 2002, Liza Weisstuch, review of *The Heaven of Mercury,* p. D8.

Kirkus Reviews, May 15, 2002, review of *The Heaven of Mercury,* p. 699.

Los Angeles Times Book Review, August 18, 2002, Mark Rozzo, review of *The Heaven of Mercury,* p. R14.

Mobile Register, October 20, 2002, review of *The Heaven of Mercury.*

National Review, February 24, 2003, Scott Morris, review of *The Heaven of Mercury,* p. 54.

New York Times, August 27, 2002, Richard Eder, review of *The Heaven of Mercury,* p. B7.

New York Times Book Review, June 9, 1996, Tom De Haven, review of *Last Days of the Dog-Men,* p. 13; November 10, 2002, Emily Hall, review of *The Heaven of Mercury,* p. 20.

Publishers Weekly, February 26, 1996, review of *Last Days of the Dog-Men,* p. 82; May 20, 2002, review of *The Heaven of Mercury,* p. 44.

Southern Humanities Review, winter, 1998, Charles Rose, review of *Last Days of the Dog-Men,* p. 98.

Studies in Short Fiction, winter, 1998, Irving Malin, review of *Last Days of the Dog-Men,* p. 98.

Times Literary Supplement, April 18, 1997, Scott Bradfield, review of *Last Days of the Dog-Men,* p. 21.

Washington Post Book World, July 28, 1996, Gregory Feeley, review of *Last Days of the Dog-Men,* p. 9.

ONLINE

BookPage, http://www.bookpage.com/ (December 12, 2002), Alex Richardson, review of *Last Days of the Dog-Men.*

Charlotte Observer Online, http://www.bayarea.com/ September 6, 2002, Polly Paddock, review of *The Heaven of Mercury.*

Identity Theory, http://www.identitytheory.com/ (July 21, 2002), Robert Birnbaum, interview with Watson.

Southern Scribe, http://www.southernscribe.com/ (December 12, 2002), Wayne Greehaw, review of *The Heaven of Mercury.**

WEISBERG, Joseph

PERSONAL: Born in Chicago, IL. *Education:* Yale University, graduated, 1987.

ADDRESSES: Home—New York, NY. *Agent*—c/o Author Mail, Random House, 1745 Broadway, New York, NY 10019.

CAREER: Writer; leader of writing seminars for high school students.

WRITINGS:

Tenth Grade, Random House (New York, NY), 2002.

SIDELIGHTS: Joseph Weisberg's first novel, *Tenth Grade,* is structured as a journal kept by an average sophomore named Jeremiah Reskin who lives in an average New Jersey suburb called Hurst Falls. The writing style is also that of an average tenth grader, with run-on sentences and other instances of creative grammar. Although several reviewers were initially skeptical of this device, "after a few pages, this strategy gets less annoying than it initially seems, and you're rather effortlessly and convincingly sucked into the slipstream of dim teenage consciousness," David Kamp wrote in the *New York Times Book Review.*

In this journal of Jeremy's coming of age, the reader hears his thoughts about important teenage firsts—his first experimentations with drugs and alcohol, his sexual initiation—and about such common experiences as hanging out with friends in basement rec rooms and struggling to master Spanish. When writing about these experiences, "Weisberg fondly and hilariously brings every tiny detail to life," Janet Maslin noted in the *New York Times.* Maslin and other reviewers also noted that Weisberg did an excellent job of actually sounding like a teenager keeping a journal. He "admirably captures the inarticulate voice of a suburban tenth-grader," observed John Green, writing in *Booklist,* even to the extent of recording the excessive "ogling of the female form" common to fifteen-year-old boys.

BIOGRAPHICAL AND CRITICAL SOURCES:

PERIODICALS

Booklist, January 1, 2002, John Green, review of *Tenth Grade,* p. 815.

Kirkus Reviews, November 15, 2001, review of *Tenth Grade,* p. 1579.

Los Angeles Times, March 10, 2002, Mark Rozzo, review of *Tenth Grade,* p. R-10.

New York Times, February 14, 2002, Janet Maslin, review of *Tenth Grade,* p. E15.

New York Times Book Review, February 3, 2002, David Kamp, review of *Tenth Grade,* p. 31.

Publishers Weekly, November 19, 2001, review of *Tenth Grade,* pp. 49-50.*

*   *   *

WELCH, Matthew

PERSONAL: Male. *Education:* Trinity University, B.A., University of Kansas, Ph.D.

ADDRESSES: Office—University of St. Thomas, Art History Department, 2115 Summit Avenue, St. Paul, MN 55105. *E-mail*—mwelch@artsmia.org.

CAREER: Art historian, lecturer, and author. University of St. Thomas, adjunct professor of art history; Minneapolis Institute of Arts, Minneapolis, MN, curator of Japanese and Korean art.

AWARDS, HONORS: Kyoto University, Japan, Fulbright scholar.

WRITINGS:

Otsu-e: Japanese Folk Paintings from the Harriet and Edson Spencer Collection, Minneapolis Institute for Arts (Minneapolis, MN), 1994.

(With Sharen Chappell) *Netsuke: The Japanese Art of Miniature Carving,* Paragon Publishers (Minneapolis, MN), 1999.

Body of Clay, Soul of Fire: Richard Bresnahan and the Saint John's Pottery, Afton Historical Society Press (Afton, MN), 2001.

Catalogue, with others, *Japanese Quest for a New Vision: The Impact of Visiting Chinese Painers, 1600-1900: Selections from the Hutchinson Collection at the Spencer Museum of Art,* edited by Stephen Addiss, Spencer Museum of Art, University of Kansas

(Lawrence, KS), 1986; contributor to *The Art of Twentieth-Century Zen: Paintings and Calligraphy by Japanese Masters,* Shambhala (Boston, MA), 1998.

SIDELIGHTS: Matthew Welch was a Fulbright scholar at Kyoto University during the 1980s. His love of traditional Asian ceramics and a ten-year friendship with preeminent Minnesota wood-firing potter Richard Bresnahan resulted in Welch's biography *Body of Clay, Soul of Fire: Richard Bresnahan and the Saint John's Pottery.*

Welch traces Bresnahan's career, from its inception as a student at St. John's University—part of the Benedictine monastery in Collegeville, Minnesota—through his apprenticeship in Japan under the innovative thirteenth-generation Karatsu-style potter, Nakazato Takashi—where he achieved the level of Master Potter—to his more than thirty years as artist-in-residence at his alma mater. Upon acceptance of his request to serve the Benedictine community in this capacity, Bresnahan designed and constructed a huge wood-burning kiln, larger and more innovative than any other in North America. Practicing a type of environmentalism that compliments the philosophy of the Benedictine order, the artist uses deadfall only to heat the kiln, digs his own clay, and uses local seeds and hulls as glazing materials.

The five-chapter book includes a foreword by Gerry Williams, illustrations and firing schedules for two multichamber wood-burning kilns, and listings of visiting artists and apprentices. Andrew McQuigg, writing for *Library Journal,* noted that Welch uses journal notes, interviews, and glorious full-color and black-and-white photographs to trace Bresnahan's "compelling story. . . . His commitment to ecology, local materials, and collective labor and the pottery's contribution to the self-sustainability of the abbey's Benedictine monks have blossomed into a highly regarded and vital community asset."

BIOGRAPHICAL AND CRITICAL SOURCES:

PERIODICALS

Ceramics Monthly, February, 2002, review of *Body of Clay, Soul of Fire: Richard Bresnahan and the Saint John's Pottery,* p. 28.

Choice, April, 2002, A. C. Garzio, review of *Body of Clay, Soul of Fire,* p. 1409.

Library Journal, March 15, 2002, John Andrew Mc-Quigg, review of *Body of Clay, Soul of Fire,* p. 77.

Utne Reader, January, 2002, Mark Odegard, review of *Body of Clay, Soul of Fire,* p. 90.*

*   *   *

WELLES, Benjamin 1916-2002

PERSONAL: Born 1916, in Japan; died January 3, 2002, in Washington, DC; U.S. citizen; married Cynthia Monteith (deceased); children: Serena Moss, Merida Holman. *Education:* Harvard University, graduated, 1938.

CAREER: Journalist. *New York Times,* New York, NY, news clerk, then reporter and journalist, 1938-72; Fletcher School of Law and Diplomacy, Tufts University, journalist-in-residence; principal deputy assistant secretary of defense for public affairs, 1981-83. *Military service:* U.S. Army, 1942-46, served with Office of Strategic Services; awarded Bronze Star.

MEMBER: Metropolitan Club (Washington, DC).

WRITINGS:

Spain: The Gentle Anarchy, Praeger (New York, NY), 1996.

Sumner Welles: FDR's Global Strategist: A Biography, St. Martin's Press (New York, NY), 1997.

SIDELIGHTS: Journalist Benjamin Welles was born into a wealthy and influential family. His father, Sumner Welles, was a major foreign-policy advisor to President Franklin D. Roosevelt. At the time of Welles's birth, his father was serving as third secretary of the U.S. embassy in Japan.

Welles did not follow his father into a diplomatic career, but chose journalism after graduating from Harvard University in 1938. He began his career as a news clerk at the *New York Times,* and worked his way up to become a reporter.

In 1942 Welles joined the U.S. Army and served in North Africa and the Middle East with the Office of Strategic Services during World War II. By the end of the war, he was a major. He was a member of the U.S. forces that liberated Paris on August 25, 1944, and earned a Bronze Star.

Welles returned to work for the *New York Times* in 1946 and worked as a foreign correspondent for the next seventeen years, traveling to China, London, and Madrid, as well as Hungary and Algeria. According to another correspondent, Paul Hofmann, Welles loved the excitement, danger, and cloak-and-dagger atmosphere of some of his assignments. Hofmann told Celestine Bohlen in the *New York Times,* "He loved having secret rendezvous with disguised army officers. He just lapped it up."

In the late 1950s and early 1960s, Welles was in Spain, and often wrote about the power of Spanish dictator Franco. He went to Washington, D.C. in 1963 to cover national security, and remained there until his retirement in 1972.

After retiring from the *New York Times,* Welles worked as a journalist-in-residence at the Fletcher School of Law and Diplomacy at Tufts University. From 1981 to 1983, he served as principal deputy assistant secretary of defense for public affairs. In January of 2002, he died of cancer in Washington, D.C.

Welles's book, *Sumner Welles: FDR's Global Strategist: A Biography,* surveys his father's influential life and career. Drawing on the senior Welles's voluminous collection of papers, interviews with people who knew his father, archives, and other sources, Welles presents a detailed and intimate look at his father. Sumner Welles's illustrious career came to an end in 1943 when he was implicated in a sexual scandal and President Roosevelt asked him to step down. In the *New York Times,* Gaddis Smith praised the book as "a candid, sympathetic portrait of a great and tragic figure." In *Presidential Studies Quarterly,* William C. Spragens noted "The diplomat's son has done a remarkable job of seeking to present a balanced picture of his father's service." Helen Delpar wrote in *Latin American Research Review* that the book presents "a detailed and sympathetic portrait," and that this volume "should stand as the definitive biography [of Sumner Welles] for a long time."

BIOGRAPHICAL AND CRITICAL SOURCES:

PERIODICALS

Latin American Research Review, summer, 2000, Helen Delpar, review of *Sumner Welles: FDR's Global Strategist: A Biography,* p. 155.

Library Journal, December, 1997, Robert F. Nardini, review of *Sumner Welles,* p. 116.

National Interest, summer, 1998, Mark Falcoff, review of *Sumner Welles,* p. 100.

New York Times, January 25, 1998, Gaddis Smith, review of *Sumner Welles,* p. 13.

Presidential Studies Quarterly, March, 2002, William C. Spragens, review of *Sumner Welles,* p. 213.

Publishers Weekly, October 27, 1997, review of *Sumner Welles,* p. 57.

OBITUARIES:

PERIODICALS

New York Times, January 4, 2002, Celestine Bohlen, p. A22.

Washington Post, January 3, 2002, p. B6.*

*   *   *

WHEELER, Richard S(haw) 1935-

PERSONAL: Born March 12, 1935 in Milwaukee, WI; son of S. Lawrence (a patent attorney) and Elizabeth Shaw (a teacher) Wheeler; married Rita Middleton, 1961 (divorced, 1965); married Sue Hart, 2000. *Education:* University of Wisconsin, Madison.

ADDRESSES: Home—219 South 5th St., Livingston, MT 59047. *Office*—219 South Fifth St., Livingston, MT 59047. *Agent*—Robin Rue, Writers House, 21 West 26th St., New York, NY 10010. *E-mail*—rwheeler@imt.net.

CAREER: Journalist, novelist, and writer. *Phoenix Gazette,* Phoenix, AZ, editorial writer, 1961-62; *Oakland Tribune,* Oakland, CA, page editor, 1963-65; *Reader's Digest,* Washington, DC, staff writer, 1966;

Billings Gazette, Billings, MT, reporter, 1968-69, copy editor and city editor, 1970-72; *Nevada Appeal,* Carson City, reporter, 1969-70; Open Court Publishing Co., Lasalle, IL, book editor, 1973-74; Icarus Press, South Bend, IN, book editor; Green Hill Publishers, Ottawa, IL, book editor, 1982-85; Walker & Co., New York, NY, book editor, 1985-87.

MEMBER: Western Writers of America.

AWARDS, HONORS: American Political Science Association award, 1969, for journalism; Western Writers of America, Spur Award, 1989, for *Fool's Coach,* 1996, for *Sierra,* and 2000, for *Masterson.;* Soyb Award, 2002, for *Drum's Ring;* Owen Wister Award, Western Writers of America, for lifelong contributions to field of Western literature.

WRITINGS:

"SKYE'S WEST" SERIES

Bannack, Tor (New York, NY), 1989.

Sun Dance, Tor (New York, NY), 1992.

Rendezvous, Forge (New York, NY), 1997.

Dark Passage, Forge (New York, NY), 1998.

Going Home, Forge (New York, NY), 2000.

Downriver, Forge (New York, NY), 2001.

Sun River, Thorndike Press (Thorndike, ME), 2002.

Far Tribes, Tor (New York, NY), 2002.

Yellowstone, Tor (New York, NY), 2002.

Santa Fe, Tor (New York, NY), 2002.

Wind River, Tor (New York, NY), 2002.

Bitterroot, Tor (New York, NY), 2002.

The Deliverance, Forge (New York, NY), 2002.

"SAM FLINT" SERIES

Flint's Gift, Forge (New York, NY), 1997.

Flint's Honor, Forge (New York, NY), 1998.

Flint's Truth, Forge (New York, NY), 1998.

The Children of Darkness, Arlington House (New Rochelle, NY), 1973.

Pagans in the Pulpit, Arlington House (New Rochelle, NY), 1974.

Bushwack, Doubleday (Garden City, NY), 1978.

Beneath the Blue Mountain, Doubleday (Garden City, NY), 1979.

Winter Grass, Walker and Co. (New York, NY), 1983.

Sam Hook, Walker and Co. (New York, NY), 1986.

Dodging Red Cloud, M. Evans (New York, NY), 1987.

Richard Lamb, Walker and Co. (New York, NY), 1987.

Stop, M. Evans (New York, NY), 1988.

Fool's Coach, M. Evans (New York, NY), 1989.

Montana Hitch, M. Evans (New York, NY), 1990.

Where the River Runs, M. Evans (New York, NY), 1990.

Fort Dance, Thorndike Press (St. Louis, MO), 1991.

Incident at Fort Keogh, Thorndike Press (Thorndike, ME), 1991.

The Final Tally, Fawcett (New York, NY), 1991.

The Rocky Mountain Company, Pinnacle (St. Louis, MO), 1991.

Cheyenne Winter, Pinnacle (St. Louis, MO), 1992.

Badlands, Tor (New York, NY), 1992.

Deuces and Ladies Wild, Thorndike Press (Thorndike, ME), 1992.

The Fate, Fawcett Gold Medal (New York, NY), 1992.

The Two Medicine River, Bantam Books (New York, NY), 1993.

Cashbox, Forge (New York, NY), 1994.

Goldfield, Forge (New York, NY), 1995.

Sierra, Forge (New York, NY), 1996.

Second Lives, Forge (New York, NY), 1997.

The Buffalo Commons, Forge (New York, NY), 1998.

Aftershocks, Forge (New York, NY), 1999.

Masterson, Forge (New York, NY), 1999.

Sun Mountain, Forge (New York, NY), 1999.

(Editor) *Tales of the American West: The Best of the Spur Award-Winning Authors,* New American Library (New York, NY), 2000.

The Witness, Signet (New York, NY), 2000.

Drum's Ring, New American Library (New York, NY), 2001.

The Fields of Eden, Forge (New York, NY), 2001.

Restitution, Signet (New York, NY), 2001.

Eclipse, Forge (New York, NY), 2002.

Cultural Gulch, Signet (New York, NY), 2003.

Exite: An Irish Rebel in America, Signet (New York, NY), 2003.

ADAPTATIONS: Several of Wheeler's books have been adapted for audiotape.

SIDELIGHTS: A prolific writer of westerns, Richard S. Wheeler has been a journalist and editor throughout his professional career. Educated at the University of Wisconsin, Wheeler has worked as an editorial writer for the *Oakland Tribune,* a staff writer for *Reader's Digest,* and a reporter for the *Nevada Appeal.* Wheeler's accomplishments also extend to book editing, where he has been an editor for publishers such as Open Court Publishing, Icarus Press, Walker & Co., and Green Hill Publishers. He has been a full-time novelist since 1987.

Wheeler, who once worked as a ranch hand, was described by *Twentieth-Century Western Writers* interviewer Dale L. Walker as "a study in contrasts. He is shy and self-effacing but imposing figure—six-foot-three, 195 pounds, with penetrating deep-blue, deep-set eyes and show-white hair." Though a westerner in all ways, Wheeler foregoes the typical garb of a westerner in favor of fashion such as "slacks, white shirt, laced shoes, and a Navy-blue sport coat," Walker observed.

Wheeler has achieved his greatest fame in the field of westerns. The author of more than fifty western novels, he is the recipient of four Spur Awards from the Western Writers of America, as well as an Owen Wister Award for lifetime achievement in western literature. Wheeler "has an enviable record, recognized by his peers, as a consistently innovative writer of off-the-main-trail novels with a sound historical under-girding, a deceptively easy style, and a born-story-teller's knack for keeping his readers glued to his pages and guessing," wrote Walker. Often eschewing the tropes and formulas of western writing—"there is not a shot fired in anger" in *Winter Grass,* Walker observed—Wheeler instead seeks to write a more original story with higher literary goals. "I haven't really varied much from my original wish to write a richer, more literate western story," Wheeler is quoted as saying in *Twentieth-Century Western Writers.*

Bushwack, Wheeler's first novel, chronicles the efforts of Linda Van Pelt, a cultured widow from the East, to deal with cattle rustlers and other unfamiliar dangers of the western landscape. There is even a bit of romance between Linda and neighbor Canada Parker, and tragedy when she realizes she cannot tolerate the western way of life. "Mr. Wheeler writes clearly, plots action scenes with skill, and has a laudable sense of values," wrote Paul Gigot in *National Review.* A *Booklist* reviewer remarked that the book has a "Solid plot, with good characterizations, too."

The main character in *Winter Grass* is Quin Putnam, a Harvard-educated Montana cattle rancher at serious odds with his neighbors over his fencing in of carefully cultivated local grassland with barbed wire. At the same time, his romance with lawyer Nicole is suffering, and it looks as though he may lose Missy, the Indian girl he has raised since childhood, because of her heritage. "The action is fast, the dialogue brisk, the characters are sharply drawn, and the descriptions often memorable," wrote Sister Avila in *Library Journal.* Janice Toomajian, writing in *Voice of Youth Advocates,* called the book "A special Western with memorable character relationships and high adventure."

The detail and historical accuracy of Wheeler's novels are frequently remarked upon favorably. A *Publishers Weekly* critic noted that *Dodging Red Cloud* "is distinguished by its depiction of life among the Crow" tribe. "Wheeler's grasp of the Old West ambience is considerable," remarked a *Booklist* reviewer, also commenting on *Dodging Red Cloud.* Charles Michaud, writing in *Library Journal,* remarked that reading *Cashbox* "is to experience life in a Western boomtown." A reviewer in *Roundup,* commenting on *Sun Mountain,* wrote, "No one can evoke the feel of grit from dirty streets on one's face and clothes, and the sounds of loud revelry of drunken miners loose on the town with bags of gold dust clutched in their hands as well as Dick Wheeler." And Susan Gene Clifford, in a *Library Journal* review of *Sierra,* called Wheeler "a real master at capturing the history, atmosphere, and romance of 1850s California."

Wheeler's talents have been recognized by his peers in the western genre, as evidence by his four Spur Awards and Owen Wister lifetime achievement award from the Western Writers of America. *Sierra,* which won the Spur Award in 1996, is "Absorbing and eventful, replete with authoritative details on the mortal risks, primitive conditions, and sometimes rich rewards awaiting those who joined the gold rush to California," wrote a critic in *Kirkus Reviews.* Ulysses McQueen leaves his prosperous ranch, pregnant wife, and domineering father to search for a rich strike in California. Stephen Jarvis, recently mustered out of the army, arrives at Sutter's Mill to make his own claim. Jarvis strikes it rich and becomes even richer by selling scarce tools and equipment. McQueen, however, arrives too late to find a claim that would even allow him to make a living, let alone become wealthy. Stung by his failure, he continually puts off contacting his wife, but she eventually finds him, though the arduous trip proved fatal to their infant

daughter. Destitute and desperate, McQueen arranges a deal with Jarvis to provide fresh vegetables for sale to the miners, bringing him full circle, back to the land. "Whether read as an adventure story, a love story, or a riveting fictional account of a watershed event in American history, *Sierra* is an outstanding novel with crackling good dialogue and unforgettable characters," commented a reviewer in *Roundup.*

Masterson, winner of the 2000 Spur Award, focuses on the fictionalized life and legend of near-mythical western lawman Bat Masterson. While working as a columnist in New York City, Masterson is interviewed by celebrated literary figures Louella Parsons and Damon Runyon. They want to know the real story behind Masterson's exploits and his association with notorious western figures such as Doc Holliday, the Earp brothers, and others. Masterson realizes that the reality of his life does not match the legend, and he sets off with his wife, Emma, to come to terms with his life as a western hero. *Masterson* "is classic Wheeler, a solid story about real people told with compassion, and a bit of whimsy," remarked a *Publishers Weekly* reviewer.

Among Wheeler's more popular books are those from his "Skye's West" series. Barnaby Skye was once on track to attend Cambridge and join his father in a lucrative merchant business. Skye is also a deserter from the Royal Navy, and though his forced "recruitment" at age fourteen through a press gang is dubious, he is still being pursued by British sailors and the Hudson Bay Company as a criminal. In the first Skye novel, *Rendezvous,* he is pursued across the wilderness from Fort Vancouver to the Rockies. After falling in with a group of friendly Shoshone, Skye is introduced to the life of the mountain man at a Rendezvous, a raucous annual gathering of fur trappers and wilderness dwellers. Though the trappers don't know exactly what to think of him, Skye's courage and grit impress them, and his knowledge of the outdoors, gained by contact with friendly Indians, saves them all during a harsh winter. Eventually, he "realizes that life in the free, open space and beauty of the mountains offers seductions and pleasures that Harvard doesn't," wrote a reviewer in *Publishers Weekly.* Skye becomes a leather-tough mountain man, "ruling his domain with his belaying pin, his Sharps and Colt .44, his two Indian wives (one a Shoshone, the other a Crow) and his ugly, vicious, battle-scarred horse Jawbone," Walker wrote. More than ten other Skye novels followed in the series. "The Skye novels are Wheeler's best pure storytelling,"Walker commented, "with all the qualities he admires in reading the works of other writers: rich characterization, well-drawn female characters, unexpected elements, eccentricities, lore, and history that never slow the pace of the story."

Wheeler's "Flint" series—*Flint's Gift, Flint's Honor,* and *Flint's Truth*—also shows him to be "a master of frontier detail and the fine points of newspapering," wrote a critic in *Kirkus Reviews.* Sam Flint is a crusading frontier journalist, determined to report the truth and unafraid of rival newspapermen or infuriated targets of his reporting. "The Flint series will be a welcome addition to the reading lists of younger western fans," remarked a *Kirkus Reviews* critic, "and a happy find for all those who prefer more traditional forms of the genre."

BIOGRAPHICAL AND CRITICAL SOURCES:

BOOKS

Twentieth-Century Western Writers, second edition, edited by Geof Sadler, St. James Press (Chicago, IL), 1991.

PERIODICALS

Booklist, March 1, 1979, review of *Bushwack,* p. 1040; September 1, 1979, review of *Beneath the Blue Mountain,* p. 27; November 15, 1987, review of *Dodging Red Cloud,* p. 539; November 15, 1987, review of *Richard Lamb,* p. 539; August, 1988, review of *Stop,* p. 1891; July, 1989, Wes Lukowsky, review of *Fool's Coach,* p. 1870; April 15, 1995, Wes Lukowsky, review of *Goldfield,* p. 1482; September 1, 1996, Wes Lukowsky, review of *Sierra,* p. 66; May 15, 1997, Wes Lukowsky, review of *Second Lives,* pp. 1564-1565; September 15, 1997, Wes Lukowsky, review of *Flint's Gift,* p. 211; December 1, 1997, Wes Lukowsky, review of *Rendezvous,* p. 610; May 15, 1998, Budd Arthur, review of *Flint's Truth,* p. 1597; August, 1998, Budd Arthur, review of *Dark Passage,* p. 1971; March 1, 1999, Wes Lukowsky, review of *Aftershocks,* p. 1155; May 15, 1999, Budd Arthur, review of *Flint's Honor,* p. 1672; October 1, 1999, Wes Lukowsky, review of *Masterson,* p. 345; February 15, 1990, Wes Lukowsky, review of *Where the River Runs,* p. 1141; June 1, 2000, Joanne Wilkinson, review of *Sierra,* p. 1848; January 1, 2001, Ted Hipple, review of *Flint's Honor,* p. 987; January 1, 2002, Ted Hipple, review of *Flint's Honor* (audiobook), p. 987; June 1, 2002, Margaret Flanagan, review of *Eclipse,* p. 1693.

Kirkus Reviews, August 15, 1973, review of *The Children of Darkness,* p. 957; April 15, 1994, review of *Cashbox,* p. 505; February 15, 1995, review of *Goldfield,* p. 182; August 1, 1996, review of *Sierra,* p. 1092; August 1, 1997, review of *Flint's Gift,* p. 1151; October 1, 1997, review of *Rendezvous,* p. 1482; April 15, 1998, review of *The Buffalo Commons,* p. 526; April 15, 1998, review of *Flint's Truth,* p. 526; September 15, 1998, review of *Dark Passage,* p. 1327; December 1, 1998, review of *Aftershocks,* p. 1696; April 1, 1999, review of *Sun Mountain,* p. 487; May 15, 1999, review of *Flint's Honor,* pp. 754-755; September 15, 1999, review of *Masterson,* p. 1443; September 15, 2001, review of *Downriver,* p. 1323; November 1, 2000, review of *Going Home,* p. 1516; April 1, 2002, review of *The Fields of Eden,* p. 458.

Kliatt Young Adult Paperback Book Guide, November, 1992, Carolyn Angus, review of *Dodging Red Cloud* (audiobook), p. 55; March, 1999, E. B. Boatner, review of *Flint's Gift* (audiobook), p. 52; March, 1999, E. B. Boatner, review of *Flint's Truth,* (audiobook), p. 52.

Library Journal, October 15, 1983, Sister Avila, review of *Winter Grass,* p. 1975; November 1, 1987, Sister Avila, review of *Dodging Red Cloud,* p. 123; November 1, 1989, Sister Avila, review of *Richard Lamb,* p. 123; February 1, 1990, Sister Avila, review of *Where the River Runs,* p. 109; June 1, 1994, Charles Michaud, review of *Cashbox,* p. 166; April 1, 1995, Sister Avila, review of *Goldfield,* p. 127; September 1, 1996, Susan Gene Clifford, review of *Sierra,* p. 212; September 15, 1997, Susan Gene Clifford, review of *Rendezvous,* p. 104; February 15, 1999, Melanie C. Duncan, review of *Flint's Gift,* p. 200; November 1, 1999, Ann E. Irvine, review of *Aftershocks,* p. 152.

National Review, June 22, 1979, Paul Gigot, review of *Bushwack,* p. 822.

New York Times Book Review, November 20, 1983, "Do as I Say, Not as I Do?" p. 46.

Publishers Weekly, October 16, 1987, Sybil Steinberg, review of *Dodging Red Cloud,* p. 69; May 5, 1989, review of *Fool's Coach,* p. 67; April 27, 1992, review of *The Fate,* p. 258; May 16, 1994, review of *Cashbox,* p. 50; March 6, 1995, review of *Goldfield,* pp. 59-60; August 5, 1995, review of *Sierra,* p. 432; April 28, 1997, review of *Second Lives,* p. 50; August 11, 1997, review of *Flint's Gift,* p. 387; October 6, 1997, review of *Rendezvous,* p. 73; February 23, 1998, review of *Flint's Truth,* p. 49; September 14, 1998, review of *Dark Passage,* p. 45; November 23, 1998, review of *Aftershocks,* p. 60; March 29, 1999, review of *Sun Mountain,* p. 90; June 14, 1999, review of *Flint's Honor,* p. 50; September 13, 1999, review of *Masterson,* p. 60; November 6, 2000, review of *Going Home,* p. 72; May 7, 2001, review of *The Fields of Eden,* p. 223; October 8, 2001, review of *Downriver,* p. 40; May 13, 2002, review of *Eclipse,* pp. 50-51.

Roundup, July, 1994, review of *Cashbox,* p. 27; October, 1996, review of *Sierra,* p. 33; August, 1997, review of *Second Lives,* p. 32; August, 1999, review of *Sun Mountain,* pp. 30-31; December, 1999, review of *Masterson,* p. 31; December, 2000, review of *The Witness,* p. 25; December, 2000, review of *Tales of the American West,* p. 26; April, 2001, review of *Restitution,* p. 30; June, 2002, review of *The Fields of Eden,* pp. 41-42.

Roundup Quarterly, spring, 1989, review of *Stop,* p. 26; spring, 1990, review of *Where the River Runs,* p. 51; fall, 1991, review of *Montana Hitch,* p. 65; fall, 1991, review of *The Final Tally,* p. 66; fall, 1991, review of *Incident at Fort Keogh,* p. 66.

School Library Journal, February, 1984, Elizabeth L. Fletcher, review of *Winter Grass,* p. 88; April, 1998, Pam Spencer, review of *Second Lives,* p. 159; March, 2002, Patricia White-Williams, review of *Downriver,* pp. 261-262.

Voice of Youth Advocates, June, 1984, Janice Toomajian, review of *Winter Grass,* p. 100; February, 1990, Joanne Johnson, review of *Skye's West,* pp. 348-349.

ONLINE

All about Romance, http://www.likesbooks.com/ (December 12, 2002), Colleen McMahon, review of *The Witness.*

Bookbrowser, http://www.bookbrowser.com/ (December 12, 2002), Harriet Klausner, review of *Eclipsed.*

My Shelf, http://www.myshelf.com/ (December 12, 2002), Jo Rogers, review of *Tales of the American West.*

ReadWest, http://www.readwest.com/ (December 12, 2002), Dale L. Walker, profile of Richard S. Wheeler.

Richard S. Wheeler Web site, http://www.readthewest.com/richardwheeler (December 12, 2002).

*   *   *

WILD, Margaret 1948-

PERSONAL: Born 1948, in South Africa; immigrated to Australia, 1972; two children. *Education:* Attended Australian National University. *Hobbies and other interests:* Music, opera, frequenting cafés.

ADDRESSES: Home—Sydney, Australia. *Agent*—c/o Author Mail, ABC Books, Allen & Unwin, P.O. Box 8500, St. Leonards, New South Wales, 1590 Australia.

CAREER: Journalist, book editor, and children's author. Editor and publisher, ABC Books, Sydney, New South Wales, Australia.

AWARDS, HONORS: Children's Book Council of Australia, Picture Book of the Year designation, 1990, for *The Very Best of Friends,* Picture Book of the Year shortlist, 1997, for *The Midnight Gang;* Australian Books of the Year Awards shortlist, 1992, for *Let the Celebrations Begin!;* Children's Book Council of Australia Award shortlist, 2002, for *Jinx;* May Gibbs Literature Trust fellowship, La Trobe University, 2001.

WRITINGS:

There's a Sea in My Bedroom, illustrated by Jane Tanner, Nelson (Melbourne, Victoria, Australia), 1984.

Creatures in the Beard, illustrated by Margaret Power, Omnibus Books (Adelaide, Australia), 1986.

Mr. Nick's Knitting, illustrated by Dee Huxley, Harcourt Brace Jovanovich (San Diego, CA), 1988.

The Very Best of Friends, illustrated by Julie Vivas, Harcourt Brace Jovanovich (San Diego, CA), 1990.

Let the Celebrations Begin! illustrated by Julie Vivas, Orchard Books (New York, NY), 1991, published as *A Time for Toys,* illustrated by Julie Vivas, KidsCan Press (Toronto, Ontario, Canada), 1992.

Space Travellers, illustrated by Gregory Rogers, Scholastic (New York, NY), 1992.

Thank You, Santa, illustrated by Kerry Argent, Scholastic (New York, NY), 1992.

The Queen's Holiday, illustrated by Sue O'Loughlin, Orchard Books (New York, NY), 1992.

My Dearest Dinosaur, illustrated by Donna Rawlins, Orchard Books (New York, NY), 1992.

All the Better to See You With, illustrated by Pat Reynolds, Allen & Unwin (St. Leonards, Australia), 1993.

The Slumber Party, illustrated by David Cox, Ticknor & Fields (New York, NY), 1993.

Going Home, illustrated by Wayne Harris, Scholastic (New York, NY), 1994.

Toby, illustrated by Noela Young, Ticknor & Fields (New York, NY), 1994.

But Granny Did! illustrated by Ian Forss, SRA School Group (Santa Rosa, CA), 1994.

Our Granny, illustrated by Julie Vivas, Ticknor & Fields (New York, NY), 1994.

Beast, Scholastic (New York, NY), 1995.

Looking after Alice & Co., illustrated by David Cox, Margaret Hamilton (Sydney, New South Wales, Australia), 1995.

Remember Me, Albert Whitman (Morton Grove, IL), 1995.

Old Pig, illustrated by Ron Brooks, Dial Books for Young Readers (New York, NY), 1996.

The Midnight Gang, illustrated by Ann James, Omnibus Books (Sydney, Australia), 1997.

Light the Lamps, illustrated by Dee Huxley, Scholastic (New York, NY), 1997.

Big Cat Dreaming, illustrated by Anne Spudvilas, Annick, 1997.

First Day, illustrated by Kim Gamble, Allen & Unwin (St. Leonards, Australia), 1998.

Miss Lily's Fabulous Pink Feather Boa, illustrated by Kerry Argent, Penguin (Ringwood, Australia), 1998.

Jenny Angel, illustrated by Anne Spudvilas, Viking (New York, NY), 1999.

Midnight Babies, illustrated by Ann James, Clarion Books (New York, NY), 1999.

The Midnight Feast, illustrated by Ann James, ABC Books (Sydney, New South Wales, Australia), 1999.

Rosie and Tortoise, illustrated by Ron Brooks, DK Publishing (New York, NY), 1999.

Bim, Bam, Boom! illustrated by Wayne Harris, ABC Books (Sydney, New South Wales, Australia), 2000.

Tom Goes to Kindergarten, illustrated by David Legge, Albert Whitman (Morton Grove, IL), 2000.

Fox, illustrated by Ron Brooks, Allen & Unwin (St. Leonards, Australia), 2000, Kane/Miller Book Publishers (La Jolla, CA), 2001.

The House of Narcissus, illustrated by Wayne Harris, ABC Books (Sydney, New South Wales, Australia), 2001.

Jinx, Walker (New York, NY), 2001.

Nighty Night! illustrated by Kerry Argent, Peachtree Publishers (Atlanta, GA), 2001.

The Pocket Dogs, illustrated by Stephen Michael King, Omnibus Books (Norwood, South Australia), 2000, Scholastic (New York, NY), 2001.

(With Jonathan Bentley) *Mr. Moo,* ABC Books (Sydney, New South Wales, Australia), 2002.

Kiss Kiss, illustrated by Bridget Strevens-Marxo, Simon & Schuster Books for Young Readers (New York, NY), 2004.

SIDELIGHTS: Margaret Wild is a prolific author of children's books whose themes sometimes address issues outside the norm of kids' literature: death and dying, grief, divorce, aging, and fears of being lost, overwhelmed, and bullied. Her realistic portrayals of these difficult subjects have been widely praised by critics and reviewers. Far from being morbid, Wild's other books are jubilant celebrations of grandmothers, babies, and childhood. Even her somber books hold the message that children can understand and cope with a sad or scary situation.

The Very Best of Friends "tells in simple, poignant language and with wonderfully vivid watercolors" the story of an Australian farm couple, James and Jessie, and their cat, William. The couple is very close; and James is especially fond of William, and Jessie tolerates the cat for his sake. When James dies suddenly, Jessie's life is in turmoil. She shuts out everything, including William, and stops caring for the farm, the animals, and herself. The neglected cat becomes thin and vicious, in his own way shut out from the world. But when William scratches Jessie, she realizes how she has let herself and her world deteriorate, and the two develop a strong friendship. This is a "story about relationships, love and loss, survival and recovery," wrote Patricia Dooley in *School Library Journal*. "The poignant tale is superbly told by Wild . . . who achieves an enviable balance of detail and simplicity," added Diane Roback in *Publishers Weekly.*

A Time for Toys—also published as *Let the Celebrations Begin!*—has the unusual setting of the Bergen-Belsen concentration camp in Germany. Miriam, an older child prisoner, can remember what life was like before the camp, when she had parents and a home and toys. Many of the younger children have known nothing but the camp. Miriam plans a very special party for the children, one that will happen when "the soldiers come to set us free" from their captivity. The women tear usable scraps of cloth from their already threadbare clothing to use to make the toys, which are indeed given when the camp is liberated. Marjorie Gann, writing in *Canadian Children's Literature* noted that the book "tells an important story well." Susan Perren, reviewing the book in *Quill & Quire,* commented that "*A Time for Toys* is about the power of hope. It is also a work of alchemy, creating something of beauty from the bleakest material."

The theme of death coupled with the hopeful message of moving on from grief while not forgetting the loved one informs two of Wild's more popular books. In *Old Pig*, the title character and Granddaughter live happily together, and have for a very long time. Old Pig carefully teaches Granddaughter how to fend for herself; the two do their daily chores together, have their meals together, and sleep peacefully together. One day, after being unable to get up and go about her routine as usual, Old Pig realizes what is coming and begins a tidying up—returning her library books, closing her bank account, paying her bills and giving Granddaughter the remainder, and feasting her eyes on nature for the very last time. The final picture in the book shows Granddaughter alone, feasting on nature the way Old Pig taught her to. "Beautiful in its simplicity, this captures the essence of a life; and children, even little ones, cannot help but feel the love that infuses it," wrote Ilene Cooper in *Booklist.*

In *Toby* the family dog is elderly and ailing, but twelve-year-old Sara is indifferent, sometimes even harsh to her lifelong pet. Her two younger brothers cannot understand her anger toward the dog, so they decide to play with Toby and comfort him. Then, the vet announces that it would be kindest to put Toby to sleep, a turn of events that makes Sara react with

hostility toward Toby. Sara's mom, however, realizes that Sara's reactions are in part due to the changes in her own life as she grows up, and in part due to the terrible sadness she feels at the prospect of losing Toby, and the entirety of her childhood that he represents. The night before Toby is to be put to sleep, Sara is found lovingly holding him and saying her last goodbyes. Michael J. Rosen, writing in *Washington Post Book World,* called *Toby* "a glorious book worth weeping over together," while Ellen Mandel, in *Booklist* declared the book "a genuinely touching illumination of a family's loss of a beloved friend."

Jenny Angel also deals with the loss of a family member. Young Davy is gravely ill and dying, but his older sister Jenny believes she can save his life by acting as his guardian angel and willing him to live. She perches protectively outside his window at night, and then spends time "flying" over the city in her imagination to bring back marvelous stories of her adventures. She even wears a heavy coat at school to hide her "wings," enduring relentless teasing and questioning in order to maintain her illusion of being Davy's guardian angel. It is only after Davy's unavoidable death and his funeral that Jenny finally takes off her coat, visits the roof one last time (with her mother), realizes that she did all she could, and accepts that Davy is gone. "Understated, honest, and ultimately hopefully, *Jenny Angel* does not simplify emotions nor does it give answers to impossible questions" remarked Nola Allen in *Magpies*. Rosemary Stores, writing in *Books for Keeps,* declared that "Wild's depiction of Jenny finding a way to accept her loss is . . . so sensitively conveyed that young readers can only be enriched by it." Margaret Dunkle, in a review in *Australian Book World,* remarked that *Jenny Angel* "is a tender, loving, beautiful story, splendidly reinforced by Anne Spudvilas' sensitive paintings. I read it with healing tears as will many others."

Optimism and exuberance, however, are not out of place in Wild's works. In *Our Granny,* she offers a celebration of well-loved grandmothers of all colors, shapes, and sizes, from all over the world. "And they can take part in any activities they like" wrote Russ Merrin in *Magpies*. "No white-haired buns pulled back from wrinkled brows here. These ladies are stirrers and doers and goers." *The Queen's Holiday* is a "royal romp" that will be "enjoyed by young and old" wrote Nancy Seiner in *School Library Journal*. The story follows the queen's trip to the beach and the steadily increasing mayhem brought about by her attendants, until the queen (who looks remarkably like Queen Victoria) declares, "This simply will not do!" and puts things right in a suitably royal manner. In *Midnight Babies,* a group of toddlers gather at the magic hour of midnight to dance, feast, and cavort before returning to bed and "normal" life. Ilene Cooper, writing in *Booklist* called it a "fantastical ode to babydom," with characters whose "actions are whimsical, bold, and delicious."

Wild's other books tackle subjects such as divorce and visitation (*Sam's Sunday Dad*); coping with homelessness (*Space Travellers*); a child's need for glasses (*All the Better to See You With!*); the aging of a relative (*Remember Me* and *Big Cat Dreaming*); and the rite of passage every child must face, the first day of school (*First Day* and *Tom Goes to Kindergarten*). Joan Zahnleitner, writing in *Magpies,* observed that with *First Day* Wild's approach "has been towards a more optimistic side of life even while acknowledging that what may seem small worries to adults can assume monumental proportions for young children."

With 2001's *Jinx* Wild steps away from the world of children's books and into a novel for teen readers. Wild wrote on the *Allen & Unwin* Web site: *Jinx* "was a new challenge for me—all those words!—but I also have a feeling of freedom as I can write about subjects that are not suitable for younger children." Told in the unconventional style of a series of interrelated poems, *Jinx* relates the story of Jen, a girl who considers herself a jinx and source of bad luck for those around her. Two consecutive boyfriends have died—the first by suicide, the second in an accident—and her parents have split up. Her sister is "born imperfect" and she has a stepmother she hates. She blames another boy for the accident that killed her second boyfriend, and she terrorizes him and his family relentlessly. Her circle of family and friends try to help her cope, but Jen adopts the Jinx name that she has been given at school. She assumes a cold-as-ice persona that won't let anyone get close, and which seems intent on turning Jen from a nice girl into a wild thing. But then she begins to feel bad about being so harsh to a boy who probably didn't mean to harm her second boyfriend, and begins to fall in love with him and shed the Jinx persona. "*Jinx* emerges as a subtly wrought, deeply affecting story dealing with friendship and familial and romantic love," commented a *Kirkus Reviews* critic. "The device of the poetry will attract many young readers; the skill with which it is fold will keep them hooked."

BIOGRAPHICAL AND CRITICAL SOURCES:

BOOKS

Children's Books and Their Creators, edited by Anita Silvey, Houghton Mifflin Company (New York, NY), 1995.

PERIODICALS

Australian Book Review, June, 1992, Meg Sorensen, review of *Sam's Sunday Dad,* pp. 60-63; April, 1995, Linnet Hunter, review of *Light the Lamps,* pp. 61-62; December/January, 1996/1997, Linnet Hunter, review of *The Midnight Gang,* pp. 91-92; October, 1999, Margaret Dunkle, review of *Jenny Angel,* pp. 43-44; February, 2001, review of *Robber Girl,* p. 52.

Booklist, November 1, 1992, Carolyn Phelan, review of *Thank You, Santa,* p. 88; July, 1993, Lisa Napoli, review of *All the Better to See You With!* p. 1978; October 1, 1993, Stephanie Zvirin, review of *The Slumber Party,* p. 355; January 15, 1994, Hazel Rochman, review of *Our Granny,* p. 925; March 15, 1994, Ellen Mandel, review of *Toby,* p. 1375; April 1, 1994, Hazel Rochman, review of *Going Home,* p. 463; February 1, 1996, Leone McDermott, review of *Remember Me,* p. 940; May 15, 1996, Ilene Cooper, review of *Old Pig,* p. 1578; February 1, 1998, Stephanie Zvirin, review of *Big Cat Dreaming,* p. 924; December 1, 1999, Michael Cart, review of *Rosie and Tortoise,* p. 715; May 1, 2000, Catherine Andronik, review of *Tom Goes to Kindergarten,* p. 1680; February 1, 2001, Carolyn Phelan, review of *The Pocket Dogs,* p. 1051; February 15, 2001, Ilene Cooper, review of *Midnight Babies,* p. 1135; September 1, 2001, Shelle Rosenfeld, review of *Nighty Night!* p. 118; November 15, 2001, Gillian Engberg, review of *Fox,* p. 585; January 1, 2002, review of *Midnight Babies,* p. 769.

Book Report, September-October, 1995, Carol Burbridge, review of *Beast,* p. 42.

Books for Keeps, March, 2000, Rosemary Stores, review of *Jenny Angel,* p. 24.

Books in Canada, December, 1997, Gillian Chan, review of *Big Cat Dreaming,* p. 35.

Bulletin of the Center for Children's Books, November, 1992, review of *Thank You, Santa,* p. 94; May, 1993, review of *Space Travellers,* p. 298; June,

1994, review of *Toby,* p. 339; February, 1995, review of *Beast,* p. 218; March, 1996, review of *Old Pig,* p. 247; September, 1991, review of *Let the Celebrations Begin!,* p. 25; March, 2001, review of *The Pocket Dogs,* p. 283; September, 2001, review of *Nighty Night!* p. 40.

Canadian Children's Literature, 1993, Marjorie Gann, review of *A Time for Toys,* pp. 34-36.

Emergency Librarian, March-April, 1987, Anne Hazell, review of *Creatures in the Beard,* p. 23.

Family Matters, winter, 2000, Carole Jean, review of *Sam's Sunday Dad,* p. 70.

Horn Book, November-December, 1989, Hanna B. Zeiger, review of *Mr. Nick's Knitting,* p. 766; March-April, 1990, Karen Jameyson, review of *The Very Best of Friends,* p. 235; May-June, 1990, Margaret A. Bush, review of *The Very Best of Friends,* p. 331; September-October, 1992, Hanna B. Zeiger, review of *The Queen's Holiday,* pp. 580-581; March-April, 1993, Karen Jameyson, review of *My Dearest Dinosaur,* pp. 241-244; September-October, 1993, Maeve Visser Knoth, review of *The Slumber Party,* pp. 593-594; May-June 1994, Hanna B. Zeiger, review of *Our Granny,* pp. 322-323.

Horn Book Guide, spring, 1996, Sheila Geraty, review of *Remember Me,* p. 50; fall, 2000, Patricia Riley, review of *Tom Goes to Kindergarten,* p. 259.

Junior Bookshelf, December, 1984, *There's a Sea in My Bedroom,* pp. 244-245; August, 1991, review of *Let the Celebrations Begin!* p. 149.

Kirkus Reviews, September 15, 1992, review of *Thank You, Santa,* p. 1195; May 1, 1994, review of *Going Home,* p. 638; November 15, 1997, review of *Big Cat Dreaming,* p. 1714; September 15, 2001, review of *Fox,* p. 1371; July 15, 2002, review of *Jinx,* p. 1048.

Los Angeles Times Book Review, December 17, 1989, Patricia MacLachlan, review of *Mr. Nick's Knitting,* p. 7; May 27, 1990, Patricia MacLachlan, review of *The Very Best of Friends,* p. 8; June 9, 1996, Michael Cart, review of *Old Pig,* p. 15.

Magpies, March, 1991, review of *Something Rich and Strange,* p. 28; July, 1991, Melanie Guile, review of *Remember Me,* p. 27; November, 1991, Margot Tyrrell, review of *Let the Celebrations Begin!* p. 29; May, 1992, review of *A Bit of Company,* p. 27; November, 1992, Lynne Ferencz, review of *The Slumber Party,* p. 31; May, 1993, Stephanie Owen Reeder, review of *Sam's Sunday Dad,* p. 27; May, 1993, Mandy Cheetham, review of *All the*

Better to See You With! p. 26; May, 1993, Robyn Shehan, review of *Beast,* p. 29; July, 1993, Stephanie Owen Reeder, review of *Space Travellers,* pp. 30-31; July, 1993, Mandy Cheetham, review of *My Dearest Dinosaur,* p. 29; November, 1993, Renya Spratt, review of *Christmas Magic,* p. 27; July, 1994, Russ Merrin, review of *Our Granny,* p. 26; March, 1995, Melanie Guile, review of *Light the Lamps,* p. 24; July, 1996, Mandy Cheetham, review of *Big Cat Dreaming,* p. 25; March, 1996, Annette Dale-Meiklejohn, review of *Looking after Alice and Co,* p. 34; May, 1998, Moira Robinson, review of *Rosie and Tortoise,* p. 27; September, 1998, Margaret Phillips, review of *Bim Bam Boom!* p. 28; September, 1998, Joan Zahnleitner, review of *First Day,* p. 24; November, 1998, Linnet Hunter, review of *Miss Lily's Fabulous Pink Feather Boa,* p. 24; November, 1999, Nola Allen, review of *Jenny Angel,* pp. 8-9; November, 1999, Joan Zahnleitner, review of *The Midnight Feast,* p. 26; July, 2000, Anne Hanzl, review of *Robber Girl,* p. 46; November, 2001, Kevin Steinberger, review of *The House of Narcissus,* p. 17.

New York Times Book Review, February 18, 1990, review of *Mr. Nick's Knitting,* p. 25.

People, November 28, 1994, review of *Our Granny,* pp. 42-43.

Publishers Weekly, October 13, 1989, Diane Roback, review of *Mr. Nick's Knitting,* p. 53; March 16, 1990, Diane Roback, review of *The Very Best of Friends,* p. 69; July 25, 1991, review of *Let the Celebrations Begin!* p. 52; August 24, 1992, review of *The Queen's Holiday,* p. 78; September 7, 1992, Elizabeth Devereaux, review of *Thank You, Santa,* p. 68; September 28, 1992, review of *My Dearest Dinosaur,* p. 78; April 12, 1993, review of *Space Travelers,* p. 63; July 19, 1993, review of *The Slumber Party,* p. 252; February 14, 1994, review of *Going Home,* pp. 88-89; September 20, 1999, review of *Rosie and Tortoise,* p. 87; February 5, 2001, review of *Midnight Babies,* p. 87; May 1, 2000, review of *Tom Goes to Kindergarten,* p. 70; April, 2001, review of *The Pocket Dogs,* p. 63; July 9, 2001, review of *Nighty Night!* p. 66; October 8, 2001, review of *Fox,* p. 65; August 5, 2002, review of *Jinx,* p. 74.

Quill & Quire, May, 1991, Susan Perren, review of *A Time for Toys,* p. 24.

Reading Teacher, February, 1991, Barbara Kiefer, review of *The Very Best of Friends,* p. 410;

October, 1992, Barbara Tolin, review of *The Very Best of Friends,* p. 146; October, 1992, Barbara Tolin, review of *Let the Celebrations Begin,* p. 146.

School Librarian, summer, 2000, Trevor Dickinson, review of *Jenny Angel,* p. 91.

School Library Journal, October, 1989, Jeanne Marie Clancy, review of *Mr. Nick's Knitting,* pp. 98-99; June, 1990, Patricia Dooley, review of *The Very Best of Friends,* p. 106; July, 1991, Susan Scheps, review of *Let the Celebrations Begin!* p. 75; October, 1992, review of *Thank You, Santa,* p. 45; October, 1992, Nancy Seiner, review of *The Queen's Holiday,* pp. 99-100; January, 1993, Cathryn A. Camper, review of *My Dearest Dinosaur,* p. 88; April, 1993, Karen K. Radtke, review of *Space Travellers,* pp. 103-104; August, 1993, Anna DeWind, review of *All the Better to See You With,* p. 154; October, 1993, Karen James, review of *The Slumber Party,* p. 114; March, 1994, Patricia Pearl Dole, review of *Toby,* p. 212; April, 1994, Karen James, review of *Our Granny,* pp. 114-115; April, 1994, Louise L. Sherman, review of *Going Home,* p. 114; February, 1995, Tim Rausch, review of *Beast,* pp. 100-101; January, 1996, Pamela K. Bomboy, review of *Remember Me,* p. 98; April, 1996, Christina Dorr, review of *Old Pig,* p. 121; February, 1998, Lauralyn Persson, review of *Big Cat Dreaming,* p. 92; September, 1999, Kathleen Staerkel, review of *Rosie and Tortoise,* p. 209; April, 2000, Ginny Gustin, review of *Tom Goes to Kindergarten,* p. 117; April, 2001, Joy Fleishhacker, review of *Midnight Babies,* p. 126; June, 2001, Lisa Gangemi Krapp, review of *The Pocket Dogs,* p. 132; September, 2001, Debbie Stewart, review of *Nighty Night!* p. 208; December, 2001, Susan Scheps, review of *Fox,* pp. 114-115.

Spectator, December 5, 1992, Juliet Townsend, review of *The Queen's Holiday,* p. 49.

Times Educational Supplement, August, 1984, review of *There's a Sea in My Bedroom,* p. 21; April 19, 1996, Robert Dunbar, review of *Old Pig,* p. B18; May 31, 1991, Ann Thwaite, review of *Let the Celebrations Begin!* p. 24.

Tribune Books (Chicago, IL), May 8, 1994, Mary Harris Veeder, review of *Our Granny,* p. 6.

Voice of Youth Advocates, April, 1995, Karen S. H. Roggenkamp, review of *Beast,* p. 29.

Washington Post Book World, May 8, 1994, Michael J. Rosen, review of *Toby,* p. 18.

Wilson Library Bulletin, April, 1994, review of *The Slumber Party,* p. 119.

ONLINE

Allen & Unwin Web site, http://www.allen-unwin.com/ (December 12, 2002).

Gold Creek School Web site, http://www.goldcreek.act. edu.au/ (December 12, 2002), review of *Jinx.*

Kane/Miller Book Publishers Web site, http://www. kanemiller.com/ (December 12, 2002).

Scholastic Australia Web site, http://www.scholastic. com.au/ (December 12, 2002).

Splatt Web site, http://abc.net.au/splatt/ (December 12, 2002), profile of Margaret Wild.

Walker & Company Web site, http://www.walkerbooks. com/ (December 12, 2002).*

*   *   *

WILLENS, Harold 1914-2003

OBITUARY NOTICE—See index for CA sketch: Born April 26, 1914, in Chemigov, Russia; died of heart failure March 17, 2003, in Brentwood, CA. Entrepreneur, political activist, and author. Willens is best remembered as an anti-nuclear weapons activist who founded the Center for Defense Information. After emigrating from the Ukraine with his parents to avoid persecution after the Bolshevik Revolution, he attended the University of California at Los Angeles and earned a B.A. in 1944. He served in the U.S. Marine Corps at the end of World War II, and visiting the Japanese cities of Nagasaki and Hiroshima after they were devastated by nuclear warheads made a lasting impression on Willens. Back in America, he founded and ran Wilshop Corp., a distributor of condiments to restaurants, working as president and chairman of the board of directors until 1975; in 1949, he also founded the textile machinery company Factory Equipment Corp. in Los Angeles, running this company until 1982; in addition, he owned and developed commercial and residential real estate. The success of his business ventures gave him the capital he needed to campaign for nuclear-freeze initiatives. He supported presidential candidates, including Eugene McCarthy, George McGovern, and Jimmy Carter, who were for nuclear arms control, but when he became disappointed by the lack of progress politicians made, he started grass-roots campaigns on his own. His greatest success was in authoring what became known as the

California Bilateral Nuclear Weapons Freeze Initiative, which was passed in 1982. He also cofounded the Businessmen's Educational Fund, which later became the Center for Defense Information, and helped found the Interfaith Center to Reverse the Arms Race. In the late 1980s Willens traveled to Russia as a business consultant and helped train businessmen there on how to run a factory. Willens book *The Trimtab Factor: How Business Executives Can Help Solve the Nuclear Arms Crisis* (1984) includes his thoughts about how citizens can influence politics for the public good.

OBITUARIES AND OTHER SOURCES:

BOOKS

Writers Directory, 12th edition, St. James Press (Detroit, MI), 1996.

PERIODICALS

Los Angeles Times, March 20, 2003, p. B15.

*   *   *

WILSON, Kenneth G(eorge) 1923-2003

OBITUARY NOTICE—See index for *CA* sketch: Born April 21, 1923, in Akron, OH; died March 11, 2003, in Mansfield, CT. Educator and author. Wilson was a longtime English professor and former dean and vice president at the University of Connecticut. His A.B. degree, earned in 1943, was from Albion College. After serving in the U.S. Army Signal Corps from 1943 to 1946, he completed his M.A. in 1948 and his Ph.D. in 1951 at the University of Michigan. Except for a year spent at the University of Bergen, Wilson's entire academic career was served at the University of Connecticut. Beginning as an instructor there in 1951, he became a full professor of English in 1963, headed the department from 1965 to 1966, was dean of the College of Liberal Arts and Sciences from 1966 to 1970, vice president of academic programs for the next four years, and vice president of academic affairs from 1974 to 1981. Returning to teaching, he retired as professor emeritus in 1989. As a university administrator, Wilson was credited by his peers for

helping to build a nationally respected life sciences department, and for generally doing the same for the university as a whole. An authority on the English language, he coedited books such as *Essays on Language and Usage* (1959; second edition, 1963) and *The Harbrace Guide to Dictionaries* (1963) and was the author of *Van Winkle's Return: Change in American English, 1966-1986* (1987) and *The Columbia Guide to Standard American English* (1993).

OBITUARIES AND OTHER SOURCES:

PERIODICALS

Chronicle for Higher Education, March 23, 2003, p. A37.

ONLINE

UConn News Online, http://www.news.uconn.edu/ (March 14, 2003).

*   *   *

WILSON, Rachel
See DUNCAN, Alice

*   *   *

WINFREY, Lee 1932-2003

OBITUARY NOTICE—See index for *CA* sketch: Born July 7, 1932, in Knoxville, TN; died March 31, 2003, in Philadelphia, PA. Journalist, critic, educator, and author. Winfrey was a reporter who became most well known for his writings as a television critic. He was a graduate of the University of Tennessee, where he earned a B.S. in 1966, and the University of Iowa, where he received a master's degree in 1968. He also attended graduate school at Harvard from 1971 to 1972. Winfrey got his start as a reporter for the *Nashville Tennessean* during the late 1950s. This was followed by stints at the *Knoxville News-Sentinel* and the *Miami Herald.* From 1966 to 1968 he worked as an instructor at the University of Iowa before returning as a journalist for the *Detroit Free Press.* In 1972 he started writing his syndicated column, "On Television," and was elected president of the Television Critics Association the next year.

OBITUARIES AND OTHER SOURCES:

PERIODICALS

Washington Post, April 7, 2003, p. B6.

* * *

WINKELMAN, Stanley J. 1922-1999

PERSONAL: Born September 23, 1922, in Sault Sainte Marie, MI; died August 19, 1999; son of Leon (a department store cofounder and president) and Josephine (Rosenblum) Winkelman; married Margaret Jayne Wallace, March 27, 1943; children: Andra Barr Winkelman Soble, Marjory Winkelman Epstein, Roger. *Ethnicity:* "Caucasian." *Education:* University of Michigan, B.S., 1943. *Politics:* Democrat. *Religion:* Jewish.

CAREER: Research chemist for California universities, 1943-44; Winkelman Stores, Inc., Detroit, MI, staff member, 1946-48, general merchandise administrator, 1948-51, vice president and general merchandise manager, 1951-57, senior vice president, 1957-60, executive vice president, 1960-65, president and chief operating officer, 1965-76, chair and chief executive officer, 1976-84; Stanley Winkelman Associates, Farmington Hills, MI, consultant to business management, 1984-99. Observer/Eccentric Newspapers, photojournalist and special writer, 1987-99; Video Billboard, Inc., marketing consultant, 1990-92; also consultant to U.S. Agency for International Development. Detroit Commission on Community Relations, member, 1962-70; Greater Detroit Chamber of Commerce, member of board of directors, 1968-71; New Detroit, Inc., member of executive committee, 1969-88, chair, 1971, honorary member of board of directors, 1986-99; Metropolitan Affairs Corp., member of board of directors, 1970-99, president, 1977-85; Detroit Citizens Education Task Force, cochair, 1972-76; Detroit Board of Education, member of Monitoring Commission, 1974-78; Detroit Economic Growth Corp., member of board of directors, 1976-90, cochair of Expenditures

Task Force, 1976-78; Detroit Renaissance, Inc., member of board of directors, 1979-84, member of long-range planning committee, 1979-88; Detroit Executive Service Corps, director, 1984-86, vice chair, 1986-95, director emeritus, 1996-99; Detroit Strategic Planning Project, member of task force on jobs and economic development, 1987-88. Economic Alliance for Michigan, member of board of directors, 1982-85; Michigan Governor's Commission on Higher Education, member, 1983-84; Michigan Commission on Art in Public Places, chair, 1986-91. Wayne State University, creator of fellowship in gerontology, 1960-80, member of advisory committee for Walter Reuther Library of Labor and Urban Affairs, beginning 1965, vice president of Wayne State University Fund, 1975; University of Michigan, creator of Memorial Lecture for Visiting Scholars in Gerontology, 1978, creator of Winkelman Memorial Chair in Retail Marketing, 1980, guest lecturer, 1986, 1988. Member of board of directors, Win Spot Co. Ltd., 1985-88, Entertainment Publications, Inc., 1986-92, Real Estate One, beginning 1987, Family Express Video, 1988-91, and Ambassador Funds, Comerica Bank, 1989-94. Member of board of trustees, Detroit Symphony Orchestra and Orchestra Hall, beginning 1985. Jewish Community Council of Metropolitan Detroit, member of board of directors, 1956-99, president, 1960-63; Jewish Welfare Federation, board member, beginning 1956, member of executive committee, 1965-84, vice president, 1969-74; Union of American Hebrew Congregations, member of National Commission on Social Action, 1958-70; Jewish Home for the Aged, member of board of directors, 1958-61; Detroit Round Table of Christians and Jews, member, 1963-88; Council of Jewish Welfare Funds, member of Urban Affairs Commission, 1977-80, 1985-88; Jewish Community Foundation, chair, 1979-88. United Foundation, board member, 1950-91, member of executive committee, 1969-91; United Community Services, member of board of directors, 1970-75; Community Foundation for Southeastern Michigan, board member, beginning 1984, cochair of Development Committee, 1984-90. National Commission for U.S.-China Relations, member, 1977-88; National Municipal League, member of council, 1977-80. *Military service:* U.S. Navy, Amphibious Forces, 1944-46; became lieutenant junior grade.

MEMBER: National Retail Merchants Association (director, 1966-85; member of executive committee, 1974-85; chair of consumer affairs, 1976-85; vice president, 1978-85), National Association for the

Advancement of Colored People (life member), Historical Society for the U.S. District Court for the Eastern District of Michigan (vice president, 1992-93), Detroit Economic Club (director, 1968-96), Detroit Club, Franklin Hills Country Club, University of Michigan President's Club.

AWARDS, HONORS: St. Cyprian Award, 1965; Amity Award, American Jewish Congress, 1968; Liberty Bell Award, Detroit Bar Association, 1968; Human Relations Award, University of Detroit, 1968; Histadrut Award, 1975; Wayne State University, Builder of Detroit Award, 1975, D.H.L., 1993; Fred M. Butzel Memorial Award, Jewish Welfare Association, 1979; Silver Plaque, National Retail Merchants Association, 1982; Great American Traditions Award, B'nai B'rith, 1982; Tree of Life Award, Jewish National Fund, 1983; Knights of Charity Award, P.I.M.E. Missionaries, 1984; Booker T. Washington Award, 1985; Mercy Medallion Award, Mercy College of Detroit, 1986.

WRITINGS:

A Life in the Balance: The Memoirs of Stanley J. Winkelman, Wayne State University Press (Detroit, MI), 2000.

BIOGRAPHICAL AND CRITICAL SOURCES:

PERIODICALS

Michigan Historical Review, fall, 2001, Kenneth Waltzer, review of *A Life in the Balance: The Memoirs of Stanley J. Winkelman,* p. 191.

[Date of death provided by wife, Margaret W. Winkelman.]

*   *   *

WOLIN, Sheldon S. 1922-

PERSONAL: Born August 4, 1922 in Chicago, IL; married, 1944; three children. *Education:* Oberlin College, B.A., 1946; Harvard University, M.A., 1947, Ph. D., 1950.

ADDRESSES: Office—Department of Political Science, Princeton University, 308 Corwin Hall, Princeton, NJ 08540.

CAREER: Political scientist, author, and educator. Northwestern University, Chicago, IL, instructor of political science, 1950; Oberlin College, Oberlin, OH, assistant professor, 1950-54, Jaszi memorial lecturer, 1962; University of California, Berkeley, instructor, 1954-58, assistant professor, 1958-61, professor of political science, 1961-71; Princeton University, professor of political science, 1961—. United States Air Force War College, lecturer, 1961. *Military service:* U.S. Army Air Forces, 1942-45, became first lieutenant.

MEMBER: American Political Science Association.

AWARDS, HONORS: Harvard University fellow, 1948-49, Sheldon fellow, 1949; Fulbright fellow, Magdalen College, Oxford, 1949-50; Rockefeller fellow, 1954-55.

WRITINGS:

Politics and Vision: Continuity and Innovation in Western Political Thought, Little, Brown (Boston, MA), 1960.
(Editor, with Seymour Martin Lipset) *The Berkeley Student Revolt: Facts and Interpretations,* Anchor Books (Garden City, NY), 1965.
(With John H. Schaar) *The Berkeley Rebellion and Beyond: Essays on Politics and Education in the Technological Society,* New York Review (New York, NY), 1970.
Hobbes and the Epic Tradition of Political Theory, introduction by Richard E. Ashcraft, William Andrews Clark Memorial Library (Los Angeles, CA), 1970.
The Presence of the Past: Essays on the State and the Constitution, Johns Hopkins University Press (Baltimore, MD), 1989.
Tocqueville between Two Worlds: The Making of a Political and Theoretical Life, Princeton University Press (Princeton, NJ), 2001.

Contributor and editor of *Democracy;* contributor to volumes such as *Reassessing the Sixties,* edited by Steven Macedo.

SIDELIGHTS: Sheldon S. Wolin is a prominent political scientist and social critic. Born on August 4, 1922 in Chicago, Illinois, Wolin served as a first lieutenant in the U.S. Army Air Force during World War II. Wolin married in 1944 and has three children. A career academic with a Ph.D. from Harvard University, Wolin has taught at Northwestern University, Oberlin College, University of California, Berkeley, and Princeton University. Highly regarded as a political thinker, Wolin is considered "our foremost theorist of the political" by critics such as Nancy L. Schwartz, writing in *American Political Science Review.*

Wolin's 1960 book *Politics and Vision: Continuity and Innovation in Western Political Thought* has influenced generations of political science students. "As an undergraduate seeking enlightenment, I asked my professor to explain to me what political theorists do," commented Steven M. Dworetz, writing in *Journal of Politics.* The professor handed Dworetz a "well-thumbed copy of Sheldon Wolin's *Politics and Vision*" and encouraged him to read it. "For once I did as I was told," Dworetz commented, "and, in awe, I began to understand."

Dworetz's reaction to Wolin's 1989 volume, *The Presence of the Past: Essays on the State and the Constitution* evoked a similar sense of awe, he said, but "there is also a chilling quality to an otherwise exhilarating experience, for here the enlightenment so generously supplied by Wolin reveals a grim view of the American Republic in the wake of its Bicentennial celebrations."

A collection of eleven essays spanning several years, *The Presence of the Past* provides a detailed critique of the American state, from the ideas of democracy promulgated by Alexis de Tocqueville to the American political culture of the 1980s. "A majority of the essays display an originality and wisdom that give new and exciting insights into the art and science of political organization as they affect the U.S. experience," wrote R. J. Steamer in *Choice.* Wolin argues that the fundamental ideas behind the U.S. Constitution and democracy, and the concomitant mechanisms for limiting political power and holding it accountable, are endangered because of a decentering of power related to "privatization of public functions," he wrote, which "immunizes power against public scrutiny and democratic control," Dworetz remarked. Privatization has created forms of power that "far exceed the power capacity envisioned in the Constitution," Wolin wrote.

Although privatization is assumed to bring about the reduction or elimination of state power, that is not its ultimate result, Dworetz said. What occurs instead, observed Wolin, "is not the elimination of power but the elimination of politics, that is, the public discussion and argument" that debates the uses and goals of power. Dworetz concluded, "Privatization of public functions—especially of *coercive* functions—must therefore be seen as *enhancing* power precisely by rendering it publicly unaccountable."

Other essays in *The Presence of the Past* provide intellectual analysis of a variety of texts in political theory. These include works by Locke, Tocqueville, Montesquieu, and even the Old Testament. "Here Wolin is graceful and illuminates old texts with new questions," Schwartz observed. "The analyses of Tocqueville on time and municipal spirit and Montesquieu on intermediary bodies . . . are brilliant." Reviewer Bin Ramke, writing in *Bloomsbury Review,* commented, "The book is elegantly written, with an awareness and investment in the theory and the practice of living in the United States of America and the world at large today. It is, in other words, a book of intelligence and passion, which, at its heart, is trying to save us."

In *Tocqueville between Two Worlds: The Making of a Political and Theoretical Life* Wolin presents a detailed biographical, political, and theoretical examination of Tocqueville, a French intellectual considered by many to be the most influential political thinker in American history. "Almost two centuries after it was written, Alexis de Tocqueville's *Democracy in America* exerts an extraordinary grip on the American imagination," wrote Alan Ryan in *New York Review of Books.* "Tocqueville is so frequently invoked in contemporary political arguments that it is hard to appreciate how extraordinary his authority is." A visitor to the newly minted United States of America, Tocqueville was a twenty-five-year-old French aristocrat when he wrote *Democracy in America,* a two-volume study of America and its political structure and institutions.

"For many, Tocqueville is primarily the French observer who traveled to America in 1830-31 and recognized the superiority of our institutions and way of life," wrote Daniel J. Mahoney in *First Things.* Tocqueville's trip to America was ostensibly to observe the American penal system, but instead it was the American system of a democratic republic that appealed to him. Tocqueville "celebrated the success of

Americans in creating and sustaining a democratic republic, praised their morals and religion, and left his French readers in no doubt that while much of this American success was fortuitous, most was not." Ryan wrote. French attempts to establish a republican government "had collapsed in bloodshed and the Terror," Ryan wrote, while the American attempt succeeded. The United States "certainly raised the question of how Americans had achieved what the French could not," Ryan remarked.

Despite Tocqueville's profound influence on American politics, however, he was not a wholehearted advocate of all concepts of democracy. In Wolin's book, he "offers a Tocqueville who is extraordinarily complex, deeply conflicted and by no means the uncritical booster of democratic possibility he is sometimes made out to be," wrote Jean Bethke Elshtain in *Washington Post Book World*. Tocqueville, wrote Mahoney, "was an observer and practitioner of politics who tried to mediate between two sets of oppositions—on the one hand, theory and practice, and on the other, democracy and what he somewhat capaciously called aristocracy (encompassing all the worlds that came before the New World of democratic consent)."

Wolin, Elshtain observed, "engages the entire body of Tocqueville's work, displaying both the historical context of his writings and their biographical urgencies; indeed, at points, *Tocqueville between Two Worlds* is as much an intellectual biography as it is a work of more abstract political thought." Stephen Holmes, writing in *New Republic,* commented that "Wolin's lengthy paraphrases, generous citations, and pungent commentaries make this a useful book for all those seeking to deepen their understanding of Tocqueville." Delba Winthrop, writing on the *Claremont Institute Web site,* observed, "Most books on Tocqueville are either biographies or studies of one, or at most a few, of his writings. Sheldon Wolin's *Tocqueville between Two Worlds* is an attempt to arrive at a coherent, comprehensive understanding of Tocqueville's political theory by analyzing and evaluating his political life and writings as a whole. It raises all the important questions, takes texts seriously—Tocqueville's as well as those of other political theorists—and is full of original and provocative readings of these texts."

BIOGRAPHICAL AND CRITICAL SOURCES:

PERIODICALS

American Historical Review, June, 1974, William L. O'Neill, review of *The Berkeley Rebellion and Beyond: Essays on Politics and Education in the Technological Society,* pp. 911-912.

American Political Science Review, December, 1990, Nancy L. Schwartz, review of *The Presence of the Past: Essays on the State and the Constitution,* pp. 1366-1367.

Bloomsbury Review, Bin Ramke, review of *The Presence of the Past,* p. 5.

Choice, June, 1990, R.J. Steamer, review of *The Presence of the Past,* p. 1755.

First Things, March, 2002, Daniel J. Mahoney, review of *Tocqueville between Two Worlds: The Making of a Political and Theoretical Life,* pp. 60-63.

Georgia Review, Summer, 1997, Sanford Pinsker, review of *Reassessing the Sixties,* pp. 362-364.

Journal of Politics, November, 1990, Steven M. Dworetz, review of *The Presence of the Past,* pp. 1283-1286.

Legal Studies Forum, winter, 1990, Lorraine K. Koc, review of *The Presence of the Past,* pp. 89-94.

Library Journal, January 15, 1971, Fay M. Blake, review of *The Berkeley Rebellion and Beyond: Essays on Politics and Education in the Technological Society,* p. 182; September 1, 2002, Thomas A. Karel, review of *Tocqueville between Two Worlds,* p. 209.

National Review, April 12, 1982, Charles R. Kesler, "Conservatism and the Founding Fathers," pp. 350-351, 375.

New Left Review, January-February, 2002, Gopal Balakrishnan, review of *Tocqueville between Two Worlds,* pp. 151-160.

New Republic, December 23, 1981, Peter Shaw, "The End of the Seventies; You Don't Need a Weatherman to Know That the Climate Has Changed," pp. 21-23; March 4, 2002, Stephen Holmes, review of *Tocqueville between Two Worlds,* p. 31.

New Yorker, October 15, 2001, Adam Gopnik, "The Habit of Democracy: Alexis de Tocqueville and the Pleasures of Citizenship," pp. 212-216.

New York Review of Books, June 27, 2002, Alan Ryan, "Visions of Politics," review of *Tocqueville between Two Worlds,* pp. 35-38.

New York Times, September 26, 1982, "The American Left Still Searches for a Clear Political Direction," p. E5.

Philological Quarterly, July, 1971, Craig Walton, review of *Hobbes and the Epic Tradition of Political Theory,* p. 441.

Political Communication, April-June 1992, Gordon Lloyd, review of *The Presence of the Past: Essays on the State and the Constitution,* pp. 143-150.

Political Science Reviewer, fall, 1981, Joseph E. Goldberg, "Sheldon Wolin's Vision of Politics: A Critical Examination," pp. 83-132.

Political Theory, November, 1990, Sanford Levinson, review of *The Presence of the Past,* pp. 701-705.

Texas Law Review, April, 1991, James M. O'Fallon, review of *The Presence of the Past,* pp. 1253-1257.

Times Literary Supplement, March 8, 2002, Biancamaria Fontana, "A Craving for New Certainties," p. 10.

Wall Street Journal, September 26, 2001, Thomas Pavel, review of *Tocqueville between Two Worlds,* p. 4.

Washington Post Book World, November 11, 2001, Jean Bethke Elshtain, review of *Tocqueville between Two Worlds,* p. 13.

ONLINE

Claremont Institute Web site, http://www.claremond. org/ (December 12, 200), Delba Winthrop, review of *Tocqueville between Two Worlds.*

Foundations of Political Theory Web site, http://www. political-theory.org/ (December 12, 2002), review of *Tocqueville between Two Worlds.*

Princeton University Press Web site, http://www.pup. princeton.edu/ (December 12, 2002).*

*   *   *

WOODCRAFT, Elizabeth

PERSONAL: Female. *Education:* Birmingham University, philosophy degree.

ADDRESSES: Agent—Annette Green, Annette Green Authors' Agency, 1 East Cliff Rd., Turnbridge Wells, Kent TN4 9AD, United Kingdome. *E-mail*—webmaster@ewoodcraft1.fsnet.co.uk.

CAREER: Barrister and author. Called to the Bar of London, England, 1980.

AWARDS, HONORS: John Creasy Memorial Dagger shortlist, Crime Writers of America, 2001, and Lambda Literary Award for best lesbian mystery, 2003, both for *Good Bad Woman.*

WRITINGS:

Good Bad Woman, Kensington Publishing (New York, NY), 2002.

Babyface, HarperCollins UK (London, England), 2003.

SIDELIGHTS: Elizabeth Woodcraft is an author and lawyer living in England. After graduating from Birmingham University with a degree in philosophy, she taught English in Leicestershire. She lived for a year in France, then worked for the National Women's Aid Federation, after which she read for the Bar. In her legal career, Woodcraft has represented a variety of protestors, activists, and laborers on strike. Among her other clients are battered women, child victims of sexual abuse, and gay parents pursuing parental rights.

Woodcraft's first novel, *Good Bad Woman,* introduces English barrister Frankie Richmond, a thirtysomething lesbian suffering from career doldrums and a lack of lucrative work. Frankie agrees to represent her friend Saskia in court on a charge of drunk and disorderly. At the conclusion of the hearing, a suspicious-looking man asks for Frankie's and her client's names, but she refuses to divulge the information. Frankie later spots the man again, and decides to follow him in her car. The man doesn't respond well to being tailed; he disables Frankie's car and gives her a black eye. When the man later turns up murdered—and clutching Frankie's license plate—suspicion turns on her as a murderer. Frankie lands in jail, charged with murder, and her situation takes an even grimmer turn when the murdered man's credit card is found in her apartment. To clear her name, she must find Saskia, but her friend is hard to locate. In the midst of her search for Saskia, Frankie meets and begins and affair with nightclub singer Margo, tries to carry on her usual relationships, and searches for rare tracks to add to her Motown collection.

A *Kirkus Reviews* critic remarked that "strong plotting, characters with depth and cunning, and a lesbian heroine who'll make readers all over the map rethink their sexual preferences mark this debut as a keeper." Belinda Meteyard, writing in *Feminist Legal Studies,* observed, "The book is enjoyable to read and was, I suspect, equally enjoyable to write." The authentic setting, featuring real streets, cafes, and restaurants, "adds an extra dimension of enjoyment of the book," Meteyard said. Rex Klett, writing in *Library Journal,* called the book "lively and imaginative."

"*Good Bad Woman* is a funky urban noir crime thriller," wrote Harriet Klausner on the *Best Reviews* Web site. "The who-done-it is very cleverly constructed and multi-layered with many interconnecting paths." Yvonne Klein, writing on *Reviewing the Evidence* online, commented that the novel suffers from faults expected from a first novel, including some inconsistent characterizations, weakness of plot, and a too-early climax. "But, as an entry in the not overly large sub-genre of lesbian crime fiction, *Good Bad Woman* has much to recommend it," Klein concluded.

BIOGRAPHICAL AND CRITICAL SOURCES:

PERIODICALS

Feminist Legal Studies, December, 2001, Belinda Meteyard, review of *Good Bad Woman,* p. 271.
Kirkus Reviews, July 15, 2002, review of *Good Bad Woman,* pp. 999-1000.
Library Journal, August, 2002, Rex Klett, review of *Good Bad Woman,* pp. 149-150.
Publishers Weekly, September 2, 2002, review of *Good Bad Woman,* p. 58.

ONLINE

Best Reviews, http://www.thebestreviews.com/ (December 13, 2002), review of *Good Bad Woman.*
Elizabeth Woodcraft Web site, http://www.elizabeth woodcraft.com (December 13, 2002).
Reviewing The Evidence, http://www.reviewingthe evidence.com/ (December 13, 2002), review of *Good Bad Woman.*

*　　*　　*

WYNORSKI, Jim 1950-

   (Arch Stanton, Jay Andrews, Noble Henry, Noble Henri)

PERSONAL: Born 1950.

ADDRESSES: Agent—c/o New City Releasing, 20700 Ventura Blvd., Suite 350, Woodland Hills, CA 91364.

CAREER: Director, producer, actor, and screenwriter. Director of films, including (also producer) *The Lost Empire,* JGM Enterprises, 1985; (also producer) *Chopping Mall* (also known as *Killbots*), Concorde/ Lightning, 1986; *Deathstalker II: Duel of the Titans,* New Horizons, 1987; *Big Bad Mama II,* Concorde, 1987; (also producer) *Not of This Earth,* Concorde, 1988; *Return of the Swamp Thing,* Millimeter, 1989; *Transylvania Twist,* Concorde, 1990; (as Arch Stanton; also casting director) *Sorority House Massacre II* (also known as *Night Frenzy* and *Nighty Nightmare*), Concorde, 1990; *The Haunting of Morella,* Concorde, 1990; (as Arch Stanton; also producer and casting director) *Hard to Die* (also known as *Tower of Terror*), 1990; (as Arch Stanton; also producer) *Scream Queen Hot Tub Party* (also known as *Hollywood Scream Queen Hot Tub Party*), WynRay Video, 1991; *976-EVIL 2: The Astral Factor,* Vestron Video, 1991; *Munchie,* New Horizons Home Video, 1992; *Sins of Desire,* Cinetel Films, 1993; *Little Miss Millions* (also known as *Home for Christmas* and *Little Miss Zillions*), 1993; *Sorceress* (also known as *Temptress II*), Triboro Entertainment Group, 1994; *Point of Seduction: Body Chemistry III,* New Horizons Home Video, 1994; *Munchie Strikes Back,* Concorde-New Horizon, 1994; *Ghoulies IV,* 1994; (also producer) *Dinosaur Island,* New Horizons, 1994; (as Noble Henry) *Virtual Desire,* Triboro Entertainment Group, 1995; (and producer and casting director) *Hard Bounty,* Triboro Entertainment Group, 1995; (and casting director, as Noble Henry) *Body Chemistry IV: Full Exposure,* 1995; (and producer) *Vamiprella,* Concorde, 1996; *Demolition High,* Astra Cinema/New City Releasing, 1996; (and producer) *The Assault,* Sunset Films International, 1996; *Against the Law,* Sunset Films International, 1997; *The Pandora Project,* New City Releasing/ Cinetel Films, 1998; *Storm Trooper,* New City Releasing, 1998; (and producer) *Desert Thunder,* New Horizons Home Video, 1998; (as Jay Andrews) *Stealth Fighter,* Artisan Entertainment, 1999; *Final Voyage,* New City Releasing, 1999; *The Bare Wench Project,* 1999; (as Jay Andrews) *Militia,* Cinetel Films, 2000; *Crash Point Zero,* New City Releasing, 2000; (as Jay Andrews) *Ablaze,* New City Releasing, 2000; (as Jay Andrews) *Rangers,* 2000; *Thy Neighbor's Wife* (also known as *Poison*), 2000; (as Jay Andrews) *Raptor,* 2001; *The Bare Wench Project 2: Scared Topless,* 2001; (as Noble Henry; and producer) *Gale Force,* 2002; (as Jay Andrews) *Project V.I.P.E.R.,* 2002; (and executive producer) *The Bare Wench Project 3: Nymphs of Mystery Mountain,* 2002; *Cheerleader Massacre,* 2003; and (as Jay Andrews) *Curse of the Komodo,* 2003.

Also producer of films *Biohazard: The Alien Force* (also known as *Biohazard II*), Trimark Pictures, 1995; *Sorceress II: The Temptress,* New Horizons Home Video, 1996; *Fugitive Rage,* A-pix Entertainment/ Royal Oaks Entertainment, 1996; *Friend of the Family II* (also known as *Hell Hath No Fury, Innocence Betrayed,* and *Passionate Revenge*), New City Releasing, 1996. Under name Noble Henry, producer of films *Storm Catcher,* New City Releasing, 1999; *Sonic Impact,* New City Releasing, 1999; *Jill Rips* (also known as *The Bone Ripper, Jill the Ripper, The Leatherwoman* and *Tied Up*), New City Releasing, 2000; *Submerged,* New City Releasing/Underwater Productions, 2000; *Captured* (also known as *Agent Red*), New City Releasing, 2000; and *Kept* (also known as *Playback*), 2001.

Also executive producer of films, including *Screwballs,* New World Pictures, 1983; *Dark Universe,* Curb Video, 1993; *The Skateboard Kid 2,* Concorde-New Horizons, 1995; (also casting director) *Midnight Tease II* (also known as *Strip Show*), New City Releasing, 1995; *Bikini Drive-in,* Metropolis Motion Pictures, 1995; *Vice Girls,* Concorde, 1996; and (with others) *Hybrid,* 1997. Also, as Noble Henry, casting director of the films *Night Eyes 4* (also known as *Midnight Hour* and *Night Eyes . . . Fatal Passion*), 1995; and *Scorned 2,* 1996.

Actor in films, including (as dying soldier; under the name Arch Stanton) *Deathstalker II: Duel of the Titans,* New Horizons, 1987; (as the man who does lunch) *Hollywood Boulevard II,* Metro-Goldwyn-Mayer (MGM), 1989; (uncredited; as porno director) *Hard to Die* (also known as *Tower of Terror*), 1990; (as Ralph) *The Bikini Carwash Company,* 1992; (as nightclub master of ceremonies) *Dragon Fire,* Concorde-New Horizons, 1993; (uncredited; as man at Denver bus ticket counter and radio voice) *Little Miss Millions* (also known as *Home for Christmas* and *Little Miss Zillions*), New Horizons Home Video, 1993; (as hanging judge) *Body Chemistry IV: Full Exposure,* New Horizons Home Video, 1995; (as drunk outside bar) *The Skateboard Kid 2,* Concorde-New Horizons, 1995; (as drunk at bar) *Midnight Tease II* (also known as *Strip Show*), New City Releasing, 1995; *Bikini Drive-in,* Metropolis Motion Pictures, 1995; (as guy who can't believe his eyes) *Attack of the Sixty-Foot Centerfold,* New Horizons Home Video, 1995; *Alien Escape* (also known as *Galaxy Girls* and *Mars Assault!*), Falcon Films, 1995; (as pig-truck driver) *Masseuse*

(also known as *American Masseuse*), Triboro Entertainment Group, 1996; (uncredited; as man with top popper) *Vice Girls,* 1996; (uncredited; as police sniper) *Demolition High,* Astra Cinema/New City Releasing, 1996; (under the name Noble Henri; as Captain Rockford) *Carnal Cruise* (also known as *Ocean of Dreams*), 1997; and (as himself) *Some Nudity Required* (documentary), Seventh Art Releasing, 1998.

Worked on made-for-television movies, including (as director) *Roger Corman Presents The Wasp Woman* (also known as *Forbidden Beauty*), Sci-Fi Channel and Showtime, 1995; (as piranha wrangler) *Roger Corman Presents Piranha,* Showtime, 1995; (as assistant casting advisor) *Roger Corman Presents Black Scorpion,* Showtime, 1995; (as production executive) *Roger Corman Presents Subliminal Seduction* (also known as *The Corporation*), Showtime, 1996. Appeared in documentary television special *Heartstoppers: Horror at the Movies,* 1992. As Noble Henry, composed score for film *Stripteaser II,* 1997; as Arch Stanton, cinematographer for film *Shreck,* 1990.

WRITINGS:

(Editor) *They Came from Outer Space: Twelve Classic Science-Fiction Tales That Became Major Motion Pictures,* introduction by Ray Bradbury, Doubleday (Garden City, NY), 1980.

SCREENPLAYS

(With Jack Hill) *Sorceress,* New World Pictures, 1982.
(With Linda Shayne) *Screwballs,* New World Pictures, 1983.
(With R. J. Robertson; and producer) *The Lost Empire,* JGM Enterprises, 1985.
(With Steve Mitchell; and director and producer) *Chopping Mall* (also known as *Killbots*), Concorde/ Lightning, 1986.
(With R. J. Robertson; and director) *Big Bad Mama II,* Concorde, 1987.
(With R. J. Robertson, Mark Hanna, and Charles B. Griffith; and director and producer) *Not of This Earth,* Concorde, 1988.
Transylvania Twist, Concorde, 1989.
(With others) *Beastmaster 2: Through the Portal of Time,* New Line Cinema, 1991.

(As Arch Stanton; with Fred Olin Ray) *Scream Queen Hot Tub Party* (also known as *Hollywood Scream Queen Hot Tub Party*), WynRay Video, 1991.

(With R. J. Robertson) *Munchie,* New Horizons Home Video, 1992.

(With R. J. Robertson) *Final Embrace,* 1992.

(With R. J. Robertson) *Little Miss Millions* (also known as *Home for Christmas* and *Little Miss Zillions*), New Horizons Home Video, 1993.

(With R. J. Robertson) *Munchie Strikes Back,* Concorde-New Horizons, 1994.

(As Noble Henri; and director and producer) *The Bare Wench Project,* 1999.

(As Jay Andrews; with Frances Doel and Michael B. Druxman; and director) *Raptor,* 2001.

(And director and executive producer) *The Bare Wench Project 3: Nymphs of Mystery Mountain,* 2002.

Also author of songs "Just Give Me Action" and "Think of the Royalties" for film *Transylvania Twist,* Concorde, 1989; and of stories on which films *Forbidden World, Think Big, Deathstalker II, House IV, Sins of Desire,* and *The Pandora Project* were based.

SIDELIGHTS: Jim Wynorski may be one of the best-known creators of so-called "B" movies in Hollywood. He began his career working for Roger Corman, the legendary director, producer, and owner of the movie production and distribution company New World Pictures. Like Corman's creations, Wynorski's films generally feature some combination of horror, action, and titillation and are usually produced on a low budget. Under one of his screen names, Jay Andrews, Wynorski has become famous for his ability to create original action movies using stock footage scavenged from other films and film companies. For example, he created the films *Extreme Limits, Militia, Desert Thunder,* and *Stealth Fighter* using stock footage from Paramount Pictures' series of films based on Tom Clancy novels, among them *The Hunt for Red October, Clear and Present Danger,* and *Patriot Games.*

Wynorski is also known for writing and directing a series of films that spoof the blockbuster independent film *The Blair Witch Project.* Wynorski's films, *The Bare Wench Project, The Bare Wench Project 2: Scared Topless,* and *The Bare Wench Project 3: The Nymphs of Mystery Mountain,* feature four young women who go out into the woods in search of the

Bare Wench, a ghost who, legend has it, was a prostitute who was run out of an old mining town and now haunts the woods surrounding it. One of the original *Bare Wench Project*'s most notable scenes, which closely parallels a scene from *The Blair Witch Project,* features the girls stumbling across a clearing in the woods which is littered with signs of the presence of the Bare Wench, including lingerie hanging from the trees and arcane symbols formed out of adult novelties.

BIOGRAPHICAL AND CRITICAL SOURCES:

BOOKS

Contemporary Theatre, Film, and Television, Volume 37, Gale (Detroit, MI), 2002.

Fischer, Dennis, *Horror Film Directors, 1931-1990,* McFarland & Co. (Jefferson, NC), 1991.

Reginald, Robert, *Science Fiction & Fantasy Literature, 1975-1991,* Gale (Detroit, MI), 1992.

Singer, Michael, *Michael Singer's Film Directors,* 9th international edition, Lone Eagle Publishing (Los Angeles, CA), 1992.

PERIODICALS

Library Journal, April 15, 1981, review of *They Came from Outer Space,* pp. 906-907.

Los Angeles Times, November 9, 1982, Linda Gross, review of *Sorceress,* p. 5.

New York Times, May 12, 1989, Vincent Canby, review of *The Return of the Swamp Thing,* p. B4.

Variety, February 13, 1985, review of *The Lost Empire,* p. 22; November 19, 1986, review of *Chopping Mall,* p. 18; October 21, 1987, review of *Big Bad Mama II,* p. 15; November 25, 1987, review of *Deathstalker II,* p. 25; May 25, 1988, review of *Not of This Earth,* p. 16; May 3, 1989, review of *Return of the Swamp Thing,* p. 13; March 14, 1990, review of *The Haunting of Morella,* p. 23; April 4, 1990, review of *Transylvania Twist,* p. 28; June 8, 1992, Lawrence Cohn, review of *Munchie,* p. 51; June 10, 1996, Godfrey Cheshire, review of *Demolition High,* p. 43.

Video Business, January 3, 2000, Ed Hulse, review of *Desert Thunder,* p. 13; March 12, 2001, Buzz McClain, review of *Rangers,* p. 17; August 6, 2001, Laurence Lerman, review of *Extreme Limits,* p. 27; August 13, 2001, Cyril Pearl, review of *Poison,* p. 17.

ONLINE

Bare Wench Project Home Page, http://www.bare wench.com/ (April 25, 2003).

Blockbuster.com, http://www.blockbuster.com/ (April 25, 2003), Mark Deming, review of *Little Miss Millions.*

Cold Fusion Reviews, http://www.coldfusionvideo. com/ (November 21, 2001), Nathan Shumate, review of *Raptor.*

DVD Talk, http://www.dvdtalk.com/ (April 25, 2003), G. Noel Gross, review of *The Bare Wench Project.*

FilmCritic.com, http://www.filmcritic.com/ (April 25, 2003), Christopher Null, review of *The Bare Wench Project.*

FilmValues.com, http://www.filmvalues.com/ (April 25, 2003), reviews of *Munchie* and *Munchie Fights Back.*

Flipside Movie Emporium, http://www.flipsidemovies. com/ (April 25, 2003), Mike Bracken, review of *The Bare Wench Project.*

MSN Entertainment, http://entertainment.msn.com/ (April 25, 2003), Cavett Binion, review of *Chopping Mall.*

Stomp Tokyo Video Reviews, http://www.stomptokyo. com/ (April 25, 2003), review of *Hollywood Scream Queen Hot Tub Party.*

Three Idiots Guide to Horror, http://www.horror.com/ (April 25, 2003), review of *Scream Queen Hot Tub Party.**

*   *   *

YAKOBSON, Helen B(ates) 1913-2002

OBITUARY NOTICE—See index for *CA* sketch: Born May 21, 1913, in St. Petersburg, Russia; died of cardiopulmonary arrest December 4, 2002, in Washington, DC. Educator, journalist, and author. Yakobson was a respected professor of Russian at George Washington University. When she was a young girl, her parents fled Russia during the 1917 revolution and ended up in China, where Yakobson attended school. She graduated with a law degree from the University of Harbin in 1934, but ended up teaching Russian language and literature for two years, before the Japanese invasion of China led her to immigrate to the United States in 1937. During World War II she worked for the Voice of America, and during the late 1940s was a script-writer and announcer for Russian programs for the U.S. Department of State in Washington, D.C. In 1951 she joined the faculty at George Washington University, where she was a professor of Russian until she retired in 1983; she was also chair of the Russian Department from 1958 to 1969. Yakobson wrote several Russian textbooks, including *A Guide to Conversational Russian* (1960) and *Conversational Russian: An Intermediate Course* (1985), and was also author of the autobiography *Crossing Borders: From Revolutionary Russia to China to America* (1994). She received several awards for her teaching, including, most recently, a 1995 award from the Russian Embassy for "preservation and development of Russian cultural and spiritual values."

OBITUARIES AND OTHER SOURCES:

PERIODICALS

Washington Post, December 6, 2002, p. B7.

*   *   *

YOUNG, Morris N(athan) 1909-2002

OBITUARY NOTICE—See index for *CA* sketch: Born July 29, 1909, in Lawrence, MA; died from a ruptured aneurysm November 13, 2002, in Norwich, CT. Ophthalmologist, magician, and author. Young had a lifelong interest in magic acts and was a world-class collector of posters, books, and other items relating to magicians, as well as a collector of books on mnemonics and of sheet music and music copyrights. He studied chemistry in college, earning a bachelor's degree from the Massachusetts Institute of Technology in 1930 and a master's degree from Harvard University in 1931. During the Great Depression he was unable to find a job as a chemist, so he continued on with his education to get a medical degree from Columbia University in 1935. Interested in magic since he was a young boy and having met the great escape artist Harry Houdini, Young was fascinated by how eyes worked and how they could be fooled; he became an ophthalmologist, working as a resident in the field at the Harlem Eye and Ear Hospital during the late 1930s. When World War II began, Young, who was already in the U.S. Army Reserve, became part of the Medical Corps and saw action in Europe and North Africa, where he performed facial reconstructive surgery on the wounded. After the war, he returned to private practice and worked at University Hospital in New York City; beginning in 1958 he was also an attending ophthalmologist and professor of ophthalmology at French & Polyclinic Medical School and Health Center in New York City. In 1970 he joined the staff of Beekman Downtown Hospital as chief ophthalmologist, and he was a consultant to Beth Israel Hospital from 1972 until 1993. Young's fascination with all things magical led him to amass an enormous collection of books on the subject, which he gathered together with his friend John J. McManus. Together, they found books dating back to the sixteenth century on such subjects as spiritualism, witchcraft, hypnotism, fortune telling, and more. The collection grew to some twenty thousand items, which Young and McManus donated to the Library of Congress in 1955. Young also collected books on mnemonics, donating his findings to the University of San Marino in Italy in 1990, and he loved to collect old sheet music, and even purchased copyrights to many songs dating back to the nineteenth century. Naturally, while researching and collecting all these works, Young became an expert on these subjects, and he wrote down his knowledge in several books, including *Presto Prestige* (1929), *Hobby Magic* (1950), *Houdini's Fabulous Magic* (1961), written with Walter B. Gibson, *How to Develop an Exceptional Memory* (1962), also written with Gibson, *Original Magicol and Indices* (1998), and *Radio Music Live: 1920-1950: A Pictorial Gamut* (1999). He was also the editor of *MAGICOL* magazine from 1949 to 1952.

OBITUARIES AND OTHER SOURCES:

BOOKS

Writers Directory, 17th edition, St. James Press (Detroit, MI), 2002.

PERIODICALS

New York Times, November 24, 2002, p. A27.
Seattle Times, November 24, 2002, p. A25.

*   *   *

ZONTA, Pat 1951-

PERSONAL: Born March 24, 1951, in Hamilton, Ontario, Canada; divorced; children: Dave, Mike. *Education:* Attended McMaster University; also studied medical radiation technology at St. Joseph's Hospital

and Mohawk College, Hamilton, Ontario, Canada. *Religion:* Roman Catholic.

ADDRESSES: Agent—c/o Author Mail, Firefly Books Ltd., 3680 Victoria Park Ave., Toronto, Ontario, Canada M2H 3K1. *E-mail*—p_zonta@hotmail.com.

CAREER: Worked as a medical radiation technologist in Ontario, Canada, including positions at St. Joseph's Hospital, Joseph Brant Hospital, York-Finch Clinic, McMaster Children's Hospital, and Gamma X-Ray and Laboratories Ltd., for twenty-five years. Also actress and singer, including a singing tour of Italy, 2001.

MEMBER: Ontario Association of Medical Radiation Technologists (education coordinator, 1996).

WRITINGS:

Jessica's X-Ray, illustrated by Clive Dobson, Firefly Books (Toronto, Ontario, Canada), 2001.

Also author of *Mikey's Endoscopy,* privately printed. Theater critic, *View.* Contributor to periodicals.

WORK IN PROGRESS: Short stories and nonfiction.

SIDELIGHTS: Pat Zonta told *CA:* "My idea for *Jessica's X-Ray* germinated when I was a student X-ray technologist, but I did not start writing the book until 1997.

"I began writing the prototype series, 'Xandra's X-Ray: Xander and Xandra Children's Learning Series' after being 'downsized' from my full-time position as an X-ray technician. I self-published the prototype series and, with the permission of Firefly Books, it is currently available exclusively to the Children's Hospital at McMaster Medical Centre in Hamilton, Ontario. The Children's Hospital provided seed funding for the series in 1997, and I have donated the series to the hospital. The 'Xandra' books are given to the children who visit the hospital. Crayola Crayons donated 500 three-packs of crayons to be attached to the black-and-white books so the children can color them.

"With *Jessica's X-Ray* I hope to allay at least a few of the fears children experience about the X-ray process in an entertaining and educational manner while speaking to them respectfully and intelligently. I hope to reach out to as many children as possible. Most people have never seen X-ray, ultra-sound, computer-assisted tomography (CT), or magnetic resonance imaging (MRI) images. I hope to give the public a little insight about how our bodies look from the inside out. I hope *Jessica's X-Ray* will reach children all over the world. I hope it will be translated into other languages. Due to the digital imaging process used to create the original diagnostic images, the book can easily be adapted to an online market or video format.

"The names Jessica and another character, Sarah, are the names of my granddaughters. Sarah, at age three, called the MRI image 'scary guy' and loved to play a game where she opened the book, screamed out his name, closed the book at lightning speed, then laughed at the fun before she repeated the process over and over again.

"Sarah, Jessica, and I are always thrilled when we see the book displayed in bookstores. I have also enjoyed reading *Jessica's X-Ray* to classrooms of children from pre-kindergarten through third grade. They were a wonderful audience and had prepared questions for me to answer after we read the book, such as 'how long did it take to write?' or 'when did you know you wanted to become a writer?' The answer to that question is—when I was in grade five.

"I thoroughly enjoy the interaction with children when I read the book to them. I designed *Jessica's X-Ray* to be interactive. I am very pleased at the fun we have reading it in the classroom. I have performed as an actor in many children's plays, and I can think of no greater thrill than participating with children—in hearing their ideas, enthusiasm, and creativity. I love helping kids in any way I can."

BIOGRAPHICAL AND CRITICAL SOURCES:

PERIODICALS

Resource Links, April, 2002, Linda Berezowski, review of *Jessica's X-Ray,* p. 58.
School Library Journal, August, 2002, Martha Topol, review of *Jessica's X-Ray,* p. 181.